LEGAL ASPECTS
of
ARCHITECTURE, ENGINEERING
and the
CONSTRUCTION PROCESS

By

JUSTIN SWEET

Professor of Law, University of California (Berkeley)

ST. PAUL, MINN.

WEST PUBLISHING CO.

1970

Library of Congress Catalog Card Number: 74–123658

Sweet, Aspects of Architecture–MCB

To

Lisa, Jonathan, Sharon, and most of all, Lesly

PREFACE

From 1963 to 1965 I gave a short series of informal lectures to architecture students at the Berkeley campus of the University of California. These lectures dealt with selected legal aspects of professional practice. Because of student and faculty interest, the Department of Architecture asked me to give a regular academic course which would treat the important legal aspects of architecture, engineering and the construction process.

The course was given in 1967, 1968 and 1969. Because I found existing published materials did not meet my needs, I prepared teaching materials. Retaining what worked well in class and eliminating what did not, I revised the materials each year. In 1968 I added reported appellate cases. This treatise is an expanded and revised version of the 1969 materials.

In planning the teaching materials and the approach to the course, I remembered a remark made by a Berkeley architect which related to the transition from school to practice. He referred to the "cold bath" a young architect receives when he moves from the world of teachers and books to the world of clients, contractors, developers, building inspectors and loan officers. An understanding of law and legal institutions may not eliminate the "bath", but it should reduce the shock and make the transition more tolerable.

Another objective of this treatise is to dispel some of the mistrust and even hostility some design professionals feel toward law and legal institutions. These architects and engineers view law as an unreasonable interference with their professional work, a device to take money out of their pockets unjustly, and a means by which unscrupulous clients avoid paying for design services.

Too often hostile attitudes are the result of limited personal contact with the law. Persons with such attitudes rarely are aware of the role allocated to law by society. The law must select from competing and often conflicting social, political and economic goals. Also, law must adjust and choose from the demands of competing interest groups.

This role is a difficult one. Even if the reader believes the legal solution to a problem to be unjust (laws and legal institutions, being created and operated by humans, are far from perfect), the reader should recognize the difficulty of the task. This recognition should reduce the suspicion and hostility with which some design professionals view law.

The described objectives cannot be met by an uncritical display of a large platter of "legal rules". Such compilations are often misleading, and even dangerous in a country with 50 states, a District of Columbia and a separate federal system. While there is considerable uniformity in American law, not infrequently the result in a case will depend upon which jurisdiction's law controls, as well the particular facts in the case.

Also, a compilation of legal "rules" makes law appear static. While relative stability is a desirable feature of a legal system, law must and often does change to meet new social, political and economic needs. The modern era is one of great change. For this reason, this treatise will focus upon trends in law and give reasons behind legal solutions, rather than simply state legal "rules".

Finally, books filled with legal rules are dry and lifeless. They do not stimulate reader interest and destroy any enthusiasm the reader may have in the subject matter.

This treatise makes suggestions designed to create and maintain a harmonious design professional-client relationship, to make the construction process more efficient and enable the design professional to avoid legal difficulties. As to the last objective, I must warn the reader that this treatise is not a do-it-yourself legal manual which will enable its owner to be his own lawyer. Legal problems require legally trained persons. But I hope that this treatise can point out the danger areas and indicate to the design professional when he needs legal advice.

Organizationally, the treatise is divided into five major parts. Part I sets forth some basic legal doctrines which are essential to an understanding of Parts II through V. Part II looks at the design process, with emphasis upon the design professional-client relationship. Part III examines briefly selected aspects of law which relate to land ownership and use. Part IV centers upon the construction process, with emphasis upon the legal relationship of those actively engaged in the construction enterprise. Part V considers a number of legal problems which often arise in the context of private professional practice.

Except for Part I, the treatise is not organized around legal concepts. Legal doctrines are incorporated into the institutional frameworks described. An institutional approach can mean occasional overlap and repetition, but it makes the law more "real" and more understandable.

The treatise is largely textual. Important legal doctrines are illustrated by examples, problems, and cases which relate to design and construction.

There is an infinite amount of material which can be included in a treatise of this type. The increasing number of legal controls on the design professions and the construction process has expanded the range of potential subject matter coverage immensely.

I have selected laws and legal institutions which are likely to enter the professional lives of architects and engineers. The model of the private practitioner was selected, despite the increasing trend toward institutional employment of architects and engineers, because the private practitioner has the greatest contact with the widest range of legal controls. This choice has meant the inclusion of material not usually included in treatises of this type.

It would be difficult to cover adequately all of the material in the traditional 30 class hour course, for architects and engineers. (Perhaps I am unbiased, but this time is inadequate.) Instructors with 30 class hours can, of course, select the material which they think most important for their students. I would suggest covering Parts I, II, IV, and Chapter 34 from Part V, dealing with the legal responsibility of design professionals. Time permitting, I would also include § 14.03, dealing with public controls on the use of land, Chapter 31, which treats licensing laws, and Chapter 40, which deals with copyrights, patents and trade secrets. (An instructor pressed for time could eliminate Chapters 3 and 4 of Part I.)

Interspersed in the treatise are reported appellate opinions. Case readings have proved popular with students. Fenerally, I have selected recent and readable opinions which show modern legal problems relevant to the design professions.

Some mention should be made of the legal citation system. When specific cases are reproduced, in whole or in part, or cited, the full legal citations are given. This is to enable the reader, whether he be an architect, engineer, or lawyer, to find the complete case if he so desires.

While legal citations often appear complicated, they are, in reality, quite simple. There are four elements to a citation. A typical citation would be *Sniadach v. Family Finance Corp.*, 395 U.S. 337 (1969). First, the name of the case is given, usually with the plaintiff (the person starting the lawsuit) first, followed by the defendant. "U. S." is the abbreviation of the reporter system from which the case is taken, in this case the United States Supreme Court Reports. The number preceding the abbreviation of the reporter system (395) is the volume in which the case is located. The number following the abbreviation of the reporter system (337) indicates the page on which the case commences. Finally, the citation concludes with the year that the court announced the decision.

Most states have official reports of the appellate court decisions of the state. Also, most state court decisions are collected in regional reports, published by the West Publishing Company. A typical state court citation would be *Weiner v. Cuyahoga Comm. Coll. Dist.*, 19

Ohio St.2d 25, 249 N.E.2d 907 (1969). "Ohio St.2d" is the abbreviation for the Ohio State Reports, Second Series. This abbreviation is preceded by the volume in the reports (19) and followed by the page number of the volume where the case begins (25). This is followed by the citation to the regional reports, Northeast, Second (N.E.2d), with the volume preceding (249) and page number following (907). Finally, the citation is concluded with the year of the decision. A list of abbreviations of the reports will be given following the Table of Cases.

Rather than employ the terms "architect-engineer", "architect or engineer", or "architects and engineers", generally I combine my reference to the two professions by employing the term "design professional". Also, I use the term "prime" contractor rather than "general" contractor. "Supplier" is favored over "materialman", but the latter term is employed on occasion.

I owe debts of gratitude to many who have, in small ways and large, participated in the creation of this book. From an institutional standpoint, I must extend thanks to the University of California School of Law at Berkeley and its Dean, Edward C. Halbach, Jr., for having given me time to teach the course in the Department of Architecture which led to this book. Also, I must give thanks to the University of California Department of Architecture and its Chairman, Professor Gerald McCue, for permitting me to experiment upon their students in the course of preparing this treatise.

I must also extend thanks to the American Institute of Architects. Members of the East Bay and Northern California Chapters were always helpful in giving me information regarding architectural practice and architectural problems. The American Institute of Architects granted its permission to reproduce a number of its forms which are found in the Appendices. Textual references to AIA Docs B131 and A201 are to the documents published in September, 1967, unless indicated otherwise.

One of the greatest debts of gratitude I owe is to Professor George P. Simonds of the Department of Architecture at the University of California at Berkeley. He was instrumental in generating the architecture law course and this treatise.

A number of my colleagues on the faculty of the University of California School of Law at Berkeley educated me in their areas of expertise. They are Professors Stephen R. Barnett, Richard M. Buxbaum, Jesse Choper, David Feller, John R. Hetland, Ira M. Heyman, David W. Louisell, Sho Sato, Lawrence M. Stone, Lawrence A. Sullivan and Jan Vetter. I owe a special debt of gratitude to my colleague Professor John G. Fleming, an outstanding international scholar in the field of torts.

PREFACE

The two major stenographic contributors to the treatise were Miss Kathryn Sommarstrom and Miss Dorothy Snodgrass. I must give a special word of thanks to the students in the three architectural courses upon whom I experimented in the course of preparing these materials.

Acknowledgments would not be complete without reference to my wife, Miriam Lesly Sweet, skillful lawyer, expert editor and patient critic.

JUSTIN SWEET

June, 1970

SUMMARY OF CONTENTS

SUMMARY OF CONTENTS

Part V

SOME PROFESSIONAL PRACTICE PROBLEMS

TABLE OF CONTENTS

CHAPTER 2. CONTRACT FORMATION PRINCIPLES—Continued

CHAPTER 3. THE AGENCY RELATIONSHIP — 54

CHAPTER 3. THE AGENCY RELATIONSHIP—Continued

Part II

THE DESIGN PROFESSIONAL–CLIENT RELATIONSHIP

CHAPTER 6. ARCHITECTURAL AND ENGINEERING SERVICES—Continued

CHAPTER 7. CLIENT OBLIGATIONS

TABLE OF CONTENTS

CHAPTER 12. INTERESTS IN LAND—Continued

CHAPTER 13. ACQUISITION OF LAND OWNERSHIP—Continued

Part IV

THE CONSTRUCTION PROCESS

TABLE OF CONTENTS

CHAPTER 23. TIME PROBLEMS—Continued

CHAPTER 30. DISTRIBUTION OF LOSSES INCIDENT TO CONSTRUCTION PROCESS—Continued

Part V

SOME PROFESSIONAL PRACTICE PROBLEMS

CHAPTER 36. DESIGN PROFESSIONAL AS AN EMPLOYER—Continued

CHAPTER 37. COLLECTION PROBLEMS 792

CHAPTER 38. FORENSIC SKILL AND THE DESIGN PROFESSIONAL AS AN EXPERT WITNESS 806

CHAPTER 38. FORENSIC SKILL AND THE DESIGN PROFESSIONAL AS AN EXPERT WITNESS—Continued

CHAPTER 40. INTELLECTUAL PROPERTY: IDEAS, COPYRIGHTS, PATENTS AND TRADE SECRETS —Continued

TABLE OF CONTENTS

TABLE OF CASES

References are to Pages

TABLE OF CASES

TABLE OF CASES

TABLE OF ABBREVIATIONS

CASE REPORTS

A.	Atlantic [2]
A.2d	Atlantic, Second [2]
A.D.2d	Appellate Division, Second (New York)
A.L.R.	American Law Reports [5]
A.L.R.2d	American Law Reports, Second [5]
Adv.Cal.App.	Advance California Appellate
All E.R.	All English Reports
App.Div.	Appellate Division (New York)
Ariz.	Arizona [1]
Ariz.App.	Arizona Appellate
Ark.	Arkansas [1]
Atl.	Atlantic [2]
C.A.	Court of Appeals (England)
Cal.2d	California, Second [1]
Cal.App.	California Appellate
Cal.App.2d	California Appellate, Second
Cal.Rptr.	California Reporter [4]
CCH, Pro.Liab.Rptr.	Commence Clearing House Products Liability Reporter
Colo.	Colorado [1]
Conn.	Connecticut [1]
Conn.Super.	Connecticut Superior
Ct.Cl.	Court of Claims (Federal)
F.	Federal [6]
F.2d	Federal, Second [7]
F.Supp.	Federal Supplement [8]
Ga.App.	Georgia Appellate
Ill.	Illinois [1]
Ill.2d	Illinois, Second [1]
Ill.App.	Illinois Appellate
Ill.App.2d	Illinois Appellate, Second
Ind.App.	Indiana Appellate
K.B.	King's Bench (England)
Kan.	Kansas [1]
L.Ed.	Lawyer's Edition (U. S. Supreme Court)[5]
L.R.A.	Law Reports Annotated [5]
La.	Louisiana [1]
La.App.	Louisiana Appellate
Mass.	Massachusetts [1]
Md.	Maryland [1]
Me.	Maine [1]
Mich.	Michigan [1]
Minn.	Minnesota [1]
Misc.	Miscellaneous (New York)
Misc.2d	Miscellaneous, Second (New York)

See footnotes on following page.

TABLE OF ABBREVIATIONS

Miss.	Mississippi [1]
Mo.	Missouri [1]
Mo.App.	Missouri Appellate
Mont.	Montana [1]
N.E.	Northeastern [2]
N.E.2d	Northeastern, Second [2]
N.H.	New Hampshire [1]
N.J.	New Jersey [1]
N.J.Eq.	New Jersey, Equity
N.J.Super.	New Jersey, Superior
N.W.	Northwestern [2]
N.W.2d	Northwestern, Second [2]
N.Y.	New York [1]
N.Y.2d	New York, Second [1]
N.Y.S.	New York Supplement [3]
N.Y.S.2d	New York Supplement, Second [3]
Ohio Abs.	Ohio Abstracts
Ohio App.	Ohio Appeals
Ohio Com.Pl.	Ohio Common Pleas
Ohio Misc.	Ohio Miscellaneous
Ohio St.	Ohio State [1]
Ohio St.2d	Ohio State, Second [1]
Okl.	Oklahoma [1]
Or.	Oregon [1]
Oreg.	Oregon [1]
P.	Pacific [2]
P.2d	Pacific, Second [2]
Pa.	Pennsylvania [1]
Pa.Common Pleas	Pennsylvania Common Pleas
Phila.	Philadelphia
R.I.	Rhode Island [1]
S.Ct.	Supreme Court (U. S.)[9]
S.E.	Southeastern [2]
S.E.2d	Southeastern, Second [2]
S.W.	Southwestern [2]
S.W.2d	Southwestern, Second [2]
So.2d	Southern, Second [2]
U.S.	United States (Supreme Court)[1]
Va.	Virginia [1]
Wash.	Washington [1]
Wash.2d	Washington, Second [1]
Wis.	Wisconsin [1]
Wis.2d	Wisconsin, Second [1]

1 Highest Court of State

2 Regional Reporter (unofficial)

3 Contains all New York Cases (unofficial)

4 Contains all California Cases (unofficial)

5 Contains cases, annotated (comments on cases)

6 Contains decisions of Federal Circuit Courts of Appeal, and some District Court opinions

7 Contains decisions of Federal Circuit Courts of Appeal, Court of Claims, Patent Court and Custom Appeals Court

8 Contains decisions from Federal District Courts (trial courts)

9 U. S. Supreme Court cases (unofficial)

TABLE OF ABBREVIATIONS

STATUTES

Civ.Code ------------------ Civil Code (California)
FLSA ---------------------- Fair Labor Standards Act (Federal)
G.L. ---------------------- General Law (Massachusetts)
Mo.Rev.Stat. -------------- Missouri Revised Statutes
P.L. ---------------------- Public Law (Federal)
R.S. ---------------------- Revised Statutes (Maine)
Stats. -------------------- Statutes (Wisconsin)
U.S.C. -------------------- United States Code (Federal)
U.S.Code ------------------ United States Code (Federal)
U.S.C.A. ------------------ United States Code Annotated (Federal)

ADMINISTRATIVE REGULATIONS

C.F.R. -------------------- Code of Federal Regulations
Fed.Reg. ------------------ Federal Register

LEGAL PERIODICALS

Baylor L.Rev. ------------- Baylor Law Review
Calif.L.Rev. -------------- California Law Review (Berkeley)
Cornell L.Rev. ------------ Cornell Law Review
Harv.L.Rev. --------------- Harvard Law Review
Ill.Law Rev. -------------- Illinois Law Review
Law & Contemp.Prob. ------- Law and Contemporary Problems
Nw.U.L.Rev. --------------- Northwestern University Law Review
Vand.L.Rev. --------------- Vanderbilt Law Review
Vanderbilt Law Rev. ------- Vanderbilt Law Review
Yale L.J. ----------------- Yale Law Journal

LEGAL ENCYCLOPEDIAS

Am.Jur. ------------------- American Jurisprudence
Am.Jur.2d ----------------- American Jurisprudence, Second
C.J.S. -------------------- Corpus Juris Secundum

OTHER

AIA Doc. ------------------ American Institute of Architects Document
N.L.R.B. ------------------ National Labor Relations Board

†

LEGAL ASPECTS OF ARCHITECTURE, ENGINEERING AND THE CONSTRUCTION PROCESS

Part I

SOME BASIC LEGAL DOCTRINES

Introduction

Chapter I provides a background to help the reader understand the court opinions included in the treatise, and gives the reader a necessary overview of the judicial process. Chapters 2, 3 and 4 explore basic contract formation principles, the agency relationship, and forms of association, respectively.

Chapter 1

THE AMERICAN JUDICIAL SYSTEM

SECTION 1.01 RELEVANCE

An overview of the American judicial system is relevant to architects and engineers. It is likely that they will come into contact with the judicial system during the course of professional practice. It may be necessary to use the judicial system to collect for professional services. Clients, and others who suffer losses, may ask that the judicial system place responsibility for these losses upon a design professional.

In addition to the possibility of being a litigant, the design professional may have other contacts with the judicial system. He may be requested to advise or assist in litigation involving architecture and engineering. He may be requested or compelled to testify as an expert witness in a court on similar matters.

Through his membership in professional groups or other civic groups, he may be interested in the outcome of litigation affecting his profession, or involving matters of general community interest.

In addition, the reader should have an overview of the judicial process to derive optimal benefit from this treatise. As mentioned in the Introduction, selected judicial opinions are included in the treatise. While these opinions have been selected and edited for the use of non-lawyers, a preliminary look at the judicial system is helpful in dealing with this material.

This treatise looks at laws and legal institutions, and their effect on design professionals. The sources of law include:

1. The Constitutions (Federal and State),

2. The Legislatures (Congress and the State Legislative bodies),

3. The many administrative agencies such as licensing boards and zoning commissions (to name a few most important to design professionals), and

4. The courts.

Even where the primary sources of law are the first three, courts play a significant role. They interpret constitutions, determine the legality of statutes and administrative regulations, and interpret statutes, ordinances and regulations.

In addition, courts directly make law. In performing their functions, judges often state that they are applying, but not making, law. Yet, in the process of determining constitutionality and applying statutes they are performing a creative, law making role.

In addition, the precedent system has made courts important lawmakers. American appellate courts generally write opinions giving the reasons for their decisions. Courts apply the reasoning expressed in prior opinions in order to produce uniformity and predictability in litigation. This gives appellate court opinions a significance beyond that of simply deciding the particular case before the court. Prior decisions also furnish guides to those who wish to know the law in order to plan their affairs, or to decide whether and how to settle a dispute without litigation. The compilation and systemization of court decisions provides a system of legal rules. Much of the law relating to contracts, torts, property and agency has been worked out by the courts through appellate decisions.

SECTION 1.02 STATE COURT SYSTEMS: TRIAL AND APPELLATE COURTS

Each state has its own judicial system. Courts are divided into the basic categories of trial and appellate courts. Within each category, there may be a further breakdown, based upon the amount or type of relief sought, or upon the nature of the matter being litigated.

The basic trial court, frequently called the court of general jurisdiction, hears all types of cases. Depending upon the state, it may be called a superior, district, or circuit court.

The bulk of the work before such courts consist of criminal cases, personal injury cases, commercial disputes, domestic matters (divorce, custody and adoption) and probate (dealing with transfer of property at death). A court of general jurisdiction may review determinations of administrative agencies (zoning, employment injuries, licensing, etc.). The presiding official will be a judge. In certain matters, there may also be a jury. The division of functions between judge and jury will be discussed in § 1.11. Courts of general jurisdiction are usually located at county seats.

Many states have established subordinate courts, with more limited jurisdiction. Municipal or city courts often have jurisdiction to try matters which involve less money than a minimum figure set for courts of general jurisdiction. There can also be a jury in such cases. As a rule, the dockets are less congested in these lower courts of limited jurisdiction than the dockets in the courts of general jurisdiction. The procedures in municipal or city courts are essentially the same as those in the courts of general jurisdiction.

Some state legislatures have established small claims courts, which provide expeditious and inexpensive procedures for disputes involving small sums. Usually the party seeking a remedy from such a court will be able to commence the action by paying a small filing fee and filling out a form provided by the clerk of the small claims court. The procedures in the small claims courts are usually informal, and there are no juries in these courts. While the judges are lawyers, attorneys are less important in such disputes, and in some states attorneys are not permitted to represent the parties.

Some states have justice of the peace courts. These are frequently run by non-lawyers with a minimum amount of legal training. In most states, the justice court has given way to the small claims court, or to the municipal or city court.

There is usually at least one appeal possible from a decision of a trial court. Usually the appeal is to the next highest court. For example, a party losing a decision in a municipal court may have a right to appeal to the court of general jurisdiction, or to an appellate division consisting of judges of the court of general jurisdiction. Appeals from courts of general jurisdiction are made to an appellate court. In the more populous states, there is usually an intermediate court which must review a case if the trial court decision is appealed. In such states the state supreme court usually is given discretion to decide whether it will hear an appeal from an intermediate appellate court. In states without intermediate appellate courts, there is an appeal from the court of general jurisdiction to the supreme court of the state.

State court judges are appointed by the governor or are elected. In most states, vacancies are filled by appointment. Usually, appointed judges are re-elected. Some states use the Missouri plan, or some variation of it. Under this system, judges submit their record to the electorate periodically, but they do not run against other candidates.

SECTION 1.03 FEDERAL COURT SYSTEM

It is basic to an understanding of the American legal system to realize that there are two parallel systems operating side by side. Each state has its own judicial system. In addition, federal courts operate in each state. The federal courts have jurisdiction to decide disputes which involve the federal constitution, or federal statutes. Presently, federal courts also have the jurisdiction to hear civil actions between citizens of different states, if the amount in question exceeds $10,000. In some cases, a plaintiff (the person commencing a suit) can bring suit in either the state or the federal court.

The federal courts operate under more modern and less formal procedural rules than most state courts. With regard to substantive law (laws which establish legal rights and duties), the federal courts use the substantive law of the state in which they sit, unless the case involves some aspect of federal law, such as a federal constitutional provision or a federal statute.

The basic trial court in the federal court system is called the district court. Each state has at least one, and the populous states have a number of district courts located in the principal metropolitan centers.

The district court is presided over by a federal district court judge. There are provisions for juries in certain types of cases. A party may appeal from a decision of the district court to a circuit court of appeals. There are eleven separate circuit courts of appeal operating in geographical areas of the United States. If a party is dissatisfied with the result of a decision by the circuit court of appeals, he may ask that the United States Supreme Court review his case. In general, the Supreme Court determines for itself which cases it will review. If it decides not to hear the case, this ends the matter. If it decides to hear the case, then the briefs and oral arguments are presented to the Supreme Court. The Supreme Court usually rejects petitions for hearings, unless the matter involves a conflict of rules between different federal courts, or unless it feels the matter is important.

Federal court judges are appointed by the President of the United States, and are confirmed by the Senate. In essence the judges serve for life, or until voluntary retirement.

Within the federal system, there are a few courts which deal with specialized matters. For example, the Court of Claims decides cases involving claims against the United States Government. Usually these cases relate to tax questions, or to disputes between government contractors and the various government agencies which award government contracts. Other examples of specialized courts are the Tax Court, which hears disputes between taxpayers and the government, and the Patent Court, which reviews disputed patent issuances.

SECTION 1.04 STATUTES OF LIMITATION: TIME TO BRING THE LAWSUIT

Most states have statutory provisions which prescribe that actions in certain types of cases must be brought within specific periods of time. The purpose of such periods of limitation is twofold. First, the longer the period of time between the acts which have given rise to the claim and the commencement of litigation, the more likely it is that people will forget what happened, documents will be lost, or witnesses may disappear or die. Secondly, a defendant is given the assurance that, after a certain period of time has elapsed, he can no longer be called upon by the legal system to respond to claims made against him.

There are two important variables in statutes of limitation. The first deals with when the statutory period commences. The second deals with the length of time during which the action may be started. Sometimes the period of time begins to run when the act complained of occurs. Sometimes the period of time will begin to run from the time when the plaintiff becomes aware of his injury or loss.

In construction litigation, this distinction may be of crucial importance. The contractor may do a defective job, but the matter may not come to the attention of the owner until a number of years after the completion of the job by the contractor. If the statutory period commences at the point the contractor has completed the defective work, the owner may lose a claim that he never knew he had. For this reason, the law must strike a balance between denying claims of the plaintiff which he did not or could not have discovered earlier, and protecting the rights of the defendant to litigate within a reasonable time after the alleged nonperformance or defective performance of the contract. Statutes and case decisions vary on this point, but the tendency is to start the period for bringing suit when the plaintiff discovered or should have discovered the loss or injury. See § 30.08 (e) for additional discussion.

The length of time to bring the action will vary considerably, depending upon the type of transaction which is the subject matter of the litigation. Periods of limitation may be as short as thirty days, or as long as twenty years. Typically, they run from one to five years. Generally, the more important or formal the transaction, the longer the time allowed to commence the lawsuit. Actions involving title to real property usually have a long period of limitation. Sometimes the statutory period will be longer for written contracts than for oral contracts. Actions for personal injury or death have a shorter period than contract actions.

The time period may be tolled (suspended) when, for various reasons, the plaintiff is unable to bring his lawsuit. For example, the time period may be tolled because the plaintiff does not have the capacity to sue. Illustrations of this would be when the plaintiff is a minor, or when the plaintiff is insane. Also, the period for commencing legal action may be tolled when the defendant is in another state and beyond the jurisdiction of the court which would normally have jurisdiction in the matter. For example, if a cause of action were to arise in State A, and the defendant moved to State B or left the country, the period of time for commencing the lawsuit would be tolled while he was outside the jurisdiction of the court.

Section 1.06 notes the modern tendency to expand the jurisdiction of a court in certain situations over persons in another state. For this reason, the tolling of the period of limitation is somewhat less likely when the defendant is in another state than when the defendant has left the country.

The important thing to remember regarding statutes of limitation is that valid claims can be lost if legal action is not brought within a time specified by law.

SECTION 1.05 HIRING A LAWYER: HIS ROLE AND COMPENSATION

Most litigation is commenced after the potential litigant has employed an attorney. While it is possible in some cases for an individual to act as his own attorney, usually the first step in commencing litigation is to engage an attorney.

Attorneys must fulfill certain requirements before they are admitted to practice. They must have completed certain educational prerequisites and, usually, must pass a bar examination. They are officers of the court and subject to professional and judicial regulation. They are retained to guide the litigant through the litigation process.

Unless the law sets the fee, which is rare, the attorney and client can determine the fee. Sometimes the fee is a flat charge for the job, such as in uncontested divorces or simple incorporations. The fee may be a designated percentage of what is at stake, such as probate of an estate. Often the fee is based on time spent by the attorney, typically computed on an hourly or daily basis. If there is no agreement on fee, the client must pay a reasonable amount.

Hourly rates charged by attorneys vary considerably. Much depends upon the attorney's skill, the amount of business he has, the amount involved, the complexity of the case, what the client can afford, and the locality in which he practices. It is not improper for a potential client to ask an attorney what he charges for his legal services. Such advance inquiry can avert possible later misunderstandings or disputes over the hourly rate. The client may wish to set a maximum figure for a particular legal job. Attorneys are reluctant to accept maximum figures, because it is often difficult to predict how much work will be involved in giving proper legal service.

Some attorneys handle cases on what is called a "contingent fee basis". This is the usual fee in personal injury cases. Under this system, the lawyer is not paid for his services if he does not obtain a recovery for the client. Usually the client agrees to pay the lawyer's fee for out-of-pocket costs for such items as deposition expenses, filing fees, and witness fees. For taking the risk that he may collect nothing, the lawyer will receive a specified percentage of any recovery. In personal injury cases, the percentage can range from anywhere from 20% to 50%, depending upon the locality, and depending upon the difficulty of the case. In some metropolitan areas, attorneys will charge 25% to 33% if they obtain a settlement without trial, and 33% to 40% if they go to trial.

A great deal of confusion can exist over what is is called a retainer. This is an amount paid at one time, or periodically, by a client to an attorney at the commencement of or during the attorney-client relationship. Retainers are used in many different ways, and for many different reasons. Rather than explore all possible arrangements which can be classified as "retainers", two principal problems will be mentioned.

First, is the retainer an advance on fees, or a nonrefundable payment made in order to have a call upon the lawyer's services? Put another way, if the value of the lawyer's services is less than the amounts paid as a retainer, does the client get a refund of the balance?

Second, is the retainer payment an agreed value for the legal services performed by the attorney? Sometimes the retainer payment is simply an advance payment on any fees which the client is obligated to pay his attorney. Sometimes it covers certain routine services, but does not include extraordinary services such as litigation. Sometimes it is an agreed valuation for all legal services to be performed for a specified period of time.

It is important for the attorney and the client to determine the function and operation of a retainer in order to avoid misunderstandings.

One other aspect of the attorney-client relationship should be mentioned. The law recognizes the need for a client to be candid in his communication with an attorney, as with his clergyman, his doctor, and his wife. For this reason, the attorney must keep confidential any communication made to him by his client, unless the communication was to plan or commit a crime, or if the client challenges the competence of the attorney's performance.

SECTION 1.06 JURISDICTION OF COURTS

Attorneys for plaintiffs must be certain that the court selected to decide the dispute has the power to give the remedy demanded or desired by the plaintiff. The defendant's attorney should determine whether the court selected by the plaintiff has the power to enter a judgment against his client. These matters are often very technical, but there are a few basic principles.

Jurisdiction (the power to grant the remedy sought by the plaintiff) may mean jurisdiction over the person who is being sued, or over subject matter that is in question. Roughly speaking, federal courts have jurisdiction where the subject is "federal", or where the parties are the citizens of different states, and the amount in question exceeds $10,000. As to the power of a particular state court, the first question relates to whether the judgment of a court will bind the defendant. The American judicial system requires that a defendant receive due process. He should be given the opportunity of knowing what the suit is about, who is suing him and where and when the suit will be brought. Usually this is done by having a summons and complaint handed to the defendant by a process server. Usually, the defendant must be physically present in the state where the court is located because the papers must be handed to him in that state. If the defendant does not come within the state, traditionally, the state court where the lawsuit is brought would not have jurisdiction over him. The plaintiff would have to sue in the state where the defendant could be physically handed the legal papers.

The requirement of physical presence in the state where the court sits can place great hardships on plaintiffs. They may be forced to commence the lawsuit in a distant state which may be far from the evidence and the witnesses. For this reason, most states have passed "long-arm" statutes. These statutes permit the plaintiff, in certain cases, to sue in his home state, despite the fact that he cannot hand the legal papers to the defendant within his state. These statutes are often used to sue defendant motorists who reside in a state other than the one where the accident occurred or where the injured party resides. Suppose an Iowa driver was involved in an accident in Illinois which injured an Illinois resident. The Iowa driver returned to Iowa after the accident. The injured Illinois resident can always sue in Iowa. Usually, he is also given the opportunity of suing in Illinois by mailing a notice of the lawsuit to the other driver in Iowa, or by filing legal papers with a designated state official in Iowa or Illinois.

Sometimes long-arm statutes are used to sue businesses which have their legal residence in a state other than that of the plaintiff. Suppose a New York company sells, directly or indirectly, electric drills to Wyoming purchasers. A Wyoming buyer would be likely to be able to sue the New York seller in a Wyoming court for injuries resulting from purchase and use of a defective drill.

The tendency of the law is to expand jurisdiction of a court over persons who are not personally served with the legal papers within the state where the court is located.

Jurisdiction may also involve the subject matter of the lawsuit. For example, if land is located in state A, and there is a dispute as to the ownership of the land, only state A will have jurisdiction, even though persons who may claim an interest in the land may not be residents of state A and may not be served with the legal papers in state A.

States usually limit their jurisdiction to matters which are of concern to that state. A state may have jurisdiction because property is located in that state, the injury occurred in that state, the plaintiff or defendant is a resident of that state, or a contract was made or performed within that state.

Another aspect of jurisdiction relates to the type of remedy or decree sought. Early in English legal history there were two sets of courts operating side by side and, to some degree, competing with each other for legal business. The two court systems were the Courts of Law and the Courts of Equity. Juries were used in Law Courts, but not in the Courts of Equity. In addition, Courts of Equity had the right to award certain remedies which were not available in the Courts of Law. The party seeking the assistance of a Court of Equity had to show that his remedy in the Law courts was inadequate. As a result of this dual set of courts, two sets of procedural and substantive rules emerged. Generally, the procedures and remedies tended to be more flexible in the Courts of Equity.

The division between Law and Equity carried over to the United States judicial system when the United States freed itself from England. However, there has been a gradual merger of the two systems in most states. For all practical purposes, there is only one set of courts. However, some vestiges of the differences between Law and Equity remain. The most important remaining difference is that certain remedies may only be given by an equity court. The most important of these remedies are "specific performance" (under which one party is ordered by a court to comply with a contract made with another party), "injunctions" (orders by the court that persons do or do not do certain things), and "reformation" (rewriting of a written document to make it accord with the parties' actual intention). Another significant difference is that there is no jury in an equity action.

SECTION 1.07 PARTIES TO THE LITIGATION

In the American system, the party commencing the action is usually called the plaintiff. The party against whom the action is commenced is usually called the defendant. When there are only two parties involved in the litigation, there is no particular difficulty with regard to the parties. However, one plaintiff may wish to sue two or more defendants, or two or more plaintiffs wish to sue one defendant. Also, the defendant may have a counterclaim against the plaintiff, or he may want to assert a claim against a third party arising from the same transaction. For example, a contractor may sue an owner for breach of contract, based upon the acts or failure to act of the architect. The owner may defend this action and also assert a claim against the architect, based upon a claimed breach of the owner-architect contract.

Such multiple actions were difficult to achieve in the Courts of Law in England, and in many early American courts. However, the Courts of Equity freely permitted a number of different parties to be involved in one lawsuit, as long as the issues did not become too confusing. It seemed sensible to the Courts of Equity to have as many different matters as possible, relating to the same transaction, disposed of in one lawsuit. Ultimately, the rules developed in the Courts of Equity prevailed, and it is generally possible to have multi-party lawsuits if jurisdiction can be obtained over all the parties, and if litigation can proceed without undue confusion or difficulty.

SECTION 1.08 PROVISIONAL REMEDIES

One problem that frequently arises in litigation is that the defendant against whom a judgment has been obtained has insufficient assets to pay the judgment. His assets may be so confused as to ownership, or so encumbered by prior rights of other creditors, that the plaintiff finds that the judgment is uncollectable. Most states have statutes creating provisional remedies. This means that the plaintiff (or the defendant, if he is asserting a counter claim) may be able, in advance of litigation, to seize or tie up specific assets of the opposing party in such a way as to insure that if he wins in the litigation he will be able to collect on any judgment he obtains. These assets may be "attached", if in the possession of the defendant, or "garnished", if in the hands of third parties. It is not uncommon for a plaintiff to attempt to tie up assets such as bank accounts or other liquid assets in advance of the litigation.

Bonds are important in the administration of provisional remedies. The party whose assets are tied up can "dissolve" (have removed) the attachment or garnishment by posting a sufficient bond.

If the party whose assets are tied up ultimately prevails in the litigation, he may have unfairly suffered damage from the seizure or tying up of his assets. To protect him from the risk of not finding assets out of which he can be indemnified for these losses, the law frequently requires that the attachment or garnishment be accompanied by a bond.

Usually, statutes limit the types of actions in which attachment or garnishment are available. Also, there is a trend towards limiting garnishment of wages, because of the hardship this can place upon lower income families. See § 36.02(c).

SECTION 1.09 PLEADINGS

The lawsuit is usually begun by handing a summons and complaint to the defendant. This is called service of process. The defendant has a specified amount of time from the time he is served to respond.

He may assert that the plaintiff has not stated the facts correctly, or that he has defenses, even if the allegations of the plaintiff's complaint are true. In some states, he may attack the legal sufficiency of the complaint by filing a "demurrer". By filing a demurrer, the defendant is saying that even if the plaintiff's facts are true, the plaintiff has no valid claim.

In addition to answering the plaintiff's complaint, the defendant, in some cases, may assert a claim against a third party by filing a cross-complaint of his own, or may file a counter claim against the plaintiff, asserting that the defendant has a claim against the plaintiff.

In some states, the plaintiff will be required to submit a reply to the answer. In most states, he will be required to submit an answer to a counter claim. In early American legal practice, there were a substantial number of other pleadings which might be filed. The tendency in American procedural law today is to reduce the number of pleadings.

The pleadings are to inform each party of the other party's contentions, and to eliminate from the trial matters upon which there is no disagreement. By an examination of the pleadings, a lawyer or a judge should be able to determine the salient issues to be explored in the litigation. The purpose is to streamline the litigation and avoid the proof of unnecessary matters. Also, trial preparation should be more efficient if each side knows the issues upon which the other party intends to present evidence at the trial.

The complaint is generally required to be a concise statement of the facts upon which the plaintiff is basing his claim, and the specific remedy he is seeking from the court. Some states permit stereotyped pleading called the common counts, which do not go into the facts.

Often the complaint contains factual statements and serious charges which the plaintiff's attorney never expects to prove, or which he has not checked out very carefully. It is important that the inexperienced litigant understand the reasons for these tactics.

The attorney may believe that the only way to get the other side to consider his client's claim seriously is to start a lawsuit and ask for a large amount of money. A lawyer who estimates that his client's claim is worth $10,000 may ask for $50,000. This gives him running room in negotiations, and it may intimidate the other party.

Often, the lawsuit is commenced before the attorney has had the time to investigate thoroughly and to employ discovery procedures. (See § 1.10.) Since he does not know how the facts will turn out, he may plead a number of different legal theories which will cover all possibilities.

Finally, he will want to be certain that his complaint is legally sufficient. He may decide to use the identical language of pleadings that have been held to be sufficient. Such pleadings may not be tailor-made for the particular case in which they are used. Also, if the form he uses is old, it may contain archaic language.

Overstatement and flexibility in handling the litigation are the lawyer's stock in trade. But if the lawyers do not explain their tactics to their clients, each party may get even angrier at the other. Increased hostility can make settlement of the dispute more difficult.

If the defendant has been served with a summons and complaint, his failure to answer, or to receive an extension of time to answer, within the time specified in the statute will mean that the plaintiff may take what is called a "default judgment". His failure to respond within the time allowed means he has lost the case "by default."

If the plaintiff obtains a default judgment, he can try to collect on this judgment in the manner described in § 1.13. Most states have statutes or case law which may enable the party against whom a default judgment is taken to have the default judgment set aside. Usually, the defendant must present cogent reasons indicating why it would be unfair to enforce the judgment against him despite his failure to respond to the pleadings in the designated time. Courts today seem more willing to upset default judgments if the defendant can show he may have a valid defense, that failure to answer was the result of excusable mistake, and if the amount of the judgment is substantial. However, generally default judgments are difficult to upset. For this reason, it is vital that a defendant who wishes to contest a claim made in a complaint have his attorney answer the complaint within the specified time.

SECTION 1.10 PRE–TRIAL MATTERS

Between the time an issue is established by the pleadings, and the time that the trial is held, there is a good deal of activity between the lawyers and the trial judge.

"Discovery" and the "pre-trial conference" are the most important pre-trial activities. Discovery is the process by which a party to litigation can learn more about the other party's case and obtain facts which will be material to the lawsuit. Uncovering facts may lead toward a settlement. There are two principal discovery methods. Written interrogatories consist of a series of written questions relating to the subject of the suit. The other method is oral questioning of the other party or his employees. For example, the plaintiff may wish to conduct an examination of the defendant in order to uncover facts. In such a case, the defendant will be put under oath and asked various questions by the attorney for the plaintiff. These statements may be used at the trial. Sometimes the demand for questioning may include a request that the person being questioned bring certain documents for examination. A proper use of discovery should avoid surprise at the trial, cut down the trial time, and encourage settlement.

Depositions are a transcription of testimony taken before trial of witnesses who will be out of the jurisdiction at the time of trial, or of witnesses who are very sick and possibly will not be alive when the case is tried. Depositions are usually taken before a court commissioner. Questioning is done by the attorneys for the parties. The depositions are likely to be taken with a view towards preserving evidence rather than assisting the parties in preparing their case.

In many states, the pre-trial conference is another step in the litigation process. Usually such a conference is conducted in the judge's chambers in the presence of the judge, the attorneys, and sometimes the parties. The main purposes of the pre-trial conference are, like the pleadings, to narrow the issues and to improve the efficiency of the trial. Another objective is to encourage settlement. The judge in a pre-trial conference has the attorneys state their legal theories, and the facts which they intend to show. Advance discussion should improve trial efficiency, and avoid surprise. If a new theory or a new demand is presented at the pre-trial conference by one of the parties, the judge may not permit it, or he may grant a delay to allow the other party to prepare for defense against the new theory or remedy.

SECTION 1.11 TRIAL

If the dispute has not been settled prior to trial, the matter will then be tried before the judge, and perhaps a jury. In some cases, the right to a jury is constitutionally guaranteed. Both parties can agree to try the case without a jury. Many civil (as opposed to criminal) trials do not have a jury. A jury usually consists of twelve persons who are selected under the rules of the jurisdiction and designated as impartial finders of fact. They will sit in the courtroom, along with the judge, the parties, the witnesses, the attorneys, and any interested members of the public.

The trial is usually commenced by an opening statement by the plaintiff's attorney. Sometimes the defendant's attorney will also make an opening statement. In his opening statement, the attorney usually states what he intends to prove, and he may also try to convince the jury that his client's story should be believed. There is less likelihood that there will be an opening statement if the trial is being conducted solely by the judge.

After the opening statements, the plaintiff presents his case. He will call witnesses, and may offer in evidence physical exhibits and documents. In civil actions, he can call the other party as a witness.

An attorney cannot ask leading questions of his own witnesses, but he can ask leading questions of the other party and his witnesses, or of any hostile witness he must call to testify. A "leading question" is a question which tends to suggest the answer to the witness. The testimony should come from the witness, and is not to be prompted by his own attorney, or the attorney for whom he is appearing. Leading questions also are permitted by the attorney calling the witness in order to establish less important preliminary matters, or in cases where the witness is of low mentality or very young.

Witnesses are supposed to testify only to those matters which they have perceived through their own senses. Usually, witnesses cannot express opinions upon technical questions unless they are qualified as experts. For further discussion of witnesses and testimony see § 38.03.

The main problem in presenting the testimony of witnesses is what is called the "hearsay rule." A witness cannot testify to what someone has told him, if the purpose of the testimony is to prove the truth of the statement. The law prefers to hear from the source of the statement, and not from the recipient. The danger in hearsay testimony is that the party who made the statement is not in court, and cannot be cross-examined as to the basis upon which the statement was made. However, there are many exceptions to the hearsay rule which permit admission of certain types of hearsay evidence.

After the attorney has finished questioning his witness, the attorney for the other side will cross-examine. He will try to bring out additional facts favorable to his client, or to discredit the testimony given on direct examination. Cross-examination can be an effective tool to catch a perjurer, or to show a witness is mistaken. However, when used improperly, it may create sympathy for the witness, or reinforce the witness's story.

Documents play a large role in litigation. Under modern rules of evidence, it is relatively easy to introduce into evidence documents to be considered by the court. Documents are hearsay testimony. They are usually writings made by persons who are not in court. However, there are many exceptions to the hearsay rule which permit the admission of documents such as official records, business entries, and others. Often the attorneys will stipulate to the admissibility of certain documents.

After the plaintiff has presented his case, the defendant will be given an opportunity to present his case. After the defendant has presented his case, the plaintiff is given the opportunity to present rebuttal evidence. After all the evidence has been presented, the judge will give instructions to the jury, if there is a jury deciding the facts. The judge may take fact questions away from the jury, if he decides that reasonable men cannot differ as to the facts. If the judge does not take away fact questions, the jury decides fact issues and evaluates the credibility of the witnesses. The judge instructs the jury on the law. The jury meets in private, discusses the case, and takes ballots. Then it decides who wins, and how much should be awarded to the winning litigant. If there is no jury, the judge will decide these matters.

American trials are conducted under the adversary system. Theoretically, permitting each side to present its case in the best possible manner ultimately will lead to the truth. In such a system, the judge has a passive role. He acts as an umpire who rules on disputes when requested by one of the attorneys. The judge is supposed to allow the attorneys to present their cases in the way that they think best, within the boundaries of the rules established for court procedure and conduct.

The adversary system assumes that each party will have a partisan or an advocate. Each advocate will try to build up his client's case, and to tear down the other party's case. In the process, some advocates are insulting, belligerent, and melodramatic. Others represent their parties capably without these tactics.

There are limits to advocacy. There are rules of trial decorum set by law and administered by the judge. The judge can punish those who violate these rules by citing them for contempt. The person cited can be fined and, in some cases, imprisoned. Also, the legal profession can discipline those who violate professional rules of conduct. As obvious illustrations, lawyers must not bribe witnesses, encourage or permit perjured testimony, or mislead the judge on legal issues. The lawyer has a dual obligation. He is the champion for his client, but he is also part of the system of administration of justice, and he must not conduct himself in any way that would subvert or dishonor that system.

There may be frequent objections by attorneys in hotly contested litigation. This is always irksome to non-lawyers, but it is often, though not always, necessary. If objections are not made at the proper time, the right to complain of errors may be lost. The judge should be given the chance to correct his errors on the spot.

The possibility of drama and tension in the litigation process can increase if a jury is used. Some attorneys employ dramatic tactics designed to influence the jury. While some enjoy the combat of litigation, litigation is at best unpleasant, and at worst traumatic, for the litigant or witness who is not accustomed to the legal setting, the legal jargon, or the adversary process. This can be intensified if the trial attracts members of the public, or is reported in the public media.

A trial is an expensive way to settle a dispute. In addition to attorneys' fees, witness fees, court costs, and stenographic expenses, there are less obvious expenses to the litigant. He must spend a good deal of time preparing for the trial and attending the trial. He may have to disrupt his business operations by searching his records. For these reasons, as well as others, most lawsuits are settled.

SECTION 1.12 JUDGMENT

What the plaintiff and the defendant are seeking in litigation is a "judgment". This is an order by the court stating that one of the parties is entitled to a specified amount of money, or to another designated type of remedy. Some judges may rule immediately after the trial. Usually, the judge takes the matter under consideration. Often the trial judge writes an opinion giving the reason for his decision.

SECTION 1.13 EXECUTION

If the plaintiff obtains a judgment for money, the defendant is supposed to pay the amount of money specified in the judgment.

However, if the defendant does not pay voluntarily, the plaintiff's attorney will deliver the judgment to a sheriff and ask that property of the defendant, in the hands of the defendant or any third party, be seized and sold to pay the judgment.

It is often difficult to find property of the defendant. In some states, the defendant can be compelled to testify as to what assets he has. Even if assets can be found, exemption laws may mean that certain assets may not be taken by the plaintiff to satisfy his judgment. Legislatures specify that certain types of property are to be exempt from judgment. Statutes usually contain a long list of items of property which cannot be seized by the sheriff to satisfy a judgment. These items are considered necessary to basic existence. Illustrations of these might be an automobile, personal clothing, a television set, tools of trade, the family bible, and other items which vary, depending upon the state and the time in which the exemption laws were passed.

In addition, there are "homestead" laws which exempt the house in which the defendant lives from execution to satisfy judgments. Financial misfortunes notwithstanding, a person should have shelter for himself and his family. Sometimes homestead rights are limited in amount, and, under certain circumstances a homestead can be ordered sold.

The mere fact that a court judgment is obtained does not mean that the judgment will be satisfied. In many cases, judgments are not satisfied because the defendant has no property, or the property in the defendant's possession is exempt. This is another reason to settle. Collection of a judgment when the defendant does not pay voluntarily may be difficult, uncertain, and costly.

SECTION 1.14 APPEALS

The losing party, or the party who thinks he has not been given an adequate amount by the trial court, may appeal the trial court decision to an appellate court or to an appropriate higher court. The appeals to an appellate court usually consist of written briefs and oral arguments, and include the transcript, if there is one, made of the proceedings in the lower court. Introduction of evidence is not permitted in appeals.

In the American system, most appellate courts write a decision stating their reasons for the way they have decided the case. Decisions vary in length. Usually, the legal basis for a decision is statutory or a prior case precedent.

Usually all the members of the appellate court agree. Sometimes there is a dissenting opinion giving reasons for not agreeing with the majority. Sometimes the majority of the court that agrees on the disposition of the case cannot agree on the reasons for the decision, and one or more majority judges may write a concurring opinion.

Generally, American courts follow precedent. One of the sources that a court will examine in determining how a current case should be decided is how the courts in its jurisdiction have decided similar cases in the past. However a court may feel that an earlier case should not control in deciding the current case, and they may "distinguish" the earlier case. Also, in rare cases the court may decide that the earlier cases were wrong, and overrule preceding cases. The precedent system operates only within a particular state. For example, an Arizona court would usually follow decisions of the Arizona appellate courts. It would not be compelled to follow a prior decision by the Supreme Court of Tennessee. A decision by the Tennessee Supreme Court might be instructive and helpful, but it would not be precedent in Arizona.

SECTION 1.15 ACTIONS AGAINST PUBLIC ENTITIES

The discussion in this chapter has assumed that the litigants are private individuals or business entities, such as partnerships or corporations. Different rules apply when the defendant is a public entity. Most of this is traceable to the desire to protect the public revenues from unjustifiable or onerous claims.

At various points in American and English legal history, public bodies were completely insulated from being sued by private citizens. This was based upon the theory of "sovereign immunity from suit." Many states, either by statute or case decision, have given up, or have lost, immunity from suit. The trend is toward limiting sovereign immunity and expanding the right of citizens to sue federal, state, and local governments. However, because of a basic governmental policy designed to protect public funds and to avoid unnecessary delay or harassment of public agencies, the party suing a governmental unit must carefully check to see that all the procedural requirements for law suits against governmental units are carefully observed.

Frequently, statutes or ordinances require that claims against a public body be made within a shorter period of time than claims that are brought against private parties. Also, statutes frequently require that claims be presented to the legislative bodies of the governmental unit within a specified period, before any court litigation can commence. For example, it is often required that claims against a city be brought before the city council for consideration before any litigation may be initiated.

For additional discussion of sovereign immunity see § 30.12.

REVIEW QUESTIONS

1. What is the difference between the function of a trial court and an appellate court?

2. Under what circumstances may an action be brought in a federal court?

3. Why does the law set time limits for the commencement of legal actions?

4. What are the ways in which attorneys are compensated for performing legal services?

5. What is the principal differentiation between courts of law and courts of equity today in the United States?

6. Give an illustration of a provisional remedy?

7. What is the purpose of the pleadings?

8. What is a pretrial conference?

9. What role does the judge serve in an adversary system of litigation?

10. In what ways are law suits against public bodies different than law suits against private persons?

Chapter 2
CONTRACT FORMATION PRINCIPLES

SECTION 2.01 RELEVANCE

The design professional will be a party to a number of different types of contracts in his professional life. If he is in private practice, he will make contracts with clients, consultants, landlords, sellers of goods, and many other persons. In addition, he will be closely involved with contracts between owners and prime contractors, prime and subcontractors, contractors and suppliers, buyers and sellers of land, and brokers and property owners. If he is an employee, he will see many of these types, and may also enter into a contract with his employer.

In other parts of this treatise, specific contracts will be analysed. This chapter will provide framework for these analyses.

SECTION 2.02 SOME BASIC POLICY CONSIDERATIONS

The basic function of contract law is to protect reasonable expectations. When agreements are made, each party expects that the other party will perform in accordance with his promise. Much of the world's commercial activity depends upon the expectation that certain things will be done as promised. Judicial enforcement of contracts helps to insure that people can plan their activities in reliance on the promised performance of others.

Generally, American law permits contracting parties to determine their rights and duties, as long as they comply with the legal requirements for a valid contract. Giving the parties such autonomy in part is predicated upon the belief that the contracting parties know best how to allocate the risks. Deciding the substantive content of all contractual relationships would cast a heavy burden on the state. Also, parties are more likely to perform if they have participated in making the rules.

However, freedom of contract assumes two parties of relatively equal bargaining power who jointly negotiate an agreement. Through the development of mass produced contracts and the emergence of large blocs of economic power, this earlier model of the negotiated contract has become the exception. If the state, through its courts, enforces "adhesion" contracts (contracts presented on a "take it or leave it" basis,) the state is according almost sovereign power to those who have the economic power to dictate contract terms. For this reason, there have been many inroads made upon contractual freedom. These inroads have been made by federal and state legislation, by the emergence of administrative agencies with the power to regulate certain types of contracts, and by courts through their power to interpret contracts and to determine their validity.

SECTION 2.03 PRELIMINARY DEFINITIONS

Frequent reference will be made to the "promisor" and the "promisee." The promisor is a person who makes the promise, and the promisee is the person to whom it is made. In most two-party contracts, each party is both a promisee and promisor. He makes promises, and he has promises made to him.

There will be reference to the terms "offeror" and "offeree." The offeror is a person who makes an offer, and the offeree is a person to whom it is made. All other definitions will be given at the time the particular term is being discussed.

SECTION 2.04 CONTRACT CLASSIFICATIONS

(A) EXPRESS AND IMPLIED

Contracts are classified in many different ways. Sometimes they are classified by the method of creation. In this sense there are "express contracts" and "implied-in-fact contracts". Express contracts are agreements in which the parties manifest their assent or agreement by oral or written words. Implied-in-fact contracts have the same legal effect, but the assent is manifested by acts rather than by express words. For example, if a person takes his suit to be dry cleaned, not a word may be exchanged between customer and dry cleaner. The customer may hand over the suit and take the receipt from the dry cleaner. Even though no words were spoken, it would be implied that the dry cleaner would clean the suit, and that the customer would pay a reasonable or the posted price for the service. Unless the agreement is one required to be in writing, the implied-in-fact agreement is just as valid as an express contract. However, it is made in a different way.

(B) BILATERAL AND UNILATERAL

Sometimes contracts are classified as either "bilateral" or "unilateral". In a bilateral contract, there is an exchange of promises, with each party promising to perform and also receiving the promise of the other. A bilateral contract is a two or more party contract, with obligations on the part of each party.

The unilateral contract does not involve an exchange of promises. Instead, it involves the exchange of a promise for an act. In unilateral contracts, the promisor requests an act but the promisee does not promise to perform the act. If the act is performed, the promisor is obligated to perform in accordance with his promise. In the unilateral contract, there is one promisor and one promisee. The promisor requests an act in exchange for his promise.

(C) SUBJECT MATTER

Sometimes contracts are classified by the type of transaction involved. Using this classification, there are sales of land, sales of goods, loans of money, leases, service contracts, professional service contracts, insurance, and family contracts. While traditionally American contract law was thought of as one unitary system, different types of transactions are treated in different ways. This tendency is manifested by regulatory legislation over certain types of contracts, as social needs develop. Also, some judicial opinions treat one type of transaction differently from another type.

(D) BARGAIN AND ADHESION

Contracts are sometimes classified as either "negotiated" or "adhered" to. The latter are referred to as "contracts of adhesion." A negotiated contract is self-explanatory. It arises when two parties with a reasonably equivalent bargaining power enter into negotiations. Each presumably will give and take, and then both parties will draw up a mutually satisfactory agreement.

In the adhesion contract, there is no bargaining. The dominant party hands the contract to the weaker party on a take or leave it basis. There is no opportunity to bargain, and, if the weaker party wishes to enter into the transaction at all, he must accept the terms of the stronger party.

Sometimes the adhesion contract is accompanied by a form of monopoly. In a competitive economy, if the weaker party does not want to accept these terms, he may deal with someone else. However, in many types of transactions he will find the same terms used by other competitors of the person whose terms he found unpalatable, or he will find no competitor. Frequently, such adhesion contracts are printed, and the person with whom the weaker power is dealing (such as a salesman or clerk) may have very little authority to vary the printed terms of the contract. While traditionally all contracts were considered to be of one type in American law, there is a strong tendency today to recognize the basic difference between the negotiated contract and the contract of adhesion.

SECTION 2.05 QUASI–CONTRACTS

Some reference should be made at this time to the doctrine of "quasi-contract". Situations develop where one party has enriched another party and asks that the latter pay for the benefit which has been conferred upon him. This form of enrichment can occur in many different contexts. It can occur in the framework of a contractual obligation. A contractor who builds a building has enriched the owner, and there are times when the contractor can measure his recovery against the owner by the benefit that has been conferred. This is unjust enrichment in a contract context.

Sometimes there is unjust enrichment because of a wrongful act (a "tort"). One illustration of this is the unauthorized removal of timber from another person's land. In such a case, the wrongdoer has been benefited by the removal of the timber. The injured party may choose to measure his recovery in a civil action not by value of the timber taken, but by the use made of the timber or by any price received by the wrongdoer. This may exceed the reasonable value of the timber. Yet it would be unjust to permit the wrongful party to retain the fruits of his wrong.

A third illustration is a benefit conferred by mistake. For example, one land owner may build an improvement on his neighbor's land, thinking it is his own, or one person may pay a bill owed by someone else because of the mistaken belief that it is his bill. The right to recover from the person benefitted does not depend upon contract or a wrongful act, but upon unjust enrichment.

SECTION 2.06 CAPACITY TO CONTRACT

Parties must have had the legal capacity to enter into contracts to obtain judicial enforcement. The difficulties in this area have involved transactions by minors, married persons, and persons of limited mental capacity. Generally, the contracts of a person under 21 are voidable at his election. The minor can choose to hold the other party to the contract by ratifying it, or he may disaffirm the contract. However, the minor is liable for contracts that he makes for necessaries. Necessaries would include at least shelter, clothing, food and medical expenses. The concept of necessaries has been expanding and would probably go beyond these basic elements today. There have been many statutory changes which have recognized the earlier maturity of young persons, with special reference to the increasing tendency for persons to marry under 21 years of age.

The same general rules apply to persons with limited mental capacity who do not understand the subject of the contract, its nature, and probable consequences. They may be responsible for necessaries, but on the whole, their contracts are voidable. The determination of whether to ratify a voidable contract often is made by a guardian, or by the contracting person himself if the disability, such as age or capacity, is removed.

Under early legal doctrines, married woman had no capacity to make contracts. However, statutes have been passed in most states giving her the right to make contracts.

SECTION 2.07 MUTUAL ASSENT

(A) OBJECTIVE THEORY OF CONTRACTS: MANIFESTATIONS OF MUTUAL ASSENT

The early history of contract law in England placed great emphasis upon the volitional or "will theory" of contracts. The law would impose a legal obligation only if a party actually, which meant, subjectively, intended to bind himself. Many cases said that there had to be a "meeting of the minds." This meant that there had to be actual agreement before there could be a valid contract.

This approach has obvious disadvantages. If one person harbors a secret intention not to be bound, and yet manifested to the other party an intention to be bound, the party who relied upon the objective manifestation should be protected. The law chose to protect the reasonable expectations of the innocent party. This was called the "objective theory". A party is bound by what is manifested to the other party, and not by secret intentions. In most cases, there is a "meeting of the minds," but there need not necessarily be actual agreement. If one party, innocently or otherwise, misleads the other into thinking that a serious contractual intention exists, there can be a contract despite the lack of actual agreement of the parties. The same principle holds true if one party is only joking when he enters into negotiations and makes an agreement with the other party. Unless the other party should reasonably have realized that the negotiations were not serious, the party who is not serious will be held to the agreement.

(B) OFFER

The mutual assent process usually involves an offer and acceptance. This is a mechanism by which people come to agreement. The mere fact that people are in agreement does not necessarily mean they have a contract. The best illustration of this is what is called "cross-offers." Suppose two parties independently manifest an identical intention relating to a particular transaction, but not to each other. Even if the two proposals match, there will not be a contract, because mutual assent usually means that there must be not merely agreement but assent to the other party's proposal.

The first analytical step usually involves the determination of whether one party has made an offer to the other. There are a number of complicated definitions of an offer. It is more useful to consider the *effect* of an offer, as part of the method of determining whether an offer exists. An offer is said to "create a power of acceptance in the offeree." This means that the offeree can close the deal without any further act of the offeror. How is it determined whether the offeree has a reasonable belief that he can form a contract by his acceptance?

Some courts place great emphasis on the language of the offer. This is more true in the case of written offers than it is in oral offers, because it is often difficult to know the exact language of an oral offer. The courts look for definite words of commitment on the part of the offeror. The courts would like to find words, such as "I offer", or "I promise." However, this is not often the case. People do not always express themselves in legal terms.

It is most likely that the court will look at the entire language of the written proposal, to see whether or not a reasonable person receiving it would think he could close the deal. They look at the certainty of the terms, any indication that the proposer will not have to take further action, the past dealings between the parties, and the person to whom the offer is made. For example, if nothing is stated on certain essential issues such as price, or quantity, or quality, the parties are probably in a preliminary stage. The first proposal is intended merely to start the negotiating mechanism, and there will be more negotiating before there will be an agreement.

Also, if the offeror is negotiating with a number of other persons at the same time, and the person to whom a particular proposal is directed knows of this, it is likely that he realizes, or should realize, that the proposer wants to have the last word rather than risk being obligated to a number of persons. In such a case, the communication is probably not an offer.

Other illustrations could be given, but the essential principle is clear. Can the offeree reasonably believe that he can close the deal without any further acts of the offeror? In addition to this, there must be sufficient certainty, so that if a dispute arose the court would have some reasonable basis for determining the exact nature of the agreement. In most cases, if the offeree can reasonably expect that he can close the deal, sufficient certainty is likely to exist. Without certainty in terms the offeree normally knows that there must be further communication on the part of the original proposer.

One of the important principles of American contract law is that offers are generally revocable. At any time before acceptance an offeror can withdraw the offer, provided he communicates the revocation directly or indirectly to the other party. This is so even if the offer itself states that the offer will be held open for a specified period of time. This rule of revocability has caused problems, and there are important exceptions to the rule.

(C) ACCEPTANCE

Suppose a written offer states that it will be open for a specified period of time such as ten days. At the expiration of this period, the power of acceptance terminates. If the offer is made by letter, it may not be clear when the time period commences. It could commence on the date of the letter offer, at the time the letter is mailed, at the time when it would normally be received or at the time when it is actually received. Usually it is held to begin when it is actually received. To avoid this problem, it is advisable to use a specific terminal date.

If no time is stated for the duration of the offer, the offer will remain open for a reasonable time. The determination of reasonableness depends upon the facts. Facts considered are the state of the market for the goods or services in question, the need of the offeror to be able to deal with others in the event the offeree does not decide to accept, and custom and usage in the particular transaction. All of this is judged from the viewpoint of the offeree. His reasonable beliefs as to the duration of the offer will usually govern. The reasonable time to accept an offer for the sale of shares of stock in a fluctuating market will usually be much shorter than the reasonable time to accept an offer dealing with the sale of land. The time to accept the offer to sell perishable goods may be considerably shorter than the time to accept an offer to sell nonperishable goods.

An offer can terminate in other ways than by expiration of a time period. One already mentioned is a revocation by the offeror. In most states, this revocation must be communicated to the offeree. When the offeree receives the revocation, he knows that he can no longer accept, and, if he is still interested, he must make another proposal to the original offeror. As has been stated, this power of revocation frequently exists despite a specified time limit in the offer. Under the Uniform Commercial Code (which governs sales of goods in virtually all states), in goods transactions a "firm" offer is irrevocable for the time stated or, if no time is stated, for a reasonable time not to exceed three months. A "firm" offer is one made between merchants, in writing, and signed separately in some cases.

In addition to revocation, an offer may terminate if it is rejected by the offeree. Sometimes the rejection is explicit. The offeree may communicate and say that he is not interested. In such a case, the offeror is free to deal with others. Sometimes rejection is implied if the offeree makes a counter offer. The normal expectation of the offeror in the event of a counter offer is that the offeree is no longer interested in doing business on the basis of the original offer. This implication may be negated, if the counter offer makes clear that the offeree would still like to have time to consider the original offer. However, in most cases a counter offer is considered a rejection of the original offer. A counter offer then has two functions: It creates a power of acceptance in the original offeror, and it terminates the power of acceptance of the original offeree. Western Contracting v. Sooner Construction, reproduced at § 2.07(j) illustrates these problems.

An offer is also terminated by the death of the offeror, whether or not the offeree knows of the death. This is an illogical rule. The purpose of enforcing contracts is to protect reasonable expectations. If the offeree does not know of the death, he may be relying upon the offer which, as far as he knows, is still open. In dealing with a corporate offeror, there is no problem, but death can present problems when offerors are partners or sole proprietors.

Also, destruction of the subject matter of the contract prior to acceptance usually terminates the power of acceptance. This is analogous to the death rule, and can operate unfairly if the offeree does not know of the destruction. In the event of these types of events occurring, it makes sense for the persons who know of the events, such as the family or business associates of the deceased offeror, or the offeror himself in the case of destruction of the subject matter, to notify the offeree that the power of acceptance no longer exists.

The acceptance must be sent or communicated while the power of acceptance still exists. Any acceptance after that time does not operate to create the contract without a further act by the offeror.

An offer must be accepted by the person to whom it was made. The theory behind this rule was that a contracting party could choose with whom he wished to contract. Today, laws in many states have limited this right by requiring that a seller or landlord of certain types of property not discriminate by reason of race, religion or national origin in the sale or rental of real property.

The acceptance generally must be absolute and unequivocal. It must not propose new terms, and must accept the terms proposed by the offeror. If the acceptance states that it is accepted *if* certain things happen, this is likely to be a qualified and not unequivocal acceptance.

Another problem relates to the suggestion of additional terms, or changes of terms, from the original offer. Generally, any modification of the original terms of the offer is fatal to the acceptance. However, in some cases, offerees accept the basic proposal but make suggestions on other matters.

The tendency is to treat the acceptance as effective and that these suggestions be considered proposals which may be accepted by the offeror. The question of whether the additional proposals or suggested changes are counter offers or merely suggestions should be judged from the position of the offeror. If the offeror can reasonably believe that these do not condition the acceptance, then the contract is formed on the terms of the original offer. He may have some obligation to reply to these suggestions. If he does not, he may find that he has acquiesced in them. However, the insertion of suggestions within an absolute acceptance will not prevent the acceptance from forming the contract. See Western Contracting v. Sooner Const. which is reproduced at § 2.07(j).

Most offerors want to know whether the offeree has accepted. For this reason acceptance, as a rule, must be communicated to the offeror. It is possible for the offeror to deprive himself of the right to receive actual notice of the acceptance. The offeror could state that "if you accept, sign the letter and you need not communicate any further with me."

(D) CONTRACTS BY CORRESPONDENCE

Generally, offers, revocations and rejections must be communicated to the other party to be valid. Since the basis for contracts is protection of reasonable expectations, it is essential that contracting parties know where they stand. However, a special rule has been developed with regard to acceptance.

When parties began to make contracts by correspondence, English courts adopted the "mailbox" or "dispatch" rule. If the offeree used the same means of communication as the offeror had employed, the acceptance would be effective when posted, and did not have to be actually received. For example, if the offeree posts an acceptance to the offeror, in response to an offer received by post, and if the address on the letter of acceptance is correct and the proper postage placed on the letter, the contract is formed at the time the letter is mailed. This rule places the risk of a delayed or lost letter upon the offeror, and protects the offeree's expectation that when he posts the letter he has formed a contract.

One aspect of this rule is often ignored. The rule only applies if the offeror has not specifically required that there be actual communication. For example, if the offeror makes his offer by mail, but states that he must receive word as to whether the offeree accepts by a specified date, then the contract is not formed unless the offeror has actual receipt of the offeree's acceptance by the stated date.

Suppose the offeree uses a different method of communication then the one chosen by the offeror. For example, the offer may come by mail, and the acceptance be sent by telegram. Also, the offer may be sent by wire, and the acceptance may be sent by airmail, special delivery. A strict application of the rule would require that only the same means of communication would enable the offeree to take advantage of the "mailbox" rule. However, this type of inflexibility has not been satisfactory, and the tendency today is to permit the offeree to form the contract at the point in time when he places his acceptance in any reasonable means of communication, provided that actual communication has not been specified in the offer.

(E) A MORE FORMAL DOCUMENT

Another area that has caused difficulty involves those transactions which are informally concluded, but where the parties expect that a more formal document will be drawn up. The basic question is whether they have intended to bind themselves, with the formal written document only to be a memorial of their actual agreement, or whether they do not intend to bind themselves until they assent to the more formal writing. This depends upon the intention of the parties.

Unfortunately, if a dispute develops, the parties are likely to have contrary intentions, depending upon the position they are trying to sustain. If there is evidence of this intention in their early agreement, the result is reasonably simple. If they state that they do not intend to bind themselves, or that they do intend to bind themselves, there is no difficulty. However, many times such specific statements as to the parties' intentions do not exist. In such cases, one can only look at the facts. If the transaction is complicated, non-routine, and the basic agreement is sketchy in form, it is likely that the parties do not intend to bind themselves until the more formal writing is drawn up and assented to. Sometimes the courts look at whether the parties have commenced performance before the more formal writing is prepared. If they have, it would tip the scales in favor of finding a contract at the earlier stage. Performance by one party would be less conclusive. In many cases, parties commence performance while not intending to bind themselves until the more formal document is prepared and signed. If no contract is made, the party receiving the other party's performance would be liable in quasi-contract, based upon unjust enrichment.

If there is any trend to be discerned in these cases, it is towards finding a contract at the earliest possible stage if the court is convinced the parties intended to be bound and only minor gaps need to be filled in.

(F) UNILATERAL CONTRACTS

Unilateral contracts are transactions where the offeror requests an act in exchange for his promised performance. Courts look at the language of the offer to see whether the offeror has asked for an act or a promise. Unfortunately, offerors do not always think precisely about the method of acceptance.

The problem that has caused the greatest difficulty is the revocability of the offer. If the court finds that the offeror has requested an act which takes a period of time to perform, problems develop when the offeror attempts to revoke after the offeree has commenced performance. The courts have solved some of these cases on a quasi-contractual basis, by requiring that the party receiving performance pay on the basis of benefit conferred. However, in some cases the performance has not enriched the offeror. For this reason, various devices have been developed to protect the offeree who commences his performance.

In such a case, the court might resolve a close question in favor of holding that the offeror was requesting a promise rather than an act. The court might find that the act itself was in the nature of a promise which obligated the offeree to continue performing, and so deprived the offeror of his power of revocation. Some cases have held that the offeror has made a collateral offer not to revoke if the offeree commences performance. Also, as has been mentioned, in the sale of goods some offers are "firm" and cannot be revoked.

(G) IRREVOCABLE OFFERS

Mention has been made of the "firm" offer in the sale of goods. Despite the normal rule of revocability there are other irrevocable offers. One of the most common irrevocable offers is the option. This is the device by which a great deal of land is marketed, and is also used in the marketing of other types of property. The normal "always revocable" rule does not apply if the offeree has paid something to make the offer irrevocable. In the sale of land, the owner may give an option to a prospective buyer. For the option, the latter may pay a nominal amount of money to the owner. If this nominal amount of money is exchanged at the time the option is created, then the option is irrevocable and the owner has no power of revocation. This creates a one-sided contract, with the owner being bound for the specified period of time or for a reasonable time, if no time is specified, and the prospective buyer not bound at all. Often, the amount of money paid for the option has no bearing on the value of the option. It is only exchanged with a view toward making the offer irrevocable.

(H) AUCTIONS

An institution that antedates modern contract law is sale by auction. An auction consists of the auctioneer asking for bids, with a view towards obtaining the best price for the property to be sold. In most auctions, the auctioneer can withdraw the item from the auction if he does not believe he has obtained a high enough price. In those cases, the high bidder has no right to receive goods. He has a right to receive goods only when the hammer is struck, which concludes the contract on the basis of the highest bid. The bidder can withdraw the bid prior to the fall of the hammer.

Some auctions are advertised as being "without reserve". If so, the auctioneer must accept the highest bona fide bid once bidding begins.

(I) OFFERS TO THE PUBLIC

Offers made to the public, such as advertisements or rewards, are another specialized type of contractual arrangement. What if the action or information requested in the reward is provided without knowledge of the offer? It has been held that the person who performed the requested act without prior knowledge of the offer cannot collect. This rule has not been followed in the case of offers made by public agencies, and has had some exceptions in private rewards.

Even more current are the problems related to advertisements. Originally, it was held that advertisements in the newspapers or by posting were not offers at all, but merely invitations to bargain. One of the reasons for this was the usual failure of the advertisement to specify any particular quantity of goods. Also, the offer was made to many persons. For these reasons, catalogs and brochures were held not to be offers.

However, a few advertisers have been held to the terms of their advertisements. If the quantity is specified, and most of the terms are set forth in the advertisement, complying with the terms of the advertisement will complete the unilateral contract as long as the announced quantity lasts. There is an increasing tendency on the part of courts to use contract liability to "punish" deceptive and fraudulent advertising.

Offers to the public raise difficult questions of revocability. It is often impossible for the offeror to withdraw his offer, since he cannot actually communicate withdrawal of the offer. In order to give the offeror some means of revoking his offer, the rule developed that the offeror could revoke the offer if he used the same means of communication as were used in the offer itself. For example, if a reward were posted in a public place in the center of town, the revocation would be effective if posted in the same place and in the same manner. If, however, the offeror knows of persons who are trying to comply with the terms of the offer, common sense dictates that he notify those persons and not rely on this useful, but still fictional, form of communicating revocation.

(J) AN ILLUSTRATIVE CASE: WESTERN CONTRACTING CORP. v. SOONER CONSTRUCTION CO.

WESTERN CONTRACTING CORPORATION v. SOONER CONSTRUCTION COMPANY

United States District Court of Oklahoma, 1966.
256 F.Supp. 163.

DAUGHERTY, DISTRICT JUDGE. This is an action by the plaintiff, Western Contracting Corporation, against the defendant, Sooner Construction Company, for breach of an alleged subcontract between the parties on a runway project at Tinker Air Force Base, Oklahoma. There was no written subcontract signed by the parties.

. . . From the evidence the Court finds that Sooner orally quoted certain unit prices on asphalt paving to Western prior to Western submitting its bid on the project for the prime contract. Western was successful on its bid. Thereafter, Sooner confirmed its orally quoted prices to Western by a letter dated March 25, 1963.[1] The oral

---

1.

Received after Bidding

Haskell Lemon Construction Co.
Road Building and Paving
Phone WIndsor 6–3357 P. O. Box 7118
OKLAHOMA CITY, OKLAHOMA

Western Contracting Corp.
Sioux City, Iowa
RECEIVED
Mar 28 1963

March 25, 1963

Western Contracting Corporation
400 Benson Building
Sioux City, Iowa
Gentlemen:
Congratulations on receiving the Tinker Field contract. I hope that it will prove to be a most successful job for you.
We would like very much to make a contract with you to do your asphalt paving work on this job. This letter is to confirm the prices which we quoted you at Forth Worth.

Item 9. Prime 48,150 gallons @ .19 Furnish, deliver and apply. .no brooming or blotting.
Item 10. Tack coat, 260 gal. @ .37
Item 11. Tack coat, 318 gal. @ .37
Item 13. Hot mix surface 17,220 T. @ $8.32, less 50¢ ton discount for payment by 10th of month
Item 14. Asphalt (85–100) 215,350 gal. @ .13
No quotation on item 12, 15, 16, 17 as they may be deleted.

We will be happy to help you in any way possible on this contract. We would appreciate your contacting us when you establish your job office here. We hope the job will prove to be both pleasant and profitable and that we will have the opportunity of working with you.

Yours very truly,
/s/ Haskell Lemon
Haskell Lemon
Haskell Lemon Construction Co.

quotes and the letter quotes were the same. Regarding the item of hot mix surface the price quote of Sooner was 17,220 tons at $8.32 per ton less a 50¢ per ton discount if payment is made by the 10th of the month. Sooner asked for the subcontract during these activities but the request was denied. During the period from March 25, 1963, the date of the above mentioned letter, until July 15, 1963, Western opened an office at Tinker and the parties had various contacts, telephone calls, and discussions regarding the possibility of a subcontract. Western was obtaining asphalt quotes elsewhere. On July 15, 1963, at Tinker a meeting was had attended by a Mr. Hastie for Western, a Mr. Lemon for Sooner, a Mr. Pybas, a superintendent of Sooner, and a representative or representatives of the United States Corps of Engineers. At the meeting discussions were had regarding the specifications, equipment and rolling stock. Hastie testified that after this meeting he for Western and Lemon for Sooner reached an oral agreement on the subcontract following which a form of subcontract, unsigned by Western, was forwarded by Hastie to Sooner for execution and return to Western for execution by Western at its home office in Iowa. On the hot mix surface this written subcontract submitted by Hastie contained a price of $7.82 per ton thereon but did not provide for payment by the 10th of the month. Rather, it provided for partial payments to Sooner, less a retained percentage of 10%, as Western was paid on estimates by the owner and final payment to Sooner upon complete performance of the subcontract within 45 days after final payment is received from the owner by Western. Lemon denied that an oral subcontract was agreed upon on July 15, 1963, with Hastie and denied that any discussions were even had whereby Sooner would agree to the $7.82 price with the retainage provision and final payment provision as above set out instead of payment for the hot mix surface by the 10th of the month. Pybas, who testified that he was with Lemon at all times going to, at and from the Tinker meeting on July 15, 1963, also denied any oral agreement on the subcontract or any discussions about the discounted price of $7.82 being agreeable without payment by the 10th of the month. Lemon testified that shortly after receiving the written subcontract from Hastie he called Hastie on the phone several times and objected to the lower price of $7.82 per ton without payment being provided for by the 10th of the month in accordance with his quoted terms. Hastie acknowledged several telephone conversations after July 15, 1963, with Lemon regarding the retainage and that Hastie suggested in one of these conversations a reduction of the retainage to only 50% of the work. Hastie further testified that Lemon never gave him an answer to this suggestion.[2]

. . .

2. This is the testimony of Hastie on these points:

"Q After you submitted Plaintiff's Exhibit A to Mr. Lemon, you say on July 18th, did you then have any further discussion with him?

A Yes, he called me on the phone on several occasions and we discussed certain of the terms of this submitted subcontract.

Q And what terms did you discuss, if you remember?

In late September, 1963, certain developments took place. Sooner sent a signed subcontract to Western to which it attached certain amendments, six in number, one of which called for full payment for each of the three phases of the work to be done by Sooner within 45 days of completion by Sooner of each phase in lieu of Sooner's requirement in its written confirmation of payment by the 10th of the month and Western's requirement in the written subcontract it prepared and submitted of the 10% retainage and the final payment in 45 days. Western wrote Sooner a letter advising Sooner that it was delinquent in the performance of its subcontract and that if Sooner did not correct this default in performance within five days Western would exercise its rights under the subcontract. Then on September 29 or 30, 1963, a meeting was held in Oklahoma City which brought a Mr. Shaller down from Iowa for Western. Shaller as manager of heavy construction for Western was over Hastie. At this meeting the six amendments were discussed one by one and Shaller disapproved the amendment about full payment in 45 days following each phase completion as well as two other amendments and in his own hand wrote "out" opposite each of the three amendments so disapproved. Shaller approved the other three amendments. In the language of Shaller, finally at this meeting "things were terminated". Under date of October 2, 1963, Western made a subcontract with Metropolitan Paving Company for larger unit prices as to all items (the price for hot mix surface—the largest item—was $8.53 per ton) and sues herein for the difference amounting to $16,957.08 plus interest, overhead and profit and other expenses.

. . .

A One of them was the retainage; he wanted the retainage reduced. The original retainage was ten percent in the total amount of the contract, and we agreed verbally to reduce that to ten percent of the first fifty percent of the contract.
Q To ten percent of the first fifty percent?
A Yes, and thereafter no further retainage.
Q And you did agree that Plaintiff's Exhibit A could be amended to that extent?
A Yes, we did.
Q And did you have any other conversation with him about any of the other terms?
A Another one of the terms that he wanted changed was that we would add a clause that he would not be responsible for keeping up with our schedule in the event of strikes, fire, flood, or things beyond his control.
Q And did you agree to that?
A Yes, we did.
Q Were there any other items that he discussed with you?
A Another one was that he wanted us at the end of each phase of the work—you understand there were three phases in this work.
Q What were the phases?
A We called them Phase One, Phase Two, and Phase Three.
Q What were they?
A They were portions of the asphalt shouldering on one of the taxiways. Phase One took a certain amount; Phase Two some more; then Phase Three the balance. And he wanted us to pay him in full for each phase of the work within forty-five days of its completion.
Q Did you agree to that?
A What I told him we could do would be if the Corps of Engineers would agree to pay us in full for each phase as it was completed, then we would pay him in full.
Q And did he agree to that?
A I don't recall he ever gave any answer to that."

15 Oklahoma Statutes, Section 71 provides:

> "An acceptance must be absolute and unqualified, or must include in itself an acceptance of that character, which the proposer can separate from the rest, and which will include the person accepting. A qualified acceptance is a new proposal."

Anderson v. Garrison, Okl., 402 P.2d 873 (1965) provides:

> "In order that a counter-offer and acceptance thereof may result in a binding contract, the acceptance must be absolute, unconditional, and identical with the terms of the counter-offer." . . .

It is true that the parties may have a binding agreement, provided they have reached one, even though they have the understanding that the agreement should be formally drawn up. This depends upon the intention of the parties.

Fry v. Foster, 179 Okl. 398, 65 P.2d 1224 (1937) holds:

> "Where parties to an agreement make its reduction to writing and signing a condition precedent to its completion, it will not be a contract until this is done, and this is true although all the terms of the contract have been agreed upon. But, where parties have assented to all the terms of the contract, and they are fully understood in the same way by each of them, the mere reference in conjunction therewith to a future contract in writing will not negative the existence of a present contract." . . .

Thus, the importance of what actually took place on July 15, 1963, between Hastie and Lemon—whether they reached an oral agreement or not—becomes apparent. Hastie says they reached an oral agreement. Lemon and Pybas say they did not. Hastie does not claim that the alleged oral agreement was reached in the presence of the representatives of the Corps of Engineers who attended the meeting, therefore, these representatives are not able to give any assistance to the problem. The Court is of the opinion and finds and concludes that Hastie and Lemon did not on July 15, 1963, reach an oral agreement on the subcontract or discuss and settle the price differential on the hot mix surface with reference to the two alternative prices quoted by Sooner and the effect of the method of payment on the same. It is believed that when Western prepared the subcontract shortly after July 15, 1963, it sought to take advantage of the lower quoted price without meeting the condition attached to the same regarding payment. To this Sooner promptly objected and Sooner did not sign and return the subcontract as requested by Western. Hastie admits that several telephone conversations immediately followed his mailing the subcontract he prepared, these telephone conversations coming from Lemon and that the subject matter of the calls had to do with the retainage provision of the submitted subcontract as it affected the price of the hot mix surface.

. . .

The Court, therefore, finds and concludes from the evidence that Sooner quoted a price of $7.82 a ton on hot mix surface provided payment was received for the same by the 10th of the month—otherwise the price would be $8.32 a ton; that the weight of the evidence indicates that this alternative quote and payment condition of Sooner was not changed or discussed on July 15, 1963; that Western in submitting a subcontract to Sooner set out the $7.82 per ton price but did not meet the payment condition attached to the same; that Sooner immediately and admittedly by several telephone conversations objected to this feature of the subcontract as submitted; . . . that while a period of several weeks lapsed before Sooner submitted its subcontract with amendments such lapse of time transpired in the face of and after objections were made by Sooner to the subcontract submitted by Western and particularly with reference to the use of the lower quoted price on hot mix surface without complying with the requested method of payment in the use of such price; that at the meeting on September 30, 1963, Western would not agree to the originally quoted alternative price of Sooner or its modification as later proposed by Sooner and terminated the matter . . . The Court is of the opinion that the parties never reached a meeting of the minds on the price and method of payment for the hot mix surface, the principle item involved. . . . In simple summary, Sooner quoted an alternative price on hot mix surface to Western, Western submitted a subcontract containing a price and method of payment different from each alternative, Sooner submitted an amended contract with still a different price and method of payment, this was not acceptable to Western and the matter was terminated by Western.

Plaintiff is, therefore, not entitled to the judgment it seeks.

The Court on p. 35 quoted an Oklahoma case which stated that the acceptance must be "absolute, unconditional, and identical with the terms of the . . . offer." Some courts are not as rigid in requiring absolute conformity. In this regard § 2–207 of the Uniform Commercial Code, which governs sales of goods, states:

(1) A definite and seasonable expression of acceptance or a written confirmation which is sent within a reasonable time operates as an acceptance even though it states terms additional to or different from those offered or agreed upon, unless acceptance is expressly made conditional on assent to the additional or different terms.

(2) The additional terms are to be construed as proposals for addition to the contract. Between merchants such terms become part of the contract unless:

(a) The offer expressly limits acceptance to the terms of the offer;

(b) They materially alter it; or

(c) Notification of objection to them has already been given or is given within a reasonable time after notice of them is received.

(3) Conduct by both parties which recognizes the existence of a contract is sufficient to establish a contract for sale although the writings of the parties do not otherwise establish a contract. In such case the terms of the particular contract consist of those terms on which the writings of the parties agree, together with any supplementary terms incorporated under any other provisions of this code.

SECTION 2.08 DEFECTS IN THE MUTUAL ASSENT PROCESS

(A) FRAUD AND MISREPRESENTATION

The negotiation process frequently consists of promises and representations made by each party. Suppose these representations or promises are made with the intention of deceiving the other party.

If there has been deception relating to factual matters or to promises, then the party who has been deceived can upset the transaction or receive damages, if the matter upon which he was deceived was important, and if he reasonably relied upon the representations. Earlier cases required that everyone check out representations for himself. However, the courts have gradually recognized that this is not always a feasible course of action. For this reason, the concept of reliance has been loosened in favor of the party who claims to have been deceived.

Sometimes the misrepresentation is not fraudulent, but merely the result of a mistake. As the conduct becomes less morally reprehensible, it becomes more difficult to upset the transaction. However, the courts have moved toward permitting cancellation of the contract if there are innocent misrepresentations. Damages cannot be collected for innocent misrepresentations.

What if one party wishes to upset the transaction, because the other party should have disclosed material facts which, if known by the former, would have induced him not to enter into the transaction. This is illustrated by the case of Kannavos v. Annino, 247 N.E.2d 708 (Mass.1969). In this case the buyer was a Greek immigrant with a high school education who had no experience in purchasing real estate. He responded to an ad in the newspaper for the sale of a large single house. The ad indicated that the house could gross a specified amount of income since it was divided into eight units.

The buyer contacted a real estate broker who showed him the property and gave him income and expense figures obtained from the seller. The buyer had no lawyer to represent him. There were no statements made by the seller or inquiries made by the buyer as to zoning or code violations.

After the plaintiff purchased the property he was notified by the city that the property was being used for multi-family purposes in violation of the building code and zoning ordinances. Also, the wiring and the plumbing were illegal. When the plaintiff found this out he attempted to "rescind" the transaction. When a contract is "rescinded" (or a "rescission" is ordered by a court), the parties are to be placed in the same position they would have been in had the contract not been made. Each party returns whatever he has received under the contract terms, and each is freed from further contractual obligations.

In prior cases, Massachusetts required that there be some representation by the seller, and that a failure to disclose would not be sufficient. But in this case the Supreme Judicial Court of Massachusetts held that the buyer could recover his money. To a substantial degree the court was assisted by the representation made in the advertisement that the property could gross a certain amount of income, but it appears that the real basis for the decision was that the seller had a duty to disclose that the multiple use violated the zoning laws, and there were violation of building codes.

(B) DURESS

"Duress" is another method of attacking the validity of a contract. In bargaining, the parties frequently try to take advantage of their bargaining power. However, if one of the parties uses an excessive amount of pressure, or uses pressure which is beyond the rules of the bargaining game, duress may invalidate the agreement. Originally duress had to be physical; the easiest illustration was someone who was compelled to make a deed while under the threat of death. However, today the concept of "economic duress" is being recognized. Some types of pressures are not proper in bargaining. This is especially so if one of the parties is not well equipped to protect himself, and if the stronger party obtains an unconscionably large economic advantage as a result of the contract.

(C) MISTAKE

The doctrine used most often in attacking the formation process is "mistake". Here again, there are no fixed or absolute rules. There may be mistakes as to the terms of the contract. One party may not read the agreement, or due to mistake or fraud the agreement may not reflect the earlier understanding of the parties. Also, parties are often mistaken as to the basic assumptions upon which the contract was made. Everyone who makes a contract has certain underlying assumptions which, if untrue, make the contract undesirable.

A few generalizations can be made. While there is always some carelessness in the making of a mistake, the greater the degree of carelessness, the less likely it is that the party making the mistake will be given relief. Also, the courts look at the values exchanged in the contract. If one party is getting something for almost nothing, the courts will look very carefully to see if mistake can be employed as a means of relieving the other party from the contract. Finally, the question of when the mistake is caught is of great importance. If the mistake is caught before there has been reliance by the other party, or before there has been performance by the other party, a court may determine that the contract should not be enforced.

Honest misunderstandings may present the formation of a contract. One famous misunderstanding case involved the sale of cotton by a seller who intended to ship cotton by the ship Peerless. The buyer intended to buy cotton which was on a different ship Peerless. There were two ships Peerless, both carrying cotton and both at the same port. Each intended a contract for the ship he had in mind. Both parties were evidently reasonable, and neither was negligent. In such a case, the court found that there was no contract because of the misunderstanding. Neither party had misled the other, and neither party was guilty of any negligence.

The mistake cases show that the courts try to equitably apportion certain types of risks. However, the law also tries to prevent parties from relieving themselves of contracts by dishonest claims of mistake, when it proves economically advantageous to do so. Steering a course between these two policies, as well as respecting the policy that persons should be able to rely upon agreements, has meant that there are few fixed legal rules that can be used to predict probable results in these cases. Courts often speak of relief being granted if the mistake is mutual, or if the mistake goes to the "essence" of the transaction. However, there are corollary rules which can be applied to give a different result.

Not all risks are assumed by contracting parties and, in some cases, a party may be relieved from a contract he has made. A determination of whether relief will be granted requires a careful evaluation of the facts and the relative degree of negligence, the assumption of risk, disparity in the exchange values in the transaction, and the likelihood that the *status quo* can be restored.

SECTION 2.09 CONSIDERATION AS A CONTRACT REQUIREMENT

(A) FUNCTIONS OF THE CONSIDERATION DOCTRINE

Before examining the definition of consideration, it may be useful to understand the function of this doctrine. No legal system enforces all promises. Some promises are not important enough to enforce. For this reason, the law usually will not enforce a promise to attend a social event. Such promises, as well as others, are not made with the intention of creating a legally enforceable obligation.

The enforcement of some promises can disrupt an important institution. For example, if a 8 year old child could go to court to enforce a promise by his father to take him to the zoo, this could affect the viability of the family unit.

Some promises are made hastily or impulsively, without due regard for the consequences. Altruistic promises are often made without regard for the burden they can place on the promisor. Some promises are best left to other sanctions. For example, the law generally does not use contract law to hold politicians to their campaign promises, relying upon the ballot box to operate as a mechanism to pressure public officials to live up to at least some of their promises.

Finally, some contracting parties have used their bargaining power to impose harsh obligations on weaker parties, promising nothing of value in return. In extreme cases, this over-reaching may be restrained by denying enforcement to the weaker party's promise.

In English and American law the consideration doctrine has been the chief vehicle for determining which promises will be enforced by the courts. It operates as a limit on complete contract freedom.

(B) DEFINITIONS: EMERGENCE OF BARGAIN CONCEPT

There have been a great many historical studies of the consideration doctrine. Some scholars in England decided that the only valid consideration was the "benefit to the promisor", the one who had made the promise. If there was no benefit to the promisor, then his promise could not be enforced. However, other scholars searching through the cases saw that there were decisions which enforced a promise where the promisor did not receive pecuniary benefit. An illustration is the case of Hamer v. Sidway, 124 N.Y. 538, 27 N.E. 256 (1891), where an uncle promised his nephew that if he gave up drinking, using tobacco, swearing and playing cards or billiards for money until he became 21, he would be paid a specified sum. The court, in that case, could find no pecuniary benefit to the uncle, but found a detriment to the nephew. The detriment consisted of forebearing from acts which the nephew had a legal right to do. The scholars had to add "detriment" to the promisee as a basis for enforcing a promise.

Finally, in the twentieth century, the concept of "bargain" developed. Rather than looking for benefit to the person making the promise, or detriment to the person to whom the promise had been made, the courts examined the transaction to see whether there had been a bargain (exchange of promises and obligations). If there had been a bargain, then there was valid consideration.

This simple test is not always easy to apply, because there are times when what appears to be a bargain is not a bargain. For example, a wealthy man makes a promise to give a specified sum to his old college. Part of the understanding is that the college will name a building after the donor. This *may* be an exchange. The donor promises to give the money in exchange for having the building named after him. In many cases, there is no bargain in such a situation, but merely a case where the donor is adding a condition to his gift. In looking for a bargain, courts usually do not examine the fairness or adequacy of the bargain. In any event, the bargain concept, although difficult to apply, seems to be the principal test which determines whether there is consideration. Some promises may be enforced without a bargain under special circumstances.

In determining whether a contract has been formed, consideration can be analyzed under three headings: present, future, and past consideration.

(C) PRESENT CONSIDERATION

One-Sided Contracts

Present consideration is what has already been described as bargain. In these cases, the promisor makes a promise in exchange for a counterpromise by the promisee, acts of the promisee or a forbearance to act by the promisee.

Generally there is consideration in most commercial transactions. The most troublesome question relates to the "one-sided" contract. One-sided is used in the sense of each party making a promise, but the promise of one party being much more onerous than the promise of the other. Both parties are "tied" but one party is much more tied than the other.

For example, contract provisons may give one party the right to terminate a contract at his own convenience, or by giving a specified notice. In an employment contract, the contract may be for three years, with the employer being given the right to terminate by giving 30-day notice. In such a case, the employee is obligated for three years, while the employer may be obligated realistically for only thirty days.

Another illustration is the contract where one party can terminate his obligation if a contingency does or does not occur. For example, a buyer of a residence may include a provision that his obligation to close the deal is conditioned upon his obtaining specified financing, or upon being able to sell his own house. The occurrence of the condition upon which his performance depends may be an event over which he has substantial control. He may not try very hard to obtain financing, or he may refuse financing which may be reasonable. He may not try very hard to sell his house, or he may turn down offers which are reasonable. In some cases, the courts would uphold such a contract by finding that the buyer, in such a case, impliedly promises to use his best efforts, or to use good faith. Commercial contracts of this type usually are enforced. Nevertheless, these types of contingency contracts, where the condition rests largely within the power of one of the parties, are one-sided contracts.

Requirement contracts for the sale of goods are another illustration. In these cases, the buyer may promise to buy his requirements from the seller, and the seller promises to ship the buyer's requirements. If there is no minimum or maximum specified, the contract may be advantageous from the standpoint of the buyer, and onerous from the standpoint of the seller. The buyer may have substantial control over the quantity of goods he requires. Whatever he requires of the contractually specified goods must be obtained from the seller. However, the buyer may, by the operation of his business, substantially control his requirements and may decide to use the contract when the market justifies it, and not use it when the market does not.

By and large, such one-sided contracts are enforcible. In rare cases the contract is so one-sided that it will not be enforced. For example, if the employer reserves the right to terminate the employment of the employee by giving one day notice, the court might find that this is no real limitation upon his freedom and that the contract is too one-sided for enforcement. Although the tendency has been to uphold the validity of one-sided contracts, there are some limits.

Pre-existing Duty Rule

Sometimes parties to an existing contract decide to modify the contract. Generally, there must be consideration for the modification. Many legal difficulties have arisen in contract modifications where one party promises to pay more money in exchange for the other party performing his "pre-existing duty"—exactly what he was obligated to do under the original contract. Since modifications involving a pre-existing duty are more easily understood in the context of the particular type of contract involved, they will be discussed in § 2.12(c), relating to employment contracts, in § 19.01(h), relating to construction contracts generally, and in § 22.03, relating to modifications based upon discovery of unforeseen subsurface conditions.

A promise may be made by a third party to induce a party to a contract to perform. For example, the owner of property may promise a subcontractor (with whom he has no contractual arrangement) that if the sub-contractor performs his obligation, he will pay him a specified bonus. What the subcontractor gives in exchange for this promise is a promise to perform or the performance of services which he is obligated to perform for the prime contractor. Some early cases held that it was wrong for the subcontractor to be able to obtain money both from the person with whom he had made the contract and from a third party for the same work. Also, there was the fear expressed in some of these court decisions that the subcontractor, or other persons in similar situations, might indicate an unwillingness to continue unless promised more money by the third party. Nevertheless, the tendency in the cases today is to enforce such promises, even though what the promisee gives is performance of a sort that he is obligated to give because of the contract he has with someone else. If there is an element of duress or over-reaching on the part of the subcontractor, then perhaps the promise will not be enforced. However, the consideration requirement is met even though the performance is something that the promisee was obligated to render to a third party. For a state with a different rule, see Bailey v. Breetwor, at § 20.02.

Forebearance to Assert a Claim

"Forebearance", or the failure to act, can be the bargained for exchange which will make a promise legally enforceable. The forebearance may consist of not asserting a particular claim. This is frequently true in the settlement of a disputed matter prior to trial. In settlements, one party agrees to pay a specified settlement figure, in exchange for the other party's promise to forebear from legal action on the claim. Generally, such promises to forbear are sufficient consideration to enforce the promise to pay the settlement figure. However, if the party agreeing to forebear suing on the claim has no good faith belief in the merit of the claim, then the promise to forebear will not be sufficient consideration to enforce the promise to pay money.

Consideration is used to accomplish a social policy which is often obscured. This policy is to preclude people from blackmailing others by asserting claims in which they themselves have no good faith belief. Persons should not be able to use the threat of the legal process as a means of extorting money from other parties. Instead of courts basing denial of enforcibility upon duress, they have employed the doctrine of consideration to prevent such extortion.

(D) FUTURE CONSIDERATION

The concept of "future consideration" is usually described as "promissory estoppel" or "justifiable reliance". The concept of future consideration was an augmentation of the bargain concept developed in certain types of cases. One area was the charitable subscription cases. In these cases, promises would be made to a charity. Because of the necessity for planning, and because of the frequent reliance upon these charitable subscription promises, various doctrines were developed to give enforceability to these promises. One was that acts of a substantial nature in justifiable reliance upon the promise would supply the necessary consideration needed to enforce the promise. In these cases, courts began to use the doctrine of "reliance" as a supplement to the bargain concept.

Another type of case in which the concept of reliance was employed was in gift cases. Generally gift promises are not enforceable, but in some cases, courts have enforced a gift promise where there has been reliance by the person to whom the gift promise was made. In other cases courts have found an exchange, or used the detriment concept (as shown in the case discussed earlier involving the promise to the nephew). However, the concept of reliance has been used to make a gift promise enforceable only if the reliance is substantial and reasonable.

Other illustrations of reliance being used to enforce a promise are promises of bonuses made by employers to employees, and promises made by manufacturers to franchised dealers. The reliance in bonus cases is the employee's remaining on the job in order to obtain the bonus. The reliance in the dealer franchise cases frequently consists of expansion of the dealer's facilities and additional investments of capital. While it might be possible to find a bargained-for exchange in these types of cases, some courts have avoided the often tortured reasoning necessary to find a bargain, and instead have used the reliance concept to make the promise enforceable.

While the reliance concept is not as accepted as is the bargain concept, it is acquiring greater respectability and recognition by the law.

(E) PAST CONSIDERATION

The final, and least important, type of consideration is "past consideration". Traditionally, past consideration was not held to be consideration at all. Suppose an employer promises an old and deserving retired employee that the latter will be paid a certain bonus because of the employee's past services. In these cases, courts frequently held that the employer's promise would not be enforced because the employer received no value in exchange for the promise, nor was there any reliance by the employee. In these cases, the only possibility was that the past services would support the promise. Generally, this was not sufficient.

However, there have been a few types of situations where past consideration has been held sufficient. One of these is where a relative works for another member of the family over a period of years with a tacit understanding that there will be compensation. A subsequent promise by the person for whom the work had been done, that the person performing the services would be paid a specified amount of money, has been held enforceable, with the past services being the justification for enforceability. This type of past consideration is not particularly important in the commercial world and is used mostly in family transactions.

The other type of past consideration which has been held to be valid consideration involves promises to pay a debt which has either been discharged by bankruptcy or barred by the statute of limitations. Normally, when a debtor is discharged in bankruptcy, the debtor need not pay most of his debts. However, subsequent promises to pay a debt which has been discharged by bankruptcy have held to be enforceable. The justification given is that the past debt is sufficient consideration.

As stated in § 1.04, a debt must be sued upon within a specified period, or the debtor can use the defense of the Statute of Limitation.

Promises to pay contract debts which would be uncollectible because of the expiration of the Statute of Limitation have been held to be enforceable.

SECTION 2.10 PROMISES UNDER SEAL

When most men were unable to write, there had to be a method for accomplishing conveyances and other legal acts. The method adopted in early English legal history was the seal. The seal was an impression placed upon soft wax which had been put upon the document. The impression would be made by a ring or other type of instrument. It emphasized the seriousness of the act being performed. There did not have to be consideration, and a sealed instrument was a powerful document.

In the United States, the seal began to lose its mystic qualities when, instead of a formal impression in wax, the seal was reduced to either putting the word "seal" on the document, or using some abbreviation such as "LS". This did not have the trappings of formality possessed by the old seal. As a result, in many states, the seal was denied any function in the preparation of the documents. In some states, if the document is under seal, there is a presumption that there is consideration, but the other party can show that no consideration existed. In other states, the fact that a contract is in writing is presumptive evidence that there was consideration. In states which still use the seal, one need not look further than the seal to find enforceability.

SECTION 2.11 WRITING REQUIREMENT: STATUTE OF FRAUDS

(A) HISTORY

If the requisites of mutual assent are met, and if there is sufficient consideration, is a written document necessary? In 1677, the English Parliament passed the Statute of Frauds. The statute set forth certain important transactions and required that there be a sufficient written memorandum signed by the defendant before there could be judicial enforceability. There are a number of justifications given for the Statute of Frauds. One is to protect litigants from dishonest claims, and protect the courts from the burden of hearing claims of questionable merit. Also, the requirement of a writing was to act as a cautionary device. It was to warn persons that they were undertaking serious legal obligations when they assented to a written agreement. The Statute of Frauds has been adopted in all American jurisdictions, in one form or another. There has been a tendency to expand the classifications to include more transactions.

(B) TRANSACTIONS REQUIRED TO BE EVIDENCED BY A SUFFICIENT MEMORANDUM

The first step in the analysis of a Statute of Frauds problem is to determine whether the particular transaction is required to be evidenced by a sufficient memorandum. The transactions set forth in the original Statute were promises by an executor or administrator to pay damages out of his own estate, promises to answer for the debt, default or miscarriages of another, agreements made upon consideration of marriage, contracts for the sale of land or an interest in land, agreements not to be performed within a year from their making, and contracts for the sale of goods over a specified value.

In some states, there are statutes requiring that enforcible contracts for the performance of real estate brokerage services must be in writing, as well as contracts to leave property by will. The question of classification has been one device by which courts have cut down the effectiveness of this statute. For example, a contract to construct a five story building might not require a writing, since the court decisions have held that if the contract *could* be performed within a year, then there need not be a writing. Many other limitations and exceptions upon the various transactions have been made by the courts.

(C) SUFFICIENCY OF MEMORANDUM

If the transaction is one required to be in writing, the next step is to determine whether there was a sufficient memorandum. The memorandum need not have been signed at the time the agreement was made. A memorandum could be made subsequent to the making of the contract. For example, if one of the parties to the agreement wrote a letter after a dispute had arisen as to performance, and acknowledged having made the agreement, this letter would be a sufficient memorandum to bind the writer if there were sufficient terms given in the letter.

The party suing under the contract need not produce the memorandum. If he can show that it was lost, he can prove the terms of the memorandum by oral testimony. Finally, the memorandum must be signed by the defendant.

As for the contents, there are great variations. About the only safe generalization is that the memorandum must contain the basic terms, but need not specify all of the terms. Finally, the memorandum can consist of a number of writings.

(D) AVOIDING THE WRITING REQUIREMENT

Sometimes oral agreements which generally require a writing are enforced despite the absence of a written memorandum. Under the Uniform Commercial Code, which governs the sale of goods in almost all American states, acceptance of or part payment for the goods is sufficient to make an oral contract for those goods enforceable. However, non-delivery of any portion of the goods ordered under the oral contract which have not been accepted or paid for cannot be the basis for a legal action.

Another concept developed in cases involving the sale of land. In these cases, what was called the "part performance" doctrine was an adequate substitute for a writing. For example, if the buyer took possession and made improvements, the court could order that the conveyance be made, despite the absence of a writing. However, part payment by the purchaser was not held to be sufficient part performance. The distinction, while not logical, has continued to be applied in sales of land.

Another device for avoiding the necessity of the writing was also initially developed in the sale of land cases, but expanded to other types of transactions. The doctrine is called "estoppel," and is a flexible legal phrase for "fairness." At first, the estoppel concept was used by courts if one party represented to the other that he would make a written memorandum, but never intended to do so. This was fraud. Then there were cases which found estoppel if one of the parties represented that there was no necessity to have this particular transaction in writing. Finally, a few jurisdictions have used the estoppel concept if one person has reasonably relied and changed his position based upon the promised written agreement, or if the other party has been unjustly enriched by the performance. This concept was employed in the leading case of Monarco v. Lo Greco, 35 Cal.2d 621, 220 P.2d 787 (1950). A young member of the family had stayed and worked on the family farm, relying upon an oral promise that upon the death of certain relatives, he would obtain the property. He worked for many years on the farm, something he would have not done had the promise not been made. In this case, the court was faced with a statute which required that contracts to leave property by will must be in writing. The court held that there was justifiable reliance and unjust enrichment, and that the oral promise would be enforced. Most jurisdictions have not gone to this extent in employing unjust enrichment and reliance as devices to avoid the writing requirement. However, the tendency is in this direction. If there has been any reliance, or if refusal to enforce the contract would involve extreme unjust enrichment, in most jurisdictions there are legal devices which can be used to enforce the contract despite the absence of a writing.

The Statute of Frauds has been eroded in certain jurisdictions. If a party has a reasonably good claim, and if he has performed or relied, his attorney may be able to find legal doctrines which would permit enforcement of the contract despite the absence of a writing. However, in some jurisdictions, the courts still rely heavily upon the Statute of Frauds, and there will still be cases where parties are denied legal enforcement when it appears that they have a good claim.

SECTION 2.12 SOME SPECIAL PROBLEMS OF EMPLOYMENT CONTRACTS

(A) RELEVANCE

Many design professionals are employed by public and private employers. There are certain aspects of employment contracts which make them somewhat different from contracts generally.

(B) CONTRACTS FOR INDEFINITE PERIODS

Many employment agreements are sketchy. If an agreement is so vague and uncertain that a court cannot determine adequate terms, a court can find that there is no contract. If performance has commenced, a court is more likely to believe that a contract was intended by the parties. If the court believes that the parties intended a contract it may imply terms to fill in gaps. Examples are such terms as "reasonable time". The employment contract often does not indicate the period of time to be covered by the agreement. The early rule was that contracts for an indefinite period of time were agreements at will. This meant that the contract could be terminated at any time by either party. In essence, the contract governed the rights and duties of the parties as long as they were both willing to continue the relationship.

This "at will" rule was justified by the courts under several rationales. There was some feeling that the employer could never effectively enforce any contract against the employee, because it was likely that the employee would not be financially able to respond to any judgment. Also, courts would not in some cases specifically order that an employee not compete with the employer, despite a promise by the employee not to compete. Finally, the courts may have believed that the "at will" rule accorded with the intention of the parties.

There were some exceptions to the "at will" rule. If the employee gave more than merely his promise to work, he might be permitted to legally enforce the contract for a reasonable period. The something "extra" might consist of the employee moving to a distant city with his family, giving up another good job, or releasing the employer from a personal injury claim held by the employee. Many cases involved actions by railroad employees who had been injured in their work and were promised a job in exchange for releasing the employer railroad from liability.

There have been variations and changes in the "at will" rule. Some cases have held that the uncertainty of time was not fatal, and that the contract period would be 1) a reasonable time or 2) as long as the employee could work properly, or 3) as long as the employer was in business, or 4) conditioning the right to end the employment upon giving reasonable notice. Also, the employee had a better chance if he could show that the agreement was that the job would be "permanent".

(C) SPECIAL PROBLEMS OF CONSIDERATION

Not only were promises in employment contracts often vague as to time, but frequently there was no express promise by the employee to work for even an uncertain period. If the employee made no promise, could the employer be held? In some cases, the courts held that the promise by the employer was enforceable because of reliance by the employee on employer promises of a bonus or retirement pensions.

Some cases have involved the enforceability of promises to pay money made by an employer to a faithful employee *after* completion of a long period of service by the employee. Such promises could not fall into the "bargain" category, because the work was already performed. For the same reason, the courts could not apply the theory of detrimental reliance. In a few cases, the courts have held the promise enforceable because of the past services of the employee, or because the promise was a benefit to the employer in that the employer received employee good will from existing employees.

Another problem that has frequently arisen in employment contracts is the enforceability of a contract modification. During the period of employment, the employee may receive an offer of a better job. Suppose he informs his employer, and the employer promises to pay him more money for the same work for the same term. Generally, the employer's promise is not enforceable, because the employer received nothing for his promise other than the performance to which his contract entitled him, and the employee did no more than he was obligated to do under the employment contract. In such cases, some courts have used the pre-existing duty rule to deny enforceability to the employer's promise.

Perhaps the real basis for this position by the courts has been the feeling that this situation inherently involved duress and taking advantage of the employer. Yet, there have been many situations where there was no duress or unfairness. As a result, the law has developed "exceptions" to the normal rule in employment cases. If the employee's duties were changed in the slightest, the promise to pay more money would be enforced. Also, the courts sometimes have held that the old contract has been cancelled by the parties, and that the pre-existing duty rule does not apply. In some states, statutes were passed, stating that the modifications did not require additional consideration to be enforceable if the modifications were in writing. Perhaps these "exceptions" reflect a judicial and statutory recognition that the employee's right to try to improve his position is more important than holding him to his contract.

(D) WRITING REQUIREMENT

The Statute of Frauds requires that contracts which by their terms could not be performed within a year be evidenced by a written memorandum, signed by the party from whom performance was legally demanded. One escape from this rule is that a writing would not be required if the work could possibly be performed within a year. This could mean that employment of an engineer for a large project which might take two to four years would not have to be in writing, because the courts have been liberal in finding that the contract could be performed within a year.

If both parties have fully performed, the contract terms for payment will be enforced. In some cases, if the employee has fully performed, the contract will be enforced. If the employee has partly performed, this is usually insufficient to enforce the unperformed part of the oral employment contract.

Suppose there is an oral contract for over a year which gives one or both parties a right to terminate at will by giving a notice which terminates the relationship in a period of less than a year. Judicial holdings vary in such cases. Some courts have held that performance was possible within a year, because the notice could have been given at any time after the term commenced. Other courts have held that termination is not performance, and have held the contract unenforceable in the absence of a writing.

(E) COLLECTIVE BARGAINING

Many of the court-made rules regarding employment contracts have been made relatively unimportant by collective bargaining. Millions of employees are covered by agreements negotiated by unions on their behalf which cover wages, hours, promotions, working conditions, and tenure of employment. Disputes are usually handled by grievance procedures or arbitration.

(F) CIVIL SERVICE

Many employees have their rights and duties regulated by civil service. Statutes are passed by legislatures, and rules issued by administrative agencies, which deal with salary, wages, hours, working conditions, promotion, and discharge. Disputes between the public agency and the employee are first resolved by the administrative agency in an informal hearing. Courts go into such disputes only if the agency has abused its discretion, or if the agency has not accorded the employee a fair hearing.

(G) GOVERNMENT REGULATION OF PRIVATE EMPLOYMENT

Private law and the law of contract is of diminished importance in the field of employment relations. Collective bargaining is, to a certain degree, controlled by federal and state legislation. State laws also directly control millions of public employees. In addition, there is greater activity on the part of state and federal governments in regulating private employment. The best illustrations are in the area of wages, hours, working conditions, and employee selection. There are laws limiting the work hours of minors, and giving the employee extra pay for work over a stated minimum of hours per day or week. Minimum wage laws set a floor for wages for millions of persons. Laws require that employers not discriminate on the basis of race, religion, national origin or sex in selection or promotion of employees. See Chapter 36 for a discussion of legal regulation of the employment relationship.

SECTION 2.13 ADVICE TO DESIGN PROFESSIONAL

Despite the fact that oral agreements for the rendering of most architectural and engineering services need not be evidenced by a written memorandum, it is desirable to express the understanding of the parties in a clear and complete agreement.

When the contracting parties express their agreement in writing, the parties must focus upon the scope of the obligations and duties of the parties. Also, misunderstandings are less likely to arise when the agreement is reduced to writing, especially if the writing is a clear and complete expression of what the parties have discussed, negotiated and resolved. Finally, parties who feel that they have jointly worked out an agreement are more likely to comply with its terms.

The design professional should be aware of the difficulties which can arise when the issue is whether the parties do not intend to bind themselves until there is a more formal writing. In the negotiation stage, it is probably advisable for the design professional to make it quite clear, preferably in writing, that while the parties may have hammered out the essential terms neither party will be bound until they both have signed a written agreement which contains the entire contract.

Also, design professionals should be aware of the frequent attacks made upon the mutual assent process. They should set forth all the representations and promises in the written agreement. The background of the transaction and the objectives of each party should be specified in the contract, to assist a court in interpreting the document, and to avoid one party attacking the formation process by claiming that other, additional or different representations were made.

During performance it is important to make written memoranda of conversations, whether these are personal conferences or conducted on the telephone. These memoranda should be sent to the client for his comment, and should be kept in the file with all the other contract documents. Careful preparation and preservation of written records is essential.

The most important objective is to have a contract which sets forth a mutually agreeable set of rules designed to foster smooth performance by all the parties. The salient problems must be discussed, and a common understanding reached on most or all of them. This common understanding should be expressed clearly, concisely and completely in the contract.

REVIEW QUESTIONS

1. What is the "objective" theory of contracts?
2. Under what circumstances are offers irrevocable?
3. What is the legal effect of an offer?
4. What are the three main types of consideration? Give an example of each.
5. Which contracts must be evidenced by a sufficient memorandum?
6. What is the effect of a counter-offer upon the power of the offeree to accept the original offer?
7. How does contract differ from quasi-contract?
8. Generally, what is the legal effect of an employment contract without a specified duration?

QUESTIONS FOR CLASS DISCUSSION

1. Should the law ever enforce a promise made by a promisor who did not intend to bind himself? If so, when?
2. Do you think all contracts should be in writing before they should be enforced?
3. Why should contracts of adhesion be treated differently from truly negotiated contracts?
4. Describe the circumstances under which you have concluded a contract.
5. Why should there be a requirement of reasonable certainty before the court finds that a particular expression is an offer?
6. Should a person be held to terms in a contract which he does not understand? That he has not read?

7. Should the seller of a house have a duty to disclose prior slide damage? Window leaks? Noisy neighbors? Plans of a neighbor to build an addition which will substantially block the view?

8. Should courts go into the fairness of contracts before they decide whether to enforce them?

9. Under what circumstances is governmental interference with freedom of contract justified?

10. Why should legislatures and the Congress regulate working conditions, selection of employees and wages?

PROBLEMS

1. Buyer and Seller were negotiating for the sale of Seller's residence. After considerable discussion, Buyer and Seller signed a piece of paper with the following words:

> We agree to buy and sell the house at 4601 N. Bay Road owned by Seller for the price of $40,000, with a downpayment of $8,000 to be made within the next 48 hours, the balance to be paid within 60 days from this date. Price includes only the house. Possession in 60 days. Escrow and other details to be agreed upon.

On the next day Buyer said he was no longer interested. Did Buyer and Seller conclude a binding contract? Would your answer be affected if Buyer had paid the $8,000 and then asked for his money back?

2. B wanted an option to buy a lot owned by A. B gave A $5.00 in exchange for a written 30-day option to buy the lot at a specified price. A week later A told B to forget about the deal as he had a different purchaser in mind. Does B have a valid contract with A?

3. A is a president of the Acme Corporation and has two years left on a four-year contract, at a salary of $75,000 a year. He has been approached by a competitor and offered $85,000 a year. A tells this to the Board of Directors of Acme, and they raise his salary to match the offer of $85,000. A agrees to this. Is this modification of the original agreement legally enforceable? If not, how can it be made enforceable?

Chapter 3
THE AGENCY RELATIONSHIP

SECTION 3.01 RELEVANCE

Agency is a legal concept vital to architects and engineers. Agency rules, and their application, determine when the acts of one person bind another. In the typical agency problem, there is a principal, an agent and a third party. The "agent" is the person whose acts are asserted by the third party to bind the "principal". Also, there can be legal problems relating to the rights and duties of the principal and agent as between themselves, as well as disputes between the agent and the third party. But because the third party v. principal part of the agency triangle is most important, and most troublesome, these problems will be used to demonstrate the relevance of agency law to architects and engineers.

The design professional, whether in private practice or working as an employee, may find himself in any of the three positions of the agency triangle.

For example, suppose the design professional is a principal partner of a large office. Suppose the office manager, whether a partner or employee, orders an expensive copying machine. In this illustration, the design professional, through his status as a partner, is a principal who might be responsible for the acts of the office manager.

Now suppose the design professional is retained by a client to design a large structure. The design professional is also engaged to perform certain functions on behalf of the client in the construction process itself. Suppose the design professional orders certain changes in the work which will increase the cost of the project. A dispute may arise between the client and the contractor, relating to the power of the design professional to bind the client. Here the design professional falls into the agent category, and the issue is the extent of his authority.

Suppose A approaches a design professional in private practice regarding a commission to design a structure. A states that he is the vice-president of the T Corporation. The design professional and A come to an agreement. Does the design professional have a contract with the T Corporation? Here the design professional is in the position of the third party in the agency triangle.

Since the design professional can fit into any of the three positions in the agency relationship, he must understand the basic concepts of agency law. In addition, the agency concept is basic to understanding the different forms by which persons conduct their business affairs, such as partnerships and corporations.

SECTION 3.02 POLICIES BEHIND AGENCY CONCEPT

(A) COMMERCIAL EFFICIENCY AND PROTECTION OF REASONABLE EXPECTATIONS

As the commercial economy expanded beyond simple person-to-person dealings, commercial necessity required that persons be able to act through others. Principals needed to employ agents with whom third parties would deal. Third parties will deal with an agent if they feel assured that they will be able to look to the principal. The agent might be a person of doubtful financial responsibility. The concept of agency filled the need for giving third persons some assurance that they could hold the principal.

Agency exposes the principal to risks. The principal might be held liable for an unauthorized commitment made by the agent. For example, the principal might authorize his agent to make purchases of up to $1,000, but the agent might order $5,000 worth of goods. From the third party's standpoint, this $5,000 purchase might seem reasonable in light of the position of the agent, or what he had been ordering in the past. The law developed doctrines which dealt with the protection of the principal from unauthorized commitments, while protecting the reasonable expectations of the third person. The fact that problems such as this could develop did not destroy the unquestioned usefulness of the agency concept. Such problems merely meant that the law had to create rules and solutions to handle such questions which would accord with commercial necessity and common sense.

(B) RELATIONS BETWEEN PRINCIPAL AND AGENT

The relationship between principal and agent concerns the design professional, since he is often an agent and may be a principal.

As a rule, the relationship of principal and agent is created by a contract, expressed in words or manifested by acts. The agent may be a regular employee of the principal. He may be an independent person hired for a specific purpose, not controlled as to the details of his activities. Several aspects of the agency relationship make it different from the ordinary commercial, "arms-length" relationship.

An arms-length transaction is one where the parties are expected to protect themselves. In such a transaction, there is no general duty imposed upon one party to protect the other party, nor any duty to disclose essential facts to the other party. While there are some qualifications, generally commercial dealings are "arms-length". On the other hand, principal and agent have a fiduciary relationship, one of trust and loyalty. For more on this see § 8.02.

Often the arrangement under which an agent performs services is sketchy, and does not delineate all the rights and duties of principal and agent. This is especially true in agency relationships which involve the performance of professional services. The law has developed rules which govern the principal-agency relationship when the principal and agent, or employee and employer, do not expressly set forth their respective rights and duties in advance.

The agent, whether an employee or independent professional, often learns a great deal about the business of his principal which can be of value to third persons, such as competitors of the principal. Fiduciary obligations of loyalty are created by law to protect the principal from the possibility that the agent will pass on such inside information. For example, sometimes a court will order that a technical employee not disclose business or industrial secrets of his employer to third persons who would benefit commercially from access to such confidential information. (See § 40.09 for more on the controls over an agent or employee relating to trade secrets.)

Since the agent has a duty of loyalty toward his principal, his conduct and advice are to be rendered without any undisclosed conflict of interest. For this reason, a design professional should not have a financial interest in any contractor's business if he will have to evaluate the adequacy of that contractor's performance.

SECTION 3.03 OTHER RELATED LEGAL CONCEPTS

Often treatment of the agency concept includes a discussion of the legal doctrine of "vicarious liability." This concept imposes liability upon one person for the acts of another. Agency includes an element of vicarious liability. However, in this treatise vicarious liability will be discussed as part of the legal problems raised when one person causes physical or pecuniary harm to another, and the injured party attempts to recover his losses from someone other than the person directly causing the loss. Confusion often occurs because of the overlapping nature of terms such as principal-agent, master-servant, employee-employer, and independent contractor. This chapter will deal only with the principal-agent relationship, and the legal concept of the power of agency under which one person may bind another to a contractual obligation. Chapter 30 will treat vicarious liability.

SECTION 3.04 CREATION OF AGENCY RELATIONSHIP

Generally, agency relationships are created by a manifestation by the principal to the agent that the agent can act on the principal's behalf, and some manifestation by the agent to the principal that he will so act. However, these elements of consent are often rather informal. There need not be a writing, except in the case where certain statutes require that the agent's authority be expressed in writing if the transaction to be consummated by the agent is one which would also require a writing. There need not be an actual agreement by principal and agent. If the manifestations of the principal reasonably lead the agent to believe that he can act on behalf of the principal, usually the agency relationship is created.

In some cases, the agent need not promise to act on behalf of the principal. The element of consent may be supplied by the agent's performance of the acts requested of him by the principal.

SECTION 3.05 ACTUAL AUTHORITY

If an agency relationship has been created, the next question is that of the scope of authority of the agent. The agent is ordinarily authorized to do only what it is reasonable for him to believe the principal wants done. In determining this, the agent must look at the surrounding facts and circumstances. If, for example, the principal has authorized the agent to purchase raw materials to be used in a particular manufacturing process, and the agent then learns that the principal has decided not to proceed with the project, it is reasonable for the agent to believe that he no longer has authority to buy the materials.

The agent must consider the situation of the principal, the general usages of the business and trade, the object the principal desires to accomplish, and any other surrounding facts and circumstances which would reasonably lead him to believe that he can or cannot do something. This is largely a matter of common sense. Sometimes the agent is given specific authority to do a certain act; this gives him authority to do those incidental acts which are reasonably necessary to accomplish his primary act. For example, when an agent is given authority to purchase a car for the principal, it is likely that the agent also has authority to buy public liability insurance for the principal.

The agent, when possible, should seek authorization from the principal to perform those acts which are not expressly included in his actual authority. The primary burden is placed upon the principal to make the agent's authority clear.

Sometimes emergencies arise, and it is difficult or impracticable for the agent to communicate with the principal. In such cases, the agent is given authority to do those necessary acts to prevent loss to the principal with respect to the interests committed to the agent's charge. Such situations may arise in a construction contract. Frequently the architect or engineer is given authority to act in certain emergencies. Even without this express authority, the design professional should have authority to bind the principal if the acts are reasonably necessary, and inferable from his other authority. This should be judged from the point of view of the design professional.

SECTION 3.06 APPARENT AUTHORITY

Most of the difficult principal-agency cases arise under the doctrine of "apparent authority." Apparent authority exists when the principal's written or spoken words, or other conduct, reasonably lead a third party to believe that the principal consents to acts done on his behalf by the person purporting to act for him. If a principal appoints a sales representative, places him in an office and cloaks him with the indicia of authority, such as a phone listing, stationery, business cards and forms, the principal may have manifested to third parties that this sales agent has authority to make certain commitments.

Sauber v. Northland Ins. Co., 251 Minn. 237, 87 N.W.2d 591 (1958), which involved an action upon an automobile insurance policy, illustrates an application of the apparent authority doctrine. The plaintiff purchased a car which had been insured by the defendant insurance company. The plaintiff testified that he telephoned the insurance company, informed the defendant's clerk that he had purchased a car which had been insured by the defendant, and asked whether it would be all right if he drove the car. He further testified that he was informed over the telephone that it would be all right to do so. (An employee of the defendant testified that she had spoken to the plaintiff but denied stating that it would be all right to drive the car.)

One of the issues in the case was whether the clerk with whom the plaintiff had spoken had apparent authority to inform the plaintiff that he would be covered by the insurance policy. The Court held that it would be *presumed* that there was apparent authority stating: "Apparent authority in cases of this kind arises by virtue of the fact that: (1) The business has invited the public to use the telephone to transact business with it; (2) the business has permitted an employee to answer the telephone; (3) such person has purported to act for the business with authority; and (4) the person calling the place of business had a right to assume that the person permitted to answer the telephone had authority to act."

The presumption put the burden of proof upon the defendant insurance company to show that the plaintiff could not have reasonably believed that the clerk had authority to make the statement in question. Such a presumption means that if no evidence rebutting a reasonable belief in the authority of the agent is introduced by the defendant, the plaintiff wins. If the defendant introduces evidence which conflicts with the evidence of the plaintiff, the jury decides the question. In most cases, a presumption of apparent authority will enable the party claiming apparent authority to win.

Suppose a construction contract between the owner and the contractor gives the architect certain authority. However, the client may have informed the architect that he no longer has this power. Unless this change in authority comes to the attention of the contractor, the architect will have apparent authority. Because of the original contract provision, while the architect no longer has actual authority, he has apparent authority to bind the principal.

Apparent authority often protects a third party who has relied upon appearances. However, a third party unsure of the agent's authority should check with the principal. Application of the apparent authority doctrine is difficult to predict, and it may be necessary to litigate in a close case. Frank Sullivan Co. v. Midwest Sheet Metal Works, reproduced at § 3.12, illustrates a typical apparent authority problem.

SECTION 3.07 TERMINATION OF AGENCY

If the authority is conferred for a specified period, the authority will terminate at the end of this period. If no time is specified, the authority continues for a reasonable time. If the authority is limited to performing a specified act, or to accomplishing a certain result, the authority terminates when the act or result is completed. Sometimes the terms of the authorization specify that the authorization is to continue until a certain event occurs. If so, the occurrence of the event will terminate the agency unless the occurrence of the event would not come to the attention of the agent. Sometimes the loss or destruction of certain subject matter terminates the agency. In certain circumstances, bankruptcy of the agent will terminate the agency. The same result can follow if the principal is bankrupt.

Sometimes the agency terminates when principal and agent consent to terminate the relationship. This can occur if either principal or agent manifests to the other that the relationship will no longer continue. In some cases, the agency can also be terminated by death of the principal, and almost always by the death of the agent. However, agency relationships sometimes are created by contract for fixed terms. The principal may, despite a fixed term contract, terminate the agency and terminate the power of the agent to bind him, but such a termination would be a breach of contract with the agent.

These events affect the actual authority of the agent. If there has been termination of the authority, but there still exist manifestations to third parties that the agent has authority, the agent may be able to bind the principal by the doctrine of apparent authority. Apparent authority will only continue as long as the third party is not put on notice that the agent does not have authority to bind the principal.

SECTION 3.08 DISPUTES BETWEEN PRINCIPAL AND THIRD PARTY

In the bulk of the cases, the legal issue is whether the principal should be bound by the acts of his agent. In such cases, the third party seeks to hold the principal, and the principal contends that there was no agency, that the act was not within the agent's authority, or that there was no apparent authority. There have been sufficient illustrations of this given in §§ 3.05 and 3.06. Also, these cases will be discussed in § 25.02 which centers around the construction project and the authority of the design professional. Also see §§ 5.04 and 5.05 which deal with scope of authority in the context of the creation of the design professional-client relationship.

Sometimes the principal attempts to hold a third party, based upon a transaction between the principal's agent and the third party. The latter may refuse to deal with the principal, claiming he did not know he was dealing with an agent. The agent may not have informed the third party that he was an agent, and the third party may not have had reason to know that the agent was acting on behalf of someone else. The undisclosed principal may disclose his status and hold the third party, unless the facts would make it unjust to permit him to assert his status as principal. (Once the principal is disclosed, the third party can hold the principal.)

If the agent acts beyond his authority, the unauthorized act may be ratified (consented to and approved) by the principal. Suppose the agent did not have actual authority to enter into a transaction but the principal discovers the transaction. In such a case, the principal may ratify the transaction within a reasonable time and bind the third party (and himself) by notifying the third party and affirming the agent's unauthorized acts. Suppose the architect orders extra work without authority. The owner-principal may ratify the transaction by informing the third party contractor of his approval of the architect's act.

SECTION 3.09 DISPUTES BETWEEN PRINCIPAL AND AGENT: AGENT HOLDING PRINCIPAL'S MONEY

Section 3.02 discussed a few aspects of the fiduciary relationship between principal and agent. Because these concepts are more understandable in context, further discussion will be deferred until § 8.02, where the relationship between the design professional and his client is discussed.

One aspect of the fiduciary relationship merits special consideration here. This concerns the legal relationships which are created when the agent or employee holds money belonging to the principal or employer.

Frequently, an agent collects or holds money for the principal. The agent may be authorized solely to hold it, or he may be authorized to spend it for certain purposes. If the agent takes this money and uses it for his own purposes, or in some other unauthorized manner, the agent has stolen the money and committed a crime. The principal also has civil remedies in such a case.

Clearly the agent is obligated to repay the money. In addition, use of the money may have resulted in a profit to the agent. For example, he may have used the money to buy shares of stock or land which increase in value. If the principal can trace his money in whole or in part into the shares or land, that proportion of the whole of the shares or land attributable to his funds will belong to the principal. The agent is not to profit from his wrongful act.

More frequently, problems arise when the agent has mixed his own money with the money belonging to the principal. There may have been no intent to steal, but merely poor judgment by the agent in not keeping the funds separated. In such cases, the law will have to decide whose money was used if the money in the mixed fund is reduced in amount or disappears, or if the investment of mixed funds turns out well. If the use of the mixed fund is profitable, the principal will receive at least the proportion of the property purchased with the mixed funds that his funds bore to the mixed fund. The principal may even be held entitled to the entire property purchased with the mixed fund. Suppose the agent mixes $1,000 of his money with $1,000 of the funds of the principal. He then uses $1,000.00 to buy shares which increase in value. Some courts would give the principal one-half of the value of the shares, while other courts would give the principal all the shares. It would be very unlikely that the agent could claim that the money used to buy the shares was all his money.

If the mixed fund decreases in value, the law will presume that what remains is money of the principal. This presumption benefits the principal at the expense of the other creditors of the agent, since in these cases the agent is usually insolvent.

The agent, or his creditors, lose either way. For these reasons, and for other obvious ones, the agent should keep his funds separate from those of the principal.

SECTION 3.10 DISPUTES BETWEEN THIRD PARTY AND AGENT

Disputes between an agent and a third party are relatively rare. If the agent is acting on behalf of an undisclosed principal, the third party will have a right to sue the agent individually. The third party may lose this right if he pursues his remedy against the principal, once the principal becomes disclosed. If the agent has misrepresented his authority and the third party is unable to hold the principal, the third party may have an action against the agent for misrepresentation of his authority. For example, if the architect or engineer misrepresents his authority to order extra work, and the contractor reasonably relies upon this manifestation, the contractor may be able to hold the architect or engineer because of this misrepresentation. See § 21.11.

SECTION 3.11 NOTICE TO AGENT CONSIDERED NOTICE TO PRINCIPAL

In many situations, knowledge of, or notice to, the agent is equivalent to knowledge of or notice to the principal. For example, if the contractor informs the design professional that there is a defect in the plans, this is knowledge which is considered communicated to the client. Also, if notices of an intention to claim an extension of time or to present a claim for damages are delivered to the design professional, these will be considered notice to the principal. See § 25.02(a) for further discussion on this point.

SECTION 3.12 AN ILLUSTRATIVE CASE: FRANK SULLIVAN CO. v. MIDWEST SHEET METAL WORKS

The *Sullivan* case provides a good illustration of the agency doctrine in the construction contract context. It also provides a review of the material discussed generally in Chapter 2 and more specifically in § 2.07(e) as well as an advance look at the measure of recovery for breach of contract, a point to be discussed in greater detail in Chapters 11 and 29. However, its main purpose for inclusion at this point is the apparent authority question. (Another interesting apparent authority case is Bayuk v. Edson, reproduced at § 11.01(b).)

FRANK SULLIVAN COMPANY v. MIDWEST SHEET METAL WORKS

United States Court of Appeals, Eighth Circuit, 1964.
335 F.2d 33.

BLACKMUN, CIRCUIT JUDGE. Midwest Sheet Metal Works, a Minnesota partnership, instituted this diversity suit against Frank

Sullivan Company, a Boston contractor, to recover damages for breach of contract. The jury returned a verdict in favor of Midwest for $85,000.

. . . The controversy arises out of the project for the extension and remodeling of the United States Post Office and Customs House at Saint Paul. Minnesota law controls. Although Sullivan asserts twenty separate points on its appeal, these come down essentially to four primary issues:

1. The identity of Midwest's Exhibit 5 as the agreement between the parties, and its effectiveness as a contract.

. . . [Second issue omitted]

3. The authority of Sullivan's agent to sign the agreement.

4. Damages.

The prime contractor on the project was Electronic & Missile Facilities, Inc., of New York City (EMF). On December 4, 1961, EMF and Sullivan executed a lengthy and detailed subcontract whereby Sullivan undertook all plumbing, heating apparatus, air conditioning, ventilation work on the job for an agreed price of $1,650,000. This contract was executed on behalf of Sullivan by Francis J. Sullivan (Frank) as its president.

In the fall of 1961, before the formal execution of the agreement between EMF and Sullivan, Frank had contact with Michael J. Elnicky, the dominant partner of Midwest, about Midwest's taking on the sheet metal and air conditioning portion of Sullivan's subcontract. Sullivan had even invited a quotation from Midwest for this work. On November 1 Midwest quoted a figure in excess of a million dollars. Frank by telephone told Elnicky that this bid was about $200,000 too high. Elnicky indicated he might reduce his price somewhat but could not approach Sullivan's suggested figure. Frank testified that he then told Elnicky, "Well, look, we have got a fellow going out there, and I will show you that these are not prices that we dreamed up, these are prices that we used in making our bid, and we got them confirmed by letters by reputable people".

Near the close of 1961 EMF told Sullivan that it was imperative that the work in Saint Paul be started. Sullivan promised EMF that it would get a superintendent, a foreman, and men and material on the job by the end of January. Sullivan sent John Sullivan (Jack) from Boston to Saint Paul in early January. On this trip he conferred with EMF's superintendent on the project. Jack was back in Minnesota later in the same month with Byers who was to be Sullivan's general superintendent on the job. Before he left Boston on this second trip Jack had been instructed by Frank to look over the labor situation in the area, to check in with prospective subcontractors, to see Elnicky and give him quotations which "will back up the reduction of his bid", and to "get the job started". Frank gave Jack the job estimates which had been prepared by Sullivan but he was not given and had not seen the prime contract.

Upon their arrival Byers called upon local union business agents, purchased material and tools, received other equipment from Boston, and placed four steamfitters on the job.

On Monday, January 22, Jack came to Midwest's office. This was the first time Elnicky saw him. Elnicky and some of his employees testified that Jack told him on this visit that he was "part of the [Sullivan] organization" and had "a piece of it". Jack denied that he made any such statement. Elnicky conceded that he made no attempt to check Jack's authority with the Sullivan home office and that he did not ask for written evidence of it.

Elnicky also testified that Jack early in this first meeting suggested that Midwest price off "the whole works"; in any event, Elnicky indicated that he was interested in taking over the entire Sullivan job. Jack did not object and said that he would try to get a copy of the prime contract for him. The two men met again on Tuesday when Jack permitted Elnicky and his people to review the bids Sullivan had received. By Wednesday Jack obtained a copy of the prime contract from EMF's office on the job. He gave it to Elnicky who kept it over night. Meanwhile, Jack talked with other prospective subcontractors. Elnicky and Jack met further, and sometimes socially, during the same week. Jack told him that Sullivan would have to have a minimum of $100,000 if Elnicky took over. On Thursday Jack told Frank by telephone of the discussions he was having with Midwest. As to this conversation Frank testified that he told Jack that this could not be done; that EMF wanted Sullivan on the job; and that Jack should "Pick up what you got and come home". Midwest finished its estimating on Saturday, January 27. That evening Jack was at Elnicky's home with Elnicky and two of the latter's men. They discussed costs and what Elnicky might offer to do the job but no conclusion was reached.

Early in the afternoon of the next day, Sunday, Elnicky came to Jack's hotel room. Jack was planning to return to Boston. Elnicky arrived with a fifth of scotch. The men were together for three and one-half hours, discussing the job and drinking the entire fifth. Byers was present but left for a time to get the copy of the prime contract which had been left elsewhere. Elnicky made an offer of $1,550,000 to perform the work. This was discussed as was the question of what to do with the equipment and materials which Sullivan already had on the job. Jack then started to write something out. Elnicky dictated part of it. Several drafts were made. Later Jack dictated a draft to a hotel typist and he and Elnicky signed it. Elnicky then took Jack to the airport. The typed draft is Midwest's Exhibit 5 *

* "Hotel Saint Paul
St. Paul, Minnesota
January 28, 1962

"The Midwest Sheet Metal Co.
340 Taft St.
Minneapolis, Minnesota

"The Midwest Sheet Metal Company of 340 Taft St., Minneapolis, Minnesota, agrees to take over Frank Sullivan Company's contract with Electronic Missile Facilities, Inc., in the amount of One Million Five Hundred Fifty and 00/100 Dollars ($1,550,000).

"The cost of the bond will be paid for by the Frank Sullivan Company.

and is the document in controversy. It was admitted in evidence over Sullivan's objection.

The testimony as to the execution of the exhibit is in sharp conflict. Jack testified that he told Elnicky that this agreement was subject to approval by Frank and EMF; that there was no sense in working out other details until this was done; that it was his intention that Exhibit 5 be merely a proposal by Elnicky to Sullivan; and that he did not intend thereby to turn the Sullivan contract over to Midwest. Byers testified that Jack told Elnicky that it had to be approved by Frank and EMF; that Elnicky acknowledged this; and that he, Byers, had expressed a hope that Frank would approve it so he "could go home". Elnicky flatly denied that Jack had said Exhibit 5 was subject to approval by Frank and EMF.

The next day, Monday the 29th, Jack called Byers from Boston to see if Elnicky had someone on the job as the writing provided. Byers called Elnicky who told him he would have someone there on Tuesday. On Tuesday Jack and Elnicky conferred by telephone. Byers then sent Elnicky's men away from the job. On the same day, January 30th, Jack, signing on behalf of the Sullivan Company, wrote Midwest that "The agreement made on January 28th, 1962, between the Midwest Sheet Metal Company and the Frank Sullivan Company is hereby cancelled", and that they would try to arrange for Midwest to quote on the job's ventilating, air conditioning, and refrigeration. Jack testified that he wrote this letter without discussion with Frank. Midwest's receipt of that letter led to the present suit.

Jack Sullivan's status is obviously of vital importance. In January 1962 he was 29 years of age. He was a high school graduate and had had one year of "night college". He held a plumber's union card and a journeyman plumber's license. He had worked for Sullivan for ten years. He had started there as a plumber and, by 1959, was a job superintendent. About mid-1960 he became an "outside superintendent". In this capacity he traveled to various jobs, examined labor and material situations and reported back to Sullivan. He did no hiring or firing. He did not order materials. He did make recommendations. He was not an officer, director, or shareholder of Sullivan. He was not related to Frank. He had nothing to do with obtaining or negotiating subcontracts. He had had no experience in sheet metal or air conditioning. He had done no estimating. He had been given no specific authority to sign any contract for Sullivan or to assign Sullivan's subcontract with EMF.

"The Midwest Sheet Metal Company will man the above mentioned project on January 29, 1962, to show good faith regarding this contract.

The above agreement is made between
Midwest Sheet Metal
Midwest Sheet Metal
M. J. Elnicky
Frank Sullivan Co.
John Sullivan"

The discrepancy between the words and the figures is readily apparent.

In January 1962 Elnicky was about 52. He had been in sheet metal and similar work for many years and had run his own business since 1947.

A. The contract. Sullivan's basic argument here is . . . that Exhibit 5 . . . is not sufficiently clear and definite to be valid and to constitute an enforceable contract. . . .

> [I]f
>
> "* * * substantial terms are left open and subject to further agreement, which is never reached, there is not only no complete agreement but no contract at all. * * * The next inquiry is whether, there being an agreement which is asserted to be a contract, it is complete. It is not unless it is in all essential terms definite and certain or capable of being made so by the aid of competent evidence and permissible interpretation. If as a contract it be incomplete, a court can no more complete it for the parties than it could make it for them in the beginning." Wells Const. Co. v. Goder Incinerator Co., 173 Minn. 200, 205–206, 217 N.W. 112, 114 (1927).

"There is no contract where there is no mutual and final assent to all the essential terms of a bargain." New England Mut. Life Ins. Co. v. Mannheimer Realty Co., 188 Minn. 511, 513, 247 N.W. 803, 804 (1933). Vagueness and indefiniteness may affect the validity of an alleged agreement. "If an alleged contract is so uncertain as to any of its essential terms that it cannot be carried into effect without new and additional stipulations between the parties, it is not a valid agreement." Ames-Brooks Co. v. Aetna Ins. Co., 83 Minn. 346, 349, 86 N.W. 344, 345 (1901). . . . And "where substantial and necessary terms are specifically left open for future negotiation, the purported contract is fatally defective." King v. Dalton Motors, Inc., 260 Minn. 124, 126, 109 N.W.2d 51, 52 (1961). But

> "A proper administration of justice does not permit an overzealous quest for subtle ambiguity to destroy the intent of the parties when the court, despite some incompleteness and imperfection of expression, can reasonably find that intent by applying the words used, with all their reasonable implications, to the subject matter as the parties themselves, under all the surrounding circumstances, must have applied, used, and understood them. This court is reluctant to invoke the principle that indefiniteness prevents the creation of a contract where a just result, consistent with a reasonably expressed intent of the parties, can be reached by upholding the agreement." Hartung v. Billmeier, 243 Minn. 148, 151, 66 N.W.2d 784, 788 (1954).

. . . Reasonable certainty is thus the standard. . . .

In the light of the foregoing authorities, we affirm on this point. We do so for the following reasons:

. . .

2. While Exhibit 5 may have been born with somewhat of an alcoholic background, this fact alone does not make it any less a contract. Evidently both Elnicky and Jack desired or were content to negotiate in that kind of atmosphere. It is not now claimed that there was duress or that Elnicky took advantage of Jack through alcohol.

3. Exhibit 5 on its face is clear and complete. It succinctly states that Midwest "agrees to take over" Sullivan's contract with EMF. It states the figure at which it does so. It leaves a $100,000 gross profit margin, less the cost of the bond, for Sullivan. It calls for immediate manning of the job by Midwest. It contains no ambiguity and Sullivan so concedes.

4. Although, as Sullivan observes, Exhibit 5 consists of but one page, as contrasted with the many pages of the subcontract between EMF and Sullivan, this difference is understandable. The document could have been more formal but it was formulated by two laymen and it in effect incorporated the detailed EMF subcontract by reference. By so doing it achieved certainty as to underlying details. Sullivan itself was originally content in this respect or it would not have made the subcontract with EMF.

5. The discrepancy between the words and the figures of Exhibit 5 is not fatal. It is true that the normal rule is that, where there is a discrepancy of this kind, the words and not the figures control. Gran v. Spangenberg, 53 Minn. 42, 45, 54 N.W. 933, 934 (1893). This usually does not invalidate a contract. The cited case also discloses that there are even situations where resort may be made to the figures. In any event, despite the facts that the difference here was a half million dollar one and that it should have been noticed by either Jack or Elnicky, there was no confusion in the minds of the two men. Each knew that the proper amount was $1,550,000. No one was misled.

6. Exhibit 5 does not have that vagueness or indefiniteness or incompleteness which, in the several Minnesota cases cited above, has served to defeat alleged contracts.

. . .

8. Jack's own letter of January 30, 1962, is almost persuasive in itself. It refers to "the agreement" of January 28 "between Midwest * * * and * * * Sullivan" and reaches out to cancel it.

C. Jack's authority. Midwest does not contend that the record supports a finding that Jack possessed actual authority to act on behalf of Sullivan. The issue is one of apparent authority. Sullivan asserts that the evidence as a matter of law was insufficient to support a finding of apparent authority and that the court's submission of this issue to the jury and its rulings and instructions consistent therewith were prejudicially erroneous.

Jack certainly assumed the mantle and the posture of responsibility and authority. There is evidence to the effect that he professed an ownership interest in Sullivan; possessed and produced the bids and the cost estimates the company has assembled; permitted Elnicky to review them; obtained a copy of the EMF-Sullivan subcontract for Elnicky; mentioned to others than Elnicky his interest in contracting out the entire Sullivan portion of the job; demonstrated a permissive attitude toward Midwest's interest in taking on the full subcontract; was in contact with Elnicky's performance bond man and asked him to confirm his comments by letter; accepted Elnicky's entertainment favors; bargained continuously for a week; and even wrote the letter of cancellation.

But apparent authority must be founded on something more than the conduct and statements of the agent himself. Liability can be imposed upon a principal only "for that appearance of authority caused by himself". 2 Williston on Contracts (3d Ed.1960), § 277A, pp. 222–24; . . . Of course, a degree of reasonableness and of diligence is required of one who deals with the agent. . . .

We find in this record adequate support for the submission of the issue of apparent authority to the jury. Accepting the evidence, as we must, in the light most favorable to the prevailing plaintiff, we have, apart from and in addition to Jack's own acts and statements, all the following: (1) Sullivan sublet part of every job it had for there were certain types of work (air conditioning and sheet metal, for example) which it never performed; (2) Sullivan sent Jack to Saint Paul to get the job started; (3) Sullivan instructed Jack to get in touch with area people in the construction industry and to obtain subcontract offers; (4) Sullivan placed Jack in possession of the breakdown of costs it had prepared and of the bids it had received; (5) Frank told Elnicky that he had a man going out to Minnesota; (6) Jack possessed the Sullivan name; (7) Jack was the highest person in authority in Sullivan's employ on the job; (8) so far as the Saint Paul job was concerned, Byers followed Jack's instructions; (9) Jack, while he was in Saint Paul the week of January 22, was in telephone communication with Boston, and, specifically, talked with Frank; and (10) Frank knew that Jack was discussing with Elnicky a complete takeover by Midwest and yet did nothing to disavow his status to Elnicky. And, for what it is worth, Jack was still with the Sullivan Company at the time of the trial.

Of course, there is an opposing factual argument, namely, that Sullivan had given Jack no instructions to turn over the entire job; that Jack was not supplied with a copy of the EMF-Sullivan subcontract and had to obtain it from the EMF man on the job; that the preliminary conversations between Sullivan and Elnicky had only to do with a limited area of work; that Elnicky knew who Frank was and was in communication with him; and that Elnicky did not inquire of Jack or of Frank as to Jack's authority. But this is just another argument for the trier of fact. The jury was not persuaded.

Sullivan places great emphasis on Elnicky's failure to make inquiry as to Jack's authority, and it urges the important nature of the contract as demonstrated by the amount involved and the time required for its performance. This argument, however, cuts both ways. If the job was so large and so important, a jury might properly infer that Sullivan's top man on the project was there with workable authority. We feel that the cases Sullivan cites in support of its argument are distinguishable on their facts. Hill v. James, supra, concerned a traveling salesman, a fact which the court stressed, and a questionably completed contract. The court readily recognized that a principal may clothe even such a salesman with apparent authority. Dispatch Printing Co. v. National Bank of Commerce, supra, concerned a Saint Paul newspaper's Minneapolis advertising solicitor-collector and his indorsing checks drawn in favor of the newspaper and depositing them in his own account. Mooney v. Jones, 238 Minn. 1, 54 N.W.2d 763 (1952) concerned a mortgagor's representation, claimed to be made on behalf of the mortgagee, to a contractor that the latter's lien waiver would not affect his lien rights for future work. Language in these opinions relative to an agent's actual authority and a third person's duty to inquire is accepted law but the Minnesota court has consistently recognized the established principles of apparent authority. Illustrative is the court's comment in Mooney itself, p. 767 of 54 N.W.2d, that "the record is insufficient to show that National Guardian did anything to hold Gustafson out as its agent". See, also, Cauger v. Gray Motor Co., 173 Minn. 370, 217 N.W. 347, 348 (1928). And in Sauber v. Northland Ins. Co., supra, Chief Justice Knutson, in speaking for the court, said, "Apparent authority exists by virtue of conduct on the part of the principal which warrants a finding that a third party, acting in good faith, was justified in relying on the assumption that the agent had authority to act." [footnote omitted]

The situation here strikes us as one where, as the negotiations developed, Jack sensed the opportunity to bring his company out of the project at a convenient profit of $100,000, without additional cost or participation, and further sensed that this would be a feather in his cap if he could bring it about. Whether Sullivan sensed this, desired it, and encouraged it, we shall, of course, never know with positive assurance. But the record supports just such an inference by the jury. We are not at liberty to overturn that body's conclusion.

D. Damages. Anticipated profits may be an element of damage where "their amount is shown with a reasonable degree of certainty and exactness" and where the nature of the business is "such as to support an inference of definite profits grounded upon a reasonably sure basis of facts". However, "This rule does not call for absolute certainty". Johnson v. Wright, 175 Minn. 236, 240, 220 N.W. 946, 948 (1928); Appliances, Inc. v. Queen Stove Works, Inc., 228 Minn. 55, 36 N.W.2d 121, 125 (1949).

Sullivan argues that there was no reasonable basis in the evidence for the jury to return any verdict for damages and certainly none for a verdict of $85,000; that the verdict is the result of speculation; and that Elnicky was not competent to give his opinion on the cost of doing the work.

Elnicky's testimony was to the effect that his anticipated gross profit was $187,000 and that this was computed on the basis that his base costs would be $1,362,000. This cost figure depended in part upon Sullivan's own estimates submitted to Elnicky. There is, naturally, a distinct element of uncertainty in all this, and an argument can be made that Elnicky's own evaluation of anticipated profit was too optimistic. On the other hand, every contractor interested in the Saint Paul project may be expected to have anticipated a profit. The week-long negotiations between Elnicky and his people and Sullivan were primarily concerned with Midwest's costs and profit. Sullivan's estimates, suppliers' bids, Midwest's computations, and Elnicky's best judgment as an experienced contractor properly provided, it seems to us, an appropriate basis on which the jury could reach its conclusion.

Elnicky's concession on cross-examination that when he figured a job "We do not know how much is going to be overhead or how much is going to be profit * * *" and that labor costs on a job are "guesstimates", do not strike us as concessions of a lack of reasonable certainty. The contracting business is hazardous and small errors or unforeseen developments can be costly. See Southern Fireproofing Co. v. R. F. Ball Constr. Co., 334 F.2d 122 (8 Cir.1964). But this does not disqualify a competent and experienced contractor's best estimate, reasonably compiled, as acceptable evidence. To hold otherwise would tend to bar recovery in all construction cases. The Minnesota court, in Johnson v. Wright, supra, pp. 240–241 of 175 Minn., p. 948 of 220 N.W., has made some revealing comments applicable to a case of this kind:

> "Johnson admits that sometimes he makes a profit and sometimes he sustains a loss in projects of this character. That is true of all work. * * * But we must assume that the price contemplates and is commensurate with a certain amount of probable disappointment, trouble, and loss. * * * Johnson has had nearly 40 years' experience as a driller. * * * Does the situation permit a jury to safely find that Johnson could make a profit having in mind the possibility of trouble and loss before reaching such depth? We think it does, though the question is a close one. * * * What is the common, usual, and ordinary experience of men in such work? It would seem to be favorable to the occupation, or else one would not continue in the work so long as Johnson has; otherwise, men would not venture the hazards of such contracts. * * * We are of the opinion that the evidence is sufficient to authorize and enable the jury to find the loss of profits with reasonable certainty, and that such determination is not conjectural or speculative."

. . .

Upon our review of the record in its entirety, we find ourselves not in accord with Sullivan's attack on damages. Instead, we agree with the trial court that the jury's verdict was reasonable when considered in the light of all the testimony and that its determination of the amount of damages is properly supported.

REVIEW QUESTIONS

1. Why is the agency concept important in commercial life?

2. What formalities are necessary for the creation of an agency relationship?

3. What is ratification, and what effect does it have?

4. What characterizes the relationship between principal and agent? Give examples.

5. Under what conditions can a third person hold the principal?

6. When can a third person hold the agent?

7. What underlies the apparent authority concept?

QUESTIONS FOR CLASS DISCUSSION

1. Why should a principal be obligated for an unauthorized contract made by his agent?

2. If agents are liable to third parties for misrepresenting their authority, should the third party be able to sue the principal on the basis of apparent authority?

3. What would be the normal authority of the office manager of an architectural firm with 10 partners and 30 employees?

4. Why not require that a third party dealing with a known agent demand evidence of the agent's actual authority?

5. Give as many illustrations of agency relationships as you can.

6. Have you ever been an agent? If so what was the scope of your authority?

7. Have you ever been a principal? If so, why did you use an agent, and what authority did you give him?

8. Have you ever dealt with an agent? Give the circumstances and discuss that agent's apparent authority.

PROBLEMS

1. A has authority to buy normal office supplies for an engineering firm. He enters into a written contract with T under which T will furnish an intercom system for the office at a cost of $825. Can T enforce this contract against the firm? What additional facts would be helpful in deciding this question, and why would these facts be helpful?

2. A was an architect who was performing services for P. P gave A $1000 and A was to purchase a stereophonic phonograph which was to be installed in a house being remodelled by P. Instead of pur-

chasing the phonograph, A used the $1000 to buy shares in Atomic Products Inc. A had a hot tip that the shares were going to double in value in the next two weeks. He did not have money of his own, but expected to buy the stereophonic equipment with the money which he hoped to receive when he resold the shares at a quick profit. He bought the shares for $1000 and ten days later sold them for $2000. He then purchased the stereophonic equipment at a sale for $900. The phonograph was installed and A gave P the difference of $100. P then found out about the unauthorized stock purchase. He brought an action against A, demanding the profits of $1000 from the unauthorized purchase. How much, if anything, should P be able to recover? Why?

3. A was an architect who was retained by P to perform design services. While attending a conference with officials of P, A learned that P was going to buy some land to be used as a plant site. P's land department was authorized to spend up to $100,000 for the site. A went to X, who owned the land. A made a deal with X under which A would give certain confidential information to X about the price P would pay, and A would then share 50% of any purchase price paid over $60,000. A gave the information to X and X sold the property to P for $100,000 (X would have sold for $60,000). X paid A $20,000.

P then abandoned the project and sold the land for $110,000. When P found out about the transaction, he demanded $40,000 from A. How much, if anything, should P be able to recover from A?

Chapter 4

FORMS OF ASSOCIATION

SECTION 4.01 RELEVANCE

The design professional should have a basic understanding of the ways in which individuals associate to accomplish business purposes. If the professional decides to enter private practice, he should know the basic elements of those forms of association professionally open to him. If he becomes an employee, or perhaps an executive in a large organization, he should understand the basic legal structure of the organization of which he is a part.

Special problems relating to dealing with various forms of business associations as clients will be discussed in Chapter 5 which covers contractual relationships with clients. When the design professional deals with a contractor on a project, he should understand corporate organization. Finally, every design professional should understand the concept which insulates shareholders from almost all liabilities of the corporation.

The most important forms of business organization are:

1. Sole proprietorship
2. Partnership
3. Corporation
4. Joint venture
5. Unincorporated association
6. Loose "association"

SECTION 4.02 SOLE PROPRIETORSHIP

The sole proprietorship, although not a form of association as such, is the logical place to begin the discussion. It is the simplest form and is the form used by many private practicing architects and engineers.

The creation and operation of the sole proprietorship is informal. By its nature, the sole proprietor need not make arrangements with anyone else for the operation of the business. Generally, no state regulations apply, except for those requiring registration of fictitious names or for having a license in certain businesses or profession. The sole proprietor need not maintain records relating to the operation of the business except for those records which may be necessary for tax purposes. He has complete control over the operation of the business, taking the profits and absorbing the losses. He rents or buys space for the operation of his business, hires employees, and may buy or rent personal property used in the business operation. The proprietorship will continue until he abandons it, or until he dies. Continuity of operation in the event of his death sometimes can be achieved through a direction in his will that his executor continue the business until it can be taken over by the person to whom he gives his business by his will. This insures that the business is a continuing operation during the handling of his estate, and that there is no costly hiatus in operation.

The proprietor may hold title to property in his own name, or in any fictitious name that he chooses. He can transfer any interest he has in the business, the only exception being that in some states his wife may have an interest in certain types of property used in the sole proprietorship enterprise.

Capital needed must be raised by his individual efforts, or by obtaining someone to guarantee his indebtedness. This differs from a corporation, which can issue shares as a method of raising capital.

The tax incidents of a sole proprietorship are relatively simple. The sole proprietor pays individual taxes on all business income, and he is allowed to take business losses. However, since he is not an employee, he cannot take advantage of certain tax advantages given to employees. In the sole proprietorship, the income is taxed only once. Because the corporation is a legal entity, it is generally taxed twice, once when the income is received, and again when it is distributed to the shareholders.

SECTION 4.03 PARTNERSHIP

(A) GENERALLY: UNIFORM PARTNERSHIP ACT

A partnership is defined as "an association of two or more persons to carry on as co-owners a business for profit". Unlike a corporation it is not a legal entity. Most states have adopted the Uniform Partnership Act, which sets forth the rights and duties between the partners themselves, and also specifies the rights and duties partners have toward third parties. The Uniform Partnership Act is a set of ground rules which, for the most part, will apply only if the partners have not specified to the contrary in the partnership agreement.

(B) CREATION

While it is not necessary that the partnership agreement be evidenced by a sufficient written memorandum, it is advisable to do so. In addition to the reasons given for having all agreements in writing, there are other reasons for expressing the partnership agreement in writing. The transfer of an interest in land must be evidenced by a sufficient written memorandum as must agreements which by their terms cannot be performed within a year. If the creation of the partnership is accompanied by a transfer of land, at least the portion of the partnership agreement dealing with the land should be evidenced by a sufficient written memorandum. Also, if the duration of the partnership expressly exceeds a year, the partnership agreement should likewise be evidenced by a written memorandum. Since agreements to answer for the debts of another must, under certain circumstances, be in writing, partnership agreements with a provision of this type should be evidenced by a written memorandum.

In stating that certain agreements must be in writing, there is a distinction frequently misunderstood. Suppose a partnership is created for a three year period. (This is rare since most partnerships are for indefinite periods.) If the agreement is not evidenced by a writing, the rights and duties of the partners will still be governed by the oral agreement, and by the Uniform Partnership Act. However, a partner has no legally enforceable obligation to perform in the future. He will have to perform those obligations that have accrued prior to his decision to terminate the oral partnership.

As for third parties, they will still have whatever rights the law would give them against the partners, without regard for the fact that the partnership agreement was required to be in writing. The fact that the law "required" the partnership agreement to be in writing, because it was to last over a year, will have a limited impact upon the "partners" and, in most cases, no impact upon third parties.

While the partnership form seems simple, its creation can involve complex legal and tax considerations.

(C) OPERATION

In the operation of a partnership, the partners decide who is to exercise control. Most matters can be decided by majority vote. However, certain important matters, such as amendment of the partnership agreement, must be by unanimous vote. Sometimes the partners desire to have something other than the majority rule apply. In a large partnership, a smaller group of partners may be given the authority to decide certain matters without requiring that a majority of the partners approve these decisions.

(D) FIDUCIARY DUTIES

The partners, as fiduciaries, have an obligation to act in good faith toward each other. A partner must account to the partnership for any secret profits he makes. He must not, through any conflict of interests, harm the partnership. For example, where the partnership acts as the owner's agent in dealing with a construction company, it would be improper for one of the partners to have a financial interest in the construction company unless he had disclosed such interest in advance to his partners, and to the owner-principal. Since the fiduciary obligation is of great importance, it may be helpful in the partnership agreement to spell out the permissible scope of outside activities of individual partners. In the absence of an understanding among the partners as to permissible outside activities, any activity which raises a conflict of interest, or competes in any way with the partnership, would not be proper.

(E) PERFORMANCE OBLIGATIONS, PROFITS, LOSSES, WITHDRAWAL OF CAPITAL AND INTEREST

In the absence of any agreement to the contrary, the partners are to devote their full time to the operation of the business and share in profits and losses equally. If a specified proportion of the profits are allocated by partnership contract to specified partners, that same percentage will apply to losses. If some arrangement other than this is desired, it must be spelled out in the partnership agreement.

Normally, partners cannot withdraw capital during the life of the partnership, unless provision is made for withdrawal. A partner may collect interest for money or property lent to the partnership, as well as for capital contributions advanced upon request of the partnership.

(F) AUTHORITY OF PARTNER

Each partner is a general agent, and his acts will bind the partnership. This is an application of the agency concept. Clearly, his authorized acts will bind the partnership. The more difficult problems arise where he acts in an unauthorized fashion.

Here, the doctrine of apparent authority discussed in § 3.06 applies. Certain extraordinary acts, such as criminal acts or other illegal acts, may not be chargeable to the partnership. However, because of the vast range of authority given to the partners, and the fiduciary obligation owed by each partner to the other, it is of great importance to consider the character of any persons with whom a partnership is being considered.

(G) LIABILITY OF GENERAL PARTNERSHIP AND INDIVIDUAL PARTNERS

A differentiation must be made between the general partnership and the limited partnership. The liability of a limited partner will be discussed in § 4.03(k). The discussion at this point contemplates a general partnership.

Creditors of the partnership can go after partnership property and, if this proves insufficient, can go after the property of individual partners. Creditors of individual partners can go after partnership property, if they have exhausted the individual property of the partner.

The creditor of an individual partner cannot attach specific partnership property. If a creditor has a judgment against an individual partner, he may ask for dissolution of the partnership. Such a request gives the partnership an opportunity to pay the debt and avoid partnership dissolution.

Unless an incoming partner assumes the obligations created before he became a partner, he is not personally liable for existing partnership debts. An outgoing partner remains personally liable for debts incurred while he was a partner, and for debts contracted after his retirement from the partnership, if third persons were not made aware of his severance from the partnership. If he is leaving a partnership, he should try to inform all persons who have dealt with the partnership that he is leaving the partnership.

A partner can recover from the partnership, and the other partners, for a liability which he incurred as the result of partnership activities. He has a right of "contribution." The partner who incurs liabilities or pays money should be indemnified by the partnership or by the individual partners. An express right of contribution should be provided for in the partnership agreement. Normal liabilities should be covered, although certain willful and malicious acts may be excluded from contribution rights.

(H) TRANSFERABILITY OF PARTNERSHIP INTEREST

A partner has some interests which are transferable. He can assign his share of profits in the partnership, but he cannot assign specific partnership property, nor his right to management and control.

(I) TERMINATION

One of the problems of a partnership is that it usually terminates upon the death of a general partner, bankruptcy of a partner, withdrawal of a partner, or by court order. The unprofitability of a partnership normally is not sufficient grounds for a court-decreed dissolution. If the business of the partnership becomes illegal, this dissolves the partnership.

If the partnership is organized for a specific time period, expiration of that time normally ends the partnership. The partnership also may be ended when a partner is expelled from the partnership for just cause.

If the partnership is dissolved, there is a "winding-up" process. The partner who performs this process is entitled to extra compensation. The partnership is not allowed to undertake any new business, but merely to conclude the business it entered into prior to the dissolution. The fiduciary duty between partners is ended when the partnership is dissolved. The assets, in the event of dissolution, are distributed first to the creditors who are not partners, then to repay loans made to the partnership by general partners, then to repay capital contributed by general partners. If anything remains, it goes to the general partners.

There are some ways of continuing a partnership arrangement that would otherwise be dissolved. The partner who desires to leave the partnership may be bought out by the partnership. Statutes may also specify provisions which may be included in the partnership agreement to ensure continuation of the partnership despite the death or retirement of a partner.

The partnership agreement may provide that the executor, or, in some cases, the wife of the deceased partner, may continue as a partner. This may be coupled with an option in the surviving partners to buy the decedent's interest. Often such an option raises problems of valuation. It may be desirable to have an agreed valuation in advance, or a method providing for valuation based on objective factors. Also, such a buy-out usually requires capital. To provide money for this purpose, it may be advisable for the partnership to carry insurance on each partner's life.

For additional treatment of the effect of a partnership reorganization, see § 10.03(d).

(J) TAXATION

The tax aspects of a partnership, like all tax matters, are complex. However, certain generalizations can be made. As mentioned before, a partnership is not an entity. This means that income to the partnership is taxable immediately to the individual partners, whether it is distributed or not. It is not taxed twice as in certain corporations.

In some instances, taxing officials can treat a partnership as a corporation. (Sometimes a corporation can be taxed as a partnership.) Since partners are not employees, many tax advantages relating to fringe benefits given to employees cannot be given to the partners. This is one of the reasons for the increased popularity of the corporate form for design professionals. This will be discussed in § 32.03.

(K) LIMITED PARTNERSHIP

A limited partnership is permitted in most states. However, it requires a filing with appropriate state authorities. A limited partner, as a rule, will be liable only to the extent of the capital he contributes. However, he is not to contribute services, nor is he to exert any management and control. Normally, the division of profits is between general partners and limited partners is provided for by contract. In the event there is no such provision, all partners share equally. A limited partner can assign only his share of the profits. Unless the articles of limited partnership provide to the contrary, the limited partner can withdraw his capital investment by giving six months notice. From a tax standpoint, a limited partnership is taxed essentially in the manner as a general partnership. The purpose of having a limited partner, or a silent partner, is to try to raise capital without surrendering management and control.

SECTION 4.04 PROFIT CORPORATION

(A) RELEVANCE

The corporate form is used by most large and medium-sized businesses in the United States, and has become the vehicle by which many small businesses are conducted. In addition, there is an increasing tendency on the part of practicing architects and engineers to choose the corporate form, where possible, for their business organization. The corporate form takes on even greater significance in light of the increasing number of architects and engineers who are employed by corporations. It should be kept in mind that the discussion will be brief and simple. There are many complexities in corporation law which cannot be discussed in this treatise.

(B) GENERAL ATTRIBUTES

While the partnership is merely an aggregate of individuals who joined together for a specific purpose, the corporation is itself a legal entity. It exists as a legal person. It can take hold and convey property, and sue or be sued in its corporate name. As shall be seen, the other important corporation attributes are centralization of management in the board of directors, free transferability of interests, and perpetual duration. In addition, the corporation offers the advantage of limiting shareholder liability for the debts of the corporation to the extent of the obligation to pay for the corporate shares purchased. Not all of these attributes are available to all types of corporations. However, as a general introductory statement, these attributes set the corporation apart from sole proprietorship and partnership.

(C) GOVERNMENTAL REGULATION

There is a great deal of government control over corporations. Statutes determine the permissible powers of a corporation, determine how the corporation is to be formed, and provide other requirements for the creation of a validly formed corporation. Both state and federal governments regulate the issuance of certain types of corporate securities. In addition the federal government, through the Clayton Act, regulates corporate mergers and acquisitions. Also, special types of corporations such as public utilities and banks, are heavily regulated by both state and federal government. In general, the corporate form is subjected to substantial governmental scrutiny and control.

(D) PRE-INCORPORATION PROBLEMS

Often, persons called promotors set into motion the creation of a corporation. They may continue in control. Sometimes they merely organize the corporation and then turn the control over to others. Promotors owe each other fiduciary duties. Usually they are compensated by the corporation after the corporation has been organized. This compensation may be in the form of cash, shares of stock, stock options, or positions within the corporation. In addition to fiduciary obligations between themselves, the promoters have a fiduciary obligation to the corporation. They must deal in good faith and make full disclosure to the corporation. They are not entitled to make secret profits. For this reason, there must be full disclosure of dealings by promoters to the board of directors and shareholders.

To promote the proposed corporation, promoters frequently make contracts with third parties. Contracts may be made by the promoters with varying obligations intended by the contracting parties. These contracts may be made:

1. not on behalf of the proposed corporation, binding only the promoters personally;
2. on behalf of the proposed corporation without the intention of binding the promoters;
3. on behalf of the proposed corporation with the intention of binding the promoters.

It is important for those dealing with promoters to discuss and spell out precisely who is to be liable on the contract, and to recognize the problems which may arise if the corporation is not formed. If the arrangement contemplates that the corporation is to be bound when it is formed, but the promoters are not to be the persons liable, it may be that the arrangement is not contractual at all, but merely a gentleman's agreement, or an offer which is to be made to the corporation when it comes into existence.

Most pre-incorporation contracts are made on behalf of the corporation, and also bind the promoters. Problems may arise regarding the continued liability of the promoter after the corporation is formed.

(E) CREATION: DE FACTO INCORPORATION

The creation of a corporation requires paper work, and some expense. Frequently organization taxes, filing fees and other fees must be paid. The pre-incorporation agreement, articles of incorporation, by-laws, minutes of organizational meetings, shareholder agreements, and stock certificates, as well as other documents connected with the organization of the corporation, must be prepared. The required number of directors must be selected, and ultimately corporate officers have to be elected.

Since the state sets up many requirements for the valid incorporation of an enterprise, problems frequently develop when the corporation has commenced operations, but there has been some technical failure in complying with legal requirements on the part of those organizing the corporation. When the corporation has complied with all the mandatory conditions, it is called a "de jure" corporation. Often a technical defect means that the corporation will be classified as a "de facto" corporation.

For most purposes, a *de facto* corporation is recognized as a validly formed corporation, although the state can attack its corporate existence. In order to be a *de facto* corporation, there must be a statute in existence under which the corporation might have been validly incorporated, a good faith attempt to comply with the statute, and some attempt to use corporate attributes or privileges.

A *de facto* corporation has the capacity to sue or be sued and has limited liability for shareholders. A defectively formed corporation which does not rise to the status of a *de facto* corporation can mean that the shareholders are liable for the debts of the corporation as if they were members of a partnership. The tendency is to hold those shareholders who have been actively participating in the business or in the organization of the enterprise. While there are no hard and fast rules, the greater his participation, the more likely it is that the individual will be held for obligations of the defectively formed corporation.

(F) SHARE OWNERSHIP

The cornerstone of corporate organization is the concept of share ownership. The corporation is a separate legal entity that is owned by the shareholders. The shareholders do not own any part of specific corporation property. They have a right against the corporation which is governed by statutes, the articles of incorporation, and the wording of the shares. One of the great strengths of modern corporation law is the variety of types of shares which can be employed by the corporation.

Usually shares are divided into a number of classes. Shares which are given a preference over other shares with regard to dividends are known as "preferred shares." Such shares may be "cumulative," "non-cumulative" or "cumulative to the extent earned." A cumulative preference entitles the preferred shareholder to unpaid dividends for all prior fiscal periods and current fiscal periods before a dividend may be distributed to shareholders having subordinate dividend rights. If the preferred shares are non-cumulative, then the preference only extends to the current fiscal period. If the shares are cumulative to the extent earned, then the preferred shareholder comes before subordinated shareholders to the extent that, in prior years, there were funds legally available to pay the preferred shareholders.

After the preferred shareholders are paid, if there is money available, and if the board of directors decides to distribute income rather than retaining it for corporate capital needs, then any dividends are distributed on a pro rata basis to common shareholders, and to preferred shareholders if their stock is denominated "participating preferred stock."

Shares are sometimes classified as "par" or "no-par" shares. Shares at a specified par value mean that the purchaser is obligated to pay the par value for the shares, and the creditors can assume that the corporation has assets in the amount of the total par value of all of the shares, at least as of the time the corporation was formed. No par shares have no set value, but the Board of Directors or the Articles of Incorporation establish a specified value for the shares which must be paid by purchasers of original shares issued, or subsequently issued shares.

Shares may be "voting" or "non-voting" shares. Those who own voting shares have the right to vote on matters such as election of a Board of Directors, corporate reorganization, mergers and dissolution. Some shares have "pre-emptive rights." Shareholders with pre-emptive rights must be offered the opportunity of purchasing newly issued shares before those shares can be sold to other persons.

Ordinarily, shares of stock in a corporation are freely transferable. This is one of the major advantages of incorporation. However, in some closely held corporations, where the shares of stock are not sold to the general public, there may be restrictions on transferability of the shares. This is to enable the shareholders to keep control of the company by eliminating the possibility of outsiders becoming shareholders. Also, restrictions on transferability sometimes accompany shares which are purchased by executives or employees as part of a stock option plan.

(G) PIERCING THE CORPORATE VEIL: HOLLAND v. JOY CANDY

One of the chief reasons for incorporating is to limit the liability of shareholders. Ordinarily, shareholders are liable for the debts of the corporation only to the extent of paying for their shares.

There are some situations where shareholders are responsible for certain special debts, such as nonpayment of wages to employees. However, generally the owners of shares are not liable for the debts of the corporation.

This limitation of liability can operate unfairly where a third party relies upon what appears to be a solvent corporation. He may find that the corporation he thought to be solvent is, in fact, merely a shell, and that the assets of the corporation are insufficient to pay the corporate obligations. Also, someone injured by the acts or failure to act of a corporation might find that the corporation is unable to pay for damages because the amount of capital paid in to the corporation was very small.

In certain cases, the corporate form will be disregarded by the law. A court may do this if unjust or undesirable consequences would result by interposing the corporation as an entity between the injured party or the creditor, and the shareholders. This is called "piercing the corporate veil." Courts are more likely to do this where a person has suffered physical harm through corporate activities, where a creditor could not reasonably have been expected to check on the credit of the corporation, and where the one-man, family, or closely held corporation is used. The latter types of corporations have been popular because they combine control with limitation of liability. Ordinarily, such corporations are valid and protect the shareholders from liability. However, this is so only if the corporation structure is used for legitimate purposes, and the business is conducted on a corporate basis. Also, the enterprise must be established on an adequate financial basis so that the corporation is able to respond to a substantial degree for its obligations. If not, circumstances such as those mentioned could result in "piercing the corporate veil".

Problems also arise when a corporation organizes a subsidiary corporation and holds all the shares of the subsidiary. This may be done to limit liability of the parent corporation for the acts of the subsidiary. In order to achieve the protection of limited liability, the two corporations must be kept separate, and the records for both corporations cannot be commingled. Formalities must be observed, and each corporation must be adequately financed in the light of the normal obligations foreseeable in a business of its type and character. In addition, the respective enterprises must be held out to the public as separate entities.

While the corporate form usually insulates shareholders from liability of the corporation, sometimes the law will "pierce the corporate veil", as shown in the following case.

HOLLAND v. JOY CANDY MANUFACTURING CORPORATION

Appellate Court of Illinois, 1957.
14 Ill.App.2d 531, 145 N.E.2d 101.

FEINBERG, JUDGE. Joy Candy Manufacturing Corporation, one of the defendants, appeals from a judgment entered against it for $6,304 upon a trial without a jury.

The action was brought against the appealing defendant and Candy Shoppes, Inc., to recover for services rendered by plaintiff, an advertising agency in the preparation and placing of advertising for the product of defendants. Defendant Candy Shoppes admitted that it owed $5,644 but denied that it owed the claimed balance of $660. Partial judgment was entered against Candy Shoppes for the admitted amount, and a trial ordered as to the balance. Defendant Candy Manufacturing Company denied any services were rendered to it by plaintiff. Upon the trial a further judgment of $660 was entered against Candy Shoppes, and judgment was entered against Candy Manufacturing Company. There is no appeal by defendant Candy Shoppes.

The evidence discloses that Alex Kanelos and Peter Stefanos operated the candy business as a partnership. In 1931 they organized both defendant corporations. Candy Shoppes was the retail outlet for the candy manufactured by defendant manufacturing company. The stock of both companies was divided equally between Kanelos and Stefanos, and both were officers and directors of the two companies. Each of them subsequently divided his stockholdings with his wife. Kanelos died in 1947, and his widow, Edith Kanelos, since 1951 acquired ownership of all of the outstanding stock of both companies, including the stock of Stefanos. She was president, treasurer and director of both corporations. Two others occupied nominal positions of secretary, directors and vice president of both corporations. After she acquired all of the stock, plaintiff continued to render the advertising service, the same as he had before her acquisition of the stock. She actively managed both corporations from the same building where both corporations had their offices. She engaged plaintiff; consulted him about advertising programs; authorized and approved plaintiff's services, as well as the advertising copy.

During the years 1953 and 1954, statements covering plaintiff's services were sent to Candy Shoppes and the Manufacturing Corporation. No objection was made by the Manufacturing Corporation to any of the statements rendered to it, and none of them were returned to plaintiff. Plaintiff received checks of the Candy Shoppes, signed by Edith Kanelos. Both companies had the same telephone number and switchboard; the same bookkeeper and time clerk, and shared a double desk in the same office. There was no lease between the two companies, and no evidence that Candy Shoppes paid any rent to the Manufacturing Corporation for its office space and facilities. The two companies had separate bank accounts.

The Manufacturing Corporation delivered the candy it manufactured to Candy Shoppes on consignment, reserving in itself title to the merchandise, to protect itself against future creditors of Candy Shoppes. The inference is clear that it refused to extend any credit to Candy Shoppes, so that in the event of insolvency or liquidation of Candy Shoppes, it could claim title to the inventory and thereby deprive the creditors of Candy Shoppes of any opportunity to enforce collection of their claims against the assets of Candy Shoppes. Under this arrangement between the two companies Candy Shoppes, except for fixtures, had virtually no assets against which creditors could enforce their claims.

Every ten days an inventory was taken by Candy Shoppes, and a check for candy sold was drawn by it, payable to the Manufacturing Corporation. The evidence further discloses that plaintiff was not informed by Edith Kanelos, and he did not know during the period of service, that the Manufacturing Corporation and Candy Shoppes were two separate corporations conducted by her.

The controlling question is whether the separate corporate entities can be used as a shield against liability, if, under all the circumstances, it would work a fraud upon creditors dealing with them.

In Dregne v. Five Cent Cab Co., 381 Ill. 594, at pages 602–603, 46 N.E.2d 386, at page 390, affirming our holding, 313 Ill.App. 539, 40 N.E.2d 739, the court said:

> "A corporation is an entity separate and distinct from its shareholders and, generally, from other corporations with which it may have relations. Indeed, the fact that the shareholders of two corporations are identical does not, necessarily, mean that the two corporations are to be considered as a single entity. Nor do the facts that one corporation owns shares in another and that they have mutual dealings require that they be regarded as one and the same corporation. Conversely, the legal fiction of distinct corporate existence will be disregarded when necessary to circumvent fraud or where the corporation is so organized and controlled, and its affairs so conducted, as to make it a mere instrumentality of another corporation. . . . In particular, it has been held that if the one corporation is merely a dummy or sham, the distinct corporate entity will be disregarded and the two corporations will be treated as one. . . ."

We think the trial court was justified in viewing Candy Shoppes as a mere instrumentality of the other corporation, and that the affairs of the two corporations were so managed and controlled by the same interlocking officers, directors and single stockholder, as to constitute one corporate entity in its dealings with creditors.

The judgment is correct and is affirmed.

(H) ACTIVITIES, MANAGEMENT AND CONTROL

The state law under which the corporation was created determines the outer limits of corporate activities and organization. Since state laws generally extend considerable latitude to the corporation on these matters, as a rule activities and organization are governed by the articles of incorporation of the corporation.

The articles of incorporation are the constitution of the corporation. They generally set forth the permissible activities of the corporation, how it is to be organized, the rights of the shareholders and how the corporation will be managed.

Sometimes these matters are phrased in general terms in the articles of incorporation, and articulated more specifically in the corporate by-laws. In large corporations there is likely to be a set of corporate documents which delineate the chain of command and spell out the authority of corporate officers and employees to handle particular corporate matters. The ultimate power within the corporation lies in the shareholders. The shareholders delegate this power to an elected Board of Directors. In theory, the Board of Directors controls long-term corporate policies, while the day-by-day operations are to be handled by the corporate officers.

This model of corporate control will vary depending upon the type of corporation. In a smaller corporation, the Board of Directors, or even large shareholders, may exert an influence upon day-to-day operations. If the corporation is a large publicly-held corporation with thousands of shareholders, the actual power is largely with the management. Even though theoretically the shareholders can displace the Board of Directors, the diffusion of share ownership often makes it difficult for this to be done and gives the Board of Directors and the officers of the corporation effective power, with the shareholders having little control over policy or corporate acts.

Some corporations have cumulative voting of shareholders for directors. This means that a shareholder who is asked to choose a slate of seven members of the board may cast all of his seven votes for one candidate. Cumulative voting is required in some states, and has the effect of protecting minority interests in the corporation.

The directors choose the officers of the corporation. Usually they will select a president, vice president, secretary, and treasurer. Larger corporations might also, through the board of directors, designate persons to serve as general counsel, controller, or as other corporate officers.

The officers are in charge of the day-by-day running of the corporation. The larger the corporation, the more likely it is that many of the details will be delegated to other employees of the corporation.

There has been a marked development in American law towards extending fiduciary obligations (fair dealing) to directors and to officers. Directors and officers owe each other fiduciary duties of fair dealing. Directors and officers owe a fiduciary duty to the shareholders. It may not be proper, for example, for a member of the board or for an officer to use his inside information to purchase shares of corporate stock from shareholders who are not aware of the inside information known by the director or officer. Also, directors and officers are not permitted to take advantage of economic opportunities which should be made available to the corporation.

The articles of incorporation usually provide for annual shareholder's meetings, as well as for periodic meetings of the Board of Directors. Minutes must be kept of all board proceedings. The administrative burden of operating a corporation can be formidable.

(I) PROFITS AND LOSSES

Usually the Board of Directors determines the disposition or distribution of profits made by a corporation. Sometimes its control is limited by the articles of incorporation, especially with regard to the rights of preferred shareholders. In addition, it may have obligations to the creditors of the corporation, based upon contracts or upon the bond agreements made between the corporation and lenders. Profits may be reinvested in the corporation, and used for corporate purposes.

While the board determines when, and how large, a share of its profits are to be paid as dividends to its shareholders, most states regulate the board in these matters. The board may pay dividends only out of certain specified funds. Sometimes, the Board of Directors may issue a stock dividend instead of a cash dividend. In such cases, the shareholders receive additional shares in the corporation instead of money. There may be statutory or other limitations relating to the redemption of shares by the corporation, and to the repurchase by the corporation of its own shares.

If the Board of Directors unlawfully issues dividends, the board members may be liable to the corporation, and to those creditors of the corporation harmed by the unlawful declaration of dividends.

Normally, individual shareholders are not responsible for losses of the corporation because of the insulation from personal liability given corporate shareholders. If the shareholder has paid for his shares in accordance with his purchase agreement with the corporation, he is not liable for any obligations of the corporation. (As mentioned earlier, under certain circumstances, shareholders may be held liable for acts of the corporation. Usually this results from specific statutes dealing with certain types of corporations.)

(J) LIFE OF CORPORATION

One of the advantages of the corporation is its "perpetual life." Sole proprietorships end with the death of the sole proprietor. Often, partnerships end with the death of any of the partners. The corporation will continue despite the death of any of the shareholders. Some jurisdictions permit a corporation to be created for a period short of perpetuity. Most corporations are formed for perpetual duration. There are methods of applying to a court to dissolve a corporation in the event of a deadlock among the Board of Directors, or under certain other circumstances.

(K) TAXATION

While the taxation of the corporations is a complicated subject, a few generalizations can be made. If the corporation is a separate entity, the use of the corporation involves what is sometimes called double taxation. This means that the corporation pays income tax upon income made, and the shareholder pays income tax when dividends are distributed to him. As has been mentioned, some smaller corporations can elect to be treated as partnerships for tax purposes. (In some instances, a partnership can be taxed as a corporation.) While there is obviously a disadvantage in the double taxation, there are many tax advantages to incorporating.

First, the first $25,000 of income is currently taxed at 22%, while income over $25,000 is taxed at the corporate rate, which is currently 48%. This could be less than the tax rate of a partnership, if the partners were in a high tax bracket. More important, the corporation and its employees can derive many tax advantages from the use of fringe benefits. The use of profit sharing plans, insurance plans, and other fringe benefits, can be advantageous to both the corporation and the employee. Deductions for such fringe benefits may be allowable to the corporation as a tax deduction in the year the contribution was made, while the employee may not be taxed at all, or if taxed, not until the fringe benefits are actually received.

In certain circumstances, shareholders can treat certain gains as capital gains, usually at a lower rate than personal income rates. This can occur if a corporation increases in value and the major shareholders sell their interests to an acquiring corporation.

(L) DISSOLUTION

The dissolution of a corporation is complicated, and is governed largely by statute. Also, the bankruptcy laws play a large role in determining what happens to assets of the corporation upon dissolution. This treatise will not go into dissolution problems.

SECTION 4.05 NONPROFIT CORPORATION

Nonprofit corporations are very similar in organization and operation to profit corporations. The major difference is that no profits can be distributed to shareholders by a nonprofit corporation. Examples of nonprofit corporations are hospitals, most educational institutions, and charities.

Capital for a nonprofit corporation is raised by donations and grants, and, occasionally, by the sale of shares. Usually there are members instead of shareholders. The members elect the Board of Directors or Trustees, who select officers to run the corporation. There are articles of incorporation, by-laws, meetings, and other similarities to a profit corporation. Generally, the shareholders are insulated from personal liability for the debts of the corporation. Such corporations are exempt from taxes, as they have no profit. Tax exemptions can be lost if certain types of political or profit making activity are engaged in by nonprofit corporations.

SECTION 4.06 PROFESSIONAL CORPORATION

One of the great advantages of the corporate form has been its flexibility. By modifications of the basic corporate structure, especially as to control, liability, and shares, the corporate form has been used in many types of business arrangements to accomplish many different purposes. Many professionals have considered, and some have adopted, the use of the corporate form.

Architects and engineers are finding the corporate structure attractive as a mode of practice. There are two basic questions which should be considered in determining the proper business organization for design professionals. First, is the corporate form permitted by state law for professional groups such as architects and engineers? Secondly, if it can be used, is the corporate form a desirable form of business organization for design professionals? These questions will be discussed in Chapter 32.

SECTION 4.07 FOREIGN CORPORATION

Usually, a corporation is organized under the law of a particular state. This means that the law of that state controls most of the requirements of the corporation's organization and operation. Often the state of incorporation is chosen because laws in a particular state are easier to comply with, or because these laws permit easier control by management or majority shareholders.

The corporation may operate in many states other than the state of its incorporation. In such cases, the corporation is a "foreign" corporation in all states in which it operates, other than its state of incorporation.

States usually assert the power to control foreign corporations which do business in their states. A state may levy franchise taxes and income taxes against the foreign corporation, based upon some stated proportion of its shares or its total business in the state. Also, many states have enacted statutes which permit certain actions to be brought against foreign corporations which do not have agents in the state, but which do business in the foreign state. Such states permit judicial actions to be commenced by mailing the summons and complaint to the foreign corporation, or to a designated state official.

States often regulate specific types of foreign corporations, such as insurance companies, by requiring that the companies comply with state laws as a prerequisite to permitting the company to do any business in the state.

SECTION 4.08 JOINT VENTURE

Joint ventures resemble partnerships, but are distinguishable from partnerships because they are created for one specific project or transaction. Frequently, joint ventures are created by large corporate enterprises which find that their capital structure does not permit projects which require a great deal of capital. Two or more corporations may band together for the operation of such a project. Usually the agreement under which the joint venture is created is complex, and sets forth in great detail the rights and duties of the joint venturers. In the absence of a detailed agreement, principles of partnership law are generally applicable. The joint venturers must be fair in their dealings with each other. Usually profits and losses are shared, and there is unlimited liability to the joint venturers, just as if they were partners. Normally, a joint venture is taxed as a partnership.

SECTION 4.09 UNINCORPORATED ASSOCIATION

Another form of association is the unincorporated association. Design professionals frequently perform services for fraternal lodges, social clubs, labor unions, churches, and other organizations of a similar nature. While many of these groups operate in the form of a nonprofit corporation many do not. It is important to understand the basic structure of unincorporated associations, especially with regard to the liability of the officers, members, and property of the association for the contractual obligations incurred on behalf of the association.

Generally, unincorporated associations are not legal entities. For this reason, under early American law they were not able to hold property in the association name, make contracts, sue in the name of the association or be sued as a group. They were merely a group of individuals who banded together to accomplish a particular purpose.

In most states, statutes have removed many of the former procedural difficulties. While they are still not legal entities, unincorporated associations are often permitted to contract, to hold property, to sue or be sued in the name of the association.

Usually such groups have constitutions, by-laws, and other group-created rules, that govern the rights and duties of the members as between themselves. They elect officers who have specified authority, such as hiring employees and running the activities of the association.

Who is liable for the contractual obligations of the association? All the members generally are responsible for those contracts entered into by the officers who were authorized by the members. This liability rests upon agency principles.

Frequently, it is difficult to establish the authority of the officers, since formalities are often dispensed with in these organizations. It may be necessary to show evidence of a meeting of members who passed resolutions authorizing the officers to make a particular contract. While the officers might have certain inherent authority by virtue of their position, important projects, such as the construction of a building, usually are beyond the scope of their inherent authority.

Officers who make the contract may be individually liable, if the contract was clearly made by them as individuals. Also, it may be possible to hold the officers on the ground that they have misrepresented their authority if the contract was not authorized. Because of the potential risk to officers and to members, many contracts contain provisions which limit liability to certain designated property, which is held in trust for the association in those states where they are not permitted to own property in the association name. A "trust" is divided ownership in which legal title is in the name of certain individuals who hold the property for the benefit of the trust beneficiaries (in this case, the association or its members). Where the association is permitted to hold property in its own name, liability is often limited to that property.

SECTION 4.10 LOOSE "ASSOCIATION"

Design professionals sometimes use the term "association" in a sense other than a group of individuals who band together as entrepreneurs. For example, a group of young architects may "associate" for practice in a common location. Each architect may be a sole proprietor in the sense that he works for himself, but each of the sole proprietors have joined together to share a suite of offices, equipment and clerical help. This "association" may look like a partnership to third parties. If so, each of the associates may find himself liable for the acts of another. Such "associations" are merely an arrangement for sharing expenses but are not true business associations as that term has been used in this chapter.

Sometimes an established architectural or engineering firm takes on a young design professional as an "associate". If he is paid a salary, and is subject to the directions of the firm, he is really an employee. The term "associate" in such a case is a professional euphemism for employee.

A third use of "associate" relates to the arrangement that may be made between two architectural firms to perform certain work. For example, a New York firm might associate a firm in Los Angeles, if the New York firm has agreed to design and administer a project in Los Angeles. There may be many reasons to "associate" with a local firm. Such an association could be a joint venture if the firms agree to share profits and losses in some manner. If the local firm merely agrees to perform certain designated functions, without any stake in the profits, the local firm is merely performing these services on a contracting, rather than an entrepreneurial, basis.

Similar to the "association" with a local firm is the arrangement under which an architect "associates" with another local architect or engineer. The purpose of this association may be to use the particular skill of the other architect or engineer. This is common in complex construction projects. Unless there is a true joint venture, this form of "association" is like hiring a local firm for an out-of-town project. Such "associations" are unlike the other associations discussed, since there is no element of joining together in an entrepreneurial sense.

Some legal aspects of such loose associations will be discussed in § 32.05.

REVIEW QUESTIONS

1. Why is the choice of a partner so important?

2. In the absence of a partnership agreement to the contrary, how do partners share profits and losses?

3. In what ways do various levels of government regulate a corporation?

4. What does piercing the corporate veil mean, and when will this be done by a court?

5. What are the principal advantages a corporation offers its shareholders?

6. Who and what determines whether a dividend shall be issued, and in what amount?

7. What is the difference between preferred and common shares?

8. What are the principal differences between organizing a hospital as a non-profit corporation and organizing a voluntary association?

9. Under what theory will members of an unincorporated fraternal organization be liable for obligations of the organization?

QUESTIONS FOR CLASS DISCUSSION

1. Why has the partnership form continued to be used, when from a liability and duration standpoint, as well as others, it is less desirable than a corporation?

2. Why should legislation regulate declaration of dividends?

3. Why should shareholders of a corporation be accorded insulation from the liabilities of the corporation?

4. Should non-profit corporations be exempt from federal income taxes? Explain.

5. The immense size of some corporations in and of itself is harmful. Do you agree or disagree? Give your reasons.

PROBLEMS

1. A and B were partners in an architectural firm. B's brother, C, was a struggling young architect, hardly able to pay his bills. B was approached by a prospective client to build a $50,000 residence at a $5,000 commission. B suggested that the client go to C, since C needed the business much more than A and B. A is unhappy with this. Does he have any legal recourse against B?

2. A and B were architectural partners under an oral agreement. A worked about twice as many hours as B did. A wants to split the profits on a 2 to 1 basis because of the difference in work time put in by the two partners. Is he legally correct? Give your reasons.

3. Alameda Engineers, Inc. was a corporation which issued 120 shares of stock. The shares were owned equally by A, B and C, all licensed mechanical engineers. Each was a member of the board of directors, with A serving as chairman. The board of directors elect-

ed A as President, B as Vice President and C as Secretary-Treasurer. They specialized in mechanical work for hospitals and schools but occasionally did mechanical work for office buildings. A was contacted by an architect regarding the mechanical work for a six-story office building. A and B then formed a separate partnership and obtained a commission in the name of the partnership to do the work. They rented office space, hired a staff and started performance. All of this was unknown to C, who was in another state on a large corporate job. A and B worked on the project at night, but did about 10% of the work during periods of time they would normally have been working on corporation matters. C has returned and has found out about this agreement. Does he have any rights against A and B? Give your reasons.

Part II

THE DESIGN PROFESSIONAL-CLIENT RELATIONSHIP

Introduction

Chapters 5 through 11 treat the significant aspects of the design professional-client relationship. Chapter 5 examines the legal aspects of establishing the relationship. Chapters 6 and 7 cover, respectively, the basic obligations of the design professional and his client. Chapter 8 extracts from those basic obligations certain specialized problems (Costs, Fiduciary Duties and Ownership of Plans). Chapter 9 treats the transfer of contractual rights to third parties and performing contractual obligations through third parties. Chapter 10 discusses termination of the relationship while Chapter 11 deals with judicial measures of recovery for breach of contract.

Parties to a professional relationship may resort to the courts where there is a breakdown in the trust and respect vital to such a relationship. Clients are more likely to seek legal relief when they think they have not been treated honestly or fairly by their architect or engineer. On occasion the client will, without provocation, turn upon his design professional when things go wrong. However, the client is far less likely to sue when he believes the design professional has acted honestly and fairly. A good professional relationship can cushion disappointments and avoid litigation.

To avoid legal entanglements, the design professional should be certain that his client is aware of the proper role of the design professional. The design professional should create and maintain a channel of communication with his client which will keep the client informed of developments. The trust and respect the client has for his design professional can be the single most important factor in influencing the client's judgment as to whether he will sue the design professional.

Chapter 5

ESTABLISHING THE RELATIONSHIP

SECTION 5.01 PROFESSIONAL STANDARDS OF PRACTICE

Many design professionals are members of professional societies such as the American Institute of Architects, the American Society of Mechanical Engineers, and similar organizations. These groups, like other voluntary associations such as the American Medical, Dental and Bar Associations, have standards of Professional Practice.

Generally, these standards, prohibit advertising or self laudatory publicity. An architect is directed not to supplant another architect "after definite steps have been taken by a client toward the latter's employment" nor to replace another architect until he has notified such other architect of the replacement in writing after conclusively determining that the original employment has been terminated. Many professional associations direct their members not to compete with each other by reduction of fees.

These standards rarely have legal sanctions behind them. The determination of whether a professional can practice depends upon the laws in his particular state, and the regulations and decisions of administrative agencies created to regulate his profession. See Chapter 31 for a discussion of state regulation of professional practice.

If membership in a professional society at state level is a condition to the right to practice one's profession, those rules of the professional association adopted by the state have legal sanctions behind them. Members of a professional association may owe an obligation to other association members to abide by the rules of the association. In Corrigan v. Cox, 254 Cal.App.2d 919, 62 Cal.Rptr. 733 (1967) a contract dispute between two dentists was resolved by reference to rules of the American Dental Association, an organization to which both disputants belonged.

SECTION 5.02 COMPETITIONS

One method of obtaining a commission is to win a competition. In competitions, a public or private owner may designate a selected number of professionals, or the profession generally, and request submission of designs for evaluation by a committee of jurors.

The rules relating to the professional competitions should be clearly defined in the invitation to competitors. Certain problems recur, and competitors should examine the terms of the competition carefully.

A competition owner may promise to designate a winner, or reserve the right not to select a winner. Obviously, in the latter type of competition, the person entering runs a substantial risk. Also, some competition invitations promise that the winner will be given the commission to design and supervise the project, in addition to a cash award. The competition terms should specify whether the designs designated as winning the competition belong to the competition owner. The absence of such a provision means that the design submitted for which a prize is paid will belong to the competition owner. (Protection of copyright should be considered at the time drawings are submitted to a competition. See §§ 40.04 and 40.05.)

The invitation to competitors may include the terms and conditions of the design professional-client relationship if the competition winner is awarded the commission. For this reason, as well as others, the terms of the competition should be checked carefully.

Aside from those arrangements where design services are performed within the client's organization, the preponderance of design commissions result from discussions and negotiations between a design professional and a prospective client. The balance of Chapter 5 will concentrate on the legal problems incident to creating design professional-client relationships in this manner.

SECTION 5.03 POWER TO ENTER INTO A CONTRACT FOR DESIGN SERVICES

(A) SOLE PROPRIETOR

There is little difficulty if the prospective client is the sole proprietor. He need account to no one, and he is not limited by articles of partnership or articles of incorporation. The only limit to his authority to enter into the contract relates to his capacity to contract generally. Persons below a certain age, or persons lacking the requisite mental capacity, cannot enter into contracts. Put more precisely, such contracts are "voidable," and can be avoided by the person who lacks the requisite capacity. Contractual capacity of sole proprietor clients is not a serious problem for design professionals.

(B) PARTNERSHIP

The power of the partnership to enter into a particular contract in question is regulated by the articles of partnership. These articles may specify the types of projects in which the partnership may engage. However, the usual articles of partnership do not go very thoroughly into this matter. It is rare that a design professional will encounter difficulty over this question when he deals with a partnership client.

(C) CORPORATION

The statute under which the corporation is organized determines the activities of the corporation. Usually, there are broad statutory authorizations. More important, the articles of incorporation establish the limits of the power of the corporation. Usually the articles give broad grants of power, and there is little difficulty in fitting the transaction into the power of the corporation.

If the corporation attempts to engage in business which is not authorized by the articles, or by a state law regulating its activities, such an engagement is "ultra-vires", or beyond the power of the corporation.

At one time the defense of "ultra-vires" was troublesome for those dealing with corporations. However, the *ultra-vires* defense has been severely restricted by the courts and by statute. As a rule, the person who deals with a corporation can assume that the corporation has the legal power to enter into the transaction. The defense of *ultra-vires* may cause difficulties within the corporate structure itself. However, as to third persons it is not a particularly troublesome problem.

(D) UNINCORPORATED ASSOCIATIONS

Without statutory authorization, an unincorporated association cannot enter into any contracts in its own name. This has been changed in some states. If the contract is made with the unincorporated association, sometimes courts hold that such a contract is a joint contract with all members of the association.

SECTION 5.04 AUTHORITY TO MAKE REPRESENTATIONS

During the negotiations, statements will be made by both the design professional and the person with whom he is dealing. Assurances will be given, promises made and factual representations given. At some later date the authority of the person with whom the design professional dealt to make these representations may be disputed.

(A) SOLE PROPRIETOR

If the person with whom the design professional is dealing is the sole proprietor himself, there is no difficulty with authority. Obviously, he has the requisite authority to make representations which will be binding upon himself. If the person with whom the design professional is dealing is an agent or employee of the sole proprietor, then the question of representation and authority will be handled by the doctrines of agency. The agent's representations will bind the principal if they are authorized, or if there is apparent authority.

Since most of the agency questions involve the scope of authority of corporate agents or employees, further discussion of the agency question will be deferred until § 5.04(c), which deals with authority to make representations, and § 5.05(c), which treats authority to make contracts.

(B) PARTNERSHIP

Each general partner is a general agent who can bind the partnership. When an architect or engineer deals with one of the partners, there is usually no agency question. It is only when he deals with an agent or employee of the partnership that there be some agency-authority difficulty. This will be covered more fully in §§ 5.04(c) and 5.05(c).

(C) CORPORATION

Usually, the potential client is a corporation. A corporation must act through representatives. Problems can arise as to the authority of the person with whom the design professional dealt directly, to make representations.

Large corporations often have detailed documents which deal with the actual authority of corporate employees to enter into contracts. Usually they do not spell out authority to make representations, because the corporation usually uses the contract itself to limit the authority of the negotiator.

Realistically, the design professional will have to rely upon appearances and common sense in determining whether the person with whom he is dealing has the authorization to make any representation which induces the making of the contract. To a substantial degree, this question will depend upon the position of the employee in the corporate structure, the importance of representation, and the size of the corporation. The more important the representation, and the more important the contract, the more likely it is that only a person higher up in the chain of command will have the authority to make representations which bind the corporation. Also, when a corporation is large, a relatively lower corporate position of the person making the representation may be sufficient to hold the corporation. For example, in a large national corporation, the head of the purchasing department may be authorized to make representations, while in a smaller company it may take a vice-president, or some other high-ranking officer, to make binding representations.

One method of avoiding the problem of unauthorized representation is to be certain that any representations made during negotiation are incorporated in the final agreement. If the corporate client objects to a provision because the negotiating agent did not have authority to make the representation, then the design professional can determine whether to proceed without the representation.

Unfortunately, many representations that are made during the negotiations are not included in any final agreement. Sometimes this occurs because of a reluctance on the part of the design professional to add to or change the final contract submitted to him by a corporate representative. Also, representations sometimes do not find their way into final agreements where the agreement is expressed in a form provided by the design professional. Frequently these forms have no provisions for representations as to factual matters, and the design professional is hesitant to change the form. The bulk of the difficulties arise when the final agreement does not contain representations that have been made during negotiations by the negotiating agent of the corporate client. In these cases, the principal question typically is not the authority of the agent, but rather how much effect a court will give to any contractual disclaimers of representations and whether these disclaimers will affect the design professional's right to prove that these representations were made. This will be discussed in greater detail in §§ 5.04(e) and 5.04(f).

(D) UNINCORPORATED ASSOCIATIONS

The same generalizations made with regard to sole proprietorship, partnerships, and corporations apply to unincorporated associations. The question is whether the person with whom the design professional deals directly has actual or apparent authority to make these representations.

(E) PAROL EVIDENCE RULE

When difficulties arise over precontract representations, they usually arise in the following manner. A dispute over the rights and duties of the parties develops, and one of the parties asserts that representations were made to him upon which he relied and which proved to be false. He may claim these representations were of existing facts or promises of future acts. Often, these representations are not included in a written agreement subsequently signed by the parties. The party who has been charged with making the misrepresentations points to the written contract and states that the written contract contains the entire agreement, and evidence of any antecedent representations or promises not contained in it are inadmissible and cannot be considered by the court. This involves what is sometimes called the "parol evidence rule".

Fraudulent or deceitful misrepresentations, either of existing facts or of promises of subsequent acts, are almost always going to be admissible if a dispute arises. This is because the parol evidence rule assumes that there has been a validly formed contract, and allegations of fraud negate this.

If there are no allegations of fraud, admissibility will depend upon whether the writing is the complete and final agreement between the parties. The resolution of this question will depend upon the appearance of completeness of the writing, the degree of variation between the asserted oral representations and the writing, the business experience of the parties, whether they were represented by attorneys, and other considerations. About all that can be said about this rule is that sometimes it is applied and sometimes it is not. If there is a provision in the writing which states that the writing is the complete and final agreement of the parties, it is likely that the supposed representations or promises not contained in the writing will not be considered unless fraud is alleged. See § 6.02(c) for further discussion of the parol evidence rule.

(F) EFFECT OF CONTRACT CLAUSES LIMITING AUTHORITY OF REPRESENTATIVE

Alleged oral representations become more complicated if the claimed representation was made by an agent of the client. Such is always the case when dealing with a corporate client, and frequently when the client is a partnership. The client may point to a provision in the writing itself, which states that any representations that have been made and not included in the final written contract were beyond the scope of authority of the person making the representations. This is a contractual attempt to insulate the principal from any unauthorized representations by agent or employees. Frequently these disclaimers of authority are buried in the fine print of a complicated written agreement. Generally these disclaimers are effective, but sometimes they are not. They can usually be attacked by allegation of fraud.

As stated earlier the design professional should incorporate representations of existing facts and promises of future conduct into the written agreement. If he does not include them in the writing, he *may* be able to show them at a later date, but he runs a serious risk of being precluded by the court from proving such representations.

SECTION 5.05 AUTHORITY TO ENTER INTO CONTRACT

(A) SOLE PROPRIETOR

The same generalization made in § 5.04(a) applies to this problem. If the design professional is dealing with the sole proprietor, clearly the latter has authority to enter into the contract. If he is dealing with an agent of the sole proprietor, the concepts of agency and scope of actual or apparent authority control. Generally, sole proprietorships are small business operations. For a sole proprietorship, it is likely that a contract for design services or construction is a serious and important transaction. For that reason, it is not likely that agents of a sole proprietor have this authority.

(B) PARTNERSHIP

The same is true of most partnership clients. Except in unusual circumstances, most partnerships are not large businesses. It is likely that only the partners have the authority to enter into contracts for design services or construction. While the partners, as between themselves, may have designated certain partners to enter into contracts, unless this matter comes to the attention of the design professional, it is unlikely that such a division of authority between the partners will affect third parties. Normally, one can expect that partners have authority to enter into most contracts (It is advisable to get *all* the partners to sign the contract for maximum protection.).

If the partnership is a large organization, it is possible that agents of the partnership will have authority to enter into a contract for performance of design services and construction. However, it would probably be best in such a case to have some written authorization from a partner that the agent has this authority.

(C) CORPORATION

Here difficulty can arise. Suppose the corporation has the power to enter into the particular contract in question. However, it is common for the Articles of Incorporation, or the by-laws, to specify *who* has the authority to make designated contracts, and how this authorization is to be manifested. The more unusual the contract, or the more money involved, the higher the authority needed. Frequently, contracts which deal with land, loans, or sales or purchases not in the normal course of business, will have to be authorized by the Board of Directors. Lesser contracts may require authorization by top management, while for contracts involving smaller amounts of money, or those in the usual course of business, subordinate officials may be authorized.

As for the administrative process, it may be required that the contracts needing board approval be passed by resolution and entered into the minutes of the board meeting. In addition, the by-laws or authority book will frequently state which corporate officials must actually sign the contract. Again, the importance of the contract will usually determine at what echelon the contract must be signed, and how many officials must sign it. The corporate by-laws or state statutes may require that the corporate seal be affixed to certain contracts.

For *maximum* protection the design professional would check the articles of the corporation, the by-laws and the authority book of the corporation. He should see who has the authority to authorize the contract and whether the proper mechanism, such as the appropriate resolution and entry of the resolution upon the minutes were made. Then he would determine whether the person who wants to or has signed for the corporation has authority to do so.

In very important contracts, it may be wise to do all of these things. It is not unreasonable for the design professional to request that the corporation attach a copy of its articles, by-laws and a copy of the resolution authorizing the particular project in question to the contract. Also, the design professional could reasonably request that the contract itself be signed by the appropriate officers of the corporation, such as the president and secretary of a smaller corporation, or the vice-president and secretary of a larger corporation.

There may be situations when these precautions need not be taken. The project may not seem big enough to warrant this extra caution. Also, the design profesional may have dealt with this corporation before and is reasonably assured that there will be no difficulty over the question of the authority to contract. However, laziness, or fear of antagonizing the client, is not a justifiable excuse.

(D) UNINCORPORATED ASSOCIATION

Dealing with unincorporated associations seems simple, but may involve many legal traps. In order to hold the members of the association, it is necessary to show that the persons with whom the contract was made were authorized to make the contract. In such cases, it is vital to examine the constitution or by-laws of the unincorporated association, and to attach a copy of the resolution of the governing board authorizing that the contract be made. Again, the persons signing the contract should be the authorized officers of the association.

It may be wise to obtain legal advice when dealing with an unincorporated association, unless the unincorporated association is a client for whom the design professional has worked in the past and in whom the design professional has confidence.

SECTION 5.06 COLLECTIBILITY OF THE FEE

In private contracts, as opposed to public contracts, the question of financial responsibility is probably more important than power to enter into the contract, authority to make representations and authority to enter into the contract. Many design professionals have spent considerable time performing design services, only to go unpaid for their efforts. Professional persons do not like to confront the question of financial responsibility openly. They prefer to assume that the clients who come to them are honorable people who will pay their obligations. Usually this is the case. However, there are many situations where this is not the case, and the design professional should seriously confront the problem of financial responsibility.

The financial condition of the client and the funding of the project are important for another reason. Where the client has financial problems, or where there is very little elasticity in the project budget, it is more likely that a claim will be asserted against the design professional when things go wrong.

(A) RETAINERS AND INTERIM FEE PAYMENTS

Most standard form contracts created by professional societies of design professionals provide for initial retainers to be paid by the client at the time the contract is signed, and for interim fee payments to be made during performance. A major purpose of such provisions is to give the design professional working capital.

Another function is to limit the scope of the financial risk taken by the design professional. If his services and efforts do not run very far beyond the amount of money which he is paid, his risk of nonpayment is substantially reduced. The difficulty is that design professionals frequently do not insist upon the client complying with these contract terms. *This is absolutely essential.* If the matter is explained properly to the client, there should be no difficulty. When the client seems to be insulted when polite requests are made for advance retainers and interim fee payments when due, this should alert the design professional to possible dangers. Clients who react adversely to such requests are often clients who either do not have the money or will not pay even if they do have the money.

(B) CREDIT CHECKS

It is not unprofessional for design professionals to try to establish the financial responsibility of the persons or business associations with whom they are dealing. A credit check may save a design professional much grief and money. It is strongly recommended that if the client is new, credit checks be made to determine the financial responsibility of the client.

(C) ONE-MAN AND CLOSELY HELD CORPORATIONS: INDIVIDUAL LIABILITY OF OFFICERS

Many small businesses are incorporated, and the shares of the business held entirely by the proprietor of the business. He is permitted to do this by law. One of his major purposes is to insulate his personal assets from the liabilities of the corporation. Also, some corporations are small, closely held corporations, with the shares owned by a family or by the persons actually running the business. In rare cases, the law will pierce the corporate veil and treat the inadequately capitalized one-man, or closely held, corporation as a sole proprietorship or partnership. If this is done, the design professional can go after the individual assets of the shareholder or shareholders. However, piercing a corporate veil is not an easy task. If the credit check reveals that the corporation is merely a shell and one that has very few assets, it may be necessary to insure that the shareholders assume personal liability. To do so, the sole shareholder or shareholders should sign in his or their corporate capacities as representatives of the corporation, and also sign individually as representing himself or themselves. If those signing individually are solvent, this is a reasonably secure method of assuring payment if the corporation is unable to pay the contractual obligations. If the individuals signing are not solvent, the individual liability will be of little value. A refusal to sign as an individual may be a warning that the corporation is in serious financial trouble.

(D) A SURETY OR GUARANTOR

Chapter 18 discusses the role of the surety in the construction phase of the project. If the design professional believes the person with whom he is dealing is not financially sound, he may want to obtain a financially sound person to guarantee the obligation of the corporation or the individual. Subject to some exceptions, promises to pay the debt, default, or miscarriage of another must be in writing. If the design professional requests and obtains a third person to act as surety for the client, he should make certain that the surety signs the contract or a separate surety contract. Legal advice should be obtained where a surety or guarantor is involved.

(E) REAL OR PERSONAL PROPERTY SECURITY

Another method of securing the design professional against the risk that the client will not pay him is to obtain a security interest in real or personal property. This may mean obtaining a mortgage or a deed of trust upon the land upon which the project is to be constructed, or upon other assets owned by the client. This may seem a drastic measure. If there is that much insecurity, it may be advisable not to deal with the client at all. However, design professionals should be aware of the possibility of personal or real property security interests in such a situation. Again, the law regarding creation of these security interests is complicated and beyond the scope of this treatise. For this reason, it is strongly recommended that legal advice be obtained if such a method is employed.

SECTION 5.07 HUSBANDS AND WIVES AS CLIENTS

(A) MARITAL PROPERTY

Often design professionals are retained by a husband or wife who owns particular property, and desires the services of the design professional. In most states, married persons can hold property separately or in various forms of co-ownership. It is possible to find that a husband with whom the design professional dealt has no property, and that all the property belongs to his wife. In such a case, the design professional may obtain a judgment against the husband but be unable to satisfy it because the husband has no non-exempt assets. It is important to be aware of this problem in dealing with married clients.

(B) AGENCY CONCEPTS: CONTRACTING PARTIES

The mere fact that two persons are husband and wife does not automatically mean that each is the agent of the other. However, the law is likely to find such agency if there is some common purpose which is being furthered by the acts of the spouse who is claimed to be the agent of the other spouse, or if unjust enrichment would result without a finding of agency. If the design professional deals with a husband, it is likely that representations made by the wife during the course of the negotiations will be binding on the husband. It is best, in dealing with a married couple, to have both husband and wife sign the client agreement. In this way they are both bound, and a design professional should not run into the problem of having an uncollectible action against one spouse because all the property is owned by the other spouse

SECTION 5.08 MECHANICS' LIEN LAWS

A mechanics' lien may furnish a method by which a design professional is able to collect for professional services rendered. Persons are sometimes given a security interest in property which they have improved, to the extent of any debt owed to the improver by the owner of the property or someone who has authority to bind the owner. If a valid lien is created, the lien claimant, if he is unpaid, can demand a judicial foreclosure of the property and satisfy his obligation out of the proceeds.

Some state statutes give design professionals mechanics' lien rights. In some states they have been brought in under general provisions granting liens to those who improve real property. However, there are a number of stumbling blocks which frequently make the lien remedy unavailable. Work usually has to commence upon the land in question. This means that the design professional is not likely to have a lien unless work has started on the land. In some states, the lien only covers services which directly benefit the land, such as supervision, but do not include design. Where design services are sufficient, they may have to be tied to supervision. Generally, the plans must be used in the project. Lien rights are rarely given on public structures, or for public improvements. There are a great many requirements for the creation of such a lien. Notices have to be given, filings have to be made, and actions have to be taken within specified time limits. Without strict compliance, there is no lien. Other persons may have equal or prior security rights in the land. The land value may not be able to pay the lien claims in their entirety.

Mechanics' liens statutes vary considerably from state to state, and are frequently changed by legislatures. Details and generalizations regarding mechanics' liens, and their availability to design professionals, could be misleading. It is sufficient to indicate that in many states such liens exist. The design professional should consult his lawyer to see whether he is within the class of persons accorded liens, and to ascertain the steps needed to perfect a lien. It is dangerous to undertake work for a client who may not be able to pay for the work with the hope that, if he does not pay, there will be a right to a mechanics' lien. The possibility of being able to assert a mechanics' lien is never a substitute for a careful consideration of the financial responsibility of the client, and collecting interim fee payments.

For more on mechanics' liens see § 24.07.

SECTION 5.09 PUBLIC AGENCIES

There has been a proliferation of public agencies in American life. There is the federal government and the various agencies which contract for it, as well as state agencies. There are, in addition, counties, cities, villages, townships, irrigation districts, water districts, park districts, pollution districts, and transportation districts. In addition, there are public schools, public hospitals and numerous other types of public agencies with which the design professional may deal at some time. Many public agencies are given limited powers by statute. Sometimes, contracts with these agencies are made on condition that there be specific appropriations or that there be bond approvals by the voters of the district. Without these conditions occurring, here may be no contract and no money for services rendered by the design professional. Power to contract can be a significant problem. In some states, there must be competitive bidding for architectural or engineering services. In other states, it is permissible for public agencies to negotiate contracts with professionals, such as architects and engineers.

On the whole, there is not much difficulty in dealing with federal public agencies. They are generally well run, and contracts that are made by contracting officers who represent the agencies usually do not run into such problems such as authority to contract, availability of appropriations, and passing of bond issues. Local agencies cause the greatest difficulty.

Taxpayers who do not approve of the project often scrutinize the transactions carefully to see if all the requisite formalities were met. They will go into the question of whether the resolution was passed by the proper legislative body of the public agency. They will examine every aspect of the transaction hoping to uncover possible corruption or graft. In addition, they may try to overturn the decision of legislative bodies such as the city council or the board of supervisors. Also, these agencies are subject to audits by all levels of government, as well as to newspaper scrutiny. About all that can be recommended is that the design professional be aware of these risks and try to reduce his exposure by not doing too much work until he is certain that the deal is valid and will go through.

In addition to these sometimes disheartening situations, the design professional may find that he cannot rely upon representations of advice given to him by agents of the public agency. Apparent authority or estoppel is rarely applied against a public body. All statutory requirements must be met when he deals with public agencies.

SECTION 5.10 RECORD KEEPING

It is essential that the design professional prepare and keep careful records of all the negotiations leading to the contract and of any post-contract discussions and negotiations with the client. Memoranda should be made of phone conversations and conferences. These memoranda should, if possible, be sent to the client for his concurrence as soon as possible.

Such memoranda are helpful to the drafter of the contract, whether it be an attorney or the design professional himself. Disputes can develop over what was stated in various conversations. Many times the careful preservation of these records will eliminate honest misunderstandings where the client has forgotten or where his recollection is faulty. In addition, they may protect the design professional from unjustified claims and fraudulent conduct on the part of some clients. The necessity for careful and detailed records cannot be over-emphasized.

REVIEW QUESTIONS

1. Under what circumstances do rules of voluntary professional associations have legal sanction?

2. What are the interpretation questions which can arise in a competition?

3. What problem is dealt with by the parol evidence rule?

4. What are the ways a design professional can protect himself from working for a client who will not pay his bills?

5. Is the wife an agent of her husband solely by virtue of her being his wife?

6. What effect does a mechanics' lien law have upon the design professional and his fee?

QUESTIONS FOR CLASS DISCUSSION

1. Why not permit advertising by professionals?

2. Why should architects not approach a potential client when "definite steps have been taken by the client toward retaining another architect"?

3. Should the law have a rule which limits the provability of oral agreements when the parties have agreed to a writing? Explain.

4. Why do so many younger design professionals have difficulty in collecting fees?

5. Can you think of any methods other than those mentioned in the treatise to protect design professionals from going unpaid for their services?

6. Why shouldn't members of an unincorporated association be generally responsible for the contract obligations of the association?

PROBLEMS

1. X comes to see you at your architectural office. You have been in practice for three months and have not designed any projects. X gives you details regarding the construction of a five-story office building which he wishes you to design. He asks you to commence work immediately. What steps would you take toward protecting the collectibility of your fee?

2. Y approaches you and asks you to perform certain design services. He tells you that he is the vice-president of the Comac Corporation, a company that makes electronic equipment. He gives you his calling card, which identifies him. He tells you that it will take some time to get the formal contracts signed by the appropriate officers of the corporation, and that you should commence work immediately. He also tells you that a written, authorized contract will

be issued shortly. You note that he is driving a new car with the words "Comac Corporation" neatly embossed upon each door.

You commence work and in three weeks you bill Comac for $1,000 for schematic design work. Comac refuses to pay since they say Y was not authorized to bind the company. Would Comac have a legal defense? Give your reasons. What other facts would you like to know?

3. Z comes to your architectural office and asks that you perform certain design work. He says that he is the vice-president in charge of construction for the Atlas Company, a large interstate corporation. You have a lengthy discussion about the laboratory building which he is asking you to design for Atlas. You inform him that customarily the architect retains ownership of the plans and specifications. He agrees with you and then asks you to sign his company's form purchase order to seal the commission. You start to read it but he tells you that everything is standard and without looking at the form very carefully you sign it. After the project is completed, the company informs you that they are going to use some of your work for another project in a different state. You tell them that they cannot do this and they show you Section 17 of their standard purchase order form which states:

> Any products resulting from the performance of services under this contract shall belong to the buyer.

You inform Atlas that you made an agreement with regard to ownership with Z. Atlas then points to Section 18 of the purchase order form which states:

> Any representation made by any agent is not authorized unless it is contained in this contract. This is the entire and complete contract between the parties.

What are your legal rights against Atlas? Against Z? What further facts would you like to know?

Chapter 6

ARCHITECTURAL AND ENGINEERING SERVICES

SECTION 6.01 SOME ATTRIBUTES OF A PROFESSIONAL RELATIONSHIP

When a client retains an architect or engineer, a professional relationship is created. The client hires the professional to assist and advise him on technical matters which the client himself cannot handle. Even if the client has technical skills, he may want independent advice from someone outside his organization, or from someone not related in any way to the prospective project. What the client seeks is the professional skill of the architect or engineer.

There are other attributes to the professional relationship agreement. As a rule, a professional is not an entrepreneur. He does not have the advantage of potentially high returns upon his investment. He performs his services, and generally he expects to be paid for his time.

The incidents of a professional relationship may not be spelled out in detail. Often, professional relationships are created without any written contract, or, if there is a written contract, there will only be the briefest description of the services to be performed by the professional. This has resulted in a great deal of judicial difficulty interpreting such agreements.

SECTION 6.02 SOME APPLICABLE LEGAL DOCTRINES

Party autonomy (freedom of contract) generally permits the parties to determine what services are to be performed. Where there are disputes relating to the extent of services, courts try to ascertain the intention of the parties. Many times the intentions and expectations of each party will vary. In such a case, the law will have to decide whose expectations are to be protected.

(A) PROTECTION OF EXPECTATIONS OF CLIENT

In most professional contracts, the client knows less about the scope of services than does the professional. The client comes to the professional expecting that the professional will perform those services which the client cannot adequately perform for himself. He relies on the professional's ability to guide him and assist him in his undertaking.

As a rule, agreements of this type are interpreted against the professional. If there are areas of doubt, the reasonable expectations of the client are likely to be protected.

The professional person is supposed to know the areas of difficulty. If he does not point out these areas to the client, he runs a substantial risk of being held to the performance of services which he himself did not intend to perform.

These principles may not be applied if the client is a large institutional entity, such as a public agency or a large private corporation. In such cases the client may prepare the contract and present it to the design professional on a "take it or leave it" basis. If the design professional has good bargaining power, the final agreement may be a carefully worked out contract between the design professional and his client. If the design professional is forced to accept the client's contract, it may be interpreted in favor of the design professional. In the negotiated contract, neither party is likely to automatically be given the benefit of the doubt in close interpretation questions.

(B) SOME INTERPRETATION GUIDES

Since more interpretation questions arise relating to the contract between owner and contractor, any detailed discussion of interpretation will be postponed until Chapter 20. However, a few general interpretation guides should be mentioned in this chapter.

As stated in § 6.02(a), contracts are generally interpreted against the party who prepares the agreement. Handwritten portions are preferred to typewritten portions, and typewritten portions are given more weight than printed provisions.

Specific provisions are given more weight than general provisions. For example, suppose a contract between architect and client states that the architect will perform his services in accordance with normal architectural professional standards. Suppose further that the same agreement provides that the architect will visit the site at least once a day. If normal professional standards would not require that the architect visit the site this often, there is a conflict between the two provisions. In such a case it is likely that the provision specifically relating to the number of site visits will control the general provision requiring that the architect perform in accordance with accepted professional standards.

Also, words are generally used in their normal meanings, unless both parties know or should know of trade usages which have grown up around the use of certain terms. This rule is important in the design professional's relationship to his client. Often a word used in an agreement will have a definite meaning to the architect or engineer, but have a different meaning, or at least an indefinable meaning, to the client. For example, architects may know that when the term "supervision" is used, that it does not involve an on-the-job, day-by-day inspection. Yet, in some cases, clients might reasonably believe that when the architect agrees to supervise, that he is obligating himself to perform such day-by-day inspection.

(C) THE PAROL EVIDENCE RULE AND CONTRACT COMPLETENESS

One aspect of the parol evidence rule (See § 5.04(e)), relates to the provability of asserted prior oral agreements when the parties have assented to a written agreement. Clients may contend that an architect or an engineer agreed to perform certain services which are not specified in the written agreement. The attorney for the architect or engineer may contend that the writing spelled out the entire agreement, and that parol evidence or oral evidence is not admissible to "add to, vary or contradict a written document." Sometimes such oral agreements are provable, and sometimes they are not.

Generally, courts do not consider that written agreements between client and design professional are complete expressions of the entire agreement. Sometimes courts will refuse to listen to *any* evidence outside the writing, if they are convinced that the writing is clear enough in meaning so that they do not need outside assistance. But most courts will permit either party, especially the client, to show prior oral agreements not contained in the writing.

Attorneys for design professionals frequently rely upon the parol evidence rule when disputes arise, and during the trial. However, such reliance is often misplaced. This is especially so if the agreement is sketchy and does not spell out the details adequately, and if the client was not represented by an attorney during the negotiations. Reducing an arrangement to writing does not necessarily protect the design professional from assertions of additional oral agreements. However, the more detail included in the agreement, and the greater the likelihood that the client understood the terms or had legal counsel, the greater the probability that the client will *not* be permitted to prove the prior oral agreement.

Also, it must be kept in mind that the parol evidence rule relates only to the *provability* of such agreements. If such agreements are admitted into evidence, the trial court or the jury, depending upon who makes the determination of fact, must decide whether the evidence shows that such an agreement was made. Very often the attorney for the architect or engineer places heavy reliance upon the parol evidence rule and does not adequately prepare for the more important question of whether the asserted agreement took place. The parol evidence rule does not apply to agreements made after the written agreement was signed by the parties.

It is common for contracts to contain what are called "integration clauses." These state that the contract is the entire agreement between the parties. Their inclusion is intended to preclude the court from finding that the writing was not complete. In the absence of an allegation of fraud, integration clauses have been successful. Until recently, AIA Owner-Architect contracts did not contain an integration clause. But AIA Doc. B131 does have an integration clause. It will be interesting to see what the courts will do with this clause, in light of past decisions regarding completeness, and the generally accepted view that in such transactions not all of the agreement is likely to be expressed in the writing.

SECTION 6.03 A LOOK AHEAD AT COMPENSATION AND LIABILITY

Sometimes it is necessary to refer to matters which will be discussed in greater detail in a subsequent section. In discussing the question of the services of the design professionals, a brief discussion of fees and liability may be useful.

(A) BASIC FEES AND EXTRA SERVICES

Services are often divided into those covered by the basic fee, and those for which the design professional is to be paid an extra amount of compensation. In most cases, the design professional will be willing to perform any services within reason, and within his basic expertise, provided he is compensated for performance of these services. Disputes may arise over whether the services requested are compensable under the basic fee, or are extra services. The discussion relating to services will assume that the question relates to whether the services in question are covered within the basic fee. This is the area where difficulties usually develop.

(B) LIABILITY OF DESIGN PROFESSIONAL

This portion of the treatise deals with the relationship between the design professional and his client. While Chapters 30 and 34 deal more directly with liability questions, it is helpful to look generally at liability before discussing the services to be performed by the design professional.

The greater the services that are to be performed, the greater the risk of liability to architects and engineers. Architects and engineers have been urged to limit the scope of their services because of potentially increased liability. The liability may relate to a loss incurred by the client, based upon a supposed breach of the design professional contract. The client may incur liability to third parties because of the failure of the design professional to use due care in his performance. The client may assert a claim against his design professional because the client has incurred this liability. Finally, third parties who suffer losses may base their claim against the architect or engineer upon the failure of architect or engineer to perform his obligations properly, obligations which may have been created by the relationship between the client and the design professional.

SECTION 6.04 RANGE OF POSSIBLE PROFESSIONAL SERVICES

The range of potential professional services has been increasing in scope. Two reasons for this are the increased control over the construction process by governmental authorities, and the increasing role of the design professional in assisting in obtaining financial support for the project. What services *might* a client expect to be performed by the design professional?

Possible services could be:

1. Consultation and preparation of analysis and planning surveys.
2. Consultation regarding restrictions upon the use of land.
3. Examination of site, sub-soil, and surroundings.
4. Preparation of drawings relating to existing construction.
5. Preparation of schematic design studies and general description of the project.
6. Assistance in procuring financing.
7. Assistance in presentation of project before governmental authorities, planning groups, or boards of directors.
8. Preparation of cost predictions at various stages of the work.
9. Preparation of design development documents, such as plans and outline specifications.
10. Consultation with client over the type of construction contract to be employed.
11. Revision of previously approved drawings and specifications.
12. Preparation of documents for alternate bids.
13. Preparation of construction documents necessary to obtain bids by contractors.
14. Filing of documents with public authorities when required to do so by law.

15. Advice in determining the contractors who will be invited to bid.
16. Evaluation and approval of samples, schedules, and shop drawings submitted by contractor.
17. Preparation of change orders.
18. Inspection of the work in progress.
19. Issuance of certificates for payment and final certificate.
20. Determination of whether the work is progressing properly.
21. Deciding disputes relating to interpretation, performance, and excuse for non-performance.
22. Consultation regarding replacement of work destroyed by fire or by other causes during construction.
23. Arranging for a new contractor to replace one whose work is inadequate, or who has abandoned the project.
24. Inspection of project prior to expiration of guarantee.
25. Preparation of as-built drawings, showing construction changes and the final location of mechanical service lines and outlets.

This list, which is taken from a number of form contracts, is not exclusive. There may be other professional services which the client may request, or which the client will assert fall within normal professional services. The length of the list indicates that there are a great number of possible services which *can* fall within the scope of professional services furnished by a design professional. It is essential to determine in advance which of these services are to be performed, and which fall within the basic fee. After this is done, the written contract should reflect the actual agreement, and performance should be in accordance with the contract requirements, or with any subsequent modifications. In this regard, the standard form contracts suggested by professional societies are helpful if properly explained to the client.

SECTION 6.05 SEPARATION OF PROFESSIONAL FUNCTIONS

The building project involves the skills and efforts of many persons. The design professional should not obligate himself to perform services which he does not have the skill or time to perform properly, services which by law he is precluded from performing, or services for which he will have to rely totally and completely upon a consultant. While he may not be an expert in each phase, he should know enough to communicate with and to check up on his consultants.

A design professional should not offer advice on essentially legal matters. He should make clear to the client that these are services which he cannot by law perform, and which should be performed by the client's legal advisers. Illustrative of these services are opinions relating to easements, rights of adjacent land owners, zoning requirements, and matters relating to liability of the owner of land.

As for other professional services, the design professional often hires consultants. This will be discussed in §§ 9.02(a) and 30.11(f). For the moment, it is sufficient to state that if the architect or engineer agrees to perform certain services, and if he hires a consultant because of the consultant's greater knowledge, normally this does not relieve the design professional from liability if the consultant does not perform his job properly. One of the basic elements of contract is that the contracting party who is responsible for certain services cannot shield himself from liability by employing others to perform the services, unless the other contracting party agrees to relieve him from this liability.

SECTION 6.06 ASSISTANCE IN OBTAINING FINANCING

Frequently, the construction of a building project necessitates obtaining financing from a lender. In order to convince a lender that a loan in a particular amount should be granted, it may be necessary to give the lender documents which will enable him to determine whether he should grant the loan, and in what amount. The lender may want schematic designs or even design development; he may want these to determine the economic feasibility of the project, and the value of the improvement.

The client often presents material prepared by the design professional to a prospective lender. But does the design professional have any obligation to do more than permit the use of his work for this purpose? Does his basic fee cover such services as appearing before prospective lenders, advising the client as to who might be willing to lend the client money, or assisting the client in preparing any information which the lender might require?

While fact situations vary, some general observations can be made. If the client is a large institution with personnel who are experienced in obtaining financing, clearly basic design services should not include participation in obtaining financing. The same conclusion should be reached even when the client does not have employees skilled in such matters. Finance is generally not an aspect of the professional training and skill of an architect or engineer and should not be considered a part of basic design services. Only if architect or engineer has *specifically* agreed to provide these services should he be obligated to do so.

It may be to the design professional's advantage to furnish assistance to the client in such matters. Clients sometimes condition their obligation to continue the project upon the obtaining of financing. If so, it may be within the self-interest of the design professional to do all he can to assist the client in procuring financing. However, in the normal case, the design professional should not have any obligation to give advice on financing, or to take any positive steps to see that financing is obtained.

SECTION 6.07 SECURING APPROVAL OF PUBLIC AUTHORITIES

Greater governmental control and participation in all forms of economic activity has meant that the design professional increasingly deals with agencies of federal, state, and local government. The same problems can arise with regard to approval by public authorities that arise in the obtaining of financing. Must the design professional as part of his normal professional services appear before the planning commission, zoning board, or city council?

Cooperation of this sort may be reasonably expected by clients. Design professionals are expected to have expertise in certain matters which are often at issue in these public hearings. Also, it may be within the client's reasonable expectations that the architect or engineer will render reasonable assistance and advise the client on these matters. Courts have found implied promises in contracts that each party will do all that is reasonably necessary to secure fulfillment of the mutual objectives of the parties. A court could find the architect or engineer obligated to make appearances before a zoning board, either on the theory that this falls within the normal professional services contracted for, or that the professional impliedly obligates himself to use his best efforts to see that the project comes to fruition. Also, it may be to the advantage of the architect or engineer to use all his best efforts to obtain permission from public authorities to construct the project.

The AIA Doc. B131, at 1.3.15, states that the architect is entitled to an extra fee for:

> Providing services as an expert witness in connection with any public hearing, arbitration proceeding, or the proceedings of a court of record.

This covers acting as an expert witness, but it does not deal with the assistance and consultation which is often requested of an architect or engineer in connection with these hearings. Since the AIA contract specifies many services for which the architect is to be paid in addition to the basic fee, perhaps a court would hold that such services are covered by the basic fee.

SECTION 6.08 SECURING APPROVAL OF CLIENT

Where dealing with large private institutional clients, authorization to construct the project may be required to be granted by a decision of the board of directors or board of trustees. The person with whom the design professional has negotiated may have authority to hire the architect or engineer to do the design work. However, the actual construction of the project may require the approval of the board of directors, or some high corporate official. In such a case, the same problem discussed in § 6.07 can arise. Does the design professional obligate himself to use his best efforts to persuade the board of directors to approve the project? If he does so, is he entitled to extra pay for such efforts?

It is difficult to answer this question categorically. However, it would seem that the implied promise to use best efforts before public authorities is not so likely to be implied where the approval must be granted by a private board of directors of the client. Again, it may be advantageous from the standpoint of the design professional to use his best efforts. However, it is not likely that normal design services include this obligation.

SECTION 6.09 CONSTRUCTION COST PREDICTIONS

Where the contract does not impose an express obligation to make cost predictions, do normal design services include the obligation to make cost predictions? Zannoth v. Booth Radio Stations, 333 Mich. 233, 52 N.W.2d 678 (1952) held that the architect was obligated to provide cost predictions under his normal design services, while Baylor University v. Carlander, 316 S.W.2d 277 (Tex.Civ.App.1958) held that this did not fall within normal design services. An earlier standard form AIA contract required that cost estimates be given only if requested. Since 1961, the standard AIA contract has required that the architect give statements of probable construction costs.

One of the reasons for hiring a design professional is to get his expert opinion on prospective costs. For this reason, the absence of any contractual provision dealing with this question should not negate an implied promise to give cost predictions. The question of how accurate these predictions must be, and the effect of inaccurate or negligent predictions upon the rights and duties of the design professional and his client, will be discussed in § 8.01.

SECTION 6.10 CLIENT DIRECTED CHANGES IN APPROVED WORK

Clients frequently change their minds and decide that the project must be redesigned. Sometimes the change is authorized after the client has approved preliminary work done by the design professional. Changes in design are costly to the design professional. The client should have the right to make changes even after design approval, but the client should pay for them. This is the result achieved in most standard contracts.

However, in the absence of any contractual provision, it may be difficult to convince a client that redesign after approvals justifies additional charges. Many of the problems discussed in this chapter should be considered as warnings that certain matters should be explored in advance with the client. If the design professional is aware of problems that may arise, and does not take the opportunity to clarify them in advance, he may be held to the reasonable expectations of the client. If the client does not know just how costly and time consuming changes in design are, he may reasonably believe that this is part of reasonable design services and that these changes fall within the basic fee. If the design professional does not wish to explore this with the client in advance, when he presents the design documents for the approval of the client, he should indicate that approval by the client means that changes ordered by the client after approval will result in additional charges by the design professional.

SECTION 6.11 SECURING A CONTRACTOR: DRAFTING OR PROVIDING THE CONSTRUCTION CONTRACT

When the design professional completes the design phase of his work, the next step is the selection of a contractor to construct the project. There are various methods of obtaining a contractor, and a number of methods under which construction can be performed. Advising his client on such matters generally are part of professional services. If the client is an experienced businessman and has had experience in this type of work, or has persons on his staff who are experienced in negotiating construction contracts, it may be that the design professional has no obligation to assist in the negotiations.

However, if the client is inexperienced, he may rely very heavily upon the advice and actual assistance from the design professional.

The design professional should not draft the construction contract, nor provide a form agreement to be used for this purpose. Some architects or engineers supply general terms and conditions, such as AIA Doc. A201, to the client to be used as part of the construction documents. It is better procedure both from the standpoint of expertise and from the standpoint of avoiding a charge that the architect or engineer is practicing law illegally to advise the client to retain legal counsel for the preparation or approval of general terms and conditions, as well as for advice upon other legal questions relating to the construction contract.

SECTION 6.12 USE OF SURETY BONDS

What about advice to the client relating to the use of surety bonds? Often the client asks for the design professional's advice on the question of whether bid, payment or performance bonds should be required. While this matter might fall within the ambit of legal advice, design professionals are often expected to have sufficient knowledge to give advice in this area. These matters should be referred to a lawyer because the law may require that certain projects have bonds. However, the lawyer may want assistance or advice from the design professional as to the need for particular bonds in particular types of construction. (Some professional liability insurance exclude coverage for liability based upon failure to advise or require insurance or bonds for a project.)

SECTION 6.13 COORDINATION OF SEPARATE CONTRACTS

One method of construction involves the use of separate contractors, rather than a prime contractor. Under this method, the client enters into contracts with the major construction trades and does not use a prime contractor-subcontractor method. Where separate contracts are used, a greater burden of coordination falls upon the client, who, in essence, is acting as his own prime contractor. He will expect that the design professional will shoulder a large share of the coordination burden. If the design professional does this, he should receive a substantially larger fee. This will be discussed under § 7.03 dealing with compensation.

What must a design professional do to coordinate the work of separate contractors? Frequently, standard contracts require that separate contractors cooperate with each other, so that each can perform his obligation economically, and within the time duration set by their contracts. The design professional should arrange scheduling, so that each separate contractor can perform his work efficiently. He should also see that schedules are followed. Without this, the client runs a substantial risk of incurring liability to separate contractors whose performance is impeded by the failure of other contractors to perform. If there is a dispute, the design professional should decide it, if he is given this function under the contract. If an arbitration clause is included, the design professional should take steps to see that the arbitration process is commenced as soon as disputes develop.

SECTION 6.14 SUPERVISION AND INSPECTION: PASTORELLI v. ASSOCIATED ENGINEERS, INC.

The design professional and the client should discuss the design professional's function in the construction process. The "supervisory" role of the design professional in the construction process has been controversial and ties into a number of legal problems.

There are those who suggest that the design professional should continue to take an active role in the construction process. They claim that the client expects it, and that the tradition of the design professions is to furnish complete service. They assert that design professionals will be judged by the completed product, and should use their best efforts to ensure that the work is properly performed. The finished product is the vehicle for getting clients and developing a reputation. Inherent in this view is the assumption that most contractors must be checked carefully to insure proper performance.

Advocates of an active role also state that the construction documents, no matter how well drawn, can never express the entire design concept. Without an active role in the construction process, they maintain, the design concepts will not be executed.

Those who oppose an active role in the construction process state that the amount of the compensation does not justify close supervision. They also state that if the design professional becomes more deeply involved in the construction process, he will be held responsible for everything that goes wrong. Implicit in their argument is the assumption that many design professionals are not skilled at construction administration and supervision.

In rebuttal, proponents of "activism" assert that the design professions will have to develop specialists who are capable administrators, that increased liability can be handled by insurance and indemnity, and that different fee structures can make active participation adequately compensated.

Form contracts have tended to limit the role and responsibility of the design professional in supervision. Phrases like "general supervision of the work" have been replaced by "on-site observation."

The proper role of the design professional during the construction process requires a professional, rather than a legal judgment. However, from a legal standpoint, several facts are clear. The more power given to the design professional in the construction process, and the more active role he takes in these matters, the greater the chance for legal responsibility being placed upon him when things go wrong.

Second, the design professional must take into account the reasonable expectations of his client. Many clients expect close supervision by the architect or engineer. If the architect or engineer wishes to limit his obligation, he should discuss the matter with his client. If he and the client agree on this, the contract should spell this out clearly.

Even if the design professional has taken proper precautions to limit his role in supervision and inspection, he should avoid performance which exceeds his contract obligations. If he does not, he may lead the client to believe that such an expanded role will continue. Contract obligations can be created by acts. Unless the design professional is willing to continue to perform beyond his contract requirements, he should stay within his contract obligations, or inform his client that any performance beyond his obligation was temporary and will not continue.

Third, what is the precise nature of the design professional's obligation to check on the performance of the contractor? Some reported appellate cases have passed on the question of whether specific acts performed by the design professional constituted adequate supervision. Chiaverini v. Vail, 61 R.I. 117, 200 Atl. 462 (1938) held that examination of the work by the architect prior to the arrival of the contractor and after departure of the contractor was not adequate supervision.

In Pancoast v. Russell, 148 Cal.App.2d 909, 307 P.2d 719 (1957) the court stated:

> There can be no serious contention that the architect's undertaking was that of an absolute guaranty that satisfactory results would ensue. On the other hand, the term "general supervision" as used in the instant agreement, must mean something other than mere superficial supervision. Obviously, there can be no real value in supervision unless the same be directed towards securing a workmanlike adherence to specifications and adequate performance on the part of the contractor.

Pastorelli v. Associated Engineers, Inc., examined in detail the question of what constitutes adequate supervision. While this case involved an injury to an employee of the owner, a point to be covered in greater detail in Chapter 30, the scarcity of cases involving disputes between owner and design professional over adequacy of supervision makes it advisable to reproduce the *Pastorelli* case at this point.

PASTORELLI v. ASSOCIATED ENGINEERS, INC.

United States District Court of Rhode Island, 1959.
176 F.Supp. 159.

DAY, DISTRICT JUDGE. In this action the plaintiff seeks to recover damages for injuries alleged to have been caused by the negligence of the three defendant corporations. . . .

The accident resulting in the injuries for which plaintiff seeks damages occurred on November 10, 1955 upon the premises of the Narragansett Racing Association, Inc. (hereinafter called "the Racing Association") in Pawtucket, Rhode Island. On said date plaintiff, an employee of the Racing Association, was lawfully upon said premises in a building familiarly known as the "clubhouse", and was engaged in the performance of his duties. While walking through said clubhouse, a heating duct suspended from the ceiling fell and struck him, causing the injuries for which he now seeks damages.

The evidence establishes that early in 1954 the defendant Associated Engineers, Inc. (hereinafter called "Associated") contracted in writing with the Racing Association to prepare plans and specifications for the installation of certain heating, ventilating and air conditioning systems on its premises (including said clubhouse). It also agreed to "supervise the contractors' work throughout the job".

The defendant Procaccini & Moroney Plumbing & Heating Corp. (hereinafter called "P. & M.") thereafter contracted with said Racing Association to erect and install said equipment; and Randall Sheet Metal Co. (hereinafter called "Randall"), as subcontractor, agreed with P. & M. to install certain heating ducts under the aforesaid contracts. Performance of the work required under said contracts was substantially completed and accepted by the owner on November 30, 1954; installation of the heating ducts in the clubhouse was completed by Randall and approved by Associated sometime in August, 1954. It is undisputed that the duct which fell upon the plaintiff was installed by Randall.

The duct which fell was approximately 20 feet long and weighed approximately 500 pounds. It was suspended from the ceiling of said clubhouse by the attachment of semi-rigid strips of metal, called hangers, to the sides of the duct, which hangers were then attached to the ceiling. This ceiling was of seven-eighths inch sheathing and was nailed to the joists of the building, leaving a considerable air space between such sheathing and the the roof of the clubhouse. The duct was not in any way affixed directly to the roof itself or to the joists of the clubhouse.

Considerable expert testimony was offered as to the quality of the duct work performed by Randall. The specifications for the heating, ventilating and air conditioning system prepared by Associated, and with which Randall agreed to comply, provided that "all sheet metal work shall be erected in a first class and workmanlike manner" and that "the ducts shall be securely supported from the building construction in an approved manner".

The credible evidence satisfies me that the securing of a duct of the weight involved here to said ceiling by the means employed was not good practice nor in accordance with generally accepted practice, and that it was not installed in a first class or workmanlike manner.

By the terms of its contract with the Racing Association, P. & M. was obligated to keep a "competent superintendent" on the job throughout the performance of the work called for by its contract so as to give "efficient supervision" thereto. It is clear that it did supervise the day to day performance of the work under its contract. Furthermore, it selected Randall to perform the sheet metal work required under its contract, made no objection to the manner in which said work was being performed, and approved it as having been completed in accordance with the contract.

Pursuant to its agreement to "supervise the contractors' work throughout the job", Associated prepared and submitted periodic "inspection reports" to the Racing Association while the work was in progress. On November 30, 1954, Associated approved the invoice of P. & M. for the balance then payable under its contract less the sum of $400 for minor items to be completed thereafter, and certified that the "performance and execution of the contractor's work has been satisfactory". Its employee, the engineer who prepared these reports, testified that his employer assigned to him the task of supervising the installation of said systems, and that in pursuance of his duties he visited the job site on one, two or three occasions each week to inspect the work of the contractor as it was being done. He also testified, however, that he never observed any of the ducts being hung from the ceiling in said clubhouse, stating that whenever he visited the clubhouse the ducts were either on the floor or already installed. He also admitted that he never climbed a ladder to determine whether the hangers by which they were suspended were attached by nails or lag screws and never tested any of the hangers to see how securely they were attached.

. . .

[Ed. note: After holding prime and subcontractor negligent, the Court continued.]

While it is true that Associated undertook to exercise only a general supervision over the installation of the several systems, including the duct work, it did at all times possess and retain the ultimate control to approve or reject all work done by the contractor and by the subcontractors. The nature and extent of the duties of an architect or engineer who is required to exercise such general supervision has been the subject of judicial consideration in several reported cases. Although each of these cases turns on its particular facts, certain general principles seem to have been clearly established. A good statement of these principles appears in Cowles v. City of Minneapolis,

1915, 128 Minn. 452, 151 N.W. 184, at page 185, where the Court held:

> "Plaintiff was an engineer and was employed as such. In performing the work which he undertook, it was his duty to exercise such care, skill and diligence as men engaged in that profession ordinarily exercise under like circumstances. He was not an insurer that the contractors would perform their work properly in all respects; but it was his duty to exercise reasonable care to see that they did so."

Pursuant to its contract, Associated assigned an engineer to supervise the work of P. & M. and of Randall; this engineer made periodic inspection reports to the Racing Association as the work progressed. He admitted that he knew that the safety of persons in the clubhouse required that the ducts be secured to the joists of that structure. He also admitted that, despite this knowledge, he made no attempt to ascertain whether they were being so installed. Moreover, he made no visits to the clubhouse at a time when he could ascertain how the ducts were being installed. In other words, he failed to see that they were properly installed and took no steps after their installation to ascertain how and by what means they were secured. In my opinion he failed to use due care in carrying out his undertaking of general supervision. It follows that his employer, Associated, failed to use due care to see that the duct work was properly and safely installed; and that the exercise of due care by it would have led to the discovery of the dangerous and hazardous condition created by Randall's work. I find that harm to persons thereafter in said clubhouse was reasonably foreseeable if Associated failed to use due care in its supervision of the work performed by Randall; that Associated was therefore negligent in failing to use due care in the performance of said supervision; and that its negligence in this regard was likewise a proximate cause of the accident and of the injuries and damages sustained by the plaintiff.

. . .

His special damages amount to $3,900.40, viz.: $2,472 for loss of wages and $1,428.40 for hospital and medical bills. In my opinion the sum of $11,000 will adequately and fairly compensate him for his injuries, pain, suffering and special damages. Judgment shall therefore be entered in his favor in the sum of $11,000 against the three defendants.

For other cases dealing with the scope of supervisory obligations see Bayuk v. Edson, reproduced at § 11.01(b) and Day v. National United States Radiator Corp., reproduced at § 34.04(c).

While case precedents often are of little value because of variant fact situations, there are some general guidelines.

Much will depend upon the nature of the project. If it is routine or small, less supervision should be required. If the project involves a large amount of money, more attention should be given because more is at stake, and the fee will justify it. Also, when the construction documents are reasonably complete, a less active role may be sufficient. Finally, if the project is at a great distance from the office of the design professional, perhaps less supervision can be expected by the client.

If the contract is a cost type, perhaps more supervision is needed. On the other hand, in a fixed price contract, the contractor may be more inclined to cut corners. If the contractor has a good reputation, there may be less need for close supervision. Also, if work has progressed well, the same result would follow.

If the client has a large technical staff, he may expect to do much of the supervision himself, and expect less from the design professional. (He may demand a fee reduction in such a case.)

To some degree, the role of the design professional will depend upon the extent to which he has retained consultants, testers, and project representatives for the projects. They may not relieve him from ultimate liability if things go wrong, but their use may indicate less was expected of the design professional personally while the project was being built.

How often, and when, should the design professional visit the site? When is more important than how often. Fewer visits, at crucial times, may be better than many visits at less important times. Obviously, it is more important to visit when a crucial step is being taken which can affect the success of the entire project. Pouring concrete would be an illustration of this.

Next, a visit at the time when work is to be covered would be important. Work should be examined carefully at this time, for reasons of economy and fairness to both owner and contractor. Finally, visits and careful inspection before payments are to be made is essential. Anything beyond this depends upon the contract terms, an understanding of the building process, the particular project and the parties involved in it. See § 34.04(c) for additional discussion of this subject.

SECTION 6.15 APPROVAL OF SHOP DRAWINGS, SCHEDULES AND SAMPLES

The architect-engineer frequently agrees to pass upon shop drawings, samples, and schedules. It may be useful to deviate from the question of what are part of basic design services to discussion of the legal implications which can be drawn from the performance of certain clearly called for acts.

The effect of the design professional's approval of shop drawings, schedules, or samples is often unclear. Does approval represent that the drawings were in compliance with the contract drawings and specifications, or only that the contract drawings and specifications were in compliance with "design and architectural effect"? Approval by the design professional should be a representation that there has been compliance with the drawings and specifications. However, shop drawings frequently contain information which is not related to the design concept or functional result. Information may relate to the fabrication process or construction techniques, and such information is frequently not called for in the contract documents.

The design professional should make clear that his approval of the shop drawings does not indicate approval of data which is not called for in the contract documents. The same caution should be exercised when approving samples.

However, if the design professional sees that the contractor intends to use an unsafe method of construction, he should make an appropriate comment and in some cases order that it not be done. While it is often stated that methods are the responsibility of the contractor, a design professional may have a duty to third parties, such as workers and members of the public, as well as to his client to exercise due care in his work. This will be discussed in greater detail in Chapter 30 and § 34.04(c).

Noting that only data called for under the contract are considered approved when the design professional approves shop drawings may put the risk of methods of construction upon the contractor. But it would be unprofessional and highly risky to ignore data on methods which, if carried out, have a reasonable likelihood of causing harm to persons or damage to property. (An appropriately worded disclaimer did work in the *Day* case reproduced at § 34.04(c).)

SECTION 6.16 ISSUANCE OF CERTIFICATES

Generally, the architect or engineer is required to issue certificates related to progress payments and completion. As in § 6.15, the main legal questions relate to what implications can be drawn from the issuance of the certificates and what the issuance represents. The design professional may not be in a position to know whether there has been strict compliance with the terms of the construction contract. For that reason, the design professional would like to avoid the representation that performance has been in accordance with the contract documents. Design professionals state that they cannot conduct detailed inspection and testing each month. They would prefer that their certificate only warrant that they have not seen any defects in the contractor's performance. AIA Doc. A201 states at 9.4.2:

> The issuance of a Certificate for Payment will constitute a representation by the Architect to the Owner,

> based on his observations at the site as provided in Subparagraph 2.2.4 [Periodic Visits to the Site and not exhaustive or continuous on site inspections] and the data comprising the Application for Payment, that the Work has progressed to the point indicated; that, to the best of his knowledge, information and belief, the quality of the Work is in accordance with the Contract Documents . . . and that the Contractor is entitled to payment in the amount certified.

Section 9.4.2 states that the issuance of the certificate does not mean that the architect has checked on how the contractor has used previous payments. Section 9.4.4 also states that a certificate for progress payment is not an acceptance of any work not done in accordance with the contract documents. The AIA Document quoted seeks to make it clear that the certificate does not mean the architect has done a thorough job of testing and inspection, and that issuance does not represent that the work to date has been done in accordance with the contract documents.

Provisions such as the AIA clause quoted attempt to employ a negligence standard. The architect is responsible only for defective work he observed or should have observed.

The standard of care spelled out in such a clause may conflict with the reasonable expectation of the client. The client may reasonably believe that the certificate implies a determination that the work to date has been properly performed. A clause of this type, while perhaps a fair one, should be pointed out to the client so there is no misunderstanding. Fortunately this standard of care is included in AIA Doc. B131, at 1.1.15, a form contract for client and architect. The client should be directed to 1.1.15 and a reasoned explanation given to him for its inclusion.

SECTION 6.17 DESIGN PROFESSIONAL'S STANDARD OF PERFORMANCE

This chapter has dealt with what the design professional is obligated to do. Section 6.17 examines *how* he must perform these obligations.

(A) SATISFACTION OF CLIENT

In a satisfaction contract, the client promises to pay if he is satisfied. The design professional may promise to satisfy the client, or at least agree he will not be paid unless the client is satisfied. Such an agreement is relatively one-sided. One party is tied much more than the other. While such an arrangement may not be a wise one for the design professional, it is generally enforceable.

To analyze a satisfaction contract, a distinction must be drawn between a promise and a condition.

In a satisfaction contract, the client's obligation to pay is conditioned upon his being satisfied with the architect or engineer's work. But generally, the design professional does not promise to satisfy the client. If he promised to satisfy the client, his failure to provide a satisfactory design would be a breach of contract. In other words, the design professional would gamble to the extent of compensation for his services, but not to the extent of responding in damages for his failure to satisfy the client. Where satisfaction contracts are made, it is likely that only the design professional's fee is at stake.

In "satisfaction" contracts there are two different standards of satisfaction which can be applied. If the performance can be measured in some objective way, courts apply the standard of reasonable satisfaction. This means that the issue will be that of whether a reasonable man would have been satisfied by the performance. Objective standards are more likely to be applied where the performance relates to mechanical rather than personal matters. For example, if an engineer-inventor agreed with a manufacturer that the manufacturer would pay if he were satisfied with the performance of a particular machine, the manufacturer would be obligated to pay if a reasonable person would have been satisfied.

If the performance is more personal, courts apply a subjective standard. For example, if an artist agreed to paint a portrait which would satisfy a person who commissioned the portrait, the test would be subjective. The court would look at whether the person commissioning the portrait, after exercising a good faith judgment, was genuinely satisfied or dissatisfied. If, for example, he refused to view the portrait or refused to give it sufficient light to judge its quality, then a court could determine that he had not exercised his judgment in good faith.

The objective and subjective standards may not be very different in operation. If a judge or jury would have thought the performance satisfactory, there is likely to be a heavy burden upon the defendant to show genuine dissatisfaction.

As for the work of a design professional, there is no unanimity among the courts. Generally, design and aesthetic performance are likely to be measured by a subjective standard. However, even in design, if the work to be performed is a standard commercial structure, a court could apply an objective standard.

As for the work of a design professional during construction itself, much will depend upon the particular aspects of the design professional's performance which is questioned. If the performance in question were the way in which the architect or engineer handled the contractor, perhaps a more subjective standard would be applied. The same would be true if the performance related to judgmental matters such as the issuance of certificates, or the determination of whether the contractor employed good workmanship or had been proceeding at a proper pace. If the performance at issue related to approval of materials or equipment, the standard of satisfaction to be applied would very likely be objective.

Roughly speaking, design is more likely to be measured subjectively while administration is more likely to be measured objectively.

Does the satisfaction have to be continuous? There are a number of stages to the design professional's performance. Must the client be satisfied at every stage? What if he is satisfied with the schematic design, but not the design development, or with the construction documents but not the finished project?

Generally, the client should be satisfied at every stage if his obligation is conditioned on his satisfaction. But some qualifications should be made. The later the dissatisfaction arises, the more likely it is that the design professional should be able to collect. If dissatisfaction occurs late in the design professional's performance, there is a greater possibility that the client is looking for an excuse and the "dissatisfaction" is not genuine. Also, the later the dissatisfaction, the greater the extent of lost fees to the design professional. Finally, if the client approves a particular detail at an early stage, it would be unfair for him to object to it at a later date. Approval may indicate satisfaction, as well as causing the design professional to rely by continuing his design plan. A client should be able to change his mind. But if he does, he should pay for any work caused by his change of mind.

When the design professional submits work to the client for his approval, the work should be accompanied by a form or letter which requests *both* approval and satisfaction. This should preclude the client from later stating that he approved the work but was not satisfied.

If the design professional has performed services under a satisfaction contract, and the client's genuine dissatisfaction is the basis for a justifiable refusal to pay, the design professional has suffered a forfeiture. He has expended time and effort and will not be paid.

Generally, law seeks to avoid forfeitures. Where possible, courts will interpret the contract in such a way as to avoid forfeiture. For example, where the forfeiture might be great, a court might be more inclined to use an objective rather than a subjective standard, if the objective standard would enable the design professional to be paid.

However, if it were clear that forfeiture was an assumed risk, the forfeiture will be enforced. Only if there is unjust enrichment will the design professional have a claim against the client.

For example, suppose there is a satisfaction contract. If the architect drew schematic designs which failed to genuinely satisfy the client, the client would not have to pay. However, if the client used those designs as the basis for construction of a project, then the architect would have a right to recover for the benefit he conferred upon the client, without regard for his inability to recover upon the contract. This would be based upon the concept of "unjust enrichment," or as it is sometimes called, "quasi-contract." It is not a relationship based upon consent, but upon benefit conferred.

A design professional who makes a satisfaction contract runs the risk that he will not be paid if his work does not satisfy the client. Design professionals should, where possible, avoid such contractual arrangements.

(B) A SPECIFIED PERFORMANCE STANDARD

Sometimes the agreed standard will be that of a designated performance. In such a case the client's obligation to pay depends upon those standards being met. For example, an engineer could enter into a contract with a manufacturer under which it was agreed that the engineer would design a machine which would turn out a designated number of units within a designated period of time.

What if the performing party finds that it is extremely difficult to meet the performance standards or that the performance standard will require an amount of time and money which was not anticipated by the performing party? In some extreme cases it is even possible that the performance standards are impossible to meet.

In such cases, two legal issues may arise. The first is whether the design professional is entitled to be paid for the effort he has made in trying to accomplish the performance specifications. This question is very much like the one discussed in the previous section. It may be an onerous contract from the standpoint of the performing party. However, if this is the risk he assumed, he is not likely to be able to collect for his performance. Like the satisfaction contracts, courts will try to resolve interpretation doubts in favor of the performing party, in order to avoid forfeiture. But if this cannot be done, the performing party will be uncompensated for his effort unless he can show that his efforts, although not fulfilling the performance standards, have contributed a benefit to the other party. While it may be beneficial to the other party to be shown that the performance standards were not possible, in most cases there will be no unjust enrichment and no right of quasi-contractual recovery for the performing party.

The second legal question may be whether the performing party has breached by not accomplishing the objective set forth in the agreement. This is again a question of whether the accomplishment of the objective is not merely a condition to the client's obligation to pay, but also a promise on the part of the performing party. In most cases, the inability to collect for his performance is a sufficient burden for the performing party. For this reason, it is not likely that he will be held to a promise to accomplish what turns out to be either an extremely difficult or impossible performance. Also, the contract doctrines of impossibility of performance or impracticability of performance may relieve him from any promise to fulfill the performance specifications set forth in the contract. Like satisfaction contracts, these agreements can be onerous to the performing party. Design professionals should think carefully before entering into such contracts. If they do enter into such contracts, they will be taking substantial risks.

(C) SUITABILITY OR FITNESS STANDARD

Clients have objectives when they enter into construction projects. The client who plans a luxury residence usually wants a house which is suitable for a person of his means and his taste. In addition to the normal requirements for any residence, such as structural stability, shelter from the elements and compliance with safety and sanitation standards, he may wish a house which is admired by those who enter it. He may also wish a residence which can facilitate closing of business deals or making business contacts. He may hope that the splendour of the residence will make his social events successful.

The client who plans a commercial office building wishes to make a profit from the rental of space. To accomplish this he hopes to find suitable tenants at an economically adequate rent. Such a client assumes that the planned use of the structure will be permitted under zoning laws, and that the structure will comply with the applicable building codes and zoning regulations relating to materials, safety, density, setback regulations and other land use controls. In addition, the client who builds an unusually designed office building may hope that his structure will be the subject of national architectural interest.

The client who desires to build an industrial plant generally assumes that the plant when completed will be adequate to perform anticipated plant activities. He also assumes that the building will comply with applicable laws relating to public health and safety.

In order to perform design services properly, the design professioned in the preceding paragraphs will be discussed and included in tioned in the preceding paragraph will be discussed and included in the client's program. Some of the matters discussed in the preceding paragraphs would be assumed and probably not discussed. One would not expect client and design professional to discuss the necessity of complying with building codes or regulations dealing with health and safety. Yet beyond these basic objectives there may have been discussions of economic and social goals less directly connected with basic design objectives.

One possible standard to measure the performance of the design professional relates to whether the project will accomplish the objectives of the client. Put another way, is the structure suitable for the client's anticipated needs, or is it fit for the purpose for which it was built? Is the building an architectural success? Has the client been able to attract good tenants? Has plant production increased? Are the social events successful?

In determining whether performance standards of this type will be used to measure compliance with the design professional's obligation, it is important to look at any antecedent negotiations, discussions, or understandings which may have preceded the client-design professional contract or may have occurred during the course of the design professional's activities.

Assuming there were discussions relating to various client objectives prior to or during the performance of professional design services two legal issues can arise. First, did the design professional warrant (promise) that his design would accomplish any particular objectives of the client, or that the finished product would be suitable for the client's needs?

Suppose that during the course of discussions, the design professional made statements on such matters. He might have indicated that in his opinion a particular luxury residence would create an artistic stir within the social circles of his client. He might have ventured an opinion that suitable tenants could be found, or that someday a particularly unusual office building would be considered an architectural landmark. If all that he has done is give his opinion on matters of this sort, generally he would not be held to any legal accountability if these objectives were not achieved.

However, if he stated that the client could conduct a certain type of activity within the building, it is likely that he is warranting that his design will enable this activity to be performed in the completed project.

In classifying a statement as a warranty rather than an expression of opinion, the law looks at the definiteness with which the statement was made, ("I am certain your cost per unit will decrease." v. "It's my considered opinion that you will improve productivity."), the degree to which the design professional's performance can bring about that objective, ("People will like the exterior design." v. "Your parties will be great successes.") and the degree and reasonableness of any reliance by the client on the statement (Using certain types of machinery in a plant v. redecorating the interior of a house at great expense for the new social season). The more definite the statement, the more within the control of the design professional is the outcome, and the more likely there has been justifiable reliance, the more likely it is the law will find there has been a warranty.

Second, what about the provability of such a statement? If the statement was made prior to the formation of a contract, a design professional might contend that such statements cannot be proved because of the parol evidence rule. See §§ 5.04(e) and 6.02(c). While results vary when parol evidence questions are raised, by and large the client will be permitted to testify as to these statements.

If the statement is made after the formation of a written contract, there is no parol evidence problem. There are other legal requirements which will have to be met by the client, but he will usually be permitted to testify regarding such statements.

In the absence of express statements by the design professional, the client may contend there has been an implied warranty by the design professional. Most courts hold that the design professional impliedly warrants that his design will comply with building codes and zoning requirements. In effect, such cases establish that the design professional warrants that his design will be suitable for the known purpose of his client. For example, in Bott v. Moser, 175 Va. 11, 7 S.E.2d 217 (1940) the Court held that the architect whose plans did not comply with setback requirements could not collect for his work.

In a similar case, Bloomsburg Mills, Inc. v. Sordoni Construction Co., 401 Pa. 358, 164 A.2d 201 (1960), the client retained the plaintiff architects to design and prepare plans and specifications for the construction of a rayon and nylon weaving mill. In order to meet the needs of its industrial purpose, a certain portion of the building was to be air conditioned to maintain a constant temperature of 80° and a constant relatively high degree humidity of 60% moisture. The design did not accomplish this purpose, and the client sued the architect. The court stated:

> While an architect is not an absolute insurer of perfect plans, he is called upon to prepare plans and specifications which will give the structure so designed reasonable fitness for its intended purpose, and he impliedly warrants their sufficiency for that purpose.

Since the court found that the architect knew of the purpose and knew it would be needed to accomplish that purpose, he in effect promised that his design would accomplish that purpose. If an implied warranty is found, the client will win if there is a breach of the implied warranty. He need not show that the design professional was negligent.

Implied warranty is sometimes found when the developer of tract homes sells his homes to a purchaser. See Humber v. Morton, reproduced at § 13.07(k). Also the manufacturer of mass-produced goods impliedly warrants that the goods are not defective when used properly. See § 30.06.

The creation of an implied warranty can place legal responsibility upon the person who is in the best position to pay for the loss. When courts imply warranties as to design, they are determining that, as between design professional and his client, design defects shall be the responsibility of the design professional.

By and large, courts have been slow to use the implied warranty concept against architects and engineers. However, as stated, courts generally imply a warranty that plans and specifications will comply with applicable building codes and other relevant land use controls such as zoning laws. Also, as seen in the *Bloomsburg* case, the design professional is likely to warrant that the structure is reasonably fit for its intended purpose. However, that purpose is likely to relate to the activities planned for the structure rather than to more remote purposes not within the expertise of a design professional. For example, a court would probably not imply a warranty that the residence would lead to successful social events, or that the client would have no difficulty obtaining tenants for a commercial building. Generally, statements of the type mentioned in the preceding sentence would not be considered warranties even if they were expressly made. If they would be considered opinions rather than warranties if made expressly, they certainly should not be the basis for implied warranty.

Generally, where a court would find an implied warranty, it is likely that the architect or engineer would be found negligent in not accomplishing the particular objective. For example, it would not be necessary to use implied warranty if the issue were whether the design would comply with setback requirements and the zoning laws. Failure to comply, in almost every situation, would constitute negligence. However, implied warranty relieves the client from having to establish negligence.

(D) PROFESSIONAL STANDARDS

Satisfaction, performance, and suitability standards, when created, are usually created by contract provisions. If these are the standards, the design professional's right to collect or his liability for damages will not depend upon whether he has exercised due care in the performance of his work.

In most cases of contracts between a design professional and his client, nothing will be stated as to standards of performance. There is an agreement that certain professional work will be done, and that there will be designated compensation for this work. In such cases, the architect or engineer will be held to a standard of due care. Put another way, he must not be negligent in the performance of his professional duties. Whether he has performed in accordance with this standard usually depends upon a comparison of the way he did the work with the way the work would have been done by other members of his profession in his locality with his general experience.

(While it has been stated that the standard of professional care is local, there is some movement toward using standards of national or regional practice. This is discussed in § 30.02(f).)

The court in the *Bloomsburg* case, cited in § 6.17(c) stated:

> An architect is bound to perform with reasonable care the duties for which he contracts. His client has the right to regard him as skilled in the science of the construction of buildings, and to expect that he will use reasonable and ordi-

> nary care and diligence in the application of his professional knowledge to accomplish the purpose for which he is retained. While he does not guarantee a perfect plan or a satisfactory result, he does by his contract imply that he enjoys ordinary skill and ability in his profession and that he will exercise these attributes without neglect and with a certain exactness of performance to effectuate work properly done.

In the design phase, use of improper materials or poor design usually is negligence. Building the structure on land not owned by the client will almost always be negligence. A case held it was not negligent for an architect to rely on a five-year-old surveyor's map furnished by a member of a school board client. Jacka v. Ouachita Parish School Board, 249 La. 223, 186 So.2d 571 (1966). (Reliance by a surveyor in such a case might be negligence.)

In Mallow v. Tucker, Sadler & Bennett, Architects & Eng. Inc., 245 Cal.App.2d 700, 54 Cal.Rptr. 174 (1966), the Court stated:

> This is the paradigm case of an architect's negligence. Architect failed to make any mention on its plans of the underground high-voltage line it knew was in the area; further, these plans called for excavation right where the buried electrical power line was located.

In the *Mallow* case, a worker was killed when he jackhammered footings at the spot called for in the plans, when the jackhammer hit the high voltage transmission line.

As for the project itself, it is negligence not to condemn defective work or material where the architect had the right to do so. Skidmore, Owings & Merrill v. Connecticut General Life Ins. Co., 25 Conn.Sup. 76, 197 A.2d 83 (1963). Inaccurate certificates, not checking on whether the prime has paid his subcontractors, failure to see defective work, failure to correct unsafe procedures—all of these are illustrations of negligent performance during supervision and inspection. Other illustrations of negligence will be found in Chapter 34.

(E) COMPLIANCE WITH STANDARD: DISPUTES WITH PUBLIC OFFICIALS

If the issue of the design professional's performance is brought before a court, the judge or jury will determine whether the design professional has complied with professional standards of care. Ordinarily there will be expert testimony of other professional persons on this question.

In disputes between design professionals and their clients, an issue which often arises is whether a design professional has complied with governmental statutes and codes relating to design. Such an issue can arise if the court determines that the design professional impliedly promised to comply with these requirements, or if compliance with these requirements is considered part of the professional standard of due care.

Such a question would be relatively simple were it not for the proliferation of governmental controls which usually require the issuance of building permits, occupancy permits and other types of government approvals before construction can begin, may continue, and before the completed project can be used. Because of increased governmental intervention, issues of compliance frequently arise before, during and shortly after construction of the project.

In order to comply with the demands of public authorities, the client may decide to comply with the demand of public officials despite the insistence by his architect or engineer that there has been compliance, and that the demands of public officials are incorrect.

While there are many factual variations possible, it may be useful to look at a few situations for guidance.

First, suppose governmental officials do not approve the design because of their stated position that it does not comply with applicable codes and land use controls. If the project is abandoned, and there is litigation between the design professional and his client, a judge or a jury will determine whether there has been compliance. If the design professional can persuade the judge or jury that he has complied, he should be able to win. The same would be true if he offered to redesign, but was prevented from doing so by the client.

If the facts establish that the client's obligation was conditioned upon issuance of a building permit, or upon the granting of a variance by a zoning board, the client should not have to pay since the design professional, perhaps unwisely, took the risk of being able to persuade the proper public authorities to grant the necessary permit or variance. However, unless the facts clearly established that the design professional warranted official approval would be obtained, he should not have to pay any damages suffered by the client because the project is abandoned. The design professional has lost his fee, and that should be sufficient.

Suppose the client makes the changes directed by public authorities in order to obtain the permit or the variance. Is the design professional entitled to be paid for the design services he performs in making the correction? Also, can the client charge the architect or engineer with any additional expenses incurred by the client because of the corrections? The same problems can arise during the course of construction or upon completion of construction. For that reason the analysis of these two difficult questions will be postponed until discussion of similar problems arising during the construction project.

Just as the owner may decide to comply with the wishes or demands of public officials before construction of the project, he may also decide to comply with similar wishes or demands during construction of the project. Here, however, the burden upon the client becomes more onerous. During construction it is often unreasonable to expect him to contest the decisions of building inspectors or other public officials. Even though his design professional may contend that there has been compliance, it is likely that the client will make the corrections demanded by the building inspector. When these corrections are made, it usually means that the design professional will have to perform additional design services. It also means that there will be cost of correction and possible losses caused by the delay in making the corrections. Just as in the preceding paragraphs, the issue should be broken down into two sub-issues. Rather than simply state the question as one of who bears the risk in such cases, it is better to ask:

1. Is the architect entitled to compensation for extra services if he does the corrective design work?

2. Does client or design professional pay for the cost of correction and other related losses?

Two relatively easy variables can be disposed of quickly. If the public official is clearly wrong and was acting arbitrarily or in bad faith, the design professional should be entitled to pay for extra design services and the client should bear the risk of the cost of correction and other possible losses. While neither design professional or client are at fault, the client should bear the entire risk. The design professional has done all that he has promised. His obligation should not be enlarged so as to encompass a performance which includes the satisfaction of an arbitrary or malicious building inspector.

At the other extreme, suppose the design professional was clearly wrong. In such a case, it is likely that he was negligent and clearly not complying with applicable codes. He should then have to bear the loss of his own services and to pay for any losses incurred by his client. He would still be entitled to the fee for his services, (except those services which consisted of correcting his own work), less any losses which his negligent conduct has cost the client.

The most difficult question arises when the question of compliance is close. Suppose that reasonable men would differ on the question of whether the design has complied with applicable codes. And suppose further the client has decided to comply with the demands of the building inspector. While arguments can be made for placing the entire risk upon the design professional or his client, it would seem fair to divide the risk. This can be accomplished by requiring each party to bear his own losses by letting the loss rest where it falls. In such a case, the design professional would not be entitled to compensation for changing the design or the work. Nor would the client be able to transfer the cost of correcting the work to the design professional. While no court opinions have been found which adopt this solution, it would seem more fair than placing the burden of the entire loss either upon the design professional or the client.

In this regard, it would be superficially attractive to place this risk upon the design professional. The client generally is caught between the building inspector and his design professional. Design is the responsibility of the design professional and ordinarily the client knows very little of design problems and applicable codes.

However, the cost of correction can be formidable. If the design professional were forced to bear this risk, he might lose a substantial portion of his fee, through no fault of his own. It is likely that the cost of correction would be a greater percentage of the total architectural fee than the cost of correction would bear to the cost of construction. Also, such losses are not likely to be covered by professional errors and omissions insurance, since there is no showing of negligence.

Under the solution suggested in this treatise, a design professional would bear the entire risk only if he is negligent. The risk would be shared (if the design professional does the corrective work) in the close cases.

SECTION 6.18 SUMMATION AND SUGGESTIONS

The design professional and his client should discuss what will be done by the design professional, and how he will do it. They should achieve a common understanding, which is expressed clearly and completely in a written contract. Honest misunderstandings as to these questions are a principal cause of a breakdown in the relationship between design professional and his client.

REVIEW QUESTIONS

1. In contract interpretation matters, does the client or design professional get the benefit of the doubt?

2. Are client-design professional contracts usually considered complete writings?

3. What services are likely to be expected by a client relating to:

   a. Procuring financing?

   b. Obtaining approval of public authorities?

   c. Obtaining approval of board of directors of private client?

4. Who must coordinate work when separate contracts are used?

5. How would "supervision" differ from "observation of the work?"

6. What legal inferences "could" be drawn from:

   a. Issuance of a certificate by a design professional?

   b. Approval of shop drawings by a design professional?

7. Is a contract with a condition of satisfaction too one-sided to be enforceable?

8. Would the design aspects of a design professional's work be judged by an objective or a subjective standard of satisfaction?

9. What is the usual standard of performance promised by a design professional?

QUESTIONS FOR CLASS DISCUSSION

1. Why interpret contracts against the design professional?

2. Why is it advisable to go over the contract with the client?

3. Will the limiting of supervisory functions gradually end the architect's role in the construction process?

4. Why should design professionals want to be involved in the construction process, if such involvement increases the scope of their liability and does not earn them a commensurate portion of their fee?

5. How many of the 25 possible services listed at § 6.04 would seem to you to be "extra services?"

6. Why should a design professional go unpaid for services performed under a "satisfaction" contract because he could not satisfy his client?

7. Can you give illustrations of negligent conduct by a design professional in the course of performing design services? In the course of performing project administration services?

PROBLEMS

1. C wants to build a new residence for $50,000. He would like to obtain a construction loan for $40,000. C has retained A to perform "usual architectural services." Would A be obligated to attend the conference with the loan officer of the bank to whom C had applied for a loan? If he did so, would this be an extra service not included in the basic fee?

2. C wants to build a large apartment building. The site is presently zoned for single family residences, but C thinks he can obtain a zoning variance. Also, C expects to obtain federal financing for the project. He has hired A to perform architectural services under a contract which states in part:

> The architect shall assist the client in applying for and obtaining the required approvals of plans, specifications and contract documents from public agencies having jurisdiction over the project.

Would A be obligated to testify as a witness before the zoning board? If he did so, would he be entitled to extra compensation? (Assume that in the contract there is a detailed list of extra services which does not include testifying.) Would the architect be obligated to assist C's attorney in preparing the matter to be submitted to the zoning board? If he did so, would he be entitled to extra compensation for it? Would he be obligated to assist in obtaining federal financing or private financing? If he did so, would he be entitled to extra services if he performed in this matter?

3. Suppose you are the architect who has been retained to design and supervise the construction of a luxury residence which is to cost $100,000. The project is to take about 4 months and you are to receive a fee of 10% of the costs. When, and how often, would you be expected to visit the site? Upon what things would the duration of your visit depend? What would you do while you were at the site? Would the frequency of your visits in any way depend upon whether the contractor has been found to be deliberately skimping on the job, or has been late in his scheduled performance?

Chapter 7

CLIENT OBLIGATIONS

SECTION 7.01 COMPENSATION BASED UPON CONTRACT

From the standpoint of the design professional, the most important client obligation is the payment of the fee. Compensation can be divided into the right to be paid, covered in §§ 7.01 and 7.02, the amount to be paid, covered in § 7.03, and when it is to be paid, covered in § 7.04. (Another related matter is the judicial measure of recovery for contract breach, a point discussed in Chapter 11.)

(A) A VALID CONTRACT

Generally the right to receive compensation requires a valid contract. The requirements for a valid contract have been discussed in Chapter 2. (It may be useful to look ahead to Chapter 31 on Licensing.) There are additional requirements for contracts with public agencies. These have been discussed in § 5.09.

(B) PROPER PERFORMANCE BY DESIGN PROFESSIONAL

The client's contractual obligation to pay is usually conditioned upon the design professional performing in accordance with his contractual obligations. See Chapter 6.

(C) CONDITION TO PAYMENT: PARSONS v. BRISTOL DEV. CO.

In addition to the existence of a validly formed contract, all the conditions which are created by contract or implied by law must be fulfilled, or excused, before the obligation to pay compensation arises. For example, if the client's obligation to pay is conditioned upon the structure being built, the structure must be built before there is an obligation to pay. If the client conditions his obligation to pay upon his being able to obtain adequate financing, the duty to pay compensation or to permit the design professional to engage in performance will not arise until adequate financing is obtained or will terminate if financing fails.

A case involving obtaining of financing as a condition to payment is reproduced at this point.

PARSONS v. BRISTOL DEVELOPMENT CO.

Supreme Court of California, 1965.
62 Cal.2d 861, 402 P.2d 839, 44 Cal.Rptr. 767.

TRAYNOR, CHIEF JUSTICE. In December 1960 defendant Bristol Development Company entered into a written contract with plaintiff engaging him as an architect to design an office building for a lot in Santa Ana and to assist in supervising construction. Plaintiff's services were to be performed in two phases. He completed phase one, drafting preliminary plans and specifications, on January 20, 1961, and Bristol paid him $600.

The dispute concerns Bristol's obligation to pay plaintiff under phase two of the contract. The contract provided that "a condition precedent to any duty or obligation on the part of the OWNER [Bristol] to commence, continue or complete Phase 2 or to pay ARCHITECT any fee therefor, shall be the obtaining of economically satisfactory financing arrangements which will enable OWNER, in its sole judgment, to construct the project at a cost which in the absolute decision of the OWNER shall be economically feasible." It further provided that when Bristol notified plaintiff to proceed with phase two it should pay him an estimated 25 per cent of his fee, and that it would be obligated to pay the remaining 75 per cent "only from construction loan funds."

Using plaintiff's preliminary plans and specifications, Bristol obtained from a contractor an estimate of $1,020,850 as the cost of construction, including the architect's fee of 6 per cent. On the basis of this estimate, it received an offer from a savings and loan company for a construction loan upon condition that it show clear title to the Santa Ana lot and execute a first trust deed in favor of the loan company.

Shortly after obtaining this offer from the loan company, Bristol wrote plaintiff on March 14, 1961, to proceed under phase two of the contract. In accordance with the contract, Bristol paid plaintiff $12,000, an estimated 25 per cent of his total fee. Thereafter, plaintiff began to draft final plans and specifications for the building.

Bristol, however, was compelled to abandon the project because it was unable to show clear title to the Santa Ana lot and thus meet the requirements for obtaining a construction loan. Bristol's title became subject to dispute on May 23, 1961, when defendant James Freeman filed an action against Bristol claiming an adverse title. On August 15, 1961, Bristol notified plaintiff to stop work on the project.

Plaintiff brought an action against Bristol and Freeman to recover for services performed under the contract and to foreclose a mechanic's lien on the Santa Ana lot. The trial court, sitting without a jury found that Bristol's obligation to make further payment under the contract was conditioned upon the existence of construction loan funds. On the ground that this condition to plaintiff's right to further payment was not satisfied, the court entered judgment for defendants. Plaintiff appeals.

. . .

. . . After providing for payment of an estimated 25 per cent of plaintiff's fee upon written notice to proceed with phase two, paragraph 4 of the contract makes the following provisions for payment:

"4. * * *

"(a) * * *

"(b) Upon completion of final working plans, specifications and engineering, or authorized commencement of construction, whichever is later, a sum equal to SEVENTY-FIVE (75%) PER CENT of the fee for services in Phase 2, less all previous payments made on account of fee; provided, however, that this payment shall be made only from construction loan funds.

"(c) The balance of the fee shall be paid in equal monthly payments commencing with the first day of the month following payments as set forth in Paragraph 4(b); provided, however, that TEN (10%) PER CENT of the fee based upon the reasonable estimated cost of construction shall be withheld until thirty (30) days after the Notice of Completion of the project has been filed.

"(d) If any work designed or specified by the ARCHITECT is abandoned of [sic] suspended in whole or in part, the ARCHITECT is to be paid forthwith to the extent that his services have been rendered under the preceding terms of this paragraph. Should such abandonment or suspension occur before the ARCHITECT has completed any particular phase of the work which entitles him to a partial payment as aforesaid, the ARCHITECT'S fee shall be prorated based upon the percentage of the work completed under that particular phase and shall be payable forthwith."

Invoking the provision that "payment shall be made only from construction loan funds," Bristol contends that since such funds were not obtained it is obligated to pay plaintiff no more than he has already received under the contract.

Plaintiff, on the other hand, contends that he performed 95 per cent of his work on phase two and is entitled to that portion of his fee under subdivision (d) of paragraph 4 less the previous payment he received. He contends that subdivision (d) is a "savings clause" designed to secure partial payment if, for any reason, including the lack of funds, the project was abandoned or suspended. Plaintiff would limit the construction loan condition to subdivision (b), for it provides "that *this payment* shall be made only from construction loan funds" (emphasis added), whereas the other subdivisions are not expressly so conditioned.

The construction loan condition, however, cannot reasonably be limited to subdivision (b), for subdivision (c) and (d) both refer to the terms of subdivision (b) and must therefore be interpreted with reference to those terms. Thus, the "balance of the fee" payable "in equal monthly payments" under subdivision (c) necessarily refers to the preceding subdivisions of paragraph 4. In the absence of evidence to the contrary, subdivision (d), upon which plaintiff relies, must likewise be interpreted to incorporate the construction loan condition (Civ.Code, § 1641), for it makes explicit reference to payment under preceding subdivisions by language such as "under the preceding terms" and "partial payment as aforesaid." Subdivision (d) merely provides for accelerated payment upon the happening of a contingency. It contemplates, however, that construction shall have begun, for it provides for prorated payment upon the abandonment or suspension in whole or in part of "any work designed or specified by the Architect." Implicit in the scheme is the purpose to provide, after initial payments, for a series of payments from construction loan funds, with accelerated payment from such funds in the event that construction was abandoned or suspended. Although plaintiff was guaranteed an estimated 25 per cent of his fee if the project was frustrated before construction, further payment was contemplated only upon the commencement of construction. This interpretation is supported by evidence that plaintiff knew that Bristol's ability to undertake construction turned upon the availability of loan funds. Accordingly, the trial court properly determined that payments beyond an estimated 25 per cent of plaintiff's fee for phase two were to be made only from construction loan funds.

. . .

Each party to a contract has a duty to do what the contract presupposes he will do to accomplish its purpose. . . . Thus, "A party who prevents fulfillment of a condition of his own obligation * * * cannot rely on such condition to defeat his liability." (Bewick v. Mecham, supra, 26 Cal.2d at p. 99, 156 P.2d at p. 761; . . . Plaintiff, however, has not shown that Bristol failed to make the proper and reasonable efforts that were contemplated to secure the loan from which he was to be paid. . . . The risk that a loan might not be obtained even though Bristol acted properly and in good faith was a risk clearly anticipated even though the reason the loan failed may not have been foreseen.

. . .

The unhappy result for Parsons was that he was not paid for 70% of his work. However, there are indications in the omitted portion of the opinion that he might have won if he had shown:

a. That Bristol did not make reasonable efforts to obtain financing or

b. That Parsons had not been notified immediately when Freeman filed his action, so that he could suspend work until title matters were cleared up, and

c. That he would have stopped work had he been notified that the construction loan had fallen through.

(The "abandonment" clause so heavily relied upon by Parsons will be discussed in § 10.04(d).)

SECTION 7.02 PAYMENT DESPITE NONCOMPLIANCE WITH CONTRACT

(A) SUBSTANTIAL PERFORMANCE

In service contracts (including construction contracts and contracts for the rendering of professional services), the nonperforming party (such as the owner or client) usually wishes to hold back his payment until the performing party (contractor or design professional) performs in accordance with the contract. To accomplish this, the paying party often conditions his obligation to pay upon full contract performance. This is a powerful device to enable the paying party to get what he bargained for.

While this is desirable for the paying party, strict application of the condition can cause hardship to the performing party. It would be unfair for the latter to almost fully perform and still deny him any payment. To do so would constitute a forfeiture and, in many cases, unjust enrichment. Often the non-performance was trivial and not at all commensurate with the money still to be paid under the contract.

One way the law has avoided such a result in construction contracts is through the doctrine of "substantial performance". In essence, substantial performance by the contractor entitles him to recover the contract price remaining to be paid, less whatever his non-performance cost the owner. See § 24.02(b) for the application of this doctrine to construction contracts. To use this doctrine courts generally require that non-performance not materially affect the basic purpose for which the project was being built.

Substantial performance has been applied in considering minor breaches by a design professional. If the professional substantially performs, he can recover the unpaid portion of the contract price, less the damages caused by the minor breaches. The most frequent use of this doctrine relates to delayed performance by the design professional. Even if the delay were unexcused, the design professional would be likely to recover the balance of the contract price, less any losses to the client caused by the delay. Also, minor errors in design, or other minor breaches, could invoke the substantial performance doctrine.

It is sometimes stated that the doctrine of substantial performance will not apply if the condition affecting the non-performing party's obligation to perform is an express condition. This means that if the contract specifies an absolutely perfect compliance as a condition to the client's obligation to pay, substantial performance will not be sufficient. There are undoubtedly cases which state this. There are also cases which have slid over this distinction, where the deviations were minor, and where forfeiture would result by a stringent application of the doctrine of conditions. Design professionals should always attempt to perform fully and properly in accordance with their obligation. But, if they do not, there is a possibility that they will be able to recover for their services, with a deduction being taken by the client for any damage caused by minor breaches of the contract.

(B) PREVENTION, HINDRANCE OR NON–COOPERATION

Generally, the client will not be able to rely upon non-performance by the design professional as a reason not to pay if the client prevented or hindered the performance. For example, the client could condition his obligation to pay upon the securing of a zoning variance. If the client did not apply for the variance, in most situations the condition would be eliminated, and the client would be obligated to pay.

Similarly, noncooperation would excuse the condition of full performance. For example, the design professional's right to be paid may be conditioned upon approval by the client of the design. The client's refusal to even look at the design would be the type of noncooperation which would enable the design professional to collect, despite nonoccurrence of the specified condition of approval.

(C) WAIVER

Sometimes a contracting party agrees expressly or implicitly to pay despite the non-occurrence of conditions, such as performance on time, performance of required services, or performance in the manner specified by the contract or by law. If the evidence is reasonably clear that the other party has agreed to give up the condition, the performing party usually is able to collect for his work despite the non-occurrence of the condition. For example, the client may state that the architect will be allowed additional time, or that he need not furnish the requisite number of copies of drawings. If so, these conditions are excused and need not occur.

Since the client may change his mind or forget what he has said, it is vital to secure and preserve any evidence that shows the non-performing party is giving up the conditions. This can be achieved by obtaining a written statement from the client, or by writing the client that it is the design professional's understanding that the objectives specified in the contract need not be accomplished. Failure to object to such a statement may assist in proving the waiver.

Waiver can be based upon reliance. If the design professional relied upon the manifestation by the client that he did not have to fully comply, such as by not performing when he could have, his reliance should enforce the client's promise to pay despite non-performance. Sometimes there is no reliance, because the time for performance has passed before the "waiver" or because the design professional could not have performed. If the waiver is held to excuse the condition, it is because the court considers that minor matters can be dispensed with or given up without reliance or bargain.

When dealing with public agencies, the concept of waiver, whether relied upon or not, generally will not be available.

(D) REPUDIATION

Usually the client's obligation to pay is conditioned upon the design professional presenting the plans and specifications to the client for the client's acceptance. There may be occasions when the client indicates that he will not proceed with the project or use the work of the design professional. This may lead the design professional to believe that presenting the plans and specifications would be a meaningless act. For this reason, the design professional may not offer the completed plans and specifications. Even though presenting the plans and specifications may be a condition, this condition will be removed from the picture if acts of the client indicate to the design professional that such a presentation would be a futile and meaningless act.

Whether such a presentation is excused is often a difficult one. To fully protect himself, the design professional should always offer performance, even though it appears that such an offer would be unnecessary and meaningless.

(E) QUASI–CONTRACT

Sometimes the design professional can recover, based upon quasi-contract or unjust enrichment. If his work has benefited the client, the absence of a valid contract, or even the absence of proper performance on the part of the design professional, may not bar recovery. For example, if the client uses the plans and specifications despite non-occurence of the condition or improper performance by the design professional, the design professional should be able to recover in quasi-contract. In such cases, courts sometimes state that the client has waived the condition and recovery is based upon the contract.

If recovery is based upon quasi-contract, the amount recoverable will be diminished by any damages caused by the failure of the design professional to perform in accordance with his agreement.

Quasi-contract is rarely available when performing work under a public contract.

SECTION 7.03 METHODS OF COMPUTING COMPENSATION

(A) EXPENSES INCURRED BY DESIGN PROFESSIONALS

Before examining the various types of methods for compensating the design professional, the design professional should know the types of expenses he will incur on a project.

One principal expense item relates to the *labor costs* of performing design services and construction project administration. The principal *direct* cost will be the salary paid to the design professional, and wages paid to his employees allocable to the project. To compute his direct design services and construction administration costs, the design professional may use several methods. He can estimate the number of hours that will be employed and multiply by the hourly rate of those performing services. He can estimate the number and size of drawings and the pages of specifications and multiply by an established cost per square foot of drawings or per page of specifications. This established cost would very likely be based upon past experience in doing work of this type. Finally, he could look at the type of project and make a cost prediction based upon cost records of other similar projects.

In addition to the direct costs connected to design services, there are *general overhead* costs which may equal the direct labor costs. Illustrations of these overhead costs would be rental for office space, clerical help, amounts allocable for promotion and good will, cost of reproduction, office machinery and equipment, costs of insurance, fringe benefits for employees and communication expenses.

Another principal item of expense which will be incurred by the design professional are *reimbursables*. These are payments which the design professional makes on behalf of the client and for which the design professional will receive reimbursement. Reimbursables can be divided into major and minor reimbursables. Under some arrangements, the design professional is reimbursed for designated consulting fees he pays, such as to a mechanical engineer, an electrical engineer, a structural engineer or a landscape architect. Another major reimbursement item can be the cost of employing a project inspector on the job.

In addition, there are smaller payments which the design professional may make on the client's behalf and which, under the terms of their agreement, may be reimbursable to the design professional. Illustrations of these types of smaller reimbursables are payments for permits, application fees for permits, inspection fees, and, in some cases, unusual costs of reproduction.

Reimbursables are expenses which are initially incurred by the design professional and paid by him. Sometimes the client incurs an expense, but the bill is sent to the design professional for payment. Under such circumstances the design professional might pay the bill and ask reimbursement by the client, or forward the bill to the client for payment.

The design professional often pays for *incidental* expenses connected to the project. These are not payments he makes on behalf of the client, such as a reimbursable. They are obligations he incurs in order to perform his services and which go beyond the normal direct costs or general overhead. Illustrations of these expenses would be travel, and cost of telephone calls and telegrams.

While, strictly speaking, profit to the design professional is not an expense, his profit should be taken into account when a fee structure is planned.

(B) TYPES OF FEE ARRANGEMENTS

The design professional and his client can agree to compensate the design professional for his services in a number of different ways. Each method has advantages and disadvantages. The role of the law in these matters is relatively limited. It consists mainly of interpreting the terms of the contract that bear upon fee computation when the parties disagree. It may also prescribe the amount of compensation where the parties have *not* agreed on a method of compensation.

The design professional and the client should mutually agree on a fee structure, and express it clearly in a written agreement. Not doing so invites the often acrimonious disputes that can develop over compensation.

Stated Percentage of Construction Costs

A method commonly used by design professionals to measure their compensation is a stated percentage of construction costs. This method has been criticized because the higher the construction costs, the higher the fee for the design professional. Some have felt that such a method discourages the design professional from reducing costs. Also, the amount of work performed is not necessarily commensurate with the construction costs. Such a system tends to subsidize the inefficient client at the expense of the efficient one. Despite criticism of the method, it is probably the most commonly used technique for computing compensation paid to design professionals. It is traditional, avoids bargaining, and is relatively easy to administer.

As for the specified percentage figure, there are recommended, but not required, percentage amounts for different types of construction work. Sometimes there is a differential based upon whether the project is residential or commercial, whether the construction contracts are single or separate contracts, and whether the construction contracts are lump sum or cost type contracts. In smaller jobs, there may be a minimum fee tied to percentage of construction costs.

There can be difficulties in determining the cost figure to which the fixed percentage is to be applied. Sometimes difficulties develop because the project is not constructed, or never reached the bid submission stage. It is even possible that the project did not get far enough for the design professional himself to have made a cost estimate.

If the contractor defaulted, part of the cost of the project may have been paid by the surety bond company. Is the fee based upon the cost to the owner, or the cost of the project?

There are other difficulties as well. Does the cost include the cost of purchasing the land or interests in other land, such as easements or rights-of-way necessary for the construction? Does it include materials and labor furnished by the client himself? If so, what measures the value? Does it include fees of the design professional or consultants? What happens if the costs are increased due to design errors caused by the design professional? What happens if the costs increase because of unforeseen sub-surface conditions? Appellate cases have gone into these questions, but there are too many different types of arrangements made, and too many different contract provisions used, to make any sensible and usable generalizations from the cases. It may be helpful to look at the definition of cost given in the AIA Doc. B131, at Art. 3. This form defines construction costs as:

> **3.1** Construction Cost to be used as a basis for determining the Architect's Fee for all Work designed or specified by the Architect, including labor, materials, equipment and furnishings, shall be determined as follows, with precedence in the order listed:
>
> **3.1.1** For completed construction, the total cost of all such Work;
>
> **3.1.2** For work not constructed, the lowest bona fide bid received from a qualified bidder for any or all of such work; or
>
> **3.1.3** For work for which bids are not received, (1) the latest Detailed Cost Estimate, or (2) the Architect's latest Statement of Probable Construction Cost.
>
> **3.2** Construction Cost does not include the fees of the Architect and consultants, the cost of the land, rights-of-way, or other costs which are the responsibility of the Owner as provided in Paragraphs 2.3 through 2.6 inclusive.
>
> **3.3** Labor furnished by the Owner for the Project shall be included in the Construction Cost at current market rates. Materials and equipment furnished by the Owner shall be included at current market prices, except that used materials and equipment shall be included as if purchased new for the Project.

Most contracts which use this method set aside two items which are added to the stated percentage of construction costs in computing the fee. They are reimbursables and extra services. During the course of the design professional's performance, he will often incur expenses on behalf of the client. Many contracts specify that these expenses are to be reimbursed by the client and do not come out of the basic fee to be paid to the design professional. It is important to spell reimbursables out carefully, if the design professional does not want to absorb them as part of his basic fee. While most reimbursables are fairly small amounts, often contracts provide for reimbursements for engineering services and other consultants. This can constitute a large amount of money, and it is important to spell out and clarify who has the obligation to pay for consultants.

The problem of reimbursement was raised in Pedersen v. Fiksdal, 185 Cal.App.2d 30, 7 Cal.Rptr. 874 (1960). The contract was on an AIA standard form, but there was a specific provision which incorporated a fixed sum for preliminary drawings, and another fixed sum for working drawings, specifications, and obtaining bids. The standard form provision dealing with reimbursements stated:

> The Owner is to reimburse the Architect the costs of transportation and living incurred by him and his assistants while traveling in discharge of duties connected with the Work, the cost of all reproductions of drawings, the cost of the services of engineers for normal plumbing, heating, electrical and other mechanical work and of special consultants and other disbursements on his account approved by the Owner.

In connection with this performance the architect incurred expenses of almost $5,000 for reproducing documents, and for consultants' fees. He did not secure approval from the owner before incurring these expenses. After the plans were completed, and some bids taken, the client abandoned the project. The client paid the fixed sums specified in the contract, but refused to pay for the costs incurred by the architect for reproducing documents and for consultants' fees. The trial court ruled for the plaintiff-architect by awarding a judgment for the reimbursables.

On appeal, the defendant-owner contended that there was no right to reimbursement unless the incurring of expense had been approved by him, and that the reimbursable items were to be included in the basic fee paid to the architect. He also stated that there was an understanding with the architect that the total amount set forth in the contract would be the absolute limit of the fee, and he would not be asked to pay any further amounts to the architect. While it seems reasonably clear from the reimbursement clause that approval of expenses is only to be required for "other disbursements on his account," the California intermediate appellate court held that the contract was reasonably susceptible to two interpretations, and that the owner's contention that his approval was required was a reasonable interpretation.

The Court also noted that there had been a fixed price set for the fee in the contract, that the contract also stated that the architect would prepare working drawings and specifications for electrical and other mechanical work, and that the fixed fee applied to working plans and specifications. The owner also testified that he was told that the architect would do all the engineering work, and there was no discussion of going outside for consultants. Also the defendant-owner testified that the job was to be performed as cheaply as possible in order for him to determine whether he could finance the project. The appellant court sent the matter back to the trial court with an instruction to listen to the extrinsic evidence, put itself in the position of the parties at the time they made the contract, and then make its decision.

The case illustrates a number of important points. First, courts often try to get at the sense of the transaction and the intention of the client. In doing so, they often pay little attention to the literal terminology of the printed form contract. Second, the reimbursement for consultant's fees can constitute an important cost item. Frequently, the client does not realize that he will have to pay something beyond the basic fee for these reimbursables. For this reason, it is essential to go over this portion of the contract with the client and make it clear as to what the understanding is regarding this expense. Third, the case shows the hazards of drafting, and the necessity to use a drafting format which makes clear whether a qualifying phrase (approved by the Owner) applies to the item immediately before the phrase, or to all items in the series. AIA Doc. B131 at 5.1.3 has substantially changed the cited paragraph and appears to require advance approval by the owner only for reimbursables connected with special consultants "for other than the normal structural, mechanical and electrical engineering services." This seems to mean that the owner's approval is not required except for special consultants other than those normally employed.

Cost Type Contracts

There is an increasing use of cost type contracts for design professional services. This may be useful where the client will make many changes. Usually, the design professional receives his costs, and in addition, a percentage of those costs or a fixed fee. This avoids some of the problems of the percentage of construction cost system but creates others. The definition of allowable costs can cause difficulty. Also, cost type contracts require more record keeping on the part of the design professional. The cost type contract has the advantage of not gearing the fee to the construction costs, but it does have the disadvantage of gearing the fee to the cost of the design professional. The cost type contract often means that the client carefully looks over the costs submitted by the design professional, and may object to certain costs as being excessive or unnecessary. It is possible to place a maximum limit on a cost type fee for the protection of the client.

Personnel Multipliers, Daily or Hourly Rates

Sometimes a design professional is paid a specific multiple (2, 2½ or 3) of designated personnel expenses. The multiplier aspect of the fee computation is to take into account administrative overhead and profit. Some design professionals may agree to work by the day or by the hour. These methods require detailed cost records which set forth:

(1) the exact amount of time

(2) the precise project upon which the work was performed

(3) the exact nature of the work

(4) who did the work

A Fixed Fee

An architect or engineer can agree with a client that he will be compensated for his services by a fixed fee. One obstacle to a fixed fee is the difficulty of determining in advance what it will cost the design professional to perform the services. Where this can be reasonably predicted, the fixed fee is often attractive to the client. He knows what his design services will cost.

The principal problem of a fixed fee in architectural and engineering contracts relates to whether the fixed fee covers all expenses incurred by the design professional, or whether the fixed fee will be augmented by certain reimbursables. Generally, design professionals attempt to be reimbursed for the smaller expenses they incur on behalf of the client such as payments for permits and inspections, and for direct expenses attributable to the work on the project, such as travel, postage, and long-distance telephone calls. It is important for the design professional and the client, under a fixed fee contract, to determine in advance whether the fixed fee is all the design professional will receive, or whether there will still be certain reimbursables allowed to him.

Handling Charges for Reimbursables

Some design professionals feel that they should be paid a service charge for the administrative costs of handling reimbursables. The design professional's overhead can be burdened by a large number of obligations he incurs for the client and which he pays for the client. In such cases the design professional might charge the client the amount paid plus a mark-up for handling. For example, if the design professional paid a consulting engineer $5,000, he might bill the client $5,000 plus $500 (10%) or $5,500. The percentage tacked on to the payment could range from 5 to 20%, depending upon the number of reimbursables and the amount of administrative overhead incurred in handling them. If the design professional wishes to add an overhead fee, this should be clearly explained to the client in advance and client approval obtained.

Reasonable Value of Services

If the parties do not agree on a method of computing the fee, then the law will apply the standard of reasonable value of the services. Also, the reasonable value of services is usually the measure to be applied for extra services not covered within the basic fee. If possible, it is advantageous to agree in advance on fees, since there are many potential areas for dispute. Determining the reasonable value of a professional's services can take into account the nature of the work, the degree of risk to the design professional, the novelty of the work, the hours performed, and other elements which are imprecise, and difficult to measure or upon which to agree. In addition, there can be problems with regard to administrative overhead and reasonable profit. If the standard is "reasonable fee," detailed cost records will also have to be kept. It is not advisable to leave open the question of fee.

If a legal issue arises as to the reasonable value of services, the design professional and, often, the client introduce evidence of the customary charges made within the locality by persons of the general qualifications of the design professional. In many cases, the design professional comes in with witnesses who inflate the reasonable value of the architect's services, and the client comes in with witnesses who deflate the value of the services. In such cases, it is not unusual for the court to make a judicial determination which falls somewhere in the middle between the testimony of the expert witnesses for both parties.

Deductions From Fee

Sometimes questions arise regarding the right of the client to deduct, from admittedly owed compensation, amounts the client claims he has or will have coming from the design professional. Acts of the design professional may result in expenses incurred by the client. For example, the client may have incurred an expense due to design errors, and wishes to deduct this expense from the fee to be paid to the design professional. Sometimes the deduction relates to a potential obligation on the part of the client. For example, design errors may have caused a claim to be made by an adjacent landowner, or by the contractor, and this claim may have been made against the client. If the client is responsible for the acts of the design professional in these cases, he may want to deduct a reserve from the admittedly owed fee to provide a fund in the event he has to pay for the acts of the design professional.

The right to take deductions or offsets in such cases can either be created by the contract or implied by law. An illustration of the first type is the frequent inclusion of provisions in construction contracts which give the owner the right to make deductions and offsets against the contractor. This type of provision is usually not found in contracts between design professionals and their clients. However, even in the absence of such provisions, the client may have the right to make deductions for expenses incurred, or likely to be incurred by the client, as a result of any contractual breach by the design professional. The amount deducted must not be disproportionate to the potential liability of the client.

(C) SUMMATION

To recapitulate, some of the principal areas of difficulty relating to compensation are: 1) Which services are included within the basic fee and which are to be the basis for an added charge? 2) Which expenditures incurred by the design professional are to be reimbursed by the client? 3) Where cost type contracts are used, what will be allowable costs? 4) If a fixed fee contract is used, will the fixed fee include all incidental expenses directly connected to the project?

SECTION 7.04 TIME FOR PAYMENT

(A) DOCTRINE OF CONDITIONS

The doctrine of conditions determines when the design professional is entitled to payment. Generally, unless there is an agreement to the contrary, the services must be fully performed before there is a right to payment.

This can raise two difficult problems for the person performing services. First, if the performance of services takes a long time, he may need some type of financing to enable him to perform. Second, the more he has to perform without being paid, the greater the risk that he will suffer a forfeiture by virtue of performing services and not being paid. For these reasons, certain judicial rules protected manufacturers and sellers of goods by giving them the right to payments as their goods were being delivered. This protection was not accorded to persons performing services. For this reason, contracts involving personal services should include provisions giving the performing party the right to be paid as he performs.

To a large degree, this rule has been modified by state statutes where the services are performed under employment contracts. Generally, statutes provide that employees are to be paid at certain fixed, short intervals. However, these statutes do not apply to those who perform design services where there is no employment relationship, and typically would not apply where the design professional is in private practice.

(B) INTERIM FEE PAYMENTS

It is common for design professionals to include contract clauses giving them the right to interim fee payments. There are obvious reasons for such clauses from the design professional's standpoint. From the client's standpoint, they can ease the financial burden by providing for payment in installments. Also, these interim fee payments can be an incentive for the design professional to begin and continue working on the project.

Usually these payments are to be made as certain defined portions of the design professional's work are completed. The use of interim fee payments brings into play the legal concept of divisibility or severability of contract provisions. This doctrine looks at whether the performance has been divided into definite segments, and whether there is an agreed valuation for these segments of performance. In some cases, contracts between design professionals and clients have been considered severable or divisible because of clauses providing for interim fee payments. Where one party has breached, does the interim fee provision preclude the other party from showing the work performed, and for which an interim payment was made, was worth more or less than the amount specified?

Section 6.1.2 of AIA Doc. B131 provides for these interim fee payments:

Schematic Design Phase	15%
Design Development Phase	35%
Construction Documents Phase	75%
Bidding or Negotiation Phase	80%
Construction Phase	100%

Suppose the client unjustifiably fires the architect after he has completed the construction documents phase. Some courts would consider the contract divisible, and would not permit the architect to recover any amount over the 75%, even if the reasonable value of the architect's services exceeded this amount. These same courts would not permit the client to show that the reasonable value of the professional services were less than 75% where the architect has, without justification, left the job. If the contract were not considered divisible, the non-breaching party could attack the 75% amount by showing that it did not reflect the reasonable value of the services. (The right to recover lost profits for the unperformed work will be discussed in §§ 10.04(d), 11.01(b) and 11.02(b).)

Courts should not consider these contracts divisible. The amounts chosen are usually a rough approximation and not a fixed and final valuation for each stage. These percentages may average out over the performance of many contracts. But it is rare that the amounts are tailored to the particular contract, especially if a form contract formula is used.

The actual cost in relationship to the stages depend upon the particular project, the client and the method of operation of the design professional. While some design professionals spend a disproportionate amount of time on design (and make up the difference on standardized construction documents), generally it is considered that the architect is overcompensated during design and undercompensated for his work on the construction project. If this is true, it may be to the advantage of the design professional to have the percentages considered agreed valuations. He will not have to prove the reasonable value of his services and may actually get more if there is a premature termination.

Since there is a distinct possibility that the percentages will be considered "fixed valuations", the design professional should try to ensure that the percentages used approximate the value of the work for each designated stage.

(C) MONTHLY BILLINGS

While interim fee payments reduce the risk of going unpaid, provide working capital, and reduce the fee "bite" on the client, they become less efficient in handling these matters in larger projects. In these projects, it may take months to finish each interim fee payment phase. To take care of the potentially long period between payments, it is useful to provide for monthly billings within interim fee periods.

> Section 6.1.2 of AIA Doc. B131 provides for monthly payments:
>
> in proportion to services performed to increase the compensation for Basic Services to the following percentages of the Basic Fee . . .
>
> [For the percentages see § 7.04(b)]

Section 6.2 of AIA Doc. B131 provides for monthly payments for additional services and reimbursables. This is also desirable.

In some public contracts it is not possible to be paid more often other than at the completion of the principal phases of performance. Also, in public contracts there may be cumbersome bureaucratic requirements which delay even the designated interim fee payments. Design professionals should take this into account when they do public work.

(D) SUGGESTIONS REGARDING INTERIM FEE PAYMENTS

Every contract between a design professional and a client should contain provisions for interim fees which are fair approximations of the value of the work as well as the right to bill monthly. It is equally important that the design professional make every effort to collect these payments as they are due. Otherwise, the design professional runs substantial risks of being unpaid for his work.

Often, payment will be made after a polite suggestion. If a polite suggestion does not suffice, the design professional should give serious consideration to suspending his performance until the fee payments are made. If the suspension continues for a substantial period of time, the design professional should consider terminating his obligation to perform further.

In cases of suspension of performance or termination of performance, it is desirable to notify the client of an intention to either suspend or terminate unless payment is received within a specified period of time. This gives the client an opportunity to make the payment and keep the contract going. It also shows the client that failure to make interim fee payments as promised will not be tolerated.

SECTION 7.05 OTHER CLIENT OBLIGATIONS

Other client obligations are expressed in design professional-client contracts or implied by law. As an illustration Art. 2 of AIA Doc. B131 sets forth one-half page of "Owner Responsibilities", some of which are:

> **2.3** The Owner shall furnish a certified land survey of the site giving, as applicable, grades and lines of streets, alleys, pavements and adjoining property; rights of way, restrictions, easements, encroachments, zoning, deed restrictions, boundaries and contours of the site; locations, dimensions and complete data pertaining to existing buildings, other improvements and trees; and full information concerning available service and utility lines both public and private.
>
> **2.4** The Owner shall furnish the services of a soils engineer, when such services are deemed necessary by the Architect, including reports, test borings, test pits, soil bearing values and other necessary operations for determining subsoil conditions.
>
> **2.5** The Owner shall furnish structural, mechanical, chemical and other laboratory tests, inspections and reports as required by law or the Contract Documents.
>
> **2.6** The Owner shall furnish such legal, accounting and insurance counselling services as may be necessary for the Project, and such auditing services as he may require to ascertain how or for what purposes the Contractor has used the moneys paid to him under the Construction Contract.

The stated obligations express the architect's view of the ideal client. This is not to suggest that the obligations placed upon the client under this contract are unfair, but there are duties expressed which may not be expected by the client. In many cases, the form contract is signed by the client, and theoretically this binds him to the terms of the form. But clients who feel imposed upon often refuse to perform, despite the contract terms. This can mean a dispute and possible litigation. If there is litigation, there is no assurance that the form will control. There are legal doctrines such as interpretation, mistake, and misrepresentation which can avoid what appears to be the plain meaning of the form.

Contract provisions work best when both parties understand them and agree to be bound by them. For that reason if the design professional wishes to make these provisions control, he should take steps to accomplish these objectives. He should:

1. Go over the contract with the client.
2. Explain the terms which may be difficult for the client to understand.
3. Give a reasoned explanation as to the necessity for the provision.

In addition to the obligations expressed in the agreement, certain other client obligations are implied by law. Contracting parties often omit provisions which they either believe to be so clear as to not require contractual expression, or which they have not considered. While courts state that they do not make contracts for the parties, but merely enforce those agreements which the parties have made, frequently courts are called upon to and do fill gaps which result from incomplete expression in the contract, or from failure on the part of the contracting parties to consider certain problems in advance.

The client impliedly promises not to interfere with the design professional's performance, not to hinder this performance, and to extend reasonable cooperation to the design professional in his performance. For example, the client should not refuse the design professional access to information which is necessary for the performance of the work. If he refuses to permit the design professional to inspect the site, this would be prevention and a breach of the implied obligation owed by the client to the design professional. Also, there are certain positive duties owed by the client. He should exercise good faith in passing upon the work of the design professional and in approving work at the various stages of the latter's performance. He should request bids from a reasonable number of contractors, and should use his best efforts to obtain a competent bidder who will agree to do the work at the best possible price. If there are conditions which will require acts of the client, such as obtaining a variance, or obtaining financing, he impliedly promises to use his best efforts to cause the condition to occur.

Since these obligations, and others of a like nature, are implied by law, they will not be implied if the contract expressly provides to the contrary.

REVIEW QUESTIONS

1. What is the best method of insuring that printed form provisions will be applied literally by a court?

2. What is the theory of quasi-contract?

3. What is the usual method for determining a design professional's compensation?

4. What are the advantages and disadvantages of such a method?

5. If nothing is stated regarding compensation, how is the design professional's compensation measured?

6. Why are provisions for interim fee payments important to design professionals?

7. Explain the doctrine of substantial performance, and give an illustration of substantial performance by a design professional.

8. What is the effect of "waiving" a condition of performance?

QUESTIONS FOR CLASS DISCUSSION

1. Should a client be held to provisions in a contract he signs that is prepared by the design professional, without regard to whether the client understands the provisions or has had them explained to him?

2. If you were a client, would the list of client obligations stated on Page 160 reflect your understanding of your obligations to the design professional?

3. Why should there be more stringent requirements in public contracts than in private contracts for the establishment of the right to collect for design services?

4. Should the design professional be able to suspend his performance if he does not receive an interim fee payment to which he is entitled?

5. Should a contracting party be able to collect when he has "only substantially" fulfilled his obligation? Why?

PROBLEM

A has undertaken to perform design services for the construction of a million dollar office building. A is to be paid six percent of the total construction cost of the project. The contract provides that there will be a deduction of $500 a day for each day of unexcused delay. Upon completion of performance, it is determined that the contractor was 50 days late, and that there is no excuse for the delay. For this reason, the client deducted $25,000 from the final balance owed the contractor. Is A's fee computed on the basis of six percent of one million, or six percent of $975,000? Explain.

Chapter 8

SOME SPECIAL PROBLEMS: COSTS, FIDUCIARY DUTIES AND OWNERSHIP OF PLANS

SECTION 8.01 COST PREDICTIONS

The relative accuracy of cost predictions is a matter of great importance to clients, whether public or private. They want to know how much money projects will cost. They may be limited to bond issues, to appropriations, or to available capital. Unfortunately, many clients think that cost estimating is a scientific process by which accurate estimates can be ground out mechanically by the design professional. For this reason, design professionals should start out with the assumption that cost predictions are vital to the client, and that the client does not realize the difficulty in making accurate cost predictions.

(A) THE INACCURATE COST PREDICTION: A SOURCE OF MISUNDERSTANDING

Design professionals frequently maintain that cost predictions are merely educated guesses which depend upon events not within the control of the design professional. They contend that the client controls the quantity and the quality of the project, and for that reason any cost predictions that architects or engineers make are only informed guesses. If these "informed guesses" turn out to be inaccurate, this inaccuracy should not have any effect on their right to be paid for their services, unless they were negligent. If the low bid substantially exceeds the cost prediction, usually architects and engineers are willing to redesign at their own expense, a costly process for design professionals.

Clients, on the other hand, frequently contend that it was part of their understanding that, unless the project could be brought in within a specified cost figure, they would not have to pay anything, including the architect's or engineer's fee. In other words, clients claim that the accuracy of the cost prediction is a *condition* to their obligation to proceed with the project and to pay the design professional for his services.

(B) CREATION OF A COST CONDITION: STEVENS v. FANNING

The principal legal question in cases involving cost predictions has been whether a cost condition was created by an agreement between design professional and his client. If there is a cost condition, generally the architect gambles that his cost prediction will be reasonably accurate. If he is wrong, whether negligent or not, he loses his fee. If it is held that he promised to be accurate, he will be responsible for any damages which result from the inaccurate cost prediction. In deciding whether a cost condition has been created, two principal questions have dominated the cases. They are:

1. Will the client be permitted to testify that there was an oral agreement or understanding not included in their written contract that the client could abandon the project and not pay for design services if the low construction bid substantially exceeded the last cost prediction by the design professional?
2. What factors, other than agreement, will courts look at to determine whether the design professional assumed the risk of an inaccurate cost prediction?

Preliminarily, some cases have held that a cost condition can be created without any agreement between design professional and his client, if the design professional knows that the client has a specified amount of money to spend.

Generally, if the written agreement is silent as to cost predictions and on the effect of their inaccuracy, the client will be permitted to try to prove that such an agreement on costs was made. In permitting him to do this, courts generally consider that such written agreements are not the complete and final repository of the entire agreement between the design professional and his client. Even if there is disclaimer language in the written contract denying the creation of a cost condition, the client stands a chance of convincing the court that he should be allowed to prove that such an agreement was made. The client must still convince the judge or the jury that an agreement was made. (The disclaimer clause may be helpful on this question.)

If the client is permitted to testify as to an antecedent agreement or understanding, and if the judge or jury believes the client, the client will win. However, often there is a conflict of testimony as to the creation of the cost condition. The client testifies that the parties agreed that the client would not have to pay if the project were abandoned because of excess costs, but the design professional testifies that there was no agreement under which he would go unpaid if the costs substantially exceeded his final cost prediction. While there are no fixed rules which can be used to predict whether a judge or jury will hold in favor of the design professional or the client, there are some generalizations which can be extracted from the cases.

In Sweet and Sweet, Architectural Cost Predictions: A Legal and Institutional Analysis, 56 Calif.L.Rev. 996, 1006–1007 (1968) the authors state:

> Courts have admitted evidence of custom in the profession. Architects have been permitted to introduce evidence that customarily architects do not assume the risk of the

accuracy of their cost predictions. Also, courts have been more favorably disposed toward holding for the architect if the project in question has involved remodeling rather than new construction, because estimating costs in remodeling is extremely difficult. The same result should follow if the type of construction involves experimental techniques or materials.

Courts sometimes distinguish between cases and justify varying results on the basis of the amount of detail given to the architect by the client in advance. Generally, the greater the detail, the easier it should be for the architect to predict accurately. However, it is much more difficult for the architect to fulfill the desires of the client within a specified cost figure if the client retains a great deal of control over details, especially if these controls are exercised throughout the architect's performance. For this reason, some courts have held that a cost condition is not created where the architect is not given much flexibility in designs or materials.

Some courts have looked at the stage of the architect's performance in which the cost condition was created. If it is created at an early stage, it is more difficult for the architect to be accurate in his cost predictions. Generally, the later the cost limit is imposed in good faith, the more likely it is to be a cost condition. But courts should recognize that if it is imposed later, creation—or, more realistically, imposition—may be an unfair attempt by the client to deprive the architect of his fee.

Occasionally the courts have applied the rule that an ambiguous contract should be interpreted against the person who drew it up and thus created the ambiguity. If the client is a private party, the contract is usually drafted or supplied by the architect. Courts have looked at the building and business experience of the client. If the client is experienced, he should be more aware of the difficulty of making accurate cost estimates. If he has building experience, the client is more likely to be aware of the custom that architects usually do not risk their fee upon the accuracy of their cost estimates.

Courts have sometimes cited provisions for interim payments as an indication that the architect is not assuming the risk of losing his fees on the accuracy of his cost estimates. However, standard printed clauses buried in a contract are not always an accurate reflection of the understanding of the party not familiar with the customs or the forms. If payments have actually been made during the architect's performance, this is a clearer indication that the client is not laboring under the belief that he will not have to pay any fee if the low bid substantially exceeds the final cost estimate. A few cases have looked for good faith on the part of the client. For example, if the client has offered some payment to the architect for his services, this may impress a court as a show of fairness and good faith. (footnotes omitted)

The professional societies have attempted, by the use of standard form contracts, to obtain different results from the usual court decisions. Contracts frequently state that cost estimates cannot be guaranteed. The AIA has eliminated the use of the word "cost estimate" and uses instead "statements of probable construction costs." The AIA Doc. B131 (1963) stated that if the client wanted a fixed cost prediction, he would be required to hire and pay for a professional cost estimator. In addition, this form stated that if the cost came in too high, the owner must give written approval of an increase in the limit, or the owner would cooperate in revising the project scope or quality, or both, to reduce the cost as required. In addition, the same form stated that "if any work designed or specified by the architect during any phase of service is abandoned or suspended in whole or in part the architect is to be paid for the service performed on account of it prior to receipt of written notice from the owner of such abandonment or suspension." This clause was interpreted by the Illinois Court of Appeals in Stevens v. Fanning, reproduced at this point.

STEVENS v. FANNING

Appellate Court of Illinois, 1965.
59 Ill.App.2d 285, 207 N.E.2d 136.

DAVIS, JUSTICE. The plaintiff, Raymond Alan Stevens, brought this suit claiming that the sum of $14,535.65 remained due him from the defendant, Edward J. Fanning, under the terms of a written contract, pursuant to which he performed architectural services for Fanning. The case was tried before the court without a jury, and the court entered judgment for the plaintiff in the sum of $2,500. The plaintiff appealed from the judgment.

Fanning, a Chevrolet dealer in Aurora, contacted Stevens in early October, 1962, for the purpose of having Stevens design a building for his dealership. At this point he had only three basic requirements for the building: first, that it contain at least 40,000 square feet; second, that it not cost over $250,000; and third, that the construction proceed with dispatch as his present lease was expiring. Fanning presented Stevens with some preliminary drawings, which he had received from an engineering company specializing in the construction of pre-fabricated type steel buildings, in order to give Stevens a general idea of the floor plan desired.

On two occasions during the latter part of October, Stevens again met with Fanning and presented a sketch plan and elevation study, after which, Fanning told Stevens he had the job. On November 5,

1962, the parties entered into a written contract, which was a standard A.I.A. form of contract between an Owner and Architect. The contract provided that the building was to be "a multiple purpose building suitable to the needs of the Owner, at an approximate estimated cost of $250,000.00."

The parties disagree as to the subsequent events insofar as they indicate the type of building to be constructed under the contract. Fanning testified that Stevens agreed that he would design a pre-stressed concrete building of the required size, which would cost no more than $250,000. While he was not certain as to when this agreement was reached, he knew that it was prior to the time they attended the first meeting at which they sought financing, in the latter part of November, 1962. Stevens testified that he never agreed to design such building for $250,000 but that a pre-stressed concrete building was at all times an alternate proposal to a steel frame building; and that he advised Fanning that the pre-stressed concrete building would cost more than $250,000, but the additional cost could, perhaps, be justified by insurance premium savings.

Stevens received the bids on the building and presented them to Fanning on December 18, 1962. The bids were based upon both steel frame and pre-stressed concrete types of construction. Those bids based on steel frame construction, totalled less than $250,000, but the bids based upon pre-stressed concrete construction, totalled $317,000. On December 21, 1962, Fanning terminated the contract stating that Stevens had failed to design a 40,000 square foot building in pre-stressed concrete at a cost of $250,000, as promised.

Stevens then filed this suit contending that he had performed the contract as required until the time of Fanning's abandonment. The contract provided that in event the owner abandoned the work, the architect was entitled to a certain percentage of the total contract price, depending on the stage to which the architect's work had progressed. Stevens alleged that he had completed the stages of work through the receipt of bids, and that under the terms of the contract he was entitled to 80% of the contract price, or $15,535.65, less $1,000 previously paid to him. Fanning contended that he did not abandon the contract under its terms permitting abandonment upon the payment of certain sums to the architect, but rather terminated the contract because of the failure of Stevens to perform as required thereunder.

Stevens here contends that he did not have an obligation to design a building to be constructed for a maximum of $250,000, in that the contract provided:

> "Witnesseth, that whereas the Owner intends to erect a multiple purpose building suitable to the needs of Owner, at an approximate estimated cost of $250,000.00 * * *
>
> "IV PROJECT CONSTRUCTION COST.
>
> "6. Since the Architect has no control over the cost of labor and materials, or competitive bidding, he does not guarantee

the accuracy of any statements or estimates of probable construction cost."

He argues that the figure of $250,000 is but "an approximate estimate" of which he made no guarantee.

The $250,000 figure did not, however, arise in a vacuum. This figure, and its accompanying phrase, was inserted in the contract as a result of the negotiations and conversations of the parties. The fundamental question in determining the meaning of a contract is always the intent of the parties. This intent is to be gathered by giving to the contract a fair and reasonable interpretation, from the language of the entire contract, considered in the light of the circumstances under which it was made. Gay v. S. N. Nielsen Co., 18 Ill.App.2d 368, 374, 375, 152 N.E.2d 468 (2d Dist.1958). A contract should be enforced according to the sense which the parties mutually understood it at the time it was made, with greater deference to be given to their clear intent than to any particular words which they may have used to express it. Keefer Coal Co. v. United Elec. Coal Companies, 291 Ill.App. 477, 10 N.E.2d 210 (3rd Dist.1937).

Stevens made no objection at the trial to the testimony of Fanning that from the time of their first contact, he, Fanning, at all times had said that the cost of the building could not exceed $250,000. This was the limitation of his budget. Indeed, it appears from Stevens' own testimony that, at all times, he knew and understood that he had a $250,000 limitation within which to work. In view of the unanimity of the testimony of the parties relative to their understanding of the cost limitation and the objects and purposes they had in mind when executing the contract, we believe that by the insertion of the clause in the contract that the building was to be of "an approximate estimated cost of $250,000.00", they intended, and manifested their intent, that $250,000 was to be the maximum cost. . . .

This construction does not conflict with the language the parties actually used to express their intent. By use of the words "approximate estimated cost", the final construction cost would have had to have been substantially within the limit set forth. The use of this language prevented the result that any deviation above the expressed limit, no matter how slight, would have been a failure to perform under the contract. Nor does this clause conflict with the printed portion of the contract which recites that the architect "does not guarantee the accuracy of any statements or estimates or probable construction cost." There is no question of a guarantee at issue. Fanning contended that under the contract, as finalized, Stevens agreed to furnish plans and specifications to the end that the cost of construction would not exceed the specified amount; and the trial court so found. Under the law, if the bids received on the type of building Stevens was to design under the contract, clearly exceeded this limit, then he failed to perform his part of the contract. . . .

Stevens contends that even if there was a limitation of $250,000 placed upon the project by the contract, he is still entitled to recover, as the bids he received for the building, based on steel frame construction, were within this limit. He contends that only the bids for the pre-stressed concrete construction were in excess of this amount and the trial court erred, as a matter of law, in finding that the parties modified the contract to provide for only pre-stressed concrete construction.

Stevens misconceives the nature of the finding of the trial court. It found that the parties, subsequent to the date of the written contract, agreed that the building was to be of pre-stressed concrete design. This finding was not a modification of, or a change in the terms of the written contract, but rather a finding of an agreement which made more definite and certain that which was incomplete in the written contract. Whether the written contract was intended to be the complete and final agreement, must be determined from the language of the contract and the circumstances of the case. "If it is silent in essential particulars, parol evidence is admissible to establish the missing parts, although inadmissible to contradict those unambiguous terms expressed in the document." Spitz v. Brickhouse, 3 Ill.App. 2d 536, 539, 540, 123 N.E.2d 117, 119, 49 A.L.R.2d 673 (1st Dist. 1954).

The written contract provided only that the owner intended to construct a multiple purpose building suitable to his needs, at an approximate cost of $250,000. The contract was silent as to the dimensions, even though it is clear that prior to the execution of the contract it was understood that the building had to contain at least 40,000 square feet in order for Fanning to meet his dealership requirements. The contract was silent as to all aspects of the nature of the building to be designed. It is apparent that it was not complete and final, but contemplated that the parties would fill this void by agreements outside the written contract. As was stated in the Spitz case supra, at page 540, 123 N.E.2d at page 119:

> "The form contract in the instant case is silent as to the style of the house to be designed, the number of its rooms, its dimensions, the quantity and quality of the materials to be used in erecting it, and so on. In Bair v. School Dist. No. 141, Smith County, 94 Kan. 144, 146 P. 347, 348, the court said: 'There must be something outside the contract to determine these questions. The architect must have had instructions outside the contract with which to undertake to comply, in the preparation of his plans.' "

Thus, where, as here, the basic written contract does not purport to be a complete expression of the whole agreement and is silent as to the nature and specifications of the building to be designed, parol evidence is admissible to more fully elucidate the agreement as finally consummated. . . . It was thus appropriate for the trial court to determine whether the type of construction was agreed to by the parties so as to fully vitalize the written contract of November 5th.

William Heckel, an architectural draftsman employed by Stevens, confirmed the testimony of Stevens that the pre-stressed concrete was always an alternate and was never promised at a cost of $250,000. Stevens accompanied Fanning to the Merchants National Bank to help Fanning secure financing. At this meeting he presented certain preliminary drawings, all of which showed pre-stressed concrete construction. The vice-president of the bank testified that at this meeting it was discussed that the building would cost approximately $250,000, and while he wasn't told that they had definitely decided on pre-stressed concrete, no other type of construction was mentioned.

About a week later the parties went to a concern called Dovenmuehle, to seek financing. Fanning's attorney accompanied them. He testified that while in the car, enroute to this meeting, no type of construction was discussed other than pre-stressed concrete. He further testified that at the meeting, the presentation to secure financing was based upon the building being constructed of pre-stressed concrete at an estimated cost of $250,000. Stevens testified that, at the Dovenmuehle meeting, they submitted the same drawings which were shown to the bank, all based upon pre-stressed concrete, and also some preliminary working drawings based upon a steel frame building. He stated that he never told the people at Dovenmuehle that he was considering only pre-stressed concrete or that he could construct the building out of pre-stressed concrete for $250,000. Apparently, however, the people at Dovenmuehle were given that impression, in that later the same day they called Fanning's attorney and suggested that he check on the architect, since the building could not be constructed of pre-stressed concrete for less than $315,000.

At the meeting of December 18th, when the bids were presented to Fanning, two acquaintances of Fanning were present. One testified that Fanning then asked Stevens whether he (Stevens) had told him (Fanning) that he could build a pre-stressed building for $250,000; and that Stevens answered, "yes". The other testified that Stevens answered that only one set of bids had been received and he thought he could reduce the final figure.

There is complete conflict in the testimony as to whether Stevens said he would design a pre-stressed concrete building under the contract for $250,000. It was the duty of the trial court to make this determination of fact, and it is not for us to set aside this finding unless it is clearly and manifestly against the weight of the evidence. Spitz v. Brickhouse, 3 Ill.App.2d 536, 542, 123 N.E.2d 117 (1st Dist. 1954). There is ample evidence to support the finding of the trial court and, thus, no basis for this Court to substitute its judgment for that of the trial court.

Stevens also contends that Fanning had a duty to alter the plans to come within the cost limit, since a printed portion of the contract provided that if the estimated construction cost exceeded the limit provided and the owner did not approve an increase in the limit, the owner "shall cooperate in revising the project scope or quality or both, to reduce the cost as required, * * *." Such contention cannot be sustained in that the trial court found that the parties contracted solely for a specific type of building at a given price, and it is undisputed that the architect did not produces (sic) such building at the agreed price.

The theory of the trial court in awarding to the plaintiff a judgment of $2,500, was that he was entitled to the reasonable value of his services up to the time the parties had definitely agreed that the building was to be pre-stressed concrete; that thereafter he failed to perform the contract as finalized; and that it was only from that time on, that plaintiff was not entitled to remuneration for his services. The trial court found that plaintiff's compensable services were worth $3,500, and that defendant had paid plaintiff $1,000.

We believe that since the understanding as to the type of construction was in fact an integral and essential part of the entire contract, as finalized, and it is undisputed that the plaintiff could not perform his part of the agreement as so-finalized, he is not entitled to any compensation under the contract. . . . However, no cross appeal was filed challenging the right of the plaintiff to the reasonable value of his services for the period of time indicated. Therefore, the judgment for the plaintiff in the sum of $2,500. is affirmed.

Judgment affirmed.

The Court looked primarily at the understanding of the client that he was to get a building to be constructed by pre-stressed concrete, even though the invitation to bidders allowed for bids on two different methods of construction. In essence, the Court disregarded the provision requiring the client to cooperate in reducing the scope of the project or increasing the cost limit.

The AIA Doc. B131, published in 1966, and continued in 1967, at 3.5 went even farther to try to protect the architect in such cases. This form states:

> When a fixed limit of Construction Cost is established as a condition of this Agreement, it shall include a bidding contingency of ten per cent unless another amount is agreed upon in writing. When such a fixed limit is established, the Architect shall be permitted to determine what materials, equipment, component systems and types of construction are to be included in the Contract Documents, and to make reasonable adjustments in the scope of the Project to bring it within the fixed limit.

In addition, this form states that the form is the entire contract, in order to attempt to avoid oral testimony by the client on any alleged "agreement" as to costs.

The professional societies are doing all they can in their printed forms to have any cost predictions considered merely cost estimates.

The courts, on the other hand, seem to be ruling in accordance with what they consider to be the basic understanding of the client rather than the language of the contract.

(C) INTERPRETATION OF COST CONDITION

Usually the courts give the design professional a tolerance of about 10% in his cost prediction. There is also the question of what should be included in the cost. This is usually worked out in the same way as the cost for determining the design professional's fee. Generally, the key cost figure is the low enforceable bid submitted by a contractor.

(D) DISPENSING WITH THE COST CONDITION

If a cost condition has been created and not performed, the next question is whether the client has dispensed with it. If the client has eliminated the cost condition, the design professional can collect. Usually this result has been reached where there have been excessive changes made by the client during the design phase. In this regard, it is helpful for the design professional to notify the client that changes which he is suggesting or ordering during the design phase will have a designated effect on any earlier cost predictions.

Sometimes the condition is removed because its occurrence is prevented or hindered. For example, if the client does not permit bidding by contractors, the condition would be excused. Also, it is arguable that if he limits bidding to an unrepresentative group of bidders, he is preventing occurrence of the condition.

Sometimes the condition is eliminated because the client indicates that he is no longer concerned with earlier projected costs. He may be so impressed by the design aspects of the structure that he is willing to dispense with the originally created cost condition. Sometimes this willingness to dispense with the condition is manifested by his taking steps to proceed with the project, knowing that the bids are higher than originally predicted. Courts have held that use of the plans removes the cost condition. This is justified if the use of the plans indicates a willingness to dispense with the cost condition. However, if the facts are clear that the project is continued for other reasons, then the condition should not be removed. Any injustice caused by the use of the plans under such circumstances should be relieved by giving the design professional a right to recover in quasi contract for the benefit conferred by use of the plans.

(E) DAMAGES

Most lawsuits which involve costs are attempts by design professionals to collect their fees when projects are abandoned because of excess costs. Sometimes the client institutes legal action to recover any interim fee payments he has made. In a few cases, the client asks for damages for breach of contract, usually where he has proceeded with the project.

Analysis of a damage claim requires that promises be differentiated from conditions. If a cost condition is created, this does not necessarily mean that the design professional promises to be accurate. He may reluctantly risk his fee upon the accuracy of his cost predictions, but he may not wish to risk an action for breach of contract.

However, courts have not made this distinction, and have frequently assumed that a fixed cost amount means the design professional has warranted or promised that the project would not cost more than a designated figure. Under such an assumption, if costs substantially exceed predicted costs, there has been a breach even if the design professional used due care in making his cost prediction. A contract breach entitles the nonbreaching party to recover damages. (See Chapter 11 for a discussion of damages.)

In most cases it has been difficult for the client to recover damages where the project is built. If he tries to recover the difference between the predicted cost and the actual cost, he is usually met with the argument that he has a project worth what it cost him. He may also be met with the contention that by proceeding with the project when he knew the costs would be in excess of predictions, he brought the damages upon himself. The client may have a chance to recover damages if he can show the diminished economic value of a commercial project.

If the client is a tenant, and not the owner of the structure, he may have a good claim against the design professional for the excess costs. In Kellogg v. Pizza Oven Inc., 157 Colo. 295, 402 P.2d 633 (1965) the client was a tenant who had made an agreement with his landlord that the landlord would pay up to $60,000 for the cost of an improvement to the landlord's building. The architect had negligently estimated costs at $62,000 but the project cost $92,000. The tenant-client had to pay the balance of approximately $30,000. The tenant recovered this amount less a 10% tolerance for errors from the design professional because of the excess cost. (The real winner appears to be the landlord, who ended up with improvements probably worth considerably more than the $60,000 he spent. If the landlord has benefited in this way, perhaps the design professional would have a good claim against the landlord based upon unjust enrichment.)

Another case, Kaufman v. Leard, 248 N.E.2d 480 (Mass.1969) held the architect, Brooks, responsible for damages in a cost case. A look at the facts may be instructive.

The clients, the Kaufmans, purchased a house after Brooks, the architect, indicated that the house could be remodeled and redecorated at a cost between $12,000 and $15,000. Brooks drew up plans which were not sufficiently detailed for a fixed price contract. After some discussion and design changes the price of $17,000 was set as a cost ceiling. Brooks upon authorization by the clients, engaged two contractors (Leard and Noel) on a time and materials basis. Ultimately the cost soared to $40,000.

The computation which was the basis for a $24,000 award against the architect was as follows:

Total of Leard's charges to the Kaufmans on time and materials basis contracted for by Brooks		$32,953.86
Total due from the Kaufmans to Noel as fair value of work contracted for by Brooks		7,000.00
		$39,953.86
Limit of cost under the Kaufmans' authorization to Brooks	$17,000.00	
Extras ordered by the Kaufmans	5,415.00	$22,415.00
Kaufmans' excess liability to the contractors, unauthorized by them.		$17,538.86
Part of architect's fee already paid		785.00
		$18,323.86
Interest		5,900.28
Par. 3 of final decree (Brooks to pay the Kaufmans)		$24,224.14
Plus costs		35.25

In commenting on the arrangement the architect had made the Court stated:

> . . . the responsibility is the architect's under this very risky and unsatisfactory arrangement. In the circumstances certain precautions to be taken by the architect were reasonably indicated. He should have made it emphatically plain to the Kaufmans that he could not be sure that the $17,000 figure would not be exceeded. His plans and specifications should have been sufficiently explicit for Leard to give a reasonably accurate estimate of cost. The architect should not have relied on his own estimate of probable painting expense. The conclusions of the master were that Brooks was negligent in failing to prepare adequate plans, in failing to submit written specifications to Leard, in failing to keep any record of the oral specifications given Leard, and in failing to tell the Kaufmans that he had only an estimate from Leard; also that Brooks exceeded his authority in ordering and directing work which he knew or should have known would cost in excess of the limit of $17,000.

The Court rejected the contention made by the architect that the clients would unjustly be enriched if they recovered the excess costs and retained the house with $40,000 worth of improvements. The Court did allow a deduction for the normal margin of error that is given an architect when he agrees to a cost condition.

The *Kaufman* case is not typical of the many cost cases. Typically, construction is never commenced, because the low construction bid substantially exceeds the cost production. This is another reason why damage claims against the architect are relatively rare in cost cases. While it might be possible to try to charge the design professional for expenses incurred before the project is abandoned, generally damage claims arise when the project is not abandoned but is completed.

(F) ADVICE TO DESIGN PROFESSIONALS

Many design professional-client relationships deteriorate or collapse because of excessive costs. The various professional societies should make every effort to try to make the cost prediction process more accurate. A well-programmed data retrieval system could help.

The chief method used by the professional societies to protect their members from losing their fees where their cost predictions are inaccurate has been the contract device. They have included many types of provisions in contracts which are supposed to insure that fees will not be lost when cost predictions are inaccurate, and that fees will be lost only where the cost predictions are made negligently. However, courts have frequently ignored these contract provisions. Reliance upon the abandonment clause may be dangerous. It would be better to expressly state that if costs are excessive and the project given up, the architect or engineer will still be paid for what he has done if he used due care in making the estimate. AIA Doc. B131 does so state.

If the design professional makes a reasonable explanation to the client, he is not likely to incur difficulty over this problem. He should inform the client how cost predictions are made, and how difficult it is to achieve accuracy when balancing uncontrollable factors. He should state that he will do his best, but that for various specific reasons the low bids from the contractors may be substantially in excess of the statement of probable construction costs. He should suggest that under such circumstances, the design professional and the client should join to work towards a design solution which will satisfy the needs of the client and his financial capabilities. In helping the client to be realistic about his desires and his available funds, the design professional should request that the client be as specific as possible as to his expectations from the project.

If these steps are taken, some clients may be lost. It may be better to lose them at the outset, rather than spend many hours and either not be paid, or be forced to go to court to try to collect.

If a realistic confrontation with the client is not achieved at the outset, the design professional must face the possible risks. He may choose to take the chance because he has to, or because he thinks that in the long run it is better. But if he does not collect for work he has performed, he should not blame the contract drafter or the law.

During performance, the design professional should state what effect any changes made by the client will have upon any existing cost predictions. Hopefully, not every change will require an increase in the cost predictions. If the client approves any design work, the request for approval should state whether there has been any change in cost predictions.

If an architect puts himself in the unfortunate position of the architect in the *Kaufman* case, discussed in the prior subsection, he should not continue the construction until he receives authorization by his clients to raise the cost limits. It should have been apparent to the architect from the bills being submitted by the contractor that the cost would substantially overrun. At the first indication of possible overrun, the work should have been stopped until approval had been given by the clients.

SECTION 8.02 FIDUCIARY OBLIGATIONS

(A) RELEVANCE

The fiduciary concept can come up in a number of ways. For example, an engineer who is on the engineering staff of a large corporation has a fiduciary relationship with his employer. Also, members of a design professional partnership have fiduciary obligations toward one another. Finally, the retention of a design professional by a client creates a fiduciary relationship. The relationship between client and the design professional is the focal point for the discussion in this section.

(B) BASIC PRINCIPLE OF FAIRNESS AND TRUST

The fiduciary concept has been mentioned in § 3.02(b). It is an imprecise concept, and one which cannot be described in great detail. Persons who owe fiduciary obligations to each other should be fair and loyal to each other. In many commercial transactions, the parties are permitted to deal at arm's length. They have no obligation to look out for each other. Within some limits, each one is allowed to do whatever is best for himself.

A fiduciary relationship requires trust and loyalty, because one party is in the position to take advantage of the other. Agreements which create these relationships are often brief, and do not detail the obligations owed by one to the other. As a result the law has had to fill in many gaps.

(C) FIDUCIARY OBLIGATION OF DESIGN PROFESSIONALS

The architect or engineer owes a duty of loyalty to his client. He must avoid any conflict of interest which could prejudice or work to the disadvantage of his client. The client relies upon the design professional's independent judgment, which can be affected by a conflict of interest. The design professional should not have a financial interest in a contractor who is bidding for construction work, or who is engaging in a construction project for his client. The design professional should not have any financial interest in any suppliers or subcontractors who may be involved in the project for which he has been retained. He should be careful to avoid endorsing products which could affect his duty of faithful performance. It may be possible for him to continue to represent and to furnish professional assistance to his client even where there is a conflict of interest, if this conflict of interest is fully and fairly disclosed to the client.

The design professional should make no profits from his position, other than the compensation paid him by his client. He should not take rebates or bribes. He should make full disclosure of all relevant information to his client, and, conversely, he must not disclose to others information which he learns as a result of his relationship to, and work for, his client. If financial opportunities come to his attention during his retention by the client, he should present these financial opportunities to his client if it is likely that this opportunity would be advantageous to the client. He must keep his funds separate from the funds of his client. If he comingles them, he will be guilty of a breach of his fiduciary obligation, and any doubts as to whom the money belongs will be resolved in favor of the client.

These, of course, are only a few illustrations of the fiduciary concept. One of its most salient features is its ability to handle many types of problems.

(D) REMEDIES FOR VIOLATION

Clearly, the client can avoid responsibility for any act by the design professional which is tainted with a breach of the fiduciary obligation. If a contract is made which could have been influenced by these considerations, the client can, if he chooses, avoid the contract. If acts have been rendered, such as the issuance of a certificate, the issuance of the certificate can be made ineffective if the client so desires.

There are a number of other significant remedies available in such a situation. A breach of a fiduciary obligation gives the client grounds for dismissal. The design professional can lose his fee if he has received bribes or gifts from other persons, such as the contractor or a supplier. Any profits which he has made as a result of such a breach can be recovered by the client, even if the efforts of the design professional substantially generated the profits. Finally, any damages suffered by the client are chargeable to the design professional, if the damages resulted from a breach of the fiduciary obligation.

(E) EFFECT OF CONTRACT UPON THE FIDUCIARY CONCEPT

As mentioned, some of the aspects of the fiduciary concept resulted from the frequently brief and incomplete agreements made between client and design professional. Today, there is an increasing use of detailed written agreements which express certain aspects of the fiduciary concept. The more detailed the written agreement, perhaps the less need for implying fiduciary obligations. However, in the normal design professional-client contract, the effect of a written, apparently complete, agreement will not eliminate the fiduciary concept. If a contract covers specific aspects of the fiduciary relationship, the contract language will control. The important thing to remember is that the law has moved, and continues to move, in the direction of obligating parties to a contract to be fair toward one another.

(F) TERMINATION OF RELATIONSHIP CREATING FIDUCIARY OBLIGATIONS

Some of the fiduciary obligations may remain even after the employment or professional relationship is concluded. Normally, the employee can compete if there is no contract provision precluding competition. Sometimes contract provisions of this sort are not enforceable if they are unreasonable. However, the employee may still be obligated not to use trade secrets which he has learned during the employment. If he uses or sells such secrets, such as customer lists, trade and technical data, and the like, he will still have a duty to account to the employer for profits. The termination of the relationship does not necessarily end all fiduciary obligations. See §§ 32.05(b) and 40.09 for further discussion of these problems.

SECTION 8.03 OWNERSHIP OF INTELLECTUAL PROPERTY: PLANS AND INVENTIONS

(A) DESIGN PROFESSIONAL-CLIENT RELATIONSHIP

Difficulties sometimes develop over the question of ownership of plans, specifications, and other documents which are developed because of the design professional-client relationship. Resolution of such difficulties depends upon the rights and duties created by the contract between the design professional and the client, and often involves rights and duties implied by law in the absence of any specific provision in the contract. In the absence of any contractual provision, the client will own all the fruits of the intellectual efforts of the design professional whom he retains. This means that the client will own the plans and specifications created as a result of the design professional-client relationship.

Sometimes the design professional asserts the existence of a custom that plans and specifications are the property of the person creating them, and that the client only has the use of these products. Unless the client is aware of this custom, or should be aware of it, such a custom will not control the question of ownership. The design professional must include a contractual provision spelling out the question of ownership, if he intends to claim that the plans and specifications are to be his property. Such provisions are commonly included in form contracts created by professional societies of design professionals, such as the American Institute of Architects.

In this regard it may be instructive to examine the provision in AIA Doc. B131 which deals with ownership of plans. Art. 9 states:

> Drawings and Specifications as instruments of service are and shall remain the property of the Architect whether the Project for which they are made is executed or not. They are not to be used by the Owner on other projects or extensions to this Project except by agreement in writing and with appropriate compensation to the Architect.

Suppose the project consists of an office building, and five years later the client decides to add a wing to the building. He chooses a new architect for the new wing. The new architect wishes a copy of the original plans in order to tie in the new wing to the old building. Under Art. 9 it would appear that the client would have to pay the original architect for the use of the old plans because of the phrase "or extensions to this Project." While most clients would have and use a copy of the plans without much fear of litigation, such a provision could, in some situations, put the client at the mercy of the original architect.

Provisions such as these crop up in form contracts created by professional societies, and make courts suspicious of their fairness. There is an economic justification for the basic ownership provision. No doubt the fee would be adjusted if it were clear from the outset that there would be multiple use of the plans, but there does not appear to be the same justification for the extensions phrase. Perhaps *some* or all of the old drawings and specifications will be copied by the new architect. But copyright laws can protect against copying. See §§ 40.04, 40.05. But where the plans are only used for information, or only in a minor way, the clause appears to be a device to discourage the client from retaining a new architect for an extension or to make him pay if he does.

In line with what has been suggested in other parts of this treatise, provisions which may be contrary to the normal expectations of the client should be carefully pointed out, and explained, to the client. Also, if possible, the reasons for the fairness of such a provision should be brought to the attention of the client. If this is done, potential disagreements may be avoided at the outset. If the design professional does not bring these matters to the attention of the client, the contract provision may protect him. But there are always possibilities of dispute if the client does not have an understanding of the clause in question, and the reason for its inclusion.

Where the client is to be the owner of the intellectual creation of the design professional, his right to ownership will depend upon his meeting his obligations under the contract. His right to ownership, where it does exist, is conditioned upon his performance of the essential parts of his contractual obligation. If he does not pay the fee, for example, he will not own the product of the design professional.

Difficulties also may develop over the ownership of correspondence and memoranda relating to the performance of contractors or consultants, and other written or electronic products, which come into being as the result of the relationship of design professional and client. These products may be of great importance in the event of litigation. Even where the client owns products which arise out of the administration of the project, communications between the design professional and members of his own staff, as well as calculations and private notes used by the design professional and his staff, should belong to the design professional. Much difficulty can be avoided if sufficient copies of correspondence are made and retained, so that both client and design professional have their interests protected and have access to the correspondence and documents which are pertinent to the project.

Ownership of plans is also important for copyright purposes. See §§ 40.04(b) and 40.07(a).

(B) EMPLOYEE–EMPLOYER RELATIONSHIP

The bulk of the discussion in this part of the treatise relates to the hiring of a design professional by a client. Often design professionals are employees rather than private practitioners. Problems sometimes develop between employee and employer over the ownership of plans, specifications, and inventions which result during the period of employment.

Ownership in such a case will depend upon contract provisions. In the absence of any contractual handling of ownership much will depend upon the purpose for which the employee has been engaged. If he has been asked to design a particular machine, or to draw up specific plans and specifications, then the employer will own these products.

However, sometimes an employee develops an invention while he is employed and while he may be using facilities of the employer. If the invention is not the specific purpose for which he has been hired, it is likely that the employee will own the rights and may patent such an invention.

If the employer's facilities are used, and if the invention is developed on the employer's time, courts have fashioned a right in the employer to use the invention called the "shop right rule." The employer will have a right to use the invention, without paying a royalty to the employee-inventor.

The shop right has limitations. It is usually non-assignable, and can be used only by the employer. Also, there may be limitations as to its use. The right to its use normally will be nonexclusive, and sometimes the right is limited to the duration of the employee's employment. Much depends on the facts and circumstances in each case, and there are no fixed rules of law which will govern this question.

Much of the law on this issue has become relatively unimportant because of agreements usually signed by employees when they enter employment. Such agreements commonly provide that the employer will have exclusive ownership of any inventions or ideas which are developed during the period of employment. Often there are interpretation questions relating to such agreements. Doubtful questions are likely to be resolved in favor of the employee.

REVIEW QUESTIONS

1. What is the difference between a cost estimate and a cost condition?

2. Are clients generally permitted to testify as to alleged oral agreements relating to cost conditions?

3. Under the AIA Doc. B131 at p. 171, what are the client's obligations if the construction bids substantially exceed any cost conditions?

4. What would be illustrations of acts or statements of a client which would eliminate a cost condition?

5. Why should there be a fiduciary relationship between design professional and client?

6. If there is no written contract between an architect and his client, who owns the right to use the design documents?

7. Who owns the rights to inventions developed by an employee while working for his employer?

8. What is the shop right rule?

QUESTIONS FOR CLASS DISCUSSION

1. Should a client be permitted to testify as to an oral agreement, when that agreement was not expressed in the written contract?

2. Should a design professional go uncompensated if his cost predictions are inaccurate, but not negligent, and the project is abandoned?

3. Can you differentiate between inaccurate and negligent cost predictions?

4. How would you avoid future misunderstandings with a client over cost predictions?

5. Differentiate a fiduciary relationship from an arm's-length relationship.

6. How does the fiduciary relationship fit into the professional life of an architect?

7. How would you justify to a client a provision in a contract giving the design professional ownership of plans and specifications?

PROBLEMS

1. A was an architect who had been retained by C to construct a small commercial building. C requested that the building contain five stories, and a specified amount of square feet. He also requested that the building have enough luxury features so that he could attract high class tenants who would pay a high rental. Since he hoped to attract law firms as tenants, he stated that sufficient space should be segregated for a law library which could be used by all of the lawyer tenants.

In the course of his design performance A had informed C that he planned to use a very luxurious type of wood paneling in the larger offices, and also that there would be murals painted in the entrance hall. He also stated that there would be a sauna bath on each floor. He planned to install piped-in music, and a number of other luxury features. All of this was agreeable to C.

The price was not to exceed $1,000,000. The construction documents were submitted to five bidders and the lowest bid was $1,300.-000. A then stated that he would replace the luxurious wood panels with a less expensive type of wall construction. He suggested that the murals and sauna baths be eliminated. He suggested elimination of the music system. Plumbing features would be of cheaper quality. In addition, he wanted to eliminate the library, and thus increase the rental area as well as cut costs. He also stated that the size of the windows would be reduced, and that a number of other features would be changed to cut the costs.

C was unhappy about all these changes. He stated that he could not charge as much rental unless the luxury features were retained. A pointed to the clause quoted on p. 171 which was part of the agreement that both A and C had signed. Does A have the right to make these changes? Are there any limits to A's rights to make deletions or substitutions? Give illustrations of changes which would be permissible, and those which would not.

2. Acme Cement Corp. is a nation-wide company manufacturing a certain type of cement. There are one million outstanding shares of common stock in Acme. Acme competes with three other large manufacturers of cement. E is an engineer retained to perform design services for the construction of a large dam. E owns 5,000 shares of Acme. Would E's selection of Acme cement for the dam constitute a breach of his fiduciary obligation to his client? Explain.

Chapter 9

SUBSTITUTIONS AND TRANSFERS UNDER A CONTRACT

SECTION 9.01 SOME PROBLEMS OF TERMINOLOGY

Generally, bilateral contracts between two or more parties create rights and duties. A party who has rights under a contract may wish to transfer those rights to a third party. Conversely, a party who has duties to perform under a contract may wish to have these duties performed by a third party. Sometimes contracts are classified as assignable or personal. This categorization does not take into account that each party typically has rights and duties.

It would be more useful to phrase the basic questions in this way:

1. Can a party with performance obligations under a contract satisfy these obligations by employing a substitute?
2. Are particular contract rights transferable?

The first question will be analyzed in § 9.02 and the second question in § 9.03.

SECTION 9.02 WHO CAN PERFORM?

(A) OBLIGATIONS OF DESIGN PROFESSIONAL

The design professional may operate through a corporation, a partnership, or be a sole proprietor. The actual performance of the work may be done by the sole proprietor, by a partner with whom the client did not negotiate, by employees of the contracting party (whether the contracting party was a sole proprietor, a partnership or a corporation), or by a consultant hired by the design professional. Are the client's obligations conditioned upon the performance being rendered by any particular person? Can certain portions of the performance be rendered by persons other than the design professional with whom the client dealt? How much of the design professional's work can be performed by others without affecting the obligation of the client to pay the fee?

Many cases have held that the drawing of plans and specifications is a highly personal performance. When the client retains a design professional, he usually does so because he is impressed with the design skill of the person with whom he is dealing. Yet most clients realize that certain parts of the performance will be delegated to employees within the design professional's organization, to partners of the person with whom the client has dealt, or to consultants retained by the design professional. In addition, licensing or professional incorporation laws may require that certain types of performance be done by, or approved by, licensed professionals.

Returning to the basic concept of the reasonable expectations of the client, the client usually expects the design professional with whom he has dealt to perform the important creative functions for which he has been retained. Many of the details will be executed by other persons. Undoubtedly, much will depend upon the size of the design professional's organization, if the client is aware of the size and nature of the design professional's organization. Also, expectations may depend upon whether the client has dealt with architects and engineers before, and, if so, under what circumstances.

The client has the right to expect that the design professional will coordinate and supervise the design. When the work is submitted to the client for his approval, the latter can reasonably expect that the design professional has checked over and approved the work of any persons to whom he has delegated portions of the performance.

Permitting a substitute to do certain portions of the design professional's performance does not relieve the design professional of responsibility for the work. There has been no transfer of the obligation from the design professional to the person who has performed the work. This cannot be done without approval of the client. The client's obligation may not be conditioned upon the requirement that the person with whom he negotiated do all of the work, unless the contract so provides. However, this does not mean that design professional has in any way relieved himself of the obligation to see to it that the work is performed in accordance with the agreement between himself and the client.

Design professionals sometimes think that if they hire a consultant to do certain portions of the work, the consultant should bear the primary and the only responsibility for deficient performance. Unless the client agrees to accept the consultant in the place of the design professional, and to relieve the design professional from this contractual obligation, the design professional will continue to bear responsibility.

Scott v. Potomac Ins. Co., 217 Or. 323, 341 P.2d 1083 (1959) illustrates this. The client claimed that a failure in the heating system was due to defective design. He asserted a claim against the architect. The architect's insurer refused to defend, claiming that the negligent act occurred in a period not covered by the policy. (See § 35.03 for a discussion of professional liability insurance.) The architect settled the claim and brought an action against his insurance company when it refused to reimburse him.

To recover, the architect found himself in the strange position of claiming he was liable. One argument made by the insurer was that the architect was not negligent because he relied upon the advice of a heating engineer. In rejecting this argument the Court stated that the architect should possess skill in all aspects of the building process and cannot shift responsibility to a consultant.

The architect was permitted to use a substitute to perform certain aspects of his work, but this did not relieve him from responsibility when the substitute performed negligently. (If the design professional is going to bear responsibility for the non-performance of the consultant, he should make certain that he can assert a claim, hopefully a collectible one, against the consultant, in the event the design professional is held responsible for the consultant's failure to perform. (See § 30.11(f).)

(B) OBLIGATIONS OF CLIENT

The client may be an individual, a partnership, or one of the various types of associations. The client has obligations under the contract, the most important being the obligation to pay compensation. However, there are other obligations, such as cooperation, good faith approval or disapproval of the plans of the design professional, and the procurement of necessary permits or licenses.

As for payment of the fee, it makes little difference to the design professional who pays the fee, as long as the fee is paid. For this reason, the client could substitute a third party to pay the fee, and performance by the third party would satisfy any obligations the client has. This is rarely a problem.

The elements of cooperation and approval of the design professional's performance can raise more difficult questions. There is a strong element of individuality involved in the performance of these obligations. The professional relationship requires give and take by both parties, since taste and judgment are so much a part of the performance of these obligations. It is arguable that the client should not be able to substitute a third party to perform these functions.

In order to evaluate this question, it is necessary to recognize that most clients are legal entities such as corporations, or aggregates of individuals, such as partnerships. The law generally regards the performance of these duties as performable by anyone selected by the contracting entity. The cooperation or approvals may be performed or given by employees of the client.

It is also possible for the client to use a substitute for such performance from outside his organization. For example, a corporation might hire another design professional to evaluate the work, and determine whether approval should be given to work submitted by the design professional retained to draw plans and specifications. Normally, this is permissible. The design professional's obligation to render professional services is not conditioned upon performance of the client's obligations by any particular individuals. If the design professional enters into the relationship relying upon the fact that he will be dealing with a particular individual, and no other person, then it is essential to include in the contract a provision specifying this. In the absence of such a clause, a client can delegate obligations to individuals within or outside of his organization.

The fact that these performances can be delegated does not relieve the client from responsibility for failure to perform by the person to whom these performances are delegated.

SECTION 9.03 TRANSFERRING CONTRACT RIGHTS

(A) TRANSFER BY DESIGN PROFESSIONAL

Can the design professional transfer his right to receive compensation for his performance under his contract with his client? He may want to transfer this right for a number of reasons. Rights to payment are usually classified as accounts receivable. He may wish to transfer his accounts receivable to a lender as security for a loan. He may wish to transfer these rights to an impatient creditor.

While earlier the law tended to set up restrictions which hampered the transfer of rights to receive money, the modern tendency is to permit such transfers. Normally, the person obligated to pay money (the obligor) is not unduly burdened if he must pay the money to a transferee rather than the other party to the contract.

There are some limitations to this general policy permitting persons who have money coming (obligees) to be able to cash in on these rights by transferring them. One cannot assign the right to receive payments of money under a contract which has not yet been made. However, under certain circumstances the law would make the assignment become effective when the contract was made.

One reason for not permitting the transfer of the right to receive payment would be a showing that the client is not likely to get the desired performance if payments are made to a third party instead of to the performing party. For example, if the design professional has transferred his right to receive his fee to a bank, a client may feel that the design professional will be less likely to be interested in properly performing his obligations. It will take a strong showing of this possibility in order to persuade a court to deny transferability.

While the law permitted transferability of rights, it also recognized that the person owing the obligation, in this case the client, should not be placed in a materially worse position than he was when he entered into the contract. If a client's obligation to pay is transferred to a third party, this obligation is conditioned upon any events which would have conditioned the client's obligation to pay the design professional. For example, if the client's obligation is conditioned upon the occurrence of certain events, or upon proper performance by the design professional, these conditions also apply if the right to receive payment is transferred. The client should be in no worse position than he would have been had the right not been transferred. The same rule applies if the client has claims against the design professional for breach. He may deduct from amounts he must pay to the assignee (the person to whom the right to payment has been transferred) any amounts which he could have deducted from amounts due the design professional.

Unless special statutes compel a different result, the transferability of contract rights can be prohibited by contract provisions precluding transferability. It is common in contracts to have provisions stating that rights under the contract are not assignable without consent of the party who would have to perform the obligation. Courts have interpreted such nonassignability clauses narrowly. Unless it were quite clear that the obligation to pay *money* could not be transferred the courts interpreted general nonassignability clauses to prohibit substituted performance but not the payment of money. But if the clause were drafted carefully such a contract provision could preclude transferability of money payment rights.

Almost all states have adopted the Uniform Commercial Code. Section 9–318(4) of the Code denies enforceability to clauses restricting transfer of rights to receive money payments, if the transfer is made to secure a loan. The Code has recognized the importance of selling rights to receive money in the commercial world. Also, the Code assumes that the person obligated to pay the money is given sufficient protection by being able to assert defenses that could have been asserted against the original party against the person to whom the right of payment was transferred (the assignee or transferee).

Most standard form agreements used by design professionals include provisions requiring consent be given to any assignments. Such provisions would not be enforceable where the right in question is the payment of money and the right is assigned as security for a loan.

(B) TRANSFER BY CLIENT

In the ordinary contract for professional design services, the client is entitled to the design services promised by the design professional. The client can transfer his right to receive these services to a third party unless such a transfer would materially change the obligation of the design professional. Normally it would not.

If the design professional's obligation is conditioned upon the cooperation and aesthetic judgment of the particular client with whom he made the contract, the right might not be transferable. It would be transferable if the original client would continue to perform these obligations, an unlikely situation.

If the transfer would only involve delivery of plans and specifications to a third party rather than the original client, then it is likely that such right is transferable by the client. This is analogous to the design professional's transfer of his right to receive payment owed to him by the client.

If, however, the client in making this transfer is also attempting to substitute the cooperation and judgment of the transferee for his own, then the question will be analyzed in the manner set forth in § 9.02(b). Can these duties be performed by a third party without materially changing the original contract? If so, then a transfer would be effective and the design professional would be obligated to perform for the third party. The obligor, in this case the design professional, is protected by the doctrine of conditions. If he is not paid in accordance with interim fee payment provisions or if necessary cooperation is not given to him, he need not continue his performance to the transferee.

This discussion assumes there is no contract clause denying transferability or assignability of the rights in question. If there is such a clause, the right cannot be transferred without consent of the other party.

(C) NEGOTIABLE PAPER

Section 9.03 stated that generally the obligor can assert against the assignee most defenses that he could have asserted against the assignor. This is to avoid putting the obligor in a substantially worse position when he must render his performance of payment to an assignee rather than to the person with whom he made the contract.

However, if the debt is expressed in negotiable commercial paper (certain types of promissory notes, checks, drafts, bills of exchange and other documents), generally the person owing the money cannot assert most defenses against the transferee of the commercial paper, even if he could have asserted those defenses against the person transferring the commercial paper. Because the law of negotiable instruments is complicated, and because it does not play an important role in design professional-client relationships, it will not be discussed further.

SECTION 9.04 NOVATION

Sometimes a party to a contract wishes to free himself of his obligation. In order to do this, he may arrange for someone to take his place. In the design professional-client relationship, the design professional may wish to relieve himself of his contractual obligation. He cannot do this without consent of the client. However, the client may be satisfied with the promised performance of a different design professional. In such a case, there can be a three-party transaction. The client and original design professional may agree to relieve the design professional from his obligation, and the client and the new design professional may agree that the second design professional be substituted for the first. This is a "novation". The first design professional is released from any further obligation. Whether there has been a novation depends upon what the evidence indicates relating to the intention of the parties. A novation can occur if the client desires to be relieved and to substitute a new client in his place, and if the new client and the design professional agree to the substitution.

A novation differs from the transfer of rights (assignment) and substituted performance. In those cases, the original contracting parties still remain obligated to perform. In a novation, there is a release of one party and he owes no further obligation to the other party to the original contract.

REVIEW QUESTIONS

1. How do licensing laws affect who can be expected to actually perform design services?

2. When the law permits the design professional to obtain a substitute to perform some design services, is the design professional relieved from responsibility?

3. What is the effect of a contract clause making the right to receive money under a contract nonassignable?

4. What is the difference between an assignment and a novation?

QUESTIONS FOR CLASS DISCUSSION

1. Should the law allow a design professional to use a consultant to perform certain of his duties? Which duties?

2. Should the design professional be allowed to assign his right to receive a contract payment to a third person?

3. Should a client who retains an architect to design a luxury residence be able to transfer his right to receive the design services to buyer of the lot on which the house was to be built? Explain.

PROBLEM

A has been hired by C to design a project at a cost of about $300,000. A is the senior partner of a five-partner architectural firm.

Later C asks what he, A, will do personally. A states that he will not draft anything but will delegate all the design work to draftsmen in his office. A states that he will look at and approve all work that will be done and will offer various suggestions to the draftsmen. As to supervision, he will send out one of his partners from time to time who has good engineering training and knows construction better than A does. C is unhappy and tells A that he wants A to participate more in the work. What are C's legal rights in this regard?

Chapter 10
TERMINATION OF RELATIONSHIP

SECTION 10.01 CONDITIONAL OBLIGATIONS

(A) RIGHT TO TERMINATE

A contract generally creates rights and duties. Often contracting parties do not wish to begin or continue performance unless certain events occur or do not occur. For example, the client may not wish to commence construction of a project until he can obtain financing, purchase the land upon which the project is to be built, obtain a zoning variance or line up prospective tenants.

A design professional may wish to condition his obligation to perform upon his being able to obtain a particular consultant, upon his being able to expand his staff to meet the needs of performance, or upon his being able to obtain a temporary permit to practice in a state in which he is not licensed.

Despite wishing not to commence performance until certain crucial events occur, contracting parties may desire to make a binding contract. However, they wish to be released from the obligation to commence performance if these important events do not occur. The creation of a condition does not affect the validity of the contract as long as the condition is described with sufficient certainty, and as long as the occurrence of the specified event is not within the absolute control of one of the parties.

If a contract does contain conditions, failure of a condition to occur, or be dispensed with, releases both parties from their obligations. Sometimes the party for whose benefit the condition was inserted may wish to perform, despite the condition not having occurred. Generally, if the condition is for his benefit, he can dispense with the condition, making the obligation unconditional.

Sometimes one or both parties will commence performance, but wish the right to be relieved from further performance if certain events occur or do not occur. For example, the design professional may commence his performance while the client attempts to procure adequate financing. If performance is commenced, nonoccurrence of any condition of obtaining financing generally terminates contractual obligations to proceed further.

(B) PAYMENT FOR PERFORMANCE PRIOR TO TERMINATION

Suppose the design professional commences performance, but the necessary financing which conditions the client's obligation is not obtained. Unless the evidence is quite clear that the design professional was assuming the risk of the inability to obtain financing, he should be paid for his work. It should be and is often covered specifically by the contract. Standard form provisions often give the client a right to terminate at any time as long as he pays the design professional for what he has done prior to the receipt of a notice of termination. (For a case showing that these clauses do not always work see Parsons v. Bristol Dev. Co., reproduced at § 7.01(c).)

SECTION 10.02 MATERIAL BREACH OF CONTRACT

Termination may occur when one of the parties commits a material contract breach, one which is an important part of the bargain. Not every breach of contract will permit the other party to cancel his obligation to perform further. However, if the breach is serious, or if the breach indicates potential future breaches, such a breach can give the other party the right to terminate his obligation to perform further.

(A) BY CLIENT

The client's failure to cooperate, his interference in the design professional's performance, or excessive delay in the payment of fees are likely to be material breaches of contract. Where the breach relates to the time of performance, the law has been less likely to classify the breach as material. If the delay relates to fee payments, damages for delay would be the interest on the payments and this often is considered sufficient. Undoubtedly this is a recognition that delays are common in the performance of these types of obligations.

However, in some cases, delay in payment of fees can constitute a material breach. If the design professional needs the payments in order to pay his employees and his rent, nonpayment of fees when due could be material enough to suspend his obligation to perform further, and perhaps to terminate his obligation to continue performing.

(B) BY DESIGN PROFESSIONAL

Negligent performance, or excessive delays by the design professional can enable the client to end his obligation under the contract.

Much depends upon the seriousness of the breach, the history of past breaches, the likelihood that past breaches can be cured or avoided, and the possible financial loss to the design professional if the contract is terminated.

(C) PAYMENT TO DEFAULTING PARTY: QUASI-CONTRACT

Can the breaching party recover for any benefit he has conferred upon the other party? Suppose the design professional has performed considerable services for which he has not yet been paid before he commits a material breach?

Early cases held that the breaching party could not recover. However, the more recent cases have awarded the defaulting party the value of any benefit he has conferred on the other party less any damages his breach has caused based upon quasi-contract.

(D) OBTAINING LEGAL ADVICE

Termination is a serious step. It is often difficult to know whether a particular breach will be considered sufficiently serious to warrant the other party's termination of the contract. If a party asserts that he has the legal justification for the termination, and a court later determines that he was wrong, he himself has committed a serious default. For these reasons, the contracting party who believes the other party has committed a serious breach justifying termination should obtain legal advice before taking a firm position that he no longer need perform under the contract.

Whether termination for material breach affects the right to recover damages for the breach will be discussed in Chapter 11.

SECTION 10.03 DISRUPTIVE EVENTS

One basic purpose of contract law is to protect the reasonable expectations of contracting parties. If a person has obligated himself to perform he should do so, and he normally bears the risk of events which make his performance more difficult or expensive. However, the law recognizes that things do occur after the formation of a contract or during its performance which would make it unfair to compel performance by one or both parties. Doctrines have been developed which may relieve a party from his obligation to perform in the event these disruptive events occur.

(A) DEATH, INCAPACITY OR UNAVAILABILITY OF KEY PERSONS: CITY OF NO. KANSAS CITY v. SHARP

There is always a possibility that one of the parties to the contract, or someone closely connected with the project, will die or be unable to perform. There is a difference between the effect of death upon the legal existence of the contracting party and upon contract obligations. If the contracting party is a corporation, the death of a shareholder, or even the sole shareholder, does not dissolve the corporation. As for a partnership, the death of a partner may in some cases terminate the partnership. However, for contract purposes the basic question is whether the continued ability to perform by a specific person is so important that his death or incapacity will terminate contractual obligations.

The death of even a sole proprietor, or of a partner, does not necessarily mean the contracts of the sole proprietorship or partnership are terminated. Performance of contractual obligations of the former may be continued by the executor, the administrator, or successor in interest, such as a purchaser. Contracts of a partnership may be continued by the remaining partners, or a successor in interest.

There is a strong policy in the law to continue contract obligations, despite death, incapacity or unavailability of persons who were connected with either the formation or the performance of the contract. However, in certain types of arrangements the personal relationship is of great significance. In the absence of a contrary contractual provision, the death of the design professional usually terminates the obligation of both parties, and recovery for work performed prior to the death would depend upon benefit conferred and unjust enrichment. Perhaps the successor in interest of the design professional (whether a sole proprietor or partnership) may offer to hire someone else to fulfill the contract duty of the design professional. This may be agreeable to the client. However, such an arrangement depends upon the consent of both the personal representative and the client. Without agreement as to this, both parties would be relieved of further obligation to perform because of the design professional's death.

Even if the performing design professional is an employee of a corporate design professional, his death could release both parties. It would take a strong showing of the reliance upon that employee's continued capacity to perform before termination because of his death would be appropriate.

As for death of the client, his performance is generally considered performable by someone else. This means that the death of the client, or if the client is a corporate entity, the death, incapacity, or discharge of a key employee or officer with whom negotiations were made, or to whom performance was to be rendered, is not likely to affect the obligations of the parties. Both parties must continue to perform. If the design professional can show the necessity for coordination and cooperation and the importance of a give-and-take relationship between client and design professional, a design professional might convince a court that he should not have to continue performance after the death of the person for whom he was to perform his services and who was to evaluate his work. This would be a difficult task.

At the time the contract is made, parties should consider the effect of death, disability, or unavailability of persons who will play important roles in the performance of the contract and include a provision which clearly states the rights and duties of the parties if anyone crucial to performance dies or for any other reason is not available.

Some form agreements deal with this question. Often such provisions are buried in fine print or are drafted in such a way as to make it difficult for one or more contracting parties to understand. An illustration of this is Art. 10 in AIA Doc. B131 dealing with agreements between clients and architects. The clause reads:

> The Owner and Architect each binds himself, his partners, successors, assigns and legal representatives to the other party to this Agreement and to the partners, successors, assigns and legal representatives of such other party with respect to all covenants of this Agreement.

It appears that a client who has hired a particular member of the partnership would be bound to continue to use that partnership even if the particular architect with whom he dealt dies, becomes incapacitated, or leaves the partnership.

While the AIA provision is not a model of clarity, it appears that if the contract is in the partnership name, a change in membership of the partnership will not affect existing contract obligations. Even without such a clause, a partnership which terminates because of the withdrawal of a partner can continue to perform an existing contract even though it may not be permitted to make new contracts.

City of North Kansas City v. Sharp, in addition to detailing some sordid aspects of municipal engineering contracts, illustrates some of the legal problems which can result when one partner leaves the partnership and there are existing contracts to be performed. That case is reproduced in part at this point.

CITY OF NORTH KANSAS CITY, MISSOURI v. P. CLIFFORD SHARP

United States Court of Appeals, Eighth Circuit, 1969.
414 F.2d 359.

BLACKMUN, CIRCUIT JUDGE. P. Clifford Sharp instituted this diversity action against the City of North Kansas City, Missouri, to recover damages for himself and as trustee for Haskins, Sharp and

Ordelheide, a partnership, for breach of an engineering contract. . . . The ultimate result was the entry of a judgment for the plaintiff and against the City for $131,262 plus interest.

. . .

The basic facts. There is no real controversy about most of the facts. Prior to November 1957 the City had employed Haskins, Riddle and Sharp, a partnership of consulting engineers, on various projects. Mr. Haskins died in 1956 but William G. Riddle and the plaintiff Sharp continued in business under the old name. On November 12, 1957, when these two were the only partners, a "Memorandum of Agreement for Professional Engineering Services" was entered into with the City. This was executed on behalf of the partnership by Riddle and on behalf of the City by R. D. Scharz, Mayor, with Blanche E. Ford, City Clerk, attesting, and with the City Attorney approving in writing "as to form and legality". The agreement called for the performance by the partnership of specified engineering services in connection with proposed sanitary sewage projects.

The contract dealt initially with "Preliminary Phase Services" to be performed by the engineers. These included surveys and studies as to existing sanitary sewage works, growth trends, the adequacy of the existing works, recommendations for improvement, cost estimates, presentation of a report to the Division of Health of Missouri and to the City, assistance in pre-bond election activities, and assistance in obtaining a federal grant.

The agreement then referred to "Design and Supervision Services." The first paragraph under this heading read:

> "6. When so instructed by the City, prepare complete contract and bid documents including detailed plans and specifications approved by the Division of Health of Missouri for the construction of recommended improvements."

Then followed provisions for assistance in obtaining bids, general supervision during the construction period and assistance to the City in overseeing and general administration of the construction, a final inspection and report, and, at the City's option, the furnishing of a competent resident engineer during construction.

The remainder of the agreement concerned the compensation to be paid the engineers.

Lorenz E. Ordelheide was admitted to the partnership in 1958.

The City admits that the partnership properly performed all the work required of it under the heading "Preliminary Phase Services." The partnership was paid for those services. A bond issue election was held in 1960 and was favorable, and a federal grant was obtained.

Then:

1. On January 24, 1961, Riddle, as first party, and Sharp and Ordelheide, as second parties, executed an agreement effective as of December 31, 1960. This described them as "co-partners doing business as Haskins, Riddle and Sharp, Consulting Engineers" and provid-

ed for "the voluntary withdrawal" of Riddle; for nonauthorization of the use of the Riddle name by Sharp and Ordelheide; for Riddle's freedom "to use his own name in any new business venture which he may hereafter undertake"; for Riddle's assignment to Sharp and Ordelheide of his interest in the partnership assets; for the assumption by Sharp and Ordelheide of the firm's liabilities; for the payment to Riddle, on or before April 1, 1961, of a stated percentage of the partnership's net profits for calendar 1960; and for the payment to him, as received, of amounts specified as Riddle's share of accounts receivable and work in progress. It also recited,

> "It is contemplated that each of the parties hereto will continue in the consulting engineering profession and will or may become competitors. As such, in the future each of the parties shall be free to serve any person, corporation, municipality or governmental agency without restriction, and regardless of whether or not such person, corporation, municipality or governmental agency may have heretofore employed the partnership of Haskins, Riddle and Sharp."

This agreement made no mention of the partnership's contract with the City. There is evidence in the record that Riddle promised Sharp and Ordelheide to hold himself available to complete the firm's outstanding contracts, that he did so work collectively with them, that he would have worked with them on the contract with the City if so requested, and that his willingness as to this was not communicated to the City.

2. On January 27, 1961, Sharp and Ordelheide sent to the City (and to other clients) a formal announcement that they "have acquired the interest of W. G. Riddle in the former firm." On the same day they also wrote a letter to Mayor Scharz, with a copy to City Clerk Ford, to the same effect and also stating:

> "* * * We further wish to advise that there has been no dissolution of the partnership and that Mr. Riddle sold his interest in the formerly existing partnership to us including any interest which he may have had in any contracts existing as of December 31st, 1960.
>
> "We further wish to advise that this office will continue to perform under our presently existing agreement with you, and that the work as required under the contract is going ahead without interruption."

3. On February 1 the City Attorney wrote the plaintiff stating that he had the letter of January 27 "relating to the dissolution of your partnership with Mr. Riddle." He went on to say:

> "* * * It is my understanding that all preliminary phase services provided for in the memorandum have been completed by the partnership, Haskins, Riddle & Sharp, but that matters relating to design and supervision of services were to be begun only upon further instruction by the City. Thus, there remains noth-

ing left to be done under preliminary phase services and nothing further to be done without further instruction by the City.

* * * * * * * *

"The City has been advised by their legal counselors that the dissolution of the partnership works a termination of any previous agreement or understanding.

"As you are aware, there are future plans relating to sewage problems in the City and it is felt that the City should be free to renegotiate any contracts or agreements involving such matters."

4. The plaintiff's attorney replied by a letter dated February 6, 1961. In it he stated (a) that the partnership of Haskins, Riddle and Sharp had not been dissolved; (b) that he did not agree that the agreement with the City had been terminated; (c) that the "present principals of the firm of Haskins, Sharp and Ordelheide stand prepared to continue their services under" the 1957 agreement; (d) that when plans and specifications and supervision under that contract were required, his clients would perform for the agreed fees; (e) that they could not comply with the suggestion that a release be executed to the City; and (f) that they did not agree that the City was free to renegotiate the contract.

5. On February 21, 1961, the City Council adopted a resolution reciting that the contract had terminated and authorizing the mayor to negotiate for the employment of consulting engineers to develop plans for sewer improvements.[1] Scharz promptly wrote Sharp a letter quoting that resolution.

6. The City Council thereafter formed a sewer committee to solicit proposals from engineering firms for completion of the work. Among those so solicited were Mr. Riddle and the firm of Haskins, Sharp and Ordelheide. Sharp, on behalf of his firm, replied by letter dated May 24, 1961, that "in our opinion we have a contractual arrangement with North Kansas City," and declined to submit a new bid. By another letter written by its attorney the partnership again asserted its willingness "to continue the performance required under the contract."

1. [Ed. note: footnote renumbered.] "In view of the fact that the partnership of Haskins, Riddle & Sharp is no longer functioning under the supervision of Mr. Riddle and Mr. Sharp collectively, it is the feeling of the Council that this works a termination of any previous understandings between said engineering firm and the City of North Kansas City. In further view of the fact that the firm of Haskins, Riddle & Sharp has completed all phases of the work contemplated in their letter of intention dated November 12, 1957, and that nothing is left to be done as contemplated in the aforesaid letter of intention without further direction of the City of North Kansas City, Missouri; the former members of the firm of Haskins, Riddle & Sharp should be notified that they will not further be required to perform any additional engineering work and that the Mayor be authorized to enter into negotiations for the employment of consulting engineers for the purpose of developing plans for the construction of storm and sanitary sewer improvements and incinerator and sewage treatment works."

Judge Collinson found:

"* * * [T]he evidence also discloses that Mr. Riddle, the retired partner, was attempting to secure a contract for the balance of the work for another engineering firm which would then make him a member. The Mayor and Mr. Riddle were evidently quite friendly and he had every assurance that he would receive the work. And the other firm, on its promise to take in Mr. Riddle, was recommended by the Mayor for employment at a substantially higher fee than that provided in the original contract.

"Before the recommendation was accepted however a City Council fight developed, there were accusations made by City Council members against the Mayor, the firm recommended withdrew their offer, and the Mayor resigned. Thereafter an engineering firm with which neither Mr. Riddle nor Mr. Sharp were connected was employed by the City to complete, and did complete, the balance of the work contemplated by the original contract."

The engineering firm employed to do the balance of the work was Black & Veatch.

. . .

The assignability of the contract. The City's argument is that the Haskins, Riddle and Sharp partnership was one of professional people; That upon the assignment of a partner's interest in a contract with a client, the client has the option to abrogate the contract; that professional service is a very personal matter; that civil engineers are to be classified, in this respect, with attorneys, citing 6 Am. Jur.2d Assignments §§ 11–13 (1963), 5 Am.Jur.2d Architects §§ 7 and 8 (1962), 50 Am.Jur. Surveyors and Civil Engineers § 3 (1944), some cases concerning lawyers, and, in particular, Smith v. Board of Educ., 115 Kan. 155, 222 P. 101 (1924), which had to do with an architects' partnership, the retirement of one of the two partners, his replacement by another, and the Board's refusal to continue with the firm.

The City would buttress this legal argument with references to (a) the testimony of Mayor Scharz to the effect that it was difficult to work with Mr. Sharp, that he was obnoxious to some people in the city government and took unfair advantage, that Sharp had had trouble with the Board of Public Works, and that the City had had difficulty with a pumping station Sharp designed, and (b) the testimony of Councilman Ellington that the City did not wish to do business with Sharp because he got into arguments with city officials.

Judge Collinson, in his memorandum said,

"The City argues that, since engineers are also professional men, this situation is analogous. This might be a difficult question to resolve if there was any evidence in the case that, first, the City had relied solely or principally upon the skill and experience of Mr. Riddle when the contract was executed, or, second,

> that Mr. Sharp was not competent, sufficiently experienced, or in some other manner not qualified to carry on the work. As to the first point the record is silent, and as to the second point, the evidence of the City's own witnesses was exactly to the contrary."

He then went on to hold that "[u]nder the particular facts of this case, and with very little precedent for guidance," the City's actions and its employment of other engineers effected a breach of the 1957 contract. The court's reference to the testimony of the City's own witnesses relates to (a) Scharz' testimony that Sharp was an able and capable engineer, that he and Sharp got along well, and that Sharp's taking advantage of people was because Sharp was strong with people and was based on hearsay, and (b) Ellington's testimony that he did not know Sharp, and that it was the mayor who said at the meeting that he could not get along with Sharp.

Despite the trial court's concern with the paucity of precedent, we have no difficulty in agreeing with its conclusion on this issue. We may, of course, generally accept the City's statement as to the law with respect to professional service contracts and, without deciding, we may assume for present purposes that professional engineers, in contracting for sanitary sewer work, come within that classification. But this acceptance and this assumption do not provide or compel an answer favorable to the City.

Missouri has adopted the Uniform Partnership Act. Section 29 thereof, Mo.Rev.Stat. § 358.290, reads:

> "The dissolution of a partnership is the change in the relation of the partners caused by any partner ceasing to be associated in the carrying on as distinguished from the winding up of the business."

Section 30, Mo.Rev.Stat. § 358.300, reads:

> "On dissolution the partnership is not terminated but continues the winding up of partnership affairs is completed."

Section 31, Mo.Rev.Stat. § 358.310, lists the causes of dissolution. Among these are death and bankruptcy of a partner and "By the express will of all the partners * * *." Although there is a presumption of a partnership's continuance, Citizens' Trust Co. v. Tindle, 194 S.W. 1066, 1068 (Mo.App.1917), we do have here the fact of the three partners' agreement as of December 31, 1960, providing for Riddle's withdrawal, and Missouri case law that partners by mutual assent may dissolve or modify their partnership relation. . . . Further, the dissolution of a partnership does not abrogate existing contracts to which it is a party. . . . Fenix v. Celebrezze, 243 F. Supp. 816, 823 W.D.Mo.1965). In the latter case Judge Becker utilized, in a case applying Missouri law, generally accepted hornbook statements that a dissolution of a partnership does not become effectual as to third persons until actual notice; that after dissolution a partnership is considered as maintaining a limited existence for the purpose of making good all outstanding engagements; that this principle is recognized in the Uniform Partnership Act; and that dissolution does not relieve the partners from their liability for performance of contracts theretofore made. . . . And Judge Collinson pointed out in his first memorandum that in Veatch v. Black, 363 Mo. 190, 250 S.W.2d 501, 508 (1952), the court observed, with respect to a partnership agreement among consulting engineers, "Surviving partners usually have an obligation to complete the executory contracts of a partnership."

It seems clear enough from these authorities that, as Judge Collinson put it, "the City could have called upon the partners to complete the contract." Of course, the City's rights against the partnership with respect to any executory contract do not necessarily measure the corresponding rights of the continuing partners against the City. But here, again, an aggregation of items convinces us of the rightness of Judge Collinson's conclusion: (1) The primary reason advanced by the City in its resolution of February 21, 1961, purporting to terminate the agreement is not the dissolution of the old partnership but something very different, namely, "the fact that the partnership of Haskins, Riddle & Sharp is no longer functioning under the supervision of Mr. Riddle and Mr. Sharp collectively." The City's theory of right to abrogate upon dissolution thus is a shift in position and it, too, has the appearance of an afterthought. (2) The trial court found, and the finding is not challenged by the City, that Riddle functioned collectively as a partner of the old firm even into 1963. (3) Although the City claims it was not so advised, there is evidence in the record that Riddle agreed to hold himself available to complete contracts outstanding between clients and the firm and that, if asked to do so, he would have worked with Sharp and Ordelheide on the city contract. (4) The 1960 agreement among the partners made no mention of the contract with the City, and it contained no purported assignment of the city contract. (5) The essence of the professional service cases is that the critical partner, for one reason or another, is no longer available to render those services. Here the critical partners were available and the record indicates, despite the weak and meager initial intimations of Scharz and Ellington to the contrary, that they were able to, and did, function collectively. (6) The record supports the trial court's finding as to the acceptable professional capacity of the plaintiff Sharp and, indeed, of his ability to get along with clients including persons in the city government. (7) Judge Collinson's findings, quoted above, as to the underlying manipulations between Scharz and Riddle tell a sorry story and reveal what was really going on. (8) The suggestions as to Sharp's incapacity and inability to get along with people in the city government are not consistent with the fact that Haskins, Sharp and Ordelheide was one of the engineering firms which the City solicited to bid for the completion of the work.

The whole deal has, for us, somewhat less than an appetizing aroma and one which is not cured by high-sounding arguments of partnership employment based on "concepts of moral values, code of professional ethics, and creativity." . . .

[Ed. note: In an omitted portion of the opinion the court held that the contract was not severable, and the city did not have the discretion to determine whether to use the engineering partnership for the design and supervision services. The language which provided that the engineer would commence design work "When so instructed by the City" would only apply if the bond issue failed or the federal grant were not obtained."]

Affirmed.

Continuity may be what the parties wish. It may be more economical and desirable to continue to use the partnership, even if the design professional who negotiated and made the contract is no longer with the partnership. However, because of the close relationship required between design professional and client, the client may not wish to continue using the partnership if the person in whom he had confidence and with whom he dealt is no longer available to perform.

(B) INSOLVENCY

What if a contracting party becomes insolvent before or during performance? Insolvency is an inability to pay one's debts as they mature, or an excess of liabilities over assets. Whichever definition is employed, an insolvent party may have trouble paying his bills. Should a contracting party be forced to continue his own performance if there is a substantial risk that he will not be paid for his work, or that the other party will not perform properly? This requires an application of the "prospective inability to perform" doctrine.

If the design professional is insolvent, his employees may leave him, he may be evicted from his office, and his line of credit may disappear. Yet mere insolvency without these things happening should not be sufficient to permit the client to terminate his obligation. Even if matters reach the point of employee resignations and eviction, the issue is still prospective inability, since presumably the design professional is still performing. In terms of risk for the client, the line between prospective and actual nonperformance is a hazy one. But on the whole, the doctrine of prospective inability is not likely to be applied when the design professional runs into financial problems.

Some of the same discussion applies to the insolvency of the client, but the problem is more serious. The design professional will be taking serious risks if it appears that the client will not be able to pay. If the client is insolvent, his line of credit will dry up and bankruptcy may be close at hand. There is a greater chance that insolvency of the client will be prospective inability to perform justifying the design professional in suspending his performance, until he is given financial assurance, or perhaps terminating his obligation in the event such assurance is not given.

This discussion assumes that the party is actually insolvent. The party who is concerned should run a credit check. Relying upon rumors or casually obtained information is risky, and can lead to a breakdown of the client relation or litigation.

(C) BANKRUPTCY

While bankruptcy will be discussed in some detail in § 37.07, it may be useful to mention certain salient features of bankruptcy law.

When an individual or business goes into bankruptcy, the bankruptcy court appoints a trustee to handle and conserve any assets of the bankrupt. The trustee collects money owed to the bankrupt and retakes property of the bankrupt which is in the hands of others. He turns over assets to those creditors who have a security interest in the assets, and retains those assets which have not been encumbered by the bankrupt. Assets or amounts conserved or recovered in this way become part of the bankrupt's estate and, subject to certain preferences, are distributed to the general creditors. (General creditors are those who have no security interest in specific assets.)

The trustee also has the power to accept or reject (decide to continue performance) any contract of the bankrupt which still has performance obligations. For example, if a client should go bankrupt, the trustee has the right to affirm the contract and the design professional will have to continue performance. This does not happen frequently, as bankrupt clients have difficulty in raising capital to continue construction projects. However, the mere fact that the client has gone bankrupt does not automatically terminate the architect's obligation to continue performance under the contract, unless the contract so provides.

The same result would follow if the architect went bankrupt. It is more likely in such a case that the design professional's trustee in bankruptcy will continue the contract performance. However, if it is not possible for the design professional himself to continue performance, and if his performance conditions the client's obligation to pay, then the client would be released.

The trustee in bankruptcy is granted a specific time by statute to decide whether he will accept or reject the unperformed portions of the contract. If he does not notify the other party to the contract within the time specified, he is presumed not to have affirmed the contract. Also, the right to affirm the contract exists only if there is no clear contractual language in the contract to the contrary.

(D) IMPOSSIBILITY, IMPRACTICABILITY OR FRUSTRATION OF PURPOSE

Other events may occur which have a substantial effect upon the performance of either party. Such events may make performance by either party more burdensome or expensive, impracticable, or impossible.

Another legal concept is called Frustration of Purpose. Although the parties can perform, something occurs which makes the bargain much less desirable and attractive than one of the parties anticipated.

There may be physical catastrophes or natural events which affect the performance of either party. Usually, this is not a problem from the standpoint of the client, since his actual part of the performance is limited to non-prevention, non-hindrance and cooperation, as well as payment of the fee. The only event which could affect these performances are death or incapacity, or financial stress. These have already been discussed.

From the standpoint of the design professional, during the design phase his building or his offices might burn down, or be flooded. However, these things would not have the type of impact which is serious enough to permit him to terminate his obligation under the contract, since he could do the work elsewhere.

Usually a substantial portion of the work will be done by the members of the design professional's staff. If there were an epidemic which affected a substantial part of his staff and made performance much more difficult, it is unlikely that even this would affect his obligation because of the possibility of obtaining others to perform the work.

Suppose a fire destroyed all the work performed by the design professional? Depending upon progress of the work, this could have a substantial effect upon the cost of his performance. However, it is not likely that a court would excuse him since, again, it would be possible for him to start over and accomplish the performance. In general, the likelihood of termination because of difficulty of performance, impracticability, or impossibility is negligible.

Suppose the project has commenced and during the course of construction a catastrophic event occurs, and destroys or nearly destroys the work in progress. This will raise serious problems between the contractor and the owner. This problem will usually be dealt with by insurance. However, very little thought is given to the effect such an event will have upon the obligations of design professional and client. In such a case, the design professional can continue his performance. However, the client can no longer supply the place of performance of the administration or supervision of the construction phase. It is likely that the law would release both parties.

When the contract was made, both parties assumed that there would be a construction project in existence. The destruction, or partial destruction, of the project, while it would not make performance absolutely impossible in that another project could be constructed, should relieve both parties from further obligation to perform.

What if the client wishes to rebuild the destroyed, or partially destroyed project? In such a case, it is likely that the law would permit him to continue to hold the design professional to the agreement as long as the project was not substantially a different one, and as long as the rebuilding would not involve too great a delay in time. In such a case, the design professional should be paid the basic fee, and an additional amount for any work which has resulted from the fact that the project was damaged or destroyed.

A more difficult problem may arise if events occur which frustrate the purpose of either party. This is more likely to be a problem with the client than with the design professional. Suppose that during the course of the design professional's work, there is a severe economic recession. As a result, the client decides to give up the project because he would not be able to rent the building at a rental which will make the project financially feasible. Here, performance by both parties continues to be possible. But the project is much less attractive to the client because of events over which neither party had any control, and for which neither party is at fault. The two tests which determine whether a party will be relieved by "frustration" are "foreseeability" and "almost total destruction of the value of the contract". In other words, would the client have been reasonably able to foresee the recession, and has the recession almost completely destroyed the value of the design professional's performance? The answers will depend upon the facts in the case.

As far as frustration affecting the performance of the design professional, it may be possible for him to obtain an opportunity to design a bigger project which would be more profitable to him, but one which would require that he discontinue performance on the project he has agreed to perform for the client. In a sense, the subsequent event has affected the value of the contract as far as the design professional is concerned. However, it is quite clear that permitting him to terminate his obligations because of such an event would be unfair to the client, and would offend the sense of fairness of most people. The twin tests for frustration would not be met in such a case, so this event would have no effect upon the obligations to perform by the design professional and the client.

As can be seen, the concepts which can relieve the contracting party have to be carefully applied to ensure that persons will not be able to walk away from contracts merely because there has been a change in circumstances which has made the contract less attractive. For this reason, courts look carefully at such excuses and, although there is greater tendency to relieve parties than there was fifty years ago, it is still not an easy matter to obtain termination because of these events.

(E) RIGHTS OF PARTIES AFTER TERMINATION

Difficulties sometimes arise when the termination occurs after one or both of the parties has commenced performance, or has acted in reliance on the agreement. In such a case, does the contract deal with the question of compensation under such circumstances? If so, then it is a matter of interpretation to determine whether the party performing is entitled to compensation from the other party, and how this compensation is to be computed.

However, in most cases, the contract will not deal with compensation for part performance or preparation prior to termination. Recovery must be based on quasi-contract or unjust enrichment. Traditionally, there had to be a tangible benefit to the other party before he could be compelled to pay for it. For example, suppose a design professional dies during the course of his performance. There have been progress payments made by the client to the design professional. However, the question of whether the partially completed performance by the design professional is of any benefit to the client depends upon whether the client makes use of the design professional's work. If he does, the answer is relatively easy. The design professional, or, in this case, his executor or personal representative, is entitled to be paid the reasonable value of his services. Also, the client is entitled to recover any interim fee payments that he has made because of unjust enrichment. In some cases, the two will cancel each other out. However, if one is greater than the other, then the person who has received more than he has given is obligated to repay the difference, based upon quasi-contract.

There is a tendency in some of the recent cases to define "benefit" loosely. For example, even if the plans and specifications are not used, it could be argued that the work did constitute a benefit to the client for which the client ought to pay. The client may have learned a great deal about the project from the work of the design professional. In such a situation, there is some chance that the design professional will be able to recover in quasi-contract.

A court may determine that the performance of the design professional can be segregated into specified portions of the work, and that he was to be paid separately for each of the portions as if each portion were a separate contract. This is a possibility where there are interim fee payment provisions in the contract. While it is a fiction to state that the parties have made a series of contracts, and that each segment of the design professional's work constitutes a separate contract, courts sometimes use this device in order to avoid a performing party being uncompensated for his work. In such a case, the interim fee provisions can assist the architect or engineer if events terminate the performance of the contract after he has partly performed certain portions of the work. However, he will not be able to recover for any portions which have not been completed.

SECTION 10.04 CONTRACTUAL RIGHT TO TERMINATE

(A) TYPES OF PROVISIONS

Many of the problems discussed in this section are of lesser significance if standard form contracts are used. This is because many standard form contracts specifically deal with the question of the right to terminate. Sometimes the contract may specify that either party can terminate by giving notice in a specific form upon a default of a substantial nature by the other party.

Sometimes contracts provide that any breach of one party will permit the other party to terminate his obligations under the contract. This does not require any inquiry into the question of the seriousness of the breach. Without such a clause, the breach would have to be serious to enable the other party to terminate his obligation.

It is also possible for contracts to provide that either party can terminate by giving a specified notice, without any breach. In a close and confidential type of relationship such as the one created when a design professional is hired by a client, such a provision makes sense. In essence, many such relationships are relationships which are called "at will" by law. This means that the contract determines the rights and duties of the parties, but does not compel them to continue performance if they do not wish to do so. Some professional associations may feel that such provisions give the client too great an opportunity to relieve himself of the obligation imposed by the contract.

In construction contracts, especially contracts with public agencies, the public agency is often given the right to terminate the contract for its own convenience. Usually such provisions give the contractor the right to be paid for what he has done, plus a designated percentage of his costs as profit. While not yet a common provision in contracts between design professionals and their clients, unless abandonment clauses (See § 10.04(d)) are considered "terminations for convenience", such clauses may become more common in the future.

AIA Doc. B131 at Art. 8 permits either party to terminate by giving a 7 day written notice when there has been a *substantial nonperformance* by the other party, not caused by the party wishing to terminate.

(B) "CURING" PROVISIONS

Many contracts contain provisions that require a party to give the other party a reasonable period of time to cure any breaches as a condition to allowing the party not at fault to end his obligations under the contract. Sometimes a party does not know that he is in default, or does not know that the default is considered serious by the other party. If the other party does consider the non-performance serious, fairness dictates that he give the defaulting party an opportunity to rectify his performance, if possible.

———

(C) INTERPRETATION OF NOTICE PROVISIONS

Interpretation questions may develop when a notice to terminate is given. What are the rights and duties of the parties during the termination period? To a degree, this will depend upon the purpose of a notice provision. Often the contracting parties do not consider the question, and when problems develop later they take differing positions.

Sometimes a notice of termination need not be based upon a default in performance by the other party. One or both parties may be given the right by the contract to terminate for any reason, but this right is often conditioned upon a notice of termination being given within a specified number of days of the effective date of termination.

The notice period may be designed to allow the parties to plan new arrangements because of the termination by allowing a short continuation of performance. The short continuation may be to avoid a costly stoppage in the project or the unavoidable expenses which can result when the design professional must stop performance immediately. For example, in a contract between design professional and client, the notice period can enable the client to obtain another architect or engineer while still keeping the old architect or engineer on the project for a short time. It can also enable the architect or engineer to make adjustments in his work force, to get his men back to their home base, to cancel arrangements he has made with third parties, and to allow him to line up other work for his employees.

A notice period can serve as a cooling-off device. Termination is a serious step for both parties. If a termination is based upon an asserted breach by the other party, an ultimate determination that there were insufficient grounds for termination can be costly to the terminating party. A short termination period can enable the terminating party to rethink his position and see whether he has grounds for termination or wishes to terminate anyway.

If the notice provision is tied to a contract breach, such as Art. 8 of AIA Doc. B131 the clause requiring notice can have an additional function. It may be a period of time designed to enable the party in default to cure past defaults and to provide assurances that there will be no defaults in the future.

If this is the function of the notice period, termination should be effective only if these conditions are not met. During the period of notice the rights and duties of the parties should continue. If it reasonably appears that there is no likelihood that past defaults can be cured and reasonable assurances be given that there will be no future defaults, performance during the notice period should continue only at the option of the party giving the notice to terminate. There is no reason to force him to continue to receive and perhaps pay for substandard performance.

Suppose the purpose of the notice period is to allow the parties to make necessary adjustments while continuing performance for a short time. In such a case, either party can justifiably insist that the other continue performing during the notice period to the extent that this purpose can be served. For example, suppose the client gives a notice to terminate. If he can show that he needs continued performance by the design professional during the notice period so that there will be no costly suspension in the project while he seeks a new design professional, the design professional should be required to continue. The same conclusion should be reached if the termination notice is given by the design professional. If he can show a real need to continue performing during the termination period, the client should be required to keep him on during this period.

One overriding consideration would change the result suggested in the preceding paragraph. If relations have so deteriorated that continued performance would be likely to mean deliberately poor performance by either or both parties during the notice period, then neither should be compelled to perform during this period.

If the notice is simply intended to allow the parties to cool off, performance should continue during the notice period but stop when the notice period ends. Only if the termination is retracted should performance continue after the termination date.

Contracting parties should decide in advance what function the notice period is to serve, and what will be the rights and duties during the notice period. Also, these issues should be considered and resolved by those who draft standard form contracts.

(It might be useful to read New England Structures v. Loranger, reproduced at § 26.07, which dealt with the legal effect of a notice of termination in a subcontract.)

(D) EFFECT OF ABANDONMENT CLAUSE

Many contract clauses give the design professional a right to be paid if the work or the project has been abandoned or suspended by the client "for any reason". Such clauses are designed to ensure that the client pays for work done by the design professional, no matter what the client decides about proceeding with the project. That this aim is not always achieved is shown by Parsons v. Bristol Dev. Co. reproduced at § 7.01(c) and Stevens v. Fanning, reproduced at § 8.01(b).

These clauses can have another effect. They have been interpreted to give the client an absolute right to abandon the contract, without such abandonment being a breach of contract. This result was reached in Furst v. Board of Education, 20 Ill.App.2d 205, 155 N.E. 654 (1959). The effect of such a conclusion means the architect could recover only for services performed prior to abandonment. This limits the normal contract remedy of profit on unperformed work. (Judicial measures of recovery are discussed in Chapter 11.)

Where a right to terminate or abandon is given by the contract, the question of compensation is usually covered by the contract. See Deuel v. McCollum, reproduced at § 11.02(b).

REVIEW QUESTIONS

1. Does any breach by the client release the design professional from the obligation of continued performance?

2. May a party collect for services performed, when he himself is in substantial default?

3. Normally, does the death of a client terminate the design professional's obligation to perform?

4. What are the requirements for invoking the doctrine of "frustration of purpose"?

5. What is a "curing" provision?

QUESTIONS FOR CLASS DISCUSSION

1. Should any breach by one party automatically terminate the other party's obligation to perform? Explain.

2. If only one party can terminate a contract "for his own convenience", why doesn't this make the contract too one-sided to be enforceable?

PROBLEM

A and C entered into a written contract, by which A agreed to perform designated design services for C. The contract contained the following provision:

> Either party may terminate the contract by giving the other party seven-day notice in writing.

What are the rights and duties of A and C, if either gives the other a written notice of termination?

Chapter 11

JUDICIAL REMEDIES FOR BREACH

SECTION 11.01 BREACH BY DESIGN PROFESSIONAL

A breach by the design professional may give the client a right to terminate his obligation under the contract. In addition, it may give him certain remedies awarded by courts for breach of contract. Traditionally, remedies for breach of contract are divided into three categories: restitution, damages, and specific performance.

(A) RESTITUTION

The objective of restitution is to place the parties in the position they were in at the time the contract was made. If there is a serious breach by a design professional, the client may seek to recover interim fee payments he has made to the design professional and be willing to return any work which he has received. Such an exchange of performance would place the parties in the position they were in at the time the contract was made. Generally, the client can use a restitutionary measure of recovery for a serious breach.

(B) DAMAGES: BAYUK v. EDSON

More commonly the client seeks to recover damages if the design professional has breached the contract. An award of damages attempts to place the innocent party (in this case the client) in the same position he would have been in had there been proper performance by the other party.

Damages can be classified into losses which are directly connected with performance, and those which are more removed from the promised performance. For an example of the first category, suppose the design professional refused to do the work, unjustifiably quit during performance, or has been negligent during performance? It is likely that the client will retain another design professional to complete the project. In such a case, the client would be entitled to recover from the design professional any excess costs which were incurred by the client, or which he will have to incur by hiring a new design professional. If the fee to the design professional would have been $10,000 and the total design professional costs incurred including hiring a substitute were $15,000, the damages would be $5,000. The client has received the promised performance and should pay only the original price. An award of $5,000 would put him in the position he would have been had there been proper performance.

Another direct damage item would be any corrective work made necessary because of the breach by the design professional. Usually, the client can recover the cost of correcting defective design work. Under certain circumstances, courts can use the difference in value of the structure as built, and as it should have been built as the measure of recovery, rather than the cost of correction of defective work. The difference in value may be appropriate if the project has been completed, and correcting the defects would require tearing down the structure or substantial rebuilding.

For an instructive case on the measure of recovery for a breach by the design professional, Bayuk v. Edson is reproduced at this point.

BAYUK v. EDSON

District Court of Appeal of California, 1965.
236 Cal.App.2d 309, 46 Cal.Rptr. 49.

PIERCE, PRESIDING JUSTICE. Plaintiffs, R. W. Bayuk and Cressa Bayuk, husband and wife, sued defendants, Jack A. Edson and Robert L. Bosworth, for alleged negligence in the performance of an oral contract for architectural services in connection with the construction of plaintiffs' home. After a court trial plaintiffs recovered judgment against defendants for $18,500 with interest and costs.[1]

The complaint pleaded, and the court found, both faulty design and supervision proximately causing damage. Defendants' arguments on appeal do not challenge the finding of faulty design nor the fact that some damage was sustained by the Bayuks thereby. Defendant Bosworth contends that there was no breach of the obligation of supervision which he had assumed and that he was not personally liable anyway because he was acting as an agent for a disclosed principal. Defendant Edson contends that Bosworth had neither actual nor ostensible authority to assume any obligation to supervise construction. Both defendants contend that the amount of the court's award of damages is unsupported by substantial evidence and that the method of measurement thereof was improper. . . .

In the summer of 1959 plaintiffs sought the services of defendant Jack A. Edson, an architect, with offices at Medford, Oregon. By telephone Dr. Bayuk informed Edson that he contemplated building a home in Yreka but could not pay the standard architect's fees for design, plans, specifications and supervision. A meeting was arranged and Edson visited the Bayuks in Yreka. He brought Bosworth with him, introducing him as an architect "out of his office." An oral contract was the product of this meeting. By its terms Edson and Bos-

1. A cause of action pleaded against Cummins, the contractor who built the home, resulted in a judgment for the contractor. That judgment is not appealed from.

worth agreed to design and prepare working drawings and specifications for a ranch-type home costing approximately $35,000. The architect's fee was to be $2,000, and it was expressly understood the contract did not include supervision. Edson had urged Bayuk to contract for supervision at an additional fee but Bayuk told him that he could not afford it. It was understood that most of the actual work would be done by Bosworth but Edson expressly agreed to check and approve his work.

Unknown to the Bayuks, Bosworth was not in the employ of Edson; in fact, he was not a licensed architect. He had had, however, considerable training as an architect and was an assistant professor at the University of Oregon.

Edson and Bosworth agreed between themselves as to the sharing of the fee to be paid by the Bayuks; a somewhat vague understanding that it would be shared in proportion to the quantity of work done by each. Of the first payment of $1,000 Edson actually received $300 and Bosworth $700. A second installment of $1,000, was paid to and retained by Bosworth.

After the meeting between the Bayuks and the defendants described above and during the preparation of plans, Bosworth held frequent conversations with Bayuk in the course of which Bosworth renewed persuasion that supervision be included in their contract. This resulted in the following understanding (as testified to by Bayuk): "I told Mr. Bosworth at that time that I had no further money and I had access to none, and that I couldn't afford it and if he wanted to supervise it, that was entirely up to him and I would accept it. And at that time also I told him that if in the future I had access to any money, I would pay him what I could afford." To that statement Bosworth had replied: "[Y]ou don't have to give me anything else; I want to supervise this house."

The house was built; Bosworth designed it, Edson approved the design, working drawings and specifications, and Bosworth did provide supervision. In this connection the trial court's findings stated: "Sometime before September 29, 1959, Bosworth and Bayuk made an oral agreement that Bosworth would supervise the construction of the home, in accordance with usual supervision standards, in consideration for the building of the Bosworth designed home by Bayuk, and for the promise to pay additional amounts to Bosworth as funds became available."

Appending to this finding is the court's useful comment: "This agreement is the crux of the problem. Depending upon whether or not Bosworth agreed to supervise, Bayuk or Bosworth has responsibility for the mistakes which were made. As I indicated in my oral decision, I credit Bayuk's testimony on this point. The language in the plans with respect to supervision, the fact of Bosworth's continual presence, the fact of money payments to Bosworth, and the impression which Cummins [the contractor] and other workers on the building had concerning Bosworth's authority all convinced me by a preponderance of the evidence that Bosworth and Bayuk had in fact agreed for supervision by Bosworth."

The court also found: "Edson was not informed by either Bosworth or Bayuk that Bosworth had made the agreement to supervise." But it also found: "During the course of construction, Edson had reason to believe that Bosworth was supervising construction and should have known that Bosworth was supervising construction by representing himself as the agent of Edson."

After stating this the court comments: "Edson was present on at least two occasions during construction and, as an experienced man in the architectural field, he should have appreciated that Bosworth was performing the services required of architectural supervision as distinct from design and occasional inspection."

As regards performance of the obligations of design and supervision the trial court found:

"The design and supervision of construction of the building was properly performed in all respects, except as follows:

"a. Design.

"1. The floor was improperly designed in that concrete tile was to be welded to plywood in a relatively large area.

"2. A number of the closets were approximately 18 inches in width and should have been at least 24 inches in width.

"3. The outside doors were constructed for a milder climate than Yreka affords, and were of an unusual type which the architect should have known could not satisfactorily be built by craftsmen in the Yreka area.

"b. Supervision of construction.

"1. Plycrate was kept on the floor after it was discovered. As indicated with respect to the cause of action against Cummins, this did not conform to specifications. The architect should have required the removal of the plycrate.

"2. Tile in the kitchen was not properly laid and has an aesthetic disfigurement of serious proportions.

"3. The outside sliding doors were not properly fitted to the building, and, as a result, do not move easily in their tracks.

"4. The fireplace was constructed so that expansion of the lintel or the flue has caused permanent cracking. (Comment: The witnesses were unable to describe with accuracy the exact cause of the cracking. There is no doubt the cracking in fact has occurred. Building a fireplace of unusual design requires close supervision. I believe that Bosworth did not exercise the kind of supervision required of a reasonably careful architect under the circumstances.)"

Appellants have not pointed out any respect in which the foregoing findings are not supported by substantial evidence. In fact, no argument whatever is addressed to the court's finding that the *design* was faulty. Argument that Bosworth, at the most, undertook only casual and superficial supervision is sufficiently answered by the trial court's observations stated above.

The contention is made that Bayuk himself interfered with and prevented Bosworth from exercising proper supervision. In this regard appellants lean heavily upon a comment by the court (appended to a finding that Bayuk had exercised reasonable care under the circumstances to insure that the building would be properly constructed). This comment is to the effect that Buyak and Bosworth did not have a proper "rapport * * * required of an owner and architect attempting to create an unusual building." But the court also went on to conclude that it could not find from the evidence that Bayuk's interference had been to an extent which was unreasonable or beyond that which an architect who had undertaken supervision should have been expected to cope with. Instances of interference in the record brought to our attention (mostly unrelated to the matters where inadequacy of supervision produced damage) would not justify us, as a reviewing court, in upsetting the finding of the trial court that Bayuk had acted reasonably.

We turn to the contention that Edson cannot be held for Bosworth's faulty supervision since the latter had no ostensible authority to contract for supervision.

An ostensible agency or authority exists when the principal intentionally, or by want of ordinary care, causes a third person to believe another to be his agent who is not really employed by him or to possess authority he does not actually possess. (Civ.Code, secs. 2300, 2316.) "A principal is bound by acts of his agent, under a merely ostensible authority, to those persons only who have in good faith, and without want of ordinary care, incurred a liability or parted with value, upon the faith thereof." (Civ.Code, sec. 2334.) Since Bayuk obviously parted with value, the question we review is whether the facts described above support a judgment founded in part upon Bosworth's ostensible authority (Bayuk himself not being guilty either of bad faith or failing to exercise ordinary care).

In California Motor Express, Ltd. v. Chowchilla Union High Sch. Dist. (1962) 202 Cal.App.2d 314, on p. 318, 20 Cal.Rptr. 768, on page 771, the court (per Stone, J.) expresses the principle in the language of the Restatement of the Law of Agency, section 261: "'A principal who puts an agent in a position that enables the agent, while apparently acting within his authority, to commit a fraud upon third persons is subject to liability to such third persons for the fraud.'" And it is noted that under section 262 of the Restatement the rule stated holds true even though the agent acts solely for his own purposes.

Applying these rules to this case, we hold that substantial evidence supports the trial court's findings. Edson led Bayuk to believe that Bosworth was an architect working for him and was to be the representative of his office with whom Bayuk was to deal.[2] At the original meeting between the Bayuks and defendants, Edson had urged the Bayuks to contract for supervision. Therefore, Bosworth's subsequent solicitations would have seemed to the Bayuks merely a continuation of Edson's entreaties. There seems no doubt, as the trial court found, that Edson was aware that Bosworth was affording general, standard architectural supervision. Moreover, the house as designed contained certain novel and untried features which, as the court found, required close supervision.[3] As an architect Edson must have been aware of this. The court therefor could logically have assumed that Edson, being aware of all of these facts, should have realized that Bosworth had contracted with Bayuk for such supervision and that Bayuk would properly assume the supervision bargained for to be a provision tacked onto the original contract.

The court made its award of damages in the sum of $18,500 on evidence which, as the trial judge himself stated, was somewhere short of a type calculated to convince a trier of fact to a moral certainty and beyond all reasonable doubt. The evidence on damages was, nevertheless, substantial: Thomas Riskas, a general building contractor, who had examined the working drawings and who had inspected the house found mistakes in both design and building which he described as "appalling" and testified that because of the extent thereof it would be economically unfeasible to repair the defects. To do so, according to his figures, tearing out and repair would cost more than the cost of rebuilding the house in its entirety. The method therefore applied by plaintiffs to compute their damage was by determination of the diminution of market value due to the defects. This was proper under the circumstances. . . To make that determination plaintiffs produced as their expert Luke Lange, a realtor and inheritance tax appraiser. Mr. Lange on direct examination fixed the value of the home without the defects at $50,000–$60,000 and the market value with the defects at $27,500 to $31,500, "somewhere in between." (The damages awarded, $18,500, represents the least of the possible remainders.) Appellants object that the expert's testimony on direct examination did not reflect values as of the date of damage and that on cross-examination it appeared that values at the time of trial had been considered. Also objected to was the fact, brought out on cross-examination, that the expert had given consideration to the reputation which the house had acquired in the community, which reputation had, at least, been contributed to by Bayuk's own publicizing of the defects.

. . .

2. For example on one occasion when the Bayuks called at Edson's office in Medford to consult him regarding some problem connected with the plans or construction, Edson referred them to Bosworth who was then at work in a back office.

3. This, indeed, was one of the respects in which the trial court found defendants to have been guilty of negligent supervision.

As regards the time as of which the appraisals were given damages should, of course, be computed as of the date when they occurred. Here, however, damages are not fixed by values but upon the difference between two values. While values between 1960 and 1963 may have changed, it does not follow that the difference or relationship between the market value of the house properly built and its value in its damaged condition would necessarily change—assuming, of course, that both values are estimated as of the same time. Since here both values *were* figured as of the same time and since no objection was interposed or showing made that a different answer would have been reached to the arithmetical problem of subtraction had 1960 values been used, we deem the defect as going to the weight of the opinion, not its admissibility. The same must be said regarding the fact that Lange on cross-examination admitted that he had taken the reputation of the house in its damaged condition into consideration in estimating its depressed value. The defects which the witness described (all of which were brought out with great particularity on cross-examination) were not only patent to the witness; they must also have been patent to any prospective purchaser to whom the house would be shown. Lange testified: "* * * The floor is screwed up [wavy]; it isn't right. You can tell that by looking at it. The doors in the glass in the front of the house are bound up they don't open and close freely * * *. The fireplace is badly cracked and it sticks right out. The beams in the roof are twisting and some are lower, some are higher. * * * They're not in line, I will put it that way. There is something wrong with them. * * * The fireplace in the kitchen, * * * [i]ts pulled away from the wall * * *. [Y]ou can't put clothes in the closets, with the exception of the master bedroom, due to the narrowness * * *." It is impossible for us to believe that reputation could have weighed very heavily when the factors upon which that reputation was based were so readily apparent to any casual observer. . . .

The judgment is affirmed.

Usually, the difference in value gives a measure of recovery which is lower than the cost of correction or completion. For this reason, some courts will use it only if they find that the breach by the design professional was not wilful or deliberate. Some courts employ the measure of recovery which produces the lowest amount. See Chapter 29 for a discussion of measures of recovery in owner-contractor litigation.

There may be less direct losses caused by the breach of a design professional. For example the building project may have been delayed, advantageous financial commitments lost, and prospective tenants may have gone elsewhere. Subject to the limitations of foreseeability, avoidable consequences and certainty, to be discussed in succeeding paragraphs, if the breach caused these losses, they are chargeable to the design professional.

In addition, the client may have been held responsible for the acts of the design professional. This will be discussed in Chapters 30 and 34. However, at this point, it is sufficient to state that if the client incurs losses because of the acts of the design professional, he may assert a claim against the design professional for any liability the client incurred to third parties as well as any costs incurred by the client in defending legal actions brought against him.

There are some limitations to the recoverability of indirect or consequential damages. These damages must have been reasonably foreseeable at the time that the contract was made. If the design professional did not know, and could not have been reasonably expected to foresee these losses when the contract was made, then the design professional would not be responsible for these losses.

The doctrine of avoidable consequences or mitigation of damages is another limitation to the right of recovery by the client for breaches of the design professional. Certain damages can be avoided by hiring a substitute design professional. For this reason, the client cannot recover those expenses which could have been reasonably avoided by him. The client cannot recover costs caused by hiring the most expensive design professional available, and certainly cannot recover for services performed by the substitute which were beyond the requirements of the original agreement.

In order to recover damages the client will have to establish his actual monetary loss with reasonable certainty. Sometimes this is difficult. In many cases the law gives the benefit of the doubt to the client when applying the need for certainty if the client can show that damages of some value were suffered.

Another difficult problem involves recovery of attorneys' fees. It often costs a good deal to use the judicial machinery to enforce a claim. Generally, recovery of attorneys' fees is not permitted unless the contract between plaintiff and defendant allows it, or a special statute provides for recovery.

Interest can constitute an important item of damage. Clearly, the plaintiff can recover interest from the date of the court judgment until the amount specified in the court judgment is paid. (In Kaufman v. Leard, discussed in § 8.01(e) the client recovered $5900 as interest on a claim of $18,300.)

More difficult questions arise when the plaintiff seeks to recover interest commencing from a time earlier than the court's judgment. Usually, the plaintiff cannot recover interest starting at a time prior to court judgment unless the claim was for a clearly ascertainable amount. Such is not likely to be the case if the claim for damages is made by the client against a design professional. Usually, "punitive damages" (intended to punish morally reprehensible conduct rather than to compensate for actual damages) are not recoverable for breach of contract. Courts frequently state that the purpose of awarding damages is to compensate the injured party and not to punish the defendant. If the court believes that the conduct of one party

was morally wrong, that party is likely to have doubtful questions resolved against him.

(C) COMBINING RESTITUTION AND DAMAGES

Historically, the law has regarded recovery of both restitution and damages as inconsistent. The traditional view would not allow the client to recover both payments made to the design professional, as well as damages incurred as a result of the breach by the design professional. The client was required to make an "election of remedies", asking for either restitution or damages. There is an increasing tendency to consider the two remedies not necessarily inconsistent, and to permit recovery for both, provided that there is not a duplication of recovery.

Suppose the total fee which would have been paid to the original architect were $10,000 and the additional cost of obtaining a substitute was $5,000. Suppose further that the client had made interim fee payments to the original architect of $4,000. It would not be proper to permit the client to combine damages ($5,000 total added cost) and restitution ($4,000 interim fee payments made) for a recovery total of $9,000. Using this combination the client would obtain design services for which he promised to pay $10,000 at an ultimate cost of $6,000. (Such a combination fails to take into account the other half of the restitution formula. It does not take into account the value of the performance of the design professional conferred upon his client.)

On the other hand, suppose the client wanted to combine restitution (recovery of the $4000 interim fee payments) with damages (delay losses caused to the project because of the hiring of a new architect). While many courts would not permit such a combination, it should be permitted.

(D) SPECIFIC PERFORMANCE

A third type of remedy is called "specific performance". This was a remedy which was available under certain circumstances in the English Courts of Equity and which could be given only under very limited circumstances. Specific performance means an order by the court to the breaching party that he is to perform in accordance with his contract. This would mean that the client could compel the design professional to perform, even if the design professional no longer wished to do so. This decree could be enforced by the court's contempt powers. Violation of the order could mean jail or a fine, until the party in contempt (refusing to perform) complies with the order.

There are many limitations on the imposition of this remedy. The party asking for a court order compelling performance must show that all other remedies would be inadequate. In addition he must show that the work is not of a personal nature. On both of these counts, it would be difficult for the client to obtain a court order awarding him specific performance. It is not likely that clients would want this. It would be difficult, if not impossible, for a client to obtain a decree for specific performance in the design professional-client relationship.

While generally specific performance is not available in a service contract such as that created by the design professional-client relationship, this result may be changed because of the presence of an arbitration clause. If the arbitrator is granted the power to award broad remedies, including ordering a contracting party to perform, there is a strong possibility that such an arbitrator's award would be confirmed by a court. This is a situation where specific performance, though not obtainable in a direct court action, might be obtainable by means of a broadly drawn arbitration clause.

SECTION 11.02 BREACH BY CLIENT

It is not necessary to repeat some of the general explanatory material in § 11.01. The emphasis in this section will be upon applying them to breaches by the client. Normally the breach by the client consists of unjustifiably firing the architect or engineer, in noncooperating, or in failing to pay compensation when it is due.

(A) RESTITUTION

The design professional may want only to recover the reasonable value of his services. If he has not completed his performance, this would be possible under a restitutionary measure of recovery. However, if the design professional has fully performed, and all that is left is for the client to pay a liquidated sum (a sum specifically determined or determinable in dollars), then the restitutionary measure would not be available. In such a case, the design professional could recover only the unpaid portion of the contract price. When using the restitutionary measure, he may not be entitled to overhead and profit if the court interprets "status quo" literally. But there is great flexibility in this area, and it is generally possible to recover overhead and profit.

The use of the reasonable value of the performance rendered as a measure of recovery may be affected by the presence of an interim fee schedule in the contract. This has been discussed in § 7.04(b). If the interim fee schedule makes the contract "severable" or "divisible" the reasonable value measure cannot be used for completed segments of work for which an interim fee payment is stated in the contract.

(B) DAMAGES: DEUEL v. McCOLLUM

In the event of a breach by the client, the design professional may want to recover damages. As mentioned before, the object of awarding damages is to place the innocent party in the position he would have been had the contract been fully performed. A breach by the client, can be measured in two ways. First, the design professional shows what he would have received had the contract been fully performed. This is done by estimating the total construction cost, and multiplying by the percentage figure, if this is the method used in the contract for compensating the design professional. If he has been employed under a different type of contract, such as cost plus a percentage of cost, or cost plus a fixed fee that contractual method is used to determine what he would have received had there been full performance. From this is deducted the amount of money which it would have cost him to complete performance of the contract, as well as any interim fee payments that have been made to him. This method is the total contract price less the expense saved the design professional as a result of the breach.

Another method is to compute the costs of part performance and preparation for part performance, and add to it the profit which would have been made had there been full performance. The latter figure is sometimes difficult to establish. The total computations would have to show what the cost of doing the entire job would have been, and deduct this from the total contract price. The design professional might also show a normally established profit figure for performing work of this sort.

Because of the difficulty of proving lost profits, the design professional may choose to recover only the cost of his preparation and part performance.

If the design professional elects to prove damages, the client will be able to deduct any losses which the design professional would have sustained had he fully performed. These "losses" were avoided by the client's breach. Showing that the design professional would have lost money had he been permitted to complete the work is generally quite difficult. Also, for historical reasons, this deduction is not permitted if the design professional asks for restitution.

If the design professional finishes the job, his damages are the added costs incurred because of any client breach. If the client did not reasonably cooperate, or hindered performance, the added costs caused by these breaches would be recoverable. Usually, the design professional shows what it cost him to perform, and what it would have cost him to perform had there been no breach. The former should be relatively easy to prove if good cost records are kept. The latter is more difficult to show. But if it is shown with reasonable certainty, the added cost should be awarded as damages. If the client can show the added cost was not caused by the breach, these costs should not be recovered.

Some design professional contracts contain "no damage" clauses. In Chas. T. Main, Inc., v. Massachusetts Turnpike Authority, 347 Mass. 154, 196 N.E.2d 821 (1964) an engineer was denied recovery for delay damages because of a contract clause limiting him to time extensions. See § 23.07 for a discussion of such clauses in construction contracts. Section 11.01 discussed recovery of attorneys' fees and interest. If the claim by the design professional is for unpaid interim fee payments or for the final fee payment, it is likely that interest will be recoverable from the time the payment should have been made, since the amount is a liquidated or ascertainable one. However, if the client contends that he is entitled to deduct unliquidated amounts because of breaches by the design professional, this may make the amount due "unliquidated" or uncertain in amount, and prevent interest from running from the time the payment should have been made. However, before the client should be able to take advantage of classifying the amount due as "unliquidated", in order to avoid interest, the court should be convinced that the claimed deductions were made in good faith and not simply to defeat a claim for interest on the liquidated amounts admittedly owed by the client to the design professional.

The design professional should be able to recover other losses he has suffered as a result of the client's breach, which were foreseeable at the time the contract was made. If he can show with reasonable certainty that he would have been able to obtain other commissions had this job been completed, or that he lost other commissions because his performance was terminated unjustifiably (if this is the case), then he will be able to recover these damages if they were foreseeable at the time the contract was made. This may be difficult to show. The design professional cannot recover damages which could have been avoided by reasonable efforts.

As stated in § 10.04(d), standard form contracts often specify that the design professional can recover for work performed if the client abandons work done by the design professional, or the project itself. Inclusion of such a clause can mean abandonment without proper cause is not a breach, and the remedy is payment for services performed prior to abandonment. This interpretation means that profit on unperformed work and consequential damages would not be recoverable.

Such a view of the contract clause rarely reflects what the parties intend when they incorporate such a provision in the contract. To avoid such a result, the contract should specify that inclusion of this clause does not exclude any other remedies which would be given by law, and that unjustified abandonment is a breach.

Other problems relating to the "abandonment" clause are illustrated by Deuel v. McCollum, reproduced at this point.

DEUEL v. McCOLLUM

Court of Appeals of Arizona, 1965.
1 Ariz.App. 188, 400 P.2d 859.

CAMERON, JUDGE. This is a suit by Glenn A. McCollum and George K. Rubel, the plaintiffs below, against E. W. Deuel, the defendant below, for breach of contract. Defendant counterclaimed, trial was held before the court without a jury, judgment was rendered against the defendant, on his counterclaim, and for the plaintiff in the amount of $3,558.43, plus $650.00 attorney's fees. From the judgment, defendant appeals.

Sometime in August, 1957, the parties hereto entered into negotiations for the subdivision of ten acres of land in Phoenix, Arizona, owned by the defendant Deuel. On or about 20 November, 1957, a contract dated 19 August, 1957, was executed by the parties. The contract was a printed form provided by plaintiffs as architects, and contained blank spaces which were filled in by typewriter, and had other portions crossed out. Paragraph A stated as follows:

> "A. *THE PROJECT AND THE ARCHITECT'S SERVICES:* The Architect's professional services consist of the necessary conferences, the preparation of the preliminary sketches and studies, working drawings, specifications, large scale and full size drawings, for architectural, plumbing, heating & cooling, structural, electrical and other mechanical work; assistance in the drafting of forms of proposals and contracts; the issuance of certificates for payment; the keeping of accounts, the general administration of the business and supervision of the Work."

Then under *"Description of the Project"* the form had been filled in by typewriter with the following language:

> "plan, design and develop a subdivision of 10 acres more or less (lot 9 Ambassador Heights, MCR, Phoenix, Arizona), prepare brochures, plan and design dwellings and appurtenant structures, and supervise construction thereof."

The contract provided for a retainer fee of $150.00 which was recited to constitute the minimum fee payable with the balance of the fee to be paid as follows:

> "Architectural & Land Planning Fee, Total Design of Project less engineering fees and less individual dwelling design & supervision fees the amount of Three Thousand One Hundred ($3100.-00) to be prorated into the release price of each lot at $100.00 per lot."

In case of abandonment of the project, the contract had the following provision:

> "8. *Abandonment of the Project*—If the Owner abandons the Project, the Architect is to be compensated in proportion to the services performed under the Contract. If such abandonment occurs prior to completion of the preliminary stage of the Archi-

tect's services, the Owner shall pay to the Architect as his compensation, in addition to the minimum fee payable hereunder: (a) the Architect's cost of technical employee's salaries employed on the Project and for the time expended by partners on the project; plus (b) two hundred percent of (a) overhead and fee. Partner's time under (a) shall be calculated at the rate of $7.50 per hour. In the event of abandonment of the project, the Architect is to be reimbursed by the Owner for all expenses incurred or for which he is committed, including the cost of mechanical and structural engineers, planners, or consultants."

The contract defined the word "abandonment" as follows:

"ABANDONMENT: The word 'abandonment' shall mean the termination of the project or operations before completion."

In addition to the architectural services, the contract provided that the owner agreed to retain an engineering firm to perform required engineering services under the direction of plaintiff. The contract also provided for reasonable attorney's fees in the event the matter should be placed in the hands of an attorney for collection. From August, 1957, until June, 1958, several plats of the area in question were drawn, some changes were made, and a trust agreement was entered into with a trust company to provide for the payment of fees and other necessary arrangements should financing be obtained. The representative from the trust company indicates that there are letters from an insurance company, February, April and May of 1958, concerning the financing of the property, and questions concerning partial release clauses as well as an alleyway on the plat. Testimony also indicates that Mr. Rubel had conferences not only with the trust company and the engineering firm, but with the County Planning and Zoning Authority although a plat was never officially filed with the County. On or about 3 June, 1958, defendants notified plaintiff that he was cancelling said contract because of plaintiff's "breach and abandonment" thereof. Plaintiff sued and defendant counterclaimed. Defendant does not urge his counterclaim on appeal. Plaintiff treats the contract as completely performed, and bases his claim as follows: $3,100.00 as provided in the contract, $17.50 for soil test, and $424.00 for engineering services, plus $650.00 attorney's fees. It is apparent that a judgment was granted as and for a completed contract, plus certain costs allegedly incurred.

This case involves the interpretation of a contract entered into between the parties which contract appears conflicting on its face. Under these circumstances, the law in Arizona is as follows:

"* * * [I]t is the law that a special provision written into a contract will prevail over the general provisions thereof, Marshall v. Patzman, 81 Ariz. 367, 306 P.2d 287, and if the written provisions in a contract are inconsistent with printed provisions, the written matter deliberately added by the parties must prevail." Wilhorn Builders v. Cortaro Management Company, 82 Ariz. 48, at 51, 308 P.2d 251, at 252 (1957).

The words added to the printed contract in this case call upon the plaintiffs to "plan, design and develop a subdivision of ten acres more or less * * * prepare brochures, plan and design dwellings, and appurtenant structures, and supervise construction thereof." The evidence below does not indicate that the contract was completed by the plaintiffs. In fact, the contrary is evident. The lower court had sufficient evidence to find the contract had been abandoned before completion by Deuel. We will look to the contract to see what remedies, if any, are available to the plaintiff in case of breach. We will not normally disturb a judgment of the trial court where there is reasonable evidence to support it, and under such circumstances the evidence will be taken in the strongest manner in favor of the court's decision. Bohmfalk v. Vaughan, 89 Ariz. 33, 357 P.2d 617 (1960). While the evidence below is sufficient to indicate a breach of this contract by the defendant Deuel, and therefore substantiate a judgment for plaintiff, there is insufficient evidence to support the amount of the judgment rendered in behalf of the plaintiff in this matter. The amount rendered could only be awarded in the event the plaintiffs had performed all acts required under the terms of the written agreement and particularly the words typed in, which required them to do many more things than were admittedly done in this matter.

Where a contract provides for the remedy or the amount of damages in the event there is a breach, the terms of the contract will control. Green v. Snodgrass, 79 Ariz. 319, 289 P.2d 191 (1955). The contract herein provided that if the abandonment occurs prior to the completion of the preliminary stage of the architect's services, the owner shall pay to the architect, in addition to the minimum fee payable, the architect's cost of technical employee's salaries employed on the project, and for time expended by the parties on the project, plus 200% of the architect's cost for overhead fee, computed at the rate of $7.50 per hour.

The same paragraph provided that in the event of abandonment of the project the architect is to be reimbursed by the owner for all expenses incurred or for which he is committed including the cost of mechanical and structural engineers, planners and consultants. Although the contract does not expressly state it would indicate that this portion of the damages would be available only if the contract were abandoned after the completion of the preliminary stage of the architect's services.

The testimony is not sufficient to indicate whether or not this contract was abandoned before or after the preliminary stage of the architect's services, but the amount of damages due to the plaintiffs would certainly be dependent upon the time at which abandonment occurred.

Judgment for plaintiff is affirmed in part and reversed and remanded for a determination of the amount of damages.

This case illustrates the result of imprecise drafting. It is likely that the last sentence of para. 8 of the contract was included to cover reimbursables, whether incurred before or after completion of the "preliminary stage of the Architect's services". When the court read it together with the prior two sentences, an ambiguity was created which was, as usual, promptly resolved in favor of the client.

If the Court's analysis was correct, the architect should not have hired the consultants until *after* the completion of the preliminary work. Yet it was likely that the consultant's work was required before that point.

(C) SPECIFIC PERFORMANCE

As for the right of specific performance, the result is the same as stated in § 11.01(d). It would be very difficult for the design professional to obtain a court decree ordering that the client continue his relationship with the architect or engineer. Sometimes the court's refusal to make such an order is justified by reference to the doctrine of "mutuality of remedy". Since the court could not award specific performance against the design professional, the design professional cannot have it against the client. But the principal reason for not awarding specific performance in such a contract is that contracts under which both parties have a continuing obligation to each other and where the performance takes time and cooperation are not those which can be readily supervised or administered by a court. For these reasons, specific performance is usually not ordered for breach of such contracts. A broadly drafted arbitration clause which gives the arbitrator the right to order a specific performance could enlarge the remedies available to include specific performance.

REVIEW QUESTIONS

1. How would you differentiate restitution from damages?

2. What can the design professional recover if he is unjustifiably fired during performance?

3. What is specific performance? Is it usually obtainable in a personal service contract?

4. What effect can contract clauses have upon measure of recovery?

QUESTIONS FOR CLASS DISCUSSION

1. Why shouldn't an architect or engineer be compelled to perform by court order if he has agreed to do so?

2. If the cost of correction of defectively designed work exceeds the difference in value between the work as designed and the work as it should have been designed, which measure is proper?

PROBLEM

A has agreed to perform design services for C. A is to be paid 6 percent of the construction cost. After the design professional had been working on schematic designs, the design professional repudiated the contract and stated that he would perform no further. Which of the following items of damage can the client recover?

1. A payment made by the client to design professional when the contract was signed.

2. The additional cost which would be incurred in hiring a new design professional.

3. Delay damages such as increased cost of obtaining construction loan, loss of rentals from prospective tenants, and increase in construction contract costs.

Part III

LAWS RELATING TO LAND

Introduction

Legal rules relating to land are important to architects and engineers. Building projects require that the client own or have the right to build upon the construction site. Also, planning and design require an awareness of those legal controls placed upon the owner or occupier of land.

Chapter 12 will discuss land ownership. Chapter 13 treats acquisition of ownership and possessory rights, with special emphasis on the marketing of land. Chapter 14 relates to public and private controls over land use.

There are many laws which relate to land and its use. Also, some of these laws are very complicated. For that reason, it will be necessary to use selectivity in the matters discussed and the extent of the treatment of problem areas.

Chapter 12

INTERESTS IN LAND

SECTION 12.01 ELEMENTS OF LAND OWNERSHIP

American property law has emphasized interests in land rather than land ownership. Ownership of land can be divided into its constituent elements. Usually the owner of land has a right to sell it or give it away, while he is alive, or effective upon his death. Also, he has the sole and exclusive right to use the land.

Where one person is the "sole" owner of land, he has all these rights. However, these constituent elements can be separated. For example, the owner of land may lease the land to a tenant. In such a case, the tenant has the right to sole and exclusive possession, while the landlord still retains the right to sell or give away the land, subject to the tenant's right to possess the land.

These rights can also become fragmented within themselves. The right to sell may be divided among co-owners or owners of successive interests in land. The right to use the land can be divided up in a number of ways. The owner of land may permit a tenant to use a portion of the land. The owner may sell subsurface or air rights to the land.

While the owner has exclusive possession of the land (a possessory interest), he may grant an easement (a nonpossessory interest). The easement holder will be able to use all or a part of the owner's land for specific purposes. The owner may give a neighbor the right to cross his land. Also, the owner of a building may grant an easement to a sign company to use part of the roof to erect an advertising sign. The advertising company has a non-possessory interest in the land upon which his sign is placed.

Finally, the owner of land can create security interests in his land. He may wish to borrow money and give a mortgage upon his land to the lender as security. The lender who takes such a security has a security interest in the land. The same is true if a court judgment is awarded against the owner of land. The person awarded the judgment can cause a judicial sale of the land in order that he be paid the amount of the judgment.

Because absolute ownership, in the sense that it has been used in this paragraph, is often divided among many persons, the American real property law has used the term "interests in land" rather than land "ownership." The purpose of Chapter 12 is to examine some of the more important interests in land most relevant to those involved in the construction process.

SECTION 12.02 TOTAL OWNERSHIP: THE FEE SIMPLE

The most common form of sole ownership is called the "fee simple." The owner of a fee simple has the right to exclusive possession of the land. He can exclude all others from entry on the land. The owner determines how the land is to be used. He may sell the land, give it away during his life, or determine how it is to pass upon his death.

None of these rights are absolute. For example, his right to absolute possession is subject to the right of state officials to enter upon his land for certain purposes if certain legal steps are taken. His right to sell the land may be subject to state-imposed formal requirements, and may be taxed by the state. His right to sell to whom he chooses may be affected by laws relating to nondiscrimination in the sale or rental of apartments or houses. His right to give away or to leave his land by will is often controlled by state laws designed to protect his creditors and his family, and may be subject to federal and state estate, inheritance and gift tax laws. Land ownership can be taken away from him by the state through its right to exercise eminent domain, or by the state through its function of protecting persons who have a security interest in that land, such as lenders or mechanics' lien claimants.

SECTION 12.03 SUCCESSIVE OWNERSHIP: LIFE ESTATES, REMAINDERS AND REVERSIONS

Absolute ownership, such as the fee simple, can be carved up into pieces which relate to the passage of time, or to the occurrence of events. This "carving" often results in one person having a present interest in the land, and others having future interests in the land. The most common illustration of a present interest in the land subject to a future interest is the "life estate". The holder of a life estate is entitled to the possession and use of the property during his lifetime, if the life estate is measured by his life, or for a period of time measured by the life of someone else. Often the owner of the fee simple determines who will get the land when the life tenancy ends. If the land will return to him, the owner has a "reversion" interest. If he decides the land will go to a third party, that party has a "remainder" interest. For example, A may leave land to B for B's life. In this case, A has a reversion. If A leaves land to B, for the life of B, and, upon B's death, to C, C has a remainder interest.

When ownership is divided into successive periods of time the law must balance the rights of the present and future owners. Various rules have evolved for the apportionment of tax assessments between life tenants and persons with remainder interests.

Generally, the life tenant cannot change the premises if the owner of the remainder interest reasonably objects to the change. The life tenant also must keep the premises in a reasonable state of repair. Nor can the life tenant, subject to certain exceptions, do anything which would cause the market value of the land to be diminished.

Sometimes the life tenant makes a permanent improvement and wishes to charge the owner of the remainder interest a portion of the cost. Usually, this cannot be done. However, if the improvement was commenced by the person who had created the life estate, the owner of the life estate can complete the improvement and charge a portion of the costs to the owner of the remainder interest. Also, if the life tenant was compelled by governmental authority to make the improvement, then a portion of the cost is chargeable to the person with the remainder interest.

These rules assume that there is no language dealing with these questions in the instrument creating the life estate. It is possible for the person creating the life estate to specify permissible conduct, state that certain repairs or improvements can or cannot be made, specify that the owner of the remainder interest pay or not pay for such improvements or give the owner of the life interest the right to sell all or a portion of the property under certain circumstances.

SECTION 12.04 MULTIPLE OWNERSHIP

(A) JOINT TENANCY

The joint tenancy's most important attribute is the right of survivorship. If A and B own real property jointly, upon the death of either joint tenant the other joint tenant takes the entire interest in the property. The estate of the deceased joint tenant has no interest in the property.

Joint tenancies have retained some popularity as forms of informal will making. No formalities are required to make the survivor the sole owner of the property, other than a simple termination of joint tenancy. However, under tax laws, inheritance taxes and estate taxes will still be due on the transfer of the property effective upon the death of the joint tenant.

Creditors can seize and have a judicial sale of the joint tenant's interest during his lifetime. Obviously, the joint tenant cannot leave his portion of the jointly-owned property by will. If creditors obtain judgments against a joint tenant, a court can make his interest in the property liable for payment of his judgment debts, and order a public sale of his interest. Older law favored joint tenancies because they tend to preserve land in larger units.

(B) TENANCY IN COMMON

Joint tenancies are often used when the land is owned by husband and wife, but today the law tends to favor tenancies in common. Under a tenancy in common, each of the tenants holds some undivided interest in the same property. One might hold a three-eighths share, another one-quarter, etc. They are tenants in common, because the property has not been divided into the individual portions. A tenant in common may sell, or divide, his interest and it can be transferred by will or inherited. Tenancies in common can be reached by creditors of the tenant during the life of the tenant, or, upon his death, by a claim against his estate.

(C) PARTITION

It may be necessary to divide land owned in multiple ownership. This problem can come up when the property is seized for the debts of one tenant, or when all the tenants wish to divide the property, or if one tenant wishes to take his share. If the parties cannot agree on a fair value and pay the proper share division, a court will order either a physical partition (a division of the property itself), or a sale of the property and apportionment of the proceeds according to the interests of each tenant.

(D) CONDOMINIUM AND COOPERATIVE

There are other forms of multiple ownership which are becoming more popular as society becomes more urbanized. One form is called the "condominium." Here, the individual units in a condominium building, whether apartments, stores or offices, are owned by the individuals. The hallways and common facilities are owned by all the individual owners, as tenants-in-common.

Another form of multiple ownership is the "co-operative". In the cooperative, the title to the land, and to the improvements, is owned by a corporation in which the residents are shareholders. Each shareholder has a long term, renewable lease interest in his own unit.

Essentially, the difference between condominium and cooperative methods is that the condominium has individual ownership and liability, while the cooperative features mutual ownership with mutual liabilities for debts.

(E) MARITAL PROPERTY

The right of a spouse in certain property of the other spouse can constitute a type of multiple ownership. In some states a wife's "dower" right gives her rights in the real property of her husband acquired during his lifetime. This and other aspects of acquiring ownership by virtue of marriage and death will be discussed in § 13.01(c).

Community property is a form of co-ownership used in eight western states. While there are some variations, generally all property acquired by either spouse during the marriage, other than property acquired by gift, will, or inheritance, is owned by the spouses equally as "community property".

In some states, the husband is given management and control of community property. However, he cannot give away the wife's interest in community property without her consent. In other states the husband may deal with the property, but he acts as a trustee for the wife when he does. In some states, both spouses are co-owners and they must act jointly in matters dealing with the property. It is common in community property states to have both spouses sign any deed of land or any transfer of personal property because of the wife's interest, or possible interest, in the property deeded or transferred.

SECTION 12.05 PHYSICAL DIVISION

The owner of land may sell part of the land itself. For example, the owner of an acre of land may sell one-half an acre. Emphasis in this section, however, is upon transactions which involve the transfer of subsurface or air rights.

Usually, the owner of land owns the subsurface of the land and the air rights above the land, subject to the public interest in permitting flights above his land. It is possible for the owner to sell or lease subsurface rights or air rights. The owner may sell the entire subsurface to persons interested in extracting minerals, oil, or natural gas from below the surface of the land. He may sell the right to extract certain minerals or gases, receiving a royalty based upon the amount extracted. He may rent, rather than sell, the surface or mineral rights.

As the population tends to concentrate in urban areas, subsurface rights and air rights are becoming increasingly valuable. As transportation tends to go underground, the right to use the subsurface becomes an important interest to the owner of the land. As space becomes scarce, an important aspect of the ownership of urban land is the power to sell or lease the use of the space above the owner's land.

SECTION 12.06 THE TRUST

Sometimes ownership is divided into "legal" and "beneficial" ownership. The deed may name one person as owner, but that person may own the land for the benefit of someone else. Such a division of legal and beneficial ownership is created by a "trust". A trust is often used as a means of holding property given to minors or to persons whom the giver does not wish to entrust with full legal ownership. Also, in some states the trust is a device for hiding the true owner of land. Where trusts are used, the person who will hold legal title is called a "trustee", and the person for whom he holds the title is called the "beneficiary". The person who creates the trust may be called the "trustor", the "settlor" or the "grantor". The laws relating to trusts are complicated, and will not be covered in this treatise.

SECTION 12.07 NON-POSSESSORY INTERESTS

(A) EASEMENTS AND LICENSES: THE FONTAINEBLEAU CASE

There are important interests in land which are non-possessory. The most important non-possessory interests for architects and engineers are "easements" and "licenses."

An easement is the right of one person to use the land of another. Examples of affirmative easements are the right to cross another's land, the right to construct and maintain underground pipes, telephone lines, and utility lines, and the right to use another's land to hold excess water.

A negative easement precludes the owner of land from using his land in a certain way. An illustration would be a promise by a landowner not to build on his land in any way which would cut off the light, air and view of an adjacent landowner.

An easement may consist of the right to enter the land of another and remove part of the land itself. For example, one party may have the right to remove top soil, minerals or gravel from the land of another. This right is sometimes called a "profit".

Party walls may create easements. A party wall is one common to adjacent structures. The wall usually sits astride the boundary line of the two pieces of adjacent property. While there are many possible methods of ownership of a party wall, the wall is usually divided longitudinally into two strips which are owned separately, with each owner having an easement in the other owner's part of the wall for the support of his structure.

Easements often are created by a "conveyance". For example, the owner of tract A may execute a deed conveying to the owner of an adjacent tract, tract B, the right to cross tract A or the right to construct a road across tract A.

Sometimes easements are created by "implication". Instead of express words granting the easement, such as "I grant A an easement to cross my land", the intention to grant the easement might be manifested by acts of the parties concerned or by other language in a deed. The most important illustration of an easement created by implication are easements of necessity. For example, A may convey part of his land to B in such a way that B will not have access to a public highway except by crossing A's land.

In such a case it is usually held that the grantor A intended to give the grantee B a right of way over A's land sufficient to reach the public highway. Without such an easement being implied, B would be land-locked and the use of his land would be drastically curtailed. The inference of an easement by necessity is stronger if there is no means of access available to the grantee without costs disproportionate to the amount paid for the conveyance.

An easement by implication can also be created if the grantor, A, would be denied access to the public highway as a result of conveying land to B. In such a case an easement by necessity might be given to A to cross B's land to reach the public highway.

Light, air and view are important considerations in construction of buildings and residences. They can be affected by how an adjacent landowner uses his land. In Fontainebleau H. Corp. v. Forty-Five Twenty-Five Inc., one luxury hotel built an addition in such a way as to cut off sun, light and view to a competing adjacent hotel. The opinion of the court is reproduced at this point.

FONTAINEBLEAU HOTEL CORP. v. FORTY-FIVE TWENTY-FIVE, INC.

District Court of Appeal of Florida, 1959.
114 So.2d 357.

PER CURIAM. This is an interlocutory appeal from an order temporarily enjoining the appellants from continuing with the construction of a fourteen-story addition to the Fontainebleau Hotel, owned and operated by the appellants. Appellee, plaintiff below, owns the Eden Roc Hotel, which was constructed in 1955, about a year after the Fontainebleau, and adjoins the Fontainebleau on the north. Both are luxury hotels, facing the Atlantic Ocean. The proposed addition to the Fontainebleau is being constructed twenty feet from its north property line, 130 feet from the mean high water mark of the Atlantic Ocean, and 76 feet 8 inches from the ocean bulkhead line. The 14-story tower will extend 160 feet above grade in height and is 416 feet long from east to west. During the winter months, from around two o'clock in the afternoon for the remainder of the day, the shadow of the addition will extend over the cabana, swimming pool, and sunbathing areas of the Eden Roc, which are located in the southern portion of its property.

In this action, plaintiff-appellee sought to enjoin the defendants-appellants from proceeding with the construction of the addition to the Fontainebleau (it appears to have been roughly eight stories high at the time suit was filed), alleging that the construction would interefere with the light and air on the beach in front of the Eden Roc and cast a shadow of such size as to render the beach wholly unfitted for the use and enjoyment of its guests, to the irreparable injury of the plaintiff; further, that the construction of such addition on the north side of defendants' property, rather than the south side, was actuated by malice and ill will on the part of the defendants' president toward the plaintiff's president; and that the construction was in violation of a building ordinance requiring a 100-foot setback from the ocean. It was also alleged that the construction would interfere with the easements of light and air enjoyed by plaintiff and its predecessors in title for more than twenty years and "impliedly granted by virtue of the acts of the plaintiff's predecessors in title, as well as under the common law and the express recognition of such rights by virtue of Chapter 9837, Laws of Florida 1923 * * *." Some attempt was also made to allege an easement by implication in favor of the plaintiff's property, as the dominant, and against the defendants' property, as the servient, tenement.

The defendants' answer denied the material allegations of the complaint, pleaded laches and estoppel by judgment.

The chancellor heard considerable testimony on the issues made by the complaint and the answer and, as noted, entered a temporary injunction restraining the defendants from continuing with the construction of the addition. His reason for so doing was stated by him, in a memorandum opinion, as follows:

> "In granting the temporary injunction in this case the Court wishes to make several things very clear. . . . The ruling is based solely on the proposition that no one has a right to use his property to the injury of another. In this case it is clear from the evidence that the proposed use by the Fontainebleau will materially damage the Eden Roc. There is evidence indicating that the construction of the proposed annex by the Fontainebleau is malicious or deliberate for the purpose of injuring the Eden Roc, but it is scarcely sufficient, standing alone, to afford a basis for equitable relief."

This is indeed a novel application of the maxim *sic utere tuo ut alienum non laedas.* [Ed. note: Use your property in such a manner as not to injure that of another.] This maxim does not mean that one must never use his own property in such a way as to do any injury to his neighbor. . . . It means only that one must use his property so as not to injure the lawful *rights* of another. . . . In Reaver v. Martin Theatres, Fla.1951, 52 So.2d 682, 683, 25 A.L.R.2d 1451, under this maxim, it was stated that "it is well settled that a property owner may put his own property to any reasonable and lawful use, so long as he does not thereby deprive the adjoining landowner of any right of enjoyment of his property *which is recognized and protected by law, and so long as his use is not such a one as the law will pronounce a nuisance.*" [Emphasis supplied.]

No American decision has been cited, and independent research has revealed none, in which it has been held that—in the absence of some contractual or statutory obligation—a landowner has a legal right to the free flow of light and air across the adjoining land of his neighbor. Even at common law, the landowner had no legal right, in the absence of an easement or uninterrupted use and enjoyment for a period of 20 years, to unobstructed light and air from the adjoining land. Blumberg v. Weiss, 1941, 129 N.J.Eq. 34, 17 A.2d 823; 1 Am. Jur., Adjoining Landowners, § 51. And the English doctrine of "ancient lights" has been unanimously repudiated in this country. . . .

[Ed. note: The doctrine of ancient lights gives the owner of land who has used and enjoyed the view from a specific window for 20 years the right to stop an adjacent landowner from building in such a way as to block the view.]

There being, then, no legal right to the free flow of light and air from the adjoining land, it is universally held that where a structure serves a useful and beneficial purpose, it does not give rise to a cause of action, either for damages or for an injunction under the maxim *sic utere tuo ut alienum non laedas,* even though it causes injury to another by cutting off the light and air and interfering with the view that would otherwise be available over adjoining land in its natural state, regardless of the fact that the structure may have been erected partly for spite. . . .

We see no reason for departing from this universal rule. If, as contended on behalf of plaintiff, public policy demands that a landowner in the Miami Beach area refrain from constructing buildings on his premises that will cast a shadow on the adjoining premises, an amendment of its comprehensive planning and zoning ordinance, applicable to the public as a whole, is the means by which such purpose should be achieved. . . . But to change the universal rule—and the custom followed in this state since its inception—that adjoining landowners have an equal right under the law to build to the line of their respective tracts and to such a height as is desired by them (in the absence, of course, of building restrictions or regulations) amounts, in our opinion, to judicial legislation. As stated in Musumeci v. Leonardo, supra [77 R.I. 255, 75 A.2d 177], "So use your own as not to injure another's property is, indeed, a sound and salutary principle for the promotion of justice, but it may not and should not be applied so as gratuitously to confer upon an adjacent property owner incorporeal rights incidental to his ownership of land which the law does not sanction."

. . .

The record affirmatively shows that no statutory basis for the right sought to be enforced by plaintiff exists. The so-called Shadow Ordinance enacted by the City of Miami Beach at plaintiff's behest was held invalid. . . .

The only other possible basis . . . is the alleged violation by defendants of the setback line prescribed by ordinance. The plaintiff argues that the ordinance applicable to the Use District in which plaintiff's and defendants' properties are located, prescribing "a front yard having a depth of not less than one hundred (100) feet, measured from the ocean, * * *," should be and has been interpreted by the City's zoning inspector as requiring a setback of 100 feet from an established ocean bulkhead line. As noted above, the addition to the Fontainebleau is set back only 76 feet 8 inches from the ocean bulkhead line, although it is 130 feet from the ocean measured from the mean high water mark.

While the chancellor did not decide the question of whether the setback ordinance had been violated, it is our view that, even if there was such a violation, the plaintiff would have no cause of action against the defendants based on such violation. The application of simple mathematics to the sun studies filed in evidence by plaintiff in support of its claim demonstrates conclusively that to move the existing structure back some 23 feet from the ocean would make no appreciable difference in the problem which is the subject of this controversy. . . The construction of the 14-story addition is proceeding under a permit issued by the city pursuant to the mandate . . . which permit authorizes completion of the 14-story addition according to a plan showing a 76-foot setback from the ocean bulkhead line. Moreover, the plaintiff's objection to the distance of the structure from the ocean appears to have been made for the first time in the instant suit, which was filed almost a year after the beginning of the construction of the addition, at a time when it was roughly eight stories in height, representing the expenditure by defendants of several million dollars. In these circumstances, it is our view that the plaintiff has stated no cause of action for equitable relief based on the violation of the ordinance—assuming, arguendo, that there has been a violation.

Since it affirmatively appears that the plaintiff has not established a cause of action against the defendants by reason of the structure here in question, the order granting a temporary injunction should be and it is hereby reversed with directions to dismiss the complaint.

Reversed with directions.

As indicated in Fontainebleau, easements for light, air and view are not created by implication but require an express grant of easement. As a rule, the owner of land can use it in any way he chooses, even if its use destroys or reduces the entrance of light, air and view to the land of his neighbor.

Public land use controls, discussed in greater detail in Chapter 14, may give some protection to light, air and view. Zoning ordinances usually contain height limitations and setback requirements which may accord some protection to light, air and view. See § 14.03.

Suppose one neighbor puts up a high unsightly fence which interferes with his neighbor's view and the entrance of light to his neighbor's land and creates an ugly eyesore. Fences put up to annoy a neighbor are called "spite fences".

The states have not been uniform in their treatment of spite fences. Some emphasize the right of a land owner to use his land as he wishes, and permit spite fences. Other states have held that if the dominant motive in erecting the fence was malicious, or if the fence serves no useful purpose, the neighbor can recover damages and be granted a court decree ordering that the fence be removed.

In some states, statutes have been passed which limit the height of any fence erected maliciously, or for the purpose of annoying a neighbor. The increasing tendency is to restrict the use of spite fences.

Easements may also be created by "prescription", or what is sometimes called "adverse use". As will be seen in § 13.04 a person may acquire title to the land of another by occupying it, under certain conditions, for a specified period of time. With regard to possessory interests, this is called acquiring title by "adverse possession". Easements may be acquired by using the land of another, without express or implied permission, for a period of time which is roughly parallel to the period of time necessary to acquire title by adverse possession.

Problems can relate to the scope of the easement. Courts examine the language of the deed creating the easement, the facts which give rise to an easement by implication, or the nature of the adverse use. If a public utility has an easement over a farmer's land to erect utility poles and wires, it is likely that the utility company has the right to enter on to the land for purposes of maintaining the utility lines. The exact nature of this right may have to take into account the right of the farmer to use his land for his own purposes.

In an easement to cross the land of another, problems can develop relating to who or what can use the crossing. If it is a foot path, can it be used by horses? If it is a road, can it be used by heavy trucks? The easement language, or the facts surrounding its creation, may indicate how these issues are resolved.

It is helpful in the granting of an easement to think carefully about the exact nature and scope of the easement, and to express the common understanding in the deed creating the easement. Courts look at whether the easement was paid for by the grantee or was given gratuitously by the grantor. If the easement is one for which the grantee has not paid, it is likely that the interpretation will be more favorable to the grantor.

Easements can expire by their own terms. A may give an easement to B for 10 years. An easement may last for the life of the holder of the easement, or for the particular purpose of the easement. In such cases, when the life of the holder ends or the purpose for which the easement was created has been accomplished, the easement rights terminate.

Most easements have a potentially unlimited duration, and some specific action is required to terminate them. Usually non-use in and of itself does not terminate an easement. However, the holder of the easement may abandon the easement. If the owner of the land upon which the easement is located makes substantial improvements to his land, relying on the abandonment, the holder of the easement may have lost his rights to the easement. Even without reliance by the owner of the land, the evidence may point to an intention to permanently abandon the easement. Non-use in this regard is a factor, but courts also look for any other acts by the holder of the easement which tend to indicate that he has abandoned the easement.

An easement may also be extinguished if a third person buys the land that is subject to the easement without any knowledge of the easement, and without the holder of the easement having recorded the deed creating the easement. Recording acts and their effect will be discussed in § 13.11.

"Licenses" are closely related to easements. A license is a less solid privilege to use someone else's land. The most important characteristic of the license is that generally it is revocable at any time by the person granting or creating the license. Because of its revocability, a license is not considered an interest in land, and is looked upon merely as a legal justification for what otherwise would be an unauthorized entry on the land of another.

(B) IMPROVING THE LAND OF ANOTHER: ENCROACHMENTS

While not technically a right to use the land of another, the rights of a person who has improved another's land merit comment.

Sometimes a person mistakenly builds a structure, or makes an improvement, upon the land of another without the latter's knowledge. Technically, the improver is a trespasser. But his trespass may not only not damage the land, but may have improved the other's land. Can the improving trespasser take back his improvement? Can he make the owner of the improved property pay some amount for that improvement? Can he force the owner to sell the land on which the improvement was made?

The traditional view refused to give the improving trespasser anything. Gradually, inroads based upon the theory of unjust enrichment were made into this rule. This change has been accomplished by case law, and by "betterment" statutes. If the owner asks for the assistance of the courts, such as to remove the improvement, the courts may order him to pay for the improvement. Sometimes the improver can recover his improvement if it can be removed, and if he pays for any damages caused by the removal. Sometimes, the court will compel the owner to sell the improved part of the land to the improver at the unimproved value. Sometimes the improver can recover the amount by which the improvement has enhanced the value of the land.

An encroachment occurs when one property owner permits or causes his property to be located upon the land of his neighbor. For example, suppose one person permits his tree to spread its branches over his neighbor's land. Another illustration would be one person mistakenly building upon the land of his neighbor. The classic cases are those where one landowner has put a few inches of his house on his neighbor's land.

The person who has encroached has committed a trespass on his neighbor's land. In such cases a neighbor usually has the right to recover any damages caused by the trespass. Often these are nominal. Also, the neighbor whose land has been trespassed upon can obtain a court decree ordering that the encroacher remove the encroachment.

But in some cases such an order would cause great hardship. If the encroachment occurred by mistake, or in reliance upon a survey, the court might refuse to order removal of the encroachment. In addition to showing he was acting in good faith, the encroacher would have to show that it would cost much more to stop or cease the encroachment than the encroachment was damaging his neighbor. For example, in Golden Press v. Rylands, 124 Colo. 122, 235 P.2d 592:

(1951) the encroacher built within his lot lines but his underground footings projected two to three inches on to his neighbor's land. Encroachment had been unintentional. In denying the decree ordering that the encroachment be removed, the court stated:

> Where the encroachment is deliberate and constitutes a willful and intentional taking of another's land, equity may well require the restoration regardless of the expense of removal as compared with damage suffered therefrom; but where the encroachment was in good faith, we think the court should weigh the circumstances so that it shall not act oppressively. . . . [R]elative hardship may properly be considered and the court should not become a party to extortion. . . . Where the defendant's encroachment is unintentional and slight, plaintiff's use not affected and his damage small and fairly compensable, while the cost of removal is so great as to cause grave hardship or otherwise make its removal unconscionable, mandatory injunction may properly be denied and the plaintiff relegated to compensation in damages.

Rozny v. Marnul, reproduced at § 30.04(h), involved an encroaching driveway resulted from a surveyor's error.

In some unusual cases, then, a person may have an interest in the land of a neighbor if he has built upon or improved his neighbor's land. This "interest" may consist of being able to remove his improvement, getting a judicial right to buy the part improved, or being able to continue on his neighbor's land while paying damages for the trespass he has committed.

REVIEW QUESTIONS

1. What are the important elements of ownership?

2. What is a fee simple? A reversion? A remainder?

3. What is the principal distinction between a joint tenancy and a tenancy in common?

4. What is the principal difference between a cooperative and a condominium?

5. How may easements be created?

6. What are illustrations of easements?

7. What is the principal difference between an easement and a license?

8. What is an encroachment?

9. What types of remedies may an improving trespasser be given?

PROBLEMS

1. A left his house by his will to his sister, B, for life, with a remainder to B's children. The house is deteriorating badly and in need of repairs. B wants to remodel the house since repairs are needed. The house is valued at $25,000, and she wants to redesign it at a

cost of $10,000. Her children state they will not pay for any major alterations. They also state they want the house retained in its present style, since the children grew up in the house. They want only those repairs made which will prevent further deterioration and repair present deterioration. B is 42 years of age and in good health. If you were a judge, would you permit B to make major changes? How should the cost of either major changes or minor repairs be allocated as between B and her children?

2. In 1933 Farmer Brown granted a 99 year easement for $1000 to Farmer Jones under which Jones could use a narrow dirt road over Brown's land. Jones wanted to transport his horses from one of his fields to another field and the shortest route was over Brown's land.

Brown graded the road in 1968 and put gravel on it, since he also used the road. Jones wants to transport tractors and oil rigging equipment over the road. (He no longer uses horses). The equipment is needed because oil was discovered on the land owned by Jones (formerly farm land). What facts would help you decide whether the easement should be interpreted to permit the use which Jones wants to make of it? How would you decide this question?

Chapter 13

ACQUISITION OF LAND OWNERSHIP

SECTION 13.01 BY DEATH OF OWNER

(A) WILLS

Most types of interests in land can be transferred by the death of the owner of the property, or by the death of someone with an interest in the property. Usually, the dispositive act is the existence and presentation of a valid will. A valid will requires mental capacity to make the will, and compliance with specified formalities for execution of wills. The states have set up formal rules for insuring that the will is authentic and that the testator, the one making the will, is aware of the seriousness of the testamentary act. Most states require that the will be witnessed by a certain number of people. It is important for the testator to read over his will to be certain that it manifests his intention as to the disposition of his property.

In some states, "holographic wills" are recognized. These are wills which are drawn up entirely in the handwriting of the testator. Such wills need not be witnessed but must be dated. Any irregularity in these requirements is likely to result in the will being declared void (of no effect) by a court.

A will can be changed or revoked at any time before death, if the testator had the requisite mental capacity to make the change and formal requirements were met.

Laws relating to wills are complex and vary considerably from state to state.

(B) DEATH WITHOUT A WILL: LAWS OF INTESTACY

If a person dies without a validly executed will, then his property will pass by the state laws of intestacy. These laws control the transmission of property upon death when the decedent does not indicate how he wishes it to be distributed. The pattern of distribution attempts to follow a "natural" distribution. While there is variation among the states, typically the widow gets one third and the children receive the remaining two thirds. If the decedent is survived by a widow but no children, the widow typically receives one half, with the remaining half going to parents if any, or to brothers and sisters. If the decedent is not survived by a widow or children, his estate will usually go first to his parents, then to his brothers or sisters, and then to other collateral relatives. If there are no relatives and no valid will, the property goes to the state.

(C) MARITAL PROPERTY

The law provides protection for the surviving spouse. Early in Anglo-American history, the wife had a "dower" interest in the real property owned by her husband. (The husband had a similar, but more limited right called "curtesy".) Upon death of the husband and survival by the wife, the widow received a life estate in one third of the land owned by her husband at any time during the marriage.

Her interest in the land attached at the time the land was acquired. This meant that a purchaser acquired only the interest of the husband, unless the wife signed the conveyance. If she did not join in the conveyance, she could still assert her life estate, if she outlived her husband. Purchasers were reluctant to buy land without consent of the wife, where she would have a dower interest.

Today dower has largely been replaced in the United States by what is known as the "widow's share." Instead of a life interest in one third of her husband's real property, the widow usually acquires total ownership of from one-third to one-half in all land and personal property, (shares of stock, bank accounts, furnishings, cars, etc.) owned by her husband at his death. In most states the widow can choose either her widow's share or the property left to her by her husband in his will.

If the property is owned by husband and wife as joint tenants, then all of the property goes to the surviving spouse because of the survivorship aspect of a joint tenancy. See § 12.04(a).

As stated in § 12.04(e) eight states classify most marital property as community property. Generally, under community property laws, most of the property acquired during a marriage is owned by husband and wife. Commonly, the will of either spouse can only dispose of the half of the community property owned by the decedent. The other half still belongs to the surviving spouse. In the absence of a will, state law determines who gets the deceased spouse's one half. In some states, if either spouse dies without a will, the other spouse becomes the owner of all the community property. In other states, the property of the deceased spouse who dies without a will will pass by the laws of intestacy. As stated, typically this means that the surviving spouse will receive one third to one half of the deceased spouse's one half, depending upon whether there are children.

(D) ADMINISTRATION

The administration of an estate is within the jurisdiction of the local probate court. The actual work of winding up and distribution of an estate is performed by the executor or the personal representative. Usually the will names an executor. If no one is named, or if the person named is unable or unwilling to serve, the probate court will name an administrator or executor. If the deceased died without a will, the court will name a personal representative to wind up and distribute the estate. Since the executor or personal representative is responsible for the estate, he will come to the court for instructions if he is at all in doubt as to what should be done regarding administration. See § 13.07(i) for discussion of the effect of death of a party or parties during the negotiation or consummation of a sale of land.

SECTION 13.02 GIFT

Sometimes the ownership of property is acquired by gift. There are three general requirements for a valid gift. They are:

1. Donative intent (intent to make a gift)
2. Delivery
3. Acceptance

Acceptance is usually not a problem since it is presumed that the recipient will accept the gift.

The difficulties center around intention to make a gift and delivery. The delivery concept originally assumed that the item which was being given could and would be manually transmitted by the maker of the gift to the receiver of the gift. This requirement demonstrated the intent to make a gift, and also impressed upon the maker of the gift that he was effectuating a final transfer of his ownership in the property. For example, to give a book, there would usually be a handing over of the book.

The requirement of delivery became difficult when the subject matter of the gift was something that could not easily be transmitted manually, such as a herd of cattle, an intangible right evidenced by a promissory note, or an intangible right not evidenced by a promissory note such as an account receivable or a bank account. Delivery of either the subject matter of the gift or something which is closely connected with the subject matter, such as a passbook or a bond or a note, is usually required.

As to gifts of real property, it is obvious that the manual transmission of the land is not possible. For this reason, the gift of land is typically made by the execution of a deed, and the delivery of the deed to the intended recipient of the gift. A deed is a written instrument by which title to real property is conveyed or transferred. See § 13.09 for a discussion of the types of deeds.

Traditionally, the law has been suspicious of gifts. Gift promises were usually not enforced. Assertions of a gift are frequently made by the recipient after the death of the maker of the gift, and proof of the facts of the transaction, and proof of the intention of the maker of the supposed gift can be difficult to find. Today, the courts are somewhat more relaxed with regard to the technical requirements of delivery. Courts are more likely to venture into the troublesome questions of intention to make a gift.

SECTION 13.03 FORCED SALES

Sometimes title to real property is acquired by judicial sale, such as tax sales and foreclosure sales. The holder of a security interest (someone who has lent money, and has been given an interest in the property as security for the loan) may have the right to have a judicial sale of the property and to be paid from the proceeds, if the borrower defaults in payments on the loan. The purchaser of the property then acquires title as a result of the judicial foreclosure sale, subject to a right to redeem the land within a certain period. See § 13.12(c).

Forced sales may also occur when there is nonpayment of taxes, or nonpayment of a court-awarded judgment. In those cases, there will be public sales, usually made by the sheriff, and the sheriff will be authorized to issue a title to the high bidder at the forced sale, subject to the owner's right to redeem within a certain period.

SECTION 13.04 ADVERSE POSSESSION

Title to land may be acquired by adverse possession. To acquire property by this method, certain conditions set by statutes (and occasionally additional conditions set by courts) must be met. To start, the one claiming an adverse title to the property must have openly occupied the property for the period of time established by law. The original owner of the property must bring a legal action to end the wrongful occupancy within a time specified by law, or the original owner loses his right to the property.

The doctrine of adverse possession has the same rationale as the law requiring that judicial actions be commenced within a certain period of time. Evidence is lost, witnesses die, memories become clouded, and the judicial resolution of the disputes becomes more difficult with the passage of time. With regard to periods of limitation dealing with ownership of land, there are additional reasons for requiring that actions be brought within a specified period of time or else title is acquired by the person adversely possessing the land. Often persons who take possession of the land believe they have a right to be on the land. They may have a document which convinces them that they are the true owners of the land. During this period they may make substantial improvements on the land. In areas where land titles are uncertain, it would often be unjust to permit someone to improve the land, rely upon it being his own, and then to eject him.

In most states, the statutory period during which the original owner may legally eject the adverse holder is twenty years. Some western states have periods which are as short as five years, but these states frequently require that the possessor pay taxes as well as occupy the land.

There are many technicalities connected with acquiring title by adverse possession. The laws vary greatly from state to state.

SECTION 13.05 EMINENT DOMAIN AND DEDICATION: ACQUISITION OF OWNERSHIP BY THE PUBLIC

If a government is to function, it must have the power to appropriate private land for public purposes. Such a power, called the "power of eminent domain", is needed to build roads, hospitals, schools and other public projects. Usually state constitutions or statutes provide for the power of eminent domain. Sometimes this power is given to private public service companies, such as power companies.

State and federal constitutions require that private property not be taken without due process of law. This usually means that the taking must be for a public purpose, and the person whose land is taken must receive just compensation. The person whose land is being taken is entitled to a fair hearing on these questions. The typical dispute in a condemnation action (the type of action under which the state exercises its rights of eminent domain), is the valuation of the property taken. This is complicated when the property is commercial, and where the property is claimed to have a value based upon prospective earnings.

One relatively recent problem has arisen regarding the right of eminent domain. May the state take land from one private owner and turn it over to another private owner who will develop the land with what is conceived to be a greater public interest? This question may come up where large areas of land are taken for public housing or redevelopment, and part of the land will be turned over to private businessmen or developers. While the answer will vary from state to state, there is an increasing tendency to permit the state to make such condemnations of private property to eliminate slums and obsolescent areas.

A public body may acquire title to property by the process of "dedication." An owner may transfer land to be used for a public use. When the public body accepts the property for present or future public use, the dedication is completed. The purpose must be of a sort that the general public can enjoy. Usually, there is public dedication for parks, streets, alleys and highways. Sometimes the person dedicating the land for public use reserves certain interests in the land. The dedication may consist of a transfer of the entire ownership, or of some lesser interest in the land. Usually dedications are made by deeds or written instruments. Dedications may occur without a written declaration, by the owner's acquiescence in the public use. A dedication may occur when a street or road is described in a plat or map which is relied upon by purchasers of lots in the immediate area.

Many states have statutes which deal with the subdividing or platting of land. These statutes often contain provisions requiring that the subdivider dedicate certain portions of land for public use.

Dedication requires that there be an acceptance. Some case decisions have held an offer of dedication may be revoked prior to acceptance. Statutory provisions may eliminate the need for express acceptance. Some statutes specify that the offer of dedication is irrevocable.

In some cases, the public right is cancelled by abandonment. Non-use of the dedicated land, or a portion of it, is not necessarily abandonment. It is an important factor which, along with other circumstances, may indicate an abandonment of the land for public use.

If the dedication is accepted, then the land itself, or a right to use the land, belongs to the public, and various incidents of liability for injuries received while on the dedicated land will result. For example, statutes may give injured persons a right to sue public bodies if a street or highway is negligently constructed or maintained.

Most land is transferred by sale. Since many legal problems relate to the marketing of land, the balance of this chapter will deal with this method of acquiring ownership.

SECTION 13.06 THE REAL ESTATE BROKER

(A) FUNCTION

While it is not necessary to hire a broker to assist a seller or buyer, typically, a person desiring to buy land, or desiring to sell land will contact a real estate broker to assist him in finding a buyer or seller. Ordinarily, the broker is hired to bring prospective buyers or sellers to his principal, and is not given the authority to actually sell the land. Sometimes brokers try to find prospective buyers or sellers without any advance agreement as to commissions. More often, there is a listing or exclusive listing made by owners of land with the real estate broker, or similar arrangements made by prospective buyers. Because it is more common for the seller to obtain a real estate broker than it is for the buyer, the discussion will center on the use of the broker by the prospective seller of property.

(B) TYPES OF LISTINGS

Under most listing agreements, the owner of land promises to pay the broker a specified commission if the broker procures a buyer ready, willing, and able to purchase the property. The owner of the property is not obligated to sell to the person making an offer to purchase. Federal, state, or local open occupancy laws may limit this seller's right if the reason for refusing to sell relates to race, religion, or national origin. If the broker does furnish a buyer ready, willing, and able to purchase the listed property at the asking price, in a typical case he has earned his right to the commission. In some listing arrangements, the owner conditions his obligation to pay the fee upon the consummation of a contract of purchase, the actual transfer of title, or upon the receipt of a specified payment.

In the exclusive listing agreement, the owner of the land agrees to use only one agent, rather than list his property with a number of brokers. Multiple listing means an arrangement where several brokers have the right to try to get a purchaser. In such cases, the fee is divided between the broker obtaining the listing, and the one finding the purchaser.

(C) LEGAL PROBLEMS

The problems which arise most frequently with regard to brokers' contracts relate to the one-sidedness of the agreement. In the typical brokerage arrangement, the broker does not promise to do anything. The promise is made by the owner, and, for that reason, the contract is typically classified as "unilateral". If it is unilateral, under older rules it could be revoked by the owner of the property at any time prior to full performance. However, various doctrines have been developed to protect the broker from expending substantial amounts of effort and spending money in performance of the contract only to find that the agreement has been revoked before he has a chance to complete his performance. There have been a substantial number of cases which have adopted the doctrine that if he commences his performance, and expends effort or money, the offer becomes irrevocable. Sometimes brokers try to protect themselves from the possibility of revocation by language in the listing agreement that binds the broker to use his best efforts to secure a buyer ready, willing, and able to buy the property. This is intended to convert the contract into a two-sided contract or a bilateral contract, where both parties to the contract have obligations.

The owner may agree to pay the broker if the broker furnishes a buyer ready, willing and able, but the owner may reserve the right to sell the property himself, without being liable for payment of the broker's commission. The court's determination of whether such an agreement has been made will depend upon the understanding of the parties as manifested by their words, acts, or by their written agreement.

(D) FORMALITIES

In some states agreements by which the owner of land promises to pay a commission if a broker procures a buyer or a renter of the land must be evidenced by a written memorandum. In most categories of transactions required to be evidenced by a sufficient written memorandum, the courts have been astute in finding exceptions which would in effect enforce an oral transaction. In contracts involving brokerage services, courts have generally refused to employ exceptions.

(E) FIDUCIARY RELATIONSHIP

The hiring of a broker creates an agency relationship between the client and the real estate broker, with fiduciary obligations on both sides. This means that the parties have an obligation to disclose pertinent information to one another, not to make profits at the other's expense without the other knowing of any such conflict of interest, and to behave fairly toward one another.

SECTION 13.07 CONTRACTS TO PURCHASE REAL PROPERTY

(A) CONFUSION WITH TERM "LAND CONTRACT"

Most of the principles which have been discussed in Chapter 2, relating to the formation of contracts, apply to contracts for the purchase of land. Contracts to purchase land should be differentiated from what are sometimes called "land contracts." A land contract, which will be discussed later in § 13.12(d), is a written agreement under which the buyer pays specified payments to the seller for a specified, usually lengthy period of time, and the buyer does not receive title until all the payments have been made. In contrast, contracts to purchase land are the first step in the process by which the buyer acquires title and ownership in real property. Usually the buyer comes to an agreement with the seller, and the parties manifest this agreement in writing.

(B) WHEN ARE PARTIES BOUND?

One problem recurs in contracts for the purchase of land. Did the parties intend to wait until a more formal writing is signed before they bound themselves? Ordinarily, the history of a contractual transaction commences with preliminary negotiations. One party puts forth a proposal, and the other party may agree or may make a counter proposal. At some stage, there is general agreement as to the basic terms of the transaction. For example, the parties may agree as to the land that is to be sold, the price, the financing terms, and the date of transfer of possession.

However, there are many other elements to this type of contract which are not likely to be considered by the parties at this stage. These other elements will be agreed upon when the agreement is transformed into a more formal written contract. The type of deed, the allocation between the parties of the risk of loss between the time the contract is formed and the execution of the deed, the furnishing of title insurance, and provisions for the forming of an escrow arrangement are not likely to be discussed at the time the preliminary agreement is reached.

Sometimes the parties may make a notation informally on a piece of paper as to the basic terms to which there has been an agreement. They may, in addition, sign this informal writing. Have they intended to bind themselves by this informal writing, so that neither party can withdraw at his own discretion? Is the informal writing only a tentative agreement, with the binding contract to be formed when both parties have assented to a more formal writing which will contain many of the details which were omitted in the informal writing?

Courts state that the determination of whether the parties are to be bound at the preliminary stage, or to be bound only upon their assent to a more formal document, depends upon the intent of the parties. However, there are other criteria which are often looked at in finding this "intention." Objective criteria are useful if the matter is disputed, since both parties are likely to state that they had contrary intentions. Courts in these cases will look at the complexity of the transaction, the custom in these matters, whether either or both parties had acted in reliance upon the earlier informal agreement, and whether the law provides sufficient guidelines to fill in the gaps which have not yet been resolved.

On the whole, the courts are likely to tip the scales in favor of a finding that the parties did *not* intend to bind themselves until there is assent to a more formal writing. This is because a transaction involving the sale of an interest in real property is usually a serious and important one. It may be better policy to delay binding the parties until they have had an opportunity to examine provisions dealing with the situations not likely to be anticipated at the time the informal agreement is negotiated. This does not mean that it is not possible for the parties to bind themselves at the time of the informal document. If there are relatively standard provisions which apply, and which seem to be accepted by the community, it may be that these standard provisions will fill in the gaps satisfactorily.

(C) AGREEMENTS TO AGREE

Another mutual assent problem which may arise relates to those agreements where the parties have manifested their assent to the major matters, but have stated that as to less important provisions, the parties will agree on them in the future. Frequently courts have stated that agreements to agree are not valid. However, much depends upon the importance of the provisions, and upon whether the agreement can be enforced without agreement on those provisions to which the parties have agreed to agree. Obviously, some provisions are less important than others, and if the major provisions have been agreed to, the fact that a few matters have been left for further agreement should not prevent the formation of the contract. This is especially so if the parties have manifested assent to a fairly complete and formal type of writing.

(D) PROTECTIVE MEASURES FOR BUYER: OPTIONS AND CONTINGENCIES

In the sale of land, the purchaser may not be willing to bind himself before inquiring into financing, costs of construction, the uses to which the property can be made, and other matters. He may, instead of binding himself, wish to obtain an option under which the seller will agree to sell, while the buyer retains the freedom of choice as to whether or not to buy.

Generally, most offers are revocable. This is so even if it is stated that the offer will not be revoked for a specified period of time. In order to make the offer irrevocable, and to create a binding option, it is necessary that the person giving the option—in this case the seller—receive something for the option. Usually this is accomplished by the buyer paying a nominal amount of money, such as one dollar or ten dollars. If this amount of money is actually paid, usually the court will not inquire into the question of whether this nominal amount was bargained for or if this was the total price actually paid for the option. Some options actually are bought for an amount of money which reflects what the option is worth. The payment of the nominal amount, such as one dollar or ten dollars, does not reflect the value of the option, but payment of this amount usually will make the option irrevocable.

The seller may not be willing to grant a one-sided option. If the buyer cannot obtain an option, the buyer may agree to buy the land, subject to being able to obtain financing, of a specified amount and at a specified rate. He might want to condition his obligation upon obtaining a variance from the zoning laws, upon selling his own home, or upon other matters which are important to him and which he wants to occur before he is obligated to purchase the land. Sometimes the buyer's promise is phrased in this way: "I will buy if I obtain financing of 80% of the purchase price for a loan not to exceed 20 years at a rate not to exceed 7½%." In such a situation, some courts might state that the buyer has not made a promise at all, but has made a conditional acceptance. This would mean that neither party is bound to perform. However, it is possible that he has made an absolute promise to perform, but has inserted a number of contingencies in the contract.

Sometimes the occurrence of these contingencies is largely within the control of the purchaser. If the contingency is his selling his own home, he may not try very hard to sell his house if he has second thoughts about the house he has contracted to buy. He may not make attempts to obtain financing if financing is a contingency spelled out in the contract to purchase the land.

Since the occurrence of the conditions is, to a substantial degree, within the buyer's power, some courts have felt that the buyer's control has destroyed the two-sidedness of the contract. They have stated that the seller is bound absolutely to perform, while the buyer can retain the power to determine whether or not he should perform. For this reason, these courts have felt that this has made the contract too one-sided for enforcement. Other courts have implied promises of best efforts, or of good faith, on the part of the buyer to make certain that the conditions occur. They have, in such a situation, found that there is a valid contract because such contingencies are relatively common and because the parties have intended that there be a valid agreement. The presence of contingencies which are substantially within the power of one party may render the contract unenforceable, but the trend is in the direction of holding such contracts enforceable.

Sometimes the seller wishes to protect himself by the use of contingencies. He may not wish to sell his house unless he is able to purchase another house or be admitted to a community for senior citizens. The same principles which have been discussed in connection with protective contingencies for the buyer would apply if the seller obtains this protection.

(E) FORMAL REQUIREMENTS

Contracts or options for the purchase of an interest in land are required to be evidenced by a sufficient memorandum, signed by the party to be charged. This requirement derived from the original Statute of Frauds enacted by the English Parliament in 1677, and adopted in all the United States. If the buyer or seller does not sign a sufficient memorandum, he cannot be made to perform, subject to certain exceptions. For discussion of this problem, see § 2.11.

(F) RISK OF LOSS

Sometimes a substantial period of time must elapse before the title is actually conveyed or possession transferred. Who bears the risk of the loss of the property between the time the contract is made and transfer of either title or possession? Suppose the house burns down during this interim period? Does the buyer still have to pay? Is the seller guilty of a breach of contract, since he will not be able to deliver the premises in the state they were in at the time the contract was made?

Such a matter should be covered in the real estate purchase contract. If it is not, the result will vary from state to state. Most states place the burden of such loss upon the purchaser, even if the seller remained in possession. Some states place the loss upon the seller, even if the purchaser has gone into possession. Some states have adopted the Uniform Vendors and Purchasers Risk Act, which places the risk of loss upon the seller if the title has not been conveyed, or if the purchaser has not gone into possession. There are slight modifications of these rules in other jurisdictions.

The parties should consider this matter at the time the contract is made. If the contract allocates the loss to one party, that party should protect himself against this loss by procuring insurance to cover this risk.

(G) FIXTURES: THINGS ATTACHED TO THE LAND

The owner of land owns not only the soil, but things which are attached to the land. For example, houses, fences, trees, and shrubbery are considered fixtures and part of the land. If these items are severed (removed), they become personal property. The contract to convey the real property does not include the personal property, unless this is expressly provided for. Usually, the test of whether a particular object is a fixture and thus, part of the land, is whether it is fastened to the land in such a way so as not to be able to be removed without substantial injury to the object, to the building, or the land. Plumbing and heating systems are illustrations of items which could not be removed without injury to the systems themselves, or to the building. Items such as an electric stove, connected only by a wire and plugged to an outlet, would not be fixtures.

Sometimes the question revolves around whether the property attached has a particular use. For example, doors, windows, and screens could be detached without any great damage, but clearly the intention is that they be a part of the house and thus, a part of the property.

The issue of whether a particular object is a fixture can, and should be, controlled by the agreement between buyer and seller.

(H) DELAYS

Another problem which occurs with some frequency is the question of delay. Usually, there is a time stated for the transfer of possession, and for the payment of money, as well as for the issuance of the deed. For various reasons, performance may be delayed.

If there is no provision to the contrary in the contract, the results vary, depending on the remedy sought. If the action were for damages, delay would terminate the other party's obligation to perform. If the suit was for specific performance, the court, in the absence of a contract provision to the contrary, would consider that time was not of the essence and, while delay was a breach, it did not terminate the other party's obligation to perform.

Usually, there are provisions in the contract specifying that time is of the essence. However, if there is substantial reliance, or substantial amounts of money paid which would be forfeited unfairly if the innocent party could terminate his obligation due to a late performance by the other party, a court might relieve against the forfeiture and not permit the innocent party to end the contract. States vary, and generalizations are precarious. About the best that can be said is that if the delay is truly minimal, not caused by fault, and if no one is particularly hurt by the delay, the decision should be against forfeiture and ending the contract. Even though late performance *may* not end the contract, the party guilty of unexcused delay will have to pay any damages caused by the delay. In the case of delayed performance by the buyer, interest is usually the measure of recovery; by the seller, it is usually loss of use or rental value.

(I) EFFECT OF DEATH

If one of the parties dies during the negotiations, any offer he may have made is revoked by his death. His personal representative (if he dies without a will) or his executor (if he dies with a will) may be interested in continuing the negotiations. However, this may involve delay in negotiations. The authority to enter into the contract may have to be ultimately approved by the probate court, which administers the estate of the deceased person. The executor or personal representative may ask for court approval in advance to avoid the risk that heirs or persons taking under the will will state that he made a bad bargain. Obtaining court approval can take time.

(J) TYPE OF TITLE PROMISED

Determining who has interests in particular real property can be extremely difficult. While a seller believes he owns the land, he generally is not willing to give absolute assurance that there are no remote interests in the land which may be asserted by third parties and which could create difficulty for the buyer. For this reason, the seller usually obligates himself to give what is called "marketable title". This means a title which is sufficiently free from dispute that it would be customarily accepted by buyers in the community.

Most interests in land are apparent from a careful study of the land records. If there are interests owned by other persons which are apparent from the land records, the seller will "except" those interests from what he promises to convey. For example, the land records may indicate that a public utility has an easement to run utility wires or underground pipes. In such a case the seller will "except" these interests from what he promises to convey. This means that the buyer will take title subject to those prior interests (usually nonpossessory interests) expressed in the land records. Easements have been discussed in § 12.07(a).

(K) IMPLIED WARRANTY: HUMBER v. MORTON

Problems sometimes develop because the buyer, after taking possession, finds defects in the house or terrain. In the area of sale of goods, courts developed the concept of an implied warranty of "fitness" or "merchantability". This meant that sellers were responsible if the goods did not accomplish what the buyer reasonably expected. It was not necessary to show an express warranty.

For various reasons, the concept of implied warranty was not used in sales of real property. One of the reasons was that the deed transferred ownership, and there were strong policies in favor of making the deed final and complete. Not only were warranties not implied in deeds, but courts even held, in many cases, that warranties made in the contract for purchase were "merged" into the deed. This meant that even express warranties were lost, if not contained in the deed.

Also, there was a feeling that the element of reliance was not found in sales of land. The buyer could inspect the premises, and he should not be given judicial protection for matters which he should have found out about himself. The buyer should and could protect himself.

The concept of implied warranty is moving slowly, but unmistakably, into land transactions. In some states, the seller of a new home impliedly warrants that the house is fit for the intended purpose of the buyer. Such a warranty is even more likely if the seller is a tract or subdivision builder. The warranty is not usually implied in the sale of a "used" home.

An illustrative recent case is Humber v. Morton, reproduced at this point.

HUMBER v. MORTON

Supreme Court of Texas, 1968.
426 S.W.2d 554.

NORVELL, JUSTICE. The widow Humber brought suit against Claude Morton, alleging that Morton was in the business of building and selling new houses; that she purchased a house from him which was not suitable for human habitation in that the fireplace and chimney were not properly constructed and because of such defect, the house caught fire and partially burned the first time a fire was lighted in the fireplace. Morton defended upon two grounds: that an independent contractor, Johnny F. Mays, had constructed the fireplace and he, Morton, was not liable for the work done by Mays, and that the doctrine of "caveat emptor" applied to all sales of real estate. . . .

It conclusively appears that defendant Morton was a "builder-vendor." The summary judgment proofs disclose that he was in the business of building or assembling houses designed for dwelling purposes upon land owned by him. He would then sell the completed houses together with the tracts of land upon which they were situated to members of the house-buying public. . . .

. . . we are of the opinion that the courts below erred in holding as a matter of law that Morton was not liable to Mrs. Humber because the doctrine of caveat emptor applied to the sale of a new house by a "builder-vendor" and consequently no implied warranty that the house was fit for human habitation arose from the sale. Accordingly, we reverse the judgments of the courts below and remand the cause to the district court for a conventional trial upon the merits.

Mrs. Humber entered into a contract when she bought the house from Morton in May of 1964 and such house, together with the lot upon which it was situated, was conveyed to her. According to Morton, the only warranty contained in the deed was the warranty of title, i. e. "to warrant and forever defend, all and singular, the said premises unto the said Ernestine Humber, her heirs and assigns, * * *," and that he made no other warranty, written or oral, in connection with the sale. While it is unusual for one to sell a house without saying something good about it, and the statement that no warranty was made smacks of a conclusion, we shall assume that such conversation as may have taken place did not involve anything more than mere sales talk or puffing, and that no express warranties, either oral or written, were involved. However, it is undisputed that Morton built the house and then sold it as a new house. Did he thereby impliedly warrant that such house was constructed in a good workmanlike manner and was suitable for human habitation? We hold that he did. Under such circumstances, the law raises an implied warranty.

. . .

. . . Does the doctrine of caveat emptor apply to the sale of a new house by a builder-vendor?

Originally, the two great systems of jurisprudence applied different doctrines to sales of both real and personal property. The rule of the common law—caveat emptor—was fundamentally based upon the premise that the buyer and seller dealt at arm's length, and that the purchaser had means and opportunity to gain information concerning the subject mattter of the sale which were equal to those of the seller. On the other hand, the civil law doctrine—caveat venditor—was based upon the premise that a sound price calls for a sound article; that when one sells an article, he implies that it has value. . .

Today, the doctrine of caveat emptor as related to sales of personal property has a severely limited application. . . .

The rapid sickening of the caveat emptor doctrine as applied to sales of new houses was exposed by the Miller-Perry-Howe-Weck-Jones-Glisan-Carpenter syndrome.[1] The history of this development is briefly set out in Carpenter v. Donohoe, 154 Colo. 78, 388 P.2d 399 (1964), and in more detail by Professor E. F. Roberts in "The Case of the Unwary Home Buyer: The Housing Merchant Did It," 52 Cornell Law Quarterly 835 (1967). See also, Williston on Contracts (3rd Ed. Jaeger) § 926A, wherein it is said: "It would be much better if this enlightened approach (implied warranty, Jones v. Gatewood, 381 P.2d 158 [Okl.]) were generally adopted with respect to the sale of new houses for it would tend to discourage much of the sloppy work and jerry-building that has become perceptible over the years." 7 Williston (3rd Ed) p. 818; . . .

The Glisan case (Glisan v. Smolenske) 153 Colo. 274, 387 P.2d 260 (1963), was factually similar to the hypothetical example heretofore set out in this opinion. Smolenske had agreed to purchase a house from Glisan while it was under construction. The court propounded and answered the implied warranty question, thusly:

> "Was there an implied warranty that the house, when completed, would be fit for habitation? There is a growing body of law on this question, which, if followed, requires an answer in the affirmative.
>
> "It is the rule that there is an implied warranty where the contract relates to a house which is still in the process of construction, where the vendor's workmen are still on the job, and particularly where completion is not accomplished until the

1. [Ed. note: Footnotes renumbered.] Miller v. Cannon Hill Estates, Ltd., [1931] 1 All E.R. 93 (K.B.); Perry v. Sharon Dev. Co., [1937] 4 All E.R. 390 (C.A.); Hoye v. Century Builders, Inc., 52 Wash.2d 830, 329 P.2d 474 (1958); Weck v. A. M. Sunrise Construction Co., 36 Ill.App.2d 383, 184 N.E.2d 728 (1962); Jones v. Gatewood, 381 P.2d 158 (Okl.1963); Glisan v. Smolenske, 153 Colo. 274, 387 P.2d 260 (1963); and Carpenter v. Donohoe, 154 Colo. 78, 388 P.2d 399 (1964).

house has arrived at the contemplated condition—namely, finished and fit for habitation. . . .

In the next year, 1964, the Colorado Supreme Court in Carpenter v. Donohoe, 154 Colo. 78, 388 P.2d 399, extended the implied warranty rule announced by it in *Glisan* to cover sales of a new house by a builder-vendor. The court said:

> "That a different rule should apply to the purchaser of a house which is near completion than would apply to one who purchases a new house seems incongruous. To say that the former may rely on an implied warranty and the latter cannot is recognizing a distinction without a reasonable basis for it. This is pointedly argued in an excellent article, 'Caveat Emptor in Sales of Realty—Recent Assaults upon the Rule,' by Bearman, 14 Vanderbilt Law Rev. 541 (1960–61.)
>
> "We hold that the implied warranty doctrine is extended to include agreements between builder-vendors and purchasers for the sale of newly constructed buildings, completed at the time of contracting. There is an implied warranty that builder-vendors have complied with the building code of the area in which the structure is located. Where, as here, a home is the subject of sale, there are implied warranties that the home was built in workmanlike manner and is suitable for habitation."

While it is not necessary for us to pass upon a situation in which the vendor-purchaser relationship is absent, the case of Schipper v. Levitt & Sons, 44 N.J. 70, 207 A.2d 314 (1965), is important as much of the reasoning set forth in the opinion is applicable here. The Supreme Court of New Jersey recognized "the need for imposing on builder-vendors an implied obligation of reasonable workmanship and habitability which survives delivery of the deed." This was a case in which a person other than a purchaser had been injured by a defective water heater which had been installed in a new house by Levitt, the builder-vendor. . . . The court placed emphasis upon the close analogy between a defect in a new house and a manufactured chattel. The opinion states:

> "The law should be based on current concepts of what is right and just and the judiciary should be alert to the never-ending need for keeping its common law principles abreast of the times. Ancient distinctions which make no sense in today's society and tend to discredit the law should be readily rejected. . . .
>
> "When a vendee buys a development house from an advertised model, as in a Levitt or in a comparable project, he clearly relies on the skill of the developer and on its implied representation that the house will be erected in reasonably workmanlike manner and will be reasonably fit for habitation. He has no architect or other professional adviser of his own, he has no real competency

to inspect on his own, his actual examination is, in the nature of things, largely superficial, and his opportunity for obtaining meaningful protective changes in the conveyancing documents prepared by the builder vendor is negligible. If there is improper construction such as a defective heating system or a defective ceiling, stairway and the like, the well-being of the vendee and others is seriously endangered and serious injury is foreseeable. The public interest dictates that if such injury does result from the defective construction, its cost should be borne by the responsible developer who created the danger and who is in the better economic position to bear the loss rather than by the injured party who justifiably relied on the developer's skill and implied representation."

In Bethlahmy v. Bechtel, 415 P.2d 698 (Idaho 1966), it appeared that the trial court had rendered judgment in accordance with the 1959 holding of the Supreme Court of Oregon in Steiber v. Palumbo, a much cited case which is relied upon by the defendant here. The specific finding of the trial court was:

> "There are no implied warranties in the sale of real property. Steiber v. Palumbo, 219 Oreg 479, 347 P.2d 978 [78 A.L.R.2d 440] (1959); Annot., 78 ALR2d 446. The sale of this home carried with it absent an express warranty, no promise that the floor would not leak."

The Idaho court was then called upon to deal with the Oregon decision and the later decisions of the Colorado Supreme Court in *Carpenter* and that of the New Jersey Supreme Court in *Schipper*. After a careful review of many decisions, including the Oregon, Colorado and New Jersey cases mentioned, the court said:

> "The Schipper decision is important here because: (1) it illustrates the recent change in the attitude of the courts toward the application of the doctrine of caveat emptor in actions between the builder-vendor and purchaser of newly constructed dwellings; (2) it draws analogy between the present case and the long-accepted application of implied warranty of fitness in sales of personal property; and (3) the opinion had the unanimous approval of the participating justices. * * *
>
> "The foregoing decisions all (except the Hoye case) rendered subsequent to the 1959 Oregon decision, relied upon by the trial court, show the trend of judicial opinion is to invoke the doctrine of implied warranty of fitness in cases involving sales of new houses by the builder. The old rule of caveat emptor does not satisfy the demands of justice in such cases. The purchase of a home is not an everyday transaction for the average family, and in many instances is the most important transaction of a lifetime. To apply the rule of caveat emptor to an inexperienced buyer, and in favor of a builder who is daily engaged in the business of building and selling houses, is manifestly a denial of justice. . . .

If at one time in Texas the rule of caveat emptor had application to the sale of a new house by a vendor-builder, that time is now past. The decisions and legal writings herein referred to afford numerous examples and situations illustrating the harshness and injustice of the rule when applied to the sale of new houses by a builder-vendor,[2] and we need not repeat them here. Obviously, the ordinary purchaser is not in a position to ascertain when there is a defect in a chimney flue, or vent of a heating apparatus, or whether the plumbing work covered by a concrete slab foundation is faulty. It is also highly irrational to make a distinction between the liability of a vendor-builder who employs servants and one who uses independent contractors. . . . The common law is not afflicted with the rigidity of the law of the Medes and the Persians "which altereth not," and as stated in Cardozo in "The Nature of the Judicial Process," pp. 150–151 (quoted in 415 P.2d 698):

> "That court best serves the law which recognizes that the rules of law which grew up in a remote generation may, in the fullness of experience, be found to serve another generation badly, and which discards the old rule when it finds that another rule of law represents what should be according to the established and settled judgment of society, and no considerable property rights have become vested in reliance upon the old rule. * * *"[3]

The caveat emptor rule as applied to new houses is an anachronism patently out of harmony with modern home buying practices. It does a disservice not only to the ordinary prudent purchaser but to the industry itself by lending encouragement to the unscrupulous, fly-by-night operator and purveyor of shoddy work.

The judgments of the courts below are reversed and the cause remanded for trial in accordance with this opinion.

GRIFFIN, J., notes his dissent.

2. In the vendor-builder situation, Professor Roberts seems inclined to agree with Mr. Bumble's estimate of the law and points out that when caveat emptor is retained with regard to the sale of new houses, the law seemingly concerns itself little with a transaction which may and often does involve a purchaser's life savings, yet may afford relief by raising an implied warranty of fitness when one is swindled in the purchase of a two dollar fountain pen. 52 Cornell L.Rev. 835. Similarly, in 111 Solictors' Journal 22, l. c. 25 (London), it is pointed out that, "the purchaser buying a new house with legal assistance is often less well protected legally than the purchaser buying a chattel without legal assistance." It is further urged that, "The legal profession should have made it their business to insure proper protection for the purchaser without waiting for building societies to take the initiative" for their own protection since most builders "try to do a good job (but) the reputation of all may be injuriously affected by the low standards of a few."

3. See, also, Holmes, Collected Legal Papers, p. 187, quoted in 16 Baylor L. Rev. 263, 277, viz.:

"It is revolting to have no better reason for a rule of law than that it was laid down in the time of Henry IV. It is still more revolting if the grounds upon which it was laid down have vanished long since, and the rule persists from blind imitation of the past."

Schipper v. Levitt & Sons, cited in the *Humber* case, involved an action for personal injury by the child of a tenant against the tract developer. In addition to being employed by courts such as the Texas Supreme Court in cases where the buyer sued the seller, it has been instrumental in some jurisdictions where there is no contract between the plaintiff and defendant. See § 30.09.

The Colorado cases cited in *Humber* show judicial lawmaking and the chance aspects of the development of legal doctrines. The *Glisan* case applied the implied warranty concept to a house purchased while under construction. It was easier to apply rules relating to the sale of goods where the work was in progress at the time of the sale. One year later, in the *Carpenter* case, the Court was faced with the sale of a tract home *after* it was completed. Noting that there was no real distinction between the two situations, the Court applied the implied warranty concept. Had the *Glisan* case not preceded *Carpenter* and opened the door, it would have been much harder to find the warranty concept in the *Carpenter* case.

While the tendency has been to find implied warranty in the most recent cases, many jurisdictions have case holdings to the contrary. But it is likely that most of the decisions which are made in the future on this question will hold as did the Court in the *Humber* case.

An interesting expansion of the warranty doctrine in the sale of tract homes occurred in Avner v. Longridge Estates, 272 Cal.App. 695, 77 Cal.Rptr. 633 (1969). In 1960 a developer sold hillside residential lots to individual purchasers. One of the purchasers built a house on his lot and several months later sold it to the plaintiff.

In 1962 and 1965 there was settling in the rear slope of the lot. The plaintiff sued the tract home developer, the soils engineer and the general engineer. The trial court sustained demurrers (a pleading which decides the case without a trial) of the defendants in which the defendants contended that there was no doctrine of implied warranty in the sale of residential lots, and that the action was barred by the Statute of Limitation.

On appeal, the District Court of Appeals held that the demurrer should not have been sustained and the plaintiff should have been given an opportunity to attempt to prove his allegations. In the portion of the opinion dealing with implied warranty and the sale of the lot the court stated:

> Here we have allegations that defendants manufactured the lot by cutting, grading, filling and compacting for the purpose of sale to the public and the construction of a house thereon, knowing that if said work was defective, it would cause damage to any improvements thereon; that the manufacturing process was defective in that it had inadequate provision for drainage, which caused water to accumulate between the fill and bedrock, in that it had organic matter beneath the fill which decomposed, causing the lot pad to settle;

and that it had not been sufficiently compacted, which also caused the lot pad to settle. The alleged defects were not visible or apparent to a purchaser; conceivably they were many feet beneath the surface of the lot pad. Information thereof could have been ascertained by subsurface soil tests and by inspections at the time of filling and grading. Is the purchaser of a manufactured lot under obligation to employ a soils engineer to make expensive and disruptive soil tests?

. . .

[W]e conclude that the manufacturer of a lot may be held strictly liable in tort for damages suffered by the owner as a proximate result of any defects in the manufacturing process.

(L) NEGOTIATION CONDUCT OF SELLER

What happens if the seller deceives the buyer by false promises or statements? What if he makes negligent misrepresentations? Does he have a duty to disclose things which he knows or suspects regarding the property, which could affect the buyer's decision?

The law is in a state of flux on these matters. Traditionally the buyer received little protection. He would be protected from outright fraud, provided he could show he had reasonably relied upon "representations of fact" by the seller. Other than this somewhat limited protection, the rule was *Caveat Emptor* or "Let the Buyer Beware."

Today the courts are taking a more active role in policing the morals of contracting parties, and also in trying to protect the reasonable expectations of the buyer. There are a growing number of cases which have:

1. Less rigidly applied the reliance requirement and other traditional elements of fraud.
2. Imposed liability for negligent misrepresentations.
3. Required the seller to disclose material matters which the buyer is not likely to discover by reasonable efforts. See Kannavos v. Annino, discussed in § 2.08(a).

As in the slowly expanding use of implied warranty, the rules relating to methods of bargaining are changing to favor the buyer's reasonable expectations.

(M) REMEDIES

Because land is regarded as unique, courts will usually grant a request for "specific performance" if the seller, without legal excuse, refuses to go through with the transaction. (As a corollary to this, the seller may be able to obtain a judgment for the purchase price if the buyer is unjustified in refusing to perform.) Specific performance means that the court orders that the seller give a deed to the property to the buyer. Failure to do so would mean that the seller would be in contempt of court, and could be put in jail until he purged himself of this contempt by executing the deed. In some states, the court can execute the deed where the seller refuses to perform. In an action for specific performance, the court will look at the fairness of the transaction, a factor that is not the subject of inquiry where the court is asked to award a money judgment for damages. There are also other requirements for specific performance.

On occasion, it may not be possible or desirable to obtain specific performance. Sometimes the rights of third parties have intervened, and the court will not order that the seller specifically perform his obligation. If the seller refuses to perform, and specific performance is either not asked for or not granted when requested, then the buyer is to be put in the position he would have been in had the seller performed. Usually this means that the buyer is entitled to the benefit of his bargain. He is entitled to the difference between the contract price at the time conveyance should have been made, and the fair market value of the property. If the contract price is $20,000 and he can show that the fair market value is $25,000, then he should receive $5,000 damages. Also, he may be able to recover additional losses caused by the seller's breach, if they are reasonably provable, and if the seller could foresee that these losses would result.

The same measure of damages will apply if the buyer is the one who refuses to perform. The seller is entitled to the benefit of his bargain, or the differences between contract price and market price, plus any other foreseeable expenses or losses resulting from the breach.

Some jurisdictions have held that there are two types of breaches. There are ordinary breaches, and bad faith breaches. Usually, ordinary breaches are caused by the seller being unable to transfer the title that he thought he had when he agreed to sell. There is no moral blameworthiness attached to the seller's nonperformance in such cases. Bad faith breaches occur when the seller refuses to sell for no particularly good reason, or, for example, if he can sell to someone else for more money. In those jurisdictions which divide the breaches in a moral fashion, the buyer could recover benefit-of-the-bargain damages only if he could show that the breach was in bad faith. If he could not show that the breach was in bad faith, he would only be entitled to recover from the seller any out-of-pocket, reliance expenses that he had incurred.

In contracts for purchase of land, the buyer may be required to give a down payment at the time of entering into the contract. Usually this amount is to be applied to the purchase price. Suppose the buyer, without legal justification, refuses to complete the transaction. The buyer may be able to show that the seller was able to sell the land for at least as much as the contract price, and on some occasions, for more. The buyer may try to compel the seller to repay any down payments made which exceed the loss suffered by the seller. For many years, courts routinely refused such requests for restitution. The courts answered the requests by stating that the buyer was himself in default, and he could not come to the court for any judicial assistance.

However, some courts permit the buyer to recover down payments he has made, if the seller has not been injured by the buyer's breach. The results in these cases are justified by the concept of unjust enrichment. It seems unfair for the seller to be able to keep the land, and sometimes even make a profit on resale, and still keep the down payment which has been paid by the buyer. Most courts still permit the seller to retain this deposit, or as it sometimes is called, "earnest money".

SECTION 13.08 ESCROW

In many transactions involving the purchase of real property an escrow arrangement is used. The seller deposits the deed, and any other documents which are ultimately to go to the buyer, with a third party, commonly a title company or a lending institution. The instructions to the third party escrow holder may be to deliver these documents to the buyer when the buyer has delivered to the escrow holder the purchase price (and perhaps has met other conditions agreed to by the parties). The escrow holder acts as a clearance house to insure that the buyer does not have to pay without getting the deed, and that the seller does not have to deliver the deed without being paid. Usually, the escrow holder is a stranger, although it may be possible to use the attorney of one of the parties as the escrow holder.

Escrows are used for a number of reasons. If both parties commence their performance by opening an escrow and making a deposit into the hands of the escrow holder, it is less likely that the deal will fall through. The advance execution of the deed makes it less likely that there will be delay and difficulty if the seller dies, as compared to those situations where the seller does not make out the deed until the purchaser has put up the money. The escrow assures each party that when he performs he takes no risk that the other party may not perform. Escrows are also useful when there are a number of interested parties to the transaction. In many transactions involving the sale of land, there will be a prior lender who will want the debt paid off, and a new lender who is advancing money to the purchaser. A substantial portion of the new loan will be used to pay off the prior lender. A number of mechanical details can be taken care of by escrow holders, especially when the escrow holders are professional escrow companies.

Sometimes problems develop because the escrow instructions, which are frequently on standard printed forms, vary from the provisions found in the agreement by which the land has been purchased and sold. Frequently courts look at all the documents as a whole, to try to find the common intention of the parties. It is advisable to compare the various instructions and the contract for the sale and purchase of land to make sure that they are consistent.

(Escrow arrangements are not necessarily limited to the purchase and sale of real property. It is possible to use an escrow arrangement when making payments to prime contractors, when the payments are partly intended to compensate subcontractors or materialmen for their work or material.)

SECTION 13.09 DEEDS

A deed is the instrument which transfers ownership from the grantor (the maker of the deed) to the grantee (the receiver of the deed). It usually contains the name of the grantor and grantee, the description of the property transferred, and language which indicates an intent to make the transfer. The deed must be in writing, and in some states it must be executed before a notary or before witnesses.

The type of deed will vary from state to state. Essentially there are two basic types. The first is the "warranty" deed. This means that the grantor warrants that he has all the interest in the land that he is granting. In other words, he personally guarantees that he will stand behind what he has promised regarding title. See § 13.07(j) on "marketable title".

The second type of deed is called a "quit claim" deed. This deed indicates that the grantor is transferring whatever interest he may have in the property to the grantee. In some states, a statutory deed called the "grant deed" is used. Under a grant deed, the grantee gets more protection than in a quit claim deed. (Buyers who take such deeds are relying more on title insurance.) See § 13.10.

SECTION 13.10 TITLE ASSURANCE

(A) DEED OF SELLER

When a purchaser of land obtains the deed, he wants to be reasonably certain that he will acquire undisputed ownership of the land, rather than a legal action. He wants the title promised by the seller, which is usually marketable title. He may be concerned with the possibility that someone will assert a claim against the land which he will either have to buy off or litigate. If he obtains a warranty deed, he has a promise by the grantor to stand behind what he promised. If it turns out that the seller does not have the title he promised, then the buyer has an action against the seller for breaching his warranty. However, the seller may be out of the jurisdiction or unable to pay any judgment awarded to the buyer.

(B) CERTIFICATION BY ATTORNEY

The buyer often wants better protection than a potential cause of action against the seller. For this reason, he may require that the seller furnish a summary of all the recorded transactions which pertain to the land. This is called an "abstract". The buyer may ask his attorney to review the abstract to see if the seller has the title that he claims, and to see if there are any encumbrances on the land. This is a system used in smaller communities in the United States.

The principal defect of such a system is that any recovery against the attorney would have to be based upon the attorney's negligence, and this may be difficult to show. Also, even if the attorney were negligent, it may be that the damages caused by his negligent performance are substantially greater than he can pay. Also, the examining attorney does not assume responsibility for the correctness of the abstract which has been compiled by an abstract company. Any action for an improper copying would have to be brought against the abstract company. Also, the abstract is not a reproduction of the original documents on record but is a condensed statement of the key facts in each transfer.

(C) TITLE INSURANCE

For these reasons, much of the title assurance work in larger cities and in many states is handled by the use of title insurance. The title insurance company issues a policy at the time of the transfer which insures the title against certain defects which appear in the land records. The staff employed by the title insurance company will check through the recorded documents pertaining to the property. If they make a mistake, the title insurance company will pay any damages.

Certain defects or "clouds on title" cannot be discovered from a search of the land records. Such title defects usually are not covered by title insurance. However, most buyers are satisfied by the title policy, because such defects are rare.

Title insurance is not absolute insurance. The policy only warrants that an expert company has checked the records and can pay if it makes a mistake. If the buyer wishes to know the scope of his insurance, he should read his title insurance policy.

SECTION 13.11 RECORDING ACTS

A potential purchaser would like to be sure that the person with whom he is dealing owns the property. He would also like to be certain that if he buys the property, he will be protected in the event the seller sells the same property to someone else. For these reasons, most states have passed recording statutes. The recording of a deed does not give any particular validity to the deed itself. As between the grantor and the grantee, recording is not necessary. But recording does assure the grantee that there is a record which potential buyers can check to show that the grantee has received a conveyance of the property. This should protect him from any assertion by a subsequent purchaser that he bought the property from the seller without knowledge that the first purchaser had already acquired ownership of the land.

SECTION 13.12 SECURITY INTERESTS

(A) PURPOSE AND TYPES

Land transactions frequently involve substantial amounts of money. Usually the purchaser is unable to put up cash for the entire purchase price. He will frequently borrow money from a lender or finance through the owner in order to buy the property.

Lenders generally want to be certain that they are repaid. They try to choose borrowers who are good credit risks, and who are likely to pay back the loan. However, lenders want further protection in the event the borrower is unwilling or unable to pay back the debt. The lender usually wants a security interest in the property in the event the borrower should fail to pay in accordance with his promise.

For example, a purchaser who wishes to buy property for $25,000 may only have $5,000 to put down on the property. He may wish to borrow $20,000 from a bank. If the bank will lend him the $20,000, he will usually sign a note for the $20,000, under which he agrees to make specified payments at specified intervals, and he will also give a security interest to the lender. The security interest may be created by a mortgage, or, in some states, by what is called a deed of trust.

(B) OPERATION OF A SECURITY INTEREST

Generally, the buyer (borrower) of the land takes title, and the lender has a security interest in the land. If the borrower does not pay in accordance with his loan obligation, the holder of the security interest has the right to foreclose on the security. In some states, this can be done without judicial participation. Generally, the lender will go to court and ask for a judicial sale of the property. The lender will be paid out of the proceeds of the property, to the extent of the unpaid debt. If the sale does not net enough money to pay off the debt, then a deficiency judgment is awarded by the court to the lender against the borrower. In some states, deficiency judgments are prohibited by law in certain types of lending transactions, and the lender can recover only the amount obtained by the judicial sale.

If the judicial sale nets more than the amount owed to the security holder, then the borrower is entitled to the remainder. Surpluses in such situations are rare. If the land is worth more than the amount owed the lender, the borrower is generally able to find another buyer, or to refinance.

The field of secured transactions is very complicated. Frequently there are many parties contending for the proceeds of the sale, and there are difficult problems of priorities. Sometimes there is a first mortgage and a second, and even a third, mortgage. There may be construction loans on the property, and mechanics' liens and tax liens may be asserted. In such cases, litigation is often necessary to unravel the competing claims.

(C) EQUITY OF REDEMPTION

In the typical mortgage situation, the mortgagor-debtor has an "equity of redemption". The foreclosure sale will not be effective to transfer ownership permanently until a specific period set by statute has elapsed. During this statutory period, the mortgagor-debtor may pay the amount owing, and redeem the property. This means that during the statutory period, the purchaser at a foreclosure sale does not have good title. This can affect the amount the buyer is willing to bid at the foreclosure sale.

(D) LAND CONTRACT

A land contract is a security device which involves the withholding of the transfer of ownership, or the delivery of the deed, until all payments have been made. It may be used when the buyer does not have enough money to make a substantial down payment. There are problems of forfeiture if he pays for a substantial period, and then is unable to continue paying. He may have put into the property more money than the value which he has received by occupying the property. He may have made improvements, and there may be reasons why it would seem unfair for him to forfeit his interest in the land for his failure to make some of the payments. For this reason, a few courts have treated the land contract as a security device, and have required a judicial sale and have given an equity of redemption. In most states, the seller under a land contract can keep payments made, and immediately retake possession.

REVIEW QUESTIONS

1. Who receives the property of a deceased person who dies without a will?

2. Why are there formal requirements for a will, such as witnesses etc.?

3. What is adverse possession?

4. What is a deed?

5. What is the function of a real estate broker in the sale of land?

6. What is an exclusive listing?

7. When is an option irrevocable?

8. What is marketable title?

9. What are the advantages of an escrow?

10. How can a buyer receive title assurance?

QUESTIONS FOR CLASS DISCUSSION

1. Why should a real estate brokerage agreement be unenforceable unless it is evidenced by a sufficient memorandum?

2. Should a seller have a duty to disclose that there has been slide damage? That a neighbor is about to build an addition which will destroy a pleasant view which is presently enjoyed by seller's land?

Chapter 14

USE OF LAND

SECTION 14.01 INTRODUCTION

(A) RELEVANCE

The most important aspect of property ownership relates to its use. To be sure, the right to sell and to give by will or by gift, are important attributes of ownership. However, for design professionals, the most important aspect of property law relates to the limitations upon how property can be used.

Normally, the design professional will know how his client intends to use the land or project which the design professional has been asked to help create. Without some understanding of limitations on the rights of the owner of land, the design professional will not be able to do a satisfactory and efficient job of counseling the client and designing the project.

(B) PRIVATE AND PUBLIC LAND USE CONTROLS COMPARED

Arrangements created primarily by private parties are one important type of land use control. The state plays an important role in such private arrangements. Its courts and laws provide an enforcement machinery and set up rules of form for such private arrangements. Yet the main source of these controls are voluntary arrangements between individuals. Easements and licenses, in § 12.07(a) are an illustration of a private land use control. An easement limits the use an owner of land subject to an easement may make of his own land. Other private arrangements will be discussed in § 14.02(f).

Private land use controls can also encompass those rules created principally by courts faced with the problem of adjusting the competing interests of persons who own land in the same vicinity. Also courts determine the nature of the duty owed by an owner or occupier of land toward those who pass by or enter upon the land. This is another form of land use control.

The primary source of public controls of land use are statutes and ordinances enacted by legislative bodies and rules promulgated by administrative agencies. Courts interpret such controls and apply them to specific fact situations. Also, courts act as a check upon the power of legislatures and administrative agencies in promulgating such controls.

SECTION 14.02 PRIVATE CONTROLS

(A) NUISANCE

The law of nuisance gives a landowner the right to enjoy his land free of unreasonable interference caused by the activities of other landowners in the same vicinity. Stated another way, the law of nuisance regulates the use of land by prohibiting uses which unreasonably interfere with the use of land by others in the same vicinity.

This doctrine seeks to balance the goals of allowing a landowner (landowner as used in this section can include a tenant) to make reasonable use of his land, without depriving landowners in the same vicinity of the reasonable use and enjoyment of their land. To a large degree, the granting of legal protection through nuisance depends upon the activity or use complained of, and the effect such activity or use will have on landowners in the same vicinity.

Looking first from the perspective of the complaining landowner, the type of interference with the reasonable use of his land can take many forms. At one extreme, there can be actual physical damage to his land. For example, blasting activities by his neighbor or the discharge of solid, liquid or gaseous matter on to his land may change the physical characteristics and shape of the complaining landowner's property and seriously affect its use.

The offensive activity may consist of disturbing the comfort and convenience of the complaining landowner. For example, activities on the offending land can result in loud noise or the omission of noxious odors which may disturb the occupants of adjacent or nearby land.

Moving to even more intangible interference, the neighbor's complaint may be based upon simply knowing the nature of the activities on the adjacent or nearby land. For example, a neighbor may have his peace of mind disturbed by the knowledge that an adjacent landowner is using his house for purposes of prostitution or as a meeting place for people whose activities are bizarre or unconventional.

Finally, moving to the outer extreme of intangible interference, one neighbor may be extremely disturbed by the looks of his neighbor's house.

The standard by which the extent of interference is measured is objective. An objective standard looks at whether the acts or activities in question would have disturbed a reasonable person and not at whether the neighbor was subjectively disturbed or deprived of the use and enjoyment of his property.

In determining whether to grant a remedy, the law looks at whether the interference could have been avoided by the person complaining if he had taken reasonable measures. For example, would closing his windows have reduced or eliminated excess noise caused by his neighbor? If so, would such protective measures unduly interfere with the use and enjoyment of his land?

Generally, the more the activity in question causes an actual physical result, such as changing the characteristics or contours of the land or makes a physical impact upon the land, the more likely it is that a court will give some relief to the landowners whose land has been affected in this way. As the interference moves toward more intangible matters, such as peace of mind and aesthetic judgments, the less likely it is that the law will accord protection. While such interests may be protected, it would take more of an interference with the use and enjoyment of the complaining landowner's property before the law will step in.

The likelihood of legal protection may depend upon the extent and duration of the interference. If the interference is temporary, or occurs only at long intervals, the law is less likely to give a remedy to the complaining landowners.

Nuisance does not require that the plaintiff show that the acts or activities in question were intended to interfere with the use and enjoyment of adjacent or nearby landowners. Nor does it require that the conduct in question be negligent. However, the more intentional and more negligent the conduct, the more likely the law will find the activity in question to be a nuisance.

Courts also look at society's interest in the activity being questioned. Certain industries and activities are necessary and are encouraged by society. The necessity for these activities may overcome any minor inconveniences to those in the vicinity. If the activity has very little social value, very slight interference with the use and enjoyment of the adjacent landowner's land can be sufficient.

One case which illustrates how the law must adjust the rights of adjacent landowners is Sans v. Ramsey Golf & Country Club, 29 N.J. 438, 149 A.2d 599 (1959). A landowner who lived adjacent to a golf course complained that the location of certain tees and greens required golfers to walk past his back yard. The conversations between golfers were frequently noisy and sometimes offensive. The court adjusted the rights of the competing landowner by ordering that certain tees and greens be relocated by the golf club in such a way as to eliminate the trek of noisy golfers past the neighbor's back yard.

As to remedy, usually the complaining party seeks a court order (an injunction) by a court of equity which commands that the activity or use cease. To do so, the plaintiff must show that his remedy at law (money damages) would be inadequate. Here, the more intangible the interference, the more difficult it is to establish a monetary value on the interference and the easier it may be to obtain an injunction. Establishing a dollar value on the effect of noise or fumes being emitted from one person's property to another's would be very difficult. Injunctions are obtainable for physical interference if there would be irreparable harm to the land if the activity continued. Finally, if the activity in question is a continuing one, a court is more likely to grant an injunction.

Under certain circumstances, activity of a landowner can constitute a public nuisance. This gives legal right to the public acting through public officials to seek an injunction, or, in some cases, penal sanctions.

It can be seen that much depends upon the character of the neighborhood and locality where the act or use takes place. The determination that acts constitute a nuisance requires a judgment that certain types of activities are inappropriate for certain localities. The regulation of use within specific localities or neighborhoods has taken on a more public character with the enactment of zoning laws. See § 14.03.

(B) SOIL SUPPORT

The excavation done during a construction project can affect the adjacent land. Legal rules have developed regarding the right of an adjacent landowner to have his land remain in the same condition and to have his buildings remain stable. The owner of unimproved land is entitled to the "lateral support" of his land by the land of his adjoining neighbor. He will have a legal remedy if this vertical support is withdrawn by excavation, without regard for whether there is any negligence on the part of the excavating adjacent landowner.

If the affected land has been improved in some way which adds weight to the soil, such as the construction of a building, the excavating neighbor is responsible only if he is negligent. Sometimes the affected landowner can show that the soil support would have been withdrawn by the neighboring excavation, regardless of the added weight to the soil. In such a case, he should be able to recover without having to show that the excavating landowner was negligent.

The excavator's primary concern will be to avoid negligence in his excavating, to use proper shoring methods, to comply with any public controls which relate to excavation (See § 14.03(b)), give notice of the excavation to the other party and to try to work out an advance agreement on the responsibility for damages which may ensue.

Sometimes underlying, or what is called "subjacent," support of the land can be affected. The owner of the land may sell the mining rights beneath the surface, and the possessor of the surface rights will be affected by the withdrawal of underlying support from his land. Usually this is covered in a conveyance by which the owner gives mining rights to another. If there is no provision dealing with this question, the owner of the surface right is entitled to have his land remain in its natural state. If the owner of the mining rights does not conduct his operations in such a way as to respect this right, he will be liable for damages to the land caused by the withdrawal of underlying support.

(C) WATER RIGHTS

The law relating to the ownership and use of water is complicated, and varies greatly from state to state. The rules relating to water in any particular state depend upon the scarcity or abundance of water at the time the legal rules were created. As a result, the rules which apply in the western, more arid, states are likely to be considerably different from those of the eastern states.

Water rights are based upon riparian ownership or upon the doctrine of prior appropriation. Some states use one, some the other, and some states apply a combination of the two.

A riparian owner is one who owns land which borders a natural water course and who has certain rights to use the waters that flow across or past his land. Under usual riparian doctrines, water belongs to the riparian owners and not to the public, except for certain navigable streams or waterways. The property interests have to be adjusted among those riparian owners who have access to the stream or lake from their own land.

The "prior appropriation" doctrine is commonly used in western or semi-arid states. Essentially, the right of prior appropriation means that an individual may acquire a right to divert and take water at certain times and at certain places for particular uses which need not be on or tied to riparian land. Where there is insufficient water to meet the claims of all appropriators, the priority among appropriators is based upon time. The earlier appropriator is favored over the later. This doctrine emphasizes the "public" nature of water, the need for maximum use, and reliance upon existing use.

While today public control over water dominates (See § 14.03 (b)), much of the litigation has involved contests between riparian owners on a natural water course, such as a lake, river or stream. Reasonable use determines the extent of the riparian owner's property right. Use by one riparian owner will have an effect upon the other riparian owners. As long as the use is reasonable, a diminution in quantity or change in the flow of the natural current is permitted. Also, under normal riparian doctrines, uses are divided into natural and artificial. Natural use relates to the existence of man, such as drinking water, household use, and water for cattle or stock. The upper riparian owner can take all the water he needs for these purposes, even if it leaves the lower riparian owner without any water. Artificial uses, such as irrigation (at least in land of reasonable rainfall), power, and propelling machinery can only be used on a reasonable basis, and one owner cannot deprive the other of a proportionate use of the water for this purpose.

An owner can change a water channel on his own land, if he returns the water to the natural channel before it leaves his land, and if it causes no damage to the lower landowner. If the diversion causes the water to miss a lower riparian owner, then the diversion is unreasonable and can result in an action for money damages or for a court order forbidding the diversion.

Pollution is not permitted, since the lower riparian owner is entitled to the same quality of water. A reasonable amount of waste may be dumped into natural water courses. (This is often controlled by special state laws, and by state agencies vested with authority to control pollution.) As for consumption, there may be problems as to priority of use between riparian owners. Courts will look at the purpose of the intended use, the injury to the complaining landowner, the possible use of substitutes, the extent, duration and necessity of the use, and the nature and size of the water course.

Ground water, or what is sometimes called percolating water, is water below the surface of the land. Some early decisions gave the owner of the land above the water absolute control over water use. This was based upon the old property concept that the owner of the land owned everything above the land to the heavens, and below to the center of the earth. This doctrine did not consider the fact that ground water, even though not in any particular physical channel under ground, does flow slowly, and the use of one landowner can materially affect the rights of adjacent landowners.

Some of the jurisdictions which gave what seemed to be absolute rights to the landowner with regard to ground water did hold that his use could not unreasonably damage the interest of other landowners. In these jurisdictions, pollution of the water can be stopped by court order or provide a basis for a money award when pollution causes injury to others.

More commonly, courts recognize the doctrine that right of use, like most property rights, is not absolute and is subject to reasonable controls.

The evolution of the law relating to *surface waters* illustrates the shift from absolute property rights to more relative tort doctrines. These tort rules try to balance interests and to consider the reasonableness of the conduct. The landowner may want to rid his land of excess surface waters. May he do so when his removal or diversion of excess surface waters may damage the property of the adjacent or lower landowner? Design professionals should be aware of drainage difficulties, especially when working on urban projects in areas of uneven contours.

Three different rules developed. These were the "common enemy" doctrine, the "civil law" rule and the rule of "reasonable use." The common enemy doctrine was predicated upon the property rights of the landowner to do what he pleased with his land. Under this rule, the landowner could divert or dispose of surface waters that come upon his land, without regard to the consequences to the adjacent or lower landowners. Adjacent or lower landowners had to protect themselves, or suffer the damage.

The civil law rule went to the other extreme. Under this rule, the lower landowner had a duty to receive naturally collecting waters from upper land in their natural flow. But the civil law rule did impose an *absolute* liability upon the upper owner who altered the amount, direction or concentration of naturally accumulating surface waters in such a way as to damage the lower property.

The reasonable use rule considers all relevant factors to determine whether the action by the party causing the damage was reasonable. If the act was held reasonable, the owner making the diversion or alteration in the flow of surface waters was not liable to the lower or adjacent owner for damage which occurred.

In Keys v. Romley, 64 Cal.2d 396, 412 P.2d 529, 50 Cal.Rptr. 273 (1966), defendant Romley built an ice rink, with a paved parking lot and graded asphalt driveway, on property above a lower lot containing plaintiffs' store. Downspouts along the rink directed rain water to the paved area. The grading and leveling of the defendant's driveway altered the level of the driveway and changed its slope.

In the rainy season, plaintiffs' property was flooded and eroded as a result of surface waters flowing onto it from defendant's land. Plaintiffs tried unsuccessfully to divert the water, first with a ditch and later with a small dam. Defendant subsequently, by agreement, and without making any legal admission of liability, built a cement curb along the boundary line.

The California Court held that the proper rule to apply would be a modified civil law rule which considered the reasonableness of the acts by both parties. Initially, loss would be allocated to whichever of the parties did not act reasonably. If *both* parties had acted reasonably, or both acted unreasonably, the civil law rule would apply and liability would be placed upon the upper landowner who interfered with the natural system of drainage.

The Court stated:

> The issue of reasonableness becomes a question of fact to be determined in each case upon a consideration of all the relavant circumstances, including such factors as the amount of harm caused, the foreseeability of the harm which results, the purpose or motive with which the possessor acted, and all other relevant matter. . . . It is properly a consideration in land development problems whether the utility of the possessor's use of his land outweighs the gravity of the harm which results from his alteration of the flow of surface waters.

While most jurisdictions have adopted either the common enemy or the civil law rule, the most recent decisions have stressed reasonableness. Reasonableness is likely to be the principal factor considered by future decisions when deciding whether to hold an owner liable for damages to other property resulting from alteration of the natural drainage patterns of surface waters.

For a discussion of public aspects of water law, see § 14.03(b).

(D) PARTY WALLS AND EASEMENTS FOR LIGHT, AIR AND VIEW

Legal doctrines relating to party walls and easements for light, air and view are other illustrations of natural rights relating to adjacent landowners. They have been discussed in § 12.07(a).

(E) DUTY OF OWNER OR OCCUPIER OF LAND

Another land use control is the duty owed by an owner or occupier of land to protect those persons who enter upon or pass by the land. Since these rules relate mainly to physical harm, they will be discussed in greater detail in Chapter 30, especially § 30.05. For present purposes, it can be stated that the owner or occupier of land must conduct his activities on the land with due care, and must keep his land in a reasonably safe condition for the protection of most persons who pass by, enter upon, or work on his land. (There is an increasing blending of private and public control in this area because of the increasing number of statutes and ordinances which deal with safety.)

(F) CREATION OF PRIVATE CONTROLS BY AGREEMENT OR ADVERSE USE

Use controls relating to water, drainage, soil support and other uses of one's land may be created by agreement between parties concerned or by "adverse use". For example, the upper landowner may make a written agreement with the lower landowner for the use of the latter's land by the former for drainage purposes. As an illustration of acquisition of such rights by "adverse use", the upper landowner may be able to obtain the right to use the lower landowner's property for drainage purposes if the former has used the latter's land for this purpose without permission, and legal steps to end the unauthorized use are not taken within the time required by the law.

Likewise, adjacent landowners may make agreements creating licenses and easements. See § 12.07(a).

The parties to a transfer of real property, can make agreements or promises as to the future use of the property. As between them, there is usually no question as to the enforceability of these agreements. The problems arise when the original parties transfer their interests in the land which is the subject of the promises. In property law, these promises are called "covenants."

Early in English legal history, the general law relating to the assignability (transferability) of contract rights was not very well developed. For this reason it was necessary for courts to develop the doctrine of "covenants running with the land," in order to bind persons who were not parties to the original covenant.

It was usually held that covenants which ran with the land were those of great importance, and not those of collateral interest to the land. Various tests have been articulated to govern the question of whether the covenants run with the land. Some illustrations of covenants which do run with the land, and are enforceable against persons not a party to the original transfer or lease are:

1. Promises by the tenant to repair, to cultivate, to reside on the leased premises, not to remove fixtures, and to deliver the premises in good condition.
2. Promises by buyers of land to build or maintain a drainage ditch, a dam or a bridge upon the purchased land, or to maintain a fence between the land of buyer and seller.

The important thing to remember about covenants is that the use of land can be restricted by an enforceable covenant which binds persons other than those who made the original agreement. Usually these restrictions are recorded in the land records, and are incorporated in the deed. Before a design professional can commence his work, it must be clear that the particular use is not prohibited by any valid antecedent agreements between prior persons who made a transaction concerning the land in question.

Covenants, as has been mentioned, frequently involve the promise to do, or not to do, a certain physical act. Many promises of this type involve building restrictions. If there is such a covenant, and it is broken by a subsequent purchaser of the land to which the covenant is attached, it is likely that the party injured by this breach of the building restrictions will resort to an action in a court of equity to compel the subsequent purchaser to abide by the building restrictions.

Such limitations became more important as cities grew, and as commercial and industrial uses began to effect the use of purely residential land. To induce expenditures of large sums of money on building residences, there should be some reasonable legal protection which can insure the continued residential characteristic of the particular neighborhood. The doctrine of equitable servitudes was developed in the English courts of equity to meet this need.

The courts developed the principle that where an owner of land enters into a contract that he will use, or not use, land in a particular way, the equity court would order any subsequent purchaser or possessor who purchased with notice of this limitation not to violate the agreement. This was done without regard for whether the covenant was one which could be enforced in an action at law as one running with the land.

This attempt to use private contract and equitable enforcement as methods of preserving or maintaining characteristics of neighborhoods has largely been replaced by public law controls such as zoning.

Suppose land use controls such as zoning are enacted which are more strict or more lenient than existing private land use controls, such as equitable servitudes. It is likely that the equitable servitude will continue to exist if it is more restrictive than the zoning laws. However, if the owner of land subject to the servitude can demonstrate that zoning has changed the character of the neighborhood drastically, the equitable servitude should end because of changed circumstances.

SECTION 14.03 PUBLIC CONTROLS

(A) ZONING: THE BROADWAY, LAGUNA CASE

The law has dealt with the use of property through voluntary contractual arrangements, such as covenants and equitable servitudes, and by tort doctrines such as nuisance and the duty of the owner or occupier of land. In nuisance cases, the courts frequently considered the utility of the use of the offending property, as well as the characteristics of the neighborhood in which it operated.

Early in the Twentieth Century there was a strong movement toward public regulation of land use through zoning. Zoning involved the creation of a master plan regulating the use of land in and around a municipality. The planners set up zones, in which use was limited to residences, commerce, or industry. These categories were frequently broken down into zones which permitted certain types of commercial establishments, while not permitting others. The same breakdown frequently occurred in industrial zones.

Sometimes zoning laws were cumulative. Cumulative zoning would allow only residences in a residential zone, but would permit residences and commercial activities in commercial zones and residential, commercial and industrial activities in industrial zones. Some ordinances were noncumulative. Under such laws, only the particular use was permitted in any given zone. For example, only residences in residential zones, commercial use in commercial zones, and industrial use in industrial zones.

Zoning has a number of objectives. The separation of industry from residences should promote public health and safety, and reduce congestion. Residential districts should be quiet, safe and enjoyable to live in. People should be encouraged to build homes in residential neighborhoods, relying upon the fact that the neighborhood would retain its residential characteristics. Planning, through zoning, should make the most sensible use of property. Whether these goals are being achieved is a matter of great controversy.

Typically, zoning ordinances regulated the use, height, and bulk of structures within these zones. Sometimes "floating zones" were set up. Under floating zones, the boundaries of districts were not set by local ordinance but were to be fixed by amendment by the planning board or city legislative body. Sometimes "contract zoning" was used. City officials would grant a permit on condition that the applicant agree to certain conditions, and post a bond guaranteeing performance. Examples of conditions for a shopping center might relate to open space, nonglare lighting, proper pavement and policed parking areas, as well as a landscaped buffer zone between the shopping center and adjacent homes.

Zones usually cover broad areas. Small zones could result in the zoning being held illegal by a court, because of the classification of the zoning as "spot zoning." Zoning was not to give a small parcel of land a use classification totally different from the surrounding areas.

In some municipalities, zoning has gone beyond use, height, and bulk regulations, and includes aesthetics. Aesthetic zoning is harder to justify from a legal standpoint than the traditional zoning dealing with use, height, and bulk. However, it has been upheld in a significant number of cases. Typical illustrations of aesthetic zoning are ordinances which deal with the use and regulations of commercial signs, elimination of eyesores such as clothes lines, and the preservation of historic structures. Sometimes a structure classified as historic cannot be substantially changed without permission of the municipal governing body. In some cities, planning commissions have established advisory art commissions to give advice on the aesthetics of certain proposed structures.

From the 1930's until relatively recent times, zoning often required that houses in the same area have generally similar characteristics. For example, zoning ordinances might require that houses not exceed one story and that garages all be attached to the house. More recently there is a trend toward avoiding look-alike developments by requiring that no house be similar in appearance to any other house within a given geographical distance. This is to avoid the dull similarity which exists in some types of suburban developments.

Zoning affects land value. In addition, people differ over aesthetics. There have been mechanisms for protecting property owners from being unnecessarily damaged by zoning ordinances. These protections have been the "special use," "variance" and the "nonconforming use." Usually, a zoning ordinance will specify that certain uses can be made of property within a specified zone. Also, the ordinance may specify that certain special uses can be made, if approval is given by the public authorities. A variance gives the property owner permission to use his property for a different purpose than that specified in the zone. To obtain a zoning variance, usually the property owner must show undue hardship or special difficulties, and that the variance will not injure or destroy the characteristics of the neighborhood. Zoning variances have been granted liberally, and many believe that the over-liberal granting of variances has destroyed many zoning plans.

The *Broadway, Laguna* case illustrates variance granting and is reproduced at this point.

BROADWAY, LAGUNA, VALLEJO ASSOCIATION v. BOARD OF PERMIT APPEALS OF THE CITY AND COUNTY OF SAN FRANCISCO

Supreme Court of California, 1967.
66 Cal.2d 767, 427 P.2d 810, 59 Cal.Rptr. 146.

TOBRINER, ASSOCIATE JUSTICE. We must decide whether the San Francisco Board of Permit Appeals exceeded the scope of its authority in granting a variance under the circumstances of this case. That variance rested upon the alleged attractiveness of the proposed building, coupled with the belated discovery of subsoil conditions requiring a more costly foundation than anticipated. We conclude that the approval of a variance on such a basis would undermine the foundation of a comprehensive zoning law.

The controversy before us arose in 1963, when a developer . . . contacted the Zoning Division of the Department of City Planning concerning a proposal to construct an 11-story, 53-unit apartment building on R-4 property located at 2030 Vallejo Street in San Francisco. The zoning division advised the developer that the proposed structure would contravene the floor area ratio regulations, which comprise the primary bulk and density control mechanism of the City Planning Code.[1] The developer nonetheless refused to modify his plans before applying for a building permit in June 1964; in July the zoning division disapproved the developer's application.

Confronted with this obstacle to the execution of his project unless he obtained a variance, the developer undertook a study of subsoil conditions on his Vallejo Street property. Although he commenced the study several months after informing the Department of City Planning that the proposed structure was already designed, the developer, and ultimately the Board of Permit Appeals, relied exclusively upon this study to support the assertion that "unusual subsoil conditions" required a variance from the floor area ratio regulations.

After completing his subsoil investigation, the developer applied for a floor area variance in August 1964. He urged that the "unusual conditions" disclosed by his study would cause unnecessary hardship if the planning code were strictly enforced. He argued further that a variance from the requirements of a "minor" code provision seemed appropriate since his building would possess "attractive features" above and beyond those required by other code provisions.

The variance requested by the developer, however, did *not* involve a relatively unimportant code provision. On the contrary, the

1. [Ed note: Some footnotes renumbered.] The developer's structure contains 80,293 square feet of floor space on a lot containing 14,575 square feet. As the developer concedes in his brief, the resulting ratio of 5.51 square feet of floor area to each square foot of lot area exceeds by approximately 15 percent the maximum authorized ratio of 4.8 to 1.0 in an R-4 zone. (City Planning Code, § 122; Zoning Bull. 63.2.)

consensus among zoning authorities is that, in terms of controlling population density and structural congestion, the technique of restricting the ratio of a building's rentable floor space to the size of the lot on which it is constructed possesses numerous advantages, both theoretical and practical, shared by no other method of controlling building bulk or density.[2] The developer in the present case thus sought more than relief from a purely technical requirement of an insignificant ordinance; he requested instead a variance from a regulation which has become a cornerstone of contemporary building codes.

To protect such crucial provisions from circumvention, the City Planning Code prohibits the granting of a variance unless the appropriate persons, beginning with the zoning administrator, have first determined that five specified conditions have been met.[3] Having concluded that the developer's application complied with *none* of those conditions, the zoning administrator denied the application in October 1964.

Recognizing the need to accord appropriate weight to the expert administrator's ruling, the draftsmen of the City Planning Code provided that his determination could be overcome only by relevant and specific findings by the Board of Permit Appeals.[4] In reversing the zoning administrator's decision in January 1965, the board purported to comply with the planning code by setting forth its findings with respect to all five code conditions. Acting under the mistaken

2. See, e. g., Toll, Zoning for Amenities (1955) 20 Law & Contemp.Prob. 266, 272–275; Comment, Building Size, Shape, and Placement Regulations: Bulk Control Zoning Reexamined (1951) 60 Yale L.J. 506, 514–519. (See also fn. 9, infra.)

3. Section 302(d) of the City Planning Code provides as follows: "The Zoning Administrator shall grant the requested variance in whole or in part if, from the facts presented in connection with the application, or at the public hearing, or determined by investigation, it appears and the Zoning Administrator specifies in his findings the facts which establish: (1) that there are exceptional or extraordinary circumstances or conditions applying to the property involved or to the intended use of the property, that do not apply generally to other property or uses in the same class of district; (2) that owing to such exceptional or extraordinary circumstances the literal enforcement of specified provisions of the Code would result in practical difficulty or unnecessary hardship; (3) that the variance is necessary for the preservation of a substantial property right of the petitioner possessed by other property in the same class of district; (4) that the granting of the variance will not be materially detrimental to the public welfare or materially injurious to the property or improvements in the vicinity; and (5) that the granting of such variance will be in harmony with the general purpose and intent of this Code and will not adversely affect the Master Plan."

4. Section 303(d) provides that, upon the hearing of an appeal from a decision of the zoning administrator, the San Francisco Board of Permit Appeals "may approve, disapprove, or modify the ruling, decision or determination appealed from or, in lieu thereof, make such other additional determination as it shall deem proper in the premises, subject to the same limitations as are placed upon the Zoning Administrator * * *. If the decision of the * * board * * * differs from that of the Zoning Administrator, it shall, in its decision, specify wherein there was error in the interpretation of the provisions of this Code, or abuse of discretion on the part of the Administrator, and shall specify in its findings the facts relied upon in making such determination. * * *"

belief that the board's ultimate conclusion was thereby insulated from judicial review, the trial court deemed itself powerless to grant a writ of mandate to compel the board to set aside its variance order. The petitioner, an association of interested property owners, then instituted this appeal.

Although the San Francisco Board of Permit Appeals possesses broadly discretionary power in passing upon permit and licensing matters, it plays a more narrowly confined role in the variance area. . . . Before granting a variance despite the zoning administrator's denial, the board must specify which aspects of the administrator's ruling it deems erroneous and must set forth in its findings "the facts relied upon in making [its] determination." (City Planning Code, § 303(d).) . . .

. . .

The basic difficulty with the board's findings in the instant case is not that they lack evidentiary support but rather that they lack legal relevance; even if they are assumed to be correct, those findings simply do not meet the requirements of the planning code.

Viewed in the light most favorable to the board and to the developer, the evidence disclosed by the record before us supports the following findings of fact: (1) After the developer had been told that the proposed building would violate the floor area ratio regulations he undertook a study of his property which revealed that unusual subsoil conditions at that location would increase foundation costs for any structure similar to the one he proposed; (2) such increased costs would render the foundation of the proposed building from two and one-half to three times as expensive as the developer had anticipated; (3) because of this unexpectedly high fixed cost, the reduction of rentable floor space in this or any similar building to a level consistent with the floor area ratio regulations would prevent the developer from realizing as high a rate of return as he had hoped to obtain from his investment; and (4) the proposed building, apart from its excessive floor area, would conform to limitations more exacting than those imposed by the planning code with respect to height, lot coverage, number of dwelling units, uncovered areas, and parking facilities. Accepting these findings as true, we have concluded that they fail as a matter of law to satisfy the statutory criteria [5].

1. *Exceptional Circumstances*

The first criterion which a variance application must meet is that there be "exceptional or extraordinary circumstances or conditions applying to the property involved, or to the intended use of the property, that do not apply generally to other property or uses in the same class of district." (City Planning Code, § 302(d).) The board purported to find two such "exceptional circumstances" here: (a) the unusual subsoil condition "applying to the property involved";

5. Since we conclude that the first three criteria have not been met, we do not pause to consider whether the last two have been satisfied. (See fn. 8, infra.)

and (b) the attractive architectural features "applying to * * * the intended use of the property." Neither of these circumstances, however, satisfies the code criterion.

a. *Unusual Subsoil Condition*

We turn first to the subsoil condition belatedly discovered by the developer. On the evidence before it, the board could make no finding, nor did it attempt to make one, linking the subsoil condition to the asserted need for a floor area variance. Unlike cases in which topographical conditions prove to be physicially incompatible with attempted adherence to a zoning provision the case before us presents no logical relationship between the condition identified and the variance requested.

Admittedly, the soil conditions beneath the developer's property restrict its income potential; but the mere fact that a floor area variance would enable the developer to increase the rate of return upon his invested capital can hardly transform the developer's subsoil problem into the sort of "exceptional circumstance" contemplated by the code. In a word, "profit motive is not and (sic) adequate ground for a variance." . . .

We recognize that virtually *any* circumstance which would lead a commercial real estate developer to seek a variance may ultimately be translated into economic terms: the developer attempts to obtain relief from a particular zoning provision in order to augment the earning power or the market value of his property. We must be careful to distinguish, however, between those circumstances which prevent a builder from profitably developing a lot within the strictures of the planning code and those conditions which simply render a complying structure *less profitable than anticipated.* If conditions which merely reduce profit margin were deemed sufficiently "exceptional" to warrant relief from the zoning laws, then all but the least imaginative developers could obtain a variety of variances, and the "public interest in the enforcement of a comprehensive zoning plan" (County of San Diego v. McClurken (1951) 37 Cal.2d 683, 690, 234 P.2d 972, 977) would inevitably yield to the private interest in the maximization of profits.

Keeping in mind this fundamental difference between circumstances which prevent a variance applicant from economically developing his property and those which simply reduce his expected earnings, we note that in the present case the board determined only that the "unusual subsoil condition" would increase the cost of the proposed building or of any similar high-rise structure. The board did not determine, however, that the subsoil condition in question would similarly increase the cost of a differently designed building.

Moreover, even if we were to assume, as did the board, that the developer could properly insist upon constructing an apartment building similar to the one he originally proposed, we would still confront a fatally defective record: The board made no finding in this case that the developer could not earn a *reasonable return* upon his investment after modifying his building to the extent necessary to comply with the floor area regulations, nor would the evidence before the board have supported any such conclusion. . . .

In this connection, we note that in July 1965 the petitioners sought a writ . . . to halt construction of the building pending appeal. The court denied the writ after the developer filed under penalty of perjury a declaration stating that if he were permitted to proceed with construction he would thereafter modify the building "by removing the top floor and two ground level apartments even after construction, to meet floor area ratio requirements of the City Planning Code if [he] should lose the appeal." Thus the developer assured the court that he would make the required modifications if the variance were later held improper. Having implied that he could proceed economically with his project even after altering it to comply with the governing floor area regulations, the developer can hardly claim now that his apartment building will yield an unreasonably low profit unless he is permitted to spread his foundation costs over a rentable floor area beyond that permitted by the code. At most, the developer may urge a reduction in expected revenue; as we have explained, however, such a claim does not rise to the "exceptional" level demanded by the code.

b. *Attractive Architectural Features*

Nor do the various architectural limitations incorporated in the developer's proposed structure constitute "extraordinary * * * conditions applying to * * * the intended *use* of the property" (italics added) within the meaning of the first variance criterion.

First, the concept of "intended use of the property" does not encompass the contemplated *design* of a building to be constructed on that property but refers only to the *activity* which is to be conducted there.[6] Second, an "intended use" does not constitute an "exceptional circumstance" unless it does not "apply generally to other * * * uses in the same class of district." In this regard, the board found only that the developer proposed "to build according to development standards which are more restrictive * * * than are the provisions of the Code themselves." The board then drew the conclusion that "[t]herefore, [the developer's] intended use of the property is unique and constitutes an exceptional circumstance." That conclusion was of course a non sequitur. The board made no finding, nor could it have done so on the evidence before it,[7] that *other* buildings in the same zone were not *likewise* built "according to development

6. A broader construction of "intended use" might bring the code provision into conflict with state law, since Government Code section 65906 authorizes variances "only when, because of special circumstances applicable to the property, including size, shape, topography, location or surroundings, the strict application of the zoning ordinance deprive such property of privileges enjoyed by other property in the vicinity and under identical zoning classification." . . .

7. The zoning administrator supplied the Board of Permit Appeals with evidence that most buildings in San Francisco, as in other cities, are designed well above planning code minimums.

standards * * * more restrictive * * * than * * * the provisions of the Code themselves."

2. *Unnecessary Hardship*

Even if the circumstances identified by the board could qualify under the first criterion, however, the variance should still have been denied since the developer did not show that, as a result of such circumstances, "literal enforcement of [the floor area ratio regulations] would result in practical difficulty or unnecessary hardship." (City Planning Code, § 302(d).) The board found: (a) that, since the building would benefit the community, enforcement of the code would work a hardship upon the surrounding neighborhood; (b) that the developer's adoption of "superior to code" building standards would impose a hardship upon him if the variance were denied; and (c) that "the subsoil condition obviously constitutes a practical difficulty for development."

a. *Benefit to the Community*

With regard to the community benefit, the board's finding was neither relevant as a matter of law nor supportable as a matter of fact. Although impact upon the surrounding neighborhood is an important factor in the variance formula, the planning code specifically provides for its consideration under the fourth and fifth criteria.[8] In requiring a showing that literal enforcement would cause hardship, the second criterion looks only to burdens upon the variance applicant.

Even if it had been legally relevant, however, the board's determination that the community would suffer if the floor area regulations were literally enforced would find no support whatever in the evidence. Accepting as true the board's finding that the "attractive features" of the developer's building would benefit the neighborhood, it does not follow that the community would sacrifice such benefits if the code were strictly enforced. Nothing in the record suggests that if his variance application should be denied the developer would forego his project or eliminate any of its beneficial features; indeed, the developer has indicated the contrary under penalty of perjury. Although a denial of a variance would cut into the developer's profit margin, the community derives benefit not from his financial gain but from his conforming building.

8. See footnote 3, supra. Indeed, in determining that the fourth and fifth criteria were met, the board expressly found that the granting of the variance would neither injure the community nor conflict with the "master plan" since the proposed building would in various ways "improve all the property in the vicinity" and "protect and enhance the character and stability of this prime residential area." We intimate no view on the extent to which the records supports these conclusions (see fn. 5, supra); we note the board's findings only to stress the fact that, in weighing the building's impact upon the community under the second criterion, the board sought to count the same factors twice. If its approach were permissible, the second criterion would ordinarily prove superfluous, since any variance application meeting the fourth and fifth would automatically meet the second. We are unwilling to eradicate an apparently significant portion of the planning code by accepting the board's argument.

b. *Superior Building Standards*

Turning to the board's inclusion of the developer's adoption of superior building standards as an element of hardship upon the developer, we need only note that such self-imposed burdens cannot legally justify the granting of a variance. . . .

c. *Practical Difficulty*

All that remains of the board's findings with regard to hardship is its observation that "the subsoil condition obviously constitutes a practical difficulty for development." But the only such "difficulty" supportable on this record must stem from the developer's claim of increased foundation cost. In this connection, the board simply concluded that *any* economic sacrifice flowing from enforcement of the floor area regulations should be deemed "unnecessary" in this case because the proposed building would more than comply with all *other* requirements pertinent to bulk and dimension. In reaching this conclusion, the board asserted that the floor area regulations merely duplicate those governing such factors as height, lot coverage, number of units, and open space. Apart from its shallowness,[9] the board's approach rests upon an impermissible assumption: that the draftsmen engaged in an idle act when they added the floor area ratio regulations as independent requirements of the planning code.

The board's characterization of any resulting difficulty or hardship as *automatically* "unnecessary" in this case must stand or fall with the broad notion that a variance applicant may earn immunity from one code provision merely by overcompliance with others. Since few buildings are designed at planning code minimums,[10]

9. Although the board referred to the floor area ratio regulations as "superfluous" and "hypertechnical," zoning authorities consider these regulations uniquely valuable. (See fn. 2, supra.) To suggest but one example of their utility, a builder who has complied with the applicable height limits, as has the developer in this case, might still evade controls on population and congestion by leaving little space between floors or by devoting relatively little room for storage and lobby areas; the planning code seeks to prevent such evasion by restricting not only the gross dimensions of a building but also the ratio of its inhabitable floor space to the area of the underlying lot.

Moreover, even if the bulk, congestion, and density objectives of floor area regulation appear to be satisfied by a design which limits size and population through self-imposed restraints on such features as height and number of dwelling units, the code's independent limitation upon floor area ratio reflects basic policy decisions which bind administrative agencies and courts alike. It has been noted, for example, that restrictions upon the *number* of dwelling units per unit of land area encourage building for large or affluent families to the exclusion of quarters for individuals, couples, or families with small means. (See, e. g., Citizens' Housing Council, Densities in New York City (1944) 21.) Floor area ratio regulations, on the other hand, are advantageous in that they permit the construction of smaller and less expensive apartment units. (Id., at pp. 21–22.) Similarly, an emphasis upon limiting *height* in order to control bulk encourages the unfortunate use of lower ceilings, whereas stressing the floor area ratio permits architects to set ceilings at optimum heights. (See, Comment, op. cit. supra, 60 Yale L.J. 506, 519.)

10. See footnote 7, supra.

variance applications based upon this open-ended theory would soon become commonplace. The board would then be empowered to decide which code provisions to enforce in any given case; that power does not properly repose in any administrative tribunal.[11]

. . .

Although a variance must be denied unless all five of the specified code conditions have been independently fulfilled, the board's findings in the present case fail to establish compliance with the first three of those conditions; the board's decision to grant a variance therefore exceeded its statutory authority.

The variance sought by the developer in this case would confer not parity but privilege; to sanction such special treatment would seriously undermine present efforts to combat urban blight and municipal congestion through comprehensive zoning codes. So selective an application of the provisions of the City Planning Code would destroy the uniformity of the zoning laws which is their essence.

The judgment is reversed and the cause is remanded to the trial court with directions to issue a writ of mandate requiring the board to vacate its order awarding a variance and to affirm the zoning administrator's original decision denying that variance, and with additional directions to the trial court to grant such further relief as is appropriate.

McComb, Justice. [dissented]

11. Discretionary power to disregard a basic planning code regulation whenever the board believes that the objectives of that regulation have been fulfilled in a particular building would probably prove impossible to control and might well undermine the entire zoning plan. We recognize that some authorities urge a compensatory application of the zoning laws, but if a "merit" or "bonus" system should be created in order to reflect the interrelationship among the objectives of various code sections, its adoption must await action by the municipal legislature. Only a detailed set of published guidelines can assure, for example, that the appropriate quantity of bonus floor area is assigned to each specific combination of other building features, and that the resulting system is uniformly and evenhandedly applied. (See San Francisco Downtown Zoning Study, Final Rpt., December 1966, pp. 21–29.)

It has been necessary to protect property owners who have used their property in a certain way before the enactment of zoning laws. This has resulted in the granting of "nonconforming uses", which permit a property owner to continue to use his property as he used it before the enactment of the zoning ordinance. Some ordinances have provided for a phasing out of nonconforming uses, while others have permitted nonconforming uses to continue. One of the reasons nonconforming uses frequently do continue is that the nonconforming user often has a monopoly in a neighborhood and has no particular desire to give it up. The liberality with which zoning officials have granted nonconforming uses has also resulted in criticism, because of the patchwork effect of planning caused by variances and nonconforming uses.

Zoning has been criticized by some as stifling creativity, and as a tool for the exclusion of undesirable persons from a particular neighborhood. Limitations on lot size hamper the building of less expensive structures. Also, certain types of activities have been looked upon with some fear by persons in the neighborhood. For this reason, ordinances have at various times excluded mobile homes, apartments, and motels from certain areas. As a particular use becomes more accepted, the restrictions are likely to disappear. However, at the outset, it may be difficult for new uses to be allowed in established neighborhoods.

The procedures under which zoning laws are enacted and administered are different than most laws. The recent movements in statutes have been toward centralization of government and greater legal control at federal and state levels. However, most zoning ordinances are local in origin and administration.

Local control is based upon the supposition that those who live in the areas directly affected by land use controls should have the major voice in determining the extent of these controls.

Generally, a legislature will pass enabling laws, which give powers to the municipalities to enact zoning ordinances and to administer them. The municipalities have generally accepted this power, and enacted zoning ordinances. Frequently, the local legislative body, such as a city council or board of supervisors or trustees, appoints a planning commission to pass upon master plans, rezoning, and zoning matters generally. The planning commission may consist of citizens who have backgrounds which should be helpful to them in city planning. They are, as a rule, not professional planners, but sometimes are assisted by planners employed by the city. However, the final decisions are usually made by the city council.

Usually cities have boards of zoning appeal. These are bodies which pass upon the granting of variances applied for by property owners.

Frequently the ordinances or statutes provide for a more direct popular control over public planning than in other areas of law. Often decisions by city authorities can be reversed if there is a petition submitted by citizens or property owners affected by the change or act of the city legislative body.

The courts have played a relatively minor role in zoning. At first, they were called upon to pass upon the constitutionality of zoning ordinances. Zoning ordinances were usually sustained. Some ordinances have been held unconstitutional for one reason or another, but on the whole the courts have stayed out of zoning.

There does appear to be a slight trend in some jurisdictions toward increased judicial control over zoning laws and administration. This may be due to the realization of the tremendous economic power in public land use controls. Much of the value of land is based upon how it can be used. Zoning can be a tool for graft, and for eliminating potential business competition. All of these may be reasons for the courts taking a more careful look to prevent zoning being used for undesirable purposes.

The *Broadway, Laguna* case, reproduced earlier in this section, illustrates this modest trend. Another case which also shows increased judicial review of zoning is Udell v. Haas, 21 N.Y.2d 463, 235 N.E.2d 897, 288 N.Y.S.2d 888 (1968). The principal issue in this case involved the validity of a building zone ordinance which reclassified a landowner's property from business to residential. The new classification would have permitted only public and religious buildings, and residences with a designated minimum size. Evidently, the event which led to the rezoning was the submission to the local authorities of a preliminary sketch for the development of a bowling alley and a supermarket or a discount house to be built on a vacant parcel that had been zoned for business use. The economic effect zoning can have on property value is demonstrated by the observation made by the New York court that more than 60% of the value of the land, or $260,000, was wiped out by the zoning change.

The New York Court of Appeals noted that a zoning ordinance to be valid must be enacted in conformity with a well-considered or comprehensive plan. It may be useful to read the portion of the court's opinion dealing with this requirement. The Court stated:

> Zoning is not just an expansion of the common law of nuisance. It seeks to achieve much more than the removal of obnoxious gases and unsightly uses. Underlying the entire concept of zoning is the assumption that zoning can be a vital tool for maintaining a civilized form of existence only if we employ the insights and the learning of the philosopher, the city planner, the economist, the sociologist, the public health expert and all the other professions concerned with urban problems.
>
> This fundamental conception of zoning has been present from its inception. The almost universal statutory requirement that zoning conform to a "well-considered plan" or "comprehensive plan" is a reflection of that view. . . . The thought behind the requirement is that consideration must be given to the needs of the community as a whole. In exercising their zoning powers, the local authorities must act for the benefit of the community as a whole following a calm and deliberate consideration of the alternatives, and not because of the whims of either an articulate minority or even majority of the community. . . . Thus, the mandate of the Village Law (§ 177) is not a mere technicality which serves only as an obstacle course for public officials to overcome in carrying out their duties. Rather, the comprehensive plan is the essence of zoning. Without it, there can be no rational allocation of land use. It is the insurance that the public welfare is being served and that zoning does not become nothing more than just a Gallup poll.

> Moreover, the "comprehensive plan" protects the landowner from arbitrary restrictions on the use of his property which can result from the pressures which outraged voters can bring to bear on public officials. "With the heavy presumption of constitutional validity that attaches to legislation purportedly under the police power, and the difficulty in judicially applying a 'reasonableness' standard, there is danger that zoning, considered as a self-contained activity rather than as a means to a broader end, may tyrannize individual property owners. Exercise of the legislative power to zone should be governed by rules and standards as clearly defined as possible, so that it cannot operate in an arbitrary and discriminatory fashion, and will actually be directed to the health, safety, welfare and morals of the community. The more clarity and specificity required in the articulation of the premises upon which a particular zoning regulation is based, the more effectively will courts be able to review the regulation, declaring it ultra vires if it is not in reality 'in accordance with a comprehensive plan.'" (Haar "In Accordance With a Comprehensive Plan", 68 Harv.L.Rev. 1154, 1157–1158.)
>
> As Professor Haar points out, zoning may easily degenerate into a talismanic word, like the "police power", to excuse all sorts of arbitrary infringements on the property rights of the landowner. To assure that this does not happen, our courts must require local zoning authorities to pay more than mock obeisance to the statutory mandate that zoning be "in accordance with a comprehensive plan". There must be some showing that the change does not conflict with the community's basic scheme for land use.

The Court held that the rezoning (which it characterized as a "race to the statute books") was not in accord with the comprehensive zoning plan and therefore invalid.

It is not uncommon for zoning ordinances to be changed after an election. This has meant that commercial enterprises and property owners may be reluctant to rely upon decisions of zoning authorities, for fear that these decisions will be changed after expenditures of money are made in reliance upon the decisions. Sometimes relief can be given to enterprisers and property owners who rely upon zoning decisions by way of making these decisions less vulnerable to attack. However, the fear of potential corruption and the strong elements of local control have made certainty and predictability in zoning difficult.

From the standpoint of the design professional, there are a number of important aspects of zoning. First, projects usually are cancelled if zoning precludes the planned project use and design. The design professional should have a clear, written understanding which covers his right to be paid if the project is abandoned for this reason. Second, the private design professional and his client should agree in advance on whether the design professional will assist the client in appearances before zoning authorities, and whether this work is an extra service not covered by the basic fee. Third, design professionals must realize that zoning ordinances do exist, and that these ordinances must be complied with in design. Obviously, the design professional must know where the structure is to be located, the limitations in the ordinance which may regulate the use of the structure, the setback lines, off-street parking facilities, height limitations, and any other regulations which affect the design aspects of the structure. Fourth, design professionals, as leaders in planning and aesthetic development and control of environment, should be aware of the problems and policies involved in zoning. Many design professionals will be called upon to advise or administer zoning laws. They must realize the strong powers they possess, and be prepared for the heated citizen reaction to decisions which affect property values and aesthetic ideas.

(B) OTHER CONTROLS

States frequently pass laws dealing with the dividing of tracts of land into smaller tracts for sale. In order to subdivide, the developer must submit a subdivision map, and receive approval of the subdivision plan by a local authority. The purposes of such laws are to secure uniform and harmonious growth of urban areas. Frequently, the laws require that the lots be of a certain minimum area, that a specified portion of the subdivision be set aside for parks and recreational facilities, and that future space be reserved for recreation uses and for open space. The street plan must be approved in advance, as well as arrangements for connection of public utility services. Frequently, fee payments are required for approval. Often subdividers are required to furnish surety bonds to assure that subcontractors and materialmen will be paid for their work. Also, performance bonds may be required to ensure that the subdivider will comply with any assurances that he has given to the local authorities.

Building codes are rules which control design, materials and methods of construction, with the object of protecting public health and safety. Special industrial regulations exist in most states for the protection of workers on construction projects. State and local regulations often control excavation. Water rights often depend upon state-issued permits, and upon drainage and pollution controls. Industrial use is often regulated by smog controls.

"Open occupancy laws" are a form of land use control. The increased concentration of members of certain minority groups in certain parts of a city has led to the ghettoization of many larger cities. Traditionally, the law permitted a property owner to sell or rent as he chose. But it is unlikely that ghettos will be broken down without positive action by federal, state and local governments. There is an increasing tendency toward federal, state or local laws which prohibit discrimination in the sale or rental of certain types of property. Some federally assisted projects require that there be no discrimination by the developers in the sale or occupancy of the residential units.

The proliferation of public land use controls plays a large part in the professional life of the design professional. These controls often determine design, materials, and methods of construction, as well as project use.

REVIEW QUESTIONS

1. From a legal standpoint, what is a nuisance?

2. Can the nuisance doctrine be applied even if the defendant did not intend to harm his neighbor, and has acted with due care?

3. When can an excavator be held responsible for subsidence of adjacent land?

4. What are riparian water rights?

5. What is the difference between the common enemy and civil law rules relating to surface waters?

6. How do covenants running with the land and equitable servitudes affect design?

7. Do courts exercise broad review over zoning matters?

8. How do subdivision laws affect the planning of the subdivision?

9. What are illustrations of public land use controls?

QUESTIONS FOR CLASS DISCUSSION

1. Application of the nuisance doctrine by courts has been called judicial zoning. Why? Should courts apply the nuisance doctrine where there is comprehensive zoning? Give your reasons.

2. Should there be open occupancy laws? Explain.

3. Do you think that increasing governmental control of design through building codes, zoning, subdivision laws, etc., will stifle creative design?

4. Should courts exercise a greater check upon local agencies who regulate the environment?

5. What are the dangers of comprehensive building codes? How can these dangers be minimized or avoided?

PROBLEM

A owns a house in the residential area of a large city. He is a writer who works late at night and cannot work when there is loud noise. B is his neighbor. B's children are 20, 16, and 14. They have a music group that plays rock music for dances. They practice late at night, often past midnight. Their music is loud, and clearly audible to A in his study. Not only is the music loud, but A despises the type of music they play. A has gone to court for an order prohibiting the group from playing their music. What ruling would you make if you were the judge? Why? What additional facts would be helpful in making your decision?

Part IV

THE CONSTRUCTION PROCESS

Introduction

Part IV centers upon project construction. Chapter 15 provides an overview of the law's role in the construction process. It emphasizes the many conflicting interests that have to be accommodated and the high likelihood of disputes which often are resolved by litigation. Chapter 16 examines types of construction contracts, while Chapter 17 deals with the selection of a contractor and the competitive bidding process. Chapter 18 discusses the role played by surety bonds in construction.

Chapters 19 and 20 deal with contract interpretation, one of the most difficult problems in the construction process. The construction documents are many and complex. There is a high probability of conflict. Also, the construction project is a complicated production with problems developing as the work proceeds. Finally, the legal controls on the construction process are significant and growing. All of these factors mean that the determination of whether a contractor has performed in accordance with his obligation is often very difficult.

Chapter 21 treats the troublesome question of changes during a construction project. Because of the complexity of a construction project, changes are common. Contractors complain that changes increase their costs, and owners and design professionals are reluctant to grant deserved price increases. Owners and their design professionals contend that changes can be a method by which some contractors make up for a deliberately low bid, by claiming every direction given during construction constitutes a "change" for which they are entitled to extra pay.

Chapter 22 deals with the recurring question of unforeseen subsurface conditions, while Chapter 23 deals with delay.

Chapter 24 treats the problems of payment. To the contractor, payment is the objective he seeks when he performs a construction project. The owner is concerned with when, and how much, he must pay. In addition, payments affect subcontractors, suppliers, lenders and surety bond companies. Finally, payments are often conditioned upon a certificate being issued by the design professional.

Chapter 25 deals with administrative problems that frequently arise during the process of construction, relating to authority and communication. Chapter 26 deals with contract termination, and Chapter 27 looks at the role of the design professional in contract interpretation and disputes. Such material could have been included in Part II, dealing with the design professional-client relationship, but it is more germane to the construction process, since it is in this setting that this function typically arises. Chapter 28 treats dispute resolution, with emphasis upon the arbitration process. Arbitration is also discussed in Chapter 39. However, in Chapter 39 the emphasis is upon the design professional as an arbitrator, while in Chapter 28 attention is directed largely to an overview of the arbitral process.

Chapter 29 treats judicial measures of recovery for contract breach with illustrations taken from the construction contract. (Chapter 11 treated the same problem but from the standpoint of the architect-client relationship.)

Chapter 30 deals with the way the law distributes and allocates losses which result during the process of construction or as the result of construction. Because of the many legal doctrines which play a role in distributing losses, Chapter 30 reviews tort law, with special emphasis upon the duty of the owner or occupier of land, misrepresentation and manufacturer's liability and other legal doctrines which relate to the distribution of losses. Because many injuries occur to workers, there will be some discussion of workmen's compensation law and its effect on employee injuries. Finally, Chapter 30 treats the increasingly important legal doctrine of indemnification and the role played by contract in the allocation of these losses.

Chapter 15

LAW AND THE CONSTRUCTION PROCESS

SECTION 15.01 THE ROLE OF LAW

This treatise deals primarily with the effect of the law upon the professional life of architect and engineer. Law encompasses the substantive and procedural rules created by legislative bodies, administrative agencies, and courts. Courts, and to a lesser degree, administrative agencies, also apply these rules to particular disputes and grant legal remedies.

In most litigated disputes between private parties, the plaintiff claims that he has suffered a loss and asks that the court transfer that loss to one or a number of defendants. The defendant or defendants often deny responsibility and may claim that they too have suffered a loss, and ask that the law transfer that loss to other defendants or perhaps the plaintiff. In deciding such cases, courts will determine the facts and apply the law to determine who will bear the loss, or, put another way, who has legal responsibility for the loss.

There may be physical harm to persons traceable to design or construction methods. For example, passers-by, visitors to the site, construction workers or subsequent occupants of the building may be injured or killed. Property may be damaged or destroyed. For example, the project may be destroyed by a catastrophic natural event or by fire. Adjacent land may subside during excavation. Faulty materials or workmanship may cause physical damage to the project itself. Pecuniary loss may occur. For example, the project may be finished late, persons may not get paid for their work, construction costs may soar because of unforeseen events, or tenants may complain when the air conditioning malfunctions.

When losses occur, the law is often asked to determine who will ultimately bear the loss. If the plaintiff loses, either the court has decided that he has not proved that he has suffered a legally recognizable loss, or that he must bear the loss himself. If the plaintiff wins, the court has shifted the loss to one or a number of defendants. Also, the court may have to decide which defendant or defendants will have to bear the loss suffered.

Contract law plays a significant role within this framework. Contract is a form of private lawmaking, under which the law gives contracting parties reasonably wide latitude to make their own rules.

To obtain this private lawmaking power, contracting parties must comply with the legal requirements for an enforceable contract. In Chapter 2, these requirements were discussed in some detail.

Mainly, they consist of manifestations of assent, consideration, proper form, contracting capacity and a lawful purpose.

Where there is litigation, the court determines whether these requirements have been met. Also, courts often are called upon to interpret the terms of a contract, to fill in contractual gaps, to determine whether a proper performance has been rendered, to decide whether performance has been excused and to select an appropriate remedy.

Even though most construction disputes are not brought to court, the presence of a potential judicial remedy is important. First, it may be a powerful sanction in obtaining promised performance. Second, parties are more likely to continue performing if they feel assured that ultimately their rights will be vindicated, if necessary, by the legal machinery of the state.

Finally, the law provides an interesting parallel which is useful in understanding the construction process. Just as the law provides rules for determining responsibility and sanctions for violation of those rules, a well-organized construction project has rules which allocate the responsibilities of the participating parties and provides methods for adjudicating disputes which arise. The former problem is treated throughout Part IV with special emphasis in Chapters 19 and 20. The latter problem is treated in Chapters 27 and 28.

SECTION 15.02 HIGH PROBABILITY OF DISPUTES AND LITIGATION

(A) PARTICIPANTS IN THE PROCESS

The owner in a construction project often is unsophisticated and unskilled in construction work. For him, the construction project is an unusual and important venture. He may be building a new residence, or investing his money in an office building.

There are some professional owners who frequently engage in construction work. State highway departments or large tract home developers are not unsophisticated and inexperienced owners.

Almost all owners have problems of finances and capital. Public agencies are frequently limited by appropriations and by bond issues. Corporate owners often are limited by their capital structure, and by the amount allocated to the construction project. Private owners building residences are often limited to the money they have available, and the money they can secure by financing. Some owners, such as subdevelopers and tract home builders, operate their venture on a limited amount of capital. Although costs are of paramount importance to owners, some owners engage in construction projects without financing adequate to cover the risks of unforeseen events or of problems which can increase the ultimate cost of the project.

The volatility of the construction industry adds to the high probability of construction project disputes. Because the fixed price or lump-sum contract is so common, a few bad bids can mean financial disaster. Contractors are often undercapitalized. They do not have adequate financial resource or equipment when they enter into the project. They spread what capital they have over a number of projects. They expect to construct the project with finances furnished by the owner (and occasionally from owners on other projects), through progress payments, or through loans obtained from lending institutions.

Labor problems are difficult for contractors. Many of the trade unions have restrictive labor practices that, to a substantial degree, control construction methods. Sometimes laborers are pulled off a job at the request of the labor unions. Sometimes the contractors themselves allocate a large share of their labor to projects which may have a higher probability of financial success, or where there is a crisis.

The construction industry also has large numbers of contractors who do not have the technological skills necessary for a successful construction project. Often the technological skill, if there is any, rests with a few key employees or officers. The skill is often spread thinly over a number of projects, and can be effectively diminished by the departure of key employees or officers for better paying jobs.

The construction industry has attracted some contractors of questionable integrity and honesty. There are contractors who will not hesitate to try to avoid their contractual obligations, and to conceal inefficient or defective performance. These contractors are skillful at diverting funds intended for one project to a different project. They are also skilled at fending off their creditors with promises that the creditors will be paid out of the proceeds of large claims which they have against the owners of certain construction projects.

It is not surprising that construction project disputes are common.

(B) THE CONSTRUCTION CONTRACT

Building a construction project is a complicated undertaking. Hopefully, the construction documents with plans and specifications will be clear and complete. At their best, they should give a good indication of the contractor's duties. Unfortunately, even the most skillful design professionals cannot do a perfect job in setting forth within the construction documents the complete construction obligations. Many of the small details may be in the mind of the design professional and not expressed in the contract documents. Often design details are not anticipated at the bid awarding stage. For these reasons, it is often necessary for the design professional to give interpretation rulings after the contract has been awarded.

Interpretation difficulties are compounded by the number of contract documents, and their possible inconsistencies. While contractual solutions for resolving potential conflicts in the documents may be attempted, inconsistencies are often troublesome.

Another reason for disputes relates to the frequent use of the fixed price or lump-sum contract. Construction projects frequently require a long period of time for performance. There is a substantial possibility that events will occur which will increase the costs of performance to the contractor. There may be labor difficulties, weather problems, unforeseen soil problems, unforeseen increases in material and labor over the length of the construction contract, and the possibility of government interference with the project. A properly developed bid proposal, and a contractor who has integrity and technological skill, can avoid difficulties caused by increases in costs. However, these ideal conditions are rare. Frequently the contractor cannot adequately absorb unanticipated increased costs.

The highly competitive nature of the construction industry often means that contractors must scale their bids down and hope for the best. Some hope to recoup by claiming that contractual ambiguities should be resolved in favor of the contractor. These contractors frequently claim that the performance demanded by the design professional is not within the contract obligations, and is an extra which must be paid for in addition to the contract price. In many projects, there is a substantial variation between the contract price and the final construction cost to the owner, due to extras. Sometimes these extras are the result of poor planning on the part of the owner and his design professional, and sometimes these extra costs result from unscrupulous contractors who seize upon the extras route as a means of making an undeserved profit on the contract.

The probability of disputes and litigation increases when the financial stakes are high. Many construction contracts involve large amounts of money. The disputes involve amounts of money that are substantial enough to merit hiring an attorney and taking disputes to court. Finally, the construction business is so competitive that many contractors are too stubborn (or cannot afford) to compromise, and insist on litigation to resolve disputes.

(C) MANY COMPETING INTERESTS

The construction project is a complex operation. There are many potentially competing interests. Along the "owner" chain, in addition to the owner, there is usually a lender who is advancing funds for the project. The seller of the land may have retained a security interest in the land. Also, the owner may be constructing a commercial structure, in which space has been leased in advance to various tenants. Finally, the creditors of the owner may have an interest in the construction project. They may hope to collect their debts from profits made by the project, or by having the land seized or sold to pay the owner's debts.

The contractor chain in the single contract system involves, in addition to the prime contractor, a large number of subcontractors and possibly sub-subcontractors. Each one of these contractors, as well as the prime contractor himself, will purchase supplies and rent equipment. The materialmen and equipment suppliers also have a substantial stake in the construction project. In addition, the use of surety bonds for prime contractors, and often for subcontractors, brings a number of surety bond companies into the picture. The creditors of the contractors, other than suppliers, are often involved. There may be various taxing authorities to whom contractors owe taxes, as well as persons who have lent money to the contractors. The contract chain would not be complete without reference to the trade unions which have a substantial stake in the construction project.

In addition to the owner and contractor chains, there is a somewhat shorter chain commencing with the architect. The architect will hire consultants, and will have his own employees engaged in the construction project, if the project is large enough. He may hire various testing organizations, and he may employ a professional estimator in the planning stages of the project. (Some of these persons could have been included in the owner chain, and they may be hired by the owner.)

Those retained by the architect also have a stake in the construction project. They are interested in being paid, and their negligence may cause damage to any of a number of persons who are also affected by or involved in the construction process.

Construction work involves a high probability of harm to persons and to property. There are the workers, and members of the public, who may be injured. There are adjacent landowners, and other owners of land in the neighborhood. There are insurance companies who insure against injuries and damage to property. The general public will be affected if persons injured do not have the financial resources to take care of themselves and are not able to collect from other parties, such as contractors or their insurance companies. If injured parties cannot pay for their own bills and take care of their families, and are unable to find other persons who will or are obligated to provide care and financial support, those injured are likely to end up as charges upon the public and cause public funds, through welfare payments, to be expended to pay their bills and to take care of their dependents.

The complexity of the construction process and the high probability of personal injuries or death, damage to property, and pecuniary loss make potential disputes almost inevitable.

(D) THE LAW

There are many laws relating to the construction process. The law of contract generally permits parties to use contracts to allocate risk assumption in the construction process. However, contract interpretations raise difficult problems.

There are many other laws which regulate and govern the construction project. Building codes are often incorporated, expressly or impliedly, in the construction documents. Building codes lack uniformity. They consist of complicated, and often cumbersome, rules which regulate the construction process. There are zoning laws and subdivision laws. There are tort doctrines, such as those relating to nuisance and soil support, which affect the use of land. Title and security problems are often difficult. The laws affecting the obligations of surety companies are governed by a specialized body of law dealing with sureties. The rights of injured persons or injured property owners are governed by tort law. The complexity of laws involved in the construction project also increases the probability of disputes and litigation between competing interests.

In addition to the large numbers of laws that are involved, many of the laws in question are in a state of transition. For example, the doctrines permitting injured persons to recover have been greatly expanded in the past 25 years.

(E) THE SITE

The physical site itself contributes to the likelihood of disputes and construction process difficulties. No two pieces of land are exactly alike. This means a high probability of subsurface difficulties. Testing methods for soil conditions are expensive, and often do not give an accurate picture of the entire site. In addition, the physical limitations of the site, together with the large number of persons and contracting parties who must perform within this limited physical area, increases the probability of difficulties. Proper scheduling is essential. If the work is not ready for a subcontractor, he incurs substantial delay costs. Workers of different contractors each claim that they are entitled to perform particular work at a particular time, and resolution must frequently be made of such claims.

As mentioned, there is a high probability that workers will be injured in the construction process. This is increased when construction involves unusual construction methods or materials.

While the site is usually a restricted physical area, work on the site itself can substantially affect adjacent land owners. Excavation always involves a risk of subsidence on adjacent land. Soil conditions may cause slides and subsidence in the excavation process. Also, transferring the materials to the site can damage adjacent owners and members of the public.

(F) CONTRACT ADMINISTRATION

Even if the general terms and conditions of the contract documents are well expressed, difficulties often develop because contracting parties often are sloppy in contract administration. Decisions are made on the site, modifications are agreed to, changes are ordered—all without the formal requirements frequently expressed in the general terms and conditions of the written contract documents. Phone conversations are often used to resolve difficulties and continue the work, but there may be a dispute at a later date as to what was said during various phone and personal conversations. In the process of the dispute, one party will often point to the contract clauses requiring that certain directions be given in writing, or that certain modifications be expressed in writing. The other party will then state that throughout the entire course of administration these formal requirements were disregarded. These are the seeds from which disputes and law suits develop.

(G) PROBABILITIES OF LITIGATION

Disputes between parties may be resolved without litigation when there is a desire to maintain good will in the parties' future dealings. This element, based upon the necessity of future relations, may be missing in many construction projects. A dispute may involve a number of parties who must consent to any settlement, such as insurance companies and sureties. The law is sometimes uncertain in these areas, and this often encourages people to litigate rather than to settle. If there is an arbitration provision, one or both of the parties may not trust the arbitration process. Even if the arbitrator makes an award, the party against whom the award is made may not perform. This means that the arbitration award must be confirmed by a court.

SECTION 15.03 HOW THIS AFFECTS THE DESIGN PROFESSIONAL

When the design professional realizes the high probability of disputes in the construction project, he should govern himself accordingly. He must organize the project carefully during the design phase. He should make the construction documents as complete and as clear as he can. He must realize that ambiguities will be seized upon by unscrupulous contractors, and are likely to be resolved against his client.

He should insist upon proper contract administration. He should familiarize himself with the general terms and conditions, and follow them. If circumstances arise which make it impossible to comply with formal requirements, immediate confirmatory memoranda should be drafted and sent to the contractor. He should realize that if the contract administration becomes casual or sloppy, it is unlikely that he will be able to point at some later date to the general terms and conditions dealing with formalities as the basis for denying a contractor's claim.

If the design professional realizes the high degree of probability that there will be personal injury or death, he will take his design work seriously. If he does not have competence in certain areas, especially in dealing with new construction methods or processes, he should obtain the advice of expert consultants.

He should be familiar with the laws that relate to the construction process. While he cannot be expected to become an expert in all these laws, there are some areas which require his careful attention. At the very least he must be thoroughly aware of the requirements of building codes. He should also have a substantial knowledge of zoning laws. As to the other areas which may affect the construction process, he must learn enough to recognize legal problems. While he is not likely to be able to solve particular problems, he will be alerted to the necessity of obtaining legal advice from the attorney of the owner, or his own attorney, depending upon the particular problem involved.

SECTION 15.04 FORM CONTRACTS

There is an increasing use of form contracts in construction work. There are good reasons for this. It is impossible for lawyers or design professionals to anticipate all the problems and to deal with them properly in each individual construction contract. Form contracts rely heavily upon the experiences of the past, and upon the expertise of persons with wide experience in construction projects. Good form contracts are often planned carefully. However, their existence does not solve the contract problems for lawyers or for design professionals.

First, some form contracts acquire the reputation for being heavily slanted in favor of one of the parties. Lawyers, when asked to pass upon these contracts, may reject them completely or make substantial modifications in them. Second, a form contract is often unread or misunderstood by the other party if he is not represented by a lawyer. This means that there is a possibility of the clauses not actually governing the relationship between the contracting parties.

This treatise will treat briefly those law doctrines which affect the construction process. One object will be to extract the principles which are the basis for the more frequently used clauses in form contracts. If the design professional can understand the basic issues involved in the construction process, he will be better able to understand and deal with provisions in form contracts. If he does not understand the underlying reasons for these provisions, his handling of the construction documents is likely to be mechanical.

Chapter 16

TYPES OF CONSTRUCTION CONTRACTS

SECTION 16.01 BASIC OBJECTIVES

(A) SELECTING A CONTRACTOR

While Chapter 17 deals principally with contractor selection, a preliminary look at contractor selection is important.

The owner, whether a private corporation, a public agency, or an individual, wishes to get the best quality of work at the lowest cost. "Cost" must take in account the indirect costs, such as the owner's administrative time, and the mental strain which can result when one deals with an incompetent or irresponsible contractor.

Timely completion is important. The owner frequently has made commitments which depend upon the project being finished at the designated time. Delay also means loss of use of funds tied up in the project. Also, the owner would like to be able to predict his ultimate costs with reasonable certainty. He needs to know how much money must be set aside for the project. The economics of a particular project frequently depends upon ultimate cost. Public agencies are concerned with cost, because they may be limited to the proceeds of a particular bond issue or a particular appropriation. Normally a fixed price contract should give this certainty, but, in construction work, the ultimate cost can far exceed the original contract price, because of costly extra work.

Also, circumstances may arise during the course of construction which make the project more costly to the contractor. A responsible contractor usually feels committed to the contract price and does not attempt to pass off every added cost to the owner. In a fixed price contract, he should be both willing and able to absorb increased costs which should be allocated to him.

It is important to have a contractor who will be financially responsible and has pride in the quality of his work. If difficulties do arise, or if the work does not meet the specifications called for, he should have the desire and the financial capability to make corrections. The financial ability of the contractor to meet his financial obligations to third parties is crucial. Unpaid subcontractors, materialmen, and laborers can place liens against the building. It may cost the owner money to remove these liens, both in terms of having to pay lien claimants and in incurring legal and administrative expenses to remove the liens.

To a large degree, the owner is in the hands of the contractor. The owner depends upon the contractor's skill, both organizational and technical, as well as upon the contractor's honesty.

A dishonest or incompetent contractor can skimp on performance or do a poor job. This can occur despite reasonable attempts to check upon contractor performance. Maximum legal protection, well-drafted contract documents, and responsible surety companies cannot substitute for a competent, intelligent, and honest contractor. The owner's basic objective is to secure a contractor who will do the job properly.

(B) CONTRACT ADMINISTRATION AND FAIRNESS

Mention has been made of the necessity for having a contractor who has both the moral commitment and the financial responsibility to absorb increases in costs. While one of the basic purposes of a fixed price contract is to place such risks upon the contractor, it is important for the design professional to take into account that there may be unusual risks which should not be allocated to the contractor. The law may relieve the contractor in certain circumstances. The contract itself may shift the costs of certain unforeseen and unusual circumstances. Whatever the contract provision specifies, or whatever the law may decide in such cases of unusual circumstances, it is important for the design professional to realize that fairness in handling such matters, both in terms of granting time extensions and additional compensation, is in the best interests of the client. Inflexible and stubborn behavior in these matters on the part of the design professional often leads to poor work, antagonism, and litigation.

SECTION 16.02 ORGANIZATIONAL VARIATIONS

Project construction can be organized in a number of different ways. The basic elements of variation lie in allocation of responsibility for coordination and in responsibility for the total project. In discussing organizational aspects, the question of costs and the method of obtaining a contractor cannot be entirely excluded.

(A) SINGLE CONTRACT SYSTEM

In the "single contract" system, the person desiring to have a project built hires a prime contractor (sometimes called the general contractor). The prime contractor is responsible for construction of the project. The only construction contract made by the owner is with the prime contractor. Because there is great specialization in the building trades, prime contractors usually hire subcontractors to do certain portions of the work. In complicated construction or engineering projects there may be sub-subcontractors and even sub-sub-subcontractors. But, from the standpoint of organization, the prime contractor stands at the apex of the pyramid. The owner and the architect deal with the prime contractor. The prime contractor must have organizational skill, as well as technological knowledge. He must coordinate the work of the subcontractors in order to complete the project within the specified time. The prime contractor takes the responsibility for late or defective performance by any of his subcontractors or their subcontractors.

One of the aspects of the single contract system which has been criticized relates to the method by which some prime contractors determine their bid proposals. Suppose the competitive bidding system is used, and that there is a lump sum, or fixed price, contract. Ordinarily the prime contractor will compute the cost of labor, materials, and equipment, (using in part bids from subcontractors) make an allowance for overhead and profit, and come up with a tentative bid proposal figure. However, in a competitive bidding system, he will have to be lower than the other bidders in order to obtain the contract. This means that after obtaining bid proposals, adding his costs and determining an allowance for profit and overhead, his bid proposal figure may seem too high. To obtain the contract, he may have to scale down the bid proposal. If he does this, he may try to compensate for this by claiming that every direction given to him during performance is an "extra", or by squeezing the subcontractors and trying to get them to take less money. Either approach can cause difficulty, and may result in a poor construction job. For this reason, some design professionals prefer some form of the separate contracting system.

One method of reducing subcontractor squeeze is to require that the prime do a specified portion of the work himself. This is to preclude his being solely a broker for the services of others, and also reduces the risk of liens being filed by unpaid subcontractors. A method of avoiding contractor incompetence, discussed in greater detail in Chapter 18, is to require that the prime contractor obtain a surety bond. If a surety will not write a bond for him, this indicates that the contractor lacks financial resources, honesty, or competence.

(B) SEPARATE CONTRACTS

Under most "separate contract" systems, the owner enters into individual contracts with the major specialized trades, such as the electrical contractor, the plumbing and heating contractor, the elevator construction contractor, as well as the contractor for construction of the building itself. The advantage of the separate contractor system is that the owner deals directly with the skilled subcontractors and avoids the possibility of subcontractor squeeze. Also, he avoids the often troublesome problem of unpaid subcontractors by paying them himself. However, in most construction projects of any magnitude, the owner will still have to be concerned with whether the separate contractors are paying their subcontractors.

In some states, certain public contracts are required to be awarded separately. This may be a recognition of the efficiency of this system, or may be merely a manifestation of the political power of certain organized subcontractor specialties.

There are some problems connected to the separate contractor system, which explain why its use is relatively limited in American building contracts. The problems of work coordination are difficult, and often exasperating. One of the advantages of having a prime contractor is that he presumably has the skill to handle these problems. The use of the separate contractor system obviously increases this responsibility on the part of the owner.

To a large degree, coordination of the work will be done by the design professional. This will mean an increased fee for the design professional. It also means that the design professional must have the skill necessary to perform an important part of a prime contractor's work. If the separate contractors are not confident that the design professional has this skill, they may submit higher bids than they would submit if a skilled prime contractor was to coordinate the work.

Under the separate contractor system, there will be additional bidding expense. The competitive bidding system is often time consuming and expensive. Multiplying this many times by competitive biddings by a number of separate contractors usually creates additional administrative expense. The requirements for coordination and supervision by the owner, exercised through the design professional under the separate contractor system, will involve additional record keeping and supervision costs which will ultimately be borne by the owner.

Delays can be troublesome in separate contracts. For example, it is usual to incorporate provisions for liquidated damages (a specified daily damage rate) for unexcused delay in construction contracts. However, if one separate contractor is late in his performance, he often contends that he was either prevented by non-performance of another separate contractor, or he contends that his late performance did not delay the project because other separate contractors also were late. In a single contract system, all that is important is whether there has been unexcused delay. In a separate contract system, allocation of responsibility for delay can be more complicated.

Sometimes owners make separate contracts with the skilled trades and then engage one of the contractors, usually the contractor erecting the structure itself, to act as prime contractor. For this service the prime contractor is paid a fee, in addition to what he is paid for the construction work he is to perform. In this way, the owner obtains the specialized skill in coordination of the prime contractor, and yet deals with the separate contractors individually, at least to the extent of entering into contracts with them. This hybrid system has some advantages, but it is still likely to involve the owner and the design professional in coordination and supervision problems generally avoided by the use of the single contract system.

Another variant of the separate contract system is sometimes called the "multiple" or "segregated contract" system. This is the separate contract system carried to its logical extreme. Under the multiple contracting system, there is no prime contractor, and the owner hires each contractor directly, with the design professional handling administration. Before this system is employed, it is important to check the state laws on licensing to see if the owner is required to be a licensed contractor.

(C) PACKAGE SYSTEM

All the methods of contracting discussed so far have assumed separate responsibility for design and building functions. Under these systems, design is the responsibility of the design professional, and the responsibility for building functions is placed on the contractor. Coordination and administration depends upon whether the single or some form of separate contract is employed. The "package system" unites design and construction functions. The owner makes one contract for all services connected with the project. This system is common in countries outside the United States. In the United States, it is used by some large engineering companies.

A package system can operate efficiently if the organization responsible for the project is expert, financially responsible, and honest. However, the owner has no independent design professional protecting his interests.

(D) DAY LABOR OR FORCE ACCOUNT

Sometimes the owner hires the laborers, buys the material, and takes responsibility for erection of the project. Under this system, he saves a portion of the fee which would be paid to prime contractors, and even to subcontractors. On the other hand, he loses the organizational and technical skills which prime contractors and subcontractors bring to a construction project. It is not used in construction jobs of any magnitude, but is occasionally chosen for minor construction or engineering jobs. Statutes sometimes prohibit this method in public contracts.

(E) SUMMATION

The determination of which type of system is best for a specific project is not a legal decision, but one within the expertise of the design professional. The single contract system is used much more commonly than the separate contract system. Anyone considering the separate contractor system should realize the problems that are likely to arise. This does not mean that the separate contractor system cannot be an efficient and economical one. The ultimate determination will lie in the question of whether a good prime contractor is available and whether the design professional is skilled at coordination and administration of the project.

SECTION 16.03 PRICING VARIATIONS

(A) LUMP SUM OR FIXED PRICE

The method used most commonly in construction projects for pricing the work is the "lump sum", or "fixed price", contract. Under this system, the contractor agrees to do the work for a fixed price. Most of the risks are placed upon the prime contractor. He takes the risk of most cost increases. He retains any savings he can make by cutting costs.

If the plans and specifications are drawn clearly and with minimal ambiguity, the lump sum system is advantageous to the owner. He knows in advance what the project will cost him, and this is of major importance. If the plans and specifications are not clearly drawn, however, there are likely to be contract interpretation problems which may result in added costs. Work which the owner expects to be performed under the contract price may be found to be an extra. Fixed price contracts usually involve fewer records than cost type contracts. (See § 16.03(b)).

The effectiveness of the lump sum method of pricing depends upon obtaining contractors who have had sufficient experience to determine bid proposal prices with reasonable certainty. If they have had little experience in this type of construction, the contractors may not be willing to bid at all on a lump sum basis, or they may include a large amount to cover the contingencies of experimental design, new materials, or new methods.

In a lump sum or fixed price contract there is an inherent conflict of interest between the owner and the contractor. When the contractor cuts the cost of his performance, he increases his profits. As long as this cost reduction does not come at the expense of the owner's right to receive the performance called for in the construction contract the owner is not hurt by such cost savings.

However, in construction projects it is often difficult to determine the exact performance required under the contract and whether such performance has occurred. In the "gray" area of compliance, the interests of owner and contractor clash. The contractor seeks to avoid performing any more than is absolutely called for under the contract while the owner would like to be certain that he is receiving the performance to which he is entitled under the contract.

The design professional often finds himself in the middle of this conflict. The owner expects the design professional to ensure that the contractor's performance meets standards set forth in the contract documents. Also, the design professional is frequently empowered to decide interpretation questions.

The tension that has been described in a fixed price contract is less likely to be a problem if the contractor wishes to protect his reputation or is looking for repeat business.

In determining the most desirable type of construction contract for a given project, the design professional should be aware of the built in conflict of interest in a fixed price or lump sum contract.

Performance frequently turns out to be more expensive to the contractor. Generally, under the lump sum contract, these additional costs are risks which are borne by the contractor. However, often the owner's best interests necessitate some flexibility on his part. If he tries to force the contractor to the line in every case, he may end up with an uncompleted building and a law suit, or with a project which does not measure up to the plans and specifications. Even though the fixed price contract allocates the risk of most increases in performance cost to the contractor, there can be situations where the increased cost is due to a circumstance which is so unforeseen and so abnormal that the contractor would be given the right to terminate the contract because of the doctrine of mistake. The architect or engineer should realize that the law does not place the risk of every increased expense upon the contractor. Sometimes contracts provide for increases in the contract price because certain circumstances arise. Even where the law would not relieve a fixed priced contractor, common sense and an awareness of the realities of the construction process may make it advisable not to demand strict performance at the contract price. If circumstances arise which cause an increased cost to the contractor, fairness and enlightened self-interest may be reasons to allow an increase in the original contract price.

Sometimes a "cash allowance" is used in a fixed price contract. This is a sum specified in a fixed price contract to cover certain designated materials to be incorporated into the contract. Cash allowances, when used, are likely to be a part of a contract to build a residence or smaller commercial work. Usually the allowance covers items such as lighting, plumbing or electrical fixtures. The actual items are determined by the owner. If the actual cost of the items exceeds the cash allowance, the difference in cost should be added to the contract price. In the unlikely event the actual cost is lower than the cash allowance fixture specified, the owner should receive a credit, reducing the contract price.

While contract interpretation problems are discussed in considerable detail in Chapters 19 and 20, it may be useful to briefly mention some interpretation problems that relate to the use of the cash allowance.

Does the cash allowance include costs over and above the purchase price of the item which is the subject of the cash allowance? For example, suppose there is a cash allowance for lighting fixtures of $5,000. In addition to the cost of the lighting fixtures, the contractor may claim that the cost of installation, the cost of delivery or other costs such as permits required for installation should be included in the cash allowance. Also, he might assert a claim for overhead or profit on the installation of the lighting fixtures. Finally, there can be a dispute over whether the cash allowance is to be the published price for the fixtures, or the price actually paid by the contractor, which is likely to be substantially less.

It is advisable for the provision creating the cash allowance to handle these problems. Generally, the contractor considers the cost of installation, other incidental costs, overhead and profit when he computes his contract bid. For this reason it would seem that the cash allowance should cover only the actual price paid by the contractor for the lighting fixtures.

(B) COST CONTRACTS

Another method of pricing a construction contract is tied to the cost of construction. There are "cost plus a fixed fee," "cost plus a percentage of cost," and "cost incentive" contracts. Cost type contracts are useful where a lump sum contract is not practical because the work is experimental or novel. The cost contract does not have the built-in-conflict of interests involved in the lump sum pricing method. Simply, a cost type of contract enables the owner to direct the contractor to do specified work for which he will be paid, based upon his costs, plus an additional amount to compensate him for overhead and profit.

There are other advantages to the cost type of contract. The degree of specificity in plans and specifications required for a lump sum contract is relaxed in a cost type contract. The contract can be formed quickly, and is of great value in an emergency situation. In cost type contracts, allowable costs should be spelled out, and a method should be devised to ensure the contractor has an adequate incentive to keep the costs down. Because of the latter problem, the federal government does not make "cost plus a percentage of cost" contracts. This is because the contractor's profit will increase in direct proportion to the cost. For this reason, a fixed fee, although sometimes difficult to determine in advance, is added to cost of construction. The obvious advantage to the cost plus a percentage of cost is that there are certain accepted guidelines for determining the percentage, such as 10 or 15 percent, while there are few convenient guides to determine the fee in a cost plus a fixed fee contract.

Sometimes the contractor is allowed a specified percentage of cost to compensate for his overhead expenses. If so, it is important to spell out that costs do not include overhead. In contracts of the type mentioned in the preceding paragraph, the percentage allowed for profit should be based upon only the cost, and not the overhead, unless the parties agree that the contractor is to make a profit on his overhead.

For example, suppose there is a cost contract where the contractor is to receive a stated percentage of cost in lieu of overhead, and an additional stated percentage in lieu of profit. It should be clear in such a contract that the base price upon which both percentages are determined are actual direct costs, unless the parties specifically agree that the contractor is to recover profit based upon both of his actual costs and the percentage of actual costs allowable as overhead.

The principal disadvantage of a cost type contract is the uncertainty of the final cost. One technique for controlling costs is used by the federal government in some of its cost type contracts. Included in such contracts is an estimated cost for the work set forth in the schedule. The contractor "agrees to use his best efforts to perform the work specified in the Schedule and all obligations under this contract within such estimated cost." These contracts go on to state:

> If, at any time, the Contractor has reason to believe that the cost which he expects to incur in the performance of this contract in the next succeeding sixty (60) days, when added to all costs previously incurred, will exceed seventy-five percent (75%) of the estimated cost then set forth in the Schedule, or if at any time, the Contractor has reason to believe that the total cost to the Government for the performance of this contract, exclusive of any fee, will be greater or substantially less than the then estimated cost hereof, the Contractor shall notify the Contracting Officer in writing to that effect, giving the revised estimate of such total cost for the performance of this contract.

(This clause is taken from the Armed Service Procurement Regulation 7–402.2(a) Oct. 1966)

If the contractor does not comply with the notice of a prospective overrun in cost, the government may, if it wishes, reimburse him for these excess costs, but has no obligation to do so. The notice of an overrun in cost provision can be useful in a cost type construction contract to keep control over the ultimate cost.

Another technique developed in federal government contracting to reduce costs in a cost type contract is the "cost incentive contract".

Under this system, there is a target cost estimate made by the owner (in this case the federal government). If the ultimate costs fall below the target estimate, the saving is shared on some prearranged basis by the contractor and the owner. This gives the contractor incentive to reduce costs, by allowing him to participate in the saving made possible by cost reduction. However, the viability of this system depends upon a reasonably realistic target cost, and a fair sharing of cost savings.

There are additional administrative costs to the owner in a cost type contract. Usually the design professional will want a higher fee than for a lump sum contract, because there are many more changes made in a cost type contract as the work progresses. Also, the design professional may have additional responsibilities for checking upon the amount of costs incurred by the contractor, and for ensuring that the costs claimed actually went into the project and were required under the contract. The determination of costs not only involves often-exasperating problems of cost accounting, but also involves the creation of record management and management techniques for determining just what costs have been incurred.

There are innumerable variations of allowable costs. Usually there is no question on certain items, such as material, labor, rental of equipment, transportation and items of the contractor's overhead directly related to the project. However, sometimes there are disputes over such matters as whether the cost of visits to the project by the contractor's administrative officials, the cost of supervisory personnel employed by the contractor, or preparatory expenses are allowable costs.

The important thing from the drafting standpoint is to try to anticipate all types of costs which can relate directly or indirectly to this project. A determination should be made as to which will be allowable costs, for the purposes of the contract. In federal government contracting, complicated formulas and lists for allowable costs are created by the government. Often this is not adequate to avoid disputes over allowable costs.

There are advantages to a cost-type contract. However, in the construction field, the owner will normally choose a lump sum contract because he is able, within limits, to predict what the project will cost him. Sometimes the cost type contract is modified by placing a ceiling price upon costs, and informing the contractor in advance that costs over a specified amount will not be paid by the owner. Obviously, while this does give some certainty to the owner as to the project costs, it defeats one of the basic objectives of the cost type contract. However, such a hybrid may be useful in certain types of projects.

(C) UNIT PRICING

Sometimes construction contracts employ the "unit pricing" technique. In such a contract, the contractor is paid a specified amount for every unit of designated work that he performs. If the construction work can be readily divided into specified units, and the number of units is reasonably predictable, it may be advantageous to specify a given price to be paid for each unit. Contractors are often able to compute their costs per unit of work quite accurately if the work is of a type that they have done in the past.

The unit pricing system is not normally used if there are many different types of work to be done, or if the units to be performed are small. But if there is a reasonably limited variety of types of work, and reasonably large numbers of units, the unit pricing technique may be useful. Sometimes a combination of unit pricing and lump sum pricing is used. The contractor may be paid a specified amount of money for each unit of certain designated types of work, and a lump sum for the balance of the work called for under the contract. Sometimes the preparatory work and other work which is not measurable in terms of the units employed in the contract is not compensated for by any separate fixed price, but is included within the unit costs specified in the contract. Usually, the contract sets forth the types of work covered under the contract, the estimated numbers of units expected to be performed, and the unit price. One advantage of the unit price system, in addition to the skill with which experienced contractors are able to bid unit price work, is that the plans and specifications need not be as detailed at the time the contract is formed, in comparison to the required amount of detail in a lump sum contract.

There are disadvantages to the unit pricing system. The owner's certainty of costs is largely dependent upon the accuracy of the estimate of quantities. If the estimate varies greatly from the quantities actually required, there is a substantial risk that the contractor may ask for an adjustment of the unit price. In such cases, the contractor may assert that his unit price was based, to a substantial degree, upon the expectation that he would perform, within reasonable tolerances, the number of units of work specified in the estimate. If the units performed vary considerably from the estimate, the contractor may claim that this is a circumstance which justifies him in using another method of pricing his work, such as the reasonable value of his services. In addition, the unit pricing system involves a substantial amount of work records, and checking the actual units that are performed.

Another frequent companion to unit pricing is the "unbalanced bid". Sometimes the contractor allocates an unreasonably high portion of the costs to those units of work which will be performed early in the construction project. This enables him to get larger progress payments earlier in the performance of his work, and is helpful to him in giving him added capital for the performance of his work. Usually the unbalanced bid does not diminish the contractor's chances of obtaining a contract in a competitive bid. This is because the lowest bid is usually determined by adding up the multiples of all unit prices by the estimated quantities of unit work. The allocation of high unit prices to portions of the work performed earlier will be balanced by low unit prices in performance of the units that are to be performed later. Such bidding can result in a greater chance of unpaid subcontractors and materialmen asserting liens if funds are diverted by the prime contractor.

The unbalanced bid is also used as a guessing device. The contractor, in effect, bets that he can guess the quantities of units that will be performed better than the owner. In this use of the unbalanced bid, the contractor bids higher unit prices on those portions of the work which he thinks will overrun. (An overrun occurs where the actual number of units exceeds the prediction). To avoid any disadvantage in the total competitive bid, the contractor in such an unbalanced bid will bid lower for portions of the work which he thinks will underrun. Since the amount of money actually paid depends upon actual quantities of work performed, an unbalanced bid will give him greater profit if his prediction of the unit quantities is more accurate than that of the owner.

(D) ESCALATION CLAUSES

In a lump-sum contract, the contractor takes the risk of most added costs that increase the cost of his performance during the course of construction. One method of avoiding the risk of increased costs is to include a price escalation provision in a lump-sum contract. In a price escalation clause, the contract price will go up (and sometimes down) if certain key cost factors change after the bid proposal is made and the contract formed. For example, it is possible to include a provision which would increase the contract price to the extent that there are price increases in the cost of designated materials, and to the extent that there are price increases in labor or other costs. Such a provision shields the contractor from the risk of certain price increases.

The drafting of a price escalation clause is more difficult than would appear. Care should be taken to include examples, because expressing a price escalation clause in words or formulas may result in uncertainty and ambiguity. It is important to specify just what items will trigger an escalation. It may be helpful to include language that requires the contractor to use his best efforts to obtain the lowest possible prices of escalatable items. Escalation clauses should consider whether the price increase relates only to those materials which are actually incorporated in the construction project, or whether it applies to increases in the general market price of the materials, without regard to whether the materials actually used cost more than the base price.

If actual incorporation is required, provision should be made for examination of records to insure that the contractor has actually incurred the cost for price increases for which he requests additional payment. Sometimes it is helpful to specify that only increases over a certain amount will be transferred by the escalation clause to the owner. Minor decimal increases under some provisions are absorbed by the contractor.

Price escalation clauses are not common in construction contracts. However, they can provide an acceptable price compromise if a skilled prime contractor wants to avoid risks of price increases during an inflationary period, or if the contract may require a long time to perform. In some cases, it is cheaper to have a price escalation clause than to have a strict lump-sum contract, because, without a price escalation, the contractors may feel that it is necessary to pad the bids in order to cover the contingency of price increases in an inflationary market. This is even more likely where the contract will take a substantial time to perform.

(E) CHANGES

Chapter 21 is devoted to this difficult problem. However, in discussing pricing techniques, it is important to consider methods of pricing additional work performed during the course of the construction project.

If possible, it is advantageous to set up unit prices for additional work, if the type of work can be predicted and falls into a measurable unit price pattern. It may be useful in drafting an agreement to provide for the possibility that there may be great variation in the units of extra work ordered by setting up a schedule of unit pricing which will be flexible, based upon the number of units of extra work ordered.

If the unit pricing technique cannot be readily adapted, or in the case where the unit pricing technique may cover some types of additional work but not others, it is important to consider how extra work is to be priced. Some contracts provide that the contractor will be paid cost plus a certain percentage of costs, in lieu of overhead and profit. A contract for cost plus a percentage of costs may mean a higher cost of performance to the owner, because the contractor's overhead and profit will be directly related to the amount of cost incurred. However, it is often difficult to arrive at a fixed fee when it is not known just what the nature of the extra work will be. For this reason, it may be necessary to use cost plus a percentage of cost. If this is done, the architect or engineer must look carefully at the cost items to see that they are reasonable, and to see that those items claimed by the contractor are directly related to the extra work. It may be helpful to use language in the contract that will specify that only material and labor, or perhaps material and labor and direct overhead costs, are to be included as cost items. If the project is likely to involve use of equipment, the direct costs of equipment used should be included with direct labor and material costs.

Sometimes parties merely state that extra work will be compensated based upon an agreed sum to be arrived at by the parties, It is important to specify whether the agreement as to costs must precede the actual performance of the extra work. Perhaps the owner will not want the extra work performed until he is certain as to his cost. Generally, the owner will want the right to order that the work be done even if there is no advance agreement on costs.

Whenever contract terms specify that extra work will be priced based upon agreement, two other problems should be considered. First, what happens if there is no agreement by the parties? Some early cases held that such cases of an agreement to perform the extra work was invalid as a mere agreement to agree. It makes more sense to hold that the absence of an agreement by the parties in such a case can either mean that the price will be determined under the arbitration clause (if there is one), or that the price will be a reasonable price. Any contract provision which uses an agreed price method of compensating extra work should specify that, in the absence of an agreement by the parties, the work is to be compensated in a specified fashion, such as cost plus a percentage of costs, or the reasonable cost, or that the dispute is one which is subject to arbitration under the arbitration clause (if there is one).

Should the contract specify a mechanism for arriving at an agreement? For example, the contract may state that the contractor will propose and support a proposed price to the owner. The owner is then free to accept this pricing proposal or to propose a price of his own based upon other supportive evidence. In some cases, contracts provide that a failure by one party to object within a specified period to a price proposal by the other party is an acquiescence to that price proposal. There are advantages to this technique. It forces the party to whom a proposal has been made to set forth his own proposal within a specified period of time. This accelerates the agreement process. Also, sometimes such a provision is included in the hope that the other party will be dilatory and forget to object to a proposal, thereby adopting it by acquiescence.

The pricing of extras is important in deciding upon the type of contract pricing technique to be used generally in a construction contract. A loose method of pricing extras often encourages a contractor to submit a low lump-sum bid, with a view towards recouping his costs on extras derived from claimed interpretation uncertainties in the plans and specifications. It is important to have clear and complete construction drawings and specifications. It is also important to recognize that there will be extra work, either caused by changes in the design or by unclear specifications. The method of pricing extra work will be a significant factor in the total price of the project.

(F) UNUSUAL SUBSURFACE CONDITIONS

Another frequent problem which increases the cost of the contractor's work is unforeseen or unusual subsurface conditions. Because this problem is so difficult, and causes so many disputes and law suits, this question will be discussed at length in Chapter 22.

In considering pricing, it is important to realize that there is a substantial chance that the contractor will discover unanticipated subsurface conditions during the course of construction. One possible solution to this problem is to set forth in the contract itself that certain types of unforeseen circumstances with regard to subsurface conditions are a risk which will be shared by the contractor and the owner, or borne by the owner. The latter has been done in federal government construction contracts. Under certain circumstances, the contractor will be entitled to an equitable adjustment of the contract price, if he runs into certain difficulties, and if he gives a specified notice to the government. This method of removing some element of the subsurface and soil risk from the contractor is used in American Institute of Architects standard form contracts. Section 12.1.6 of AIA Doc. A201 is reproduced in the Appendix.

The bid proposal by the contractor may reflect his awareness of how this particular risk is to be handled. The reasonable likelihood of subsurface difficulties may mean that the contractor will have to pad his bid with a certain percentage contingency figure in order to avoid this risk, provided such padding does not make his bid uncompetitive.

However, if the contractor realizes in advance that the risk for certain types of subsurface conditions will be borne by the owner, this contingency for a subsurface problem may not be included in the bid. While it is not clear that this plays much of a role in bidding, these clauses may create a spirit of good will in contract administration and avoid bitter disputes over such costs. These results themselves may justify inclusion of such a risk shifting clause in the contract, even if the contract lump sum will be exceeded if such events occur.

(G) COST OF CONTRACT ADMINISTRATION

Standards of performance, measurement of compensation, and specifications generally should be made as clear as possible to lighten the burden of administering the contract. Administrative convenience can be the justification for using certain pricing provisions. An easily administered contract reduces the likelihood of disputes and time-consuming negotiations.

REVIEW QUESTIONS

1. What are the basic objectives in selecting a contractor or contractors to perform a construction project?
2. How are the risks allocated in a fixed price contract?
3. What can cause actual costs to exceed the fixed price?
4. What are the ideal conditions for a fixed price contract?
5. When is a unit price contract most desirable?
6. What are the advantages of a cost type contract? The disadvantages?
7. What is an escalation clause?

QUESTIONS FOR CLASS DISCUSSION

1. If you were building a residence for yourself, would you prefer a fixed price contract or a cost type contract? Why?

2. What would determine the fee amount in a cost plus a fixed fee contract?

3. Do you think the package system is more efficient than dividing the functions of design and construction?

4. Do you think there should be requirements in public contracts that separate contracts be used for the major trades? Give your reasons.

PROBLEMS

1. Your client is about to secure a contractor for the construction of a 10 story commercial office building. He wants to know whether he should use a single or separate contract system. He also wants to know whether he should use a fixed price or cost type contract. He asks you how "fixed" is a fixed price contract, and whether he should set aside a reserve above any fixed price figure in the construction contract. How would you advise him? What would be the considerations which would bear upon any advice you would give?

2. C entered into a contract with O, under which C would construct a residence and O would pay "cost plus 10% in lieu of overhead and 10% in lieu of profit". Cost was not defined. C claims that he is entitled to the cost of long distance phone calls from his main office to the site some 100 miles away. He also claims he should be reimbursed for his expenses in submitting his bid. He wants reimbursement for a $2000 payment he made to an adjacent landowner, whose plants were destroyed by the negligence of C's men when they excavated. C also claims that the 10% in lieu of profit should be computed by multiplying the allowable costs and the amount in lieu of overhead by the additional 10% to determine his profit. Which, if any, of C's claims are justified?

Chapter 17

SELECTING A CONTRACTOR: EMPHASIS ON COMPETITIVE BIDDING

SECTION 17.01 RECONSIDERATION OF BASIC OBJECTIVES

The basic objective in selecting a contractor, as in selecting the type of contract, is to obtain maximum quality at the best price. "Price" must take into account administrative cost, potential litigation costs, the possibility of defective work being concealed, and any other aspect of the construction process which can cost money. Some methods of contracting appear to be most attractive, but appearances are often deceptive. The lowest competitive bid may make it appear that the owner will save money by using the bid of the lowest contractor. However, if the lowest bidder does not have the capability nor the desire to do a good job, it may be more costly to use him on the project.

Also, the owners are sometimes deluded by what appears to be the certainty of a lump-sum bid arrived at through the competitive bidding process. Such a bid price may be unrealistically low and may be based upon the hope that subcontractors can be squeezed and upon the expectation that extras can be profitable. It cannot be overemphasized that the basic objective is to obtain a contractor who can do the job properly at the lowest "total" cost.

SECTION 17.02 COMPETITIVE BIDDING: THEORIES AND SOME PITFALLS

Most construction contracts are awarded through the use of competitive bidding. The basic theory of the competitive bid is that competition will enable the owner to get the best price. To a certain degree this is true. Often the competitive bid is the only way that the owner has to determine what is a fair price for the construction work. The bids themselves give him a good indication of the actual job cost, when allowances are made for overhead and profit. In addition, the competitive bidding system should avoid favoritism and corruption in awarding contracts. This is especially true in public contracts. In many countries, and in some states and cities of this country, the methods by which public contracts are awarded have been scandalous. A competitive bid gives everyone an equal chance to bid and receive the award.

The objectives of fairness in making the award and the best price would be sufficient to tip the scales in favor of competitive bidding if the item which is purchased or the services which are to be rendered can be objectively evaluated or compared. If the item which is being purchased can be tested scientifically to see whether it measures up to certain performance standards, competitive bidding would be the best method of obtaining the lowest price without favoritism to anyone.

On the other hand, the buyer may be purchasing goods or services which are highly technical and experimental. In such a case the buyer wants more security than a mere assurance that the job will be done properly. The buyer wants performance. While it is true that the successful bidder obligates himself to perform in accordance with the contract, this does not insure proper performance. Nonperformance may create a legal right to damages. If the bidder is financially solvent, or if there is a surety, this cause of action may be collectible. However, proper performance was not achieved as planned. For this reason most of the research and development contracts of United States Government agencies are not subjected to the requirement of competitive bidding. In such cases, the agency stresses the need for the contractor to have the technological skill to do the job properly. In such contracts, the competitive bidding system may not be the best method to select a contractor.

Most construction work is not as sophisticated or experimental as military missile work or space projects. However, it is often difficult to determine whether the owner is getting the promised for performance, because plans and specifications, however well drafted, cannot thoroughly and clearly delineate the obligation. There are opportunities for the contractor to skimp on the job if he wishes. Even careful inspection, testing and supervision cannot assure proper compliance with the contract. Obtaining an honest contractor does not necessarily mean the work will be properly performed. He may not have the technological skill, or the organizational ability, to perform properly. Determination of proper workmanship and contract compliance is often subjective. For this reason, owners should give careful thought to using systems other than the competitive bidding system if they are private owners, and if they are not compelled to use the competitive bidding process.

Admittedly, the competitive bidding process can be protected by various techniques. The invitation to bidders may state that the contract will be awarded only to the lowest responsible bidder. There may be methods of prequalification to screen out bidders who do not have the requisite competence or capacity. Nevertheless, despite these protective provisions, a good share of the likelihood of success of the construction project depends upon the integrity and the ability of the contractor. This may be difficult to measure in the competitive bidding process, where the tendency is to look solely at price.

The competitive bidding system is likely to predominate despite the difficulties mentioned. It is likely to continue to be used, because it is traditional, and, when run honestly and efficiently, can accomplish its purposes of obtaining proper performance at the lowest cost to the owner.

The competitive bid system assumes free bids and true competition. In some industries, these are lost because of price-fixing agreements by "competitors". Also, some bidders may use "turn bidding", in which the bidders agree to rotate the low bid among the various bidders, over a specified number of contracts. These agreements are violations of civil and criminal antitrust laws. Such agreements to avoid competition are rare in the construction industry. But design professionals should be aware of the possible loss of competition by agreement between "competitors".

Another aspect of the competitive bidding system which should be taken into account is that usually the competitive bidding system involves a lump-sum contract. Some of the disadvantages that are mentioned in evaluating various pricing techniques become aggravated when competitive bidding is used. For example, bids may be scaled down to be competitive, with the expectation of squeezing subcontractors and obtaining profitable extras. It is not always easy to anticipate whether a contractor is likely to use these techniques to make up for a low bid. In some cases, it may be possible to require that he show the subcontractor bids, and then determine whether the subcontractors have contracts at these prices. Unfortunately, often this is not determinable until the contract has been awarded and the performance has been commenced.

To sum up, the competitive bidding system is presently, and is likely to continue to be, the major method of obtaining construction contractors. However, design professionals should be aware of the pitfalls in competitive bidding, and, in the proper circumstances, they should give serious thought to another method of obtaining a contractor.

SECTION 17.03 THE COMPETITIVE BIDDING PROCESS

(A) OBJECTIVES

The principal justifications for the competitive bidding system are that competition produces the best price, and that contract awards are made fairly, without regard to favoritism. In order for the competitive bid to function properly, efforts must be directed toward the fulfillment of these goals. For example, non-conforming bids are usually disregarded because conformity is needed for a proper comparison of bids, and to give each bidder an equal opportunity to win the award. Also, the competitive bidding system cannot function properly unless honest and capable bidders have enough confidence in the fairness of the system to submit bids. Submitting a bid proposal is an expensive and time consuming operation. The bidders are entitled to reasonable assurance that they will be treated fairly, and that the owner will stick by his own rules. The owner, or more realistically his design professional, who conducts a fair and proper competitive bidding arrangement is likely to impress bidders as the type of owner whose efficiency and fairness is likely to result in a successful building project operation for all parties concerned.

(B) INVITATION TO BIDDERS

In the following discussion there will be no effort to cover every possible aspect of the competitive bidding process. Most public agencies have standard forms for the competitive bidding process, and they are often regulated by statutes, regulations and ordinances. Also, private owners often have engaged in substantial construction work and have also developed their own forms and methods. Most design professions have developed standard or recommended forms for bidding documents. They are usually available to the design professional. The balance of the chapter examines the process, and how the law fits into the framework of the competitive bid.

Sometimes competitive bidding is initiated by public advertising. Frequently, public contracts are required to be "advertised." This means that the agency which wishes to erect a project must give public notice that it is requesting bids on the project. This is sometimes done through trade newspapers, professional journals, and other media likely to reach the bulk of the potential contractors. Government publications put out by the Department of Commerce list public bid invitations for many federal agencies. The advertised bid is a method of permitting as many people as possible to submit bids on the proposed work. It is supposed to give everyone a chance to bid and, through open competition, obtain the lowest price.

While inviting the maximum number of competitors should result in a lower price, there are dangers in having too many bidders. Good bidders may be discouraged if the large number of bidders make their chances of winning quite remote.

Also, owners and design professionals who are knowledgeable about the construction industry know that nothing can replace a skilled contractor who has the integrity, equipment and personnel to do the job properly. For this reason, the "prequalification system" is sometimes used. The owner, through his design professional, selects a group of bidders, all of whom are likely to have the capability of doing a competent job. The design professional may request information from specific contractors on prior jobs completed, capital structure, machinery and equipment, and personnel (including supervisory personnel). After evaluation of this information, the design professional determines which contractors should be permitted to receive an "Invitation to Bid".

The advantage to prequalification is that there is a better chance of finding a good contractor. However, there will be administrative time and expense expended in making this preselection or prequalification, and the competitive aspect is likely to be diminished. Such a method should be used where the project is of great magnitude, or involves new construction techniques, and where cost is less important than ensuring the quality of performance.

Bidders should be given adequate opportunity to study the bidding information, to make tests, to inspect the site and to obtain bids from subcontractors and suppliers. Even when there is adequate time, bidders often wait to complete their bids until the bid closing deadline is imminent. Generally, this is due to reluctance on the part of subcontractors to give sub-bids to bidders until shortly before the deadline for bid submissions. The reasons for this reluctance is explored in § 17.05. Even if bidders do not make proper use of the time available to them, having allowed reasonable time for bid preparation can be helpful to the owner if a dispute arises over claimed computation errors or unforeseen subsurface conditions.

While it used to be relatively standard for the invitation to state that bids could not be changed, corrected or withdrawn after submission, there is some move in the direction of more flexibility in permitting changes, corrections, and withdrawals of submitted bids before bid opening. This may be due to the tendency of modern courts to release a low bidder who has made computation errors even *after* opening of bids, but while there is still an opportunity to award the contract to the next lowest bidder. Also, permitting changes can help the owner by permitting and encouraging reduction of bids in a changing market. However, over-liberality in permitting changes, corrections, and withdrawals may cause bidders to lose confidence in the honesty of the bidding competition.

Where the right to change is given, it may be limited to reducing the bid. If changes, corrections, or withdrawals are to be permitted, the invitation can limit such a right to a designated time period, and require that any change, correction, or withdrawal be expressed in writing and received by the owner by a designated time.

The invitation to bidders usually gives the owner a right to reject any and all bids, and usually obligates the owner to award the contract to the lowest responsible bidder if he is going to accept any bid. The invitation usually states that the bidder must put up some form of security to insure that he will enter into the contract if the award is made to him. The security could be a security interest in real property, certain types of personal property, a cashier's or certified check, cash, or a bid bond. It is relatively rare to use property or cash as a security, as this ties up capital during the period from the submission of the bid until a short time after award. For the same reason, bid bonds are becoming more popular than cashier's or certified checks.

The invitation should also state how long the securities will be held, since this is a matter of considerable importance to the bidder. It is usually advisable for the owner to hold all the bid securities for a short period after bid awards, but then to release all the securities except for the lowest three or four bidders. Perhaps the person who submits the low bid will not enter into the contract, and it still may be possible under some circumstances to hold the next low bidder. However, there is no justification for holding the securities of bidders who are not likely to be awarded the contract.

Usually the bidders must make a small monetary deposit when they request information in order to study a possible proposal. Sometimes this has the effect of discouraging persons who are not serious about making a bid proposal from obtaining the plans and specifications merely out of curiosity. The deposit is usually refunded when the bidding documents are returned. (For the effect on such a deposit on the common law copyright in the drawings, see § 40.05(e).)

It is important for the owner to retain all the records connected to the bidding process. Time logs should be kept which show exactly when the bidder obtained the bidding information. If there are changes in bidding information, they should be sent to all persons who have picked up bidding information, with copies of the changes kept for future reference. Changes after the bidding information is disseminated should be kept to a minimum.

Sometimes the invitation to bidders contains a provision that bidding technicalities can be waived by the owner. This means that minor non-compliances, and perhaps minor non-conformity, may be disregarded by the owner. Advance notice to bidders that technicalities can be waived may mean sloppier proposals, and also may induce bidders to believe that there is a possibility that favoritism will be shown to certain bidders by waiving any defects in their bid proposals. In some cases, this flexibility in disregarding minor bid variations may be possible, without language in the invitation to bidders expressly reserving this right to the owner.

As shall be seen in § 17.03(j), waiver of procedural defects is permitted only rarely in public competitive bidding.

Sometimes larger projects can be divided into designated stages. The owner may decide not to build the entire project if he does not have the money, or if bids are too high for certain portions of the work. For this reason the invitation to bidders can be divided into the stages, or project alternatives. The difficulty with alternatives is that it may mean that favoritism can be accomplished by the award. For example, there may be an invitation to bidders involving a hospital, a dormitory for nurses, and a parking structure. One alternative could be the hospital alone. A second alternative could be the hospital with the parking structure, and a third alternative could be the hospital with the nurses' dormitory. One bidder may be low on the total bid. Another bidder may be low on the first alternative, another on the second, and another on the third. The determination of which alternative is to be awarded could be based upon favoritism to one of the bidders. To avoid this difficulty, the invitation to bidders should state what are the preferred alternative choices. The first choice could be the entire project, provided the total cost comes within a certain specified limitation. If the total cost for the entire project does not meet this specified limitation, then the next choice could be the hospital with the parking structure, again provided that the cost of this alternative falls within the amount of money available. The next preference could be the hospital with the nurses' dormitory, subject to the lowest responsible bid being within the money available. The last choice might be just the hospital.

The same type of award manipulation is possible if the alternates consist of different methods of construction or materials. A list of preferences within price limits may avoid suspicion of favoritism.

(C) INFORMATION TO BIDDERS

Information to bidders usually consists of plans, specifications, drawings, contract terms and conditions, and any other documents which will be part of the contract. Soil test reports may be included in the bidder's information. Sometimes the bid information states that certain information is available in the office of the soils engineer or a design professional, if the bidder wishes to make use of the information. Inclusion of soil information may make the owner liable to the successful bidder for extra costs incurred in reliance upon incorrect soil information. See Chapter 22.

The information to bidders should be as detailed as possible, so that the bidders have sufficient information to make an intelligent bid proposal. If the information is too vague, and if too much discretion is left in the hands of the design professional, bidders may be discouraged from submitting any bid. Also, vagueness of information may encourage bidders of doubtful integrity to make a low proposal, in hopes that they will be able later to point out ambiguities and to set up large claims for extras. It may be helpful in the information to bidders to specify that any ambiguities that the bidder believes to exist must be resolved by a written request for a clarification to the design professional, before award of the bid. The clarification itself should also be in writing, and should be sent to all persons to whom invitations have been sent.

It is customary to include many disclaimers in the bidding information, and sometimes in the invitation to bid as well. A soil disclaimer, for example, is a provision which may warn the bidder to inspect the site himself, to make his own tests, and to check the accuracy of his bid proposal. The purpose of disclaimers is to try to place certain risks upon the bidder, and to preclude subsequent contentions of mistake either in computation or subsurface conditions. See § 22.05 for a discussion of the effect of such disclaimers.

(D) BID PROPOSALS

It is important that the bid proposals be submitted on the forms provided by the owner. This is to insure that the bids can be properly compared, and that all the bidders are proposing to do the same work under the same terms and conditions. The bid proposal form provided by the owner should also contain disclaimers such as those mentioned in the preceding paragraph. These disclaimers do not furnish absolute protection against a contention by the bidder that he made mistakes caused by misrepresentations made by the owner, or by someone employed by him. However, disclaimers do materially reduce this risk.

The methods used by contractors to determine their bids are relevant for a number of reasons. First, it can be seen how difficult cost estimating can be, a point made in § 8.01 dealing with cost predictions by design professionals. Second, the design professionals are frequently called upon to advise the owner as to whether a bidder should be released for bidding mistakes, or whether a bid should be accepted. Understanding the pricing techniques employed by contractors should assist the design professional in determining whether or not a particular bid was made in error, or is so unrealistically low that satisfactory completion at the bid price is unlikely. Third, design professionals, especially engineers, may become contractors or work for contractors, and prepare bid proposals.

The two major items used by the contractor in determining his bid are material and labor. The contractor must estimate the quantities and costs of materials required. The contractor must also estimate the hours and types of labor necessary, multiplying this by the applicable labor rate for the various trades. In addition to materials and labor, there are other important items which must be considered. Illustrations are:

1. Supervisory and office staff in the field
2. Engineering costs
3. Rental of site office space and sometimes of site housing
4. Equipment
5. Storage facilities
6. Power and the means of getting it to the places where it is needed
7. Transportation of materials and personnel
8. Allowances for contingencies which have not been directly considered in the other items, such as encountering difficult subsurface conditions and administrative costs which may be increased because of working with an unreasonable design professional or owner
9. Overhead
10. Profit

11. Interest on money needed to finance the operation
12. Insurance such as Workmen's Compensation, Public Liability and Property insurance
13. Bonds
14. Taxes
15. Cost of permits and other fees
16. Legal expenses.

After these items are taken into account, the contractor must determine whether the tentative bid proposal will be competitive. He must also consider whether the invitation to bid has any fixed limitation, beyond which the bids will not be considered. There may also be consideration of whether there are adequate appropriations or bond issues to cover his tentative bid proposal figure. This is usually reflected in the invitation to bidders in public work.

Much of the estimating of costs of material and labor can be accomplished by the use of bids by subcontractors and materialmen. Subcontractor bids can reduce the work of making bid proposals, and, if good subcontractors are chosen, can result in a more realistic bid.

Another factor which must be taken into account is the contractor's need to employ his work force, even if the job will not be a profitable one. Also, a busy and efficient contractor may increase his bid, because he knows that his reputation is good enough to get certain jobs whether he is the low bidder or not.

For these and other reasons, large bid variations are common.

The bid proposal should be signed by an authorized person. If the bidder is a partnership, the entire name and address of the partnership should be given. If the bidder is a corporation, the bid should be signed by appropriate officers, and the corporate seal should be attached. It may be desirable to attach to the bid a resolution of the board of directors approving the bid. The invitation to bidders often contains directions on the formal aspects of the bid proposal.

(E) BID OPENING

Usually the contractors' bid proposals are sent in sealed envelopes to the design professional, and are not to be opened until the time and place specified in the invitation to bidders. At the time specified, the design professional or the owner will open all bids and read aloud the bid proposals submitted. Usually the award is not made at that time. Bid proposals will have to be studied and evaluated to determine who is the lowest responsible bidder. Usually the invitation to bidders gives the owner a specified period of time to evaluate the bids. Care must be taken not to make it look as if the low bidder has been awarded the contract merely because his bid is lowest at the bid opening. A design professional should make it clear that there must be an evaluation of the bids. The successful bidder, as well as those who are unsuccessful, should be notified within the specified time set forth in the invitation.

(F) EVALUATION OF BIDS

The design professional is frequently called upon to evaluate the bids, and to make recommendations to the owner, public or private, upon the bid award. First, he should determine whether or not the bids are in conformity. If they are not in conformity, the non-conforming bids should be rejected and not considered. (A non-conforming bid is a proposal based on performance not called for in the information or in the invitation, or offers performance different than that specified in the information or invitation.) Non-conformity may relate to the work, the times of completion, the bonds submitted, or any part of the contractual arrangement.

In considering who is the lowest responsible bidder, the design professional and the owner can take into account the following factors, as well as any others which bear upon who would be the bidder most likely to do the job properly:

1. Expertise in type of work proposed
2. Capital structure
3. Organization
4. Reputation
5. Technological skill and integrity
6. Past performance.

These illustrations relate to the basic objectives of obtaining a contractor who is likely to do the job properly at the lowest price, and with the least administrative cost to the owner.

In contracts for the purchase of machinery, bid evaluation should take into account:

1. Length and extent of warranty
2. Availability of spare parts
3. Service and maintenance
4. Cost of replacement parts
5. Cost of installation
6. Durability.

Price should not be the sole criteria for selecting the contractor.

As stated in § 17.03(b) bidders may be asked to bid separately on project alternatives. Sometimes, in such cases, bidders make an "all or nothing bid". Such a bid means they will not obligate themselves to perform any individual part of the project, but submit the bid on the assumption they will be given the entire project or none of it. Usually such a bid is not considered nonconforming, unless so specified by the invitation to bidders.

If the owner changes the contract terms after the bid has been awarded, and the change makes the obligation less burdensome to the successful bidder, this can be unfair to the other bidders. For this reason, changes of this type should be done with caution. It may be necessary to do so, but the possibility of a law suit by a disappointed bidder should be considered if such a step is taken.

Good administration requires evaluation of criteria other than price in selecting a contractor, but there is a substantial risk of legal action if the bid is awarded to someone other than the low bidder. Sometimes bid awards in public contracts can be taken to court. This should not deter the design professional from advising the client, even a public client, that someone other than the low bidder should be awarded the contract. However, the record should show compelling reasons for not awarding it to the low bidder.

(G) NOTIFICATION TO BIDDERS

When the decision is made to award the contract to a particular bidder, the unsuccessful bidders should be notified. However, the design professional should realize that sometimes the successful bidder will not enter into the contract awarded to him. He may have legal justification for not doing this. For this reason, it is advisable when notifying the unsuccessful bidders of the bid award to state that their bids still remain available for acceptance by the owner for the period of time specified in the invitation to bid. This should be done to avoid any later contention that awarding the contract released the unsuccessful bidders.

(H) SIGNING THE FORMAL CONTRACT

The successful bidder is notified and requested to meet at a specified time and place to sign the formal documents. Records of all correspondence should be kept, in event there are subsequent disputes between the owner and the contractor relating to the bidding process and awarding of the contract.

(I) RE-ADVERTISING

Sometimes the bids are all too high, and the owner decides to re-advertise the project. In public contracts, there are procedures for re-advertising. Re-advertising requires time and administrative expense. Some feel that re-advertising without reducing the scope or quality of the project is unfair, because it is an attempt to beat down the bids of the contractors, often resulting in deficient workmanship and substandard materials. Frequently, re-advertising means higher bids from all bidders, because the less skillful bidders have seen what the better bidders have bid.

(J) SPECIAL RULES FOR PUBLIC CONTRACTS: WEINER v. CUYAHOGA COMMUNITY COLLEGE

Competitive bidding rules may depend upon whether the owner is a public agency. Some statutes require that certain types of contracts be awarded by competitive bidding, and that there be public advertising of the proposed contract award. This means that a negotiated contract cannot be used. Pre-qualification is less common, although it is sometimes used in some state contracts and certain types of federal contracts. Some federal public contracts must be set aside for small business, in furtherance of a public policy to encourage smaller businesses. This can mean a loss of competition. Sometimes small businesses may be given preference, if the price differential does not exceed a specified amount.

Many public contracts require that contractors and subcontractors not discriminate in employment, not use convict labor, abide by certain fair labor standards and wage rates, and use only American-made goods. These are particularly important in federal public contracts, but they are becoming more common in state and local public contracts. Weiner v. Cuyahoga Community College Dist., illustrates this trend.

WEINER v. CUYAHOGA COMMUNITY COLLEGE DISTRICT

Supreme Court of Ohio, 1969.
19 Ohio St.2d 35, 249 N.E.2d 907.

This is a taxpayer's action brought in the Court of Common Pleas of Cuyahoga County to enjoin the Cuyahoga Community College District from awarding or expending funds in furtherance of a contract for heating, ventilating and air-conditioning work on the Cleveland campus of the college, to a contractor other than the lowest and best bidder. The development and construction on the campus necessitating such contract is a joint project of state and federal entities. The invitation for bids on the contract contained specifications which required the contractor to submit an *Affirmative Action Plan* intended to "have the *result of assuring* that there is minority group representation in all trades on the job and in all phases of the work." (Emphasis original.) The specifications further provided detailed principles of affirmative action, steps to be taken for a program, a guideline for the contractor's program and established a *pre-award* meeting one week after bid opening for discussion of such program. It was also specified: "A written affirmative action plan by each such apparent low bidder must be approved by the federal government prior to the contract execution. Such affirmative action plan is to be submitted by such apparent low bidder not later than 15 days after the above mentioned pre-award meeting * * *."

There were two bidders for the contract involved in this suit. Reliance Mechanical Contractors, Inc., submitted the low bid and an Affirmative Action Plan of some 100 pages. Reliance conditioned its proposed minority representation in jobs, however, with the words "Subject to availability and referral to Reliance Mechanical Contractors, Inc. of qualified journeymen and apprentices from Pipefitters Local No. 120," referring to the union with which it had an exclusive hiring hall contract. At the pre-award meeting, the college objected to the foregoing condition in Reliance's plan, and other forms of wording were tried and rejected. The final submission of Reliance stated: "* * * this company will continue to make every reasonable effort to see to it that Negro apprentices are employed and placed on this project. However, this company cannot and, therefore, does not guarantee that it will have Negro apprentices on this project."

Thereafter, Reliance's bid was formally rejected by the college for failure to include submission of an Affirmative Action Program acceptable to the federal government. The contract was awarded to the second low bidder, whose assurance of equal employment opportunity and minority group representation on the job was expressed in its statement: "You are hereby advised that we will have Negro representation in all crafts employed on this project."

Plaintiff contends that the college and federal officials who rejected Reliance's Affirmative Action Plan were seeking an unlawful guarantee that the contractor would have Negroes on the job, that Reliance's bid was lowest and best, that its Affirmative Action Plan was consistent with state and federal law and the specifications of the invitation to bid, and that the rejection of Reliance's bid in favor of a higher bidder was, accordingly, an abuse of discretion and unlawful.

The trial court found that Reliance was never requested or expected to hire Negroes or any other persons on a quota basis, but that the invitation to bid and appellees' position during discussions thereafter did lawfully require an unequivocal assurance of positive equal employment opportunity efforts. It found from both oral testimony and documentary exhibits that Reliance at no time gave such assurance and rendered judgment for defendants. Upon appeal on questions of law and fact, the Court of Appeals took additional documentary evidence, adopted the findings of the trial court and rendered the same judgment.

HERBERT, JUDGE. The issue at the heart of this dispute is whether the policies of the United States and the State of Ohio against discriminatory employment practices may be positively enforced by a public body through the medium of public improvement contracts. The public policy is clearly formulated in the legislation proscribing racial discrimination in employment. *See* Civil Rights Act of 1964, Section 2000e–2, Title 42, U.S.Code; Section 4112.02, Revised Code. Public construction contracts requiring employment in their performance must contain provisions by which the contractor promises that he will not engage in any discriminatory hiring practice (Section 153.59, Revised Code; Presidential Executive Order No. 11246, Section 202[1], 30 Fed.Reg. 12319), but more important, both state and federal executive orders implementing civil rights legislation enjoin upon public contractors affirmative duties with respect to seeking, hiring, training, promoting and paying employees, and in regard to their dealings with subcontractors, unions and employment agencies, all to the end that nondiscrimination in the performance of the contract will be assured. *See* Presidential Executive Order No. 11246, *supra,* Parts II and III; Ohio Gubernatorial Executive Order, June 5, 1967 (unnumbered and unreported).

Plaintiff does not question the requirement that public contractors promise not to discriminate in employment. Exacting such a promise from a contractor does little more than provide a contract remedy for practices already condemned by law. Rather, he contends that the community college district, as a public body of the state, and the federal agency, through the college (*see* Section 3354.09[H], Revised Code), attempted to exact contractual obligations from the successful bidder which were not authorized by law.

It may be argued that requiring public contractors to take affirmative action to forestall discriminatory employment practices in the performance of their contracts will tend to raise the cost of such contracts. Increased costs impair another governmental interest, that of economy. It must be noted, however, that neither state nor federal contracts are secured only to the lowest bidder, but to the lowest *and best* bidder (Section 3354.16, Revised Code) and lowest *responsible* bidder (Section 112[b], Title 23, U.S. Code). Moreover, the alternative of securing a like degree of compliance with equal employment opportunity laws by means of public prosecutions and administrative proceedings is also costly and, in addition, is both *post hoc* [Ed. note. "Post hoc" literally means "after this". In this context, it probably means that public prosecutions and administrative proceedings occur *after* the time compliance is needed, such as during construction.] and punitive. Indeed, it might reasonably be supposed that the governmental objectives of equal employment opportunity and low-cost public construction would be better served by requiring public contractors to undertake affirmative duties in practicing nondiscrimination in their dealings with and through others in the performance of the contract, thereby denying the benefits of public contract expenditures to those who would discriminate.

In addition to economics as a reason for requiring public contractors to assure nondiscriminatory performance, the strong moral commitment of both state and federal governments to fair employment practices is reflected in their respective legislation. A government which has declared discriminatory employment practices unlawful should not then finance them indirectly by binding only its direct contractor, and not the entire contract performance, to a promise of attempted compliance. We conclude that the capacity to assure a performance which complies with antidiscrimination laws is reasonably a part of the standard of a best or responsible bidder on a contract involving the expenditure of public funds. Accordingly, a bidder for a construction contract to be awarded by a public body of this state may be required to assure, by appropriate promises contained in contract provisions or related instruments, nondiscrimination in employment in the entire performance of the contract.

The remaining issue is the propriety of the particular promise sought in this case.

Plaintiff contends that a *guarantee* of *Negro* employment was sought. The only use of those terms occurred in Reliance's negation of what it could assure. The factual determinations of both of the courts below are that neither the invitation to bid nor the negotiations with respect to Affirmative Action Plans were directed at securing either an absolute guarantee of the actual results of such a plan or a result pertaining solely to Negroes. The establishment of a quota of employment of any particular minority would also be discriminatory in violation of the Civil Rights Act of 1964 (Section 2000e-2[j], Title 42, U.S.Code). It is no answer that the successful bidder promised Negro representation on the job. The record contains no evidence that such a promise was either required or solicited, or that the promise would be enforced to the exclusion of all other persons. The findings of the courts below are supported by the record and we are not disposed to disturb them from this distance. . . .

The courts below also found that what was sought was an unequivocal statement by the contractor which would assure equal employment *opportunity*, and that Reliance's posture throughout the discussions included only equivocal assurances. The record supports the conclusion that all parties to the bid understood what was required by the federal government through the college, but that Reliance found itself in the position of being willing but unable to make a contractual commitment of full nondiscriminatory performance. We have determined that such a commitment may validly be exacted and, therefore, Reliance's bid was lawfully rejected.

It is unfortunate that Reliance, whose submitted Affirmative Action Plan reflected the company's equal opportunity employment practices, should have lost this contract for failure to satisfy the government that racial discrimination would not be practiced. However, it must be remembered that while the public entity was interested in Reliance's compliance with the letter and spirit of fair employment laws, it was also vitally concerned that the entire job be conducted in compliance with such laws. Toward this end, it properly sought the prime contractor's unequivocal assurance that it would deal with others involved in the performance in a manner which would secure such compliance, and was entitled to judge the best or responsible bidder accordingly.

The record supports the findings and conclusion that defendants did not abuse their discretion in rejecting the low bid of Reliance and awarding the contract to the second bidder. The judgment of the Court of Appeals is therefore affirmed.

Judgment affirmed.

TAFT, CHIEF JUSTICE (dissenting). As stated in the majority's statement of the case, "the invitation for bids on the contract contained specifications which required the contractor to submit an *Affirmative Action Plan* intended to 'have the *result of assuring* that there is minority group representation in all trades on the job and in all phases of the work'" and "Reliance's bid was formally rejected by the College for failure to include submission of" such a plan.

I fail to perceive any distinction between such a "Plan intended to 'have the *result of assuring* * * * minority group representation'" and a guarantee of such representation. Counsel for the College conceded that such a guarantee would be a discrimination against others that is prohibited by the Civil Rights Act of 1964 (Section 2000e-2 [j], Title 42, U.S.Code).

Likewise, the majority opinion concedes that "[t]he establishment of a quota of employment of any particular minority would * * * be discriminatory in violation of" that Act. Certainly, such an unlawful establishment of a quota would necessarily be a part of any *"Affirmative Action Plan* intended to 'have the *result of assuring* that there is minority group representation in all trades on the job and in all phases of the work.'"

In addition to provisions on hiring practices, such as in the *Weiner* case, there are other requirements for public contract bidders, that set them apart from private contracts. The bidder may have to certify that he has not employed anyone on a contingent fee basis to help him procure the contract. He may have to certify that he has not paid any government official for assisting him in obtaining the contract. There are other statutory provisions, such as conflict of interest laws, which are designed to protect the integrity of the public bidding processes. Public contracts involve policies and considerations that go beyond obtaining the best product at the best price. As seen in *Weiner*, public contracts may be a device to assist minority group employment, or to give protection to small businesses, or to American industries. In addition, the fear of graft and corruption is greater in public contracts. This is manifested by the various provisions dealing with influence peddling and conflicts of interest.

As to the competitive bidding process itself, everything has to be done more carefully in public contracts. There is always the possibility of audit, of newspaper investigations, and of investigations by legislative or administrative bodies. Public officials usually try to avoid any appearance of irregularity. Sometimes they seem overly-rigid and unreasonable. However, public officials may be personally responsible if they do not obey all the rules relating to the contract award process. For this reason, public officials are reluctant to waive defects, or to permit corrected or withdrawn bids, unless they clearly have the power to do so.

A court opinion expressed the philosophy behind requiring absolute compliance with all requirements in public contracts. The bidding agency attempted to accept a bid made one minute late. In holding that the agency could not do so, the Ohio Common Pleas Court of Lake County stated in H. R. Johnson Construction Co. v. Board of Education, 16 Ohio Misc. 99, 241 N.E.2d 403 (1968):

> The argument is made that even if the bid was one minute late this deviation is so minor that it should be disregarded out of consideration for the larger interests of the school population and the community. But it cannot be disregarded. The language of Section 3313.46, Revised Code, is clear and unequivocal.
>
> ". . . sealed bids must be filed with the clerk by twelve noon of the last day . . ."
>
> A court has a duty to adhere to a statute as it is written and enforce its literal terms. Where the language is clear it may not be interpreted. It must be enforced.
>
> So where a statute provides that an act must be performed by a specific time, a court may not, no matter how desirable it may be in a given situation, declare that the statute really means "at or near" the time. Where the language is free of ambiguity there is no judicial latitude whatsoever.
>
> But it is said that the board has discretion to waive the noon requirement and did so in this case; that the exercise of this discretion should not be upset without evidence of fraud or collusion, I cannot agree. There is no evidence of fraud or collusion here. But a school board has no discretion to waive a statutory command. The procedures set forth in this statute must be followed for a contract to be valid. Its provisions are mandatory upon the board. . . . .
>
> I deny, as some will, that the effect of this ruling is to administer justice by barren technicality. There is sound reason for adhering strictly to the deadline. The evidence demonstrates the advantage to a bidder who submits a bid even a few minutes late. He can wait later than his competitors to assemble his bid and benefit from last minute price "shopping." To allow a waiver of a deadline would certainly prejudice the rights of other bidders.
>
> More than this, it would ultimately injure the taxpaying community by destroying competitive bidding altogether. If this board has discretion to allow a one minute deviation, then all boards have discretion to allow a 15 minute or even an hour deviation. And if they have discretion on the subject then they are free to exercise it or not as they choose. The question then arising is what responsible contractors will spend the time and money preparing and submitting bids knowing that a board is free to accept a late bid; knowing

> also that it is likely to be the lowest bid by virtue of its very lateness?
>
> I suppose only those contractors who are friendly with the boards and have some confidence that the deadline will be waived in their cases.
>
> Or, perhaps even more likely, if this court declares that a bid deadline may be disregarded, what contractor will risk submitting his bid on time knowing that others can undercut him by waiting longer? The result of this will be that all bids will be late and thus the effect will be not merely to modify the statutory requirement by judicial fiat but to rescind it altogether.

Also, public contracts and payments for work often depend upon the availability of designated funds. There are more likely to be conditions in the invitation to bidders, based upon availability of appropriations or bond money. Winning a public contract award is more speculative because there are greater possibilities that no contract will be awarded at all. Rejection of all bids is more common in public contracts because of the financial contingencies.

SECTION 17.04 SOME LEGAL ASPECTS OF COMPETITIVE BIDDING

(A) INVITATION TO BIDDERS

Ordinarily, the invitation to bidders is not an offer and does not create a power of acceptance in the bidders. The invitation to bid is merely a request that the bidder make an offer to the owner, which the owner can accept or reject. This does not mean that the invitation to bidders is not an important document. It sets up the ground rules for the competitive bid. If a contract is formed with one of the bidders, the invitation to bid can be considered as part of the arrangement between the parties, unless it is modified by the final contract made between the successful bidder and the owner. The invitation to bidders by itself does not in any way obligate the owner.

(B) BID PROPOSAL

The proposal submitted by the bidder is an offer, and does create a power of acceptance in the owner. This means that the owner has the right to close the deal and bind the bidder without any further act of the bidder. Offers are normally revocable, even if they are expressly stated to be irrevocable for a specified period of time. In early English legal history the irrevocable offer could only be made by the use of a sealed instrument (a device which has largely been abandoned in this country) or if the owner gave something of value to the bidder and thus made the bid an irrevocable offer (sometimes called a binding option). Despite the general doctrine of revocability of offers, for all practical purposes the bid proposal is irrevocable for the period of time stated in the invitation to bidders or the proposal itself. In public contracts, this result is achieved by statute, or by local ordinance. In private contracts, some courts have held that the bidder is exchanging his irrevocable bid in order to obtain consideration of his bid by the owner. This is a fiction, but it has sometimes assisted courts in holding that the bid is irrevocable. Generally, the bid proposal made by the bidder cannot be revoked for the period of time specified in the invitation or in the proposal. (The doctrine of mistake may be used to relieve the contractor-bidder from his bid. This is not because his bid is revocable, but because there exist sufficient grounds to permit him relief from his bid.)

(C) MUST A BID BE ACCEPTED?

Is the owner obligated to accept any of the bids? This depends upon the language used in the invitation to the bidders. It is possible to word an invitation in such a way as to obligate the owner to accept the low bid, or the lowest responsible bid. In such a case, the invitation to bid would be an offer conditioned on there being a low bid or a low responsible bid. As stated previously, most invitations to bidders are not offers.

The right to reject all bids is frequently given by statute to public agencies that conduct competitive bidding for public contracts. In private projects, the right to reject any and all bids is usually expressed in the invitation to bidders. Usually the bid is an offer, but the formation of the contract depends upon the acceptance of a particular bid by the owner, and awarding of the contract to the particular bidder.

(D) DURATION OF POWER TO ACCEPT BID

Is the power of acceptance of the owner affected by the awarding of the contract to one bidder who does not enter into the contract? The low bidder may be awarded the contract but refuse, without justification, to enter into the contract, or may have grounds to be relieved from his bid because of the doctrine of mistake. Can the owner take the next low bid, or does his award of the contract to the low bidder terminate his power of acceptance? Court results differ on this question. The power of acceptance should not expire until the time specified in the invitation. This time should take into account the possibility that the bidder awarded the contract will not execute the contract. This possibility should be covered by the invitation to bidders.

(E) WITHDRAWAL OR CORRECTION OF MISTAKEN BIDS: ELSINORE UNION v. KASTORFF

The bid opening may reveal a substantial variation between the low bidder and the other bidders. Great variations in bid proposals are common, because of the unscientific way costs are predicted and the variant pricing factors. Sometimes, contractors refuse to enter into a contract because they claim their bid was the result of a mistake. There may be computation errors, such as omitting a large item, or making a mistake in adding the tally sheet. The mistake may be caused by poor judgment in estimating quantities, labor, or other elements of the bid proposal.

Sometimes prime contractors seek relief because one (or more) of their subcontractors claims that he need not perform in accordance with his sub-bid because the sub-bid was revocable, or the sub-bid itself was arrived at through mistaken computations. (For special discussion of subcontractor problems see § 17.05.)

The tendency of earlier cases was to deny relief because of such mistakes. The mistake was "unilateral", one made only by the prime contractor, and not a mutual mistake shared by both prime contractor and owner.

Courts began to moderate the strictness of this doctrine by use of the "snap-up" theory. A person to whom an offer has been made cannot accept the offer if he knows, or should have known, that there has been a mistake. For example, if the owner or his design professional knows that an entire item composing a substantial part of the bid has been omitted, or if he knows that there has been a mistake in adding the total, it would be unfair for him to accept the mistaken figure and try to bind the prime contractor to his contract. This "snap-up" theory has been the wedge by which many prime contractors have obtained relief from their bids, where the court thought it fair to give them relief.

However, even a large variation in bids may not necessarily be held to put the owner or his design professional on notice that there has been some antecedent mistake. Often the design professional calls attention to the variation which becomes apparent at the time of the bid opening, and asks the bidder if he would like to check his figures. Frequently the prime contractor says that he will stand on his bid, and he is certain that the bid has been properly computed. It is only when he returns to his office and thinks about the prospects of a losing contract that he decides he would like relief from his bid.

If the mistake is clerical, involves a substantial portion of the total bid or a large amount of money and if the owner has not relied to his detriment upon the mistaken bid, the bidder has a good chance of being relieved. There is less likely to be judicial relief from a mistaken bid if the error related to matters of judgment, if the error was causd by a high degree of negligence, and if the owner is not able to award the contract to the next lowest bidder.

Even those courts which have been willing to permit a bidder to withdraw a bid will not permit the bidder to submit a corrected bid after the bids have been opened.

An illustrative modern case is Elsinore Union Elementary School District v. Kastorff.

ELSINORE UNION ELEMENTARY SCHOOL DISTRICT v. KASTORFF

Supreme Court of California, 1960.
54 Cal.2d 380, 353 P.2d 713, 6 Cal.Rptr. 1.

SCHAUER, JUSTICE. Defendants, who are a building contractor and his surety, appeal from an adverse judgment in this action by plaintiff school district to recover damages allegedly resulting when defendant Kastorff, the contractor, refused to execute a building contract pursuant to his previously submitted bid to make certain additions to plaintiff's school buildings. We have concluded that because of an honest clerical error in the bid and defendant's subsequent prompt rescission he was not obliged to execute the contract, and that the judgment should therefore be reversed.

Pursuant to plaintiff's call for bids, defendant Kastorff secured a copy of the plans and specifications of the proposed additions to plaintiff's school buildings and proceeded to prepare a bid to be submitted by the deadline hour of 8 p. m., August 12, 1952, at Elsinore, California. Kastorff testified that in preparing his bid he employed worksheets upon which he entered bids of various subcontractors for such portions of the work as they were to do, and that to reach the final total of his own bid for the work he carried into the right-hand column of the work sheets the amounts of the respective sub bids which he intended to accept and then added those amounts to the cost of the work which he would do himself rather than through a subcontractor; that there is "a custom among subcontractors, in bidding on jobs such as this, to delay giving * * * their bids until the very last moment"; that the first sub bid for plumbing was in the amount of $9,285 and he had received it "the afternoon of the bid-opening," but later that afternoon when "the time was drawing close for me to get by (sic) bids together and get over to Elsinore" (from his home in San Juan Capistrano) he received a $6,500 bid for the plumbing. Erroneously thinking he had entered the $9,285 plumbing bid in his total column and had included that sum in his total bid and realizing that the second plumbing bid was nearly $3,000 less than the first, Kastorff then deducted $3,000 from the total amount of his bid and entered the resulting total of $89,994 on the bid form as his bid for the school construction. Thus the total included no allowance whatsoever for the plumbing work.

Kastorff then proceeded to Elsinore and deposited his bid with plaintiff. When the bids were opened shortly after 8 p. m. that evening, it was discovered that of the five bids submitted that of

Kastorff was some $11,306 less than the next lowest bid. The school superintendent and the four school board members present thereupon asked Kastorff whether he was sure his figures were correct, Kastorff stepped out into the hall to check with the person who had assisted in doing the clerical work on the bid, and a few minutes later returned and stated that the figures were correct. He testified that he did not have his worksheets or other papers with him to check against at the time. The board thereupon, on August 12, 1952, voted to award Kastorff the contract.

The next morning Kastorff checked his worksheets and promptly discovered his error. He immediately drove to the Los Angeles office of the firm of architects which had prepared the plans and specifications for plaintiff, and there saw Mr. Rendon. Mr. Rendon testified that Kastorff "had his maps and estimate work-sheets of the project, and indicated to me that he had failed to carry across the amount of dollars for the plumbing work. It was on the sheet, but not in the total sheet. We examined that evidence, and in our opinion we felt that he had made a clerical error in compiling his bill. * * * In other words, he had put down a figure, but didn't carry it out to the 'total' column when he totaled his column to make up his bid. * * * He exhibited * * * at that time * * * his worksheets from which he had made up his bid." That same morning (August 13) Rendon telephoned the school superintendent and informed him of the error and of its nature and that Kastorff asked to be released from his bid. On August 14 Kastorff wrote a letter to the school board explaining his error and again requesting that he be permitted to withdraw his bid. On August 15, after receiving Kastorff's letter, the board held a special meeting and voted not to grant his request. Thereafter, on August 28, *written notification* was given to Kastorff of award of the contract to him. Subsequently plaintiff submitted to Kastorff a contract to be signed in accordance with his bid, and on September 8, 1952, Kastorff returned the contract to plaintiff with a letter again explaining his error and asking the board to reconsider his request for withdrawal of his bid.

Plaintiff thereafter received additional bids to do the subject construction; let the contract to the lowest bidder, in the amount of $102,900; and brought this action seeking to recover from Kastorff the $12,906 difference between that amount and the amount Kastorff had bid. Recovery of $4,499.60 is also sought against Kastorff's surety under the terms of the bond posted with his bid.

. . . Judgment was given for plaintiff in the amounts sought, and this appeal by defendants followed.

In reliance upon M. F. Kemper Const. Co. v. City of Los Angeles (1951), 37 Cal.2d 696, 235 P.2d 7, and Lemoge Electric v. County of San Mateo (1956), 46 Cal.2d 659, 662, 664 [1a, 1b, 2, 3], 297 P.2d 638, defendants urged that where, as defendants claim is the situation here, a contractor makes a clerical error in computing a bid on a public work he is entitled to rescind.

In the Kemper case one item on a worksheet in the amount of $301,769 was inadvertently omitted by the contractor from the final tabulation sheet and was overlooked in computing the total amount of a bid to do certain construction work for the defendant city. The error was caused by the fact that the men preparing the bid were exhausted after working long hours under pressure. When the bids were opened it was found that plaintiff's bid was $780,305, and the next lowest bid was $1,049,592. Plaintiff discovered its error several hours later and immediately notified a member of defendant's board of public works of its mistake in omitting one item while preparing the final accumulation of figures for its bid. Two days later it explained its mistake to the board and withdrew its bid. A few days later it submitted to the board evidence which showed the unintentional omission of the $301,769 item. The board nevertheless passed a resolution accepting plaintiff's erroneous bid of $780,305, and plaintiff refused to enter into a written contract at that figure. The board then awarded the contract to the next lowest bidder, the city demanded forfeiture of plaintiff's bid bond, and plaintiff brought action to cancel its bid and obtain discharge of the bond. The trial court found that the bid had been submitted as the result of an excusable and honest mistake of a material and fundamental character, that plaintiff company had not been negligent in preparing the proposal, that it had acted promptly to notify the board of the mistake and to rescind the bid, and that the board had accepted the bid with knowledge of the error. The court further found and concluded that it would be unconscionable to require the company to perform for the amount of the bid, that no intervening rights had accrued, and that the city had suffered no damage or prejudice.

On appeal by the city this court affirmed, stating the following applicable rules (at pages 700–703 of 37 Cal.2d, at pages 10, 11 of 235 P.2d):

> "[1] Once opened and declared, the company's bid was in the nature of an irrevocable option, a contract right of which the city could not be deprived without its consent unless the requirements for rescission were satisfied. [Citations.] * * * [2] * * * the city had actual notice of the error in the estimates before it attempted to accept the bid, and knowledge by one party that the other is acting under mistake is treated as equivalent to mutual mistake for purposes of rescission. [Citations.] [3] Relief from mistaken bids is consistently allowed where one party knows or has reason to know of the other's error and the requirements for rescission are fulfilled. [Citations.]
>
> "[4] Rescission may be had for mistake of fact if the mistake is material to the contract and was not the result of neglect of a legal duty, if enforcement of the contract as made would be unconscionable, and if the other party can be placed in statu quo. [Citations.] In addition, the party seeking relief must give prompt notice of his election to re-

scind and must restore or offer to restore to the other party everything of value which he has received under the contract. [Citations.]

"[5] Omission of the $301,769 item from the company's bid was, of course, a material mistake. * * * [E]ven if we assume that the error was due to some carelessness, it does not follow that the company is without remedy. Civil Code section 1577, which defines mistake of facts for which relief may be allowed, describes it as one not caused by 'the neglect of a legal duty' on the part of the person making the mistake. [6] It has been recognized numerous times that not all carelessness constitutes a 'neglect of legal duty' within the meaning of the section. [Citations.] On facts very similar to those in the present case, courts of other jurisdictions have stated that there was no culpable negligence and have granted relief from erroneous bids. [Citations.] [7] The type of error here involved is one which will sometimes occur in the conduct of reasonable and cautious businessmen, and, under all the circumstances, we cannot say as a matter of law that it constituted a neglect of legal duty such as would bar the right to equitable relief.

"[8] The evidence clearly supports the conclusion that it would be unconscionable to hold the company to its bid at the mistaken figure. The city had knowledge before the bid was accepted that the company had made a clerical error which resulted in the omission of an item amounting to nearly one third of the amount intended to be bid, and, under all the circumstances, it appears that it would be unjust and unfair to permit the city to take advantage of the company's mistake. [9, 10] There is no reason for denying relief on the ground that the city cannot be restored to status quo. It had ample time in which to award the contract without readvertising, the contract was actually awarded to the next lowest bidder, and the city will not be heard to complain that it cannot be placed in statu quo because it will not have the benefit of an inequitable bargain. [Citations.] [11] Finally, the company gave notice promptly upon discovering the facts entitling it to rescind, and no offer of restoration was necessary because it had received nothing of value which it could restore. [Citation.] We are satisfied that all the requirements for rescission have been met."

In the Lemoge case (Lemoge Electric v. County of San Mateo (1956), supra, 46 Cal.2d 659, 662, 664 [1a, 1b, 2, 3]) 297 P.2d 638, the facts were similar to those in Kemper, except that plaintiff Lemoge did not attempt to rescind but instead, after discovering and informing defendant of inadvertent clerical error in the bid, entered into a formal contract with defendant on the terms specified in the erroneous bid, performed the required work, and then sued for reformation. Although this court affirmed the trial court's determination that plaintiff was not, under the circumstances, entitled to have the contract reformed, we also reaffirmed the rule that "Once opened and declared, plaintiff's bid was in the nature of an irrevocable option, a contract right of which defendant could not be deprived without its consent unless the requirements for rescission were satisfied. [Citation.] Plaintiff then had the right to rescind, and it could have done so without incurring any liability on its bond." . . .

The rules stated in the Kemper and Lemoge cases . . . appear to entitle defendant to relief here, ...

Further, we are persuaded that the trial court's view . . . that "Kastorff had ample time and opportunity after receiving his last subcontractor's bid" to complete and check his final bid, does not convict Kastorff of that "neglect of legal duty" which would preclude his being relieved from the inadvertent clerical error of omitting from his bid the cost of the plumbing. . . . Neither should he be denied relief from an unfair, inequitable, and unintended bargain simply because, in response to inquiry from the board when his bid was discovered to be much the lowest submitted, he informed the board, after checking with his clerical assistant, that the bid was correct. He did not have his worksheets present to inspect at that time, he did thereafter inspect them at what would appear to have been the earliest practicable moment, and thereupon promptly notified plaintiff and rescinded his bid. Further . . . Kastorff's bid agreement, as provided by plaintiff's own bid form, was to execute a formal written contract only after receiving written notification of acceptance of his bid, and such notice was not given to him until some two weeks following his rescission.

If the situations of the parties were reversed and plaintiff and Kastorff had even executed a formal written contract (by contrast with the preliminary bid offer and acceptance) calling for a fixed sum payment to Kastorff large enough to include a reasonable charge for plumbing but inadvertently through the *district's* clerical error omitting a mutually intended provision requiring Kastorff to furnish and install plumbing, we have no doubt but that the district would demand and expect reformation or rescission. In the case before us the district expected Kastorff to furnish and install plumbing; surely it must also have understood that he intended to, and that his bid did, include a charge for such plumbing. The omission of any such charge was as unexpected by the board as it was unintended by Kastorff. Under the circumstances the "bargain" for which the board presses (which action we, of course, assume to be impelled by advice of counsel and a strict concept of official duty) appears too sharp for law and equity to sustain.

Plaintiff suggests that in any event the amount of the plumbing bid omitted from the total was immaterial. The bid as submitted was in the sum of $89,994, and whether the sum for the omitted plumbing was $6,500 or $9,285 (the two sub bids), the omission of such a sum is plainly material to the total. In Lemoge (Lemoge Electric v. County of San Mateo (1956), supra, 46 Cal.2d 659, 661–662, 297 P.2d 638) the error which it was declared would have entitled plaintiff to rescind was the listing of the cost of certain materials as $104.52, rather than $10,452, in a total bid of $172,421. Thus the percentage of error here was larger than in Lemoge, and was plainly material.

The judgment is reversed.

[Ed. Note: Footnotes omitted.]

Frequently state statutes which regulate public bidding and federal procurement regulations which perform a like function in the area of federal public contracts provide for relief from mistake under certain circumstances. For example, in Massachusetts a bidder can be relieved, and his bid deposit returned to him, if there has been a "bona fide clerical or mechanical error of a substantial nature" Massachusetts General Laws, Chapter 149, Section 44B(2).

Another illustration of statutory relief given to bidders in public contracts, is shown in Section 14352 of the California Government Code. This section gives relief if "the mistake was made in filling out the bid and not due to error in judgment or to carelessness in inspecting the site of the work, or in reading the plans or specifications." Also to obtain relief the bidder must give notification within five days after bid opening of the mistake, and must specify how the mistake occurred. Finally, Section 14350 of the Government Code of California specifically denies the public agency the authority to relieve a bidder, but requires that the bidder bring a lawsuit to obtain relief.

What if the invitation to the bidder states that the bidder will be bound even if there are errors of computation? Theoretically, the bidder can, by assenting to the invitation to bid, assume the risk of all types of mistakes. However, if the mistake is caught quickly, and if the court is convinced it was an honest mistake, there are good possibilities of relief despite any contractual provisions to the contrary.

Design professionals should realize that the tendency is toward relieving bidders for honest mistakes. If the mistake is detected early enough, and if the owner can be placed in status quo without any difficulty, attempted enforcement of the bid may be unwise. If the equities are in favor of the contractor, the contractor stands a good chance of being relieved by a court. Even if he does decide to perform the contract, he is not likely to do a good job.

(F) FORFEITURE OF BID DEPOSIT

The bidders are usually requested to submit deposits with their proposals. A number of legal problems relate to deposits. First, is the deposit merely a security deposit out of which the owner can take whatever damages he has incurred by an unexcused failure of the contractor to enter into the contract after it has been awarded to him? Is the payment an attempt to limit the damages to a specified figure that still obligates the owner to prove damages up to that figure? Is the deposit submitted in an attempt to set damages in advance by agreement of the parties?

This can be illustrated by a hypothetical example. Suppose bidder A submits a proposal for one million dollars, and the invitation to bidders requires him to submit a bid bond for 5% of his bid. A bid bond for $50,000 is deposited. The bids are opened and A is low. The next highest bidder has submitted a bid of $1,100,000. A is offered the contract but without any legal justification declines to enter into it. The contract is offered to the next high bidder for $1,100,000. In this case, is the owner entitled to $100,000 damages, with $50,000 being a security deposit out of which he can assure himself that he will be able to collect at least a part of his damages? Or is he limited in his damages to $50,000 because this is what the parties have agreed will be the agreed damage figure, without regard to actual damages being higher or lower?

What if the next high bidder had been $1,025,000 instead of $1,100,000? In such a case can the owner keep the entire $50,000 or be limited to $25,000?

To a certain extent the parties are free by their contract to determine whether the amount submitted or the bid bond deposited "liquidates" (agrees in advance on the amount) damages, is a security deposit, or is a limitation of liability. A "security deposit" is merely an amount of money deposited with one party, out of which he can satisfy whatever damages to which he is entitled. It insures he will have money in his possession which he can use to satisfy any claim he has. If the 5% deposit is merely a security deposit, then he can retain this amount and sue for any balance to which he is entitled, or he must return the excess of the deposit over his damages.

If the 5% deposit is an attempt to "liquidate" damages, the parties have agreed that no matter what the damages are, they have limited the liability to 5%, or, as in the illustration, $50,000. Technically, the owner has the right to retain the $50,000, whether his damages are $200,000 or $1. In order to have a valid liquidation of damages clause, there are generally two requirements. First, the damages must be difficult to ascertain at the time the contract is made; secondly, the amount agreed upon must be a genuine pre-estimate of the potential damages. Stated more realistically, the amount agreed upon must be reasonable. Some states require that there be actual damages before a liquidation of damages provision is effective.

If the amount is disproportionate to the actual or anticipated damage, and is merely a coercive device to compel performance, the provision is a penalty and unenforceable. For example, if the deposit were 50% of the bid, and if it were beyond the realm of probability that there would be damages resembling this amount, the clause would be a penalty and unenforceable. This would mean then that the owner would be entitled to only actual damages without regard for the amount of the deposit, and he would have to refund the excess of the deposit over his actual damages.

Sometimes ordinances or statutes are drawn up in such a way as to give the public agency the right to sue for the difference between low bid and the next highest bid if the low bidder does not enter into the contract when it is awarded to him. In such a case, it is clear that the amount designated is a security deposit, and not an attempt to liquidate damages. If it were a truly liquidated damages clause, the specified figure would be the damages without regard to actual damages, and there would be no possibility of collecting anything in excess of the designated figure.

Some statutes provide that the public agency can retain the amount deposited only to the extent of the difference between the bid of the bidder who has forfeited his deposit and the next high bid. For example, if the amount deposited were $50,000 or five per cent of the million dollar bid, and the next high bidder bid $1,025,000, then the owner would be entitled to retain $25,000. Under statutes of this type, the provision for a deposit sets up a liquidation of damages which will apply only if the actual damages are greater than the amount deposited. If the actual damages are less, then the deposit is for security.

Opinions differ as to whether it is better to set up an agreed damage figure, or merely use the deposit as a security deposit. From the owner's standpoint, the chances are very unlikely that he will be able to collect much from the contractor over and above the bid deposit. On the other hand, he would like to retain the 5 or 10% without having to show that he had been actually damaged to that extent. For that reason, in most cases it is probably preferable to create liquidated or agreed damages rather than using the deposit requirement solely as a security deposit. It is true that the pure security deposit does protect the right to recover larger damages if there is an extremely great variation between the low bidder and the next high bidder, but the greater the variation between the two bids, the greater the likelihood that there may have been a mistake which would release the bidder. Also, contractors often are not able to respond or pay very large judgments. This is one of the reasons for providing for a security deposit. The use of the agreed damages figure as indicated does relieve the contractor from excessive damages, and guarantees the owner that he will have a reasonable amount of collectible damages.

This treatise has suggested that the parties *can* make the deposit serve as a liquidated damages clause. Some courts might not enforce such a clause. While it is frequently stated that the uncertainty of the amount of damages must exist at the time the contract is made, many courts, especially in cases involving the sale of land, have looked at whether the amount of damages will be easily ascertainable at the time of breach. In the sale of land cases, some courts have often held that the usual formula for ascertaining damages, the difference between contract price and market price, is sufficiently certain at the time of breach to deny enforceability to any clause liquidating damages.

Looking at the competitive bid deposit, at the time the amount of the deposit is established, the amount of damages in the event the bidder does not enter into the contract is not known. This is because the usual measure of recovery, that is, the difference between the bid of the breaching bidder and the next highest bidder, is not known until the bids are open. However, at the time of breach, that is when the low bidder refuses to enter into the contract, damages are ascertainable. Because of this, some courts might not enforce the deposit amount as a liquidated damage clause.

However, the clause should be clearly enforceable if it is necessary to rebid the entire project. Rebidding entails additional administrative expense.

Even if it is not, there are substantial administrative expenses that are involved when the low bidder, without justification, refuses to enter into the contract. The loss suffered by the person conducting the competitive bid is not limited to the difference between the two bids. These additional costs and administrative problems could furnish a legal justification for enforcing the deposit amount, provided it is reasonable.

What if there are liquidated damage deposits and both the low bidder and the next low bidder unjustifiably refuse to enter into the contract? Can the owner retain the deposit by both bidders? While is may seem unfair for him to retain both bidders' deposits, it is not logically indefensible. Each bidder has breached, and each has been to some degree relieved from the risk of excessive damages by the use of an agreed damage provision. However, good will and the avoidance of litigation may necessitate some solution such as retaining one-half of each, rather than trying to retain both deposits.

(G) OWNER'S DUTY TO DISCLOSE

There is an increasing tendency in the law to require that owners in a competitive bidding context disclose all the relevant information at their disposal to the bidders. This trend was illustrated by Helene Curtis Industries, Inc. v. United States, 312 F.2d 774 (Ct.Cl.1963). In this case the plaintiff successfully entered competitive bidding for the supply of a disinfectant for the federal government. The plaintiff incurred unanticipated costs. It had expected to use a certain process, but found it necessary to use a more complicated process. The plaintiff claimed that the government knew that the more complicated process would be needed, and did not disclose this to bidders. While the court would not find that the government owed a fiduciary obligation toward its contractors, it held for the plaintiff stating:

> . . . the Government—where the balance of knowledge is so clearly on its side—can no more betray a contractor into a ruinous course of action by silence than by the written or spoken word.

In most construction contracts, it is not likely that the owner will have the balance of knowledge so clearly on its side. However, if it does, there is a strong possibility that the owner will be held to the duty of disclosing important information which it had reasonable grounds to believe the bidders did not possess.

(H) ILLEGAL PUBLIC CONTRACTS: GERZOF v. SWEENEY

What if the public contract award is made illegally? Problems involving unjust enrichment to the public owner can occur if the contractor has partially or fully performed, and seeks to be paid for what he has done. Also, even more difficult problems can arise if the contractor has been paid for his work, and then the illegality is discovered. The next case illustrates the flexibility courts can use in solving these difficult problems.

GERZOF v. SWEENEY

Court of Appeals of New York, 1968.
22 N.Y.2d 297, 239 N.E.2d 521, 292 N.Y.S.2d 640.

FULD, CHIEF JUDGE. On this appeal—the case was previously before us three years ago (16 N.Y.2d 206, 264 N.Y.S.2d 376, 211 N.E. 2d 826)—we are concerned only with the question of remedies. However, to place the issues in proper perspective, it will be helpful to summarize the facts established not only by the present record but by the earlier one as well.

The Village of Freeport having decided, in 1960, through its regularly authorized officials that there was a need to supplement its power plant by the acquisition of a 3,500 kilowatt generator, advertised for bids for the purchase and installation of such an engine. In early 1961, two bids were received, one from Enterprise Engineering Co. and the other from Nordberg Manufacturing Co. Enterprise's bid was $615,685, while Nordberg's, higher by some $58,000, was $673,840. The Village Water and Light Commission (the agency which initially passed on the matter), following the recommendation of its engineer, urged the Board of Trustees to accept Enterprise's lower bid. However, before further action was taken, a new Mayor and two new trustees were elected and, upon the request of the former, the matter was deferred.

When, a short time later, the reconstituted Board of Trustees met, it summarily dismissed the members of the Water and Light Commission, accepted Nordberg's higher bid and awarded the contract to that company.[1] Enterprise thereupon brought suit to rescind

1. [Ed. note. Some footnotes renumbered.] The members of the Commission who had been replaced by new appointees challenged their dismissal and subsequently obtained a court order directing their reinstatement. (Matter of Amatulli v. Sweeney, 33 Misc.2d 324, 224 N.Y.S.2d 330, affd. 17 A.D.2d 631, 230 N.Y.S.2d 677.)

the award and succeeded in having the contract set aside. Then, despite the court's direction that it "award the contract as provided by law", the Board of Trustees arranged, over the objection of a majority of the Water and Light Commission, for the drawing up of new specifications for a larger generator of 5,000 kilowatts. These specifications, . . . were prepared "with the active assistance of a representative of the defendant Nordberg" and were "so slanted as to make impossible a bid on the second contract by any other manufacturer."

As had been anticipated, Nordberg was the only bidder. Its bid, of $757,625, was accepted and it was awarded the contract.

These were substantially the facts which led us to hold in 1965 that there was such "unlawful manipulation" in preparing and submitting the specifications as to render the contract illegal . . . We remitted the case for rendition of a judgment in favor of the plaintiff. The trial court, after a hearing, held that the Village should retain the generator, which was installed and in full operation, and should, in addition, recover from Nordberg the purchase price of $757,625 which it had paid. In reaching this conclusion, the court declared that the defendants, before "final determination of litigation and with full knowledge of the possible consequences of an ultimate reversal * * * elected to proceed under the contract, make the installation and make payment." And, the opinion continued, "[a]s a result of this perseverance in the face of uncertain consequences the Village now * * * is in the intolerable position of being faced with the payment of higher costs for every facet of the project were the Court to make an attempt to restore the parties to their original positions" (52 Misc.2d, at p. 507, 276 N.Y.S.2d 485, at p. 488). The judgment rendered also directed that the defendant Nordberg and the individual defendants, the Mayor and the trustees, pay counsel fees of $25,000.

On cross appeals by all parties, the Appellate Division 29 A.D.2d 646, 286 N.Y.S.2d 541, modified the judgment by providing that, while Nordberg was to pay back the purchase price of the generator, it could retake the machine upon posting a bond of $350,000 to secure the Village against any damages stemming from the removal and replacement of the equipment. . . .

We have not previously been called upon to fashion a remedy appropriate to a case such as this, where an illegal and void contract for public work, entered into in defiance of the competitive bidding statute (General Municipal Law, Consol.Laws, c. 24, § 103) has been performed in full on both sides. We have, however, dealt with the situation, one step removed, in which the municipality has consumed or had the full benefit of illegally purchased goods or services but the vendor or supplier has not been paid. We have repeatedly refused, in such cases, to allow the sellers to recover payment either for the price agreed upon or in quasi-contract. One of our salient purposes in adopting this rule has been to deter violation of statutes governing the spending of public moneys for goods and services. The restrictions imposed by such legislation, we recognized, are designed as a safeguard against the extravagance or corruption of officials as well as against their collusion with vendors. If we were to sanction payment of the fair and reasonable value of items sold in contravention of the bidding requirements, the vendor, having little to lose, would be encouraged to risk evasion of the statute; by the same token, if public officials were free to make such payments, the way would be open to them to accomplish by indirection what they are forbidden to do directly. . . .

There should, logically, be no difference in ultimate consequence between the case where a vendor has been paid under an illegal contract and the one in which payment has not yet been made. If, in the latter case, he is denied payment, he should, in the former, be required to return the payment unlawfully received—and he should not be excused from making this refund simply because it is impossible or intolerably difficult for the municipality to restore the illegally purchased goods or services to the vendor. In neither case can the usual concern of equity to prevent unjust enrichment be allowed to overcome and extinguish the special safeguards which the Legislature has provided for the public treasury. Although this court has not had occasion to pass on the question, appellate courts of at least two other states have so decided, holding that the vendor must pay back the amount received from the purchaser even though the items sold are not capable of being returned (see County of Shasta v. Moody, 90 Cal.App. 519, 523–524, 265 P. 1032; McKay v. Town of Lowell, 41 Ind. App. 627, 638, 84 N.E. 778),[2] and we strongly favor this view. Only thus can the practical effectiveness and vigor of the bidding statutes be maintained.

There was, therefore, justification—and precedent—for Special Term's decision directing Nordberg to repay the full purchase price of $757,625 and allowing the Village to retain the machinery which had been installed and was in operation. We conclude, nevertheless, though the patently illegal conduct of the defendants entitles them to little consideration, that the amount to be awarded should be less than that. We may adopt this course, in the unusual circumstances of the present case, without disturbing the salutary rationale and policy underlying such decisions as Albany Supply & Equip. Co. v. City of Cohoes, 18 N.Y.2d 968, 224 N.E.2d 716, affg. 25 A.D.2d 700, supra, 268 N.Y.S.2d 42. The sheer magnitude of the forfeiture that would be suffered by the defendant Nordberg, as well as the corresponding enrichment that would enure to the Village of Freeport, under Special Term's determination adds an element to this case not to be found in any of those in which the principles we have been discussing have been applied.

Ordinarily, the application of the law to particular cases may not, of course, vary with the sums involved. But we must recognize

2. The courts of several other jurisdictions have reached a contrary result. (See Vincennes Bridge Co. v. Board of County Comrs., 8 Cir., 248 F. 93, 98–102; Grady v. City of Livingston, 115 Mont. 47, 141 P.2d 346; Scott Twp. School Dist. Auth. v. Branna Constr. Corp., 409 Pa. 136, 185 A.2d 320.)

that the rule with which we are concerned has unique aspects that make it appropriate for us to take into account the severity of its impact in cases as extreme as the present one. The purposes of our competitive bidding statutes may be fully vindicated here without our rendering so Draconian a decree as to subject the defendant Nordberg to a judgment for over three quarters of a million dollars. Justice demands that even the burdens and penalties resulting from disregard of the law be not so disproportionately heavy as to offend conscience. This, more than likely, was the reason for the Appellate Division's modification of the judgment, affording Nordberg the option conditioned on posting a sufficient bond, of removing the engine from the power plant. In our view, though, there is no warrant for allowing Nordberg this opportunity to recoup its loss or for subjecting the Village power system to the disruption and uncertainty that would result from dismantling the present installation. The courts should not invite unpredictable consequences of this kind. We must regard the machinery as unreturnable, . . .

Nor would it be sufficient to limit the judgment to the alternative amount proposed by Nordberg. Pointing out that its own bid on a 3,500 kilowatt machine exceeded the bid of its competitor, Enterprise, by 8.6%, the defendant suggests that it be required only to refund to the Village a sum equal to 8.6% of the price paid for the illegally purchased 5,000 kilowatt machine. This would result in the entry of a judgment against Nordberg of about $65,000 which, the defendant states, is what the court "could presume to be a reasonable profit plus selling expenses." Such a disposition, which would do little more than deprive the seller of its profit, would reduce to negligible proportions the hazard of selling to a municipality in violation of the bidding regulations.

A more appropriate alternate remedy is available on the record before us, a remedy which takes into account both the wrong done to the village by the defendants' callous disregard of the competitive bidding statutes and our policy of depriving sellers of any incentive to participate in such a violation. In point of fact, the remedy, lying well within the domain of equity, impresses us as one uniquely suited to the circumstances of this case.

The Board of Trustees, it is to be noted, had originally decided that a 3,500 kilowatt generator—such as the one for which specifications had been prepared—met the Village's reasonable needs, and bona fide competitive bidding established that such an engine could be purchased for the sum of $615,685. The Village was diverted from that purchase by the persistent efforts of Nordberg to persuade the trustees, in disregard of the determination of their own Water and Light Commission, to rewrite the specifications in a way that would prevent any other manufacturer from submitting a competing bid. The successful result of this cynical maneuver—in the course of which a Nordberg employee became, to all intents and purposes, the author of the specifications—was the illegal purchase of the far more costly Nordberg engine.

We may estimate the ensuing loss to the Village by taking the difference between the $757,625 paid to Nordberg and the $615,685 which the Village would have paid if it had accepted the low bid of Enterprise for the 3,500 kilowatt engine the Village had earlier set out to procure. That difference is $141,940. To the sum just mentioned we should add the difference between what it cost the Village to install the Nordberg machine and what it would have cost it to install the one offered by Enterprise. The trial court's finding that none of the construction and related costs incurred by the Village could be allocated to the installation of the engine must be stamped as error. The defendant Nordberg itself introduced into evidence the expert opinion of qualified engineers that the cost of installing its engine was $36,696 greater than the amount the Village would have had to expend for installing the Enterprise machine, and no one else testified to a lesser figure. We may assume that the amount furnished by Nordberg's own witness is conservatively stated. The total of the two items mentioned is $178,636, and the judgment against the defendant Nordberg should be modified so as to direct payment of this sum to the Village, together with interest at the rate of 3% per annum—which is consistent with the rate (3.2%) payable by the Village on the bonds it issued to finance the acquisition of the generator—computed from December 16, 1964, the date on which Nordberg received the final installment of the purchase price.

The order appealed from should be modified, without costs, in accordance with this opinion and, as so modified, affirmed.

SECTION 17.05 SUBCONTRACTOR PROBLEMS

Prime contractors often base their bids upon quotations given to them by subcontractors. Subcontractors base their bids upon bids by sub-subcontractors and materialmen. As specialization grows, these techniques of passing the risks of bidding on to the contractor below are likely to be more common. There are a number of legal problems that relate to the frequent use of subcontractors in the competitive bidding process.

The use of the single contract system, with many subcontractors, means that there is no direct contractual relationship between owner and subcontractor. There are advantages to this absence of a contractual relationship between owner and subcontractor. The owner does not want to deal with individual subcontractors, and, from an organization standpoint, the owner may prefer to deal only with the prime contractor. Also, the owner would prefer insulation from liability for the failure of prime contractors to pay their subcontractors, and for negligence of subcontractors. (The former is not always possible because of Mechanics' Lien Laws, which protect unpaid subcontractors and materialmen.) Also, the owner does not wish to be responsible to subcontractors for delays caused by the design professional, or for injuries incurred by subcontractor employees. Both from the standpoint of legal relations and from the standpoint of operational efficiency, there are reasons why the owner chooses not to have a contract with subcontractors.

Yet, it is vital to have skilled subcontractors. If the owner were to dictate the subcontractors that were to be used, he might find himself responsible for breaches or negligence of the subcontractor. In addition, the prime's bid might be higher if he were not allowed to use the competitive bidding process to obtain the lowest responsible subcontract price. Again, a balance must be struck between the price and the probability of project success, both from an administrative and from a quality standpoint.

Two problems which frequently plague the subcontractor relationship are "bid peddling" (or as it is called by prime contractors, "bid shopping") and "bid chiseling." Bid peddling consists of the prime contractor disclosing bids made to him by some subcontractors, to other subcontractors, to get a lower subcontractor bid and improve his competitive bidding position. Bid chiseling can occur after the prime contractor has been awarded a fixed price contract. The prime contractor may try to beat down the subcontractors' price so that he can make the largest possible profit. He often does this by holding an informal competition of his own, with interested subcontractors, with a view toward getting the lowest possible price once he has obtained the prime contract.

Bid peddling and bid chiseling are obviously distasteful to the subcontractors. Also, they can operate to the detriment of the owner. Where there is a good deal of bid peddling before the submission of proposals, subcontractors often refuse to submit their bids until just before the deadline for bid submission by the prime. This can increase the risk of computation errors in the bid proposals, because many items have to be added up at the last minute. Bid peddling can, by competition, reduce prime contractor bids. But not much can be said for bid chiseling from the owner's standpoint, unless the prime contractor passes on to the owner savings made by beating down the prices of subcontractors, a rare occurrence.

Subconstractors sometimes inflate their bid proposal, because they know they are going to be beaten down after the bid opening or award. This can reflect itself in higher bid proposals generally. Some good contractors do not like to bid on subcontractor work, because they have no assurance that they will get the job at their bid price even if they are the low bidder and even if their bid is used by the successful prime contractor. This can reduce competition. Finally, bid peddling and chiseling can mean price cutting and substandard work by contractors who do not have technological skills.

Some of the worst evils of bid chiseling can be avoided by the ground rules of the competitive bidding. The contract may provide that the bidder must agree to do a specified portion of the work himself. This reduces, to some degree, the scope of subcontracting and eliminates the possibility that the prime contractor will merely be a broker who wants to make money from the services of subcontractors and runs very little risk himself. Also, the invitation to bidders may state that the bidder must submit the names of the subcontractors he proposes to use, and agree to use those subs he names if he is awarded the contract, subject to substitution with permission of the owner. This can protect against incompetent subcontractors, and also assist subcontractors from having their bids chiseled down after the prime contract has been made. It is possible, although uncommon, to require that bidders enter into binding contracts in advance with their subcontractors, conditioned upon the bidder being awarded the prime contract.

As a rule, prime contractors have superior bargaining power over subcontractors until the subcontractors have a binding subcontract. The law, in many states, has given the prime contractor additional bargaining power by holding that the subcontractor's bid becomes irrevocable if the prime contractor makes his bid relying upon the sub-bid. While some earlier decisions would not make the bid under these conditions irrevocable, the recent trend has been toward making the subcontractor bid irrevocable when the prime contractor bases his bid upon it.

This means that the prime contractor can hold the subcontractor, while in most cases the subcontractor cannot hold the prime contractor.

One case which held the subcontractor's bid irrevocable, Drennan v. Star Paving Company, 51 Cal.2d 409, 333 P.2d 757 (1958), gave some protection to the subcontractor when it stated:

> . . . a general contractor is not free to delay acceptance after he has been awarded the general contract in the hope of getting a better price. Nor can he reopen bargaining with the subcontractor and at the same time claim a continuing right to accept the original offer.

There are some ways the subcontractor can give himself some protection from being held himself without being able to hold the prime contractor. He can denominate his bid as a "price quotation" and not as a firm bid. In such cases, it has been held that the subcontractor's bid is revocable. He may not be in a bargaining position to do this. Also, less than firm subcontractor bids can hurt the owner by causing the prime contractor to inflate his bid to cover the possibility that the prime may have to pay more to his subs than the original sub bid proposal.

Another method would be for the subcontractor to submit a bid, and to make it expressly conditioned upon the prime contractor agreeing to use him at the specified price if the prime contractor is awarded the contract. The difficulty with these methods is that subcontractor bidding is often done haphazardly, and without the benefit of any writings at all. Often subcontractor bids are made by telephone, and entered on a tally sheet kept by employees of the prime contractor. Also, subcontractors may not have sufficient bargaining power to bind the prime contractor, or to insure that they themselves are not bound.

Subcontractors in some states have been successful in improving their bargaining positions with prime contractors through legislation. Some states require that designated public contracts employ the separate contractor system. Some states have enacted Subcontractor Listing Acts, which require prime contractors to list their subcontractors. Only under certain designated circumstances and with permission of the public agency can a prime contractor use a sub other than the listed subcontractor. This gives the subcontractor bargaining advantages if the prime contractor attempts to reopen bargaining.

State governments and the federal government have passed anti-trust laws. These laws are intended to protect competition by prohibiting agreements which unreasonably restrain trade. The most obvious illustration of a restraint on trade is a price-fixing agreement between competitors. But there are many less obvious ways of restraining trade and limiting competition. Serious anti-trust violations can lead to fines and imprisonment. Persons who have been injured financially because of a violation of anti-trust laws can bring civil actions for treble damages or obtain court orders restraining the illegal conduct.

A California case illustrates the anti-trust problems involved in the use of bid depositories. The Inland Bid Depository operated in two California counties. Members of the depository could not submit bids to prime contractors who did not use the depository. Prime contractors who wanted to receive bids submitted to the depository had to agree not to use bids from non-members, unless these bids were processed through the depository.

Bids were submitted by members to the depository four hours before the time specified for submission of prime bids to the public authority or the owner. The bids would be tabulated by the depository and given to the prime. Prime contractors were required to use the low bid submitted. The successful prime bidder paid ½ of 1% of the bid price to the depository. A member could withdraw a bid from one contractor bidding on a given contract if he withdrew his bid from all contractors bidding on this contract, and if he paid a fine. The rules were enforced by fine, suspension, or expulsion of the members.

In State v. Inland Bid Depository, 233 Cal.App.2d 851, 44 Cal. Rptr. 206 (1965), the California Court of Appeals held that the depository, under its existing rules, was an unreasonable restraint of trade. The court ordered that it be dissolved unless it filed rules approved by the court. Some courts have ruled the other way.

Another example of an illegal contract in a subcontractor setting, was illustrated in Premier Electrical Construction Co. v. Miller-Davis Co., 291 F.Supp. 295 (Dist.Ct.Ill.1968). One of the grounds for not granting recovery to a sub-bidder against a prime bidder for alleged breach of contract was that part of the arrangement between sub and prime was that the sub would give high sub bids to other prime bidders, to help the defendant prime bidder get the prime contract. The court held that this made the contract illegal, and that the sub-bidder could not collect damages for not being given the subcontract.

SECTION 17.06 NEGOTIATED CONTRACTS

Another method of obtaining a contractor is to select a contractor who has the integrity and ability to do the job, and enter into negotiations with him. Unsophisticated owners are hesitant to use the negotiated contract method because it does not furnish a comparison, and they are fearful that they are not in a position to negotiate a price with sufficient information. On the other hand, sophisticated owners who know a good deal about construction methods and prices may feel competent to sit at the bargaining table with a contractor.

As for the legal aspects of the negotiated contract, there are no problems of mutual assent comparable to the problems that arise under competitive bidding. The parties enter into their negotiation and, if they have reached agreement on the major terms, they will usually enter into a written contract. Because the construction contract usually is complex and involves substantial amounts of money, it is not likely that the parties intend to bind themselves until there is assent to a final written contract. Even in smaller construction projects, it is likely that the parties do not intend to bind themselves merely by a handshake.

One important legal problem in the negotiation of construction contracts relates to the duties of disclosure each party owes toward the other during the negotiations. Information as to subsurface and soil conditions, a fertile breeding ground for disputes, will be discussed in some detail in Chapter 22. As to general information known by the contracting parties, the more traditional legal doctrines refuse to require parties who are dealing at arm's length to disclose relevant information which the other party might be able to obtain himself. There is an increasing tendency to require that parties act in good faith during negotiations, even though the parties are not in any fiduciary relationship. See § 17.04(g).

If one party has information about matters which will materially affect the other party's performance, and he can reasonably believe that the other party either cannot or is not likely to acquire this information, he should disclose this information to the other party. Some courts, perhaps, would not require him to do so, but good relations during performance and the possibility of litigation if he does not disclose this sort of information should be sufficient reasons to make disclosure advisable.

In certain types of federal government negotiated contracts, the contractors must submit cost or pricing data prior to the award of the prime contract. The contractor may be required to certify that to the best of his knowledge and belief the data submitted was accurate, complete, and current. Under federal law, the price of a negotiated contract can be adjusted to exclude any significant sums found to have resulted from inaccurate, incomplete or noncurrent data. Congress was concerned with the inaccuracy of cost data that was sometimes used as the basis for negotiation leading to negotiated contracts. This concern led in 1962 to the Truth in Negotiating Act expressed in P.L. 87–653, 10 U.S.C.A. § 2306(f). This statute, like other material discussed (See § 17.04(g)) reflects this increasing tendency toward requiring good faith in negotiations.

REVIEW QUESTIONS

1. What are the objectives of competitive bidding?

2. How are these objectives accomplished?

3. Can a bidder withdraw a bid before opening, if the invitation to bidders states he can not do so?

4. Can a prime contractor hold a subcontractor whose bid he uses if the sub revokes before the prime accepts?

5. Under what conditions can a bidder be relieved from his bid after bid opening?

6. What are the reasons to require that a bidder post a bond or certified check with his bid?

7. What are the advantages and disadvantages of competitive bidding?

8. When would a negotiated contract be desirable?

QUESTIONS FOR CLASS DISCUSSION

1. Should a public owner be able to waive minor defects in the bid proposal?

2. Should a bidder be able to withdraw a bid after acceptance, because of a mathematical error of large proportion? What facts are crucial in such a situation?

3. Is it fair to hold the sub to his bid, but not compel the prime to use the sub?

4. Do you think that bid peddling is harmful to the interests of the owner? Give your reasons. What about bid chiseling?

5. Should public contracts for architectural services be awarded by competitive bidding? Give your reasons.

6. Should competitive bidding be the normal method of selecting public contractors?

7. Would a contractor have the duty to disclose that he had been fired from his last job?

PROBLEMS

1. O decided to construct a building and to obtain competitive bids. He selected five contractors and sent them invitations to bid, as well as bidding information. The invitation stated that bids would be irrevocable until 30 days after bid opening. It also stated that the bid would be awarded to the lowest responsible bidder. Bids were to be submitted no later than 2:00 p. m., on June 10. Each bidder was to accompany his bid with a certified check, or bid bond, for 10% of his bid. This amount would be "forfeited" if the bidder were awarded the contract but did not sign it.

When the bids were opened, they disclosed that four of the bids ranged from $1 million to $1.4 million. The fifth bid by Acme Construction was for $840,000. The owner asked Acme if there had been some mistake. Acme said that he was certain that this was the correct bid. The owner then told Acme that the job was his, and that he did not have to evaluate Acme's responsibility because he knew that Acme had an excellent reputation.

A week later Acme came in and stated that his bid was under bid by $120,000. There was a computation error of $80,000 caused by his bookkeeper, who did not add the columns correctly. Also, the electrical sub-contractor had claimed that he left a $40,000 item out of his bid figures and he canceled his bid.

a. Would you release Acme?

b. Would you let him "correct" his bid?

c. Would a court permit Acme to cancel? To correct?

d. Can the owner accept the next lowest bid if Acme refuses to perform?

e. If Acme unjustifiably refuses to perform, can the owner retain his damages for the difference in bids, or is he limited to the 10% deposit?

2. O wanted to build a residence on a lot he owned. He asked three contractors to give him a fixed bid price on the project. None would do so, because experimental methods of construction were called for, and because the architect was considered difficult to get along with. O asked C to make a fixed price bid. He did not tell C that three other contractors had refused to do so. C gave a written bid of $100,000 which O accepted. Three days later C found out that the three contractors had refused to bid on the job. He claims O should have told him of this. Does C have a legal defense if he refuses to go through with the contract? Explain.

Chapter 18

SURETY BONDS

SECTION 18.01 SCOPE OF DISCUSSION: FUNCTION OF SURETY

Design professionals should understand the basic purpose of a surety, and the role that he plays in the construction process. However the laws and practices of suretyship are complicated, and only a brief outline will be given. Emphasis will be placed upon the functional role of the surety in the building process.

A surety's function is to assure one person that a person with whom he is dealing will be backed up by someone who is financially responsible. Sureties are used in many different types of transactions. A person may be asked to post a bond to assure that he will appear at a certain time in court to answer a criminal charge. Banks may require that their employees be "bonded", so that if the employees steal money, the banks will have a solvent person from whom they can recover their loss. Sureties and surety bonds are used where persons deal with individuals or organizations of doubtful financial capacity.

SECTION 18.02 MECHANICS AND TERMINOLOGY

The surety bond transaction is a peculiar arrangement, and differs procedurally from an ordinary contract. In the typical surety problem, there are three primary parties. The first is the "surety." He obligates himself to perform or to pay a specified amount of money, if the "principal debtor," usually called the "principal", does not perform. The person to whom this performance is promised is usually called the "obligee", (sometimes called the "creditor"). In the building contract context, the surety is usually a professional bonding company. The principal is the prime contractor, or, in the case of subcontractor bonds, a subcontractor. The obligee is the owner or, in the case of a subcontractor bond, the prime contractor.

If required by the owner, the prime contractor (the principal) applies for a bond from a bonding company. Usually the cost of the bond is paid indirectly by the owner, since the bidder adds the cost of the bond to his costs when computing his bid. The bond will be issued to the owner (the obligee). It is said that the bond runs to him. This means that the performance by the surety has been promised to the owner, even though the application for the bond has been made by the prime contractor.

Another difficulty in dealing with the surety bonds results from the antique way in which bonds are written. The earliest bonds were called "penal" bonds. The surety made an absolute promise to render a certain performance, or to pay a specified amount of money. Then there would be a paragraph which would state that the bond would be void if the principal promptly and properly performed under the contract between principal and obligee. This format can cause problems. Often the language of bonds is vague and does not go into problems of coverage, problems of notices, and other things which are normally part of any contract. There has been some improvement in this regard, and bonds today do contain specific provisions which inform the interested parties of their rights and duties under the bond. (The Appendix includes some sample bonds used in construction.)

SECTION 18.03 JUDICIAL TREATMENT OF SURETIES

There has been a change in the judicial attitudes towards sureties. Prior to the development of professional sureties, the surety would be a private person (perhaps a relative of the principal) who wanted the principal to obtain a contract, and who was willing to obligate himself to perform if the principal did not. The surety was frequently not paid and received no direct benefit for undertaking performance in the event the principal did not. For these reasons the surety was considered a "favorite" of the law.

One of the best illustrations of the protection given the surety is illustrated by the Statute of Frauds. The Statute of Frauds specified that certain types of promises must be evidenced by a written memorandum. In 1677 the original Statute of Frauds included promises to answer for the debts, defaults, or miscarriage of another. Without a writing, the surety was not held liable. This was to protect him from the enforcement of an impulsive oral promise often made without due deliberation. Also, any minor change in the contract between the principal and obligee would "discharge" the surety (relieve him of liability).

The personal, unpaid surety could not handle the surety needs in a complex economy. The personal surety himself might not be financially responsible. For this reason, the professional, paid surety has developed as an important institution in both economic life generally and in building contracts.

Once professional sureties came into the picture, it was obvious that the protective rules which were developed largely when sureties were uncompensated would be modified. While it is true that some of the rules have carried over, it is clear that the professional surety is not regarded with the tender solicitude that the personal, uncompensated surety once was. This changeover from a legally favored position to one of neutrality, and perhaps even to one of disfavor, has created a great deal of difficulty in litigation. Older cases are sometimes cited as precedents to protect sureties, but these precedents may be of limited value, because the surety business has changed.

Surety companies are regulated by the states in which they operate. In addition, sureties who wish to write bonds for certain types of federal projects must qualify under regulations of the United States Treasury Department. Sureties are limited by their capital structure in the size of the projects they can bond. One reason for bond limits is to have a limit on their exposure. In larger projects, there may be co-sureties, or the surety may be required to reinsure a portion with another surety. Surety rates are usually regulated, and are based upon a specified percentage of the limit of the surety bond. Careful bond issuance, and skillful management of projects that do go into default, can lead to reasonable premium rates. Generally it is considered that surety bond premiums are reasonable in terms of the total construction cost. It is the one cost that has tended to remain stable, or even to decline, in direct contrast to most other construction costs.

SECTION 18.04 SURETY BONDS IN CONSTRUCTION CONTRACTS

Surety bonds play a vital part in the construction process. The contracting industry is volatile. Bankruptcies are not uncommon, and a few unsuccessful projects can cause financial catastrophe. Estimation of costs is difficult, and requires a great amount of skill. Lump sum contracts place many risks upon the contractor, such as price increases, labor difficulties, subsurface conditions, and changing governmental policy. Many construction companies are poorly managed and poorly supervised. They are often under-capitalized, and rely very heavily upon the technological skill of a limited number of individuals. If these individuals become unavailable, it is likely that there will be difficulties. Credit may be difficult to obtain for many construction companies. Some contractors do not insure against the risks and calamities which can be covered by insurance. Finally, anti-inflationary government policies such as tight money policies almost always hit the building industry first.

Design professionals must be aware of the economic realities in the construction industry. In most construction projects, there is a need for a system of bonding to protect the owner. By and large the owner would like to be able to look to a financially solvent surety in the event the successful bidder does not enter into the construction contract (bid bond), the prime contractor does not perform his work properly (performance bond), or the prime contractor does not pay his subcontractors or suppliers (payment bond).

If none of these difficulties arise, the amount paid for a surety bond may appear wasted. Some design professionals believe there is no need for a surety bond system if the prime contractor is chosen carefully and if a well-administered payment system is used which eliminates the risk of unpaid subcontractors and suppliers. Also, some large-volume owners may choose to be self-insurers and not obtain bonds. They, too, may believe they can select good prime contractors and set up good payment systems. They realize that there may be losses, but believe that the losses over a long period will be less than the cost of bond premiums.

Even where a bond is not required, it is best to include a provision in the prime contract which will require the prime contractor to obtain a bond before or during his performance if the owner so requests. Usually the cost of a bond issued after the price of the project is agreed upon is paid by the owner.

If the owner chooses not to use a bonding system, the design professional should send him a written memorandum explaining the risks of such a course of action. The design professional should retain a copy of this memorandum.

Some professional liability insurance policies (see Chapter 35) exclude from policy coverage failure to advise or require surety bonds. Where such a policy is in effect, the design professional should realize that he may have to pay for any losses suffered if he cannot establish that he advised his client properly on the need for surety bonds, and that any decision not to use surety bonds was made by the client with full knowledge of the risk.

Some public projects require a surety bond. The most significant federal law requiring bonds is the Miller Act. The Miller Act states that most federal government construction contracts must contain provisions requiring that the prime contractor obtain a surety bond to a certain designated percentage of the contract price, for the protection of certain designated subcontractors and materialmen. Many state codes require that contractors obtain surety bonds. In addition, certain acts, such as state Subdivision Map Acts, may require that a subdivider furnish bonds to protect the prime contractor, the subcontractor, and materialmen. It is vital to determine whether a bond is required by law for any specified type of construction work. This will change depending upon the type and amount of the contract, and depending upon the applicability of particular state laws.

The surety bond requirement serves another purpose. It can act as a preliminary screen for incompetent or financially irresponsible contractors. A contractor who cannot get a bonding company to write a bond upon him is likely to be a poor risk. This can be a good reason to require surety bonds.

The invitation to bidders usually states whether the contractor is required to obtain a surety bond, the type or types of bonds, and the amount of the bonds. In some cases, the owner wishes to approve the form of the bond and the surety that is used. Also, the owner may want to have the right to refuse any substitution of surety without his express written consent, given in advance of substitution.

Should the owner specify which surety bond company is to be used? The choice will depend upon rates, bond provisions, and the reputation of particular bonding companies for efficient operation and for fairness in adjusting claims. If there is relative standardization on these matters, it is probably advisable to give the contractor the freedom to choose the bonding company. He may have worked before with one bonding company, or he may owe a favor to a particular bonding company. In most cases it is probably sufficient to permit the bonding company to be chosen by the contractor, as long as the bonding company selected is licensed to practice in the state where the project will be built.

There may be occasions when a designated bonding company will not be satisfactory to the owner. This may be based upon suspicion of financial instability, or a past record of arbitrariness in refusal to settle claims. One method of exercising some control over the selection of the bonding company is to provide in the contract that the contractor submit to the owner the bond of a proposed bonding company for the owner's review. If the owner, in the exercise of his best judgment, determines that it is inadvisable to use that bonding company, the owner can veto the proposed bonding company and designate the bonding company to be used.

SECTION 18.05 BID BOND

The main function of the bid bond is to give the owner assurance that if the contractor does not enter into the contract when it is awarded to him, there will be a financially responsible person who will pay the damages. Section 17.04(e) discussed the legal problems incident to a failure of a contractor to enter into the contract when awarded. The face value of the bond may be a liquidation of damages, a limitation of liability, an unenforceable penalty, or simply a security device.

Another problem relating to bid bonds involves the relationship between forfeiture of the bid bond, and relief given to the contractor for a mistake in bid. Suppose a contractor who has posted a bid bond makes a computational error, or leaves a large item out of his computation which results in his submitting a bid substantially lower than any other bidder. Suppose that the facts are such that a court would give him relief from any obligation to perform under the contract. Is the owner entitled to keep any deposit he has given or collect upon the bond?

It can be contended that the bid bond merely relates to his breach of promise to enter into the contract if awarded to him, and that while he cannot be compelled to perform for the mistaken price or pay damages for failure to perform, he ought nevertheless forfeit the bid bond or deposit as long as that amount is reasonable. Under this analysis he is breaching his promise to enter into the contract, rather than breaching the construction contract itself. If this rationale were followed, the owner would be permitted only to keep the amount of the bond, and not to sue for any damages which might exceed the deposit or the bond. This would seem to be a fair solution to the mistake in bid problem.

The contractor's exposure would be limited to the five to ten per cent he is asked to deposit, or the face amount of any bid bond he is asked to deposit. However, courts have not made this distinction, and have generally held that the contractor is relieved from his performance entirely if he brings himself within the requirements of mistake or any statutory provision for relief. In such a case, he is entitled to recover his deposit, and the owner cannot collect on the bid bond. While the amount involved may be only five or ten percent of the contract bid, in large jobs this amount is substantial. In addition, where the facts are sufficient to allow the mistake doctrine to be applied, perhaps it is unfair to make the bidder lose even the deposit.

SECTION 18.06 PERFORMANCE BOND

The performance bond provides a financially responsible party to stand behind the prime contractor if he does not perform properly. For an illustration of a performance bond see AIA Doc. A311, reproduced in Appendix E.

Bonds usually state a specified dollar amount as a limit to the liability of the surety. A performance bond does not give absolute assurance that the construction project will be built as specified for the contract price. It indicates a financially responsible person stands behind the contractor, to the limit of the face amount of the bond.

Bonds can be obtained with a face value of 50 or 100% of the contract price. Some statutory bonds require that the face value be 50% of the contract price. It is useful to inquire as to whether there is any difference in bond premiums between 100% and 50% bond. In many cases there is no essential difference in bond premiums.

Bonds usually contain provisions which permit the surety to remedy the default and complete the contract itself, or pay to the limit of the bond. The surety company usually chooses whichever route it thinks will cost less money.

Sometimes there is confusion as to the coverage of the bond and as to the types of risk for which a surety stands behind the prime contractor. Generally, the surety's risk relates to getting the project built properly. During the course of construction, losses may be suffered by third parties. For example, there may be damage to adjacent land, or injuries to employees of the contractors, or to persons who enter onto the project or pass by it. Injuries to these persons may result in liability to the owner, and often are a breach of the prime contract by the prime contractor. However, such risks are usually handled by public liability insurance taken out by the contractor or the owner or both. Perhaps the bonding company will be responsible on the bond if the prime contractor fails to live up to any contract obligation he may have to provide and maintain adequate public liability insurance. Much will depend upon the language of the bond.

SECTION 18.07 PAYMENT BOND

The payment bond (See AIA Doc. A311 in Appendix F) gives protection to the owner, in the event subcontractors and suppliers (sometimes called materialmen) are not paid by the prime contractor. It is important to differentiate private from public work in regard to the rationale for payment bonds.

The private owner desires a project which is free and clear of liens. Because of the instability of the construction industry, and the fact that prime contractors sometimes do not pay their subcontractors or suppliers, almost all states have legislation which gives unpaid subcontractors and suppliers liens against the construction project if they are unpaid. Sometimes this is based upon the benefit conferred on the owner by the inclusion of labor and materials in the structure. However, as a result, mechanics' lien laws can require the owner to pay twice, once to the prime contractor, and again to the unpaid subcontractors and suppliers, in order to remove their lien.

If a lien is perfected, the lien claimant has a right to have a judicial foreclosure sale on the property, and to have his claim satisfied out of the proceeds. In most cases, the owner will prefer to remove the lien rather than have his property foreclosed upon. To do this, he will have to pay the lien claimant. While the owner has a claim against the prime contractor for not paying the subcontractors and suppliers, the claim is often worthless because of the insolvency or bankruptcy of the prime contractor. For these reasons, the owner wants to insure as best he can that there will be no liens placed against the building.

While there are other ways to avoid this problem, the principal method used is to require that the prime contractor obtain a payment bond. Under a payment bond, the bonding company pays the subcontractors and suppliers if they are not paid by the prime contractor. The owner wishes to avoid liens, and he also wishes to avoid any claims being made against him, justified or unjustified. The owner is, as a rule, not in any contractual relationship with these unpaid subcontractors or suppliers. So far as the owner is concerned, he wants to be able to tell them that they are to look to the bonding company rather than to him for payment.

There are other reasons why it is advisable to have a payment bond. Subcontractors are more likely to make bids if they can be assured that there will be a surety to whom they can go if they are unpaid. Also, sub-bids, where there is a bonded prime, should not have to include as an expense item the contingency of not being paid without the expense of asserting a lien. This should lead to lower subcontractor bids. Subcontractors and suppliers may be more inclined to perform properly, and to deliver the material as quickly as possible, if they have some assurance that they will be paid. Even though they have a right to a mechanic's lien, the procedures for perfecting the lien and satisfying the unpaid obligation out of foreclosure proceeds are cumbersome, and filled with many pitfalls. Subcontractors and suppliers would prefer payment bonds to going through mechanics' lien procedures.

Generally, subcontractors and suppliers are not permitted to obtain liens against public structures. In some states, they can file "stop notices", discussed more fully in § 24.07. A stop notice informs the owner that a subcontractor has not been paid, and the owner is required to hold up payments to the prime. Even though unpaid subcontractors and suppliers have no lien rights, they often present claims against public bodies through requests for special legislation to Congress, state legislatures, or city councils. Requiring that the prime be bonded provides a mechanism whereby they can be paid. This can relieve public legislative bodies from troublesome and time-consuming claims. Some of the other reasons mentioned when private projects were discussed also apply to public jobs.

It is important to both public and private owners that there be a healthy construction industry. If competent subcontractors are not provided with a mechanism to collect for their work through bonding, there are strong possibilities of substantial numbers of subcontractors going out of business. This can reduce the number of subcontractors, and have the unfortunate effect of reducing competition or eliminating skilled subcontractors.

SECTION 18.08 SUBCONTRACTOR BONDS

In large construction projects, it is common for the prime contractor to require that his subcontractors also obtain payment bonds and performance bonds. If a subcontractor does not perform as obligated, the prime contractor wants to have a financially responsible person to stand behind the subcontractor. This is the justification for a subcontractor performance bond. The justification for the subcontractor payment bond is similar to the justifications given for prime contractor payment bonds. If a subcontractor does not pay his sub-subcontractors or suppliers, the prime contractor is likely to be responsible, since he obligates himself to erect the project free and clear of all liens. In many cases, unpaid sub-subcontractors and materialmen of subcontractors have lien rights against projects. In a large construction project, there may be a substantial number of bonding companies who have written bonds on the various contractors in the project. This makes the litigation in such cases complicated, and often the principal participants in a litigation are bonding companies who are trying to shift the responsibility to other bonding companies.

SECTION 18.09 SOME LEGAL PROBLEMS

(A) WHO CAN SUE ON THE BOND?

Before surety bonds were generally divided into performance and payment bonds, the owner typically would require that a prime contractor obtain one bond called a faithful performance bond. Unpaid subcontractors and suppliers often were denied the right to sue the bonding company directly. The bonding company contended that it was obligated only to perform to the owner, and the unpaid suppliers and materialmen were not named or designated in the faithful performance bond. In order to meet this problem, some courts used the third party beneficiary doctrine. Under certain circumstances, a plaintiff can sue when he has suffered damage because of the defendant's failure to perform in accordance with a contract to which the plaintiff was not a party. In determining whether to give the right to sue to a third party, courts held that such a right existed if the promise, in this case by the surety, were made for the benefit of the plaintiff, in these cases, unpaid contractors and suppliers, or if the bond was intended to give the latter persons a right to sue on the bond.

Realistically, the principal intention of the owner obtaining the bond is to benefit himself. He wants the lowest possible price, and he wants to ensure that there are no liens placed against the building. To accomplish this, he may desire that the subcontractors and suppliers be paid, and in a sense his intention is to benefit them. Struggling with this "intention to benefit" concept made the law cloudy when faithful performance surety bonds were used. This area of doubt was even greater in the area of public bonds, because the subcontractors and suppliers generally cannot assert a lien against the public structure.

Some courts would permit direct action by subcontractors on the faithful performance bond, but others would not. This was one of the factors that led to the development of the payment bond as a separate bond from the performance bond. Where payment bonds were used, it was much easier for courts to hold that there was an intent to benefit subcontractors and suppliers, and that they should have a direct right of action. Payment bonds frequently spell this out. Most courts permit action against the bonding company by unpaid subcontractors and suppliers on payment bonds.

(B) VALIDITY OF BOND

What if the contractor makes misrepresentations when he applies for the bond? He may state that he has capital that he does not have, or that he has not had any other difficulties with other jobs. This would be misrepresentation by the applicant, not by the obligee-owner. In such a case, the bond is generally valid, and the surety bond company must pursue any remedies it has against the contractor-applicant. However, if there is fraud on the part of the obligee-owner, then the surety can avoid having to perform under the bond. For example, suppose the obligee-owner participates in, or knows about, the fraudulent statements made by the applicant contractor or misleads the bonding company in some other way. In such a case, the bond would not have been validly obtained, and could not be legally enforced.

Sometimes the principal contract itself, that is, the contract between the owner and the contractor, is not valid or enforceable. For example, suppose the building contract was to construct an enemy spy net. To permit the owner to sue upon the bond in such a case would further an illegal activity. For that reason, the bond could not be enforced. This is because enforcement of the bond would require that the court take part in an illegal act.

There are lesser degrees of illegality. Perhaps there has been no building permit, and yet construction begins. Or perhaps the contractor is not licensed to build this particular structure. As the illegality becomes less socially objectionable, there are greater possibilities that the surety bond will be enforced.

(C) DEFENSES GIVEN TO SURETY

Certain defenses may arise during the course of performance. For example, the owner may not make payment, despite the issuance of progress payment certificates. He might unjustifiably interfere with the work of the contractor. The design professional might not approve shop drawings in sufficient time to permit proper performance. The contractor's performance may be rendered impossible because of a court order, death of the contractor, or some natural catastrophe. The performance might be rendered impracticable due to discovery of unforeseen subsurface conditions. If the contractor had a defense if he were sued by the owner, then this defense would be available to the surety.

When the surety undertakes the stand behind the contractor, the surety would like to be able to assume that the deal between the contractor and the owner will remain substantially the same. What if the owner and the contractor modify the construction contract, or the owner directs changes in the work? The total exposure can be limited by putting a fixed limit on the bond. However, as to other modifications, problems did develop as a result of earlier rules that had developed when the surety was unpaid. Many cases held that changing the basic agreement was sufficient to release the surety. However, the advent of the paid surety has made inroads on these earlier cases. Frequently, bonds provide that the surety "waives notice of any alteration or extension of time made by the owner." Without such a provision, it may be possible for the surety to be released because the principal obligation has been changed.

Sometimes a dispute arises between the contractor and the owner, and is settled by the owner releasing the contractor from any further performance under the contract. In such a case, the surety's obligation as to unperformed work may be terminated because the principal debtor, the contractor, has been released. Sometimes, such a settlement between owner and contractor may attempt to save the owner's rights against the surety by reserving to the owner the right to sue the surety for nonperformance by the contractor. Sometimes such a reservation in a settlement between owner and contractor is effective.

(D) BANKRUPTCY OF CONTRACTOR

If, during the course of performance by the contractor, the contractor is adjudicated a bankrupt, the trustee in bankruptcy (the person who takes over the affairs of the bankrupt contractor) may be able to determine whether or not to continue the contract. Usually he does not. If he does not, then the bankrupt contractor is released from any further obligation to perform under the contract. The owner may have a provable claim against the bankrupt contractor in bankruptcy, but he is not likely to recover much. Here, ending the contractor's obligation will not release the surety. This is the very risk contemplated when the surety bond is purchased.

(E) ASSERTING CLAIMS

The ground rules for asserting claims against a surety on payment bonds may be different from basic contract rules. For example, payment bonds frequently state that a subcontractor or supplier must notify the surety if he has not been paid within a specified time from the completion of his work, and give data as to the amount claimed, and the person to whom the materials or labor were furnished. Sometimes bonds contain periods of limitation, stating that actions cannot be brought on the bond later than a specified time after completion of the principal contractor's performance under the job. This may be a period shorter than the normal period of limitations which govern the time in which action can be brought under most state laws. Also, the bond may be limited to claims which comply with mechanics' lien laws. The bond may contain provisions limiting action under the bond to a particular court. Sometimes such provisions are enforceable.

Performance bonds also contain limitations of the type specified in payment bonds. It is important for the design professional to familiarize himself with the conditions which must be fulfilled before actions can be brought on the bond.

(F) REIMBURSEMENT OF SURETY

If a surety must pay the principal's obligations or complete the principal's performance, he tries to reimburse himself for his loss. One method is to attempt to recover from the contractor for any losses incurred by the surety because of the contractor's nonperformance. This is not likely to be worth much, because the principal reason for having to take over the work is the financial difficulties of the contractor.

The surety frequently tries other methods to reimburse himself. Various legal doctrines give him the right to go after the owner for any claims which the principal contractor may have against the owner. Often the contractor claims damages against the owner based upon claimed interference with the contractor's performance or for extras. In addition, the surety frequently goes after the retainage that is held by the owner to secure the owner against losses that may result from the contractor's nonperformance. In seeking to recover all, or a portion, of the retainage, the surety bond company frequently finds that it must compete with other claimants for the retainage. Often state and federal taxing authorities contend that the retainage should go to them where the contractor has defaulted in the payment of taxes. Also, if the contractor has gone bankrupt, the trustee in bankruptcy frequently attempts to assert ownership to the retainage held by the owner.

When these situations arise, the owner takes from the retainage enough to satisfy any claims he may have against the contractor, and pays the balance into court. He notifies all claimants, and the court decides who is to get the money.

REVIEW QUESTIONS

1. Which of the parties in the construction process is the obligor of a surety bond? The obligee? The principal?

2. What is the function of a surety?

3. What are the principal types of bonds used in a construction project, and what is their major purpose?

4. Generally, can an unpaid subcontractor sue a surety on a payment bond?

5. What defenses can the surety assert when sued on the bond by the owner?

6. Normally, is the promise of a surety required to be in writing?

QUESTIONS FOR CLASS DISCUSSION

1. Under what conditions might it be advisable not to use surety bonds?

2. Should an unpaid subcontractor be able to sue a surety on a payment bond? Explain.

3. Should public contracts require surety bonds? Explain.

PROBLEM

C was a contractor in Idaho. He also did jobs in other nearby states. There was no requirement that contractors be licensed in Idaho. However, C undertook a job for O in Utah, which did have a licensing law. C did not apply for a license. C applied for and received a bond from S. C defaulted, and now S refuses to perform its obligations under the bond. S has offered to refund the premium to O. But S claims that the contract between C and O was illegal, since C was not licensed. Should this defense be allowed? What would be your conclusion if Idaho had a licensing law, and C's license had been revoked for fraud and incompetence? Would your conclusion be influenced by whether O knew of the revocation? If so, in what way?

Chapter 19

SOURCES OF CONSTRUCTION CONTRACT RIGHTS AND DUTIES

SECTION 19.01 CONTRACT DOCUMENTS

(A) INVITATION, INFORMATION AND PROPOSAL

The invitation to bidders, accompanied by the information to bidders, normally does not create any power of acceptance in the invited bidder. Yet the language in the invitation and the information can have legal significance if a contract is finally concluded. The major purpose of the invitation to bidders is to set up the ground rules under which a competitive bid will take place. However, there can be substantive statements in the invitation, the information, and the instruction to bidders, which can be significant. For example, instructions to the bidders which require that the bidder check the site and make his own test of soil conditions will be relevant in the event that subsurface conditions turn out to be different from that anticipated or represented in instruction documents, and a claim of fraud or misrepresentation is made by the contractor.

(B) BASIC AGREEMENT

The basic agreement is the document which contains the essential contract provisions. This document can be the culmination of competitive bidding or negotiation. At minimum, it will contain provisions dealing with price, payments, and time of commencement and completion. It may contain other provisions.

The basic agreement will frequently "incorporate by reference" other contract documents, such as the drawings, specifications, general terms and conditions, and any other data. Proper incorporation by reference makes documents which are not physically fixed to the signed writing legally binding, just as if the referred-to documents were contained in or attached to the signed writing. Another method of making certain that these ancillary writings form part of this owner-contractor obligation is to physically affix them to the basic agreement itself. Attaching the ancillary writings physically may be clumsy or impractical if the documents are bulky plans and specifications.

(C) PLANS OR DRAWINGS

The contract drawings express design concept data which can best be communicated by pictorial language rather than by written description. Sometimes drawings have notes on them, making the drawings a combination of graphic and word description.

The drawings are usually incorporated by reference or attached to the basic agreement. The drawings should be clear, accurate, and complete. If drawings submitted to contractors are vague and incomplete, honest bidders may be discouraged from bidding because of uncertainty as to the extent of the proposed obligation, and dishonest bidders may be encouraged to submit low bids and then seize upon ambiguities as a basis for charging costly extras.

The drawings play a significant role in spelling out the rights and duties of the owner and the contractor. The drawings, along with the other contract documents, determine whether the contractor has performed in accordance with his obligation. Also, compliance with the drawings may often relieve the contractor if the project is unsuccessful, or does not accord with the wishes of the owner or the purposes of the project. Finally, deficient drawings can result in liability being imposed upon the design professional for damage caused to the owner, the contractor, and to the subcontractor or members of the public. Faulty or incomplete drawings can result in higher costs of construction to the owner and liability to the design professional.

(D) SPECIFICATIONS

Specifications express the obligation of the contractor relating to workmanship and material in words. Like any tool of communication, specifications should be certain, complete, and reflect technical accuracy and skill.

Sometimes specifications indicate materials and methods. Other specifications may call for an end product or a specified result. Also, there may be specifications which deal with combinations of materials, methods, and results.

The differing types of specifications are of basic importance to the design professional. If the specifications indicate both the material and the method, there is greater risk upon the owner and ultimately upon the design professional. If the contractor is told just what he is to use, and how he is to use it, the risk of any failure of the project is likely to be assumed by the owner if the contractor can show that he complied with the specifications. In addition, there will be an increased chance of liability upon the owner and design professional for personal injury or damage to property caused by the structure or the method of construction.

This requires a brief explanation of the independent contractor rule. Generally, one who employs an independent contractor is not responsible for the acts of the independent contractor. Suppose a home-owner calls a technician to install a television antenna on his roof. If the technician drives negligently and injures a pedestrian, the technician and his employer will be liable, but not the owner who has called the technician. For more discussion see § 30.08.

There are many exceptions to the independent contractor rule, but if the exceptions do not control, the basic legal test in determining its applicability is the degree of control the person hiring has over the person whose negligent acts have caused the loss. The greater the degree of control over how the work is to be done, the greater the risk that the person causing the injury will be considered an employee and not an independent contractor. For this reason, and for others, it is often advantageous for owners to hire persons who would be classified as independent contractors. Where they are used, there is less risk that the person hiring the independent contractor will be liable if the independent contractor causes injuries to third parties. If the contractor is controlled as to choice of materials and methods, there is an increased risk that he will not be called an independent contractor. This can result in a greater potential range of liability to the owner.

On the other hand, design professionals should realize that the independent contractor defense is weakening, and, while not dead, is less important than it once was. This means that use of greater control may not expose the owner to increased legal responsibility. In addition, the increased use of public liability insurance can diminish the need for the independent contractor protection. While it is true that the public liability insurance will only cover whatever liabilities the law imposes upon the policy holder, the owner will be protected in most cases. Either he will be found to be not liable, or, if he is liable, payment will be made by the insurance company.

If legal responsibility for damages resulting from the contractor's acts or omissions is a diminished factor, it may be worthwhile to look at the advantages to the owner and the design professional of greater control over methods and materials. Specifying a result, and permitting the contractor to decide on how it should be accomplished means that greater reliance is being placed on the technological skill of the contractor. While it is true that if he does not perform properly, the use of sureties may give relief to the owner, this should not obscure the basic objective. The basic objective is to have the project performed properly the first time. This objective may be accomplished more readily if the owner and the design professional provide greater detail, with a view to controlling methods and materials, unless the contractor has more technical skill in this area than does the design professional. The decision, then, on whether the specifications should emphasize materials and method as well as the desired result, should be based upon which method is most likely to get the project completed promptly and properly. It should not be based upon the greater or lesser risk of liability on the part of the owner to third parties.

Associations of design professionals, through form contracts, are attempting to reduce the scope of liability of the design professional by placing greater risks upon the contractor. This can cause a conflict of interest for the design professional. By advising the owner to transfer as many risks as he can to the contractor, he may be able to relieve himself of liability. However, by transferring these risks to the contractor, he may be reducing the likelihood that the project will be accomplished successfully.

Another important basic consideration relates to economics and competition. The greater the flexibility given to the contractor, both in terms of method and materials, the greater the likelihood of a better competitive bid by the contractor. If he is limited to certain materials, or to certain equipment specified by manufacturer's name or brand name, he will have less flexibility and his bid is likely to be higher. If he is given more latitude, he will be able to shop around for more economical materials and equipment, and this saving can be passed on to the owner by way of the bid proposal.

Specification writing requires an awareness of the role played by construction unions in determining how, and by whom, the construction work is to be performed. While as between owner and contractor, construction methods are primarily the responsibility of the latter, the design professional can become involved in disputes relating to methods by which the work is done. This involvement can be illustrated by the legal questions that have been generated by the increased use of prefabricated materials.

National Woodwork Manufacturers Ass'n v. N.L.R.B., 386 U.S. 612 (1967) involved a dispute between a contractor and a construction union. The collective bargaining agreement between the contractor and its union contained a provision by which the union sought to preserve work for its members. The provision in this agreement excused union members from having to handle door units which had been assembled prior to being delivered to the job site. While the specifications in the job in question did not call for prehung doors, the contractor decided to use them. When the doors were delivered to the site, union members refused to handle the doors.

The contractor complied with the wishes of the union, but a trade association whose members made premachined doors asserted that the union was guilty of an unfair labor practice. The United States Supreme Court held that the clause in the collective bargaining agreement was enforceable because it was an attempt by the union to preserve its work and not an illegal secondary boycott of goods to be furnished by a third party. A subsequent opinion by the Federal 8th Circuit Court of Appeal, American Boiler Manufacturers Ass'n v. N.L.R.B., 404 F.2d 547 (8th Cir. 1968) expanded traditional work which could be protected by such an agreement to include all work which union employees have performed, or are still performing, at the time the work preservation clause was negotiated.

The design professional can be involved in such disputes in a number of ways. First, he may be called upon to determine whether the contract permits prefabricated material. His role in resolving interpretation questions will be discussed in Chapter 27.

If there is a union walkout or labor dispute because of the attempted use or use of such materials, the design professional may be empowered to decide whether the contractor is to receive an extension of time. This will be discussed in Chapter 23.

However, the design professional can be involved in such disputes due to his function of drafting specifications and issuing change orders.

In drafting specifications, the design professional should consider whether prefabricated materials should be designated. He should also consider whether prefabricated materials would be permitted under the specifications, if not specifically designated.

In making these judgments, he should take into account that the designation of prefabricated materials or drafting the specification in such a way as to permit prefabricated materials may cause a labor dispute. Even if, as will be suggested, his specifying prefabricated materials may legally avoid the impact of any work preservation clause in the collective bargaining agreement, the design professional may decide that it is better in the long run not to specify prefabricated materials or even to make certain that prefabricated materials will not be considered acceptable, even though those materials might reduce the construction contract price. This is not to suggest that these materials should never be designated. However, the legal difficulty and operational problems that may result should be considered in making this determination.

If the contractor would prefer to use prefabricated material, he might approach the design professional and suggest that the specifications designate prefabricated material. If the union objects to the use of prefabricated material as a violation of the collective bargaining agreement, the contractor could contend that he is not in control of the matter, and that he is not violating the collective bargaining agreement.

Whether the union will be able to exert economic pressure, such as a walkout, if the contractor attempts to use the prefabricated materials, is not clear. While some cases have sustained the contractor when the specifications required prefabricated materials, and have held that the union has no right to refuse to handle the materials or to strike, the law in this question is still unsettled. Even if the contractor does not suggest to the design professional that the original specifications list prefabricated materials, the contractor might approach the design professional after the project has been awarded and request a change order designating prefabricated material. If he does this openly, he may not be able to contend that it is a matter that is "beyond his control". For this reason a request for a change order may be made indirectly or very subtly.

The design professional must realize that the designation of prefabricated materials can cause difficulty on the construction site. He must be aware of the sensitive nature of such specifications and, that the law relating to these matters is, as yet, unsettled. Even if the law is on the side of the contractor, unions often take strong action if they feel it necessary to protect their jobs. One of the reasons the law is unsettled in this area is the difficulty of balancing the interests of construction workers in protecting their jobs against the interests of the owner, the contractor, and the public in using more efficient methods of construction.

(E) GENERAL CONDITIONS

Disputes often arise on construction projects. It is necessary to have a set of guidelines which will spell out clearly and completely the rights and duties of the parties, with special reference to payment, administrative control, changes, and claims.

For these reasons, most construction documents include "standard terms and conditions", or "general conditions of the contract". These are the basic ground rules under which the building will be constructed. They are often lengthy and quite detailed. They deal, as a rule, with the following subjects:

1. Scope of contract documents and resolution of conflicts between them
2. Roles and responsibilities of the principal participants in the project
3. Subcontractors and separate contractors
4. Time
5. Payments and completion
6. Protection from and risk of loss to persons and property
7. Changes
8. Corrections
9. Termination
10. Disputes.

See AIA Doc. A201, reproduced in Appendix D, for an example of terms and conditions.

In smaller contracts, these problems may be covered in a short form contract which will contain the basic terms and a lesser number of general terms and conditions. In larger projects the general terms and conditions may be physically separate from the basic agreement.

As general terms and conditions become longer and more complicated, there is a greater risk that there will be conflict between the various contract documents, resulting in misunderstanding once the project is underway. The risk of such misunderstanding is enhanced when there is physical separation between the basic agreement and the general terms and conditions on the one hand, and the drawings and specifications on the other. The problems of inconsistency and contradictory documents will be discussed in § 20.03.

It is desirable for the design professional to go over and explain the general conditions of the contract to his client before such an agreement is signed. The standard terms and conditions in a construction contract are detailed and complicated, and many clients have never had experience with them. As for going over them with the contractor, the latter is more likely to be experienced in construction and more likely to understand general terms and conditions than is the often inexperienced client. If the contractor chooses not to read the terms and conditions, he is still bound by them. If the contractor chooses to read the terms and conditions, he should be able to understand them. For these reasons, the contractor's rights and duties are likely to be measured by the standard terms and conditions.

However, it may be useful to explain to a contractor any standard terms and conditions which deviate from generally accepted contract clauses. This is especially true when recently published standard terms and conditions are used, and where it is unlikely that the contractor has previously dealt with the form. While the contractor should protect his interests by reading the form himself, it may be useful to go over key provisions which deviate in some meaningful way from prior forms or customary practices.

In dealing with most public agencies, the contractor will have to accept the general terms and conditions given to him by the agency. Such terms are part of adhesion contracts, and are not bargained contracts. In such a setting, a contractor is more likely to persuade a court that he should receive the benefit of any interpretation questions which may arise. The necessity for going over and explaining standard terms and conditions in such contracts seem less compelling, because it is unlikely that much could be done to change the contract. However, even in such agreements, it may be useful to point out to the contractor terms and conditions which may be different from earlier terms and conditions, or vary in some meaningful way from accepted practices. While the contractor may still be bound, if he understands his obligations there is a greater likelihood that he will perform them.

(F) SOIL AND SITE TEST REPORTS

Frequently, construction documents will contain soil test reports or site data, or contain a reference that such data is available in the office of the design professional or a soil consultant engaged by the design professional or the owner. The information and data contained in these documents is of great importance in the construction project. Mention has already been made of the possible disputes which can occur if the subsurface conditions are not accurately reflected in data furnished, or made available, to the contractor. This will be discussed in greater detail in Chapter 22. However, for present purposes, it should be noted that information furnished to the contractor regarding subsurface and site conditions must be considered as part of the basic over-all deal between contractor and owner.

(G) PRIOR NEGOTIATIONS AND THE PAROL EVIDENCE RULE

The parol evidence rule relates to the provability of oral agreements which are made before, or at the same time, as a written contract. This rule is based upon the concept of "completeness of writings." If the written agreement, and other written documents incorporated by reference or attached to it, is the complete agreement of the parties, then prior or contemporary oral agreements are not binding on the parties. Even if they were made, they were integrated, or merged, into the written, complete document. See §§ 5.04(e) and 6.02(c) for more on this rule.

Most construction contracts are complete. Nevertheless, there is a possibility that oral agreements have been made before, or at the same time, as the final written agreement. If the written agreement contains a clause specifying that the written agreement is the complete and final agreement, it will be difficult for either party to prove a prior oral agreement. It will not be impossible, because there are various doctrines which can permit proof of an oral agreement even if there are provisions specifying that the written agreement is the complete document.

If there is no contract provision dealing with the question of completeness, all that can be said is that the law is uncertain. Sometimes courts will admit the testimony of oral agreement, and sometimes they will not. It is important at this stage to emphasize the necessity of putting the entire agreement into the writing. Even if the writing is prepared and ready for execution, the design professional, and certainly the owner's legal advisor, should insist on incorporating any changes or additions into the writing itself. The entire document need not be retyped if there is a time problem. If the oral agreement is not included in the writing, there is a substantial risk that it cannot be proved.

If there is a dispute as to the meaning of certain terms used in the writing, and if a court determines that the words chosen by the parties were ambiguous, the court can look at the surrounding facts and circumstances to determine how the parties used those particular words. These circumstances include the setting of the transaction, the contracting parties' objectives in making the contract, and any conversations they may have had. Even if a writing is considered complete, antecedent or subsequent conversations may be admissible to interpret the writing.

(H) MODIFICATIONS

"Modifications" should be differentiated from "changes". "Changes" occur frequently during a construction project and are discussed in detail in Chapter 21. They are generally governed by carefully drawn and complete provisions under which the owner has the right to order changes, and the contractor must perform them, with appropriate contract language dealing with compensation for deletions or additions caused by the changes. A "modification" is a change in the basic obligation not based upon any contractual provision giving the owner right to order changes.

In most jurisdictions, a modification requires consideration to be binding. (See § 2.09 for a discussion of consideration.)

Suppose there is a construction project for $100,000. The obligations of the contractor are spelled out in the contract documents. If, during the life of the agreement, the parties mutually agree that the contract price will be increased to $110,000, this increased obligation on the part of the owner must be exchanged for something received by the owner, or some detriment suffered by the contractor. If, in exchange for this, the contractor agrees to an increase in the quality or quantity of the building, or to shorten the time for completion, then there is an appropriate exchange and the modification agreement is binding. Difficulties arise when the modification agreement encompasses an increase in price without any change in the contractor's obligation. Such an agreement can run afoul of what is called the "pre-exising duty rule". Unless one of the many exceptions applies, the agreement is not binding if the party, in this case the contractor, is obligating himself to do no more than he was previously obligated to perform under the original contract.

This pre-existing duty rule has come under a great deal of criticism. It limits the autonomy of the parties, by denying enforceability of agreements voluntarily made. Implicit in the rule is an assumption that an increased price for the same amount of work is likely to be the result of expressed or implied coercion on the part of the contractor, as if the contractor is saying "pay me more money or I will quit and you will have to whistle for the damages". However, there are circumstances where the parties have arrived at a modification of this type voluntarily, and there seems to be no particular reason for not giving effect to their agreement. For this reason, there have been a number of exceptions which have developed in order to relieve against the sometimes harsh effect of the pre-existing duty rule.

In the construction contract, minor changes in the contractor's obligation have been held sufficient to avoid the rule, even if it was quite clear that the increase in price was not at all commensurate with the change in obligation on the part of the contractor. This means that the contract modification would be enforced if the parties have had enough foresight or legal knowledge to provide for some minor and relatively insignificant change in the contractor's obligation as a means of enforcing the increased promise. In addition, courts have sometimes employed the fiction that by making the agreement for increased price, the parties have abrogated or rescinded the old agreement. If they have "rescinded" the old agreement, then there are no existing contractual obligations which justify application of the pre-existing duty rule. Under this approach, courts proceed as if the parties had torn up the original agreement, both parties being free to perform or not as they choose, and then entered into a new agreement at the increased price for the same performance promised under the original contract. This is obviously a fiction, but its use has shown some judicial dissatisfaction with the pre-existing duty rule.

Another indication of dissatisfaction with the requirement of consideration for a modification is manifested by the Uniform Commercial Code, a set of laws dealing with sales of goods. Under Section 2–209 of the Code, modifications are valid without consideration, but a modification obtained through "bad faith" is not valid.

Curiously, despite the movement toward abolition of the requirement of consideration for a modification, the rule is applied vigorously in federal public contracts. Many cases hold that unless the government receives something for an increase in price or a reduced price for a deletion, the modification is not valid. Sometimes this rigid adherence to the consideration requirement is justified as a means of insuring that there be no gifts of public funds. Also, the rule may be justified as a means of preventing corruption and collusion between contractor and public official. Finally, giving some advantage to a contractor without the government getting anything in return may be unfair to the other bidders.

Statutes in a few states require that written contracts be modified by written contracts or by executed oral agreements. California has grafted upon this statutory rule a court-made rule: if there is consideration for the modification, then the executed performance need only be by the party who is asserting the modification. For example, if, during the course of construction, the contractor and the owner agree to use a different method of measuring concrete work payable under a unit price schedule, this agreement need not be in writing despite the statute. Since there is consideration (the changed method of measurement), all the contractor must show is that he performed in accordance with the alleged oral modification. He will still have to convince the court that there was a modification, but it need not have been in writing to be enforcible.

Contractual provisions requiring that modifications be in writing generally are not valid. In enforcing oral modifications despite such clauses, the courts have stated that by making a subsequent oral modification, the parties have changed the agreement requiring that modification be in writing. However, under Sec. 2–209 of the Uniform Commercial Code (dealing with sales of goods), oral agreements modifying the written agreement are not effective if the written agreement contains a provision requiring that modifications be in writing. There are some exceptions to this, but the Code does express the policy that such contractual provisions requiring a writing as a condition to enforcement of an asserted modification agreement should be given more effect than the courts have given them in the past. It remains to be seen whether this change in the law relating to the sale of goods will have any impact upon judicial thinking in cases not related to the sale of goods.

To sum up, modification of construction contracts usually requires consideration, and sometimes requires that modification be in writing. A valid modification extinguishes that portion of the original agreement with which the modification is inconsistent, and creates new rights and duties.

SECTION 19.02 JUDICIALLY DETERMINED TERMS

(A) NECESSITY TO IMPLY TERMS

The sources of contract rights and duties go beyond the contract documents. When making a contract, parties frequently do not consider all problems which may arise. Some matters may have been considered, but the parties believed the resolution of the matters to be so obvious that contract coverage would be unnecessary. There may have been matters discussed by the parties during negotiations but the parties may not have been able to agree on a contract solution to the problem. Yet these parties may intend to have a binding contract despite their inability to resolve all problems during negotiation. In such cases, the parties may state in the contract that they will agree in the future on certain less important contract matters, or merely omit the matter from the contract entirely.

In these cases, it may be necessary for the courts to fill in the gaps not covered by the contract or decide matters left for future agreement where the parties could not agree. Courts are more likely to perform these functions if they are convinced that the parties intended to make an enforceable agreement, especially where performance has commenced.

Sometimes courts try to adjust extreme disparity in bargaining power by implying terms which favor the weaker party. Nineteenth century and early twentieth century English and American judges were hesitant to imply terms. To these judges, the function of the judge was to apply the existing law or enforce a contract, rather than create law or "make contracts for the parties". Today, courts seem less insecure about their role in contract disputes. They are beginning to recognize that they do make law, and that they do "make" contracts for the parties. They are beginning to recognize the need for implication of terms because of poorly drafted contracts and inequality of bargaining power. For these reasons courts today feel relatively more free to imply terms than did courts fifty years ago.

Courts should exercise some restraint in implying terms, especially if the contract is one truly negotiated by the parties. In such cases, it is likely that most of the major problems were considered, and the absence of contract coverage may be deliberate. For a court to imply a term in such cases may disrupt the bargain.

Where there are negotiated contracts, it still may be necessary to imply terms which were so obvious that the parties did not think it necessary to express them. Also, a court should "complete" the deal by filling in gaps where parties intended to make a contract, left minor terms for future agreement, but have not been able to agree.

In dealing with "to be agreed upon" provisions, courts will examine whether the parties intended to conclude a binding agreement, or whether their leaving matters open for further negotiation meant that they were making tentative agreements but were withholding final agreement. The Uniform Commercial Code has led to a weakening of the older, more rigid doctrines. Under Section 2–204 of the Code, parties can leave minor matters open without affecting the validity of the contract. Even though the Code does not apply to construction contracts, Code thinking is likely to spill over to other types of contracts. (The Code section may apply to the sale of goods, machinery and equipment for a construction project.) In determining whether and how to fill gaps, courts consider the provisions expressed in the contract document. Often, in construction contracts, parties use forms or negotiated contracts which are very detailed and reasonably complete. Generally courts will not imply terms if the implication would produce a result directly contrary to the expressed language.

For example, in Weber v. Milpitas County Water District, 201 Cal.App.2d 666, 20 Cal.Rptr. 45 (1962), the contract specified that the contractor would obtain all necessary permits. Work was delayed due to the failure of the highway department to issue an encroachment permit. Because of the delay, the contractor was given an extension of time. However, he also sought delay damages because much of his work had to be done during the rainy season. The District Court of Appeals reversed a holding of the trial court which awarded delay damages to the contractor. In doing so, the court made short shrift of the contractor's argument that it should be implied by law that the owner would obtain such a permit. The court would not imply a term which would change an express term in the contract.

However, what if the subject matter is covered, but the contract does not deal in detail with the problem? For example, a contract may cover some aspects of delivery but not deal with size of containers, numbers of deliveries per month, or other similar matters.

The issue in such cases is whether the coverage by the parties of the general question of delivery should preclude the court from implying any terms relating to delivery.

While generalizations are difficult in this area, whether a court will imply a term will depend, to a large degree, upon the amount of detail in the contract itself. If the contract is detailed, courts are less likely to imply additional terms, even if the additional terms are not directly at variance with the expressed terms.

Some generalizations can be made regarding the terms that will be implied in construction contracts. However, such generalizations must be made cautiously. As has been stated, express contract provisions are likely to control implied terms. Also, as shall be seen, custom will be preferred to terms which might be implied.

As examples on the contractor's side, he impliedly promises to use proper workmanship and materials. He usually impliedly promises to have the project constructed free and clear of liens by other parties. He promises that the work will be in a state of readiness which will permit subcontractors to perform their work in accordance with work schedules. If there are separate contractors, each promises to cooperate reasonably with the others, so that the project can be completed in accordance with contract obligations and with reasonable efficiency.

The owner promises that the site will be ready for the contractor's performance when performance is to commence. He usually impliedly promises to obtain any easements or rights in the land of others necessary for the project. He also impliedly promises that he and his designated representative, usually the design professional, will perform in such a way as to expedite the contractor's performance. For example, he will usually be held to have impliedly promised that the design professional will pass upon the sufficiency of shop drawings within a reasonable time.

In addition to these illustrations, there are some general implied terms. Each party impliedly promises not to prevent or hinder the other party and to cooperate reasonably. There may be limits to these implied terms. For example, suppose there is a contract for repair work on a plant which will continue to function during construction. What if the contractor is ordered off the job for short periods because the entire plant assembly line is needed to fill a rush order? This "prevention" may be permissible if the facts and circumstances indicate that it was an assumed risk by the contractor.

With regard to cooperation, courts use a rule of reason. The parties are not usually required to undertake heavy burdens to help the other party. But clearly cooperation would be implied if, without cooperation, the other party could not economically perform, or if a small effort by one party would substantially assist the other party.

Another area where terms can be implied relate to the time for completion. Usually a specified time is given in the contract. If there is no express provision dealing with this question, courts hold that the contractor must complete performance within a reasonable time. Reasonableness will be determined in light of all the surrounding facts and circumstances.

Courts should be cautious in applying a reasonable time for performance if performance has not yet commenced, and if the failure to agree on a time for performance indicates that the parties have not yet intended to conclude a contract. The absence of agreement on such an important question may mean the parties are still in a bargaining stage.

(B) CUSTOM

Custom plays an important role in both interpreting contract terms and filling in contract gaps. Sometimes courts state that when they use custom they are merely finding the agreement of the parties because parties contract with reference to existing customs. In that sense, courts can be said to be simply giving effect to the actual intention of the parties. However, in many cases parties have not thought about the problem, and courts find that custom is a more convenient or efficient method of filling gaps than having the court itself deciding what is reasonable and fair.

For example, if the custom in a particular locality is that the contractor obtain a building permit, the court is likely to place this responsibility upon the contractor. This would be so even if the judge's own experience would lead him to believe it would be more reasonable for the owner to obtain the building permit.

In order to fill a gap by custom, courts generally require that the custom exist within the area and within the particular type of business in question, and that the parties knew or should have known of the custom.

Courts will not imply custom if that custom is different than an expressed contract term. In Weber v. Milpitas County Water District, a case discussed in § 19.02(a), the court rejected the contention by the contractor that customarily the water district was responsible for the issuance of an encroachment permit by the highway department. Rejection was based upon an expressed term in the contract, specifying that the contractor would obtain all necessary permits.

(C) COMPLIANCE WITH LAWS

There are many laws which regulate the construction process itself. In many construction contracts, it is implied that the project, as constructed, will comply with the requirements of the local building codes. There is nothing to preclude the parties from agreeing to construct a project which goes beyond the requirements of the building code but they must at least conform to the standards set forth in the building codes. The same would be true of zoning ordinances regulating the population density, off-street parking, or height and bulk limitations.

These are primarily the responsibility of the design professional. However, the contractor should object to a building project which he knows does not accord with the building codes or the zoning ordinances. If he built such a structure, he would be violating the law, and could incur obligations to persons who might be harmed as a result of construction not in accordance with building codes and standards. The contractor might contend that he is only undertaking to construct a building in accordance with the plans and specifications, and he need not concern himself with potential violation of building codes or zoning ordinances. However, it is likely that a court will imply that the contractor should bring to the attention of the design professional, or the owner, anything which indicated to him that the plans and specifications would deviate from the requirements set forth by building codes or by zoning ordinances.

There are other laws which affect the construction process. They relate to workers' safety, safety to the general public, and laws protecting the rights of adjacent landowners. Since most of these relate to construction methods and the project site, the primary responsibility for compliance will rest with the contractor. The absence of provisions in the contract dealing with allocations of responsibilities regarding compliance with these regulations and laws does not mean that the contractor need not perform in accordance with these laws and regulations.

Most federal contracting agencies have extensive and complicated regulations. In addition, form contracts used by government agencies are quite detailed. Christian v. United States, 312 F.2d 418 (Ct.Cl.1963), involved a contract for construction of military housing which did not contain a provision permitting the government to terminate at its convenience. Regulations required such provisions in almost all government contracts, including the *Christian* contract, but for some reason it was not included. Despite this omission, the Court of Claims held that the regulation had the force and effect of law, and that the provision for termination for convenience was implied in the contract because the regulation required that it be inserted there.

This decision can mean that a federal contractor cannot know the scope of his obligation until he consults and evaluates the formidable body of regulations of the federal agency. On the other hand, perhaps the decision only means that provisions which are commonly included, and of which the contractor is likely to have knowledge, are going to be a part of the total obligation of the contractor and the public agency, despite a failure to physically include the provisions in the contract.

Increasing governmental control over construction means that permits issued by public authorities often are required before, during, and at the end of construction. It may be necessary to obtain a special use permit or zoning variance to construct the project. Local officials generally must issue a building permit before the project can be commenced. During performance, public officials may be required to inspect the project to determine whether there is compliance with employee safety rules, and compliance with building codes relating to excavation, structural work, electrical work, and other aspects of the project. Permission may have to be obtained from public utilities to connect the utilities of the project to lines of the public utility. Drainage rights of way may have to be obtained, as well as permits from state highway officials for certain types of construction. Upon completion of the project, it is usually necessary to obtain an occupancy permit from local officials. To obtain permits of the type described, it may be necessary to submit design data to public officials, to arrange for and permit that inspections of the project be made, and to pay fees for issuance of such permits. Is the owner or the contractor required to obtain such permits?

Generally, construction contracts cover these matters. If the contract does not deal with the question, there are likely to be customs which allocate the responsibility for obtaining various permits. In the absence of an express contract provision or accepted custom, the law will be likely to imply that the owner will obtain the more important types of permits such as land use control permits, building permits, and occupancy permits. The contractor is likely to be required, by implication of law, to obtain permits from public officials or others which are less important and more operational in nature, such as utility hookup permits and arrange for inspections by public officials concerned with employee safety and building code compliance.

REVIEW QUESTIONS

1. What are the contract documents?

2. What are the advantages and disadvantages of specifications which dictate materials and method of construction?

3. What are the legal requirements for a contract modification?

4. How does the pre-existing duty rule affect contract modifications?

5. When will the court imply terms?

6. Under what circumstances will custom be part of a contract?

QUESTIONS FOR CLASS DISCUSSION

1. Why should the court imply terms in a contract?

2. Should a contracting party be held responsible for a custom of which he had no knowledge?

3. Why should a party be precluded from proving an earlier oral agreement after he assents to a writing?

PROBLEMS

1. A agreed to design a residence for O, which C was to build. Nothing was stated in the contract documents about sealing the basement so that it would be waterproof. The drawings and specifications merely gave the dimensions and materials. The basement leaked. Would C be liable? Give your reasons.

2. A agreed to design a residence for O which C was to build. The specifications stated that the basement was to be made waterproof. The contract documents set forth the materials and the method. C complied but the basement leaked. Who assumed this risk, O or C? What if C knew that the materials and method would not do the job, but said nothing? What if C told A he did not think the materials and method would work, but A told him to go ahead anyway?

3. Would your conclusions in 1 and 2 be affected if the reason for the leaking was a defective batch of material warranted to be waterproof?

Chapter 20

CONTRACT INTERPRETATION

SECTION 20.01 BASIC OBJECTIVES

The basic objective in contract interpretation is to determine the intention of the parties. However, within this relatively simple standard lie many problems. Some of these are:

1. What can be examined to ascertain the intention of the parties?
2. Once the relevant sources are examined, how is the intention of the parties determined?
3. What if each of the parties had different intentions?
4. What if one party knew of the other party's intention?
5. What if the parties had no particular intention about the matter in question?
6. Can the court go beyond these presumed intentions of the parties and interpret in accordance with what the court thinks they would have intended had they thought about it?
7. Can a court disregard the intention of the parties test and base determination of the rights and duties of the parties upon judicial notions of proper allocation of risk?

The list is given merely to indicate that phrasing the test as the process of ascertaining the intention of the parties is deceptively simple, often hiding difficult interpretation problems.

SECTION 20.02 MEANING OF CONTRACT LANGUAGE: BAILEY v. BREETWOR

Words have no inherent meaning. Yet words develop commonly accepted meanings because people who use them as tools of communication attach meanings to them. A judge asked to interpret contract terms could decide all interpretation questions simply by using a dictionary and choosing the dictionary meaning which seemed most appropriate to him. However, the parties to the contract may have used the words in a way which is not found in a dictionary. Also, the choice of which dictionary meaning to be selected can be a formidable one. For these reasons, the determination of the meaning of the terms in question by the parties who use them in the contract should take into account the setting and function of the transaction, and other matters not found in the contract or the dictionary. Often, courts state that they put themselves in the position of the contracting parties and determine what the contracting parties meant or intended when they used the language in question.

The law has been reluctant to give judges or juries absolute freedom to determine the meaning of words. Some of this reluctance may be traceable to the fear that juries, and sometimes trial judges, will be unduly sympathetic to a hard luck story, and too inclined to protect the party in the weaker bargaining position. Also underlying this reluctance is the skepticism the law has toward the ability of the trial process to separate truth from falsehood. Not infrequently contracting parties differ in their testimony as to what transpired during the negotiations.

Reluctance to give absolute discretion in interpretation questions to the fact finders may also be traceable in part to the fear that juries, and sometimes trial judges, may not realize the importance to the commercial world of attaching consistent, commercially accepted, meanings to terms.

The method employed to limit interpretation powers of juries and trial judges has been the "plain meaning" rule. A judge must first determine whether the words used by the parties to a contract had a plain meaning. If he determined that the meaning seemed plain to him, he could not look beyond the document itself to determine what the parties meant when they used those particular words. (In the process of interpretation, a court may have to interpret acts of the parties, as well as the language they have chosen. However, this section deals with interpreting the words used by the parties.)

If the judge determines that the meaning to be attributed to the words used by the contracting parties cannot be determined solely by looking at the writing, then he will look outside the writing. He may look at the surrounding circumstances which led to the making of the contract, the preliminary negotiations and statements of the parties, any special "codes" the parties may have adopted, custom and usage, and the interpretation the parties placed upon the words as shown by their acts. In many cases, judges state that the words are plain on their face and require no outside help. Yet the judge may have already looked at those elements outside the writing and had his initial reaction confirmed, or found that outside sources were not helpful. Yet the judge may say that the meaning must be determined from the contract itself.

There is one significant exception to the plain meaning rule. Most courts will look at evidence of custom and usage, even though the custom and usage seem to be at variance with the apparently plain meaning of the terms employed. For example, the contract might specify that meat to be delivered must not have a fat content of over 50%. Yet suppose custom in that particular industry was that the seller is permitted to deliver meat which has a fat content of 50.5%. The seller would be permitted to show this custom.

Also, the plain meaning rule applies only to litigation. For example, an arbitrator could examine evidence outside the writing, without first deciding that the language being interpreted was ambiguous.

While courts still give lip service to the plain meaning rule, application of the rule today may mean only that judge will have to make a preliminary finding that the meaning is not plain on its face before he openly looks at other indications of how the parties used the crucial language.

Assuming that the judge determines that the meaning of the crucial language cannot be established without outside assistance, what will he examine to determine this meaning? He will look at surrounding circumstances, statements of the parties, and acts of the parties. Frequently, what parties do gives a good indication of what they intended when they made the agreement.

With regard to statements and acts of the parties, it is important to differentiate those statements and acts which occur after a dispute has developed. Once the dispute has developed, the parties' statements and their acts are not very informative as to their intentions at the time they entered into the contract. Often their statements and acts result from their desire to improve their case.

There are limits to outside sources or assistance to the court. For example, the uncommunicated intention of a party is normally not considered relevant in determining intention. His intention is relevant only if he informs the other party of his understanding.

Sometimes rejection of this intention evidence is based upon the "objective" theory of contracts. Under this theory, persons are contractually obligated by their manifestations of intention, rather than by their actual, but undisclosed intention. One of the purposes of contract law is to protect the reasonable expectations of contracting parties. If one person leads another to believe that certain performance will be rendered, his actual intention to render or not to render that performance is irrelevant. For this reason, courts normally do not listen to uncommunicated statements of one party's intention.

Often a court finds little assistance in the surrounding circumstances, the statements of the parties, or their acts. In such cases, courts sometimes employ what are called "canons of interpretation." There are many such interpretation guides. A few are used frequently. One is based upon the Latin maxim of *expresio unius est exclusio alterius.* (The inclusion of particular things means that things not expressed are excluded.) For example, if a party is excused from performance in the event of fire, rainstorm, drought, earthquake, and flood, a court might hold that the occurrence of some event not mentioned, such as a tornado, does not terminate the performing party's obligation. If the parties went to the trouble of expressing five justifiable excuses, they must have intended to exclude all other excuses for failure to perform. This guide is sometimes harshly applied, and does not give realistic recognition of the difficulty of drafting a complete list of events.

The "guide" called *ejusdem generis* states that the meaning of a general term in a contract is limited by the specific illustrations which accompany it. Anything not specifically mentioned must be similar in meaning to those things which are mentioned. For example, damages payable for harm to crops, trees, fences, and premises, probably would not include depreciation in market value of the land. The particular item in question is too unrelated to those items listed to be covered by the contract terms.

There are other interpretation guides. A court should give an interpretation which does not lead to an absurd result. If possible, the interpretation should be fair and reasonable, unless it is clear that the parties intended the result under which one party clearly made an unreasonable contract. Generally, courts hesitate to decide questions of reasonableness in contracts, and prefer to leave this to the bargaining of the parties.

There is a guide to interpretation which is used more frequently than some of the others mentioned. Courts interpret a contract against the person who drafted the contract, or against the party who caused the ambiguity to exist. Often, it is difficult to determine who actually chose the language, if the contract is one which is jointly negotiated by the parties. However, many contracts are created entirely by one party to the contract, and presented to the other party on a take-it-or-leave-it basis. In such cases, courts are likely to construe ambiguities against the party who created the form.

Sometimes this legal interpretation approach is based upon negligence in spelling out the terms. The party who was not careful enough to avoid the ambiguity is penalized for his lack of care.

More often, the underlying rationale is a policy of protecting the underdog in a contract. This "guide" had its genesis in the interpretation of insurance contracts. In many insurance cases, the courts gave the insured protection and coverage above and beyond what would appear to be reasonable from a neutral reading of the terms of the policy. Part of this was a recognition of the social utility of insurance, and protection of the normal expectations persons have when they take out insurance.

The special rules relating to interpretation of insurance policies recognize the difficulty insureds have in reading the entire contract, let alone understanding it. Interpretation against the drafter can also be employed against design professionals who use contract documents put out by their professional societies. Frequently, the client does not read the agreement, nor does the design professional explain the crucial provisions to the client. In such a case, doubtful questions of interpretation are very likely to be resolved in favor of the client.

Another interpretation guide employed by courts relates to provisions by which one party to a contract attempts to "exculpate" or relieve himself from responsibility for his negligent acts. Courts require a high degree of specificity before they will interpret the clause to cover the negligence of the party seeking exculpation. The same is true when one party seeks indemnification from another person for acts of negligence of the party asking indemnification.

Such provisions are common in construction contracts. Owners often include provisions by which the contractor promises to indemnify or "hold the owner harmless" for all injuries occurring in the construction process. Prime contractors often demand and obtain a corresponding provision from subcontractors. These clauses will be discussed in greater detail in § 30.13(b), dealing with accidents during construction. These provisions usually are not interpreted to relieve a person from his active negligence, unless the clause expressly states this agreement.

Usually courts prefer to apply the ordinary meaning of a term, unless the term has a technical meaning, and the contract deals with technical matters. Custom and trade usage of the locality in which the contracting parties are located are very persuasive in interpretation matters.

A typical contract interpretation case, Bailey v. Breetwor is reproduced at this point.

BAILEY v. BREETWOR

District Court of Appeal, California, 1962.
206 Cal.App.2d 287, 23 Cal.Rptr. 740.

BURKE, PRESIDING JUSTICE. . . . The case was tried without a jury and judgment was entered . . . in favor of plaintiff Phillip Bailey doing business as Bailey Construction Co. ("Bailey") in the sum of $3,818. Defendants, owners of the property, Saul J. Breetwor and Beverly Breetwor ("Breetwor"), appeal from the judgment.

Viewed most favorably to the plaintiffs, the following is a summary of material facts. Breetwor entered into a contract with Colich to grade and compact Breetwor's building site as per plan, including compacting available fill material to the approximate profile shown on the grading plan for a contract price of $2,600. The contract included the securing of a report by an engineering firm acceptable to the city of Inglewood ("City") Building Department "that all work has been done to City specifications." Colich subcontracted the grading and compacting work to Bailey, with Bailey agreeing to perform the work in accordance with the provisions of the Colich-Breetwor contract and with Colich reserving to himself the installation of certain drainage structures.

There had been a natural drain running across the property at its lowest point, and upon commencing the work and scraping the surface of this area Bailey uncovered an extensive amount of wet clay.

This was called to the attention of the company engaged by Bailey to report to the city of Inglewood and Bailey was advised that all of this wet clay material would have to be removed in order to permit proper compaction of the soil in accordance with City requirements. Bailey notified Breetwor of the condition, the necessity for its correction and that such work was not included in his subcontract with Colich; further, that if the work was to be done it would have to be paid for as an extra. When Breetwor inquired as to the cost of doing the extra work Bailey advised him that it was not possible to give him an estimate without knowing the extent of the underlying wet clay strata and suggested that Breetwor contract with an engineering company to conduct soil tests to determine the extent of the condition. Breetwor insisted that the compaction of the muddy soil was within the terms of his contract with Colich. Bailey advised him that unless Breetwor agreed to pay for the work as an extra he would stop work on the contract. Breetwor urged him not to stop work because he had plans to construct an apartment building on the site and did not want the job delayed. Bailey offered to do the extra work on a cost plus 10 per cent to cover overhead basis. Breetwor told him, "Until I get this straightened out with Colich Construction Co. I will authorize you to go ahead and I will assume responsibility for the costs." Breetwor's version of this conversation was more favorable to himself but that conflict in the testimony must be resolved on appeal in favor of the prevailing parties.

Bailey proceeded with the special work and segregated the cost of doing it from the work which he originally subcontracted to do for Colich. Upon the completion of the entire project he billed Breetwor direct for the extra work which amounted to $3,213, . . . Bailey . . . filed a lien and a complaint to foreclose it, to which Breetwor answered and cross complained, alleging that Bailey's work was done pursuant to the Colich-Breetwor contract; that there existed no contractual relationship between Bailey and Breetwor; that the alleged oral agreement sued upon was without any consideration whatever . . .

On appeal defendants contend that the Colich-Breetwor contract required Colich to compact the wet clay which was uncovered in the doing of the work; that Bailey obligated himself under the Colich-Bailey subcontract to do the same thing that Colich had agreed to do and that since any promise that Breetwor would have made to Bailey would have already covered under a pre-existing contract, such promise was not enforceable against Breetwor for lack of consideration.

In referring to the compaction to be engaged in under the contract, the Colich-Breetwor contract included the phrase, "No import or haul-away included." The trial court permitted the testimony of expert witnesses in order to be enlightened as to the meaning of this phrase. It also permitted expert testimony on the meaning of the words "grading," "compaction," "fill," and by the phrase "compacting available fill to the profile shown on the grading plan." Technical words are to be interpreted as usually understood by persons in the profession or business to which they relate unless clearly used in a different sense. (Civ.Code, § 1645.)

"Where any doubt exists as to the purport of the parties' dealings as expressed in the wording of their contract, the court may look to the circumstances surrounding its execution—including the object, nature and subject matter of the agreement [citing case]—as well as to subsequent acts or declarations of the parties 'shedding light upon the question of their mutual intention at the time of contracting.' [Citing case.]" (Barham v. Barham, 33 Cal.2d 416, 423, 202 P.2d 289, 293.)

There was no error in permitting expert testimony as to the proper interpretation of technical words used in these construction contracts. From the testimony it was apparent that a considerable amount of loose fill material had been dumped from the street over an embankment onto the subject property, which material was readily visible to anyone inspecting the property, and there could be no doubt but that the contractor was responsible under the contract to work over this particular material in order to compact it in such a manner as would form a firm base for the construction of the contemplated apartment house building. However, the wet clay condition was not readily apparent from the surface and was exposed only after the work of grading had commenced. While the contract contemplated that certain soil would be removed from the high ground and compacted on the lower level, there was nothing in the contract which required an excavation at the lower level below the natural contour of the ground in order to remove an underlying wet clay condition, and it was this condition which the plaintiffs asserted was beyond the work contemplated in the original contract or subcontract. Once this condition was noted there was no obligation on the part of the contractor or subcontractor to proceed.

The authorization given by Breetwor to Bailey to proceed to do the work on a cost plus basis constituted, in the eyes of the trial court, a special verbal contract establishing a contractual relationship between Breetwor and Bailey directly upon which the latter was entitled to recover. The evidence showed that Breetwor remained in constant attendance as the work progressed and was advised by Bailey from time to time as to the costs being incurred. Having authorized the work to proceed, it was up to Breetwor to terminate this arrangement as and when he saw fit. He could not, however, wait until the completion of the work to repudiate his oral contract with Bailey.

The rule is established in California that a promise of extra compensation for completion of a contract to a promisee who has at the time a pre-existing legal duty to perform the contract is without consideration. . . . (p. 103.) Also a promise by one to fulfill his own contract with another is no consideration for a promise by a third party. . . .

However, if the duty of performance under the subsequent contract is different from the duty owed under the prior contract, then the promisor is not promising to perform a pre-existing legal duty. His promise imposes upon him a new detriment and confers upon the promisee a new benefit and is sufficient consideration for the promise of another to pay for his costs. (Civ.Code, § 1605.)

In the instant case the duty of performance owed by Bailey under the original subcontract, which incorporated the terms of the contract between Colich and Breetwor, was to grade and compact Breetwor's building site according to certain plans and specifications, "import or haul-away excluded." Under the subsequent contract with Breetwor, Bailey's duty of performance included correcting the wet clay condition requiring excavation below the natural contour line of the ground and importation of additional fill material. This performance was clearly beyond the scope of the original contract. Bailey thus incurred a new detriment and Breetwor received a new benefit constituting sufficient consideration for Breetwor's promise to cover Bailey's costs. (Civ. Code, § 1605; also see Restatement of Contracts, § 84, subd. c.)

Judgment for plaintiffs affirmed.

The preexisting duty rule has been discussed in §§ 2.09(c) and 19.01(h). Bailey was met with the contention that his performance was not sufficient consideration to enforce Breetwor's promise, because Bailey had obligated himself to render this same performance in his agreement with Colich.

In most states, such an agreement would be enforceable because the duty of performance was owed to a third party (Colich) and not to the promisor (Breetwor) but in California it has been held that even if the performance was owed to a third party (Colich) it could not be the basis for enforcing a promise by Breetwor to Bailey. But the court enforced Breetwor's promise by holding that the performance rendered by Bailey in exchange for Breetwor's promise went beyond the obligation Bailey owed Colich.

SECTION 20.03 RESOLVING CONFLICTS AND INCONSISTENCIES

(A) WITHIN THE WRITTEN AGREEMENT

Interpretation of contracts is a difficult process. A court must try to put itself in the position of the parties and try to determine their intentions when they made the agreement. This process is complicated by the fact that the tendency today is to have longer agreements which contain many different provisions. Often such agreements are not scrutinized with great care, and there may be a conflict requiring a choice of whether emphasis is to be given to particular portions of the agreement rather than other portions of the agreement. Various priorities of interpretation have been developed by the court in resolving these inconsistencies.

Sometimes the contract has a clause generally dealing with one problem, and another clause which deals more specifically with that problem. In such a case, the more specific clause will take precedence over the general clause. This is because the specific clause is likely to give a better indication of what the parties intend than a general clause.

For example, suppose a building contract specified that all disputes were subject to arbitration, but also specified in a different paragraph that disputes as to artistic effect were to be resolved by the design professional, and that his decisions were not arbitrable. In such a case, it is likely that the parties intended that the specific clause would control over the general on the question of artistic effect. If the parties have expressed themselves specifically on the question, their failure to change the general clause is likely to be due to their belief that the specific handling of the problem would not make a change in the general clause necessary, and that the contract would become cluttered up with exceptions and provisos if general clauses were changed to reflect exceptions created by specific clauses. Sometimes the parties have not noticed the discrepancy.

Sometimes conflicts result because of an inconsistency between printed provisions, typed provisions, and handwritten provisions. Usually, the courts will prefer the handwritten provision over the typed provision, and the typed provision over the printed provision. This scale of priorities is based on the assumption that people express themselves more accurately when they take the trouble to write out the language as opposed to typing or printing the expression. Also, specially typed provisions on a printed form are more likely to be an indication of the true intention of the parties.

There are other guides which are employed in resolving inconsistencies within the document. Sometimes courts hold that the later clause takes precedence over the earlier clause. These methods of priority are only guides, and not rules. They are merely employed to assist the court in resolving interpretation questions. Often one party points to one guide to support his view and the other party points to an equally applicable guide to support his view. Courts sometimes gives these guides as justifications for the decision which they have already reached by common sense, or by their sense of fairness. Nevertheless, a close case may be resolved by use of one of these guides.

(B) BETWEEN DOCUMENTS: DUNLAP v. WARMACK–FITZ STEEL CO.

Construction contracts present difficult interpretation questions because the parties express their agreement in a number of different documents. There is a basic agreement, the general terms and conditions, the plans, the specifications, and even the invitations or information to bidders. Often there will be documents which call for certain work to be done which is not called for in another document. For that reason, it is essential to set up priorities between documents and a method of resolving inconsistency between the contract documents.

Which document controls when one document calls for certain work while others do not? AIA Doc. A201 at 1.2.3 states that ". . . what is required by any one shall be as binding as if required by all." Sometimes the contract will specify a set of priorities as between the various contract documents. This relates to the concept of the specific controlling the general. It might be possible to specify that in the case of conflict the order of priorities could be (1) the basic agreement; (2) the specifications; (3) the drawings; (4) general terms and conditions.

In Graham v. Commonwealth, 206 Va. 431, 143 S.E.2d 831 (1965), the Supreme Court of Appeals of Virginia supported its holding in favor of the contractor by pointing to a provision that stated that in the event of conflict, the specifications controlled over the general conditions, and the basic agreement should control over specifications, drawings and the general conditions. Also, the court employed the "guide" that the document was to be construed against the person creating the document, in this case the public owner. *Graham* involved pricing of extra work not the required performance.

Another method of handling this is to delegate to the design professional responsibility for determining which document controls in the event of conflict, or even giving him the right to call for any work which falls within "the intent" of the contract.

The method of handling potential conflicts should consider the contractor and his bid. If too much discretion is given to the design professional, the contractor may feel he must inflate his bid to compensate for the risk that the interpretation given will cost him money. This is a problem, even if the discretion of the design professional is limited to merely determining which of the contract documents is to control. It may be best to specify that if the work is called for under any of the documents, it is required to be performed. This at least informs the contractor that he must look carefully at all documents and base his bid upon the likelihood that if work is called for under any documents, performance of the work will be required under the contract.

Because of this problem, the design professional should take great care to see that the documents are made as consistent as possible, and that if changes are made in any of the contract documents, the changes will be reflected in the others.

Another problem relates to documents which are directly inconsistent. One calls for certain work, and another says something else must be done. This differs from one document saying something must be done, while another is silent.

AIA Doc. A201 at 1.2.3 states:

> The Contract Documents are complementary, and what is required by any one shall be as binding as if required by all. The intention of the Documents is to include all labor, materials, equipment and other items as provided in Subparagraph 4.4.1 necessary for the proper execution and completion of the Work. It is not intended that Work not covered under any heading, section, branch, class or trade of the Specifications shall be supplied unless it is required elsewhere in the Contract Documents or is reasonably inferable therefrom as necessary to produce the intended results . . .

This clause, detailed as it is, does not specifically cover conflicting documents, nor set up a priority among documents.

For a case illustrating the result of a conflict between the bid proposal and the specifications, as well as the importance of checking over the contract documents, Dunlap v. Warmack–Fitts Steel Co. is reproduced at this point.

DUNLAP v. WARMACK–FITTS STEEL COMPANY

United States Court of Appeals, Eighth Circuit, 1967.
370 F.2d 876.

MATTHES, CIRCUIT JUDGE. Warmack-Fitts Steel Company, hereinafter referred to as contractor, is a general contractor specializing in erection of steel and construction of plants requiring steel construction work. Homer Dunlap and the other parties named in the caption as appellants will hereinafter be referred to as owners. They contemplated the erection of a 200 ton per day lime plant in Marble City, Oklahoma. Kennedy-Van Saun, hereinafter referred to as KVS, is a large manufacturer of machinery for the production of finished lime products. KVS designed the Marble City plant, supervised construction of the assembly work involved, and supplied the necessary KVS equipment to owners under separate contract.

The owners and contractor entered into a series of three written contracts for the erection of the plant. Contractor substantially completed the plant on June 26, 1964, over two months beyond the completion date of April 22, 1964 set forth in the third contract. A dispute arose as to the balance due under the written contracts and for labor and materials furnished by contractor which allegedly was not encompassed by the contracts. The contractor claimed that the owners were indebted to it in the sum of $48,231.21. The owners by counterclaim prayed judgment against appellee for $55,000.00 as damages for unnecessary delay in completion of the project. After an extended trial, the court, Honorable John E. Miller, found that the contractor was entitled to recover the sum of $45,303.21, and interest at 6% from June 26, 1964. Judgment was entered for that amount and for dismissal of the counterclaim.

. . .

The contractor claimed and the court allowed $9,455.62 for extra labor and use of rigs in assembling parts of the KVS equipment which was installed in the lime plant. Owners contend that all of the items forming the basis for this extra charge were embraced in the original bid information, the contract plans and specifications, and that therefore the court's findings in regard to this charge are clearly erroneous. We agree and reverse this allowance.

The record shows and contractor concedes that prior to the time it submitted its bid it was furnished with data which included a number of drawings prepared by KVS relating to the assembling of the equipment. The bid forms and drawings which became a part of the contract referred to additional reference drawings. It is likewise without dispute that the reference drawings contained detailed information, that is, the drawings submitted with the bid forms, together with the reference drawings, clearly revealed what was required to be done in order to assemble and erect the KVS equipment. Included in the bid forms was this provision which played a key role in the trial court's decision:

"For detail information on drawings prior to bidding contact

Mr. Robert Shandry

Kennedy Van Saun Mfg. & Eng. Corp.

Danville, Penna."

Although Bill Fitts was fully aware of the existence of the reference drawings he did not avail himself of these documents. Instead, according to his testimony, he contacted Shandry "as to what effect these drawings would have, did they have enough effect on the steel erection for it to be necessary for him to send them to me and he said, no, in his idea it didn't because it was strictly for shop reference."

Relying solely on the information contained in the drawings actually submitted, and on the statement of Shandry, contractor submitted a bid of $17,500.00 for the assembly work.

The ensuing contract of December 24th provided:

> "Where any conflicts occur between proposal and bid of Contractor and plans and/or specifications furnished by Owner or Engineer, said plans and/or specifications shall control.
>
> * * * * * * * * *
>
> "Engineer will furnish to the Contractor such additional drawings or explanations as may be necessary to detail and illus-

trate the work to be done, and the Contractor shall conform to the same as a part of this contract, the same as if they were originally attached hereto as contract documents so far as they may be consistent with the drawings and specifications referred to in Article II above."

Contrary to its expectations contractor found, upon the arrival of the KVS equipment, that it consisted of many small, unassembled pieces. The assembling of the KVS equipment was then carried out by contractor under the supervision of an engineer of KVS employed by the owners.[1]

Contractor made no claim for the extra labor until March 6, 1965, more than nine months after the project had been completed. The bill submitted showed the total cost of "equipment setting and erection" to be $26,955.62. Credit for $17,500.00, the bid price, left a balance of $9,455.62, the amount allowed by the court.

Careful analysis of the record convinces us that the trial court fell into error in sustaining this charge. It is clearly evident that contractor, through its agent, Bill Fitts, chose to completely ignore the reference drawings which contained detailed specifications. Rather, it assumed solely on the basis of Mr. Shandry's statement that the KVS equipment would arrive largely assembled. Since the detailed specifications in the reference drawings could have been readily ascertained by referring to the drawings in the bid information, and became in fact a part of the December 24th contract, we cannot escape the conclusion that it was encumbent upon contractor to probe into the matter more than it did before submitting its bid.

In summary, the allowance in question, supported only by the uncorroborated testimony of Bill Fitts, is contrary to the bid information, the plans and specifications, the testimony of Terry Dunlap, an engineer, who detailed in great length the information available in the reference drawings, and the testimony of the KVS engineer. We conclude that a mistake has been committed and that the court's allowance of this item must be reversed.

. . .

There is a controversy as to whether contractor was required to paint the exterior and interior of eight storage bins or tanks with an oxide primer and one coat of enamel. Contractor concedes that it painted the interior of the tanks with only a primer coat and only partially painted the exterior with a primer coat. Owners' position is that it is entitled to an additional credit of $4,000.00 because the contractor defaulted in regard to this phase of the construction. The trial court declined to allow the credit, apparently on the theory

1. [Ed note. Footnote renumbered.] Mr. Scott Kipping, the KVS engineer who supervised the assembling, testified, without contradiction, that KVS shipped the components of the equipment to the Marble City site in as large pieces as was permitted by railroad specifications; that similar KVS components were assembled and shipped to five other identical plants in the same manner.

that the disagreement with respect to painting, which arose subsequent to the execution of the written contract, had been compromised by the parties. Our examination of the relevant evidence convinces us that the court's finding and its disallowance of the extra credit is clearly erroneous and must be reversed.

Contractor asserts that the invitation for bids on the eight tanks called only for a "shop coat of red oxide primer," and that its bid was responsive to that information. Owners dispute this and argue that the document upon which the contractor relied was merely an invitation to bid only on the *fabrication* of the eight storage bins whereas the "Owners' Specification for Fabrication and *Construction*" constituted the actual contract entered into on December 24th. Regardless of the purport of the first document, the conceded fact is that the contract—the controlling document—expressly provided:

> "After complete fabrication, each unit will be cleaned both inside and out, and will be painted inside and out only one shop coat of green oxide primer and one coat enamel, our [owners'] choice."

. . ., [T]he December 24th contract unequivocally provided that the specifications controlled where a conflict occurred between the proposal and bid on the one hand and the specifications on the other.

Accepting contractor's interpretation of the bid proposal document, it is self-evident that there was a conflict between that document and the contract specifications which, without more, would compel a decision in favor of the owners. The question remains as to whether the parties modified or amended the written specifications by a subsequent oral agreement. On this issue Bill Fitts, representing contractor, and Terry Dunlap, representing the owners, were the key witnesses. Fitts testified that he did not read the portion of the December 24th contract relating to the painting of the tanks until December 26th, two days after he signed it. He further stated, in substance, that after he discovered the discrepancy between the bid proposal and the contract specifications, he and Terry Dunlap mutually agreed that contractor would be relieved from its contractual obligations and that one coat of primer paint on the exterior and interior of the tanks would suffice. Dunlap denied this and stated, in effect, that there had been no deviation from or modification of the written contract. Dunlap's version of the matter has appealing logic. It is difficult for us to comprehend that Dunlap would agree to cancel out a $4,000.00 item and receive nothing in return.

In summary, we do not believe contractor should be relieved from its written obligations because of the negligence of its president in failing to read the contract before signing it. Written and binding contracts should not be cast aside on the uncorroborated and contradicted testimony of an interested party. We conclude that more proof was required than appears in this record before a court is justified in holding that the contract specifications do not control.

The evidence shows that the fair and reasonable value of the painting was $4,000.00. Owners are entitled to credit for that amount.

. . .

(C) DOCUMENTS v. IMPLICATIONS OF LAW

The law frequently has to fill in contractual gaps which result from omission. Generally these implications will not be made if the implication would conflict with the contract. This rule is relatively simple, but there are difficulties in determining what is actually a conflict. As mentioned in § 19.02, sometimes a given subject will be mentioned and the implication of law will amplify the language in the contract. These are difficult questions to resolve. About all that can be concluded is that the courts are less likely to imply terms if the subject matter is reasonably well covered.

(D) SEQUENCE OF AGREEMENTS

Frequently a construction project covers a long period of time. There may be a series of modifications of the contract. The rule is again a simple one. The later controls the earlier. A modification discharges that portion of the antecedent agreement which is inconsistent with the subsequent agreement.

(E) ANTECEDENT ORAL AGREEMENT v. CONTRACT DOCUMENTS

Antecedent agreements are usually irrelevant when the parties assent to a final and complete writing. However, written agreements are not necessarily complete agreements. The parties may have an agreement which is partly written and partly oral. If it is determined that the writing is not the complete agreement, then antecedent or contemporaneous agreements will be effective provided that they do not conflict with the written agreement. The written agreement controls the earlier agreement. The difficult question is to determine whether the written agreement is the complete and final agreement of the parties. See § 19.01(g).

Most construction contracts of any magnitude include a clause stating that the written contract is the final and complete agreement. See AIA Doc. A201 at 1.1.2. While there may be some doubts as to the effectiveness of such clauses when they are contained in design professional-client contracts, they are likely to be effective in contracts between the owner and the contractor. Contractors are usually experienced in making these contracts, and are likely to be held to a high standard of care in contract making. However, if either party can show that the "integration" or completeness clause was obtained by fraud, then he will be permitted to show any antecedent oral agreement he claims was made.

Design professionals should be aware of the increasing suspicion courts are showing toward printed standard form contracts, where one of the parties has no opportunity to bargain over terms. There are techniques which can deny effectiveness to integration clauses in such a contract-making context. However, generally such clauses will be effective in construction contracts.

SECTION 20.04 REFORMATION OF CONTRACTS

Sometimes parties to a contract reduce their agreement to a writing and, for various reasons, the writing does not truly express the intention of the parties or a party to the contract. The Courts of Equity developed a remedy called "reformation" which "rewrote" the contract to make the writing conform to the actual agreement of the parties. Because there were no juries in equity cases, the equity courts felt freer to go into the difficult questions of intention and mistake.

Most of the cases have involved simple clerical errors. An illustration would be an improper description of land in a deed. Such descriptions were complicated, and often taken from old deeds and old tax bills. It was not unusual for the person copying the old description to make a mistake. If it could be shown by fairly reliable evidence that there had been a mistake, then the court would reform the contract. This would be a judicial declaration that the contract covered the particular land that the parties actually intended to buy and sell, rather than the land covered in the description.

In addition to the cases of mutual mistake in description, other types of mistake would justify reformation. Usually, these mistakes would involve the process by which the actual agreement was reduced to writing.

In addition to these mistakes, sometimes courts have been asked to reform a writing which did not express the understanding of one party, because of the other party's fraud. For example, one party might state that something had been included in a written agreement when it was not, or that something was not included in a written agreement when it was included. In such a case a court might reform the document to coincide with the understanding of the innocent party. Courts felt less free in such cases to reform, because there was often a strong element of carelessness on the part of the other party. The party asking for reformation would have to show that he reasonably relied on the representations made by the other party that the particular clause was either omitted or included. This necessity for reasonable reliance made granting of this remedy somewhat more limited than those cases involving a mutual mistake. However, there have been cases where courts have reformed the writing to coincide with the understanding of the innocent party.

There have been a few cases where courts have ordered reformation where the fraud or mistake in question did not relate to the process by which the earlier agreement was reduced to writing. Here again the court's role is more limited than in the simple clerical error case. For example, a court in New York reformed a salesman's commission agreement where the salesman contended that he signed an agreement for a lower commission rate under representation of the employer that he would be paid a higher commission, and that the necessity for specifying the lower figure was to make certain that other employees did not know that he was being paid more than they were. Brandwein v. Provident Mut. Life Ins. Co., 3 N.Y.2d 491, 146 N.E.2d 693, 168 N.Y.S.2d 964 (1957). Here there was no mistake in the process of reducing the agreement to writing. However, the court felt that there was fraud on the part of the employer in promising to pay a higher commission when the employer did not intend to do so. This type of case also involved the doctrine developed in the Courts of Equity called "clean hands". This meant that the equity court has the discretion not to award a remedy if it feels that the party asking for the remedy did not come to the court with clean hands. If the court believes that the reason for the writing not expressing the real agreement was morally wrong, it could refuse to grant the remedy.

The important thing to realize is that writings are not sacrosanct. The law recognizes that writings sometimes do not reflect the actual agreement of the parties. Nevertheless, courts grant the remedy of reformation only if the facts are very compelling. Parties should never rely upon the possibility that the law will bail them out of a written agreement. If they consciously realized that the written agreement did not reflect their actual agreement, it will be most unusual for courts to grant relief. For this reason, signing a written contract which does not express the true agreement of the parties is risky. Under certain limited circumstances, there are methods by which contracts can be reformed or rewritten.

SECTION 20.05 SOME COMMON INTERPRETATION PROBLEMS

(A) GENERAL PERFORMANCE REQUIREMENTS

Just what has the contractor obligated himself to do by way of performance? The plans usually contain a graphic depiction of the contractor's obligation. The specifications indicate the contractor's obligation in words. The general terms and conditions frequently contain clauses which deal with the standard of performance which is to be met. Some questions that can arise are:

1. What are the standards of workmanship?
2. What quality of materials are to be used?
3. Is the owner's obligation to pay conditioned upon the final structure accomplishing a particular purpose or upon meeting designated performance standards?
4. Is the contractor to perform to the satisfaction of the owner or of any designated third person?

The answer to any particular question requires an examination and interpretation of the agreement of the parties. Sometimes the parties do not spell out their understanding on these crucial questions. Certain generalizations can be made.

At a minimum, the obligation of the owner will be conditioned upon conformity with the plans and specifications, proper workmanship and materials, and a complete project free and clear of liens. If the owner wishes to show that performance is to be satisfactory to himself or to third parties, he will have to supply proof that the parties agreed to this standard. If he wishes to demand compliance with certain performance standards or insists that the structure must accomplish his desired purpose, the owner will have to point to these standards in the contract document or in an admissible oral agreement or show surrounding facts and circumstances clearly manifesting that this was impliedly agreed upon.

Performance standards may be specified. For example, the specifications may state that the building shall be waterproof and prescribe materials, and sometimes methods, for accomplishing this result. Does this mean that the contractor assumes the risk that the suggested methods and materials will accomplish the purpose? By and large, courts have not been sympathetic to owner claims that the contractor assumes the risk of performance standards when the owner has specified materials and methods (See § 30.11 for a case discussing this problem.)

How should this problem be resolved? First, look at the contract to see whether it expresses any intention of the parties as to whether the contractor or the owner assumes the risk that the materials and methods prescribed will not accomplish the desired result. If there is no clear expression of this, the risk should be allocated to the owner. Design is a function of the owner and his design professional. If the contractor knew, or should have known, that the results could not be accomplished using the materials and methods prescribed, he should bear the risk unless he conveys this information to the owner or the design professional. This discussion assumes that the contractor's performance was in accord with the contract documents. Often the reason for the failure is non-compliance, not design errors.

If there are conditions of satisfaction, the standard which will usually be applied in construction contract satisfaction clauses is objective satisfaction, and not subjective satisfaction. However, if the standard relates to aesthetics rather than mechanical criteria, it is likely that a subjective standard (good faith) will be the method of measuring compliance. (See § 6.17(a) for a discussion of satisfaction clauses.)

(B) COMPLIANCE WITH CODES

Usually the contract document will contain a provision requiring the contractor to comply with applicable laws relating to construction. Even without such a provision, the contractor impliedly promises to comply with applicable state and local building codes. If the design as expressed in the contract documents, or any construction methods are prescribed in the contract documents, are not in accord with building codes, the contractor should call this to the attention of the design professional. He should not be able to proceed with construction which he knows or believes to be out of conformity with building codes or safety regulations. He should not be able to shield himself behind errors of the design professional. If the design professional insists that he perform despite non-compliance with legal requirements, complying with this directive is likely to subject the contractor, as well as the design professional, to criminal sanctions, to civil liability for harm which results from non-compliance, and an inability to use the courts to collect for work which he has performed.

(C) BRAND NAMES OR EQUIVALENTS

Interpretation questions often relate to the issue of compliance with material or equipment requirements. If the design professional specifies certain designated material or equipment by trade name, he limits the discretion of the contractor to supply less expensive material or equipment which may, nevertheless, be as good. For this reason, it is common in public construction, and often in private construction, to accompany designated materials or equipment with the performance alternative of an approved equal or, more sensibly, an approved equivalent. Approved usually means by the architect or engineer.

The contractor may plan to use less expensive material or goods under an equivalent clause, and may submit a lower bid based upon this expectation. If he does so, generally he assumes that the design professional will be reasonable in determining whether the material he proposes to use is the equivalent of the designated material. If he believes he will face an unreasonable design professional, he may not plan to use "equivalent" material. This will deprive the owner of possible cost savings and a better price.

The design professional should use every reasonable effort to determine whether materials and equipment proposed by the contractor will accomplish the desired purpose. Unreasonable demands that the contractor install or use materials and equipment which are most expensive causes hostility and, in the long run, may be disadvantageous to the owner. On the other hand, if there is a functional or aesthetic difference between the designated material and equipment and that proposed by the contractor, the design professional should insist that the designated material or equipment be used.

Contractors frequently complain that architects and engineers are unreasonably insistent that certain brand name materials and equipment be used, because the manufacturers' representatives who sell the designated brand name materials or equipment have provided free engineering service for the architect or engineer. Architects and engineers should avoid unreasonable partiality to a designated brand name product in order to repay a manufacturer's representative who has been helpful during the design phase.

SECTION 20.06 ROLE OF THE DESIGN PROFESSIONAL

Difficult interpretation questions are frequent in construction contracts. The design professional should do his best to eliminate ambiguities and conflicts in all contract documents. He should try to anticipate the difficulties that are likely to arise and provide for a contractual solution for them. The drafting of the specifications and the drawings are primarily his responsibility. He should check all the contract documents to eliminate potential inconsistencies, and he should have at least a working knowledge of the general conditions of the contract. The general conditions are essentially "lawyer clauses", but the design professional will have to deal with them and should understand them. He must understand the reason for the clauses. When disputes arise and the design professional is asked to give interpretations or decide disputes involving interpretation, he must know the ground rules under which he is to interpret the contract.

He should keep careful and complete records of all conversations with both his client and the contractor, as well as copies of letters sent to him and letters sent by him in the course of the construction project. He should have records which indicate the dates communications sent to him were received. Construction project disputes are common, and the design professional should conduct his internal affairs with the realization that he may be called upon at any time either by the client, the contractor, or a court to justify what he has done or to determine facts relating to the transaction. For this reason detailed record-keeping is essential for the design professional.

For a detailed discussion of decisions by the design professional, see Chapter 27.

REVIEW QUESTIONS

1. What is the basic objective in interpreting contracts?

2. What is the plain meaning rule?

3. Do courts consider the uncommunicated intention of one of the parties in interpreting contracts?

4. Why is a contract interpreted against the drafter?

5. Why should handwritten terms be preferred over printed terms?

6. What is reformation of a written contract? When is it done?

QUESTIONS FOR CLASS DISCUSSION

1. Why should a court look at custom if the meaning of a term appears to be clear to a judge?

2. Is it best to let the other party draft the contract? Explain.

3. Which is a better indication of intention, the specifications or the general terms and conditions? The basic agreement or the general terms and conditions? The specifications or the basic agreement?

4. Should the design professional be given the right to decide which document governs in the event of conflict?

PROBLEM

O owned a large house. He entered into negotiations with C regarding the painting of the house. They both signed a written contract, under which it was agreed that C would receive $2,000. C drafted the contract. In part the contract stated:

C will do a first class job of painting O's house.

(Garage not included.)

A dispute arose over the number of coats of paint to be used and whether C was to paint the cement steps leading to the house. C claimed two coats were adequate, while O stated that three coats were needed for a first class job. C claimed the contract did not include the cement steps. O states that he pointed to the steps when they inspected the house, and that he said that the steps needed a coat of paint. C admitted O said this, but C contends that when it was not included in the contract, he assumed he would not have to do it. The steps would cost about $50.00 to paint. How should a judge decide this dispute? Give your reasons.

Chapter 21

CHANGES

SECTION 21.01 FUNCTION OF A CHANGES CLAUSE

Before, and during, a construction project, frequently it becomes necessary to order changes in the work to be performed by the contractor. The contract documents are at best an imperfect expression of what the design professional and the client intend to be performed by the contractor. Circumstances during the construction process sometimes develop which make it necessary or advisable to revise the plans and specifications.

Methods and materials which were called for in the specifications sometimes become undesirable or unavailable. Changes may be needed because of natural events over which neither party had control, or because of poor design on the part of the design professional. Changes may be required because of defective work performed by the contractor, or by one of the subcontractors. Whatever the reason, it frequently becomes necessary to make changes after the contract has been awarded to the contractor.

(Changes which relate to, or affect, the time for completion of the project will be considered in Chapter 23, which deals with time problems.)

"Changes" questions can arise in at least two contexts. In most litigated cases involving changes, the contractor contends that he has performed work which went beyond his contract requirement and for which he should be paid "extra". This is the principal issue in Watson Lumber v. Guennewig, discussed in § 21.12.

Sometimes contractors defend an action brought against them by the owner, based upon nonperformance, with a contention that the original contract requirements were changed and that the contractor had complied with his obligations.

"Changes" must be contrasted with modifications and waivers. Modifications are two-party agreements by which owner and contractor mutually agree to change certain portions of the work. The basic difference between a modification and a change, as the latter term is usually used in construction contracts, is that the owner usually has the power by contract to unilaterally direct that changes be made, while a modification is a voluntary two-party arrangement between owner and contractor.

The owner may decide, or lead the contractor to reasonably believe, that the owner is willing to give up his right to have certain required work done. He may decide that he will pay the full contract price, even if the project does not measure up to every aspect of the plans, specifications, or schedule. This is often called a "waiver", and will be discussed in § 24.02(e).

Changes are sometimes classified by how, and if, they affect the contract price. A minor change often does not affect the contract price. An "addition" or "extra" will increase the contract price. A deletion will decrease the contract price.

This chapter deals principally with changes which result when the owner changes his mind. Emergency situations and extra costs due to design defects will be mentioned briefly. Changes caused by unforeseen conditions such as subsurface problems or catastrophic natural events will not be discussed.

SECTION 21.02 CHANGES AS A PART OF COST CONTROL

One of the major complaints made by owners is that the ultimate cost of the construction project substantially exceeds the fixed contract price because of excessive changes. Some of the fault must be attributed to the design professional. If the plans and specifications are not properly drafted and drawn, ambiguities may result in extra costs. Also, design professionals may not warn owners that changing their minds on project details increases the contract cost. Some contractors of questionable integrity bid low deliberately to get the job because they think that they can make a tidy profit on extras. These contractors may seize upon interpretive instructions or directions given by the design professional, or by the client, as the basis for a long list of extra items submitted upon completion of the project.

SECTION 21.03 RIGHT TO ORDER CHANGES

Inclusion of a changes clause in a contract permits the owner to order changes without the necessity of obtaining approval or consent by the contractor. Even without advance agreement on price, some clauses require the contractor to perform the work as changed, with various formulas given in the contract for determining compensation. Such flexible "one-sided" provisions do not invalidate the construction contract.

The changes clause gives the owner a right to order work which the contractor must perform. This broad power can operate unfairly. Contract clauses and court interpretation have limited the effect of "changes" clauses to work which falls within the general scope of the contractor's promised performance under the contract. If the contractor has been engaged to erect a residence, the owner should be able to order a carport, or perhaps even a garage, under the changes clause. However, the owner could not unilaterally order that the contractor construct a beach house twenty miles away. There should be physical and functional connection between work which is ordered as a change, and the subject matter of the construction contract.

SECTION 21.04 DUTY TO ORDER EXTRA WORK FROM CONTRACTOR

The power to order changes is one usually given to the owner. Does the contractor have a "right" to do any extra work?

There is an advantage to the contractor in being able to preclude the owner from either using the owner's own construction forces or hiring another contractor to perform extra work. If the owner is negotiating over the price of extras with the contractor, the right to place the work with someone other than the contractor can give him a substantial bargaining advantage. Usually, the right to order changes does not preclude the owner from awarding the extra work from someone else. However, for practical reasons, he is not likely to do so.

SECTION 21.05 WHO CAN ORDER A CHANGE?

In the absence of any contract clause dealing with the question of authority to make changes, the question of who can order a change is controlled by doctrines of agency. The owner can order changes. Members of the owner's organization may also have the authority to order changes expressly, impliedly, or by the doctrine of apparent authority. Usually carefully thought out construction contracts specify just which members of the owner's organization have the power to order changes.

The design professional, by virtue of his position alone, does not have the authority to order changes.

A typical judicial statement of this rule is the following statement from Kirk Reid Co. v. Fine, 205 Va. 778, 139 S.E.2d 829 (1965):

> [It] is clear that the authority of the architects and the engineer to act as agents of the defendant was of a limited

scope, confined to those areas set forth in the contract and where, in special instances, their powers might be broadened. It is equally as clear that changes in the work, except of a minor nature, could only be made on the written order of the defendant or the written order of the architects or engineer stating that the defendant had authorized such changes.

If the architect or engineer has no authority solely by virtue of his position to order changes, clearly the project representative (formerly known as the Clerk of the Works) does not have this authority.

However, difficulties can develop over asserted changes by the project representative. It is important to inform the project representative that he is on the site to observe and report, but not to give directions. Normally, he should not interfere with the construction process. If his directions are followed and things do not go well, the contractor may deny responsibility. The project representative often does not have a full picture of the design. Changes which he might direct or directions he might give might not integrate with other aspects of the project.

The project representative is often in a difficult position. The contractor may wish to obtain authority to deviate from the contract documents or to obtain an interpretation of the contract documents. If he cannot contact the architect or engineer, he may request the project representative to authorize a change or render an interpretation. Project representatives should be instructed to transfer such requests to the architect or engineer. In addition, contractors should be told that project representatives have no authority to give directions, make changes or render interpretations.

The construction contract can give the design professional authority to order changes under certain circumstances. AIA Doc. A201 at 12.1.2 gives authority to owner and architect jointly to order changes. In addition, a written change order can be issued by the architect alone, provided he has written authority from the owner for such a procedure, and provided that a written copy of such written authority is furnished to the contractor upon request.

The architect may be given express authority in some other way, or the owner may cloak him with apparent authority. The owner might pay for architect-ordered work, which could lead the contractor to believe that the architect has this authority. Apparent authority is much less likely to be used by a court if the contract is one with a public agency.

There may not be sufficient time to get an authorization from the owner, or another authorized person, where work is needed immediately, due to a reasonable likelihood of danger to person or property. The contractor should have authority to do the work necessary to avoid such losses. Form contracts usually provide that extra work in emergencies can be performed without an authorization. (It would be better to require that the contractor do so.) Even without express or implied authority, the contractor should be able to recover for work done in an emergency, upon the principle of unjust enrichment. Even if the architect or engineer does not have authority to order changes, it might be sensible to give the design professional authority to deal with emergency problems which may develop.

Minor changes are those which do not affect the contract price. Some contract documents give the design professional authority to make minor changes. For example, the AIA Doc. A201 states at 12.3.1:

> The Architect shall have authority to order minor changes in the Work not involving an adjustment in the Contract Sum or an extension of the Contract Time and not inconsistent with the intent of the Contract Documents. Such changes may be effected by Field Order or by other written order. Such changes shall be binding on the Owner and the Contractor.

Even if the architect has this authority, he should, where feasible, check with the owner before making even minor changes. If it is necessary to order that changes be made before the owner can approve, it is advisable to inform the owner of this at the earliest possible time.

It may be useful for the design professional to meet the contractor and his job superintendent immediately after award of the contract or, at the very latest, before commencement of the contractor's performance. At this meeting, authority questions should be discussed and worked out. It may be useful at such a meeting to point to provisions in the construction contract which spell out who has the authority to make changes and how this authority is to be manifested. It might also be useful to conclude such a meeting by having the contractor and his superintendent sign a memorandum which expresses the matters discussed and resolved at the meeting.

A meeting of the type suggested takes time and may appear to belabor the obvious. Such a meeting does not guarantee the absence of difficulties over changes, but it can be helpful to the owner by drawing the lines early and setting up a record of mutual understanding.

SECTION 21.06 FORMAL REQUIREMENTS

Unscrupulous contractors often use any direction given by the architect as the basis for a claim that they are entitled to additional compensation. Also, the design professional may order a minor change which he does not intend to affect the contract price. Since disputes frequently develop over whether particular work is within the contract, and whether work ordered or directions given constitutes an extra, contracts usually require an express change order in writing. Usually, the writing must be signed by the owner. In some cases it may be signed by the design professional, if the owner has given him express written authority to do so. It is possible to require that both owner and design professional must sign change orders. The important thing is to decide who is to have the authority, express it in the contract, and follow the requirement in contract administration.

Sometimes the contract specifies the form this writing must take. Most well-run construction projects have forms for change orders. They are numbered and issued consecutively. Often construction projects employ "field orders", a written record of orders given at the site, which serve the same function as a change order.

Changes issued by change or field orders are a clear indication that the architect or engineer issuing the order considers that the work is a change.

During the course of the project, the architect or engineer may give a written direction that work is to be done in a certain way. This may be an exercise by the design professional of his power to interpret the contract documents. It may not constitute a manifestation that the design professional has considered the direction he has given to be a change. If directions of this type are given, many contracts provide that the contractor must indicate whether he considers that the direction will constitute a change for which he will be entitle to additional pay. (See 12.2.1 of AIA Doc. A201 in Appendix D.) In addition to a contract clause of this type, it may be useful for the design professional to make it clear in any writing given to the contractor relating to the work that the writing should not be considered a written change order.

Does the written change order have to be issued before the contractor performs the extra work? This is obviously the desired solution from the standpoint of the owner. If he wants to keep his costs down, he would like to know whether a direction will increase his cost and, if possible, how much, before he authorizes that it be performed. Often, contracts are unclear as to whether a change order issued after the work has begun is sufficient to fulfill the writing requirement under the contract. AIA Doc. A201 states at 12.1.2:

> A Change Order is a written order to the Contractor signed by the Owner and the Architect, issued after the execution of the Contract, authorizing a Change in the Work or an adjustment in the Contract Sum or the Contract Time.

This does not make it clear that the change order must be executed before the work is begun. The AIA contract does provide that the contractor must submit, in writing, a statement of intent to make a claim for the increase in contract price or for an extension of time. Such a notice must be given before the work constituting the extra is performed, except in cases of emergency. If this provision is in the contract and followed, the owner should be able to control his costs in an effective way. If written notice must be

given in advance of doing work, the written authorization for the change is more likely to be issued before the work is performed. Also, doing the work without a manifestation of an intention to claim an extra may indicate that the contractor thought it was called for by the contract, and the claim for an extra was either trumped-up or an afterthought.

SECTION 21.07 EXCUSING FORMAL REQUIREMENTS

Parties often disregard the construction contract formalities carefully created in the contract documents. Pressing time problems, and the casualness with which many contractors conduct their affairs, often mean sloppy contract administration. Many claims for extras made by contractors are opposed by the owner because of failure to comply with the writing requirement as to changes or notice of an intention to claim an extra. In such cases, most courts have held that the owner, by ordering extra work, orally "waives" the writing requirement. Unfortunately, courts do not always differentiate between those cases where the owner admits ordering the work but claims it was within the contract requirement, from situations where he admits that the work was extra and that he ordered it. One principal purpose of having a requirement for a written change order is to obviate these proof difficulties. However, if the court finds that the work is extra and that the owner ordered it, the absence of a writing is not likely to prevent the contractor from recovering.

The more difficult problem centers around oral change orders by the design professional. Here, finding waiver is more difficult. If the work is made necessary by an emergency, there may be no necessity for a writing. In some cases, the owner's conduct in systematically disregarding the formal writing requirement may lead the contractor to believe that it is no longer necessary. If the owner paid for work orally ordered by the design professional in the past, this may lead the contractor to believe that the writing requirement has been dispensed with.

In Rivercliff v. Linebarger, 223 Ark. 105, 264 S.W.2d 842 (1954) the Court found a waiver of the writing requirement, stating:

> For a second ground, appellant contends that . . . the trial court should not have made any allowance to the contractor because the extra work was not authorized in accordance with the terms of the contract. This contention appears to be supported by the terms of the contract, which provides that extras must be approved in writing prior to execution. This provision was not complied with but it does not constitute a defense available to appellant, because, as we

> hold, a strict compliance with this provision of the contract was waived by appellant in this instance. It is not disputed that the extra excavation was done with the knowledge and at the direction of Smith who was not only the architect supervising the work for Rivercliff but was also a part owner of the appellant corporation. From his testimony we gather that he refused to approve an allowance for extras mainly because he did not think the contractor was entitled to anything as a result of the changed method of constructing the foundation. It appears that other changes in construction had been made and paid for where no written change order had been previously issued. Although it was shown that several such changes had been made and paid for during the construction of the four buildings, yet Mr. Smith testified that only one written change order had been made.

A court is likely to hold that there has been a waiver of the writing requirement if the architect gave an oral change order in the presence of the owner, who stood by silently while the work was ordered, knowing the work was extra.

Sometimes the extra work is made necessary by design errors of the design professional. In those cases, some courts have held that the work made necessary because of the design errors is not an extra within the formal requirements of the Changes clause. The courts have regarded recovery for the work as a form of remedy for defective plans which were originally given to the contractor, and have not required a written change order or, for that matter, even that the work be ordered orally.

In general, courts are likely to disregard the necessity for a writing if it would seem unfair to permit the owner to have the benefit of extra work without paying for it. Unfortunately, courts do not always look carefully at whether the work claimed to be an extra is, in fact, an extra. The very reason for the omission of a written order may be because the design professional ruled that the work came within the requirements of the contract documents. If this is the case, it would be unfair for the contractor to collect for the work. If the contractor feels a change order should be issued, he should either perform work under protest and later resolve the question of whether it is extra, or he should invoke any arbitration clause in the contract to decide whether the work is extra.

SECTION 21.08 EXCESSIVE CHANGES

What if the changes ordered are within the scope of the work, but are so extensive that they change the nature of the basic construction contract? If the contractor performed the changes, a court might consider these changes as an abrogation of the basic construction contract and permit the contractor to recover the reasonable value of the services without regard to contract pricing provisions. Also, contractors should not be compelled to perform excessive changes which go beyond the work originally contemplated by the parties. In such a case, a direction for extensive and unforeseeable changes would then be merely a proposal by the owner which would have to be agreed to by the contractor before there could be any obligation on his part to perform the work.

SECTION 21.09 EFFECT OF CHANGES ON PERFORMANCE BONDS

When sureties were usually uncompensated individuals, courts held that any changes in the contract between the principal and the obligee would discharge the surety. This would be unjust where a professional surety bond company is used, especially since changes and modifications are common in construction contracts. Most surety bonds provide that modifications made in the basic construction contract will not discharge the surety. Some changes clauses permit changes up to designated percentage of the contract price without notifying the bonding company.

SECTION 21.10 COMPENSATION: ADDITIONAL COMPENSATION FOR UNCHANGED WORK

Section 16.03 (e) discussed the problems of pricing changed work. This section should be reread at this point. One additional aspect of pricing should be mentioned. Extensive changes may have a substantial effect upon the cost of performing unchanged work. Sometimes such additional costs can be recovered.

SECTION 21.11 MISREPRESENTATION OF AUTHORITY

Misrepresentation of authority will be discussed in § 25.02 (d). However, it can raise particularly difficult problems in the area of changes and should be mentioned briefly.

Sometimes construction contracts give the architect a right to direct changes, provided he has written authorization from the owner, and that this written authorization is furnished to the contractor upon the latter's request. Suppose the owner has not given the authorization, but the architect states that he has authority to order the change orally and is able to persuade the contractor to perform the changed work without showing a written authorization from the owner. Or suppose the architect or engineer misrepresents his authority, and is able to persuade the contractor to perform in accordance with the directions given by the architect or engineer.

The threshold question is whether the contractor reasonably relied upon the misrepresentation. In many cases, any reliance would not be reasonable because typically architects and engineers are not given authority to direct changes, or the contractor should have checked with the owner. However, there may be cases where it would be reasonable to comply with a change directed by the design professional, even though the design professional has misrepresented his authority to make the change.

If the case is one of simple misrepresentation of authority, the contractor can collect his losses from the design professional. These losses can consist of the cost of performing the changed work, and the costs of any correction necessary to make the work conform to the contract documents.

Suppose the change enhanced the value of the project. If it can be removed without materially injuring the project, there is no benefit to the owner. However, if it is not feasible to remove the work from the project, arguably the owner has received a benefit from the extra work. However, if the benefit was received because of misrepresentation of authority, it would be very difficult for the architect or engineer to collect from the owner on an unjust enrichment basis.

However, suppose the design professional does not have actual authority to make a change, but the acts of the owner have cloaked him with apparent authority. In such a case, the contractor can collect from the owner. Suppose the owner seeks to transfer this loss to the design professional, because the design professional has misrepresented his authority to make the change.

The loss was caused both by the design professional's misrepresentation of authority, and the acts of the owner which made it appear to the contractor that he had authority. Since the more culpable act is the misrepresentation of authority, the loss should be borne by the design professional.

However, if the misrepresentation resulted in extra work enhancing the value of the project, the question becomes more difficult. The owner in such cases does receive a benefit. While the law generally refuses to divide losses of this type, it would seem fair to do so where the work has enhanced the value of the project. Another method is to give the owner a claim for the difference between what the owner had to pay the contractor, and the enhanced value of the project due to the additional work. This method could "divide" the loss.

SECTION 21.12 AN INSTRUCTIVE CASE: WATSON LUMBER CO. v. GUENNEWIG

WATSON LUMBER COMPANY v. GUENNEWIG

Appellate Court of Illinois, 1967.
79 Ill.App.2d 377, 226 N.E.2d 270.

EBERSPACHER, JUSTICE. The corporate plaintiff, Watson Lumber Company, the building contractor, obtained a judgment for $22,500.00 in a suit to recover the unpaid balance due under the terms of a written building contract, and additional compensation for extras, against the defendants William and Mary Guennewig. Plaintiff is engaged in the retail lumber business, and is managed by its president and principal stockholder, Leeds Watson. It has been building several houses each year in the course of its lumber business.

. . .

[Ed. note: The project was a four bedroom, two bath house with air conditioning for a contract price of $28,206. The total amount claimed as extras and awarded by the trial court was $3840.09.]

The contractor claimed a right to extra compensation with respect to no less than 48 different and varied items of labor and/or materials. These items range all the way from $1.06 for extra plumbing pieces to $429.00 for an air-conditioner larger than plaintiff's evidence showed to be necessary, and $630.00 for extra brick work. The evidence, in support of each of these items and circumstances surrounding each being added, is pertinent to the items individually, and the evidence supporting recovery for one, does not necessarily support recovery for another.

. . .

Most of the extras claimed by the contractor were not stipulated in writing as required by the contract. The contractor claims that the requirement was waived. Prior to considering whether the parties, by agreement or conduct dispensed with the requirement that extras must be agreed to in writing, it should first be determined whether the extras claimed are genuine "extras". We believe this is an important area of dispute between these parties. Once it is determined that the work is an "extra" and its performance is justified, the cases frequently state that a presumption arises that it is to be paid for. Adams v. Tri-City Amusement Co., 124 Va. 473, 98 S.E. 647. No such presumption arises, however, where the contractor proceeds voluntarily; nor does such a presumption arise in cases like this one, where the contract makes requirements which any claim for extras must meet. Buckingham Routh Co. v. Wuesterfeld Co., 114 Conn. 720, 157 A. 414. In 17A C.J.S. Contracts § 371(4), it is stated:

> "Where the contract provides that there shall be no charge for extra work unless a written agreement is made therefor, the

builder cannot recover compensation as for extra work on account of alterations made at the oral request or consent of the owner but for which no agreement to pay additional compensation is made."

and,

"Where at the request of the owner, the builder makes alterations from the original contract which are such that the owner is justified in thinking that there will be no extra cost therefor, he should notify the owner that there will be extra cost if such is the case, otherwise he will be precluded from claiming extra compensation."

The law assigns to the contractor, seeking to recover for "extras", the burden of proving the essential elements. . . . That is, he must establish by the evidence that (a) the work was outside the scope of his contract promises; (b) the extra items were ordered by the owner, . . . (c) the owner agreed to pay extra, either by his words or conduct, . . . (d) the extras were not furnished by the contractor as his voluntary act, and (e) the extra items were not rendered necessary by any fault of the contractor. . . .

The proof that the items are extra, that the defendant ordered it as such, agreed to pay for it, and waived the necessity of a written stipulation, must be by clear and convincing evidence. The burden of establishing these matters is properly the plaintiff's. Evidence of general discussion cannot be said to supply all of these elements.

The evidence is clear that many of the items claimed as extras were not claimed as extras in advance of their being supplied. Indeed, there is little to refute the evidence that many of the extras were not the subject of any claim until after the contractor requested the balance of the contract price, and claimed the house was complete. This makes the evidence even less susceptible to the view that the owner knew ahead of time that he had ordered these as extra items and less likely that any general conversation resulted in the contractor rightly believing extras had been ordered.

In a building and construction situation, both the owner and the contractor have interests that must be kept in mind and protected. The contractor should not be required to furnish items that were clearly beyond and outside of what the parties originally agreed that he would furnish. The owner has a right to full and good faith performance of the contractor's promise, but has no right to expand the nature and extent of the contractor's obligation. On the other hand, the owner has a right to know the nature and extent of his promise, and a right to know the extent of his liabilities before they are incurred. Thus, he has a right to be protected against the contractor voluntarily going ahead with extra work at his expense. He also has a right to control his own liabilities. Therefore, the law required his consent be evidenced before he can be charged for an extra. Booher v. Williams, 341 Ill.App. 504, 95 N.E.2d 518; and here the contract provided his consent be evidenced in writing.

The amount of the judgment forces us to conclude that the plaintiff contractor was awarded most of the extra compensation he claims. We have examined the record concerning the evidence in support of each of these many items and are unable to find support for any "extras" approaching the $3,840.09 which plaintiff claims to have been awarded. In many instances the character of the item as an "extra" is assumed rather than established.[1] In order to recover for items as "extras", they must be shown to be items not required to be furnished under plaintiff's original promise as stated in the contract, including the items that the plans and specifications reasonably implied even though not mentioned. A promise to do or furnish that which the promisor is already bound to do or furnish, is not consideration for even an implied promise to pay additional for such performance or the furnishing of materials. The character of the item is one of the basic circumstances under which the owner's conduct and the contractor's conduct must be judged in determining whether or not that conduct amounts to an order for the extra.

The award obviously includes items which Watson plainly admits "there was no specific conversation". In other instances, the only evidence to supply, even by inference, the essential element that the item was furnished pursuant to the owner's request and agreement to pay is Mr. Watson's statement that Mrs. Guennewig "wanted that". No specific conversation is testified to, or fixed in time or place. Thus it cannot be said from such testimony whether she expressed this desire before or after the particular item was furnished. If she said so afterward, the item wasn't furnished on her orders. Nor can such an expression of desire imply an agreement to pay extra. The fact that Mrs. Guennewig may have "wanted" an item and said so to the contractor falls far short of proving that the contractor has a right to extra compensation. See, 17A C.J.S. Contracts § 371(1), p. 401, where the rule is expressed thus:

> "* * * he (the owner) is not rendered libel by the mere fact that he has knowledge that the builder is doing extra work, if he does not know that the builder expects additional pay * * *.
>
> "* * * as a general rule, a builder or contractor is not entitled to additional compensation for extra work or materials voluntarily furnished by him without the owner's request, or knowledge that he expects to be paid therefor."

1. We cite as some examples: An extra charge was made for kitchen and bathroom ceilings, concerning which Watson testified that he was going to give these as gifts "if she had paid her bill". According to the testimony, the ceilings were lowered to cover the duct work. We consider it unlikely that the parties intended to build a house without duct work or with duct work exposed. Likewise an "extra" charge was made for grading, although the contract clearly specifies that grading is the contractor's duty. An "extra" charge is sought for enclosing the basement stairs, although the plans show the basement stairs enclosed. An extra charge is sought for painting, apparently on the basis that more coats than were provided in the contract were necessary.

Many items seem to be included as "extras" merely because plaintiff had not figured them in the original cost figures.

It is clear that the contractor does not have the right to extra compensation for every deviation from the original specification on items that may cost more than originally estimated. The written contract fixes the scope of his undertaking. It fixed the price he is to be paid for carrying it out. The hazards of the undertaking are ordinarily his. McKay Engineering & Construction Co. v. Chicago Sanitary Dist., supra.

> "If the construction of an entire work is called for at a fixed compensation, the hazards of the undertaking are assumed by the builder, and he cannot recover for increased cost, as extra work, on discovering that he has made a mistake on his estimate of the cost, or that the work is more difficult and expensive than he anticipated." 17A C.J.S. Contracts § 371(6), p. 413.

Some so called "extras" were furnished, and thereafter the owner's agreement was sought.[2] Such an agreement has been held to be too late. . . .

The judge, by his remarks at the time of awarding judgment, shows that the definition of extras applied in this case was, indeed, broad. He said,

> "substantial deviation from the drawings or specifications were made—some deviations in writing signed by the parties, some in writing delivered but not signed, but nevertheless utilized and accepted, some delivered and not signed, utilized and not accepted, some made orally and accepted, some made orally but not accepted, and some in the trade practice accepted or not accepted".

While the court does not state that he grants recovery for all extras claimed, he does not tell us which ones were and were not allowed. The amount of the judgment requires us to assume that most were part of the recovery. It can be said with certainty that the extras allowed exceeded those for which there is evidence in the record to establish the requirements pointed out.

Mere acceptance of the work by the owner as referred to by the court does not create liability for an extra. Mueller v. Rosen, 179 Ill. 130, 53 N.E. 625. In 13 Am.Jur.2d 60, "Building & Cont." § 56, it is stated, that : "The position taken by most courts considering the question is that the mere occupancy and use do not constitute an acceptance of the work as complying with the contract or amount to a waiver of defects therein". Conversation and conduct showing agreement for extra work or acquiescence in its performance after it has been furnished will not create liability. . . . More than

2. The drain tile around the foundation of the house, according to the evidence, was already in place when it was disclosed to the owner that it was more expensive material. It was only then that the contractor secured the owner's consent to pay for one-half the cost of the more expensive material.

mere acceptance is required even in cases where there is no doubt that the item is an "extra". . . .

The contractor must make his position clear at the time the owner has to decide whether or not he shall incur extra liability. Fairness requires that the owner should have the chance to make such a decision. He was not given that chance in this case in connection with all of these extras. Liability for extras, like all contract liability, is essentially a matter of consent; of promise based on consideration. . . .

The Illinois cases allow recovery for extra compensation only when the contractor has made his claim for an extra, clear and certain, before furnishing the item, not after. They are in accord with the comments to be found in 31 Ill.Law Rev. 791 (1937). There the author, after reviewing the cases, makes the following analysis:

> "The real issue in these cases is whether or not the contractor has, at the time the question of extra work arises, made his position clear to the owner or his agents and that would seem to be the true test in situations where a written order clause is sought to be disregarded. If he does expressly contend that work demanded is extra, the owner certainly cannot be said to be taken unawares, and if orders are given to go ahead it is with full knowledge of the possible consequences."

The contractor claims that the requirement of written stipulation covering extras was waived by the owner's conduct. The defendants quite agree that such a waiver is possible and common but claim this evidence fails to support a waiver of the requirement. There are many cases in which the owner's conduct has waived such a requirement. . . . In all the cases finding that such a provision had been waived thus allowing a contractor to collect for extras, the nature and character of the item clearly showed it to be extra. Also, in most cases the owner's verbal consent of request for the item was clear beyond question and was proven to have been made at the time the question first arose while the work was still to be finished. The defendants' refusal to give a written order has in itself been held to negative the idea of a waiver of the contract requirement for a written order. . . . We think the waiver of such a provision must be proved by clear and convincing evidence and the task of so proving rests upon the party relying upon the waiver. . . .

[Ed. note: The Court ordered a new trial, stating that the contractor could recover only for those extras he could prove were ordered as such by the owner in the proper form, unless he could show that the owner waived the requirements of a writing by clear and convincing evidence.]

REVIEW QUESTIONS

1. What is a change order?
2. Normally, who has the authority to order changes?
3. Why is it important to comply with formal requirements for ordering changes?

QUESTIONS FOR CLASS DISCUSSION

1. Why are changes important in cost control?

2. Is it desirable for the design professional to have authority to order changes?

3. Should the contractor be compelled to perform a written change order before there has been an agreement on price?

PROBLEM

A was the architect for a construction project being built by C for O. The specifications called for soundproof tile for certain room ceilings. C wanted to put in tile of a certain brand, which was represented by the manufacturer to be soundproof. A insisted that another, more expensive, brand be used. C claimed that this would be an extra, and demanded a change order. A claimed that as judge of performance, he was ruling that the tile which the contractor wanted to use did not meet the contract requirements. C used the tile specified by A, and, after completion of performance, demanded that he be paid extra for the tile he had used. A instructed O not to pay, because the tile used was required under the contract, and because the contract required that a written change order be issued before there could be extra payment for any work. Is A correct in his position? (Assume that no tiles are actually soundproof, but that the tile demanded by A resisted sound better, and cost more, than the tile which C wanted to use.)

Chapter 22

SUBSURFACE PROBLEMS

SECTION 22.01 SOME BACKGROUND

Many disputes in construction projects involve soil and subsurface conditions. There is a great variety of subsurface conditions, even within small areas of land. Test borings of one area of the project will not necessarily reflect the composition of the subsurface in the entire project area. Soil testing is expensive, and only a limited number of borings are usually taken. Soil reports must be evaluated carefully to see whether a sufficient number of test borings have been taken at representative places.

Contractors sometimes ask for additional compensation, or for relief from performance, because, during performance, they discover that the subsurface conditions differ from what they had expected, or differ from what they had been led to believe by the owner. Is the contractor entitled to relief when he runs into subsurface conditions which were unforeseeable or unexpected?

SECTION 22.02 RISK OF UNFORESEEN SUBSURFACE CONDITIONS IN FIXED PRICE CONTRACTS

This section assumes that the owner has not furnished subsurface or site information, or that, if he has, he is able to disclaim responsibility for the accuracy of the information furnished. How does the law allocate the risk of additional costs incurred when subsurface conditions in a fixed price contract are not as anticipated by one or both parties of the contract?

Usually, unexpected subsurface conditions mean added costs to the contractor. The subsurface condition may be on the construction site or at areas intended to furnish compaction material for grading (borrow pits). Added costs may result from the need for additional labor or for more expensive excavation techniques or equipment. In the case of a borrow pit problem, the contractor may incur substantial expense to find a different source of compaction materials. Usually, the law places risk of such added costs upon the contractor. Only if the contract affords him relief will he be entitled to recoup some, or all, of his additional unanticipated costs from the owner. See § 22.06.

If the circumstances are such that the costs are *many* times more than the anticipated costs, the doctrine of mutual mistake might give the contractor a right to terminate his obligation to perform further, along with the right to recover for the reasonable cost of what he has done. This result is more likely if both parties anticipated that the subsurface conditions would be different from what was discovered during the contractor's performance. Also, much would depend upon the added costs in relationship to the total cost of contract performance. If the contractor is successful in asserting the doctrine of mutual mistake, his only remedy will be to be relieved from any further obligation to perform. He will not be entitled to any additional costs, unless he can establish that the owner has warranted that the subsurface would conform to the information furnished, or if the owner deliberately misrepresented the nature of the subsurface conditions. In most cases, the law places the risk of differing subsurface conditions upon the contractor, unless he can point to contractual language which gives him a right to additional costs.

The problem becomes more difficult if the building slides or settles because the subsurface conditions turn out to be different than anticipated. If the owner has specified both materials and methods relating to excavation and construction of the building, he is likely to be held to have assumed the risk of sliding or settling after the construction has been completed. If the owner specifies material and methods, only an express promise by the contractor that the building will not settle unreasonably or slide will enable the owner to transfer any corrective costs or diminished value to the contractor. As indicated in § 20.05, without a clear contractual assumption of this risk, courts are hesitant to saddle the contractor with performance standards when the owner has designated materials and methods.

Where the owner has not designated the method of excavation, it is likely that the contractor will have to pay damages based upon the corrective work necessary, or upon the diminished value of the premises. The contractor might be given relief, if he can establish that the settling or sliding occurred because of an unforeseeable and unusual event. See Chapter 26.

SECTION 22.03 PROMISES BY THE OWNER TO PAY MORE MONEY

The discovery of unusual subsurface conditions may cause the contractor to ask the owner for additional money. The owner may have no viable choice other than to give this assurance. In some of these "requests" by the contractor, there is implied coercion. The contractor may be saying that if the owner does not pay, he will walk off the job and leave the owner with a lawsuit.

On the other hand, the owner may make the promise voluntarily because he wants to be fair. Usually, promises to pay additional amounts for the same work are unenforceable, because of the pre-existing duty rule. In exchange for his promise, the owner receives only what he was already entitled to get under the contract. However, in a substantial number of subsurface condition cases, courts have relaxed the doctrine enough to permit the promise to pay additional compensation to be enforced. Sometimes the courts have stated that the facts would have permitted the contractor to rescind the contract. The contractor gave up his right to rescind in exchange for the new promise by the owner to pay more. This "fiction" allows the courts to give relief if they can find a new promise by the owner to pay more money.

SECTION 22.04 REPRESENTATIONS BY OWNER

In many construction contracts, the owner furnishes a soil report to the bidders, prepared by a soils engineer. The report states what tests were taken, what the tests showed, and opinions by the tester relating to subsurface conditions. Also, the engineer might give advice on the type of methods to be used to excavate or extract compaction material.

Suppose the information furnished to the contractors turns out to be inaccurate. The "inaccuracy" may relate to the test results, or to the observations or inferences which the soil tester has drawn from the tests. The soil tests may be inaccurate due to negligence on the part of the soil tester, or the tester may be "wrong" in his conclusions, despite the use of due care.

In the absence of valid disclaimers, the contractor is entitled to rely upon the representations. Certainly negligent or fraudulent misrepresentations, and possibly innocent misrepresentations, which are reasonably relied upon, can be the basis of an action on the part of the contractor. He would be able to rescind the contract and recover the reasonable value of what he has performed, or he would be able to recover damages caused by the misrepresentation. Damages, in most cases, would be the additional expense incurred because the work requires a different technique or more expensive machinery because of the unanticipated subsurface conditions.

Also, the contractor who suffers these losses may have a valid claim against the soils engineer, despite the absence of any contract between them. In the past, absence of "privity" (a contractual relationship directly between the parties—here the contractor and the soils engineer) shielded the engineer, but this "shield" is weakening today. It will be easier to recover if the tester is negligent or guilty of fraud, but there is a possibility of recovery for innocent misrepresentation. See § 30.04.

The owner has an action against the soils engineer if the soils engineer is negligent in his work, and possibly if he is wrong despite the use of due care. Unless the tester has promised to be accurate, he should not be liable unless he is negligent. Soils engineers often attempt to avoid any liability by the use of disclaimers. See § 22.05.

SECTION 22.05 EFFECT OF CONTRACT DISCLAIMERS

What effect do contract "disclaimers" have upon the contractor's misrepresentation claims? Almost universally, when soil information is furnished to the contractor, the owner contractually denies any responsibility for the accuracy of soil reports. He may demand that the contractor visit the site, observe the terrain, and make his own tests. The owner wants to place the risk of unusual soil conditions upon the contractor, despite furnishing him with inaccurate information. His efforts to do so have been generally, but not entirely, successful.

Most of the cases involving contract disclaimers have upheld such disclaimers. If no reports were made available, the owner can argue, the contractor would have the risk. Why penalize the owner when he does furnish information he was not obligated to furnish? Yet, the owner benefits by having the tests made and used by the contractor. Also, the owner knows that the contractor does rely. In a few cases, the contractor has won, especially if there was no time to check or make his own tests. Also, there have been cases where the contractor has been able to circumvent the disclaimer clauses by showing that it was economically unreasonable to make his own tests.

Fraud, or bad faith, by the owner is not shielded by contract disclaimers. In the City of Salinas v. Souza and McCue Construction Co., 66 Cal.2d 217, 424 P.2d 921, 57 Cal.Rptr. 337 (1967), the City of Salinas hired a construction company to build a sewer line. The contractor claimed that the city materially misrepresented the soil conditions by failing to inform the contractor and other bidders of unstable conditions known to the city. Also, it was asserted by the contractor that the city engineer in charge of the project knew that particularly difficult conditions were likely to be encountered in the site area. The contractor alleged that the chief engineer directed an independent testing firm to take borings at "preselected spaces and locations which avoided the area of the greatest unsettled conditions; that the method of taking the tests was misleading; that the reports of these boring tests were sent to bidders only a few days before the opening of bids, and that while it would have been proper practice to warn bidders of anticipated difficult conditions, the city did not do so."

The court in the *Salinas* case held that, if the contractor could prove his allegations, he could recover damages from the city for fraudulent misrepresentation and non-disclosure. The contract specifications requiring that the bidders examine the site would not excuse the government agency for active concealment of conditions. The *Salinas* case is a strong argument for imposing a duty upon the owner to disclose relevant subsurface information, if this data is not likely to be discovered by the contractor. While cases have not gone very far in this direction as yet, this duty seems only fair, and likely to be the rule in the future.

While disclaimers are usually upheld, there is a slight movement toward protecting the contractor who relies upon information provided by the owner. The difficulty of predicting the effect of disclaimers is illustrated by two cases decided by the Supreme Court of California on the same day. In one case they upheld the disclaimer, and in the other case they did not.

In Wunderlich v. State of Cal., 65 Cal.2d 777, 423 P.2d 545, 56 Cal.Rptr. 473 (1967), the contract involved the construction of a highway. The alleged breach of warranty related to the composition of compaction material in borrow pits. The state's soil testers took samples of the material, and permitted bidders to see the results. The contractor was required to examine the site. The terms and conditions stated that the state would not guarantee or accept responsibility for the accuracy of the preliminary investigations. The contractor ran into difficulties, and had to expend considerably more money to extract the material at the source made available for him by the state. The factual information as to test results was accurate. The issue was whether the conclusions suggested by the tester were a representation of fact that sufficient suitable material extractable at a reasonable cost would be available at the borrow pit. In finding for the state because there was no justifiable reliance by the contractor, the Court stated:

> The Special Provisions state simply that samples had been taken from the pit, and that they appeared to point to the fact that there was suitable material in the pit. There was no representation as to quantities in the source, or that a consistent proportion of materials would be found throughout the source. If we consider the memorandum as embracing the whole of the representations made, it does not purport to disclose the average of overall conditions of the Wilder pit. It purports to explain, rather, that the pit was composed of sand and gravel, and expressly states that "some test holes encountered considerable coarse material, while others were practically all sand." It forewarns bidders that there might be more sand than anticipated, ...

> Although the memorandum accurately reported the fact that borings results ranged from 55 per cent to 88 per cent sand, this would hardly seem to warrant the conclusion that the pit would average the median of that range, as claimed by plaintiffs.

Also, other bidders made their own tests. Relieving the contractor in *Wunderlich* could encourage sloppy preparation for bidding.

While the court found no justifiable reliance on the contractor in the *Wunderlich* case, they did find justifiable reliance in the case of E. H. Morrill Co. v. State of Cal., 65 Cal.2d 787, 423 P.2d 551, 56 Cal. Rptr. 479 (1967). In the *Morrill* contract, the state had stated:

> *Boulders* which may be encountered in the site grading and other excavation work on the site *vary in size from one foot to four feet in diameter. The dispersion of boulders varies from approximately six feet to twelve feet in all directions, including the vertical.* (Emphasis by the court.)

It turned out that the boulders were substantially larger and more concentrated than represented. Plaintiff contractor had visited the site, but relied upon the representations in submitting his bid. The court held that the plaintiff contractor could recover despite general disclaimer conditions which required that the bidder examine the site of the work and satisfy himself as to the character, quality and quantity of surface and subsurface materials to be encountered. Here, the court held that this it was not merely a matter of reporting the results of investigation, as in the *Wunderlich* case. The court held that the state had made a positive assertion of fact as to condition. In the *Wunderlich* case, the disclaimer provisions were placed in the very section in which the alleged representation had been made. This was not the situation in the *Morrill* case. In effect, the court stated that contractors are more likely to rely upon representations where there is no disclaimer stated together with the representation itself. The court also held that the responsibility of a government agency for its positive representations cannot be overcome by general clauses requiring the contractor to check the site and resume responsibility for the work. The court compelled the trial court to take evidence in the matter to see whether the contractor could justify his complaint that the state knew, or should have known, that the representation as to the size of the boulders was false.

SECTION 22.06 CONTRACTUAL PROTECTION TO CONTRACTOR

Federal construction contracts now include "differing site conditions clauses." Such clauses provide:

> (a) The Contractor shall promptly, and before such conditions are disturbed, notify the Contracting Officer in

writing of: (1) subsurface or latent physical conditions at the site differing materially from those indicated in this contract, or (2) unknown physical conditions at the site, of an unusual nature, differing materially from those ordinarily encountered and generally recognized as inhering in work of the character provided for in this contract. The Contracting Officer shall promptly investigate the conditions, and if he finds that such conditions do materially so differ and cause an increase or decrease in the Contractor's cost of, or the time required for, performance of any part of the work under this contract, whether or not changed as a result of such conditions, an equitable adjustment shall be made and the contract modified in writing accordingly.

(b) No claim of the Contractor under this clause shall be allowed unless the Contractor has given the notice required in (a) above, *provided,* however, the time prescribed therefore may be extended by the Government.

(c) No claim by the Contractor for an equitable adjustment hereunder shall be allowed if asserted after final payment under this contract. (Armed Service Procurement Regulations, 7–602.4, Feb. 1968).

AIA Doc. A201 states at 12.1.6:

Should concealed conditions encountered in the performance of the Work below the surface of the ground be at variance with the conditions indicated by the Contract Documents or should unknown physical conditions below the surface of the ground of an unusual nature, differing materially from those ordinarily encountered and generally recognized as inherent in work of the character provided for in this Contract, be encountered, the Contract Sum shall be equitably adjusted by Change Order upon claim by either party made within a reasonable time after the first observance of the conditions.

It appears, although it is by no means clear from the clauses, that the purpose of both the federal and AIA clauses dealing with subsurface problems, were intended to shift the added cost from contractor to owner. Another possible interpretation is that, by the use of the term "equitably adjusted", the added cost could be shared. If neither party is at fault, perhaps it is equitable to split the added cost equally. If the job required expenditures of $10,000 more than it would have taken had the subsurface been as anticipated or represented, there is no reason why the amount of adjustment could not be $5000. Also, it is possible to stay within the clause language and split the added cost on some bases other than 50-50, if there is some equitable reason why one party should bear more of the loss than the other.

SECTION 22.07 TWO ILLUSTRATIVE CASES: O'CONNELL'S SONS AND HERSEY

DANIEL O'CONNELL'S SONS, INC. v. COMMONWEALTH

Supreme Judicial Court of Massachusetts, 1965.
349 Mass. 642, 212 N.E.2d 219.

KIRK, JUSTICE. This is a petition under G.L. c. 258, §§ 1 and 2, to establish the petitioner's right to damages as the result of costs incurred for alleged extra work in the performance of a road building contract with the Commonwealth. In the Superior Court the case was referred to an auditor who found for the petitioner (contractor). Thereafter the case was heard by a judge who, upon the auditor's report and other evidence, made findings of fact and an ultimate finding for the Commonwealth. The judge reported the case to us with two questions for our determination.

We set out certain facts, mainly uncontroverted, which appear in the judge's report. The contract with the Commonwealth, executed on April 21, 1959, called for the contractor to build a two mile stretch of highway in Greenfield and Bernardston at a cost of more than $2,000,000. The project included the construction of a bridge over a stream in Bernardston. This involved the excavation of the riverbed for pier construction.

Several provisions of the "Standard Specifications for Highways and Bridges" (specifications),[1] incorporated into the contract, related to the building of cofferdams. Thus, Article A3.30 D of the specifications provided, in part: "The Contractor will be required to construct suitable cofferdams for the foundation work whenever the nature of the work requires them. Before starting this work the Contractor shall submit for comment by the [Commonwealth's] Engineer sketches and details of the cofferdam construction he proposes to use. The full responsibility for their safety and construction will rest with the Contractor. Each cofferdam shall be sufficiently tight to prevent the flow of water through the area in which the work is to be done, and shall be built to adequate strength to withstand all pressures to which it may be subjected. The top of the cofferdam shall be sufficiently above the water to prevent flooding the interior by any reasonable rise in elevation of the water during the use of the cofferdam. The bottom of the cofferdam shall be a sufficient depth below the proposed foundation grade to permit a reasonable change (at least 2 feet) in depth of the foundation within the cofferdam, if directed."

Article 4 provides: "Statements as to the condition under which the work is to be performed, including plans, surveys, measurements, dimensions, calculations, estimates, borings, etc., are made solely to

1. The specifications comprised a printed volume of 500 pages.

furnish a basis for comparison of bids, and the * * * [Commonwealth] does not guarantee or represent that they are even approximately correct. *The Contractor must satisfy himself by his own investigation and research regarding all conditions affecting the work to be done and labor and materials needed, and make his bid in sole reliance* thereon" (emphasis supplied).

The geological data provision states: "An interpolated line, purporting to show boulder or rock obstruction, is plotted on the cross-sections where limited geologic data based on seismic explorations or punchings indicate such obstructions. These lines are in no way guaranteed by the Department as truly representative of existing conditions. The seismic data shown on the plans was taken for design purposes only and may not represent materials actually encountered during construction. This information is available for the bidders to see at Room 640, Department's Main Office at 100 Nashua Street, Boston, Mass. *Any reliance placed on such information will be solely at bidders risk. The bidder shall have no redress against the Department for any loss sustained if his prosecution of work or submission of his bid prices are based on this data*" (emphasis supplied).

Item A3–5 of the contract obliged the contractor to avoid causing "boiling or other disturbance of the ground in the foundation area," and to use such means of excavation as would prevent water seepage. It also provided that "[t]he contract price for Bridge Excavation shall include full compensation for whichever means are required to attain the foregoing requirements."

Although, under Item A3–5 of the contract, a unit price covered all means employed for bridge excavation, Article A3.41 of the specifications provided, in part, for payment above the unit price for extra work in the following language: "If any change in depth of foundation or in other dimensions of the foundation is directed by the [Commonwealth's] Engineer after the controls have been provided, and if such change is greater than can be accommodated by the controls as constructed by the Contractor with the approval of the Engineer, then any changes made as directed by the Engineer will be paid for in accordance with the contract provisions for Extra Work."

The judge found that the contractor began construction of piers for the bridge over the stream in August, 1959. The plans of the Commonwealth indicated that solid ledge would be reached about two feet below the stream bed which the Commonwealth plotted at elevation 319.4 and that a westerly pier at elevation 311 and an easterly pier at elevation 312.5 were to be constructed. Based on these figures, excavations of about 8.4 feet on the westerly side and 6.9 feet on the easterly would be necessary. These figures were relied upon by the contractor in preparing his bid. He chose to control the waters by means of a simple earthen cofferdam to permit excavation.

The judge found that, from the beginning of the cofferdam construction, the Commonwealth's engineer was at the site at least once and sometimes twice daily. The engineer knew of the contractor's plans and intentions for water control and observed the installation and construction of those controls. He never objected to the methods employed by the contractor or to the manner in which the work was being carried out.

After work had begun, the contractor discovered that ledge was more than two feet beneath the bed, and that additional methods of control were needed. He thereupon dredged the bed of the stream and lowered the headgates of a downstream dam at a cost of over $6,000. (The contractor seeks no extra compensation for this expenditure.)

Despite the additional methods of control undertaken by the contractor, it became clear that the westerly pier required four more feet of excavation before ledge would be encountered. The contractor's representative and three of the Commonwealth's engineers, namely, the resident engineer and two of his superiors, conferred at the site of the bridge and decided that the earthen cofferdam and other controls were inadequate to meet the change in the depth of the excavation. The engineers then directed the contractor to install a steel sheeted cofferdam. The contractor's superintendent said that the contractor would be entitled to "extra compensation" for the installation. The engineers told him to keep a separate account of his costs for the installation, and said that they would discuss the extra charge at a later date.

The footings for the two piers as finally constructed were, on the westerly side, at elevation 307 and, on the easterly side, at elevation 309.3. The excavations were, respectively, 4 feet and 3.2 feet greater in depth than had been originally plotted.

The contractor incurred costs attributable to the construction of the steel sheeted cofferdam at the direction of the engineers amounting to $12,030.14.

The Commonwealth refused to pay the alleged extra costs, and in consequence, the petition was brought. In addition to the findings already stated, the judge found that "the earthen cofferdam methods originally employed by the * * * [contractor] were not economically feasible, nor were they adequate to provide the dry working area necessary under the original specifications." The judge found for the Commonwealth.

We need discuss only the first question reported by the judge, since the answer to it is decisive of the case. . . . The question was: "Whether on the foregoing facts the petitioner is entitled by the provisions of Article A3.41 of the Standard Specifications to recover the costs incurred by it in the construction of the steel sheeted cofferdam in accordance with the contract provisions for Extra Work."

The findings clearly show that the contractor relied upon geological data provided by the Commonwealth, despite the Commonwealth's express disclaimer of responsibility for the accuracy of the data, and the provision that "the Contractor must satisfy himself by his own investigation and research regarding all [such] conditions." Specifically, the original decision to use an earthen cofferdam to control the waters was the contractor's alone. No responsibility for it was shared by the Commonwealth. The decision of the contractor was made in ignorance of ascertainable geological data which he had the duty to establish, namely, the depth to the ledge below the stream bed. The discovery during the construction of the earthen cofferdam of the actual depth demonstrated that the cofferdam was inadequate chiefly because the contractor had failed to determine, by his own investigation and research, the location of the ledge. The subsequent direction by the engineers to build a steel sheeted cofferdam did not entitle the contractor to payment for extra work under Article A3.41, but merely required him to perform his part of the contract as provided in Article A3.30 D of the specifications.

The contractor's case is not strengthened because the resident engineer was daily at the site, was aware of the contractor's plans, and made no objection. Whatever the plans were, they rested upon an error of fact concerning the depth to ledge which the contractor had the exclusive responsibility to establish. See Benjamin Foster Co. v. Commonwealth, 318 Mass. 190, 199, 61 N.E.2d 147, 166 A.L.R. 925.

The answer to the quoted question is: No. Judgment must be entered for the respondent.

So ordered.

HERSEY GRAVEL CO. v. STATE

Supreme Court of Michigan, 1943.
305 Mich. 333, 9 N.W.2d 567.

BUSHNELL, JUSTICE. This is an appeal by defendants State of Michigan and Michigan State Highway Department from a judgment entered in the Court of Claims in favor of plaintiff Hersey Gravel Company in the sum of $16,155. The total amount claimed by plaintiff is $59,622.27, and it has taken a cross-appeal from the disallowance by the court of the remainder of that amount.

On July 7, 1938, the State advertised for bids for the construction of 5.17 miles of highway on U.S. 41 and M-28, between Michigamme and Lake George in Spurr township, Baraga county. This advertisement came to the attention of William S. Allswede, vice-president and manager of plaintiff, on July 10th. He obtained plans and specifications from the Highway Department and spent two days examining the proposed right of way and "borrow pits." The blueprints which he examined contained notations of soil conditions upon which he claims his company based its bid, which was filed and opened on July 20th. This bid in the sum of $266,324.19, being the lowest of those tendered, was accepted, and a contract dated August 8, 1939, [1938?] was executed covering the project. The contract required the work to be completed by July 1, 1939. Delays were encountered and the work was not actually completed and accepted until July 1, 1940, but no delay penalty was exacted by the State.

The contract called for 373,086 cubic yards of earth excavation and 17,007 cubic yards of rock excavation, but an extra construction estimate shows that the contractor completed an additional 32,175 cubic yards of earth excavation and 11,390.08 cubic yards of rock excavation. The amount allowed plaintiff for additional construction, including these items and others, totalled $35,111.67.

The verified claim filed by plaintiff in the Court of Claims states that: "If the material to be encountered had been of the character indicated by the drawings and as represented directly or impliedly, the claimant could have completed the work at the contract price and would have earned a reasonable profit. By reason of the fact that the material actually encountered was not the kind indicated in the drawings and directly and impliedly represented to be, but of a kind vastly more difficult and expensive to move as above set forth, the cost of completing the work of the contract was $59,622.27 in excess of the cost anticipated."

These alleged representations and warranties of fact as to subsoil conditions, for the breach of which plaintiff seeks damages, consisted of certain descriptive phrases on the blueprints, such as "Baraga fine sandy loam," Crystal Falls loam," and "Diana stony loam." As stated in the opinion of the circuit judge presiding in the Court of Claims:

"There is no real difference, under the testimony, between the three soil designations above quoted. The Baraga formation denotes a formation which, generally, had three layers or horizons. This formation is, generally, topped by a thin covering of top soil and then by a few inches of sandy loam. Below that is another layer of earth which is apt to be very, very firmly compacted and to contain more or less rocks and boulders running from comparatively small sizes up to considerable dimensions. The third zone differs from the middle zone in that it is harder and may have more rock and is more difficult to handle.

"The term 'Crystal Falls' indicates a formation which mostly contains the same material but the bed rock underlying it is nearer the surface and there is less of the looser material.

"The Diana formation does not differ materially from the other two in the contents of the soil found but it does differ in that it is wetter and that its water-table is nearer the surface of the ground. * * *

"The words 'Baraga,' 'Crystal Falls,' and 'Diana' are part of the technical terminology of soil experts and have arbitrary meanings attached to them. Under the testimony 'Baraga' is described as, 'Well drained, moderately stony loam. Bed rock four to eight feet. Fine grading difficult due to stoniness. Surface of the bed rock is very irregular.' 'Crystal Falls:' 'Thin stony loam and rock outcrops. Fine grading difficult due to stoniness.' 'Diana:' 'Three to eight feet, wet stony loam over bed rock.' "

The soil notations on the blueprints were made as a result of investigations conducted under the supervision of the district soils engineer of the Highway Department in the winter of 1937, when a crew of men dug test holes down to the ditch grade and took soundings at points where cuts were shown on the plans.

Plaintiff's testimony is that the actual soil conditions encountered were of an entirely different character from those indicated on the plans, far more difficult and costly to handle, and destructive to its equipment. For example, although plaintiff claims its equipment was in good working order, 17 sets of steam shovel dipper teeth were used in the west "borrow pit" in three months, and 16 sets in other pits in less time, although it takes, ordinarily, only one set of dipper teeth a season to handle 200,000 yards of material.

The State denies that the material encountered was more difficult and expensive to handle than that described in the plans, and, although it maintains that the notations thereon were accurate, insists that the plaintiff should have been aware of the difficult and rocky nature of the terrain because of the outcroppings of ledge rock and boulder formation readily discernible to prospective bidders. The State admits that the work progressed slowly, but charges that this was because of the dilatory methods employed by plaintiff and its lack of enough good equipment. It is asserted that, if plaintiff's representative had made the proper kind of investigation, the exact nature of the soil could have been ascertained and its bid made accordingly.

The trial judge held, under the authority of Atletwed v. City of Marysville, 295 Mich. 102, 294 N.W. 110, that plaintiff was entitled to rely upon the contract, blueprints, plans and specifications prepared by the State, and upon the engineering practice in that connection, and he stated that it was the duty of public authorities, when preparing proposals, to provide all available information and data in unmistakable and clear-cut terms. He absolved the State and the Highway Department of any bad faith, but held that, so far as the excavations along the length of the highway were concerned, there was a warranty in connection with the nature of the subsoil, and that this warranty had been breached because of a misstatement of the conditions actually existing. He declined to hold that an implied warranty existed with respect to the nature of the soil in the "borrow pit," or that there was any conclusive testimony that plaintiff's equipment was not in good condition. . . .

The State . . . relies upon the accuracy of the representations on its plans and specifications, and also insists that plaintiff is precluded from recovery because the blueprints upon which its bid was based are supplemented by specifications which say: "Soil notations shown on the plans are for information only and shall not be construed to relieve bidders of their responsibility to satisfy themselves by examining the site of the proposed work as to actual soil conditions."

This provision put plaintiff on notice, but the notations on the plans had the effect of also advising plaintiff that an investigation had been made by the Highway Department of the character of the soil along the entire proposed highway. The testimony shows that this investigation extended over a considerable period of time. The period between the time the advertisement appeared asking for bids and the date upon which bids were to be submitted and opened, would not suggest to any reasonable bidder that it was necessary for him to make a more extended investigation of soil conditions than was made by plaintiff's manager, Allswede, who spent two days examining the proposed right of way. Plaintiff complied with the requirements of the proposal and carried out the responsibility to satisfy itself as to actual soil conditions by the examination of its manager of the site of the proposed work.

"Undoubtedly the commission's knowledge of subsoil conditions was superior to that of the plaintiffs, and they tried to acquire this knowledge from it. It is equally true that these facts were not within the fair reasonable reach of the plaintiffs, and there was lack of time for them to obtain this information by an independent investigation before the letting. * * *

"The duty rested on the sewer commission to furnish to the plaintiffs in this case all the material information it had in its possession, obtained either by borings or from past experience, as to subsoil conditions in the sewer line, and if it failed to do so, and as a result thereof the plaintiffs were put to large additional expense in completing the contract, they are entitled to recover the reasonable damages sustained by them." Davis v. Commissioners of Sewerage, D.C., 13 F.Supp. 672, 681.

In United States v. Atlantic Dredging Company, supra, the court said: "The case is therefore within the ruling of United States v. Spearin, 248 U.S. 132, 136, 39 S.Ct. 59, 63 L.Ed. 166 [169] where it is stated that the direction to contractors to visit the site and inform themselves of the actual conditions of a proposed undertaking, will not relieve from defects in the plans and specifications, citing Christie v. United States, 237 U.S. 234, 35 S.Ct. 565, 59 L.Ed. 933; Hollerbach v. United States, 233 U.S. 165, 34 S.Ct. 553, 58 L.Ed. 898, and United States v. Utah, N. & C. Stage Co. 199 U.S. [414], 424, 26 S.Ct. 69, 50 L.Ed. 251, [255]."

. . .

Plaintiff's cross-appeal is from the trial court's refusal to allow its claim in connection with material excavated from "borrow pits." A "borrow pit" is "a bank or a pit from which earth is taken for use in filling or embanking." Webster's New International Dictionary, 2d Ed. The court held: "As to the claims in connection with the borrow pits, I can find no ground for raising any implied warranty in this contract except the one that the material from those pits were reasonably suited to use as fill material in the making of grades. In point of fact the material was suitable for that use as such material. It was difficult to excavate with shovels but it was excavated with shovels. One pit became impracticable after about 14,000 cubic yards were removed but another pit was substituted. One pit was difficult of excavating and presented some compacted formation that could not be excavated after some 97,000 cubic yards had been taken from the pit with the equipment claimant had. I am not able to see where there is any implied warranty to be drawn from the contracts in connection with the borrow pits which has been violated. The conclusion that I do reach is that the petitioner is entitled to compensation for highway excavations, but not for excavations in the pits."

Plaintiff contends that there is an implied warranty that the kind of soil noted on the plans at specified stations is the same kind of material to be encountered in the borrow pits corresponding to such stations. It bases this contention upon a claimed custom of contractors to consider the "borrow" to be of the same material as the roadbed itself. It also contends that the State failed to furnish proper borrow pits. The evidence offered in support of these contentions does not justify a determination that the trial judge was in error in his conclusion, and that his finding should be set aside. "We are unable to say in the instant case that 'the evidence clearly preponderates in the opposite direction.'" Hanson v. Economical Cunningham Drug Stores, Inc., 299 Mich. 434, 437, 300 N.W. 153, 154. The court did not err in disallowing plaintiff's claim for additional compensation for material excavated from the borrow pits.

. . .

The judgment of the Court of Claims is affirmed, . . .

BOYLES, CHIEF JUSTICE (dissenting). Plaintiff bases its claim on statements made by the State Highway Department in certain plans and specifications attached to and apparently made a part of a highway construction contract. The statements relied upon by plaintiff were notations of soil conditions in connection with blueprints. When plaintiff relies for recovery on the lack of accuracy of these notations in the plans, it must accept the plans in their entirety. Plaintiff cannot base its claim for recovery on a part of the plans and ignore other provisions in the same plans which are to its disadvantage when they fail to suit its purpose. The notations of soil conditions in the plans on which plaintiff relies were subject to this provision: "Soil notations shown on the plans are for information only and shall not be construed to relieve bidders of their responsibility to satisfy themselves by examining the site of the proposed work as to actual soil conditions."

Plaintiff did examine the site of the proposed work as to actual soil conditions. There is no sound basis in law for plaintiff's present claim that it was misled by the plans. In the absence of fraud, deceit, misrepresentation, or subsequent change of contract by agreement by someone authorized to make the change, the written agreement controls. Plaintiff cannot now recover for unanticipated soil conditions.

The judgment must be set aside and the cause remanded to the claims court for entry of judgment of no cause for action, with costs to defendants.

The differing attitudes of courts in the subsurface cases is reflected by the two opinions reproduced. The *Hersey* case split the court 5 to 3. More courts would permit the owner to furnish the information and then disclaim responsibility for its accuracy. But a significant number of state courts would hold as did the Michigan court in *Hersey*. Much depends upon the facts, such as the time available for an independent check, the cost of such a check, the language of the representations, and the language and placement of the disclaimer.

REVIEW QUESTIONS

1. Who usually bears the risk of added costs of excavation under a fixed price contract?

2. If an owner makes representations as to soil conditions, can he successfully disclaim his responsibility for the accuracy of the information?

3. How does AIA Doc. A201 deal with subsurface problems?

QUESTIONS FOR CLASS DISCUSSION

1. Should the owner try to transfer the entire risk of differing subsurface conditions to the contractor?

2. If the owner promises to pay more money for the same work when differing subsurface conditions are discovered, should the promise be enforced?

3. Should an owner be able to furnish inaccurate information and divest himself of responsibility for its accuracy? Should the result depend upon whether the owner is a public or private body?

PROBLEM

O hired A to design a house and prepare construction drawings and specifications, but not to supervise or inspect. A did his work and was paid. O then hired C to build a residence for $35,000.

O thought the soil might be spongy in the area of his lot, since a neighbor encountered some minor slide problems. However, he made no soil tests, and did not call in a soils engineer for an inspection. Shortly after the house was completed, the exterior steps began to crack. The house settled, causing some wall cracks and a mildly tilting floor in the living room. Does O have a valid claim against C? If so, how would his damages be computed? (To avoid these settling problems, it would be necessary to rebuild the house.)

Chapter 23

TIME PROBLEMS

SECTION 23.01 AN OVERVIEW

The date of project completion determines when it can be used. While use is an important part of the value of a project, time delays are treated differently than other types of breaches. Time is not generally considered part of the basic exchange of values in a construction contract. The basic exchange is money given by the owner in exchange for the structure built by the contractor. In addition, the law has recognized that delays are common, if not inevitable, in construction projects. For these reasons, if the contractor is delayed in his performance without a justifiable excuse, he should pay for whatever his delay has cost the owner, but should not lose his right to complete the contract or to be paid for what he has done.

As for delays caused by the owner, the courts have given effect to provisions under which a contractor is entitled to an extension of time but not to delay damages caused by the owner. Where "no damage" clauses are given effect, it is a recognition both of the commonness of delays, and the difficulty of proving exactly what a delay has cost.

The law has assisted the owner in the difficult task of proving what a contractor delay has cost the owner. Generally, the parties are permitted to specify in advance how delay damages chargeable to the contractor will be computed. As for owner-caused delays, while it would be possible to establish agreed figures for these delays, typically the contracting parties do not do so. Owners who are concerned with this question often seek to avoid liability entirely by the use of "no damage" clauses.

SECTION 23.02 COMMENCEMENT, SCHEDULING AND COMPLETION DATES

Construction contracts usually contain a completion date, as well as specified dates for completion for designated stages of the project. Sometimes difficulties arise because, at the time the contract documents are signed, it may be difficult to know exactly when the contractor can commence performance. Permits may have to be obtained, land or easements may have to be secured, financing may have to be obtained, and other matters disposed of before the contractor can be given site access. For this reason, it is ordinarily helpful to allow a specified number of total days for completion of the project or for any of its stages (starting with site access), rather than set specified completion dates. It is common to see time expressed as "______ days from the date the contractor is given access to the site".

Such a method of computing the completion obligation relieves the owner of possible liability for delays in furnishing the site to the contractor, yet does not make the contractor assume this risk. Even this method should not relieve the owner, if the delay in furnishing the site is excessive and beyond the normal expectations of the parties or due to the owner's fault. In such a case, the contractor would, in the absence of a valid "no damage" clause (see § 23.07), be entitled to delay damages.

It is possible to set a specific completion date. In such case, the contractor has accepted the risk of short delays which may preclude him from commencing work. However, in the normal case, he does not assume this risk, and does not expect to have the time of his performance begin to run until he has been given access to the site.

The *Bloomfield* case, reproduced at § 23.08, explores this question with a somewhat unsatisfactory result. The *Bloomfield* case does show the difficulty that can result because it is unclear when the stated number of days for performance commences. In that case, the contract was dated, and sent unsigned to the contractor. The contractor was requested to sign it and return it to the school district for its signature. Despite the fact that there was approximately six weeks between the time the contract was dated and the receipt by the contractor of the contract finally signed by the school district, the court held the time for performance would commence when the contract was pre-dated.

In determining the time allowed for completion, the contract should specify a designated number of days and make clear when that designated number of days will commence and conclude.

Sometimes construction contracts give the owner a right to accelerate the completion date. Any such right should be limited to reasonable acceleration, unless the contract makes it clear that the contractor is accepting the risk of even unreasonable acceleration of the completion date.

While changes clauses give the owner a right to make certain types of changes, these clauses are not always clear on whether this includes the right to accelerate the completion date. For example, AIA Doc. A201 at 12.1.1 permits a change:

> consisting of additions, deletions or other revisions.

If the right to accelerate is desired, it should be spelled out clearly in the agreement and not left to the general wording of a changes clause.

If acceleration is properly ordered, the contractor should be entitled to added costs caused by the speed up, unless he has assumed the risk of these costs by contract.

If there is no agreed schedule for completion of various stages of the work, the contractor must proceed at a reasonable pace.

Sometimes a schedule is part of the contract documents. The contract may give the design professional the right to set up schedules or to revise them. Unexcused failure to comply with the schedule can, in some cases, give the owner a right to terminate the contract. See § 26.04.

Whether the work has been completed, and when it was completed, is often determined by the design professional through issuance of a certificate of completion. See § 24.04.

SECTION 23.03 CAUSE OF DELAY

(A) ACTS OF THE OWNER OR SOMEONE FOR WHOSE ACTS OWNER IS RESPONSIBLE

Sometimes delays are caused by the owner's inability to furnish the site to the contractor by the agreed date. Site access may depend upon the issuance of permits, or upon obtaining easements or rights of way. Sometimes delays are caused by the owner's failure to furnish owner-supplied materials to the contractor by specified dates. Delays may be caused by poor coordination by the owner or by the design professional. Some delays are caused by the necessity for correction of work caused by faulty design, or by incomplete plans and specifications. There may be delays caused by separate contractors, or by failure of the design professional to approve shop drawings, make tests, or inspections within a reasonable time. Delays may be caused by the design professional's unreasonable delay in issuing certificates, or by the owner's failure to pay progress payments despite issuance of certificates. Finally, delays almost always result from additions to the work.

(B) ACTS OF THE CONTRACTOR OR SOMEONE FOR WHOSE ACTS CONTRACTOR IS RESPONSIBLE

Sometimes delays are caused by poor planning on the part of the contractor. He may not have enough men on the site at particular times. He may have to redo work because of inferior materials, or poor construction workmanship. His supervision may be inadequate, and there may be delays caused by his subcontractors.

(C) EVENTS CHARGEABLE TO NEITHER PARTY

The contractor's performance may be delayed by events which are not the fault of himself or the owner. There may be fires, strikes, or extremely bad weather conditions. Public authorities may interfere with the work. There may be labor or material shortages which go beyond what was expected at the time the contract was made.

(D) MIXED CAUSES

Even the events under (c) often result in part from acts or failure to act on the part of owner or contractor. A substantial part of the delay for poor weather conditions may be caused by failure of the contractor to take proper preventive measures. Fires sometimes result from negligence of the contractor. Delays may be caused by acts of the contractor and the owner. The shop drawings may be submitted late, and they may not be passed upon as quickly as they should have been.

In many delay problems, the cause of the delay is not easy to trace. Some delays are caused solely, or at least principally, by the fault of one party. Many others are caused by concurrent fault. Others are not caused principally by the fault of either party, but may be due in part to the acts of one party. Allocation of risk, and responsibility for delays, must consider the complicated problems of causation.

SECTION 23.04 ALLOCATION OF RISK FOR DELAYS

If nothing is stated in the contract regarding possible disruptive events delaying performance of the contractor, the law generally places most of those risks upon the contractor. If he has agreed to perform by a specific time, he has assumed the risk of most events which delay his performance.

Even in the absence of contractual protection, the contractor might get some relief. He would not normally assume the risk of delays caused by the owner. However, even this risk may be assumed by contract. For example, an owner might be constructing an addition to an existing plant. The parties could agree in the contract that the owner could order the contractor off the site, if the owner's operation so required. This contractual assumption of risk might be held not to cover an inordinate amount of such interferences, or interferences with the contractor not made in good faith.

The contractor is likely to be excused for any delay caused by a devastating fire or a calamitous natural catastrophe. If the soil conditions were different from those reasonably anticipated by the contractor, he might receive some relief. Such relief would be given only in extreme cases of hardship, if at all.

Usually contracts contain what are sometimes called "force majeure," or acts of God, clauses. These consist of a catalog of events such as floods, tornadoes, earthquakes, strikes, fires, lockouts, etc. If these events occur and have a specified (make performance "impossible", "impracticable", substantially hamper or interfere) effect upon the performance of the contractor, then he will be excused to the extent that these acts have delayed his performance.

The result in any particular case will depend upon the language of the clause, the gravity of the event, its unforeseeability, the impact on the contractor's performance and whether the event was an assumed risk. Rains in certain parts of the country, at certain times of the year, can be quite heavy. For this reason, even rains which substantially exceed the normal expectations may be risks which are assumed by the contractor. Courts often go into the question of whether the particular risk could have been prevented by the exercise of reasonable care. The impact of the event upon the performance will be significant. For example, inclement weather may hamper the contractor's performance, and make it more expensive. However, the impact upon his efficiency may not be extreme. In such a case, he is not likely to be given relief, despite some delay caused by the reduced efficiency.

SECTION 23.05 MECHANISM FOR TIME EXTENSIONS

As has been mentioned, contracts frequently provide for a mechanism by which extensions of time can be given. The determination of whether particular events and their impact on contractor performance should justify an extension is often placed in the hands of the design professional.

The decision as to whether an extension should be given usually requires a determination of the facts and an application of these facts to the force majeure clause.

Sometimes the parties agree on the effect of excused delay. For example, if the owner orders a change, it is advisable for the parties to try to agree both upon how the change will affect the contract price, and upon the extension of time justified by the change order. If they cannot agree, the determination is usually made by the design professional. Contract clauses frequently provide that the contractor must notify the design professional, in writing, within a specified period of time after the occurrence of the event causing a delay, if the contractor intends to claim an extension of time. This notice is usually considered a condition precedent to awarding the extension. Even if the events were such as to merit an extension, failure to give notice often means that no extension of time will be given.

Some courts seem to consider conditions of notice to be technicalities. For this reason, courts, on occasion, have found a waiver of the condition. Conditions of notice do serve a useful function. They frequently inform the design professional, or owner, that persons for whom they are responsible (separate contractors, consultants) are delaying the contractor. This may be the only way in which the owner or design professional can discover that delay is occurring, providing an opportunity to take timely corrective steps. Also, claims are sometimes invented when it appears that late performance will cost the contractor money because of liquidation of damage clauses. The requirement of notice should eliminate such spurious claims by the contractor. Also, a timely notice should permit the design professional to make an evaluation of what occurred while the evidence is still reasonably obtainable, and witnesses still remember what actually happened.

If one of the parties is dissatisfied with the determination of the design professional on a delay question, often contracts give that party the right to demand arbitration. Chapter 27 discusses the role of the design professional in making decisions and Chapter 28 treats the arbitration process.

SECTION 23.06 UNEXCUSED DELAY BY CONTRACTOR: LIQUIDATED DAMAGES AND THE BETHLEHEM CASE

What remedies are available to the owner if the contractor has not met progress schedules which are included within the contract documents, or are created by the design professional in accordance with the contract documents? What if it seems reasonably clear that, without justifiable excuse, the contractor will be unable to complete the project in accordance with time requirements?

If the delay is serious, it can constitute a material breach, justifying the owner in terminating his obligations to the contractor and in ordering the contractor to cease work. Sometimes contracts specify that this can be done, and that the owner can get a replacement contractor. The owner may be given the right to order that the contractor work overtime, or put on added manpower. The owner is entitled to damages if he terminates. The damages would consist of any additional costs (including added design professional fees) incurred in obtaining a substitute contractor. In addition, the owner could recover any prospective business advantages lost because of the delay, which were reasonably foreseeable by the contractor, and any other damages directly relating to the delay which could not be avoided by reasonable efforts on the part of the owner.

What if the contractor completed the project, but without excuse, exceeded the completion date? In such a case, the owner could recover the same delay damages which he could have recovered had he terminated the contractor's performance during the course of the project. Usually, the owner deducts from the balance of the contract price an amount which will cover the damages that have occurred because of the delay, as well as damages which are likely to be incurred. The owner must be careful not to retain an excessive sum for delay damages likely to be incurred.

Establishing the economic loss caused by unexcused delay is difficult. For this reason, it is common to include contractual provisions under which the parties agree that certain types of unexcused delay will cost the contractor specified sums of money. These are usually known as "liquidation of damage clauses."

Early in American legal history, courts were suspicious of contract-created measures of recovery. Part of this suspicion was based upon a feeling that remedies were matters belonging exclusively to the courts.

Also, such clauses often set an amount of damages which would be considerably higher than the potential or actual damages. This was often the result of extreme inequality of bargaining power. To give effect to such "penalty" clauses would punish contracting parties for breaches of contract rather than providing an award of damages based upon compensation.

The courts in this early period grudgingly approved liquidated damages in some cases, but only when the clauses met at least two tests. These tests were:

1. Were the damages difficult to ascertain at the time the contract was made?
2. Was the amount agreed upon a genuine pre-estimate of the damages which might incur from the breach?

In addition, some courts required that the plaintiff show that he suffered some damage.

Modern courts seem more willing to give effect to liquidated damages clauses for unexcused delay. They realize that proving actual damages in delay cases is extremely difficult. However, the clauses must still meet the requirements that the damages be difficult to ascertain and that the amount be a genuine pre-estimate of the damages. Also, some modern courts still require that the plaintiff show that he has suffered some damage.

While the stated tests look principally at the situation which existed at the time the contract was *made* (damages difficult to ascertain and a genuine pre-estimate), some courts take into account the actual damages at the trial. If there is a large discrepancy between what appears to be the actual damage and the figure agreed at the time the contract was made, the court may find the clause invalid. In that case the plaintiff recovers his actual damages.

Courts sometimes differentiate between what they call a "penalty" and "liquidation of damages." A penalty is a sum of money which does not bear any relationship to the predictable or actual damages, arbitrarily chosen by the dominant party to the bargain to coerce performance. If the court determines that the clause in question is a penalty, it will be disregarded. In such a case, the owner will have to establish his actual damages. If the liquidated damages clause is upheld, it is applied to both parties. The owner cannot prove damages over the agreed figure, while the contractor cannot prove damages were less than the agreed figure (except to show by such evidence that the clause was not valid).

In determining enforceability, the label chosen by the parties is not conclusive. Even if the clause is labelled a penalty, it may be upheld. Calling it a clause for liquidation of damages will not give validity to the clause if it is a penalty. Sometimes, parties insert penalty-bonus clauses. This means that a contractor will receive a bonus for every day ahead of schedule he completes the project, and he will lose a specified amount of money for every day he is late. It is not necessary to tie a liquidation of damages clause to a bonus provision. It may help to persuade a court that the figure is reasonable and likely to have been bargained for on an equal basis by both the parties. Also, a clause liquidating damages will not be enforced unless it is the sole and exclusive money damage remedy. If the owner is given a choice of either suing for his actual delay damages or claiming under the liquidation of damages clause, then the clause will not be enforced. Generally, liquidation of damage clauses for delay in building contracts are enforced.

A typical case, Bethlehem Steel Corp. v. City of Chicago, is reproduced at this point to illustrate judicial attitude toward such clauses.

BETHLEHEM STEEL CORPORATION v. CITY OF CHICAGO

United States Court of Appeals, Seventh Circuit, 1965.
350 F.2d 649.

GRANT, DISTRICT JUDGE. Plaintiff-Appellant (Bethlehem) brought this action to recover an item of $52,000.00, together with certain items of interest, etc., withheld by the Defendant (City), as liquidated damages for delay in furnishing, erecting, and painting of the structural steel for a portion of the South Route Superhighway, now the "Dan Ryan Expressway", in the City of Chicago. . . . [T]he District Court concluded that Plaintiff's claims on the items in controversy should be denied and entered judgment accordingly. We agree and we affirm.

The trial court's findings included the following uncontroverted facts:

* * * * * * * * * *

"The work which Bethlehem undertook was the erection in Chicago of structural steel for a 22-span steel stringer elevated highway structure, approximately 1,815 feet long, to carry the South Route Superhighway from South Canal Street to the South Branch of the Chicago River. Bethlehem's work was preceded and followed by the work of other contractors on the same section.

"The 'Proposal and Acceptance' in the instructions to bidders required the bidders to '* * * complete * * * within the specified time the work required. * * *' Time was expressly stated to be the essence of the contract and specified provisions were made for delivery of the steel within 105 days threafter, or a total of 195 days after commencement of work, which was to be not later than 15 days from notification. The successful bidder was to submit to the Commissioner of Public Works a 'Time Schedule' for his work and if 'less than the amount * * * specified to be completed' were accomplished 'the City may declare this contract forfeited. * * *' The work had to be completed irrespective of weather conditions.

"The all important provision specifying $1,000 a day 'liquidated damages' for delay is as follows:

> 'The work under this contract covers a very important section of the South Route Superhighway, and any delay in the completion of this work will materially delay the completion of and opening of the South Route Superhighway thereby causing great inconvenience to the public, added cost of engineering and supervision, maintenance of detours, and other tangible and intangible losses. Therefore, if any work shall remain uncompleted after the time specified in the Contract Documents for the completion of the work or after any authorized extension of such stipulated time, the Contractor shall pay to the City the sum listed in the following schedule for each and every day that such work remains uncompleted, and such moneys shall be paid as liquidated damages, not a penalty, to partially cover losses and expenses to the City.
>
> 'Amount of Liquidated Damages per Day * * * $1,000.00.
>
> 'The City shall recover said liquidated damages by deducting the amount thereof out of any moneys due or that may become due the Contractor. * * *'

"Provision was made to cover delay in a contractor's starting due to preceding contractor's delay. Unavoidable delays by the contractor were also covered, and extensions therefor accordingly granted."

Bethlehem's work on this project followed the construction of the foundation and piers of the superhighway by another contractor. Bethlehem, in turn, was followed by still another contractor who constructed the deck and the roadway.

Following successive requests for extensions of its own agreed completion date, Bethlehem was granted a total of 63 days' additional time within which to perform its contract. Actual completion by Bethlehem, however, was 52 days after the extended date, which delay the City assessed at $1,000.00 per day, or a total of $52,000.00 as liquidated damages.

Bethlehem contends it is entitled to the $52,000.00 on the ground that the City actually sustained no damages. Bethlehem contends that the above-quoted provision for liquidated damages is, in fact, an invalid penalty provision. It points out that notwithstanding the fact that it admittedly was responsible for 52 days of unexcused delay in the completion of its contract, the superhighway was actually opened to the public on the date scheduled.

In other words, Bethlehem now seeks to re-write the contract and to relieve itself from the stipulated delivery dates for the purposes of liquidated damages, and to substitute therefor the City's target date for the scheduled opening of the superhighway. This the Plaintiff cannot do.

In Wise v. United States, 249 U.S. 361, 365–67, 39 S.Ct. 303, 304–05, 63 L.Ed. 647, the Supreme Court said:

> "* * * [T]he result of the modern decisions was determined to be that * * * courts will endeavor, by a construction of the agreement which the parties have made, to ascertain what their intention was when they inserted such a stipulation for payment, of a designated sum or upon a designated basis, for a breach of a covenant of their contract * * *. When that intention is clearly ascertainable from the writing, effect will be given to the provision, as freely as to any other, where the damages are uncertain in nature or amount or are difficult of ascertainment or where the amount stipulated for is not so extravagant, or disproportionate to the amount of property loss, as to show that compensation was not the object aimed at or as to imply fraud, mistake, circumvention or oppression. *There is no sound reason why persons competent and free to contract may not agree upon this subject as fully as upon any other, or why their agreement, when fairly and understandingly entered into with a view to just compensation for the anticipated loss, should not be enforced.*
>
> "* * * *The later rule, however, is to look with candor, if not with favor, upon such provisions in contracts when deliberately entered into between parties who have equality of opportunity for understanding and insisting upon their rights, as promoting prompt performance of contracts and*

> *because adjusting in advance, and amicably, matters the settlement of which through courts would often involve difficulty, uncertainty, delay and expense.* * * *
>
> "* * * It is obvious that the extent of the loss which would result to the Government from delay in performance must be uncertain and difficult to determine and it is clear that the amount stipulated for is not excessive * * *.
>
> "The parties * * * were much more competent to justly determine what the amount of damage would be, an amount necessarily largely conjectural and resting in estimate, than a court or jury would be, directed to a conclusion, as either must be, after the event, by views and testimony derived from witnesses who would be unusual to a degree if their conclusions were not, in a measure, colored and partisan." (Italics supplied.)
>
> . . . [Ed. Note: Footnotes omitted.]
>
> Affirmed.

What about delays partially caused by the owner, and partially caused by the contractor? If the clause does not apportion the loss between those delays which are not the responsibility of the contractor, and those delays which are, the entire clause will be disregarded. The courts will not make an apportionment unless the parties have done so.

There are certain interpretation questions which can arise when a liquidation of damages clause is used. Are only normal working days included, or all days? What happens if the contractor either abandons the work when he is behind schedule or past the completion time, or is ordered from the work for the same reason by the owner? One solution is to enforce the liquidation of damages clause until the project has either been abandoned by the contractor, or he has been removed from the premises. Another method is to charge those days, plus any delay caused by the hiring of a substitute contractor.

In most cases the unexcused delay will end when the owner occupies the premises. It is at this time that there is a determination of the number of days of unexcused delay. This number is multiplied by the per diem figure to give an amount of damages for the delay.

However, sometimes the owner occupies the premises, but is not able to make full use of the premises because certain portions have not yet been completed, or there are defects which develop shortly after he occupies the premises. It is not always easy to determine whether the liquidation of damages clause will be applied in such cases.

In Hungerford Const. Co. v. Florida Citrus Expo Inc., 410 F.2d 1229 (5th Cir. 1969) the contract involved a construction of an exhibition center for the citrus industry. The building was to have a concrete dome 170 feet in diameter as its roof. The roof was designed to be waterproof without independent waterproof covering. The completion time was 180 calendar days, and the liquidated damages were specified to be $200 per calendar day of delay.

The project was completed within 180 days and the owner moved into the project. However, from the beginning the roof leaked and it was necessary to do corrective work. The corrective work did not require that the owner leave the premises, but it did preclude the owner from making the premises available on a rental basis to those who might want to use it for exhibition purposes. The court referred to this use as a secondary use. Even after the corrective work, the secondary use was diminished because there was unsightly discolored plaster across the roof caused by the leaking and correction.

The court held that the liquidated damages clause would not be applied in this case. The court stated that the building was available to the owner for its primary use and that the loss of secondary use was entirely speculative. The court stated:

> One auto show may have been lost but there is no evidence as to the amount of rent which would have been realized out of this transaction or whether the loss occurred during the period in suit. The only other loss of use claimed was in the form of a daily admission charge to the public to see the building and its contents. The proof demonstrated only that this use did not rise above a suggested use. In any event, such loss of secondary use as there may have been is capable of proof. The proof that was offered was entirely disproportionate to the sum of $200.00 . . . per day. It is thus clear that the claim for liquidated damages was far in excess of such compensatory damages as would be indicated from the slight deprivation of secondary use claimed by the owner.

It would have been better in this case, and in many others, to provide two daily rates. The first would apply to periods of time during which the building cannot be occupied. The second would apply to periods of time after occupancy during which uncompleted work or corrective work make the building predictably less useful or profitable to the owner.

Usually, the owner can deduct liquidated damages from final payment. It is best to specify not only that the contractor will pay a specified amount per day, but also that the owner will have a right to deduct this amount from the final payment. If the liquidated damages amount exceeds the retainage, or if the owner does not deduct the liquidated damages from the retainage, the owner will have to sue the contractor for the damages. If, for any reason, the liquidated damages are not to be set off against the final payment, the owner should make it clear when he makes the final payment that he is not thereby waiving any claim for delay damages which he would have under the terms of the contract.

SECTION 23.07 UNEXCUSED DELAY BY OWNER

What if the contractor is delayed unjustifiably in his performance by the owner, or someone for whom the owner is responsible? If the acts causing the delay are serious, the contractor may terminate further performance. The acts of the owner, or someone for whom he is responsible, may increase the contractor's cost of performance. He may have men who are unable to work, machinery he has rented that he is unable to use and other expenses caused by the owner's acts. (Delay in making progress payments will be treated in § 24.03(k).)

Even if the contractor is entitled to stop performance, he generally continues performance, requests a time extension, and sometimes asks for delay damages. He should be given a time extension if he complies with formal requirements. Whether he can also obtain delay damages depends upon a number of considerations.

Some courts have held that the inclusion of a provision giving him an extension of time where he is delayed by unexcused acts of the owner means that he is giving up his right to delay damages. The mere fact that he is given the right to an extension should not mean that he is thereby giving up his right to delay damages. Even an asked for, and accepted, extension should not operate as a waiver of delay damages.

AIA Doc. A201 at 8.3.4 provides that the contractor will be entitled to delay damages, even if he obtains an extension of time.

Some private contracts contain "no damage clauses." Under such clauses a contractor is not entitled to delay damages, and can obtain only an extension of time where he is delayed by unexcused acts of the owner. Where such clauses are a part of the contract, they are generally given effect. But because the effect of such clauses is to force a contractor to absorb losses caused by the conduct of the owner, they are interpreted narrowly. For example, it may be possible to hold that the particular cause of the delay did not come within the ambit of the clause, or to hold that such clauses protect the owner only when he is not negligent, or when he has operated in good faith.

Public contracts raise more obstacles to the contractor who attempts to collect delay damages. He is more likely to be met by a "no damage" clause. Since delay damages increase the total cost of the project, he may also face the hurdle of an insufficient appropriation, or public revenue bonds which are inadequate to cover the delay damages.

In federal public contracts, a rule developed which tended to preclude delay damage claims, but inroads have been made into this rule. A federal contractor may recover for delay damages if the federal contracting agency was negligent, or, as is common, the construction contract contains a "suspension of the work clause". Under such a clause the contractor is entitled to both delay damages and an extension of time when the government suspends the work.

Where the contractor can overcome the obstacles of "no damage clauses", he can recover only for the damages which were caused by the delay. He must also establish, with reasonable certainty, the amount of the loss. Finally, the owner will have a defense if he can show that the loss claimed could have been avoided if the contractor had taken reasonable steps.

SECTION 23.08 THE BLOOMFIELD CASE: A TYPICAL DELAY CASE

BLOOMFIELD REORGANIZED SCHOOL DISTRICT v. E. M. STITES

Supreme Court of Missouri. 1960.
336 S.W.2d 95.

BARRETT, COMMISSIONER. In 1955 the appellant, E. M. Stites, and the respondent, Reorganized School District R–6 of Stoddard County, entered into a contract in which Stites agreed to construct a combination gymnasium-music building in Bloomfield for the price of $276,-247. . . .

In substance the trial court found that the district was entitled to the possession of the building as of July 24, 1957, that Stites had breached the contract in that he had failed to complete the building within the time provided in the contract and therefore the district was entitled to $7,000 liquidated damages. . . .

One issue with some bearing on several matters is the effective date of the contract. The contract provided that the building was to be "substantially completed" in 395 calendar days; it is dated August 8, 1955, and so the district contends that the contract period elapsed and that liquidated damages accrued from and after September 6, 1956. The contract, however, was mailed to Stites by the architect on August 17, 1955, it was signed by Stites and then delivered by him to the school superintendent for execution by the board. The superintendent mailed the executed contracts to the architect in St. Louis September 14 and on September 21 the architect mailed an executed copy to Stites who received it on either September 22 or 23. The superintendent in transmitting the contracts admonished the architect, Lorenz, to not deliver the contracts until Stites delivered his "performance bond," and although Stites delayed sending his bond and certificate of insurance he wrote Lorenz on September 15 asking for a "proceed order." In sending a copy of the contract Lorenz wrote Stites two letters on the same day, the second one correcting his first statement that the 395 calendar days would run from September 21,

1955. On his part Stites ordered 9000 bags of cement for the Bloomfield school, August 15, 1955, but did not actually start the initial work of grading and hauling dirt until October 3, 1955. In these circumstances Stites argues that the contract was not "operative" until September 22 or 23 when as he says "the last act necessary for its completion was performed." 1 Restatement, Contracts, Sec. 74.

The chief difficulty with his position is that all these matters are outside the contract terms; this contract does not contain a provision for a "work order," and its date was not left blank to be filled in upon signing. When signed by the parties this contract unambiguously said, "This Agreement made the *eighth* day of *August* in the year Nineteen Hundred and *fifty-five*" (the italicized words being typed into the contract) and there was then no objection to the date or suggestion that it be changed. Furthermore, in Article 2 it was provided that the work to be performed under the contract "shall be commenced *immediately*" and "shall be substantially completed *in three hundred and ninety-five calendar days*." In these circumstances, the parties having elected that their mutual rights and obligations are to be determined according to the letter of the contract, its effective date was August 8, 1955. "It is of first importance that a contract shall have definitely ascertainable dates of commencement and termination. To that end, those dates should be determinable from the recitations in the contract itself; there should be no room for conjecture or speculation. If, however, the intent of the parties becomes material, it should be gathered from the language of the contract and resort to extraneous facts is justified only if the contract itself creates a patent ambiguity, * * * Obedient to that rule, the courts have generally construed contracts to run from the date they bear and not from the date of delivery." Greer v. Stanolind Oil & Gas Co., 10 Cir., 200 F.2d 920, 922.

One of the substantial, controverted issues upon this appeal is "liquidated damages." Article 2, after providing that the work was to be commenced immediately and substantially completed in 395 days, that the date of beginning, rate of progress and time for completion were "essential conditions" also contained this provision which was also typed into the printed form: "If the said Contractor shall neglect, fail or refuse to complete the work within the time herein specified, then the said Contractor does hereby agree, as a part consideration of the awarding of this contract, to pay to the Owner the sum of $50.00, not as a penalty but as liquidated damages for such breach of contract as hereinafter set forth for each and every calendar day that the Contractor shall be in default after the time stipulated in the Contract for completing the work, not including Sundays." As indicated, the effective date of the contract was August 8, 1955, and its completion date September 8, 1956. 685 days later, June 24, 1957, 290 days beyond the promised completion date, "the work," admittedly, was not "complete." Pursuant to the quoted provision of the contract and beginning with the contractor's estimates submitted after September 8, 1956, the school board deducted $50 a day from its payments to Stites, withholding as liquidated damages, according to the court, the sum of $10,300. In this connection the court found, without explanation, that the contractor was liable to the district for liquidated damages in the sum of $7000 although the contract according to these figures was 290 days in default. But the district has not appealed and unless for some reason the contractor is entitled to a reduction in that item or unless the contract provision is invalid the sum found due by the court has finally determined the matter.

The contractor contends that the contract provision is not one for liquidated damages as the contract recites but instead is a penalty provision and therefore invalid. If the provision is valid the contractor contends that the school district finally elected to terminate the contract and therefore could not also pursue the remedy of collecting liquidated damages. It is his position, furthermore, that any delays in completion of the work were "excusable" delays under the contract or were delays caused and brought about by the district or its architect, Lorenz, and therefore he is entitled to credit on the liquidated damages claim for the excusable delays, which, according to him, is the entire period

. . . [I]n this particular contract between these particular parties and in the circumstances of this case, the liquidated damage provision is valid and enforceable and the amount provided is not unreasonably disproportionate to the "actual injury suffered." . . . And also in this connection, the district's claim and assertion of liquidated damages as of September 8, 1956, under Article 2 of the contract did not constitute an election of remedies and prevent the district's termination of the contract 290 days later. East Arkansas Lumber Co. v. Swink, 128 Ark. 240, 194 S.W. 5. Upon this subject Article 18 of the specifications provides that "This article does not exclude the recovery of damages for delay by either party under other provisions in the contract documents."

Mr. Stites testified that there were delays due to a cement and steel shortage and to the weather, over which neither party had any control. He claimed that there were numerous delays attributable to the misconduct of the architect: denial of permission to fabricate his own steel, delay in approving various shop drawings, delay in furnishing a paint schedule, delay in supplying information as to light fixtures, refusal to answer inquiries as to two stairways and, in short, just about every item in the plans and specifications. Some of these matters for which Stites claims credit were not specifically covered by the contract . . . the architect was not obligated under the contract to furnish some of the information and as to some of the items the architect was inexcusably dilatory and some of the matters were not a substantial cause of failure to complete within the specified time. Gillioz v. Missouri State Highway Commission, supra. On the other hand, Mr. Stites was often exasperatingly dilatory and his testimony as to several matters is not too convincing. One item over which there was the greatest controversy was whether Stites could fabricate his own steel, particularly for the most important structural part of the building, the steel trusses. The matter was not specifically covered in the contract, Mr. Lorenz first denied and then granted permission subject to certain conditions. Mr. Stites was most uncooperative as to the conditions but in the end the fabrication in process was inspected by professional testers, the trusses were likewise inspected and their installation was entirely satisfactory and so this one item illustrates the useless bickering and waste of time. . . .

Also typed into Article 2 of the contract, however, was this sentence: "Extensions of time will be granted for delays beyond the control of the Contractor." Stites seizes upon this sentence and urges that extensions of time for these various delays, especially those beyond his control, were automatic and excused his own delicts and prevented the application of the liquidated damages provision. In so arguing he again contends that the typewritten sentence prevails over all other provisions, particularly over Article 18. But Article 18 of the general plans and specifications plainly covers the subject of delays and extensions, particularly delays "beyond the Contractor's control" or due to the "neglect of the Owner or the Architect." In a separate paragraph this article plainly states that "No such extension shall be made for delay occurring more than seven days before claim therefor is made in writing to the Architect. In the case of a continuing cause of delay, only one claim is necessary." As with liquidated damages and election of remedies, there is no irreconcilable conflict in Article 2 of the contract and Article 18 of the specifications, and they are to be construed together with respect to delays and extensions of time as well as with respect to other relevant subjects. . . . From their mere recitation it is obvious that the several claims of delay were not "continuing" in character and Mr. Stites, admittedly, made no attempt to comply with this contract provision. On September 27, 1956, nineteen days after the agreed completion date, he did write the school board a letter in which he asked for an extension of 120 days stating that there had been delays beyond his control consisting in the delivery of cement from August 15, 1955, to November 14, 1955; "indefinite delivery of steel," 45 days delay in progress in January and February due to cold weather, and delay of door frames and hardware,—he said that "some of the hardware has not been delivered yet." All of these listed delays had occurred in the past, not "seven days before claim therefor is made," and they extended far beyond 120 days both before and after the request. There was no reply to this letter and there was no other request for an extension of time and the architect did not grant an extension. While the contractual provision, Article 18, may have been intended for the contractor's benefit, he did not comply with it and he is therefore not to be excused for the delays. . . .

Unfortunately, the figures do not add up in the *Bloomfield* case. According to the Supreme Court of Missouri, the contractor was 290 days late. At fifty dollars a day, the school district would have been entitled to $14,500 as delay damages. Yet the Court noted that the amount deducted by the school district was $10,300. Perhaps this amount was used before the exact number of days of unexcused delay became known. In any event, the trial court had found that the contractor owed the school district $7,000. The Supreme Court noted that the school district did not appeal from this determination and it, the Supreme Court, would not go into the variance in amounts.

Perhaps this explains the rather harsh holding of the court on when the time period for completion would commence. If the contractor had been sustained in his contention that the time period should not begin until September 22, there would have been a reduction in the unexcused delay of approximately 45 days. This would have reduced the amount owed by the contractor to the school district by $2250. This amount was less than the unexplained $3300 difference in the award made by the trial court. However, this is merely speculation.

What would have happened had the contractor appeared at the site after he signed the contract and returned it to the school district, but before the school district had signed the contract? Undoubtedly, the school officials would have expelled him from the site until they had signed the contract. Also, what would have happened had the contractor incurred large expenses after he signed the contract, but before it had been signed by the school district? He did order 9,000 bags of cement for the job. If the school district had decided not to enter into the contract because the contractor did not deliver a performance bond, would the contractor have had any claim against the school district for losses he might have suffered by procuring goods or making other commitments? It is likely that he would not.

It can be seen, then, that the time for performance may have commenced on August 8, but neither party was bound to perform until the school district signed the agreement. The only way out of this possible paradoxical result is to hold that the parties had made a binding contract before either party had signed the written agreement and that the signatures were merely confirmation of an already formed contract. It is not likely that either party thought this was the case.

REVIEW QUESTIONS

1. In the absence of contractual provisions relieving the contractor, who assumes the risk of most events which delay the contractor?

2. What are the requirements for a valid liquidated damages clause?

3. What effect does the creation of a valid liquidated damages clause have upon the recovery of delay damages?

4. What is a "no damage clause"?

QUESTIONS FOR CLASS DISCUSSION

1. Why is delay treated differently from other breaches?

2. Should the law enforce a liquidated damages clause? Explain.

3. Why not enforce a penalty clause?

4. Under what circumstances, if any, should a contractor be granted a time extension if he fails to comply with a provision which requires him to give notice of an intention to present such a claim?

PROBLEM

C and O contract for C's construction of a five story office building for $500,000. The completion date is December 1. The contract provides that for every day of unexcused delay C shall be chargeable with liquidated damages of $3000 a day. The building was completed 20 days late, and the delay was not excused by any events set forth in the force majeure clause. What can O recover for the delay? What added facts would be helpful in answering this question?

Suppose the agreed damage figure had been $1000 a day, and C abandoned the project on December 30. O obtained a replacement who completed the project 25 days later. The substitute contractor cost $60,000 over the contract price. What can O collect from C?

Chapter 24
PAYMENT PROBLEMS

SECTION 24.01 RELATIONSHIP TO MATERIAL DISCUSSED PREVIOUSLY

Payment problems are intertwined with much of the material already discussed in this treatise. Interpretation problems (Chapters 19 and 20), changes (Chapter 21), subsurface problems (Chapter 22) and delays (Chapter 23) relate to if, when and how much the contractor is entitled to be paid for his work. Chapter 24 emphasizes payment for the labor and materials incorporated into the project, the mechanism by which payment is made and remedies for nonpayment.

SECTION 24.02 PAYMENT FOR WORK DESPITE NONCOMPLIANCE

In Chapters 19 and 20 reference was made to the performance obligations of a contractor. This section examines whether the contractor can collect for his work when he has not performed strictly in accordance with his contract obligations.

(A) THE DOCTRINE OF CONDITIONS

A condition is a fact which must occur or be excused before a promise to perform matures. Conditions may be expressed in the contract, implied from the acts of the parties or created by law.

In the construction contract, the promise by the owner to pay is usually conditioned upon the contractor complying with all the contract obligations. Unless the owner, or someone for whose acts the owner is chargeable, excuses this condition, or unless there are provisions for progress payments (See § 24.03), the doctrine of conditions permits the owner to refuse to pay until the contractor has performed all his obligations.

The doctrine of conditions, if strictly applied, helps the owner get what he bargained for under the contract. The legal right not to pay until the contractor performs is a strong weapon to obtain promised performance.

However, in all contracts, and especially construction contracts, strict application of the doctrine of conditions can cause hardship to the contractor. If he is not paid for what he has done, the contractor may suffer a loss which is disproportionate to the economic loss occasioned by his nonperformance. In addition, such a result can unjustly enrich the owner since he, as a rule, is occupying the structure. To strike some balance between the interest of the owner in getting what he bargained for, and the interest of the contractor in not being unduly penalized for nonperformance, the law has fashioned a number of devices.

(B) SUBSTANTIAL PERFORMANCE: PLANTE v. JACOBS

Absolute compliance in a construction contract is unusual. Contract documents are often very detailed, and there is usually some deviation during the performance. The prime contractor, to a large degree, relies upon work performed by subcontractors. Ambiguities in the contract agreements frequently crop up, and it is difficult to get an authorized interpretation. It is often difficult to find someone with authority to make a change or approve "equal" or "equivalent" material.

One of the principal devices developed by the law to protect a contractor from being unpaid for work despite minor deviations is the doctrine of "substantial performance." Successful application of this doctrine permits the contractor to collect, despite minor deviation from the plans and specifications. The deviation must not be "willful" or "intentional," although these requirements are not applied rigorously by the courts. Kirk Reid Co. v. Fine, 205 Va. 778, 139 S.E.2d 829 (1965) involved the installation of an air conditioning system. The major deviations were:

1. the system was 46 to 50 tons short in capacity
2. the primary air unit was of a lower rating by 7850 cubic feet per minute
3. the condenser water pump was 120 gallons per minute short of capacity.

The contractor attempted to collect some $14,000 left unpaid under the contract. The owner claimed $75,000 damages. The court held that the owner's damages were $24,000, based upon the difference in value of the work as built and as it should have been built. But it allowed the contractor to collect the $14,000 balance. The Court used substantial performance, despite the finding that the deviation had occurred knowingly.

Usually the issue of substantiality of performance arises when the project is essentially completed, the owner occupies the building, and minor deviations from contract requirements become evident. The contractor demands the unpaid balance of the contract price, and the owner defends by asserting he need not pay until every deviation is eliminated.

The leading case applying this doctrine, Jacob and Youngs v. Kent, 230 N.Y. 239, 129 N.E. 889 (1921), involved installation of one brand of pipe, when another was called for in the contract. The court held that the contractor had substantially performed.

Another case illustrative of this doctrine involved the construction of a church. In this case, Pinches v. Swedish Evangelical Lutheran Church, 55 Conn. 183, 10 A. 264 (1887), the deviation consisted of a two-foot lower ceiling, windows which were shorter and narrower than called for, and seats narrower than designated by the specifications. The court held that the contractor had substantially performed.

The question of whether there has been substantial performance cannot be reduced to mathematical certainty. Some courts compare the cost of making the work conform to the total contract price, to determine percentage of completion. The greater the percentage of non-completion, the less likely it is that there has been substantial performance. In evaluating the desirability of considering such a ratio as the measurement standard, it may be useful to keep in mind that the amount in question is usually the final payment. Except in the case of a very small construction project, most of the contract price has been paid by progress payments by the time the dispute over substantial performance arises. If, as suggested by some, 10 percent is a proper cut off, the contractor would always get the balance if the final payment did not exceed 10 percent. A more useful standard takes the ratio of cost of correction to total contract price into account, but places a greater emphasis upon the particular nature of the defect or deviation, and how it affects the basic purpose of the project.

For example, if specifications state that a machine is to turn out 1,000 units per hour, a manufacturer who builds a machine which turns out 900 units probably has substantially performed. But, if the assembly line upon which the machine was to be located was geared to take 1,000 units, and it would not be economical to handle 900 units, it is likely that 900 would not be substantial performance.

Suppose the plans for an apartment building called for bedrooms which were 10 x 13 feet. If the contractor constructed rooms which were 10 x 12′ 9″ it is likely that he has substantially performed. See Plante v. Jacobs, reproduced later in this subsection.

Generally, the smaller the degree of deviation, the more likely there has been substantial performance. But even a small degree of deviation could result in a finding that there has been no substantial performance. Suppose an air conditioning system in a humid climate would bring the temperature down to 72° rather than the specified 70°? If this deviation would seriously hamper the use of the building for its intended purposes, the doctrine of substantial performance would not be available for such a relatively slight deviation.

Kirk Reid Co. v. Fine, discussed earlier in this section, involved the installation of an air conditioning system. In holding that the contractor had substantially performed, the Court stated:

> It appears from the . . . finding that "there was a workable air conditioning plant installed and operating

by May 1, 1959," the time called for by the contract. It further appears from the record that the system so installed and operating has been used, since that time, by the defendant without complaint by him that it is insufficient to perform its task.

Deviations which relate to aesthetics rather than function, health, or safety are more likely to permit the use of the substantial performance doctrine. Summing up, the owner must receive, in essence, the bargained-for performance.

While some cases have held that the doctrine cannot be used where there is an express condition of strict compliance, the doctrine is applied in most construction cases.

The application of the doctrine of substantial performance gives the contractor a right to the contract price balance, but the owner can set off any damages caused by the contractor's failure to perform in accordance with the contract documents. If the corrective work would not be extensive, the owner will be entitled to deduct the cost of correction. If the defective work cannot be corrected except by the expenditure of large amounts of money out of proportion to the difference in value between the work as done and the work as it should have been done, such as in the *Jacobs* or *Pinches* cases, the court will use the difference in value as the measure for the owner's set-off. The court would determine what the structure is worth as built, and what the structure would have been worth, had it been built in accordance with the contract. The difference between these two figures would be the amount of money which could be deducted by the owner from the balance of the contract price. Often the difference in measure of recovery will produce a very small damage amount, or none at all.

The contractor is given some leeway in his performance, to enable him to collect the full contract price. However, the doctrine of substantial performance is designed to avoid forfeiture, and not to relieve the contractor from all responsibility for his defaults.

Plante v. Jacobs, reproduced at this point, illustrates the substantial performance doctrine and the judicial attitude toward minor deviations.

PLANTE v. JACOBS

Supreme Court of Wisconsin, 1960.
10 Wis.2d 567, 103 N.W.2d 296.

Suit to establish a lien to recover the unpaid balance of the contract price plus extras of building a house for the defendants, Frank M. and Carol H. Jacobs, who in their answer allege no substantial performance and breach of the contract by the plaintiff and counterclaim for damages due to faulty workmanship and incomplete construction. . . . After a trial to the court, judgment was entered for the plaintiff in the amount of $4,152.90 plus interest and costs, from which the defendants, Jacobs, appealed and the plaintiff petitioned for a review. . . .

The Jacobs, on or about January 6, 1956, entered into a written contract with the plaintiff to furnish the materials and construct a house upon their lot in Brookfield, Waukesha county, in accordance with plans and specifications, for the sum of $26,765. During the course of construction the plaintiff was paid $20,000. Disputes arose between the parties, the defendants refused to continue payment, and the plaintiff did not complete the house. On January 12, 1957, the plaintiff duly filed his lien.

The trial court found the contract was substantially performed and was modified in respect to lengthening the house two feet and the reasonable value of this extra was $960. The court disallowed extras amounting to $1,748.92 claimed by the plaintiff because they were not agreed upon in writing in accordance with the terms of the agreement. In respect to defective workmanship the court allowed the cost of repairing the following items: $1,550 for the patio wall; $100 for the patio floor; $300 for cracks in the ceiling of the living room and kitchen; and $20.15 credit balance for hardware. The court also found the defendants were not damaged by the misplacement of a wall between the kitchen and the living room, and the other items of defective workmanship and incompleteness were not proven. The amount of these credits allowed the defendants was deducted from the gross amount found owing the plaintiff, and the judgment was entered for the difference and made a lien on the premises. . . .

HALLOWS, JUSTICE. The defendants argue the plaintiff cannot recover any amount because he has failed to substantially perform the contract. The plaintiff conceded he failed to furnish the kitchen cabinets, gutters and downspouts, sidewalk, closet clothes poles, and entrance seat amounting to $1,601.95. This amount was allowed to the defendants. The defendants claim some 20 other items of incomplete or faulty performance by the plaintiff and no substantial performance because the cost of completing the house in strict compliance with the plans and specifications would amount to 25 or 30 per cent of the contract price. The defendants especially stress the misplacing of the wall between the living room and the kitchen, which narrowed the living room in excess of one foot. The cost of tearing down this wall and rebuilding it would be approximately $4,000. The record is not clear why and when this wall was misplaced, but the wall is completely built and the house decorated and the defendants are living therein. Real estate experts testified that the smaller width of the living room would not affect the market price of the house.

The defendants rely on Manitowoc Steam Boiler Works v. Manitowoc Glue Co., 1903, 120 Wis. 1, 97 N.W. 515, for the proposition there can be no recovery on the contract . . . unless there is substantial performance. This is undoubtedly the correct rule at common law. . . . The question here is whether there has been substantial performance. The test of what amounts to substantial performance seems to be whether the performance meets the essential purpose of the contract. In the Manitowoc case the contract called for a boiler having a capacity of 150 per cent of the existing boiler. The court held there was no substantial performance because the boiler furnished had a capacity of only 82 per cent of the old boiler and only approximately one-half of the boiler capacity contemplated by the contract. In Houlahan v. Clark, 1901, 110 Wis. 43, 85 N.W. 676, the contract provided the plaintiff was to drive pilings in the lake and place a boat house thereon parallel and in line with a neighbor's dock. This was not done and the contractor so positioned the boat house that it was practically useless to the owner. Manthey v. Stock, 1907, 133 Wis. 107, 113 N.W. 443, involved a contract to paint a house and to do a good job, including the removal of the old paint where necessary. The plaintiff did not remove the old paint, and blistering and roughness of the new paint resulted. The court held that the plaintiff failed to show substantial performance. The defendants also cite Manning v. School District No. 6, 1905, 124 Wis. 84, 102 N.W. 356. However, this case involved a contract to install a heating and ventilating plant in the school building which would meet certain tests which the heating apparatus failed to do. The heating plant was practically a total failure to accomplish the purposes of the contract. See also Nees v. Weaver, 1936, 222 Wis. 492, 269 N.W. 266, 107 A.L.R. 1405 (roof on a garage).

Substantial performance as applied to construction of a house does not mean that every detail must be in strict compliance with the specifications and the plans. Something less than perfection is the test of specific performance unless all details are made the essence of the contract. This was not done here. There may be situations in which features or details of construction of special or of great personal importance, which if not performed, would prevent a finding of substantial performance of the contract. In this case the plan was a stock floor plan. No detailed construction of the house was shown on the plan. There were no blueprints. The specifications were standard printed forms with some modifications and additions written in by the parties. Many of the problems that arose during the construction had to be solved on the basis of practical experience. No mathematical rule relating to the percentage of the price, of cost of completion or of completeness can be laid down to determine substantial performance of a building contract. Although the defendants received a house with which they are dissatisfied in many respects, the trial court was not in error in finding the contract was substantially performed.

The next question is what is the amount of recovery when the plaintiff has substantially, but incompletely, performed. For substantial performance the plaintiff should recover the contract price less the damages caused the defendant by the incomplete performance. Both parties agree. Venzke v. Magdanz, 1943, 243 Wis. 155, 9 N.W.2d 604, states the correct rule for damages due to faulty construction amounting to such incomplete performance, which is the difference between the value of the house as it stands with faulty and incomplete construction and the value of the house if it had been constructed in strict accordance with the plans and specifications. This is the diminished-value rule. The cost of replacement or repair is not the measure of such damage, but is an element to take into consideration in arriving at value under some circumstances. The cost of replacement or the cost to make whole the omissions may equal or be less than the difference in value in some cases and, likewise, the cost to rectify a defect may greatly exceed the added value to the structure as corrected. The defendants argue that under the Venzke rule their damages are $10,000. The plaintiff on review argues the defendants' damages are only $650. Both parties agree the trial court applied the wrong rule to the facts.

The trial court applied the cost-of-repair or replacement rule as to several items, relying on Stern v. Schlafer, 1943, 244 Wis. 183, 11 N.W.2d 640, 12 N.W.2d 678, wherein it was stated that when there are a number of small items of defect or omission which can be remedied without the reconstruction of a substantial part of the building or a great sacrifice of work or material already wrought in the building, the reasonable cost of correcting the defect should be allowed. However, in Mohs v. Quarton, 1950, 257 Wis. 544, 44 N.W.2d 580, the court held when the separation of defects would lead to confusion, the rule of diminished value could apply to all defects.

In this case no such confusion arises in separating the defects. The trial court disallowed certain claimed defects because they were not proven. This finding was not against the great weight and clear preponderance of the evidence and will not be disturbed on appeal. Of the remaining defects claimed by the defendants, the court allowed the cost of replacement or repair except as to the misplacement of the living-room wall. Whether a defect should fall under the cost-of-replacement rule or be considered under the diminished-value rule depends upon the nature and magnitude of the defect. This court has not allowed items of such magnitude under the cost-of-repair rule as the trial court did. Viewing the construction of the house as a whole and its cost we cannot say, however, that the trial court was in error in allowing the cost of repairing the plaster cracks in the ceilings, the cost of mud jacking and repairing the patio floor, and the cost of reconstructing the non-weight-bearing and nonstructural patio wall. Such reconstruction did not involve an unreasonable economic waste.

The item of misplacing the living room wall under the facts of this case was clearly under the diminished-value rule. There is no evidence that defendants requested or demanded the replacement of the wall in the place called for by the specifications during the course of construction. To tear down the wall now and rebuild it in its proper place would involve a substantial destruction of the work, if not all of it, which was put into the wall and would cause additional damage to other parts of the house and require replastering and redecorating the walls and ceilings of at least two rooms. Such economic waste is unreasonable and unjustified. The rule of diminished value contemplates the wall is not going to be moved. Expert witnesses for both parties, testifying as to the value of the house, agreed that the misplacement of the wall had no effect on the market price. The trial court properly found that the defendants suffered no legal damage, although the defendants' particular desire for specified room size was not satisfied. . . .

On review the plaintiff raises two questions: Whether he should have been allowed compensation for the disallowed extras, and whether the cost of reconstructing the patio wall was proper. The trial court was not in error in disallowing the claimed extras. None of them was agreed to in writing as provided by the contract, and the evidence is conflicting whether some were in fact extras or that the defendants waived the applicable requirements of the contract. The plaintiff had the burden of proof on these items. The second question raised by the plaintiff has already been disposed of in considering the cost-of-replacement rule.

It would unduly prolong this opinion to detail and discuss all the disputed items of defects of workmanship or omissions. We have reviewed the entire record and considered the points of law raised and believe the findings are supported by the great weight and clear preponderance of the evidence and the law properly applied to the facts.

Judgment affirmed.

(C) DIVISIBILITY

Suppose there is a construction project with five well-defined stages and designated payments for each stage. What if the contractor completes three stages, but does not complete the remaining two stages? Sometimes contractors contend that they should be paid for the stages they have completed, because the project is divided into five separate contracts. The owner can take a deduction for damages caused by the failure to perform the last two stages.

This does not succeed often in construction contracts because, as a rule, the payments of portions for designated stages of the work are generally rough approximations, and not intended to be agreed figures for each stage. If the payments are clearly agreed equivalents for the clearly set-forth stages, then the contractor should be able to apply the divisibility doctrine.

(D) QUASI-CONTRACT

Another concept applied to avoid forfeiture and prevent unjust enrichment is quasi-contract. What if the contractor has stopped work, without legal justification, after part performance? He has not gone far enough to use substantial performance, but he wants to be paid for what he has done.

The law traditionally has not been sympathetic to defaulting parties. Many cases have held that the party in substantial default could not collect for work performed. However, there has been some relaxation of this harsh doctrine. Some contractors have been able to recover in quasi-contract, despite their own breach, in order to avoid unjust enrichment to the other party. For example, suppose that the contract involves a structure which is to cost $100,000. Without proper justification, the contractor walks off the job during the middle of construction. The defaulting contractor has already been paid $20,000, and the replacement contractor finishes the work for $75,000. In this unlikely situation, the defaulting contractor should have the right to recover $5,000. Without the original contractor being given this right, the owner would get his structure for $95,000. The defaulting contractor's performance benefitted the owner to the extent of $25,000, and he has paid only $20,000.

Such cases are relatively rare, because contractors who default have usually spent a good deal more money than they expected, and are usually involved in a losing contract. Also, replacement contractors almost inevitably cost the owner a greater total than the project would have cost him had the first contractor finished the work. But, in the unlikely event that the work of the contractor who is in default has created a benefit to the owner in excess of what the defaulting contractor has been paid, the contractor in default should recover this excess. The owner should not be put in a better position than he would have been had there been completion in accordance with the contract by the original contractor.

(E) WAIVER

Contractors sometimes use the theory of "waiver" to justify a claim for payment of the unpaid balance of the contract price, when they have not fully performed. When the owner asserts noncompliance, the contractor may assert that the owner has, by expressed words, or by acts, "waived" exact compliance with the contract.

Waiver is often defined as an intentional relinquishment of a known right. It may be based upon a manifestation by the owner (or someone with authority to bind the owner) that the owner will pay the full contract price, despite certain designated noncompliances with contract obligations. For example, suppose the contractor requests permission to deviate in some way from the contract specifications during the course of performance. He may request, for example, that he be permitted to substitute a different floor covering, or different light fixtures. If he indicates that he proposes to do this, and the owner acquiesces, either expressly or by acts which indicate acquiescence, the owner will have to pay, despite noncompliance with the original contract, once the contractor has relied by making the substitution.

It would be possible to classify such an arrangement as a contract modification. If so, the normal requirements for contract modification would have to be met. In the case of a substitution, there is rarely a problem (See § 19.01(h)).

If the new arrangement consists of the owner promising to pay the full contract price despite an omission as opposed to a substitution, there could be a consideration question. The owner is giving up something without getting anything for it, other than what he was entitled to receive under the contract. It is for this reason that courts often call such an arrangement a waiver, which often avoids a necessity of finding consideration.

Waiver, unlike modification, can be retracted. For example, if the owner changes his mind before the contractor has relied, the owner is usually permitted to revive the original obligation.

Such an arrangement could be classified as a change. While changes usually involve decisions by the owner to change the work in some way, it is possible to classify a change made at the request of a contractor as falling within any changes clause in the contract. If so, the requirements for a change, such as requisite authority and proper formality, would have to be met. Again, it is often easier to classify this type of transaction as a waiver and avoid the requirements for a change.

Waiver questions are more difficult when the owner's act rather than an *express* statement of waiver is the basis for the waiver. An express waiver would be the owner stating "You may make the substitution or leave out certain required work and I will still pay." A waiver can consist of an act by the owner which reasonably leads the contractor to believe that the owner will pay, despite noncompliance with the contract. For example, the owner might observe the contractor deviating, and make no objection. Suppose it is apparent to the contractor that the owner knows that there is a deviation. The contractor may reasonably believe that not objecting to the deviation manifested a willingness by the owner to go along with the deviation, and waive certain contract rights. The important question is whether the contractor can reasonably believe that the owner is going along with the substitution or omission.

With the exception of waiver by making a progress payment (to be discussed in § 24.03(k)), generally waivers during performance of the work are predicated upon "estoppel" or "justifiable reliance." The law will not permit the owner to go back on his word when the contractor has justifiably relied.

Waivers are often predicated upon an act of statement of the owner *after* the deviation from the contract obligation occurred. For example, if the owner inspects the work during the project or after its completion, and indicates either that he is satisfied with the work despite the deviation or raises no objection to an obvious deviation, it is likely that the owner has waived strict compliance with the contract provisions. Finding a waiver in such a case is not based upon reliance. Instead a waiver is given effect because the law permits the owner to give up relatively minor contract obligations if he so desires, without the necessity of showing reliance by the contractor.

There have been cases where the courts have not given effect to a waiver unless there has been justifiable reliance. However, if the evidence of the waiver is relatively clear, such as the owner stating that he is satisfied and will pay despite a minor deviation, it is likely that most courts would hold that the owner has waived full compliance with the contract obligation. When the owner's waiver is predicated upon acts, it is more difficult to find waiver, because acts are often ambiguous and do not clearly manifest to the contractor that the owner will pay despite noncompliance.

Two other criteria often determine whether a court will find that the owner has waived defects in the contractor's performance. The longer the delay between the asserted waiver and the attempted retraction of the waiver, the more likely it is that the court will find that there has been a waiver. Secondly, the more trivial the deviation or the nonperformance, the more likely it is that there has been a waiver. For example, if the contractor attempted to assert that the owner had "waived" one story of a five story building, it is unlikely that the court would give effect to the waiver claim.

For a discussion of waiver of defects not included in a final list of defects, see § 24.04.

Waiver differs from substantial performance in one important aspect. Substantial performance entitles the contractor to the balance of the contract price, less what his deviation has cost the owner, either measured by cost of correction or diminished value. If a waiver is found, the contractor is entitled to the full contract price, without deductions.

SECTION 24.03 PROGRESS PAYMENTS

(A) FUNCTION

Bilateral contracts which involve performance of services and payment, usually require that the work be performed before there is any obligation to pay. Such a rule can operate harshly in most construction contracts. Most contractors cannot afford to erect the entire structure before they are paid any money. Unless he can borrow, the contractor must be paid as he goes along. Also, non-payment until completion would place a substantial risk on the contractor that he would not be paid.

Ordinarily, construction contracts contain provisions under which the contractor is entitled to progress payments to be made at specific time or performance intervals. Without such provisions, the contractor would not be entitled to payment until he had substantially performed.

(B) APPLICATION FOR CERTIFICATE

Usually, the contractor makes an application for progress payment a certain number of days before payment is due, or upon completion of certain stages of the work. He usually must accompany the application with his estimate of what amount is due, and how it has been computed. Also, he may be required to submit evidence which will show that no liens will be filed by subcontractors and suppliers. See § 24.07.

The application is usually submitted to the design professional, or to the construction lender, such as a bank or savings and loan association. The certificate for payment, if any payment is due, is issued by the architect or engineer within the specified time period set forth in the contract or within a reasonable time. If a lender is handling the payments, he will pay the contractor. The time allowed should permit a reasonable opportunity for the design professional or lender to check the site, verify submitted data, determine the amount due, and request any further supporting data.

(C) COMPUTATION OF AMOUNT DUE

In a fixed price contract, the contractor is to receive a specified amount for the entire performance. The progress payment should be the proportion of the total contract price earned at particular stages by the contractor, less any amount the contract allows the owner to withhold for security purposes. Suppose there is a fixed price contract of $100,000. If the contractor has completed 20% of the work, he should receive $20,000, less any retainage amount specified, minus any other amounts for claims which the owner has, or will have, against the contractor. Suppose the contract states that the owner has the right to withhold 10% as retainage. In the example, the amount of the progress payment would be $20,000 less 10% or $2,000, making the amount due the contractor $18,000.

In the above example, the proportion of the work completed is stated. If this fact is known, and if progress payments are based upon a percentage of the contract price, the computation is simple. However, the proportion of the entire contract performance that has been completed is often difficult to ascertain. Also, some contracts use actual cost or value of the work performed as a test for computing progress payments. These standards involve a difficult valuation question, as well as a difficult quantity determination. Also, the example assumes no difficulty in determining whether material must be incorporated into the structure, whether materials at the site are counted, or whether material fabricated, but not yet delivered, may be considered.

One method of resolving some of the difficult computation questions is to base the progress payments upon completion of certain specific stages of the performance of the project. For example, a contract for $100,000 could be divided into four stages. The contract might provide that the contractor is to receive $20,000 at the end of Stage I, $25,000 at the end of Stage II, $30,000 at the end of Stage III and the balance of $25,000 at the end of Stage IV. This provision requires the determination only of whether the designated stage has been completed, but the pre-performance determination of the amounts to be paid at each stage requires an advance determination of the value that each stage bears to the total performance, as well as consideration of retainage.

For example, a contract pricing based upon stages of completion would require an evaluation of the proportion of the total project represented by Stage I. If Stage I were 25%, the contractor would be paid $25,000 less any retainage. If retainage were 20% ($5,000) the amount to be paid would be $20,000. The same analysis would be made of the other stages. Doing this in advance of performance can save the design professional from resolving difficult questions. However, the amounts selected should take into account the approximate portion of the total contract price allocable to each specified stage.

Most projects of any size specify that there will be monthly progress payments. There are important contract variations. First, is the amount to be based upon actual value, actual cost, or value proportionate to the contract price? Second, will there be a retainage, and, if so, how much? Third, how far must performance have gone before it is paid for? (Ordering beams, fabricating them, delivering them to the site, erecting them?)

The most difficult problem in monthly progress payment contracts concerns the proportion of the total contract price earned by the contractor. At any given point in the construction, this is difficult to measure. In order to avoid difficulty, contracts often provide that there will be agreed valuations by owner and contractor in advance of performance. For example, the AIA Doc. A201 states at 9.2.1:

> Before the first Application for Payment, the Contractor shall submit to the Architect a schedule of values of the various portions of the Work, including quantities if required by the Architect, aggregating the total Contract Sum, divided so as to facilitate payment to Subcontractors in accordance with Paragraph 5.4, prepared in such form as specified or as the Architect and Contractor may agree upon, and supported by such data to substantiate its correctness, as the Architect may require. Each item in the schedule of values shall include its proper share of overhead and profit. This schedule,

when approved by the Architect, shall be used only as a basis for the Contractor's Applications for Payment.

It is not the actual value of the work and materials that determines the progress payments, but the proportionate value of the total contract price represented by the work done. Some construction contracts use the actual value or cost to contractor as a measurement. In a losing contract, this often results in the contractor receiving more money at an early stage than he would receive if the proportion of the total contract price standard is used. This, while helpful to the contractor in paying his obligations as he incurs them, has the unfortunate effect of shrinking the owner's retainage. For example, suppose the contract price is $100,000 with payments of 90% to be based upon actual cost (or value) of the work as performed. If the contractor has put in $20,000 on the project, he would be entitled to $18,000. Yet, in a losing contract this work may represent only 15% of the total work to be performed. In such a case, the 10% retention amount will not be 10% of the total, as intended by the owner. For that reason, it is better to use proportion of the total price rather than the actual value or contractor cost.

Part of the confusion in method of valuation may stem from the requirement that the contractor show that he has paid his subcontractors and suppliers. This is to protect the owner from mechanics' liens. The actual amounts paid to subcontractors should not necessarily be the basis for the progress payment.

(D) WHEN MATERIALS ARE ALLOCABLE TO THE CONTRACT

From the contractor's standpoint, the earlier the payment, the better. He may be paying for the materials as he gets them, so he would prefer an early determination point. Some contracts may give him a right to payments in advance, to assist him in performing. Even without such a provision, the owner may find it necessary to help finance the contract by paying for work before it is performed, or material before it is purchased.

There are dangers in paying in advance, or in paying before the material is physically incorporated into the project. If the contractor is in financial difficulty, his creditors may claim that material left in his possession should be subject to their claims, even if paid for by the owner. If the contractor becomes bankrupt, the trustee in bankruptcy may claim that the materials "belong" to the contractor, and that any security interest asserted by the owner in the material for which he has paid has been lost because it was a "secret lien," and invalid. The owner's payment to the contractor for the material may not give the owner title to the material. An agreement between the owner and the contractor as to who owns title is not likely to bind third parties. Failure of the contractor, in such a case, to repay the owner will give the owner a legal claim for non-payment. But there may not be any assets out of which the owner can satisfy this claim.

But the owner may be considered the owner for other purposes. If the material is lost, destroyed or stolen, the owner may have the risk of loss. It is necessary that the material be insured against such loss. Even if the material is stored in an independent warehouse, insurance is usually necessary. Even though warehouses may be liable for non-delivery, often they are permitted to limit their liability to an amount which may be substantially below the actual value of the material.

If possible, it is best not to pay for work until it is incorporated into the structure. Payment for material delivered to the site is less dangerous than payment while the goods are still in the possession of the contractor. But payment for material delivered to the site usually means the risk of loss or theft or destruction will be upon the owner. With regard to risk of loss, the advice of a good insurance counsellor is vital. If advance payments involve security in specific property, legal advice should be obtained.

The discussion has involved construction contracts where payments are not usually made until the work is incorporated into the project at the site. Design professionals, especially engineers, may become involved in contracts for the construction of industrial machinery or equipment. Such contracts often call for progress payments to be made by the purchaser to help finance the manufacturer-seller. In such contracts, the security for repayment or protection from attack by creditors is more pressing than in the construction contract. In manufacturing contracts, the seller usually has possession of the work in progress. The risk of paying the contractor and leaving the materials in his possession are even greater when progress payments are made to the manufacturing seller. Protecting the buyer who is advancing money for the manufacture of the machinery is complicated and requires legal advice.

(E) DEDUCTIONS FROM PAYMENTS

The retainage is a security device for the owner. The owner would like to have in his possession funds out of which he can satisfy his claims against the contractor. Illustrations of such claims would be: (1) liquidated damages for unexcused delay, (2) cost of repairing defective work, (3) liability incurred to third parties because of the acts or failure to act by the contractor, (4) payment of lien claimants who assert liens because they have not been paid for their work. The percentage may vary and may slide. It might be anywhere from 5–25%. Also, it may decrease as the work progresses.

In addition to the retainage amount specified by the contract, the owner may want to deduct other amounts to protect himself from the claims mentioned in the preceding paragraph. Even without a contract provision permitting such set-offs, a contracting party has the right to deduct amounts from money he is obligated to pay if the payee (the person to whom the payment is to be made) does owe, or will very likely owe, the paying party money. If the paying party (the owner) were not given this right of set-off, he would have to pay the full amount, and then sue for the amount he had coming from the payee.

It is advisable to specify in the contract when amounts can be set-off, and who makes the determination. AIA Doc. A201 states, at 9.5.1, that the architect may deduct amounts from the payment due which, in his opinion, are necessary to protect the owner from loss due to: (1) defective work not remedied, (2) claims filed or reasonable evidence indicating probable filing of claims, (3) failure of the Contractor to make payments properly to Subcontractors or for labor, materials or equipment, (4) reasonable doubt that the Work can be completed for the unpaid balance of the Contract Sum, (5) damage to another contractor (6) reasonable indication that the Work will not be completed within Contract Time, or (7) unsatisfactory prosecution of the Work by the Contractor. Such a provision broadens the right given by law for set-off. The design professional should always use his best effort to avoid excessive or unjust deductions.

(F) ADJUSTMENT OF TOTAL CONTRACT PRICE

The total contract price should be adjusted as changes increase or decrease the total price. The important objective is to maintain the constant retainage percentage. It is advisable to state in the contract provision dealing with progress payments that payments are to be based upon the total contract price, as adjusted during performance.

(G) COST CONTRACT

In a cost type contract, the design professional may have to pass upon cost problems, if he administers progress payments. In cost contracts, the costs incurred should be reasonable in amount, and have been required under the contract. The owner does not want to pay unreasonable costs, pay for work which was not called for under the contract or pay for work which went to another project of the contractor. Another major question in cost type contracts is whether any, or what proportion of, indirect costs, such as office overhead, visits to the site by executives of the contractor and advertising costs, are to be included.

If the contract form is cost plus a fixed fee, the design professional may have to evaluate the portion of the fee allocable to the work performed, which is the basis for the application for payment. If possible, this should be decided in advance in the contract.

(H) UNIT PRICING

In unit pricing, the progress payment certificates usually involve the units of work performed. As a rule, the evaluation has been provided for in the contract. There may be a deduction for retainage or set-offs. This should be spelled out in the contract.

(I) DIVISIBILITY OF CONTRACT

The determination of how much a contractor in a fixed price contract is to be paid when there are provisions for progress payments must be a rough approximation. The evaluation of labor and material which has gone into the product is rarely susceptible to precise measurement. Even where contracts provide for a schedule of agreed evaluations to determine the amount due at various stages of work, the amounts are estimates. Since the amount determined to be payable is a rough approximation, it should not, and normally is not, regarded as an agreed figure for the work done, except for progress payment purposes. It can be adjusted as additional work is done and if mistakes are discovered. It is subject to a final adjustment when the project is completed.

(J) PAYMENT AS A WAIVER OF DEFECTS

Waiver has been discussed in § 24.02(e). Sometimes the contractor will claim that by making a progress payment after a contract deviation, the owner has "waived the defect".

In such cases, there is usually no reliance, since the deviation is made before the payment. Perhaps the contractor relied by not making a correction until it became more expensive, because the payment led him reasonably to believe that he would not have to make the correction. Usually this is not the case.

To avoid claims of waiver by the making of progress payments, construction contracts often contain provisions to negate waiver. For example, AIA Doc. A201 at 9.4.4 states:

> No Certificate for a progress payment, not any progress payment . . . shall constitute an acceptance of any Work not in accordance with the Contract Documents.

Courts should not find a waiver simply by the issuance of a payment certificate or making a payment. Only if there is evidence of an express waiver through statements or other unambiguous acts, should waiver be found.

(K) FAILURE TO MAKE PROGRESS PAYMENTS

If the owner fails, without legal justification, to make a progress payment, the effect nonpayment has upon the contractor's obligation to proceed may be governed by express contract provisions. For example, AIA Doc. A201, at 9.6.1, gives the contractor the right to suspend his performance by giving a 7 day notice if he is improperly denied a certificate of payment 7 days after application or if the owner does not pay within 7 days after a payment certificate has been issued by the architect or awarded by arbitration. For a discussion of notice provisions, see § 10.04(c).

If there is no contract provision which deals with a contractor's remedy when he is not paid, the contractor should be able to suspend his performance until he is paid, and he should be entitled to obtain an extension of time equivalent to the suspension period. Nonpayment will make it difficult for him to continue his performance and increase the risk that he will go unpaid.

In any case, the contractor is entitled to interest on the payment which he should have received. If he can show any damages caused by the failure to make the payment which could not have been reasonably avoided, and which were reasonably foreseeable by the owner at the time the contract was made, the contractor can recover these damages. Such damages will be rare. If the contractor were going to use the money to obtain another project, losses which might be incurred because of a failure to obtain the project or complete it could very likely have been avoided by borrowing money. If he had to pay more interest to borrow money, he should be able to recover the added cost of borrowing. These damages assume that the owner knew, or should have known, that the contractor was relying upon the payment for the purpose claimed for recovery by the contractor. This is usually difficult to prove. As a rule, the non-payment of progress payments when due allows suspension, an extension of time, and interest on the amount due.

Nonpayment may also give the contractor a right to terminate his contract obligations. See § 26.04(b). Usually the right to terminate gives the contractor a right to collect for what he has done, and the profit on unperformed work. See § 29.04(a).

SECTION 24.04 COMPLETION, ACCEPTANCE AND FINAL PAYMENT

Completion of the project is important for several reasons. It controls the outer limit of time obligations. Also, completion may control the time for asserting mechanics' liens. It also gives the contractor a right to the final payment, unless an amount is retained to cover subsequently discovered defects or claims or warranties for time periods after completion.

Completion may be divided into substantial completion, and final completion. The former occurs when the building is ready for occupancy or the use for which it was constructed, despite defects which must be corrected or minor aspects of the work which are yet uncompleted. Substantial completion is roughly the same as substantial performance as discussed in § 24.02(b).

Some contracts provide that the contractor is entitled to be paid for what he has done, less any justifiable retainage after "substantial" completion. This is a contractual recognition of the substantial performance doctrine. Since the retainage in part is to cover costs which may have to be incurred by the owner to complete the project, the contractor should not receive the retainage upon substantial completion. Also, substantial completion normally should limit the extent of liability for any unexcused delay.

Sometimes the project may be considered "complete" if the owner "accepts" the work. In the past, often completion was claimed when the owner occupied or used the project. The contractor would contend that occupation or use was acceptance, and that acceptance was evidence of completion. Sometimes such claims were successful. This would give the contractor his final payment, and might mean that the owner "waived" any claim for defects or for incomplete work. Today, most contracts state that occupation is not acceptance. The mere fact that the owner occupies or uses the project should not cost him his claim for defective work.

Much of what has been stated about progress payments applies to the issuance of the final payment. However, the amount of the final payment is not merely an approximation, as are the progress payments. Final payment should be the balance of the contract price, less any deductions which, by contract or by law, are permitted to the owner. As stated, the provisions for progress payments usually allow the owner to withhold a specified percentage as the work progresses. Frequently he will withhold a small amount, even after acceptance of the project, to take care of possible future liabilities, or to protect him against the possibility that the contractor will not live up to any warranty which extends past the time when the owner takes possession. In addition, contracts usually provide that an amount may be withheld, in addition to the retainage, for present or future claims the owner may have against the contractor.

Final payment requires a careful inspection of the work to see that it has been performed in accordance with the contract documents. Usually, the contractor notifies the design professional that the project is substantially completed. Upon such notice, the design professional makes his inspection. If the work is accepted, final payment should be made. As will be seen in § 24.07, it is important to get substantiating evidence that subcontractors and materialmen (used interchangeably with suppliers in this treatise) have been paid, or have filed waivers of liens. In some cases, the contractor may be permitted to furnish a bond to indemnify the owner against the imposition of liens after acceptance.

Acceptance and final payment may have other consequences. There is a strong policy in the law to wind up transactions as quickly as possible. For that reason, sometimes claims which have not yet been settled or paid for are lost when the final payment is made and accepted by the contractor, or when the owner "accepts" the contractor's work. What effect do these acts have upon:

1. Claims by the owner for damages against the contractor for revealed defective work?
2. Claims by the owner for damages based upon defective work revealed after acceptance?
3. Claims for damages by the contractor against the owner?

Paragraph 9.7.5 of AIA Doc. A201 states that final payment shall constitute a waiver of all claims by the owner, excepting those arising from unsettled liens, faulty or defective Work appearing after Substantial Completion, failure of the Work to comply with the requirements of the Contract Documents or terms of any special guarantees required by the Contract Documents. This language seems to indicate that the owner, by accepting and making the final payment, does not give up any claims for defective performance appearing after completion or which appeared before completion.

Another method of avoiding the possibility that completion and acceptance will bar claims for defective workmanship which appear subsequently is to incorporate a warranty clause in the construction contract. Such clauses are designed to obligate the contractor to repair any defects which appear within the warranty period. Warranties will be discussed in § 30.11(d).

Acceptance or final payment is often accompanied by a list of defects in the work as determined by the final inspection. Some courts hold that the listing of specific defects shows an indication that the owner intends to give up any defects which are not on the list of defective work. One justification for finding a waiver is that the contractor may rely upon the list as exclusive, and it would be unfair to make him make corrections when he could have made the corrections much more cheaply before the final acceptance. Also, waiver can be predicated upon the desire to put an end to transactions as quickly as possible, or to give effect to the intention of the owner. In any event, the furnishing of a list may constitute a waiver of any items not on the list. It should not operate to waive any defect which could not have been reasonably discoverable. The language in the AIA Doc. A 201 seems to preclude waiver, but there is always the risk that the use of a list, despite the language in A201, will constitute a waiver. In such a case, it may be helpful to specify in the list that the listing covers only defects which were observable by ordinary inspection, or, if desired, that nothing is waived by the use of the list.

For a case involving the question of whether a notice of termination for one reason waives other grounds for termination see New England Structures v. Loranger, reproduced in § 26.07.

Paragraph 9.7.6 of the AIA Document A201, states that "The acceptance of final payment shall constitute a waiver of all claims by the contractor except those previously made in writing and still unsettled." The effect of such a provision means that contractor claims not submitted in writing are waived by contractor acceptance of final payment.

Upon completion of the project, there may be a dispute over the ownership of the retainage. What if a specified amount of money has been retained, and that this amount exceeds whatever damages are owing or will be owing to the owner? In such a case, problems can develop when the prime contractor is in financial trouble. If he has been unable to finish the project, and the work was completed by the surety, the surety frequently wants to obtain the retainage. If the surety has had to pay materialmen and subcontractors under payment bonds, he will also make a claim to the retainage.

In addition to the surety company, the trustee in bankruptcy of the contractor (if he has gone bankrupt) will frequently try to claim the funds belong to the contractor, and that the trustee should take these funds. The contractor, in such a situation, is not likely to have paid his taxes. As a result, federal, state, and local tax authorities may assert that they have tax liens on these funds. Finally, any lending institutions that have lent money to the contractor often come in and assert that the contractor has assigned those payments to them as security for any loans made by the lenders to the contractor. In most cases, the owner will pay the money into court and start a lawsuit in which he names as parties all persons who have claimed the retainage. In such a lawsuit (called an "interpleader" action), the court will resolve the frequently difficult questions of ownership of retainage.

SECTION 24.05 TO WHOM PAYMENT SHOULD BE MADE

(A) ASSIGNMENTS OF RIGHT TO BE PAID

The contractor may transfer his right to payment to third parties by making an assignment. Assignments were discussed in § 9.03, in connection with contracts between the design professional and his client. They are important in connection with owner-contractor contracts since contractors assign their rights to be paid more frequently than do design professionals.

When a contractor transfers his right to be paid, he usually does so to satisfy an obligation he owes a creditor, or to provide security to obtain a loan.

Early in American legal history, it was difficult to transfer such intangible rights. However, the law soon recognized the necessity for contracting parties to be able to sell their "rights" to be paid. In recognizing this "right", the law attempted to protect the person who would owe the money (the obligor). As a basic principle, the obligor was not to lose anything by virtue of the transfer, other than having to pay to the person to whom the transfer had been made (the assignee), rather than the person making the transfer (the assignor).

The obligor could assert any defenses against the assignee that he could have asserted against the assignor. This means that the owner can assert against the assignee (the lender or creditor) that no valid contract had been formed, that the events which conditioned his obligation to pay have not occurred or been excused, or that he has valid set-offs against the assignor (the contractor). Also, if the obligor is not notified of the assignment, he can pay the assignor contractor, despite the assignment. He is entitled to rely upon appearances when he makes the payment. If he reasonably believes he can pay the assignor, he cannot be made to pay twice.

Despite substantial protection given by the law to the obligor-owner, many contracts contain provisions which require that the owner consent to any assignment made by the contractor. This was to protect the owner from having to deal with strangers, as well as reflecting the fear that an assignor-contractor might lose interest in performing properly if he transferred his right to be paid. Prior to the enactment of the Uniform Commercial Code such provisions protected the owner. However, if the assignment is made as security for a loan, § 9–318(d) the Commercial Code states that the owner's consent is not necessary, despite a contract clause requiring his consent.

If the owner has been notified of an assignment as a security for a loan, he must pay the assignee. But he need not pay any more than he would have had to pay the assignor-contractor.

(B) SUBCONTRACTORS AND SUPPLIERS

In a single contract, payment will usually be made only to the prime contractor. To avoid liens, methods may have to be set up to ensure that subcontractors and suppliers have been paid. Normally, payments are not made directly to subcontractors and suppliers. (As shall be seen in § 24.07, payments may be made *jointly* to prime and subcontractor). The owner tries to avoid having to deal directly with a potentially large number of other parties for convenience reasons, to avoid liability for the acts of such parties, and to avoid responsibility for acts which delay or damage subcontractors and suppliers. The owner often attempts to accomplish these goals by not contracting or dealing with these parties. Yet the owner tries to maintain quality control over them and preclude them from asserting liens. Such a tightrope is often difficult to walk.

SECTION 24.06 LEGAL EFFECT OF ISSUANCE OF CERTIFICATES

Participation by a design professional in the payment process raises a number of legal questions. The principal question involves the implications which can be drawn from the issuance of a payment certificate. This is a matter which relates principally to the relationship of a design professional to his client. It has been discussed in § 6.16 and need not be repeated in this chapter. It may be useful to noting the increasing tendency on the part of form contracts to limit the implications which can be drawn from the issuance of a certificate relating to the quality of performance. The conclusiveness of the payment certificate as between owner and contractor will be discussed in Chapter 27. Liability to third parties because of negligently issued certificates of payment will be treated in § 24.08.

SECTION 24.07 UNPAID SUPPLIERS, SUBCONTRACTORS AND LABORERS: THE MECHANICS' LIEN

(A) LEGISLATIVE PROTECTION

A "mechanics' lien" is a security device by which unpaid design professionals, laborers, prime contractors, subcontractors, and suppliers who have improved land may collect for their work and materials through the lien process. Where such a lien is created, the lien claimant can cause a judicial sale of the property subject to the lien. Usually, the owner will pay to remove the lien. Liens by persons with whom the owner has contracted can be avoided by the owner paying his bills. This section treats liens which may be asserted by persons who are not paid by contractors and sometimes subcontractors. Payments to contractors, both progress and final, must consider possible lien claimants. One of the conditions of the owner's obligation to pay is that the contractor keep the structure free of such liens.

In the United States, state statutes have created lien rights for unpaid subcontractors, suppliers, and laborers. There is no uniformity in state laws, and the laws frequently change. At the outset, it is likely that these statutes were enacted to give special recognition to the financial problems of laborers and small artisans. This is indicated by the term "mechanics' " lien. Such persons needed a speedy and efficient remedy to insure that they would be paid for their work. The "legal" justification for such laws came from the analogy to the "equitable lien", a concept based upon unjust enrichment. A person who could trace his material or labor into the property of another might, under certain circumstances, have a lien upon the property. Today these original beneficiaries of mechanics' lien laws (laborers and small artisans) rarely use them. The principal users of lien laws are unpaid suppliers and contractors.

Lien laws also reflect a recognition of the financial instability of the construction industry. There is a righ risk that prime contractors either will not or cannot pay their subcontractors and suppliers. Expansion of the category of those entitled to liens also reflects the realities of the legislative process. Once some groups were given liens, other groups used their legislative power to get liens for the members of their groups.

Whatever their original purpose, granting such liens has sped up the construction process. Lien rights often encourage persons to invest their time and materials in a project without the necessity for checking upon the credit of the prime contractor or, in the case of prime contractor liens, of the owner.

Lien laws have been greatly criticized. They are extremely complex, involve many technical requirements, and change often. This means that many lien claimants find that they have not complied with the technical requirements to obtain a lien. Secondly, often lien rights are worthless because of the priorities given to other security holders in the project, such as sellers who have taken mortgages or deeds of trust on the property as security for part of the purchase price, and construction lenders. Thirdly, the lien laws have come in for criticism because often unsophisticated owners find that the lien laws require them to pay twice. Without any awareness of the lien laws or methods of protecting against liens, owners may pay prime contractors, and then find out that suppliers and subcontractors have lien rights which can be extinguished only by paying the lien claimants. Recently there has been legislative activity in some states directed toward protecting small owners from having to pay twice.

There are no lien rights against public structures. But some states have accorded protection to unpaid contractors, materialmen and laborers through the device of a "stop notice". This permits an unpaid subcontractor (the term "subcontractor" will be used to cover materialmen and laborers) to notify a public or private owner (or lender) that he has not been paid, and to demand that no further payments be made to the contractor until the claimant is paid. Also, many public contracts require that there be surety bonds which operate for the benefit of unpaid subcontractors, laborers and materialmen.

States vary as to who can assert liens. Usually subcontractors, laborers, and suppliers of subs or prime contractors can claim a lien. Some states limit the total liens to the prime contract price. In others, the total amount of liens can exceed the contract price between the owner and the prime contractor. In those states, the owner can limit his lien obligation to the contract price by filing a copy of the contract and posting a bond, something done rarely.

Owners of property generally can avoid liens resulting from improvements ordered by tenants by posting a notice of non-responsibility within a specified time after the owners learn that the improvement is being made. In most cases, the lien operates only upon improvements on the land. This means that if the project does not commence, or if the project itself is destroyed, the lien right is destroyed with it. There have been a few cases where liens have been permitted where the project was abandoned because of the acts of the owner. However, as a general principle, there must be improvements on the land before the lien will be created.

Some states uphold "no lien" contracts, under which the contractor agrees not to assert a lien. In some states, this may be binding upon subcontractors if such a contract is filed.

There are often difficult questions with regard to priorities. As between themselves, all lien claimants share equally, except that liens of prime contractors may be subordinated to other lien claimants. Laborers may be given a preference. However, there may be prior rights in persons who have a security interest in the land, such as lenders or sellers who have taken a mortgage or deed of trust on the land, and who have made a public recording of their interest before commencement of any improvements on the land.

Since the owner can be forced to pay twice, it is important that the owner assure himself that the contractor is paying those persons who would have liens against the structure. See § 5.08 for a discussion at mechanics' liens for design professionals.

(B) REDUCING RISK OF SUBCONTRACTOR AND SUPPLIER LIENS

In some states, the risk of such liens can be substantially eliminated by the use of what is called a "no lien" contract. Under such a contract, the contractor gives up his right to a lien in advance. In some states a no lien contract given by the contractor can be properly worded to preclude liens being asserted by subcontractors and materialmen. In some states, statutes permit filing of a "no lien" contract which precludes subcontractor liens. It is possible, although cumbersome, to require that subcontractors and materialmen waive their liens in advance of performance before being allowed to furnish services or material.

Typically, contracts require that the contractor give satisfactory evidence that he has paid the subcontractors and materialmen. Should a design professional accept an affidavit or sworn statement by the contractor that he has paid his subcontractors? If the contractor is lying, the lien may be asserted, and any claim against the contractor is likely to be worthless. It is risky to accept the word of the contractor in such a case. If the contractor is a person of exceptionally good reputation, and a person who is financially responsible, problems may never develop. However, merely accepting the contractor's word is dangerous.

Section 484b of the California Penal Code makes it a crime for the prime contractor to wilfully divert funds given to him for payment of his subcontractors and materialmen. Section 484c makes it a crime to submit false vouchers to obtain construction loan funds. Perhaps reproduction of such statutes in the Application for Payment might cause a prime contractor to have second thoughts before submitting a false voucher or application, or not paying his subcontractors.

The design professional could require additional evidence such as paid bills, or statements of the subcontractors and materialmen that they have been paid. If the statements and bills are authentic and not tampered with, then this eliminates the possibility of liens. This method assumes that the design professional knows the subcontractors and materialmen.

R. D. Reeder Lathing Co. v. Allen, 66 Cal.2d 373, 425 P.2d 785, 57 Cal.Rptr. 841 (1967) held that a subcontractor was precluded from asserting a lien where the prime and subcontractor concocted a scheme under which the subcontractor would perform services on the project without the owner knowing it. If the owner did not know that the subcontractor was working on the project, he would not demand either a waiver of lien from the subcontractor or some evidence that the prime had paid the subcontractor before making the progress payment.

Requiring the prime to pay his subcontractors before issuance of progress payments to him means that the prime contractor must have enough money to pay off the subcontractors and materialmen before he is paid. Often contractors do not have sufficient funds to do this. They intend to use the progress payments to pay off subcontractors and materialmen. An alternative is to require that the contractor submit waivers of liens by subcontractors and materialmen. Contractors often tell subcontractors and materialmen that unless they furnish a waiver of the lien, they will not be paid. If a contractor can convince them to give up their lien rights in advance and get them to sign the waiver of lien, this usually eliminates the possibility of liens being asserted against the building. Again, it is important to know who the subcontractors and materialmen are. If there are persons who have furnished labor and material on the structure, and they are not known to the design professional, they may come in later and assert liens if they are unpaid. However, the major subcontractors and materialmen are usually known to the design professional.

Sometimes, owners try to insure that subcontractors and suppliers are paid by issuing a check jointly to the contractor and the subcontractor or supplier. This requires that both of them endorse the check before there can be payment by the bank. This method had a rather unusual twist in Ferry v. Ohio Farmers' Insurance Co., 211 Cal.App.2d 651, 27 Cal.Rptr. 471 (1963). In this case, the owner drew a check payable jointly to the contractor and to the materialman, after the materialman gave a written waiver of his lien rights. Both parties endorsed the check and proceeds were paid to the prime contractor. The prime contractor then gave his personal check to the materialman. The check was dishonored by the bank, because the contractor did not have sufficient funds in his checking account. The materialman then sued the contractor, and received a judgment from the court for the entire amount of the debt. However, the materialman could only collect $10,000 of the $18,000 judgment. He then instituted an action against the surety bond company for the balance. The court held that by executing a waiver of lien, the unpaid materialman did not lose his right to sue the surety bond company. In such cases, much will depend upon the exact language of the surety bond. However, the court's opinion reflected a strong concern for unpaid materialmen, and the feeling that this is the very risk which the surety assumes.

Another method of avoiding liens is not to pay the prime contractor until the time for filing the liens has elapsed. Usually, contractors must file their liens within a specifed time. If the owner can, by contract, delay progress payments until the time for filing liens has expired, he would have foolproof protection against the filing of liens. The contractor may not be able to wait the 30, 60, or 90 day period which must elapse before it is certain no lien claim will be filed. Since as a rule liens must be filed within a designated number of days from completion, this technique would be useful only on the final payment.

Another technique is to insist upon a reasonable retainage percentage in the contract, and keep it constant throughout the payments. This should cover small liens of unknown subcontractors and materialmen.

It is helpful to include a provision that the contractor will pay each subcontractor as his work is accepted and the contractor is paid for this work by the owner. Some contractors try to wait until all the subcontractor work is accepted. Such delay can lead to a lien being asserted by an unpaid subcontractor who completed his portion of the work early in the construction.

The function of the payment bond is to protect the owner from liens. For a premium a surety company will pay materialmen and subcontractors if the prime contractor does not pay them. Requiring a bond from prime and major subcontractors can avoid liens.

(C) LAW OF DEFAMATION

This chapter emphasizes the owner's interest in insuring that subcontractors and suppliers are paid. What if the subcontractor or supplier (or anyone else) informs a third person, such as the owner or design professional, that he had not been paid when he had been paid? A communication of this type may injure the credit and reputation of the person falsely charged with non-payment. Such a communication can make the communicator liable for defamation. The person defamed is entitled to recover from the defamer the actual financial losses caused by the defamation, an amount to compensate for any loss of reputation suffered and, in cases of malicious acts, punitive damages.

Diplomat Electric, Inc. v. Westinghouse Electric Supply Co., 378 F.2d 377 (5th Cir. 1967) involved a communication by a supplier of a subcontractor made to the prime contractor and owner which stated that he had not been paid by the subcontractor. The court held that if the plaintiff subcontractor could prove that the communication was false, he would be able to recover for defamation against the defendant supplier.

SECTION 24.08 LIABILITY OF DESIGN PROFESSIONAL IN PAYMENT MATTERS

Chapters 30 and 34 treat actions against design professionals in more detail, but it may be useful to discuss his role and legal responsibility in the payment process in this section.

The design professional may lead the owner to believe by the issuance of the certificate for payment that the work has been performed properly. If so, the design professional could be liable if the owner has either lost his claim against the contractor, or if the claim turns out to be uncollectible. The same can be true if the design professional submits an incomplete list of corrections, and the owner loses his claim against the contractor because of waiver.

What if the design professional does not use due care in the issuance of certificates for payment? He may cause losses to the owner, the surety, and possibly to the contractor. The owner can suffer a loss by the failure to use due care in the issuance of certificates. Liens may be asserted and amounts paid out prematurely. Underpayments can injure the contractor.

A surety may have to make payments to subcontractors and materialmen under the terms of the payment bond. If so, they may claim that the design professional should be responsible if his negligence enabled the contractor to divert funds. Also, the surety often looks to the retainage as a fund out of which to cover its losses if it has to pay. If the carelessness of the design professional has reduced the retainage, the surety company may, and did in one case, recover against the architect. See State ex rel National Surety Corp. v. Malvaney, 221 Miss. 190, 72 So.2d 424 (1945).

Much of the discussion in this section assumes that the payments are being disbursed by the owner through the mechanism of payment certificates issued by the architect or engineer. There have been some references to the construction lender making the payments to the prime contractor out of construction loan funds. In major construction projects, the owner rarely has enough money to pay for the project. Usually he obtains a construction loan from a bank or savings and loan association. In such cases, the lender, like the owner when the latter is making payments, will want to insure that payments are not being diverted, and are going to the subcontractors and suppliers. For this reason, lenders often develop a voucher system for insuring that funds are not diverted. The lender pays based upon vouchers of subcontractors and suppliers which are submitted to the lender by the contractor. While lenders get fooled on occasion, lenders who do a large amount of construction lending are likely to develop a better system to insure that prime contractors are paying their subcontractors and suppliers than can a design professsional. A recognition of this is the expanded use in many states of what are called "joint controls". Joint controls are companies which specialize in paying contractors during the course of a construction project.

The increasing use of lenders and joint controls is likely to mean a diminished use of architects and engineers in the payment process. This may be a good thing for architects and engineers who wish to relieve themselves of this complicated, and often costly, role. It may be advantageous for architects and engineers who do not have a trained and efficient administrative staff to be relieved of the responsibility of making payments to the prime contractor.

REVIEW QUESTIONS

1. How does the doctrine of conditions affect the contractor's right to be paid?

2. Under what circumstances will the contractor be able to recover despite noncompliance with the contract obligations?

3. Can a contractor assign his right to a payment to a lender without consent of the owner?

4. What is the function of progress payments? Of a retainage?

5. How do the rights of unpaid subcontractors and suppliers affect payments to the prime contractor?

6. What are methods for avoiding subcontractor liens?

7. Can a subcontractor obtain a lien against a public building?

8. What is the danger in specifying a list of defects?

9. What risks of liability does a design professional assume when he participates in payment processes?

QUESTIONS FOR CLASS DISCUSSION

1. Why give an unpaid subcontractor a mechanics' lien?

2. Should the design professional avoid being a part of the payment process because of potential liability?

3. Should the law require more than substantial performance on the part of the contractor?

4. Will giving breaching contractors a right to be paid for the net benefit they confer upon the owner encourage them to quit when they are in a losing contract?

5. Should occupation of the building operate as a waiver of known defects?

PROBLEMS

1. A construction contract called for oak panelling in certain rooms. Because oak was unavailable, a subcontractor installed birch panel. The prime did not notice this deviation. The cost of oak and birch panelling is the same. When the owner saw the panelling, he told the prime contractor he liked it. The next day the owner told the prime contractor he wanted oak panelling installed. Is the contractor obligated to replace the panelling? If he does not, what, if anything, can the owner recover?

2. On February 1, C was entitled to a progress payment of $10,000 based upon a certificate issued by the architect. The owner informed the contractor on February 2 that payment would be delayed for about a week because the proceeds of the construction loan had run out, and the owner was in the process of getting a new loan. What are the contractor's rights at this point? What additional facts would be helpful in resolving this question?

Chapter 25

ADMINISTRATIVE PROBLEMS: AUTHORITY AND COMMUNICATIONS

SECTION 25.01 RELEVANCE

Before, during and sometimes after construction of a project the parties to the construction contract must communicate with each other. These communications may consist of modifications of the contract, changes, notice of a time for inspection, notice of termination, approval of shop drawings, notice of claims, to mention only a few. Communications are made by or given to the design professional, the project representative, and other employees or representatives of owner and contractor. In a properly run construction project the participants know who has authority to do what acts, and to whom notices are to be directed. When these matters are not clearly set forth in the contract, or followed during contract administration, legal problems can develop. The purpose of this chapter is to explore some of them.

SECTION 25.02 PROBLEMS OF AUTHORITY

(A) AUTHORITY OF DESIGN PROFESSIONAL

Under what circumstances will the acts of the design professional bind the owner? A differentiation should be made between design professional acts chargeable to the owner by virtue of agency, from those situations where the design professional is given power to bind not only the owner, but both parties, when he makes certain determinations during the administration of the contract. For example, the design professional is frequently given the power to decide interpretation questions and to judge performance. In theory, his exercise of these functions does not bind the owner by agency. Instead, the design professional is exercising the power given to him by both parties to the contract. However, courts frequently consider such powers given to the architect under the contract as manifestations by the owner of the express authority of the architect to bind the owner, rather than as a manifestation by both parties to the contract that the architect is given the power to bind both parties when he interprets the contract, judges contract compliance, or makes other similar quasi-judicial determinations. Much of the emphasis upon the architect as agent is based upon the fact that he is usually selected and paid by the owner. Also, traditionally, the architect or engineer is considered to be the professional advisor of the owner and acts to protect the owner's interest. While sometimes courts distinguish the two roles of the architect-engineer, that of professional advisor and that of dispute decider, these roles often become blurred.

There is another way of testing whether the powers conferred by the owner-contractor agreement are based upon agency, or are a jointly conferred power by both parties. Suppose the owner removed the architect? If the powers given to the architect are jointly conferred by both contracting parties, this removal could not be accomplished without the consent of the contractor (unless the contract also gave the owner the power to remove and replace the architect unilaterally).

It is generally assumed that the owner has the power to remove and replace the architect-engineer. The architect is often referred to as the owner's architect. In any event, whether it is an agency power or a jointly created contract power, the design professional does have the power to bind the owner (and the contractor) in certain situations when the owner-contractor contract gives him this power.

In a true agency question, there are three major issues. First, is there an agency relationship? Second, what was the scope of the agent's actual or implied authority to act for the principal? Third, if the agent was not authorized, did the principal lead the third party (the person attempting to bind the principal through the acts of the agent) to reasonably believe the agent had authority to do the act in question?

The power of the design professional to order a change was discussed in § 21.05. Other issues relate to the authority of a design professional to make contracts or modify them, and whether notices to or knowledge of the design professional shall be considered knowledge of or notice to the owner.

Generally, the architect or engineer does not, solely by virtue of his position, have authority to make or modify contracts. Sometimes he will be given express authority to perform these acts. Some changes clauses give him authority to direct certain types of changes. See § 21.05. The primary roles of the design professional are to act as the professional advisor to the owner, to give contract interpretations, and to judge performance. Unless he has actual authority, or unless the owner in some way has cloaked him with apparent authority, generally he has no authority to make or modify contracts of the owner.

During construction of the project or, in some cases, after it has been abandoned or completed, it may be necessary for the contractor to communicate certain information to the owner. For example, during performance it is often required that the contractor give notice of an intention to claim an extra or a time extension. Also, he is frequently required to give notice of any acts which he will use as the basis for a damage claim. Frequently the contract will specify that such notices can be given to the architect or engineer. Clearly, in such cases notice to these designated persons is sufficient.

But what if the contract does not specify that notice can be given to architect or engineer? Often courts hold that facts known to the architect or engineer is the same as knowledge to the owner. The law speaks of such knowledge as being imputed to the owner. Also, the law frequently holds that notices given to the architect or engineer are the same as if these notices were given to the owner. Courts often hold that the architect or engineer has authority to receive these particular notices.

A case illustrating the imputation doctrine is Trane Co. v. Gilbert, 267 Cal.App.2d 720, 73 Cal.Rptr. 279 (1968). In this case the owner sued the manufacturer of air conditioning equipment for the cost of material and labor in replacing a burned out component. The manufacturer claimed that the warranty on the equipment was limited to one year, and the component burned out more than one year after installation. The one year limitation of the warranty was contained in an equipment manual delivered to the mechanical contractor and to the mechanical engineer who had been retained by the architect. The limitation was also contained in a form submitted to both the mechanical contractor and the mechanical engineer. The equipment manufacturer's salesman stated that he pointed out this limitation to the mechanical engineer.

The court held that the mechanical engineer was a sub-agent of the owner and that information that came to his attention was imputed to the owner-principal. The court noted that the construction project was a "turn key" project, with the architect being given authority to handle negotiations with third persons relating to the construction of the project. The court further noted that the information in question, the one-year limitation on the warranty, was acquired by the mechanical engineer while he was acting within the scope of his authority and related to a matter to which his authority extended.

Perhaps the case was influenced by the court's classification of the transaction as having been one which was a "turn key" contract. This would seem to give the architect, and any consultants he appoints, more authority than is usually found in a construction project. The information which was imputed to the owner in this case related to an important term of the contract under which the equipment was purchased by the mechanical contractor. It is unlikely that the mechanical engineer would have had the authority to purchase the equipment and bind the owner. Yet his knowledge controlled the owner's warranty claim.

Some statutes, such as mechanics' lien laws, require that certain notices be given to the owner. Often such statutes specify that the architect is an agent of the owner for this purpose. Even without such a statutory rule, often notices given to the architect are considered as having been given to the owner.

The design professional must communicate relevant information that comes to his attention to his client. Also he should forward all notices given to him, to his client.

(B) OTHER EMPLOYEES OR AGENTS

As for the other employees or agents of the contracting parties, their authority is governed by the rules of agency which have been discussed in Chapter 3. It is helpful for both parties, especially if they are large organizations, to designate in the contract a person and an alternate with authority to make certain decisions during contract administration. Performance is often impeded when it is difficult to find someone who has authority or is willing to take responsibility for decisions.

(C) USE OF A PROJECT REPRESENTATIVE

Frequently the design professional is not obligated to furnish continuous supervision during the construction project. He may suggest to the owner that a project representative, or what used to be called a "clerk of the works", be hired. If this is done, the project representative is usually paid for directly or indirectly by the owner. Often the project representative is an employee of the design professional.

Problems may arise as to the authority of the project representative. Usually, he does not have authority to modify the contract, or to perform any of the functions of the design professional. See § 21.05. His function is to observe the progress of the construction project, and to report to the design professional at periodic intervals.

(D) MISREPRESENTATION OF AUTHORITY

What if the design professional misrepresents his authority to modify the contract? Acting upon this representation, the contractor might perform work which does not come within the contract documents. What recourse does the contractor have in such a case?

First, he might try to assert that the design professional had apparent authority to make the modification. Unless the owner in some way led the contractor to believe that the design professional had this authority, the contractor is not likely to be successful. Next, the contractor might assert that he should recover from the owner on the basis of quasi-contract. He could contend that by performing the work he has enriched the owner. In some cases this might be successful. In most situations, a claim based upon unjust enrichment would not be recognized by the law.

If the contractor cannot recover from the owner, he should be able to recover his damages from the design professional because of misrepresentation of authority. If the design professional is held responsible for misrepresentation, he might try to recover from the owner on the basis of unjust enrichment. However, it is unlikely that a court would find the owner to be unjustly enriched in such a case. See § 21.11 for a more full treatment of this question in the context of Changed Work.

(E) PUBLIC CONTRACTS

If the owner is a public agency, agency problems can be more difficult. Courts rarely apply the concept of apparent authority in public contracts. Usually a public contract will designate a particular person who is to represent the public agency. In federal public contracts, this individual is called the Contracting Officer. Sometimes the Contracting Officer can delegate authority to subordinate agency employees, especially if the contracting agency is a large one. Usually these delegations are made in writing.

SECTION 25.03 COMMUNICATIONS

(A) COMPUTATION OF TIME REQUIREMENTS

If no specific time is designated, a communication must be made within a reasonable time. More commonly, a contract will set a time requirement. For example, a clause in the contract might require that a contractor notify the owner of an intention to claim a time extension. Such a notice may have to be given within a specified time. Does the time begin to run when the event occurred, when the contractor knew of its occurrence, or when he should have known of its occurrence?

Other questions can arise relating to when a specified time period begins. For example, the design professional might notify the contractor that the contract will be terminated unless he pays certain subcontractors within 10 days. What if the letter to the contractor is dated on September 1, mailed on September 2, and received on September 4? Does the time period begin when the letter is dated, mailed, or received?

Problems may arise relating to compliance with a time requirement. What if the contractor must respond to a communication within 10 days. If he posts the letter on the 10th day but it is not received until the 12th, has he complied? What if a communication is placed in the means of transmission but never arrives?

Such problems can be avoided by drafting contracts and communications carefully. Exact dates should be set as deadlines and actual receipt required.

What if the contract or the letter does not precisely cover these issues? As stated, if no time period is set, the act will have to be performed within a reasonable time. If a demand letter or a contract is unclear, the issue will often be resolved against the party who could have clarified the matter. For example, if the party writing the letter does not make clear when the period is to commence, or whether a reply must be received, a court would resolve ambiguities against the letter writer. The period would begin when the letter is actually received, and posting a reply within the time period will comply. If the issue is when an acceptance is effective, American courts generally follow the mailbox rule. When the acceptance is placed in a reasonable means of communication, the contract is formed. Only if the offer requires actual receipt by the offeror is this rule changed. This concept, although developed in contract formation cases, can be applied to construction project communications.

The mailbox rule can be created by the construction contract. The contract can make communications effective when properly addressed and placed in a designated means of communication.

The mailbox rule, whether created by law or contract, places the risk of a lost or delayed communication upon the person to whom the notice is sent. If it is desired to change this result, the contract should specify that the communication is not effective until actually received by the person to whom it is directed.

(B) TO WHOM COMMUNICATIONS SHOULD BE DIRECTED

Section 25.02 discussed the problems of authority and noted that it is essential to have designated persons with authority for each party, to make decisions and to take responsibility. With regard to communications, each party should know to whom he should direct any particular communication. The authorized person should be designated by name in the contract, and his address given. It is important to notify the other party if there has been a change in personnel, and notices are to be sent to someone else. See § 25.02(a) for discussion of authority to receive notices and communications.

(C) FORM OF COMMUNICATION

A communication can be made personally, by telephone or by a written communication. Generally, written communications should be required where possible. If it is not possible for a written communication to be made, at the very least, a person making the oral communication should give a written confirmation as soon as possible. If the contract provision which deals with communications of notices does not state how communications are to be made, the communication can be made in any reasonable manner.

Contracts frequently set forth formalities to avoid difficult proof problems. During the course of contract administration, parties often dispense with formal requirements. If they do, there is a serious risk that the formal requirements have been eliminated by the conduct of the parties. For this reason, formal requirements should be complied with throughout contract administration. If the formal requirements must be dispensed with, it is important for the party who wishes to rely on the formal requirements at a later date to notify the other party that the dispensation of the requirements on this occasion will not operate as an elimination of the formal requirements for the balance of the contract. Sometimes contracts contain provisions in the standard terms and conditions which state that waiver as to formal requirements in one or more instances will not operate to eliminate formal requirements in the future. These clauses may not mean much if the parties, by their conduct, show an intention to generally dispense with formal requirements.

(D) PROOF PROBLEMS

What about false claim of dispatch or receipt of a particular notice? It is important to select a means of communication which is reliable. It may be helpful to send important notices certified or registered mail, and request that a return receipt be obtained from the receiver. This is proof that the communication was received. If a communication is claimed not to have been received, the party who claims that the communication was sent may have to prove that the communication was placed in the means of communication. This often requires a showing of a standard operating procedure for mailing letters or sending telegrams. It is rare that an employee actually remembers having sent a particular communication. Usually the method of operation is introduced into evidence to show that in the normal course of operations the communication would have been sent.

It is desirable to have copies of all communications which are sent out, and notices received, in a readily accessible file. Such records should be kept for a reasonable time after the contract performance has been completed, since claims may be made long after performance is terminated, or the project completed.

Similar procedures can be used to avoid false claims that communications *were* sent.

It may be helpful to set up a system of recording how and when communications are received. If these records do not show a particular communication was received, it may be difficult to persuade a fact-finder that such a communication was sent. Absence of a signed return receipt may also assist in showing that a communication was not sent.

(E) STATUTORY NOTICES

The rules regarding time, form, and persons to whom notices are to be sent in a contract context can be created by contracting parties in the contract. However, certain rights, such as the right to assert a mechanics' lien, may depend upon compliance with statutory requirements. There is variation from state to state with regard to the types of requirements for communications in perfecting mechanics' liens. The attorney for the party who intends to perfect a mechanics' lien should check the statutory procedures carefully to insure that all communication requirements are met.

REVIEW QUESTIONS

1. Is the design professional normally authorized to modify a contract?

2. Under what circumstances will the owner be responsible for any modifications made by a design professional?

3. Give some illustrations in construction contracts of situations where notices and communications are required.

4. What is the mailbox rule?

5. If a communication states that an answer must be received within a specified period of time, does the specified period commence on the date of the communication, when the communication is mailed, or when the communication is received?

QUESTIONS FOR CLASS DISCUSSION

1. Is it desirable, from the design professional's standpoint, to have authority to modify a contract?

2. When a design professional is given authority to interpret the contract documents, is he in the position of an impartial "judge", or is he really representing the owner?

3. Why should it be more difficult to apply the concept of apparent authority in public contracts than in private contracts?

4. Is it best to have a communication effective when mailed or when received?

5. Why should the parties set up requirements that certain communications be made in writing?

6. Why are contract formalities difficult to comply with in construction contracts?

PROBLEM

A construction contract between O and C stated that completion of the project would be no later than December 1. A provision of the contract stated that O could accelerate the completion date, not to exceed sixty days, if he notified C of this in writing no later than April 1.

C's main office was in Chicago. O's main office was in New York and the construction project was in Toledo, Ohio. On April 1, O drafted a letter requesting a 45 day time acceleration. The letter was mailed on April 1, and was directed to C's office in Chicago. The normal course of post between New York and Chicago is one day air-mail and two days regular mail. By mistake the clerk placed regular mail postage on the letter and the letter did not arrive in Chicago until April 3. The employee receiving the letter at C's Chicago office did not know that it pertained to the Toledo job and, for that reason, actual notice to the Toledo employees of C was not received until April 5. Does O have the legal right to accelerate the construction date 45 days? What would your answer be if, on April 1, an employee of O called the project supervisor of C at Toledo and told them to accelerate the performance 45 days and then sent the letter?

Chapter 26

TERMINATION OF A CONSTRUCTION CONTRACT

SECTION 26.01 DEFECTS IN CONTRACT FORMATION

Chapter 2 discussed the requirements for the proper formation of a contract. After what appears to be the formation of a valid contract, one of the parties may assert that the contract was not properly formed. He may assert that there was a mutual mistake, a mistake by one party known by the other party, fraud, misrepresentation, or a lack of consideration. Other types of formation defects which could invalidate the contract are failure to comply with the requirement of form (the Statute of Frauds), lack of capacity to contract, illegality or duress. However, most of the formation attacks that are made on construction contracts center around claims of fraud, misrepresentation or mistake.

(A) FRAUD

A deliberate misrepresentation of the contents of the contract if reasonably relied upon is one type of fraud. This is called "fraud in the execution" of the contract.

Fraud also may consist of one party falsely stating facts, or falsely promising to do something in the future. If these statements or promises are relied upon reasonably by the other party, and if the statements or promises relate to important matters, the innocent party can call off the contract. Also, it may be fraudulent not to disclose important facts, when the person with knowledge knows, or has reason to know, that the other party will not, or cannot find out these facts.

Most modern courts are willing to examine the tactics used to obtain a contract in order to determine whether one party went beyond the bounds of permissible bargaining and fair play. Earlier technical rules which made fraud difficult to establish are weakening. Courts still require that proof of the fraud be clear and convincing, but they are more willing to go into the question and are not hesitant to upset a contract obtained by sharp practices or unfair methods.

Sometimes one party inserts contract language to try to avoid the charge of fraud. For example, an owner may include a provision in a contract which states that the contractor will not rely upon any representations as to soil conditions made by the owner, or that statements made are not factual, but only opinions. Usually, such provisions will not preclude an attack upon the contract based upon fraud. The purpose of such a provision is to negate the element of reliance needed for fraud, but the courts have held that enforcement of such a clause would be against public policy and would encourage fraudulent conduct. Also, some courts consider that such clauses are often inserted by the stronger party, and that, in fact, there may have been reliance despite the clause.

Clauses attempting to negate reliance may be effective in a close case. They are not iron-clad assurance against a court finding fraud, and they will not preclude a party from trying to establish fraud to upset a contract.

If fraud is to be the basis of canceling obligations under a contract, the party asserting fraud must give prompt notice of discovery of the fraud, of his intent to call the deal off, and offer to restore anything of value he has received under the contract. In some states, these requirements are technical, and often constitute a trap for the defrauded person. Legal advice should be consulted where fraud is to be the basis for relieving one from obligations under a contract.

In addition to fraud terminating a contract, fraud may be the basis for an action for damage, both compensatory (to make up for losses) and punitive (to make an example of the wrongdoer).

(B) MISREPRESENTATION

Sometimes representations of fact, or future promises, are made which are not fraudulent, because of an absence of an intent to deceive. Yet they may be untrue, and they may be relied upon reasonably by the other party. Can they be the basis for canceling a contract?

The law has been reluctant to interfere with the bargain in this area, but there has been an increasing tendency to recognize that the effect on the relying party may be the same whether or not there is intent to deceive. For that reason, courts sometimes will permit a party to relieve himself from a contract where he has relied upon negligent, or even innocent, misrepresentations by the other party. If the party relying wants to use the misrepresentation affirmatively, such as asking for damages, he will find it difficult. But if he merely wants to call the deal off, he may be successful. For example, if the owner negligently or innocently misrepresents the condition of the subsurface, there is a good chance that the contractor can avoid the contract if there has been reasonable reliance. It would be difficult for the contractor to get damages by way of added costs if he performed after discovering the misrepresentation.

(C) MISTAKE

The other major defect involves mistake. The concept of mistake may relate to subsurface conditions, discussed in Chapter 22, or mistake by the submission of bids by bidders, § 17.04(e). There may be a mistake by the contractor as to the specific location of the site. If the mistake was solely that of the contractor, he would have difficulty, unless the mistake was honest, not extremely negligent, and there was no substantial reliance by the owner.

If both parties assumed that the work was to be performed at a certain site, and it turned out the site that both had in mind was not owned by the seller, or was a different site owned by the seller, this would be sufficient mutual mistake to enable the parties to cancel the contract and terminate any further performance.

Just as there can be fraud in the actual reduction of the agreement to writing, there may be a mistake in the contract drafting process. Parties may insert an incorrect land description in a contract to purchase land, in a deed, or in a construction contract. There may be other technical errors in the contract. In such cases, if both parties made the same mistake, either party can terminate his obligation to perform because of the mistake. But if both parties had the same intention, the contract can be "reformed". "Reformation" is a judicial declaration that the actual agreement was not reflected in the written agreement because of the mutual mistake. The court then gives an order which, in effect, rewrites the agreement. The parties are then to perform in accordance with the judicially rewritten agreement. See § 20.04.

SECTION 26.02 SUPERVENING EVENTS

There is a reasonable likelihood that events may occur during the performance of a construction contract which will have a substantial impact upon the performance of either or both parties. Sometimes these events will merely make performance more costly and difficult. Other events may make it impossible to comply with completion dates, but otherwise not affect the obligation to perform. Other events may make performance impossible by either or both parties.

Which events will cancel contract obligations when the contract does not deal with the particular event which occurs?

(A) DEATH

Generally, the death of a person closely connected to the project will not affect the continuation of the contract. The obligation on the part of the owner is to pay for the work and perform other duties relating to the construction project. His death would not normally have any effect on contract obligations. This would clearly be so where the contracting owner is a corporation or public body. If the owner is a partnership or a sole proprietor, the death of the partner or the sole proprietor will usually not affect the continuation of the contract. The partnership will still be responsible, and the executor or personal representative of the sole proprietor will still be obligated to continue performance. If a key executive or employee of a corporate or public owner dies, this should not affect the continuation of the contract.

If the contractor or key employee of the contractor dies, the results are generally the same. While it is true that there is a more personal element in performance by a construction contractor, as contrasted to payment of money and the other obligations owed by the owner, the construction contract usually continues despite the death of a sole proprietor contractor or a partner in a construction partnership. The same result follows if the contractor is a corporation. The death of a key executive or employee does not affect the obligation to perform.

Unless the contract provides to the contrary, the death of someone closely connected with the performance of the construction contract generally does not terminate the contract.

(B) DESTRUCTION, TOTAL OR PARTIAL, OF THE PROJECT BEFORE COMPLETION

In construction contracts, some rather unsatisfactory rules have been developed by the courts. If a partially completed structure is destroyed by fire or acts of nature, the contractor is not relieved from his obligation to construct the building. He must start again and perform in accordance with the original obligation. Courts have frequently stated that termination requires strict impossibility, and have determined that it was not strictly impossible for the contractor to start over and complete the project. Sometimes this result has been tempered with the suggestion that the contractor should be given an extension of time to perform. Some relief has been accorded a contractor where he did not undertake to construct the entire building by himself. For example, if he were merely repairing an existing structure, destruction of the existing structure would terminate his obligation to perform. Also, if the work had been divided among a number of contractors, with the owner exercising coordination responsibility, destruction of the partially completed project would terminate the obligation of each contractor to perform.

A better result would be to look at the effect of the destruction of the partially completed project. If the project involved a substantial period of time, compelling the prime contractor to start over would cause a great deal of hardship. His original bid may have been based upon prices and conditions existing at the time the bids were submitted. His subs may be relieved by the destruction, and the prime may have to renegotiate.

Whether the prime contractor has been paid for what he has done should be taken into account. If the contractor will be compensated for the work that he has performed, either through already having received progress payments, or through insurance proceeds, the failure to terminate his obligation may not be unfair. But the rule of "no discharge" did not turn on these distinctions. For this reason, the contract should provide language dealing with the possibility of destruction of the premises during the course of performance by the contractor.

Even if the owner can require the contractor to start over, the project itself may be of considerably diminished value to the owner. The time delay alone may mean hardship to the owner, if the contractor wishes to start over and continue performance. The proper solution would be to incorporate a provision in the contract which would give either party a right to terminate if the project is totally or nearly totally destroyed during the contractor's performance.

(C) INCREASED COST OF PERFORMANCE

The contractor's performance may become more expensive or onerous than anticipated at the time of making the contract. The cost of materials may go up considerably, labor costs may increase because of new labor contracts, and other events may occur which make his performance more expensive. Generally, these are risks which are borne by the contractor, and occurrence of these events will not end his obligation to perform. Perhaps catastrophic labor or material price increases or shortages would relieve him from his obligation.

Unusual weather conditions may occur during performance. This has been discussed in § 23.04 dealing with extensions of time. However, unusual weather may cause unforeseen increase in the cost of performance. Without contract clause relief, the contractor generally is not relieved from performance. For a discussion of problems resulting when weather destroys the work in progress, see § 26.02(b).

(D) LABOR DIFFICULTIES

Labor disputes can disrupt performance. The union employees of one subcontractor may refuse to work with non-union workers of another subcontractor. Two unions may have a jurisdictional dispute. Employees may object to the construction methods they are asked to use. They may refuse to cross a picket line set up by employees of the owner. In the absence of a contract provision dealing with these questions, such risks will be upon the contractor. He will not be relieved, or even given an extension of time. He has assumed the risk of events which make his performance more difficult or costly.

There is some weakening of the doctrine. There are occasional cases which have relieved the contractor where there are labor disputes over which he has no control, and even for those in which he is involved. However, these matters usually are covered in the contract. It is common to include strikes in the extension of time provisions. Unfortunately, drafters do not always phrase the clauses broadly enough to cover the types of situations which may occur. For example, the clauses may include strikes by employees of the prime, but not cover strikes by the subcontractors' employees, or others. They may include all strikes, but not other labor disputes, such as boycotts.

(E) GOVERNMENTAL INTERFERENCE

Sometimes government authorities interfere with performance. A building inspector, or other public official, may obtain a court order compelling the project to be stopped until certain conditions are met. If the project is shut down for an appreciable period of time, the party not causing the shutdown may be relieved from further obligations. He may also have a cause of action against the other party. For example, if the shutdown is due to improper design on the part of the owner's design professional, the contractor may have a cause of action for damages, or perhaps be relieved from further performance. If the shutdown is due to poor construction methods or to failure to comply with the contract documents, the owner, in addition to being able to order the contractor off the site, may have an action against the contractor for breach. The mere fact that the performance is stopped by a governmental official does not necessarily negate breach by one of the parties. If the stoppage is due to the unexcused nonperformance by one of the parties, there is a breach as well as a possible termination.

Sometimes important equipment rented by the contractor is retaken by the equipment owner, or seized by a creditor of the contractor. This is clearly a risk assumed by the contractor, and the fact that the creditor or owner has obtained a court order which interferes with his performance does not bring the situation into the governmental act category for purposes of terminating his obligation to perform.

There may be situations where governmental acts may stop performance, and the stoppage may not be the responsibility of either contracting party. The site may be condemned by the state's power of eminent domain. A governmental rationing program may make it impossible to obtain materials. These acts, as well as other governmental acts which truly preclude performance, would be sufficient to relieve both parties from any further contract obligations. Recovery for performance rendered would be based on benefit conferred, or determined by any applicable contract clauses.

(F) FINANCIAL PROBLEMS

Once a project has begun, either the owner or the contractor, or both, may have financial difficulties. They may have trouble paying their bills, they may become insolvent, or go bankrupt. Such financial reverses will not give the financially distressed party a right to terminate his obligations under the contract. If he goes bankrupt, he can no longer be compelled to perform. His nonperformance does give the other party to the contract a claim for damages. If he is bankrupt this claim is not likely to be worth much.

Financial reverses of the type discussed may be the basis for a claim by the solvent party that he can terminate his obligations under the contract when the other party is in financial difficulty. The owner may want to employ a different contractor if the prime contractor is insolvent. The prime contractor may wish to leave the work if the owner is insolvent.

If there is nothing in the contract which deals with this question, the party who wishes to terminate must resort to the doctrine of "prospective inability to perform". What are his rights when it appears that the other party will not be able to perform?

If the owner is insolvent, the contractor has a right to demand some reasonable form of security. Perhaps the owner will have to post a bond or obtain a responsible guarantor. Arguably, the owner should not have to post a security, since the contractor will have a right to a lien on the structure. But this "right" may not be worth much, and may be expensive to assert. The contractor's obligation to continue performance in the event the owner is insolvent or in deep financial trouble should be conditioned upon compliance with a contractor demand for reasonable security. If the owner refuses, the contractor is relieved from further obligation, and may also be able to sue for damages.

What about financial troubles of the contractor? Frequently, contract clauses permit the owner to terminate if the contractor has been adjudged a bankrupt, is insolvent, or has made an assignment for the benefit of creditors. Sometimes the contract gives such a right to the owner if he is "insecure." Also, if the contractor is committing a present breach by not paying his subcontractors and suppliers, this may be grounds for termination, either under a specific clause or because such a breach is material. The contractor should be given a chance to cure these breaches in a specified time period, prior to terminating the contract.

In the absence of a contract clause, the owner may have the right to demand that the contractor post reasonable security if the contractor is insolvent. If there already are performance and payment bonds, the owner may not need added security. If the contractor is bankrupt, the same result would follow as when the owner is bankrupt. The trustee may affirm the contract within a specified time. This is analyzed in greater detail in § 37.07. Section 26.06

deals with contractual power to terminate. Contract clauses sometimes cover the effect of events of the type discussed in this section.

(G) FRUSTRATION OF PURPOSE

Each party to a contract has certain assumptions when he enters into the contract. Sometimes these assumptions turn out to be wrong or untrue. Events may occur which greatly affect the desirability or value of the other party's performance. Normally such risks are assumed by the contracting parties. Contract rights would not be worth much if a party could get out of a contract simply because the deal does not look as good because of events occurring after the contract was made.

There may be occasions where the frustrating events have so changed the deal that the law will terminate the contract. For example, a person rented rooms in London at a very high price to view the coronation of King Edward VII. The coronation was called off because of the illness of the king. The party renting the rooms was relieved from any further obligation to pay.

Frustration affects the desirability of the contract, but not the ability of the parties to perform. Each party can perform, but performance is much less desirable or valuable to one party. The tests which are used in American cases are "foreseeability" and "almost total destruction of subject matter". The party seeking to be relieved must show that the event which occurred was not reasonably foreseeable at the time the contract was made, and that the value of the other party's performance was destroyed or almost destroyed.

The leading American case in Lloyd v. Murphy, 25 Cal.2d 48, 153 P.2d 47 (1944). In this case a tenant leased commercial space in 1941, for use as a new and used car salesroom. When World War II was declared, there were no new cars to sell. But the court held such an event was reasonably foreseeable at the time the contract was made, and the leased premises still had substantial value. As a result the tenant received no relief.

Events may occur which make the construction project much less desirable to the owner. A depression may occur. Rents may plunge. The owner may run short of funds. Usually, the owner bears such risks. But if the event is not reasonably foreseeable, and the value of the project to the owner becomes almost destroyed, relief might be given.

For example, suppose there were a contract for the construction of a race track and then the state banned horse racing. The owner would have a good case for termination of the construction contract, if there had been no move to ban racing at the time the contract was made, and if a race track could not be used for other commercial purposes. If it could be used for auto racing, the case for frustration would be weaker.

It is rare for frustration of purpose to be used as a justification for terminating a construction contract.

SECTION 26.03 NON–OCCURRENCE OF CONDITIONS

Conditions are events which must occur, or be excused, before an obligation to perform arises or continues to exist. For example, the owner may condition his continuing obligation to perform upon his being able to obtain satisfactory tenants for the projected commercial structure, or his ability to obtain new or extended financing. If these conditions do not occur, the owner could terminate his obligation to continue his performance under the construction contract.

Perhaps the owner will want to continue performance under the construction contract. If the conditions are substantially for the benefit of the owner, he can continue performance under the contract despite the non-occurrence of the condition. In such case, the condition would be excused and both parties are obligated to perform.

As for the contractor, he might have conditioned his obligation to perform upon his being able to make a particular type of agreement with his labor union, or upon being able to rent certain equipment for a later stage of the project. If these conditions do not occur, and the contractor does not decide to dispense with them, the contractor would be able to terminate his obligation to proceed further under the contract.

SECTION 26.04 BREACH

(A) MATERIALITY OR IMPORTANCE OF BREACH

If one party does not perform in accordance with his obligation, and the non-performance relates to an important matter, or bears upon the likelihood that the non-performing party will be able to perform in the future, such non-performance may terminate the other party's obligation. Such a breach is called a "material breach". The determination of whether a particular breach gives the right to terminate may depend upon contract provisions which deal with this question. In the absence of any provisions dealing with this question, courts look at forfeiture possibilities (the contractor will be burdened with materials and equipment he cannot use elsewhere, or will be unpaid for work he has done), the importance of the breach, whether it is likely to occur again or has occurred before, and the reasons for the breach. Not every trivial defect or non-performance is sufficient to release the other party. Courts often look carefully at these matters, and try to determine whether the party claiming he need no longer perform has merely been looking for an excuse to get out of a bad contract.

(B) SUSPENSION v. TERMINATION

A breach may suspend the obligation to perform, but not terminate the obligation. For example, the failure of an owner to make progress payments when due should be sufficient to suspend the contractor's obligation to perform further. If this failure to pay continues for a substantial period, the contractor may be relieved from the obligation to perform further. AIA Doc. A201 at 14.1.1 gives the contractor the right to terminate after seven days notice, if he has stopped work for thirty days because of an improper refusal to issue a certificate for payment, or refusal by the owner to pay after issuance. It is unclear whether the owner can make the payments during this seven-day period and keep the contract in force. See §§ 26.06 and 26.07.

(C) PROSPECTIVE BREACH

Subsections (a) and (b) of this section relate to breaches which have already occurred. This subsection deals with breaches which may occur in the future. One party will not be able to perform when the time for performance arrives, or one party may state that he will not perform when the time for performance arrives.

Prospective inability has already been discussed in § 26.02(f), which dealt with the financial problems of parties to the construction contract. However, prospective inability to perform can relate to other problems. The contractor may lay off some of his employees, or a number of his employees may quit. The contractor may cancel orders for supplies, or his suppliers may indicate that they will not perform when the time for performance arises. In such cases, it may appear to the owner that the contractor will be unable to perform.

Such inability, whether it is on the part of the owner or the contractor or subcontractors, may be a breach. Each party owes the other party the duty to appear to be ready to perform when the time for performance arises. Even if no such promise is implied, under certain circumstances events may permit one party to terminate the contract unless the party who appears to be unable to perform can, in some way, give assurance or security that when the time for performance arrives he will be able to perform.

Prospective inability involves probabilities. In the examples given, the question is whether the owner should have to wait to see whether there will be actual nonperformance or defective performance, or whether he can demand assurance and, in the absence of this assurance, legally terminate his obligation to use the contractor.

Usually there are contract provisions which deal with this question. See § 26.06.

In the absence of such contract provisions, it will take a strong showing on the part of the owner to terminate the contractor's performance on the grounds that the contractor may not be able to perform in the future. In many cases, there is a combination of present and prospective non-performance. If there is present non-performance, such as the installation of defective materials or poor workmanship, the likelihood that this will continue will be a strong factor influencing the court to allow the owner to terminate the contractor's performance. Pure prospective inability without present breach is likely to be held to be insufficient grounds unless the probabilities are very strong, or unless there is a contract provision giving the owner this right.

A breach by anticipatory repudiation occurs when one party indicates to the other that he cannot or will not continue his performance. Both parties are entitled to reasonable assurance that the other party will perform in accordance with the contract. If one of the parties indicates that he will not, or cannot, perform, the other party loses this assurance. Should he be required to wait and see whether the threat or the indication of inability to perform will come to fruition?

The law has expanded the rights of a party to terminate a contract because of the other party's repudiation. The law will protect his feeling of assurance, since this is one purpose of making the contract. Sometimes a party who indicates that he does not feel that he is bound, or that he does not care if he is bound, or that he will be unable to perform, is merely jockeying for position. If he is the owner, he may be trying to pay less, or obtain more than the called for performance. If either party does repudiate, the other party will be given the right to terminate the obligation.

The party to whom the repudiation is made need not terminate the obligation immediately. He may state that he intends to hold the other party to the contract. If the repudiator relies upon the statement that the contract will be continued, the nonrepudiating party will lose his right to terminate because of the earlier repudiation.

The right to continue one's performance despite repudiation by the other party is qualified by the rule against enhancing damages. One party cannot recover damages caused by the other party's breach, when those damages could have been reasonably avoided by taking reasonable steps to cut down or eliminate the loss.

For example, if the contractor repudiates the contract, the owner cannot recover for those damages caused by breach which could have been avoided by hiring a replacement contractor. Suppose the contractor states unequivocally that he will walk off the job in three days, and there is no legal justification for a walkout. It might be reasonable for the owner to insist that he will hold the contractor to the contract for a short period, such as until the date of the walkout, or even for a few days after the walkout. But when it is clear that the contractor will not return to the project, the owner should take reasonable steps to replace the contractor, if the owner wishes to continue the project. A replacement should be obtained when the repudiating contractor has committed his men and machinery to another project, and it appears that he has neither the willingness nor the capacity to return to the job. Any damages that could have been avoided by the hiring of a replacement will not be assessable against the repudiating contractor.

Some contracts require that a notice to terminate be given in these situations. If the contractor contends that there is no valid contract (a contention often made in the context of a repudiation), it is arguable that such a notice need not be sent since the contractor has not recognized the existence of a contract. Nevertheless, it is desirable to send such a notice. See § 26.07.

Repudiation may accompany present or prospective breach. The greater the scope of any present or prospective breach, the greater the likelihood that the court will find that the innocent party will be released by reason of both the breaches and the repudiation. Even a small breach, plus a repudiation, may be enough to terminate the innocent party's obligation to perform further.

SECTION 26.05 TERMINATION BY AGREEMENT OF THE PARTIES

Just as parties generally have freedom to make a contract, they also have the freedom to cancel the contract. The exercise of this power may be called "rescission", "cancellation", or "mutual termination". Whatever it is called, it means that the parties have agreed to call the deal off. The requirements for such a consentual cancellation are generally the same as for formation of any contract. There must be manifestations of mutual assent, consideration, and fulfillment of any requirements of form required by law. By and large, there is no difficulty in finding manifestations of mutual assent. The evidence must show the parties agreed to call the deal off. Sometimes problems are raised when one party says nothing. In most cases, silence is not acceptance of the proposal for cancellation. However, silence, plus other acts which lead the proposer to believe that there has been agreement on cancellation, could be sufficient.

Usually, there is no difficulty over the question of formalities. Most construction contracts do not have to be in writing. For that reason, cancellations need not be in writing.

If both parties still have obligations to perform under the contract, the consideration consists of each party giving up his rights to the other. However, if one party has fully performed, there may be consideration difficulties.

For example, suppose a contractor has been paid the full contract price, but has not finished his performance. If the parties agree to cancel any remaining obligations of the contractor, the owner is not receiving anything for his promise to cancel. However, the courts are easier on enforcement of agreements to cancel than they are in treating questions of formation of contracts. The court may enforce such an agreement by calling it a waiver, or by calling it an executed (completed) gift. Some difficulties may arise, but generally agreements to cancel by both parties are enforceable.

SECTION 26.06 CONTRACTUAL POWER TO TERMINATE

A contract may give one, or both, parties the right to terminate if certain events occur. At the outer extreme, contracts may give the owner a right to terminate at his own convenience. This means that if he complies with notice requirements specified in the contract, and complies with payment requirements for work performed, he is able by his own act to terminate his obligations under the construction contract. This is common in contracts and subcontracts made for federal work.

More frequently, contracts contain provisions that, if certain events occur, the contract will be terminated. For example, AIA Document A201 at 14.2.1 permits the owner to terminate if the contractor is adjudged a bankrupt, makes a general assignment for the benefit of creditors, or has a receiver (a person by a court to handle the financial affairs of someone in financial trouble) appointed, because of the contractor's insolvency. In addition, the owner can terminate if the contractor persistently or repeatedly refuses to provide enough properly skilled workmen or proper materials. He is also given the right to terminate if the contractor is not making prompt payment to the subcontractors or materialmen or workers, or if he persistently violates laws and ordinances. The AIA contract requires that such right to terminate be exercised by a certificate issued by the architect that just cause exists for termination under the contract.

AIA Doc. A201 at 14.1.1 permits the contractor to give a seven day notice of termination, if he has ceased work for thirty days because he has not been paid. He is also given the right to terminate if work has been stopped for a period of thirty days by any court or public authority having jurisdiction, when the stoppage occurs without the fault of the contractor or of anyone for whose acts he is responsible.

SECTION 26.07 CURING DEFAULTS, AND NOTICES OF TERMINATION: THE LORANGER CASE

As stated in § 26.06, contracts often provide that the occurrence of an act or event may give one party a right to terminate the contract. Often such clauses specify that termination is conditioned upon the party intending to terminate giving a written notice to the other party. The contract may provide that the notice to terminate must be given within a specified time after the occurrence of the act or event. More often, the contract specifies that the notice will make the termination effective a designated number of days after the notice is given.

In addition to problems common to all notices and communications, see § 25.03, other legal problems frequently arise relating to such notices. What are the rights and duties of the parties during the notice period? Can the defaulting party cure the default during the period and keep the contract going? Is the party giving the notice entitled to continued performance or even accelerated performance during the notice period? The answer to these questions depends upon the reason for giving a notice to terminate.

The notice may simply create a cooling off period. Performance problems often generate animosity, and the time gap between notice and effective date of termination may be designed to permit the parties to rethink their positions.

Another purpose of a notice to terminate may be to permit the defaulting party to cure any defaults which are curable, with a view towards keeping the contract going. This may depend upon the nature of the event or act which gave rise to the right to terminate, and on the curability of any default.

Finally, the reason for the time gap may be to allow both parties, especially the non-breaching party, to make other arrangements. If so, the party serving a notice to terminate based upon the other party's default should have the option of stopping performance of the defaulting party immediately, or of permitting the other party to continue performance until the effective date of termination.

Such questions should be answered by the clause setting forth the notice requirement, but often are not. New England Structures v. Loranger, reproduced at this point illustrates this problem.

NEW ENGLAND STRUCTURES, INC. v. LORANGER ET AL.

Supreme Judicial Court of Massachusetts, 1968.
354 Mass. 62, 234 N.E. 888.

CUTTER, JUSTICE. In one case the plaintiffs, doing business as Theodore Loranger & Sons (Loranger), the general contractor on a school project, seek to recover from New England Structures, Inc., a subcontractor (New England), damages caused by an alleged breach of the subcontract. Loranger avers that the breach made it necessary for Loranger at greater expense to engage another subcontractor to complete work on a roof deck. In a cross action, New England seeks to recover for breach of the subcontract by Loranger alleged to have taken place when Loranger terminated New England's right to proceed. The actions were consolidated for trial. A jury returned a verdict for New England in the action brought by Loranger, and a verdict for New England in the sum of $16,860.25 in the action brought by New England against Loranger. The cases are before us on Loranger's exceptions to the judge's charge.

Loranger, under date of July 11, 1961, entered into a subcontract with New England by which New England undertook to install a gypsum roof deck in a school, then being built by Loranger. New England began work on November 24, 1961. On December 18, 1961, New England received a telegram from Loranger which read, "Because of your * * * repeated refusal * * * or inability to provide enough properly skilled workmen to maintain satisfactory progress, we * * * terminate your right to proceed with work at the * * * school as of December 26, 1961, in accordance with Article * * * 5 of our contract. We intend to complete the work * * * with other forces and charge its costs and any additional damages resulting from your repeated delays to your account." New England replied, "Failure on your [Loranger's] part to provide * * approved drawings is the cause of the delay." The telegram also referred to various allegedly inappropriate changes in instructions.

The pertinent portions of art. 5 of the subcontract are set out in the margin.[1] Artlicle 5 stated grounds on which Loranger might terminate New England's right to proceed with the subcontract.

1. "The Subcontractor agrees to furnish sufficient labor, materials, tools and equipment to maintain its work in accordance with the progress of the general construction work by the General Contractor. Should the Subcontractor fail to keep up with * * * [such] progress * * * then he shall work overtime with no additional compensation, if directed to do so by the General Contractor. If the Subcontractor should be adjudged a bankrupt * * * or *if he should persistently * * * fail to supply enough properly skilled workmen* * * * or * * * disregard instructions of the General Contractor or fail to observe or perform the provisions of the Contract, then the General Contractor may, by *at least five * * * days prior written notice to the Subcontractor* without prejudice to any other rights or remedies, *terminate the Subcontractor's right to proceed with the work.* In such event, the General Contractor may * * * prosecute the work to completion * * * and the Subcontractor shall be liable to the General Contractor for any excess cost occasioned * * * thereby * * *" (emphasis supplied).

[Ed. note: Balance of footnotes omitted.]

There was conflicting evidence concerning (a) how New England had done certain work; (b) whether certain metal cross pieces (called bulb tees) had been properly "staggered" and whether joints had been welded on both sides by certified welders, as called for by the specifications; (c) whether New England had supplied an adequate number of certified welders on certain days; (d) whether and to what extent Loranger had waived certain specifications; and (e) whether New England had complied with good trade practices. The architect testified that on December 14, 1961, he had made certain complaints to New England's president. The work was completed by another company at a cost in excess of New England's bid. There was also testimony (1) that Loranger's job foreman told one of New England's welders "to do no work at the job site during the five day period following the date of Loranger's termination telegram," and (2) that, "if New England had been permitted to continue its work, it could have completed the entire subcontract * * * within five days following the date of the termination telegram."

The trial judge ruled, as matter of law, that Loranger, by its termination telegram, confined the justification for its notice of termination to New England's "repeated refusal * * * or inability to provide enough properly skilled workmen to maintain satisfactory progress." He then gave the following instructions: "If you should find that New England * * * did not furnish a sufficient number of men to perform the required work under the contract within a reasonable time * * * then you would be warranted in finding that Loranger was justified in terminating its contract; and it may recover in its suit against New England * * *. [T]he termination * * * cannot, as * * * matter of law, be justified for any * * * reason not stated in the telegram of December 18 * * * including failure to stagger the joints of the bulb tees or failure to weld properly * * * or any other reason, unless you find that inherent in the reasons stated in the telegram, namely, failure to provide enough skilled workmen to maintain satisfactory progress, are these aspects. Nevertheless, these allegations by Loranger of deficiency of work on the part of New England Structures may be considered by you, if you find that Loranger was justified in terminating the contract for the reason enumerated in the telegram. You may consider it or them as an element of damages sustained by Loranger * * *." Counsel for Loranger claimed exceptions to the portion of the judge's charge quoted above in the body of this opinion.

1. Some authority supports the judge's ruling, in effect, that Loranger, having specified in its telegram one ground for termination of the subcontract, cannot rely in litigation upon other grounds, except to the extent that the other grounds may directly affect the first ground asserted. See Railway Co. v. McCarthy, 96 U.S. 258, 267–268, 24 L.Ed. 693 ("Where a party gives a reason for his conduct and decision touching * * * a controversy, he cannot, after litigation has begun, change his ground, and put his conduct upon * * *

a different consideration. He is not permitted thus to mend his hold. He is *estopped* from doing it by a settled principle of law" [emphasis supplied]); . . . .

Our cases somewhat more definitely require reliance or change of position based upon the assertion of the particular reason or defence before treating a person, giving one reason for his action, as estopped later to give a different reason. See Bates v. Cashman, 230 Mass. 167, 168–169, 119 N.E. 663, 664. There it was said, "The defendant is not prevented from setting up this defense. Although he wrote respecting other reasons for declining to perform the contract, he expressly reserved different grounds for his refusal. While of course one cannot fail in good faith in presenting his reasons as to his conduct touching a controversy he is not prevented from relying upon one good defense among others urged simply because he has not always put it forward, when it does not appear that he has acted dishonestly or that the other party has been misled to his harm, or that he is estopped on any other ground." . . .

We think Loranger is not barred from asserting grounds not mentioned in its telegram unless New England establishes that, in some manner, it relied to its detriment upon the circumstance that only one ground was so asserted. Even if some evidence tended to show such reliance, the jury did not have to believe this evidence. They should have received instructions that they might consider grounds for termination of the subcontract and defences to New England's claim (that Loranger by the telegram had committed a breach of the subcontract), other than the ground raised in the telegram, unless they found as a fact that New England had relied to its detriment upon the fact that only one particular ground for termination was mentioned in the telegram.

2. As there must be a new trial, we consider whether art. 5 of the subcontract (fn. 1) afforded New England any right during the five-day notice period to attempt to cure its default, and, in doing so, to rely on the particular ground stated in the telegram. Some evidence summarized above may suggest that such an attempt was made. Article 5 required Loranger to give "at least five * * * days prior written notice to the Subcontractor" of termination.

If a longer notice period had been specified, one might perhaps infer that the notice period was designed to give New England an opportunity to cure its defaults. An English text writer (Hudson's, Building and Engineering Contracts, 9th ed. p. 530) says, "Where a previous warning notice of specified duration is expressly required by the contract before * * * termination [in case of dissatisfaction], the notice should be explicit as to the grounds of dissatisfaction, so that during the time mentioned in the notice the builder may have the opportunity of removing the cause of objection. * * *" This view was taken of a three-day notice provision in Valentine v. Patrick Warren Constr. Co., 263 Wis. 143, 164, 56 N.W.2d 860, without, however, very full consideration of the provision's purpose. In

Corbin, Contracts, § 1266, p. 66, it is said of a reserved power to terminate a contract, "If a period of notice is required, the contract remains in force and must continue to be performed according to its terms during the specified period after receipt of the notice of termination." See Simons v. American Dry Ginger Ale Co. Inc., 335 Mass. 521, 524–525, 140 N.E.2d 649.

Whether the short five-day notice period was intended to give New England an opportunity to cure any specified breach requires interpretation (see Valentine v. Patrick Warren Constr. Co., 263 Wis. 143, 155, 56 N.W.2d 860) of art. 5, a matter of law for the court. . . It would have been natural for the parties to have provided expressly that a default might be cured within the five-day period if that had been the purpose. See e. g. Mad River Lumber Sales, Inc. v. Willburn, 205 Cal.App.2d 321, 322, 325, 22 Cal.Rptr. 918 (contract specifically gave period in which to cure default).

Strong practical considerations support the view that as short a notice period as five days in connection with terminating a substantial building contract cannot be intended to afford opportunity to cure defaults major enough (even under art. 5) to justify termination of a contract. Such a short period suggests that its purpose is at most to give the defaulting party time to lay off employees, remove equipment from the premises, cancel orders, and for similar matters.

Although the intention of the notice provision of art. 5 is obscure, we interpret it as giving New England no period in which to cure continuing defaults, but merely as directing that New England be told when it must quit the premises and as giving it an opportunity to take steps during the five-day period to protect itself from injury. Nothing in art. 5 suggests that a termination pursuant to its provisions was not to be effective in any event at the conclusion of the five-day period, even if New England should change its conduct.

If Loranger in fact was not justified by New England's conduct in giving the termination notice, it may have subjected itself to liability for breach of the subcontract. The reason stated in the notice, however, for giving the notice cannot be advanced as the basis of any reliance by New England in action taken by it to cure defaults. After the receipt of the notice, as we interpret art. 5, New England had no further opportunity to cure defaults.

Exceptions sustained.

SECTION 26.08 RESTITUTION WHERE CONTRACT TERMINATED

Termination problems often involve the right to recover for performance made before the contract is terminated. Where the contract gives a party the right to terminate for "convenience," or by a notice period, the contract often provides for a method of paying for performance rendered prior to termination. The contractor is usually allowed the reasonable value of what he incorporated into the project, the value of materials which have been allocated to the contract but not incorporated if the materials cannot be used elsewhere, expenses which cannot be avoided, and a reasonable or specified allowance for overhead and profit on work performed.

If the termination results from breach of the other party, the non-breaching party has a right to be paid for what he has done. This will be covered in Chapter 29, dealing with judicial remedies for breach of contract. The value of the work performed may be a permissible measure of recovery for the other party's breach.

Sometimes termination occurs by mutual consent of the parties, by the occurrence of acts or events which end performance, or by some defect in the mutual assent process such as fraud, mistake or duress. In such cases, any recovery must be based upon restitution or benefit conferred. If either party has conferred a benefit on the other, the party conferring the benefit can recover the benefit itself or its value. If the termination is because of the wrongdoing of one party, such as fraud or duress, close benefit questions will be resolved in favor of the innocent party.

Where the reason for termination is destruction of the project, many of the restitution questions are handled by insurance. The contracting parties should be aware of the risks of such losses and should insure against them.

REVIEW QUESTIONS

1. What are the principal formation defects that can terminate what appears to be a valid contract?

2. As a rule, can a contractor terminate his obligation to perform if his costs are higher than expected?

3. What are the possible functions of a notice of termination?

4. Under what conditions will a breach by one party terminate the obligation of the other party?

QUESTIONS FOR CLASS DISCUSSION

1. Why should it be easier to terminate a contract because of fraud than because of negligent or innocent misrepresentation?

2. If one party has a right to terminate at his own convenience, is the contract too one-sided for enforcement?

3. Should the law terminate a contract if the cost of excavation turns out to be 10 times what both parties expected, and excavation costs are 50% of the entire contract cost?

4. Would the owner be released from his obligation to build a residence if he were fired from his job and had to leave the area? If he were laid off work and had to take a lower paying position?

If he were transferred to another city? What added facts would be helpful in resolving these questions?

PROBLEM

P was the prime contractor for the construction of a 5-story office building. When the building was half completed, it burned down. The prime and subcontractors were paid through progress payments or insurance for the work incorporated into the structure. Are the prime and subcontractors obligated to start over? Can the owner be legally compelled to let them start over if they so desire?

Chapter 27

DESIGN PROFESSIONAL DETERMINATIONS AND DECISIONS

SECTION 27.01 RELEVANCE

During the course of a construction project, the design professional may make a number of decisions affecting performance and the rights and duties of owner and contractor. Usually, the right to make these decisions is created by the contract. For example, the architect issues certificates for both progress and final payments. He makes a determination of whether there has been substantial completion of the project. He has the power to condemn improper materials and faulty workmanship. He can, if certain circumstances occur, order the contractor to leave the project. He has the right, within certain limits, to interpret the contract documents and determine what is called for under them. He may have the right to uncover covered work and make inspections. He is usually given the right to grant time extensions, approve substitution of subcontractors, and pass upon the sufficiency of shop drawings submitted by the contractor. This chapter deals with the legal aspects of decision making by the design professional during the course of the construction project.

SECTION 27.02 DOCTRINE OF CONDITIONS

Parties to a contract can condition their obligations upon the occurrence of events. Normally, unless these conditions are eliminated, the duty to perform does not arise, or may be terminated if the condition does not occur.

It is common for parties to a construction contract to give the design professional power to make certain decisions. If a determination by the third party conditions an obligation of a contracting party, the duty to perform will not arise unless the determination is made by the designated third party. For example, if a certificate by an architect or engineer is necessary for payment, without that certificate the payment need not be made by the owner.

While the law permits a condition to consist of a decision of a third party, there will be considerable caution when that third party is not truly independent. One basic prerequisite of a legal system is the selection of an impartial third party to decide disputes which parties cannot resolve themselves. Normally, a court provides this impartial forum. While the law permits parties to designate third persons to decide certain disputes and often makes such decisions conclusive, if it appears that the third party is largely within the control of one of the parties, such third party decisions will be scrutinized carefully.

Also, if it appears that acceptance of the third party was forced unilaterally on the weaker party to the bargain, there is a greater likelihood that the court will accord less finality and conclusiveness to the decision of the third party.

SECTION 27.03 ELIMINATION OF CONDITION

A condition may be eliminated. Suppose a certificate by an architect is a condition precedent to an obligation by either party to perform. If the architect dies, or becomes incapacitated, the condition will be eliminated. The contract could make a provision for a substitute architect to be agreed upon by both parties. However, if no substitute were designated by contract, and if the parties could not agree upon a substitute, then the condition would be removed. If the parties themselves could not agree on the matter that was to be decided by the architect, then the matter would have to be decided by a court or by arbitrators (if there were a clause for arbitrating such disputes, or if the parties agreed to submit the dispute to arbitration).

Sometimes a condition is excused if both parties manifest an intention to give it up. Suppose the contractor and owner agree that the system by which the architect exercised certain powers was not working well. In such a case, the parties could modify the contract to eliminate the need for an architect's certificate. This might be a breach of the architect-client contract. (If the client did not reduce the fee, it is not likely that the breach would give the architect any damages.) In any event, the owner and the contractor could decide to eliminate the necessity of an architect's certificate.

Collusion on the part of the design professional, and either the client or the contractor, would also excuse the condition. If the owner and the architect conspire to deny the certificate arbitrarily, the issuance of the certificate would no longer be a condition. The same would be true if there were a conspiracy between the architect and the contractor.

The condition is excused if one party prevents the condition from occurring. For example, if the owner would not permit the architect to visit the site to determine the amount of progress payments due, such an act would excuse the condition.

The principal reason for giving these decisions to the design professional is for protection of the owner. He is usually unskilled in matters of construction, and relies heavily upon the professional advice and skill of the design professional. Since the condition is generally for the protection of the owner, the owner may dispense with, or "waive", the occurrence of the condition. If so, then the condition would be eliminated.

The contractor could contend that one of the reasons he entered into the contract was his reliance upon the expertise and fairness of a particular design professional. He might contend that the owner could not, by his own unilateral act, waive the condition of the architect certificate or architect determination. It would take a strong showing of this to deny the owner the power to waive the architect's decision as a condition precedent. However, if the contractor were able to make a clear showing of this reliance upon the particular design professional, the condition should continue to exist unless both parties wish to dispense with it.

SECTION 27.04 JURISDICTION OF DECISION-MAKING POWERS

The jurisdiction of the design professional to make decisions and determinations is created by the contract between owner and contractor. For this reason, jurisdictional questions depend upon an interpretation of this contract. It is likely that courts will examine the contract carefully to determine the jurisdiction of the design professional to make certain decisions. This is due to the general feeling on the part of courts that the architect or engineer, selected and paid by the owner, may not be impartial in making these decisions.

A court is more likely to grant jurisdiction to the design professional if the contract includes an arbitration mechanism for appealing decisions and determinations by the design professional. Since arbitration can act as a check upon possible arbitrariness of the design professional, an arbitration clause may persuade a court to decide that the dispute is within the jurisdiction of the design professional.

On the other hand, a court may be persuaded that customarily design professionals are given power to decide certain types of disputes. This may lead the court to grant broad jurisdiction to the design professional. As shall be seen, these considerations, as well as certain others, are likely to play a role in determining the degree of finality given to decisions by the design professional. See § 27.10.

SECTION 27.05 WHO CAN MAKE THE DECISION?

Sometimes the particular design professional empowered to decide questions is a partner or a principal shareholder in an architectural or engineering partnership or corporation. If so, it is unlikely that he can delegate his decision making power to someone else in his organization, without the permission of the contracting parties. If he has been given quasi-judicial powers by the contract, these powers should be exercised only by him.

In Huggins v. Atlanta Tile & Marble Co., 98 Ga.App. 597, 106 S.E.2d 191 (1958) the contract designated the architect as "A. Thomas Bradbury". The work in question had been inspected by another architect who was associated with Bradbury. This other architect, while an employee, did participate in the profits of the firm. The court stated:

> An architect is selected and agreed upon to exercise his personal skill, discretion and judgment and his duty to exercise [these skills] cannot be delegated.

SECTION 27.06 THE CONTRACT AS A CONTROL ON DECISION-MAKING POWERS

In addition to jurisdiction, there are other limits to the decision making powers of the architect or engineer. If he is given the power to grant time extensions, usually the contract provides a clause which sets forth standards for determining whether an extension of time should be given. He may have to decide whether the particular event specified occurred, what effect the occurrence of the event had upon the performance of the contractor, and the remedies which should be given to the contractor. There may be a clause which states that unusually inclement weather will entitle the contractor to an extension of time, if his performance is materially hampered by such weather. In such a case, the person having the right to grant the extension would have to determine whether this were unusually inclement weather, whether the weather had the specified effect upon the contractor's performance, and how many days of extended time should be given to the contractor. As a rule, the contract will set up general principles, but application of these principles will be left to the person who is given the power to make the decision.

SECTION 27.07 STANDARD OF INTERPRETATION

Interpreting construction contract documents is a difficult task. Words, and even drawings, are often an imprecise means of communication. Also, the very number of construction contract documents can result in confusion and contradiction. These difficulties are compounded when the design professional who must interpret the contract documents has participated in their drafting.

Should he interpret the documents to give effect to what he was intending (or what he thought or wished he had intended) at the time he drafted the plans and specifications? Some design professionals believe this to be the proper interpretation standard. One justification for the design professional having interpretation power is the inherent difficulty of drafting contract documents which contain all of the design details that ultimately go into the construction project.

Yet using his interpretation powers in this fashion can be unfair to the contractor. In N. E. Redlon Co. v. Franklin Square Corp., 89 N.H. 137, 195 A. 348 (1937), the issue was the proper interpretation standard to be applied by the architect as interpreter of the construction documents. The court held that the architect must not take into account the intention of owner or contractor, nor was he to take into account the intention he had at the time he drafted the documents in question. According to the court, he should first look at the contract documents to see whether they have provided any guidance in interpretation matters. In the *Redlon* case the contract specification stated that terms were to be used in their trade or technical sense. After applying whatever guides were given in the contract documents, he was to determine the meaning of the contract terms by using an objective standard.

Yet eliminating the actual intention of the parties or the drafter and even specifying an objective standard does not end the matter. There are a number of possible interpretation standards.

The architect could interpret the contract documents by putting himself in the position of a reasonably prudent contractor and determining what the contract document terms would have meant to such a hypothetical contractor.

He could interpret ambiguous or contradictory terms against the drafter. This is done in litigation, especially in cases involving interpretation disputes in federal public contracts. Using this technique, the contractor would be given the benefit of the doubt once it was determined that specifications or drawings are ambiguous.

Giving the contractor the benefit of the doubt places the design professional in a delicate position. Such a technique involves a determination that the specifications and drawings were ambiguous. As a rule, the design professional drafted the drawings and specifications. Construing the language against the drafter because of ambiguity is making a concession that he did not exercise proper professional skill in drafting. This concession, if it is brought out into the open, can place him in a difficult position with respect to his client, the owner. If this were the standard, many design professionals would simply avoid responsibility by making a determination that the contract documents were not ambiguous. It is difficult for a creative person to step away from his own work and make honest judgments about its clarity and accuracy. Perhaps this reality is one justification behind the position of courts such as the New York Court of Appeals in Arc Electrical Construction Co. v. George A. Fuller Co., reproduced at § 27.10, which would not accord finality to the architect's refusal to issue a certificate.

Another possible standard is strict objectivity. This would mean the interpretation which would be given to the term by a reasonably competent design professional. This is the standard suggested in the *Redlon* case. Using this standard, the design professional should forget his participation in the drafting and administrative processes, and give an interpretation similar to one which would be rendered by a design professional with his comparable skill and knowledge without prior contact with the project.

While in theory this might appear to be the best solution, it is difficult to achieve. It is hard for the design professional to put himself in a position of absolute neutrality in interpreting the contract documents.

What should the design professional do when faced with an interpretation question? Perhaps the best analysis would require that he first try to put himself in the position of a reasonable and honest contractor looking at the contract documents and submitting a bid or making a negotiated contract. If such a hypothetical contractor would have had a particular interpretation, then this should be the interpretation that should be given by the architect or engineer. If a reasonably prudent and honest contractor would have noted an ambiguity or contradiction in the contract documents, and if it would have been reasonable to have clarified this ambiguity or contradiction in the bidding or negotiations stage, then the interpretation can be rendered against the contractor. Just as contracts are often interpreted, where ambiguous, against the person drafting the contract, so can contract documents which could have been clarified be interpreted against the party who could have reasonably clarified the ambiguity. (As will be mentioned later in this section, it is not always reasonable to expect advance clarification.)

But suppose these steps are not fruitful in solving the interpretation question. What if the design professional cannot honestly put himself in the position of the contractor? Perhaps it is too difficult to determine whether the contractor should have requested a clarification. If this is the case, the best solution is to be as objective as possible. Perhaps the design professional can put the interpretation question to a colleague with whom he is associated who had not had contact with the project and solicit his view. Maybe he can submit the matter on an informal basis to a trusted colleague outside of his own organization.

If he uses the advice of outsiders, he must be certain not to delegate decision making powers to them. He should seek their advice in order to help them render his interpretation. However, he should not delegate his decision making power.

If he cannot or will not use the advice of outsiders, he may have to simply put himself in the position of the outsider and render the best objective judgment he can.

Sometimes the invitation to bidders includes a statement that bidders are to study the specifications and drawings and request clarifications of anything they feel to be ambiguous or contradictory. The clarification is to be given to all bidders in sufficient time for them to use it in submitting their bids.

In light of the realities of the competitive bidding process, this technique is not likely to be very successful in actually culling out the ambiguities. Construction documents are immense in size, and asking bidders to specify all matters which they think to be ambiguous would force contractors to spend endless hours going over specifications and drawings and then drawing up a list of "ambiguities." Also, the work involved in issuing clarifications where there are many bidders could be staggering.

Perhaps this technique may have some value in negotiated contracts, or smaller projects. Also, it may be useful if there is subsequent litigation over the meaning of contract documents. The owner in such cases might point to such a direction in the invitation to bidders as a reason not to apply the usual rule that ambiguous contract documents are to be construed against the drafter.

The method used by a design professional to interpret contract documents will largely be a matter of his own individual conscience, style, and taste. Hopefully, design professionals will be aware of the problems in standards of interpretation and do their best to be fair to both contractor and owner.

SECTION 27.08 FORMAL REQUIREMENTS

Generally, the law looks at the contract and the facts to determine whether and how the design professional exercised the power given to him under the contract. The contract may specify the form of the decision. If the facts show that the design professional did exercise his power, courts are less likely to require that he manifest this exercise of power by a formal writing.

When formal requirements are specified in the contract, can both parties, by their words or acts, eliminate any required form? What happens if one party leads the other to believe that he will not insist on a formal writing? Must the writing be made contemporaneously with the decision, or can it follow an orally made decision? Most of these matters should be handled by the contract, but often they are not.

Design professionals should exercise their power to make decisions and determinations by a clear and complete writing executed at the time the decision or determination is made. The writing should be sent by some reliable means to both contractor and owner, preferably by certified or registered mail. Time limits for arbitration may depend upon when one party receives notice of an adverse decision which can be appealed to arbitration. The design professional should keep records which indicate when such notices were sent out, and how they were sent out. If it is not possible to give a written decision at the time, the oral decision should be confirmed in a written memorandum, prepared with the same degree of care mentioned above, and sent by a reliable means of communication which furnishes proof of mailing and receipt.

SECTION 27.09 COSTS

Decisions made by architects or engineers during the performance of a construction contract involve time and effort. The architect's or engineer's compensation for this function is part of his basic fee. The costs of presenting witnesses, attending any informal hearings, or any other costs attendant to the decision making process itself, will be borne by the parties who incur them, unless the contract prescribes a different result. Usually the costs of inspection or testing are borne by the owner.

In order to make a determination, the architect or engineer charged with decision making responsibility may have to order that work be uncovered. This is a costly process. For this reason, work should be checked before it is covered. The contract usually gives the owner and and the design professional the right to uncover covered work, and, in some instances, may specify who will pay for the cost of uncovering and recovering work.

Article 13 of the AIA Doc. A201 deals at length with uncovering and correction work. It provides that work which is covered contrary to the request of the design professional must be uncovered at his request, at the contractor's expense. As for other uncovering, if the work has been performed in accordance with the contract documents, the cost of uncovering and replacing is borne by the owner. (A time extension may also be justified in such a case.) If not, the contractor shall pay for the costs "unless it be found that this condition was caused by a separate contractor . . . and in that event the Owner shall be responsible for the payment of such costs."

What happens under the AIA contract if there is a small deviation from the plans and specifications in relation to the scope of the work uncovered? Perhaps the parties should share the cost if the minor deviation was unintentional.

SECTION 27.10 CONCLUSIVENESS OF DECISION: THE ARC CASE

There have been many cases dealing with the finality or conclusiveness of a determination by a design professional.

Conclusiveness or finality relates to the scope of judicial review of the decision made by the architect or engineer. At one extreme his decision could be conclusive. If he has jurisdiction, and it is determined that he has complied with the rules set forth in the contract which gave him jurisdiction, his decisions would not be reviewed by a court at all. At the other extreme, his decisions could simply be advisory, and not bind either party. Between these extremes, his decision could be attacked only if it were dishonest, fraudulent, or corruptly obtained. Another possible solution is to make his decision final, unless there is an appeal to a court, or an arbitrator, selected by the parties. If the design professional's decision is appealed, the arbitrator or judge would start over in handling the dispute.

Generally, unless the contract clearly specifies that his decision is to be final, his decision is not final. Much of this is based upon the feeling by courts that the design professional is primarily, if not solely, interested in his client's welfare and is not a truly impartial third person. Admittedly, many contract provisions state that in exercising certain functions, the design professional is not a representative of either party, but is an independent "arbiter." Yet some courts feel this cannot be the situation under the facts. For these reasons, some courts have held that his decision is not final, and either party can have the matter redetermined in court.

There is no unanimity on the finality to be accorded decisions of the design professional, even where the contract language "appears" to make his decision final. Most courts have accorded finality to determinations by the architect or engineer which, even if erroneous or even negligent were honestly made. These courts would look only at the question of the honesty of the decision, with special reference to the process by which it was made. If the parties, or, more realistically, the contractor or the subcontractor, had the opportunity to present their positions, these courts would not go into the merits of the decision, but would simply affirm it. In addition some courts would go into the merits of the decision if they felt that it were grossly negligent. Finally, some courts would review the merits of the decision, with varying degrees of weight being given to any determination made by the architect or engineer.

New York applies one standard where the certificate is issued by the architect, and another standard where the architect refuses to issue the certificate. Arc Electrical Construction Co. v. George A. Fuller, a case stating this rule is reproduced at this point.

ARC ELECTRICAL CONSTRUCTION CO. INC. v. GEORGE A. FULLER COMPANY, INC.

Court of Appeals of New York, 1969.
24 N.Y. 99, 247 N.E.2d 111, 299 N.Y.S.2d 129.

FULD, CHIEF JUDGE. The plaintiff, Arc Electrical Construction Company, was the electrical subcontractor for the construction of a sugar refinery in Cayuga County. It brought the present action against George A. Fuller Company, an intermediate contractor, alleging that the latter had failed to pay for work performed. After a trial without a jury, the Supreme Court awarded the plaintiff the full amount of its claim and, on appeal, the Appellate Division unanimously affirmed. On this appeal, here by our permission, the defendant seeks reversal on the ground that, under the terms of its contract, the plaintiff was not entitled to be paid since the project architect had not approved the work performed.

The contract—a standard form printed agreement prepared by the defendant Fuller—provided for two different methods of computing the payments due to Arc. The first method, contained in article XXXI, was intended to apply while the contract was in effect. It provided for regular monthly progress payments constituting 90% of the amount due Arc for work performed during the preceding month, with the remaining 10% to be withheld pending completion of the project. In order to receive these monthly payments, Arc was required to submit a requisition, "[s]ubject to the approval by the Contractor [Fuller] and the Architect". The second method of payment was set forth in article XXXIII; a provision which gave Fuller the right to terminate the contract at any time prior to completion. Unlike the progress payments under article XXXI—pursuant to which 10% was to be withheld pending completion of the job—Fuller was required, if it terminated the contract prior to completion, to pay Arc the entire amount due it at that time. There is no mention, in article XXXIII, of any requirement for the architect's approval.

Arc commenced work on the project in March of 1965, and the first eight requisitions submitted, totaling about $1,400,000, received the necessary approval and were paid in due course. In December, 1965, however, the architect failed to approve Arc's requisition for the preceding month and, even though the work had been approved by Fuller's own project manager, no payment was made. Following this, four more requisitions were submitted, all of which lacked the signature of the architect's representative and none of which were paid by Fuller. Meanwhile, on February 18, 1966, Fuller's representative instructed Arc that it was exercising its option to terminate the contract and told it to cease all further work. The following May, Arc instituted the present suit for the amount due on all work it had performed since November, 1965, plus the 10% reserve that had been withheld from its previous payments.

In awarding judgment to the plaintiff, the trial judge indicated that recovery was not based upon article XXXI, which provided for progress payments of only 90% subject to the approval of the architect, but upon article XXXIII, which contained no such limitations. He rejected the argument that the requirement for the architect's approval should be read into the provisions of article XXXIII, stating that such a construction of the statute "would require the rewriting of Article XXXIII" and that, in any event, the enforcement of such a condition after the contract had terminated would constitute an unenforcible "forfeiture." We agree with this conclusion.

Although the provisions for computing payments under articles XXXI and XXXIII are quite separate and distinct, Fuller contends that, at least where payment is being sought for the same work, the requirement for the architect's approval must, by necessary implication, be applied to both provisions. Otherwise, it is said, Arc would be able to obtain payment under the termination provision for work which had already been found to be defective and had been properly rejected. "There is nothing to indicate", Fuller asserts in its brief, "that the mere passage of time would transform a bad claim into a good one."

There is considerable difference between the rejection of a claim for a progress payment and the refusal of payment after the contract has been terminated and all work has ceased. When the architect failed to approve Arc's requisition for a progress payment, this did not mean that its efforts would go permanently uncompensated. Arc was still on the job and could make whatever changes or corrections were necessary to satisfy the architect and qualify for payment. The withholding of approval, though it may have postponed, did not eliminate Arc's right to compensation for the work it had performed. However, once the contract was terminated, preventing the subcontractor from curing any defects, it is reasonable to construe the contract as providing for payment for all work actually performed, even though it may not have been entirely completed. If there were any deficiencies in performance, they would merely diminish the amount to which Arc would be entitled and would not (and should not) result in the forfeiture of its entire right to be compensated.[1] Such a construction of the contract, which adequately protects the interests of both parties, comports best with its language and we see no reason to rewrite article XXXIII of the contract—drafted, as we have noted, by Fuller—to eliminate any obligation to pay for work performed in the absence of approval from the architect.

Indeed, even if a requirement for the architect's approval was expressly incorporated in article XXXIII, it would not be enforceable. It was Fuller's own act, in terminating the contract, which rendered it impossible for Arc to take any necessary steps to satisfy the architect. The law looks with disfavor on contractual provisions that would allow one party, by its own unilateral act, to avoid its obligations by preventing or hindering the other party from fulfilling one of the conditions to the contract. . . . "[T]he defendant cannot rely on [a] condition precedent", this court wrote in the *O'Neil Supply* case (280 N.Y., at p. 56, 19 N.E.2d, at p. 679), "where the non-performance of the condition was caused or consented to by itself".

It is also significant that there was no showing in this record of any defects in performance which could have justified the architect's failure to approve Arc's requisition. Although such approval, if given, would have been conclusive on the question of satisfactory completion of the work (see 20 East 74th St. v. Minskoff, 308 N.Y. 407, 412–415, 126 N.E.2d 532, 534–536), it is well established that, where work has, in fact, been substantially performed in accordance with the provisions of a contract, the withholding of approval does not bar recovery.[2] . . .

The leading case of Nolan v. Whitney (88 N.Y. 648, *supra*) applied this principle in circumstances not too unlike those in the present case. There, as here, a contractor had brought suit to recover for work performed under a construction contract, and the defendant asserted the failure to obtain the architect's approval. A trial was held before a referee, who decided that, except for a trivial defect valued at $200, the work had been substantially performed and awarded judgment despite the lack of an architect's certificate. Our court affirmed the award, stating that, "When [the plaintiff] had substan-

1. In fact, Fuller was unable to show any defects in Arc's performance and the trial court awarded the full amount claimed.

2. The rule is based upon the fact that the architect, in contracts of this sort, rarely a disinterested arbiter, is usually the representative of the party, often the owner, who must ultimately bear the cost of the work. In the case before us, the architect was the Vitro Corporation of America, the prime contractor from which Fuller was to receive its compensation. Since approval, when given, constitutes an admission that the work is acceptable, it may be relied upon as a good indication that the contract was, in fact, properly performed. On the other hand, there is no denying that the architect has some incentive to delay approval or even withhold it entirely, and the fact that, in this case, Vitro may have been reluctant to pay Fuller for Arc's work does not necessarily mean that Arc failed in any way to perform properly under its contract with Fuller.

tially performed his contract, the architect was bound to give him the certificate, and his refusal to give it was unreasonable, and it is held that an unreasonable refusal on the part of an architect in such a case to give the certificate dispenses with its necessity" (p. 650).

In sum, then, the trial court was entirely correct in applying the contract as it was written, without reading into it a requirement for the approval of the architect after the contract had been terminated. It is undisputed that the work had, in fact, been substantially performed by Arc and the fact that an architect, for some undisclosed reason, had failed to approve the work should not prevent the plaintiff from receiving compensation for its labors.

. . .

Order affirmed.

The discussion in the Court's opinion relating to the finality of an architect's certificate or his refusal to issue a certificate, is called "dictum" because the main thrust of the opinion was that the architect's certificate was not necessary where the defendant terminated at its own convenience. Also, the court emphasized that the condition of proper performance had been dispensed with because the defendant prevented the plaintiff from complying.

The conclusiveness or finality of a design professional's decision may relate to the type of dispute involved. In the AIA contract, as an example, architect decisions on artistic effect are to be conclusive if "consistent with the intent of the Contract Documents". Also, if the decision is one which is particularly within the expertise of the design professional, it is more likely to be accorded finality. Some courts feel that decisions can be divided into those which involve questions of fact, those which involve questions of law, and those which involve mixed questions of fact and law. These lines of demarcation are often difficult to understand, and are not very precise. However, as a generalization, the court is less likely to give finality to a decision of the design professional if that decision is one which has traditionally decided by law-trained people. A court is more likely to give finality to a decision of the design professional which concerns technical factual matters. Some clauses which vest the right to make decisions in the hands of third parties draw a distinction between question of law and questions of fact.

A case decided only a few months after the decision in the *Arc* case illustrates the importance of the type of decision as a factor in determining the degree of finality to be accorded a decision by a design professional. This case, Yonkers Contr. Co. v. New York State Thru. A., 25 N.Y.2d 1, 250 N.E.2d 27, 302 N.Y.S.2d 521 (1969), involved a contract to construct a portion of a New York freeway. The contract provided that the materials were to be measured "in place" by the engineer on the job and that his "measurements . . . shall be accepted as final, conclusive and binding on the contractor".

The contractor contended he should be allowed to recalculate the measurement on the basis of truckloads supplied. The court rejected this contention, stating:

> . . . the engineer adopted the method of measurement prescribed in the contract and that, in the absence of fraud, bad faith or palpable mistake, his final estimate is, in the language of the contract, 'conclusive and binding on the contractor'.

In the *Yonkers* case the court was willing to employ the contract to make the engineer's measurement conclusive in the absence of fraud, bad faith, or palpable mistake. Yet, the court stated in the *Arc* case that if the architect's refusal to issue a payment certificate was "unreasonable", the contractor could collect despite the absence of the architect's certificate.

Perhaps the cases can be reconciled. In the *Arc* case, the question was whether the contractor could be paid without the architect having approved the work. In the *Yonkers* case, the question related to the method of measuring the amount of materials that had been incorporated in the freeway. The former is a more discretionary decision, while the latter tends to be more mechanical.

The finality of the decision, as well as the right of the design professional to make the decision, may depend upon whether the matter in dispute involves self-interest of the design professional. For example, there have been cases where courts have refused to permit design professionals the right to make a decision where there is a cost condition (See § 8.01). If the cost is exceeded, a design professional could lose his fee, and might have to pay damages as well. For that reason, if there is a dispute over interpretation, and the contractor contends he is to do the work in one manner, and the owner wants work done in a different manner, a resolution of the dispute in favor of the contractor would mean an extra, and ultimately an increase in cost. For this reason, it would be difficult for the design professional to be impartial.

What if the design professional is asked to determine whether the contractor should be granted an extra or an extension of time, when the determination of these questions depends upon whether the contract documents contain faulty design? In such a case, the design professional cannot truly be impartial. If the work has been designed poorly, he may be liable for any damages incurred by his client, as well as damages which may be incurred by other parties. For that reason, it would be unfair to permit him to make this determination, and certainly unfair to have any determination made by him final. It is unlikely that a court would find any such determination final if this type of conflict of interest were present.

Some criteria for determining the degree of finality to be given to a design professional's decision can be illustrated by two court decisions. Walnut Creek Elec. v. Reynolds Const. Co., 263 Cal.App.2d 511, 69 Cal.Rptr. 667 (1968), involved an action by an electrical subcontractor against the prime contractor and the bonding company of the prime contractor. The dispute related to whether conduit pipes laid in gravel fill were required to be wrapped. The specifications, according to the court, were ambiguous. The contention made by the defendants was that the school district's architect made a determination, and that this determination should be conclusive. The subcontract provided that the work was to be done in accordance with the plans and specifications, and "to the satisfaction of the architect". The court held that the satisfaction language dealt only with the quality and quantity of performance, and did not give the architect to make a final decision on a legal interpretation of the subcontract, or to resolve ambiguities in the plan and specifications. The court stated that if he were to be given this power, it must be "unequivocally expressed". The court went on to hold that the specification was ambiguous and would be resolved against the school district which created it.

This case illustrates court reluctance to accord finality to architect decisions which relate to contract interpretation, a matter which courts frequently think of as involving legal questions. Secondly, the case also illustrates the tendency to accord less finality to decisions which may affect the obligation of the subcontractor. While it is true that the subcontractor agreed to terms which gave certain powers to the architect, it is likely that he had very little bargaining power, and had to accept the provision. For this reason, doubtful questions as to the conclusiveness of the architect's decision are likely to be resolved in his favor.

John W. Johnson, Inc. v. Basic Construction Co., 292 F.Supp. 300 (Dist. Ct. Dist. of Columbia 1968) illustrates the attitude of at least some courts regarding the necessity for a reasonably fair hearing process, before the design professional determinations will be given some form of finality. In this case, the subcontractor brought an action against the prime contractor and the architect. The action against the architect was based upon a dispute over the question of whether the subcontractor had enough workers on the project to finish his work on schedule. The architect directed the prime contractor to cancel the plaintiff's subcontract. The trial judge stated:

> This amazing directive was issued by the architect's office without notice to the plaintiff and without giving the plaintiff any opportunity to be heard, orally or in writing, formally or informally. This action on the part of the architect's office was contrary to the fundamental ideas of justice and fair play. The suggestion belatedly made at the trial that it was not appropriate for the architect to maintain any contacts with subcontractors is fallacious in this connection. Any such principle as that did not bar the architect's representative from according a hearing to the subcontractor before directing that his subcontract be cancelled.

However, the subcontractor left the job for other reasons. Since the directive was not carried out, the court held that there was no claim against the architect, even though the court seemed to conclude that the architect's action had been arbitrary.

The *Johnson* case indicates that the finality and weight to be given to any decisions by the architect may depend upon the fairness of the process used by the architect in making his determination.

SECTION 27.11 LIABILITY OF DESIGN PROFESSIONAL

Chapter 34 discusses the problems relating to legal responsibility of architect and engineer. However, it may be useful to consider the question of whether persons displeased with decisions by the architect or the engineer have any legal recourse against the architect or the engineer. Determinations by the architect or engineer can injure the owner, the contractor, subcontractor, sureties, or lenders. They may contend that the decision was wrong, that it was improperly made, that it was motivated by spite or bad faith, or that it was corrupt or dishonest. In § 27.10 emphasis was upon the degree of finality or conclusiveness of these decisions. This section deals with the possibility that persons who are displeased with the decision may decide to bring civil action against the architect or engineer who has made the decision.

The modern tendency in litigation has been to institute civil action against anyone who can be connected with the acts or decisions which cause a loss to a plaintiff. For this reason, an increasing number of civil actions against architects or engineers are based upon decisions they have made during the administration of a construction contract.

There have been two basic legal problems. The absence of any contractual relationship ("privity") between the design professional and any of the parties, other than the owner, has proved to be a stumbling block in many cases. This will be discussed more fully in Chapters 30 and 34, which deal with damage claims against design professionals.

Second, the law sometimes accords immunity from civil liability to persons exercising judicial or quasi-judicial functions. The prime example is the judge. The law accords him absolute immunity from being sued by litigants who are unhappy with his decision. This is so even if the decision was fraudulent or corrupt. In the case of corruption, the judge may be removed from office by the state, or subject to criminal action, but the parties cannot sue him. The purpose of such a rule is to protect judges from being harrassed by vexatious litigants, and to permit judges to decide cases without fear of being sued personally.

Immunity, in varying degrees, is given to other public officials. Sometimes they are protected from suit if they acted honestly and in good faith. The law tries to steer a line between placing liability upon decision makers who injure persons by their decisions, and the policy that a good system of government requires that decision makers have freedom to act without an inordinate fear of civil actions being brought against them.

Judicial immunity has been applied by analogy to the design professional's decisions. Some courts have held that the design professional, when he makes certain decisions, should be accorded quasi-judicial immunity. This means that he can be sued only if his decision is corrupt, or obtained by fraud. Merely showing that he was negligent or wrong is not sufficient. Other courts have held that he can be sued for his negligence in decision making, and they have refused to give him quasi-judicial immunity.

Some courts accord immunity when the decision involves the issuance of a final certificate for payment, but refuse immunity when the decision concerns the issuance of a progress payment certificate. Some courts have looked at whether the decision was one which would be conclusive on the parties. If so, they have felt that this was analogous to the position of a judge, and that for this reason the design professional should be given immunity from being sued unless he was corrupt or dishonest. Such courts seem to pay very little attention to the fact that giving both immunity to suit and finality to the decision of a design professional precludes the owner or the contractor from attacking either the decision or the person making the decision. A judge may be immune, but usually his decisions can be appealed. These courts give the design professional more power than either the owner or the contractor, or, for that matter, the design professional, would intend or want.

Courts sometimes look at whether the contract provided an opportunity to arbitrate decisions and determinations by the design professional. If so, there is less conclusiveness to the latter's decisions. In such cases, the design professional looks less like a judge and cannot obtain quasi-judicial immunity. (If there is a chance to arbitrate, the design professional's decision should not injure the parties significantly, since they can go to an impartial forum for a final decision.)

Sometimes courts draw a distinction between factual determinations and contract interpretation decisions. An illustration of a factual determination would be the measurement of the quantity of work made in order to determine the amount of a progress payment certificate. This would be contrasted with the design professional determining whether there has been compliance with the contract documents. In the latter role, the design professional appears to be more like a judge than in the former role. However, an evaluation of the different types of decisions and determinations which may be made by the design professional shows the difficulty of drawing this line.

Early English decisions gave the design professional immunity. More recent cases have left the rule in doubt. The earlier Ameriican cases adopted a rule denying immunity, but a few recent cases have been impressed by the judicial immunity analogy and have granted immunity in some types of determinations. The results have varied, depending on some of the fact variations that have been mentioned.

Some contractors have sued architects for decisions or determinations, upon the theory that the architect wrongfully induced the owner to breach the owner-contractor contract. Courts have held that such an interference with the contract is "privileged", because the owner-contractor contract gives the architect the power to make these determinations and decisions. "Privilege" is a defense to an action for interference with a contract, because the interference is considered legitimate and for a proper purpose.

The legitimate purpose is the contractual responsibility given the architect or engineer to make these determinations. However, the privilege is "qualified", and the architect or engineer will not be able to use it as an absolute defense if his interference with the contract is in bad faith, or with the intention to injure the contractor. Whether the architect is given a qualified immunity from suit, or the privilege defense to an action for wrongful interference with contract, the issues are the same. Should he be accorded protection from being sued when he makes honest determinations or decisions in accordance with the power given to him by the contract? There is no clear-cut answer in the American cases to this question.

One case illustrates the complexity of immunity. Lundgren v. Freeman, 307 F.2d 104 (9th Cir. 1962) resulted from a school district terminating a contractor's performance on the advice of the architects. In addition to suing the school district for an alleged wrongful termination, the contractor brought an action against the architects. The contractor claimed that the architect wrongfully interfered with his construction contract, wrongfully induced the school district to breach the contract, and damaged the contractor's reputation by assertions as to his competence. In addition, the contractor sought punitive damages against the architects.

The Court stated that the architect could have been acting in one or more of three capacities. He could have been the agent of the owner, a quasi-arbitrator, or acting on his own. If he acted as an agent, he would not be liable, since the contractor brought an action against his principal, the school district. Only if the judgment were uncollectible against the school district, would the contractor have a claim against the architects, and then only for those damages that "he can prove to be the result of willful and intentional misconduct by the architect".

If the acts of the architect were in his capacity as quasi-arbitrator, the architect would be immune if his decisions were made in good faith. Only if he acted fraudulently, or with an intent to injure the contractor, would the architect be liable.

As for acts of architects which are outside the scope of their powers as agents or quasi-arbitrators, they will be held liable for those damages which naturally flow from those acts. The contractor must show that the acts were wilful and intentional, but need not show a specific intent to injure him. If the contractor can show wrongful assertions relating to his credit and his reputation as a builder, he can recover foreseeable damages from the architect. If these acts were done maliciously, he can recover punitive damages.

Unfortunately, in *Lundgren*, the court did not go into which acts of the architect fall into which categories. This was because the decision dealt only with the question of whether the contractor should be given an opportunity to have a trial on these questions. The court concluded that he should be given this opportunity, and that the trial court was incorrect in granting a motion by the architects for a summary judgment. (A summary judgment concludes litigation without an actual trial.)

SECTION 27.12 FINALITY AND IMMUNITY: SOME SUGGESTIONS

(A) FINALITY

If the parties to a contract voluntarily designate a third party to make certain determinations or decide certain disputes, and also agree that these determinations or decisions shall be binding on both parties, the law should give effect to such an agreement. Parties who genuinely agree to abide by such third party decisions, and who are satisfied that the decision was honestly made, are likely to perform in accordance with the decision. The third party may be better equipped, in the view of the contracting parties, to give a fair and quick decision. Finally, failure to make such agreements final may discourage parties from agreeing to submit determinations and disputes to third parties, or encourage them not to live up to such agreements. The result can be an increasing burden on an already burdened judicial system.

Contract language and courts often state that, in making certain determinations, the architect or engineer is acting in a quasi-judicial function, and not as a representative of one of the contracting parties. This does not change the realities of the situation. The architect performs professional services for, and is the professional advisor of his client, the owner. His functions are to perform services for which his design training qualifies him, and which the owner cannot do for himself. Also, he protects his client's interests in the construction process, and tries to insure that his client gets the performance to which he is entitled. Many times architects are referred to as "the owner's architect".

The architect or engineer cannot shed these primary roles and suddenly become a neutral, expert judge when called upon to make certain determinations and decide certain disputes. This, coupled with an inherent conflict of interest, should lead to the conclusion that the design professional should not be considered a judge, and his determination should be reviewable on the merits by arbitration or litigation.

If the contractor or subcontractor voluntarily agrees to accept the architect or engineer as a quasi-judge, then it might make sense to accord honest decisions finality. But the contractor and, certainly the subcontractor, rarely has a choice in the matter.

Generally, determinations and decisions by the architect or engineer are followed by the parties. This may be because the parties (mainly the contractor) are satisfied, because it is too costly to arbitrate or litigate, or because of the need to retain the good will of the design professional. In most cases, this will mean that giving him decision making powers, in the first instance, will provide a quick method of handling construction disputes. According his decisions some degree of finality simply gives effect to the superior bargaining position the owner frequently enjoys at the time a construction contract is made.

Taking all these factors into account, most decisions and determinations by the design professional should not be accorded any finality if appealed. Until appealed, they control. But if appealed, they should be reviewed on the merits ("Was he right?") and not simply affirmed if honestly made.

Such a conclusion avoids specious distinctions such as the differentiation between a progress payment and a final certificate, between a question of interpretation and a determination of quality or quantity, or any of the other differentiations often made by courts. In drafting contracts, especially in drafting the standardized forms used in many transactions, it may be useful to recognize the realities and fairness of the situation. Language should make it clear that the architect or engineer's decision is binding, unless and until it is appealed to an arbitrator or to a court.

(B) IMMUNITY

The tests for determining immunity are hopelessly complex. It may be more useful to focus upon the different persons who may wish to institute legal action against the design professional, based upon his decision making. In looking at potential plaintiffs, emphasis should be upon the type of duty owed by the design professional, rather than upon comparison to the judicial model.

The design professional should not be given immunity from actions brought against him by his client. If he makes a negligent or fraudulent decision, he should be held accountable to his client. Designating a particular architect or engineer to make these determinations should not mean the owner has assumed the risk of negligent decisions.

Nor should the design professional be given immunity from actions brought by the contractor. If the design professional is not given immunity from actions brought against him by his client, he should certainly not be given immunity in actions brought against him by the contractor. Realistically, the contractor does not have much choice as to who will be the architect or engineer. If the suggestion in § 27.12(a) is adopted, the scope of exposure of the design professional will be relatively limited. If his decision can be appealed either to arbitration or to the courts, the loss to the contractor because of a negligent or fraudulent decision will be limited.

Also, even where immunity has been granted, it has not protected the design professional from being sued where he has been dishonest or corrupt. Actually, what is primarily involved is the question of a negligently made decision. The suggestion in this subsection would make the design professional responsible for negligently made decisions and determinations, but only for those losses which could not have been reasonably avoided by the contractor.

The design professional should not be given immunity from actions brought against him by third parties such as sureties, lenders, or security holders who may be injured by a negligently issued payment or completion certificate. In such cases, it is highly unlikely that the third parties have played much of a role in picking the design professional and giving him decision making powers. Perhaps, in some cases, the lender will be able to exert some control in this regard. Nevertheless, the person chosen should not be given immunity simply because he has been chosen to perform these functions.

Third parties should be able to recover any losses they have suffered because of the negligence of the design professional which were reasonably foreseeable by the design professional, both as to the persons who might be injured, and the type and scope of injury which could arise.

If the architect's certificate is given greater finality than suggested in § 27.12(a), this is a greater reason for eliminating immunity. If the decision is difficult to attack, there should be a way for an injured party to pursue the maker of a negligent decision. Even in these cases, the contractor who has suffered a loss can only recover for those losses which could not have been avoided by the use of reasonable care. If the architect has made a negligent decision, most construction contracts provide that his decision is subject to arbitration.

While professional liability insurance should protect against this type of liability, some professional liability insurance policies exclude coverage for liability for negligently made decisions.

REVIEW QUESTIONS

1. Under what circumstances will the decision of a design professional be excused?

2. Under what circumstances is the decision of a design professional conclusive?

3. Can a design professional be sued by the owner for a negligent decision? By a contractor?

QUESTIONS FOR CLASS DISCUSSION

1. Should a design professional be immune from suit based upon any decisions he is required to make under the contract?

2. If a design professional dies during the performance of the contract, should the owner be given a right to replace him with anyone he chooses?

3. If design professional decisions are not conclusive, why have him make these decisions?

PROBLEM

Under the terms of a construction contract between O and C, A, the architect, was given the power to terminate C's performance if C was not making reasonable progress. A informed C that his progress was not satisfactory, and that he was to leave the job. C tried to show A records of weather conditions to prove that unseasonably cold weather cut down his efficiency, that there had been a jurisdictional strike between the unions of two subcontractors, and that A had taken too long to approve shop drawings and render interpretations. A refused to look at the evidence, or to consider these contentions. He also refused to give any time to the contractor to catch up. C left the site. There was no arbitration provision.

C sued O for firing him without just cause. He also sued A for firing him. Does C have a good claim against O if he can prove what he contends? Should A be given immunity from suit?

Chapter 28

DECIDING DISPUTES: EMPHASIS UPON ARBITRATION

SECTION 28.01 METHODS OF RESOLVING DISPUTES

Disputes in building construction projects are common. In the absence of contractual provisions which designate specific persons to decide disputes, disputes which cannot be resolved by the contracting parties may have to be decided by a court.

There are many disadvantages to litigation. Often, court calendar congestion causes a substantial time delay. Litigation requires an attorney, and a complex lawsuit can mean substantial attorneys fees. In many law suits, it is necessary to take "depositions" (testimony of the parties and prospective court witnesses) in advance. While these depositions can save trial time, reduce the probability of surprise at the trial, and often assist in getting parties to settle, they can be time-consuming and costly. To take a deposition usually requires lengthy preparation by the attorney, and an expensive transcript (typed record) of the testimony.

Some persons do not want to go to court, because court procedures are public and sometimes involve unwanted publicity. Some contracting parties do not trust the fairness of the decision obtained in court. This is especially so when the matter involves technical problems which contractors and design professionals feel are beyond the competence of a judge and jury. Even if a court judgment is obtained, it is often difficult to collect.

To avoid litigation, and provide for an expedient method of handling disputes, the contract may direct that certain matters be resolved by third persons. As seen in Chapter 27, the design professional is often given the power to make determinations under a construction contract. Also, in a cost-type construction contract, it is possible that the parties will designate a specified public accounting firm to determine whether certain costs are to be included. The determination of whether certain performance standards have been met may be submitted to professional independent testers or laboratories. Where a lender or a governmental institution plays a large role in the construction project, it may be possible to specify that the work must be done to their satisfaction, or that they will have authority to decide certain disputes.

Chapter 28 assumes that such determinations are not submitted to these third parties (design professional, accountant, tester or other third party), or have been decided by those persons, with one party wishing to appeal the determination.

Arbitration is the method used most frequently in construction contracts to handle disputes in which one or both parties are not satisfied with the determination of the design professional, an accountant, or a tester.

SECTION 28.02 IS ARBITRATION DESIRABLE?

Opinions differ on the desirability of arbitration for construction contracts. When arbitration first came into general use, it was thought that arbitration was almost always preferable to going to court. Arbitrations were thought of as a quick and economical method of solving disputes, especially where speed was essential. Also, many people felt that arbitrators with technical skills were better qualified to make determinations than courts. However, there has been some shift in attitudes toward arbitration.

As arbitration has become more institutionalized, occasionally it has acquired some of the worst attributes of judicial dispute settling which made arbitration a desirable substitute. Arbitration can be quite expensive. The arbitrator may not make a quick, fair decision. Many persons feel that arbitrators tend to compromise. When a party has a good case, he may feel that compromise is unjust to him.

Also, courts have begun to be more efficient in the resolving of disputes. Many of the technical rules which exasperated litigants and caused skepticism about the fairness of the judicial process have been modified or eliminated. The courts have tried to expedite litigation. Today, much litigation delay results not from flaws in the judicial system, but from the failure of the litigants, or their attorneys, to bring the dispute to trial. Courts have developed methods of digging into the facts in advance, through discovery and depositions, which makes litigation more efficient and encourages settlement.

Another complaint frequently made of arbitration, especially in terms of its comparison to courts, is that arbitrators do not feel obligated to conduct a fair and impartial hearing. Arbitrators may feel that they have been hired as technical experts to decide a dispute, based on their own knowledge. Many contracting parties and attorneys have become disillusioned with the arbitration process because they have had arbitrators who did not give them a proper opportunity to present their case.

Another weakness of arbitration is that it is often difficult to separate factual and technical questions from legal questions. Often the arbitrator is not an attorney, and may be unable to understand and apply relevant legal concepts. Also, many judges have had sufficient experience with construction projects themselves, either as attorneys or through their work as judges to give them some expertise in both technical and legal matters.

Another significant difference lies in the right to appeal. In arbitration, there is no meaningful appeal. Where the matter is appealed to a court, the court generally does not examine the merits of the decision. It merely determines whether the arbitrator had jurisdiction, and whether the award was honestly made. In litigation, if a party is dissatisfied with the decision of the trial court, he will have the right to appeal to a higher court. While the scope of review is limited to a degree, it is broader than the review given an arbitration award.

Another disadvantage of arbitration of construction contracts is that it is often difficult to bring all the parties before the arbitrator. There are many persons involved in the project, some of whom are tied by contract, but not all are parties to the same contract. Today, it is relatively easy to get all the interested parties in the same lawsuit.

A judge has power to order that witnesses appear and testify (subject to the right not to testify based upon constitutional protections against self-incrimination) and to require that relevant documents be brought before the court. In some states, an arbitrator is given this power by state arbitration laws. However, without this specific statutory power, an arbitrator cannot compel witnesses to appear nor order that they produce documents.

In Lesser Towers Inc. v. Roscoe-Ajax Construction Co., 271 Adv. Cal.App. 776, 77 Cal.Rptr. 100 (1969), the court noted that arbitration "is not always a simple, expeditious or inexpensive method of adjudicating commercial controversies". This case involved an action to confirm an arbitrator's award which related to a construction contract for a twenty story apartment building.

The total elapsed time for arbitration was 19 months, of which 202 days consisted of hearings, and three days consisted of oral arguments. It took 25,000 pages of a reporter's transcript to record the oral proceedings. 1500 exhibits were introduced. Over $400,000 in arbitration expenses, *exclusive* of attorneys fees, were incurred.

Before the arbitration even began, each party went to court to obtain rulings relating to the arbitration. After the owner had put in his claim in the arbitration, the contractor sought to introduce evidence of a counterclaim. At this point, the owner refused to arbitrate and went to court to restrain the arbitrators from considering this claim. Ultimately, the arbitrators ruled for the owner, but the owner had to go to court again to get an order confirming the award. While he was doing this, the contractor went to the federal court to try to reverse the award of the arbitrator. Without comparing the quality of the arbitrator's decision to the quality of the decision which would have been rendered by a court, one wonders how much money was saved by arbitrating this particular case.

The *Lesser* case illustrates that arbitration works best when the parties accept the decision and do not go to court. In construction, good will and a continuing relationship, matters which discourage appeal, are often absent. Arbitration may not be appropriate for all disputes which may develop on the construction project. There is a proper use for arbitration, but it is important that the determination of whether arbitration is to be used takes into account the nature of the dispute to be arbitrated, the arbitrator who will be used, and whether, in the long run, arbitration is the preferable solution. For example, it might be advantageous to specify that disputes which occur after performance is terminated, or after a contractor has been removed from the project, not be subject to arbitration. This would preserve the right to arbitrate those matters which need quick resolution. There can be other possible lines of demarcation between arbitration and the courts. These are matters which should be carefully analyzed by the parties and their attorneys when determining which, if any, disputes should be subject to arbitration in a construction contract.

Arbitration clauses have become common, and are usually drafted to cover most types of disputes. This is often done without proper evaluation of whether arbitration is the best solution in the particular case. It also should be kept in mind that arbitration can take place by submission, which is an agreement by the parties to submit an existing dispute to arbitration.

SECTION 28.03 VALIDITY OF ARBITRATION AGREEMENTS

At one time courts were openly hostile to arbitration. Some states did not permit arbitration at all, on the theory that arbitration ousted the courts from their proper jurisdiction. Other courts placed limits on the right to arbitrate. Arbitration was permitted only by submission of existing disputes in some jurisdictions. Sometimes courts gutted arbitration provisions by not according the arbitrator's decision the type of finality necessary to make arbitration work. However, the recent trend has been towards giving a broad scope to arbitration, and to accord the arbitrator's decision substantial finality and conclusiveness. Sometimes this has been done by arbitration statutes. The judicial interpretation of these statutes has been favorable to arbitration. While it still may be difficult to arbitrate certain types of disputes in some states, and while some courts still consider that an agreement to arbitrate is revocable, the strong tendency in America today is to accord arbitration a dominant role in the resolution of construction contract disputes.

SECTION 28.04 JURISDICTION OF ARBITRATOR: WAIVER OF ARBITRATION

The arbitration agreement must be interpreted to see whether the particular dispute in question falls within the arbitration clause. If the arbitration clause is drawn broadly to cover all types of disputes, this will not be much of a problem. However, anything less than a broad mandate to the arbitrator can mean that the arbitrator or the judge must determine whether the arbitrator has jurisdiction, under the contract in question, to arbitrate the particular dispute.

Sometimes, one party decides that he does not want to arbitrate. He may prefer going to court, or wish to use delaying tactics. He will look for excuses not to arbitrate. He may not appoint an arbitrator, despite his promise to do so under the contract. (In many states, and under many arbitration provisions, a court may appoint the missing arbitrator. Some provisions permit the one arbitrator selected to pick a second, who can pick the third.)

In order to avoid arbitration, one of the parties may contend that the arbitration procedure has been "waived." He will emphasize any conduct on the part of the other party which may tend to show that the other party did not intend to arbitrate the dispute. If one party states that he will not arbitrate, and the other party agrees to give up arbitration, arbitration is eliminated.

However, what usually happens when one party tries to avoid arbitration is that he will seize on anything the other party has done and claim that the arbitration clause has been "waived." For example, one party may file a mechanics' lien. He may have to do this, because the time for filing the lien may be nearing expiration. The other party may then seize upon this as an indication that the party filing the lien has decided to use the judicial route, and thus has given up arbitration. (Whether the filing of a mechanics' lien claim does waive arbitration varies from state to state. It certainly should not waive arbitration where the filing of the lien claim was necessary to protect the lien, and where there is no indication that the party filing was intending to give up arbitration.)

If a party wants to use arbitration, his actions should be consistent with an intention to arbitrate the dispute. If he wishes to do anything which may appear to be inconsistent, he should seek legal advice on whether what he intends to do will waive arbitration. All the requirements for arbitration procedure should be met promptly and correctly.

There are other methods that have been used to try to avoid the arbitration procedures. One is to claim that the entire contract, including the arbitration clause, was procured by fraud, or some other defect in the contract formation process. If this can be done successfully, then the disputed matters in question will not have to be arbitrated. Some courts have required that there be a showing that the arbitration clause itself was obtained through fraud, or through a mistake, before there can be a submission of disputes to a court rather than to arbitrators.

SECTION 28.05 ARBITRATION PROCEDURES

After determining whether the dispute is arbitrable, the next questions are: (1) who are to be the arbitrators and (2) where is the arbitration to be held? The former problem will depend largely upon the arbitration clause. Sometimes arbitration clauses provide for three-man arbitration boards. They usually consist of one member appointed by each party, and a third member appointed by the two other arbitrators. A particular arbitrator, or a panel of arbitrators in a specified priority, can be agreed to in advance by the parties. The panel obviates the difficulty of a specific person being appointed and not being able to serve. Some procedures permit a third party, such as the American Arbitration Association, to designate arbitrators, if the parties cannot agree. A person should not serve as an arbitrator if he has a stake in the outcome of the arbitration, or if he is closely connected with one of the parties, unless the parties know of these facts and still want him to serve.

The United States Arbitration Act authorizes and regulates certain interstate arbitrations. The United States Supreme Court reviewed an arbitrator's award made under this statute in Commonwealth Corp. v. Casualty Co., 393 U.S. 145 (1968). The "neutral" arbitrator was the owner of an engineering firm that had provided services to construction companies in the past, including services to the prime contractor who was a party to the arbitration. Despite the fact that there was no evidence of partiality in the award, the Court invalidated the award because the neutral arbitrator had not disclosed information regarding his past dealings with one of the parties to the arbitration at the time the arbitration commenced.

A rule of the American Arbitration Association requires a prospective arbitrator to disclose any circumstances "likely to create a presumption of bias or which he believes might disqualify him as an impartial arbitrator." Parties to the arbitration can determine to proceed with that arbitrator after they have been given information which might bear upon his impartiality.

Arbitration is most likely to work successfully if the parties have respect for the arbitrator or arbitrators. For this reason it is advisable, where possible, to designate a specific arbitrator or arbitrators in advance, or use a panel of arbitrators with a designated set of priorities. This is usually better than having each party select one arbitrator, and having these two arbitrators select a third, or accepting as an arbitrator someone designated by an association such as the American Arbitration Association or the American Institute of Architects. While these groups do have able arbitrators among their panels, sometimes parties are reluctant to accept decisions of persons with whom they have had no prior contact, or in whom they have no particular reason for confidence. Some parties may prefer a decision by an absolute outsider. However, generally arbitration works best when the parties respect the arbitrator and are willing to accept his decision.

The arbitrators can designate the place of arbitration, unless the contract limits this power. In some arbitration clauses, the dominant party will designate a place of arbitration which is convenient to the dominant party, and inconvenient to the weaker party. Central Contracting Co. v. Maryland Casualty Co., 367 F.2d 341 (3rd Cir. 1966) involved a large subcontract which was to be performed in Pennsylvania. The subcontractor was a Pennsylvania corporation, and the surety bond company from which the subcontractor was attempting to recover was a Maryland corporation. The contract provided that the subcontract would be construed in accordance with the laws of New York; that any legal action brought pursuant to it would be limited to the courts of New York County in New York. Also the contract specified that the arbitration would be held in the City of New York. The Third Circuit Court of Appeals held that the contract provisions determining where litigation must be brought would be given effect by the court, as long as the provisions were reasonable. The court noted that the three general contractors on the project were New York corporations, and that the New York court specified was only 400 miles from the plaintiff's home office.

The court only gave effect to the provision controlling the place of litigation after determining that it was reasonable. The same test could apply if the issue were the place of arbitration.

The parties should have reasonable freedom to select the place of arbitration. But if the purpose of the selection is to substantially frustrate any opportunity to get an impartial ruling on a dispute, such a provision should not be effective. Often arbitration must precede court action. The use of an extremely inconvenient place for the arbitration can effectively frustrate any remedy as far as the weaker party is concerned. While it would take an extreme case for the courts to upset a clause dealing with place of arbitration, it is not likely that the courts would accord the contracting parties complete autonomy in determining this question.

Once it is determined who are to be the arbitrators, and where the arbitration is to be held, the next question is to determine the procedural process which will be followed by the arbitrators. The objective is to have a fair, and yet expeditious, settling of the dispute. The matter should be disposed of quickly, without an unnecessarily lengthy and time-consuming hearing. Each party should have an adequate chance to present his case.

The arbitrator can do some things in advance of the hearing to make the hearing process more efficient. He can request that each party make a written statement of his position, to assist both the arbitrator and the other party to prepare for the hearing. Such advance statements of position also can narrow the issues.

In advance of the hearing, the arbitrator can permit each party to question the other party and any witnesses the other party intends to present at the hearing. Also, the arbitrator can suggest or order that the parties exchange documentary evidence that will be presented at the hearing. Such preliminary techniques are more likely to be used where the arbitration involves a substantial amount of money and a large number of issues.

The parties should have proper notice of the hearing, and an adequate time to prepare and present their case.

When witnesses testify, usually they will be examined by the party who presents them or his attorney, and cross-examined by the other party or his attorney. They may be examined by the arbitrator as well. The formality of a court hearing is usually not found in an arbitration hearing. Usually, the legal rules of evidence need not be applied. The arbitrator is free to listen to any testimony he thinks is relevant, without regard to whether the testimony would have been admissible in a court hearing. He can consider writings or documentary evidence, without determining whether those documents would have been admissible in a court of law.

There is normally no requirement that there be a transcription of the testimony nor that a written transcript be made. Some arbitrators have the testimony taken down and reproduced for their own use, and to settle any disputes which may arise between the arbitrators and the parties as to what was said by witnesses.

Usually the arbitrators have a specified time in which to make their decision. The decision need not be in writing, nor reasons given for the decision, although often it may be advisable to give a written decision with the reasoning used because this adds to the dignity of the proceeding and is more likely to satisfy the arbitrating parties.

(Chapter 39 examines arbitration in considerable detail from the viewpoint of the arbitrator. The discussion in this chapter is designed to present an overview of the arbitration process.)

One of the difficulties with arbitration involves the fact that many disputes concern a number of parties. It is helpful to bring all the interested parties together in one arbitration, and then to try to allocate risk and responsibility. Arbitration is not always flexible enough to permit joining all the parties in the same arbitration. On many occasions, the parties involved are not all parties to the same contract.

The amount of the arbitration fee, and who pays it, can be determined in advance by the parties in the arbitration clause. The American Arbitration Association provides a service by which it will furnish arbitrators and will act as a clearing house for papers and notices. It charges a fixed percentage of the claimed amount, as an administrative fee. If the hearing goes over a specified period of time, the arbitrators are paid a fixed per diem fee. The arbitration clause can provide that the losing party will pay for the cost of arbitration, or that the parties will share the cost. Sometimes the contract permits the arbitrator to decide who is to pay for costs. The costs include not only the fees to the arbitrator, but the possible cost of a written transcript (if one is desired), and fees for any neutral witnesses who may be called. Also, it may be necessary to hire offices for holding the hearing. The parties can make an advance determination as to these matters, or they can leave them to the discretion of the arbitrator.

The Construction Industry Arbitration Rules administered by the American Arbitration Association are reproduced in Appendix G.

SECTION 28.06 SUBSTANTIVE QUESTIONS

Arbitrators generally apply and interpret the contract documents. Usually, they do not follow case precedents, but they can, if they so wish. Sometimes, though rarely, the arbitration clause or submission agreement may state they should "do equity" or base their decision upon general notions of fairness. If so, they can, if they desire, ignore the contract, and base their award on these broad standards.

Sometimes contracting parties attempt to employ contract language to limit the power of the person deciding the dispute. In one commercial lease, the parties specified that if there were litigation, only the lease itself would be considered in determining the intention of the parties. This was an attempt to exclude consideration of any evidence outside of the written agreement. When the matter went before a court, the court held that such an agreement would not bind the court. Garden State Plaza Corp. v. S. S. Kresge, 78 N.J.Super. 485, 189 A.2d 448 (1963). When parties come to the courts to resolve their disputes, they must accept the court procedures for determining how these disputes are to be solved. Would an arbitrator feel bound to follow any such contract limitation? Many arbitrators believe that their powers are strictly limited by the agreement which created the arbitration, and that they should follow any directions given by the contracting parties.

There are other questions which can become difficult, both because of the differences and similarities between arbitration and litigation. For example, in some states a contractor cannot use the courts to collect on a construction contract if he is not licensed. However, what if there were an arbitration provision in a contract between an owner and an unlicensed contractor? What if the matter is arbitrated, and the arbitrator awards a specified amount of money to the unlicensed contractor. If the owner does not pay, the unlicensed contractor may have to come to court to have the award confirmed. Would a court in such a case confirm this award? This would depend upon the licensing statute. The statute may state that the contractor cannot bring action to collect for services performed when he is not licensed. However, a confirmation of an arbitration award is not, strictly speaking, an action to collect. Despite this, courts generally refuse to confirm such awards, because to do so would be to frustrate the policy of the licensing laws.

Another problem area relates to the remedies which can be ordered by the arbitrator. Often, the arbitration clause states that the arbitrator can award a money judgment for damages, or order that the parties perform in accordance with the contract. The latter power is essential in certain disputes, especially if the contractor is still working on the project. Grayson-Robinson Stores, Inc., v. Iris Const. Co., 8 N.Y.2d 133, 168 N.E.2d 377, 202 N.Y.S.2d 303 (1960), involved the construction of a shopping development. The arbitrator ordered that the developer build a large shopping center in accordance with his contract. (The latter contended he had a legal defense to his obligation, but the arbitrator did not agree.) When the developer refused to comply, the matter was taken to court. The court held that the arbitration award would be confirmed and enforced, even though the court itself would not have awarded specific performance of this particular contract. (Courts usually refuse specific enforcement of construction contracts because of the difficulty of administering the performance and determining compliance.) In this sense, then, the arbitration award went further than the remedy which could be given by a court. For a closer look at the substantive and procedural aspects of arbitration from the standpoint of the arbitrator see Chapter 39.

SECTION 28.07 JUDICIAL ATTITUDE TOWARD ARBITRATION: CHILLUMS–ADELPHI CASE

Today, courts take a relatively hands-off attitude toward arbitration. The jealousy with which courts regarded arbitration, and the feeling that the courts should be the sole method and forum for deciding disputes, is disappearing. Courts are recognizing that the parties should have contractual freedom to have their disputes decided in some way other than bringing these matters to litigation. It is true that the court will look at the validity of the arbitration clause, and may not force the arbitration if the contract in which the arbitration clause was contained was not validly formed. They will also refuse to confirm any arbitration, if the arbitration was a result of fraud or collusion between the arbitrators and one of the parties. But they are not likely to go into the question of whether the arbitrator was correct in his decision. On the whole, they will let the arbitrator decide the dispute.

The typical judicial attitude toward arbitration can be illustrated by the following case.

CHILLUM–ADELPHI VOLUNTEER FIRE DEPARTMENT, INC. v. BUTTON & GOODE, INC.

Court of Appeals of Maryland, 1966.
242 Md. 509, 219 A.2d 801.

BARNES, JUDGE. This suit was brought by Button & Goode, Inc. (appellee) to enforce an arbitration award entered after Button & Goode and Chillum-Adelphi Volunteer Fire Dept. Co. (appellant) had submitted to arbitration proceedings in regard to a dispute which arose concerning whether Chillum-Adelphi could keep certain sums due Button & Goode under a contract for the erection of a fire house. This money was retained by Chillum-Adelphi as liquidated damages occasioned because of Button & Goode's delay in completing construction of the building. Button & Goode was granted summary judgment in its suit to enforce the arbitration award. This appeal followed.

On April 30, 1962 Button & Goode (contractor) and Chillum-Adelphi (owner) entered into a construction contract whereby Button & Goode agreed to erect two buildings for Chillum-Adelphi. Plans and specifications had been drafted by the owner's architect, Philip W. Mason. The arbitration proceedings and this suit are concerned only with one of the two buildings, the other having been fully completed as required by the contract.

Article 2 of the construction agreement provided that work to be performed under the contract was to commence upon written notice; and the building was to be substantially completed 180 calendar days from the date of such notice. Article 45 of the American Institute of Architects' General Conditions of Contracts, made part of the construction agreement in this case by Article 1 of that agreement,[1] provided that the time in which the contractor agreed to complete the work was of the essence of the contract, and failure to complete the work within the time specified would entitle the owner to deduct as liquidated damages out of any money which may be due the contractor under the contract, the sum of $50.00 for each calendar day in excess of the 180 days until the building should be substantially completed.

The owner's architect specified that one of the buildings was to be constructed of pre-cast concrete framing. Button & Goode could not commence work until that material was delivered to the building

1. All the articles of the American Institute of Architects' General Conditions of Contracts were made a part of the construction agreement between the parties in this case by virtue of Article 1 of that agreement.

[Ed. note: Balance of footnotes omitted.]

site, and the long and protracted delay of Nitterhouse Concrete Products, Inc. (Nitterhouse) in delivering the concrete frames caused a delay in completing the building beyond the 180 days agreed upon as the time within which construction was to be substantially completed. Chillum-Adelphi retained $21,426.48 of the contract price as damages occasioned because of Button & Goode's delay in substantially completing the building.

Article 40 of the General Conditions of Contracts provided that the owner and contractor would submit all disputes, claims or questions arising under the contract to arbitration under the procedure then obtaining in the Standard Form of Arbitration Procedure of the American Institute of Architects (AIA). Button & Goode filed a demand for arbitration with the American Arbitration Association (AAA). Chillum-Adelphi objected to the arbitration procedure provided by the AAA; however, the parties agreed to submit their dispute to arbitration by the AAA provided that the procedure complied with that of the AIA whereby the parties would be given the opportunity to examine and cross-examine all witnesses and introduce exhibits at any time during the hearing.

It was agreed between Button & Goode and Chillum-Adelphi that the issues to be decided by the board of arbitrators would be: (1) What damages, if any, should be assessed against the contractor in this case, and (2) Was the building completed at the time of arbitration?

A hearing was held by the board of arbitrators on August 26, 1964. The arbitrators found that the owner's architect had specified that pre-cast concrete materials of Nitterhouse's manufacture be used in construction of the building, that the contractor had made repeated attempts to have some other company substituted for Nitterhouse to supply the pre-cast concrete frames, but the architect refused to authorize a change because he expected delivery from Nitterhouse sooner than from another company since the order had been pending there for such a long time. Furthermore, a change of suppliers would have necessitated a change in the plans of the building.

Article 18 of the General Conditions provided that the owner's architect should extend the time for the completion of the building if the contractor be delayed in the progress of the work "for any cause beyond the contractor's control". The arbitrators found that Chillum-Adelphi was bound by the decision of its agent, its architect Mr. Mason, to use a product in the construction of the building which proved to be unavailable. The contractor was therefore not responsible for any delay in construction until January 11, 1963, the date Nitterhouse delivered the concrete frames. Under the circumstances, the delay was "beyond the contractor's control" and the architect should have extended the time for completion of the job.

After the pre-cast framing was delivered, Button & Goode proceeded promptly to resume work on the job. The building was substantially completed on August 10, 1963, 211 days after the framing was received from Nitterhouse.

The arbitrators found that Button & Goode was entitled to 180 days from January 11, 1963 for the completion of the job. Since the contractor required 211 days to substantially complete the building from the date the pre-cast frames were delivered, Chillum-Adelphi was entitled to $1,550.00 as liquidated damages, or $50.00 per day for 31 days. Chillum-Adelphi had retained $21,426.48 from the amount due the contractor under the construction agreement. The board of arbitrators therefore awarded Button & Goode $19,876.48 and divided the costs equally between the parties.

Button & Goode filed a petition for judgment on the arbitration award . . . Thereafter, a motion for summary judgment was filed. The trial court entered summary judgment on the arbitration award. . . .

An arbitration award is the decision of an extra-judicial tribunal "which the parties themselves have created, and by whose judgment they have mutually agreed to abide." Continental Milling & Feed Co. v. Doughnut Corp. of America, 186 Md. 669, 674, 48 A.2d 447 (1946). When suit is brought to enforce the award, a court will not review the findings of law and fact of the arbitrators, but only whether the proceedings were free from fraud, the decision was within the limits of the issues submitted to arbitration, and the arbitration proceedings provided adequate procedural safeguards to assure to all the parties a full and fair hearing on the merits of the controversy. . . .

In City of Baltimore v. Allied Contractors, Inc., supra, Judge Hammond, for the Court, said:

> "Mistakes by an arbitrator in drawing incorrect inferences or forming erroneous judgments or conclusions from the facts will not vitiate his award. (citations omitted)
>
> . . . the decisive primary question is not whether the judgment was right or wrong but whether impropriety, to a significant extent, brought about its obtention." (Pages 546–547 of 236 Md. pages 552–553 of 204 A.2d).

Although a court may modify an arbitration award for a mistake of form such as an evident miscalculation of figures . . . an arbitrator's honest decision will not be vacated or modified for a mistake going to the merits of the controversy and resulting in an erroneous arbitration award, unless the mistake is so gross as to evidence misconduct or fraud on his part. . . .

In short, where parties have voluntarily and unconditionally agreed to submit issues to arbitration and to be bound by the arbitration award, a court will enter a money judgment on that award and enforce their contract to be so bound unless, notwithstanding that the arbitrator's decision may have been erroneous, the facts show that he acted fraudulently, or beyond the scope of the issues submitted to him for decision, or that the proceedings lacked procedural fairness. A court does not act in an appellate capacity in reviewing the arbitration award, but enters judgment on what may be considered a contract of the parties, after it has made an independent determination that the contract should be enforced.

. . .

We hold on this appeal that the trial court properly granted Button & Goode's motion for summary judgment on the arbitration award.

There is no merit in Chillum-Adelphi's contention that the arbitrators went beyond the issues submitted to them for determination. Chillum-Adelphi and Button & Goode had agreed that one of the issues to be submitted to arbitration was what damages, if any, should be assessed against the contractor in this case. The architect had refused to extend the time for completing the construction since he did not feel that the delay was occasioned by circumstances beyond the contractor's control. Since the gravamen of the arbitration proceedings was the fact that because of a delay in completing the contract, Chillum-Adelphi had withheld monies otherwise due the contractor, the arbitrators were clearly authorized to determine whether the architect was correct in his determination that the time for completing the contract should not have been extended. It was essential to review the architect's decision before a determination could be made as to what damages, if any, would be assessed against the contractor.

Chillum-Adelphi's second contention is likewise without merit. The fact that arbitrators may fail to follow strict legal rules of procedure and evidence is not a ground for vacating their award. Continental Milling & Feed Co. v. Doughnut Corp. of America, supra. The procedure followed at the arbitration hearing was fair and in full compliance with the AIA procedural rules which the parties agreed would govern the determination of their dispute. The record in the arbitration proceedings remained open for a full six months before the final award was entered. Additional evidence could have been presented to the arbitration board at any time during that six month period, and upon good cause shown the hearing could have been reopened.

Finally, we must discount Chillum-Adelphi's bald assertion that the determination of the arbitration board was unsupported by the evidence. There is no showing of lack of good faith or fraud on the part of the arbitration board, and we will not review the award on the merits. . . .

A modern court might accord less respect to an arbitrator's award if it concludes that the arbitration was not truly the result of a reasonable, bargained-for provision. Many arbitration clauses are inserted in the contract without any bargaining being involved. The dominant party may require that the other party take the arbitration clause, whether the other party wants to or not.

The court have not ventured much into these matters. If the facts show that the arbitrators were to be hand-picked by one of the parties, that the arbitration was to be held at a very inconvenient place, and that the rules specifying procedures were largely in favor of the stronger party, then it is possible that the courts would not enforce the arbitration award.

Within reasonable limits, today contracting parties are given the opportunity of setting up a separate method outside the courts for deciding their disputes. Judicial attitude does vary from state to state. In the large commercial states which have had considerable experience with arbitration, the courts are likely to give a wide scope to the arbitration process. In less commercial and industrial states, there still may be a residue of some judicial suspicion and apprehension about the arbitration process.

SECTION 28.08 PUBLIC CONTRACTS

(A) USE OF ARBITRATION: CITY OF MADISON v. WRIGHT

In some states, it is not possible to arbitrate a dispute involving a public agency. This problem is illustrated by the following case.

CITY OF MADISON v. FRANK LLOYD WRIGHT FOUNDATION

Supreme Court of Wisconsin, 1963.
20 Wis.2d 361, 122 N.W.2d 409.

On July 5, 1956, the city of Madison, a municipal corporation (hereinafter "city") entered into a contract with the Frank Lloyd Wright Foundation (hereinafter "Foundation"), a non-stock, non-profit corporation.

This contract was entered into as a result of a $4,000,000 bond issue approved by the electorate of the city for the purpose of building an auditorium and civic center in the city of Madison at the Monona Terrace site. The election took place on November 2, 1954, and at the same election an advisory referendum endorsed the employment of Frank Lloyd Wright as the architect for the project. The common council of the city of Madison, on June 28, 1956, authorized the city clerk and the mayor to enter into the architectural services contract with the Foundation, and the contract was executed on July 5, 1956.

The contract provided that the cost of the auditorium and civic center was not to exceed $4,000,000, (plus parking facilities of $1,500,000) and that the architect was to receive an overall seven percent on the cost of the auditorium and civic center, (plus $40,000 for engineering fees and four percent of the cost of the parking facilities) but in no event was the fee to be based on an amount in excess of $4,000,000 for the auditorium and civic center and $1,500,000 for the parking facilities.

Clause 11 of the July 5, 1956, contract provided as follows:

> "Arbitration of questions in dispute under this agreement shall be submitted to arbitration at the choice of either party in accordance with the provisions then obtaining, of the standard form of Arbitration Procedure of the American Institute of Architects."

The city approved preliminary plans submitted by the Foundation on June 11, 1959, and in accordance with the contract, the Foundation was paid $122,500 for these plans.

Bids on the project were solicited as per final plans and specifications and the only bid received was $12,112,805. On March 9, 1961, the city rejected all bids.

The Foundation did not make any further claim on the city for architectural fees or any other monies, but did, on November 15, 1961, serve on the city a "Demand for Arbitration."

William Wesley Peters, as vice president for the Foundation, (Frank Lloyd Wright having passed away in the meantime) demanded in the name of the Foundation as follows:

> "We hereby make demand on you to arbitrate our claim against you [city] for our architect's fees already earned for the completed plans and specifications on the Monona Terrace Civic Center drawn and completed in accordance with your directions and accepted by you.
>
> "We demand that said arbitration shall be administered in accordance with the Standard Form of Arbitration Procedure of the American Institute of Architects."

In response, the city, on November 27, 1961, commenced this present action for declaratory relief seeking a declaration that the contract was invalid and also seeking to enjoin all further arbitration proceedings as per the "Demand."

. . .

On May 10, 1962, the city council terminated the contract claiming a breach by the Foundation in that the costs had exceeded the limits placed in the contract and the Foundation had failed to design facilities within those cost limits. This followed another advisory referendum in April, 1962, in which a majority of Madison voters approved termination of the Monona Terrace project.

Further hearings were held by the trial court and finally the court, on November 23, 1962, entered an order which recited, in part, as follows:

. . .

> "* * * that the temporary restraining order heretofore entered by this Court, restraining the defendant from proceeding with arbitration, be and it is hereby dismissed.

"* * * that the trial of this action be stayed until arbitration has been had between the parties pursuant to the Standard Form of Arbitration Procedure of the American Institute of Architects."

. . .

WILKIE, JUSTICE. This is the third time in recent years that the so-called Monona Terrace controversy has been brought to the supreme court. In 1957 the court ruled in Madison v. State, 1 Wis.2d 252, 83 N.W.2d 674, that the city of Madison could constitutionally proceed with the construction of a civic center and auditorium at the Monona Terrace site using Lake Monona frontage filled in as per authority granted by ch. 301, Laws of 1931.

After the so-called Metzner act was adopted by the 1957 session of the legislature, effectively prohibiting the erection of the civil center and auditorium on that site, the validity of the Metzner law was challenged in the case of Frank Lloyd Wright Foundation v. City of Madison and Stewart G. Honeck, Individually and as Attorney General of the State of Wisconsin, and the case was dismissed as moot by the supreme court because in the meantime the Metzner law had been expressly repealed in 1959.

After these several years of controversy and delay, bids were finally requested and rejected (when over two times the original contemplated cost). The Foundation in its demand for arbitration sought to be paid for work done since receiving payment on February 22, 1960, for the preliminary plans. The city (under new administration) countered by starting the present action in late November, 1961.

. . .

Issue I. (2) *Is the contract invalid because the city cannot tie itself to an arbitration agreement that (a) calls for arbitration of future disputes; or (b) calls for arbitration of the whole subject matter of the contract and not just particular items?* Although the city concedes that city governments may validly contract to arbitrate disputes it insists that the disputes must be present disputes, not future disputes, and the arbitration must cover specific items and must not cover the whole subject matter of a contract.

The annotation at 40 A.L.R. 1370, entitled "Power of municipal corporation to submit to arbitration" discussed the power of cities to arbitrate and states, at p. 1370: "It is well established that a city has the power to submit to arbitration any claim asserted by or against it, whether based on contract or tort, in the absence of a statutory prohibition. This power is based on the right to contract and the right to maintain and defend suits." At p. 1372: "It follows that a city has the power, when making a contract, to include a provision for arbitration of future disputes or claims which may arise under it. Such a clause is valid and of the same effect as a similar provision between private parties." There is no statute prohibiting the city of Madison from agreeing to arbitration on an architectural contract such as this.

In Kane v. The City of Fond du Lac (1876), 40 Wis. 495, this court held at p. 499:

> "That a municipal corporation may, unless restricted by its charter, lawfully submit a disputed claim against it to arbitration, and that the common council of the defendant city had ample power to do so in the present case, we cannot doubt."

. . .

The city asserts that arbitration is permitted only as to present disputes, and paragraph 11 contemplates "future disputes." The city argues extensively that under municipal corporation law, one governing body cannot tie the hands of the administration that will succeed it by entering into contracts or passing laws "which would restrict the exercise of discretion by a legislative body with respect to governmental matters entrusted to it." . . .

The city contends that the common council of Madison in existence in 1956 could not contract to submit matters to arbitration arising out of a dispute under said contract, which dispute may arise when another administration is in office.

3 Am.Jur., Arbitration and Award, p. 851, sec. 24, states:

> "Within the limits of its charter powers, a municipal or a quasi municipal corporation, unless restricted by positive law, may submit any dispute to arbitration and *may stipulate in its contracts for arbitration of disputes arising thereunder.* * * *" (Emphasis added.)

5 Am.Jur.(2d), Arbitration and Award, p. 570, sec. 68, states:

> "Municipal corporations *may also stipulate in contracts for arbitration of disputes arising thereunder.*" (Emphasis added.)

In neither of these sections is any distinction drawn between arbitration of *present* disputes and *future* disputes.

If the city is correct that only present disputes can be arbitrated then there would be no valid agreement to arbitrate disputes that may arise under a contract. In short there would never be any reason for incorporating an arbitration clause since the only type of dispute that could be arbitrated would be one that already existed at the time the contract was executed. This, of course, would render nugatory the well-established Wisconsin law that cities may agree to arbitrate disputes.

. . .

The city's final assertion is that it [is] illegal to have an arbitration clause under which arbitration may be had of disputes involving the whole contract as distinguished from arbitration merely of individual precise questions. The decisions of arbitrators quite frequently include mixed questions of fact and law. The Foundation here demands additional fees. The city raises a host of questions about the performance of the Foundation under the contract, and about the contract. It denies that any fees are due. All of these questions presumably will be examined in detail under arbitration. The fact that the contract requires the submission of disputes to arbitration procedure rather than resorting to normal court litigation is a decision that was within the power of the common council to make.

. . .

Issue III. *Is the arbitration agreement statutory or is it an agreement at common law, which would permit the city to cancel the arbitration at will at any time before an award is made?* The question of whether common law or statutory arbitration is called for by paragraph 11 is probably the most important issue in the case. This is because of the effect that would follow should there be a determination that this was common law arbitration. In 3 Am.Jur., Arbitration and Award, p. 899, sec. 70, it is stated:

> "Generally.—Generally speaking, at common law it is a well-settled rule that until it is consummated by a valid award, an executory agreement, not made a rule of court, that the substantial rights and liabilities of the parties respecting present or prospective questions in difference shall be determined by arbitrators, will not be enforced by the courts except in an action for breach of the agreement, against a party who revokes or fails or refuses to perform it. * * *"

Thus, if the contract calls for common law arbitration, the Foundation would not be able to have specific performance of the arbitration clause, but would be only entitled to sue for breach of the agreement.

The disputed arbitration clause in the contract reads as follows (clause 11):

> "Arbitration of questions in dispute under this agreement shall be submitted to arbitration at the choice of either party in accordance with the provisions then obtaining of the standard form of Arbitration Procedure of the American Institute of Architects."

The Wisconsin Arbitration Act, enacted in 1931, obviously was intended to make arbitration agreements subject to Wisconsin law specifically enforcible. Thus sec. 298.01, Stats., provides as follows:

> "Arbitration clauses in contracts enforcible. A provision in any written contract to settle by arbitration a controversy thereafter arising out of such contract, or out of the refusal to perform the whole or any part thereof, or an agreement in writing between two or more persons to submit to arbitration any controversy existing between them at the time of the agreement to submit, *shall be valid, irrevocable and enforcible save upon such grounds as exist at law or in equity for the revocation of any contract;* provided, however, that the provisions of this chapter shall not apply to contracts between employers and employes, or between employers and associa-

tions of employes, except as provided in section 111.10 of the statutes." (Emphasis added.)

The whole purpose of arbitration is to substitute a less expensive and less formal method of settling differences between parties for normal court litigation. In arbitration greater use may be made of persons who have a particular expertise that may permit them to adjudicate and settle differences that may exist on highly technical matters.

Every contract that is subject to Wisconsin law and which contains an arbitration agreement, and which does not clearly negate the application of the provisions of the Wisconsin Arbitration Act, incorporates the provisions of that act and those provisions shall apply. Parties entering into a contract that is subject to Wisconsin law and which contains an arbitration agreement, may, as here, prescribe that the arbitration procedure of the American Institute of Architects (or of some other comparable authority) shall apply and the arbitration shall be considered subject to ch. 298, Stats. If one or more of the provisions of the agreed arbitration procedure is in conflict with the provisions of ch. 298, then the provisions of ch. 298 shall apply.

. . .

Issue IV. (2) *Is the Foundation barred from demanding arbitration to determine additional fees because the bid cost of the project exceeded the maximum figure ($5,500,000) allowed in the contract?* Paragraph 1 of the contract between the Foundation and the city provided in part as follows:

> "1. *Cost of the Work.* The project shall be planned and designed so as to not exceed the cost of $4,000,000, plus the cost of parking facilities in the amount of $1,500,000, * *"

The bids on final plans and specifications were over $12,000,000.

The city claims that the Foundation not only breached its contract by not coming in under the cost figure, but also by failing to revise its plans and specifications to bring that result. The city contends that it could terminate the contract for these reasons and also since the contract itself was invalid. The Foundation has countered with explanations of the cost increase which negate any breach on its part and it also has contested the claim that the contract is invalid. The city's real point is that because of this breach the Foundation cannot proceed to arbitration, especially since the arbitration of its claim for fees will lead the arbitrators into considering the legal questions involved in determining whether the city had the right to terminate the contract. These questions, the city argues, the courts and not the arbitrators should resolve.

. . .

Although the city claims here that the Foundation has breached the contract, the Foundation claims that it has not and that it is entitled to additional architectural fees. The affidavit of William Wesley Peters, in support of the Foundation's application for a stay of action, states that building costs rose some 21.3 percent between March, 1955, and March, 1960; that the city of Madison had requested changes from the original plans, namely an auditorium to seat 2,400 people instead of 2,000, a larger floor in the exhibition hall than was originally called for in the contract, seating in the exhibition hall for 3,800 instead of 3,500, seating capacity of 460 persons in the "little theatre" instead of the 300 initially called for, 13,731 square feet of art exhibition area instead of the original 3,000 square feet, a parking area to provide for 840 to 940 cars instead of the original 750 cars, and 19 committee rooms occupying 19,000 square feet instead of the original 15,000 square feet. It is very apparent that there is a very real dispute arising out of the contract which . . would properly be the subject for arbitration proceedings.

It is not fatal that the arbitration process here will lead to a consideration of mixed questions of law and fact. On the contrary, this is to be expected and is entirely consistent with the basic purpose of arbitration proceedings as a substitute for normal litigation.

. . .

Orders dated November 23, 1962 and December 28, 1962, affirmed,

. . .

[Ed. note: Footnotes omitted]

The portion of the City of Madison v. Wright reproduced is only a small part of the 17 page, double-columned full court opinion. A substantial number of major issues have been omitted.

The case illustrates some of the controversy that surrounded the work of Frank Lloyd Wright. As can be seen, proponents and opponents of his work went to the courts, and to the legislature, on a number of occasions in order to stop the project or to enable it to be built. Also, the case illustrates what can happen to a project when there is a change in city administration. A reading of the full opinion shows that Madison, the city Wright considered as his "home town", spared no effort to raise every possible point to defeat the arbitration.

The contract was made in 1956. The opinion reproduced was issued in 1963. Unless the matter has been settled by agreement among the contending parties, the opinion of the Wisconsin Supreme Court is only a step toward the arbitration which will determine whether Wright's successors are entitled to be paid. Looking at the setting of the judicial opinion, it is likely that any arbitrator's award would have to be fought again through the courts.

(B) DISPUTES CLAUSES

Federal construction contracts contain Disputes Clauses. Under a Disputes Clause, the "Contracting Officer" is given authority to decide disputed questions of fact which arise during performance of the contract. The Contracting Officer is usually an administrative official of the agency which has awarded the contract. His decisions are conclusive, subject to a right to appeal to the head of the agency awarding the contract within 30 days from the contracting officer's decision.

If an appeal is taken, the matter is heard by a Board of Appeals which is appointed by the head of the agency. Boards of Appeal meet in Washington, and occasionally hear cases elsewhere. There is a hearing before the Board issues its decision. The Board's decision is final on questions of fact, if supported by substantial evidence. Issues of law, or questions of whether its factual conclusions were supported by substantial evidence, can be appealed to the Court of Claims in Washington. Usually there is no new trial before the court. The court considers only the transcript made before the Board of Appeals. Appeals from Court of Claims decisions go to the U. S. Supreme Court, which has the discretion to consider cases appealed to it. The Supreme Court rarely reviews Court of Claims' decisions in these matters.

Increasingly, provisions in state public contracts specify that disputes between the state agency and private contractors shall be resolved by a state appointed hearing officer or an employee of the state contracting agency. These decisions will be final if made honestly and supported by substantial evidence.

REVIEW QUESTIONS

1. What determines the jurisdiction of the arbitrator?

2. If an arbitration award is taken to court, what will the court look at in deciding whether to confirm the award?

3. Must the arbitrator have a written transcript made, or write an explanation of his decision?

4. Who pays the costs of arbitration?

QUESTIONS FOR CLASS DISCUSSION

1. Which disputes are best to arbitrate?

2. Who would be good arbitrators in a construction contract dispute?

PROBLEM

The arbitration clause in a contract between O and C provided:

> The parties agree to arbitrate all disputes under this contract.

C refused to perform under the contract, because he claimed that O defrauded him into making the contract by telling him that he would award two other construction contracts to C, when O knew he had already awarded them to another contractor. C claimed he relied on the promise by making a much lower bid than he would have ordinarily made. O denied making the promise, and demanded arbitration. C refused to arbitrate and started a court action for fraud. O insists upon arbitration. Must this dispute be resolved by arbitration?

Chapter 29
JUDICIAL REMEDIES FOR CONTRACT BREACH

SECTION 29.01 FLEXIBILITY OF STANDARDS

The court's computation of the measure of recovery to be awarded the plaintiff for the defendant's breach of contract is not controlled by mechanical formulas. While there are certain principles which play a significant role in this determination, there is sufficient "play" in the principles to permit a court to take certain factors into account which can be roughly characterized as "fairness".

If it appears that one party has been attempting to take unfair advantage of the other, doubts may be resolved against the former. The way parties conduct themselves, both before and after a dispute develops, is often an important factor. For example, if the defendant has not been conducting himself in a fair manner, the court may say that damages do not have to be proved with mathematical precision by the plaintiff. On the other hand, if the defendant has done his best to perform, and has conducted himself sensibly and reasonably in negotiations, the courts may hold that the plaintiff has not established the monetary value of his claim with sufficient certainty.

SECTION 29.02 SOME PRELIMINARY MATTERS

(A) CAUSATION

In contract cases, courts sometimes have difficulty in determining whether the breach by the defendant has caused the loss claimed by the plaintiff. For example, the owner may unreasonably delay approval of shop drawings. Suppose, the contractor proves the project cost him a specified amount more than he expected. However, it is often difficult to determine whether the delay by the owner caused the increased costs to the contractor.

(B) FORESEEABILITY

Also, the law limits damages to those which were reasonably foreseeable at the time the contract was made. For example, if the owner unjustifiably terminates a contractor's performance, it would be difficult for the contractor to recover lost profits on other jobs which the contractor claims he would have obtained had he been permitted to finish this job. Only if the owner had reason to know that successful completion of a particular job would have given other profits to the contractor would these items be recoverable, assuming the contractor can show the owner's breach caused him to lose other jobs.

(C) CERTAINTY

It is often difficult to prove with mathematical precision just what a particular breach has cost the claimant. Courts often state that they do not require mathematical certainty, but merely that damages of some sort be established, and that it will be the task of the defendant to establish that the amounts are too uncertain and speculative.

Certainty and foreseeability requirements are also a method of controlling irrational decisions by juries. Since these issues are considered "legal" questions, a judge's determination that the evidence does not prove damages with sufficient certainty, or were not foreseeable, means that the issue of damages will not be submitted to the jury.

(D) CONTRACT AUTONOMY: FREEDOM OF CONTRACT

How much contract autonomy will the court give contracting parties to predetermine the amount of damages for breach of contract? Section 23.06 treated liquidation of damages in the context of delays. Generally, the courts permit contracting parties to predetermine the amount of damages if it appears that both parties voluntarily agreed to do so, and if the amount selected is reasonable in light of potential or actual damages. If the amount selected bears no relationship to actual or potential damages, and is merely a device to coerce performance by setting forth a harsh remedy for nonperformance, courts will not enforce the clause.

(E) RELATIONSHIP TO LIABILITY

It is often difficult to separate liability from the measure of recovery. If the court feels that it can award a lower amount of damages, it may resolve liability questions in favor of the plaintiff. If, on the other hand, the measurement will result in a large and unusual amount of damages, the court may decide liability questions in favor of the defendant, and adversely to the claimant.

SECTION 29.03 MEASURES OF RECOVERY GENERALLY

In a construction project, most parties engaged in the project are connected by contract with another party participating in the construction work. Usually there are contracts between the owner and the design professional, the design professional and the consultant, the owner and the contractor, the contractor and the subcontractor, as well as other contracts up and down the chain. This chapter assumes there has been a validly formed contract, that one party has, without legal justification, failed to perform in accordance with his obligations, and that any conditions precedent to recovery for damages have either been performed or excused. How much will the breach cost the breaching party?

(A) COMPENSATION AND RESTITUTION

In contract law, there are two basic measurement principles. The first is compensation, and the second is restitution. Compensation places the claimant in the position he would have been in had the contract been properly performed by the other party. Restitution places the parties in the same positions they were at the time the contract was made, but before any performance was commenced.

(B) AVOIDABLE CONSEQUENCES

The "rule of avoidable consequences" (or, as it is sometimes called, "the duty to mitigate damages") prevents a claimant from collecting damages from the breaching party which could have been avoided by the reasonable efforts of the claimant. For example, suppose the contractor unjustifiably abandons a shopping center project in the middle of construction. If the owner were to do nothing toward completion of the contract by another contractor, the owner might suffer severe losses. He might be liable for breach of contract damages to any tenants who have contracts which entitle them to possession by specified time. He might also lose profits which he would have been able to make had the project been completed. He might also be forced to default on loans, and lose any security he has had to give to obtain these loans. It is clear that these losses, in a sense, have been caused by the contractor's breach. However, most of them could have been avoided if the owner had hired another contractor within a reasonable time to finish the project. For that reason, those losses which could have been reasonably avoided are not chargeable to the breaching contractor. Those losses were caused not by the contractor's breach, but by the owner's failure to hire a replacement contractor.

(C) ATTORNEY'S FEES, COURT COSTS AND OTHER LITIGATION EXPENSES

The winning party in a law suit is entitled to recover certain direct court costs, such as filing fees and witness fees. However, he cannot recover the costs of his own attorney's services unless recovery of attorney's fees is expressly provided for by the contract or by an applicable statute. He cannot recover the often expensive cost of deposition taking, nor the cost of paying his expert witnesses. For costs recoverable in arbitration, see § 28.05.

(D) INTEREST

See § 29.04(a) and (b).

(E) PUNITIVE DAMAGES

In contract claims, punitive damages are usually not awarded. Punitive damages are awarded for the purpose of making an example of the wrong-doer, and deterring others from committing similar wrongs.

(F) SPECIFIC PERFORMANCE

Equity courts have the power to grant specific relief called "specific performance". This is an order by the court that a contracting party perform in accordance with his contract obligation. Failure to comply with this order is contempt of court, and may be punished by the non-complying party being fined or sent to jail.

Specific performance is used in sales of land, where a seller has unjustifiably failed to convey real property. Instead of a money judgment for damages, the buyer usually can get a specific decree from the court ordering that the seller convey the property in question. However, the use of specific performance is rare in construction contracts. Such decrees are difficult to administer by a court, and it is generally considered that a money judgment for damages is adequate. For that reason, decrees for specific performance will not be discussed further.

SECTION 29.04 CONSTRUCTION CONTRACTS

The contract between owner and prime contractor will be used as an illustration. Many of the principles would apply to the contracts between other parties in the construction project.

(A) CONTRACTOR'S MEASURE OF RECOVERY

Uncompleted Project

If the project is never commenced, the contractor is entitled to recover his loss of profit. He usually establishes this by deducting from the contract price the cost he would have incurred in building the project. Sometimes courts permit the profit to be computed by applying a generally accepted profit ratio on the designated type of work, such as five to fifteen per cent. For a case involving the measure of recovery by a sub-subcontractor against a subcontractor where the work was never commenced, see Frank Sullivan Co. v. Midwest Sheet Metal Works, reproduced in § 3.12.

Suppose the contractor justifiably ceases performance on the project because of a material breach of contract by the owner, or suppose the owner unjustifiably orders that the contractor cease performance. For the measure of recovery for work performed, see §§ 24.02 and 24.03. Generally, the contractor can collect the cost of part performance plus profit on the whole project, or the contract price less cost of completion. Using restitution, he can collect the reasonable value of his goods and services that went into the project. Some courts use a percentage of the completion of the project. If the contractor completed 70% of the project, he would receive 70% of the contract price. This would give him profit only on the percentage of his total obligation actually performed.

In some jurisdictions lost profits may not be given if the breach consists of an unjustifiable failure to make progress payments. An illustration is Palmer v. Watson Construction Co., 265 Minn. 195, 121 N.W.2d 62 (1963). The trial court had awarded the plaintiff subcontractor his loss of profits for unperformed work. The Minnesota Supreme Court held this was incorrect, stating:

> . . . it is our opinion that the evidence does not sustain the verdict in so far as it includes damages for loss of the profit anticipated in the event of full performance. A party to a contract who is entitled to progress payments may treat the failure to make such payments when due as a breach of the contract which will justify him in refusing to perform further and which will give legal basis for a claim for the reasonable value of the services performed or material supplied pursuant to the contract. . . . His alternative course is to continue with performance and recover the contract price in full upon completion. . . . It is true that a party ready, willing, and able to perform may recover damages for breach of contract, as distinguished from the reasonable value of the services rendered or material supplied, if he is *prevented* from performance by an act or omission of the other contracting party. . . . We are committed in this state, however, to the rule that nonpayment of installment obligations is not in and of itself such prevention of performance as

will make possible suit for loss of profits even though the party entitled to payment may lack working capital. . . .

Although the letter written by plaintiff's attorney on March 20 stated that nonpayment was interfering with the discharge of Palmer's obligation to his subcontractor and thus preventing completion, there is nothing in the testimony of the subcontractor, who was called as a witness in behalf of plaintiff, to support this argument adequately. While the parties to a construction contract could make nonpayment of progress payments such an event as would empower the party entitled to the money to discontinue performance and sue for that which he would have earned had the contract been completed, we find no such provision in the agreements here involved. It is conceivable that refusal to make progress payments without justification and under circumstances where the refusal is intended to make performance by the contractor impossible could be considered such prevention of performance as would justify recovery of profits for breach of an indivisible contract. For the present, it is sufficient to say that this is not such a case.

Showing prevention is generally difficult. In jurisdictions which have a rule like that of Minnesota, contractors who wish to recover profit on unperformed work should attempt to include a provision in the construction contract giving them the right to such damages.

Completed Project: Luria Bros. v. United States

If the contractor has completed the project, the measurement problems are relatively simple. He is entitled to the contract price, less what he has already been paid. Usually, he is not entitled to recover the reasonable value of his services when all that remains is for the owner to pay the balance of the contract price.

After the contract is completed by the contractor, he may have claims relating to additional costs which he alleges were caused by breaches of the owner or by someone for whom the owner is responsible, such as the design professional. In addition, he may also have claims for extra work which he asserts went beyond the requirements of the contract. Delay damage claims were discussed in Chapter 23 and extras in Chapter 21.

However, it may be instructive to look at a delay damage case at this point.

LURIA BROTHERS & COMPANY, INC. v. THE UNITED STATES

United States Court of Claims, 1966.
369 F.2d 701.

Whitaker, Senior Judge

[Ed. note: The following is digested from the court opinion:]

This case involved a contract for the construction of a hangar for an aircraft maintenance facility. Because of the unusual design of the building, the foundation footings for the arch columns were of utmost importance. The original specifications stated that these footings were "to bear on rock good for a safe load of 15 tons per square foot". The specifications also indicated that the footings would have to be eight or nine feet below the ground surface.

During construction, government officials became concerned about the bearing capacity of rock at certain crucial points. Work had to be halted on a number of occasions while the government made additional tests. The additional tests showed that it would be necessary to revise the design of the foundations and the footings. Ultimately, using a trial and error process, both as to the depth of the footings and the length of the footings, the footings for the arch columns required excavation five to ten feet more than originally designed. This required that the dimension of the footings be enlarged because of the additional depth.

The court held that the original specifications were defective, that they misrepresented the nature of the bearing value of the material underlying the foundation of the structure, and that the government impliedly warranted that if its specifications were complied with, satisfactory results would follow. In addition, the court found that the defendant was dilatory in recognizing the need for making appropriate revisions to the defective foundation plans. There were other acts of the defendant which increased the plaintiff's costs and delayed his performance.

The court found that the various breaches by the defendant resulted in 420 days of unexcused delay for which the plaintiff was entitled to delay damages. The total delay period was 518 days, and the plaintiff recovered 81% (420/518) of the overrun period costs for "idle equipment, field supervision, winter protection, rehandling materials, maintaining excavations, and wage and material price increases plus 100% of an insurance premium plaintiff was required to pay."

However, there was dispute over two additional items demanded by the plaintiff. The first related to home office overhead. The court held that the plaintiff was entitled to a designated proportion of home office overhead.

The second item in controversy related to the loss of productivity caused by the delay. The trial commissioner, an official appointed by the Court of Claims to make factual determinations and recommendations, did not allow any amount for loss of productivity.]

Loss of Productivity. The second item of damage, not allowed by the trial commissioner, claimed by plaintiff to have been caused by defendant's delay was loss of productivity of its labor force. First, it says the delay required it to work during severe winter weather between December 1, 1953 and March 10, 1954, and again between November 25, 1954 and January 19, 1955; second, from March 11 to August 11, 1954, it had to work under adverse water conditions; and, third, the constant revisions in the contract drawings resulted in confusion and interruption of the orderly progress of the work.

For this loss of productivity of its labor, it claims damages in the aggregate amount of $131,116.66. . . .

The testimony on loss of productivity is far from satisfactory. Plaintiff's sole witness on this point was John Crawford, who had been in plaintiff's employ for about 10 years and who was its chief of construction at the time the work on this job was being done. However, at the time of his testimony he had left plaintiff's employ and was then chief engineer in the New York area for the Frouge Corporation of New York City and Bridgeport, Connecticut, a company with which plaintiff had no connection. It was a large company, with $50 million worth of building construction in that area, consisting of housing developments, apartments, and office buildings. Mr. Crawford had graduated as a civil engineer from Columbia University in 1924, since which time he had been engaged in both heavy and building construction work.

He was a competent witness, well-qualified to express an opinion on the loss of productivity of the labor. But, strangely, plaintiff offered no corroboration of his testimony. But, stranger still, defendant did not cross-examine him on this point and offered no testimony in rebuttal. His testimony stands unchallenged.

The defendant's sole reply to plaintiff's request that the trial commissioner find the facts as testified to by this witness was in its exceptions to plaintiff's proposed findings of fact. In this document, defendant made only this reply:

> Plaintiff's productivity losses, so-called, were based on estimates, entirely unverifiable.
>
> Defendant considered this item unproved. It entirely neglects allowances for time consumed by strikes, plaintiff's own delays, and other nongovernment delays.

That loss of productivity of labor resulting from improper delays caused by defendant is an item of damage for which plaintiff is entitled to recover admits of no doubt, Abbett Electric Corp. v. United States, 162 F.Supp. 772, 142 Ct.Cl. 609 (1958); nor does the impossibility of proving the amount with exactitude bar recovery for the item.

. . .

It is a rare case where loss of productivity can be proven by books and records; almost always it has to be proven by the opinions of expert witnesses. However, the mere expression of an estimate as to the amount of productivity loss by an expert witness with nothing to support it will not establish the fundamental fact of resultant injury nor provide a sufficient basis for making a reasonably correct approximation of damages. . . .

Crawford's testimony is unrebutted. Defendant, out of whose pocket the money must come to pay the large sum testified to by

him, did not undertake to discredit his testimony, and so, while it is the sacred duty of this court to protect the Government from unrighteous demands as well as to protect the citizen from imposition by the Government, we cannot wholly reject this witness's testimony on the question of amount of damage.

However, we cannot ignore the fact that he was plaintiff's former employee and had been over a period of 10 years. While he was not in plaintiff's employment at the time he testified, he quite properly had a certain predilection for his old employer and wanted to "help them out" all he could. His sympathy was naturally with his former employer rather than with the Government. We do not mean the witness was dishonest, but we do think he made his estimates as high as he could to the extent his conscience would permit.

Crawford testified that between December 1, 1953, and March 10, 1954, the productivity of plaintiff's labor force was reduced inasmuch as the men had to work outside on trench excavations and foundation construction in winter weather. This required them to wear gloves and warmer clothing, and to work on ground which was frozen and/or extremely wet because of the rising ground water during that time of year. Based on his over-all experience in construction work and his observation of this particular job, he estimated that the average loss of productivity of labor during this period was 33⅓ percent. With regard to the period between March 11, 1954, and August 11, 1954, Crawford testified that the labor productivity was reduced 25 percent because of adverse water conditions encountered at the construction site. During the period from August 12, 1954, to November 24, 1954, Crawford estimated that the average loss of productivity of plaintiff's labor force was 20 percent because of confusion and interruption of normal job progress as a result of several revisions by defendant of the contract drawings for the leanto building. Crawford also estimated that the loss during the period from November 25, 1954, to January 19, 1955, was 20 percent due to cold weather conditions when the men had to work in an only partially completed structure.

That winter weather and adverse water conditions reduce the efficiency of a labor force in the performance of construction work only stands to reason. It has been held by this court that when loss of productivity brought about by these conditions results from defendant's breach of contract, the plaintiff is entitled to recover its additional costs occasioned thereby as damages. . . . However, with respect to the loss of efficiency caused by the revisions to the leanto plans during the period from August 12, 1954, to November 24, 1954, there is no testimony that there was a loss of efficiency on this account other than Crawford's estimate of the amount thereof. Proof of damage is essential before estimates can be received of the amount thereof. Plaintiff's claim for loss of productivity during that period must therefore be rejected. . . .

Notwithstanding the fact that Crawford's estimates regarding the other three periods are unrebutted, we cannot ignore the fact that the percentages testified to were merely estimates based upon his observation and experience. Furthermore, his estimates are much higher than those testified to in other cases in which the conditions were not materially different from those present here. Taking these things into consideration and in view of the fact that no comparative data, no standards, and no corroboration support his testimony, we are constrained to reduce his estimates based on the record as a whole and the court's knowledge and experience in such cases to 20 percent, or $11,091.02 for the period from December 1, 1953, to March 10, 1954; to 10 percent, or $13,014.87 for the period from March 11 to August 11, 1954; and to 10 percent, or $925.50 for the period from November 25, 1954, to January 19, 1955.

The total additional cost to plaintiff during the 518-day overrun period because of loss of productivity of its labor force was thus $25,031.39. . . . Because of a duplication of costs included in another of plaintiff's claims, $4,550.63 must be deducted from this total figure. This results in a net cost to plaintiff of $20,480.76 because of loss of productivity of its labor force. Since the defendant was responsible for 420 days of the 518-day overrun, plaintiff is entitled to recover 81 percent of this amount, or $16,589.42.

We have found that the plaintiff is entitled to recover $62,948.33 for excess home office overhead. Adding these two items to the $85,544.92 found by the trial commissioner makes a total of $165,-082.67. A judgment for this amount is entered in favor of plaintiff against defendant.

Richter Contracting Co. v. Continental Cas. Co., 230 Cal.App. 2d 491, 41 Cal.Rptr. 98 (1964), involved the issue of whether the restitutionary measure could be used by a subcontractor where he completed performance because of a clause in the subcontract which required him to continue work despite any disputes during his performance. It is common in public contracts to require that the contractor continue performance despite disputes over matters such as extras, what constitutes proper performance, and other disputes during the course of construction.

In *Richter*, there were difficulties at the outset of performance. However, because of the contract clause, the subcontractor continued his performance to completion. He then attempted to use the restitutionary measure to recover the reasonable value of the services, which would have given him considerably more than the balance remaining of the contract price. The court held that by agreeing to continue performance despite the dispute, the subcontractor had given up his right to use the restitutionary measure of recovery. The restitutionary measure can be beneficial if the contractor or, as in this case, the subcontractor has entered into a losing contract. To protect their rights to restitution, subcontractors and contractors may expressly provide in the contract that by agreeing to continue their performance despite disputes they are not automatically giving up their right to a restitutionary remedy.

Interest

Usually the owner's breach consists of the failure to pay money to which the contractor is entitled. The normal measure of recovery for failure to pay money is the legal rate of interest. In a large claim, interest can constitute a substantial amount of money.

If the contractor must sue to recover money to which he is entitled, clearly he can collect interest from the date of the court's judgment. Often he seeks to collect interest starting at an earlier point in time. Generally, the interest on contract claims is recoverable from the time the money should have been paid if the amount in question is clearly established, or if the contract provides that interest can be recovered starting at some earlier time than the date of the court judgment.

In construction contracts, if the amount is clearly ascertained, interest is recoverable. Usually, this means that the contractor can collect interest from the time he should have received a progress or final payment for a definite amount, based upon an established price in the contract. However, if the contractor is trying to collect the reasonable value of extras or delay damages, he will not be entitled to interest until the amount is established. Usually this is not established until the court judgment.

Special rules relating to interest often apply in public contract law. In some jurisdictions, contractors cannot recover interest on claims against a public agency.

(B) OWNERS' MEASURE OF RECOVERY

Uncompleted Project

If the contractor never commences performance, the owner is entitled to recover the difference between the contract price and what it will cost to obtain another contractor to do the same work.

If the contractor unjustifiably quits performance, in the middle of the project, the contractor is liable for the reasonable value of completing the project. If the contract price is $100,000, and the owner has paid $60,000 in progress payments, the contractor is liable for any reasonable costs or losses in excess of $40,000 which the owner incurs or would have to incur to complete the project.

Usually, a contractor breach of this type causes unjustifiable delay in the completion of the project. The owner is entitled to recover delay damages, and often incorporates a clause liquidating such damages in the construction contract. See § 23.06. Additional damages will be discussed in § 29.04(d).

Completed Project: Baldwin v. Alberti

If the contractor completes performance, but has not done so in accordance with plans and specifications, the owner is entitled to the cost of the correction of the defective work, unless the defective work correction will involve unreasonable economic waste. If the cost of correction is $50,000 but correction would increase the value of the project only $10,000, and the defects do not affect the structure or use of the building, it is likely that the owner's measure of recovery will be limited to $10,000, or the difference between what the building should have been worth if it had been built in accordance with the contract, and what it is worth as built. Diminished value recognizes that most owners will not use the $50,000 to correct the defects, and that an award of $50,000 would be a windfall. If used to correct the defect, this would be economic waste. Some courts will let the contractor use diminished value only if his breach was in good faith. Measurement problems of this type often arise in substantial performance cases. See § 24.02(b) and Plante v. Jacobs, reproduced in that section.

A case illustrative of this problem is reproduced at this point.

BALDWIN v. ALBERTI

Supreme Court of Washington, 1961.
58 Wash.2d 243, 362 P.2d 258.

WEAVER, JUDGE. Defendant contracted to build a house for plaintiff on his land. The house was built and plaintiff paid defendant in full for its construction.

The contract provided, among other things:

> "The contractor * * * shall remedy any defects due to faulty materials or workmanship which appear within *a period of one year* from the date of completion of the contract." (Italics ours.)

Within a year, numerous defects appeared in the house. In the main, the defects were: (a) the grounds, which had been graded, did not drain properly and caused moisture to collect under the patio and house; (b) a portion of the roof sagged; (c) a concrete wall had not been built properly; (d) certain water pipes, instead of being one inch, were only one half inch; (e) the septic tank drain field failed to function properly; (f) the garage ceiling light required relocation, an additional electrical switch was necessary, and the garage door had to be rehung.

This is an action for breach of the contract; the defendant did not remedy the defects. *Plaintiff appeals* from a $3,000.96 money judgment in his favor. Defendant neither appeals nor cross-appeals. Liability is not an issue—only the amount of damages.

The amount of plaintiff's judgment is based upon the trial court's finding that this sum is the *reasonable* cost of correcting the defects chargeable to defendant. Plaintiff, on the other hand, contends that he is entitled to the difference between the value of the house for which he contracted and the value of the house as actually constructed.

The term "damages" means the compensation the law will award for an injury done. State ex rel. Macri v. City of Bremerton, 1941, 8 Wash.2d 93, 101, 111 P.2d 612. In Spokane Truck & Dray Co. v. Hoefer, 1891, 2 Wash. 45, at page 51, 25 P. 1072, at page 1073, 11 L.R. A. 689, this court said that

> "* * * 'damages are given as a compensation or satisfaction to the plaintiff for an injury actually received by him from the defendant. They should be precisely commensurate with the injury, neither more nor less; and this whether it be to his person or estate' * * *"

The purpose of money damages is to put the injured party in as good a position as that in which full performance would have put him.

The rule applicable to the instant case is succinctly stated in 1 Restatement, Contracts, § 346:

> "§ 346. Damages for Breach of a Construction Contract. (1) For a breach by one who has contracted to construct a specified product, the other party can get judgment for compensatory damages for all unavoidable harm that the builder had reason to foresee when the contract was made, less such part of the contract price as has not been paid and is not still payable, determined as follows:
>
> "(a) For defective or unfinished construction he can get judgment for either
>
> "(i) the reasonable cost of construction and completion in accordance with the contract, if this is possible and does not involve *unreasonable economic waste;* or
>
> "(ii) the difference between the value that the product contracted for would have had and the value of the performance that has been received by the plaintiff, if construction and completion in accordance with the contract would involve *unreasonable economic waste.*" (Italics ours.)
>
> *"Comment on Subsection* (1a)," following the above-quoted section of the Restatement, states:
>
> "* * * Sometimes defects in a completed structure cannot be physically remedied without tearing down and rebuilding, at a cost that would be imprudent and unreasonable. The law does not require damages to be measured by a method requiring such economic waste. *If no such waste is involved, the cost of remedying the defect is the amount awarded as compensation for failure to render the promised performance."* (Italics ours.)

In the instant case, the evidence discloses, and the trial court found, that the defects could be "adequately and reasonably" repaired. In other words, the court found that the defendant substantially performed the contract and that the defect could be repaired without unreasonable economic waste; hence, our disposition of this case is controlled by the rationale of 1 Restatement, Contracts, § 346(a) (i), quoted supra, and Bernbaum v. Hodges, 1953, 43 Wash. 2d 503, 261 P.2d 968, and cases cited. . . . We conclude that the trial court applied the proper rule for the determination of damages.

The testimony is conflicting in many areas; it appears, however, that the court's findings of fact are within the ambit of the evidence. We cannot disturb them.

. . .

The judgment is affirmed . . .

Usually, the contractor attempts to use the difference in value as the measure of recovery rather than cost of correction. However, in the *Baldwin* case the contractor evidently preferred cost of correction, while the owner argued for the difference in value.

Interest

Usually, in the absence of a contract provision giving the owner a right to recover interest, the owner will not be able to collect interest prior to the date of the court judgment. Most of the claims by the owner against the contractor are for unliquidated or uncertain amounts. For this reason, pre-judgment interest is generally not recoverable. See § 29.04(a).

(C) BURDEN OF PROOF

Since proof of damages is often difficult, the result is often controlled by allocation of burden of proof. Usually, the plaintiff has the burden of showing that a contract was formed, that the defendant breached, that a specified amount of damages were suffered by the plaintiff, or that there was a valid liquidation of damages. Matters which would reduce or prevent recovery must be proved by the defendant. Usually, the defendant must show that the plaintiff would have suffered a loss if the defendant had performed, if plaintiff uses compensation as his measurement principle. Also, the defendant would have to prove that plaintiff could have avoided the loss by reasonable effort.

(D) CONSEQUENTIAL DAMAGE: FORESEEABILITY

Either party may suffer losses which do not relate directly to correction of defective work, delay, or non-payment of money, but are caused by improper performance.

Charging the nonperforming party with all the damages caused by his breach would place a large risk upon him. For this reason, as stated in § 29.02(b), the English and American courts have adopted a foreseeability test for determining the collectability of damages not directly related to the transaction itself.

Hadley v. Baxendale, a leading English case, involved an unexcused breach by a carrier in shipping a defective shaft to the factory. The English court would not permit the shipper to recover profits lost because the shipper's plant had to be shut down when the shaft was not returned as promised. The court held that the carrier could not reasonably foresee that a delay in the delivery of this shaft would shut down the plant nor was he advised of this by the shipper at the time the shipping contract was made.

If a party states in advance to the other party that certain damages will be incurred, he will be able to collect for them if he can show that the losses were caused by the breach. For example, if the contractor makes clear to the owner that if he constructs the project, he has a reasonable likelihood of obtaining other jobs, an unjustifiable termination of the contract by the owner should subject the owner to liability for lost profits on other jobs, as well as damages directly caused by the breach. It may be difficult for the contractor to show with reasonable certainty that he would have been able to obtain the other jobs. However, if he makes a persuasive showing of this, he should be able to recover. The same holds true for similar indirect damages incurred by the owner because of the contractor's breach.

If one of the contracting parties believes that breach by the other party will cause indirect damages of the type mentioned, he should incorporate provisions in the contract which make it clear that he is likely to suffer these losses in the event of nonperformance by the other party.

Contracts frequently contain clauses which attempt to exclude recovery for consequential damages. This may be done directly by a contract provision stating that consequential damages are not recoverable, or it may be done indirectly by prescribing a measure of recovery which limits recovery to certain items and by implication excludes consequential damages. For example, it is common in contracts for the sale of equipment or goods for the seller to limit his liability to the repair and the replacement of defective equipment or goods. Generally, such clauses between buyer and seller are effective, unless the buyer is a consumer who suffers physical injury because of a defective product. If the latter is the case, there is a reasonable likelihood that the limitations expressed in the contract will not be given effect.

REVIEW QUESTIONS

1. How does the foreseeability test limit the liability of the party who has committed a breach of contract?

2. What is the difference between compensation and restitution?

3. Under what circumstances may attorneys fees be recovered as an item of damage for breach of contract?

4. What is the usual contractor's measure of recovery if the owner breaches and the contractor does not complete performance?

5. What are illustrations of consequential damages in a construction contract?

QUESTIONS FOR CLASS DISCUSSION

1. Should foreseeability be determined as of the time the contract is made or at some time before the breach of contract? Why?

2. Should fault be taken into account in determining the measure of recovery for breach of contract?

3. Should contracting parties be given the power to determine in advance the measure of recovery for breach?

PROBLEMS

1. O and C entered into a construction contract under which C was to construct a commercial office building and was to receive a total of $100,000. C had completed approximately 50% of the project when he was wrongfully dismissed from the job by O. C had been paid a total of $40,000 in progress payments. The reasonable value of the material and services which C had put into the project were $60,000. It would take approximately $50,000 to complete the project. What would be C's measure of recovery? Explain.

2. Suppose O's dismissal of C was legally justified. Would C be entitled to anything from O based upon quasi contract (unjust enrichment)? See § 24.02(d).

Chapter 30

DISTRIBUTION OF LOSSES INCIDENT TO CONSTRUCTION PROCESS

SECTION 30.01 INTRODUCTION

One function of the legal system is to distribute losses by the process of determining legal responsibility for these losses.

Losses and injuries of various types can occur incident to the construction project. Workers or others who enter upon the site may be injured or killed. The site owner, or adjacent landowners, may suffer damage to their land, to structures on their land, or to personal property located on their land. The owner, or those persons performing work on the project, may find their expenditures are greater than anticipated because persons with whom they have contracted, or third persons, have not acted in accordance with duties created by law or by contract. Those who invest in the project or who execute bonds relating to contract performance may suffer financial losses.

After the project is completed, persons who enter upon or live in the project may be injured or killed because of defective design, poor workmanship, or improper materials. Those who put their money in the project may find their property damaged or may suffer economic losses for like reasons.

The construction project is a complex undertaking involving many contracting entities. There is a strong likelihood of human error or unavoidable accidents which cause injuries, death, or other losses. Because of the many entities engaged in the project, and the complex network of laws, regulations, and contracts, the placing of legal responsibility is a complicated undertaking. In addition, legal responsibilities become even more complicated because the duty owed the person who suffers the loss may depend upon the status of the person who suffers the loss. His reason for being on the land may bear heavily on this issue. Finally, the laws relating to legal responsibility for such losses vary considerably from state to state.

The purpose of this chapter is to bring together the legal rules which allocate responsibility for losses incident to the construction process. Section 30.02 will deal with tort principles, the method by which the law allocates responsibility for losses generally. Section 30.03 will examine some aspects of contractual methods of handling losses. Sections 30.04, 30.05 and 30.06 treat aspects of tort law which are particularly important to construction projects. These doctrines are misrepresentation, the duty owed by the owner or occupier of land, and the liability of manufacturers for defective products.

Section 30.07 examines the legal doctrines relating to employment injuries, with special reference to workmen's compensation laws.

The balance of the chapter will apply these principles to the types of losses which occur incident to the construction process.

Earlier chapters have dealt with loss allocation. More particularly, Chapter 23 dealt with time problems, Chapter 22 with subsurface conditions and Chapter 24 with payment problems. Those chapters generally relate to losses suffered by parties to a construction contract which they attempt to transfer to the other contracting party. Chapter 30 encompasses the entire project, the participants and those affected by it.

SECTION 30.02 SOME PRINCIPLES OF TORT LAW

(A) DEFINITION

Legal scholars have had difficulty defining tort law. Usually they find definitions either too broad, and thereby meaningless, or too limited to include newly emerging forms of tort liability. However, one working definition which may prove useful defines a tort as a breach of a duty imposed by law, in contrast to duties created through contract principles (consent), or through quasi contract principles (unjust enrichment). As shall be seen, there is an overlap between the three doctrines, but the division between the three can be useful as a preliminary working definition. Tort liability, then, can be predicted upon the violation of a duty created by law, rather than a duty created by consent, or liability based upon unjust enrichment.

It is less difficult to express the function of tort law. A primary function of tort law is to distribute the losses which arise through human activity. While tort law has some punitive aspects, its principal function is to determine whether a person who suffers a loss can shift that loss to the person whose conduct or activity has substantially caused the loss.

(B) SELECTIVITY OF DISCUSSION

It would not serve any useful function to classify the many types of wrongs labeled by the law as "torts", nor to describe and discuss them. Emphasis will be on those tort doctrines which most directly relate to the construction process. Some torts of lesser importance will be mentioned where they relate to a specific problem. For example, defamation has been mentioned in connection with payment problems in § 24.07(c). Also, the intentional tort of trespass relates to the duty owed by the owner or occupier of land to those who enter upon or pass by his land and will be discussed in § 30.05. A major emphasis in § 30.02 will be upon rules for allocating losses which are most relevant to the construction process.

(C) FAULT (NEGLIGENCE) AS DOMINANT TORT PRINCIPLE

Generalizations regarding tort law are particularly dangerous, because tort law consists of a heterogeneous collection of legal doctrines, many of which are related to one another solely because of the basic tort law function of distributing losses. In addition, many areas of tort law presently are in a state of flux. Nevertheless, some generalizations may be useful.

Modern Anglo-American tort law developed in the 19th century. This period saw the rise of modern industrialism, as well as the glorification of rugged individualism. This era also witnessed the deification of science and industrial progress as the hoped for vehicles for creating a better life.

Ever since its modern development in the 19th century, tort law has oscillated between attempting to insure that persons who suffer losses are compensated by the person who caused the loss, and protecting those persons whose activity caused losses from the imposition of onerous financial burdens, especially if those persons were engaged in commercial or industrial activities.

The policy of protecting those engaged in commercial and industrial activities was a dominant one during much of the developmental period of tort law. Lawmakers of the period, mainly judicial, formulated a number of rules designed to protect commercial and industrial activities from the potentially crushing burden of legal responsibility for all losses which might result from the manufacture of their products, or from their other commercial activities. These protective rules were articulated as rules of law, a device which controlled the potentially irrational and anti-defendant jury. To accomplish this protection in the tort area, a number of legal doctrines developed which will be mentioned later. But for present purposes, it should be noted that the fault theory required a finding of negligence by the defendant, in addition to the defendant having actually caused the loss. This contrasted with prior law which, in many types of cases, imposed liability without fault.

This development was parallel to the 19th century contract doctrines which limited contract damages to losses which were foreseeable at the time the contract was made. See §§ 29.02(b) and 29.04(d).

There were strong moral overtones to the development of the fault doctrine. Liability without fault seemed antithetical to the concepts of rugged individualism. People were expected to take care of themselves. If someone suffered a loss, he could transfer that loss to the person causing it only if the latter had deviated from reasonable conduct.

Paradoxically, 19th century tort law was moving in two opposite directions at the same time. New forms of liability were being created, while older rules of liability without regard to fault were being questioned and modified. Both of these trends found the fault doctrine a compromise which was often better than violent shifts from nonliability to liability without regard to fault or from the latter type of liability to nonliability.

The fault doctrine also squared with the 19th century view that law could be used as a means of channeling people into socially acceptable conduct. Persons would be more likely to act carefully if they were made legally responsible for their negligent conduct.

(D) PROTECTION FOR DEFENDANT: PROXIMATE CAUSE, DUTY, AND PRIVITY

In addition to making liability depend principally upon fault, other doctrines protected the defendant from open-ended liability and possible crushing financial burdens. Even if the plaintiff could show that the defendant was negligent, the plaintiff had to show that the defendant's conduct was the "proximate" (principal) cause of his loss. In addition, the law held that the defendant could not be liable if he did not owe a duty to the plaintiff to conduct himself in accordance with the legal standard of care. The doctrines of "proximate cause" and "duty" could relieve the defendant from liability if the plaintiff's injury occurred at a place and time substantially removed from the act of the defendant which caused the injury, unless the defendant could have reasonably anticipated that the plaintiff would suffer the very loss which occurred.

Duty also was expressed in the privity rule. If the defendant's act was a breach of contract, persons injured who were not a party to the contract were not allowed to recover from the defendant. Courts stated that since there was no privity of contract between the injured plaintiff and the defendant, the defendant would not be held liable.

Proximate cause, duty, and privity could be applied where the injury was the end result of an unusual sequence of events, or where there were a number of factors which substantially caused the loss. For example, suppose an electrical contracting company sends an electrician to a 30 story commercial office building to repair an electrical circuit. The electrician installs an electrical cable which is not sufficient to carry the electric current. This causes an overload and a short circuit. This short circuit causes the electricity of the office building to fail for three hours. The failure of the electricity shuts down the elevators for a two hour period, until emergency power sources can be employed. An employee of a large contracting company enters the building to submit a bid on the 28th floor for the construction of a $20,000,000 construction project. When he enters the building, he finds that the electricity is off and the elevators are not running. Since he does not know how long it will take to repair the elevator, and since he does not wish to walk 28 flights of steps, he waits. When the elevator is finally repaired, he takes the elevator to the 28th floor but finds that he is too late to submit his bid. His employer loses a $20,000,000 job upon which he could reasonably be expected to make $2,000,000. Should the electrician or the employer of the electrician be liable for the $2,000,000 loss?

In a sense, the original negligent repair job started the chain of events and caused the $2,000,000 loss. But, in addition to the series of unusual events, perhaps the loss was caused by the building owner not having an adequate emergency power source which could be instituted immediately upon failure of the basic electrical system. Perhaps the loss would not have occurred had it not been for the negligence of the janitor whose acts caused the necessity to repair the wiring in the first place. Perhaps the cause of the loss was the employee's reluctance to walk the 28 flights of steps rather than wait for the elevator to be repaired. And if the facts are slightly changed so that the cause of the short circuit was defective wire, rather than use of inadequate wire, perhaps the loss was caused by the manufacturer of the electrical wire.

This illustration could be complicated further by assuming that the employee of the bidder did try to walk the 28 flights of stairs and died at the 20th floor because of a heart attack. In addition of the possible causes that have been mentioned in the preceding paragraphs, was his death caused by his unwise decision to walk 28 flights?

What if he did not realize that he had a weak heart, but had been informed two months earlier by his doctor that his heart was in excellent condition, when in fact his heart was deteriorating? The possibilities are infinite, and loss allocation problems of this sort can be hopelessly confused when issues of proximate or substantial cause and duty are injected. Liability can become even more complicated if two or three negligent acts can be said to have substantially caused the injury. In such a case, the plaintiff may be able to recover from two or three defendants, who will then in turn sue each other trying to establish that one's negligence was either more causal, or one's negligence was more culpable than the other.

The imposition of liability in such a complicated chain of events or concurrently caused cases is often an uncertain matter. About all that can be said is that sometimes a person whose negligence sets the chain into motion is held liable, and sometimes he is not. Sometimes the result will depend upon whether the risk is one which was paid for and contemplated in the original transaction. If the electrical job in question involved a trifling amount of money, it would seem unfair to place huge losses upon the electrical contractor. If, on the other hand, the electrical project was a sizable one, imposition of such liability may seem less unjust. Coupled with these considerations is the increasing use of public liability insurance. While it is true that the insurer only has to pay if the insured is held liable, the recognition by judges and juries that such losses are often insured against by the defendant has had a bearing in expanding liability through the device of denying defenses based upon lack of proximate or substantial cause, or absence of a duty owed by the defendant to plaintiff.

Causation questions are not uncommon in construction contracts. When a roof collapses, the injured parties may contend that the design was defective, or that supervision was inadequate, and charge the architect or engineer with liability. The plaintiff may also contend that the contractor or a subcontractor was negligent in the way he did the work. The plaintiff may also contend that any equipment or materials used were defective and sue the manufacturer of materials, or the person who supplied the equipment. It is often difficult to determine whose acts substantially caused the injury in such cases. This problem will be discussed in more detail in §§ 30.07 and 30.08.

(E) LIABILITY WITHOUT FAULT

Exceptions to Fault Doctrine

Even though the fault doctrine dominated the developmental period of Anglo-American tort law, there were a substantial number of exceptions. Keepers of animals, those engaged in ultra-hazardous activities, (such as selling explosives or blasting), and persons who sold dangerous products, were held liable for losses their activities caused without regard to whether they were negligent.

Also, "vicarious liability" was a type of liability without fault which developed in the 19th century as an exception to the dominant fault doctrine. The employer of an employee whose negligence injured the plaintiff would be held liable for those injuries if the negligent employee was acting within the scope of his employment. Such liability would not depend upon negligence on the part of the employer in selecting, training, or allowing a known careless employee to continue working. Such liability, like the agency doctrine, recognized the realities of business activities, and the fact that most of the persons who were in the position to act negligently, injuring others, were not the actual entrepreneurs or proprietors of the business. This recognition was reinforced by the growing dominance of the corporation as the organizational form through which commercial activities were performed. Corporations operate through employees. Vicarious liability also implicitly recognized a social policy of insuring that persons who were injured could collect from financially responsible defendants. Often, the employee actually causing the injury was not in an economic position to make good the loss suffered by the plaintiff. The doctrine of vicarious liability was a precursor to the mid-twentieth century emergence of liability without fault based upon theories of enterprise liability.

Modern Development of Liability Without Privity or Fault

While this trend will be discussed in greater detail in § 30.06, it merits some mention in this subsection. Despite the fact that there is no direct contract relationship between an injured consumer and the manufacturer of a defective product causing the injury, courts recognize the desirability of giving injured persons the right to sue manufacturers in such cases. The law has moved in the same direction, although perhaps more slowly, where the ultimate user of a defective product suffers an economic loss because of the product defect. When persons buy consumer goods, they often are encouraged to do so by national advertising of the manufacturers. Persons who buy under these circumstances often assume that the manufacturer will stand behind his product and will be responsible in the event products are defective and cause injuries or other losses.

In addition to this reliance element, courts, through notions of enterprise liability, are recognizing the economics of pricing and the increased use of public liability insurance. In large scale mass production of goods, statisticians and economists can ofter predict the number and types of injuries that will result from the use of the products. The costs of these injuries can be included in the price of the product and passed on to the consumer. If pricing of injuries is too difficult or exposure too great, a manufacturer can insure against such losses, and pass the cost of insurance on to the consumer. When insurance is used, the insurance company must make predictions based upon experience and, in effect, price the cost of such injuries. In addition, the immediate seller of the product to the consumer who is injured may not be financially responsible or able to pay a claim made by the injured party.

These considerations have led to a virtual obliteration of the privity defense formerly given to manufacturers of mass produced goods. In addition, the difficulty of proving negligence of the manufacturer, as shall be seen in § 30.06, has tended to cause the law to hold the manufacturer liable for injuries caused by defective products, without requiring that the injured party prove that the manufacturer was negligent.

(F) VIOLATION OF APPLICABLE LEGAL DUTY

In subsections (c), (d), and (e), discussion centered around the standard of care owed by defendant to plaintiff. In this subsection, emphasis will be upon a more particular definition of the standard of care owed and methods by which the plaintiff can prove that the defendant has violated the applicable standard of care.

An Objective Standard

Various formulas or definitions have been created by courts and scholars for the purposes of ascertaining whether the defendant has been negligent. Sometimes it is said that the defendant must "act with due care", that he must act as a "reasonably prudent man", and that he must not expose the plaintiff to "unreasonable risks of harm." Sometimes it is stated that he is responsible for "the natural and probable consequences of his act."

First, the standard that is applied is usually objective. It is not a matter of determining whether the particular defendant *knew* that his act would expose someone to an unreasonable risk of harm. His conduct is usually measured by a standard of reasonableness. What would a reasonable man have anticipated and foreseen at the time of the asserted negligent act? The standard of reasonableness is diluted somewhat by looking at the particular point in time when the act occurred, as well as at what the particular defendant knew at the time of the act. Also, the law looks at the age, experience, and skill of the particular defendant. When this is done, a youthful or inexperienced defendant may be held to a lower standard of care, while a particularly experienced or trained defendant will be held to a higher standard of care.

Custom

Sometimes the plaintiff in construction accident litigation attempts to prove that the defendant did not act in accordance with "customary" conduct. Conversely, the defendant may try to show that his conduct did comport with custom.

Evidence that the defendant's conduct conformed to custom is relevant to the question of negligence but it is not conclusive on that issue. If the defendant can show that his act was performed in a generally accepted manner, this is evidence tending to show that he used due care. In the absence of any showing to the contrary by the plaintiff, this evidence may be sufficient to have a judge direct a verdict for the defendant. However, the plaintiff will be permitted to show that complying with custom was not sufficient to relieve the defendant from a finding of negligence. The fact that all builders use the same unsafe construction methods should not relieve a builder from a finding that he did not act with due care. Evidence that the defendant did not act as others in similar situations usually act could be quite persuasive that he was negligent. Under such circumstances, it is likely that the defendant will have to make a strong showing that his acts or failure to act were justifiable under the circumstances to show he acted with due care.

Professional Standards

In suits against doctors, lawyers, architects, engineers, surveyors and other persons with technical education and training, it may appear that custom is almost conclusive on the question of negligence. Professional persons are often held to the standard of good professional practice. Such a standard takes into account the learning and skill possessed by members of his profession in good standing, the location where the defendant practices, the facilities available to him, and whether the defendant held himself out as a specialist (in which case the standard will be higher).

It used to be generally accepted that a professional person would be held to the standard of professional practice in his specific locality. The law would inquire how a professional person in the same or similar city or town would have acted under the same circumstances.

The law is beginning to look beyond the specific locality where the professional practices. There is an increasing standardization of education in the professions. Testing for competence tends to be on at least a state-wide basis, with moves in some directions toward national testing. Post-school training and education tend to be at least state-wide, and often national. For these reasons, professionals within a specialty should be able to function at the same level of competence as others in the specialty, at least on a state-wide basis and, in the case of some professions, on a national basis.

Some states have expanded the standard to a state or even national standard. This is likely to become the rule in all states.

Using the customary standard of care used by a profession does tend to permit the profession to set its own standards for liability purposes. This means that the law has delegated professional standards to the profession.

The degree of delegation given to the profession to establish the legal standards may depend to a substantial degree upon the respect generally accorded to the profession by the community at large. If the profession is thought to do a thorough job of training its members, maintaining professional discipline and developing the knowledge in the profession, for all practical purposes this is likely to mean that the standards of that profession will be conclusive on the question of negligence.

The degree to which a profession is permitted to set its own standards may also depend upon the confidence the legal system has in dealing with technical questions, such as professional standards. For example, in complicated medical questions, the legal system, with its law-trained personnel and lay juries, is likely to accord a healthy respect to the standards of practice of the medical profession. For these reasons, the autonomy accorded medical practice will be greater than that accorded legal, architectural, and engineering practices. In hotly contested medical malpractice cases, the principal issue will be what are accepted medical practices and whether the defendant lived up to them.

Also, the finality accorded professional practices may depend upon the issue. A judge or jury may feel just as competent in the field of aesthetics as the architect, but these same judges or jurors will respect engineering practices when the issue relates to the collapse of a roof or bridge.

Statutory Standards: Effect of Violation or Compliance

More difficult questions relate to the effect of showing that the conduct of the defendant violated statutory standards. There are many statutes, ordinances, and regulations which relate to building materials, construction methods, and design.

The first step in analyzing the effect of a statutory violation is to determine whether the plaintiff was in the group of persons intended to be protected by the legislation. Generally, this hurdle is not difficult to overcome in the ordinary construction injury case.

Next, it must be determined whether the violation of the statute was a substantial cause of the injury. For example, in Hazelwood v. Gordon, 253 Cal.App.2d 178, 61 Cal.Rptr. 115 (1967) an employee fell down a flight of stairs. The evidence showed that the steps were too narrow at the bottom, and that this, together with an inadequate handrail, violated a city ordinance. However, the court held that the injured party could not recover from the owner of the property because her injury was not caused by a violation of the ordinance, but was due to her negligently placing her foot on the top step of the staircase knowing that the stairs were dangerous.

If it is shown that the plaintiff was in the class to be protected by the statute, and that the violation of the law caused her injury, what effect does a violation of the statute have? It is at this point that there is a great variation in case decisions.

Some statutes state that failure to comply is conclusive on the negligence question. If a statutory violation has been proved, nothing further is needed to prove negligence. The defendant cannot overcome a statutory violation by showing he acted with due care. Some statutes go even further by providing that contributory negligence by the injured party will not constitute a defense. Similarly, some courts have given the same conclusive effect to the violation of certain statutes.

Frequently, courts hold that a statutory violation makes the defendant negligent *per se.* This means that the plaintiff wins, unless the defendant can show that his violation of the statute should be excused. It will take a very strong showing by the defendant to relieve himself from a finding of negligence. Without a showing of this sort, it is likely that the judge will direct that the jury find that the defendant was negligent.

Some courts have held that the statutory violation is evidence of negligence, and must be taken into account with other evidence of whether the defendant acted with due care. Finally, a few courts hold that the violation of the statute is not even evidence of negligence.

Generally, a showing by the plaintiff that the defendant has violated a statute which was designed to protect the plaintiff, and that violation of the statutory standard caused the plaintiff's injury, will lead to a finding that the defendant was negligent. In some extraordinary circumstances, the defendant will be able to show that his violation of the statute was justifiable, and that he was not negligent.

A somewhat different problem arises when the defendant attempts to show that he complied with the statutory standard, and that this should relieve him from the finding that he was negligent. The effect of showing compliance with statutory standards is less than the effect of showing that the defendant violated statutory standards.

For example, if a city ordinance provides that a fence surrounding a private swimming pool should be six feet high, have certain locks, and be composed of certain materials, the defendant who complies could conceivably be negligent, if he knew, or should have known, that a neighbor's four year old child was very skillful at climbing over such a fence, or picking the lock. The statutory standard may set a minimum which may not be sufficient, when other circumstances are known, or should be known, to the defendant. Evidence that the defendant has complied with the statute will help him on the question of negligence. However, the plaintiff will be given an opportunity of showing that the defendant's conduct did not constitute due care.

Some other generalizations can be made. A federal or state statute is likely to be more influential in determining the applicable legal standard of care than a local ordinance. State administration regulations generally fall between state statutes and local ordinances.

Also, violation of employee safety laws are likely to be more influential in determining the applicable legal standard of care than violation of the typical building code. In Major v. Waverly & Ogden, Inc., 7 N.Y.2d 332, 165 N.E.2d 181, 197 N.Y.S.2d 165 (1960), the plaintiff, a social guest of a tenant, sued the landlord when she fell down a flight of stairs. She based her claim upon a violation of the building code which required that there be a light and hand rail for the staircase.

The New York Court of Appeals held that the violation of the code was evidence of negligence, but barred the plaintiff from recovery because of her contributory negligence.

The Court refused to follow earlier cases which had held that violation of certain laws went beyond merely being evidence of negligence and precluded the contributory negligence defense. The Court stated that those cases had involved violations of employee safety laws and stressed the need to give special protection to workers because of the unavoidable hazards of their occupation.

For more discussion of statutory violations, see § 30.08(d).

Res Ipsa Loquitur: Circumstantial Evidence of Negligence

It is often difficult for the plaintiff to prove that the defendant was negligent. Before the advent of modern discovery procedures (techniques for examining the other party to the litigation, his employees and his records), it was difficult to obtain information which could be used as evidence to establish the defendant's negligence. For this reason, the law developed a doctrine called *res ipsa loquitur*. Literally, this means that the act speaks for itself. It originated in a case in 1863, which involved a barrel of flour rolling out of a warehouse window and falling on a passing pedestrian. In a sense, it was simply part of the theory of circumstantial evidence. While there may have been no direct evidence of negligence, the case stood for the principle that it was likely that the barrel rolled out of the window because of the fault of the defendant. It soon expanded into many other types of cases. It enabled a plaintiff to establish negligence from the objective facts surrounding the occurrence of the injury, and enabled him to get his case to the jury. It is usually stated that the doctrine can be used when the event is of the type which does not ordinarily occur in the absence of negligence, and the injury to the plaintiff was caused by an agent or instrumentality within the exclusive control of the defendant. As shall be seen in § 30.06, it often has been used in cases involving actions against manufacturers of defective products.

Negligence cases may involve the use of expert witnesses to prove that the defendant acted negligently. This is especially true in actions against manufacturers, and in construction site accidents. It is often necessary to establish that the defendant did not use safe methods, or that the injury was caused by poor workmanship or defective materials. For a discussion of expert testimony see § 38.04.

(G) A LEGALLY RECOGNIZABLE LOSS: DAMAGES

In addition to the requirements mentioned, the plaintiff must show he has suffered a legally recognizable loss.

Pecuniary Losses Incurred or to be Incurred

Where someone is injured, either during or after the construction project is completed, the injured person usually seeks to recover for out of pocket losses, such as his medical expenses, and his lost earnings prior to the law suit. Usually such items are recoverable. Sometimes such losses are reimbursed by a third party, such as an insurance company, or a workmen's compensation carrier. If so, this usually does not affect recovery. The third party may be able to claim reimbursement in some situations.

The injured person is also entitled to recover for losses which he is likely to incur or suffer in the future. Illustrations of these are future medical expenses, and future loss of earnings. Projections into the future are often guess work. What will the injured person be able to earn in the future, and how long will his disability or diminished earning power continue? The plaintiff may recover these items of economic loss if he can establish them with reasonable probability.

Pain and Suffering

More difficult questions are involved where the issue is that of recovery for damages which are difficult to assess monetarily, and which are often easy to fabricate, such as pain and suffering. An injured person is entitled to recover for pain and suffering which occur both before trial and after trial. Courts have looked with some suspicion upon pain and suffering. However they are recoverable items if the court or jury can reasonably believe that they have been incurred, or will be incurred, and can place some monetary value upon them.

Disfigurement

What if the injured party is disfigured by an injury which causes him to have a permanent scar upon his face? There is no doubt of the occurrence of the injury. But what of the economic valuation of such disfigurement, and the possibility that such disfigurement can be eliminated by plastic surgery in the future? Despite these difficulties, damages for disfigurement are recoverable if they can be established with reasonable certainty.

In addition, the injured party may be able to recover for loss of use of certain parts of his body which resulted from the injury. Again, there is a question of economic valuation. Such items are recoverable if they can be established with reasonable certainty.

Attorneys Fees and Interest

A personal injury claim usually requires the services of an attorney. Usually an attorney will take personal injury cases upon a contingent fee. In such agreements, the injured party may agree to pay the attorney's out of pocket expenses, whether or not the suit is successful. However, he does not pay for the attorney's time unless the suit is successful. The attorney will take a stated percentage of the recovery, depending upon the difficulty of the case, and the stage at which the recovery is reached. If there is a settlement prior to trial, the attorney will receive anywhere from 25 to 40% of the recovery. If the matter must be tried in court, the corresponding percentage will go up to approximately 33 to 50% of the recovery. Although there is a movement toward establishing recoverability of attorney's fees, at present the injured party is not entitled to recover his attorney's fees as part of the judgment against the defendant. If the "tort" is also a breach of contract, attorney's fees are recoverable only if the contract calls for it, or a special statute authorizes recovery of attorney's fees. The injured party can recover court costs, which are usually quite small. He cannot recover interest on the claim. Since the amount recoverable in a personal injury case cannot be established until settlement, or until the case is tried, interest is usually recoverable from the date of settlement or the date of judgment.

Emotional Distress

The law has had difficulty in awarding damages for emotional or psychic distress. For example, a worker on a construction project may suffer emotional injury, despite the absence of any physical injury. He may be on a building roof which partially collapses. He may suffer emotional trauma because of the fear that he will fall from the roof, even though he does not actually fall. Another illustration of emotional distress would be the horror experienced by a construction worker when he sees someone else fall from the roof of a building. Courts have been very hesitant to grant recovery for emotional distress which is not tied to some form of physical injury.

What if a shock or emotional fright is followed by physical harm, such as a miscarriage? Many courts have denied recovery for such physical harm unless there was also some physical impact upon the plaintiff. More recent decisions have eliminated the requirement for impact in such cases.

Where the emotional stress is connected to injury or prospective injury to a third party, persons suffering emotional distress have had considerable difficulty in recovering. Those courts which require that there be an impact deny recovery. Even in those cases which do not insist upon impact, recovery has been difficult.

Some courts have granted recovery to the plaintiff for "physical" injury if the plaintiff has been in the zone of risk, such as being in the path of a vehicle which has struck the plaintiff's child. One case, Dillon v. Legg, 68 Cal.2d 728, 441 P.2d 912, 69 Cal.Rptr. 72 (1968) allowed the plaintiff mother to recover when she suffered a physical harm ("great emotional disturbance and shock and injury to her nervous system") when she witnessed a fatal accident involving her child, even though the plaintiff herself had not been in danger. Where courts have permitted recovery, the emotional shock or stress has caused great trauma and a lasting effect upon the mental health of the plaintiff.

Losses Suffered by Persons other than the Injured Person

Can third parties recover when they have suffered a loss because of the injury? For example, the children of an injured worker may lose the companionship of their father, or the wife of the injured workman may be denied companionship and marital services. Generally, these third parties can recover, unless the recovery to the injured party included those items of damage. For example, it would not be proper to permit a child to recover for pecuniary loss relating to injury to his father, where the recovery by the father includes those items. Also, it may be difficult to establish the economic value of loss of consortium (marital companionship and services). In the latter cases, the law differentiates between husband and wife. It is usually possible for a husband to recover for the loss of his wife's consortium, but it is difficult for the wife to recover for the loss of her husband's consortium. This distinction is gradually being eliminated. It seems likely that in the future either party will be able to recover for this loss, provided that some economic value can be placed upon it.

Punitive Damages

Punitive, or exemplary, damages are not based solely upon a loss suffered by the plaintiff, but are predicted upon punishing the person causing the injury. Also, it is hoped that such "punishment" will deter others from committing similar acts of wrongdoing. In most injury cases, punitive damages are not recoverable. However, if the act is particularly blameworthy, there is a possibility of recovering punitive damages. The type of tort cases where punitive damages are most frequently recovered are defamation (libel or slander) cases. In such actions, it may be very difficult to establish actual damages suffered. However, if the defamation is malicious, courts sometimes will permit juries to award punitive or exemplary damages, even where actual damage was nominal.

Survival of Legal Claim: Wrongful Death Statutes

In early Anglo-American legal history, the cause of action died with the death of the person injured, and there could be no recovery. Today all states have wrongful death statutes which permit the near relatives, or the person handling the estate of the deceased, to recover from the wrongdoer. The statutes vary considerably. Sometimes the statutes permit recovery by the relatives, based only upon their loss. Other statutes also will permit recovery for the losses suffered by the deceased prior to his death. Many wrongful death statutes set monetary limits to recovery for wrongful death.

(H) DEFENSES

Contributory Negligence

If the defendant can show that the plaintiff's injury was substantially caused by the plaintiff's own negligence, the defendant will be relieved from liability. Usually the burden is upon the defendant to establish contributory negligence, although in some states the plaintiff has the burden of showing that he was free from fault. To avoid the harshness of this doctrine where the plaintiff's negligence is much less than the defendant's negligence, sometimes juries permit the plaintiff to recover by deciding that the plaintiff's negligence did not substantially cause the injury.

To avoid the often harsh result a finding of contributory negligence can cause, an increasing number of states have adopted the comparative negligence doctrine. While there are variations among the states which have adopted comparative negligence, essentially this doctrine involves a comparison by the jury of the negligence of plaintiff and defendant on a percentage basis. For example, a jury might find the plaintiff 20% negligent, and the defendant 80%. The plaintiff would recover the percentage of his damages attributable to the negligence of defendant. In the example given, the plaintiff would recover 80%. In a pure comparative negligence system, even if the plaintiff were 90% negligent and the defendant 10%, the plaintiff would recover 10% of his damages. Most states which have comparative negligence bar the plaintiff from any recovery if his negligence is over a specified percentage, typically 50–66⅔%. Comparative negligence is used in admiralty law (losses which occur incident to maritime activity), and for injuries to the employees of certain common carriers under the Federal Employers Liability Act.

Assumption of Risk

Another important defense is "assumption of risk." The plaintiff cannot recover if he gave his consent to the defendant's act, knowing of the risks involved. If he knows of the risks and voluntarily engages in the activity, he may have assumed the risk of injury or loss.

Independent Contractor Rule

Sometimes defendants can avoid liability by use of the "independent contractor rule." Generally, the employer of an independent contractor is not liable for the negligent acts of the independent contractor. For example, if a home owner hires a contractor to do remodeling work, in most situations the owner will not be responsible for injuries caused by the negligence of the contractor. The traditional test for determining the status of the contractor is whether the employer of the contractor has controlled, or had the right to control, the details of how the work was to be done by the contractor.

The law has developed many exceptions to the independent contractor rule, because independent contractors frequently are not financially able to respond for injuries caused by their negligence. Also, a financially solvent employer might choose to insulate himself from liability by hiring an independent contractor to do work for which he would normally use his own employees. For more discussion see § 30.08(c), (e) and (f).

(I) IMMUNITIES

Sometimes a particular defendant is given immunity from suit. The two principal beneficiaries of immunity are public bodies and charitable organizations.

The law has moved slowly but surely toward abolishing the immunity of charitable organizations. There is no particular reason to insulate charities from liability, especially in light of the availability of public liability insurance. It makes no difference to an injured plaintiff whether his injury is caused by an ordinary private citizen, or by a charitable organization. His loss is the same. Immunity was originally given to encourage activities of charitable organizations, as most of them perform useful functions. While there still may be states which are said to still have charitable immunity because of older case decisions, it is unlikely that charitable immunity would be a good defense today even in those states. Very few modern decisions have granted charities immunity from tort liability.

Because claims against public bodies are important in the contract context, as well as in the tort context, detailed discussion of this immunity will be postponed until § 30.12. Generally immunity in this area is stronger than charitable immunity, but many states have removed the immunity, or have created special rules for tort actions against public entities.

Sovereign and charitable immunity are largely court-created doctrines. Another immunity which is significant in construction project loss allocation relates to the statutory immunity given employers from tort action when their employees are injured in the course of employment. Generally, the employee is limited to his workmen's compensation claim and cannot institute a tort action against his own employer. This is discussed in greater detail in § 30.07.

SECTION 30.03 THE ROLE OF CONTRACT LAW IN LOSS ALLOCATION

(A) AS THE BASIS FOR A CLAIM

When two or more parties make a contract, they may agree in the contract that losses will be borne by one party or the other, or will be shared by the parties. In addition, the parties may agree that if one party is forced to settle or pay a judgment for injuries due to acts of the other party, the party actually causing the loss shall indemnify the paying party. Particular types of contract loss allocation questions will be discussed in greater detail in § 30.11, and a special section, § 30.13(b) will be devoted to indemnity actions.

In addition, a contracting party may be held liable for a loss caused by his breach of contract incurred by a person who was not a party to the contract, if the latter can be classified as a "third party beneficiary". In determining whether he is a third party beneficiary, generally the test is whether the contract was made for his benefit. For example, a subcontractor who incurs a loss which is caused by the negligence of an architect might be successful in a suit against the architect, based upon the contract between the architect and the owner, if he can persuade the court that this contract was made for his benefit.

For use of the third party beneficiary doctrine in the surety bond context, see § 18.09(a).

Under certain circumstances, contract and tort doctrines can be relevant to the same fact situation. For example, if the architect or engineer has not used due care in the performance of his work, the owner may be permitted to sue either in contract or in tort.

(B) AS A DEFENSE

Sometimes contract can operate to give a defense to a party whose acts have caused an injury or loss to someone. For example, a "no damage" clause in a construction contract may relieve the owner from any damages which result from an unjustified act of the owner, or design professional which interferes with the performance of the contractor. A "no damage" clause usually limits the contractor to an extension of time.

Another illustration of the contract furnishing a defense was seen in Independent School District #877 v. Loberg Plumbing and Heating

Co., 266 Minn. 426, 123 N.W.2d 793 (1963). In this case, the plaintiff school district sued a plumbing contractor for damages caused by a fire allegedly resulting from the defendant contractor's negligence. The contract provided that the owner would obtain fire insurance on the building, and would insure the interests of all contractors working on the project. The contract also specified that the owner and the contractor would be liable to each other for damage caused by the other's negligence, except for damage caused by fire or vandalism. In an action by the school district against the contractor, the court held that the contract exonerated the defendant contractor from any liability for fire caused by his own negligence.

Finally, the contract may give the owner a defense if the contractor discovers unusual subsurface conditions. As seen in § 22.05 disclaimers in the contract documents often relieve the owner from liability for any added expenses incurred by the contractor traceable to unusual subsurface conditions.

The effectiveness of contractual loss allocation will depend to a large degree upon the realities of the contract making process. As emphasized throughout this treatise courts are increasingly becoming aware of the adhesive, one-sided nature of many contracts. While still according a substantial amount of autonomy to the contracting parties to allocate losses and place responsibility as they see fit, where it is clear that there is very little bargaining over contract terms because one party can more or less dictate the terms due to its superior bargaining power, courts have tended to favor the weaker party. While contracts related to the construction process are often entered into by experienced businessmen, there is still a possibility that a court will attempt to achieve a fair allocation of responsibility for losses rather than follow the literal language of the contract. This is even more likely to be the case when the party with dominant bargaining position attempts to place the risk on the other party for losses caused by the negligence of the dominant party to the bargain. An illustration of this will be seen in the judicial treatment of indemnity provisions. See § 30.13.

SECTION 30.04 MISREPRESENTATION

(A) SCOPE OF DISCUSSION

While misrepresentation problems can occur in the contract formation process, this section treats the liability of persons whose business it is to make representations. A surveyor makes representations as to boundaries, a soils engineer as to soil conditions, an architect or engineer as to costs, or a lawyer as to legal rights.

(B) REPRESENTATION OR OPINION

At the outset, representations should be distinguished from opinions. For example, an architect may give his best considered judgment on what a particular project will cost. However, his prediction may not be intended by him, or understood by his client, to be a factual representation which will give the client some legal claim in the event the prediction turns out to be inaccurate. If the statement is merely an opinion, and not a representation of fact, it is reasonably clear that the person making the representation will not be liable simply because he is wrong.

(C) CLASSIFICATIONS OF CONDUCT

The person making the misrepresentation may have had a fraudulent intent. He may have made the representation knowing it was false, and with the intention of deceiving the person to whom the representation was made. His representation may not have been made with the intention to deceive, but may have been negligently made. Finally, his representation may have been made with due care, but turned out to be wrong. This is sometimes referred to as an innocent misrepresentation.

(D) PERSON SUFFERING THE LOSS

Another classification relates to whether the harm was suffered by the person to whom the representation was made, or by some third party. For example, the soils engineer may make a representation as to soils conditions to a client. If the representation is incorrect, the harm may be suffered by the client, or, in some cases, by third parties such as a subcontractor or the contractor.

(E) TYPE OF LOSS

Finally, misrepresentation cases can also be classified by the particular type of harm which resulted from the misrepresentation. A misrepresentation with regard to soil conditions may result in a cave-in which kills or injures workers. It may also cause damage to property. Finally, it may also cause economic loss. The owner may have to pay for damage caused to an adjacent land owner's property. A subcontractor may incur additional costs during the excavating because of the misrepresentation.

(F) RELIANCE

Generally, the misrepresentation must have been relied upon reasonably by the person suffering the loss. If there is no reliance, or if the reliance is not reasonable, then there is no actionable misrepresentation. A principal application of this doctrine has been discussed in Chapter 22. Often the owner makes representations as to soil conditions to the contractor, and then attempts to disclaim responsibility for the accuracy of the representation. The disclaimer is an attempt to transfer the risk of loss for any inaccurate representations to the contractor. It is intended to negate the element of reliance, which is a basic requirement of misrepresentation. As has been seen, in most circumstances such disclaimers are successful in placing the risk of loss upon the contractor. However, such disclaimer cannot relieve the person making the representation from liability for fraud, and it may not be effective if the representations were negligently made.

(G) SOME GENERALIZATIONS

Generally, the more wrongful the conduct by the person making the representation, the greater the likelihood of recovery against that party. For example, fraudulent misrepresentation always creates liability. Negligent misrepresentation usually provides the basis for a valid damage claim for misrepresentation. Innocent misrepresentations, being the least culpable, are the most difficult types of cases for the person relying on the representation to recover damages. He is not likely to have a valid claim against the person making the misrepresentation unless that person has promised to be accurate.

Liability to third parties often depends upon the type of harm suffered. If the harm suffered relates to death or personal injury, it is not likely that the absence of a contractual relationship between the person suffering the harm and the person making the misrepresentation will constitute a defense. For example, an injured worker will be able to recover from a soils engineer whose negligent misrepresentations cause a cave-in injuring the worker, despite the lack of any contractual relationship between the injured worker and the soils engineer. If the loss suffered by a third party relates to economic loss, the lack of privity (contractual relationship) between the persons suffering the loss, and the person making the misrepresentation, in many jurisdictions may preclude recovery against the latter party.

Courts have looked at foreseeability in determining whether third parties could sue persons making the misrepresentation. If reliance by a third party is reasonably foreseeable, or if the person making the representation intended to influence a third party, absence of privity is not likely to bar recovery.

In addition, the extent of the risk is another criterion which may be applied in determining whether a person making a misrepresentation will be held responsible to third parties who suffer losses. A misrepresentation may set off a chain of events which cause substantial losses to many persons. If the person making the misrepresentation is held accountable for all these losses, he would be exposed to enormous liability, often with a remuneration not commensurate with such risks.

For example, a certified public accountant may make an audit report which causes thousands of investors to invest in a particular company. If the certified public accountant were negligent in his representations, holding him accountable to all these investors could place an enormous liability upon him. Applying both foreseeability and extent of risk, a soils engineer is more likely to be held liable than a certified public accountant.

The rights of persons who are injured because of misrepresentations have been expanding, especially if those misrepresentations are negligent and certainly if they are fraudulent. However, there are some limitations. If the loss is purely economic, and not reasonably foreseeable by the person making the misrepresentation, there may be a chance to avoid liability on the part of the person who has made the misrepresentation.

(H) A RECENT IMPORTANT CASE: ROZNY v. MARNUL

ROZNY v. MARNUL

Supreme Court of Illinois, 1969.
250 N.E.2d 656.

UNDERWOOD, JUSTICE. Plaintiffs Raymond A. Rozny, Jr. and Catherine M. Rozny, husband and wife, purchased a house and lot which was described in a plat of an admittedly inaccurate survey prepared by defendant for S. & S. Builders, apparently a firm engaged in real-estate development. Plaintiffs brought this action for damages in the circuit court of Cook County and recovered a judgment entered on a jury verdict in the amount of $13,350. . . .

Defendant made the original, inaccurate "spot" survey of this vacant lot on August 27, 1953. Subsequently, a house was erected on this lot, and on August 21, 1955, defendant issued a written location "plat of survey" for the same property, this time apparently simply showing on the original plat the location of the building. Defendant did not know the person for whom he did this survey but believed it was for a builder, one Harold Nash, who had apparently purchased the property from S. & S. Builders subsequent to the original survey.

Plaintiffs first saw the property in January, 1956, when the builder, Nash, showed it to them. They agreed to purchase the property. . . .

In September, 1956, the existing driveway leading to the back of the house was extended and plaintiffs constructed a garage on the rear of the lot, relying upon an iron pipe in the backyard fence and a mark on the front sidewalk shown by the plat as the *indicia* of their boundary limits. That plat shows an iron pipe at each of the back corners of the lot and a mark on the sidewalk two feet north of each of the front corners. Had these markers been correctly located, adequate space would have existed for the driveway. In fact, these markers had been placed in accordance with the inaccurate survey, and, as a result, portions of the existing driveway and the new driveway extended over the west lot line, and the west edge of the garage encroaches on the adjacent lot from 2″ to 1′ 2″. Plaintiffs testified that the first time their attention was called to any possible encroachment or survey errors was about two years before the trial, which occurred in September, 1964.

The August 21 survey was signed by defendant and had his Illinois surveyor's seal affixed thereto. . . Printed on the survey plat was the following:

"IMPORTANT

"Before starting any excavating or building, excavators and builders are requested to compare all measurements and should any discrepancies be found, report same to our home office at once.

"This plat of survey carries our absolute guarantee for accuracy, and is issued subject to faithful carrying out of the above and foregoing instructions and conditions before any liability will be assumed on part of the Jens K. Doe Survey Service.

"State of Illinois
County of Cook } ss

I, John Marnul, hereby certify that I have resurveyed and located the building on the property above described and that the plat above is a correct representation of said survey and location. Chicago, August 21st, A.D. 1955.

Licensed Surveyor with

JENS K. DOE SURVEY SERVICE"

At the trial, Olaf Nilsen, a housemoving and shoring contractor, testified that the estimated cost of moving the house 2 feet and garage 6 feet and rehabilitating both would be $13,030.

The jury returned a verdict against defendant in the sum of $14,000, which was later reduced to $13,350, and judgment entered in that amount. . . .

The principle that performance of a private contract can give rise to duties in tort seems to have been first articulated in the 19th century . . . While attempts to recover by third parties injured by negligent performance of contractual duties had generally failed because of a lack of privity . . . this restriction in cases involving physical injuries was lifted in cases such as MacPherson v. Buick Motor Co., 217 N.Y. 382, 111 N.E. 1050, and Heaven v. Pender, 11 Q.B.D. 503. These extensions of liability, however, generally involved negligence resulting in tangible physical harm and not merely loss to intangible economic interests. . . . Further extension to the intangible economic interests soon resulted. (Glanzer v. Shepard, 233 N.Y. 236, 135 N.E. 275, 23 A.L.R. 1425.) There, liability was predicated upon the fact that the public weigher of beans at a seller's request was liable to the buyer damaged by negligent overstatement of the weight because the weigher knew the buyer would rely on the erroneous weight statement. While the later case of Ultramares Corp. v. Touche, Niven & Co., 255 N.Y. 170, 174 N.E. 441, 74 A.L.R. 1139, held an auditing firm which negligently certified an inaccurate audit not liable to one who, in reliance upon the audit, loaned money to the actually insolvent firm, the court carefully distinguished *Glanzer* on the grounds that there the weight statement was "primarily" for the use of the purchaser while the *Ultramares* audit statement was only "incidentally" for the use of third parties. However, the facts of the two cases are such that it seems clear that the more persuasive factor was the existence in *Ultramares* of potential "liability in an indeterminate amount for an indeterminate time to an indeterminate class."

It is apparent that many of the courts which have considered analogous situations have thought the potential liability of one who negligently supplies inaccurate information to be such as to militate against imposing liability when the person ultimately damaged was one whose reliance on the information might have been called "foreseeable". . . . but have been willing to impose liability when the reliance of the third person might have been said to be "known". . . . Although the absence of privity may have been the stated reason for denying liability, it seems likely that the virtually unlimited and unknown potential responsibility of the defendant weighed heavily in the courts' thinking. . . .

An excellent article by Dean Prosser, Misrepresentation and Third Persons (1966), 19 Vand.L.Rev. 231, discusses a number of the factors which have affected the decisions in third-party misrepresentation cases. In the class of cases where "plaintiff is an unidentified member of a group or class [and] defendant has special reason to expect that any member of it may be reached and influenced" by his representation, the liability for negligent misrepresentation resulting in pecuniary loss has been mixed. (19 Vand.L. Rev. at 246.) The article discusses the *Ultramares* case and notes that other decisions concerning accountants are in accord. It is then stated: "But what if the defendant is informed that his representation is to be passed on to some more limited group, as a basis for action on the part of one or more of them? In M. Miller Co. v. Central Contra Costa Sanitary District, [198 Cal.App.2d 305, 18 Cal. Rptr. 13] a California decision, an engineering company was hired to prepare a soil report, knowing that it was intended to be made available to all bidders for work on a sewer system and to be used by the successful bidder to do the work. It prepared the report negligently and the bidder lost money; accordingly it was held liable for negligent misrepresentation. . . .

We agree that the unknown and unlimited liability factor, as so ably stated by Mr. Justice Cardozo in the *Ultramares* case, is not to be lightly discounted. But we deal here with a defendant who has included on his inaccurate plat an "absolute guarantee for accuracy." As might reasonably have been foreseen by defendant who admitted he knew the plats were customarily used by lending agencies and others, that plat was subsequently relied on to his damage by a third party in connection with the financing and purchase of the surveyed property. Under these circumstances it seems to us the fortuitous circumstance that the ultimate loss resulting from the faulty survey fell upon one other than the person for whom the survey was made should not absolve defendant from responding in damages. The situation is not one fraught with such an overwhelming potential liability as to dictate a contrary result, for the class of persons who might foreseeably use this plat is rather narrowly limited, if not exclusively so, to those who deal with the surveyed property as purchasers or lenders. Injury will ordinarily occur only once and to the one person then owning the lot.

. . .

And, even in the accounting field where the potential liability argument is much more persuasive than here, two recent cases have held liability could exist to third parties whose reliance was foreseeable by the negligent accountant. (Rusch Factors, Inc. v. Levin (D.R.I., 1968), 284 F.Supp. 85; Fischer v. Kletz (S.D.N.Y., 1967), 266 F.Supp. 180.) The basis of liability in *Fischer* was defendant's failure to disclose after-acquired information which invalidated the accuracy of facts earlier certified to be correct. . . . While we believe it unnecessary here to consider the questions of existence and scope of a duty on defendant's part to disclose to those whose earlier use of the plat was foreseeable the fact that it was incorrect, it is not without significance that the record contains no proof that anyone was actually informed by defendant of the error.

As is apparent from the foregoing discussion, the factors we consider relevant to our holding are:

(1) The express, unrestricted and wholly voluntary "absolute guarantee for accuracy" appearing on the face of the inaccurate plat;

(2) Defendant's knowledge that this plat would be used and relied on by others than the person ordering it, including plaintiffs;

(3) The fact that potential liability in this case is restricted to a comparatively small group, and that, ordinarily, only one member of that group will suffer loss;

(4) The absence of proof that copies of the corrected plat were delivered to anyone;

(5) The undesirability of requiring an innocent reliant party to carry the burden of a surveyor's professional mistakes;

(6) That recovery here by a reliant user whose ultimate use was foreseeable will promote cautionary techniques among surveyors.

Based upon a consideration of these factors as presented by this record we hold plaintiffs may recover. . . . To the extent that this holding may be thought contrary to prior decisional law of this State, particularly National Iron and Steel Co. v. Hunt, 312 Ill. 245, 143 N.E. 833, 34 A.L.R. 63, and Albin v. Illinois Crop Improvement Ass'n, Inc., 30 Ill.App.2d 283, 174 N.E.2d 697, such decisions are no longer the law.

[Ed. note: In the balance of the opinion the court examined the statute of limitations problem. The court held that the applicable statute was one which applied to "all civil actions not otherwise provided for", a five year period of limitations. Noting that the plaintiffs purchased the property in 1956 but did not become aware of any discrepancies in the location of the lot, driveway and garage until 1962, the court held that the five year period would commence to run at the time they knew or should have known of the defendant's error. The action was brought within a sufficient period of time. The court noted that the passage of time did not increase the problems of proof in this particular case.]

The judgment of the circuit court of Cook County is accordingly affirmed and that of the appellate court is reversed.

In its haste to eliminate the privity requirement in all tort actions, the Supreme Court did not draw a clear distinction between negligent and innocent misrepresentation. While most of the authorities cited by the court dealt with negligent misrepresentations, the plaintiff's original complaint in the *Rozny* case was based upon negligence and contract. Before the case went to the jury, the negligence count was stricken and the case proceeded based on a "guarantee" contained in the plat. It appears, then, that the basis for recovery in the trial court was an innocent misrepresentation since the negligence count had been stricken. Yet, the Supreme Court, while indicating that the "guarantee" should be taken into account, appeared to predicate its decision upon a negligent misrepresentation, glossing over the distinction by using the term "tortious" misrepresentation.

SECTION 30.05 DUTY OF THE OWNER OR OCCUPIER OF LAND

(A) RELEVANCE

Tort law determines the duty owed by the owner or occupier of land to those persons who pass by the land or enter upon it. Before, during, or after completion of a construction project, members of the public will pass by the land or, with or without permission, enter upon the land and may be injured or killed by a condition on the land, or by an activity engaged in by the owner or occupier of the land. In addition to members of the public, workers may suffer injury or death because of the condition of the land, or activities on it. Also, persons who live in, or enter, a completed project may suffer injury or death because of something related to the land or the construction process. Liability for such harm depends upon the duty owed to the plaintiff by the owner or occupier of land near which or upon which the physical harm was suffered. The duty owed often depends upon the status of the person who has suffered harm. The law often looks at whether the injured party had permission to be near or on the land, and his purpose for being there.

The terms "owner, occupier or possessor of land" will be used in this section without exploring the troublesome question of whether the owner, the prime contractor or subcontractors fall into this category during the construction process. This will be treated in § 30.08 (c).

(B) TO PASSERSBY

The owner of land or occupier must use due care to protect those outside the premises. He has the duty to take reasonable steps to keep his premises in good repair, and injuries to passersby which result from defective buildings or attachments to buildings are chargeable to him.

Some earlier cases held that there was no duty on the part of the landowner to remedy conditions of natural origin upon his land, such as falling rocks, spreading of weeds, or accumulation of snow and ice. But even the decisions which stressed the strong right of the owner to use his land as he chose limited this "natural conditions doctrine" if the owner or occupier altered the condition of the premises. This rule of natural conditions was better suited to a rural society, and has less significance in an urban community. For example, the landowner will be liable if he negligently permits a tree to fall or to remain on the ground in an urban area and this causes property damage, or physical injury, to another person. Statutes and local ordinances may also place liability upon the owner or occupier of land.

(C) TO TRESPASSING ADULTS

A trespasser is one who enters on the land of another without permission. In doing so, he is committing an injury to the owner's right to possession. Intruders upon the land of another were not treated very kindly by early English law. They were generally expected to take care of themselves. The possessor was not liable for injury to trespassers caused by his failure to put the land in reasonable condition, or by his activities or the activities of his household members, his employees, or by those persons whom he permitted to use the land.

There were some limitations to this insulation given landowners. If the landowner knew trespassers came in substantial numbers at a particular place, he had a duty of reasonable care to discover and protect them from activities which he carried on. An illustration would be persons frequently crossing over a specified portion of railroad track.

A few jurisdictions have protected trespassers on railroad property, on the theory that running the railroad is a dangerous activity, and reasonable care is required of the railroad company.

(D) TO TRESPASSING CHILDREN

Special rules have developed for trespassing children. Frequently they do not realize that they are entering on the land of another, or, if they do, they do not realize the dangerous characteristics of certain natural and artificial conditions on the land. The law has begun to realize that a different standard should be applied when the trespasser is a child. The general tendency today is to apply the standards of due care to possessors of land when their land is entered by trespassing children. The Restatement of Torts, Second, which reflects the law in most jurisdictions, states in Section 339 that there is liability to the possessor of land for injuries to trespassing children, caused by artificial conditions upon the land if:

(a) the place where the condition exists is one upon which the possessor knows or has reason to know that children are likely to trespass, and

(b) the condition is one which the possessor knows or has reason to know and which he realizes or should realize will involve an unreasonable risk of death or serious bodily harm to such children, and

(c) the children because of their youth do not discover the condition or realize the risk involved in intermeddling with it or in coming within the area made dangerous by it, and

(d) the utility to the possessor of maintaining the condition and the burden of eliminating the danger are slight as compared with the risk of children involved, and

(e) the possessor fails to exercise reasonable care to eliminate the danger or otherwise protect the children.

These limitations apply only to artificial conditions upon the land, and not to activities of the possessor. Activities highly dangerous to constant trespassers, whether they are children or not, are likely to require a standard of due care by the person conducting the activity on the land.

The problem of trespassing children is important to the design professional. There have been numerous cases of injuries or death to children who drown in swimming pools, or who are injured when they play with construction materials or equipment on a construction site. Often city ordinances and state statutes require that certain safety measures be taken.

The bulk of the cases have involved subteenage children. As a child reaches 13 or 14, he should begin to realize that certain activities are going to involve physical danger, and the quoted section from the Restatement recognizes the necessity for showing that the children could not appreciate the kind of danger that their activity involved.

A case which demonstrates the difficulty of the child trespasser cases is reproduced at this point.

PATTERSON v. PROCTOR PAINT AND VARNISH COMPANY

Court of Appeals of New York, 1968.
21 N.Y.2d 447, 235 N.E.2d 765, 288 N.Y.S.2d 622.

BERGAN, JUDGE. Defendant was engaged in the manufacture of paint and varnish in a Yonkers residential area. Adjoining its plant was an open yard, unfenced on one side. On the outer wall of the plant facing the yard were a number of fill pipes available to tank trucks supplying the plant with fluids for paint and varnish manufacture. Dripping of the fluid from some of these pipes was caught in cans placed by defendant on the ground. The fluid which drained into these cans was a form of paint solvent. It was white in appearance, looked like water, but was described by a chemist as "a flammable liquid commonly known as mineral spirits" with a flash point at 103 degrees Fahrenheit and both "combustible" and "explosive". Since the yard was not entirely enclosed, and was in a residential area, children played there and the defendant had knowledge they played there.

On October 29, 1961 the infant plaintiff, Matthew Patterson, then 12, and his younger brother John, 9, came onto the lot by climbing over a wall opposite the building. Matthew picked up a drip pail containing fluid that looked like water from under one of the pipes and carried it back toward the wall on the other side of the yard. As he did so he spilled some of it on his clothing.

He then lighted a fire and, playing "fireman", poured some of the fluid on the fire which then flared up. The flame caught onto his clothes where the fluid had spilled. He was severely burned.

This outline of events assumes the most favorable view of the facts in support of plaintiffs' action for damages, a view that must be taken in this court upon appeal from the dismissal of the complaint at the end of proof for legal insufficiency by the trial court, affirmed at the Appellate Division. Two Justices dissenting in that court were of opinion a case prima facie had been made out by plaintiffs.

Respondent [defendant] argues in this court that the relevant New York decisions bar the cause of action asserted and that the complaint was properly dismissed without sending the case to the jury. There is some stress placed by defendant in its argument that "since infant plaintiff was concededly a trespasser, as matter of law" the cases which might otherwise support plaintiffs' argument cannot be relied on validly to sustain it.

There are, indeed, New York cases which, treating a child injured by a dangerous condition in a place to which he was without legal right of access, as a trespasser, have denied recovery on this ground alone. The turntable case, Walsh v. Fitchburg R. R. Co., 145 N.Y. 301, 39 N.E. 1068, 27 L.R.A. 724 [1895], is a protean example and was followed literally in Flaherty v. Metro Stas., 235 N.Y. 605, 139 N.E. 753 [1923], and Morse v. Buffalo Tank Corp., 280 N.Y. 110, 19 N.E.2d 981 [1939].

But as a rigid concept by which all such cases are to be at once dismissed, the "trespass" theory applied to children injured by dangerous conditions on land of owners having notice of the presence of children and the existence of danger has lost force as the law in New York has developed.

This is to be seen in cases of injury by dangerous static conditions on land and by volatile substances dangerous in themselves, since in this trespass aspect—the right to get to the danger—the same rule governs both situations.

The present direction of the New York case law in this area is readily demonstrable. First, as to nonvolatile danger. In 1938, the court decided Collentine v. City of New York, 279 N.Y. 119, 17 N.E. 2d 792. There a boy climbed onto the roof of a building in a park which was closed to the public. He had no legal right to be there. He fell from the roof when he tripped over an iron bar. The roof had once been open to the public but was then closed and the main access barricaded. However, there was proof access could be had by another means. A case was held made out based on the dangerous condition of the roof.

Nor has public ownership of premises been deemed decisive on the rule of liability. A similar rule was applied to entirely private premises in 1954 in Mayer v. Temple Props., 307 N.Y. 559, 122 N.E.2d 909, where liability was sustained when a 12-year-old boy crawled under a gate to gain access to defendant's property where he had no legal right to be and was killed when wooden slats placed over an opening in a platform gave way when he walked on them.

Even a broken and twisted railing on a public stairway, manifestly not designed or intended for climbing, was held a sufficient ground for municipal liability when a child, climbing on it, was injured (Levine v. City of New York, 309 N.Y. 88, 127 N.E.2d 825 [1955]). And in Soto v. City of New York, 9 N.Y.2d 683, 212 N.Y.S. 2d 418, 173 N.E.2d 238 [1961], the roof of a condemned building had an unfastened door which made it possible for children to reach the roof. A loose brick from the chimney caused a child to fall. It was held there was a case prima facie.

It will be observed that in each of these cases the injured child was in greater or lesser degree a "trespasser" in the classic sense that he had no right to be there, but this alone was not held a sufficient ground to bar recovery. Thus the court has moved away from an automatic and literal application of the trespass doctrine to the children injured by dangerous conditions on land.

The situation as to dangerous volatile substances has, of course, an added element: that the active intervention of the child, usually the ignition of the substance, is itself ingredient to the injury. In addition to the "trespass" (wrong) in getting to the substance, there has been an additional trespass or wrong in activating it dangerously. But this has made no difference in the decisions.

In Travell v. Bannerman, 174 N.Y. 47, 66 N.E. 583 [1903], children went on the private, but open, lot of the defendant's gun factory and took away black material resembling asphalt and containing brass. In attempting to extract the brass the black material exploded, a child was injured, and a recovery was allowed. Defendant, in Kingsland v. Erie County Agric. Soc., 298 N.Y. 409, 84 N.E.2d 38, 10 A.L.R.2d 1 [1949], stored fireworks in an enclosed and fenced-in place. Boys climbed over the fence and stole some of the fireworks, taking them off the premises. One of the boys was later injured when a bomb exploded. A case prima facie was held made out.

When a substance, somewhat similar to that involved here and used in connection with painting, was stored in a recessed room under an archway in Brooklyn Bridge, to which children were able to gain access, a case prima facie was held to be made out when a child lighted a match causing an explosion (Carradine v. City of New York, 13 N.Y.2d 291, 246 N.Y.S.2d 620, 196 N.E.2d 259 [1963]).

In none of these cases was there a showing of any legal right in the children either of access to the place or of access to the material which caused injury.

In Parnell v. Holland Furnace Co., 260 N.Y. 604, 184 N.E. 112 [1932], affg. 234 App.Div. 567, 256 N.Y.S. 323, an employee of defendant left his old and then unused Ford car in an open space utilized by defendant, adjoining defendant's plant. The space was not exclusively controlled by defendant. There was gasoline in the car tank. Children removed a properly secured cap from the tank and caused an explosion. A case was held made out against defendant, and although right of access to the land by another tenant made it possible to say, as Sears, P. J., did for the Appellate Division, that the children playing in the space were not trespassers by being there, they had no right to open up the gas tank and thus expose the gasoline to explosion, as Crane, J., noted in dissent in this court (pp. 606, 608, 184 N.E. 112). Still a case was held made out against defendant.

A somewhat similar situation existed in the most recent case in this court (Burdeau v. Burdeau, 21 N.Y.2d 677, 287 N.Y.S.2d 413, 234 N.E.2d 452), where the child, although not literally a trespasser on the defendant's land itself, nevertheless ignited a can of gasoline left near defendant's house and was injured. A judgment for plaintiff was sustained.

Thus the cases which would suggest a dismissal of the complaint in the present action have not been followed and are not controlling. The most important of them is Morse v. Buffalo Tank Corp., 280 N.Y. 110, 19 N.E.2d 981, decided in 1939 and cited above. A drum of gasoline was kept by defendant in its open yard. Some of this was taken by boys and ignited. Plaintiff, 10 years old, running by the flame, was injured. It was held defendant was not liable, Lehman and Loughran, JJ., dissenting.

The majority opinion distinguished *Parnell* on the difference in the cases on the right of access to the land; and distinguished *Bannerman* on the difference between gasoline and "inherently dangerous materials" (p. 116, 19 N.E.2d 981). To read the decision made 10 years later (1949) in *Erie County Agric. Soc.* is to see the rule as it has evolved that "trespass" does not alone bar recovery, given other essential conditions; and to read *Carradine, Burdeau* and, indeed, *Parnell,* is to see that volatility of the material has been treated as a matter of degree and hence as a question of fact. Nor does Flaherty v. Metro Stas., cited above and decided in 1923, lead to a different end.

The main body of decisions in this court instructs us that the rule today is that if the owner of land leaves it open and accessible to children; if he knows that children use it for play; and if he leaves accessible to them highly volatile substances, a case prima facie is made out if a child is thus injured.

The order should be reversed; the motion to dismiss denied, and a new trial ordered, with costs to abide the event.

BREITEL, JUDGE (dissenting).

The court by its present decision is imposing a marked extension of liability on the occupants of land, and the wisdom of the extension is dubious. In all of the cases on which it relies the act or omission of the occupant was not necessary or even desirable to the proper use of the land, or the simplest of corrective devices would have corrected the condition, as in the turntable cases. Indeed, the acts or omissions in these cases were careless and inexcusable even if done in a vacuum in which no injury to anyone occurred. In the present case, on the other hand, the liability is extended to reasonable conduct in controlling drippings from a fill pipe without any showing that the drippings were not a natural result of the permitted use of the occupant's facilities. The means employed by the occupant to collect drippings on its own partially enclosed land was a reasonable use, even though children could misuse the means to cause themselves injury.

Cases very recently decided by this court point to the correct principle (Cuevas v. 73rd & Cent. Park West Corp., 21 N.Y.2d 745, 287 N.Y.S.2d 889, 234 N.E.2d 843, affg. 26 A.D.2d 239, 272 N.Y.S.2d 41; Conway v. St. Gregory's Parochial School, 21 N.Y.2d 755, 288 N.Y.S.2d 230, 235 N.E.2d 217, affg. 27 A.D.2d 555, 277 N.Y.S.2d 371). The principle is that children who use another's facilities to injure themselves may not thereby occasion liability for the occupant, merely because the unlawful presence of children and the general likelihood of their engaging in self-injurious mischievousness is known. As in so many areas of the law, a balance of convenience must be struck between the risk of injury to others who misconduct themselves and the reasonable use of one's premises. Only if an unreasonable risk of injury to children outweighs the utility to the occupant does liability arise (Restatement, 2d, Torts, § 339, subd. [d], Comment *n*).

In this case, the children concerned did not enter defendant's land by the open ways but over a wall and on a Sunday when defendant's plant and yard were unattended. So that even if the yard had been fully enclosed, the accident would have happened anyway. Most important, while children had been known to invade the yard, there were no prior incidents of children playing with fire, although the plant's workers during the week often burned rubbish in the yard within sight of neighboring children.

Finally, even a 12-year-old boy, as this infant plaintiff, knows that if he plays with fire he exposes himself to an untoward risk. Thus, in a slightly different and yet relevant context, the Restatement says:

"There are many dangers, such a[s] those of fire and water, or of falling from a height, which under ordinary conditions may reasonably be expected to be fully understood and appreciated by any child of an age to be allowed at large. To such conditions the rule stated in this Section ordinarily has no application, in the absence of some other factor creating a special risk that the child will not avoid the danger, such as the fact that the condition is so hidden as not to be readily visible, or a distracting influence which makes it likely that the child will not discover or appreciate it.

"Where, however, the possessor knows that children too young to appreciate such dangers are likely to trespass on his land, he may still be subject to liability to such children under the rule stated." (Restatement, 2d, Torts, § 339, Comment *j*.) Accordingly, I dissent and vote to affirm.

FULD, C. J., and BURKE and KEATING, JJ., concur with BERGAN, J.

BREITEL, J., dissents and votes to affirm in a separate opinion in which SCILEPPI and JASEN, JJ., concur.

Order reversed, with costs to abide the event, and a new trial granted.

[The principal issue in the *Patterson* case was whether the trial judge was correct in withdrawing the case from the jury. When the court frames the issue in terms of whether there was a "prima facie case" or that the issue is one of "law", it is deciding whether the jury will be permitted to decide who wins. [Ed. note]

This case demonstrates the differing conclusions judges reach when they must balance the owner's right to use his land in the manner he chooses with the desired objective that owners of land make their land reasonably safe for small children who enter their land without permission. The trial judge took the matter from the jury. The Appellate Division agreed with him but only by a 3 to 2 vote. The Court of Appeals held by a 4 to 3 vote that the trial judge should have submitted the matter to the jury.

(E) TO LICENSEES

A licensee has a privilege of entering or remaining upon the land of another because of the latter's consent. But the licensee comes for his own purposes rather than for the interest or purposes of the possessor of the land. Examples of licensees are persons who take short cuts over property with permission, persons who come into a building to avoid inclement weather or to look for their children, door to door salesmen and social guests.

There are some anomalous exceptions, such as the fireman who enters a building at night to put out a fire, or the policeman who enters to apprehend a burglar. Logically they should be considered as benefitting the possessor of land, but many cases hold they are simply licensees.

Early cases held that the only limitation on the possessor's activity was to refrain from intentionally or recklessly injuring a licensee. However, most modern courts require that the possessor of land conduct his activities with due care for the physical safety of licensees.

As for conditions of the land, the possessor has a duty to repair known defects or dangerous conditions, or to warn licensees of dangerous conditions which they would not be able to discover by themselves. Unlike the invitee, who will be discussed in the next subsection, the license cannot demand that the land be made reasonably safe for him, and the possessor is not obligated to inspect the premises, discover dangers unknown to the possessor, or to warn the licensee about conditions which are known or should have been known to the licensee.

(F) TO INVITEES

The most favored person under the law is the invitee. He enters at the invitation, and for the benefit, of the owner or occupier. The line between licensee and invitee is blurred. The tendency has been to increase protection, and expand the invitee category. The major difference between the invitee and the licensee is that the invitee is entitled to affirmative acts on the part of the occupier of land to protect him, not only against dangers of which the occupier is aware, but also against those which the possessor could have discovered with reasonable care. While he is not an insurer of the safety of invitees, the occupier of the land is under an affirmative duty to inspect and make sure his premises are reasonably safe. Sometimes he is permitted to satisfy his obligation to make the land reasonably safe by warning the invitee of dangers which would not have been apparent to the invitee.

There are limitations to this obligation. The area of invitation may be limited. The public part of a store may be included, but the area reserved for employees is not likely to be covered.

To some degree the possessor is protected by the doctrine of "assumption of risk". If the injured party consciously chooses to enter into an activity or to do something which he knows is likely to cause great harm to him, the landowner or occupier will not be liable. But, on the whole, the increasing tendency is to place liability on the occupier of land. Sometimes this is done under the enterprise theory (part of the cost of doing business), and sometimes on the theory that he is in a better position to bear the risk, as a self-insurer or through public liability insurance.

(G) MOVEMENT TOWARD ONE GENERAL STANDARD OF CARE

Some courts believe that the various categories which determine the standard of care are too difficult to administer. Exceptions develop within the categories, and the application of the categories is often uneven.

For this reason there is some movement toward a rule which would impose upon the owner or occupier of land the duty of due care to all those who enter upon the land. The Supreme Court of California stated in Rowland v. Christian, 69 Cal.2d 108, 443 P.2d 561, 70 Cal.Rptr. 97 (1968):

> Without attempting to labor all of the rules relating to the possessor's liability, it is apparent that the classifications of trespasser, licensee, and invitee, the immunities from liability predicated upon those classifications, and the exceptions to those immunities, often do not reflect the major factors which should determine whether immunity should be

> conferred upon the possessor of land. Some of those factors, including the closeness of the connection between the injury and the defendant's conduct, the moral blame attached to the defendant's conduct, the policy of preventing future harm, and the prevalence and availability of insurance, bear little, if any, relationship to the classifications of trespasser, licensee and invitee and the existing rules conferring immunity. . . .
>
> We decline to follow and perpetuate such rigid classifications. The proper test to be applied to the liability of the possessor of land in accordance with section 1714 of the Civil Code is whether in the management of his property he has acted as a reasonable man in view of the probability of injury to others, and, although the plaintiff's status as a trespasser, licensee, or invitee may in the light of the facts giving rise to such status have some bearing on the question of liability, the status is not determinative.

(H) LANDLORD LIABILITY

In many instances there is a division between ownership and occupancy of land. This section deals with the liabilities of an owner or occupier of land. In many situations, a lease transfers possession or occupancy from the landlord to the tenant. Generally, the landlord is not liable for injuries caused to persons who enter upon the leased premises. However, in some cases the tenant, especially a residential or small business tenant, may not be financially able to pay judgments for serious personal injury and may not have had the foresight or the financial capacity to insure against this risk.

For this reason, there have been some exceptions to landlord nonliability. Sometimes this has been done by statutes obligating the landlord to repair and keep the premises in good condition. Other exceptions have been developed by cases. The landlord is under a duty to disclose to the tenant concealed conditions of which he has knowledge, except for those conditions which are obvious to the tenant himself. Another exception relates to the landlord's responsibility continuing for at least a reasonable time after the actual transfer of possession of the land, if the land involves a condition of unreasonable risk of harm to others outside of the land. These cases have usually involved minor private nuisances, dangerous to passersby.

A third exception covers premises leased to those who will admit the public. In such cases, the landlord has the affirmative duty to exercise reasonable care to inspect and repair the premises before they are transferred to the tenant, and to prevent unreasonable risk of harm to those who enter. Examples of these cases are those involving amusement parks, theaters, beaches, and hotels. Sometimes a differentiation is made based upon whether the public enters in large numbers.

Another exception is those areas of leased premises which are still in control of the landlord. Examples of this are common hallways in an apartment building or office building. The tenants can use them, but do not occupy them, and responsibility for their condition rests upon the landlord. The obligation imposed is that of reasonable care, and the landlord is not liable merely because an injury takes place there. However, the increasing tendency is to find lack of due care on the part of the landlord, if there is an injury that is not caused solely by the acts of the injured person. Here again, legislative bodies have enacted ordinances and statutes which may impose a specific standard. For example, a landlord may be obligated to light certain passageways, and to remove snow and ice from the steps. The effect of a violation of compliance with such standards has been discussed in § 30.02(f).

If the landlord has an obligation to repair, his failure to do so will make him liable to the tenant, or to other persons who enter the building with the status of licensees or invitees.

Commonly, landlords attempt to use the lease to transfer risks from landlord to tenant. Leases often require the tenant to agree that he will indemnify the landlord for any expenses incurred by the landlord as a result of litigation over injuries occurring on the premises. This is more likely to occur in commercial leases. Also, landlords frequently try to have tenants agree to hold the landlord harmless for injuries to the tenants for which the landlord might be responsible.

Should such contract clauses be enforced? Frequently they are buried in printed forms which are difficult to read or understand. In many residential, as well as commercial, leases even if the tenant objects he may not be able to do very much about it from a bargaining standpoint. There is some tendency to recognize this problem of unequal bargaining powers, and to hold that such provisions are not enforceable if they are not reasonable.

(I) NON-DELEGABILITY OF LEGAL RESPONSIBILITY

Has the landowner fulfilled his obligation if he hires someone to perform acts which would discharge his duty, and the person hired does not do so? Suppose the owner of a swimming pool hires a contractor to build a fence around the swimming pool. Clearly the landowner will be liable if he knowingly picks an incompetent contractor. He will be liable if he does not remove an incompetent contractor, or if the owner does not inspect the work with due care.

Generally, the employer of an independent contractor is not liable for the latter's negligence. However, the duty owed by the owner or occupier of land is considered so important that many states do not permit him to transfer his responsibility to an independent contractor. As a result, in the case of the swimming pool fence, the landowner may be liable for harm to trespassing children if the independent contractor fails to install the fence, installs it badly, or uses improper materials. This liability is not based upon the negligence of the landowner, but upon his duty to maintain the land in a reasonably safe condition.

If the independent contractor has been negligent, the landowner, and usually the person harmed, will be able to recover from the independent contractor. The right of recovery against the independent contractor may not be worth much if the latter is in financial difficulty, or is not insured. For these reasons, it is advisable for the landowner to have public liability insurance against such risks, or to make certain the independent contractor is solvent or insured.

SECTION 30.06 LIABILITY OF MANUFACTURER FOR DEFECTIVE PRODUCTS

(A) RELEVANCE

It may be useful to briefly consider the historical development of rules relating to the liability of a manufacturer for harm caused by his products. First, the development of this rule of law manifests the clear shift from doctrines which protect commercial ventures toward doctrines which attempt to insure that persons who suffer harm can find a financially responsible economic enterprise which can and should bear the loss.

Second, the doctrine of manufacturer's liability has become an important aspect of distributing losses incident to the construction process. Often losses are caused by defective equipment or materials. There can be a resultant harm to persons, damage or loss to property and economic loss.

The development of manufacturer's liability has been done by the courts on a state-by-state basis. This means that the applicable rules will vary, depending upon the state law which governs the litigation. The discussion in this section will stress trends rather than detailed statements as to the current state of the law in any particular jurisdiction.

(B) PRIVITY AND THE STANDARD OF CARE: TOWARD LIABILITY WITHOUT FAULT

The two principal legal questions that have troubled the law relating to manufacturer's liability for defective products have been the relationship between the injured party and the manufacturer in a legal sense, and the duty of care owed by the manufacturer. The first is sometimes phrased in terms of "privity of contract". If there is no contractual relationship between the ultimate purchaser of the defective product or the person injured and the manufacturer, (as is usually the case) the manufacturer often argues that there is no duty owed by him to the injured party, and therefore no right on the part of the injured party to recover from him. Secondly, where lack of privity has been surmounted, the legal battleground has been over whether the manufacturer must be shown to have been negligent, or whether the manufacturer is liable if the injured party can establish that he has been injured because of a defective product made by the manufacturer.

In 1842, the famous English case of Winterbottom v. Wright, required that the injured party have a contractual relationship with the maker of the product which caused the injury. Without contractual "privity" between the injured party and the person against whom the claim was made, the injured party could not win, even if he could show that his injury or loss was caused by the negligently made product of the defendant.

Privity was sometimes justified as a means of protecting an infant manufacturing industry developing out of the Industrial Revolution. Also, there was a feeling that parties should know the limits of their exposure. One effect of the privity rule was that the manufacturer would know that he could not be held responsible to persons other than those with whom he dealt. Also, one could not take protective measures by contract with a person with whom there was no privity. Along with this "privity" protection, even under a contract the manufacturer was relieved from losses which his failure to perform might have caused, if it could be shown that the injury was not foreseeable at the time the contract was made. These rules protected manufacturers and sellers from substantial risks.

Even in its strongest period, the privity rule had exceptions. Sometimes the injured party could assign his claim to a person who was in privity with the defendant. Also, by use of a series of lawsuits, the manufacturer might have been held responsible. For example, the purchaser of a defectively-constructed tool could sue the retailer from whom he purchased the drill. The retailer then might be able to sue the wholesaler (who could sue the manufacturer), or the manufacturer if the retailer had dealt directly with the manufacturer. In this way, the manufacturer might bear the ultimate loss. A chain of suits, or one suit with a number of parties suing each other, was a wasteful process. Also, if the dealer who sold the defective drill was insolvent or could not respond to any judgment, it might have been futile for the injured purchaser to sue him.

The twentieth century brought change. No doubt some of this was due to a feeling that injured parties ought to have a solvent party from whom they could recover for their losses. The change also may have been due, in part, to the development of insurance as a method by which manufacturers could spread extraordinary risks. In 1916, the New York Court of Appeals decided MacPherson v. Buick Motor Co., 217 N.Y. 382, 111 N.E. 1050 (1916). Cases prior to the *MacPherson* case had held that a negligent manufacturer could be liable to someone with whom he was not in privity if there was a latent defect in the goods sold, or if the goods sold could be considered dangerous. The *MacPherson* case expanded this category to automobiles by holding that the exception for dangerous goods included goods which were dangerous if made defectively. In effect, the *MacPherson* case eliminated the privity rule.

The plaintiff still had the difficult problem of proving negligence by the manufacturer. The injured party also had to show that the particular product or goods caused the accident. To assist the injured party, the courts permitted him to use the doctrine of "res ipsa loquitur". This meant that "the act speaks for itself", and the injury could not have occurred without negligence of the defendant. To use "res ipsa loquitur", the plaintiff had to show the accident could not have happened without a negligently made product, that the manufacturing process was within the control of the defendant and the goods were not mishandled by the plaintiff or third parties after it left the manufacturer's control. If he did bring his case within "res ipsa", the plaintiff did not have to show negligence on the part of the manufacturer.

From "res ipsa loquitur", it was a small jump to imposing liability without requiring a showing of fault. The means to this result was the "warranty" concept. This doctrine was borrowed from cases involving the sale of goods. The seller "warrants" (promises) that his goods were manufactured properly, and in certain situations, are fit for the purposes for which a buyer is going to use them. Liability through warranty came first in the food and drug cases, and it has begun to be the standard rule for most manufactured goods. Liability without fault means that, as between the manufacturer and the injured party, the former will bear the loss. Presumably, the manufacturer can anticipate these types of losses, compute their cost, insure the risks, and include the cost in the price of the manufactured product.

A few courts have recognized that the "warranty" concept was simply a device to avoid the privity requirement, and to eliminate the necessity for proving negligence. Also, such courts have pointed to the essentially commercial nature of warranty and have found it inappropriate when the issue is who will bear the loss when someone is injured because of a defective product. In addition the warranty concept carries along with it certain technical rules which are more appropriate to transactions between businessmen rather than to purchases by consumers. These courts have classified the right of an injured party against the manufacturer of a defective product which causes his injury as one based upon tort. For purposes of this treatise, no differentiation will be made between liability without fault based upon warranty, and liability without fault based upon tort.

A general summation of the law is given in the Restatement of Torts, Second. While not as yet followed in all jurisdictions, it reflects the existing law in most jurisdictions. Section 402(a) states:

(1) One who sells any product in a defective condition unreasonably dangerous to the user or consumer or to his property is subject to liability for physical harm thereby caused to the ultimate user or consumer, or to his property, if

(a) the seller is engaged in the business of selling such a product, and

(b) it is expected to and does reach the user or consumer without substantial change in the condition in which it is sold.

(2) The rule stated in Subsection (1) applies although

(a) the seller has exercised all possible care in the preparation and sale of his product, and

(b) the user or consumer has not bought the product from or entered into any contractual relation with the seller.

Comment J to Section 402(a) states:

[T]he seller may be required to give directions or warnings, on the container, as to its use. . . .

A seller is not required to warn with respect to products, or ingredients in them, which are only dangerous, or potentially so, when consumed in excessive quantity, or over a long period of time, when the danger, or potentiality of danger, is generally known and recognized. . . .

Where warning is given, the seller may reasonably assume that it will be read and heeded; and a product bearing such a warning, which is safe for use if it is followed, is not in defective condition, nor is it unreasonably dangerous.

(C) SOME UNANSWERED QUESTIONS

There are still problems in the manufacturer's liability field. How effective are disclaimers of responsibility which are included in contracts or put on containers in which goods are shipped? To avoid this problem, some courts have moved from warranty, a type of contract action, to tort. Is the manufacturer liable to members of the ultimate purchaser's family, his friends, or his social guests? Does liability without fault extend to the manufacturer of components of the product, and those who assemble the product? Will the plaintiff be barred if he "assumed the risk" or was guilty of contributory negligence?

Another significant unanswered question relates to the extent of manufacturer's liability for injuries received because the product was the result of faulty design. Most cases involve poor workmanship or material. However, the courts have been reluctant to impose liability on manufacturers for defective design. Some feel that complicated design determination should not be second guessed by inexpert juries. A case which details the variant holdings on this question is Larsen v. General Motors Corp., reproduced at § 30.06(h).

(D) SELLERS OF SERVICES

Courts have been reluctant to extend these product liability rules to persons who engage in the performance of services, such as architectural or engineering concerns. Some of the factors that have been persuasive in cases which have involved mass produced goods, sold through advertising in mass media do not apply to those persons who sell services.

(E) ECONOMIC LOSSES

Also, the law has been more charitable to manufacturers where there has been economic loss, as opposed to harm to persons. Courts have been willing to grant recovery for economic loss to ultimate users where the manufacturer has breached an express warranty as to product performance. There is some reluctance to extend manufacturer's liability without fault for economic losses, where the claim is based upon a warranty implied by law, such as merchantability, or fitness for a particular purpose. In the area of economic loss, the law has also been somewhat reluctant to grant recovery by the ultimate user of a product against the manufacturer where the goods have not been goods or equipment specially prepared for the ultimate consumer by the manufacturer, and have been sold through an intermediary, such as a jobber. Where goods are specially manufactured, there is more likely to be an express warranty. The manufacturer knows what is expected, and the extent of his risks.

(F) SELLERS OF TRACT HOMES

Liability without fault has found a foothold in cases where the defendant makes mass-produced houses. The law has not gone as far in those latter areas as it has in manufactured goods. However, there is a trend toward finding liability without fault, based solely upon the fact that the injured party has suffered a loss as a result of a house manufactured by the defendant. See Kriegler v. Eichler Homes and Schipper v. Leavitt in § 30.09.

(G) SHOULD JUDGE OR JURY DECIDE?

Legislatures and appellate courts may create generally accepted rules of law. However, controversy may exist over who should apply these laws to specific disputes involving given fact situations.

In litigation, this often takes the form of determining whether the trial judge or the jury will decide whether the plaintiff suffered a legally recognizable loss, what the loss is worth and whether the defendant will have to pay. For example, in law suits involving the duty of an owner or occupier of land (see § 30.05) who will determine whether the defendant fulfilled his obligation? In cases involving the liability of a manufacturer for a defective product, who will determine whether the products were defective and whether the defective products caused the injury to the plaintiff?

Cases appealed to appellate courts often concern whether the jury should decide these questions. If the case had been submitted to the jury and the jury ruled for the plaintiff, the defendant on appeal often contends that the facts were so clearly in favor of the defendant, that it was improper to send the case to the jury. Conversely, if the trial judge would not submit the case to the jury, the plaintiff may contend on appeal that he should have.

The same questions are raised when the defendant attempts to have the case resolved by procedural devices such as a demurrer, a motion to dismiss or a motion for summary judgment. These are devices to keep these questions from the jury.

Generally, modern courts have been willing to submit questions of manufacturer's liability to the jury. It is more likely that a trial judge will be reversed if he refuses to submit the question to the jury than if he does so. There are cases where courts have held that juries should not have considered a particular case, as the facts were clearly in the favor of the defendant. But the preponderance of the appellate cases conclude with the holding that it was a proper case for the jury. This does not necessarily mean that the appellate court agreed with the jury's determination. However, if the case is close enough to merit submission to the jury on factual questions, appellate courts generally do not interfere with the determination of the jury.

The strenuously contested judge-jury questions reflect the generally accepted view that juries are more favorably inclined toward persons who have suffered personal injury. For this reason, much of the litigation strategy of the defendant is designed to keep such cases away from the jury.

(H) A CASE ON DESIGN DEFECTS: LARSEN v. GENERAL MOTORS

LARSEN v. GENERAL MOTORS CORPORATION

United States Court of Appeals, Eighth Circuit. 1968.
391 F.2d 495.

FLOYD R. GIBSON, CIRCUIT JUDGE. The driver of an automobile claims injury as a result of an alleged negligent design of the steering assembly of the automobile. The alleged defect in design did not cause the accident, and the manufacturer asserts the law imposes no duty of care in the design of an automobile to make it more safe to occupy in the event of a collision. The trial court agreed, rendering summary judgment in favor of the manufacturer, reported at 274 F. Supp. 461 (D.C.Minn.1967). We reverse and remand.

The plaintiff-appellant,[1] Erling David Larsen, received severe bodily injuries while driving, with the consent of the owner, a 1963 Chevrolet Corvair on February 18, 1964 in the state of Michigan. A head-on collision, with the impact occurring on the left front corner of the Corvair, caused a severe rearward thrust of the steering mechanism into the plaintiff's head. The Corvair was manufactured by General Motors Corporation and liability is asserted against General Motors on an alleged design defect in the steering assembly and the placement or attachment of the component parts of the steering assembly to the structure of the Corvair.[2]

The plaintiff does not contend that the design caused the accident but that because of the design he received injuries he would not have otherwise received or, in the alternative, his injuries would not have been as severe. The rearward displacement of the steering shaft on the left frontal impact was much greater on the Corvair than it would be in other cars that were designed to protect against such a rearward displacement. The plaintiff's complaint alleges (1) negligence in design of the steering assembly; (2) negligent failure to warn of the alleged latent or inherently dangerous condition to the user of the steering assembly placement; and (3) breach of express and implied warranties of merchantability of the vehicle's intended use.

General Motors contends it "has no duty whatsoever to design and manufacture a vehicle * * * which is otherwise 'safe' or 'safer' to occupy during collision impacts," and since there is no duty there can be no actionable negligence on its part to either design a safe or more safe car or to warn of any inherent or latent defects in design that might make its cars less safe than some other cars manufactured either by it or other manufacturers.

. . .

General Motors contends that it has no duty to produce a vehicle in which it is safe to collide or which is accident-proof or incapable of injurious misuse. It views its duty as extending only to producing a vehicle that is reasonably fit for its intended use or for the purpose

1. The parties will be referred to as designated in the trial court or by name.

2. The plaintiff alleges that the design and placement of the solid steering shaft, which extends without interruption from a point 2.7 inches in front of the leading surface of the front tires to a position directly in front of the driver, exposes the driver to an unreasonable risk of injury from the rearward displacement of that shaft in the event of a left-of-center head-on collision. So positioned it receives the initial impact of forces generated by a left-of-center head-on collision. The unabsorbed forces of the collision in this area are transmitted directly toward the driver's head, the shaft acting as a spear aimed at a vital part of the driver's anatomy.

for which it was made and that is free from hidden defects; and that the intended use of a vehicle and the purpose for which it is manufactured do not include its participation in head-on collisions or any other type of impact, regardless of the manufacturer's ability to foresee that such collisions may occur. . . .

The plaintiff maintains that General Motors' view of its duty is too narrow and restrictive and that an automobile manufacturer is under a duty to use reasonable care in the design of the automobile to make it safe to the user for its foreseeable use and that its intended use or purpose is for travel on the streets and highways, including the possibility of impact or collision with other vehicles or stationary objects. . . .

There is a line of cases directly supporting General Motors' contention that negligent design of an automobile is not actionable, where the alleged defective design is not a causative factor in the accident. The latest leading case on this point is Evans v. General Motors Corporation, 359 F.2d 822 (7 Cir. 1966), cert. denied, 385 U.S. 836, 87 S.Ct. 83, 17 L.Ed.2d 70 (1966). A divided court there held that General Motors in designing an "X" body frame without perimeter support, instead of an allegedly more safe perimeter body frame, was not liable for the death of a user allegedly caused by the designed defect because the defendant's design could not have functioned to avoid the collision. The Court reasoned at pp. 824 and 825 of 359 F.2d:

> "A manufacturer is not under a duty to make his automobile accident-proof or fool-proof; nor must he render the vehicle 'more' safe where the danger to be avoided is obvious to all. Campo v. Scofield, 1950, 301 N.Y. 468, 95 N.E.2d 802, 804. Perhaps it would be desirable to require manufacturers to construct automobiles in which it would be safe to collide, but that would be a legislative function, not an aspect of judicial interpretation of existing law. Campo v. Scofield, supra, 805.
>
> * * * * * * * * * *
>
> "The intended purpose of an automobile does not include its participation in collisions with other objects, despite the manufacturer's ability to foresee the possibility that such collisions may occur. * * *"

A strong dissent was written by Judge Kiley in which he contended that General Motors had a duty in designing its automobile to use such care that reasonable protection would be given a user against death or injuries from foreseeable yet unavoidable accidents. . . .

Since MacPherson v. Buick Motor Co., 217 N.Y. 382, 111 N.E. 1050, L.R.A.1916F, 696 (1916), the courts have consistently held a manufacturer liable for negligent construction of an automobile. . . .

The Courts, however have been somewhat reluctant to impose liability upon a manufacturer for negligent product design in the automotive field. . . .

Accepting . . . the principle that a manufacturer's duty of design and construction extends to producing a product that is reasonably fit for its intended use and free of hidden defects that could render it unsafe for such use, the issue narrows on the proper interpretation of "intended use". Automobiles are made for use on the roads and highways in transporting persons and cargo to and from various points. This intended use cannot be carried out without encountering in varying degrees the statistically proved hazard of injury-producing impacts of various types. The manufacturer should not be heard to say that it does not intend its product to be involved in any accident when it can easily foresee and when it knows that the probability over the life of its product is high, that it will be involved in some type of injury-producing accident. O'Connell in his article "Taming the Automobile," 58 Nw.U.L.Rev. 299, 348 (1963) cites that between one-fourth to two-thirds of all automobiles during their use at some time are involved in an accident producing injury or death. Other statistics are available showing the frequency and certainty of fatal and injury-producing accidents. See footnote 4. It should be recognized that the environment in which a product is used must be taken into consideration by the manufacturer. Spruill v. Boyle-Midway, Inc., 308 F.2d 79 (4 Cir. 1962).

We think the "intended use" construction urged by General Motors is much too narrow and unrealistic. Where the manufacturer's negligence in design causes an unreasonable risk to be imposed upon the user of its products, the manufacturer should be liable for the injury caused by its failure to exercise reasonable care in the design. These injuries are readily foreseeable as an incident to the normal and expected use of an automobile. While automobiles are not made for the purpose of colliding with each other, a frequent and inevitable contingency of normal automobile use will result in collisions and injury-producing impacts. No rational basis exists for limiting recovery to situations where the defect in design or manufacture was the causative factor of the accident, as the accident and the resulting injury, usually caused by the so-called "second collision" of the passenger with the interior part of the automobile, all are foreseeable. Where the injuries or enhanced injuries are due to the manufacturer's failure to use reasonable care to avoid subjecting the user of its products to an unreasonable risk of injury, general negligence principles should be applicable.[3] The sole function of an automobile is not just to provide a means of transportation, it is to provide a means of safe transportation or as safe as is reasonably possible under the present state of the art.

3. As aptly and concisely phrased by Noel, "Manufacturer's Negligence of Design or Directions for Use of a Product," 71 Yale L.J. 816, 818 (1962): "The manufacturer does not have to make a product which is 'accident-proof' or 'fool-proof'. Liability is imposed only when an unreasonable danger is created. Whether or not this has occurred should be determined by general negligence principles, which involve a balancing of the likelihood of harm, and the gravity of harm if it happens against the burden of the precautions which would be effective to avoid the harm."

We do agree that under the present state of the art an automobile manufacturer is under no duty to design an accident-proof or fool-proof vehicle or even one that floats on water, but such manufacturer is under a duty to use reasonable care in the design of its vehicle to avoid subjecting the user to an unreasonable risk of injury in the event of a collision. Collisions with or without fault of the user are clearly foreseeable by the manufacturer and are statistically inevitable.[4]

The intended use and purpose of an automobile is to travel on the streets and highways, which travel more often than not is in close proximity to other vehicles and at speeds that carry the possibility, probability, and potential of injury-producing impacts. The realities of the intended and actual use are well known to the manufacturer and to the public and these realities should be squarely faced by the manufacturer and the courts. We perceive of no sound reason, either in logic or experience, nor any command in precedent, why the manufacturer should not be held to a reasonable duty of care in the design of its vehicle consonant with the state of the art to minimize the effect of accidents. The manufacturers are not insurers but should be held to a standard of reasonable care in design to provide a reasonably safe vehicle in which to travel. . . . Our streets and highways are increasingly hazardous for the intended normal use of travel and transportation. While advances in highway engineering and non-access, dual highways have considerably increased the safety factor on a miles traveled ratio to accidents, the constant increasing number of vehicles gives impetus to the need of designing and constructing a vehicle that is reasonably safe for the purpose of such travel. At least, the unreasonable risk should be eliminated and reasonable steps in design taken to minimize the injury-producing effect of impacts.

This duty of reasonable care in design rests on common law negligence[5] that a manufacturer of an article should use reasonable care in the design and manufacture of his product to eliminate any unreasonable risk of foreseeable injury. The duty of reasonable care in design should be viewed in light of the risk. While all risks cannot

4. National Safety Council, Accident Facts 40 (1966 ed.) reports: In 1965 motor vehicle accidents caused 49,000 deaths, 1.8 million disabling injuries. In automobile accidents since the advent of the horseless carriage up to the end of 1965, 1.5 million people have been killed in the United States. In 1966 the annual toll of those killed in automobile accidents rose to 52,-500 and 1.9 million suffered disabling injuries.

5. The Michigan case of Piercefield v. Remington Arms Company, Inc., 375 Mich. 85, 133 N.W.2d 129 (1965) applied the doctrine of strict liability in tort, and gave effect in a case involving a defective shotgun shell, to an implied warranty that a product is reasonably fit for the use intended. We, however, think the duty in this evolving field of the law should and can rest, at this time, on general negligence principles, with each state free to supplement common law liability for negligence with a doctrine of strict liability for tort as a matter of social policy expressed by legislative action or judicial decision. The National Traffic and Motor Vehicle Safety Act of 1966 will result in the establishment of minimum safety standards the violation of which may constitute negligence *per se*.

be eliminated nor can a crash-proof vehicle be designed under the present state of the art, there are many common-sense factors in design, which are or should be well known to the manufacturer that will minimize or lessen the injurious effects of a collision. The standard of reasonable care is applied in many other negligence situations and should be applied here.

The courts since MacPherson v. Buick Motor Co., 217 N.Y. 382, 111 N.E. 1050, L.R.A.1916F, 696 (1916) have held that a manufacturer of automobiles is under a duty to construct a vehicle that is free of latent and hidden defects. We can perceive of no significant difference in imposing a common law duty of a reasonable standard of care in design the same as in construction. A defect in either can cause severe injury or death and a negligent design defect should be actionable. Any design defect not causing the accident would not subject the manufacturer to liability for the entire damage, but the manufacturer should be liable for that portion of the damage or injury caused by the defective design over and above the damage or injury that probably would have occurred as a result of the impact or collision absent the defective design. The manufacturer argues that this is difficult to assess. This is no persuasive answer and, even if difficult, there is no reason to abandon the injured party to his dismal fate as a traffic statistic, when the manufacturer owed, at least, a common law duty of reasonable care in the design and construction of its product. The obstacles of apportionment are not insurmountable. It is done with regularity in those jurisdictions applying comparative negligence statutes and in other factual situations as condemnation cases, where in some jurisdictions the jury must assess the value of the land before and after a taking and then assess a special benefit accruing to the remaining property of the condemnee.

General Motors in arguing against what it views as an expanded duty of a care in design makes the statement that this duty "must be considered in its application to all products. Automobile manufacturers cannot be made a special class." With this we quite agree. We think the duty of the use of reasonable care in design to protect against foreseeable injury to the user of a product and perhaps others injured as an incident of that use should be and is equally applicable to all manufacturers with the customary limitations now applied to protect the manufacturer in case of an unintended and unforeseeable use. The courts have imposed this duty, perhaps more readily against other manufacturers than against the automotive industry.[6]

6. See, Brandon v. Yale & Towne Manufacturing Co., 342 F.2d 519 (3 Cir. 1965)—failure to equip a forklift truck with adequate safety devices; Rosin v. International Harvester Company, 262 Minn. 445, 115 N.W.2d 50 (1962)—a defectively designed inner grease seal that resulted in a brake malfunctioning; Phillips v. Ogle Aluminum Furniture, Inc., 106 Cal.App.2d 650, 235 P.2d 857 (1951)—an inadequately designed chair; Simpson Timber Co. v. Parks (9 Cir. 1965), CCH Pro.Liab.Rptr. ¶5498—inadequately packaged doors for shipment (see comment herein for later developments in this case).

We, therefore, do not think the automotive industry is being singled out for any special adverse treatment by applying to it general negligence principles in (1) imposing a duty on the manufacturer to use reasonable care in the design of its products to protect against an unreasonable risk of injury or enhancement of injury to a user of the product, and (2) holding that the intended use of an automotive product contemplates its travel on crowded and high speed roads and highways that inevitably subject it to the foreseeable hazards of collisions and impacts. Neither reason, logic, nor controlling precedents compel the courts to make a distinction between negligent design and negligent construction.

The manufacturer's duty to use reasonable care in the design and manufacture of a product to minimize injuries to its users and not to subject its users to an unreasonable risk of injury in the event of a collision or impact should be recognized by the courts. The manufacturers themselves have, in various public utterances in discussing automotive safety, expressed their concern for making safer vehicles.[7] And General Motors admits the foreseeability of accidents which are matters of public and common knowledge over a long period of time.[8] Legal acceptance or imposition of this duty would go far in protecting the user from unreasonable risks. The normal risk of driving must be accepted by the user but there is no need to further penalize the user by subjecting him to an unreasonable risk of injury due to negligence in design.

7. C. A. Chayne, then vice-president in charge of the engineering staff of defendant General Motors, made a statement before the Subcommittee on Interstate and Foreign Commerce, House of Representatives, 84th Cong., 2nd Sess., on Investigation of Highway Traffic Accidents, Traffic Safety (1956), pp. 325–327:

"* * * it is always relatively easy to come up with a new design of an old part, or the design of a new feature or part, but until we are able to adequately test this part and have a pretty clear picture of what it will do under the circumstances to which it is subjected, we are exposing ourselves, the users of our products, and frequently others on the highways to risks."

K. A. Stonex, Automobile Safety Engineer for General Motors in an article "Vehicle Aspects of the Highway Safety Problem," appearing in TRAFFIC SAFETY, National Safety Council, Chicago, Illinois, June 1962, at p. 22, said: "The two-car collision * * is so important statistically that car structure has to be evaluated under these conditions."

The president of General Motors in Hearings on the Federal Role in Traffic Safety Before the Subcommittee on Executive Reorganization of the Senate Committee on Government Operations, 89th Cong., 1st Sess. pt. 2 at 667 (1965), stated: "We recognize that the increasing movement of people and goods by motor vehicles contributes naturally to a higher possibility of accidents. This imposes new responsibilities on all of us. Automobile manufacturers must continue to seek all possible ways in which the built-in protection for car occupants can be improved."

8. Goddard & Haddon in their article "Passenger Car Design in Highway Safety" published by Consumers Union of U.S., Inc. make the statement that: "Between one-fourth and two-thirds of all vehicles manufactured are at sometime during their subsequent use involved in the tragedy of human injury and death. Consequently the anticipation of this result by both designer and manufacturer is mandatory."

[Ed. note: Last footnote omitted.]

On the second count of plaintiff's petition alleging negligence in failure to warn of an alleged dangerous condition in vehicle design the same principles would apply. We think a cause of action is alleged and that under the law the manufacturer has a duty to inspect and to test for designs that would cause an unreasonable risk of foreseeable injury. Ford Motor Company v. Zahn, supra. The failure to use reasonable care in design or knowledge of a defective design gives rise to the reasonable duty on the manufacturer to warn of this condition.

The duty of a manufacturer to test and to warn of defects in its product needs little elaboration. The Restatement (Second), Torts, § 395, comment (f) (1965) reads:

> "* * * The particulars in which reasonable care is usually necessary for protection of those whose safety depends upon the character of chattels are * * * (4) the making of such inspections and tests during the course of manufacture and after the article is completed as the manufacturer should recognize as reasonably necessary to secure the production of a safe article. * * *"

. . . Almost any chattel or commodity is capable of inflicting injury; knives cut, axes split, dynamite explodes, food spoils, poison kills. Where the danger is obvious and known to the user, no warning is necessary and no liability attaches for an injury occurring from the reasonable hazards attached to the use of chattels or commodities; but where the dangerous condition is latent it should be disclosed to the user, and non-disclosure should subject the maker or supplier to liability for creating an unreasonable risk.

In Blitzstein v. Ford Motor Company, 288 F.2d 738, at p. 744 (5 Cir. 1961) the court held the evidence was sufficient to present a jury issue on whether the supplier Ford Motor Company was negligent in failing to exercise reasonable care to warn of a dangerous condition caused by designing a non-ventilated motor car trunk in which an undetectable leaky gas tank was located, stating:

> "We think that a jury could reasonably have found that the American Ford Company was negligent in marketing a product which was inherently dangerous, of which danger it should have been aware from its long experience in the design and manufacture of automobiles, and that American Ford failed to exercise reasonable care to inform the buying public of this dangerous condition. * * *"

If, because of the alleged undisclosed defect in design of the 1963 Corvair steering assembly, an extra hazard is created over and above the normal hazard, General Motors should be liable for this unreasonable hazard. Admittedly, it would not sell many cars of this particular model if its sale's "pitch" included the cautionary statement that the user is subjected to an extra hazard or unreasonable risk in the event of a head-on collision. But the duty of reasonable care should command a warning of this latent defect that could under certain circumstances accentuate the possibility of severe injury.

. . .

For the reasons set forth, we reverse and remand for proceedings not inconsistent with this opinion.

When federal jurisdiction is based upon diversity of citizenship, as in the *Larsen* case, the federal court applies the law of the state in which it sits or, in some cases, the law of another state. In the *Larsen* case, the court applied the law of Michigan, since the parties agreed that Michigan law applied.

When the federal court applies state law, it is often reluctant to go beyond what the state has actually held in its decisions. In an omitted portion of the *Larsen* opinion, the federal court stated that it was uncertain as to the Michigan law on the liability of a manufacturer for defective products without regard to fault. Since the court felt that negligence would give the plaintiff a fair opportunity, it did not go into the question of whether the manufacturer would be liable without a showing of fault. A state court which had gone a considerable distance in recognizing manufacturer's liability without fault might have also held the manufacturer on a warranty or a liability without fault basis.

In another omitted portion of the opinion, the court rejected the defendant's contention that compliance with the National Traffic and Motor Vehicle Safety Act of 1966, P.L. 89–563, 15 U.S.C.A. § 1381 a federal statute on automobile safety, gave the manufacturer a defense to any negligence actions.

The crucial issue in the *Larsen* case was a legal question. What duty does a manufacturer of an automobile owe to make his car reasonably safe after a collision? After this opinion, there will have to be a trial to determine whether the manufacturer designed the car negligently and, if so, what portion of any recoverable damages to the plaintiff were due to negligent design.

While this case does not directly relate to construction, it is important for design professionals. The opinion at footnote 6 reflected the court's feeling that in the area of other machinery and equipment, the law has gone far toward putting a burden on the manufacturer to anticipate accidents due to misuse of his machine when he designs it. Also, the manufacturer must warn the user of any dangerous conditions which would not be apparent to the user. To the extent that these standards are followed in other federal courts and in state courts, they have a serious impact on renters, sellers, and manufacturers of material and equipment used in construction.

Also, the *Larsen* case shows the increasing concern of courts and legislatures over product safety. Design professionals, mainly engineers, deal constantly with design and product safety.

(I) TREND TOWARD PLAINTIFF'S RECOVERY

Product liability cases reflect the general trend in the tort area toward permitting injured parties to recover from the person whose negligence causes the loss, or whose economic enterprise ought to bear the risk of such losses. This is a recognition, too, of the increasing use of insurance to cover many types of tort risks. In injury cases, the principal issue is that of which of the defendants will actually bear the loss. The injured party can usually recover. The person from whom a recovery is made will frequently look to someone else for indemnification or reimbursement. The concept of enterprise liability, which assumes that the costs of injury are, or can be, computed, insured against, and included as part of the cost of manufacturing the product, is slowly dominating the tort field.

SECTION 30.07 EMPLOYMENT INJURIES: EMERGENCE OF WORKMEN'S COMPENSATION

By and large, the nineteenth century employee did not fare very well in English and American courts. The expansion of the Industrial Revolution caused a substantial increase in the number of employees injured during the course of employment. The law did require that the employer furnish a safe place for the employee, safe appliances, tools, and equipment, and required that the employer warn the employee of any danger connected with the work of which the employer knew, or should have known. But there were many obstacles to recovery by the employee.

First, he had to show that the employer had in some way been negligent. Many accidents occurred due to the nature of the work, and not to any specific acts of negligence on the part of the employer.

In addition to having to show negligence, there were three defenses which were frequently employed by the employer when sued by the employee. Those defenses were "contributory negligence", "assumption of risk", and "the fellow servant rule". "Contributory negligence" required the employee to exercise due care for his own safety. If the injury were caused substantially by his own negligence, he could not recover, unless the conduct of the employer was willful or wanton.

"Assumption of risk" barred recovery if the employee, by taking the job, assumed the risk of injuries as an incident of his employment, or at least those risks which were normally incident to his employment. In some cases, remaining on the job after he knew or appreciated the danger would constitute an assumption of risk. This was so even if he protested, or if he were given a direct order to continue, the violation of which would have meant he would have been fired.

In addition to these obstacles, there was "the fellow servant rule". If the injury occurred due to the negligence of a fellow servant, the employee could not recover against the employer. American cases developed an exception to the fellow servant rule. The employee causing the injury might have been sufficiently high up in the hierarchy of the employer's organization to be considered a "vice principal" of the employer. In such a case he would not be considered a fellow servant and the injured employee would not be barred by the fellow servant rule.

In any event, the employee frequently went uncompensated for injuries which occurred during the course of his employment. As a result of this, in the early twentieth century states began to enact workmen's compensation laws which substantially changed the rules relating to employment injuries. Generally, an employee can recover for injuries incurred in the scope of or arising out of his employment.

All states today have workmen's compensation laws which apply to employment injuries. There are great variations among the states. However, there are certain common issues and general rules.

Is the employer covered by the act? Many statutes exclude from workmen's compensation coverage employers of agricultural workers and domestics, as well as employers with only a few employees.

Did the injury arise out of, or in the course of, employment? Many cases have explored the question of whether various activities fell within the statute. There have been injuries on company picnics, injuries while the employee was in the parking lot, and injuries caused by horseplay of fellow employees. The law has generally been protective of the employee in deciding whether the injury was sufficiently related to the employment to be covered.

In most states, the law requires that the employer obtain workmen's compensation insurance. A few states set up state funds for injury insurance. It is also possible in some states to be a self-insurer, if adequate proof of financial responsibility is made. The important thing is that the state requires that there be a financially responsible entity which will be able to pay any valid claim.

The need for financial responsibility was recognized in the construction industry. Some 41 states have what are called *subcontractor under* or *statutory employer* provisions. This means that the prime contractor will be considered the employer of any employees of a subcontractor under certain circumstances, such as a showing that the subcontractor did not procure the required insurance. Under these statutes the employee of a subcontractor may be able to recover from the insurance carrier of the prime contractor. These special rules relating to subcontractors recognized that many subcontractors were not financially sound and might not obtain the requisite insurance for employee injury. Also compensation coverage could be diluted if a prime contractor subcontracted out work which he would ordinary perform to reduce the number of employees for whom he would have to obtain insurance coverage. Usually "subcontractor under" provisions do not apply to the owner when he hires a prime contractor. The employee of the prime contractor will not be able to consider the owner a statutory employer.

If the injury occurred during the course of employment, the employee would not have to show any negligence on the part of the employer, nor would he be precluded from recovering if he were negligent or would have been considered to have assumed the risk. The fellow servant rule would not affect his recovery. Some states denied recovery if employee was guilty of wilful misconduct or was drunk. However, ordinary negligence, assumption of risk, or the fellow servant rule would not bar recovery by the employee.

If the injury is one which is covered under workmen's compensation, typically the employee receives a proportionate amount of his normal wages, as well as reimbursement for medical expenses incurred. In addition to lost wages, he may receive a specific monetary award for specific injuries.

Generally, disfigurement is compensable if it affects earning capacity and in some states, even if it does not. The award to the employee will not include an amount for pain and suffering.

Some states require that the injury be physical, and do not recognize occupational diseases. The tendency has been to extend the coverage to occupational diseases as well as to physical injury.

By and large, workmen's compensation rights have replaced whatever liability the employer might have had for employment injuries to his employees. Statutes usually stated that a workmen's compensation claim was the only remedy an employee had against his employer. This was done to give the employers something in exchange for giving up existing legal protection in employment accidents. Also, making the compensation remedy exclusive avoided litigation and kept the cases within administrative agencies charged with responsibility for handling these claims.

States vary considerably in whether they permit the employee, or the employer's insurance carrier who pays the claim to sue third parties whose negligence caused the injury. In some states, the employee can recover under workmen's compensation, and then sue any third party whose negligence caused the injury, such as a manufacturer of a defective product, or even a fellow employee. Compensation claims, although relatively easy to obtain, are smaller than may be recovered from a tort claim. Because of the many different parties connected with a construction project, these third party claims are becoming common in construction site injuries. The injured employee of a subcontractor will, if he can, sue the prime, the design professional, the owner, and any other third party whom he claims caused his injury.

The major legal questions in third party cases involve the same types of issues which plagued the employee before the advent of workmen's compensation laws. He will have to show that the third party was negligent, and that this negligence caused his injury. He may be aided by various presumptions, such as "res ipsa loquitur", if the work was in the control of the defendant. (See § 30.02(f). This doctrine will be useful if the injured employee is bringing a legal action against the manufacturer of the product which caused the injury where strict liability (liability without fault) for defective products is not recognized.

Typically, workmen's compensation claims are handled by an administrative agency rather than a court. The hearings are informal, and are usually conducted by a hearing officer or examiner. The employee can represent himself, or can be represented by a nonlawyer or a lawyer. Fees for representation are usually regulated by law. The awards given by the agency can be appealed to a court, but the court review is limited. Usually, the court will look only to whether the agency had jurisdiction to make a determination, and whether there is any evidence to support the award.

Third party actions based upon negligence are handled by courts, not by administrative agencies.

SECTION 30.08 HARM TO PERSONS

This, and subsequent sections, will apply the doctrines discussed in preceding sections. Since liability may depend upon the type of loss suffered, this section will discuss harm to persons, § 30.09 will discuss harm to things, and § 30.10 will discuss economic harm.

(A) POTENTIAL LITIGANTS

Persons who suffer physical harm can be classified into two groups. They are persons who suffer physical harm during the construction process, and those who suffer physical harm after a project is completed.

A second important line of demarcation relates to the employment status of the injured person. During the construction project, employees of those engaged in the construction project may be injured or killed. After the project is completed, employees of the person owning the completed project or leasing space in the completed project may be injured.

On the other hand, persons not employed on the project may be injured during construction. Children may trespass on the construction site, mailmen may deliver the mail to the site during the process of construction, members of the public may walk by the project and be injured, and persons on adjacent land may suffer physical injury due to activities on the construction site. After completion of the project, customers of a business located in the completed project may suffer physical harm, as may tenants or their social guests in a completed residential project.

When persons suffer physical harm related to a construction project, there is a wide range of potential defendants. Defendants in these actions may be prime contractors, subcontractors, design professionals, owners of the project, those who finance the project or participate in its planning, and those who sell or make equipment or material which goes into the project.

(B) SOME SPECIAL ASPECTS OF EMPLOYMENT INJURIES

Section 30.07 briefly outlined laws relating to employment injuries. Generally, an employee who is injured in the course of his employment can recover workmen's compensation from his employer or his employer's workmen's compensation insurance carrier. However, recovery under workmen's compensation, while relatively certain and quick, is often inadequate.

Under workmen's compensation law the injured employee cannot institute a negligence action against his employer. His sole remedy against his own employer is under the workmen's compensation laws. In many states he can recover from third parties whose violation of some legal duty caused his injury. In some states an employee of a subcontractor cannot sue the prime contractor if the prime contractor is considered a statutory employer for the purposes of the workmen's compensation law. In some states, the injured employee cannot sue anyone engaged in a common employment. But generally the injured employee has considerable latitude in suing third parties. The basis for his action against a third party is usually negligence. However, if the injury resulted from a defective product, the employee may be able to recover from the manufacturer without any showing of negligence by the latter.

Wagner v. Grannis, 287 F.Supp. 18 (Dist.Ct.Pa.1968), involved an action by the estate of the deceased worker against the owner of the site on which the deceased worker's employer was erecting a building, the owner of an adjacent building whose wall collapsed, the architect employed by the owner of the construction site, and a demolition contractor who had previously demolished part of the former building on the construction site. The trial judge stated:

> This is a diversity negligence action for wrongful death under Pennsylvania law. Its difficulties arise out of an attempt to impose liabilities on third parties for the death of a workman where statutory liability has been placed upon the employer regardless of negligence on his part. The awards under such compensation acts are often considered inadequate, and less than can be realized in a suit based upon negli-

gence tried before a jury. The beneficiaries of the deceased plaintiff risk nothing, because they are entitled to the statutory award; the employer or his insurance carrier is frequently a highly interested party because he may . . . recover what he has been required to pay; and the counsel for the workman or his beneficiary is entitled to his fee by statute for any recovery that he has achieved on behalf of the employer, regardless of the extent to which his client has been benefited. The excess recovery over the compensation paid, goes to the employee or his beneficiaries. . . . All this leads to highly complex theories of liability to hold third parties responsible, and frequently great confusion to the jury, which cannot be told and which is often unable to understand why a party shown by the evidence before them to be guilty of negligence which proximately caused the accident, is not before them. In the Federal Courts such employer is frequently joined as a third party defendant to protect rights of contribution or indemnity which the defendants may try to assert, although his liability has been fixed, determined and limited to that imposed by the Pennsylvania Workmen's Compensation Act. In this case, the employer, whose negligence was apparent, was not joined as a third party defendant, making the task of the jury more difficult.

In addition, these cases are often complicated by indemnity actions brought between the various defendants. This will be discussed in greater detail in § 30.13.

The discussion for the balance of this section will assume that if the plaintiff is an employee, he is asserting a third party action against the person whom he claims caused his injury. As stated in the *Wagner* case, the employee is often joined in his law suit by the compensation carrier of his own employer.

(C) LEGAL RESPONSIBILITY: THE DUTY CONCEPT

Legal responsibility for the plaintiff's injury is complicated in the construction accident because of the many possible causes of the injury, the multitude of legal entities engaged in the construction process and the complex blending of contract, tort and construction safety laws.

A brief review of the organization of construction projects is useful. The "typical" construction project centers around an agreement between owner and prime contractor, under which the owner will pay a designated sum of money in exchange for the contractor building a project in accordance with the contract documents. The owner furnishes the site, and retains an architect or engineer as his technical advisor and representative for the project. The architect or engineer is often given the power to interpret the agreement and resolve disputes relating to performance. The architect or engineer may engage consultants to advise him on the project such as a structural engineer, a mechanical engineer, or a landscape architect.

The prime contractor does a portion of the work and hires subcontractors to perform the balance. In complicated projects the subcontractor may sublet portions of their performance. Prime and subcontractors usually purchase supplies and rent equipment from suppliers.

Ordinarily, the prime contractor is given a specific result to accomplish and much of the detail as to construction methods is left to him. However, the owner retains significant power over the prime contractor during performance. Ordinarily, the owner, through the design professional, has the right to inspect the work, determine whether there has been proper performance, determine whether it appears that performance will be as promised, terminate the performance under certain circumstances and require that the contractor correct nonconforming performance.

To some degree the prime contractor retains parallel controls in his subcontracts. He may give himself the same powers in the subcontract that the design professional has in the prime contract or he may give the same powers to the design professional over subcontract performance that the design professional has over prime contract performance.

In addition to the "typical" organization for a construction project, there are other types of arrangements. First, there may be a separate contracting system. The owner may contract directly with a number of prime contractors rather than contract with one prime contractor who subcontracts much of the work. In such a case, a higher degree of coordination responsibility will belong to the owner rather than to the prime contractor. In some separate contracts the owner delegates coordination to one contractor although he still enters into the contract with a number of contractors.

Another atypical arrangement involves the owner furnishing materials, equipment or labor to the contractor. In these arrangements the owner will play a more active role than in the typical arrangement.

There are other atypical arrangements. For example, a construction project can involve an addition to an existing structure belonging to the owner. Under such an arrangement, the owner is likely to have more general control and supervision over the construction site and work because there may be existing safety rules and regulations which apply on the site. The same can result if the project involves remodeling of an existing structure. In additions and remodeling the owner is more likely to have more control over construction operations than if the owner simply has purchased land, given construction documents to the contractor and requested that he build a particular structure.

Another arrangement which must be differentiated from the "typical" project organization arises when the design professional is a salaried employee of the owner. Such a design professional is a person over whom the owner will generally have more control.

In the typical construction accident claim, someone is injured during construction or after the project is completed. If he is an employee, he usually recovers workmen's compensation and searches for a third party against whom he can make a claim. Usually the injured party can find a number of causes for his injury. He may have been injured by defective material supplied by a manufacturer or defective equipment furnished by an equipment supplier. He may have been injured because of negligent acts of employees engaged on the project.

He may base his claim upon failure to comply with safety requirements imposed by law. For example, an injured employee who falls from a scaffold may base his claim on the failure of prime or subcontractor to supply a guard rail or to require that safety belts be worn at all times.

Sometimes the negligence is less direct, but nevertheless causal. For example, the injured party may claim that the prime contractor or design professional permitted an incompetent subcontractor to continue on the project after it became clear that he could not do the work properly. A claim might be based upon the failure by the design professional or prime contractor to inspect the work as often as it should have been inspected, or upon careless inspections. The negligence may relate to the failure to furnish proper instruction to a sub or prime contractor.

In a construction project, then, there can be a number of causes of the injury. It can be the direct acts of workers or supervisors, defective products or equipment or faulty design. Other acts can contribute in a less direct way to the injury, such as failure to inspect, negligent inspections, or permitting incompetent workers to continue on the project.

Usually there are contract provisions in the prime and subcontract which bear upon these questions. For example, prime and subcontractors typically will promise to comply with all applicable laws and regulations and in some contracts there will be specific provisions upon certain aspects of safety. For example, in West v. Atkinson Construction Co., 251 Cal.App.2d 296, 59 Cal.Rptr. 286 (1967) a case to be discussed in greater detail in subsection (f), a contract for the construction of a highway contained a provision that "the contractor shall comply with all applicable federal, state and local laws governing safety . . . [and] shall provide all safeguards, safety devices and protective equipment and take any other needed action, on his own responsibility reasonably necessary to protect the life and health of employees on the job and the safety of the public." Also there may be provisions in the prime contract under which the prime contractor agrees to take responsibility for any negligent acts or failure to act on the part of the subcontractor.

In addition, it is common for construction contracts to contain indemnity provisions. They will be discussed in greater detail in § 30.13.

Finally, construction contracts frequently contain provisions requiring that the contractors procure and maintain adequate public liability insurance.

The legal rules relating to construction accidents are a complex blending of court-made and statute law. It may be useful to commence with a general picture of the statutory safety controls on the building process.

Almost every construction project is subject to state and local laws relating to safety. In addition, there may be federal laws which bear upon safety matters. Sometimes these laws are very general. It may only require that every contractor or person in control of a construction project make the project reasonably safe for those engaged in the project, persons who come on the site or passersby.

Some statutes do not expressly deal with construction projects but are phrased in terms of obligating an employer to furnish a safe place of employment.

Statutes, administrative regulations and local building codes often set forth in detail particular health and safety measures.

Usually, these statutes specify who must comply with safety statutes and administrative regulations. While statutes vary and often are unclear, as a rule, statutory requirements are the responsibility of the person who has overall control of the project. In the typical construction project, this will be the prime contractor. Sometimes these statutes provide sanctions for noncompliance by the person charged with the responsibility for compliance. There can be penal sanctions, such as fines and imprisonments. A violation may be considered negligence *per se*. In such cases the violator will be held liable in a civil action for harm to persons caused by his failure to comply unless he can show compelling reasons excusing his noncompliance. See § 30.02(f).

Statutory requirements may involve the application of the independent contractor rule. This rule will be discussed in greater detail in this section. However, it may be useful to consider this rule as it relates to statutory violations.

Unless one of the many exceptions to the rule applies, the independent contractor rule absolves the person who hires an independent contractor from responsibility for the negligence of the independent contractor. Suppose the prime contractor is responsible for compliance with safety rules. Suppose he hires an independent contractor to actually fulfill his obligation. For example, what if the prime contractor is responsible for the installation of a sheltered walkway around the project, and the subcontractor hired for this purpose does not perform, or performs it negligently? It is likely that the prime contractor would not be given the benefit of the independent contractor rule. One of the principal exceptions relates to nondelegable duties. Statutory safety obligations are usually considered nondelegable. The person who has the obligation cannot relieve himself of the obligation by hiring an independent contractor. Usually safety matters are considered too important to be delegable to an independent contractor. In addition, independent contractors sometimes lack the financial responsibility of the person hiring them. To permit the person with legal responsibility to substitute an often financially weak independent contractor could result in uncompensated injured parties.

In addition to allegations of statutory violations, plaintiffs who are injured sometimes contend that the defendant should pay for their injury because the defendant, or someone for whom he is legally responsible, acted negligently and caused his injury. Persons engaged in a construction project should not expose others to unreasonable risk of harm. For example, if the employee of a subcontractor is injured by the negligent act of the employee of another subcontractor or the prime contractor, generally, the latter employee would be liable for the harm suffered. In addition, the employer of the negligent employee is likely to be liable based upon vicarious liability. If the employer of the negligent employee had the right to control or did control the activities of his employee, then the employer is liable for his employee's negligent act.

The negligence action, then, may be directed against the negligent party himself or, more likely, against persons vicariously liable for the negligence of the person actually causing the injury. In addition to these direct acts of negligence being the basis of the claim by the injured party, there are some of the less direct causes of the injury which have been mentioned earlier in this section. For example, § 30.05 discussed the duty owed by the owner or occupier of land. While the duty owed may depend to a large degree upon the status of the injured party, the growing tendency in the cases is to require that the owner or occupier of land maintain the land in such a way as to avoid the unreasonable risk of harm to those to enter upon it or pass by.

In the typical construction project, the owner is not considered for these purposes the possessor of the land. He has turned over the entire site to the prime contractor and has left the methods of performance to the prime contractor. Ordinarily, the owner will not be liable for injuries which result from the prime contractor's failure to make the land reasonably safe for those who enter upon it.

There are some cases which hold that the owner is responsible for the prime contractor's failure to keep the land reasonably safe for those who enter upon it. These cases look at the amount of control that the owner, through the design professional, may have even in typical construction projects. As stated, the design professional may have the power to order the prime contractor off the job, to order that defective work be corrected, to speed up performance by ordering that a designated number of laborers be placed on the project and other operational controls. See the case of Associated Engineers Inc. v. Job, discussed in § 30.13(d).

However, as a rule the fact that the owner, through the design professional, possesses these powers does not make the owner responsible to those who are injured because of the prime contractor's failure to make the land reasonably safe for those who enter upon it.

If the owner has operative presence, such as the opportunity to find and correct unsafe conditions, he may be found to be the possessor, with the responsibility to maintain the land in a safe condition. This would be more likely if the project were within the owner's existing plant or were an addition to an existing plant. Also, if the owner used one of his own employees as a design professional, this might take the case out of the usual rule that the owner, during the course of construction, is not considered an owner or occupier of land.

Another important doctrine is the independent contractor rule. It has been briefly discussed earlier in this section. Subject to many exceptions, a person who hires an independent contractor is not liable for the negligence of the independent contractor. The test for determining whether a person is an independent contractor is the control or right to control by the hirer of the contractor over the details of the work to be performed by the contractor.

Often contracts contain provisions stating that the performing party is an independent contractor and that the person engaging him to perform services is not responsible. Such clauses will not control if an injury occurs to a third party. The court is likely to look at the economic aspects of the transaction, the financial capacity of the negligent party, and the traditional tests of control or the right to control.

The independent contractor doctrine can be applied in a construction project accident. For example, if the injured party sues the owner, he is likely to base his action upon the alleged negligence of the architect or engineer. In rare cases, he may allege that the owner is responsible for the negligence of the prime contractor.

By and large, the owner will not be held for the negligent acts of the architect or engineer, and almost certainly not for the negligent acts of the prime contractor. Only if the owner himself is negligent is he likely to be held. The independent contractor defense for negligent acts of the design professional is given the owner because the owner generally does not control or have the right to control the details of the design professional's work. The same is even more true if the negligence is that of a prime or subcontractor.

Where courts do consider the owner to be vicariously responsible for the negligence of architect or engineer, it is more likely that the negligence relates to the role of the architect or engineer during construction project administration, rather than in the design services performed prior to the commencement of construction itself.

As indicated, there are exceptions to the independent contractor rule. The most important relates to inherently dangerous activity which the hirer of the independent contractor should recognize as likely to create a peculiar, unreasonable risk of physical harm to others unless special precautions are taken. Illustrations of inherently dangerous activity would be excavation, structural repairs and wall demolition. If the activity falls into this category, the prime contractor will be liable if the injury has resulted from the negligence of a subcontractor even if the latter is an independent contractor.

The other exception to the independent contractor rule has been mentioned. If the duty is an important one imposed by statute relating to safety, it is likely that the party with the ultimate responsibility for compliance with the designated standard cannot divest himself of this responsibility by hiring an independent contractor to perform it.

Judicial holdings on these issues vary considerably from state-to-state. Much will depend upon statutory language applicable to the case, any relevant contract language and the particular facts in the case. Yet it may be useful to attempt a brief summary. If a prime is sued because of the negligence of the sub or if the owner is sued because of the negligence of the prime, primes and owners in such cases are likely to claim that they are not responsible for the negligence of the sub and prime respectively. Generally, the independent contractor rule will provide a defense unless the plaintiff can establish any duty violated was nondelegable to an independent contractor. If so, the prime or the owner may be held liable for the negligence of the sub or the prime respectively.

Sometimes the plaintiff claims his injury resulted from the violation of the duty owed by the possessor of land to those who enter upon the land. In such a case it must be determined whether the defendant was the possessor of the land. If the actual negligence is that of the sub, sometimes the prime has been successful in claiming that he did not have the type of control over the sub's operation to be classified an owner or occupier of land. Generally, this defense has not been very successful. However, if the owner is sued on the basis of being the owner or occupier of land, he stands a good chance of convincing a court that when he turns over the entire operation to the prime contractor, the latter, and not the owner, is the possessor of land. This is more likely to be the case in a "typical" construction contract as that term has been defined in this subsection.

Also, the plaintiff frequently asserts that his injury was caused by the violation of a statutory or administrative safety regulation. In such cases he often attempts to sue the prime when the more directly responsible party was the sub, especially if the subcontractor was the plaintiff's employer. Sometimes the plaintiff sues the owner or design professional when the more culpable party was the prime or the subcontractor. While much depends upon the statutory language and the facts of the case, it is likely that the prime contractor will be considered the overall "employer" on the project and be responsible for safety violations. There are and are likely to be cases where the prime contractor will be relieved if there is very little to connect him, either through action or inaction, with the injury. As for the owner, in some states he will be held to be the "employer" because of the extensive powers given the design professional. However, it is more likely that the owner in a typical construction project will not be considered the person responsible for safety violations. In atypical arrangements, such as separate contracts, additions or repairs to existing buildings or projects where the design professional performs close supervision, the owner could be the possessor of land and responsible for compliance with statutory safety laws.

For case histories of construction accident litigation, see §§ 30.08 (f) and 30.13(d).

This subsection has assumed that the legal standard is one of due care. If the plaintiff is injured by a defective product, or by defective material or equipment, the action against the manufacturer or supplier may be based upon a failure by the defendant to supply products, material or equipment free of defects. This is liability without fault, which has been discussed previously in § 30.06. Also, liability without fault may result under the provisions of certain statutes which require that the employer or owner of a building make the building safe. If this is the standard, it is not necessary to show that the employer or owner was negligent. A showing of lack of compliance with the statutory standard is sufficient to justify imposing liability on the defendant.

(D) PROOF OF THE VIOLATION OF THE APPLICABLE LEGAL DUTY

Assuming that a court determines that a duty was owed by the defendant to this plaintiff, the next issue is whether the defendant has violated that duty. Many statutes, regulations, and codes are designed to protect workers on the construction project, persons who live in completed projects, and members of the public. On the whole, proof that these laws have been violated are likely to decide the question of negligence. See § 30.02(f).

Unlike plaintiffs in actions against manufacturers of mass produced goods, plaintiffs in construction site accidents are generally not given the benefit of "res ipsa loquitur". Gobel v. General Building Service Co., 26 Wis.2d 129, 131 N.W.2d 852 (1965), involved an action by the employee of a subcontractor against a prime contractor. The plaintiff claimed that the defendant was negligent in letting a stone fall from a state owned building he was repairing. The plaintiff claimed that despite the absence of direct evidence of negligence, the trial judge should have submitted the issue of negligence to the jury based upon *res ipsa loquitur*.

The owner of the building continued to occupy it and, through the right to inspect, the architect and state representative had control over the work. Since *res ipsa* requires exclusive control, it was not applied in this case. Even when the owner does not occupy the project, it will be difficult for the plaintiff to use *res ipsa* because of the many persons and entities involved in a construction project and the right to direct operations often retained by the owner and exercisable through the design professional.

Sometimes a defendant contractor claims he was not negligent because he complied with the plans and specifications, custom, or applicable law regulating construction methods or materials. See § 30.02(f). Compliance is evidence of due care, but will not be conclusive, and may not be very persuasive.

As noted in § 30.02(f), to use a statutory violation to show negligence the plaintiff must show that the statute was intended for his protection. Some cases hold that an employee of a subcontractor cannot use a statutory violation by a prime contractor as a basis for a negligence action. On the other hand, some states have statutes imposing liability on employers which are broad enough to consider the prime contractor as the employer where there are injuries to employees of the subcontractor. Again, about all that can be said is that there are variations in state laws. But the modern tendency has been for a broad application of safety rules for the protection of anyone whose injury could be reasonably foreseen by the prime contractor, or by anyone else charged with responsibility for the injury.

(E) DEFENSES

Absence of Privity

Assuming that the plaintiff can show that the defendant or defendants violated a duty of care owed, the defendant often asserts a number of defenses. In earlier construction injury litigation, defendants asserted the lack of privity between the injured party and the defendant. While the privity defense has retained more of its original force in construction injury cases than in manufacturer's liability cases, it is gradually disappearing.

Inventive plaintiffs' attorneys constantly expand the possible defendants in these cases. Public liability insurance carriers usually have the right to inspect the site to determine whether there is compliance with safety rules. Such a right may be part of a loss prevention program, or designed to determine the appropriate premium rate.

In a number of cases, plaintiffs have sued public liability insurance carriers, claiming that the failure on the part of the carriers to inspect, or to inspect properly, caused the injury to the plaintiff. This approach was successful in Nelson v. Union Wire Rope Corp., 31 Ill.2d 69, 199 N.E.2d 769 (1964), but in most cases the insurance company has been given a defense based upon lack of privity. Gerace v. Liberty Mutual Ins. Co., 264 F.Supp. 95 (Dist.Ct.Dist.Col. 1966).

The privity doctrine has somewhat more vitality where the injury occurred after completion of the project. These cases usually involve tenants or persons who enter a completed building and have accidents attributable to defective design, materials, or methods of construction. Even in these cases, the privity doctrine is slowly disappearing.

Acceptance

Another defense which still has some vitality is the "acceptance doctrine". As stated in § 30.02(d), the defendant will be relieved if he can show that the injury was caused by some subsequent intervening instrumentality. Many earlier cases relieved contractors from liability for losses or injuries which occurred after the building had been accepted by the owner. In such cases, the defense of acceptance was based upon the owner's negligence in accepting a defective structure. The longer the time gap between completion of the project and the injury, the more difficult it is to show that the injury was substantially caused by the contractor, subcontractor, or design professional. Too many other factors may have entered the picture. The plaintiff has a more difficult time proving by preponderance of the evidence that the substantial cause of his injury was negligence of the contractor. While the acceptance device is somewhat stronger than the privity defense, it, too, is weakening and is likely to disappear.

Contributory Negligence

If the plaintiff is guilty of contributory negligence, and this negligence was a substantial cause of the injury, he is generally barred from recovery. There are some specialized statutes which provide that contributory negligence is not a bar or, if it is proven, it simply reduces the amount of recovery. As has been noted, contributory negligence is not a bar to an injured employee in a workmen's compensation action.

Assumption of Risk

Assumption of risk is sometimes asserted as a defense in construction project accidents. If the defendant can establish that the plaintiff voluntarily assumed the risk of the injury which resulted, he will have a defense unless the action is based upon workmen's compensation. One interesting case involving the assumption of risk was Demarest v. T. C. Bateson Construction Co., 370 F.2d 281 (10th Cir. 1966). In this case, the employee of the subcontractor sued the prime contractor for injuries suffered in a fall at the site. The plaintiff had been sent to the attic area to assist in the installation of air conditioning units. The floor of the attic was composed of "a rigid decking of expanded metal mesh, suspended some 20–25 feet above the main floor. Running the length of this decking were five parallel gaps or openings, each about two feet wide and separated by uniform intervals". The employee complained to his foreman about the dangers posed by the openings, and asked that they be covered. Nevertheless he crawled upon a scaffold, worked for two or three hours, and then fell.

The court held that the prime contractor owed the plaintiff employee a duty to provide him a safe place to work, and that he negligently breached that duty. Since the accident occurred in New Mexico, the federal court applied New Mexico law. The trial court ruled that the plaintiff had assumed the risk, and would not submit this question to the jury.

From the plaintiff's own testimony, it was clear that he knew he was engaged in dangerous work and that he fully appreciated the danger of going up in the attic with the openings mentioned. The plaintiff contended that the fact that he knew and appreciated the risk should not bar recovery because "he was economically coerced into assuming it, i.e., he either had to work in the attic or 'go home' ". The court was sympathetic to the contention that there was a type of economic coercion, and not a free assumption of the risk. However, they felt bound by New Mexico law, which does not recognize economic coercion as bearing on the question of voluntariness in an employment relationship. Only if the employee complains, and relies upon the employer's promise to repair, can he avoid the defense of assumption of risk.

The court noted that the coercion, if there were any, did not come from the defendant, since the plaintiff worked for a subcontractor and not for the defendant prime contractor. The court held that the trial judge was correct in not submitting the assumption of risk issue to the jury and in deciding the matter in favor of the defendant prime contractor.

The *Demarest* case might have come out a different way in other jurisdictions. However, assumption of risk may bar recovery if it is established that the plaintiff voluntarily consented to assume the particular risk which caused his injury.

Independent Contractor Rule

Another defense often used in construction contracts is the "independent contractor rule." Subject to a number of important exceptions, the hirer of an independent contractor is not liable for the negligent acts of the independent contractor. See the discussion of this doctrine in § 30.08(c).

Statute of Limitations

Another defense frequently asserted is the statute of limitations. By law, certain legal actions must be commenced within a specified period, or else the right of legal action is lost. The purpose of such a rule is to avoid the difficulty of defending a case when the witnesses have died or are no longer available, and when the evidence is difficult to collect because of the passage of time. Its positive purpose is to encourage people to commence litigation when the trial can be reasonably efficient. Also such statutes are designed to put an end to potential litigation and to permit persons to be secure in the knowledge that after a certain period of time they will not be sued. See § 1.04 for a discussion of this subject.

Generally the period is longer in contract actions than in tort actions. Sometimes a plaintiff can sue either in tort or contract. For example, a client may be able to sue his architect or engineer for negligent design (tort) or breach of contract based upon an implied promise to use due care in design. While there may be advantages in suing in a tort action, a tort claim may be barred by the statute of limitations, while a contract claim may not be.

It is often difficult to determine when the time period commences. In a construction accident case, it could begin when the faulty work is done, when the work is accepted, when the loss occurred, or when the plaintiff knew, or should have known, of the loss. Much depends upon the language of the statute, and the judicial attitude toward the statutes of limitation. Some courts seem to be reluctant to use the statute to bar a valid claim, and they use considerable ingenuity to avoid the statute.

The Illinois Supreme Court in Rozny v. Marnul, reproduced at § 30.04(h) held that the statute of limitations in an action against a surveyor commenced at the time the surveyor's error was discovered or when it should have been discovered.

There have been some recent legislative changes which have shortened the period of limitations, or which have specified the period begins to run when the defective work has been done or accepted. These changes are designed to protect design professionals and contractors from claims made after the project is completed.

(F) TWO CASE HISTORIES

West v. Atkinson Construction Co., 251 Cal.App.2d 296, 59 Cal. Rptr. 286 (1967) involved an action by an injured employee of a subcontractor against the prime contractor who had been engaged by the State of California to construct a road. The plaintiff's employer had been hired to install girders for an overpass. The plaintiff was working on top of a "float" or hanging scaffolding at the time of the accident. A crane operated by the plaintiff's employer was rearranging some hinge plates attached to girders for the overpass. The negligently operated crane cut the float in two, causing the plaintiff to fall. None of the employees of the prime contractor were involved in this aspect of the project, nor had they played any part in the installation of the girders.

The prime contractor asserted that he was not liable because the injury was caused by the negligence of a subcontractor who was an independent contractor. The defendant prime contractor moved for a summary judgment in order to avoid the jury. The trial court and the California District Court of Appeals agreed that the independent contractor rule gave the prime contractor a defense.

The court would not apply the recognized exception to the independent contractor rule relating to inherently dangerous work, and would not apply other exceptions to the independent contractor rule.

The plaintiff asserted that a California safety statute required that the employer furnish a safe place for all employees engaged in the project. The court held that such a general obligation would not make the prime contractor liable to the injured plaintiff.

The court also rejected contentions by the plaintiff that the prime contractor had breached his prime contract obligation to take all reasonable measures to protect the life and health of employees on the job. The court held that the injured employee was not a third party beneficiary of any such promise made by the prime contractor to the state. The language of the court reflected a feeling that third party actions brought by injured workers are windfalls and should not be granted too liberally. The court stated that considering the activity in question to be an exception to the independent contractor rule would:

> . . . create an extension of the exceptions to the general rule of nonliability and would effectually make the owner-general contractor an insurer providing the employees of subcontractors double coverage. Such employees already receive workmen's compensation, and, generally speaking, workmen's compensation benefits are those which the state seeks to afford every workman. Why should the employee of the independent contractor recover greater benefits than the employee of the general contractor?

On its face, the opinion in the *West* case would seem to make it difficult for an injured employee of a subcontractor to use a violation of a general safety statute or the breach of a contract promise as the basis for recovery against the prime contractor. However, there was no proof that safety orders or contract obligations had been violated.

Six days after the opinion of the California Intermediate Appellate Court in the *West* case, the Supreme Court of California handed down their opinion in Alber v. Owens, 66 Cal.2d 790, 427 P.2d 781, 59 Cal.Rptr. 117 (1967). (The close proximity of the dates of the opinions indicate that it is likely that neither court knew of the opinion by the other court. The cases are discussed not to evaluate the effect of a subsequent opinion of the highest appellate court upon the opinion of an intermediate appellate court, but simply to show the differing attitudes of two courts toward employment accidents.)

In *Alber,* the plaintiff was the president and co-owner of a cement subcontractor for an apartment project. The subcontractor was a small company and the plaintiff often worked on jobs. The defendants were the parties who owned the land, developed it and acted as general contractors for the project.

The plaintiff on the day of the accident was assisting a laborer employed by the plaintiff's company. The laborer needed some tin snips to cut wire mesh. The plaintiff brought them to him on the second story of the apartment building. Both men then started to cut the mesh and nail it to the platform. In the course of this work the plaintiff fell off the balcony and suffered serious injuries. The plaintiff predicated his claim against the owner-prime contractor on the defendant's statutory violations in failing to provide guard rails on the second story platform.

The Supreme Court had no difficulty placing liability upon the defendant. It stated:

> . . . the record before us establishes a duty on the part of defendants respectively to furnish plaintiff a safe place to work, either on the theory that as a result of an invitor-invitee relationship they owed him a common law duty to provide him with a safe place to work or to warn him of dangers not obvious . . . or on the theory that they were employers within the meaning of the Labor Code (§ 6304) and therefore under a non-delegable duty to comply with the applicable safety provisions found therein.

The court unhesitatingly extended the protection of the statute to an employee of a subcontractor and would not permit the prime contractor-owner to assert the independent contractor rule as a defense.

The principal argument made by the defendant was that the plaintiff himself was an employer and had a duty to provide a safe place. Since he did not do so, he was guilty of contributory negligence and barred from recovery. The court rejected this contention and in doing so noted that the provisions relating to safety expressed in the Labor Code were part of a broad legislative program "designed to improve the position of the working man." The court stated that the statutory safety provisions directed "the employer to furnish a safe place of employment and forbade him to permit or require an employee to be in any unsafe place of employment".

The court also noted that construction safety orders imposed by the Division of Industrial Safety imposed specific duties such as requiring that railings be provided on all built up scaffolds, runways, ramps, etc. The court stated that violation of such a statute was negligence *per se* if the plaintiff was in the class intended to be protected and the harm which occurred is of the type intended to be prevented.

The court felt that safety in the construction industry required a broad statutory definition of an employer. But because of the many small subcontractors often engaged in a construction project, there are likely to be a number of construction workers who could fall within the employer category. Holding that their failure to comply would be contributory negligence barring their recovery would deny protection, according to the court, to a significant number of workers engaged in the project. The court stated that:

> Such elimination of employer's liability would remove a great incentive to assume seriously the responsibilities for safety imposed by statute. We believe it would constitute a regression in the advances made by legislatures and courts in the past half century to correct one of the

chief reproaches to the law, the uncompensated industrial injury.

Finally, the court stated that, as a practical matter, the general contractor is in the best position to coordinate the work and provide expensive safety features that protect employees on the project. The court noted that often subcontractors and supervisory employees are aware of safety violations, but they are unable to rectify the situation themselves, or are in too poor an economic position to compel their superiors to do so.

The court concluded by stating that the prime contractor was in the best position to make sure that such safety regulations were followed, and they would not deny recovery to an injured employee simply because he was also an employer along the chain of prime and subcontractors.

In the *Alber* case there was a clear violation of the statute relating to guard rails. There was no statutory violation in the *West* case. In the *Alber* case the defendant was the owner-prime contractor, while in the *West* case the defendant was simply the prime contractor. These distinguishing aspects taken aside, it is still apparent that there is a different attitude expressed by the Supreme Court of California in the *Alber* case from the attitude of the District Court of Appeals (the intermediate appellate court) in the *West* case. The District Court of Appeals was much more willing to accord a defense to the prime contractor based upon the independent contractor rule. This court was concerned with the absence of direct fault on the part of the prime contractor. It would not look to liability based upon who can best afford to pay, or who was in the best position to comply with the requirements. Also, the attitude of the court expressed in the *West* opinion was that workmen's compensation laws are adequate and giving the injured employee an additional negligence claim against the third party is providing him with a windfall.

The California Supreme Court was much more concerned with extending as much protection as possible to employees on a construction project. They were willing to extend this liability to the prime contractor, on the theory that he is more likely to be financially responsible, more likely to have adequate public liability insurance and ought to be given primary responsibility during the project. Also the court did not seem to be concerned with the possibility that holding the prime contractor would give the employer of the subcontractor a windfall above and beyond his workmen's compensation recovery.

Generalizations in this area are perilous because there are so many contradictory court opinions even within a particular state. However, if there can be any trend discerned from case opinions, it would appear that the philosophy reflected in *Alber* is more likely to be dominant than the philosophy in *West*. While there are undoubtedly many cases which still reflect the attitude of the court in the *West* case, the trend seems to be toward expanded rights to injured parties on construction projects to recover for injuries from third party defendants, such as prime contractors and owners in the case of an injured employee of a subcontractor, and owners and design professionals in the case of an injury to the employee of a prime contractor.

SECTION 30.09 DAMAGE TO PROPERTY: EXPANSION OF POTENTIAL DEFENDANTS

During the course of a construction project, or after its completion, a number of persons may suffer property damage. An adjacent land owner may find that his soil support has been weakened or eliminated by the excavation for the construction project. The owner himself may suffer property damage during the course of construction. The ultimate buyers of the project may suffer property damage after they have purchased the property, because of defective design, materials, or construction methods.

The party who suffers the loss looks for as many defendants as possible. He may not believe that he can recover against all the defendants, because the duties owed by the defendants may vary. However, his primary concern is to name as many defendants as possible, so that he does not face the situation of obtaining a judgment against an insolvent defendant. His search for defendants may also be for the purpose of finding a defendant who will be within the jurisdiction of a convenient court.

Legal results vary, depending upon the type of injury. As indicated, the contractors' defenses of privity and acceptance by the owner are diminishing in significance, when the cause of action is based upon personal injury or death. However, these defenses may still be successful when the injury is pecuniary or economic. Injuries to property fall between personal injuries and pecuniary loss cases.

The law generally gives the injured party a liberal range of potential defendants in the property damage cases. Also, the necessity for showing negligence may not be as great in property damage cases as it is in pecuniary loss cases. For example, the owner of adjacent unimproved land is entitled to a soil support without having to show negligence by the excavator. Nor will the owner of the construction project be able to rely in such a case upon the independent contractor rule. The owner of the construction project has an absolute liability to preserve the soil support of unimproved adjacent land.

As discussed in §§ 30.02 and 30.06, two of the principal problems faced by plaintiffs who attempt to shift their loss to a defendant have been lack of contract privity and the necessity of showing negligence.

In the products liability field, privity has more or less disappeared. Manufacturers of mass produced goods have been held liable in many cases where there has been a showing that the injury resulted from defective goods, without any necessity to show negligence on the part of the manufacturer. While most of the cases where these doctrines have developed have involved harm to persons, there has been a tendency to apply these product liability rules to cases where the harm suffered has been injury to property, and, to a lesser degree, where there has been pecuniary loss.

An illustration of the use of product liability rules in construction cases is found in Kriegler v. Eichler Homes, Inc., 269 Adv.Cal. App. 224, 74 Cal.Rptr. 749 (1969). In this case, the defendant built and sold a large number of tract homes in 1951. In 1957, the plaintiff suffered property damage because of the failure of a radiant heating system to work properly. There was no contractual relationship between plaintiff and defendant, because the plaintiff had purchased the house from a party to whom the defendant had sold the house in 1952. The California District Court of Appeals affirmed a trial court judgment in favor of the plaintiff home owner against the defendant tract developer. This judgment held the defendant liable without any showing that the defendant had been negligent. The defendant according to the court, had impliedly warranted that the house was reasonably fit for its intended purpose. It is interesting to note that the court in the *Kriegler* case quoted extensively from Schipper v. Levitt & Sons, Inc., 44 N.J. 70, 207 A.2d 314 (1965), an action against a developer by a plaintiff who had suffered physical injury when excessively hot water came out of the tap. While most courts have struck down privity and many have imposed liability without fault where there has been physical injury, many of those courts have been reluctant to do so when the damage relates to harm to property or to pecuniary loss. However, the *Kriegler* case drew no such line. For another illustration of the application of product liability principles to tract home developments, review the *Avner* case, at § 13.07(k).

In Connor v. Great Western Savings and Loan Association, 69 Cal.2d 850, 73 Cal.Rptr. 369, 447 P.2d 609 (1968), the purchasers of tract homes suffered losses from cracking caused by negligently designed foundations that could not withstand the expansion and contraction of adobe soil. Among a number of defendants, the plaintiffs sued the savings and loan association that had played a large part in financing the development. The Supreme Court of California stated:

> . . . Great Western became much more than a lender content to lend money at interest on the security of real property. It became an active participant in a home construction enterprise. It had the right to exercise extensive control of the enterprise. Its financing, which made the enterprise possible, took on ramifications beyond the domain of the usual money lender. It received not only interest on its construction loans, but also substantial fees for

making them, a 20 percent capital gain for 'warehousing' the land, and protection from loss of profits in the event individual home buyers sought permanent financing elsewhere.

The court held that the savings and loan association was negligent, because it knew that the developers were inexperienced and operating on a dangerously thin capitalization. The court went on to state that the savings and loan knew, or should have known, that damage "from attempts to cut corners in construction was a risk reasonably to be foreseen." The court went on to state:

> It knew or should have known of the expansive soil problems and yet it failed to require soil tests, to examine foundation plans, to recommend changes in the prepackaged plans and specifications, or to recommend changes in the foundations during construction. It made no attempt to discover gross structural defects that it could have discovered by reasonable inspection and that it would have required Conejo to remedy. It relied for protection solely upon building inspectors with whom it had had no experience to enforce a building code with the provisions of which it was ignorant.

The court concluded by holding that the savings and loan association had a duty to the buyers of the homes to exercise reasonable care to protect them from damages caused by major structural defects.

(Much of the sting of the *Connor* decision was removed by the enactment of § 3434 of the California Civil Code in 1969.)

Many of the cases mentioned in this section were decided by California courts. Other state courts may not have reached the same results as did the California courts. However, California has been a leading jurisdiction, and it is likely that other jurisdictions will follow the lead of the California courts in rejecting privity as a defense, and in using the analogy of manufacturer's liability in the sale of tract homes.

Sometimes property damage results from acts of nature, or from fires. Such losses are usually covered by insurance. Insurance companies that pay for such losses often try to find someone whose negligence has caused the loss. This is often true when fires result, or if losses due to natural events could have been avoided by the use of reasonable care. An insurance company is usually not permitted to sue its policy holder for such losses. (If the policy holder sets the fire, he cannot collect.) However, when the insurance company pays an insurance claim, it may succeed to the rights of the person to whom the insurance proceeds have been paid. If the fire is caused by a negligent subcontractor, the insurance company may try to recover its losses from the subcontractor. Some insurance policies provide that the insurance company may not recover in such cases. It is important for those who participate in the construction project to know whether they can be subjected to these claims by the insurance carrier, and whether their own insurance covers such liability.

SECTION 30.10 PECUNIARY LOSSES

Usually pecuniary losses result from increased expenses of performance, loss of use of property, liability to third parties, and diminished or lost profits. This section examines attempts by parties suffering pecuniary losses to transfer them to the person causing them, where there is no direct contractual relationship. For example, one separate contractor may claim that he suffered pecuniary loss because of the acts of another separate contractor. The subcontractor may want to transfer losses which he claims were caused by the owner or the design professional. In addition to the direct parties to the construction contract, there are other potential claimants, such as a bonding company, a lender, and patent holders. The potential defendants in such pecuniary loss cases, in addition to contractors, design professionals, and owners, could include manufacturers of products and materials, distributors of products and materials, and lending institutions such as banks and savings and loan associations.

(A) MISREPRESENTATION

One basis for liability is misrepresentation. The plaintiff may assert that the defendant, usually someone who is in the business of making investigations or representations, has misrepresented certain facts upon which he has relied. For example, a subcontractor may claim that the soils engineer has misrepresented the soil conditions in the report submitted by the soils engineer to the owner or to a prime contractor. The first hurdle which the claimant must overcome in such cases is the absence of privity between himself and the soils engineer. In some cases, privity remains a bar, especially if the action is based upon warranty rather than negligence. The privity doctrine still has vitality in pecuniary loss cases. Even if the claimant can overcome the absence of privity, he will usually have to show that the misrepresentation was a negligent one, rather than merely an inaccurate one. Also, he will usually have to show that he reasonably relied upon the representation of the soils engineer.

In many cases, soil information is given to contractors with specific disclaimers. This has been discussed in detail in § 22.05. The disclaimer is usually made as part of the contract relationships between the parties making the representations, such as the soils engineer, and the person who pays for the work done by the soils engineer, (the owner or prime contractor). The disclaimer usually negates the element of reliance needed for misrepresentation.

For a case involving misrepresentation based upon a survey, see Rozny v. Marnul, reproduced at § 30.04(h).

(B) THIRD PARTY BENEFICIARY

Sometimes a person who is not a party to a contract may be able to recover damages caused by a breach of that contract. For example, a prime or subcontractor who may have difficulty recovering from a soils tester based upon misrepresentation, may be able to persuade a court that he is a "beneficiary" of the contract between the soils tester and the person who has hired him to make the test. To accomplish this the plaintiff will have to show that the breached contract was intended for his benefit or was intended to confer a legal claim upon him. (§ 18.09(a) examines this doctrine in the context of a surety bond.)

In the construction project, there are often many contracting parties. Sometimes one contracting party attempts to transfer his loss to another party with whom he has no contractual relations. For example, a subcontractor may attempt to recover from the owner, the design professional or another subcontractor. A separate contractor may attempt to recover from another separate contractor, or from a subcontractor of a separate contractor. Generally, courts have held that the absence of a contractual relationship will be a bar in such cases. However, there have been some cases where the plaintiff has successfully invoked the third party beneficiary doctrine, and escaped "no privity of contract" defense.

In Aetna Casualty and Surety Co. v. Kemp Smith Co., 208 A.2d 737 (Dist. of Col. Ct. of App. 1965) a sub-sub-subcontractor recovered from a sub-contractor on the basis of the latter's promise to the prime contractor to pay for all supplies and materials. In another case, a separate contractor was successful in his suit against another separate contractor, based upon the latter's promise to the owner to perform in accordance with a certain schedule. In this case, Visintine & Co. v. New York, Chicago, St. Louis R. Co., 79 Ohio Abs. 753, 155 N.E.2d 682 (1958) affirmed 169 Ohio St. 505, 160 N.E.2d 311 (1959) the separate contractor could not bring a contract action against the owner, because the owner in this case, the State of Ohio, had sovereign immunity and could not be sued for breach of contract.

Some public entities are precluded from incurring bonded indebtedness. To avoid these limitations, often such entities create quasi-public corporations to build projects. The land is leased to the newly created quasi-public "authority", and the latter enters into the building contract. After the project is completed, the building is usually leased to the public entity.

Such an arrangement was used in the Cox v. Fremont County Public Building Authority, 415 F.2d 882 (10th Cir.1969). When the skylight leaked, both the county and the building authority created by the county sued the contractor and his surety. In holding that the county could sue both the contractor and the surety, the court stated:

> The obligation for the benefit of the County is inherent in the contract documents and the surrounding circumstances. Under the Leasehold Agreement, the Authority's obligation to the County to construct the courthouse building was recognized, and the plans and specifications for the building were subject to the approval of the County. Under the Construction Agreement, the County had the right to approve the form of the performance bond. The contractor was not entitled to final payment until completion of the building and final acceptance of work by the Authority, the County and the architects. The land belonged to the County and was leased to the Authority to have the courthouse built and to lease the land and building back to the County. Thus, the agreements and the circumstances show that the benefit of faithful performance of the Construction Agreement and the bond were intended to flow to the County. Such contractual benefit to the property owner is enforceable by him.

If recovery as a third party beneficiary is not available, the injured party must sue the person with whom he made the contract. Often the latter brings a legal action against the person who owed him the contractual duty. For example, if the design professional is unreasonably dilatory in approval of shop drawings, the subcontractor may have an action against the prime contractor, the prime contractor against the owner, and the owner against the design professional. Permitting a direct action by the subcontractor against the design professional can avoid multiplicity of actions, and save time and expense for all the intervening parties. This is one justification for permitting an action based upon the concept that the contract breached is for the benefit of the third party. While intention to benefit is perhaps a legal fiction, it can prove useful. Ultimately, the third party beneficiary theory may be discarded in these situations in favor of a tort principle. As between the design professional who is dilatory in approving shop drawings, and the injured subcontractor, the loss should be borne by the design professional.

Generally, it has been difficult to invoke the third party beneficiary doctrine in these types of cases. However, there is a slight movement toward applying it, especially where the plaintiff would not have an adequate remedy against the party with whom he had contracted, or if a direct right to sue would avoid circuity of action.

(C) INTERFERENCE WITH CONTRACT

"Interference with contract" is another theory which occasionally has been used to justify a recovery for pecuniary loss where there is no contractual relationship between the party suffering the loss and the party who caused the loss. For example, if an adjacent landowner prevented the contractor from entering the construction project site, the latter would have an action against the adjacent landowner. Precluding entry would interfere with his contract. Using the same reasoning, a subcontractor might have a direct action against the owner if the owner breached his contract with the prime contractor, and if this breach caused the subcontractor additional expense.

However, courts have generally required that interference with a contract be intentional, and not merely negligent. Also, interference with the contract may be privileged. For example, one of the purposes of having an architect during the construction project is to provide professional advice to the owner. If the architect advised the owner to terminate the contractor's performance because the latter had not been furnishing sufficient manpower and was falling behind on his schedule, this advice would be an intentional interference with the contractual rights of the contractor.

However, the purpose and function of the architect is to perform this function, and his interference may be sanctioned by contractual provisions which give him this right or, even in their absence, by classifying his advice as privileged. He should be able to advise the owner without risking action being brought against him by the contractor for interference with the contractor's contractual rights.

However such privilege, whether conferred by law or contract, must not be abused. If the interference with the contractor's rights were motivated by malice or bad faith, then the architect would be liable for any pecuniary loss caused the contractor by his interference. The same reasoning would apply to architects' determinations that certain amounts of money were due as progress payments, or that certain work had or had not been completed in accordance with the contract requirements. This has been discussed in § 27.11 dealing with design professional decisions.

(D) ASSIGNMENT

Sometimes the party suffering pecuniary loss can obtain an assignment of the rights of a person who had entered into a contract with the person who caused the loss. For example, if a subcontractor has suffered losses due to the dilatory conduct or interference by the owner or the design professional, it may be possible for the prime contractor to assign to the subcontractor whatever rights the contractor has based upon his contract with the owner. Sometimes the prime contractor may bring an action for the benefit of the subcontractor who has actually suffered the loss.

(E) PATENT AND COPYRIGHT LAW

Patent and copyright laws may furnish the basis for a legal action against a person with whom the party instituting the action has no contractual relationship. Such laws give protection to persons who own the rights to inventions or processes, or to written materials such as plans and literature. Infringement of patents and copyrights give the party whose rights have been infringed a civil action against the infringer. In Baut v. Pethick Construction Co., 262 F.Supp. 350 (Dist.Ct.Pa.1966), the owner of a patent for the construction of stained glass panels instituted an infringement action against a general contractor and a subcontractor who had used his patented invention in the construction of a church. The general contractor and subcontractor instituted a cross action against the architect who had drawn the plans and specifications. The court held that all three had infringed the patent.

For a more detailed discussion of patent and copyright see Chapter 40.

(F) MECHANICS' LIENS

Another statutory method of transferring a loss is the mechanics' lien. An unpaid supplier or subcontractor may be able to assert a mechanics' lien upon the land and structure which his work has benefited. See § 24.07.

SECTION 30.11 CONTRACT CONNECTED PARTIES

In construction projects, there are a number of contracts entered into by participating parties. There is usually an agreement between the owner and the prime contractor or the separate contractors, between prime contractors and subcontractors, between the contractors and their suppliers, between the owner and the design professional, and frequently between the design professional and his consultants. Sometimes contracting parties make claims against one another based upon breach of contract. In such cases there is no privity problem. However, there are other legal questions which may arise.

(A) PERFECTING CLAIMS FOR BREACH OF CONTRACT

A party seeking to sue for breach of contract must show the existence of a valid contract. The requisites for formation of contract were discussed in Chapter 2. The claimant must establish, usually by interpretation, the rights and duties of the parties. Next, he will attempt to establish that he has substantially performed, and that any conditions have occurred or been excused. Contracts frequently contain clauses which set forth conditions which must occur before claims can be collected by judicial action.

Time to Bring Legal Action

In § 30.08(e), statutes of limitation were discussed. Sometimes contracts contain clauses which attempt to shorten the statutory period for the institution of legal action. Such provisions are generally upheld if they are reasonable.

Notice of Claim: Surety Bonds

Contracts frequently state that before claims may be sued upon the party claiming the damage must give a written notice indicating the nature of the claim and the fact that he intends to make a claim for damages. Sometimes such requirements will be excused, if it is clear from all the facts that the owner was well aware of the acts which gave rise to the claim and that the other party intended to make a claim for damages.

In making claims upon surety bonds, it is often required that the party making the claim give notice to the surety bond company within a specified time, or a reasonable time if no time is specified. Also, bonds may require that the obligee (the person to whom the bond is written) institute an action against the primary party before the surety can be held. In such situations, the surety's obligation may be to pay any judgment which is obtained against the person behind whom the surety is standing. Surety bonds often contain clauses requiring an action be brought on a bond in a shorter time than the normal period of limitations.

Arbitration

Arbitration is one of the most important conditions which may have to be met before resort to the courts is permitted. See Chapter 28. A properly drafted arbitration clause makes arbitration a condition precedent to any legal action. Parties may, by their conduct, give up this condition. Illustrations of waivers of arbitration could be instituting a legal action on the part of one party, and a failure to demand that arbitration be held on the part of the other.

Statutory Conditions

As mentioned, the law usually sets a time limit for the commencement of litigation. In construction contract litigation, two other requirements may have to be met before the courts can be used. First, many states require that a contractor have a valid license before he can use the courts to collect his claims. Licensing in general will be discussed in Chapter 31. Second, if the party seeking assistance of the court is a corporation organized under the laws of a state other than the state where the law suit is being brought, the foreign corporation frequently must register and pay fees to the state whose courts it seeks to use, before it can sue in those courts.

(B) TORT OR CONTRACT

Sometimes a claimant may have an action either in contract or tort. An illustration of this would be a claim against an architect or engineer by the owner, based upon the design professional's failure to use due care in the performance of his professional duties. Since there is a contractual relationship between the design professional and the owner, the owner can sue for breach of contract. However, in some cases he may also be able to sue for tort. This is more likely to be the case if the breach of contract is a negligent act, and if the damage incurred is injury to person or to property. However, even in cases where there is only pecuniary loss, it may be possible to sue in tort as well as contract.

(C) FOLLOWING PLANS AS A DEFENSE

A defense sometimes asserted in an action based upon breach of contract is that the contractor followed the plans and specifications, and that any difficulty which resulted should not be chargeable to him. Suppose some aspect of the project does not work out as planned and the owner asserts that the contractor should pay for any cost of correction or diminished value. An illustration of this problem occurred in Kurland v. United Pacific Insurance Co., 251 Cal.App. 2d 112, 59 Cal.Rptr. 258 (1967). In this case, the contract involved the construction of an apartment building in Nevada. The defendant was the surety for a subcontractor who had undertaken to install an air conditioning system in an apartment building. The plans and specifications designated the equipment to be used as well as stating:

> System is to establish at least a 30 degree variation from outside temperature for cooling and a 50 degree variation from outside temperature for heating.

The subcontractor performed in accordance for the plans and specifications, but the air conditioning system did not function as required. It was determined that the subcontractor had followed the plans and specifications and installed equipment in a workmanlike manner, but the system did not function because it had been incorrectly and inadequately designed. In affirming a judgment for the surety of the subcontractor, the court stated:

> Since the plans and specifications were prepared by the owners' architect and not by the subcontractor, and since the subcontractor undertook to do the work in accordance with his specific proposal, we cannot reasonably conclude that the subcontractor assumed responsibility for the adequacy

of the plans and specifications to meet the purpose of achieving a '30 degree variation from outside temperature for cooling'. The language upon which the plaintiff relies constituted a statement of the purpose sought to be achieved by means of the owners' plans and specifications rather than an undertaking on the part of the subcontractor of responsibility for the adequacy of such plans and specifications as the design of a system capable of producing the desired result.

The plaintiff pointed to the provision in the specifications under which the contractor would guarantee that the equipment installed would satisfactorily cool and heat the building, and that if it did not do so the contractor would remedy the defect. This provision had been incorporated by reference by the subcontract. Despite this, the court interpreted the guarantee as an undertaking on the part of the subcontractor that he would work as effectively as possible to achieve the desired results, rather than holding that the contractor had warranted the performance adequacy of contractually specified materials.

Another case involving the defense of compliance of plans and specifications was Havard v. Board of Supervisors, 220 Miss. 359, 70 So.2d 875 (1954). This was an action by the owner against the contractor and his surety, based upon a one year warranty provision covering defects in workmanship. An installed floor buckled from dampness within the one year period. The Supreme Court of Mississippi reversed a judgment in favor of the owner, because it had not been established whether the buckling was due to defective design, defective material, or improper workmanship. The court also stated that if the contractor had followed the plans and specifications, he would be given a defense unless it were shown that he was negligent or that he had made a guarantee that the design was suitable. See also Luria v. U. S., reproduced in part at § 29.04(a), for a similar result in a soils case.

Suppose the contractor knew, or should have known, that the plans and specifications were defective. In such a case, the contractor should inform the owner or his design professional that he does not think the design is proper. It is arguable that the design is not his business, and that he has no duty to inform the owner of any design defects which appear to him. However, it would seem to be better practice to point out design defects to reduce the risk of having assumed responsibility for defective plans and specifications.

(D) WARRANTY CLAUSES

Often it is difficult to establish the cause of the defect or the failure of the project to meet specified performance standards. Was there poor workmanship, defective material, improper construction methods or improper design? Usually the burden of establishing that the contractor is responsible is upon the owner, and it is a burden which is often difficult to sustain.

One method of avoiding this difficult burden of proof is to specify that the contractor will have the burden of establishing that the defect which results was caused by design, and not by poor workmanship or material.

Insertion of a warranty clause is another method of coping with this problem. Warranty clauses were discussed in § 24.04, in the context of the legal effect of making a final payment, issuing a certificate of completion or moving into the project. A warranty clause in that setting is a method of insuring that defects which appear after completion are the responsibility of the contractor, and that certificates of completion, final payment, and moving into the project do not automatically absolve the contractor from responsibility.

Warranty clauses can serve the additional function of eliminating the necessity to establish that the defect was caused by the contractor's noncompliance with the plans and specifications rather than design. Also, a warranty clause, if drafted carefully, can place the risk of even defective design upon the contractor by clearly obligating the contractor to repair *any* defects which appear after completion. The warranty clause that does not clearly place this risk upon the contractor is not likely to succeed. This is illustrated by the *Havard* case which involved a clause covering only defects resulting from defective workmanship. Courts are not anxious to place the risk of defective design upon the contractor.

Warranty clauses can have unexpected results. In Independent Con. Sch. Dist. # 24 v. Carlstrom, 277 Minn. 117, 151 N.W.2d 784 (1967) a contract for the construction of a school contained a provision stating that the contractor would remedy any defects which appeared within a year from the date of substantial completion. Defects traceable to poor workmanship and material appeared more than a year after substantial completion. The court held that the warranty provision constituted the exclusive remedy for subsequent appearing defects, and that the contractor was not responsible for even defects relating to material and workmanship which appeared after the expiration of the one year warranty period.

Warranty clauses generally are not intended to limit the remedy for defective workmanship and materials to those defects which appear within the warranty period. The *Carlstrom* case appears to give the warranty clause such an unintended effect. If the owner wishes to be able to hold the contractor responsible for defects due to poor workmanship or material which occur after the warranty period, it is advisable to make this clear in the warranty clause. For example, liability can include *any* defect which appears within the warranty period and defects which are traceable to poor workmanship and material which occur at *any* time after completion.

It will be more difficult to recover for defects which appear a long time after completion, because it will be difficult to establish noncompliance. However, it is probably better to retain the right to hold the contractor accountable for those defects relating to workmanship and material that occur after expiration of the warranty period.

(E) SUBCONTRACTS

Often the subcontracts are brief, and incorporate by reference many of the provisions of the prime contract. For example, the prime contract may contain a provision requiring that disputes be arbitrated, that the owner disclaims any responsibility for inaccurate soil tests furnished, that the sub indemnify the prime (see § 30.13), as well as other provisions. Often the subcontract incorporates these provisions by merely referring to the prime contract, without expressly including them in the subcontract. Subcontractors should check the provisions of the prime contract when provisions are incorporated by reference. Unfortunately, subcontractors do not always do this, and may find that they have agreed to provisions in the prime contract of which they were unaware at the time of signing.

Sometimes subcontractors are given judicial protection from this burden. Unless the provisions of the prime contract are clearly incorporated into the subcontract, it may be held that the reference to the prime contract was merely for information, but did not become part of the obligation between subcontractor and prime contractor. Nevertheless, in many situations subcontractors will be held to provisions in the prime contract.

In Beacon Construction Co. v. Prepakt Concrete Co., 375 F.2d 977 (1st Cir.1967), Prepakt entered into a contract with Beacon under which Prepakt would do piling work in connection with the construction of a postal facility which was being built by Beacon. There was no arbitration clause in the contract between Prepakt and Beacon. However, that contract stated that Beacon intended to assign the entire post office job to another contractor. If such an assignment were made, the terms and conditions in the contract under which the assignment were made would become the contract between Prepakt and the assignee.

Beacon assigned the prime contract and the subcontracts to Ameco, including the subcontract with Prepakt. The agreement between Beacon and Ameco contained an arbitration clause.

When a dispute arose, Prepakt sued both Beacon and Ameco, and Beacon insisted that the dispute be resolved by arbitration. Beacon contended that Prepakt agreed in advance to any general terms and conditions contained in any agreement Beacon might make with Beacon's assignee of the post office contract.

This argument convinced the trial court, but not the Circuit Court of Appeals. It held that under the terms of the original agreement any assignment Beacon might make could not substantially change the subcontract. The court stated ". . . we cannot say that a provision requiring arbitration with an unknown party, as a precondition to suit, is so inconsequential a change in obligation as to be ignored".

In the *Prepakt* case, there was an attempt not merely to bind the subcontractor to clauses contained in the prime contract, but to bind the subcontractor to clauses which might be contained in a future prime contract. Fortunately, the subcontractor was not held to have assumed this risk.

Payments under subcontracts can cause legal problems. Often the subcontract specifies that payments to the subcontractor will be tied to payments to the prime. If possible, the prime will try to avoid paying the subs until he has been paid. Interpretation questions can arise relating to such payment provisions. Do they mean that the sub will be paid when the prime is paid, or only if the prime is paid? If the former, the provision affects only the time of payment and if the prime is not paid, he will still have to pay the sub. If the latter, the sub assumes the risk of not being paid unless the prime is paid. In order to avoid forfeitures, the judicial preference is the former interpretation. But, if the language chosen and the surrounding facts and circumstances show the intention was the latter, the sub will be held to assume the risk of not being paid unless the prime is paid.

International Erectors v. Wilhoit Steel Erectors and R. Serv., 400 F.2d 465 (5th Cir.1968) illustrates the complexity of the multi-party construction contract. The project involved construction of a plant for Sunbeam Electronics Company. Sunbeam contracted with a prime contractor, who subcontracted the work of fabricating and erecting the structural steel portion of the project to Southern Engineering. Southern, as subcontractor, sub-subcontracted the labor part of its undertaking to Wilhoit. Wilhoit sub-sub-subcontracted the labor work to International Erectors. International incurred delay damages because the steel had not been delivered as scheduled. International sued Wilhoit, the party with whom it made the contract, and sued Southern, one step removed on the contractual chain, claiming that it, International Erectors, was a third party beneficiary of the promise Southern had made to Wilhoit.

Southern was to supply the steel for the project. The contract between Wilhoit and International stated that International would supply the labor, and that Wilhoit's obligation was specified as "None". The court held that this indicated that Wilhoit was not responsible for the delivery of the steel. While it is true that Wilhoit was not going to supply the materials, it is plausible that in such a contract Wilhoit impliedly promised that the materials would be available when scheduled, even though Wilhoit was not obligated to supply the materials.

The court rejected the contention that Wilhoit, by virtue of a general clause under which it assumed Southern's obligations, had undertaken to be responsible in the event Southern did not deliver the structural steel as scheduled. The court also rejected the contention that it was inconceivable that an experienced steel erector would enter into an agreement to erect the steel for a large complicated building within thirty-five days without obtaining an assurance from the party with whom it dealt that the steel would be ready for erection as scheduled. In rejecting this, the court stated:

> Prudence and perhaps foresight might have insisted that a provision creating such an obligation be included in the written contract, but the written memorial of the parties' intention expressly and unequivocally negated any such obligation. This was an arms-length transaction between contractors of considerable experience in such matters and we cannot rewrite the contract just because one of the parties would in retrospection have written it differently.

After rejecting International's claim against Wilhoit, the court considered International's claim against Southern. Southern had promised to have the steel available by a certain time. Yet, Southern's promise had been to Wilhoit and not International. The court rejected International's claim against Southern, since it held that this promise was not made to International nor was it for International's benefit.

The end result is that, through judicial rigidity and careless contract making, International was held to have assumed the risk of delay damages caused by the steel not being at the site on schedule.

(F) CONSULTANT CONTRACTS

The design professional may be liable for the acts of his consultants, such as the landscape architect, the structural engineer or civil engineer. The design professional impliedly promises his client that all services will be performed properly. That the design professional may satisfy his obligations by obtaining others to perform normally does not relieve him from liability when these obligations are not performed properly. See § 9.02(a). If the client selects the consultant, the design professional may be absolved.

If the design professional is liable, he will usually have a valid claim against the consultant who has not performed properly. The design professional should insure that the consultant is obligated to him in the same manner as he is obligated to the owner. It would be unfortunate from the design professional's standpoint to find that he is responsible for certain nonperformance on the part of the consultant, and that the consultant has not promised him that he will perform these exact duties.

The design professional should evaluate the financial responsibility of his consultants. Having a good claim against the consultant may be meaningless if the consultant is not able to pay the claim. It may be important to require that the consultant carry adequate professional liability insurance. If the consultant is a small corporation, it may be necessary to bind the individual shareholders to the contract, so that they will be personally liable.

If the design professional wishes to escape responsibility for the work of his consultant, he should request that the client contract directly with the consultant, or obtain an agreement from the client to relieve the design professional of liability for mistakes of the consultant.

SECTION 30.12 CLAIMS AGAINST PUBLIC ENTITIES

The concept of sovereign immunity, established early in England and adopted in the United States, precluded any legal action against public bodies for either breach of contract or for tort claims. While the origin of the doctrine may have been in the ancient concept that the king can do no wrong, where it continues today, it is based upon the financial burden upon public entities if they are held accountable for injuries or losses caused by their contract breaches or by their negligent acts. Allowing an action against some public agencies permits judicial intrusion into the running of government. For example, the city of New York was sued by a woman who had requested police protection from a disappointed suitor. This protection was not provided, and the rejected suitor hired a thug to throw lye in the plaintiff's face. (After the assault, she was given round the clock protection for three and a half years.)

The New York Court of Appeals in Riss v. City of New York, 22 N.Y.2d 579, 240 N.E.2d 860, 293 N.Y.S.2d 897 (1968) granted immunity to the city and denied the plaintiff's claim. In doing so, the court stated:

> The amount of protection that may be provided is limited by the resources of the community and by a considered legislative-executive decision as to how those resources may be deployed. For the courts to proclaim a new and general duty of protection in the law of tort, even to those who may be the particular seekers of protection based on specific hazards, could and would inevitably determine how the limited police resources of the community should be allocated and without predictable limits. This is quite different from the predictable allocation of resources and liabilities when public hospitals, rapid transit systems, or even highways are provided.

While there has been a diminution of sovereign immunity, some courts feel imposition of liability on public agencies would violate the separation of powers between executive and judicial branches.

Sometimes cases have differentiated between public entities acting in their governmental capacity and acting in their proprietory capacity. For example, the government in fighting fires or doing police work is clearly acting in its governmental function and has been held immune. On the other hand, when the government has performed activities frequently performed by private bodies, it would be acting in its proprietory capacity, and amenable to legal action. Illustrations of these would be operation of hospitals, wharfing facilities, or amusement parks. As governments, especially local governments, have become more active and more varied in activity, the line between proprietory and governmental has become increasingly more difficult to draw.

At the federal level, Congress consented to being sued for breach of contract in 1887 by the Tucker Act. The Court of Claims hears these disputes. In the tort field, Congress passed the Federal Tort Claims Act in 1946, permitting lawsuits against the United States for certain types of legal wrongs. There are exceptions expressed in the statute, and there has been a considerable amount of litigation determining the extent of the government's liability for tort claims.

Those who advocate limitation of sovereign immunity contend that when a citizen is injured as the result of the negligent conduct of a public entity or persons for whom the entity is responsible, it is more just that the loss be shared by the taxpayers of the entity rather than borne entirely by the injured person.

While sovereign immunity is clearly weakening, claims against public entities are treated differently than claims against private persons.

Abolition of state sovereign immunity has moved slowly, and in narrow areas. But, within the past ten years, there has been a significant movement in state courts to abolish, or severely limit, the doctrine of sovereign immunity. In reaction to some of these decisions, some legislatures have enacted statutes which include a comprehensive set of rules for determining when the state can be sued, and when it cannot. Some statutes spell out defenses which the state may have when sued. For example, California enacted a statute which gave the state a defense if the trial judge found that the design was properly prepared and approved by designated state officials. In Cabell v. State of Calif., 67 Cal.2d 150, 430 P.2d 34, 60 Cal.Rptr. 476 (1967), a student dormitory resident put his hand through the glass pane in a lavatory door. The student sued the state, since the injury occurred in a state-constructed and owned dormitory. However, the state was given a defense based upon the statute. The court rejected the contention that the state knew that the glass was inadequate because other accidents had occurred after the dormitory had been constructed and prior to the occurrence of the injury sued upon.

This treatise has emphasized the increased participation of governmental authorities in the construction process. It is usually necessary to obtain a building permit before construction, and an occupancy permit after construction. Issuing a building permit may involve the approval of drawings and specifications, while an occupancy permit usually necessitates an inspection to insure compliance with building code standards.

Usually, when such permits are issued the issuing agency disclaims responsibility for any injuries or losses which may result because of faulty design or construction. Municipalities seek to avoid being sued by injured parties who claim that the city should have noticed the faulty design or failure of the project to conform to safety or health standards. Even if there is municipal immunity, generally municipalities seek to relieve themselves from any possible liability by disclaimers at the time such permits or approvals are given. Usually, they accomplish their purpose.

In addition to immunity problems, the procedures for making claims against public bodies are often complicated. Failure to comply can mean no recovery, even on a meritorious claim. There is great variation from state to state, but a few generalizations can be made.

Claims usually have to be presented to a legislative body of the local governmental unit before the claim can be taken to court. If a person intends to sue a city, typically that person will have to present the claim to the city council. If the city council denies the claim, then the claimant will have a specified time in which he can appeal the decision to either the regular courts, or to a court or agency with jurisdiction to hear these claims. There are usually shorter time limits for bringing legal actions against public agencies than against private parties.

What is the extent of sovereign immunity? Design professionals are frequently hired by public agencies to perform design or supervisory services for construction projects. If someone incurs a loss, or there is an injury during the course of the project, the injured party may try to recover from the design professional. The public agency may have sovereign immunity. This immunity sometimes extends to employees of the public agency, or the private contractor, and to private design professionals who may be retained by the public agency. If a person is sued, it may become important to ascertain whether the state agency is required to defend the action, or to indemnify the defendant for any loss he may suffer.

For a discussion of procedures in contract claims, review § 28.08 (b).

SECTION 30.13 RISK SHARING AND SHIFTING

Generally, persons who suffer physical injuries or death as a result of defective design, materials, equipment or construction methods are likely to recover from someone for their loss. Persons who suffer pecuniary loss may have somewhat greater difficulty, but, on the whole, they will also recover for any loss which may result from similar causes. More important is the question of which of all the parties potentially liable will have to ultimately bear the loss. Also, can these risks be transferred, either through contract or quasi-contract?

(A) CONTRIBUTION

How has the law dealt with multiple defendants? Early English cases held that two parties who were jointly liable would not have any right of contribution against the other. For example, if there were two defendants, and both were liable for the commission of a joint wrong, neither party could look to the other to share the financial burden of the plaintiff's loss. This meant the plaintiff could collect from either party. And even if the party selected by the plaintiff had to pay the entire judgment, he would have no action against the other defendant. There was some recognition of the right of contribution if one of the defendants was guilty of a wilful and conscious act. (Ultimately England adopted a statute which provided for contribution between joint wrongdoers.)

The American decisions generally refused to permit contribution where both defendants were guilty of negligence. A few decisions permitted contribution, but it took general legislation to plant the doctrine of contribution in the United States. Most states permit contribution.

A defendant who pays a judgment can usually obtain contribution from other defendants who are also liable. Usually, the total judgment is divided equally among all defendants found liable. In some states, a comparative fault basis is used. Where there is no contribution, there may be a right to indemnification.

(B) INDEMNIFICATION

If injury occurs, or loss results, during or because of the construction process, typically the plaintiff sues any solvent party whose acts or failure to act played some part in causing the injury or loss, as well as anyone who has supplied material or equipment which can in any way be connected to the loss or injury. For example, an injured employee of a subcontractor, while typically barred from suing his own employer, will sue the prime contractor, the owner, the design professional and, where appropriate, another subcontractor. In addition, he is likely to sue the manufacturer or seller of any material or equipment which in any way contributed to his injury. A person injured after completion of the project is likely to sue the owner of the building, the prime contractor, the design professional and anyone else he can connect to his injury. A subcontractor who has suffered delay damages might sue the prime contractor, other subcontractors, the design professional and even the owner.

The plaintiff may not be successful against all the defendants. Each defendant typically contends he is not liable but that if he is, someone else is more liable than he is. To protect against the possibility that he will lose, each defendant is likely to turn upon the other defendants. The process by which one defendant seeks to relieve himself for any money he pays the plaintiff, either by way of court judgment or settlement, and for any expenses he incurs in defending himself, is indemnification.

Because injuries are reasonably foreseeable in the construction process, one method of obtaining indemnification is to obtain a promise of indemnification by contract. Typically, the owner obtains a promise from the prime contractor that the latter will indemnify the owner and, in some cases, the design professional. The prime contractor typically obtains a promise of indemnification from a subcontractor. In larger projects, a subcontractor may obtain a promise of indemnification from a sub-subcontractor. When one of the participants is sued, he often seeks indemnification based upon an indemnity clause in his contract. Even without contractual indemnification, there may be indemnity claims based upon quasi-contract. What results is an incredibly complicated lawsuit, both on the question of who is liable to the plaintiff, and even more so on who will ultimately bear the loss as between the defendants. This complexity is illustrated by the cases described in § 30.13(d).

Generally, courts enforce contractual indemnification provisions. However, often the party who is attempting to invoke the indemnification clause has caused, or has played a significant part in causing the injury or loss. For example, if an injured employee of a subcontractor sues the prime contractor, his claim against the prime contractor may be based upon negligent acts of the prime contractor, or upon the prime contractor not using due care to correct improper construction methods used by other participants in the project. If the prime contractor seeks indemnification from the subcontractor, giving effect to the clause may have the result of relieving the prime contractor from his own negligence. In some jurisdictions, the courts appear to require that such an indemnification clause expressly state that the subcontractor will indemnify the prime contractor even if a substantial cause of the injury is the prime contractor's negligence. In some jurisdictions, the language need not be that explicit. However, courts are hesitant to permit a party to use indemnification where that party's acts have played a major role in causing the loss.

In addition, an indemnification provision is often thrust upon the weaker party to the bargain. At the time a construction contract is made, typically the owner has more bargaining power than the contractor. He exercises this by obtaining a broad indemnification from the prime contractor. At the same time the prime contractor generally has superior bargaining power over the subcontractor and exacts a correspondingly broad indemnification promise from the subcontractor. Because of the often unequal bargaining power, some courts are hesitant to give indemnification provisions their literal effect.

Some courts interpret such clauses literally. They look at indemnification as a means of allocating risks so that these risks can be covered by public liability insurance. Buscaglia v. Owens-Corning Glass is one such case. For this reason, and because it treats a typical indemnity arrangement, it is reproduced at this point.

BUSCAGLIA v. OWENS–CORNING FIBERGLAS v. CATALYTIC CONSTRUCTION COMPANY v. SNELL

Superior Court of New Jersey, Appellate Division, 1961.
68 N.J.Super. 508, 172 A.2d 703.

CONFORD, S. J. A. D. This action originated with a complaint by Buscaglia against . . . Owens-Corning Fiberglas ("Owens" hereinafter) to recover damages for injuries he sustained at its Barrington plant on April 8, 1957 while doing electrical wiring as an employee of . . . William E. Snell and May Snell ("Snell" hereinafter) in the course of the latters' performance of a subcontract for electrical work under a contract [between Snell] . . . and . . . Catalytic Construction Company ("Catalytic" hereinafter) with Owens to do certain construction work in Owens' plant aforementioned. Owens claimed over against Catalytic in respect of the Buscaglia action on the basis of an indemnification clause, and another provision of the agreement with Catalytic allegedly breached by the latter; Catalytic, in turn, claimed over against Snell on an indemnification clause of the subcontract.

When the case came to trial, Owens settled Buscaglia's claim against it for $20,000, which the other parties have stipulated was a reasonable settlement of Buscaglia's claim of negligence against Owens. The other claims were then submitted to the late Camden County Judge Dzick, sitting in the Superior Court, Law Division, to be decided by him without a jury, on the basis of a stipulation of facts and pretrial depositions. The court held for Owens against Catalytic in the amount paid Buscaglia plus costs and counsel fees incurred in that regard. . . . But Judge Dzick found the provisions of the Catalytic-Snell subcontract too vague to ground Catalytic's claim over against Snell. Catalytic appeals both determinations.

Under the Owens-Catalytic contract the latter undertook to install machines and apparatus in the Owens plant to be used in its manufacturing operations. Specific work was ordered by "owner's purchase orders." In January 1957 Owens ordered from Catalytic, among other items, the installation and wiring of a "Process 20" machine and a monorail at its Barrington plant. When completed, the monorail would serve as a track for the movement of a traveling overhead hoist crane to transport heavy parts of the Process 20 machine to other parts of the plant for cleaning. Power for the operation of the hoist crane was transmitted through contact with an electrically charged and exposed "buss" running along the monorail. The parts and fittings of the machine and monorail were supplied by Owens, and it also specified the design. The electrical work, including the wiring of the machine and electrifying the monorail, was subcontracted by Catalytic to Snell. The arrangements between Catalytic and Owens concededly contemplated that Owens' manufacturing operations would proceed while the contracted equipment was being installed.

On April 5, 1957 installation of the monorail was completed. Owens' personnel tested it and found it satisfactory. It was "green-tagged" as a finished part of the contract, turned over to the owner and accepted by it for its use. It was actually used by Owens each day thereafter prior to the accident to the plaintiff on April 8, 1957, and specifically on the Owens night shift the night before the morning of April 8, 1957. On that day plaintiff, an employee of Snell, and engaged on the Owens job but a short time, was wiring the Process 20 machine under the contract and subcontract aforementioned. He was working on top of the machine, high off the floor, near the energized monorail, when he either lost his balance or tripped upon catching his trousers cuff, and came into contact with the monorail, suffering burns and falling to the floor.

From the testimony it appeared that neither Catalytic nor Snell, nor their agents or employees, notified plaintiff that the current in the monorail was or may have been turned on. Nor did they make any effort to determine whether or not it was on. Buscaglia testified that although he knew the monorail was there and was operated by electricity, his foreman had told him at the time that "it was O.K. and everything was safe in that area to work." A field superintendent of Catalytic was present when the monorail was turned over to Owens on April 5, 1957. It was then tested and the power shut off. After that Catalytic had no more to do with the monorail.

Resolution of the issues herein depends upon construction and application of the contract language. Two sections of the Owens-Catalytic contract are particularly material to the dispute between those parties. They follow:

> "15. *Use of Premises*
>
> "Catalytic shall perform all work in such manner as not to interfere with use of premises by Owner or other contractors. Catalytic agrees that there shall be no interruption of Owner's manufacturing operations except as approved by Owner. Catalytic shall take all necessary precautions (including those required by Owner's safety regulations) to protect the premises and all persons and property thereon from damage or injury and shall assume responsibility for the taking of such precautions by Contractor's and subcon-

tractor's employees, agents, licensees, and permittees and subcontractors. * * *

* * * * * * * * *

"19. *Indemnify and Save Harmless*

"Catalytic shall, subject to the limits of insurance provided in Section 18, indemnify Owner and hold it harmless from and against all liability claims and judgments or demands from damages arising from accidents to persons or property occasioned by Catalytic, its agents or employees, and against all claims or demands for damages arising from accidents to Catalytic, its agents or employees, whether occasioned by Catalytic or its employees or any other person or persons and Catalytic will defend any and all suits that may be brought against the Owner on account of any such accidents and will make good to, and reimburse the Owner for any expenditures that said Owner may make by reason of such accidents."

Under section 18 of the contract Catalytic was required to maintain, in addition to workmen's compensation and employers liability insurance, comprehensive "general liability insurance" with bodily injury limits of $1,000,000 each person and $1,000,000 each accident, as well as property damage limits in the same amount. "This shall include Contractor's Protective Liability and Completed Operations Insurance, also Contractual Liability * * *." Catalytic was released as to any claims of Owens, including for bodily injuries, in excess of the limits of the insurance coverage specified.

Quotation of the Catalytic-Snell contract is reserved for the treatment hereinafter of the claim over against Snell.

I.

We consider first Owens' claim against Catalytic as based upon the express agreement of indemnification. . . .

Catalytic argues that the agreement should not be construed to cover the instant claim because Owens had designed the monorail, with its exposed busses, and had exclusive possession and control of it at the time of the accident. It is argued that Catalytic had no right to shut off the power or interfere with use of the monorail by Owens. These circumstances, however, do not derogate from the fact that it was the direct responsibility of Catalytic, as against Owens, under the companion section 15 of the agreement, to see to the safety of the procedures being employed by its own and its subcontractor's agents and employees in carrying out the work contracted to be done. Catalytic knew the nature and dangerous propensity of the electrified monorail, having just finished installing it, and should have realized the hazard of inadvertent contact with it by a workman who would be as close to it as plaintiff was in performing the job assigned to him. Catalytic could easily have conferred with the Owens people for arrangements to turn off the monorail power current while the Process 20 machine was being wired, or to defer the wiring until a time convenient to Owens to turn off the current. Even a warning to Buscaglia of the danger might have averted the accident.

The circumstance that Owens retained control of the mechanism which directly effected the workman's injury will not derogate from Catalytic's continuing liability under an express indemnification agreement covering claims for injuries on the job occasioned by it if that circumstance and the possibility of some inadvertent neglect by the Owens personnel or by the workman contributing to the injury could fairly have been within the contemplation of the parties as not lessening the obligation of indemnity, looking not only to the contract language but also to all the surrounding circumstances. Stern v. Larocca, 49 N.J.Super. 496, 501, 502, 140 A.2d 403 (App.Div.1958); Cozzi v. Owens Corning Fiber Glass Corp., 63 N.J.Super. 117, 164 A.2d 69 (App.Div.1960); . . . The Stern and Cozzi cases, supra, are particularly reflective of the present-day judicial view that indemnity clauses of construction contracts are to be viewed realistically as efforts by business men to allocate as between them the cost or expense of the risk of accidents apt to arise out of construction projects on a fairly predictable basis, rather than upon the generally debatable and indeterminate criteria as to whose negligence, if any, the accident was caused by, and to what degree. See Dayton Fabricated Steel Co. v. Dayton Town & Country, Inc., 99 Ohio App. 309, 133 N.E.2d 423, 425 (Ct.App.1954). It is generally contemplated, as was here specifically arranged for in the contract, that the risk of accident claims will be covered by insurance, and the only practical feature of the bargain, ordinarily, is the decision as to who is to bear the cost of the insurance. Here was Catalytic. It is significant here that Catalytic was required to carry contractual liability insurance, presumably to cover its liability to Owens on the very type of claim here in litigation. Note the cross-reference in section 19 to the insurance coverage provided in section 18.

We have no difficulty in agreeing with the late trial judge that, viewed in the light of the foregoing principles, it was the intention of the indemnity clause quoted above to place the risk of such a claim as this upon Catalytic and to require it to indemnify Owens therefor.

Section 19 of the agreement is seen to express two distinct obligations of indemnity. Catalytic agrees to indemnify Owens and save it harmless from damages "arising from accidents to persons or property occasioned by Catalytic." Additionally, Catalytic undertakes such indemnification of Owens against claims "arising from accidents to Catalytic, its agents or employees" no matter by whom such accidents may be occasioned. We need not resolve the doubtful question whether Buscaglia was an "agent" (he clearly was not an employee) of Catalytic, within the meaning of the second category of indemnification mentioned, as we are firmly of the view that the indemnity clause is activated by reason of the fact that Catalytic "occasioned" the accident, within the proper meaning of that term in this context.

Accidents "occasioned by," in the light of the purposes and objects of an indemnity clause of a construction contract like this, means "accidents caused by," and more particularly, in this context, "caused by the work being performed by." . . . Causation, not negligence, is the touchstone. There was a direct causal relation between Catalytic's or its agents' carrying on of the work and the occurrence of the accident; the condition for indemnification has therefore occurred. It makes no difference, in the light of the purpose and function which this clause was to play in regulating the allocation of costs and expenses as between Owens and Catalytic, that some causal contribution to the accident may have also emanated from the action or inaction of Owens' employees as well, or, for that matter, from the injured workman himself. It was in fair contemplation that such contribution might play a part in an accident covered by the indemnity. The accident was still "occasioned" by Catalytic, within the meaning of the agreement.

If there were any doubt concerning the soundness of the foregoing construction of section 19 from what appears therein (together with the surrounding circumstances), it is dispelled by section 15 . . . . Catalytic was to "take all necessary precautions * * * to protect the premises and all persons * * * thereon from * * * injury" as well as assume responsibility for such precautions by those working under it, including subcontractors. There was evidence that a Snell foreman had assured Buscaglia of the safety of the working conditions. These considerations fortify the conclusions that Owens was looking to Catalytic to save it harmless from any claim for personal injury arising out of the prosecution by or under Catalytic of the work contracted for and that this specific claim was covered by the indemnity clause.

There remains for determination the question whether Catalytic is entitled to shift its liability to Owens over to Snell by virtue of the Catalytic-Snell contract, which reads:

"16. *Risk of Loss:*

"It is further understood and agreed that all risks of loss and/or injury to personnel of Subcontractor and/or to the construction or automotive equipment involved hereunder, shall be for the account of the Subcontractor and Catalytic and Catalytic's Customer are hereby released and held harmless from any and all costs arising out of the damage or injury to said equipment or personnel."

We would be reasonably clear that a claim based upon this language might be sustained, were it one by Owens against Snell because of the claim it settled with Buscaglia, or one by Catalytic against Snell after satisfying a claim against it by Buscaglia. But we are unable to find that the provision clearly contemplates and covers a claim by Catalytic arising only by reason of its collateral agreement of indemnification of Owens. Catalytic drew this contract, and it must be construed against it in case of fair doubt as to its scope, . . ., particularly since it is a contract of purported indemnity. . . . We are constrained to resolve the doubtful issue of coverage of this claim by the contract language against Catalytic.

Judgment affirmed.

(The opinion was affirmed by the New Jersey Supreme Court in 36 N.J. 532, 178 A.2d 208 (1962).)

The court applied a broad interpretation of the prime contract indemnification, based upon risk allocation and insurance, but fell back to the traditional, narrow interpretation when dealing with the subcontract indemnification. This may be based upon the general tendency to place responsibility for accidents upon prime contractors.

Courts are often called upon to interpret indemnity clauses. As stated, they will narrowly interpret clauses of this type if one party is seeking to obtain indemnification for his own negligence. In addition to this question other interpretation problems can arise.

Which losses are covered by an indemnification clause? Suppose an injured employee of a subcontractor sues a prime contractor and recovers a substantial court judgment. If the prime contractor seeks indemnification from the subcontractor based upon an indemnification clause, does the indemnification clause cover attorneys' fees and other court costs incurred by the prime contractor in defending the lawsuit? Generally, clauses are specific on this question and include such expenses.

However, suppose the prime contractor is held not liable? Can he recover his attorneys' fees and costs in defending the lawsuit in an indemnification action against the subcontractor? Generally, he can. See Titan Steel Corp. v. Walton, discussed in § 30.13(d).

Most lawsuits are settled without litigation. Usually indemnification clauses cover amounts paid and expenses incurred in making the settlement, even though the party against whom the indemnification is sought claims that the plaintiff would not have succeeded in the lawsuit. Only if the settlement were made without proper investigation of the claim, or made in bad faith, would the person against whom indemnification is sought be able to avoid paying.

Indemnity clauses are often interpreted narrowly, if indemnity is part of an "adhesion", one-sided contract. Pacific Gas & E. Co. v. G. W. Thomas Drayage etc. Co., 69 Cal.2d 33, 442 P.2d 641, 69 Cal.Rptr. 561 (1968) involved damage to the property of a public utility that had hired the contractor to repair one of its steam turbines. There was an indemnity provision, under which the contractor performing the work agreed to indemnify the public utility "against all loss, damage, expense and liability resulting from injury to or death of person, or injury to property, arising out of or in any way connected with the performance of this contract." The court held that the defendant should be permitted to show that the indemnity provision was intended to apply only to losses suffered by the public utility because of liability incurred to third parties, and not to losses to the public utility's own property.

If an injury occurs after completion of the structure and acceptance by the owner, the owner may be held responsible. If the owner attempts to assert an indemnification against the prime contractor, indemnity may depend upon whether the indemnification clause covers injuries that occur after completion of the project and acceptance by the owner.

In General Accident, Fire & Life Assurance Corporation, Ltd. v. Finegan and Burgess, 351 F.2d 168 (6th Cir. 1965), a sign subcontract included a broadly-drawn indemnity provision. After completion of the sign subcontractor's work, a project engineer for the owner went to inspect the sign, accompanied by an employee of the sign subcontractor. After inspection, the engineer indicated he wished to check a particular switch that had been installed by another subcontractor. The employee of the sign subcontractor indicated the location of the switch and then left. On his way to inspect the switch, the engineer fell from a walkway which had no railing, because of the prime contractor's negligence. The injured engineer sued both prime and sign subcontractor. The jury in this case found the prime contractor had been negligent, but the sign subcontractor had not. The prime contractor's insurance company paid the claim, and then sued the sign subcontractor on the indemnity provision.

The court noted that the purpose of the inspection was to enable a tenant to move in earlier and was not directly related to the sign subcontractor's performance. The court also noted that the area where the injury had occurred was under the general control of the prime contractor. For these reasons the court interpreted the indemnity provision in favor of the sign subcontractor.

Sometimes there are attempts to transfer a loss under a contract that does not contain an express indemnification clause. For example, suppose the prime contractor promises to use proper workmanship in the construction of the project. The owner may contend that the prime contractor should indemnify him for any losses suffered by the owner which result from failure on the part of the prime contractor to use proper workmanship. While it is somewhat more difficult to obtain indemnification in such cases, there have been decisions which have permitted indemnification in such situations.

There is another growing area of indemnification which is not based upon contract, but upon "quasi-contract" or unjust enrichment. Between two wrongdoers, the one who is more wrong should bear the loss. Sometimes the courts have classified the conduct in question as "active" or "primary", as opposed to "passive" or "secondary".

For example, an injury to a subcontractor's employee may be caused by improper construction methods of the prime contractor, as well as by a negligent failure to discover these methods or to take proper corrective measures by the owner, through his design professional. It is arguable that the owner is only passively negligent, while the prime contractor is actively negligent. In such a case, the owner who might be held liable to the injured employee would be able to recover the amount he paid from the prime contractor, because the owner's negligence has not been as blameworthy as the negligence of the prime contractor.

The owner of land may be liable because he did not make the land reasonably safe for invitees. If he had hired a contractor to repair an unsafe condition, he might have a claim for quasi-contract indemnification if the contractor was negligent in the performance of the work.

(C) EXCULPATION

"Exculpation" does not attempt to share losses, as in contributions, nor does it attempt to transfer losses between one wrongdoer and another, as in indemnification. Exculpation is the process by which a party who may suffer loss agrees not to institute legal action against the party who may cause the loss and who would have legal responsibility. It places the loss upon the party who suffers it.

An illustration of an exculpatory clause would be a provision included in a hospital admittance form, under which the patient agrees not to institute any legal action against the hospital, or against any of the doctors, in the event he suffers any injury or death because of acts of the hospital or the doctors. Another example would be a clause in a contract between an owner and a soil tester, under which the tester would not be liable for any losses caused by an inaccurate, or even a negligent, soil test report.

If parties are accorded maximum contractual freedom, there is no reason why one party cannot agree to take the risk that acts of the other party will cause him damage. However, often such clauses are the result of extreme inequality of bargaining power. The patient who is being admitted to a hospital is not likely to be able to bargain away such an exculpatory clause, even if he were so inclined to do so. For that reason, the courts have been reluctant to give full effect to some exculpatory clauses, especially those involving harm to persons. Where there is no realistic possibility of bargaining, there is a good chance such a clause will not be held valid. Where only pecuniary loss is involved, the public policy against such clauses is not as strong.

(D) SOME CASE STUDIES

Some of the principles stated in § 30.08, and in this section, can be illustrated by reference to specific cases. Titan Steel Corporation v. Walton, 365 F.2d 542 (10th Cir. 1966), involved an action by the estate of a deceased employee of a subcontractor against the prime contractor and the owner for wrongful death resulting from a fall by the employee from the roof of the owner's building. The owner, in addition to defending the action generally, asserted a claim of indemnification against the prime contractor, based upon an indemnification provision in the contract between owner and prime contractor. The owner asked for indemnification against the subcontractor, (the employer of the deceased employee) based upon the provision of indemnification in the subcontract. The prime contractor asserted indemnification against the subcontractor based upon the same indemnification provision in the subcontract.

The court exonerated the owner, because the court held that there was no duty owed to the employee of the subcontractor by the owner. However, the court held that the prime contractor had a duty to the deceased employee of the subcontractor to keep the premises in a safe condition, and to warn of latent or concealed perils of which the prime contractor knew, or should have known, and which the deceased would not know. The employee's estate was allowed to recover against the prime contractor, even though the prime contractor had notified the subcontractor of the dangerous condition.

The owner, although absolved from liability, asked to be indemnified for all the legal expenses and costs he had incurred in defending the action. Also, the prime sought indemnity from the subcontractor. The subcontractor claimed it would be unfair and unconscionable to impose substantial liability risks upon someone who agreed to perform only a small part of the work. The court held that while such a contract of indemnification is not favored by the law, it will be enforced if made at arm's length, without undue disparity of bargaining power. The court rejected the contention that any indemnification against the subcontractor would subject the subcontractor to tort liability, despite workmen's compensation statutes denying the employee a direct right against his employer based upon negligence. The end result of the *Titan* case is that the entire loss was borne by the subcontractor, at least to the extent of the ability of the subcontractor to respond to the judgment. If the subcontractor cannot pay, or if his insurance is not adequate to pay the judgment, the loss will have to be borne by the prime contractor.

Another case dealing with the same problem was Associated Engineers, Inc. v. Job, 370 F.2d 633 (8th Cir. 1966). In this case, an employee of the prime contractor, injured when a power line was reenergized while he was working near it, recovered workmen's compensation from his employer, and then instituted action against the engineer and the owner. The owner asked for indemnification against the prime contractor and the engineer. The engineer asked for indemnification against both the owner and the prime contractor.

The jury found that the injured employee had been negligent. But under the rules of comparative negligence applicable in that state (South Dakota), they held that his negligence was not sufficient to bar him from recovery, because the defendants had been considerably more negligent.

The court found that the owner and the engineer had been negligent in hiring a prime contractor with inexperienced personnel, and in permitting that contractor to remain on the job and use unsafe procedures.

The contract between the engineer and owner required the engineer to supervise the construction, and make diligent efforts to make sure that the work was performed in accordance with the construction contract. The engineer also had the right to inspect materials and workmanship, as well as maintain a resident engineer with full authority to act. The court pointed to the powers given to the engineer to effect changes in the number of employees, and to suspend the work if the prime contractor was not proceeding in accordance with safety standards.

In holding the engineer responsible to the injured employee, the court recognized that there had been cases which had relieved the design professional from responsibility for injury where the latter had the power to act but did not. However, the court felt that, in this case, the obligation of the design professional went beyond the obligations involved in the cases which had relieved the design professional from responsibility.

Both owner and engineer were held liable to the injured employee of the prime contractor. This complicated case became even more complex when indemnity entered the picture.

In the trial court, the engineer sought indemnification from both the owner and the prime contractor. The trial court did not grant him indemnity against either party. On appeal, the engineer abandoned his claim of indemnity against the prime contractor but did assert that he should have been granted indemnity against the owner.

The engineer contended that the act of the owner in re-energizing the lines was active negligence, while his negligence was passive. However, the court concluded that the owner's negligence consisted of its failure to compel the prime contractor to employ competent personnel and to use reasonable safety procedures, or, in the alternative, to halt the work. The court found that the negligence of owner and engineer were of a similar nature. For that reason, the engineer could not receive indemnification from the owner.

The owner claimed indemnification from the prime contractor, based upon an express indemnification provision. The court sustained the position of the owner based upon contractual indemnity. Unlike quasi-contractual indemnity, the court held that there was no need to make any comparative evaluation of the negligence of owner and prime contractor, despite the argument by the prime contractor that the indemnification provision did not expressly provide for indemnification where the owner himself was negligent. The court held that the indemnification provision need not expressly state that indemnification would be paid even if the owner were guilty of negligence. The court noted that in the absence of such a provision, the owner would have been entitled to indemnification based upon quasi-contract, because the owner's negligence was passive while the prime contractor's negligence was active.

The injured employee received a judgment against the owner and the engineer, and the owner was entitled to indemnification against the prime contractor for whatever the owner would be obliged to pay to satisfy the injured employee's judgment against the owner. The loss was to be borne by the prime contractor and the engineer with the owner being relieved because of indemnification.

The interaction between indemnification and the independent contractor can be seen in Muth v. Urricelqui, 251 Cal.App.2d 901, 60 Cal.Rptr. 166 (1967). A subsequent purchaser of a house recovered a judgment against the general contractor-owner for damage resulting from landslides and soil subsistence. The general contractor-owner then sued a number of parties, among them the grading subcontractor. The general contractor-owner did not base his claim against the grading subcontractor upon an indemnification provision, but upon the doctrine of quasi contract. He claimed that as between himself and the grading subcontractor, the latter should bear the loss, because the latter's negligence was primary or active, while the general contractor-owner's liability was passive or secondary.

The subcontractor claimed that there was negligence on the part of the soil engineer and the civil engineer, and that their negligence should be chargeable to the general contractor-owner. However, the court held that the soil and civil engineers were not employees of the general contractor-owner, even in an indemnification action for the negligent acts of soil and civil engineers. The court noted that the fact that the general contractor-owner had the right to inspect and specify changes did not mean that the latter's failure to do so constituted active negligence.

One of the most difficult areas in these indemnification cases relates to the owner's power to condemn defective work, or to stop the construction project. If the prime or subcontractors are not performing properly, the owner's inaction may constitute active negligence. In the *Job* case, the extensive powers given the design professional were the basis for the successful action by the injured employee of the prime contractor against the design professional. However, in the *Muth* case the fact that these powers were present, and that failure to exercise them might be negligence, was held not to preclude the right of indemnification of the general contractor-owner, when he sought to transfer the risk of loss to the negligent subcontractor.

The unbelievable complexity and often bizarre assertions made in these cases is illustrated by Palier v. Dreis & Krump Mfg. Co., 81 Ill. App.2d 1, 225 N.E.2d 67 (1967). The employee of the subcontractor was injured when he fell from a scaffold. The scaffold violated the Illinois Structural Work Act (commonly known as the Scaffold Act) because it did not have guardrails. The Scaffold Act places liability for injuries traceable to defective scaffolding upon the person in charge of the construction project. After recovering workmen's compensation from his own employer, Palier sued the owner of the building, claiming that the owner was in charge of the construction and had violated the Scaffold Act. The Scaffold Act provides that contributory negligence by the employee shall not bar recovery.

In the same case, the owner asserted a claim against the employer of the injured employee based upon implied indemnity. The employer then, to complete the chain, asserted a claim based upon implied indemnity against its own employee, the plaintiff employee. The culmination of these cross actions saw A sue B, B sue C and C sue A. The basis for such a circular lawsuit was implied indemnity based upon negligence. The owner claimed the employer-contractor was negligent, and the employer-contractor claimed its own employee was negligent. The court would not permit implied indemnity against the employee, since to do so would be to frustrate the Scaffold Act's provision that contributory negligence on the part of the employee would not bar his recovery.

These illustrative cases demonstrate the complexity of construction project accident litigation. It would seem that the proper solution to such loss allocations questions would be limiting the injured employee to a more fair and adequate workmen's compensation recovery. If such were the case, these complicated, and often frustrating, lawsuits could be substantially eliminated.

SECTION 30.14 ROLE OF INSURANCE IN CONSTRUCTION LOSS LITIGATION

In many loss allocation cases, the real litigants are insurance companies. In employee claims, for example, the employee recovers workmen's compensation payments from the workmen's compensation insurance carrier of his employer, and then joins with the latter in suing a third party whom he claims caused the injury. That third party may be covered by a public liability insurance policy, and the liability, if any, will be borne by the insurance company to the limits of the policy. When there is loss or damage to real or personal property, the person suffering the loss is often covered by property damage insurance. He may be able to collect from his insurance company, and the insurance company paying the claim often looks for someone to charge with legal responsibility for the loss.

Insurance policies are long, often difficult to understand, and frequently filled with exclusions from coverage. While courts have tended to favor the insured when interpreting coverage and exclusions in insurance policies, it should not be automatically assumed that property damage insurance will cover all types of property damage, or that public liability insurance always means that the insurance company will pay if the insured is liable.

All persons connected with the construction process should check their coverage and exclusions to make certain that their actual insurance protection and their expectations of insurance protection coincide. They should make certain that the amount of property damage coverage is adequate. Above all they must make certain that they comply with applicable laws which require insurance for certain risks (e.g. Workmen's Compensation Insurance), and that the amount of public liability insurance is high enough to cover potential liability.

The amount of protection must take into account the great increase in settlement amounts and court judgments in injury and death cases.

REVIEW QUESTIONS

1. What types of losses can occur incident to a construction project?

2. What is the principal function of tort law?

3. What principle of loss allocation dominated tort law in the 19th century?

4. What principle of loss allocation is becoming more predominant in the 20th century?

5. What are the doctrines developed in tort law to reduce the scope of risk for defendants?

6. What effect does the showing of a statutory violation have in a negligence action?

7. What is the principal difference between contributory negligence and comparative negligence?

8. How does contract law affect loss allocation?

9. What has been the trend in misrepresentation cases?

10. What duty does an owner or occupier of land owe an invitee?

11. What was the principal effect of workmen's compensation law on employment injuries?

12. What is the independent contractor rule? Name some exceptions to it.

13. Which statutes deal with the allowable time to bring a lawsuit?

14. What theories have been used by plaintiffs to attempt to transfer economic losses to defendants?

15. How do claims for losses against public agencies differ from claims against private parties?

16. How has indemnification affected loss allocation in construction contracts?

17. Under what circumstances can a person successfully indemnify himself from losses caused by his own negligent acts?

QUESTIONS FOR CLASS DISCUSSION

1. Which is a more equitable loss allocation principle, fault or enterprise liability?

2. Should the showing by the defendant that he has complied with a safety regulation absolve him from any finding that he was negligent? Explain.

3. Should the law allow recovery for pain and suffering? For disfigurement? For emotional distress?

4. Are there any circumstances when contracting parties should not be allowed to determine loss allocations between themselves?

5. Should those professionals in the business of making representations, such as soils engineers, be accountable for any losses caused by negligent representation? Losses caused by non-negligent misrepresentation?

6. Should a manufacturer of products be responsible for all losses caused by defective products when he has not been negligent in designing the product, selecting the materials, or putting the product together? Explain.

7. Should a prime contractor be able to require that a subcontractor indemnify him for losses caused substantially by the negligence of the prime contractor?

PROBLEMS

1. A was the architect commissioned by O to design a luxury residence and swimming pool. The applicable building code required that the perimeter of the pool area be surfaced with a non-skid material. However, the specifications drafted by A did not require that a non-skid material be used at pool side.

C was hired to construct the residence and swimming pool. He noticed that the specifications did not require a non-skid material but said nothing to O or to A. He assumed that A had checked the most recent building code and had found that non-skid material was not required.

Three months after O went into possession of the house, he held a cocktail party for business associates and social acquaintances. Drinks were served on a terrace adjacent to the swimming pool. One of the social guests accidentally spilled a cocktail along the edge of the pool. X, a business associate of O, did not notice the wet area along the pool. He slipped in the moist area adjacent to the pool and injured himself.

Does X have a valid claim against O? Against A? Against C? If X does have a valid claim against any of these persons, how would the law apportion final responsibility for the loss as between O, A and C?

2. Suppose A had specified a non-skid material but C had failed to comply with the specifications. A issued a final certificate of completion, but did not notice that C had deviated. From whom should X collect?

3. Suppose the materials were warranted to be non-skid by the manufacturer but the material supplied by a jobber was not what would be considered non-skid material in the trade. How would this fact change any conclusions reached in Problem 1?

4. Suppose the contract between O and C contained a provision under which C agreed to indemnify O for "claims, liability or losses suffered by O or A resulting from any acts of C". Would this provision change any of the conclusions set forth in Problem 1?

5. Would any of the conclusions given for any of the above problems be different if O operated a public outdoor swimming pool and charged admission?

Part V

SOME PROFESSIONAL PRACTICE PROBLEMS

Introduction

Part V consists of a residue of legal problems often faced by a design professional not discussed in any of the preceding parts of the treatise. The emphasis in Part V is on the architect or engineer in private practice. However, some of the chapters in Part V will be important to design professionals who become employees. For example, while the main emphasis of Chapter 36 is upon the design professional as an employer, the legal protection given employees would be available to design professionals who are employees. Also, some of the material covered in Chapter 40 dealing with intellectual property would be important to design professionals who are employees. However, the main emphasis of Part V is upon the design professional in private practice.

In Part V, Chapter 31 will deal with the state control over professional practice by licensing and registration laws. Chapter 32 will deal with forms of association for practice. Chapter 33 will highlight some of the legal problems incident to renting space. Chapter 34 will discuss professional liability problems. Chapter 35 will look at the role of insurance, mainly professional liability insurance, in professional practice. Chapter 36 looks at the legal controls over the design professional when he is an employer. Chapter 37 will deal with collection problems, Chapter 38 with the design professional as an expert witness and Chapter 39 with the design professional as an arbitrator. Finally, Chapter 40 will look at intellectual property with emphasis on patents, copyrights and trade secrets.

Chapter 31

LEGAL REQUIREMENTS FOR PROFESSIONAL PRACTICE

SECTION 31.01 PUBLIC REGULATION OF ARCHITECTURE AND ENGINEERING

The importance of the design professional's role in construction has meant increased governmental regulation of the design professions. This is manifested by expanded professional liability, to be discussed in Chapter 34, and direct governmental control through licensing and registration laws. The constitutional power to enact licensing and registration laws rests upon the police powers of the state, and upon the state's right to protect the general welfare.

Laws have been enacted which determine who can enter into the practice of architecture and engineering, establish the conditions for remaining in practice and provide penalties for violation of such laws. The major purpose of licensing and registration laws is to insure that only qualified and competent persons perform architectural and engineering work. Also such laws should assist members of the public in selecting competent design professionals. To the layman, a licensed professional meets minimum standards of competence and honesty. A license does not insure that professional work will be done properly and honestly. However, it may be the only guide a client has when he desires to retain an architect or engineer.

Political considerations play a part in licensing laws. When professional groups come to the legislature and request enactment of statutes dealing with licensing and registration, groups inside or outside the profession often contend the laws are intended to restrict competition, and to "fence in" those already admitted to practice. For these reasons, and because licensing and registration laws affect the right to use what one knows to earn a livelihood, such legislation is often a compromise. Also, the treatment these laws receive in the courts may vary, depending on whether a particular judge looks upon these laws as a method of elevating standards and protecting the public, or as a technique for reducing competition and for giving a monopoly to certain professional groups.

The federal government, except as it may set up standards for those persons who are to perform professional work for its agencies, has left licensing to the states. This has meant great variation in legal requirements for practice. As a result, generalizations as to what constitutes unauthorized or unlawful practice are dangerous. The result often depends on the language of the statute, the case decisions within a particular state, and the facts of the case. Also, problems have been generated by the tendency for design professionals to engage in interstate transactions, and by the growth of larger organizations. The state can regulate professional activities within the state, even though interstate commerce is affected. But the regulations must be reasonable, and must not unreasonably discriminate against nonresidents of the state.

Municipalities generally have only that power to tax or regulate which is given to them by the state. Often municipalities impose an occupations or professional tax upon practicing professionals. As a rule, the purpose of these taxes is to raise revenue, and not to regulate the profession for the protection of the public.

SECTION 31.02 TYPES OF REGULATING STATUTES

Statutes regulating professional practices fall essentially into two categories. They are "practice" and "holding-out" statutes.

The "practice" statutes require a license to practice architecture or engineering. The "holding-out" statutes regulate the use of professional practice titles by prohibiting a person from calling himself an architect or engineer, unless he is licensed or registered. The purpose of the holding-out statutes is to avoid misleading the public. Most persons would believe that a person who holds himself out as an architect has demonstrated certain competence to the state. An indirect goal of a holding-out statute is to encourage professionals to become licensed, in order to be able to call themselves architects or engineers.

There is frequent legislative activity in the licensing area. The tendency has been to make the statutes more comprehensive, and to change from holding-out statutes to practice statutes. Most statutes today are practice statutes.

There is an increasing tendency to break down registration laws by well recognized specialties. For example, some states have special registration for landscape engineers. Also, there is a tendency to break down engineering into its established specialties. Surveyors are often set apart for special registration requirements. Finally, about one fourth of the states have licensing requirements for contractors.

SECTION 31.03 REGISTRATION, SUSPENSION AND REVOCATION

The details of registration and license requirements vary considerably from state to state. Generally, statutes require a specified number of years of college, plus a period of candidacy, or a lengthy period of office practice. Most states also require a written, and occasionally an oral examination.

States vary on the question of whether corporations are permitted to practice architecture or engineering. Generally, architects are not permitted to incorporate. However, because of tax considerations which make it advisable to practice as a corporation rather than as a partnership, a few, but commercially significant, states permit corporate practice. There is a greater tendency to permit engineers to incorporate. These questions will be explored in Chapter 32.

Generally registration laws contain grandfather clauses. Such clauses are designed to protect those who have been practicing lawfully prior to the enactment of, or change in, registration laws. Sometimes grandfather clauses permit those who are practicing to continue to practice, even though they have not met current standards. Some grandfather provisions allow them to practice for a designated period designed to permit them a reasonable time to comply with new requirements. The passage of time should eliminate those who are practicing under grandfather clauses. However, the frequency of change in registration and licensing laws has meant that there are likely to be architects and engineers who are permitted to practice, despite noncompliance with current registration laws.

State licensing agencies are often given the power to suspend or revoke licenses, as well as the power to determine who can enter the profession. Usually, the laws relating to suspension or revocation require that there be serious misconduct before these sanctions can be imposed. It may take gross incompetence or dishonesty before a license can be suspended or revoked.

Even where there is a revocation or suspension, the scope of judicial review of these actions is generally broad. A court is more likely to look carefully at a suspension or revocation than at an administrative determination not to license someone initially.

Also, the administrative agencies given these powers seem reluctant to exercise their power to suspend or revoke. The hesitation to invoke these sanctions is traceable, to some degree, to the reluctance to deprive a person of his principal means of livelihood. While this is a commendable, humanitarian feeling, often the public and the profession suffer when incompetent or dishonest persons are permitted to continue in professional practice.

SECTION 31.04 WHAT CONSTITUTES A VIOLATION?

Many court cases have involved the question of whether an individual was practicing without a proper license, or was holding himself out as an architect or engineer, without having complied with the legal requirements. Case holdings are often deceptive. The question of whether there is a violation frequently depends upon the precise wording of the applicable statute. Secondly, a court may be motivated to go one way or the other by considerations of the particular issue in the case. For example, a case may involve criminal liability for unlicensed practice, a negligence action where failure to obtain a license was considered evidence of negligence, or an attempt by an unlicensed professional to collect for his services.

The result in any particular case may depend upon what is at stake. If the sanction is criminal, with its attendant seriousness, a court is likely to read such statutes narrowly. This is a manifestation of the respect due the presumption of innocence, and the necessity of establishing criminality beyond a reasonable doubt.

If the issue relates to professional liability for personal injury, damage to property or economic losses, the stakes are often high, but do not involve potential imprisonment. The stakes are less high when the issue is whether the architect or engineer can collect for his work. While the amount of money at stake may be substantial in the latter cases, it is still less important on the whole, than when the issue is his professional responsibility for harm, or whether he has committed a crime.

In those cases where an unlicensed design professional is trying to collect for work he has done, sustaining the no-license defense by the client may unjustly enrich the client. The absence of a license may only be an excuse. The determination by the court in such cases requires a delicate balancing of the policy of requiring licensing to eliminate incompetence and protect the public, and permitting the client to enrich himself by using the services of the unlicensed professional without paying for them. The precise issue in question may determine whether a court will find that the conduct in question falls within architecture or engineering registration laws.

There are many exceptions to general licensing laws which relate to the type of work done. Single family homes, decoration of store fronts, farm structures, and other types of work may be exempt from a requirement that they be performed by licensed professionals, but there may be a licensing violation even though the basic licensing statute does not cover the particular activity in question. For example, California, prior to 1963, had a "holding out" statute. However, another statute required that all hospitals be designed by licensed architects.

While case results vary considerably because of differing statutes, differing judicial attitude toward the usefulness of such statutes and the particular issue in the case, some generalizations can be made.

(A) TYPE OF ACTIVITY

While there are differentiations between the practice of architecture and engineering (see State v. Beck, reproduced at § 31.04(e)), it may be useful at the outset to focus upon those attributes of professional practice common to both. Architecture and engineering can be divided into those services which relate to design, and those which relate to construction project administration. Design can be further subdivided into plans and specifications which are sketchy and obviously preliminary, and work which is more detailed. For example, anyone with minimal artistic and design ability can sketch the exterior of a residence or lay out a floor plan. It would not be likely that these activities would constitute the practice of architecture. Similarly, a person without engineering training or skill might draw a rough sketch of a conveyor machine layout or a dam without violating engineering practice statutes.

But as the broad concept and the simple sketch are translated into construction drawings and specifications which can be the basis for a construction contract, the activity becomes subject to the registration laws and must be performed or at least checked by a licensed design professional. His knowledge of mathematics, the physical sciences, materials (both natural and man-made), construction methods, and legal controls over construction such as building codes, are needed to perform these activities with the skill necessary for the protection of the public.

These professional skills carry over into the construction phase of the project. Many design decisions have to be made during construction. Also, traditionally, the role of architects and engineers includes acting in a quasi-judicial function during project administration. The architect or engineer is frequently given the power to determine whether the contractors are performing properly. He issues certificates of payment and completion. He may be given the power to terminate the contractor's performance if it appears that the contractor will not perform properly, or has not been performing properly. In these roles he is called upon to use his special training and knowledge in aesthetics, design, materials, methods, and the legal controls over the construction process. While his role during the construction process is perhaps less purely architectural or engineering than is his role before construction begins, there are still sufficient elements of his specialized training and skill connected to his role to classify these activities as the practice of architecture or engineering.

Again, the wording of the registration statute may be crucial. In some states, certain services relating to contract administration may not constitute the practice of architecture or engineering. For a discussion of out-of-state consultations, see § 31.05.

Architectural and engineering practice can be defined as those activities for which architectural and engineering education and training are required to achieve minimal competence. The more technical the activity, and the more the activity requires specialized architecture and engineering training, the more likely it is that a license will be required.

(B) TYPE AND SCOPE OF PROJECT

The nature of the project for which the work is being done also affects the determination of whether the services fall within the registration laws. As stated, certain types of projects are specifically exempt from the registration requirements. Some states exempt single family homes, farm structures, minor remodeling, and less important projects. Even if the project does not fall within the stated exemption, the smaller and less public the project, the less likely it will be that the design services will constitute architectural or engineering practice. For example, drafting plans for the remodeling of a kitchen in a private residence is not likely to constitute architectural practice. Remodeling of the kitchen in a hotel would be more likely to fall within the registration laws.

(C) BUILDING AND OCCUPANCY PERMITS

Municipalities often require that an architect sign design documents before a building permit will be issued. While the municipality should not make this a requirement unless the performance of these design services will fall within the registration laws, some municipal officials take an inflexible position that it is always necessary to have a licensed design professional approve any work for which a building permit is to be issued. Perhaps minor work would not necessitate a building permit. However, there is a greater degree of public control over all aspects of building, and through the requirements for building and occupancy permits, the municipality often imposes another legal control of architecture and engineering.

(D) ENGINEERING

Moving into the engineering field, differentiations may relate to whether the services are primarily related to machinery or products, rather than construction. The design of a conveyor machine, or engineering advice made by a salesman, might not fall within the engineering statute, while design or administration incident to the remodeling of the plant necessary to install the equipment would probably constitute engineering services. Where there is substantial structural or support work connected with an industrial project, the design services will probably have to be performed by a registered architect or engineer.

(E) ARCHITECTURE OR ENGINEERING? STATE v. BECK

The line between architecture and engineering is often narrow. Sometimes emphasis is placed upon all-around environmental control and aesthetic skill as grounds for differentiating architecture from engineering. While architectural work may include the safety and utilitarian aspects of engineering, there may be certain types of work which fall mainly within engineering, due to the tangential aspects of aesthetics or environmental control. Dams, roads, tunnels and works of this type are likely to be considered engineering projects, even though they may have aesthetic aspects to them. Industrial plants are likely to be architectural, while power plants could be engineering. A good discussion, both of the difference between architecture and engineering and the roles of architect and engineer, is contained in State v. Beck, reproduced at the this point.

STATE v. BECK

Supreme Judicial Court of Maine, 1960.
156 Me. 403, 165 A.2d 433.

SULLIVAN, JUSTICE. On exceptions. Respondent was prosecuted and found guilty by jury verdict upon a complaint for the offense of appropriating the title of architect by publicly erecting and maintaining upon the building housing his professional quarters a sign with the legend, "Melvin W. Beck, Engineer & Architect", when he had not been registered by the Maine State Board of Architects in compliance with the provisions of R.S. (1954), c. 81.

Respondent at the time of his imputed misdemeanor was a professional engineer registered in accordance with R.S. c. 83.

At the trial it was stipulated that the respondent who was not a registered architect owned the sign and that it had been displayed at his direction.

. . . [T]he law forbids the assumption of the title of practicing architect by one who is not qualified by state registration although he be a registered professional engineer. But the latter may, nevertheless, engage in architecture to the contained extent that such is incidental only to his engineering.

The respondent assails the constitutionality of R.S. c. 81 upon plural grounds. . . .

The particulars of the controverting of the constitutionality of R.S. c. 81 by the respondent may be summarized as follows:

The Legislature distinguishes no efficacious difference between professional engineering and architecture other than the aesthetics of the latter but aesthetics without more are not a proper or adequate object of police power. The act essays to control, by licensing requirements, the practice of art, and such the Legislature can not do. The statute is an arbitrary and unwarranted interference with the right of a citizen to pursue a lawful livelihood. More schooling or training is required by the Legislature for professional engineering than for architecture. An architect is basically an engineer with training in art. The respondent's qualifications as a professional engineer are at least the equivalent of an architect's and, notwithstanding, the Legislature discriminates against the former and prevents him from applying art to his profession. If an engineer by the statute is qualified to practice architecture as it may be "incidental to his engineering work," then the stricture against such engineer holding himself out as an architect has no reasonable relationship to the stability of the public health, welfare or safety. The definition of the practice of architecture in R.S. c. 81, § 8 is a hodgepodge of statutory criminality and so vague as to lack that certainty requisite in a criminal law. R.S. c. 81, § 9 violates the principle of equal application of the law in excepting employees who need have no special education or qualifications but who may design a building, provide specifications and supervise construction although the safety of a large segment of the public may be jeopardized. Respondent queries as to how a trained and qualified engineer might endanger the public by merely advertising that he performs architectural service while an employee without particular qualification may practice architecture without danger to the general public.

R.S. c. 81 as to architects and R.S. c. 83 as to professional engineers are exercises of the police power.

. . .

The Legislature first regulated by licensing, engineering practice, P.L.1935, c. 189, and subsequently, architecture, P.L.1945, c. 356, and must be assumed to have been cognizant of the provisions of P.L.1935, c. 189 (R.S. c. 83) when it adopted P.L.1945, c. 356 (R.S. c. 81). The Legislature must be considered as having entertained a consistent design and policy embracing both acts.

. . .

Professional engineering and architecture in the Legislative estimation are patently regarded as separate *species* of the engineering *genus* and such a judgment seems objectively valid. While categorically an engineer, the architect—without disparagement toward the professional engineer—is required to demonstrate that he possesses and utilizes a particular talent in his engineering, to wit, art or aesthetics, not only theoretically but practically, also, in coordination with basic engineering. R.S. c. 81 prescribes that an engineer verify that he has such special talent to a sufficiently cultivated degree before he may publicly solicit patronage as an architect.

Professional engineering and architecture are not mutually separable and can never be completely disassociated. They are overlapping vocations. Nonetheless the Legislature in reason was justified in not regarding them as coextensive but as occasioning individualized attention for the public weal.

In the education of architects Massachusetts Institute of Technology informs us that:

> "The prerequisites for the study of architecture are sympathy for human institutions, aesthetic perception, and the ability to utilize effectively the methods of science in arriving at specific solutions of building problems. At bottom perhaps a special 'constructive' aptitude (important for various other careers as well) is, if not actually necessary, extremely desirable. The course of study must provide in different ways for work along various lines—humanistic, artistic, and technical. * * * In this the elements of function, of structure, and of design in the layman's sense—that is form and expression—are combined and ultimately integrated. Like any other student, the student of architecture must proceed some distance analytically with the study of the separate aspects of his world before he can hope to reach a successful synthesis * * *" Education of Architects and Planners (M.I.T.) P. 15.

In Goldschlag v. Deegan, 135 Misc. 535, 238 N.Y.S. 3, 4, 5, the court said:

> "* * * But I think it may be safely said that, speaking of to-day, there are many elements of service in the prep-

aration of plans for the construction of a building of whatever type, and the superintendence of construction, that may be more properly left to what we now know as an architect than to what we now know as an engineer. Certainly, an engineer is not to be presumed to be 'one who understands architecture.' * * *"

In People v. Babcock, 343 Mich. 671, 73 N.W.2d 521, 526, it is said:

> "While it is a fact that the definitions of architects and engineers are somewhat similar, yet there is a distinction. The services of an architect requires the application of the principles of architecture or architectural design, while the services of an engineer requires the application of engineering principles."

We quote from Rabinowitz v. Hurwitz-Mintz Furniture Co., 19 La.App. 811, 133 So. 498, 499:

> "In the Encyclopedia Britannica we find the following with respect to the profession of engineering: 'Specialization has brought about separate grouping of those interested in mechanical, electrical, mining, etc. engineering. Underlying all groups is the work of the civil engineer, whose field particularly is that of structures. Foundations, simple or extremely complicated, are within his realm. He designs and supervises the construction of bridges and great buildings, tunnels, dams, reservoirs and acqueducts.' From the same work we excerpt the following definition of an architect: 'One who, skilled in the art of architecture designs buildings, determining the disposition of both their interior spaces and exterior masses, together with the structural embellishments of each, and generally supervises their erection.'"

In McGill v. Carlos, Ohio Com.Pl., 81 N.E.2d 726, 729, the Ohio Court said:

> "Primarily, an architect is a person who plans, sketches and presents the complete details for the erection, enlargement, or alteration of a building or other structure for the use of the contractor or builder when expert knowledge and skill are required in such preparation. The practice of architecture may also include the supervision of construction under such plans and specifications * * *"

In Architectural Research: Its Nature and Practice, by Robert W. McLaughlin, FAIA, Director, School of Architecture, Princeton University, (1958), we find the following:

> "* * * Man's decision to live in groups in stable locations led to the building of towns and cities. The ways in which men organize society determine the nature of our cities, and in turn the nature of our cities has a profound effect on the nature of society. An extreme example of this

is the slum. *Architecture unrelated to the interests of society produces a slum as soon as it is built.* The study of human ecology, which is concerned with the relation of society to physical environment, and vice versa, holds keys to the understanding of the nature of our cities which can lead to wise planning. The methods and findings of the social scientists are applicable to this area. Urban research, which is architectural research in its widest aspects, leads to principles badly needed for understanding and conditioning the growth and deterioration of cities. * * *

"History records man's constant effort to change and improve his environment. He has changed it through building, and improved it through architecture. *He has also damaged his environment through architecture—bad architecture."* (Italics supplied.)

We conclude that, while all architects may be engineers, all engineers are not architects. To restate these truths in one proposition, some engineers are architects. The Legislature confirmed these inferences when in 1945 it made requisite a special and classificational licensing of architects as such and enacted a separate statute for such a purpose in addition to the earlier engineering licensing act of 1935. While the respective functions of an engineer and those of an architect as recited in the two statutes superficially appear parallel and equivalent as predicated for each group they are designedly not so. Notably in the instance of architects studies, plans, specifications, etc., are coupled conjunctively with "a coordination of structural factors concerning the aesthetic." That element is absent from the engineering law. And although the architect licensing act states that it regulates as to the performing of:

"* * * any other service in connection with the designing or supervision of construction of buildings located within the state, regardless of whether such persons are performing any or all of these duties * * *,"

architecture connotes the fulfillment of such duties—which are fundamentally done very well by engineers—in an ulterior manner and with certain finesse not indispensable to the vocation of basic engineering.

It is self-evident from mere definition that the practice of both the professional engineer and the architect directly relate to the public health and welfare.

Architects are commonly engaged to project and supervise the erection of costly residences, schools, hospitals, factories, office and industrial buildings and to plan and contain urban and suburban development. Health, safety, utility, efficiency, stabilization of property values, sociology and psychology are only some of the integrants involved intimately. Banking quarters, commercial office suites, building lobbies, store merchandising salons and display atmospheres, motels, restaurants and hotels eloquently and universally attest the decisive importance in competitive business of architectural science, skill and taste. A synthesis of the utilitarian, the efficient, the economical, the healthful, the alluring and the blandished is often the difference between employment and unemployment, thriving commerce and a low standard of existence. Basic engineering no longer suffices to satisfy many demands of American health, wealth or prosperity.

R.S. c. 81 is necessary to assure the public in these times of expanding and mobile populations that one who publicly offers himself in the role of an architect may evidence his competence by due registration with the State Board.

. . .

Exceptions overruled.

Judgment for the State.

SECTION 31.05 INTERSTATE PROBLEMS

Problems often arise where the professional is licensed in one state, but performs services which have a relationship to a state in which he is not licensed. For example in Johnson v. Delane, 77 Idaho 172, 290 P.2d 213 (1955), an engineer licensed in the state of Washington obtained a commission to prepare plans and specifications for a project to be built in Idaho. The engineer was not to perform any supervisory function. He obtained the commission while visiting in Idaho. He performed the requisite design services in Washington and delivered the plans and specifications to the client in Idaho. The court held that he was not practicing architecture in Idaho, and he was able to collect for his services.

If the purpose of Idaho licensing laws is to protect Idaho clients from retaining unqualified architects and to protect Idaho citizens from being exposed to risk of harm due to structures which may not comply with local building laws and codes, it would seem that the project being constructed in Idaho for Idaho clients should necessitate the licensing of the architect under Idaho laws.

The *Johnson* case is supportable if the architectural registration requirements for Washington and Idaho are generally similar and if there are no peculiarities of Idaho building codes which might make them substantially different than those in effect in Washington. As to the interests of Idaho in insuring that structures met Idaho building code standards, the defendant client would have had a defense to any action by the architect, whether licensed in Idaho or not, had there been a failure to comply with local building codes.

Also, the decision can be supported on another ground. It is likely that the architect could have complied with Idaho laws by applying for a nonresident or temporary license to perform the services for one project. If so, granting him recovery despite his not being registered in Idaho would relieve him of a forfeiture and prevent unjust enrichment of the client by in effect excusing his failure to use this method of complying with Idaho law.

Sometimes a design professional licensed in one state performs design services as a consultant for a project to be built in a state in which he is not licensed. If the performance of these services violates the licensing laws of the state in which the project is located, sometimes the unlicensed consultant can collect for his services and sometimes he cannot. For a detailed discussion of this problem, see § 31.07.

Conderback v. Standard Oil of California, 239 Cal.App.2d 664, 48 Cal.Rptr. 901 (1966) involved the application of a California contractors licensing statute to a project in Washington. The contractor was not licensed in California, his principal place of business. Despite the fact that the negotiation took place in California and the fact that the contractor was located in California, the court held that the failure of the contractor to have a California license did not preclude the use of the California courts to collect for work performed in Washington. According to the court, the State of California would be giving its law effect beyond the borders of California if these laws were applied to a project in another state.

Architects and engineers who intend to perform direct professional services or consulting services for projects which are located in states where they are not licensed should first determine whether a license is required in that state. In some states consultation services may not constitute the type of activity which requires a license. If the out of state architect or engineer is to have the primary design responsibility, he will probably have to be registered in the state. If he does not register, it may be possible to have a local architect as the primary architect with the out of state architect performing consulting services.

If the type of services he intends to perform requires registration, he should ascertain whether there are exceptions set forth in the registration statute or in case decisions for isolated single projects, whether on a direct design professional basis or on a consulting basis. If there is no such exception, the design professional should determine whether reciprocity exists between the state in which he is registered and the state where he intends to perform design services. Often it is a simple procedure to obtain a temporary license for one project if reciprocity exists.

SECTION 31.06 TIMING PROBLEMS

What if the professional was not licensed when the contract was made, but became licensed during the performance of his work? What if the architect or engineer was not licensed until after the work was performed, but before he had to use judicial assistance in collecting his fee? What if the professional was licensed at some time during the performance of his work, or even throughout the performance of his work but, before he sues for his fee, his license has been suspended, revoked, or not renewed?

The result will often depend upon statutory language, the judicial feeling that the client may be seeking an escape from paying a properly earned fee and whether the failure to obtain or maintain a license resulted from inadvertence. In Latipac, Inc. v. Superior Ct., 64 Cal.2d 278, 411 P.2d 564, 49 Cal.Rptr. 676 (1966), the failure to renew was due to the inadvertence of an office manager who had a mental breakdown. The contractor was allowed to recover. The license should be obtained at the earliest possible time, kept current throughout the performance of the work, and be operative at the time legal action may have to be brought to collect for work performed.

SECTION 31.07 SANCTIONS: DENYING RECOVERY OF FEES

There are various sanctions against unlicensed practice. There are usually criminal sanctions of a fine or imprisonment. This may be so whether the licensing laws are "practice" or "holding-out" statutes. In addition, there may be civil penalties, such as civil fines, for unauthorized practice. There may be injunctive powers in the administrative agency which administers the profession in question, which may permit the agency to go to court to stop the unlicensed professional from either practicing or holding himself out as licensed to practice.

The greatest and most frequently used sanction against unlicensed practice is to give a defense to the client if he is sued for not paying the fee. Most of the cases have involved attempts by an unlicensed design professional to collect for his services. While recovery has been allowed in some cases, unlicensed professionals have usually been denied recovery. They may even be denied recovery for undeniably non-architectural work, where there was some element of architectural work in the performance. Most courts view the architectural and engineering licensing laws as being so important that the fact that the client may have known that the architect was not licensed will not assist the unlicensed architect in collecting his fees, unless the architect is in one of the few "holding-out" states.

In denying recovery to the unlicensed professional performing services, courts have stated that these contracts are illegal and that to permit recovery in such a case would frustrate the operation of the statutes. When contracts are found to be illegal, the courts generally leave the parties in *status quo*. They do not assist one party in collecting from the other, nor do they, as a rule, require that the unlicensed professional return payments that may have already been made. Also, courts generally deny recovery on an unjust enrichment theory because to permit recovery on unjust enrichment would also frustrate the operation of the statute.

While some decisions have permitted an unlicensed architect to collect without obtaining a license, the unlicensed professional runs serious risks of being uncompensated for performing professional services.

The case decisions are more uncertain where a design professional licensed in one state performs consulting services related to a project which is to be built in a state in which he is not licensed. Two cases of this type illustrate the unpredictability of legal results in these cases.

In Markus & Nocka v. Julian Goodrich Architects, Inc., 250 A.2d 739 (Vt.1969) the plaintiff was an architect licensed in Massachusetts who specialized in hospital design. The defendant was a Vermont architect who had been retained to perform design services for hospital facilities in Vermont. The hospital directed the Vermont architect to hire a specialist in hospital architecture and he hired the plaintiff.

The plaintiff made a study of the design needs, consulted with the Vermont hospital staff and prepared revisions of preliminary sketches and specifications. The plaintiff's staff made numerous trips to Vermont in performing these services. Ultimately, the design recommendations of the plaintiff were not accepted by the hospital staff and the project was put out to bid based on the design work of the defendant.

The court held that the Massachusetts architects had violated the Vermont registration laws. Since the architectural contract between plaintiff and defendant violated Vermont law, the contract was illegal and the provision for the payment of compensation was unenforceable. The court noted that the construction was to be undertaken in Vermont and that many visits had been made to the Vermont site, along with consultations with Vermont hospital personnel.

Since the consulting contract was found to be illegal, the question was whether the plaintiff consulting architects could collect for their services. The court held that they could not. In denying recovery the court stated that:

> The underlying policy is one of protecting the citizens of the state from untrained, unqualified and unauthorized practitioners.

The court would not apply an exception used by some states which permit a consulting architect to recover if his performance was one single, isolated act. The court noted that such an interpretation would weaken the registration laws. The court pointed out that the Vermont registration laws were phrased in broad, positive terms and provided no exception of this type.

The court also noted that the registration laws for medicine and engineering *specifically* authorized consultant services in Vermont by those properly licensed out of state but that there was no corresponding provision relating to out of state architectural consultants.

The court stated that Vermont law provided that architects licensed in another state whose standards were not below those of Vermont could be admitted in Vermont without examination.

The court made it clear that consultations across state lines on Vermont projects would not necessarily violate Vermont registration laws. The court emphasized this by concluding:

> . . . when the nonresident architect presumes to consult, advise and service, in some direct measure, a Vermont client relative to Vermont construction, he is putting himself within the scope of the Vermont architectural registration law.

Costello v. Schmidlin, 404 F.2d 87 (3rd Cir. 1968) involved an action for consultation fees by Costello who was licensed in New York but not licensed in New Jersey, the state in which the project was being built. Costello was an engineer who specialized in the construction of swimming pools. In addition to being licensed in New York, his principal place of business, he was licensed in Maryland, Illinois and New Mexico. He agreed to perform consulting services for a New Jersey municipal swimming pool complex through a consulting contract with the New Jersey architect.

When he was not paid, Costello sued in federal court.

The trial judge, applying New Jersey law, ruled that the services were performed under an illegal contract because the plaintiff was not licensed in New Jersey and therefore the plaintiff could not collect.

The Circuit Court of Appeals reversed, holding that the plaintiff could collect despite the consultation contract having violated New Jersey law.

The court noted that registration laws protect general members of the public, not persons engaged in the same business or profession as the unlicensed professional. The court also noted that the New Jersey professional engineers licensing act contained no express provision denying enforcement of claims by nonlicensed engineers.

In reviewing prior decisions, the court noted that in most cases where the out-of-state engineer was denied the right to recover for his services, the engineer is not licensed in any state, and was performing services as a direct professional engineer rather than as a consultant through a licensed architect as in the *Costello* case.

The issue in these cases is whether the unlicensed engineer can collect for consultation services. Even in the *Costello* case, where he was permitted to collect, he still violated the New Jersey law by consulting on a New Jersey project.

In the Federal court opinion there appears to be a recognition of the difficulty that specialists who practice on an interstate basis would have if they had to meet the registration standards of all states in which they practice. This is indicated by the fact that the court noted that the plaintiff was licensed in four states. One can infer that he would have had the necessary qualifications to become licensed in New Jersey as well.

As mentioned, approximately one fourth of the states license contractors. Since these statutes are not nearly as universal as registration statutes for architects and engineers, it is possible for a contractor who does interstate business to engage in a project without realizing that he should obtain a license in the state where the project is located.

While the *Markus* and *Costello* cases involved somewhat different facts and somewhat different statutory language, there are different attitudes expressed by the two courts toward licensing laws in general.

The Vermont court emphasized the need to insure that all persons who performed design services for Vermont clients on Vermont projects meet minimal Vermont standards of competence. In the view of the Vermont court, it is most important that these design professionals register under Vermont law and one method of insuring this is to deny them recovery for services they performed when they had not registered under Vermont law.

The federal court in the *Costello* case appears more concerned with doing justice between the two parties to the case, the out of state consultant and the local design professional. It does not seem just to them to deny the out of state consultant the right to be paid for his services. The federal court also seems to believe that the basic purpose of licensing laws is to protect laymen when they deal with professionals. In the *Costello* case the contract was between design professionals and not between a design professional and a layman. While the same was true in the *Markus* case, the court was less willing to look at these other considerations in determining whether the design professional could collect for his services. Again, it must be emphasized that in the *Costello* case the court did not hold that Costello had not violated the New Jersey law. Its only concern was whether this violation would preclude his right to recover for his services.

Some state laws do not require a license for performance of services by an out-of-state design professional if he is licensed in the state where he practices principally and as long as there is a licensed design professional in overall charge of the project. However, the licensed local design professional must not be a figurehead, but actually perform the usual design professional functions. Sometimes out of state architects or engineers "associate" a local architect as a means of insuring that they will be able to collect their fees.

In Food Management, Inc. v. Blue Ribbon Beef Pack, Inc., 413 F. 2d 716 (8th Cir. 1969) plaintiff was an Ohio engineering corporation that had entered into a written "turn key" contract with the defendant for the design and construction of a meat packing plant to be built in Iowa. The plaintiff was not licensed in Iowa, but entered into a written contract with an Iowa architect-engineer. This agreement designated the Ohio corporation as the "Principal Consultant" and referred to the local architect-engineer as the "Associate Engineer." The contract stated in part:

> "C. Consideration of the Associate Engineer's Work: The Principal Consultant shall give thorough consideration to all reports, sketches, drawings, specifications, proposals and other documents presented by the Associate Engineer, and shall inform the Associate Engineer of his decision within a reasonable time so as not to delay the work of the Associate Engineer.
>
> "D. Standards: The Principal Consultant shall furnish the Associate Engineer with a copy of any design and construction standards he shall require the Associate Engineer to follow in the preparation of drawings and specifications for This Part of the Project."

The project was ultimately abandoned because of excessive cost. When the plaintiff sued for the services performed, it was met with the defense that it was not licensed to practice in Iowa. One of the contentions made by the plaintiff was that the engineering or architecture performed in Iowa had actually been performed by the Iowa architects and engineers. The court held that the Iowa architects were not actually in charge of the project and the plaintiff was not simply executing the plans of the Iowa architect. The case denied recovery for design services.

SECTION 31.08 ADMINISTRATION OF LICENSING LAWS

The licensing and practice laws are administered mainly by administrative agencies. Until the end of the nineteenth century, generally rulemaking in American states was accomplished by statutes enacted by the legislature. Disputes generally were handled in courts. However, gradually legislatures began to recognize that they could not enact adequately detailed laws in the many regulated areas. For this reason, legislatures began to spell out the basic principles or rules by statute, and then created administrative agencies to administer and implement these laws.

Usually, agencies created to regulate professions are given power to make rules and regulations designed to fill in gaps left by the statutes or to make particular the general principles articulated by the legislature. Frequently they are given authority to render advisory opinions, if requested, on the statutes and regulations. They also have the power to obtain court orders requiring that persons stop violating the licensing statutes and regulations. Finally, they often have the power to make initial administrative decisions, in particular license violation cases.

Such agencies and commissions have great power over the professions they regulate. This power is even greater when courts take a passive role in reviewing agency actions. On the whole, administrative decisions and regulations are generally free from judicial scrutiny. In the area of decisions, courts usually look at whether the agency had jurisdiction and whether there was substantial evidence to justify their decision. As to the regulations, courts look at whether the procedures of the agency were proper and whether regulations fell within the statutes which authorized them.

Some states provide a broader scope of judicial review where the agency revokes or suspends a design professional's license, but very little judicial review where the issue is whether the agency should have registered an applicant. Generally, there is a slightly increasing tendency for courts to take a more active role in regulating these administrative agencies.

REVIEW QUESTIONS

1. What is the difference between a "practice" statute and a "holding out" statute?

2. What are the criteria for determining whether particular services fall within those services required to be performed by a registered design professional?

3. Compare engineering and architectural services.

4. What are the available sanctions against unlicensed professional practice?

5. Generally, can an unlicensed design professional collect for his services?

QUESTIONS FOR CLASS DISCUSSION

1. What are the advantages and disadvantages of increased governmental control over the design professions?

2. With the increased interstate activity of design professionals, should there be a national registration system?

3. If an unlicensed design professional performs properly, should he be deprived of his fee?

4. Should a client who knowingly hires an unlicensed architect or engineer be able to assert the lack of license as a defense in any legal action by the unlicensed architect against the client for his fees?

PROBLEM

A was registered as a licensed architect in the state in which he had his offices. In that state licenses must be renewed every five years. Renewals are usually granted unless there have been a large number of complaints made with the licensing board.

Three months before A's license was required to be renewed he entered into a written contract for the performance of design services for C. A was paid approximately 60% of his fee through interim payments. When the time came for final billing after the services were completed, A discovered that he had forgotten to renew his registration. He called the licensing board and they informed him that he would have been renewed had he applied at the proper time and A then took steps to renew his registration.

However, C discovered that A had not renewed his registration and now refuses to pay the balance of the fee. He also demands that A return to him the interim fee payments made.

Should A be entitled to recover the balance of the fee? If your conclusion is that he should not, should he be obligated to repay any interim fee payments made? Give your reasons.

Chapter 32

FORMS OF ASSOCIATION FOR PRACTICE

SECTION 32.01 FORMS OF ASSOCIATION AVAILABLE

In all states, the private architect or engineer can practice as a sole proprietor, or in a partnership. In an increasing number of states, the corporate form for practice is available.

An "association" may be merely an arrangement for practice under which the members agree to share space and expenses and occasionally do work for one another.

SECTION 32.02 SHOULD PROFESSIONAL INCORPORATION BE PERMITTED?

Before discussing the advantages and disadvantages of using the corporate form where it is permitted, (see § 32.03), it may be useful to look briefly at the essentially non-legal question of the desirability of permitting the corporate form to be used by design professionals.

This question has been controversial within the design professions as it has within the medical and legal professions. The main issues relate to tax advantages of incorporation as opposed to the claimed adverse effect of incorporation upon the design professions and design services.

While those who favor permitting corporate practice point to the corporation as a more efficient organizational form and means of raising capital, the principal justification for professional incorporation relates to tax advantages. These will be discussed in § 32.03.

As design professionals, mainly engineering organizations, grow in size, there is a need for a more efficient organization. However, the partnership form, if handled and planned carefully, can provide a high degree of organizational efficiency.

As for raising capital, this has not been used much by professional corporations. While it is true that large amounts of capital may be necessary for large design professional organizations that engage in costly long-term projects, such capital can be raised by borrowing rather than by issuing shares of stock. Lenders may not get the degree of power over the affairs of the borrower that the shareholders get over the affairs of the corporation. Where incorporation by design professionals is permitted, it is likely to be used by small design professional organizations not for purposes of better organization or raising capital, but for the purpose of obtaining tax advantages.

Those opposed to the corporate form feel that permitting incorporation ultimately will drive smaller practitioners out of the profession. They also maintain that the corporate form through its profit-making image and its use to limit liability will downgrade the professional status of architect and engineer and can result in poorer professional services. Some feel that the corporate form will interfere with the close relationship necessary between client and professional and that the profit seeking nature of a corporation will be harmful to the service aspect of the design profession. Finally, those opposed to permitting incorporation point to the possibility that final authority and responsibility for professional decisions can fall into the hands of businessmen rather than design professionals. Those opposed to the corporate form feel that if there is inequity in the tax laws which make it more desirable to incorporate rather than practice as a partnership, there should be tax reform.

In rebuttal, those who favor permitting incorporation state that the professional corporation can be tailored by statutes permitting it to meet some of the objections raised by opponents of incorporation. Professional incorporation statutes frequently require that the control of the corporation be in the hands of registered professionals, that the management be limited to such professionals or that professional work shall be the responsibility of a registered professional and signed by him.

Professional incorporation statutes often place restrictions on the transferability of shares so that nonprofessionals do not gain control.

As for the use of the corporate form to insulate design professionals from responsibility for their work, proponents of incorporation state that professional incorporation statutes can be drafted to deny shareholders the usual liability protection given to shareholders in a business corporation. Also, proponents of incorporation state that the risk of liability for professional acts can be met by the use of professional liability insurance and the normal business corporation insulation from liability is not necessary. If a design professional is properly insured, the issue of corporate insulation for shareholders is not likely to arise. (In Chapter 35 it will be seen that professional liability policies often exclude coverage for important types of liability.)

Finally, those who favor incorporation say that the realities of legislative process are likely to preclude correction of tax inequities that have led to increased use of the corporate form.

SECTION 32.03 WHERE PERMITTED, SHOULD THE CORPORATE FORM BE USED?

(A) ADVANTAGES

A partnership is not a separate legal entity. The income to the partnership is taxed once, at the individual rates specified by law. Also, the partners are principals, and not employees.

A corporation is a separate legal entity which operates through employees. In this way, unlike a partnership, the shareholders can also be employees. Fringe benefits with tax advantages can be given to the professional architects and engineers in their capacity as employees of the corporation. These benefits with equivalent tax advantages are not available to sole proprietors or partners.

For example, a corporation may set up a profit sharing plan or pension plan which can postpone payments to employees until a period of time when the employee retires, when his income is usually lower and taxed at a lower rate. A corporation can give other fringe benefits to its employees, such as group life insurance, and group health plans. The expense of contributions to such profit-sharing and pension plans and the cost of group insurance are deductible to the corporation. Such contributions are either not income to the employees, or are not taxed until received.

There has been some progress in changing tax laws to permit self-employed persons, such as sole proprietors or partners, to set up pension plans with tax advantages corresponding to those that are given to employees of corporations. Since 1968, a self-employed person can set aside up to 10% of his income, not to exceed $2,500, in a pension plan. He can also deduct this amount as a business expense, thus reducing his income. However, he must make this pension plan available to all of his employees, although he can place some restrictions on the rights of employees to participate in a pension plan.

A capital asset is one held for investment or use and not for sale in the ordinary course of business. For example, if a design professional owns shares in a corporation, this is a capital asset. If he has held it for six months before selling it, any profit on the sale is a long term capital gain. Generally, such capital gains are taxed at a lower rate than income received from the performance of services or the sale of goods in the ordinary course of the taxpayer's business. If the corporate form is used, a design professional who is a shareholder in the corporation may sell his interest in the corporation by selling his corporate shares. In such a case he may be able to obtain the advantage of long term capital gains rates.

In addition to tax advantages, there may be other advantages to the corporate form. Large engineering organizations may need to raise capital. The corporate form lends itself more readily to raising capital than does the partnership form. Also, long-term projects may be more successfully accomplished if the corporate form is used. This is because the corporate existence can be unlimited, while, under partnership law, certain events may dissolve the partnership.

Another possible advantage is the limitation of liability. In the normal corporate structure, individual shareholders are not liable for most debts of the corporation. This "advantage" may be considerably limited by the state laws which permit professionals to incorporate. Sometimes these statutes change the normal corporation rule, so that individual shareholders are liable for the debts of the professional corporation.

(B) DISADVANTAGES

The initial organization and creation of a corporation require articles of a corporation be drafted. There are usually by-laws to govern the corporation's activities. Franchise taxes will have to be paid and, in some states, a permit will have to be issued by a state agency charged with the responsibility of regulating corporations. After the corporation is properly organized, the corporation must have a specified number of corporate directors' meetings during the year. Minutes must be kept of these meetings, and any acts of the corporation will be governed by the laws regulating the corporations, the articles of the corporation, and the by-laws. All of this involves some legal and administrative expense.

In addition to initial expense in organizing the corporation, there are small continuing expenses in keeping it going. If the formalities of the corporate form are not followed, there is always a chance that the corporate form will be disregarded by a court. This may have adverse consequences to the shareholders, both from tax and liability standpoints.

Limited liability, if it exists, is less important than it once may have been. Professional liability risks should be handled through the use of professional liability insurance. Clients may insist that a corporate design professional obtain professional liability insurance. The use of the corporate shield, where possible, may cause ill will. If a corporate structure were used, and if the corporation were not properly capitalized, there would be a substantial possibility that the individual shareholders would be held individually liable. If they were naive enough to believe that the corporation would shield them from liability, they might make the mistake of not having adequate professional liability insurance. In such a case, their private assets could be lost if a large judgment were obtained against them.

Since professional incorporation laws often require that the work be performed or checked by designated persons, professional incorporation can require a readjustment of normal design professional methods of operation.

Sometimes taking in new shareholders raises problems. A partnership can take in new partners, without the new partner having to make a contribution to capital. However, it sometimes is more complicated to give a proprietory stake to a former employee when the corporate form is used. (The possible entry of new shareholders into the corporation should be provided for when the corporation is created.)

There are other expenses when a corporation is used. There are likely to be additional accounting and legal expenses, because separate returns have to be made out for the corporation and for the individual shareholders. This usually must be done both at the state and federal levels.

Another disadvantage of the corporate form is that some clients do not feel as comfortable in seeking and obtaining professional advice when they are dealing with a corporation, as opposed to a partnership. As the use of the corporation becomes more prevalent, this may change. However, some architects and engineers feel that the use of the corporation can destroy some of the confidential relationship and trust between the design professional and his client.

(C) DELAYING THE DECISION

There are advantages and disadvantages in using the corporate form. A determination as to what form should be used need not be made at the time a number of individual architects or engineers band together for professional practice. When they begin practice they may not have the necessary funds to hire a lawyer and put the corporate structure into operation. Their income may not be at a high enough level to find tax advantages in incorporating. The entry of new people into a corporation is easier when the architectural or engineering group has more or less stabilized. At the beginning there may only be a few partners and employees. In five or ten years, if the association is a successful one, there may be many more people involved in the operation. This may be the time to choose whether to incorporate.

SECTION 32.04 PARTNERSHIP

For a discussion of the legal aspects of a professional partnership review § 4.03. Section 10.03(a) treats the effect of a change of partners on existing partnership contracts.

SECTION 32.05 "LOOSE" FORMS OF ASSOCIATION

(A) TYPES

The terms "association" or "associated with" are sometimes employed in describing certain types of arrangements which vary considerably in function and effect from the partnership and corporate forms of association that have been discussed.

A recently licensed design professional may become an employee of a sole proprietor, a partnership, or a corporate employer. Sometimes the term "associate" is used to describe his status. He is usually paid a salary, or an hourly wage, for his work. Calling him an "associate" in such an employment situation is simply a euphemism for an "employee".

Sometimes the recently admitted design professional either is unable to obtain a job as an employee, or does not wish to be an employee. He may wish to be a sole proprietor, but may not have sufficient funds to rent space or to pay for the overhead necessary to be a sole proprietor. In these cases, certain types of "loose association" may be open to him.

Sometimes a number of architects and engineers join in an office and share expenses. They may desire to be independent, and not form a partnership or corporation. In such a "share expense" association, design professionals are essentially on their own, but share rental, clerical, and supply expenses. In such an arrangement, one design professional may do work for another in the association.

Sometimes a design professional may be essentially on his own out of choice or necessity. To supplement his income he may do work for another design professional. For reasons of economy and convenience, the two design professionals may share the same office.

For example, an established architect may rent office space in his suite of offices to a younger architect. There may be an arrangement between the two under which the younger architect will perform services for the established architect at a designated fee. As for clients brought to the office by the young architect, the latter may pay a portion of the fees earned from such clients to the other architect as his contribution to the overhead of the office paid by the established architect. Such payments may be in lieu of any fixed monthly share of overhead attributable to the space occupied by the younger architect and the clerical assistance used by him. Payment of a percentage of fees earned permits the younger architect to avoid any obligation to pay a fixed monthly overhead payment when he may not have clients or fees.

(B) LEGAL PROBLEMS

A number of legal problems may result from these "loose" forms of association. What are the rights and duties of persons who share space and overhead expenses? Who pays for what, and how much? When are payments to be made? What is the duration of the relationship? Contract arrangements could answer these questions but frequently such associations are created without any formal or detailed contracts, and many of the gaps have to be filled in by custom or common sense.

Payment for Work

If one design professional does work for another, what governs their rights and duties? As between themselves, the applicable principle is the law of contract. Usually, they agree in advance on the amount of compensation. They should consider reimbursable expenses, as well as an hourly rate. They should clarify whether the amount of work is to be limited by time, or by a fixed monetary limit. Is payment to be conditioned upon the client paying the design professional for whom the work is being done? How soon is the work to be completed?

If possible, these matters should be settled in advance. Where they are not, the law will award the design professional the reasonable value of his services, probably reimbursement of out-of-pocket expenses, not place any time or monetary limit on the amount of work other than good faith, and obligate the performing party to finish within a reasonable time. If nothing is stated as to conditioning payment upon payment by the client, and if no custom or usage to contrary exists, the performing party will be entitled to be paid within a reasonable time, without regard to whether the client pays for the work.

Client Problem: Termination of Association

The most difficult questions in "loose" associations relate to clients. For example, a client may be brought to the office by one design professional. Another design professional may, at the request of the design professional who brought in the client, do certain work for this client. This work may put the client in direct contact with the design professional who is doing this work.

While the association continues, in the sense that the same office sharing arrangement is maintained, disputes may arise when a client decides to take work from one professional and give it to the other, or when a client brings future work to the person other than the one who brought him to the office. More common, and more difficult, are the disputes which can develop if the loose association is terminated and one or more design professionals move to a new location. The professional who has left may want to take clients whom he did not bring to the old association to his new location.

To do this, he may want to send announcements of his new location to all clients for whom he did work while he was with the old association. Often these clients were not brought to the old association by him. He may decide to actively solicit these clients.

Sometimes informal "solicitation" is made before he terminates the old association and goes into a new location. He may want to know whether he can take certain clients with him before he decides to terminate the old association.

To build up his new practice, the outgoing associate may desire to take client lists with addresses, copies of work done for clients in the past, and copies of plans, specifications, and drawings which may have been done for jobs which are not yet completed. These records may be useful to him and, in some cases, he may find that some of them are essential to his being able to perform professional services for clients of his own and for clients whom he hopes to attract.

If he succeeds in taking clients with him, or if he copies or takes records other than his own, the remaining associate might: (1) seek a court order precluding the former associate from representing certain clients, based upon interference with an existing contract or with a prospective client relationship, (2) seek a court judgment for money damages caused by the solicitation and taking of his clients, (3) take the matter to a grievance committee established by a professional organization to which both may belong, (4) sue clients for breach of contract if they leave him or (5) take a complaint to the licensing board of the state in which the departing associate practices.

While case precedents on "loose" associations are scarce, there are analogies from the law of employee-employer relationships, the law of principal-agent, and partnership law. Usually, in the absence of any contractual provision to the contrary, the agent or former employee can compete with his former employer or former principal. However, he can be precluded from making use of trade secrets or special lists of customers or clients which he surreptitiously takes from his old employer or former principal. Those clients or customers whose names he has memorized, he can approach. Usually he is not precluded from using the skills and the ability to service clients or customers that he developed while working for his former employer or his former principal.

In the dissolution of a partnership or the sale of a partnership to a purchaser, similar problems can arise. In the absence of any contractual provisions to the contrary, the withdrawing partner or the members of the old partnership where there is a sale of the partnership business, are permitted to compete with the old partnership, the former partners, or the purchaser of the partnership. They are permitted to solicit the customers of the prior partnership, provided they do not engage in unfair competition. Unfair competition usually consists of representing in some way that they are dealing on behalf of the old partnership.

There can be liability for deliberately tampering with existing contracts or relatively stable relationships. Liability can result from a misrepresentation as to who is being dealt with, or a misuse of trade secrets learned during the employment relationship or during the partnership.

While the law favors free competition, promises not to compete are generally enforced, either by an injunction against competition or by damages, providing the promises are reasonable and if there is a sufficient social justification for their enforcement.

The loose association does not involve partners who have bound themselves together in a form of shared ownership, nor the close relationship of an employee and his employer. Despite the resemblance of the loose association to the employment relation, because of the frequent work done by one loose associate for another, the loose association is not an employment relationship. Certainly, what is permissible under the laws of employment relations and partnership would be permissible under the loose association.

If the withdrawing associate's activities relating to seeking or obtaining clients would not be permitted under closer relationships such as partnership or employment relationships, they might be permissible under a loose form of association. Much will depend upon the degree to which there is deceptive or dishonest conduct. For example, even under a loose form of association, taking client records belonging to another associate without permission would not be permitted. On the other hand, a statement by the withdrawing associate that he can provide better service is likely to be permissible.

In addition to the general policy of fostering free competition, the law must also take into account the desirability of permitting clients to select their own professional advisors. This is true in the fields of architecture and engineering, as well as in medicine and law. Legal rules which inhibit a client from retaining a design professional who has left an old association can frustrate that objective.

Corrigan v. Cox, 254 Cal.App.2d 919, 62 Cal.Rptr. 733 (1967), while not involving a loose association of design professionals, may be instructive. This case involved litigation between two dentists who had been loosely associated. The plaintiff was an established dentist who had taken in a younger dentist to handle his overflow patients. The younger dentist generally worked on patients who had been attracted to the office by the established dentist and received a percentage of the fees generated by his work.

While the method of operation of a dental "loose" association is somewhat different from a loose association of design professionals, the case is instructive on two points. First, the court looked to the rules of the American Dental Association because both dentists were members of that group. The issues in the case were whether the departing dentist could send announcements to all patients he had treated while a member of the association and whether the withdrawing dentist could make copies of the dental records of patients whom he had treated.

The rules of the American Dental Association permitted a dentist who was changing his location to send an announcement to other dentists, to members of the other health professions and to patients of record. The court held that patients who had been treated by the withdrawing dentist, were "patients of record" of the departing dentist despite the fact that they may have been initially attracted to the dental office by the established dentist. The court also held that the departing dentist was entitled to copies of the records for these patients.

The remaining dentist also contended that the departing dentist was his "employee" and that as a former employee he would not be permitted to compete with his old employer.

Without noting that generally employees can compete with their old employer as long as they do not take trade secrets, disparage the old employer or mislead customers as to whom they are dealing with, the court held that the departing dentist was not an employee. The court noted that the established dentist did not withhold federal income taxes on amount earned by the departing dentist, did not pay social security taxes or unemployment taxes on amounts earned and generally treated the withdrawing dentist as an independent contractor.

If the design professionals in an association are both members of the same professional association, a court might apply the rules of the professional association.

The standards of professional practice of the American Institute of Architects contain a number of provisions dealing with clients. Architects are not to compete for clients based upon fee. An architect should not knowingly, falsely or maliciously injure the professional reputation or prospects of another architect. Architects are prohibited from attempting to supplant another architect after definite steps have been taken by a client toward the latter's employment. Nor is an architect supposed to replace another architect until he has notified the other architect of that fact in writing, and can determine conclusively that the original client relationship has been terminated. There is some similarity between professional rules of conduct and the legal rules which have been developed relating to prohibitions against interfering with existing contracts or with potential clients. However, the rules or principles promulgated by the professional association frequently go beyond the legal rules.

Applying the rules of a professional association to settle the disputes of this type between its members who practice in a "loose" association has some merit. These "rules" may be customs within the profession that are understood and accepted by the members. Also, the law often has very little else with which to decide these disputes.

Yet courts should be cautious before automatically applying these rules to handle disputes of the type described. Clearly, it is a fiction to suppose that members of the association expect that these rules will govern such disputes. Often these rules were not designed for this use. While members of the association may be generally aware of such rules, they may not know their precise nature.

On the question of whether a loose design professional association has created an employment relationship, most courts would come to the same conclusion as did Corrigan v. Cox. In architectural or engineering "loose" associations there is probably less control exercised by the established design professional over the others with whom he shares offices than there would be in a "loose" dental association. This matter is discussed in greater detail later in this section.

A design professional who leaves a "loose" association should be able to send out a dignified announcement when he has terminated his association and has moved to a new location. He should be able to send this announcement not only to other professionals, but also to persons for whom he has rendered professional service. This should be so even if the persons for whom he has rendered professional service were initially brought to him by another member of the loose association.

Greater difficulties arise when he attempts to solicit clients who have an existing relationship, contractual or otherwise, with another professional. Much would depend upon the way this solicitation is made, and whether the solicitation involves an unfair disparagement of the other professional.

As stated previously, courts should not automatically apply the rules of a professional association to fill in the gaps of the relationship. These rules can help if they are generally known and accepted by the members of the association and if they do not contradict anything agreed to by the disputants or the customs in the community in which the disputants practice.

Many of the legal difficulties could be eliminated if the professionals who associated themselves in a loose association would agree in advance on the question of the right to contact or solicit clients when the association is terminated. However, it is not realistic to expect that persons who associate themselves in these ways are likely to go into this question when the loose association is created. Bringing up such a matter is likely to make each party suspicious of the possibility that the other party will steal his clients, either while the association is operating, or after it terminates. Also, advance discussion of this problem can result in onerous conditions being imposed upon the younger and less established professional. He may be so desperate for an association that he will agree to provisions at this time which can severely limit the future prospects of his professional success if he abides by them. Also, there is more likely to be litigation if onerous provisions are imposed upon him and he decides that he will not abide by them because they were imposed upon him in this fashion, and because they would effectively destroy or materially hamper his professional practice.

Perhaps little can be done to resolve these problems in advance, and problems of this sort will have to be worked out by the parties at the time they arise.

Is Associate an Employee?

Other legal problems can arise when there is a loose office association. As shall be discussed in Chapter 36, there are many legal obligations imposed by law when there is an employment relationship. Employee taxes must be deducted or paid. Workmen's compensation requirements must be met. There are legal controls which relate to wages, working conditions, and termination of the employment relationship.

The existence of an employment relationship depends upon the facts and the reason for making the determination. But there are some generalizations.

If the alleged employer has considerable control over how the work is done and when it is to be done, it is more likely to be considered an employment relationship. The existence of other controls over the alleged employee may lead to a similar result. Also, if the alleged employee is paid on an hourly, daily or salaried basis as opposed to a commission or "job" basis, it is more likely that there is an employment relationship.

Also, the law looks at whether the asserted employer complied with laws which govern the employment relationship. For example, in Corrigan v. Cox, discussed at p. 717, the court noted that the person claiming to be an employer did not deduct withholding and did not pay social security or unemployment insurance taxes.

Liability Questions

Suppose a client retains an architect in a loose association and requests that he perform certain design services. What if the architect is too busy to perform some of these services and requests that another architect in the loose association perform them? If the work is not done properly, the issue should not be whether the performing associate is an employee or agent of the original architect. While it might be permissible for the original architect to have these services performed by someone else, a point which would not necessarily be true in every case, this would not relieve the original architect from responsibility if the associate does not do the job or does it improperly. See § 9.02(a).

What if the associate does a negligent job of design? Is the associate himself liable to the client or to third parties who may suffer losses because of his negligence?

Suppose the design professional had hired a consultant to perform services for him. If the consultant is negligent and reasonably foreseeable losses occur to others, the consultant is likely to be liable. The same would be true if instead of an outside consultant being used, the negligence were that of an associate in a loose association.

It is likely that the original architect in the problem would be sued rather than the associate. Also, if the associate were sued, he might be entitled to indemnification from the principal architect on the same theory that an employee may be entitled to indemnification from his employer if the employee is sued because of acts performed within the scope of his employment.

An Apparent Partnership?

Are the members of the loose office association liable if one of the associates makes unauthorized financial commitments for the office? If the association "appears" to the world to be a partnership, the members of the association will be treated as a partnership. Each may be liable for most contractual commitments entered into by the other.

The result may depend upon whether the creditor has relied upon the appearance of a partnership or whether he has advanced goods or services relying solely upon the credit of the person with whom he dealt.

If the association calls itself Jones, Smith, and Brown, and uses this partnership-like name in its dealings and stationary, it may find that for contract and tort purposes it will be treated as a partnership. This would also mean that the negligent acts by the "associate" could be charged to the "association."

REVIEW QUESTIONS

1. What forms of association are generally available to design professionals?

2. What is the principal reason for incorporation?

3. What are the disadvantages of using the corporate form where permissible?

4. What are the legal risks where three design professionals associate for the purpose of sharing expenses, but hold themselves out to the public as a partnership?

5. When an employee leaves his employer, may he generally compete with his former employer?

QUESTIONS FOR CLASS DISCUSSION

1. Will the professional stature of architects and engineers suffer if incorporation becomes a prevalent mode of professional practice?

2. If businessmen can use the corporate form to insulate their personal assets from liability, should professional incorporation laws deny professionals this same protection?

3. Should a withdrawing member of a loose association be able to perform design services for a client whom he met while he was a member of a loose association if these services relate to an entirely new project unconnected with any work performed by the loose association?

4. Suppose there is litigation between two former members of a loose association over clients. If both architects are members of the American Institute of Architects, should the dispute be resolved by applying the Rules of Professional Practice of that Association?

PROBLEM

Smith and Jones were young architects who decided to share expenses and office space. Smith was wealthy while Jones was barely able to make ends meet. Their offices were in the Atlas Building and painted on the door was the inscription "Smith and Jones, Architects". This was also the listing in the telephone directory and in the office directory of the Atlas Building.

Actually, each had his own clients and neither did any work for the other. They hired a secretary who also acted as a bookkeeper. Each income item was allocated to the person who had performed the services and expenses were allocated based upon who used the services or supplies. Each had a separate checking account and there was a third account in the name of Smith and Jones. The latter account was used to pay for the rent, the cost of the secretary and other office expenses.

On occasion each would consult the other with regard to professional design matters. It was not uncommon for one to call the other in while a client was present in order to get informal advice on a design question.

(a) Jones ordered an expensive copying machine at a cost of $700. The order was placed in the name of Smith and Jones. Jones did not pay for the machine and the seller claims that they have a legal right to collect from Smith as well as from Jones. Do you agree? Give your reasons. Would your answer depend on any way upon whether the copier machine company knew of Smith's wealth and supplied the machine based upon his good credit?

(b) Jones designed an exclusive residence for Client. His negligence in design required that certain work be redone at an expense of $2,000 to the client. Client's lawyer ascertained that Jones had no assets or professional liability insurance and that any judgment against him would be uncollectible. Client's lawyer now asserts that he has the right to recover from Smith because Jones and Smith appear to the world as a partnership. Is he correct? Would your conclusion be changed or reinforced if it could be shown that during a conference between Jones and his client, Smith was called in to offer some suggestions relating to design? (Assume that the suggestions did not relate to matters which ultimately were the basis for the claim and that Smith was not negligent in any way).

Chapter 33

RENTING SPACE

SECTION 33.01 RELEVANCE

Because most architects and engineers who enter private practice will rent office space, a brief treatment of office leases should be useful.

SECTION 33.02 LEGAL REQUIREMENTS

Generally, the legal requirements for a lease are similar to the requirements for the making of a valid contract. There must be manifestation of mutual assent, consideration, or one of its substitutes, and the necessary form. Most states require that leases for a period of over a specified length, such as one year, must be in writing.

Generally, American law does not require that leases be recorded or registered in order to be valid. However, it is advisable for the tenant to record his lease at the public office where land records are kept in his county. If he does so, then anyone who purchases the property from the landlord will be obligated to honor the existing lease. (Failure to record the lease does not necessarily mean that the lease will not be effective against third parties who purchase without knowledge of the existing lease.)

In some states it may be necessary to comply with certain formalities, such as having the signature notarized or acknowledged before a lease can be recorded.

SECTION 33.03 RENTAL AMOUNT

Rent may be fixed, or flexible. In a fixed rental, the tenant will agree to pay a specified sum, usually per month, for the term of the lease. Sometimes the rental is determined by a specified multiple times the square footage that is being rented.

Since leases often run for a long period of time, both landlord and tenant are interested in the possibility that events will occur which will make the rental price disadvantageous to either or both parties.

From the landlord's standpoint, there may be a substantial increase in real property taxes which, if absorbed entirely by the landlord, will diminish his profit from the rental of the space. It is not uncommon for leases to contain escalation provisions, under which the tenant agrees to pay all or a specified proportion of any increased taxes that are assessed during the term of the lease.

In business leases a fixed rental for a long term may operate to the disadvantage of the tenant, in the event of a business slump or recession. In such leases it is common to provide that the lease will be a specified percentage of the gross receipts taken in by the tenant. This enables the tenant to reduce his rental if his business declines. Often, the "percentage of gross receipts type lease" is accompanied by a minimum, and sometimes a maximum, provision. The minimum rental usually covers fixed charges incurred by the landlord, such as taxes and the payment of principal and interest. This is to insure that the landlord will be able to meet those fixed charges even if the business conditions which affect the tenant deteriorate. The maximum rental figure is usually for the benefit of the tenant, since it sets a ceiling on the amount of rent which he will have to pay if business is very good.

Suppose a tenant rents office space under a ten year lease. If the rental market shifts downward, it is possible that the landlord will rent comparable space to another tenant for a lower rental amount. Sometimes tenants obtain provisions in leases under which the landlord agrees that he will reduce the rent to an amount which is equal to the rental amount he gives to subsequent comparable tenants for comparable space. This is called a "most favored nations" clause. Obviously it will take good bargaining power on the part of the tenant to obtain such a clause.

If the tenant has sufficient bargaining power to obtain a most favored nations clause, he may have sufficient power to obtain a provision under which the landlord agrees that if the tenant has the opportunity of getting equivalent space in another building at a lower rent, the landlord will either reduce the rental to the lower amount available to the tenant in another building, or release the tenant from any further obligations under the lease. Such a clause is called a "meeting competition" clause. Its chief use is in the area of sale of goods, but it could be appropriate in a long-term lease.

SECTION 33.04 DURATION

(A) PERIODIC TENANCIES

Sometimes office space is leased on a month to month or year to year basis. These are called periodic tenancies. While there is some variation in the state laws relating to the duration of a periodic tenancy, typically the lease continues until one party has given a written notice of termination. The notice of termination usually must be given within a specified period of the effective date of the termination. For example, if the lease is month to month and the rent is paid monthly, either party can terminate by giving one month's notice. Often the effective date of termination must be at the end of a rental period. For example, suppose there is a month to month tenancy which begins at the first of each month and rent is paid on the first of each month. Such a tenancy generally can be terminated effective on August 31 by delivering a written notice of termination on July 31.

(B) FIXED TERM LEASES

Most office space is leased on a fixed, long-term basis. In such leases the lease will expire at the end of the time designated in the lease. While location is not as important in the lease of office space for design professionals as it is in a business lease, location can be important. As indicated, if the term will be for a long period, both landlord and tenant often seek provisions which will protect them from events which will affect the desirability of the lease. In addition to flexibility in the rental amount, the tenant often wishes flexibility in the duration of the lease.

This can be accomplished through an option given the tenant to extend his lease. Options to extend the lease are enforceable as long as they are spelled out with sufficient certainty. Key items are rent, space, and duration.

Usually if the tenant receives an option for additional time, he must exercise this option in a specified manner and in a specified time period. For example, if the lease is to be for ten years with an option given to the tenant for five additional years, as a rule, the lease will specify that the tenant must give written notice to the landlord within a specified period, such as six months, prior to the termination of the basic lease period if he decides to exercise the option to extend the lease period.

Entering into a lease for a long period is a serious obligation from the standpoint of the tenant. Unless he has certain protective provisions, he may find that he is responsible for rent when he can no longer afford it, or when he needs additional space or a different location. Sometimes tenants hedge the long-term lease by having a provision included under which they can terminate the lease at any time by the payment of a specified sum of money. It is important that it be clear that this payment relieves the tenant of any further obligation he may have under the lease. Often, such "buy-out" payment is keyed to the rental price. For example, the tenant may enter into a ten-year lease with a provision enabling him to terminate his obligation under the lease if he pays six months or one year rental.

These buy-out provisions can raise problems. For example, if the tenant pays the buy-out payment, and then the landlord is able to rent the space without any loss to himself, the tenant may argue that the landlord has been unjustly enriched and demand that the payment be returned to him. While this argument would be unlikely to be successful in most states, there is an increasing tendency on the part of courts to preclude the landlord from collecting the buy-out payment and also being able to rent the space, at the same or higher rental. While it is true that there is a gamble inherent in such a provision, in that if a landlord is not able to rent the space he may take a substantial loss, it often appears to courts to be unfair to permit the landlord to keep the payment if he has suffered no loss.

Sometimes such provisions state that the amount paid for the buy-out provision must be returned to the tenant to the extent that it exceeds the landlord's actual loss. Such a provision would be difficult to include if the landlord is in a superior bargaining position.

(C) TERMINATION PRIOR TO EXPIRATION OF TERM

Independent Covenants (Promises)

For historical reasons promises made by landlord and tenant were considered "independent covenants". Under this rule, each party must continue to perform under a lease despite nonperformance by the other. Only if the lease gave either or both parties the right to cease performance or to remedy the other's nonperformance, could this be done. For example, suppose the landlord did not perform in accordance with his lease obligations to keep the premises in a specified condition. Without specific contract language giving the tenant the right to withhold his rent payments, to terminate the lease or to repair the defective condition and deduct it from the rent, the tenant had to continue to pay rent. He had a claim for damages against the landlord for nonperformance. Often such a claim was not much of a remedy if the litigation costs were much greater than the amount of damages caused by the breach. The doctrine of independent covenants effectively deprived the tenant of the powerful weapon of holding back his rent in order to get the landlord to live up to his lease obligations. Only if he had sufficient bargaining power to obtain protective rights in the lease, was he given this protection. (In some jurisdictions this rule has been changed by case decision or statute.)

Where the tenant has sufficient bargaining power, he should include provisions in the lease which give him the right to suspend his rental payments until the landlord complies with important contract provisions. Also, the lease should terminate his obligation to pay rent if the landlord's nonperformance continues beyond a specified or a reasonable time. If the tenant has sufficient bargaining power, he should attempt to include provisions which give him the right to remedy any defects which the landlord has not remedied after he gives specific notice to the landlord of the defect and the right to deduct the cost of remedying the defect from his rental payments.

There have been inroads made by some courts in this doctrine of independent covenants. As seen in other contexts, one party to a contract often has the right to terminate his obligation to perform when the other party commits a serious breach. The doctrine of independent covenants stemmed largely from the early classification of a lease as a conveyance rather than a contract. Some courts are beginning to recognize the contractual aspects of leases. Where this is done, courts are more likely to follow the contract rules rather than the doctrine of independent covenants. In Medico-Dental Building Co. v. Horton & Converse, 21 Cal.2d 411, 132 P.2d 457 (1942), the court held that a tenant did not have to continue to pay rent where the landlord breached by leasing space to a competing business in the same building. This is standard contract doctrine, but this doctrine has only recently been applied to leases where the lease did not specifically cover this question.

Constructive Eviction

If the landowner physically evicts a tenant, the tenant need no longer pay rent and has an action for damages against the landlord. However, if the non-performance by the landlord is serious, sometime courts hold that there has been a "constructive eviction." The word "constructive" means that the particular categorization made by the court did not, in fact, occur; but, in law, it is just as if it had occurred. Simply put, this means that although the landlord does not physically evict the tenant, under circumstances constituting a constructive eviction, the law holds that it is just as if he had physically evicted the tenant. An illustration of constructive eviction occurred when the tenant abandoned his premises because parts of the building were rented to tenants who were using their premises for immoral purposes and created disturbances which prevented the abandoning tenant from sleeping. Another illustration is the failure of the landlord to make, or permit the tenant to make, repairs required by public authorities in order for the tenant to continue his business. Any substantial interference with the tenant's right to possession or enjoyment could constitute constructive eviction.

Surrender and Acceptance

The landlord's "acceptance" of the tenant's "surrender" is another device to relieve against the harshness of independent covenants. Suppose the tenant moves out, either because he can no longer pay the rent or because the landlord has failed to live up to the lease. If the landlord's breach is not sufficient to constitute constructive eviction, the lease obligation is not terminated by the tenant's surrender of the premises. But if the landlord reenters to clean up or make repairs or the landlord rerents the premises to another tenant, the landlord may have accepted the "surrender" by the tenant. If so, the landlord can no longer hold the tenant for rent for the balance of the term of the lease. Nor can he charge the tenant with damages if any reletting was for a smaller sum than the agreed rental under the original lease. If the landlord can show that he did these things for the benefit of the tenant, he may still be able to hold the tenant to the rent, or for damages. Many leases state that it is presumed that if the landlord re-enters, he does so for the benefit of the tenant. The concept of acceptance of the surrender developed to relieve tenants from the harshness of long term leases, where there has been failure by the landlord to fully perform. It can constitute a trap for the unsuspecting landlord who has performed his obligations.

Frustration of Purpose

A fixed rental for a long-term lease obligates the tenant to pay rent despite the occurrence of events which can make the leased premises much less valuable to the tenant and events which make it more difficult for him to pay the fixed rentals. A depression can occur which hurts the tenant's business or brings the rent much below the rental market price. Marketing methods and public tastes change. Laws may be passed which may make the premises unsuitable or unuseable for the purpose anticipated by the tenant. For example, prohibition laws affected permissible business activities and often reduced the economic value of leased premises. Finally, wars occur which can have a severe impact on the use, suitability or economic value of the premises.

The doctrine of "frustration of purpose" has been mentioned in §§ 10.03(d) and 26.02(g). Courts hesitated to apply this concept to leases because the tenant still had the possession of the premises that he had sought and received. Also, leases typically permit a broader use of the premises than the use for which the premises were sought. This means that the tenant can make other use of the premises.

For these reasons, courts were reluctant to relieve tenants from obligations under leases when even extremely disruptive events occurred. If the tenant could establish that the particular event was unforeseeable and that the event rendered the premises almost valueless, then he could be relieved from any further obligations under the lease by the doctrine of frustration of purpose. As has been stated in § 33.03, percentage leases can diminish the risk of economic cycles in commercial leases.

SECTION 33.05 RENTAL SPACE, FURNISHINGS AND UTILITIES

Sometimes questions can arise regarding the extent of space included in the lease. In office leases, there is usually no question as to the office space itself. However, problems sometimes develop relating to the tenant's right to use parking facilities, and whether the tenant will have to pay extra for the parking facilities. Tenants in office buildings should consider the availability of parking space for their clients as well as themselves. Matters relating to parking should be discussed, agreed upon and expressed clearly in the lease.

One problem faced by design professionals who lease office space is the need for flexibility in amount of space. When large projects are completed, the design professional often wishes to reduce rented space. When large projects are obtained, it may be necessary to obtain additional space. It is possible for the lease to specify that the space leased shall be the space required by the tenant. Requirements contracts are commonly used in the sale of goods and are generally considered enforceable despite their flexibility. Fisher v. Parsons, 213 Cal.App.2d 829, 29 Cal.Rptr. 210 (1963) involved a lease for office space which covered the space required by the tenant to the extent of the landlord's ability to furnish the space. The court held that such a lease provision was enforceable. Where the tenant has the bargaining power to get such a flexible provision and he can anticipate the need for reducing or increasing his space, he should give careful consideration to the use of a "requirements" clause.

As to furnishings, ordinarily office leases are for bare space and nothing else. However, furnishings which are permanently or semi-permanently affixed to the space are likely to go along under the lease. For example, permanently affixed carpeting or drapes can be part of the leased premises, especially if they were present at the time the tenant inspected the office space. Only if there are clear disclaimers in the lease should the landlord be released from having to furnish these furnishings. As to furnishings such as desks, chairs, office equipment and pictures, these are likely not to go along with the office space, especially if it is relatively clear that these things belong to the prior tenant. In any event, landlord and tenant should carefully delineate those furnishings which will be a part of the rented space and express their agreement in the lease.

What about heat, water, gas, electricity, air conditioning, telephone and other utilities that are important to office space? While there will be variations based upon local custom, where the leased space is part of an office building, the landlord usually provides at his expense heat, water, gas, electricity and air conditioning. It is likely that the tenant will be obligated to provide and pay for telephones. (As for building maintenance, see § 33.07)

Persons leasing office space again should discuss, agree upon and express in the lease who will furnish and pay for these utilities.

SECTION 33.06 ACTIVITIES OF THE TENANT

Frequently leases provide for some restrictions on how the leased premises may be used. These may be limited to what is lawful, or may attempt to limit the tenant to a narrower range of conduct. If the landlord is trying to establish a building which has largely professional people, he may include a provision under which only certain activities can be performed within the leased space. Without such a limitation, the tenant can generally use the premises in any reasonable way which does not violate public land use controls, such as zoning.

Sometimes tenants want to insure that competitors will not be in the same building or the same shopping center. For example, a liquor store may want a provision under which any tenants who are in the building or shopping complex will not sell liquor, or other goods which he sells. While this is not common for professional activities, it is possible for an architect or engineer to obtain a provision under which the landlord will not rent space in the building to other architects or engineers. Since this is rather unusual, such a provision, if agreed to, should be expressly included in the lease. (While earlier cases would not have given the tenant a right to move out if the landlord violated such a provision, the tendency in recent cases is to consider such a breach to be sufficiently important to allow the tenant to terminate his obligation, if he so chooses.)

The prospective tenant must take into account not only what activities he will be permitted to engage in, but the other activities in the building. For example, an architect or engineer who leases second floor space in a commercial building should determine the types of businesses which are on the ground floor of the building. It would be disconcerting to discover after entering into the lease that the main floor of the building contained a night club, especially if the design professional expected to work in the evenings. Legally, it is not likely he could do much about the night club, unless it was violating a law or were a public nuisance. If it was reasonably clear at the time he entered into the lease that such a night club did operate on the main floor of the building, he is unlikely to have a legal remedy.

Generally, the landlord and sometimes the tenant, will have fire insurance covering the leased premises. Such policies often contain provisions which limit coverage or increase the rates if certain things are done on the premises which affect the risk of fire. Often lease provisions control activity by stating that any activity which would affect fire coverage or fire insurance rates is prohibited. If the activity would merely increase the rate, it is likely that the landlord will consent if he is informed of the changed activity, and if the tenant agrees to pay the increased fire insurance premium.

SECTION 33.07 MAINTENANCE, ALTERATIONS, AND CONDITION OF PREMISES AT THE TERMINATION

Disputes can arise over who must maintain the leased premises. Much depends upon whether the tenant takes over an entire building or leases a portion of space within a building. If he takes over the entire building, it is likely that he has the obligation to maintain the premises. If he occupies a portion of the building, the landlord is likely to have the obligation to keep the halls and entrance ways clear and unobstructed and insure that the elevator system functions properly. However, as to portions of the lease premises which are exclusively within the control of the tenant, such as the offices themselves, the tenant is likely to have the obligation to maintain them in a proper condition.

Disputes often develop relating to the right of the tenant to make changes in the leased space, or to do anything which could injure the premises. For example, the tenant may wish to hang pictures in the office, or to lay permanent carpeting. He may wish to put in room partitions, or to knock out a wall and make a larger office. Usually, the landlord reserves the right to approve any structural changes. Even if the tenant wishes to pound a nail into the wall, the lease may require landlord approval.

The reason the landlord reserves these rights is twofold. First, he wants to make certain that any alterations or changes, or even pounding of nails, are done in such a way as to avoid damaging the premises. For this reason, minor requests by the tenant are usually granted if the landlord is reasonably certain that the tenant will do a decent job, or if the tenant agrees to have the work done by someone acceptable to the landlord. In addition to worrying about how the work is going to be done, the landlord will worry about the proposed changes causing a diminution in the utility and looks of the leased premises. For that reason, the landlord may give the tenant the right to redecorate at specified intervals, but make it clear that the type of decoration has to be approved by the landlord. A tenant in a strong bargaining position may compel the landlord to redecorate in a manner which is suitable to the tenant.

Disagreements may develop over decoration, repairs, and structural changes. It is vital to obtain agreement on these matters during the negotiations and express the agreement in the lease. If the agreement is different than the prepared, often printed, lease, the latter should be changed to conform to the common understanding.

Questions may arise at the conclusion of a lease as to who owns certain improvements which the tenant, or the landlord, has made. For example, the landlord may have permitted the tenant to install permanent bookcases, or reasonably permanent wall partitions. If nothing is stated in the lease, improvements which are affixed in some way to the leased premises and cannot be removed without damaging the premises or without abnormal expense, will belong to the landlord. It is frequently provided in the lease that the tenant may remove these types of improvement if removal does not materially damage the premises, or as long as the tenant is willing to pay for any damage which is incurred as a result of these improvements being removed.

At the termination of the lease, the tenant is usually obligated to return the premises to the landlord in the same condition in which he received them, less fair wear and tear. In a long-term lease it is quite clear that the premises will not be exactly the same as they were five or ten years before. The determination of what is fair wear and tear often depends upon the term of the lease and the type of activity engaged in by the tenant. The fair wear and tear concept is most difficult to apply where the leased premises include furniture, carpets, drapes or any type of equipment.

In some states, the tenant is given the right to make certain repairs himself, if he notifies the landlord to do so and the landlord does not make them. If he does make these repairs, the tenant is often given the right to deduct the cost of such repairs, up to a specified amount, from his rent. If the tenant has sufficient bargaining position, he should try to incorporate a provision under which he can make certain repairs and deduct the cost of these repairs if the landlord does not do so within a reasonable period of time. Unfortunately, even in states which give the tenant this protection by statute, it is common for the landlord to incorporate a provision in the lease under which the tenant gives up his right to make the repairs and deduct them from the rent. Generally, such provisions are enforceable. If, however, it is part of a take-it-or-leave-it contract, there is a chance of persuading a court that it violates public policy and should not be enforced.

SECTION 33.08 HARM TO PERSONS

Sometimes persons are injured while on the premises leased by the tenant. The persons injured may be the landlord, the tenant, employees of either, customers, or other third parties who enter into the leased premises. If the injury occurs in parts of the premises which are in control of the landlord, such as hallways, entranceways, and elevators, the landlord is generally liable if he has not used due care in maintaining the premises. If the injury occurs in the office rented by the tenant, the legal problems are usually going to be those of the tenant. In some cases, the injury may be caused by a structural defect or some other condition which was the responsibility of the landlord if his attention was drawn to it by the tenant. In such a case the injured party may sue both landlord and tenant, and the landlord may point to an indemnity provision under which the tenant agrees to indemnify the landlord for any injuries, losses, or expenses incurred by the landlord for injuries which occur in the space rented by the tenant. There is a possibility of indemnity based upon quasi-contract if the landlord is held responsible for something which should really have been the responsibility of the tenant. It is important for both landlord and tenant to carry public liability insurance.

SECTION 33.09 SUBLETTING AND ASSIGNING

During the lease term the tenant may wish to relieve himself from the burden of paying rent. One of the most important ways he can do this is to sublet the premises, or to assign the premises to a third party. While there are many technical legal distinctions between subletting and assigning, there are two major differences. First, a subletting occurs for less than the remainder of the term of the lease. Secondly, the person who takes under a subletting, the subtenant, does not obligate himself to the landlord. His obligation is to the tenant, and tenant still retains his obligation to the landlord. The subtenant cannot be sued by the landlord if he does not make payments to the tenant. In some cases, landlord, tenant, and subtenant may agree to a "novation". This relieves the old tenant from any liability, and substitutes the new subtenant for him. A novation usually requires consent of all three parties. Certainly the landlord must consent if he is to be divested of any rights that he may have against the tenant. Also, the subtenant clearly must consent if he is to have an obligation to a new party, the landlord.

If there is an assignment, the assignee (subtenant) will be obligated to pay the rent to the landlord. This is caused by the peculiar doctrine of "privity of estate," a doctrine which obligates the assignee of a lease to pay the landlord with whom he may not have had any direct contractual dealings. The effect of an assignment is to create a new right in the landlord against the assignee subtenant, while still retaining for the landlord the rights he had under the original lease against the tenant.

The right to sublet or assign is very important to both landlord and tenant. For that reason, landlords usually spell out in the lease that they must consent to any assignment or sublease. Sometimes the tenant is in a sufficient bargaining position to incorporate a provision under which the landlord agrees to be reasonable in exercising his consent to a sublease or an assignment. In some cases, the tenant may demand and receive a provision which allows him to sublet or assign without the landlord's consent, if the assignee or sublessee is in the same business or profession as the original tenant. There is also a novation possibility in an assignment. If the landlord is satisfied with the assignee (the one to whom the assignment is made), he may agree to accept him in place of the original tenant.

SECTION 33.10 PARTIAL OR TOTAL DESTRUCTION OF PREMISES

The leased premises may be partially or totally destroyed by fire, explosion, natural causes, or by eminent domain (condemnation). Increased governmental urban renewal means an increasing possibility that in a long term lease part, or all, of the premises may be condemned under the state or municipality's power of eminent domain. It is important to consider the possibilities which can arise during a long term lease which relate to partial or total destruction of the premises.

A fire which destroys the building is likely to terminate the lease. Perhaps some older cases considered that such a destruction did not relieve the tenant from the obligation to pay rent in the absence of a contract clause so providing. Such a result would be based upon the assumption that when possession was transferred to the tenant at the commencement of the lease, he got all that he bargained for when he made the lease. It is not likely that this rule would be applied today. In the case of fire, it is likely that both parties will be relieved from any further obligation. Also, clauses dealing with this problem are common.

Both landlord and tenant generally insure their property interests against fire. If the building is destroyed by fire or other cause which falls within the fire insurance policy, the landlord will be paid for his interest, and the tenant will be paid for his. From the tenant's standpoint, there is a real risk of what is called "subrogation."

After the landlord's fire insurance company pays the landlord, the insurer may look for someone who caused the fire to charge him with this loss. By the concept of subrogation, the insurer steps into the shoes of the policy holder when the latter is paid, and has any rights that the latter would have against any third party causing the fire. For example, if the tenant, in violation of the lease, stored an amount of flammable materials on the premises, or if the storage of such flammable materials was a violation of city ordinances, then the fire insurance company could try to make up its loss by suing the tenant.

There are a number of ways that the tenant can protect himself from such subrogation claims. The first is to make certain that the policy with the landlord includes a provision under which the fire insurance company waives its right to subrogation. The second method is to make both the landlord and the tenant parties to the fire insurance policy. Usually, the doctrine of subrogation cannot be employed against those who are insured under the fire insurance policy.

If the premises are partially destroyed, there are a number of possibilities. If the tenant wishes to continue occupancy of the premises, he should be able to do so, and it would be helpful to him if there were a provision in the lease which specified that there be an appropriate rental deduction for the diminished usefulness of the leased premises. In the absence of such a provision, he is unlikely to be able to obtain a rental reduction unless the landlord agrees. If the premises are untenantable for a designated period of time while repairs are made, the lease should contain a provision under which he is absolved from the obligation of paying rent during this period. This would seem to be common sense. However, common sense is often absent from landlord-tenant law. For this reason, it is better to specify that inability to use the premises, in addition to possibly terminating any further obligation under the lease, would at the very least give the tenant the right to withhold rental payments during the time the premises were not suitable for his use.

Condemnation raises a great many difficult legal questions. As for continued obligations to perform, these will usually be ended by the condemnation. However, each party may want to seek damages from the condemning authority for the loss of his interest. It is clear that the landlord will be losing the building and potential income. On the other hand, the tenant may want to assert a claim for a loss of the value of a long-term lease. However, whether he can recover for such loss depends upon the condemnation laws and cases in his jurisdiction.

SECTION 33.11 REMEDIES

Generally, without protective provisions in the lease the tenant's remedies for the landlord's nonperformance are generally ineffective. Usually the tenant must continue to pay rent despite the landlord's failure to perform in accordance with the lease obligations. His sole remedy is the right to sue for damages caused by the landlord's breach.

The tenant's position has been improving. Where he has sufficient bargaining power, it is becoming more common for leases to give the tenant the right to cease or suspend rental payments or to terminate his obligation under the lease if the landlord does not perform. He may also be given the right to make certain repairs and deduct the costs of those repairs from the rent.

Also, courts are beginning to emphasize the contractual aspects of the lease rather than the conveyance aspect. They have been adopting principles taken from contract law which have enabled the tenant to relieve himself from any further obligations under the lease in the event the landlord commits a serious breach.

As for the landlord's rights, these were generally broader than those of the tenant. If the tenant did not pay rent, the landlord frequently was able to evict him. Most states provide for a quick proceeding, under which the landlord can evict the tenant when the tenant refuses to pay rent.

As for damages, the landlord can sue for rental payments which are due and owing. He can let the premises sit unoccupied if the tenant moves out, and sue for the unpaid rent. Sometimes he has been precluded from suing for rent installments which have not yet matured, since some courts felt that permitting such an action would be inconsistent with the position that the lease continued. Also, such actions would require determining damages well in advance. For example, if the tenant moves out after five years of a twenty year term, to permit the landlord to sue for the difference between the rental price and the fair rental value would require a difficult look into the future. However, some states permit the landlord to sue for damages (the difference between lease price and fair market value of the lease) for the balance of the term if there is a provision in the lease giving the landlord this right.

As stated, usually the landlord reserves the right under the lease to re-enter the premises if the tenant abandons them, and to re-let the premises for the benefit of the tenant. This gives the landlord the right to sue for any difference which results from re-renting.

Another illustration of the landlord-oriented law relates to the contract concept which refuses to charge the breaching party with damages which could have been reasonably avoided by the non-breaching party. This is sometimes known as "mitigation of damages." For example, if the tenant abandons the premises, most states do not require that the landlord make any effort to re-let the premises. (Generally, he will not let the premises lie vacant, because the premises could fall into disrepair and collection of such rents where a tenant abandons is often difficult.) However, the law is gradually recognizing that it is easier for the landlord than the tenant to re-rent in most cases. For that reason, there is an increasing tendency on the part of the courts to hold that the landlord cannot collect for any damages which he could have reasonably avoided by re-letting the premises.

SECTION 33.12 FORM LEASES AND LEGISLATIVE ACTIVITY

Almost every landlord of commercial space will present the tenant with a form lease. Such leases are frequently purchased at stationery stores, or stores which sell legal supplies. They may be drafted by the attorney for the landlord. It may be difficult for the tenant to get such leases changed. He may not have the bargaining power, or he may have to content himself with a verbal arrangement with the rental agent.

If he takes the trouble to read the lease, he should try to get rid of objectionable and unfair provisions. If he can get a variation, he should get this variation put in the lease and eliminate any conflicting lease language. Often such precautions cannot or will not be taken.

In recent years there has been a greater tendency on the part of state legislatures to go into the fairness of the leases. Provisions regulating the contents of leases, while not common in state laws, are beginning to become more significant. For example, statutes have been passed dealing with notice of termination, right of the tenant to make repairs, and provisions for allocation of risk. Also, open occupancy laws affect the right to obtain a lease. There will be a greater control over private autonomy in leasing where the balance swings too heavily in favor of one party. Where that party uses its economic power to secure a socially undesirable and unfair objective, there is a possibility that the legislature may step in and cut down the power of the stronger party.

REVIEW QUESTIONS

1. Under what circumstances must leases be in writing?

2. What type of rental provision can be included in a long term business lease if the tenant does not wish to have to pay the same monthly rental despite economic fluctuations in his business?

3. What is the reason for the development of the doctrine of constructive eviction?

4. Normally, can a tenant get out of a lease because events occur which make the location less desirable to him?

5. What is the tenant's obligation with regard to the condition of the premises at the end of the lease?

6. Usually, can a tenant assign his lease or sublet without consent of the landlord?

7. What remedies are available to the landlord if the tenant abandons the premises during the term of the lease?

QUESTIONS FOR CLASS DISCUSSION

1. Should legislatures make up the rules for residential leases or should they permit the parties to do so?

2. Is there a need for state regulation of residential leases? For business leases? Explain.

3. If the landlord does not repair a defective toilet in an apartment, what right should be given to the tenant?

4. Who should have the obligation to perform repairs not caused by a residential tenant?

5. If an apartment house burns down, should the tenant still have to pay rent for the balance of the term?

6. What types of improvements in an apartment should the tenant be able to make without consent of the landlord?

PROBLEM

A was an architect who had entered into a two-year lease with X. A occupied a suite of offices on the second floor of X's five-story commercial building. There are 18 months remaining on the lease. X rented the street floor part of the building to a tenant who ran a small nightclub which featured rock and roll music. The nightclub was open from 8:00 p.m. to 2:00 a.m. A frequently worked in the evening. He stated that the noise level precluded him from working properly. A moved out and now X maintains that A is still obligated to make rental payments. Is X correct?

Chapter 34

PROFESSIONAL LIABILITY OF ARCHITECTS AND ENGINEERS

SECTION 34.01 TREND TOWARD INCREASED LIABILITY

In recent years there has been an unmistakable trend toward holding professional persons responsible for their negligence. Increasingly, doctors, lawyers, accountants, architects and engineers find themselves enmeshed in litigation commenced by persons who have suffered losses which they claim resulted from a professional person failing to use due care or not complying with contract obligations.

Those who support such a trend argue that it is long overdue. They contend that professional persons have enjoyed a type of immunity from responsibility for their acts which is not accorded others. Those who favor such a trend contend that it has made professional persons exercise a higher degree of care than they would have without such legal accountability. They also argue that professionals often operate through highly organized and profitable associations which can and should respond for losses caused by their conduct in furnishing professional services. This trend can also be supported as a method of eliminating incompetent professionals who somehow manage to continue to practice because of the laxity of enforcement of licensing and registration laws.

Many professional groups feel that such increased liability in the long run hampers proper professional practice. Opponents of increased professional liability state that it has forced professionals into large organizations which have not always produced imaginative professional work. They also contend that increased liability has caused the rates for professional liability insurance to soar astronomically and places an unreasonable burden on younger professionals. They also contend that increased professional liability will inhibit professionals from using new or unconventional techniques for fear that they will be held liable if things go wrong. While some professionals are willing to accept legal responsibility for their negligence, they feel that in reality they will be held to a standard of perfection by judges and juries. If anything goes wrong, they fear they will be held responsible.

SECTION 34.02 WHO SUE ARCHITECTS AND ENGINEERS?

Commencing with those who suffer physical or emotional harm, architects and engineers can anticipate the possibility of being sued by construction workers on the project. They may also anticipate being sued by those who enter upon the project during construction such as child or adult trespassers, mailmen, tenants, policemen, customers, and others. After the project is completed those who enter the structure or pass by it and are injured because of something connected to the construction process may choose to sue the architect or engineer connected with the project.

Moving to economic harm and harm to property, the design professional might find himself the defendant in an action by an adjacent landowner whose land or property has been adversely affected by the construction project. The architect or engineer may find himself sued by his client when the project does not meet the client's expectations. Also the design professional may be sued when the client has been sued by others, such as the contractor or injured employees, for acts or nonaction by the architect or engineer.

The design professional may find himself sued by participants in the construction project. These can include contractors, subcontractors, suppliers, surety companies and lenders.

This list is not exclusive and there may be other types of plaintiffs who bring legal actions against architects or engineers. However, it is sufficiently detailed to indicate that there is a substantial risk that the design professional will find himself a defendant in a lawsuit.

SECTION 34.03 REASONS FOR MORE LAWSUITS

In the past a number of legal doctrines and economic facts tended to protect architects and engineers from litigation. First, if the injury occurred during the construction process, the absence of a contractual relationship (lack of privity) between the design professional and the injured party often provided a legal defense. If the injury occurred after acceptance of the structure by the owner, the design professional, as well as contractors, had, in addition to the privity defense, a defense based on acceptance by the owner. The justification for this rule was that the act of the owner in accepting the project was an intervening cause which relieved contractors and design professionals from liability.

Both of these defenses have weakened substantially in the past decade. In rejecting the absence of privity, the court in Miller v. DeWitt, 37 Ill.2d 273, 226 N.E.2d 630 (1967) stated:

> It appears that the parties agree that architects must exercise reasonable care in the performance of their duties and may be liable to persons who may foreseeably be injured by their failure to exercise such care, regardless of privity.

(For a more detailed comment on this case, see § 34.06.)

In the injury cases absence of privity is not likely to be a defense. The same is true of acceptance. While there are still some decisions which give a defense on the basis of the owner's acceptance, these too are diminishing and are likely to be of little future protection. An omitted portion of Pasterelli v. Assoc. Eng. Inc., reproduced at § 6.14 held that acceptance by the owner would not be a defense.

The privity rule still provides some protection where the loss is economic rather than personal. For example, in Peyronnin Construction C., Inc. v. Weiss, 137 Ind.App. 417, 208 N.E.2d 489 (1965) a contractor sued a soils engineer based upon the latter's misrepresentation of the amount of dirt to be excavated and the fill which would be needed for a construction project. This estimate was relied upon by the excavation subcontractor (who was not a party to the lawsuit) and by the plaintiff-contractor. However, the estimate varied considerably from the facts. The court ruled that the engineer would not be responsible even if he were negligent because his responsibility and duty was to the excavation subcontractor who had paid for and received the estimate and not to the prime contractor who had based his bid upon the excavation subcontractor's bid proposal. (But in Rozny v. Marnul, reproduced at § 30.04(h), a surveyor was held liable to the subsequent purchaser of property.)

In addition to the lack of privity defense, the court in the *Peyronnin* case noted that the contractor himself was negligent in failing to investigate the discrepancy between the excavation subcontractor's bid and the bids of other excavation subcontractors.

In the past there have been economic factors which have minimized the likelihood of the architect or engineer being sued. Traditionally architects and engineers practice as sole proprietors or in small partnerships. Professional liability insurance was rare. If a potentially high judgment could not be collected, there was very little sense in suing. However, whether the cause of the trend of increased liability or a result of it, architectural and engineering firms are becoming larger and more able to respond to judgments and there is a much greater likelihood that even smaller design professionals will carry professional liability insurance.

Another reason architects and engineers find themselves sued more often relates to the tendency of the plaintiffs to sue all those who had any connection with the construction project. Joining a number of defendants in one lawsuit is relatively easy today. Typically, an injured subcontractor employee will sue the prime contractor, the owner, the design professional and anyone else who may have had some connection with his injury. As a rule it does not cost much more by way of litigation expense or attorneys fees to bring in a few more defendants.

While it is difficult to measure, it appears that clients are less reluctant to resort to legal action against their architect or engineer when things do not go as planned and the client suffers economic losses. Some of this may be traceable to the more impersonal relationships created when the client is a large corporate entity and the design professional is a large organization. Also, the client may be more likely to sue his design professional if he believes the ultimate payout will be made by an insurance company rather than the design professional himself. These factors, coupled with the apparent willingness with which more people litigate their claims, have contributed to the greater likelihood that architects and engineers will be sued in the course of their professional practice.

SECTION 34.04 BASIS FOR LEGAL ACTION

(A) BREACH OF CONTRACT

Some claims against design professionals are based upon breach of contract. Typically, these are claims brought by the client against his architect or engineer. The rights and duties of design professional and his client were discussed in detail in Part II of this treatise. Contract claims of the client against the design professional can be based upon design. Design errors can cause additional construction cost to the client, can diminish the economic value of the project or can cause losses to the client because of claims of third parties. Some claims are based upon inaccurate or negligent cost predictions. See § 8.01.

Clients also may have claims which result from inadequate or negligent administration during the construction project. Illustrations are failure to condemn defective work, improper issuance of progress payment certificates or certificates of completion and delay in approving shop drawings submitted by contractors.

A design professional might also be sued based on breach of contract by a person who is not a party to the contract between client and his design professional. For example, a prime or subcontractor who suffers losses because of the failure on the part of the design professional to live up to his agreement with the client might attempt to predicate his action against the design professional upon the breach by the design professional of his agreement with the client. For example, if the design professional is obligated expressly or impliedly to pass upon shop drawings submitted by the contractor within a reasonable time, failure to do so could be the basis of a claim by the contractor against the design professional if the contractor can persuade a court that this promise was made for his benefit.

In such a case the contractor who suffers a loss because of the unjustified delay by the design professional might and often does choose to make his claim against the client-owner. (See Chapter 23 on delays generally). However, in some cases it may be difficult to obtain damages from the owner. There may be a "no damage" clause in the agreement between owner and contractor. Also, an owner that is a public agency may have immunity from such suits. For these and other reasons the contractor may choose to try to recover from the design professional. While recovery against the architect or engineer is difficult, sometimes contractors have been successful.

Even if the action is brought against the owner, the owner may assert a claim over against the design professional if the owner's liability is based upon a breach of the client-design professional contract.

(B) MISREPRESENTATION OR WARRANTY

While breach of warranty or misrepresentation is sometimes used to describe actions by a client against a design professional, it is better to reserve "warranty" to describe actions brought against the design professional by persons with whom the design professional has no contractual relationship. As has been seen, actions are sometimes brought against surveyors by those who have relied upon an inaccurate survey. See Rozny v. Marnul, reproduced at § 30.04(h). Also, lawsuits are sometimes brought against soils engineers based upon inaccurate description of soil conditions. Those design professionals who are in the business of giving professional opinions or making representations as to existing facts or conditions may find themselves sued, sometimes successfully, by third parties who have reasonably relied upon these representations. See the discussion in § 30.04 relating to misrepresentation.

(C) PROFESSIONAL NEGLIGENCE: ERHART AND DAY CASES

Most claims brought against design professionals are based upon professional negligence, a failure on the part of the design professional to use due care to avoid exposing others to unreasonable risks.

Professional negligence can relate to any aspect of the design professional's performance. It may relate to defective design, selection of inadequate or improper materials or equipment, and any other part of the design services furnished by architect or engineer. For example, in Mallow v. Tucker, Sadler and Bennett, Architects and Engineers, Inc., 245 Cal.App.2d 700, 54 Cal.Rptr. 174 (1966) the court held that an architect's failure "to make any mention on its plans of the underground high-voltage line it knew was in the area" when "these plans called for excavation right where the buried electrical power line was located" was negligence on the part of the architect.

Professional negligence can occur during the construction process itself. For example, failure by the design professional to condemn defective work or to stop unsafe practices is likely to be considered professional negligence. Miller v. DeWitt, to be discussed in § 34.06, held that this was a jury question. Because this problem is so important to design professional, it may be instructive to reproduce another case of this type at this point.

ERHART v. HUMMONDS

Supreme Court of Arkansas, 1960.
232 Ark. 133, 334 S.W.2d 869.

HOLT, JUSTICE. This appeal comes from a judgment against appellants, architects, on a jury verdict awarding substantial damages to one injured workman and to the representatives of three other workmen who were killed. The record reflects that the Seventh & Main Street Realty Company, owner of the premises at Sixth and Main Street, entered into an agreement with J. C. Penney and Company to erect a building suitable for Penney to house and sell merchandise. Pursuant to this agreement, Seventh & Main Street Realty Company negotiated with the architectural firm of Erhart, Eichenbaum & Rauch to design and draw the necessary plans for a suitable building. This was done and a contract was let by Seventh & Main Street Realty Company to the J. A. Jones Construction Company of Shreveport, Louisiana. After this contract was let, it developed that Penney was not going to furnish supervision of the construction work, contrary to the owner's prior understanding that they would. Seventh & Main Street Realty employed the present appellants, architects, to guard its interest by supervising construction of the building, in addition to their architectural duties. For this additional work, appellants were to receive an additional fee over and above their architectural fee. Work under the contract proceeded and the Jones Construction Company subcontracted the excavation to one Claude Machen. Due to the depth of the excavation and because of danger to adjacent buildings and workmen, the plans for the excavation were set out in some detail in the contract. As the excavation proceeded in depth, it became necessary to shore the walls to prevent sliding and caving of the earth. Serious questions were raised by the field supervisor of the architects, Vance A. Davenport, as to the adequacy of the shoring on the east wall, then 17 feet deep and perpendicular. Comments by Davenport were to the effect that the shoring of this wall was no better than a "whitewash" and "it wasn't worth a d. . . ." With some dispatch, a call was placed by Mr. Eichenbaum, one of the architects, to the general office of Jones Construction Company at Shreveport, requesting that a new job superintendent be brought to the job at once; otherwise, they would ask the owners to stop work on the job immediately, as allowed under the contract. The next day, Friday, the new superintendent arrived on the job and promised to make shoring of the east wall the first order of business Monday morning. There was evidence that a slow drizzle of rain fell over the weekend causing the excavation walls to soften. Monday morning, as Vance Davenport, appellants' supervisor and superintendent, drove his automobile [which weighed 4,600 lbs.] into the alley near the edge of the east embankment wall, this wall caved in killing three employees and seriously injuring a fourth. It was stipulated: "It is further stipulated and agreed by the defendants Erhart, Eichenbaum & Rauch that Vance Davenport was their agent, servant, and employee and acting within the scope of his employment on the J. C. Penney Company job site at the time of the accident and prior thereto.

Suit was filed by the injured workman on behalf of himself and by the personal representatives of the three estates of the three workmen who were killed alleging, in effect, that appellants, architects, were negligent in failing to inspect and direct the erection of the contractor of the necessary protection for the workmen according to the plans and specifications, in failing to require compliance in accordance with Little Rock Ordinance # 2801 and that the negligence of the agent and supervisor, Vance A. Davenport, in driving his automobile through the alley above the excavation when he knew vibrations therefrom might cause the wall to fall, was imputable to them, and that appellants were negligent in failing to stop the work under their powers set forth in the contract until the dangerous conditions had been corrcted. Appellants answered, in effect, with a general denial.

Upon a trial of the issues, as indicated, the jury found in favor of appellees and the following judgments rendered accordingly:

"Benjamin Hummonds – $10,000.00
Monteen Criswell – 48,000.00
Lucy Lewis – 48,000.00
Vernie Lowman – 12,000.00."

The points for reversal may be summed up as follows: (1) The appellees have no cause of action on the basis of contract provisions (2) The architects did not breach any contractual duty to the owner . . . ..

Appellants' contention under point one has been settled adversely to them in our recent case of Hogan v. Hill, Ark., 318 S.W.2d 580, 584. Hogan, a contractor, entered into a contract with the Arkansas Highway Commission to do certain work. Hogan violated the safety clause contained in a provision of the contract and as a result, Hill, not a party to the contract, was injured. We there stated: "It will be noted that Hill's complaint states a cause of action in tort based not only on the common law of negligence, but based also on Hogan Company's failure to comply with the regulations in the contract relative to public safety. This, we think he had a right to do. . . .

Assignment two presents the question of whether the architect breached any duty to the owner, and further the issue if there was a duty whether it did not arise until the excavation was completed. The issue here, we think, is not whether the architect breached any duty to the owner, but whether there was a breach of duty owed to the workmen by the architect arising out of the safety provisions of the contract. In the Hogan case above, Hogan did not breach any duty to the highway commission, but did breach a duty which it owed to the traveling public and for whom the safety provisions were intended. In the case here presented, we hold that there was substantial evidence that appellants, architects, breached a duty owed to the workmen whom the safety provisions of the contract specifically named. Appellants were further obligated to inspect the excavation upon completion and prior to the commencement of concrete work. Section 1–02 (d) of the contract, dealing with inspection and excavation, provides: "Upon completion of excavation, and prior to commencement of concrete work, excavations will be inspected by the Architect to insure that suitable earth foundation conditions have been obtained, and that compliance with the requirements of the specifications and the drawings have been maintained. No concrete shall be placed until this inspection has been made and approval of the Architect has been obtained."

Mr. Davenport, appellants' employee and supervisor, testified that the east wall footings were poured Friday afternoon before the accident on Monday; that he was the architects' inspector or supervisor to see that the plans and specifications were followed; that he did not approve making a vertical cut on the wall, that it was a dangerous thing to do and dangerous to workmen underneath; that the vibrations of any vehicle in the alley would be a contributing factor to the cave-in; that he was familiar with the effect of rain on the banks of an excavation, that the dirt around the excavation was saturated with rain which created a greater tendency for cave-ins; it was his opinion that the wall was dangerous and the shoring inadequate and that one should have people trained to detect a dangerous wall like that, that it would not be noticeable to the average layman or citizen. Section 2801 of the Little Rock Building Code provides: "All excavations for buildings and excavations accessory thereto shall be protected and guarded against danger to life and property."

As indicated, the architects were paid, in addition to the fee for preparing the plans and specifications, $12,000 by the owners to see to it that the terms of the contract between the owners and the contractors were complied with. The contract provides that the general contractor "shall erect such protection as may be required, or as directed by the architect, maintain same, and maintain any existing protections, all in accordance with the governing laws, rules, regulations and ordinances." And, further, the "contractor shall do all shoring necessary to maintain the banks of excavations, to prevent sloughing or caving, and to protect workmen." The contract further provides: The architect "shall have general supervision and direction of the work—. He has authority to stop the work whenever such stoppage may be necessary to insure the proper execution of the contract." It was a question for the jury as to whether the architect was negligent in failing to stop all work until the shoring on the east wall was made safe for the workmen.

On the whole case, finding no error, the judgment is affirmed.

WARD, JUSTICE (dissenting).

On Thursday afternoon Davenport detected the unstable condition of the excavation, inquired of the contractor's representative whether or not he had obtained the approval of the Safety Department of the Department of Labor, expressed his disapproval, and then very promptly telephoned Mr. Pugh, Vice President of the Prime Contractor at Shreveport, Louisiana. Davenport told Mr. Pugh of the condition and advised immediate action on his part. The result was that Mr. Pugh sent their regular Superintendent to Little Rock, arriving on the following morning (Friday) to take over the management of the job. At that time there had been no collapse. The new representative of the Prime Contractor (a Mr. Wright) immediately conferred with an agent of appellant who pointed out the defects of the work, and Mr. Wright promised to take care of the situation. The following day, Saturday, no work was done on the excavation, and none was done on Sunday. On Monday morning, at 8 o'clock, work was resumed under the supervision of Mr. Wright who had all the shoring removed without telling Davenport. A short time later that morning, about the time Davenport appeared on the scene, the wall caved in on the workmen.

What I cannot understand, and the majority do not point out, is how any negligence can be imputed to Davenport or the appellants. The majority do point out that appellants were paid a substantial fee and thereby appear to infer that Davenport should have taken over the operation, but in this connection two other things must be considered. One is that appellants had many other duties to perform under its contract of employment. The other is that the Prime Contractor, under the terms of its contract, was specifically charged with the duties which the majority would impose on appellants. In part this contract reads: "Each contractor shall be responsible for his own work and every part thereof, and all work of every description used in connection therewith. He shall specifically assume, and does assume, *all risk of damage or injury from whatever cause to property or persons* * * *." (Emphasis supplied.) Not only so, but a witness for appellees (the Chief Safety Engineer for the Arkansas Department of Labor) stated that he looks to the Prime Contractor to make the job safe and not to the architects or a subcontractor.

Since there is no substantial evidence in the record to contradict the above factual situation it was, in my opinion, error for the trial court to permit the jury to base a finding of negligence on this point.

. . .

Another issue in the *Erhart* case was whether the injuries were caused by Davenport's (an employee of the architect) negligence. The majority and the dissenting judge both concluded that there was sufficient evidence to submit to the jury the question of whether Davenport was negligent in driving his automobile close to where the excavation gave way when he knew the ground was soaked by excessive rains. However, the dissenting judge was of the opinion that the matter should be retried solely on the question of Davenport's negligence in driving the car and not on the question of the defendant's negligence in not immediately stopping the work while the unsafe excavation methods were being used.

The *Erhart* case confronted the question which has been troublesome in cases like Miller v. DeWitt, to be discussed in § 34.06. Who has legal responsibility for safety on the construction project? The dissenting judge in the *Erhart* case said it was the contractor's responsibility. The majority opinion in the *Miller* case felt that to a large degree it was the responsibility of the architect.

The issue before the Supreme Court of Arkansas was whether the case should have been submitted to the jury. The opinion should not be taken to mean that the Appellate Court considered the architect to have been negligent. Its holding is limited to the point that there was sufficient evidence of negligence to submit it to the jury.

Many of these cases are divided by split courts. This indicates the inability of the law to determine with some uniformity whether the architect will be responsible for construction safety.

Permitting incompetent contractors to continue on the project or at the very least failure to point this out to the owner, is likely to be professional negligence.

A design professional can be negligent in the issuance of certificates of payment or completion. This negligence could relate to the measurement of the quantity of work performed or a finding that the work was in accordance with the contract documents. It could also relate to failure to use due care in ascertaining whether subcontractors and suppliers have been paid or have executed waivers of lien. Professional negligence can consist of undue delay in giving interpretations of the contract documents or in passing upon shop drawings submitted by contractors.

Who is liable where someone is injured because of faulty construction methods which had been set forth in shop drawings approved by the design professional? This troublesome question, as well as others, was faced in *Day* case reproduced at this point.

DAY v. NATIONAL U. S. RADIATOR CORPORATION

Supreme Court of Louisiana, 1961.
241 La. 288, 128 So.2d 660.

HAWTHORNE, JUSTICE. Mrs. Cecilia LeBlanc Day instituted this suit on her own behalf and as natural tutrix of her minor children,

Judy Dianne Day and Randall Joseph Day, to recover damages for the death of Willie Day, her husband and the father of her children. Day was fatally injured as a result of a boiler explosion which occurred while his employer, Vince Plumbing & Heating Company, a subcontractor, was installing a hot water system in a new building of the tuberculosis hospital at Greenwell Springs, Louisiana. Several persons, firms, and corporations, with their insurers, were named defendants. The district court gave judgment for plaintiff against Wilson & Coleman, the firm of architects on the building, and its insurer, and held the other defendants relieved of any liability. The Court of Appeal likewise gave judgment for plaintiff against the architects and their insurer, . . .

The Louisiana State Building Authority entered into a contract with defendant Wilson & Coleman, a firm of architects, to prepare plans and specifications for the construction of the New Patients' Building at the Greenwell Springs Tuberculosis Hospital. Upon completion of the plans and specifications by the architects a contract was entered into with Charles Carter & Company, Inc., a general contractor, for construction of the building. The contractor in turn negotiated a subcontract with Vince Plumbing & Heating Company, in which the latter undertook to perform all mechanical work as per plans and specifications (which were made part of this subcontract), including heating, plumbing, etc., necessary to complete the central heating system and the domestic hot water system. The boiler which exploded was a part of the domestic hot water system. After installation the boiler was lighted by an employee of Vince to test its operation. The explosion occurred shortly afterwards, and Willie Day, plaintiff's husband, who was standing near by, was scalded to death.

In their contract with the building authority the architects' services were to consist, among other things, of "supervision of the work" as indicated by a schedule set forth in the contract. According to this schedule they were to prepare "complete working drawings, and specifications for architectural, structural, plumbing, heating, electrical and other mechanical work". In this schedule they further bound themselves to exercise *"adequate supervision of the execution of the work to reasonably insure strict conformity with the working drawings, specifications, and other contract documents"*, and this supervision was to include, among other things, "* * * (b) inspection of all samples, materials, and workmanship * * * (d) checking of all shop and setting drawings (e) frequent visits to the work site * * *". (Italics ours.)

Pursuant to the authority given them by this contract the architects employed a firm of consulting engineers, Chesson, Forrest & Holland, at a fee of 3 per cent of the cost of mechanical and electrical work, to be paid from the proceeds of the 6 per cent fee which the architects were to receive from the owner. Under their contract with the architects the consulting engineers, among other things, prepared for the architects plans and specifications for all mechanical and engineering equipment to be incorporated in the building. It was the duty of these engineers to consult with and advise the architects about the proper mechanical and electrical equipment for the building. They were to examine all *shop drawings* submitted by the contractor or the subcontractor and report to the architects, and make a final inspection and report to the architects when the general contractor had completed the work. The architects admitted that they relied on the consulting engineers' technical ability for the installation of the mechanical and electrical equipment, of which the boiler that exploded was a part, because they themselves were without the specialized knowledge to determine whether the mechanical equipment was installed in a safe way.

The architects' specifications plainly stipulated that the hot water heater or boiler was to be provided with a thermostat, and that the contractor was to "equip hot water heaters with temperature and pressure relief valves".

The specifications further provided that in the installation of the domestic hot water system the contractor before proceeding with the work "shall make complete shop and working drawings of such apparatus or connections as directed by the Architects and/or hereinafter required. These drawings shall show construction details and dimensions of each piece of equipment so drawn". The provision quoted was found in that part of the specifications dealing with plumbing. In Section 1 of the general contract specifications under the heading "Shop Drawings" it was provided that four copies of shop drawings or data for all mechanical work should be submitted, and two corrected or approved copies returned to the contractor, and that no shop drawings should be submitted by any subcontractor directly to the architects or to the architects' consulting engineers. This section further specifically provided: "Shop drawings marked 'Approved as Noted', are assumed to be *approved for fabrication or placing orders.*" (Italics ours.)

. . .

After obtaining the subcontract Sam Vince, sole owner of Vince Plumbing & Heating Company, furnished to the architects through the general contractor, as provided in the specifications, a *brochure* for their approval of certain equipment. The terms "brochure" and "shop drawing", as shown by this record, are interchangeable and mean the same thing. In other words, a brochure was considered by all as a shop drawing, as that term was used in the specifications. This brochure was submitted by the architects to the consulting engineers, who approved it with certain exceptions. This qualified approval, according to the evidence, was tantamount to rejection in toto. Vince then submitted a second brochure. This brochure also was referred to the architects' consulting engineers, and on the advice of the engineers was likewise disapproved by the architects. These two brochures were disapproved for causes which were in no way related to the subject of the boiler explosion. A third brochure was submitted to the architects, who, without submitting it to their consulting engineers, endorsed it "Approved as Noted" and returned it to Vince. All these brochures were prepared for Vince by Amstan Supply Division of American Radiator and Sanitary Corporation. The approved brochure did not specify or list a pressure relief valve for the hot water boiler which subsequently exploded.

After receiving the approved brochure or shop plan Vince ordered the material and equipment shown in it, and proceeded with the installation of the domestic hot water system. In making the installation of the hot water heater, a part of this system, Vince failed to follow the plain provision of the specifications that the hot water heater or boiler should be equipped with a thermostat and with a temperature and pressure relief valve. He installed the hot water boiler without a pressure relief valve, and instead of putting the thermostat and the temperature relief valve on the boiler he installed these safety devices on a hot water storage tank. After the installation of the hot water system Vince, to check his own work, caused the boiler to be lighted for a preliminary testing, and the explosion ensued which resulted in the death of Vince's employee Day.

At this point it may be well to note that Vince made this preliminary test without informing either the architects or the consulting engineers that the hot water system was ready for inspection, and did not request any of these persons to make an inspection at any time before the explosion.

It is clear from this record, as shown by the testimony of the experts, that because of the method of installation the explosion of the boiler was inevitable. Among other things, it was not equipped with a pressure relief valve as called for by the specifications, and, further, if this boiler had been equipped with such a valve, the explosion could not have occurred. As said by the Court of Appeal, the experts "all stated that, assuming all component parts performed their respective functions, the explosion would nevertheless have eventually occurred because of the absence of a pressure relief valve on the system".

. . .

Let us . . . consider the holding of the Court of Appeal that the terms and conditions of the architects' contract with the State Building Authority imposed upon the architects the obligation of supervising the installation of the domestic hot water system, that the architects breached this obligation because neither they nor their agents, the engineers, were aware that this system was being installed and neither they nor the engineers inspected the system during installation or after completion, and that all of this constituted negligence by the architects.

. . . [W]e should point out that we do not have here a case where the architects failed to provide in the specifications for a pressure relief valve on the boiler and for other safety devices; or a case where they inspected and approved the installation, or even where they had knowledge of the installation and stood by and permitted the boiler to be tested without having proper safety devices; or a case where they visited the site after the completion of the installation and, knowing that the boiler was to be tested, failed to observe that the boiler was not equipped with the safety devices stipulated in the specifications. Under such circumstances we should not hesitate to say that they breached a duty and that they reasonably should have foreseen that this breach would cause damage.

The narrow question here presented is whether the architects' contract with the owner imposed upon them the duty to be aware that the boiler was being installed by Vince, the plumbing subcontractor, and whether they were required by their contract to inspect the hot water system, of which the boiler was a part, during installation and before the boiler was tested by the subcontractor Vince.

In their contract with the owner the architects bound themselves to exercise "adequate supervision of the execution of the work to reasonably insure strict conformity with the working drawings, specifications and other contract documents", and this supervision was to include "frequent visits to the work site". If this provision of the contract required the architects to know that the boiler was being installed and required them to inspect the installation while it was in progress and before the system was tested, then the decision of the Court of Appeal may be correct. We therefore must determine the meaning of the above quoted provision of the contract.

As we view the matter, the primary object of this provision was to impose the duty or obligation on the architects to insure to the owner that before final acceptance of the work the building would be completed in accordance with the plans and specifications; and to insure this result the architects were to make "frequent visits to the work site" during the progress of the work. Under the contract they as architects had no duty to supervise the contractor's method of doing the work. In fact, as architects they had no power or control over the contractor's method of performing his contract, unless such power was provided for in the specifications. Their duty to the owner was to see that before final acceptance of the work the plans and specifications had been complied with, that proper materials had been used, and generally that the owner secured the building it had contracted for.

Thus we do not think that under the contract in the instant case the architects were charged with the duty or obligation to inspect the methods employed by the contractor or the subcontractor in fulfilling the contract or the subcontract. Consequently we do not agree with the Court of Appeal that the architects had a duty to the deceased Day, an employee of Vince, to inspect the hot water system during its installation, or that they were charged with the duty of knowing that the boiler was being installed.

We might add that the record discloses that as the work progressed over a period of some nine months before the explosion, the architects in performance of their duty to the owner made frequent visits to the work site in order to determine that the work in progress was being executed in conformity with the plans and specifications and other contract documents, all in accordance with what was considered by other architects who testified in the case as good and accepted architectural practice.

We finally consider the question of whether the architects were negligent in approving Vince's shop drawing or brochure which did not specify the pressure relief valve for the boiler and, if this was negligence, whether such negligence was a proximate cause of the accident.

. . .

It is to be noted that according to the specifications a shop plan "Approved as Noted" was assumed to be approved for fabrication or placing orders. The architects contend that the brochure approved by them was submitted by Vince to obtain their approval only for the purchase of the items listed and designated therein; that it was not approved for fabrication or as a detailed plan for the installation of the boiler.

Vince testified that these shop plans were made for him by Amstan to be presented to the architects and engineers for their approval, which had to be secured before the plumbing supply house would accept an order for the items listed. A representative of the plumbing supply house which prepared them stated that such documents are usually prepared for a contractor who wants to order from the company certain equipment, and do not necessarily list all items called for in the specifications because the supply house only furnishes the contractor that part of the equipment which he needs.

The plans and specifications required many items to be incorporated in the domestic hot water system and listed them in detail, whereas the brochure prepared by Amstan listed only a few of the items required by the specifications to be installed in the system. A comparison of the items of equipment listed in the brochure with those called for in the specifications shows beyond doubt that the brochure was not intended to include all of the equipment required for the installation of the boiler, a part of the domestic hot water system.

As we view the matter, the architects' approval of the brochure was only an approval for Vince to place the order with Amstan for the purchase of the items listed in it, and the brochure was not intended as a shop plan for fabrication or a plan showing construction details.

There is still another convincing reason why plaintiff cannot recover because of the architects' approval of the brochure. Let us assume a position most favorable to the plaintiff and concede that the brochure was in fact a shop plan submitted by Vince for installation of the boiler, purporting to show all construction details and all connections and safety devices to be installed thereon, but not listing or calling for a pressure relief valve, and that the architects were negligent in approving the shop plan for the installation of the boiler.

Even if we should concede all this, however, it was established beyond any question by plaintiff's own witnesses that Vince, the subcontractor, did not use or rely on this brochure in his installation of the boiler. Accordingly its approval by the architects had no causal connection with, and was not a proximate cause of, the explosion. We therefore conclude that plaintiff's suit against the architects should be dismissed.

. . .

For the reasons assigned the judgment of the Court of Appeal insofar as it awarded plaintiff damages against the architects and their insurer is reversed and set aside, and plaintiff's suit is dismissed at her costs.

There are some troublesome aspects of the *Day* case. It is questionable whether the approval of shop drawings is merely to permit the subcontractor to place an order for material. Approval of shop drawings can serve an additional function of informing the architect how the subcontractor intends to perform. Also, it is difficult to agree with the court's conclusion in the last paragraph of the opinion that even if the architect were negligent in approving the shop plans for the boiler installation, the architect should not be held liable. A substantial cause of the plaintiff's injury could be traceable to the architect's approval of a dangerous construction method. Approval of shop drawings and their legal effect was discussed in § 6.15.

In negligence cases design professionals frequently assert that they have complied with customary standards of professional practice and ask that they be relieved from liability for this reason. As stated in § 30.02(f) compliance with customary standards of conduct is taken into account in determining whether there was negligence but would not be conclusive on that question. Also, in that section it stated that customary practice would be more persuasive in professional negligence cases but still not be conclusive. This can be illustrated by Holt v. A. L. Salzman & Sons, 88 Ill.App.2d 306, 232 N.E.2d 537 (1967). In this case injured workers instituted legal action against an architectural firm that participated in the design phase of a project in which they were injured. The plaintiffs charged that the architects had been negligent. The defendants contended that its expert witnesses had established that the conduct of the defendant "represented good architectural and engineering practice, and was in accord with what was customarily done in the construction of other buildings". The court treated this as indicating that the architects had complied with local custom, a test often applied in determining whether a professional person has been guilty of malpractice. However, the court held that custom could never be conclusive and it so stated:

> In Darling v. Charleston Community Memorial Hospital, 33 Ill.2d 326, 211 N.E.2d 253, in considering a similar conten-

tion, the Supreme Court, at page 331, at page 257 of 211 N.E.2d, said: "Custom is relevant in determining the standard of care because it illustrates what is feasible, it suggests a body of knowledge of which the defendant should be aware, and it warns of the possibility of far-reaching consequences if a higher standard is required. . . . But custom should never be conclusive. As Judge Learned Hand said, 'There are, no doubt, cases where courts seem to make the general practice of the calling the standard of proper diligence; we have indeed given some currency to the notion ourselves. * * * Indeed in most cases reasonable prudence is in fact common prudence; but strictly it is never its measure; a whole calling may have unduly lagged in the adoption of new and available devices. It never may set its own tests, however persuasive be its usages. Courts must in the end say what is required; there are precautions so imperative that even their universal disregard will not excuse their omission'. The T. J. Hooper, (2d Cir.1932) 60 F.2d 737, 740."

(D) LIABILITY WITHOUT FAULT FOR DESIGN DEFECTS

Most claims against design professionals are predicated upon negligence. Some have contended that the trend toward imposing liability without fault for defective products should be expanded to those who perform design services. Adoption of such a standard would relieve a plaintiff from the burden of showing that the design professional was negligent. He would simply have to show that he suffered a loss caused by defective design.

While some courts have been willing to employ liability without fault in the sale of tract homes and to a lesser degree in the sale of individual homes, (see Humber v. Morton, reproduced at § 13.07(k)) they have not as yet employed the liability without fault principle to those who perform services such as architects and engineers.

However, it is possible that at least some courts will expand enterprise liability to those who perform services just as they have to those who sell goods or, in some cases, sell homes.

SECTION 34.05 LEGAL PROTECTION GIVEN DESIGN PROFESSIONALS

The lack of privity and acceptance doctrines are of very limited value in injury cases although they still may have some value where the losses are purely economic. However, there are other doctrines which may prove of assistance to design professionals when they are sued.

To recover in a negligence action the plaintiff must show that the defendant's negligence was the substantial cause of the plaintiff's injury or loss. Because of the many entities involved in a construction project and the likelihood that a number of these entities played some part in causing the injury or loss, causation questions are very difficult in construction litigation.

For example, in some cases the architect or engineer may concede he was negligent but assert that the loss was caused principally by the contractor's deviation from the construction documents or by improper construction practices. The design professional might assert that the principal cause of the injury or loss was defective material or equipment supplied by someone else. He might also assert that the owner, or someone for whom the owner is responsible, was the principal cause of the injury or loss.

One of the difficulties in establishing lack of causation as a defense is the overall power the architect or engineer has over a construction project. His extensive powers to condemn defective work, stop incompetent contractors from performing and the other powers that given to him often make it difficult to assert that the principal cause were acts of others. His extensive powers often mean that he has the last word. This may make it difficult for him to point to the conduct of others as the principal cause when he had the power to condemn defective work or order that unsafe practices be discontinued. See the discussion in § 34.06 relating to the case of Miller v. DeWitt.

If the injured party is a worker on the project, he generally cannot sue his own employer. Typically, the injured worker sues others whom he claims caused his injury. While technically it is possible for the architect or engineer to show that the principal cause of the injury was the negligence of the employer of the injured worker, (or the negligence of the worker himself), juries are not likely to relieve the architect or engineer from liability because they can not impose direct liability on the employer. If the party sued, such as the design professional or in some cases the owner, asserts an indemnity action against the employer of the injured worker, the negligence of the contractor will be relevant to the indemnity claim.

Generally, architects and engineers have not been very successful in using lack of causation as a defense.

Statutes of limitation require that legal actions be brought within a designated period of time after the legal claim arose. They have been of some assistance to architects and engineers, especially where the injury occurs after completion of the project. However, the efficacy of such statutes has been considerably reduced by the tendency of most courts to start the statutory period at the time the negligent act is discovered or the injury occurs. See § 30.08(e). In such jurisdictions the design professional may find himself sued for allegedly negligent acts committed many years before commencement of the lawsuit. Defense in such cases can be very difficult. This is one of the reasons why some courts and some statutes start the time period for bringing legal action at the time of the negligent act or when the project was completed rather than at the time the negligent act was discovered or when the injury occurred.

In some cases the architect or engineer is given a defense based upon quasi-immunity if the act complained of related to the exercise of quasi-judicial functions on the part of the architect or engineer. See § 27.11.

The principal legal protection for architects and engineers is indemnification. In many cases the principal wrong-doer is a contractor and the architect or engineer is held accountable because he did not take reasonable steps to correct improper construction methods or to condemn improper work. Design professionals who are liable in such cases may have a valid claim against the contractor or anyone whose negligence was greater based upon express or quasi-contract indemnification. See § 30.13(b). This will be illustrated in § 34.06 dealing with the leading case of Miller v. DeWitt.

SECTION 34.06 MILLER v. DeWITT, A LEADING CASE

In Miller v. DeWitt, 37 Ill.2d 273, 226 N.E.2d 630 (1967), the contractor was hired to expand and remodel an existing gymnasium. It was necessary to remove a proscenium truss, as well as two steel columns in the old wall. During the removal, the gymnasium roof collapsed and several workers were severely injured. These workers sued the architects and the school district. The basis for the action against the architects was that they had failed to provide adequate support for the roof, that they had not calculated a safety factor in the tubular steel scaffolding used to shore the trusses, that they had failed to oversee and inspect the scaffolding to determine whether it was safe, and that they had failed to apply to the work the degree of skill which would have been customarily brought to such work by competent architects.

To preclude these issues going to the jury, the architects asked the trial judge to direct a verdict in favor of the architects, because the method of work was within the province of the contractor and not the architects. The trial judge refused to do this, and he was upheld by the Illinois Supreme Court. The court held that a jury should decide whether the architect was negligent in failing to oversee and inspect the scaffolding and to see that the work was done properly by the contractor.

In addition, the architect was held to be in charge of the structure under the Illinois Scaffold Act, and liable on that basis as well.

The architect had the usual powers given to architects to condemn defective work and stop the work if performance was not proceeding in accordance with the contract. The court stated that usually the architect is obligated to see that the building meets the plans and specifications. However, they pointed to the architects' right to condemn defective work as evidence that the architects' powers were enlarged under this contract. The court stated that the architects had no duty to specify the method used, but that they had the right to insist upon a safe and adequate use of any method selected.

In Miller v. DeWitt, the dissenting judge argued that imposition of this liability was not proper, because the construction industry had functioned well without imposing liability upon architects and engineers who design but do not build.

Other cases have resulted in holdings similar to that in Miller v. DeWitt. But some cases in other jurisdictions have not imposed the same responsibility upon the design professional. For example, in C. W. Regan, Inc. v. Parsons, Brinckerhoff, Quade & Douglas, 411 F.2d 1379 (4th Cir.1969) a contractor on a tunnel project sued the engineer for damages suffered because of flooding of the tunnel. In holding that the trial judge should have directed a verdict for the engineer, the court stated:

> Parsons is not charged with the creation of any condition nor with any active conduct. Parsons is charged with negligence in the approval of plans for a temporary bulkhead which four months later proved to be leaky. There was no evidence of any duty on the part of Parsons to specify how the bulkhead should be caulked nor how it should be fitted against the surrounding masonry walls. No defect in the plans was suggested nor shown. All the evidence showed that the manner of fitting the bulkhead against the masonry and the manner of caulking to prevent leaks were field details which were the responsibility of the contractor. No damage resulted from any defect in the plan. Such damage as may have resulted arose either from improper installation or from changes in the shape and fit of the bulkhead in the four months from the time it was installed until the time of the flood. The duty of the engineer to obtain for the owner a tunnel according to plans and specifications does not carry with it a duty to see to it that one contractor's negligence does not damage the property of another contractor, and does not create a continuing duty of inspection as to temporary details of construction of temporary structures. This theory is also inconsistent with the express provisions of the contract documents themselves, . . .
>
> It is no doubt true that engineers and architects have a duty of care in drawing plans and in carrying out duties which they have accepted. It is possible, of course, for an engineer to assume such sweeping duties of supervision and

control over all details of construction that nothing else appearing he may be held to have assumed a duty to parties outside his contract. See, for example, Associated Engineers v. Job, 370 F.2d 633 (8th Cir.1966) (rehearing denied Feb. 21, 1967), where although the engineer was held liable the Court . . . said:

"We are not, as Associated suggests, converting every supervising engineer into a safety engineer as a matter of law. *We are simply construing a contract.*" (Emphasis added.)

(The *Job* case was discussed in § 30.13(d).)

Cases such as *Miller* and *Regan* may indicate the desirability from a liability standpoint of reducing some of the overall powers given a design professional in a construction project. As for predicting judicial results in such cases, while there will be variations depending upon contract language, it appears that the holding in the *Miller* case will set the trend.

In Miller v. DeWitt the architect asserted a cross action against the contractor who was the employer of the injured workers. The trial judge ruled that the architect had no cross action against the employer, and would not submit the case to the jury. The reasoning of the judge was that workmen's compensation laws prohibited any direct or indirect action for negligence against the contractor when the injured parties were employees of the contractor.

The Supreme Court of Illinois held that such an action could be brought against the employer of the injured workers, and that the trial court erroneously ruled for the contractor. The basis of such a cross action is quasi-contractual, since there was no contractual relationship between the architect and the contractor. The court held that the cause of the injury to the workers was the active negligence of the contractor in using improper shoring methods, while the basis for liability against the architect was passive negligence in not taking steps to make certain that the contractor used proper shoring methods. In such a case, the architect should have a valid cross action against the contractor, based upon quasi-contract.

SECTION 34.07 SOME ADVICE TO DESIGN PROFESSIONALS

Unquestionably, the tendency toward more professional liability lawsuits against architects and engineers is likely to continue. However, there are some methods for reducing the risk of such litigation being brought and for reducing the likelihood that such litigation will result in a judgment against the design professional.

The question of liability may depend to a substantial degree upon the contractual obligations of the design professional. The greater the scope of his obligation and the greater his power on the construction project, the more likely he is to be held accountable when things go wrong. The proper role for the design professional in construction projects should not be dictated by legal considerations although they are relevant. Whatever the scope of the obligation of the design professional, the obligation should be clearly and completely expressed in a written contract. Also, the design professional should make every effort to perform in accordance with his contractual obligations. If he goes beyond his contractual obligations, he may not only be going beyond his expertise but he may, in addition, be creating an expectation on the part of the client and others that he will continue to exceed his contract obligations, creating the possibility of increased legal responsibility.

The design professional should make every effort to obtain and maintain proper professional liability insurance. This will be discussed in greater detail in Chapter 35.

Design professionals may be held accountable for the negligence of their consultants. Consequently, a design professional hiring a consultant should make certain that the consultant owes him the same obligation that he owes his client. It would be unfortunate for the design professional to find that his contract with his client covered certain services and then find that his consultant did not obligate himself to perform these services. Also, in retaining consultants design professionals should make every effort to determine whether the consultant has the professional skills to do the work properly and the financial ability, either directly or through liability insurance, to pay for any liability incurred by the design professional as the result of the acts of the consultant.

Just as it may be possible to transfer losses to the consultant, the design professional should carefully consider the use of indemnity against contractors. Since there usually is no direct contractual relationship between design professional and contractor, such indemnification may have to be obtained in the construction contract between the owner and the prime contractor. Paragraph 4.18 of AIA Doc. A201 provides in part:

> **4.18 INDEMNIFICATION**
>
> **4.18.1** The Contractor shall indemnify and hold harmless the Owner and the Architect and their agents and employees from and against all claims, damages, losses and expenses including attorneys' fees arising out of or resulting from the performance of the Work, provided that any such claim, damage, loss or expense (a) is attributable to bodily injury, sickness, disease or death, or to injury to or destruction of tangible property (other than the Work itself) including the loss of use resulting therefrom, and (b) is caused in whole or in part by any negligent act or omission of the Contractor, any Subcontractor, anyone directly or indirectly employed by any

of them or anyone for whose acts any of them may be liable, regardless of whether or not it is caused in part by a party indemnified hereunder.

. . .

4.18.3 The obligations of the Contractor under this Paragraph 4.18 shall not extend to the liability of the Architect, his agents or employees arising out of (1) the preparation or approval of maps, drawings, opinions, reports, surveys, Change Orders, designs or specifications, or (2) the giving of or the failure to give directions or instructions by the Architect, his agents or employees provided such giving or failure to give is the primary cause of the injury or damage.

Indemnification covers only claims relating to personal harm and to "tangible property" other than the project itself. This would exclude indemnification for purely economic losses and physical harm to the project itself, neither of which have been principal areas of difficulty in liability cases.

Paragraph 4.18.3 sets up some exceptions to the general scope of indemnification provided for in 4.18.1. It excludes from indemnity those losses suffered by the architect which relate to design services and under certain circumstances "the failure to give directions or instructions by the Architect".

Apparently paragraph 4.18.3(2) is directed toward those lawsuits like Miller v. DeWitt which are brought against architects based upon their failure to discover unsafe construction practices or their failure to correct those that are discovered. If the liability falls into this category, the clause requires a comparative causal evaluation.

The architect will be denied indemnity against the contractor if the architect's negligence is the *primary* cause of the injury or damage. Apparently, if a worker is injured partly due to poor construction methods used by the contractor and partly due to the failure on the part of the architect to discover and correct these methods, this clause would require the law to determine which is the primary cause of the injury or damage. If the contractor's conduct is the primary cause, he will have to indemnify the architect. If the architect's conduct is the primary cause, then the contractor will not have to indemnify the architect.

As noted in § 30.13, some states employ quasi-contractual indemnity between two wrongdoers. If one wrongdoer can establish that his liability is based upon secondary or passive negligence, he may be able to recover indemnity if the other wrongdoer is guilty of active or primary negligence.

The use of clauses such as 4.18 will assist in those states which have not as yet recognized quasi-contractual indemnification. In those states where it is recognized, it is likely that the courts will apply the clause with its determining factor of "primary cause" and not resort to quasi-contractual indemnity. When contracting parties provide in detail for how certain contingencies are to be handled, the use of quasi-contractual principles based upon unjust enrichment are less likely to be applied by the courts.

Obviously, one of the main purposes of 4.18 is to benefit the architect. This would mean that the architect should be classified as a third party beneficiary, giving him a right to sue upon the contract between owner and prime contractor. However, it might have been better to specify in the indemnification clause that it is for the benefit of the architect.

Another technique for minimizing liability relates to disclaimers. Those design professionals in the business of making representations, such as soil testers, structural engineers, and in some cases architects should make best efforts to disclaim any responsibility for the inaccuracy of these representations unless it can be shown that they were negligent in making them. Disclaimers of this sort may not always be possible because those who hire design professionals to perform these services may not be willing to hire those who use disclaimers. However, if the design professional employed to make these representations explains to the person retaining him some of the difficulties that can cause inaccurate representations, the person hiring the design professional may be willing to agree to disclaimers.

There are no iron clad guarantees that design professionals will not be sued. Some of the methods described in this section may minimize the risk and may give the design professional a better chance if he is sued. In any event, it is important for design professionals to keep careful records relating to the performance of their services. These records should relate to conversations with clients and contractors, directions given during the performance of the project and records which indicate the number of visits to the site and the things done while visiting the site. Since claims are often brought a substantial period of time after the work is performed, it is important to have a carefully planned records retention system under which these records are kept and are available at any time prior to the expiration of the applicable statute of limitations.

REVIEW QUESTIONS

1. What is the present trend in liability of design professionals?

2. Who are the persons who might institute legal action against a design professional?

3. What are the legal grounds for suits against architects and engineers?

4. What are possible defenses?

5. What types of acts can be the basis for legal action against architects and engineers?

QUESTIONS FOR CLASS DISCUSSION

1. Is the present trend of expanded liability for architects and engineers a desirable one?

2. Should a soil engineer be able to disclaim responsibility for any economic losses or injuries which occur because of an inaccurate soils test?

3. Should the architect be responsible for injuries which result from improper construction methods when those methods were stated in the shop drawings?

4. What is your opinion of the holding in the *Erhart* case? The *Day* case? Miller v. DeWitt?

PROBLEM

A was the architect for a large office building. When he selected material to be used for wall construction, he did not realize the fire insurance rates were dependent upon the type of wall construction material. He specified wall material based upon cost, safety factors and aesthetics. Had he specified different materials of approximately the same cost, there would have been a reduction in the fire insurance rate. When the owner found this out, he claimed that the additional insurance premium should be borne by the architect because the architect should have known that insurance premiums are based upon materials used in construction. Is the owner correct in his statement? What additional facts would be helpful in resolving this problem?

Chapter 35

INSURANCE

SECTION 35.01 RISKS AND RISK PROTECTION

Architects and engineers must be aware of the types of risks to which they may be subjected, and develop methods of protecting themselves from those risks. Insurance plays a vital role in risk protection.

(A) DEATH

Life insurance is a protective device dealing with the risks of death. In addition to its importance as a method of protecting one's family, it has other uses for the design professional.

When a partner or a shareholder in a closely held corporation dies, often the remaining partners or shareholders would like to buy out the persons to whom the share or partnership ownership would succeed upon the death of the partner or shareholder. This is done in order to avoid dissolution of the partnership, or losing control of the corporation, as well as to provide cash to the estate. Often there is insufficient cash available to make this large purchase. If the partnership or corporation has insured the life of a major shareholder or partner, the proceeds from the life insurance are available to purchase the shares or to purchase the partnership interest.

Life insurance may be useful to ameliorate the sometimes adverse effect caused by the death of a partner, a major shareholder, or even a key employee. Often the business success of an enterprise depends upon the continued ability of an individual to direct the enterprise. When such a key individual dies, business may suffer permanently or temporarily.

Employers often provide group life insurance for employees. This can be done at low, tax-deductible, cost to the employer, and generally without the employees having to pay income tax on the employer contribution. Group insurance can help create good employment relations.

(B) LOST OR DAMAGED PROPERTY AND BUSINESS INTERRUPTION

There are other risks. For example, property belonging to an enterprise may be stolen, lost, or destroyed. Insurance can protect against these risks. Also, a business may be unable to function for a specified period because of catastrophic events such as fire, an act of nature, death, or illness to a key employee, or because projects upon which the enterprise have been working have to be cancelled or suspended. It may be possible to purchase insurance which can insure against the risk of business loss due to those interruptions.

(C) ACCIDENTS AND ILLNESS

Accidents and illness to proprietors and employees and their families can cause serious financial hardship. The risk of high medical expenses and lost salaries and wages can be protected against by health, accident and disability insurance. This protection, like group life insurance, can often be bought economically through group plans. Such protection, provided in whole or part by the employer, can boost employee morale.

(D) LIABILITY

The law often imposes liability upon an employer for the acts of his employees, and upon a manufacturer for losses caused by defective products he makes. Architects and engineers, as employers, need protection from risks incident to normal employer activities such as operating automobiles. In addition, they need insurance for liability resulting from professional activities. Public liability insurance provides protection for normal employer activities, and professional liability insurance provides protection against professional liability. See § 35.03 for a more complete discussion of professional liability insurance.

(E) OTHER RISKS

Fire insurance covers the risk of damage or destruction to a project caused by fire or other related causes. Workmen's compensation insurance may be required to handle the risk of employee injuries received in the course of employment.

SECTION 35.02 SOME BASIC PRINCIPLES OF INSURANCE LAW

(A) UNILATERAL CHARACTER OF POLICY

There are legal problems which recur in insurance disputes. Usually, an insurance policy consists of promises by the insurance company to pay a specified amount of money if certain things occur. In a life insurance policy, the obligation to pay arises upon the death of the insured. In a fire insurance policy, the specified occurrence is fire of a certain type, causing losses. Usually, the insured is not obligated to continue to pay premiums. In this sense, the insurance contract is one-sided. However, the payment of premiums is the condition, among others, which controls the obligation on the part of the insurance company to pay.

(B) POLICY APPLICATION

The policy application contains many questions which must be answered by the insured. In life insurance, the application will make a searching inquiry into the past medical record and history of the applicant. All questions asked on the application must be answered honestly. If the applicant does not know certain facts, he should state so on his application.

Generally, a material misrepresentation in the policy application relied upon by the insurer will enable the insurer to avoid any obligations under the policy. A material misrepresentation usually relates to some fact which is relevant to the risk taken by the insurance company. For example, a misrepresentation as to the past medical history of an insured applying for life or health insurance is likely to be material. In a fire insurance policy a material misrepresentation as to the activities which will take place on the insured property would very likely be material.

Generally life insurance policies contain incontestability clauses. Such clauses provide that the insurance company cannot raise defenses of the type mentioned in this subsection after a certain period has elapsed from the time the policy is issued.

(C) COMMENCEMENT AND CONTINUATION OF COVERAGE

One of the problems which occurs frequently relates to commencement of coverage. Often the policy states that the coverage will commence after the first premium is paid and the insurance company has notified the insured of the commencement of coverage. Disputes may arise because an insurance agent makes a representation that the coverage will commence immediately because of what he calls a "binder." The law may compel the insurance company to live up to the representations of the insurance company agent, if the agent raised a reasonable expectation on the part of the insured that he was covered. Usually the insured will rely to his detriment by not obtaining other insurance. If possible, the insured should obtain representations in writing from the company. If an agent makes a representation as to coverage, it is best to get this representation in writing. If it is not possible, it is advisable to send a letter to the company stating what the agent has informed the insured.

Often the initial policy is for a specified period. When that period expires, the insured will contact the agent and request that the policy be renewed for a specified period. Again it is important to get a written confirmation of the renewal, and to be certain that the premium is paid at the time of the renewal. To avoid problems, the insured should keep a record of written notes and memoranda of conversations in which he has been informed that the policy commences on a specific date, or that an existing policy has been renewed.

Another problem relates to the payment of continuing premiums. Usually insurance companies or their agents send out notices stating when premiums are due. It is essential to pay when the premium is due, and to keep a record that such payment has been made. It may be helpful to set up a payment schedule which has suspense dates for the payment of all important insurance premiums. This insures against the possibility that premium notices may not be received or become lost.

Most insurance policies contain grace periods. This is to protect the insured from losing his coverage if he does not pay by the due date of the premium. Frequently these periods are thirty days, and during this period he may pay without losing his coverage. However, it is never advisable to rely on grace periods.

(D) COVERAGE AND EXCLUSIONS: COURTS FAVOR INSURED

Coverage, even where broadly stated, is often qualified by exclusionary provisions which often make the insurance policy lengthy and almost unreadable. But it is important to know what is excluded. If losses of certain types are excluded, these exclusions can make the policy useless. Sometimes exclusions can be eliminated by a rider to the policy. If the insured wishes coverage that would be excluded, he should so indicate at the time he applies for the policy. The insurance company may not issue the policy, but in many cases it will.

Examination of coverage and exclusions are important from another standpoint. Sometimes a comparison of existing policies of the insured will reveal overlapping coverage. Also, these policies may provide that they will apply only if the loss is not covered by another insurer. This can mean that the insurer is paying for more coverage than he has or needs.

While the insurance policy is a type of contract, the laws relating to other types of contracts are often not applied in insurance contract disputes. This is because insurance policies are usually difficult to read and to understand. Also, courts increasingly try to protect the reasonable expectations of the insured, despite language in the policy which seems to contravene those expectations. Nevertheless there are cases where the insured loses. The policies should be carefully checked to see whether they cover what the insured wants to be protected against. If they do not, he should try to negotiate this question with the insurance company, or look for a policy which covers those risks which he wants to cover.

(E) NOTICE OF LOSS INCURRED OR CLAIM AGAINST INSURED

The insurance company's obligation to pay is usually conditioned upon the insured giving notice by a specified time, or by a reasonable time after the occurrence of the loss or making of the claim. There should be strict compliance with the notice requirements of the insurance policy. For this reason, it is important to keep copies of all the insurance policies in the office of the design professional or his insurance advisor. Courts sometimes excuse a notice period where the absence of the notice did not materially injure the rights of the insurance company, but it is never safe to rely on such a possibility.

Sometimes disputes arise relating to the amount of money the insured should receive when he has suffered a loss. Frequently the insurance policy itself sets forth a measure of recovery which is not advantageous to the insured. Sometimes it is helpful to compare policies of different companies with regard to how they will measure a loss. If this is done, it may be possible to get better coverage by insuring with one company rather than another.

(F) OTHER CONDITIONS

There are other conditions which are included in insurance policies relating to the risk which the insurance company undertakes. For example, in fire insurance policies there is usually a provision which states that ordinances relating to the storing of flammable materials will be complied with at all times. For that reason, it is important that the insured make certain that he is not doing anything that violates any conditions of the policy.

(G) RELIABILITY OF INSURER

The reliability of the insurance company may be a factor in an insurance policy. Occasionally insurance companies go bankrupt and are unable to pay the claims asserted against them. Most states restrict who can write insurance within the state. Usually the statutes create administrative agencies which are empowered to regulate insurance companies. The agencies may have power to control the insurance policies. If the insured is at all in doubt about the reliability of the company, he should contact the state administrative agency which regulates insurance.

(H) VARIATION IN POLICIES

There are many different types of policies, and many insurance companies. Premiums frequently vary, coverage varies, as do other important aspects of the insurance policy. An independent insurance advisor can be helpful in policy selection. He also may be able to convince the company to pay a claim, even though certain technical requirements set forth by the policy were not met. He may be able to inform the insured that he had coverage for certain types of risks which the insured himself did not realize.

(I) CONTRACTS REQUIRING INSURANCE

It is becoming more common for one contracting party to require that the other have insurance coverage. For example, the owner may want the contractor to carry public liability insurance. To effectuate this, the owner could obtain a promise that the contractor will carry this insurance. But if the promise is not performed, the owner may be left with an uncollectable claim against the contractor for breach, instead of insurance coverage.

To protect himself against this risk, the owner could require that the contractor show or deposit the policy with him. This, however, would not take care of the possibility that for one reason or another the policy may expire or be cancelled during the period when the contractor may incur liability to a member of the public. To take care of this problem, the owner can request the insurance company to notify the owner if the policy is about to be cancelled or expire, in order to give the owner a chance to continue or reinstate coverage.

The same cautionary steps might be advisable if the architect or engineer intends to hire a consultant for whom the architect or engineer might be responsible.

(J) SPECIAL PROBLEMS OF GROUP INSURANCE

There has been a great expansion in the use of group insurance, mainly in the area of life and health insurance. Sometimes the employer has a detailed master insurance contract with the insurer. As a rule, the employee does not see the group master policy and bases his expectations upon literature and brochures prepared by the insurer or the employer and distributed by the latter.

There may be a conflict between the actual terms of the master policy and expectations raised by such literature. While technically the master policy controls, the law is beginning to pay more attention to the more informal type of literature distributed to employees, which often is the only written statement on important insurance matters they receive.

Where feasible, the employer should distribute to the employees actual copies of the master insurance contract negotiated by the employer and the insurance company. If this is not feasible, the employer should make certain that the information given to the employees accurately reflects the important provisions in the master insurance agreement.

Increasingly, group insurance programs are being regulated by statute and administrative regulations enacted by state insurance regulatory agencies.

SECTION 35.03 PROFESSIONAL LIABILITY INSURANCE

(A) COMPARISON TO PUBLIC LIABILITY INSURANCE

Because of the increasing tendency for design professionals to find themselves defending law suits, professional liability insurance (also known as errors and omissions insurance), is important. It is important to differentiate public liability insurance from professional liability insurance. If the architect or engineer is an employer, and his employee causes an accident by driving negligently, the liability of the architect or engineer can be covered by the architect or engineer's public liability insurance. Professional liability insurance covers those risks which relate to the performance of professional services by the architect or engineer.

The distinction between public liability insurance and professional liability insurance is illustrated by Shaw v. Aetna Cas. and Surety Co., 407 F.2d 813 (7th Cir.1969). This was an action by an architect on his public liability insurance policy. The policy provided that coverage was excluded for injuries which arise "out of defects in maps, plans, designs or specifications, prepared, acquired or used by the insured, or due to the general supervision of the insured in connection with the operations of any contractor".

The architect and the public owner were sued for an injury to a worker who had been struck by the outrigger of a hoist. Liability was predicated upon a violation of the Illinois Scaffold Act. This law places liability upon those in charge of a project for injuries caused by a violation of safety rules set forth in the statute.

The architect requested that the insurance company defend the case. It refused, claiming that the acts upon which liability was predicated was excluded from coverage. The architect settled the suit and sued the insurance company. He asked for reimbursement for the money paid under the settlement and his legal fees.

A tortured judicial comparison of the complaint of the injured worker and the policy (the complaint alleged the architect placed and operated the hoist improperly) enabled the architect to recover. It is likely that the architect thought his public liability policy covered any liability. The policy language chosen shows that the insurance company attempted to exclude liability based upon professional acts. The decision in favor of the architect does not lessen the likely error of the architect in thinking his public liability policy was designed to protect him from all liability, including negligent design or supervision.

(B) REQUIREMENT OF PROFESSIONAL LIABILITY INSURANCE

The law in general does not require that a design professional carry professional insurance. But increasingly owners require that the architect or engineer have or procure, and maintain professional errors and omissions insurance in a designated amount. When such owners consider that they may be sued as a result of negligent acts of their architect or their engineer, they want to be sure they have a collectible claim over against the architect or engineer. For this reason, they may require that the architect or engineer carry professional liability insurance. Also, if the architect on a project is financially solvent or carries adequate professional liability insurance, anyone injured as a result of his negligence may choose to sue the architect rather than the owner.

Even if not required, many design professionals carry this insurance. They do so to protect their assets from being taken by the law if they are held liable. Also, most design professionals do not wish to see persons who are injured because of their professional mistakes go uncompensated.

(C) COVERAGE AND EXCLUSIONS

The design professional should examine the policy carefully. Will his policy cover claims that are made against him for negligence after policy issuance which relate to projects completed before issuance of the policy? When does coverage end? Which risks are included and which are excluded?

Some coverage questions relate to the location of the project. Within the United States the extent of exposure to liability may depend to a substantial degree upon which state law will govern the lawsuit. This is usually determined by location of the project. The variation of liability exposure may be even greater if the project is located in a foreign country.

Some professional liability insurance policies exclude coverage for work undertaken outside the United States. Some policies will cover such work if the litigation has been commenced in the United States or Canada.

Generally, the policies cover liability for professional negligence. In addition, the professional negligence must relate to tasks commonly undertaken by design professionals. Certain types of hazardous work may be excluded. One policy excluded work not customarily performed by an architect. Negligence relating to boundary surveys, subsurface conditions, ground testing, tunnel and bridge activities, dams, failure to advise or require insurance for surety bonds, failure to complete contract documents on time, or to act upon shop drawings on time were also excluded in that policy, unless the loss was due to negligence in design. Also, excluded were express warranties, guarantees, and estimates of probable construction cost, as well as indemnity liability assumed by the architect by contract, and liability for copyright, trademark, or patent infringements.

Exclusion for contractually created liability can raise difficulties for the design professional. In some jurisdictions the owner bears the risk of defective plans. If the owner is liable for defective plans, he might assert that the design professional owes him a corresponding obligation to turn out a set of plans which will do the job properly. This obligation may be based upon the design professional knowing or being in the position to know that the owner was taking this risk in his dealings with the contractor or upon express or implied provisions in the agreement between the owner and design professional. (Section 6.17 analyzes the types of arrangements which can be made between design professional and his client relating to the standard of performance by the design professional.) If the undertaking goes beyond an agreement to use professional due care, any losses suffered by the design professional because of a breach of such an agreement may not be covered by such a professional liability policy.

In addition, design professionals may be held liable for inaccurate cost predictions, or inaccurate soil representations. Such liability would not be covered by most professional liability policies. The exclusion for a contractually assumed liability can discourage the use of arbitration. For example, suppose the design professional and his client have an arbitration clause in their contract. If a dispute arises, the design professional might hesitate to invoke arbitration because of a fear that any award by the arbitrator would be considered "contractually created" since the contract created the jurisdiction for the arbitrator to decide the dispute. The insurance company might contend that their liability exposure is limited to those awards which are made by courts and not awards made by arbitrators. An exclusion for contractually created risks should not apply to arbitration awards. If the dispute relates to negligent conduct on the part of the design professional, a liability generally covered by such contracts, submission of the dispute to arbitration should not relieve the insurance company from liability. (The insurer should be notified of any intention to arbitrate.)

Insurance coverage is severely limited by a policy with the types of exclusions mentioned earlier in this subsection. When presented with such a policy, the architect or engineer should attempt to get a rider changing some of these exclusions, if they are risks which are likely to be incurred. If this cannot be done, the architect should consult an insurance advisor to see if another company offers a better policy, or if the excluded risks can be covered by other types of insurance. If not, the architect should realize that he will have to bear those risks himself.

As insurance becomes more essential, the professional services performed and contractual obligations undertaken by architects or engineers may be determined to a large degree by insurance companies. This is more likely to be so if one or only a small number of companies will issue professional liability insurance.

Whose negligence is covered under the policy? The design professional often uses consultants to do work on projects. It is important to determine whether the policy will cover acts of consultants, as well as the design professional himself.

(D) DEDUCTIBLE POLICIES

In addition to excluding certain types of claims, insurance companies frequently try to reduce their risks by having deductible policies. Losses up to a specified amount must be borne by the insured, or divided in some predetermined way between the insured and the insurance company. There has been a tendency to raise the deductible amounts. Deductibles cause a number of problems.

Does the insurance company have to defend a claim that is below the deductible amount? While this depends upon the language of the policy, usually it must defend the claim. To a degree, this is based upon the self interest of the insurance company. It may be fearful of letting the insured litigate even small claims, because the case may set a precedent disadvantageous to the insurance company. In addition, the insured may justifiably think that the financial burden of defense will not fall upon him even if the claim is small. It can cost a great deal to litigate a small claim.

Deductible policies may cause a conflict of interest between the insurance company and the insured. When small claims are made, the insurance company may choose to settle and pay the claim rather than incur the costs of litigation. Yet the architect may oppose such a settlement because he believes a settlement is an admission that he was negligent, reflects upon his professional skill, and comes out of his pocket. The policy should cover this question.

(E) POLICY LIMITS AND CONFLICT OF INTEREST

Most insurance policies contain dollar limitations on insurance coverage. Questions similar to those discussed in § 35.03(d), relating to deductible policies, can arise when there are policy limits.

Is there an obligation to defend the claim if the insurance company is willing to pay the policy limit? For example, suppose that the policy limits are $100,000 and the claim is for $200,000. Any recovery over $100,000 will have to be paid by the insured. Generally, professional liability insurance policies require the insurer to defend even though the insurance company is willing to pay to the policy limits.

Suppose the claimant is willing to settle for $50,000 but the insurance company refuses to settle. Suppose the case is litigated and the plaintiff recovers a judgment for $125,000. The insured might contend that had the insurance company settled, he would not have had to pay any amounts in excess of the $100,000 policy limit. While the law is in a state of flux on this question, courts tend to hold insurance companies liable for amounts over the policy coverage if their refusal to settle was unreasonable in light of all the circumstances.

(F) NOTICE OF CLAIM

Usually insurance policies state that the insured must notify the insurance company when a claim is made against him. The purpose of the notice is to enable the insurance company to evaluate the claim, and collect evidence for a possible lawsuit. If a clear claim is asserted against the architect or engineer he does not, as a rule, hesitate to notify his insurer. Sometimes it is unclear whether a claim is being made. Someone may make a vague complaint. If the design professional is in any doubt, he should notify the insurance company.

On occasion, the insured will settle the claim and then ask for reimbursement from the insurance company. This is dangerous. If the settlement appears to the insurer to have been reasonable, and if it is saved the expense of negotiating a settlement or litigating, it may pay the claim for reimbursement. But it may not pay if it believes there was no liability, or if it believes the settlement was overgenerous. The insurer may not go into the merits of the settlement, but simply refuse to pay based upon the contract language which requires that it be notified. Architects and engineers should not settle a claim first and then notify the insurance company.

Sometimes the policy does not make clear whether the claims that are made below the deductible figure must be reported to the insurance company. Insurance companies generally desire to receive this information to determine whether the design professional is a good insurance risk, even if they do not have to pay the claim.

(G) DEFENSE OF THE ACTION

One of the important aspects of insurance protection is the cost of handling the claim and any resulting litigation. Usually the insurance company furnishes legal counsel. But there are significant expenses in addition to attorney's fees.

Who pays for the preparation of exhibits, expert witnesses, transcripts of testimony taken in advance of trial and other costs of preparation of litigation? The policies should make this clear. Often they do not.

The insured may wish the case handled by his attorney, rather than the attorney furnished by the insurance company. This may be acceptable to the insurance company, if it feels the attorney is skilled in such matters, and if there is some advance understanding on fees and the right to settle the claim.

The design professional may wish to use his own attorney even if the insurance company wishes to use its own attorney. For example, in claims which are in excess of the policy limits, the architect or engineer may have an interest which conflicts with that of the insurance company. In such cases, it may be advisable for the insured to have his own attorney representing him in the matter. While this will cost the insured legal fees, it may be worthwhile if the liability exceeds the policy limits. Usually claims of this sort are not made unless the insured has property or assets and can satisfy a large judgment.

After notice of a claim, the insured and the insurance company may disagree on coverage. The insurance company may insist that even if the architect or engineer is liable, it is not. But the insurer may not be certain. In such a case, it may choose to refuse to defend the claim and take its chances on its liability. But if a settlement is made, or if the litigation is lost, the insurer may have to pay. See Shaw v. Aetna Cas. and Surety Co., discussed at § 35.03(a).

To avoid this risk, the insurance company may offer to defend the claim "with reservations". This means it wishes to reserve the right to contend that the liability does not come within the coverage of the policy. Courts have looked askance at these "with reservation" defenses, and they are not always successful. Once the insurance company takes charge of the defense, it may have a difficult time avoiding liability if the insured is found liable.

Usually the policy requires that the insured cooperate in his defense. He is usually obligated not to make statements to the other side, or to compromise the case in any way.

REVIEW QUESTIONS

1. What types of insurance are important to design professionals? Why?

2. Why is it generally stated that insurance contracts are unilateral?

3. What are the most important conditions precedent to the insurance company's promise to pay?

4. What is the principal difference between public liability insurance and professional liability insurance?

5. What are the types of exclusions from coverage from professional liability insurance?

6. What is a deductible liability policy?

7. Why is it important that the insured give notice to the insurance company that a claim had been made or an accident has occurred?

QUESTIONS FOR CLASS DISCUSSION

1. Should the courts favor an insured when there is a question of interpreting an insurance policy?

2. In what way can insurance coverage exert a significant influence upon professional architectural and engineering practice? Is this desirable?

PROBLEM

Suppose A were insured under a professional liability insurance containing the exclusions set forth in § 35.03(c). During the period of insurance coverage A sent a letter to his client stating that the prime contractor had not been paying his subcontractors and suppliers. Copies of this letter were also mailed to the prime contractor's bonding company. But the prime had paid his subs and suppliers. The prime contractor brought a libel action against A. Would A's liability be covered under his professional liability insurance policy?

Chapter 36

DESIGN PROFESSIONAL AS AN EMPLOYER

SECTION 36.01 RELEVANCE: TREND TOWARD LARGER ORGANIZATIONS

While the architectural and engineering professions are still generally centered around the small practitioner, there is an increasing tendency for architectural firms, and especially engineering firms, to develop large organizations. When an architect or engineer is a small practitioner, many of the specialized services needed are performed by persons outside his organization. He may hire an accountant to take care of his financial records, an attorney to handle his legal affairs, an insurance counselor to advise him on insurance matter, and he may even use an independent secretarial service.

As his organization grows in size, there is a tendency to have the services performed by his own employees. He usually finds it is more convenient and more economical to have people on his staff who can perform these services. For that reason, larger organizations are likely to have secretaries, accountants, draftsmen, and even an attorney as employees.

However, in considering whether to have these functions performed by employees rather than by persons who are outside the organization and who specialize in this work, a design professional must take into account the heavy governmental regulation placed upon employers, and the fact that having employees will raise legal problems which may not be faced by the design professional when he uses outside specialists to perform these services. He may still find the advantages outweigh the disadvantages but he must be aware of how the law regulates employers.

While emphasis in this chapter is upon the design professional as an employer, the legal controls described are important to the large number of architects and engineers who will work as employees. Generally, these legal controls protect employees. Knowledge, even in a general way, of their existence is important to those who are employees.

SECTION 36.02 GOVERNMENT REGULATION: BROADENING OF LEGAL CONTROLS OVER THE EMPLOYMENT RELATIONSHIP

There are increasing legal controls over the employment relationship. Some early attempts by state and federal legislative bodies to regulate employment conditions were held unconstitutional by state and federal courts. However, it can be assumed that the state, through the exercise of its police powers, and the federal government, through the exercise of its right to regulate interstate commerce, have the power to pass laws which govern wages, hours and working conditions.

Through labor unions, millions of employees bargain collectively with employers on matters such as wages, hours, fringe benefits, working conditions, employment security, and promotions. For government employees, such matters are frequently determined by state laws and administered by civil service administrative agencies. However, there are still large numbers of private employees who have to depend upon protective legislation.

(A) JURISDICTION: STATE AND FEDERAL

Historically, the employment relationship was regulated by the states. However, as American business and industry developed more interstate characteristics, there has been an increasing tendency for the federal government to enter this field. Usually, this power given to the federal government is derived from its right under the Constitution to regulate interstate commerce. It is not difficult to find contacts between more than one state in most types of businesses. There may be some very local businesses which sell in a limited area and could be considered as being involved only in intrastate commerce. However, the likelihood is that the goods which are purchased by these small businesses may have traveled through interstate commerce at some time, in one form or another. For this reason, the federal government has the power to regulate most businesses.

However, the federal government does not always exercise its full constitutional power. There may be some elements of regulation that the states can handle more efficiently. Also, there are practical limits to the federal power. Extensive jurisdiction requires large administrative organizations and payrolls, with a concomitant increase in the cost of the federal government expenses. For this reason, many statutes giving the federal government control over certain businesses and transactions define the jurisdictional limits so as to cover businesses with a particular gross dollar volume or a specified profit derived from interstate commerce. This means that larger businesses are more likely to be regulated by the federal government than are smaller businesses. But the tendency has been to lower the dollar limits of these jurisdictional lines. Also, the degree to which full federal jurisdiction is exercised varies from statute to statute.

The most important governmental controls on the employment relationship relate to wages, hours, and working conditions. Legal controls relating to these aspects of the employment relationship vary considerably from state to state. Also, such laws frequently change in details. However, it is important for architects and engineers to have some general idea of the nature of governmental control over employers.

(B) WAGES, HOURS AND CONDITIONS OF EMPLOYMENT: THE *LUBLIN CASE*

The most important limitation relates to minimum wages. State governments and, to an increasing degree, the federal government, have passed laws which specify that persons are to be paid a stated minimum wage. Often these laws have exceptions for domestic workers, farm workers, and employees in other specialized industries.

In 1966 Congress raised the minimum wage for employees covered under the Fair Labor Standards Act to $1.40 per hour for the first year of the change, and to $1.60 per hour thereafter. The 1966 Act also brought certain employers and employees under federal law who had not been previously covered. As to these employers and employees, the federal minimum wage begins at $1.00 per hour and after a series of graduated steps, reaches $1.60 per hour after the fourth year of the enactment of the statute.

In addition to setting minimum wages, the Fair Labor Standards Act (FLSA) requires that covered employees be paid time and a half for any work over 40 hours a week. Again, the 1966 Act provided for a gradual adoption of the time and a half rule for hours over 40 for employees who are brought under the Fair Labor Standards Act by the 1966 amendments to the Fair Labor Standards Act. There are a great many exceptions, qualifications, and exemptions from this general rule.

It is in the area of time and a half for overtime that many architects and engineers can get into difficulty. Often employees of architects and engineers work long work weeks or long days when there are peak loads of work in the office. It is important for architects and engineers who are in private practice to determine whether their activities fall within the scope of the Fair Labor Standards Act and, if so, to comply with the requirements of the act in terms of wages paid and working hours. (There are exceptions for work performed under certain collective bargaining agreements with unions, and for professional and executive employees.)

The FLSA requires the employer to keep detailed records dealing with wages and hours. Penalties for non-compliance with FLSA requirements can be a fine of up to $10,000, six months imprisonment, double payment of the proper amount for wages as damages, and attorneys' fees. If the action is brought by the Secretary of Labor, the employee receives only the wages he should have been paid.

A leading case dealing with the applicability of the FLSA to design professionals is reproduced at this point.

MITCHELL v. LUBLIN, McGAUGHY & ASSOCIATES

United States Supreme Court, 1959.
358 U.S. 207.

MR. CHIEF JUSTICE WARREN delivered the opinion of the Court.

Petitioner, the Secretary of Labor, brought this action under § 17 of the Fair Labor Standards Act, 29 U.S.C. § 217, 29 U.S.C.A. § 217, to restrain respondent from violating the record-keeping and overtime provisions of the Act. . . . The complaint was dismissed basically on the lower court's conclusion that the activities of respondent, an architectural and consulting engineering firm, were local in nature and not within the Act's coverage. . . .

Respondent is hired to design public, industrial and residential projects and to prepare plans and specifications necessary for their construction. It has offices in both Norfolk, Virginia, and Washington, D. C., and it employs some sixty-five or seventy persons. Respondent does considerable work for the armed services. The District Court estimated that approximately 60% of the work in the Norfolk office has been done for the Army Engineers or the Navy Department while 85% of the work in Washington has been performed for similar agencies or for subdivisions of local governments in the District and nearby States. Many of respondent's projects and clients are located outside Virginia and the District of Columbia. A typical project undertaken in the past was the design of a standard mobile Army warehouse with the attendant preparation of detailed plans and specifications. In addition, respondent has designed various construction projects including the widening of streets at a naval operating base, the extension and paving of airplane taxiways and parking aprons at a naval air station, a local sewerage system in Maryland, the alteration of various hangar facilities at military air bases, the relocation of radio and television facilities, the improvement of state roads and turnpikes, and the repair of government buildings at shipyards. The balance of respondent's activity has consisted of preparing plans and specifications for the construction of private projects such as homes, commercial buildings, bus terminals, shopping centers and the like. Respondent has performed certain supervisory functions in connection with the construction of some of the private projects but almost none where governmental agencies were involved.

The government contracts required respondent to produce plans and specifications, copies of which were sent by the governmental agencies to prospective bidders, many of whom were located outside Virginia and the District of Columbia. These plans consisted of drawings and designs and were supplemented by explanatory specifications which contained the information necessary for estimating cost and guiding contractors in bidding and construction. They were prepared under the supervision of respondent's professional members and associates by draftsmen employed by respondent. In many cases, the information necessary to prepare the plans and specifications was gathered on the site of the projects by fieldmen employed by respondent. These fieldmen included surveyors, transitmen and chainmen who often traveled across state lines to get to the projects. On one project, fieldmen from the Washington office went daily to nearby Maryland to gather data for a sewerage project. In addition to the draftsmen and fieldmen, various clerks and stenographers employed by respondent participated in the mechanical preparation of these plans and specifications.

The parties are agreed that respondent's professional employees—architects and engineers—are exempted from the coverage of the Act by § 13(a) (1), 29 U.S.C. § 213(a) (1), 29 U.S.C.A. § 213(a) (1).[1] Therefore, the Secretary's injunction action is directed at some fifty employees mentioned above: draftsmen, fieldmen, clerks and stenographers. The stenographers, in addition to their connection with the plans and specifications, manned respondent's private phone wire connecting the Norfolk and Washington offices, prepared and typed substantial numbers of letters concerning the described projects which were mailed to persons in places other than Virginia and the District of Columbia, and prepared payrolls in the Virginia office for employees at the Washington and Norfolk locations.

The question at issue is whether these non-professional employees are "engaged in commerce" as that term is used in §§ 6 and 7 of the Act, 29 U.S.C. §§ 206, 207, 29 U.S.C.A. §§ 206, 207.[2] To determine the answer to this question, we focus on the activities of the employees and not on the business of the employer. . . . We start with the premise that Congress, by excluding from the Act's coverage employees whose activities merely "affect commerce," indicated its intent not to make the scope of the Act coextensive with its power to regulate commerce. . . . However, within the tests of coverage fashioned by Congress, the Act has been construed liberally to apply to the furthest reaches consistent with congressional direction. Thus the Court stated in Overstreet v. North Shore Corp., 318 U.S. 125, 128, 63 S.Ct. 494, 496, 87 L.Ed. 656, "* * * the policy of Congressional abnegation with respect to occupations affecting commerce is no reason for narrowly circumscribing the phrase 'engaged in commerce.' "

1. [Ed. note: footnotes have been renumbered.] The section provides:

"The provisions of sections 206 and 207 of this title shall not apply with respect to (1) any employee employed in a bona fide executive, administrative, professional, or local retailing capacity, or in the capacity of outside salesman (as such terms are defined and delimited by regulations of the Administrator.) * * *"

2. Section 6 provides:

"(a) Every employer shall pay to each of his employees who is engaged in commerce or in the production of goods for commerce wages at the following rates * * *."

Section 7 provides:

"(a) Except as otherwise provided in this section, no employer shall employ any of his employees who is engaged in commerce or in the production of goods for commerce for a workweek longer than forty hours, unless such employee receives compensation for his employment in excess of the hours above specified at a rate not less than one and one-half times the regular rate at which he is employed."

Where employees' activities have related to interstate instrumentalities or facilities, such as bridges, canals and roads, we have used a practical test to determine whether they are "engaged in commerce." The test is "whether the work is so directly and vitally related to the functioning of an instrumentality or facility of interstate commerce as to be, in practical effect, a part of it, rather than isolated local activity." Mitchell v. C. W. Vollmer & Co., supra, 349 U.S. at page 429, 75 S.Ct. at page 862. Coverage in the instant case must be determined by that test for, as the parties stipulated below, the draftsmen, fieldmen, clerks and stenographers all worked intimately with the plans and specifications prepared by respondent for the repair and construction of various interstate instrumentalities and facilities including air bases, roads, turnpikes, bus terminals, and radio and television installations. In our view, such work is directly and vitally related to the functioning of these facilities because, without the preparation of plans for guidance, the construction could not be effected and the facilities could not function as planned. In our modern technologically oriented society, the elements which combine to produce a final product are diffuse and variegated. Deciding whether any one element is so directly related to the end product as to be considered vital is sometimes a difficult problem. But plans, drawings and specifications have taken on greater importance as the complexities of design and bidding have increased. Under the circumstances present here, we have no hesitancy in concluding that the preparation of the plans and specifications was directly related to the end products and that the employees whose activities were intimately related to such preparation were "engaged in commerce."

. . .

The judgment is reversed and the case is remanded to the District Court for proceedings not inconsistent with this opinion. It is so ordered.

Reversed and remanded.

[JUSTICES WHITTAKER and STEWART dissented].

In the *Lublin* case, the courts faced the question of whether particular employees were "engaged in commerce" and held that the test was the activities of the employees.

The Fair Labor Standards Act also covers employees who are "engaged in . . . the production of goods for commerce". In Wirtz v. A. S. Giometti and Associates, Inc., 399 F.2d 738 (5th Cir. 1968) the issue was whether draftsmen who make plats and maps of land boundaries are "engaged in the production of goods for commerce". In holding that the trial court was incorrect when it ruled in favor of the employer, the court stated:

> As a physical matter these papers on which the plats appear are "things." Likewise the paper is changed from an unrevealing blank piece of paper to one which is not only a

"thing" but a thing on which something else has been added—perhaps two things, (a) the artistic-engineering concept of the scrivener-artist-draftsman, and (b) the lines, squares, angles, curves making up the drawing plus the physical ingredients of India ink or other mediums in which they are sketched. What is it then, which makes something less than "goods" out of physical material which in the operation is changed from a blank nothing into something significant?

This is what leads us to the Employer's contention so successfully pressed below. With conceptualistic ingenuity which perhaps rivals our own efforts to describe the Employer's work product, it contends and the District Judge found, that these drawings and plats are nothing more than physical embodiments of professional conclusions concerning title, area, ownership, etc., and therefore do not come within the definition of "goods" contained in 29 U.S.C.A. § 203(i).

As we view it, an Act meant to operate directly in the very practical matter of hourly, daily, and weekly pay of non-owner wage-earners cannot tolerate such metaphysical dialectic as the basis for its application. Getting it out of these heady heights, the decisions so far reject it.

. . .

The idea that these line drawings with dimensions and boundary indicators are but the embodiment of a professional opinion is hardly an answer. The elaborate blueprints for a modern bridge or skyscraper are but the professional judgment of architects-engineers that the structure can be built to such specifications and if so it will serve its intended purpose. Likewise, in what an outsider can only guess as to its magnitude, the thousands of pages of specifications, blueprints, test and launching schedules frequently in the most esoteric erudition of the scientific world covering the launch of Apollo represent in the final analysis professional opinions of the most sophisticated kind. Yet surely such bulk, sent by interstate mail, from NASA at Houston to Red Stone to the Cape would constitute "goods."

State laws also deal with wages, hours, and working conditions. There are usually minimum wages and limitations on hours, State laws often require that wages be paid at short, specific time intervals. Usually states extend special protection to child labor, and to female employees. Such protection may relate to prohibiting their working at all, prohibiting their doing certain types of work, limiting the hours of their employment, or regulating other conditions of employment. State and federal law often regulate employment conditions relating to health, sanitation, and safety.

Some state laws regulate the tenure of an employment relationship. If an employee does not have a fixed period established by an individual employment contract, a collective bargaining contract, or state personnel rules, some states have laws which require that an employee cannot be discharged unless he is given a notice of termination and paid wages until the expiration of the notice period.

(C) PROTECTION OF WAGES AND CONSUMER CREDIT

There are other legal aspects of the payment of wages. One deals with wage assignments. When an employee borrows money, the lender may ask him to assign any wages which he has coming, or will have coming, under an existing employment relationship, as security for the loan. Such an employee may do this, without the realization that all of his salary, or at least most of it, will be needed to furnish the basic necessities for himself and his family. For this reason, most states regulate wage assignments.

Statutes specify that not over a given percentage of the wages can be assigned. Some states require that a spouse consent to the wage assignment. Sometimes wage assignment statutes state that assignments can be made for only goods or services which are important to the employee and his family. If an architect or engineer is given an assignment of wages by a lender or creditor, he should check to see whether state laws limit in any way the right of the employee to assign his wages.

Sometimes an employer is served with a garnishment by a creditor of one of his employees. Garnishment is a device by which creditors can collect a debt or a court judgment by taking property of the debtor which is in the hands of a third party. Because many debtors have only exempt property (property which cannot be seized by a creditor) creditors often look to wage garnishment to satisfy a debt or court judgment.

The same policy that protects employees by limiting their power to assign wages led to state laws limiting the power to garnish wages.

In some states wages can be garnished without a prior court hearing. This can place a powerful weapon in the hands of the creditor. The Supreme Court of the United States has held that those statutes which permit wage garnishment prior to a court hearing without a showing of a special need by the creditor are unconstitutional. Sniadach v. Family Finance Corp., 395 U.S. 337 (1969).

Sometimes an employer will discharge an employee who has his wages garnished. Some states have laws which preclude discharge for this reason.

The Federal Government has also been active in protecting wage earners from garnishment. Section 303 of the Consumer Credit Protection Act of 1968, Public Law 90–321, 15 U.S.C.A. 1671–7, limits the percentage of wages that can be garnished for those who work for employers covered under the act. Section 304 of the same statute provides that an employer may not discharge an employee because his earnings have been subjected to garnishment "for any one indebtedness".

While legislative controls over wage assignments and garnishments often are compromises, there is an unmistakable movement toward limiting the right of an employee to assign his wages and restricting the right of a creditor to garnish them. Employers must be aware of the legal controls over wage assignments and garnishments and comply with them.

(D) DISCRIMINATION IN EMPLOYMENT PRACTICES

State and federal governments have taken an active role to prevent certain types of discrimination in job hiring, promotion and security. Many states forbid employment discrimination based upon race, religion, sex or national origin. The Civil Rights Act of 1964, Public Law 88–352, Title VII, was a major move by federal government to implement fair hiring practices. This act applies to employers engaged in interstate commerce. Realistically, this means that almost all employers whose operations directly or indirectly touch upon more than one state and who have twenty-five or more employees. The act makes it an unfair employment practice (subject to certain exceptions):

> to fail or refuse to hire or to discharge any individual, or otherwise to discriminate against any individual with respect to his compensation, terms, conditions, or privileges of employment, because of such individual's race, color, religion, sex or national origin. (42 U.S.C.A. 2000(e)–2).

The act also created the Equal Employment Opportunities Commission, which hears complaints. The commission is empowered to use methods short of litigation (conciliation, mediation, etc.) to obtain compliance. If these efforts fail, the aggrieved person can institute a lawsuit charging unfair discrimination. In such a case, the court has the power to order that the employer cease any unlawful practices, grant affirmative relief to the plaintiff (hiring him, promoting him and paying him back pay), and pay the reasonable attorneys fees of the plaintiff.

Also, there have been governmental attempts to eliminate racial discrimination from the operations of labor unions. It is likely that there will be an increasing governmental control over the hiring, promotion, and lay-off aspects of the employment relationship.

In addition to direct laws and regulations which prohibit discrimination in employment, the federal government, and some state governments, have specified that persons who do business with the government must agree not to discriminate on the bases of race, religion or national origin. Often contractors must obtain agreements from their suppliers and their subcontractors not to discriminate.

(E) EMPLOYMENT TAXES: INDEPENDENT CONTRACTORS

Another area where design professionals can have difficulty relates to taxes which are based upon the employment relationship. The federal government, and most states, have statutes which require that employers withhold a certain percentage of wages which are to be applied to any income taxes which are owed by the employee. In addition to withholding taxes, employers are required to pay unemployment compensation taxes to the state. When an employee is laid off, or is unable to work, most states permit him to collect a designated portion of his salary, or a certain designated amount, as unemployment benefits. These benefits come from a fund which consists of payments made by employers to the state.

Sometimes attempts are made to circumvent these employer obligations. Some design professionals would like to consider almost all who perform services for them as independent contractors. In addition to avoiding some of the employer obligations mentioned, these design professionals think that by classifying these persons as independent contractors they can avoid liability for their mistakes. See § 36.04.

Some persons are clearly independent contractors. Certainly the design professional need not withhold amounts for state or federal income taxes from fees he pays his attorney, his accountant or a consultant he hires for a specific project.

However, those who perform services which do not fall into these highly skilled professional categories are likely to be considered employees if the bulk of their fees or wages are earned by performing services for the same design professional and if they appear to be under the general organizational control of the design professional.

(F) PENSION AND PROFIT-SHARING PLANS

There is another way in which the government indirectly regulates the employment relationship. Employers can create pension plans and profit sharing plans, under which employees will receive certain benefits upon retirement or when they leave the employment. One of the advantages of profit sharing plans and pension plans is that any contributions made by the employer to such plans are deductible to the employer when the contributions are made. However, these amounts are not income to the employee until they are received. This permits the employee to receive the money and pay taxes upon it when he is subject to a lower tax rate.

For such plans to accomplish these purposes, they must meet certain requirements set forth in the federal tax laws. Such plans must not be discriminatory in favor of the highly paid employees. They must provide that at certain stages the employee has an absolute right to the money, even if he leaves the company. To receive the tax advantages, employers submit such plans to the Internal Revenue Service for its approval. If these plans are approved, it usually assures that the plan will accomplish the tax objectives sought.

An employer can have a plan which does not qualify under the federal tax laws. However, a non-approved plan will not have tax advantages for employer and employee. For this reason, the power of the government to set conditions for qualifications, and the power of the government to approve or disapprove plans, is a control over the employer in the payment of wages to his employees.

SECTION 36.03 EMPLOYMENT INJURIES AND WORKMEN'S COMPENSATION

As discussed in § 30.07, most states have laws requiring that employers carry workmen's compensation insurance, or show adequate financial responsibility sufficient to be designated as a self-insured employer. This is to protect against the possibility that an employee will be injured, and that the employer will not be able to respond to any workmen's compensation award to which the employee is entitled. The employer must keep his workmen's compensation insurance in effect, or continue to comply with any requirements for self-insured employers.

SECTION 36.04 VICARIOUS LIABILITY

One person may be liable for the negligence of another. "Vicarious liability" may be based upon a master-servant or, more accurately, an employer-employee relationship. If an employee was acting in the scope of his employment, anyone injured by his negligence will be able to recover from the employer, as well as the employee. See § 30.02(e)

One of the asserted justifications for holding the employer for the negligent acts of his employee which occur in the scope of employment is that the employer controls or has the right to control the activity of his employee. However, a more justifiable rationale for vicarious liability is enterprise liability. The employer is in a better position to pay and the cost of these injuries must be taken as a part of the total cost of running his enterprise.

Often the employee causing the injury cannot pay for the losses suffered by the injured person nor is he likely to have public liability insurance. If the injured party cannot collect from the employee and cannot recover from the employer unless the employer himself was negligent in some way, the injured party will have to bear the loss himself. Often injured persons do not have the money to bear these losses and ultimately the burden would fall upon the state. Enterprise liability assumes that the cost of such losses, usually handled by insurance, can be calculated in advance and ultimately placed upon the consumer of the goods or services supplied by the enterprise. A more realistic reason for enterprise liability is that the enterprise is likely to insure against these risks, while the individual who is injured may not.

Business entities generally are responsible for injuries that are caused by their employees, as long as some rational connection can be established between the act causing the injury and the business itself. For example, suppose an architectural firm employs a draftsman to draft plans and specifications. If this draftsman is directed to drive his car to pick up supplies, it is likely that any accident caused by his negligence which occurs while he is driving on this errand will be the responsibility of his employer as well as the driver.

What if the draftsman deviates from the prescribed or normal route? He may decide that on the way home he would like to stop at his apartment and pick up some records. Earlier cases relieved the employer for the responsibility for accidents which occurred during a marked deviation from the employer's business. However, such deviation today has to be very marked and totally unconnected with the employer's affairs.

There are other laws which create vicarious liability in auto accidents. For example, some states have laws which place liability upon owners of motor vehicles when those vehicles are driven negligently by someone driving with consent of the owner. Other statutes place similar liability upon the person who endorses an operator's license issued to a minor, when the minor's negligence caused an accident. Frequently statutes creating ownership or endorsement liability are limited to a designated dollar amount.

Liability can be placed upon the employer because of his own negligence, rather than the negligence of someone for whose acts he is responsible. For example, if the employer hires a driver whom he knows, or should know, drives recklessly, the hiring itself is a negligent act. Also, permitting a driver to continue to drive, when the employer knows that he is reckless, is negligence. In these situations, accidents caused by the negligence of such drivers will be chargeable to the employer.

Generally, injuries or losses caused by employees will be the responsibility of the employer. Most of the risk imposed by the law for such injuries can be covered by public liability insurance. See § 35.01(d).

SECTION 36.05 AGENCY

Agency is a legal concept by which one party's acts can bind another. See Chapter 3. The employer may be held responsible for the contracts of his employee which are actually or apparently authorized.

SECTION 36.06 FIDELITY BONDS

Fidelity bonds can be obtained which will reimburse employers if employees steal money. Since fidelity bonds cost the employer money, some employers who are confident in their employees choose to become self-insurers. The wisdom of this approach depends upon the size of the organization, and the amount of money that is handled by the employees.

SECTION 36.07 UNIONS AND COLLECTIVE BARGAINING AGREEMENTS

The past thirty years has seen a marked increase in unionization of certain industries. The construction trades are highly unionized. There is, as yet, no comparable high degree of unionization among office employees and draftsmen. However, there is a likelihood of increasing unionization of these types of employees. Consequently, the design professional who is an employer should be aware of the government's role in collective bargaining.

State and federal labor laws encourage collective bargaining. First, the law provides a mechanism to determine whether the employees want a collective bargaining representative and, if so, who is to represent them. If such a bargaining representative is selected, the employer must deal with the representative on wages, hours, seniority, and working conditions. Also, the collective bargaining representative must represent all of the workers of the collective bargaining unit in good faith. Grievance procedures are created to handle disputes during the life of a collective bargaining agreement.

The law also designates certain acts as unfair labor practices. An important unfair labor practice is the refusal to bargain in good faith. Another is coercion by an employer, intended to frustrate worker attempts to organize.

Unions can be divided roughly into three types. A "closed shop" exists when employees must join the union before they can be hired by the employer. Closed shops are prohibited for employers subject to federal law. Some states permit closed shops. Generally, state law applies to smaller, intrastate employers. Under federal law, certain exemptions given to construction trades (the employee must join within 7 days of employment, hiring halls are permitted, and the employer and the union can make a pre-hire agreement), while not directly permitting a closed shop, create an arrangement which operates very much like a closed shop.

A "union shop" is an arrangement under which the union and employer agree that the worker must join the union within a designated period of time after he is hired. The federal law requires that the period of time to join must be at least 30 days, which is the typical time period in which the worker must join under such agreements.

An "open shop" is one which does not require the worker to join the union. A variation of the open shop is a collective bargaining agreement which contains a "maintenance of membership" clause. Under this type of contract, the worker must remain a member for a specified period of time if he joins the union.

Labor law is a complex blend of statutes, (both state and federal), case-made law, and administrative law (regulations and decisions of administrative agencies such as the National Labor Relations Board and comparable state administrative agencies). Only a cursory overview is possible in this treatise. But the design professional must be cognizant of the trend toward unionization, and increased state and federal participation in labor-management relations.

REVIEW QUESTIONS

1. What factors must be taken into account in determining whether specialized work should be performed by an employee or an independent contractor?

2. Traditionally, has the state or federal government regulated the employment relationship?

3. What are the important governmental controls on the employment relationship?

4. Which portion of the Fair Labor Standards Act is important to architects and engineers?

5. What is garnishment?

6. What controls exist on wage assignments?

7. Which employers are subject to the Civil Rights Act of 1964?

8. What is vicarious liability?

QUESTIONS FOR CLASS DISCUSSION

1. Should the federal government take a more active role in regulating employment relationships? Explain.

2. Do you believe that the state (state or federal government) should make it unlawful to discriminate on the basis of race? On the basis of sex?

3. Should there be substantial limitations on the right of a creditor to garnish wages? Explain.

4. Do you believe that minimum wage laws are desirable? Explain.

Chapter 37

COLLECTION PROBLEMS

SECTION 37.01 DESIGN PROFESSIONAL AS A CREDITOR

Some design professionals perform services for a client but subsequently have difficulty in collecting for those services. While the legal doctrines which relate to collection questions can be relevant to the design professional as a "debtor" (a person who owes money), this chapter assumes that the design professional is a creditor who wishes to collect for his work.

SECTION 37.02 PREVENTIVE MEASURES

There are measures which can be taken to reduce the risk of uncollectible accounts.

First, the design professional should be certain that he has a valid contract. This is especially true when he deals with local public agencies. See § 5.09.

Second, he must anticipate the reasons a client will give when he refuses to pay. The principal reasons given are:

1) He understood he would not have to pay unless the project could be brought in below a designated amount of money (See § 8.01), or,
2) He would not have to pay unless he could obtain adequate financing (See § 7.01), or
3) He would not have to pay unless he was completely satisfied with the design (See § 6.17(a)).

In order to reduce the risk of these and other reasons being asserted, the design professional should, where possible, obtain a clearly expressed, written agreement from the client that the design professional is not risking his fees on the occurrence of these events.

Third, the design professional should do his best to insure that his client will have the financial resources to pay for the services rendered. If the client's credit is questionable, measures should be taken to reduce the risk of having a valid claim against a client who cannot pay. See § 5.06.

Fourth, an architect or engineer should perform in accordance with his contractual obligations, and with the professional skill required by law. While there are undoubtedly clients who refuse to pay without justification, often the client's refusal to pay is based upon a belief by the client that he has not received the professional services he expected, or to which he was entitled. Each party must agree on what the other party will do. This is central to a good design professional-client relationship. The establishment of such a relationship, and the trust and good will which go along with it, are among the most important preventive measures a design professional can take to protect his fee.

Fifth, the design professional should bill and collect for all his work as he performs it. At a minimum, the contract should contain provisions for interim fee payments, based upon designated stages of the work. If the job is of any magnitude, the contract should contain provisions for monthly payments of the interim fees.

SECTION 37.03 ESTABLISHING THE AMOUNT DUE: ACCOUNTS STATED

(A) PROCESS OF STRIKING A BALANCE

Often debtor and creditor have a substantial number of transactions between them. Sometimes the number of transactions, and the often inaccurate way in which some persons keep their accounting records, makes it advisable periodically for debtor and creditor to compare their records, discuss the matter and, by an arithmetic process, agree upon the current balance.

For example, a retailer may buy on credit from a wholesaler. During any month, the retailer may make a substantial number of purchases, may return some merchandise for credit, and may make some payments. Entries will be made on the account records of the wholesaler and the retailer. At the end of a billing period, the wholesaler may send a bill to the retailer, indicating the charges for merchandise supplied, the credits for payments and merchandise returned, and a current balance. If the retailer disagrees with the figures, retailer and wholesaler may get together, compare their records, correct mistakes, and agree upon a proper balance. This balance is an "account stated."

Sometimes the creditor hopes to create an "account stated" by sending a bill to the debtor, indicating that this is the creditor's position on the balance owed, and stating that unless the debtor responds within a designated period of time, it will be assumed that the debtor agrees with the balance stated by the creditor.

Sometimes the debtor, such as a bank, will send a monthly bank statement for a checking account which includes a notation that failure to raise objections to the bank's computation of the account within a designated period of days will make that determination conclusive. These are attempts to create accounts stated by acquiescence or by silence of the person to whom the statement is sent.

Since an account stated is a contract, it usually requires assent by both parties. Usually, one party cannot create a contract by stating that the other party's silence will constitute acceptance. This doctrine is applicable to the attempts to create an account stated by acquiescence or silence. However, if the person attempting to create the account stated can show that he relied in some way on silence, such as destroying important records, the silence could constitute an acceptance. Also, the longer the time before an objection is raised to an account, the more difficult it will be to challenge the accuracy of the account.

The fact that it may be difficult to create an account stated by silence should not encourage laxity in responding to statements of account sent by debtor or creditor. It is better procedure to check accounts for accuracy and respond immediately if it is determined that the stated account is erroneous.

(B) ENFORCEABILITY OF AN ACCOUNT STATED

Where there is an account stated, generally the debtor promises to pay the amount agreed to, and the creditor promises to accept this amount as full payment for the account. Most promises require consideration. In the case of a true account stated, (agreement by debtor and creditor on a balance determined by an arithmetic process of comparing debits and credits), the consideration is the past debt owed. The promise to pay the account stated cannot rise above the amount actually owed by the debtor to the creditor.

For example, suppose a supplier has been delivering goods to a contractor for a three month period. At the end of that period the supplier and the contractor compare their records, agree that the contractor owes $5,000, the contractor promises to pay this amount, and the supplier agrees to accept it as full payment. The promise to pay $5,000 is supported by past consideration, consisting of the goods delivered by the supplier. If, upon a recheck, the contractor determines that he only owed $4,000, his promise to pay the $5,000 is enforceable only to the extent of the actual debt, or $4,000. Conversely, if the supplier rechecks his records and finds that he is entitled to $6,000, he should be able to collect that amount, unless his agreement to accept $5,000 has been relied upon by the contractor to the latter's detriment.

(C) PURPOSE OF AN ACCOUNT STATED

If the account stated is always subject to the actual amount owed, why set up an account stated? There are a number of reasons. First, and probably most important, the burden of proof will be on the person who attempts to establish an amount different than the agreed account stated. For example, suppose the contractor in § 37.03(b) wishes to assert that the actual debt is only $4,000. He will have the burden of proving the actual amount of the debt. If he cannot sustain this burden, he will lose.

Secondly, litigation strategy may be a reason for creating an account stated. Suppose the debtor and creditor entered into a transaction in the home state of the creditor. Suppose the creditor would like to attach or garnish property that is within the state of the debtor. Sometimes the laws which give creditors the right to attach or garnish require that the contract which is the basis of the garnishment or attachment have been made in the state where the creditor wishes to attach or garnish funds. To shift the place of contracting from the creditor's home state to the debtor's home state, the creditor may send a statement of account to the debtor and hope that either the debtor will agree in some way, or will not respond. If so, it is arguable that there has been an account stated in the home state of the debtor, and the creditor may use attachment or garnishment in that state.

(D) "APPARENT" ACCOUNT STATED

There are certain types of transactions which are called "accounts stated" but are not truly methods by which debtor and creditor use an arithmetic process of comparing accounts in order to strike a balance of what is owed. For example, an architect may render professional services without any specific agreement as to fee. By law, he would be entitled to the reasonable value of his services. However, it would take an agreement of the parties as to value, or a determination by an arbitrator or a court to establish the reasonable value of his services. To avoid this possibility, or at least to assist him if he must arbitrate or litigate, the design professional may send a bill to the client for a specified amount. If the client does not respond, or if the client agrees to this amount, courts often call this bill an "account stated". While strictly speaking it is not a mathematical process of comparing debits and credits, it may operate in a similar fashion. If the client agrees that this is a reasonable amount, it is likely that this agreement will be binding. The consideration for such an agreement would be the giving up of the right to contest the reasonable worth of the services.

If the client does not respond to the bill, this may constitute an admission by him that the amount specified in the bill is the reasonable value of the architect's services. While this admission may not bind him, or shift the burden of proof as in a true account stated, it may be very helpful if there is arbitration or litigation.

SECTION 37.04 CASHING CHECKS SENT BY CLIENT: ACCORD AND SATISFACTION

(A) DEFINITION

Another legal concept relevant to bill collection is "accord and satisfaction." An "executory accord" is an agreement by two parties to accept a different performance from what is owed under a contract or under some other legal obligation. For example, the architect and the client may agree that the architect is to be paid $5,000 for design services for the building of a luxury house. Subsequent to the agreement, architect and client may agree that the architect will design a small commercial building instead of the residence. The second agreement changed the original obligation substantially, and would be considered an executory accord.

If the executory accord is performed, then the original obligation is terminated. Suppose the design services for the commercial building are performed. The original obligation then is terminated. The performance is called "satisfaction". There has then been an executory accord followed by satisfaction. If the architect did not perform the executory accord, that is, he did not perform the design services relating to the commercial building, the client would be able to sue either for the original obligation, the luxury residence, or upon the executory accord, the commercial building.

An "accord and satisfaction" often occurs in two steps. First there is the executory accord, and then satisfaction by virtue of performance of the executory accord.

If the parties intended to supplant the original obligation by the act of making the second obligation, the second obligation is a "substituted contract". A substituted contract differs from an executory accord, since making of the latter does not automatically terminate the original obligation. It is only performance, or satisfaction, which terminates the original obligation. The determination of whether the second agreement is a substituted contract or an executory accord requires an inquiry into the facts to ascertain if the parties intended to supplant the original deal by the making of the second deal.

(B) VALIDITY OF EXECUTORY ACCORD: CONSIDERATION

An executory accord is a contract, and requires consideration. If the executory accord constitutes the substitution of one type of obligation for another, there is no consideration problem. In such a case, the client gives up his right to have a residence designed, in exchange for receiving design work for a commercial building. The design professional gives up his right to fulfill his obligation by performing services connected to the residence, and he can fulfill his obligation by performing design services connected with the commercial building.

A Dispute Context

Most executory accords occur in the context of a dispute. An architect may contend that he has $5,000 coming from the client, and the client may contend that the correct amount is $3,000. Suppose the client agrees to pay $4,000, and the architect agrees to accept this amount. Since both parties are giving up their right to seek a legal determination of the true amount owed, there is sufficient consideration to enforce the agreement.

A Liquidated, Matured Obligation

Consideration causes difficulty where the amount owed by the debtor to the creditor is liquidated (reduced to a fixed amount) and matured (presently due and owing). For example, suppose the contract between architect and client expressly states that the architect is to receive $5,000. The architect has performed all the services, and the money is due and owing. However, for various reasons the parties may agree that the client will pay and architect will accept $4,000 in full and final settlement of the debt.

If such an agreement is made, it may run foul of the "preexisting duty rule". In such a transaction, the architect is receiving no more than he is entitled to get under the original agreement. Also, the client is paying no more than he is obligated to pay under the original agreement. The architect may agree to accept a lesser sum in full settlement because it will avoid the necessity of having to litigate. Most state courts hold there is no legal benefit to the creditor and no legal detriment to the debtor in such a transaction. For this reason, most state courts have held that such agreements are not enforceable. This means that if the client pays the $4,000, the architect may still sue for the balance of $1,000.

There are a few jurisdictions which enforce such agreements. Additional jurisdictions have modified the rule by statute. Some statutes have made such agreements enforceable. Others enforce them where the creditor has agreed in writing to receive the partial payment as full payment, and receives part payment from the debtor. For example, under these statutes, if the debtor owes $1,000, and makes a written agreement with the creditor that upon payment of $500 the full amount will be considered paid, such an agreement will be enforceable if the $500 is paid and received.

Protecting Employees: Amounts Admittedly Owed

Some states have held that payment of the amount admittedly owed by the debtor to the creditor is not good consideration, while other states have come to a contrary conclusion. Suppose an employer admits that he owes the employee $100 for wages. However, the employee asserts a claim to an additional $50 for additional services performed. In such a situation, suppose the employer refuses to pay the amount admittedly owed, that is the $100, until the employee agrees to accept it in full and final settlement of the entire claim. There can be a great deal of economic pressure on the employee to make such an agreement. Recognizing this, some states have enacted statutes making such agreements unenforceable.

Cashing Checks as Accord and Satisfaction

Earlier discussion noted that an accord and satisfaction can arise in two steps. First there is the executory accord and then, if there is performance under the executory accord, there is satisfaction. Sometimes the debtor receives a bill on a disputed claim and submits a lesser amount by check, with a notation on the check or an accompanying letter of transmittal that the amount is tendered in full and final settlement of the account.

Generally, if the creditor knows, or should know that the amount is tendered in full and final settlement, his cashing of the check, or his retention of it for an unreasonable period of time, constitutes an accord and satisfaction. In this type of accord and satisfaction, the cashing of a check constitutes both assent to the accord and the satisfaction. The cashing of the check, then, is a single step which replaces the two-step method of an accord and satisfaction. When the check is cashed under such circumstances, the original obligation is terminated. The creditor cannot sue for the balance.

Submission of a check under such circumstances puts the creditor in a dilemma. Generally, he would like to retain the proceeds of the check, and still have a right to assert a claim to the balance of the account. He may feel that the money tendered is his, and that he can take it without giving up his claim. To accomplish, or to at least to try to accomplish this result, he may scratch out the restrictive language on the check or letter of transmittal, or replace it with the notation that he takes it only on account. Or, he may cash the check and simultaneously notify the debtor that he cashed the check without intending to give up his claim to the balance, simply taking the amount tendered as a part payment of the money owed. Usually, such attempts are not successful. If the person receiving the check knows, or should know, that it is tendered in full and final settlement, his cashing of the check, or retaining it for an unreasonable period of time, is likely to cost him the balance of his claim. On a few occasions, creditors have been successful in asserting the right to demand the balance from the client after they have cashed the check. However, it is very risky to cash the check and expect to be able to sue for the balance.

The harshness of the check cashing rule has been softened where there is a fiduciary relationship between debtor and creditor.

In Hudson v. Yonkers Fruit Co., Inc., 258 N.Y. 168, 179 N.E. 373 (1932) the owner of a quantity of apples asked a broker to find a purchaser for him. The broker did this, and collected the money from the buyer. He remitted a check for the amount of money that he had received, less an amount he claimed he had coming as commission. The seller of the apples cashed the check, protesting that the services were to be gratuitous. When the seller sued the broker for the amount deducted, the broker claimed that by accepting the check the seller had completed an accord and satisfaction.

The New York Court of Appeals held that there was no accord and satisfaction because the defendant broker was an agent and owed a fiduciary obligation to his principal. The agent was merely accounting for money which belonged to the principal.

Such a holding could be applicable if the design professional remitted money owed to his client by check and indicated on the check or in a letter of transmittal that the money was in full and final settlement of their account. If the rule in the *Hudson* case were followed, the client could cash the check and still contest the amount owed. However, it is not likely that the *Hudson* rule would be applicable if the client sent a check to the design professional marked "full and final settlement". This would not be a case of an agent remitting money to his principal. Arguably, persons in a fiduciary relationship should not be able to use the check cashing method of creating an accord and satisfaction. Using this rationale, a court could extend the *Hudson* rule to cover a tender of a check by a client to the design professional. If a design professional is considered an employee, in some states tendering what is admittedly owed would not create a good accord and satisfaction.

About all that can be stated is that if the design professional receives a check marked "full and final settlement", and if he intends to try to collect the balance, he should obtain legal advice. Generally, cashing a check will divest him of the right to sue for the balance.

SECTION 37.05 COLLECTION AGENCIES

Sometimes persons who cannot collect from their customers or clients turn the account over to collection agencies. This is a common practice in ordinary commercial relationships, but professional persons often hesitate to do so. This reluctance may be based on a feeling that it is "unprofessional" to interject a third party into a professional relationship. This is similar to the reluctance on the part of many architects and engineers to sue for fees. Implicit in this reluctance is the feeling that turning the matter to a collection agency, or bringing legal action, is a confession of professional incompetence. Architects and engineers often pridefully state they never have had to refer an account to a collection agency or to sue a client.

Another reason for such reluctance is the commonly known fact that many collection agencies use high-pressure tactics to obtain payment. While there are some legal limitations on what they can do, their methods seem morally objectionable to some design professionals.

Finally, a more prosaic reason may exist for refusal to turn the matter over to a collection agency. Usually collection agencies take a substantial fee for doing their work. It is not uncommon for the collection agency to take 50% of whatever it can recover. Sometimes professionals feel that they would rather give the debtor a longer time to pay, and perhaps he will pay the full amount.

While referring an uncollectible account to a collection agency may be a last resort, in some cases it is done. It may be useful for the design professional who does turn the matter over to a collection agency to use a collection agency that has the reputation for firm, but not outrageous, bill collecting tactics.

SECTION 37.06 LITIGATION: POSSIBILITY OF JUDICIAL ADJUSTMENT

Sometimes the architect or engineer institutes legal action against the debtor for failure to pay on a bill. In a way, this is perhaps even more drastic to the design professional than is turning the matter over to a collection agency. Some of the hazards of litigating matters have been mentioned in Chapter 1.

Many times judges informally will make an adjustment in the debt. For example, sometimes judges will suggest to the plaintiff creditor that he either compromise or "stretch out" the obligation. If the debtor owes $1000, the judge may suggest that the creditor agree to accept fifty dollars a month. While as a rule, the creditor is not obligated to agree with these suggestions made by the judge, he often does. In effect, the judge in such a situation acts as a kind of arbitrator.

While the law may entitle the plaintiff-creditor to his full thousand dollars, the judge may take into account the fact that the debtor is having difficulty with his financial affairs, the fact that the debtor may be an honest debtor and not simply trying to avoid paying a just obligation, and the desirability of avoiding the use of the legal machinery to collect. For this reason, informal settlements, either in terms of amount or stretched out period for payment, are made during the litigation. In making settlements, creditors should take this into account. It is cheaper to make such adjustments before litigation.

SECTION 37.07 BANKRUPTCY: ITS EFFECT ON COLLECTION

(A) FUNCTION

Bankruptcy is often the culmination of financial difficulties. The function of bankruptcy laws is two-fold. They create a process for orderly distribution of the bankrupt's assets to his creditors, and they provide a method by which an honest debtor may be able to wipe his financial slate clean and, hopefully, start over.

(B) BANKRUPTCY PROCEEDINGS

Bankruptcy is controlled mainly by federal law, and is administered by the federal courts. Federal district court judges appoint referees. The referees are analogous to judges. Their decisions are appealable to the federal district court judge.

There are two types of bankruptcy petitions. The first is a "voluntary" petition filed by the debtor himself. The second is an "involuntary" petition, under which a designated number of creditors may petition the court to start the bankruptcy proceedings.

Voluntary petitions occur when the debtor himself sees no way out, and would like to be discharged from his obligations. An involuntary petition usually occurs when a number of creditors are fearful that the debtor's situation is likely to deteriorate even further. Rather than permit him to continue running his business, or to ask that there be a reorganization or arrangement under federal law, they choose to start the bankruptcy proceedings.

The requirement for bankruptcy is that the debtor be "insolvent". Insolvent in the sense of the bankruptcy laws means that the debtor's liabilities exceed his assets.

(C) PARTICIPATION BY CREDITORS

The unsecured creditors (those who do not have security interests in property possessed by the bankrupt) play a large role in bankruptcy administration. After the filing of the petition, there is a meeting of these creditors. They elect a trustee who administers the property of the bankrupt. The creditors can examine the bankrupt in order to find concealed assets, discover illegal transfers made prior to the bankruptcy, and obtain information which might make certain debts nondischargeable by bankruptcy.

(D) THE TRUSTEE IN BANKRUPTCY

One of the most important functions of the trustee is to take possession of the bankrupt's property, as well as the bankrupt's books and records. Money owed to the bankrupt will be collected by the trustee, or by a court appointed receiver. Property of the bankrupt in the hands of other parties will be reclaimed. The trustee will have to give property in the possession of the bankrupt to those who own it, or to those who are entitled to possession, because they have a security interest in it. Under certain circumstances, the trustee may prosecute or defend suits by or against the bankrupt.

Another function of the trustee relates to the power to affirm (accept) or reject existing contracts of the bankrupt. At the time of bankruptcy, the bankrupt usually has existing leases and contracts. Unless the leases or contracts contain provisions which state the contract is terminated by bankruptcy, the trustee can decide within a designated time period whether to continue performance under the lease or contract. If he disaffirms, the other party to the lease or contract is entitled to damages out of the bankrupt's property. (Usually only a small portion of the allowable damages are actually collected.)

The determination of whether to affirm or reject is based upon whether the contract seems to be a favorable one, and whether enough money can be obtained to continue performance.

One of the functions of bankruptcy is to provide for an equitable distribution of the bankrupt's funds. One creditor is not to be favored over another. For this reason, one of the functions of the trustee is to set aside "preferences". A preference is a transfer of money or property by the bankrupt, made within four months of the adjudication of bankruptcy. However, the transfer is not a preference if the bankrupt has received assets such as property, goods, securities or money in exchange for the transfer.

(E) LIQUIDATION AND DISTRIBUTION

Ordinarily, the bankrupt's property will be "liquidated" (reduced to cash) in order to make a distribution to the creditors. The trustee is generally not empowered to continue the bankrupt's business unless the trustee is ordered to do so by the court.

Expenses of administration (trustee's fee, legal fees, expenses of collection and liquidation) are taken out of the money obtained through liquidation. Such expenses are often formidable.

After expenses of administration are paid, what remains is distributed to the unsecured creditors on a pro rata basis. For example, if there are $200,000 of unsecured debts, and the liquidation brings $20,000, each unsecured debtor receives $.10 for each dollar of his debt. The percentage paid on each debt is usually small.

(F) DISCHARGEABLE DEBTS

As stated, one of the functions of bankrutpcy is to discharge an honest debtor from most of his obligations. When the bankrupt files his petition for bankruptcy, he is required to list all his creditors. One of the reasons for doing so is to notify these creditors of the bankruptcy proceedings. Only those debts which are listed are dischargeable by bankruptcy.

By statute, certain debts are not dischargeable by bankruptcy. Some of the more important debts not dischargeable are:

1. Taxes
2. Obligations owed because of obtaining property, services, or money under false pretenses.
3. Intentional tort obligations
4. Alimony and child support
5. Debts created by the bankrupt's fraud or embezzlement while acting in a fiduciary capacity.
6. Debts for wages earned within three months before bankruptcy.

Generally, honest debts are discharged unless special protection is needed for certain debtors (employees, wives and children) or unless the debts are owed to society in general (taxes).

(G) ADVICE TO DESIGN PROFESSIONAL

First, if one of his debtors is in serious financial trouble, it may be advisible to join with other creditors to file a petition for involuntary bankrutcy. This may mean recovering very little, rather than nothing.

Second, to get even the small distributions out of bankruptcy, the creditor must file his claim within 6 months after the first meeting of creditors.

Third, it may be advisible to include provisions in a client contract which negate the trustee's right to affirm the contract. Affirmation can mean more difficulties. If the design professional wishes to continue his performance, he usually will be able to work something out with the trustee, if the latter also wishes and can continue contract performance.

Fourth, payments made by a debtor who is in a precarious financial position may turn out to be a preference which can be set aside by the trustee. While it may not be improper to take the payment, it might not be wise to assume it cannot be taken back.

Fifth, bankruptcy for an architect or engineer who is in a desperate financial situation may be the best financial step to take. It is no crime to be bankrupt, and it may be the best way out of a bad situation.

SECTION 37.08 REORGANIZATIONS, ARRANGEMENTS, AND WAGE EARNER PLANS

In addition to bankruptcy, federal law provides other vehicles for handling the affairs of a financially distressed business or individual. These other vehicles, unlike bankruptcy, do not have the objective of liquidating the bankrupt and making a final distribution to creditors. Instead, the objective is to work out a plan for realigning the interests of shareholders, bondholders, secured and unsecured creditors, with a view toward effectuating a sounder financial basis for the debtor. Also a reorganization may install new and hopefully better, management.

"Arrangements" and "wage earner plans" are less comprehensive. Usually the creditors are all unsecured creditors who may do better in the long run if debts are adjusted, or payments postponed, in order to enable the debtor company or wage earner to get back on a sounder financial basis.

SECTION 37.09 CREDITOR COMPOSITIONS

A "composition" of creditors is a voluntary plan, agreed to by all or most of the debtor's creditors. Like a bankruptcy, the objective of a creditors composition is to enable the creditors to recover as much as they can from the debtor. In a composition, the creditors agree not to take any steps to legally enforce their claims against the debtor. This is to avoid a race to the courthouse by the creditors, with each trying to collect his debt. Also, the creditors try to sell the debtor's business as a going business. If a purchaser can be found to purchase the debtor's business, generally more will be obtained by the creditors than if the assets of the business are sold piecemeal, as is typically done in a bankruptcy.

If the creditors can cooperate, a composition often gets them a greater return than does the bankruptcy. In addition to a better chance to sell the debtor's business as a going business, much of the often crushing administrative expenses of a bankruptcy are avoided by a well-run composition of creditors.

REVIEW QUESTIONS

1. What steps can design professionals take to reduce the risk of uncollectible accounts?

2. What is an account stated?

3. How does the pre-existing duty rule affect settlements of claims?

4. What is the risk of cashing a check marked full and final payment?

5. What are the major purposes of bankruptcy laws?

6. What types of claims are not discharged by bankruptcy?

QUESTIONS FOR CLASS DISCUSSION

1. Should a creditor be precluded from asserting the right to collect the balance of a disputed account because he has cashed a check marked "full and final settlement"?

2. Should the law permit most types of honest debts to be discharged by bankruptcy? Explain.

PROBLEM

A hired a draftsman, D, to work on a three-month project. For all but the last week of the project, A paid D weekly at a rate of $4.00 an hour. D did not work over eight hours a day or over 40 hours a week.

At the conclusion of the project, D came to see A and requested payment for the final week. He also requested payment of $500 which he claims he was promised at the commencement of employment which would be a bonus if he worked the entire three-month period.

A denied that such an agreement had been made. He wrote out a check for $160 for the last week's work. He typed on the check the phrase "payment in full for all of D's services performed to date". D took the check but stated that he was going to sue A for the $500 he claimed as a bonus.

D cashed the check and then started a lawsuit demanding the $500 bonus. A claimed that D lost whatever rights he had to sue for the bonus because his cashing of the check amounted to an accord and satisfaction. There are no specific statutes dealing with the effect of tendering the amount admittedly owed to an employee. Would A's defense be effective? Give your reasons.

Chapter 38

FORENSIC SKILL AND THE DESIGN PROFESSIONAL AS AN EXPERT WITNESS

SECTION 38.01 FORENSIC SKILLS IN PROFESSIONAL PRACTICE

The emphasis in this chapter will be upon the design professional as an expert witness in the litigation process. However, forensic architecture and engineering go beyond the role of a design professional in the litigation process. In the course of professional practice, architects and engineers must communicate and persuade. These are the important skills of forensic architecture and engineering.

Obtaining a commission and performing design services involve communication skills. In both, the architect or engineer should communicate to his client or potential client the salient design features he proposes and their rationale. He should also explain to the client the function served by the design professional in the construction project. The same communication skills are helpful when the architect or engineer presents his work to the client for the latter's approval.

The design professional may be obligated by the agreement with his client or may find it within his self interest to persuade public officials to grant a zoning variance or to rezone land upon which the project is to be built. For these same reasons he may want to persuade a lender to advance funds for the project.

As interpreter of the contract documents and the judge of proper performance, the design professional will find it helpful to convince both his client and the contractor that any decision he makes was preceded by a careful and honest evaluation of all the relevant information.

Design professionals who are employees of business or professional organizations may be requested to make presentations regarding the feasibility of particular projects to boards of directors or officers of their employers. Correspondingly, such employees may be requested to persuade lenders that funds should be advanced for certain projects. Similar activities may have to be performed by architects and engineers who work for public agencies.

An understanding of the legal rules relating to expert witnesses and the reasons behind them, as well as an appreciation of the skills needed to do a good job of being an expert witness, can assist a design professional when he must perform forensic architectural or engineering services in these other contexts.

SECTION 38.02 RETAINING AN EXPERT WITNESS

(A) NATURE OF SERVICES

If an architect or an engineer is approached by a party to an arbitration or litigation, it is important that the design professional ascertain his function. He may be employed solely to examine the premises, examine the plans and specifications, and then give a professional opinion to the party requesting his services or the attorney for that party.

He may be asked to go further and actually participate in the resolution of the dispute. He may be requested to accompany the attorney or person requesting his services during the arbitration or litigation, with a view toward providing ideas and insights in the area of his professional competence. He may be asked to go one step farther, to appear and testify. In such a case, he does not merely observe and provide information. He also presents his opinion to those charged with the responsibility of deciding the dispute in order to influence the resolution of the dispute.

(B) COMPENSATION

The expert witness should clarify in advance, and preferably expressly in writing, when and how much he is to be paid. Typically, expert witnesses are paid on a *per diem* basis. There should be a clear understanding on the *per diem* amount, the number of hours which will make up a compensable day, and whether the number of days is to include only the time spent in court or include time spent in preparing for court. There should be advance agreement on whether the expert witness is to receive travel expense and how this expense is to be computed. Also, will the expert be paid a *per diem* allowance while he is travelling? Finally, often the expert witness prepares exhibits and documentary evidence to assist in making his presentation. There should be an advance agreement on whether, and to what extent, the party retaining the expert witness will pay for these expenses.

(C) CONTINGENT ARRANGEMENTS: ADVANCE RETAINERS

The design professional should avoid making his fee contingent upon any particular result being reached.

Such agreements should not be made because they tend to impugn the impartiality of the witness. His testimony is more like to be discredited if facts are brought out which show that he will recover for his efforts *only* if the party hiring him is successful.

There will be too great a temptation on the part of the architect or engineer to give a dishonest or misleading opinion if his fee is dependent upon a particular result.

There is another reason to make it clear that the expert witness is not performing services on a contingent fee basis. A losing litigant sometimes refuses to pay his expert witness. Frequently he will claim that there was an understanding that the expert would not be paid unless the case were won. A clear written expression negating any such arrangement will make such a contention difficult to sustain.

The expert witness should try to get an advance retainer to reduce the risk of the client not paying if the result is unsatisfactory.

SECTION 38.03 SOME RELEVANT ASPECTS OF THE JUDICIAL PROCESS

Chapter 1 provided a brief description of the American judicial system. To understand the role of an expert witness in litigation it is important to review briefly some of that material and to elaborate upon certain portions of it.

(A) JUDGE AND JURY: EXPERTISE IN CONSTRUCTION MATTERS

In most civil litigation, either of the litigants can request a jury. While the use of juries in civil matters is decreasing, a substantial number of trials still employ a jury. Generally, a jury is composed of twelve laymen, selected at random from the community. They are not selected for any particular skill or expertise in the matter being litigated.

Trial judges vary considerably in their expertise in construction matters. Some will know very little, while others may be quite knowledgeable. Much will depend upon the trial judge's legal experience before elevation to the bench, and upon the types of cases he has presided over while a judge.

Generally, the jury decides disputed questions of fact, especially credibility matters. Questions of fact typically relate to the events which have occurred which bear upon the lawsuit. Credibility matters arise when there is contradictory testimony of witnesses.

The trial judge can withdraw factual questions from the jury and decide them himself, if he believes that reasonable men could reach but one conclusion based upon the evidence. Such withdrawals are uncommon, especially in the credibility area.

(B) THE RULES OF EVIDENCE

The rules of evidence determine how and which matters will be proved in court. These rules are found in statutes and appellate case decisions. An important principle of the rules of evidence is that those who must resolve the dispute, such as the judge and the jury, will base their decision upon the evidence presented in court.

Generally, the evidence consists of the testimony of witnesses, depositions of witnesses taken in advance of trial, and documentary evidence. In construction disputes, judge and jury sometimes visit the construction site, if a viewing of the premises will help resolve the dispute.

(C) QUESTIONING WITNESSES

Most of the questioning is done by the attorneys for the litigating parties. Under the "adversary system", each side tries to present its case in the best possible way, and also tries to discredit the evidence presented by the other side. Generally, the judge is the referee. He steps in where there are disputes, and makes rulings where necessary. Some judges take a more active role in running the trial and questioning the witnesses.

Generally, the testimony consists of questions propounded by the attorney and answers given by the witness. Some have proposed that witnesses testify in a narrative fashion. These proponents believe narration is a more natural and efficient way of getting the facts to the judge and jury. Some lawyers are suspicious of the narrative method, because they feel that the witness will state matters which are inadmissible, or which are prejudicial to their side. For these reasons, and because lawyers are not accustomed to making changes in procedures that they have used for a substantial period of time, most of the questioning is likely to be specific, and the answers are likely to be limited to the specific question asked. There are ways of framing a question which can lead to a narrative answer.

Questioning can be divided into "direct questioning" and "cross examination". When an attorney calls a witness, usually he must use direct questioning. This means that after certain preliminary matters are established, he is not permitted to "lead" the witness. A "leading question" suggests the answer which the lawyer wishes the witness to give.

Suppose an architect has sued his client when the latter has refused to pay for the architect's services. Suppose the client defends by asserting that there had been an agreement that the work would be performed to the client's absolute satisfaction. If the client is a witness, it would be improper for his attorney to ask "Isn't it true that the plaintiff (the architect) told you that he would perform his services to your absolute satisfaction?" Such a question obviously suggests the answer to the witness. Any objection by the architect's attorney would very likely be sustained and the client's attorney would be asked to rephrase the question. He would very likely rephrase the question in this fashion:

> Pointing your attention to a meeting between yourself and the plaintiff which took place on January 15th, 1970, please state as best you recall the nature of the conversation?

Generally, lawyers skilled in examining witnesses, develop the technique of gently leading the witness by including something in the question which puts the witness on the track while not leading in the obvious manner given earlier.

The purpose of cross examination is to test the veracity and accuracy of what the witness has testified to under direct examination. By the use of leading questions, and by emphasizing the weaknesses in the direct testimony, the attorney using cross examination tries to show that the witness is lying, that his memory is bad, or that he does not have any basis for the statements he has made on direct examination. Cross examination can be very rigorous. Insinuations are made. The attorney may hammer relentlessly at the witness with a series of rapid questions. The attorney may suggest that the witness has given different answers at other times. Going through severe cross examination can be a trying process. While the attorney is given a wide latitude in cross examination, there are some limitations. There are occasions when the judge must step in to protect the witness from harrassment and intimidation. However, the witness testifying must be prepared to face uncomfortable, and often exasperating, cross examination.

There may be a long delay between the events upon which the lawsuit is based and the trial. In some metropolitan areas, it may take five years to get a case completed after it is filed. These delays make it difficult for the witness to remember what transpired many years before. It is common in American judicial procedure for the attorney to prepare his witnesses. He will tell them what he proposes to ask, and may refresh their recollection as to what happened. An attorney should discuss the case in detail with the witnesses he proposes to call. If an attorney does a careful job of preparation prior to trial, the witness' recollections will be refreshed and he will be in a position to testify with reasonable assurance.

Sometimes the opposing attorney will ask if the witness has discussed the case with attorney before trial. Often a witness will think there is something dishonest about doing so, and deny having done so. Such a statement can easily be proven false, which may discredit the witness. The witness should respond truthfully to such questions.

There are methods that can be used during the course of the testimony for refreshing the witness' recollection. This may be done by giving documents or other memoranda to him to examine during the course of his testimony. After he has had a chance to look at them, and after the attorney for the other party has had a chance to look at this documentary material, the witness may be permitted to testify that his recollection has been refreshed.

(D) COMPENSATION OF WITNESSES

Witnesses are compensated in various ways. Courts and sometimes arbitrators generally have what is called a power of "subpoena". This is the authority to demand that witnesses within the jurisdiction of the court appear and testify. If a witness is a friendly witness, the subpoena is usually not necessary. The attorney merely requests the witness to testify.

Sometimes a subpoena is issued for a friendly witness because witness fees are costs paid by the losing party only when a witness is compelled to testify. In most jurisdictions, witnesses who are not expert witnesses are compensated only by payment of a small per diem fee and travel allowance. Some witnesses are hesitant to testify unless they are promised additional compensation beyond that authorized by law. While theoretically they are all subject to subpoena, attorneys may feel they will have to pay a witness additional compensation because "reluctant" witnesses are often poor witnesses.

Expert witnesses are usually paid on a "per diem" (daily) basis. Witnesses such as doctors, architects, and engineers often receive substantial fees for their testimony. The opposing attorney in cross examination may stress that the witness is receiving a high fee for testifying. Some expert witnesses admit only with the greatest reluctance that they are being paid a large fee. The fact that a witness is being paid a large amount of money to testify may make his testimony less credible to the jury or to the judge. Jurors, and certainly judges, realize that this is common, and for that reason are not likely to take very seriously attempts to discredit the testimony based upon fee amount.

(E) PERMISSIBLE TESTIMONY OF WITNESS: ROLE OF JUDGE

Generally, witnesses can testify only to the things they have perceived through their own senses. The judge and the jury are to draw the proper inferences from their testimony. For example, a witness might testify that he observed a wall collapse. However, unless he were an expert witness, he would not be permitted to testify that the reason for the collapse was poor construction methods. The ultimate determination of this latter question will be made by the judge or jury.

In the litigation process, almost nothing can be assumed. If any facts must exist before other facts can be determined, or before certain conclusions can be drawn, those underlying facts should be admitted into evidence. The exceptions are those areas where the court can take "judicial notice" of certain elementary or basic facts. For example, it would not be necessary to have evidence produced that there are thirty days in the month of September or that the earth is round. But a trial judge would run a risk of being reversed if he took judicial notice that tract home developments are unimaginative and ugly. If tract home appearance were relevant to the lawsuit, it is likely that there would have to be testimony of witnesses to establish this fact.

(F) WEIGHT OF TESTIMONY

Even if testimony is admitted, it may not be very probative. It may be considered, but may not be very persuasive. The witness who testifies as to what he saw may have poor eyesight, or may have been at a substantial distance from the object of his senses. Perhaps he has too much to gain, and his testimony is not impartial. For that reason not all evidence is likely to be considered persuasive by the fact finders.

(G) COMMENTING ON EVIDENCE

Judges generally have the right to comment on the testimony. The trial judges in the federal court system freely comment on the weight of the evidence. This means that they may instruct the jury that certain evidence, although admitted, should not be considered as very trustworthy by the jury. This is less likely to be done in state courts. In state courts, the function of commenting on the weight of the evidence is usually the function of the attorneys.

(H) TENDENCY TO ADMIT TESTIMONY FREELY

The modern tendency is to admit most relevant evidence. If the evidence is not very persuasive, the trial judge may control the jury by either commenting on the weight of the evidence or withdrawing issues from the jury where the evidence is one-sided. Some relevant evidence will not be admitted. For example, particularly gruesome photographs of homicide victims may not be received in evidence, even though they may be relevant, because they may inflame the jury against the defendant. Likewise, evidence of repair of a structure after an accident is not permitted, because to permit admission of repairs might discourage persons from making such repairs.

Generally, appellate courts give considerable discretion to the trial judge on the questions of admissibility. There is a decreasing use of the jury in civil cases. For that reason, there are likely to be fewer limitations on the admissibility of evidence. Presumably the trial judge, where there is no jury, will be able to separate the weighty from the flimsy. Trial judges are inclined to listen to any testimony which they believe will help them resolve the dispute. They are less likely to feel limited by any strict rules on admissibility of evidence.

(I) OPINION TESTIMONY BY NON–EXPERTS

"Opinion" testimony should be differentiated from "fact" testimony. Generally, witnesses testify to only what they have seen, touched, tasted, smelled, or heard. Only qualified experts can give opinions.

But sometimes opinion evidence by non-expert witnesses is admissible. Usually these are questions upon which the average person can express an opinion which has reasonable reliability and does not require any specialized training, education, or skill. For example, any witness is usually permitted to testify as to whether a particular person was in a state of intoxication. One reason for permitting this opinion testimony is that the line between fact and opinion is very difficult. For example, a witness might testify that a certain person had bloodshot eyes, slurred his words, walked with an uneven gait, and had an alcoholic smell on his breath. Some of these observations are expressions of opinion. Often non-expert witnesses are permitted to testify on questions of insanity, the value of their own property, handwriting, speed of a vehicle, and other matters of a similar nature.

A non-expert person should be able to give an opinion on whether a particular structure is aesthetically pleasing. He might also be able to give an opinion on whether the physical arrangements of a building will permit the activity within a building to function efficiently. Whether he can give an opinion on whether a particular community was a well planned one is more questionable. Usually, it will be necessary to be an expert if the issue is the reason for the collapse of a particular structure or whether a structure was designed in accordance with proper engineering standards.

SECTION 38.04 OPINION TESTIMONY BY EXPERTS

(A) FUNCTION OF EXPERT

The function of the expert witness is to assist the finders of fact in matters beyond the normal jury or trial judge competence. Since the judge is law trained, and the jury are lay persons selected from the community at large, it is likely that they will not have much knowledge about certain matters which may become issues in litigation. It is the function of the expert witness to assist them in resolving these matters.

(B) PREPARATION OF EXPERT

The lawyer will determine whether a particular expert he has in mind has the technical skill needed. A design professional should not undertake to testify if he lacks such skill.

The expert should prepare carefully prior to litigation. He should be aware of the issues in the case, and should be given a simple explanation of the legal and factual issues that are likely to arise. In architecture and engineering expert testimony, he should almost always make a careful inspection of the site. He should not rely upon what others tell him about the site, or upon any documentary evidence. He should also review those documents which appear in the file of the attorney, in order to gain a clear picture of the litigation, and also to anticipate the type of arguments which will be made by the other side. He should prepare any visual aids that will be helpful in explaining his position, and which will be persuasive to the finders of fact. He should make certain that the visual aids are easily seen and understood by the jury and the trial judge, and that the visual aids are accurately and honestly prepared. If the visual aids will depend upon certain evidence being admitted in the litigation, he should advise the attorney that this is so, and request that the attorney make certain that these matters are introduced in evidence. Otherwise the visual aids may not be admissible.

The attorney will usually spend a good deal of time instructing the witness on matters of dress, tactics, presentation, and other matters which will make his testimony more persuasive. He will try to anticipate the arguments that will be made by the other side, and prepare his expert witness for these attacks. Frequently the expert witnesses are questioned as to whether or not they have read certain standard treatises in their field. Careful preparation also means the careful reading or rereading of standard treatises in the field. Some expert witnesses who are very experienced need not be prepared with the care required for expert witnesses who are less experienced.

(C) THE COURTROOM: QUALIFICATION OF WITNESS

Moving to the courtroom scene, the first question relates to the qualification of the expert to give an opinion on the matter at issue. The trial judge determines the qualifications of the expert. The attorney places his expert on the witness stand. The attorney questions the witness on his occupation, education, degrees, professional licenses, membership in professional societies, experience, employment, and publications.

Increased professional specialization can cause problems in qualifying an expert witness. As a body of scientific knowledge becomes more fragmented and specialized, should a generalist be permitted to give expert testimony in specialized areas? A witness trained in soils engineering will not be qualified as an expert in matters of mechanical engineering. Even well-developed specialities, such as mechanical engineering, have their sub-specialities. Perhaps a mechanical engineer will not be qualified to give an expert opinion upon air conditioning. As specialization grows, the law must resolve whether it will take the time to listen to someone who has expertise in a broader field of which the specialized field is a sub-category. Obviously, it is best to get a witness who is an expert in the particularly narrow issue which is before the court.

However, it is not always easy to obtain these types of expert witnesses. Litigation may involve a scientific area which does not have many specialists. It may be difficult to obtain a specialist as an expert witness where the professional judgment of another is the major issue. This is especially true in medical malpractice cases. Doctors are reluctant to testify for the plaintiff against a defendant doctor. Where it is difficult to obtain expert witnesses who possess expertise in the narrow sub-specialty which is at issue in the litigation, courts are likely to permit experts in the general area to testify, even though they do not have the specialized expertise which might prove more helpful. Where the judge admits testimony by such an expert witness, the lack of specialized education and training may affect the weight which the judge will give to such testimony.

(D) PRESENTATION OF OPINION

If the expert witness has been qualified and the judge is willing to receive his opinion, how is his opinion presented?

Basis for Opinion

The judge and jury must know the factual underpinnings for expert opinion. If the factual underpinnings are not those which have occurred in the particular case, the opinion is irrelevant. Also, the finders of fact will want to know the basis for his opinion. The best way for an expert to give his opinion is for him personally to have seen the observable facts which are the basis for his opinion. In a construction project dispute, it is essential for the expert to have made a careful inspection of the site. He should not rely upon what he is told by third parties, as this will, in some cases, render his opinion inadmissible. Not only might it render inadmissible, but even if admissible, the weight of his opinion wlil be substantially reduced if he has not personally inspected the site in question. If he has done so, then by his own direct testimony he can establish the underpinnings for his opinion.

Hypothetical Question

If the expert has not himself seen the observable facts, he may have to give his opinion based upon a hypothetical question. The hypothetical question is a long, and often involved, question propounded by the attorney to the expert witness. In this hypothetical question are included all the factual underpinnings, which should coincide with the facts as they have been or will be established at the trial. For example, suppose the issue relates to why a roof has collapsed. The hypothetical question should include all the details as to the materials and methods which were used in constructing the building, the physical facts relating to the building's collapse, the use which had been made of the roof, atmospheric or weather conditions, or any other facts upon which his opinion as to the cause of the collapse are based.

Communication of Opinion

Communication is an essential element of testimony, and especially important for an expert witness. If he is not able to communicate in terms understandable to the judge and jury, he is not going to be a persuasive witness. He should try not to talk down to the judge and jury. He should educate them on the scientific matters upon which he is testifying. He should convince them that his testimony is impartial and honest, as well as expert. He should use whatever visual aids are necessary and helpful in the presentation of his testimony. He should be courteous to the judge and to the opposing counsel.

The expert witness must consider his audience. If an architect is asked to testify as an expert witness in litigation, he should realize that he is invading, to some degree, an area which is largely dominated by law-trained persons. Sometimes he is invading the province of the jury when he attempts to persuade the jury that a particular result should be reached. For these reasons, his testimony may be received suspiciously by the persons who must evaluate it. Also, the persuasiveness of the testimony, to a very large degree, may depend upon the expert witness realizing his function. He is there to assist persons who do not have his professional training. In order to do this, he must show sufficient respect for their intelligence, and he must communicate in a way which can be understood by persons who have not had his education or his background.

Cross Examination

An attorney who has called the witness to testify usually prepares the witness for the cross examination he will receive from the other attorney. The witness should realize that the function of cross examination is to determine how much weight should be accorded to his testimony. He should realize that the cross examiner is given a wide license to try to show that the testimony should not be believed, or should not be accorded much weight. There are some limits to cross examination and, if he feels harrassed, he should hesitate to answer a question, in order to give the attorney for the side calling him an opportunity to object to the testimony.

While leading questions are freely permitted in the cross-examination, the questioning must be fair. The questioning should not be repetitious, and the witness should not be made to go over material and to give answers which are already given. The questions should not be "loaded". A loaded question is one which cannot be answered by a straight "yes" or "no," because a "yes" or "no" conveys a misleading impression. The classic example is, "Do you still beat your wife? Either "yes" or "no" will admit that at least on some occasion the witness has beat his wife. Sometimes a cross-examiner will insist that the witness give a yes or no answer. If the question is a loaded one, a judge will, upon proper objection on the part of the other attorney, ask the cross-examiner to rephrase his question or to withdraw it. Even where the question is not a loaded one, it may be very difficult for a witness to give a straight "yes" or "no" answer. In such cases, he should refuse to give a "yes" or "no" answer. Generally, if his refusal is fair, the trial judge will order the attorney to rephrase the question or permit the witness to qualify his answer.

The witness should not try to bluff. He should be willing to admit that he does not know the answer to a question. He should show impartiality, even though he may be forced to admit that he is being paid well by one side for his testimony. While he should not attempt to bluff or to give a categorical answer where one cannot be given, a good expert witness is willing to try to answer a crucial question without too many qualifications. If he equivocates unnecessarily, his testimony may not be very persuasive to the jury or to the trial judge.

(E) CRITICISM OF SYSTEM

There has been much criticism of the expert witness system in American litigation. A lawyer may consult five experts, seeking expert opinion favorable to his client. He will choose the two who will be favorable, and then pay them substantial expert witness fees to act as his advocates in the courtroom. The other attorney will do the same thing, selecting witnesses who will be favorable to his case. The battle of the experts is often one which is difficult for a lay jury, or even a trial judge, to resolve. The jury and the judge do not know who to believe. Each side may present witnesses of outstanding qualifications who reach opposite conclusions on the analysis of the same facts.

There have been suggestions for reform of this system. Most of the reform is centered around the idea of a court-called expert witness.

Some proposals have suggested that only court-appointed expert witnesses should be used. Others have suggested that it would be wrong to deny each side the right to present its own expert witnesses, but that it would be advisable to have a system under which court-appointed expert witnesses would be common. In such cases, the jury and the trial judge would accord more weight to the testimony of the impartial expert witness called by the court. However, it appears that the present system is likely to continue, except for occasional experiments with court-appointed experts.

REVIEW QUESTIONS

1. What are the principal advantages and disadvantages of the question and answer technique used in examining witnesses?

2. What are and who determines the qualifications of an expert witness?

3. What is the function of an expert witness in a lawsuit?

4. What is the principal difference between direct and cross examination?

5. Generally, does a trial judge have a right to comment on the credibility of the testimony?

6. What is a hypothetical question?

QUESTIONS FOR CLASS DISCUSSION

1. How can the present system used for obtaining expert testimony be improved?

2. Should an expert witness be permitted to be hired on a contingent fee basis (his pay depends upon the litigation success of the person retaining him)?

3. Should a judge be able to comment on the weight of testimony given by a witness?

Chapter 39

THE DESIGN PROFESSIONAL AS AN ARBITRATOR

SECTION 39.01 ARBITRATION: A MECHANISM FOR DISPUTE RESOLUTION

While arbitration is occasionally used in the labor relations field as a method for forming a collective bargaining agreement, its principal use in the commercial world is a mechanism for dispute resolution. Some industries and some trade associations prefer arbitration for handling their disputes rather than the alternative of using the judicial process. Where arbitration is accepted and used frequently, there are usually skilled arbitrators knowledgeable in the customs of the industry and capable of resolving disputes quickly and inexpensively. If the disputants accept arbitration and the arbitrator's decision, resort to the judicial process is rarely needed.

In the construction industry, arbitration clauses are common in contracts between owner and contractor, between contractor and subcontractor, and often between the design professional and his client. While arbitration is not used as universally in construction disputes as it is in some other commercial fields, it still plays a significant role in resolving disputes incident to a construction project.

Chapter 28 dealt extensively with the desirability of using arbitration, the arbitral process and the legal controls over it. Since design professionals are frequently called upon to serve as arbitrators, this chapter focuses upon the design professional's role as an arbitrator.

In understanding the role of the arbitrator, and in offering suggestions on how the arbitrator should proceed, the analogy to litigation is useful. Why is arbitration being used increasingly as a substitute for litigation? Arbitration should be a quick, informal, and cheap method of resolving disputes. In addition, arbitration should provide an expert outsider who brings to the arbitration skill and knowledge which will enable him to render a better decision than a judge in a court.

By and large, the correctness of the arbitrator's decision is not subject to review. In litigation, the losing party can appeal to a higher court. These points are emphasized because the arbitrator should try to maximize the advantages of arbitration, such as an expert decision arrived at quickly and informally, while keeping in mind that the parties want a process which is roughly similar to the due process which litigation should provide. Due process means a reasoned, impartial, decision arrived at after notice and a fair hearing. The arbitrator must realize that his decision in essence is final.

SECTION 39.02 SOME PRE-HEARING MATTERS

(A) SELECTION OF AN ARBITRATOR: NEUTRALITY

Methods of selecting an arbitrator have been discussed in § 28.05. Typically, there will be a single arbitrator or a panel of three arbitrators. Sometimes specific arbitrators will be named in the agreement creating the arbitration. More commonly, a method for determining the arbitrators is set forth in the contract. For example, often contracts provide that each party will appoint an arbitrator and the two arbitrators appointed in this fashion will select a third arbitrator.

Generally, single arbitrators are more efficient and less expensive. However, it is often difficult to get both parties to agree upon a single arbitrator. This may be the principal reason for the three-man arbitration panel. In three-man arbitration panels, the arbitrators appointed by the parties usually act as advocates for the party selecting them while the decision is made by the neutral arbitrator.

However selected, the arbitrator should be neutral. If he is connected in any way, by family, by business venture, or by owing favors to a party, he should not serve as arbitrator. The arbitrator should disclose any of these possible conflicts of interest at the outset.

As stated in § 28.05, the United States Supreme Court held that an arbitration award under the United States Arbitration Act was invalid because the neutral arbitrator had not disclosed information regarding his past dealings with one of the parties to the arbitration. Commonwealth Corp. v. Casualty Co., 393 U.S. 145 (1968).

If any prospective arbitrator discloses any facts which could impugn his neutrality or expose any conflict of interest, the parties may still choose to permit him to serve. But the arbitrator himself may and should excuse himself if he believes he could not render an impartial decision.

Each party to the arbitration should be given the opportunity at the outset of the arbitration to question the arbitrators to determine if there are any facts which would make it difficult for the arbitrator to make an impartial decision. It is good procedure for the arbitrators themselves to suggest that the parties ask them any questions relating to possible bias.

An arbitrator cannot be compelled to serve, even if chosen by the parties or the other arbitrators. The arbitrator may be too busy to serve, or may feel that he lacks sufficient expertise in the particular dispute being arbitrated to be able to function efficiently as an arbitrator. Under either circumstance, he should decline to serve. If he is busy, and will not be able to render a speedy decision, he should make this matter known to the arbitrating parties. If they wish to use him nevertheless, then he may stay on as arbitrator. The same holds true if he feels he does not have the requisite scientific, technical, or legal knowledge to arbitrate a particular type of dispute. He should make this known to the parties. If they wish to use him, then he may proceed if he so chooses. If he is both busy and also feels that he lacks knowledge in the particular type of dispute being arbitrated, it is probably better for him to remove himself from the arbitration. The fact that he may lack legal or technical skill does not necessarily mean he should not serve. There are ways in which the arbitrator can educate himself when he is asked to decide a dispute where he lacks certain specialized knowledge.

(B) ARBITRATOR'S INQUIRY INTO HIS JURISDICTION

While generally courts have taken a "hands-off" attitude when asked to review arbitration awards, one area which they have examined relates to the jurisdiction of the arbitrator. Initially, the arbitrator should determine whether he has jurisdiction over the dispute submitted to him. This is determined by the terms of the arbitration clause or any submission agreement by which parties agree that a particular dispute is to be handled by arbitration.

While there has been a tendency for arbitration clauses to be drawn so broadly so as to include almost any type of dispute, there is an increasing awareness on the part of drafters that not every dispute is best handled by arbitration. For example, the drafters may decide that arbitration should be used only where the parties are still performing, and not after performance has been completed, or after the contractor for one reason or another has left the job site. Some arbitration clauses may exclude disputes which the parties thought were not a proper subject for arbitration. For example, the parties may decide to exclude what they consider questions of law if the arbitrator is likely to be a non-lawyer.

(C) ARBITRATION v. OTHER METHODS OF FACTUAL DETERMINATIONS

The arbitration process is a method of resolving disputes through a hearing process. It is much like litigation except that the arbitrators are not actually judges, there is no jury, and the rules of evidence need not be applied.

Arbitration must be distinguished from other contract-created methods of determining facts. What appears to be an arbitration clause may be a method by which the parties have designated a third party to make factual determinations. For example, the clause may state that in the event of a dispute over whether certain performance standards have been met, the determination will be made by a particular testing organization. If there is a dispute over whether certain expenses of a contractor in a cost-plus contract are allowable costs, the parties may agree that this matter is to be decided by a certified public accountant. Valuation of property may be referred to real estate appraisers. In these illustrations, the parties are not creating an arbitration process. If the clause has not created an arbitration process, the party given the power to make the determination may, if he wishes, conduct a hearing to assist him. However, more typically, he has been asked to resolve the question based upon his own expertise and he may do so without going through the hearing process.

(D) PARTIES TO THE ARBITRATION

At the very least the parties to the contract will be parties to the arbitration. However, in an enterprise as complicated as a construction project, there are many parties who may be involved in the dispute who are not parties to the contract under which a particular dispute is being arbitrated.

If possible, all the parties who are involved in the dispute should be parties to the arbitration. Sometimes this can be done by a series of interrelated arbitration clauses, which can create jurisdiction to arbitrate among a number of parties to different contracts. This may also be accomplished if all interested parties agree to participate in the arbitration and be bound by the arbitrator's award.

(E) PRELIMINARY WRITTEN STATEMENTS BY PARTIES

An arbitration is usually commenced by one party giving notice that he is demanding arbitration in accordance with the arbitration clause or the rules incorporated into the contract which deal with arbitration. Often these rules or contract provisions state that he must give some brief summary of his claim.

For example, Section 7 of the Construction Industry Arbitration Rules published by the American Arbitration Association requires that the initiating party file "a statement setting forth the nature of the dispute, the amount involved, if any, and the remedy sought". (The amount involved often determines the arbitration fee charged by groups which conduct arbitration.) Section 7 also provides that the other party may, if he desires, file "an answering statement". If no statement is filed, it is assumed that the claim is denied.

In complicated arbitrations, it may be useful to permit, or even suggest, that the arbitrating parties submit in advance a written statement giving the position and support for the position being taken by each party. Often such an advance submission of summary of the facts, the issues, and the positions of the parties can eliminate a good deal of irrelevant testimony at the hearing. Such advance statements can serve the same function as pleadings in the litigation process. The purpose is to give each side some idea of what the other side is contending. This can assist the opposing party in preparing his case, and can also make the proceedings more expeditious by eliminating the issues upon which there is no essential dispute.

SECTION 39.03 THE HEARING

(A) WAIVER

Usually there is a hearing. The parties can agree to submit the matter to the arbitrator or arbitrators solely on the basis of written statements, the contract documents, and any other written data which either party feels is relevant. This type of submission can save time in relatively minor disputes. However, paper record submissions are often deceptive and, in many cases, may be insufficient as the basis for an arbitrator's decision. Even if the parties have agreed that no hearing is necessary, an arbitrator may request a hearing and the presence of both parties, if he feels he can not resolve the dispute solely upon the paper record submitted to him. If the parties refuse to have a hearing, the arbitrator will either have to render a decision based upon what he has, or decide that he must remove himself from the arbitration.

(B) TIME AND PLACE

Where and when will the arbitration hearing be held? The contract provision dealing with arbitration may state where arbitration will be held. If so, this determines the place of the arbitration hearing, unless the parties agree to a different place. If the place of hearing would make it virtually impossible to submit the dispute to arbitration, such a locality selection provision might not be legally enforceable. If this were true, the entire arbitration clause might be disregarded, and a court would resolve the dispute. Perhaps the portion of the arbitration provision dealing with locality would be eliminated, and the arbitration could proceed at a locality designated by the arbitrator.

If there is no provision relating to the place of arbitration, the arbitrator is usually given discretion to determine the place of the hearing. He should take into account convenience and expense. He should also take into consideration where the particular work was performed, where the witnesses are likely to be, and where a proper place for a hearing can be arranged. It may be useful to conduct an arbitration at the building site, if an appropriate place can be found for the hearing (which can be relatively informal), and if such a place would be convenient to the witnesses and the arbitrators.

The arbitrators should attempt to schedule the arbitration hearing as soon as possible for a quick, fair disposition of the matter. One of the advantages of arbitration should be its speed. The arbitrator should consider the wishes of the arbitrating parties. (Scheduling problems with a three man arbitration panel may be a reason for preferring a single arbitrator.) The arbitrator should not put up with dilatory tactics on the part of one of the arbitrating parties. If there are sensible reasons for any of the delays requested by one of the parties, the arbitrator should go along with the request.

Often requests for delays are merely bargaining tactics used to get a better settlement. Delay is often used by a party who feels the other party's financial position is weak, and delay may force a settlement on the stronger party's terms. In determining time of the hearing, the arbitrator should be patient and yet resolute. He must get the process started within a reasonable time, or the arbitration loses much of its advantage. The arbitrator should take into account the time needed to prepare for the hearing when he sets the hearing. A complicated dispute may require the opinions or services of engineers, architects, accountants, attorneys, photographers and others. If he does not allow adequate time for preparation, there will be requests for continuances and adjournments once the hearing process has commenced.

On the other hand, if the matter is relatively simple, the arbitrator should not permit dilatory tactics by one party. If both parties are slow, it is somewhat different. Perhaps they can still settle the matters themselves. But if one wishes to proceed, and the other drags unreasonably, the arbitrator must be firm. The arbitrator should notify the arbitrating parties and their attorneys of any hearings, or of any time deadlines which the arbitrator proposes to set. The arbitrator should ask each party to give him the address of a person to whom notices can be sent. See § 25.03 dealing with communications.

(C) THE ARBITRATORS

As stated in § 39.02(a) it may be useful at the outset to permit the parties to direct any questions to the arbitrators relating to matters which could affect their impartiality.

The arbitrators should comply with any state arbitration laws requiring that arbitrators take an oath. Even if not required, it may be helpful for the arbitrators to take an oath that they will conduct the hearing and render their award impartially and to the best of their ability.

(D) RULES FOR CONDUCTING THE HEARING

Generally, arbitration clauses do not prescribe detailed rules relating to the method of conducting the hearing. Certain arbitration statutes give general directives, such as requiring that the arbitrator permit each party to present his case and to cross-examine witnesses for the other party. Arbitration associations or trade groups which conduct arbitration often have simple rules relating to the conduct of the hearing. For example, Section 28 of the Construction Industry Arbitration Rules of the American Arbitration Association provides:

> The Arbitrator may, at the beginning of the hearing, ask for statements clarifying the issues involved.
>
> The complaining party shall then present his claim and proofs and his witnesses, who shall submit to questions or other examination. The defending party shall then present his defense and proofs and his witnesses, who shall submit to questions or other examination. The Arbitrator may in his discretion vary this procedure but he shall afford full and equal opportunity to the parties for the presentation of any material or relevant proofs.

If the arbitration is being conducted in accordance with specific arbitration rules, the arbitrator should follow these rules. If there are no rules, the arbitrator generally determines how the hearing is to be conducted.

The actual conduct of the hearing will depend greatly upon the complexity of the dispute, the amount of money involved, whether attorneys are present and the individual style of the arbitrator.

(E) OPENING STATEMENTS

In a complicated arbitration, or even in matters which may not appear to be complicated, it is often helpful to permit the parties, or their attorneys, to make a brief opening statement. If the statement is not too long or involved, it can help the arbitrator determine what evidence is relevant to the dispute, and may also serve the function of reducing the number of issues by having the parties agree to certain facts and to the issues.

(F) PRODUCTION OF EVIDENCE: SUBPOENA POWERS

Some states give arbitrators the power to issue a *subpoena.* In these states, he can compel witnesses to appear and testify, as well as require that persons bring in relevant records. Without such a statutory power, the arbitrator cannot compel that witnesses appear or that documents be produced.

Usually, the arbitrating parties are more than willing to produce witnesses and to supply whatever records are advantageous to their position. If issues can be resolved more easily if certain witnesses are produced or certain documents are presented, the arbitrator can resolve those questions against the party who refuses to produce these witnesses or records within his control. If the arbitrator indicates this to a reluctant party, the latter is likely to produce the witness or the records.

(G) LEGAL RULES OF EVIDENCE

The rules of evidence applied in courts need not be followed by the arbitrator. However, certain principles which form the basis of the legal rules of evidence should guide the arbitrator when he determines whether material submitted by the parties should be considered. These principles relate to *relevance* and *administrative expediency.*

As to relevance, the arbitrator should not go into matters which are not germane to the dispute. This is often difficult to determine. At the outset, the arbitrator should not cut off a line of testimony which may not appear to be relevant at the moment it is presented. Perhaps this testimony will become relevant as the hearing proceeds. However, the arbitrator should ask the party presenting the evidence what he intends to establish. If it is then determined that what he intends to establish is not germane to the dispute, the evidence should be disregarded, and testimony cut off.

The hearing should be run efficiently. The arbitrator should avoid testimony and arguments which do not add any light to the dispute. This is usually easier if the parties are represented by legal counsel, and the attorneys are prepared for the hearing. When this is done, the evidence presented should be relevant, and should not be cumulative. Once a fact has been established, it is usually not necessary to establish it again.

Often arbitrating parties not represented by counsel, or represented badly by counsel, will attempt to present irrelevant and cumulative evidence. While giving them a chance to present their cases is extremely important, the arbitrator should refuse to hear evidence which does not bear on the dispute, or which has already been established. He should, however, take into account that the arbitration process, in addition to being a search for truth and a method of resolving disputes, has value as a therapeutic device to the parties. By the time there is an arbitration, there may be much hard feeling and acrimony between the parties. They may feel it important to present their side of the story, even if it takes a good deal of time. For that reason, it may be useful to permit a certain amount of repetition, and even an occasional excursion into irrelevancy, if it appears that the party presenting the evidence is seriously insisting upon its being considered. Obviously there are limits to the therapeutic value of listening to irrelevant and repetitive testimony. However, the arbitrator should not move too quickly to suppress presented evidence unless he is firmly convinced that it would serve no useful function to have this evidence presented.

(H) DOCUMENTARY EVIDENCE

There are many technical rules of evidence used in courts which relate to the admissibility of documentary evidence. Fortunately, the arbitrator need not follow these rules. He should consider any documentary evidence submitted by the parties, provided that it is relevant and not cumulative. The authenticity of the document can be taken into account. An excessive preoccupation with form, notarial seals, witnesses to the document, etc. can slow down the hearing. Unless a party questions the authenticity of a document, the arbitrator should consider it.

As for the weight to be accorded the documentary evidence, the arbitrator should be skeptical toward documents and written statements made *after* the dispute has arisen and which appear to have been made with a view toward supporting a position which will be taken in the arbitration. Also, the arbitrator should view cautiously documentary evidence prepared by someone with a strong motive toward self interest, such as to cover up his mistakes or to prepare for arbitration or litigation.

(I) QUESTIONING OF WITNESSES

While there is no requirement that witnesses be put under oath, arbitrators often do so. Some state laws require an oath if one of the parties demands it. The requirement of a simple oath often adds dignity to the hearing and may induce truthful testimony.

In litigation, the party who presents a witness is not permitted to ask leading questions. The other party is permitted to ask leading questions by cross-examination, and to ask any questions which bear upon the credibility of the witness. In litigation the judge may question the witness, although many judges tend to leave questioning to the attorneys.

In arbitration, the arbitrator is free to use the question and answer technique, or he may permit the witness to present his information in narrative form. It is better procedure to permit thorough examination by the opposing party or opposing counsel. The purpose of cross-examination is to determine whether the statement being made, or the evidence presented, is worthy of belief. Cross-examination in court can be a useful tool to separate the truthful witness from the liar or from the witness whose recollection may be faulty. The arbitrator should not hesitate to question the witness if he feels that the questioning by the parties, or the witness's statement, has not brought out matters which he believes to be pertinent to the dispute.

(J) KEEPING CONTROL OF HEARING

The hearing should be conducted in a dignified manner, and the arbitrator should not permit the parties, or their attorneys, to take control of the hearing process. Sometimes attorneys try to dominate an arbitrator who is not an attorney. It is often uncomfortable for a non-attorney arbitrator to be caught in a cross-fire between two attorneys. Nevertheless, many arbitrators develop skills at arbitrating disputes, and are capable of handling themselves when caught in such a cross-fire. An attorney who seeks to control an arbitration hearing being conducted by a nonlawyer often finds that he has prejudiced his client's case.

(K) VISITING THE SITE

Generally, the hearing will be conducted in a hearing room or in an office. It is possible, and often helpful, to conduct a hearing at the site where the evidence is available to the arbitrator or arbitrators. Even when the hearing is not conducted at the site, the arbitrator, either on his own motion, or when requested by a party or the parties, may view the premises. Preferably, the viewing of the premises should not be done without the presence of the arbitrating parties or their attorneys.

(L) *EX PARTE* COMMUNICATIONS

Ex parte communications are information or arguments communicated by one party to a dispute or by a third party to the person deciding the dispute without the knowledge of the other party. For example, it would be improper for a judge to receive privately communicated information relative to a pending case from one of the parties, one of the attorneys for the parties or a third party not connected with the case. The attorneys who represent the litigating parties should know what communications are being made to the judge in order to respond to them or to point out inaccuracy. This is one reason why arbitrators should notify the parties if they plan to view the premises and set a time which will enable the parties to be present.

Section 30 of the Construction Industry Arbitration Rules requires that all evidence "be taken in the presence of all of the Arbitrators and all of the parties, except where any of the parties is absent in default or has waived his right to be present." Section 39 of these Rules prohibits any communication between the parties and the arbitrator except at the oral hearing.

The problem of *ex parte* communications relates to the need the arbitrator may have to obtain information in order to render a proper decision. An arbitrator who is an attorney may need to learn about engineering principles, mathematics and the physical sciences. He may be asked to determine why a building collapsed or whether proper construction techniques were used.

An architect or engineer called upon to arbitrate a dispute may be faced with questions which relate to the validity of a contract, contract interpretation, or whether one party was legally justified in terminating his own performance. Either an attorney or a design professional could be faced with a complicated accounting problem in the course of an arbitration.

If the hearing is well run and the arbitrator is experienced, these problems may not be difficult. The parties, or their attorneys, should present evidence on these matters to assist the arbitrator. If the lawyer arbitrator is experienced in construction, he may be knowledgeable in technical matters. The design professional arbitrator may acquire adequate knowledge about law. But there will be occasions where the arbitrator feels he does not know enough about a particular subject to make a fair decision.

The arbitrator who is not a lawyer might suggest to the parties in the hearing that he is having a particular difficulty with a legal question. He could ask permission of the parties to consult a particular attorney to help him decide the legal issue. If this were agreeable to the parties, he could consult the designated person without the presence of the arbitrating parties or their counsel. If this is not satisfactory to the parties, or to either of the parties, it might be possible for the arbitrator to call a lawyer to act as an expert witness on the legal question. He can do this without the consent of the parties. He should, if he uses this approach, give the expert sufficient information and enough time to enable him to prepare. (If he decides to call in an expert, the arbitrator should look at the rules of the arbitration association under which he is serving, or the arbitration clause, to determine who pays the cost of the expert witness. Sometimes this is an expense borne by the party or parties to the arbitration, depending upon how costs are to be assessed.)

No doubt there are arbitrators who seek advice from persons outside the arbitration process, and on an *ex parte* basis. It seems more expeditious to do so. However, the arbitrator should, if at all possible, keep *ex parte* communications to a minimum, if he uses them at all. He should try, whenever possible, to obtain a stipulation by the arbitrating parties that he be permitted to do this.

(M) CONTINUING THE HEARING

Some arbitrations take a number of hearings. It may be necessary to adjourn a hearing in order to get further information, or because the hearing itself has not been completed. Hopefully, the hearing process will not be prolonged. The parties should prepare their case well, and thereby avoid the possibility of adjournments and postponements. The arbitrator should agree to postponements, if the parties agree.

SECTION 39.04 SOME POST-HEARING MATTERS

(A) SUBMISSION OF BRIEFS

At the end of the hearing, or at any other time, the arbitrator may request that the parties submit written briefs which contain statements of their positions. This will lengthen the decision process, especially if the attorneys move slowly. However it is sometimes useful if the dispute is a difficult one, and the hearing is complicated.

(B) MAKING THE DECISION

If there is a panel of arbitrators, they should meet in closed session and deliberate upon their decision. If a transcript of the testimony has been taken, they can review the transcript. The award should be signed by all the arbitrators, or at least by a majority of them. In making their determinations, they need not follow precedent. They should look carefully at the remedies they can award. If the parties are hostile to each other, and are no longer working together, it is likely that the best remedy is to order that one pay the other money. The remedy may also require that certain work be done, or that certain performance be rendered by one party to the other. This may be proper while the parties are still performing. However, it may be asking for trouble if there is extreme hostility, or if they are no longer working together. Sometimes arbitration agreements provide for time deadlines for decisions. These deadlines should be followed by the arbitrator.

The virtual nonappealability of his decision should make the arbitrator carefully weigh all the evidence submitted before rendering his award. An arbitrator need not give reasons for the award, unless the rules under which he is operating require him to do so. Arbitrators sometimes find that given a reasoned explanation for an award is helpful in getting the parties to accept the arbitrator's award without the need for judicial confirmation.

(C) COSTS

The arbitration clause, or the rules under which the arbitration is conducted, should state who pays costs, and how much the arbitrator will receive. The major costs are arbitrator's fees, the cost of expert witnesses, and stenographic expenses. Sometimes costs are paid by the losing party. This may tend to discourage submission of weak or frivolous claims. In close cases, it may be difficult to tell who won the arbitration. Costs may be shared by the parties, or the arbitrator may be given the power to decide who pays the costs.

REVIEW QUESTIONS

1. What determines the jurisdiction of the arbitrator?
2. What determines the time, place and manner of the arbitration?
3. What is the role of the arbitrator?
4. What are *ex parte* communications?

Chapter 40

INTELLECTUAL PROPERTY: IDEAS, COPYRIGHTS, PATENTS AND TRADE SECRETS

SECTION 40.01 RELEVANCE TO DESIGN PROFESSIONALS

Design professionals use their training, intellect and experience to solve design, construction or manufacturing problems of their clients or employers. Usually design professionals reduce the proposed design solution to written form. The tangible forms, which may be sketches, renderings, drawings, models and specifications, communicate the design solution to the client or employer and others concerned with the project. Often the design solution is followed by the completed project. The three essential steps are the intellectual effort by which the solution is conceived, the communication of the solution and the development of the end product; that is, the completed project.

The creator or owner of the design solution may wish that the ideas, their tangible manifestations (drawings, etc.) or the end product of the creative process not be copied, used or duplicated without his consent. The client may not want another residence or building of an identical design constructed in order to preserve the uniqueness of his residence or building. The manufacturer of a product, or the developer of a manufacturing process, may not want others to be able to copy his product or process without his permission. He may wish to recoup the money he has invested to develop the process or project by retaining any competitive advantage his research or his skill has given him.

An architect or engineer who performs design services may wish to obtain the maximum economic value from these services. He may want to retain the right to use the drawings he has drafted, and to be able to preclude his client or anyone else from using them for a similar project without paying an additional fee. If the architect or engineer knows that his drawings and specifications will be used many times, he may adjust his fee accordingly.

For these, and other reasons, design professionals, and those who pay for their work may be concerned with the legal protection given to them when persons copy or use their work without their permission.

SECTION 40.02 AN OVERVIEW OF THE CHAPTER

(A) RELATIONSHIP TO MATERIAL PREVIOUSLY DISCUSSED

The ownership of a design solution can raise legal questions between the design professional and the person who pays for his work. Section 8.03(b) dealt with the ownership of design documents as between employer and employee. Section 8.03(a) treated the ownership and use of drawings and specifications as between the design professional and his client.

(B) DEGREE OF SPECIFICITY OF DISCUSSION

Certain aspects of the law relating to intellectual ideas will be explored in greater detail than others. For example, patents, though of great importance to engineers, will be discussed only briefly. Patent law is a highly technical area. Inventors who wish to obtain a patent, or to enforce a patent, require a patent lawyer. For this reason, only the basic principles and certain salient features of patent law will be mentioned.

Obtaining copyright protection, on the other hand, is a relatively simple process. Persons who wish to *acquire* copyright protection, in contrast to legal *enforcement* of copyright remedies, can generally do so without the assistance of an attorney. For this reason, more detail will be given to copyright law than to patent law.

The degree of specificity given in the text also depends upon whether the legal protection is based upon state or federal law. For example, much of the legal protection of trade secrets and common law copyright is given by state law. Often legal precedents vary from state to state. For this reason, when legal protection is accorded by state law, only principles and trends which can be extracted from the cases will be mentioned.

(C) PROPOSED REVISED COPYRIGHT LAW

Copyright law is under constant congressional study. Annually bills are introduced to change the copyright law, yet copyright law has remained largely unchanged since 1909. There is a great deal of congressional activity in copyright because of new methods of reproduction and new communication techniques. A comprehensive revision of the copyright law is now before Congress, and there are indications that it may be passed in the future. The copyright discussion will center upon the existing copyright law. However, some mention will be made in § 40.06 of the salient features of the Proposed Revised Copyright Law.

(D) SOME PRELIMINARY POLICY QUESTIONS

This chapter deals with the legal protection given to persons who, through their training, ability, and experience, create design solutions for structures, manufacturing processes and products. One method of encouraging creativity in this work is to reward creative people by protecting them from those who use their work without their permission.

On the other hand, society can suffer from excessive protection. Much intellectual and industrial progress depends upon free interchange of ideas and free use of the work of others. Medicine and law profit enormously because most doctors and lawyers freely communicate their professional ideas to others in their profession. Also, commercial and industrial ventures can be frustrated or impeded if entrepreneurs are compelled to pay tribute to persons who claim that their ideas, designs or inventions have been used in some way by the entrepreneur. The law attempts to reward truly creative and inventive work, without unduly limiting the free flow of ideas and use of industrial and scientific technology. Patent law, for example, gives a seventeen-year monopoly to the inventor of a novel, original and non-obvious invention in exchange for his disclosure to the public of his invention. The seventeen-year period was chosen as a compromise which adequately rewards the inventor, but does not unduly perpetuate the stagnation which can accompany monopoly.

(E) EXCLUSIONS FROM COVERAGE

The creation of an effective and universally recognized trademark or tradename is an intellectual act. However, architects and engineers are not as concerned with trademarks and tradenames as they are with patents and copyrights. For this reason there will be no discussion of common law or statutory trademarks or tradenames. (The Lanham Act, a federal statute, permits registration of tradenames, trademarks and service marks.)

Also, the doctrine of "unfair competition", another legal concept designed to protect intellectual creativity, will not be covered in this chapter.

SECTION 40.03 PROTECTION OF AND TRADING IN IDEAS

(A) GENERAL UNPROTECTIBILITY OF IDEAS

Generally, if ideas are communicated by one person to another, the person to whom the idea is communicated may make whatever use of the idea he wishes, without having to pay the person who communicated the idea to him. For example, if an architect told another architect that he thought a particular type of material would be useful for exterior walls in a certain climatic area, the architect to whom the idea was communicated could use it without having to pay the architect who gave him the idea. In this sense it is often stated that disclosure of ideas is "unprotectible." (As shall be seen in § 40.04, copyright law does not protect ideas, but protects against copying the tangible manifestation of these ideas.)

(B) BARGAINING FOR IDEAS

Contracting parties can bargain for undisclosed ideas. For example, a motion picture producer may agree to pay a writer for an unknown, at least to the producer, idea for a movie. The producer may be dissatisfied when the idea is disclosed to him, but if this is the bargain he made, the law will generally enforce it.

Usually, courts hold that the law will not inquire into the "adequacy" of the bargain. The law is concerned only with whether there was a bargain. Some courts have held that if an idea is bargained for, it must have "value."

A New York case involved a bargain for an undisclosed idea designed to increase profits. The bargain was made between a manufacturer of a product and a person who claimed to have an idea which would increase the manufacturer's profit. The idea consisted of raising the price of the product to wholesalers in an amount that would not justify the wholesaler's passing the price increase to the retailers. This would mean the same sales to consumers, but a greater profit margin to the manufacturer. In this case, Soule v. Bon Ami Co., 201 App.Div. 794, 195 N.Y.S. 574 (1922), affirmed, 235 N.Y. 609, 139 N.E. 754 (1923), the court refused to enforce the promise, even though the manufacturer used the idea. The court held that it was assumed that the information for which the manufacturer promised to pay would not be generally known, and would to some degree be new or original. The court protected the manufacturer from an unwise bargain.

Contrasted to the *Soule* case is High v. Trade Union Courier Pub. Corp., 31 Misc.2d 7, 69 N.Y.S.2d 526 (1946), affirmed, 275 App.Div. 803, 89 N.Y.S.2d 527 (1949). The *High* case involved an agreement between the plaintiff and the defendant labor union newspaper, under which the defendant agreed to pay the plaintiff 35% of any savings of federal excise taxes on telephones used by the union newspaper. To perform his end of the bargain, the plaintiff simply pointed out that there was a federal statute which exempted newspapers from telephone excise taxes. The defendant refused to pay, claiming that the information was "not valuable," and was generally known. The court held that the parties can bargain for generally known information, and ruled for the plaintiff.

(C) UNSOLICITED IDEAS

Sometimes persons send unsolicited ideas to businesses. The idea may deal with product design, manufacture or merchandising. If the idea is used, the person submitting the idea may demand compensation. Usually he contends that by using the idea the user has impliedly promised to pay for it. Sometimes the person submitting the idea demands profits he claims were made because of the use of his idea.

Businesses which receive unsolicited suggestions devise techniques for avoiding these claims. Sometimes they return the letter immediately. Sometimes they send the letter to the legal department and try to avoid having the letter get into the hands of the manufacturing or sales departments. Sometimes they send a form letter to the person submitting the letter stating that the idea cannot be considered until the submitter agrees to accept a specified amount of compensation in the event the idea is used.

Generally courts have not been sympathetic to the claims of persons submitting unsolicited ideas. They have held that even if the idea is used (which can be taken as an implied promise to pay), the promise is not supported by consideration. They point to the fact that the idea was disclosed before the promise to pay could be implied and therefore there was no exchange of the promise for the information.

There have been some recoveries where it was relatively clear that the idea was used, and the manufacturer benefitted substantially by its use. However, the disclosure of unsolicited ideas, without obtaining a promise to pay for it by the manufacturer (usually a difficult thing to do), is risky. Generally, the person submitting the idea must take his chances, and will have to content himself with whatever the manufacturer will pay for the idea.

SECTION 40.04 COPYRIGHT PROTECTION GENERALLY

(A) COMMON LAW COPYRIGHT

Common law copyright gives the author the right of first publication for his written work. He can determine when, how and if his work is to be published. The term "common law copyright" is used because:

1. Protection is given by state law rather than federal law;
2. Protection generally comes from court decisions rather than statutes;
3. Protection is against unauthorized copying.

To be protectible, the work must be original. Originality, in terms of common law copyright, means that the work must have resulted from the independent labor of the author and must not have been copied from someone else. The fact that someone earlier had written the same thing would not affect common law copyright, as long as the person asserting the common law copyright did not copy the earlier work.

In addition to originality, the work must be reduced to tangible form. Usually, this means that the intellectual concept must be reduced to writing, or some other tangible form such as a model, a painting or the like.

The principal legal problem relating to common law copyright is whether the author has "published" the work. Publication, in the common law copyright sense, cannot be given its usual meaning. It has become a complicated legal doctrine, both in common law copyright, where publication divests the owner of his common law copyright, and in statutory copyright, where publication without complying with statutory requirements can also divest the owner of his statutory copyright.

An author may make a limited distribution of his manuscript without having the work considered published. For example, he may send the manuscript to his literary agent, send a number of copies to friends for their criticism and send a number of copies to publishers, all without losing his common law copyright. However, if he were to reproduce a substantial number of manuscripts and make them available to anyone who might wish to see them, then the work would very likely be considered published, ending his common law copyright. Since publication has caused the most difficulty in the area of work by architects and engineers, publication will be discussed in § 40.05.

Unlike statutory copyright (see § 40.04(b)), the copier is not accorded the "fair use" defense, which permits some copying for certain purposes.

If the owner of the common law copyright can show an infringement, he is entitled to a court decree ordering that the defendant cease using the work, cease selling the work, and, in some cases, destroy any unauthorized copies. Also, the plaintiff will be able to recover for any losses suffered by virtue of the infringement of his common law copyright, and, in some cases, will be able to recover any profits which the defendant has made by infringing the common law copyright.

The potential duration of a common law copyright, unlike a statutory copyright, is unlimited. As long as the work remains unpublished, as that term is defined by the law, the common law copyright continues. For authors of literary works, a common law copyright is not of much value. The way they will realize profits from literary work is to publish. However common law copyright has been important to architects and engineers. See § 40.05.

(B) STATUTORY COPYRIGHT

Federal Law

Statutory copyright is governed by federal law. The principal source of federal copyright law is the Copyright Act of 1909. The federal nature of statutory copyright law avoids some of the variations in state-created common law copyright. However, there are still areas of doubt because of the ambiguity of statutory language and the fact that certain difficult questions have not as yet been resolved by the courts. However, there is a greater degree of uniformity in statutory law than in common law copyright law. Also, the fact that statutory copyright law is governed by federal law means that statutory copyright infringement actions are brought in federal rather than state courts.

Purpose of Copyright Law

Copyright law encourages people to express their ideas in tangible form by giving them protection against people copying their work. Yet such protection should not unreasonably hamper the interchange of ideas. To encourage expression without unreasonably hindering the expansion of knowledge, statutory copyright generally gives certain protection to authors for a specified period of time in exchange for the authors' making their works public. In this sense, it differs from common law copyright which is predicated upon the right of authors to decide when, if, and how to publish their work.

Copyrightable Material

The copyright law lists thirteen categories of material which can be copyrighted. For the purposes of this chapter the two most important categories are *designs and models for works of art,* and *drawings or plastic works of a scientific or technical nature.* Clearly, most written work executed by architects and engineers is copyrightable under federal law. (Sec. 40.05 will discuss the special problems of protection to architects and engineers.)

In addition to fitting within one of the thirteen categories, the work must have resulted from the independent labor of the author, and must have been reduced to tangible form. Ideas, in and of themselves, are not copyrightable. It is only the tangible manifestations of the ideas which can receive protection under copyright law. As for originality, the statutory copyright laws are similar to common law copyright. Originality means that the work must not have been copied from someone else, and must have been the result of the independent efforts of the author.

A work of art, or the design or model for a work of art, must manifest minimal creativity. Also, the work must be ornamental rather than functional or utilitarian. For a further discussion of models or designs for works of art, see § 40.05(f).

Securing Copyright Protection

In order to receive statutory copyright protection, there are two principal requirements. First, the proper copyright marking must be made upon the material copyrighted. Second, the work must be deposited with the Office of Copyright in Washington.

The first requirement is much more important than the second. The material can be registered and deposited with the Office of Copyright at any time before an infringement action is commenced. (The author is subject to a $100.00 fine if he does not register the material after it has become published, and after a demand for deposit has been made upon him by the Register of Copyrights.) In order to deposit or register copyrighted material, the copyright owner must deposit two complete copies of the best edition then published. If the Register of Copyrights determines that it is impractical to deposit copies because of size, weight, fragility or monetary value, he may permit a substitute such as a photograph in place of actual copies.

The most important act to create a statutory copyright is the proper marking on the material to be protected. Subject to some exceptions, the copyright notice must appear on the original and upon each authorized copy, and contain the word "copyright", or a prescribed substitute or symbol, the name of the copyright proprietor, and the date of publication. The authorized substitute for the word "copyright" is the abbreviation, "copr.". The symbol is ©. (While all three are acceptable, the use of © gives certain types of international protection under the Universal Copyright Convention. If any international protection is likely to be sought, the latter type of abbreviation should be used.)

Unpublished Work

Generally, copyrighted materials are published. However, unpublished material can be copyrighted. Section 12 of the Copyright Act provides for a copyright for unpublished works. Among the categories of unpublished work which can be copyrighted are ". . . photographs, works of art, and plastic works and drawings." Section 12 requires deposit of one complete copy of the work, together with a registration certificate rather than two copies of the best edition as is required for published materials. The *availability* of federal copyright protection for unpublished works has no effect upon the common law copyright of the author. Probably, *registration* of unpublished material under Section 12 will divest the author of his common law copyright.

Extent of Copyright Protection

Generally a copyright protects against others copying the copyrighted material. The person claiming infringement (an impermissible copying) usually has the burden of showing that the alleged infringer actually copied the copyrighted material. If the defendant can establish that he never knew of, nor used, the copyrighted material, he will not be liable. In this sense, it is usually important to determine whether the defendant had access to the copyrighted material. Also, the degree to which the infringer's material is identical, or nearly identical, to the copyrighted material will be very persuasive in determining whether there has been an infringement. The more the alleged infringing copy is an exact copy of the copyrighted material, the greater the likelihood that there has been an infringement.

Infringement by copying may be indirect. An infringer may have memorized the copyrighted material and later committed what he had memorized to tangible form. If he has done so, he has infringed the copyright even though he has not directly copied the material. He may also have infringed even though he had not seen the original plans if he makes a copy of the copyrighted designs under the instructions of someone who had seen them. Infringement may also occur if a person innocently copies something which itself was an infringement of copyrighted material. While this may be an infringement even if the conduct of the infringer is innocent, the judicial remedy will be less harsh.

For all categories of copyrighted material, the copyright owner is given the exclusive right ". . . to print, reprint, publish, copy and vend" his copyrighted works. In addition, if the material is a model or a design for a work of art, the copyright owner has the right ". . . to complete, execute, and finish" the work of art. If the copyrighted material is, for example, a "drawing or plastic work of a scientific or technical character," the only statutory protection is against copying the drawing itself.

An important limitation on the protection given the owner of a copyright is the "fair use doctrine." The courts have created the fair use doctrine to avoid the unreasonable limitation on free interchange of information which could result if copyright protection against copying were absolute. Generally, fair use means that relatively small portions of copyrighted works may be used without authorization from the copyright owner if the user has a valid reason to use such portions and if the use does not adversely affect the owner's interests. For example, portions of copyrighted material may be quoted in book reviews and scholarly treatises, or used in the classroom. To determine whether there has been fair use, the courts look at the extent to which the use competes with the copyright owner and affects his market, the relative size and importance of the part used, the nature of the copyrighted works, and the user's reason for using the works without requesting permission. (If someone wishes to use portions of the copyrighted work for even the noncompetitive uses mentioned, it is wise to obtain permission of the copyright owner. Usually this is not difficult to secure.)

Ownership of Copyright

A copyright may be secured by the author or by someone taking under him such as his executor, administrator or someone to whom he has assigned his rights. The law also provides, that "an employer in the case of work made for hire is the author." For example, if a draftsman (employee) draws plans and specifications for an architect (employer) the employer has the right to the copyright, unless there is an agreement between employee and employer giving the employee copyright ownership.

While not expressly set forth in the statute, the majority of the cases have come to a similar conclusion where the works have been commissioned. The right to obtain a copyright generally belongs to the person who commissions and pays for the work, unless the parties have agreed that the author will have copyright ownership. To determine the latter question, courts look at any express agreement the parties have made as well as the surrounding facts and circumstances. However, the person who commissions the work will have ownership only for the first twenty-eight year term of the copyright, and not to any renewal term. This contrasts with works created as part of an employment relationship. In employment cases, the employer will have both the copyright for the original term and have the right to apply for a renewal term.

As stated in § 8.03(a) the work of an architect or engineer will become the property of his client unless there is an agreement to the contrary. For copyright reasons, as well as the reasons given in that section, it is important for the design professional to have a written agreement specifying that the client is merely paying for the right to use the work of the design professional, rather than becoming the owner of the work of the design professional.

Duration

The copyright term is twenty-eight years, with the right to an extension for another twenty-eight year period. (As will be seen in § 40.06, the Proposed Copyright Revision would make a substantial change in copyright duration.)

Remedies

The remedies against infringement of a statutory copyright are generally similar to the remedies for infringement of a common law copyright. The plaintiff can obtain a court decree ordering that the defendant infringer not sell or make an improper use of the copyrighted material. He may also obtain damages for both losses to himself and any profits made by the defendant infringer.

Statutory copyright does give some additional protection when the plaintiff seeks profits that are not obtainable under common law copyright. The copyright law states ". . . in proving profits the plaintiff shall be required to prove sales only, and the defendant shall be required to prove every element of cost which he claims." In addition, the copyright law gives the plaintiff the option of seeking statutory damages rather than proving his losses or the profits of the infringer. With some qualifications, the statutory damages are not to be less than $250 and not to exceed $5,000. The trial court is given discretion within the statutory amounts.

The federal copyright law permits the judge to award attorneys' fees to the prevailing party. This is an important differentiation from common law copyright.

Foreign Protection

Generally, the copyright laws of the United States protect only against infringements occurring in the United States. Legal protection for American authors for infringements in foreign countries depends upon bilateral agreements between the United States and foreign countries, or American ratification of international copyright agreements. These agreements are usually called copyright "conventions." The countries which agree to abide by and enforce these conventions have copyright protection for their authors in those countries which agree to the conventions.

The United States has multilateral agreements with some thirty-eight countries, and has ratified the Universal Copyright Convention, which adds a number of countries where American authors have some protection. The United States is not a "Berne Union" country (another international convention) which would have added more countries where American authors would be protected. Sometimes American authors are able to achieve protection under the Berne Union by simultaneously publishing in the United States and in a Berne Union country, such as Canada or the United Kingdom.

SECTION 40.05 SPECIAL COPYRIGHT PROBLEMS OF DESIGN PROFESSIONALS

(A) ATTITUDE OF DESIGN PROFESSIONALS TOWARD COPYRIGHT PROTECTION

Design professionals vary considerably in their attitude toward the desirability of legal protection for their work. Some design professionals want their work imitated. Imitation may manifest professional respect and approval of work. When credit is given to the originator, imitation may also enhance the professional reputation of the person whose work is copied. Also, many design professionals are messianic about their design ideas and would be distressed if their work were not copied. Finally, many design professionals feel that free exchange and use of architectural and engineering technology is necessary for design progress.

Even design professionals who desire imitation, or who do not object to it, draw some lines. Some design success is predicated upon exclusivity. Copying the exterior features and layout of a luxury residence or putting up an identical structure in the same neighborhood is not likely to please the original architect or his client. Also, the same architect or engineer who might want his ideas to become known and used might resent someone going to a public agency and without authorization copying his construction documents which were required to be filed there. This same design professional is likely to be equally distressed if a contractor were to copy plans made available to him for the limited purpose of making a bid. Much depends upon what is copied, who does the copying, and whether appropriate credit is given to the originator.

(B) WHAT MIGHT BE COPIED?

It may be useful to look at the types of work of design professionals which conceivably could be the subject of legal protection. The design professional makes rough sketches of projects. He may proceed further by doing schematic and design drawings. He may draft floor plans and elevations. He may create two-dimensional renderings, or three-dimensional models of his project. The usual culmination of design work are the construction documents which are sufficiently detailed to enable contractors to bid and to build. Finally, there is the completed project itself.

(C) AGAINST WHOM MIGHT LEGAL PROTECTION BE SOUGHT?

The work mentioned in the preceding paragraph can come into the hands of many persons. Clients, lenders, contractors, subcontractors, suppliers, consultants and employees of these persons have access to various products of the design professional at various times. These products may be submitted to persons or groups conducting an architectural competition. They may be filed with public officials who must examine them in order to determine whether a proposed subdivision will be approved, or whether a building permit will be issued. Sometimes these documents are public records available to anyone who wishes to see them. The design professional may submit his work to professional journals for publication. He may also submit models or plans or simple designs to newspapers or magazines of general circulation. Design professionals sometimes distribute their work to other design professionals to seek advice, or to demonstrate new materials or techniques. Members of the public may see the design professional's design work displayed publicly at an exhibition. Finally, the general public often sees a completed project from the outside and often from the inside.

(D) TYPES OF UNAUTHORIZED USE

What are the types of unauthorized use which may be made of the work of a design professional? The writings, or, for that matter, the completed project, could be copied, completely or substantially. Substantial design features of the design professional could be incorporated in another project. The work of the design professional could be used without having been copied to construct an identical project. Finally, the work of the design professional could be reproduced and sold.

(E) COMMON LAW COPYRIGHT AND PUBLICATION: THE *WOOD* CASE

The most troublesome question in common law copyright relates to whether there has been a sufficient general publication to end the common law copyright. As stated earlier, the word "publication" has acquired a special legal meaning, both in common law and statutory copyright. The *Wood* case, reproduced at this point, discusses most of the publication cases.

EDGAR H. WOOD ASSOCIATES, INC. v. ALEX J. SKENE

Supreme Judicial Court of Massachusetts, 1964.
347 Mass. 351, 197 N.E.2d 886.

REARDON, JUSTICE. . . .

. . . Wood is a Massachusetts corporation comprising an association of architects. The corporation is a duly licensed architect. One Thomas Moylan retained Wood to draft plans for the erection of two sections of buildings, each section to contain 110 apartments, in Woburn. After acceptance of the plans by Moylan they were filed with the building department of Woburn and approved. Filing was required in order to obtain a building permit. Moylan then commenced erection of one of the two sections. He and Wood had entered into an agreement under the terms of which Wood retained "all * * * [its] property rights, title and interest to the said plans for all times." Moylan employed the defendant Portugal to supervise construction of the building in accordance with the plans. About the same time the defendant Skene desired to erect on land owned by him in Norwood apartment houses similar to those of Moylan. As the result of a conspiracy between Skene and Portugal, Portugal left Moylan's employ, entered that of Skene, and took with him to Skene plans of the Woburn buildings. Other defendants, the Wallaces, organized a real estate trust under the name of Windsor Gardens Co. of Norwood, Massachusetts. The trust bought Skene's Norwood land. Skene transmitted the plans to the Wallaces who in turn gave them to the defendants, Alonzo B. Reed, Inc. and its employee Vincent Sullivan, to be copied. Reed's name and that of Sullivan were affixed to the copied plans. These plans were presented to the building commissioner of Norwood and to others. In sum, Wood's plans were copied and are being or were used to construct in Norwood buildings identical in design and specifications to the Woburn buildings being erected.

Wood did not resort to statutory copyright, and we are concerned solely with an examination of its rights under the common law. Common law copyright exists in this Commonwealth. "That the right of property which an author has in his works continues until by publication a right to their use has been conferred upon or dedicated to the public, has never been disputed." Tompkins v. Halleck, 133 Mass. 32, 35. . . .

The principal issue in dispute is whether Wood lost whatever common law rights it had in its plans (1) when they were filed with the Woburn building department, or (2) when Moylan constructed a building from them. We deal with a matter of first impression in this Commonwealth. Only six cases are in point from other jurisdictions, none by a court of last resort. They are in conflict and so is such literature as exists on the subject.

THE REPORTED CASES.

The first of the reported cases is Gendell v. Orr, 13 Phila. 191 (Pa.Common Pleas), decided in 1879. An architect and builder erected a porch "of a new and novel design and artistic beauty" (13 Phila. p. 191) along the front of his house, which stood bordering a highway. Later he sought to enjoin the construction of copies of his porch. The court held that the completion of such a design and its exposure to public gaze for three years constituted a general publication of the work.

There followed in 1903, Wright v. Eisle, 86 App.Div. 356, 83 N.Y.S. 887. An architect had prepared plans for a private residence which were "duly filed with the building department of the city of Mt. Vernon" (86 App.Div. p. 357, 83 N.Y.S. p. 888). After the residence was built, the defendant sought to procure a duplicate set of plans from the architect. He declined to meet the architect's price and thereafter retained a third party whose plans led to the erection of a building "conforming substantially" (86 App.Div. p. 357, 83 N.Y.S. 887) to the first residence. The architect sought recovery for the value of the second set of plans. The New York court held that when the architect had filed the plans in a public office, he had "published his work to the world" (86 App.Div. p. 358, 83 N.Y.S. p. 889) and lost his exclusive right to them.

In Kurfiss v. Cowherd, 233 Mo.App. 397, 121 S.W.2d 282 (1938), an architect drew plans to modernize an old house. As modernized the house was opened to public inspection. The pleadings indicate that the defendants made copies of the plans and used them in the construction of other houses. The original plans were not filed in a public office. It was held that "this unrestricted exhibition" (233

Mo.App., p. 408, 121 S.W.2d 282) of the modernized house was a publication of the plans.

In 1959, on the authority of Wright v. Eisle, supra, the Supreme Court of New York held that the filing of plans with a building department in connection with the erection of one house precluded the architect from recovery of compensation from one defendant who erected additional houses from the same plans which came to him from his codefendant for whom the first house had been built. Tumey v. Little, 18 Misc.2d 462, 186 N.Y.S.2d 94.

The earlier cases were reviewed in an extended dictum in DeSilva Constr. Corp. v. Herrald, 213 F.Supp. 184 (M.D.Fla.1962). The court was of opinion that the filing of plans with a building department in order to obtain a construction permit was a publication that terminated the common law copyright (213 F.Supp. pp. 194–195). But the court stated that a completion and exhibition of the building did not constitute such a publication of the plans (213 F.Supp. pp. 195–196).

The final case, Smith v. Paul, 174 Cal.App.2d 744, 345 P.2d 546, 77 A.L.R.2d 1036 (1959), differs from those already discussed. Smith was not a licensed architect but was "in the business of designing homes" (174 Cal.App.2d p. 746, 345 P.2d p. 547, 77 A.L.R.2d 1036). He brought an action against the owner of a house and the contractor who built it on the ground that the plans employed in its construction had been drawn by him for a third person. The plans had been originally filed in a county office as required by law in order to obtain a building permit, and a house had been constructed from them. Smith had preserved his ownership in the plans in his contract with his client. Paul had copied them. The court held that there had been only a limited publication of the plans and hence that the designer had not lost his common law copyright in them. It pointed out that "[t]he purpose of the requirement of filing the plans in a government office is to protect the public from unsafe construction—not to take away from the architect his common law property rights. * * * The architect derives no profit from the deposit of his plans with the building department. He does not thereby sell his work and has no intention of dedicating it to the public" (174 Cal. App.2d p. 750, 345 P.2d p. 550, 77 A.L.R.2d 1036). The court emphasized that a filing was necessary in order to build. The court also held that a mere viewing of the house by guests of the owner, limited in number, constituted no general publication of the plans. The reasoning was that while exhibition of the exterior to the public might cause a loss of the common law copyright to the exterior design, "it * * * [was] not a general publication of the detailed plans themselves" (174 Cal.App.2d p. 758, 345 P.2d p. 555, 77 A.L.R.2d 1036).

General and Limited Publication.

The concepts of general and limited publication alluded to in Smith v. Paul, supra, were defined in the leading case of Werckmeister v. American Lithographic Co., 134 F. 321, 326 (2d Cir.). Only a general publication terminates a common law copyright. It is "such a disclosure, communication, circulation, exhibition, or distribution of the subject of copyright, tendered or given to one or more members of the general public, as implies an abandonment of the right of copyright or its dedication to the public" (134 F. p. 326). A limited publication is "one which communicates a knowledge of its contents under conditions expressly or impliedly precluding its dedication to the public" (134 F. p. 324). Further, to be general a publication must be such "' * * * as to justify the belief that it took place with the intention of rendering * * * [the] work common property.' " . . . As more recently stated, "a * * * publication which communicates the contents of a manuscript to a definitely selected group and for a limited purpose, and without the right of diffusion, reproduction, distribution or sale, is considered a 'limited publication,' which does not result in loss of the author's common-law right to his manuscript, but * * * the circulation must be restricted both as to persons and purpose, or it cannot be called a private or limited publication" . . . While the test is properly one of intention, it is clear that the unexpressed, subjective intention of the creator cannot be allowed to govern . . . rather the implications of his outward actions to the reasonable outsider are controlling.

The Federal cases thus recognize fully that there may be a fairly substantial but limited distribution of material susceptible of statutory copyright without putting the material in the public domain and without forfeiture of the author's common law copyright in it. It remains to determine whether a general publication has occurred here.

FILING OF PLANS.

We have already noted that the New York decisions have held that a filing with a building department does release architectural plans into the public domain. . . . In both New York cases it appears that a further reason for denying recovery was the absence of an agreement between the architect and his client that the ownership of the plans should not pass to the client by virtue of the commission. The substitute bill before us alleges that Wood specifically retained its property rights in the plans in its agreement with Moylan. . . .

There is no basis for concluding that, by filing with the Woburn officials, Wood made manifest any objective intention to publish the plans generally. . . . On the contrary, the protective clause in Wood's contract with Moylan indicates that the intention was to preserve Wood's common law rights in them. The sole reason for the filing of the plans was to procure official approval of them. The filing was a publication to but a single entity for a limited purpose. To hold that, in filing, an architect makes a general publication would be to limit his ability to effect a sale of more than one set of plans.

As already pointed out, this view was recognized in Smith v. Paul, 174 Cal.App.2d 744, 345 P.2d 546, 77 A.L.R.2d 1036. That case held that a necessary filing of architectural plans was not a general publication, despite a general statutory right to inspect and secure copies of "any public writing" on the part of the general public. This Commonwealth has a similar statutory provision: "Every person having custody of any public records shall, at reasonable times, permit them to be inspected and examined by any person, under his supervision, and shall furnish copies thereof on payment of a reasonable fee. * * *" G.L. c. 66, § 10. The filed plans are without question "public records." The argument is advanced that in G.L. c. 66, § 10, the Legislature has in effect decreed that a filing of plans with a building department shall constitute a general publication. The power to copy public records has been said to be not limited by the use sought to be made of the copies. . . . It must be clear, however, that the principal objective of Woburn in compelling a filing is to insure that the public will be protected from unsafe construction. . . . There is no indication that a second and unrelated objective, one to compel an architect to divest himself of the fruit of his labor as a condition precedent to obtaining a building permit, is within the purpose of the filing requirement or of G.L. c. 66, § 10. . . .

In the light of what has been said, we hold that the filing requirement and G.L. c. 66, § 10, give the public the right to inspect and, if necessary, to copy the filed plans for purposes reasonably related to the objectives behind the filing requirement, for example, to determine whether a building constructed in accordance with plans will comply with zoning and safety laws. That right does not extend to making copies which will impair the architect's common law copyright and property in the plans. It is not the purpose of the filing requirement to facilitate and permit architectural plagiarism, or enable one to obtain free of charge the benefit of another's work and thus "to reap where it has not sown." . . .

We conclude that the public filing of plans in the circumstances alleged is only a limited publication of them. No objective intention to make a general publication appears.

Construction of a Building.

We next consider whether the completion and exposure of the building which is the product of the plans constitutes such a general publication as will justify a copying of the *plans*. . . . In Kurfiss v. Cowherd, supra, a house was modernized in accordance with plans and thereafter opened to general public inspection. The court reasoned although "it was not intended that the public could or would take measurements * * * [of the house] the fact remains that there were no restrictions to keep any one from so doing" (233 Mo.App. at 408, 121 S.W.2d at 288), and that there had been a general publication of both the house and the plans. We regard the correct rule as having been suggested by Tabor v. Hoffman, 118 N.Y. 30, 23 N.E. 12. In that case a repairman made copies of the construction patterns used in the manufacture of a pump. The issue was "whether there is a secret in the patterns that yet remains a secret, although the pump has been given to the world" (118 N.Y. p. 35, 23 N.E. p. 12). The court held that "the patterns were a secret device that was not disclosed by the publication of the pump * * *. While the defendant could lawfully copy the pump, because it had been published to the world, he could not lawfully copy the patterns, because they had not been published, but were still, in every sense, the property of the plaintiff, who owned not only the material substance, but also the discovery which they embodied" . . .

The rule of Tabor v. Hoffman, supra, can be, in our opinion, soundly extended to the facts in this case. It has been so extended in Smith v. Paul, 174 Cal.App.2d 744, 750, 345 P.2d 546, 550, 77 A.L.R. 2d 1036: "[T]he fact that a building is built from the plans and is open to the gaze of the public * * * may be a publication of the general design or idea of the building but not a publication of the exact plans whereby another may without effort other than that of tracing the work of the architect completely duplicate the latter's effort." It is contended that Smith v. Paul, supra, cannot serve as a guide in resolving this case because access there to a private home afforded to a limited number of people was quite different from access to the Woburn apartments afforded to the general public. The argument is inapposite: "An architectural plan is a technical writing. It is capable of being copied only by similar technical writings, that is, by other plans, etc. A structure is the result of plans, not a *copy* of them. It follows that building a structure and opening it to public gaze cannot be a publication of its plans." . . .

Observation or measurement of the exterior and the interior of a completed building can hardly be said to approach an accurate copy of a set of plans. We do not suggest that a common law copyright in the plans is infringed by a drawing made from observation of the interior or exterior of the buildings. Such a doctrine could lead only to a multiplicity of law suits between parties who had erected successively structures of somewhat similar design. On the other hand, the right fully to reproduce plans is a far more substantial aid to a builder unwilling to pay for architectural services than the right to make sketches or drawings of a completed structure.

We thus hold that the construction of the building from the plans constitutes no publication of them at all.

. . .

THE EXTENT OF PERMISSIBLE RELIEF.

The facts stated in the substitute bill, if established at a trial on the merits, set forth a case for equitable relief. In a proper case injunctive relief against future use of the plans might be appropriate. If it should appear that the Norwood apartments are in process of construction or completed, then, assuming that Wood is entitled to some relief, an injunction should not be granted. Rather, considerations of relative hardship should limit Wood to the recovery of the fair market value of a set of its plans. . . . Any value assigned should reflect the fact that at the time of the conversion and the copying of the plans they had already been used in the Woburn apartment project and hence were not novel. . . . No recovery should include any amount normally allocable as a fee for architectural supervision of the construction project. . . .

The substitute bill of complaint does state a cause of action in equity, and the plaintiff's motion for leave to file it should have been allowed. The final decree is reversed and the case remanded to the Superior Court for further proceedings on the substitute bill. Wood is to have costs of appeal.

So ordered.

[Ed. note: Footnotes omitted.]

As indicated in the *Wood* case, the three principal areas of difficulty relate to:

1. Publication by completion of the project
2. Publication by filing design documents by a public authority
3. Publication by general distribution of the design.

As to the first two problems, the more recent and better reasoned cases have favored the design professional. It is likely that future cases will not hold that the design professional loses his common law copyright in his drawings if he files his design documents with a public authority, or if the ultimate project is completed and displayed to the public. The third category, that of general distribution, is likely to prove a more serious obstacle to common law copyright protection.

The *Wood* case should be supplemented by other cases. In Shanahan v. Macco Constr. Co., 224 Cal.App.2d 327, 36 Cal.Rptr. 584 (1964), the plaintiff tract home developer sued the defendant for copying the plaintiff's plans and specifications and building a number of homes from these plans and specifications. The plaintiff had built a number of model homes, distributed brochures depicting the floor plans, invited public visitors to model homes, submitted plans of the homes to a number of magazines of general circulation which had published pictures and floor plans of the homes, and sold well over a thousand homes—all before the defendant copied the plans and specifications. In addition, 250 copies of the plans and specifications had found their way into the hands of third parties, mainly subcontractors. An expert designer or draftsman could visit the model home, take measurements, and draw detailed floor plans essentially similar to those copied by the defendant.

The court in the *Shanahan* case held that there had been general publication. While noting that some courts have stated that the question of general limited publication is one of intention, the court stated that the test is objective. It will not be sufficient for a design professional to state that he did not intend to make a general publication. The court will look at the objective evidence relating to the general dissemination of the drawings, the specifications and the completed project.

The court distinguished Smith v. Paul, discussed in the *Wood* case, by noting that in Smith v. Paul, the plaintiff had designed one set of plans for one client, while in the *Shanahan* case over 1400 homes had been built and sold to the public. The *Shanahan* case demonstrates that tract home design and marketing methods are likely to preclude enforcement of common law copyright.

In Read v. Turner, 239 Cal.App.2d 504, 48 Cal.Rptr. 919 (1966), the plaintiffs were a husband and wife who had developed a floor plan for a split-level, four bedroom residence and caused their design to be expressed in a drawing. Turner was a subcontractor who had obtained a copy of the plans and specifications in order to bid on construction of the residence. Turner was told that the plans and specifications were to be returned to the plaintiffs but evidently was not told that the floor plan was not to be copied. Turner was awarded the subcontract and did the work on the plaintiffs' house.

Later, Turner decided to build a number of homes in the same tract where the plaintiffs' house was located. He even planned to build a house next to the plaintiffs' house. He asked Fulmer to draw floor plans for the houses he proposed to build. He furnished Fulmer with copies of the plaintiffs' floor plans, and suggested using them as a guide, a suggestion which Fulmer followed.

The trial court awarded the plaintiffs compensatory and punitive damages. On appeal the court sustained the defendant's contention that there had been a general publication of the floor plan. A general publication ends common law copyright protection while a limited publication preserves it. The court noted that the plaintiffs' house was sold on a multiple listing (a large number of brokers can show the house under a multiple listing), that there had been open house exhibitions, that the plaintiffs had invited the general public to view the floor plan, and that characteristics of the floor plan were recordable by casual observation. Taken together, the court found an intention by the plaintiffs to make their floor plan public. The court also pointed to the fact that the plaintiffs had given a copy of the floor plan to the ultimate buyers of their house.

However, the court held that Turner had infringed the common law copyright when he had the floor plan copied by Fulmer, something that had been done before the general publication of the floor plans in the manner indicated. Showing the drawings to Turner for the purpose of allowing him to bid was a limited publication, and did not terminate the common law copyright.

From Read v. Turner, it appears that building a "spec" home, putting it on a multiple listing, and showing it to the public ends the common law copyright in the floor plan. Other language in the opinion indicated that such conduct would not end the common law copyright in the construction documents if they are more than rough floor plans.

There is a disquieting statement in *Read* that, under some circumstances, construction of the project "publishes" certain aspects of the design. While these are likely to be aspects which are of minimal economic value, such as floor plans, the statement demonstrates the questionable value of a common law copyright in comparison to the statutory copyright. See § 40.07.

Ashworth v. Glover, 20 Utah 2d 85, 433 P.2d 315 (1967) illustrates another potential pitfall in common law copyright. *Ashworth* involved the copying of plans for a drive-in restaurant. A sharply divided court followed the *Wood* case and held that filing of the plans did not end the common law copyright, nor did distribution of the construction documents to a number of bidders. In *Ashworth*, the argument was made that the bidders could obtain a copy of the drawings and specifications by a deposit of $25, which was forfeited if they did not return the contract documents. The defendant contended that this meant that the construction documents were, in effect, sold for $25 to the bidders. The *Ashworth* court correctly rejected this argument.

(F) STATUTORY COPYRIGHT

Ownership of Copyright

Without an agreement between the design professional and his client which clearly states that the design professional is the owner of all documents, instruments of service, and other copyrightable material which is prepared by the design professional or his employees, the client will have the right to receive copyright protection.

Scope of Protection

The principal protection given a copyright owner is to print, reprint, publish, copy and vend his copyrighted work. An additional exclusive right to complete, execute and finish a work of art is given to the copyright holder of the model or design for the work of art.

Usually, the construction documents and other writings copyrighted by the design professional fall into the category of technical drawings. The protection accorded these writings precludes copying the documents, but not completing the project. For example, if an architect copyrighted drawings and three-dimensional models for a commercial building, the copyright would not be infringed if someone else constructed a similar building without directly copying the drawings or models. However, if the drawings or model were of an unusual structure which could be classified as a work of art, such as the Lincoln Monument or the Eiffel Tower, then copyright protection would give the copyright owner the exclusive right "to complete, execute and finish it." For this reason, it would be advantageous for a design professional to copyright designs and models as designs and models for a work of art, rather than as technical drawings. If the project is purely ornamental, it is likely to be a work of art. If it is purely utilitarian, clearly it is not. The troublesome cases are when ornament and utility are blended in various proportions. (While most buildings and residences are not works of art, the Taj Mahal should qualify.)

Generally, the Copyright Office takes the position that the works of architects and engineers are copyrightable as technical drawings, and not as works of art. The most recent regulation of the Copyright Office, 37 C.F.R. § 202.10(c) states:

> If the sole intrinsic function of an article is its utility, the fact that the article is unique and attractively shaped will not qualify it as a work of art. However, if the shape of a utilitarian article incorporates features, such as artistic sculpture, carving, or pictorial representation, which can be identified separately and are capable of existing independently as works of art, such features will be eligible for registration.

Under this regulation, only limited aspects of a building may be the subject of a copyright as a work of art. If the building contains an unusual exterior frieze or unusual aspects of design, these aspects might be copyrightable as a work of art. Under some circumstances, such features can be the subject of a design patent. See the *Blumcraft* case reproduced at § 40.08(c). Since it is difficult to copyright drawings as designs for works of art, this discussion will cover the copyright protection accorded to the author of technical drawings.

The principal protection accorded by copyright law is against copying the copyrighted documents. If a third party, without permission, copies plans and specifications which have been copyrighted, there is an infringement. However, if the contract documents are merely used to execute the project, there is no copyright infringement. It is difficult to construct an identical project without copying the plans and specifications or at least substantial portions. Only in the most simple type of construction is it likely that the design could be duplicated without some direct copying.

In some countries, the project itself can be copyrighted. However, under American copyright law the structure cannot be copyrighted. Even if the project is considered to be a work of art, the copyright owner has the right only to complete the project. Anyone can copy the completed project. Sometimes certain design features of a completed project are novel enough to be patented as a design patent. See the *Blumcraft* case reproduced at § 40.08(c).

Some mention should be made of the protection against others selling copyrighted material. If the copyright owner publishes his work, the work can be sold by anyone to anyone, at a price determined by buyer and seller. However, if someone sells an unauthorized copy of copyrighted material, then the seller has infringed the copyright. This is so even if he did not know that the copies were illegally made. As applied to the drawings and specifications of a design professional, if a contractor has obtained copies of the construction document solely for the purpose of bidding, and if he sells these documents to a third party, the contractor has infringed the statutory copyright.

Effectiveness of Copyright Protection

Neither statutory nor common law protection for architects and engineers has been effective. The law seems more anxious to foster free dissemination of design ideas and concepts than to reward the creator of copyrighted material.

SECTION 40.06 PROPOSED REVISED COPYRIGHT LAW

The present copyright law is largely the result of the Copyright Act of 1909. Copyright law is constantly under congressional scrutiny. Almost every session of Congress sees the introduction of changes in the copyright law. However, changes have been infrequent.

At present Congress has before it a completely revised copyright law. The impetus for major reform has come from a recognition that there have been new methods of reproduction and new forms of communication. Also, there has been dissatisfaction with certain aspects of the existing copyright law. Detailed studies were prepared and published in 1961. These studies examined every aspect of copyright law, and the authors of these studies made proposals for change. The present bill, which has passed the House and is before the Senate, is Senate Bill 543. The report of the House of Representatives accompanying this bill, and giving reasons for its recommended changes, is Report No. 83 of the 90th Congress, 1st Session. If enacted, the Proposed Revised Copyright Law will make substantial changes in the present copyright law. The purpose of this subsection is to note some of the changes which would be made if the Proposed Revised Copyrighted Law is enacted.

(A) RESTRUCTURING OF CLASSIFICATIONS OF COPYRIGHTABLE MATERIAL: MORE FLEXIBILITY

One major change relates to the classification of copyrightable material. Instead of the thirteen categories set forth in the present law, the revised law sets forth seven categories. From the standpoint of design professionals, most of their copyrightable material would be "pictorial, graphic or sculptural works." The Proposed Revised Copyright Law states:

> Pictorial, graphic and sculptural works include two-dimensional and three-dimensional works of fine, graphic and applied art, photographs, prints and art reproductions, maps, globes, charts, plans, diagrams and models.

The Proposed Revised Copyright Law would make the categories of copyrightable material non-exclusive. As new methods of communication are developed, the courts can extend copyrightability without being limited to the categories expressed in the statute. This desire for open-endedness and flexibility is also manifested by the definition of "pictorial, graphic and sculptural works" using the term "include."

(B) ELIMINATION OF COMMON LAW COPYRIGHT

The enactment of the Proposed Copyright Law would virtually end common law copyright. If adopted as proposed, common law copyright would be abolished as of January 1, 1971. See § 40.07 for a comparison of common law and statutory copyright.

(C) DURATION

Another change would be the substitution for the twenty-eight year plus an additional twenty-eight year term of copyright protection by a term measured by the life of the copyright owner plus fifty years. Where the copyright owner is not an individual, the copyright period will be seventy-five years from the term of its first publication, or for one-hundred years from the year of its creation, whichever occurs sooner.

(D) CODIFICATION OF FAIR USE DOCTRINE

The Proposed Revised Copyright Law would codify the "fair use" doctrine which has been created by the courts. In determining fair use, the following factors would be considered:

1. The purpose and character of the use;
2. The nature of the copyrighted work;
3. The amount and substantiality of the portion used in relation to the copyright work as a whole, and
4. The effect of the use upon the potential market for or value of the copyrighted work.

These are the considerations which have been taken into account by the courts in determining whether there has been fair use.

(E) STATUTORY DAMAGES INCREASED

The Proposed Revised Copyright Law would increase the statutory damage amounts that can be awarded by the court for infringement.

SECTION 40.07 SOME ADVICE TO DESIGN PROFESSIONALS

(A) COPYRIGHT OWNERSHIP

To protect copyright ownership in his work, the design professional should have a written agreement with his client, reserving ownership rights in all documents to the design professional.

(B) STATUTORY v. COMMON LAW COPYRIGHT PROTECTION

Under the present law, the design professional can choose whether to employ statutory or common law copyright. Most architects and engineers seem to choose common law copyright protection. This is unwise. Statutory protection is better, and easy to obtain.

Common law copyright is too easily lost by "publication." Despite some of the recent decisions more favorable to architects and engineers on the question of publication, there is a real risk that in some jurisdictions filing the plans with a public agency or completing the project will divest the author of his common law copyright. Even in jurisdictions which have been more favorable to architects and engineers, it is likely that the usual methods by which tract homes are sold such as newspaper ads, broadsides of advertising brochures and gala open houses, will end common law copyright in at least the readily observable details, such as floor plans. Common law copyright can be lost by selling even a single home, where many real estate agents bring numerous prospective buyers to view the premises. Even a broader than absolutely necessary distribution of construction documents could end common law copyright. In most of these situations, statutory copyright protection would be available.

In addition, statutory copyright remedies offer more protection than common law copyright remedies. There is a possibility of recovering attorneys' fees in statutory copyright. When the plaintiff in a statutory infringement action seeks to recover profits, he is given burden of proof advantages. He also has the right to statutory damages where he cannot show losses to himself or gains to the infringer.

Also, the likely enactment of the Proposed Revised Copyright Law will end common law copyright protection. This may not happen immediately, but ultimately it will be enacted. Architects and engineers may not know that the law has been changed and may continue to expect the protection of common law copyright. It is more sensible to develop a procedure for employing statutory protection, even in advance of common law copyright elimination. This avoids the risk of relying on common law copyright protection after it has ceased to exist.

Sometimes design professionals do not use statutory copyright because they do not wish to incur the expense and inconvenience of depositing and registering the copyrighted material. As has been stated, under the present law, the material can be deposited and registered at any time prior to an infringement action, at least during the first twenty-eight year period. It is not necessary to deposit the two copies required for published works until it is clear that infringement litigation will be necessary. Also, if the copyrighted materials are bulky, or if it would be expensive to require deposit, there are provisions under the Copyright Regulations under which a substitute can be deposited, rather than the copyrighted material.

Finally, perfection of a statutory copyright is relatively simple. It is important to properly mark the copyrighted material with the word "copyright," or its authorized abbreviation or symbol. This is followed by the name of the copyright owner, and the year. There are circumstances when the copyright owner need not put his true name on the copyrighted material as long as the name with which the copyright owner is identified is used within the copyrighted material. It is possible to use a tradename, or a fictitious name, as long as there is sufficient identification. (Some states require filing of a fictitious name with state authorities. It is advisable to comply with such fictitious name statutes, if a fictitious name is going to be used on the copyright marking.)

The copyright owner's "initials, monogram, mark or symbol" may be used in the copyright notice instead of the copyright owner's name if the copyrighted works are maps, works of art, reproductions of works of art, drawings or plastic works of a scientific or technical character, photographs, labels and pictorial illustrations.

The date is usually given in arabic numbers. In the case of printed literary material and dramatic works, the year which must appear is the year of first publication. In other types of copyrighted material, the year need not be given. For example, it is not necessary to include the year where the copyrighted materials are models or designs for works of art or technical drawings. However, it is advisable to include the year, even though it is not required. Design professionals should use the copyright symbol, ©, the copyright owner's name and the year of publication. For example, © John Jones 1970.

(C) PROTECTION OF COMMON LAW COPYRIGHT

For those design professionals who wish to rely on common law copyright, there are a number of steps which should be taken. Again, it is important to reserve ownership in the work to be protected by an agreement between the design professional and his client. Also, it is important to limit the distribution of drawings and specifications. Only the number absolutely required should be reproduced at the outset. Those that must be distributed to contractors, subcontractors, and others who need to see them should be clearly marked in some fashion to indicate that there is no general distribution. Some of the markings that can be used are:

1. All rights reserved.
2. Solely for the purpose of preparing bids.
3. Not for general use or publication.
4. To be returned to John Jones, Architect, within ______ days.

In addition to markings which indicate that only a limited publication and distribution is intended, design professionals should keep track of the copies that have been distributed and check to insure that copies are returned when the purposes for which they have been distributed have been accomplished.

SECTION 40.08 PATENTS: SOME OBSERVATIONS AND COMPARISONS

(A) SCOPE OF COVERAGE

The discussion of patent law will be brief. Whether the design professional wishes to institute legal action for infringement of a patent or a copyright, he will have to retain an attorney. While the steps for perfecting a copyright are simple, if an inventor wishes to obtain a patent, he must secure the services of a patent attorney. A patent attorney is needed to guide the inventor through the maze of patent law and the complexities of a patent search. Perfection of a copyright, as a rule, will not require the services of an attorney.

(B) PATENT AND COPYRIGHT COMPARED

Generally the subjects of patents are products, machines, processes and designs. See the *Blumcraft* case reproduced in § 40.08(c). Copyright generally protects writings.

The principal protection accorded by copyright law is the exclusive right to copy and vend the copyrighted material. Copyright law does not protect against someone who, without knowledge of the copyrighted work or access to it, creates a similar work. A patent gives the patent owner a monopoly, since he can exclude anyone from the field covered by his patent, even if the same invention has been developed independently, and without any knowledge of the patented device.

The most important difference between patent and copyright law is the higher degree of originality required for issuance of a patent. Copyright law requires only that the work be the independent labor of the author. Patent law requires that the work be original, inventive, useful, novel and not obvious from the prior art in the particular field.

Protecting an invention commences with the issuance of a patent. Issuance of a patent is supposed to presumptively establish that the patent is valid. But in the bulk of patent infringement cases, the defendant attacks the validity of the patent by trying to show that the invention is not novel, is obvious, non-inventive, and an insufficient advance on the prior art. The defendant has a good chance of establishing that the patent is not valid.

Patent infringement suits are lengthy, complicated and expensive. However, the potential gains to the plaintiff are often worth this type of litigation. The plaintiff can recover his damages, the profits made by the defendant, and, in some cases, can obtain compulsory royalty for infringement of his patent. In some flagrant infringement cases, the plaintiff can recover treble damages and attorneys' fees.

The duration of a patent is seventeen years. Like copyright law, the limited duration of monopoly protection reflects a compromise between rewarding inventiveness and the economic stagnation and abuse of power which often accompany monopoly.

Generally, patent protection is harder to acquire than copyright protection, but the scope of protection is greater and the remedies are more lucrative.

(C) THE *BLUMCRAFT CASE*: A TYPICAL DESIGN PATENT CASE

It may be instructive to reproduce a typical design patent case at this point.

BLUMCRAFT OF PITTSBURGH v. CITIZENS AND SOUTHERN NATIONAL BANK OF SOUTH CAROLINA

United States Court of Appeals, Fourth Circuit, 1969.
407 F.2d 557.

BUTZNER, CIRCUIT JUDGE. This appeal is taken from the district court's ruling that two patents, D–171,963 for design and 2,905,445 for a mechanical device, owned by Blumcraft of Pittsburgh were valid and infringed by railings produced by Architectural Art Manufacturing Co. We hold that both patents are invalid under 35 U.S.C. § 103.

I.

Blumcraft's design patent, D–171,963, was granted April 20, 1954 to Louis Blum for a railing styled for use in buildings of contemporary architecture. His application contained a single claim for the design "as shown" in a drawing. The railing consists of multiple parallel rails offset from vertical posts. The handrails are generally flat with slightly curved gripping surfaces. The posts are rectangular. Inconspicuous L-shaped brackets attach the undersides of the rails to the posts, leaving the gripping surfaces of the rails unobstructed. The multiple, offset, and parallel handrails set up a horizontal plane in opposition to the vertical plane formed by the parallel posts. The result, with the connections between the two planes minimized, is the visual illusion that the handrails are floating free.

The law authorizes the grant of a patent to "[w]hoever invents any new, original and ornamental design for an article of manufacture * * *." 35 U.S.C. § 171. Architectural Art urges that the design patent is invalid under 35 U.S.C. §§ 102 and 103 because it was anticipated by the prior art and its subject matter was obvious to a person having ordinary skill in the art of creating ornamental railings. The Court of Claims recently found Blum's design patent valid. Blumcraft v. United States, 372 F.2d 1014, 178 Ct.Cl. 798 (1967). We agree with it and with the district court that Blum's design was novel because the prior art did not disclose multiple rails offset from posts by inconspicuous connectors presenting the illusion of the rails floating in space. But a design must be more than novel. As Judge Soper wrote in Glen Raven Knitting Mills v. Sanson Hosiery Mills, 189 F.2d 845, 851 (4th Cir. 1951):

> "[T]here must be an exercise of the inventive faculty, and if the design lacks this quality, it will not suffice to say that it is new, original and ornamental, and has received wide public acceptance."

Title 35 U.S.C. § 103 denies patentability to a novel design if the differences between the design and the prior art are such that the design would have been obvious to a person skilled in the art of designing ornamental railings. The test for obviousness, which must be applied as critically to designs as to other inventions, is: "the scope and content of the prior art are to be determined; differences between the prior art and the claims at issue are to be ascertained; and the level of ordinary skill in the pertinent art resolved. Against this background, the obviousness or nonobviousness of the subject matter is determined." . . .

Multiple parallel rails offset from their supporting posts were known to the prior art. Two examples are Hollaender's stair rail, 1949, and Wallach's Jamaica store, 1950. However, neither of these designs, nor the many examples of multiple rails that intersect their posts, gave the floating effect which the district court found in Blum's patent. Prior art also discloses that architects who custom designed railings, not Blum, first appreciated and met the requirements of contemporary architecture for modern railing design. In a church built in the early 1940's, Eliel and Eero Saarinen achieved a floating effect with a single rail offset from balusters by inconspicuous brackets. The rail follows the stairwell from flight to flight with unbroken lines. A similar illusion was obtained in a sanatorium built in the mid-1930's. Photographs of the Kansas City Auditorium, published in 1937, and of a W. T. Grant store, published in 1940, disclose relatively flat, single handrails offset from posts and walls by subdued brackets.

A Chicago savings and loan office contains a railing installed in 1952 that follows and reinforces the lines of a curved staircase. The architect accentuated the separation between the horizontal and vertical lines of the railing by offsetting the top rail with brackets.

The differences between the prior art and Blum's design are minor. His predecessors offset multiple rails with prominent connectors and single rails by inconspicuous connectors. Blum merely offset multiple rails by inconspicuous connectors to achieve with several rails the floating effect that had previously been imparted to a single rail. It is apparent from the sophistication of the prior art that designers of ornamental railings, including manufacturers and architects, were highly skilled. Therefore, the fact, which the district court emphasized, that prior art would have to be redesigned to achieve Blum's railing is not decisive. The joining of known components usually requires skill, but this does not necessarily negate obviousness. . . .

Graham v. John Deere Co., 383 U.S. 1, 17, 86 S.Ct. 684, 15 L.Ed.2d 545 (1966), also directs inquiry into secondary indicia of obviousness or nonobviousness, including commercial success and long-felt but unsolved needs. Blumcraft's commercial success lay in the fact that it was the first to offer a railing of acceptable modern design as a prefabricated product. Both Blum and an architect testifying in his behalf stressed this point, and Blumcraft's advertising emphasized the utilitarian advantages of its railing. However, commercial success that results from the prefabrication of a known architectural style, and not creative artistry, fails to support patentability. . . .

To prove long-felt, unsolved need, Blumcraft says, "The need for a commercially available railing system compatible with modern architecture had existed for some time prior to the Blum invention." This observation illustrates both Blum's success and the invalidity of his patent. There was no unsolved need for attractive modern railings. Architects were capable of supplying them through custom design. There was a need, however, for a prefabricated railing system embodying modern design. Blum met this need by adapting known custom designs to a prefabricated railing system. Blum's product enabled architects to specify the number and location of posts and the number and spacing of rails to create designs compatible with the architecture of many modern buildings. Blum's contribution to the art was not his design; this was obvious. It was his railing system which was unique. But Blum's railing system is not the proper subject of a design patent. The statutory grant of a design patent is for appearance and not for a method of manufacture or assemblage function, or utility.

. . .

[Ed. note. The Court also held that the mechanical patent was invalid because it also was obvious from the prior art.]

[Ed. note. Footnotes omitted.]

The judgment of the district court is reversed, and this case is remanded for entry of final judgment in favor of the defendants.

SECTION 40.09 TRADE SECRETS

(A) DEFINITION

The Restatement of Torts has defined a trade secret as:

> . . . any formula, pattern, device, or compilation of information which is used in one's business, and which gives him an opportunity to obtain an advantage over competitors who do not know or use it. It may be a formula for a chemical compound, a process of manufacturing, treating or preserving materials, a pattern for a machine or other device . . . A trade secret is a process or device for continuous use in the operation of the business. Generally it relates to the production of goods, as, for example, a machine or formula for the production of an article.
>
> Restatement, Torts, Sec. 757 comment b.

In order for information to be protectible as a trade secret, it must be kept generally secret and not be generally known. The Restatement continues:

> The subject matter of a trade secret must be secret. Matters of public knowledge or of general knowledge in an industry cannot be appropriated by one as his secret. Matters which are completely disclosed by the goods which one markets cannot be his secret. Substantially, a trade secret is known only in the particular business in which it is used. It is not requisite that only the proprietor of the business know it. He may, without losing his protection, communicate it to employees involved in its use. He may likewise communicate it to others pledged to secrecy.

The Restatement sets forth these factors which are considered in determining whether particular information is a trade secret:

(1.) the extent to which the information is known outside of his business;

(2.) the extent to which it is known by employees and others involved in his business;

(3.) the extent of measures taken by him to guard the secrecy of the information;

(4.) the value of the information to him and his competitors;

(5.) the amount of effort or money expended by him in developing the information;

(6.) the ease or difficulty of which the information could be properly acquired or duplicated by others.

(B) CONTEXT OF TRADE SECRET LITIGATION

Trade secret litigation can arise when an employee leaves his employer, either to go into business for himself or to work for a new, and often competing, employer. If the employee has commercial or technical information, the prior employer may seek a court decree ordering the former employee not to disclose any trade secrets, "belonging" to the prior employer and a decree ordering the new employer not to use the secret information. Such a court order can be justified by a confidential relationship between the prior employer and the former employee, or the breach of an employment contract between the prior employer and the former employee.

Trade secret litigation can result when the proprietor of a trade secret learns that someone to whom he has disclosed his trade secret on a basis of confidentiality intends to make, or has made, an unauthorized use of the information. For example, the developer of a new product may give technical information relating to the product to the contractor building the plant in which the product is to be manufactured, or to the manufacturer who is to build the machinery needed to make the product. Trade secret litigation may result if the person to whom the disclosure is made intends to, or has made, unauthorized use of the information. Similarly, a confidential disclosure of the information may be made to a manufacturer by an inventor who desires to interest the manufacturer in a process or product developed by the inventor. The unauthorized use of such a "pre-contract" disclosure can lead to trade secret litigation.

Finally, developers of technology sometimes try to recover research costs by licensing others to use the data. In order to protect the secrecy of the technology and to enable them to sell the data to others, they usually obtain a promise from the licensee not to disclose the data to anyone else. Breach, or a threatened breach, of such a non-disclosure promise may cause the proprietor of the trade secret to seek a court decree forbidding any unauthorized use or disclosure.

(C) CONTRAST TO PATENTS: DISCLOSURE v. SECRECY

It may be useful to contrast the legal protection accorded trade secrets with the legal protection accorded patents. First, patent law requires public disclosure of the process, design, or product which is the subject of a patent. In exchange for this public disclosure, the patent holder obtains a seventeen year monopoly. Trade secret protection, on the other hand, requires that the data asserted to be a trade secret be kept relatively private and non-public.

A patent requires that the invention be novel, unique, useful and not obvious from the prior art. The trade secret need not meet these formidable requirements. While the courts are not unanimous on the point, it seems clear that the person who asserts ownership of a trade secret must show that he has made some advance on what is generally known. If the information is generally known, or generally available, then the information is not a trade secret.

Roughly, trade secret protection has the same relationship to patent protection that common law copyright has to statutory copyright. Both the doctrine of common law copyright and the doctrine of trade secrets are predicated on extending legal protection to creative people by giving them the right to determine when, how, and if the fruits of their intellectual labor should be made generally available. Patent and statutory copyright are predicated upon disclosure. Finally, trade secret protection is accorded by state law, and suffers from the same lack of uniformity as common law copyright. On the other hand, patent law is governed by federal law, resulting in general uniformity throughout the United States.

(D) ADJUSTING COMPETING SOCIAL VALUES

The doctrine of trade secrets, like many other legal doctrines, must consider and adjust various desirable, yet often antithetical, objectives. This can be shown by examining these objectives from the points of view of the various persons affected.

Those who seek trade secret protection, primarily inventors and research-oriented organizations, want to be rewarded economically for their creativity. Restricting others from using the information and technology they have developed can make their information more valuable. Without adequate economic incentives, perhaps scientific and industrial progress would be impeded. Also, protection of trade secrets can discourage industrial espionage and corruption.

Trade secret protection restrains the freedom of choice and action for research employees. It can immobilize a creative employee, and preclude him from making the best economic use of his talent. In addition, failure by his employer to consider or develop his research ideas can destroy his creativity. Many space age industries developed when creative people banded together to start new companies. Had they been tied to an older established company unwilling to engage in experimental research, many of these industries might not have developed, or might have taken considerably longer to do so.

Over-zealous protection of trade secrets can hamper commercial, scientific, and industrial progress. To a large part, such progress is made possible by the free dissemination of technical and scientific information. Dissemination of such information can avoid costly duplication of research efforts.

Over-protection of trade secrets can also have an anti-competitive effect. Protection of trade secrets can give the developer a virtual monopoly which can hinder the development of competitive products and can result in higher prices to consumers.

Trade secret law has had to consider and adjust all these competing objectives. The task has not been easy.

(E) AVAILABILITY OF LEGAL PROTECTION

Duty Not to Disclose or Use: Confidential Relationship and Contract:

The circumstances surrounding the disclosure, and the nature of the information disclosed, are relevant in determining whether there is a duty not to use or disclose the information. If the disclosure is accompanied by an express promise not to use or disclose, there is a general duty not to disclose. It may still be necessary to interpret the agreement to determine what cannot be disclosed, to whom disclosure is prohibited and the duration of the restraint.

For example, suppose there is a licensing agreement by which the licensor permits the licensee to use technological data disclosed by the licensor to the licensee. Does the restraint on disclosure include information which the licensee knew before the disclosure? Does it include information developed by the licensee from the disclosed information? Does the restraint include parts of the technological data disclosed which are known at the time of disclosure or become generally known? Can disclosure be made to an affiliated or successor company? Is there a continuing obligation for either or both parties to communicate new technology? These questions should be and usually are covered in the licensing agreement. If not, courts must interpret the agreement and, if necessary, imply terms.

However, in some circumstances there is no express provision prohibiting unauthorized use or disclosure. The method by which the information is acquired will often determine whether the disclosure is made in confidence and whether the person to whom it is disclosed obligates himself not to disclose it to others. This is similar to the process by which the law implies certain promises between contracting parties which are not expressed in the written contract. The communication may be part of a contractual arrangement. For example, the possessor of the information may communicate it to a consulting engineer who has been retained to advise the possessor on the type of machinery to be used in the process. If there is a written contract, the possessor will usually require a promise by the consulting engineer not to divulge certain specified information. Even without such an express promise not to disclose, the law would probably imply such a promise, based upon surrounding facts and circumstances. The same is true if the disclosure is made to the manufacturer of the machine or to a building contractor.

However, there are circumstances where there is no contractual relationship between the possessor of the information and the person to whom it is disclosed. For example, an inventor may disclose information to a manufacturer in order to interest the manufacturer in buying the information. It is possible for the inventor to obtain a promise from the manufacturer not to disclose the information. However, even without such a promise, if it is apparent from the surrounding facts and circumstances that the disclosure is made in confidence, then any disclosure of the information by the manufacturer would be a breach of the confidence and would give certain remedies to the inventor.

Nature of Information

If the person to whom the information is disclosed, whether a contractor hired to build a plant, a manufacturer hired to build a machine, or a consulting engineer hired to furnish technical services, knows that the information is not generally known in the industry, this is likely to persuade a court that a confidential relationship was created, or that a non-disclosure promise should be implied.

The nature of the information will also determine the legal remedy for a breach of confidence or a breach of contract. Under American law, the normal remedy for a breach of contract is a judgment for money damages. Only if that remedy is inadequate will the law specifically order that a defendant do or not do something. This is of crucial importance in trade secret cases. Typically, if the information is truly valuable, and not generally known, the most important remedy is the court decree ordering that the person who has the information not disclose it to anyone else. Violation of such an order is punishable by a fine, or even imprisonment, under the contempt powers of the court. Also, such a decree puts the plaintiff in a good position to demand a substantial royalty or settlement price if the defendant needs to use the trade secret information.

To obtain such an extraordinary remedy, the plaintiff must show that there would be irreparable injury without such a court order, and, as mentioned, that a judgment for money damages would be inadequate. In a trade secret case, the plaintiff tries to show that he would suffer irreparable economic harm if the information which he claims is a trade secret is broadly disseminated. He usually asserts that such broad disclosure will enable competitors to draw even with him despite his research expenditure to turn out a better product or develop a better process. He will also claim that it is difficult, if not impossible, to establish the actual damages he will suffer by general dissemination of the information he calls a trade secret.

If the court concludes that the information is a trade secret, it is likely that it will give injunctive relief.

The principal defense asserted by defendants in trade secret cases is that the information was not secret. Often they point to the existing literature in a given scientific or technical area, with a view towards showing that a person diligently searching for this information could put it together and arrive at the process independently. Courts have not been particularly receptive to this defense. Usually the defendant has not gone through the literature to ferret out the secret himself. He obtained the information from an employee of the trade secret proprietor, paid for its disclosure by virtue of a licensing agreement, or received it through a confidential, limited disclosure. While the defense has occasionally worked, on the whole it has not been successful. Part of the difficulty in arguing for this defense is that sometimes information and data is available, but not in a collected, organized, convenient and usable form. These factors are the principal advantages of the trade secret. Sometimes the data is collected and organized in readily accessible form but most people in the industry are unaware of this fact, or unable to locate the material easily.

Employee Cases: The Goodrich case

There are special aspects to the cases where the information has been learned or developed by an employee, and that employee goes into business himself, joins in a venture with others, or is hired by an existing or potential competitor of the prior employer. In addition to the use of the confidentiality theory, the former employer often points to an employment contract under which the employee agreed not to disclose the information after he leaves the employment. Sometimes the limitation on disclosure far exceeds what is reasonable. Often, the employee has little bargaining power in deciding whether to sign such an agreement. Some courts have recognized the adhesive (non-bargain) nature of such agreements, and have refused to give these agreements literal effect. However, the employer who has an agreement by the employee not to divulge information is in a somewhat better position if he seeks to obtain a court decree ordering the employee not to disclose particular information.

In addition to recognizing the adhesive nature of most employment contracts, some courts feel that agreements under which an employee cannot practice his trade or profession, or use the information which is his principal means of bettering himself, are unduly oppressive to employees. Such courts are not likely to be sympathetic to claims for trade secret protection. On the other hand, other courts manifest great concern with immorality and disloyalty on the part of employees, and look upon employee attempts to cash in on information of this type as morally indefensible. These courts are likely to deal harshly with employees in trade secret cases.

At this point an employee trade secret case will be reproduced.

B. F. GOODRICH CO. v. WOHLGEMUTH

Court of Appeals of Ohio, Summit County, 1963.
117 Ohio App. 493, 192 N.E.2d 99.

DOYLE, JUDGE. . . .

The B. F. Goodrich Company, appellant, seeks a permanent injunction against Donald W. Wohlgemuth, a former employee, from doing any of the following things:

"a. From performing any work for any corporation, business employer or party other than plaintiff, relating to the design, manufacture and/or sale of high-altitude pressure suits, space suits and/or similar protective garments, hereinafter called 'products,' and

"b. Disclosing to any person or party other than authorized employees of plaintiff [Goodrich], any information or data relating to the design, manufacture and/or sale of such products, and

"c. Consulting or conferring with any person or party other than authorized employees of plaintiff with reference to trade secrets, experimental research or development work of plaintiff, secret processes, techniques, data and information used or developed by plaintiff, future plans of plaintiff, data concerning materials used or rejected by plaintiff, sources of supply for materials insofar as the foregoing pertain to the design, development, manufacture and/or sale of such products, and

"d. Contacting, either directly or indirectly, any present or future employee of plaintiff engaged or experienced in the design, development, manufacture and/or sale of such products for the purpose of obtaining information from him or her related to the design, development, manufacture and/or sale of such products, or endeavoring, either directly or indirectly, attempting to induce or encourage any of plaintiff's said employees to leave the employment of plaintiff."

It appears from the record that Donald W. Wohlgemuth graduated from the University of Michigan in the year of 1954 as a bachelor of science in chemistry; soon thereafter he obtained employment with The B. F. Goodrich Company; following a short period of service in the United States army, he returned to the Goodrich Company in the year 1956, and was assigned to work in the pressure-space suit department; as his technical knowledge increased, he was appointed successively in this highly specialized department to the positions of materials engineer, product engineer, sales engineer, technical manager, and finally manager of the department.

In November, 1962, Wohlgemuth was offered a position of employment by the International Latex Corporation, of Dover, Delaware, which corporation operates in the pressure-space equipment field, and is a competitor in this field of operation with The B. F. Goodrich Company; the offer of employment by Latex to Wohlgemuth resulted in his resignation from Goodrich and his employment soon thereafter by Latex.

The B. F. Goodrich Company, as the record shows, has been in the high-altitude, full-pressure space suit business since the year 1934, and over the years it has acquired, through experiment and development of processes, a high degree of scientific knowledge and advanced technology required in the research, design, construction, and testing, of space suits. It may be concluded from the evidence, as stated by appellant, that "Each phase of this business must be meticulously accomplished, because a failure of a minute part of the finished product would probably result in the loss of the life of the user. In the production of the final product—a suit to protect man in space—there are involved countless secrets which one must either create or acquire from someone who has already done so."

The International Latex Corporation (present employer of the litigant, Wohlgemuth), is a manufacturing company with about 6,000 employees, which first entered the pressure-space equipment field in the year 1948, or approximately fourteen years after the entry of Goodrich. It first developed a pressure breathing mask, and later a full-pressure helmet. In the spring of the year 1962, the National Aeronautics and Space Administration awarded a contract known as the Apollo (man-on-the-moon contract), for the development of a space vehicle. (Project Apollo, in general terms, is "the first space project of the United States aimed at putting a man on the surface of the moon and bringing him back.") This contract was awarded to Hamilton Standard Division of the United Aircraft Corporation, with International Latex Corporation as subcontractor to develop the space suit.

Neither time nor space permits a discussion of the present development of the space suit, nor an analysis of the approximately 1600 parts from which it is created. Suffice it to say that Goodrich has produced, up to the present time, more than 2300 full-pressure space suits. Let it also be noted that each day, through research and development, the acquiring of advanced know-how and techniques, with attendant progressive changes in plans, costs and other aspects of information, the area of operation for the development of a space suit safe and suitable for future space travel is rapidly expanding and reaching new and more advanced scientific levels.

There is no doubt that Wohlgemuth was one of a few top executives and developers in this field of operation with the Goodrich Company, and that he had, and has, full knowledge of many of the secrets, and confidential facts which have come into existence through not only his own work, but also that of his fellow scientists and engineers with whom he has been closely associated. In fact, he stated that he was (1) technically responsible "for complete engineering of pressure suits and ancillary equipment, both the development and production phases"; (2) "responsible for the co-ordination between development engineering and The B. F. Goodrich's research center's effort in pressure suit research design and development"; (3) responsible for keeping himself and subordinates abreast of the latest advancements and "state of the art in the space suit field"; (4) responsible for the direction of proposal writing aimed toward further space suit development.

It further appears that Wohlgemuth, while employed by Goodrich, was in technical charge of practically all research in space suits, and as a result had detailed knowledge of the scientific and engineering principles involved in the production of space suits for use in space flight. The evidence also shows that he was required to, in the course of his employment with Goodrich, "co-ordinate the activities of the research center and the development engineering group in the space-suit field"; "approve or veto new designs and direct changes in designs"; "approve or direct changes to new manufacturing specifications and revisions, standard operating procedures, suggestions and new simplifications"; "review and direct technical action on customer specifications, requests to quote, purchase order inquiries, contracts and contract modifications"; "direct compounding operations on pressure suit items"; "check out new materials and designs"; and, "check out changes in product engineering policies."

. . .

Throughout the voluminous record of testimony can be found evidence establishing Goodrich trade secrets used in the manufacture of space suits presently in use, and trade secrets resulting from research and process development for use in the later manufacture of equipment, to make possible the continuance of human life in future space travel, as for instance in the present Apollo project.

Evidence further establishes the fact that Goodrich's former employee, Wohlgemuth, is in possession of many of these secrets; in fact, he was a part of the various Goodrich teams of highly-skilled men, which, through research and development, brought them into existence. The evidence further establishes the conclusion of fact of the Court of Common Pleas (which court, nevertheless, denied the injunction) that:

> "There isn't any doubt that the Latex Company [in hiring Wohlgemuth] was attempting to gain his valuable experience in this particular specialized field for the reason that they had this so-called 'Apollo' contract with the government, and there isn't any doubt that if he is permitted to work in the space suit division of the Latex Company he could not only give the Latex Company valuable experience and skill in this specialized field, which he has a right to do, but he would have an opportunity to disclose confidential information of The B. F. Goodrich Company."

There is testimony in the record indicating the mental attitude of Wohlgemuth at the time of the severance of his Goodrich employment. When objection was made, by a member of the Goodrich staff, to his accepting employment with a competitor in the highly-specialized field of space equipment, he said that "he would like to state his side" of the case.

He explained that he had been contacted "by an employment agency regarding this new job," and that he subsequently visited International Latex, where he was then offered an "increase in salary and a better position." It was then said to Wohlgemuth that in leaving Goodrich "he was taking with him a body of information which did not belong to him or to any individual, but did belong to the company, and that there was a matter of company loyalty and ethics involved." Wohlgemuth replied that "loyalty and ethics had their price;

insofar as he was concerned, International Latex was paying the price."

In further conversation, Wohlgemuth said that Latex knew of him because of his pressure-suit work, and when he was asked if he felt that he "could go into this position with a competitor and not use information which was proprietary to Goodrich," he replied that: "Once he was a member of the Latex Team, he would expect to use all of the knowledge that he had to their benefit."

. . .

We adopt, for the purposes of this case, the elements of trade secrets as they are set forth in 4 Restatement of the Law of Torts, Sec. 757b:

> "A trade secret may consist of any formula, pattern, device or compilation of information which is used in one's business, and which gives him an opportunity to obtain an advantage over competitors who do not know or use it. It may be a formula for chemical compound, a process of manufacturing, treating or preserving materials, a pattern for a machine or other device, or a list of customers. * * * A trade secret is a process or device for continuous use in the operation of the business. Generally it relates to the production of goods, as, for example, a machine or formula for the production of an article. * * *"

. . .

We have no doubt from the testimony of many witnesses, and the exhibits, that Goodrich possessed a number of trade secrets in the space-suit area which resulted from a multitude of experiments and expensive research, and that it had put into practice close security measures for maintaining the secrecy of many of the processes and scientific knowledge employed in space-suit manufacture and its future development.

The subject matter of a trade secret must be secret, and matters of public knowledge or of general knowledge in an industry cannot be classified as trade secrets; however, the fact that a number of engineers, scientists and technicians employed by a corporation for research and development in an area pertinent to the manufacture of an article, such as a space suit, are possessed of knowledge of the secret processes and devices discovered and created by their joint or individual efforts, does not make their knowledge general or public knowledge; and the processes and devices, if they are in fact trade secrets, remain trade secrets of their employer.

We find from the evidence that Wohlgemuth is possessed of knowledge of Goodrich trade secrets, and that any revelation of them to a Goodrich competitor is in equity a breach of faith and reprehensible to a court of equity.

There is no evidence before this court that Goodrich trade secrets have been revealed by Wohlgemuth; however, the circumstances surrounding his employment by Latex, and his own attitude as revealed by statements to fellow Goodrich employees, are sufficient to satisfy this court that a substantial threat of disclosure exists. We have no doubt that an injunction may issue in a court of equity to prevent a future wrong although no right has yet been violated.

In cases of this character the law does not require an agreement between an employer and employee restricting the employee from securing employment with a competitor before an injunction may issue.

It is a rule in equity jurisprudence that, if an employee gains knowledge of his employer's trade secrets as a result of the confidential relationship existing between employer and employee, and, in violation of the confidence, discloses such secrets to competitors after the termination of his employment, such abuse of confidence may be enjoined. The basis for equitable intervention is the employee's wrongful conduct in violating the confidence. Equitable intervention is sanctioned when it appears, as it does in the instant case, that there exists a present real threat of disclosure, even without actual disclosure.

While we could base the decision in this case upon the general rules of equity stated above, there is an additional ground for injunctive relief. When Wohlgemuth re-entered his employment with Goodrich, following his army service, he entered into a contract with his employer in which he promised "6. To keep confidential all information, records and documents of the Company of which I may have knowledge because of my employment with the Company, and, except as required by my employment, not to remove from the property of the Company any record or other document relating to any business of the Company, or make copies thereof; all such records and documents whether made by me or by others being recognized as the property of the Company and not to be used for my own or another's benefit or communicated to another, either before or after termination of my employment with the Company, without the written consent of the Company."

This written contract expressly binds the employee not to breach the trust and duty accepted by him—that is, not to misuse special confidential knowledge of trade secrets secured by him while the contractual relationship of employment existed. Injunction may be employed to prevent such abuse.

We have no doubt that Wohlgemuth had the right to take employment in a competitive business, and to use his knowledge (other than trade secrets) and experience, for the benefit of his new employer, but a public policy demands commercial morality, and courts of equity are empowered to enforce it by enjoining an improper disclosure of trade secrets known to Wohlgemuth by virtue of his employment. Under the American doctrine of free enterprise, Goodrich is entitled to this protection.

In conclusion, we find by clear and convincing evidence that Goodrich's former employee is possessed of Goodrich's trade secrets made known to him by virtue of his employment with Goodrich; that a disclosure of trade secrets to a competitive company is seriously threatened; and that, unless a restraining order is issued, Goodrich may suffer irreparable injury. As a consequence of this finding, we direct the issuance of an injunction not inconsistent with this opinion.

Injunction granted.

(The court used the "American doctrine of free enterprise" to protect Goodrich. Yet the holding of the case may have the effect of limiting Wohlgemuth's opportunity of bettering his employment status, another "American Doctrine".)

The technical employee whose knowledge and skill is largely limited to one narrow area will find it very difficult to find another job unless he can use the information he has learned while developing his skill. While the court does state that he can work for a competitor, the injunction limits him from using information considered to be a trade secret of Goodrich. It would be most difficult for Wohlgemuth to draw a line between what information he is permitted to use and what information he has been ordered not to use. Under these circumstances, his employability in a narrowly specialized area will be sharply curtailed. This can mean that Goodrich is in the position to take advantage of him unless he is willing to start on a different type of career.

(F) SCOPE OF REMEDY

If the trade secret claimant can show an infringement, he is entitled to recover damages he has suffered, profits made by the infringer resulting from the infringement, and a court decree prohibiting him from using or divulging the information. The injunctive relief usually does not exceed the protection needed by the plaintiff. Some courts have made the injunction last only for a period of time commensurate with the advantage gained through the technological information improperly acquired or used. If the defendant could have ascertained the information within a designated period, the court decree may require that he not use the information for that period of time. Also, some courts hold that unless the defendant has made the information public himself, the court order for non-disclosure will apply only until the information is generally known. Other courts take a more punitive attitude, and will order that the trade secret not be used even if it becomes generally known. Generally, the more reprehensible the conduct by the defendant, the broader the injunction.

(G) DURATION OF PROTECTION

Like a common law copyright, the trade secret is protectible as long as it is kept relatively secret. This unlimited time protection has caused some to advocate protecting trade secrets for a limited period of time by according a patent-like monopoly to the developer of a trade secret.

Some trade secrets are patentable. Unlimited duration of protection for a trade secret can frustrate the 17-year patent monopoly policy. To the extent that states, through protection of trade secrets, frustrate patent law, it is likely that such trade secret protection will be unconstitutional. In Sears, Roebuck & Co. v. Stiffel, 376 U.S. 225 (1964), the United States Supreme Court held that Illinois could not preclude copying a pole lamp where the pole lamp was unpatentable. While there is some doubt as to the effect this decision will have on trade secrets (the case involved copying and not a trade secret), the case may lead to a narrowing of trade secret protection.

(H) ADVICE TO DESIGN PROFESSIONALS

Design professionals who invent processes, designs, or products should, wherever possible, use contracts to give them protection against the possibility that persons to whom they divulge the information may disclose the information to others, or use it themselves.

Design professionals who occupy managerial positions in companies where trade secrets are important should use all methods possible to keep the information secret. Only those who have an absolute need to use the information should be given access to it, and these persons should expressly agree, in writing, not to disclose the information. Management should also realize that employee loyalty is probably the best protection against the loss of trade secrets. Reasonable treatment of employees is likely to be a better method of preserving trade secrets than litigation.

Finally, design professionals who are technical employees, and who wish to take their technological information to start their own business, join in a business venture, or work for a competitor of their present employer, should realize that their departure under these circumstances may result in litigation, or at least the threat of litigation. Legal advice should be sought in order to examine the legality of any asserted restraints, and to determine the scope of risk involved to the employee if he chooses to leave his present employment.

REVIEW QUESTIONS

1. Which categories of copyrightable materials under the Copyright Act are most important to design professionals?

2. What is the advantage of copyrighting a model as a model or design for a work of art?

3. What is the extent of copyright protection given to technical drawings?

4. What are the principal differences between common law copyright and statutory copyright?

5. What is the most important step necessary to perfect a statutory copyright?

6. How does publication affect statutory and common law copyright protection?

7. What are the principal differences between patent protection and copyright protection?

8. How do remedies for infringement of common law copyright and statutory copyright differ?

9. In what ways is trade secret protection analogous to common law copyright?

10. What would be the major changes which would be made by the enactment of the Proposed Revised Copyright Law?

11. When is a disclosure confidential?

12. Why is it generally stated that the disclosure of ideas is unprotectable?

QUESTIONS FOR CLASS DISCUSSION

1. Do you believe the law should give copyright protection to structures? Explain.

2. When should common law copyright be lost?

3. What would be fair use of architectural or engineering drawings?

4. Should common law copyright protection to floor plans be denied when the floor plans are generally displayed to the public even though the defendant has actually copied drawings containing the floor plan?

5. Would it be better to require that trade secrets be disclosed in exchange for a monopoly for a designated period of years than the present trade secret protection accorded by law?

6. Should an employee be free to use any information he has acquired by working for an employer that has not been reduced to tangible form? Explain.

PROBLEMS

1. A drew a set of drawings and specifications for a ten-story office building. He made 20 copies of the documents at the request of his client. His client took 15 copies of this document and left them with 5 prospective lenders, 5 prospective prime contractors and 5 public officials who would have to approve the design before the issuance of the building permit.

In addition, A distributed 5 copies to a seminar conducted at an architectural school because the design incorporated novel features in design and materials.

The plans and specifications were neither marked in accordance with statutory copyright law nor gave any indication that the use was limited to the purpose for which the distribution had been made.

D, an architect operating in another city secured a copy of the plans and specifications from a member of the architectural seminar. He thought the design was attractive and he decided to use it to construct a more or less identical building in his city.

D made five copies of the documents and used them for his own purposes.

Does A have any legal rights against D? Give your reasons.

2. The P company conducted an advertising campaign in which it emphasized that many improvements on its product were suggested by housewives who used the product. X, a housewife who had used the product, wrote to the P company stating that the product would be better if it had a more efficient handle. She enclosed a rough drawing for what she considered to be an improvement in the handle.

The P company sent the drawing to its research department. The department, after making some changes, incorporated the suggested change. Prior to this being done, P company wrote a letter to X stating that they appreciated her interest in the product and it was because of suggestions like hers that P's products dominated the field.

When X saw that the change had been made in accordance with her suggestion, she wrote to the P company stating that they should pay her either the reasonable value of the design suggestion or one half of the additional profits which would be made because of the improved handle. Does X have a valid claim against the P company? If so, how would her claim be measured in terms of dollars?

APPENDIX A

AIA Document B131*

Standard Form of Agreement Between Owner and Architect

on a basis of a

PERCENTAGE OF CONSTRUCTION COST

AGREEMENT

made this day of in the year of Nineteen Hundred and

BETWEEN

the Owner, and

the Architect.

It is the intention of the Owner to

hereinafter referred to as the Project.

The Owner and the Architect agree as set forth below.

I. THE ARCHITECT shall provide professional services for the Project in accordance with the Terms and Conditions of this Agreement.

II. THE OWNER shall compensate the Architect, in accordance with the Terms and Conditions of this Agreement, as follows:

a. *FOR THE ARCHITECT'S BASIC SERVICES,* as described in Paragraph 1.1, a Basic Fee computed at the following percentages of the Construction Cost, as defined in Article 3, for portions of the Project to be awarded under

A Single Stipulated Sum Contract	per cent (%)
Separate Stipulated Sum Contracts	per cent (%)
A Single Cost Plus Fee Contract	per cent (%)
Separate Cost Plus Fee Contracts	per cent (%)

b. *FOR THE ARCHITECT'S ADDITIONAL SERVICES,* as described in Paragraph 1.3, a fee computed as follows:

Principals' time at the fixed rate of dollars ($) per hour. For the purposes of this Agreement, the Principals are:

Employees' time computed at a multiple of ( ) times the employees' Direct Personnel Expense as defined in Article 4.

Additional services of professional consultants engaged for the normal structural, mechanical and electrical engineering services at a multiple of ( ) times the amount billed to the Architect for such additional services.

c. *FOR THE ARCHITECT'S REIMBURSABLE EXPENSES,* amounts expended as defined in Article 5.

d. *THE TIMES AND FURTHER CONDITIONS OF PAYMENT* shall be as described in Article 6.

TERMS AND CONDITIONS OF AGREEMENT BETWEEN OWNER AND ARCHITECT

ARTICLE 1

ARCHITECT'S SERVICES

1.1 BASIC SERVICES

The Architect's Basic Services consist of the five phases described below and include normal structural, mechanical and electrical engineering services.

SCHEMATIC DESIGN PHASE

1.1.1 The Architect shall consult with the Owner to ascertain the requirements of the Project and shall confirm such requirements to the Owner.

1.1.2 The Architect shall prepare Schematic Design Studies consisting of drawings and other documents illustrating the scale and relationship of Project components for approval by the Owner.

1.1.3 The Architect shall submit to the Owner a Statement of Probable Construction Cost based on current area, volume or other unit costs.

DESIGN DEVELOPMENT PHASE

1.1.4 The Architect shall prepare from the approved Schematic Design Studies, for approval by the Owner, the Design Development Documents consisting of drawings and other documents to fix and describe the size and character of the entire Project as to structural, mechanical and electrical systems, materials and such other essentials as may be appropriate.

1.1.5 The Architect shall submit to the Owner a further Statement of Probable Construction Cost.

CONSTRUCTION DOCUMENTS PHASE

1.1.6 The Architect shall prepare from the approved Design Development Documents, for approval by the Owner, Working Drawings and Specifications setting forth in detail the requirements for the construction of the entire Project including the necessary bidding information, and shall assist in the preparation of bidding forms, the Conditions of the Contract, and the form of Agreement between the Owner and the Contractor.

1.1.7 The Architect shall advise the Owner of any adjustments to previous Statements of Probable Construction Cost indicated by changes in requirements or general market conditions.

1.1.8 The Architect shall assist the Owner in filing the required documents for the approval of governmental authorities having jurisdiction over the Project.

BIDDING OR NEGOTIATION PHASE

1.1.9 The Architect, following the Owner's approval of the Construction Documents and of the latest Statement of Probable Construction Cost, shall assist the Owner in obtaining bids or negotiated proposals, and in awarding and preparing construction contracts.

CONSTRUCTION PHASE—ADMINISTRATION OF THE CONSTRUCTION CONTRACT

1.1.10 The Construction Phase will commence with the award of the Construction Contract and will terminate when final payment is made by the Owner to the Contractor.

1.1.11 The Architect shall provide Administration of the Construction Contract as set forth in Articles 1 through 14 inclusive of the latest edition of AIA Document A201, General Conditions of the Contract for Construction, and the extent of his duties and responsibilities and the limitations of his authority as assigned thereunder shall not be modified without his written consent.

1.1.12 The Architect, as the representative of the Owner during the Construction Phase, shall advise and consult with the Owner and all of the Owner's instructions to the Contractor shall be issued through the Architect. The Architect shall have authority to act on behalf of the Owner to the extent provided in the General Conditions unless otherwise modified in writing.

1.1.13 The Architect shall at all times have access to the Work wherever it is in preparation or progress.

1.1.14 The Architect shall make periodic visits to the site to familiarize himself generally with the progress and quality of the Work and to determine in general if the Work is proceeding in accordance with the Contract Documents. On the basis of his on-site observations as an architect, he shall endeavor to guard the Owner against defects and deficiencies in the Work of the Contractor. The Architect shall not be required to make exhaustive or continuous on-site inspections to check the quality or quantity of the Work. The Architect shall not be responsible for construction means, methods, techniques, sequences or procedures, or for safety precautions and programs in connection with the Work, and he shall not be responsible for the Contractor's failure to carry out the Work in accordance with the Contract Documents.

1.1.15 Based on such observations at the site and on the Contractor's Applications for Payment, the Architect shall determine the amount owing to the Contractor and shall issue Certificates for Payment in such amounts. The issuance of a Certificate for Payment shall constitute a representation by the Architect to the Owner, based on the Architect's observations at the site as provided in Subparagraph 1.1.14 and on the data comprising the Application for Payment, that the Work has progressed to the point indicated; that to the best of the Architect's knowledge, information and belief, the quality of the Work is in accordance with the Contract Documents (subject to an evaluation of the Work as a functioning whole upon Substantial Completion, to the results of any subsequent tests required by the Contract Documents, to minor deviations from the Contract Documents correctable prior to completion, and to any specific qualifications stated in the Certificate for Payment); and that the Contractor is entitled to payment in the amount certified. By issuing a Certificate for Payment, the Architect shall not be deemed to represent that he has made any examination to ascertain how and for what purpose the Contractor has used the moneys paid on account of the Contract Sum.

1.1.16 The Architect shall be, in the first instance, the interpreter of the requirements of the Contract Documents and the impartial judge of the performance thereunder by both the Owner and Contractor. The Architect shall make decisions on all claims of the Owner or Contractor relating to the execution and progress of the Work and on all other matters or questions related thereto. The Architect's decisions in matters relating to artistic effect shall be final if consistent with the intent of the Contract Documents.

1.1.17 The Architect shall have authority to reject Work which does not conform to the Contract Documents. The Architect shall also have authority to require the Contractor to stop the Work whenever in his reasonable opinion it may be necessary for the proper performance of the Contract. The Architect shall not be liable to the Owner for the consequences of any decision made by him in good faith either to exercise or not to exercise his authority to stop the Work.

1.1.18 The Architect shall review and approve shop drawings, samples, and other submissions of the Contractor only for conformance with the design concept of the Project and for compliance with the information given in the Contract Documents.

1.1.19 The Architect shall prepare Change Orders.

1.1.20 The Architect shall conduct inspections to determine the Dates of Substantial Completion and Final Completion, shall receive written guarantees and related documents assembled by the Contractor, and shall issue a final Certificate for Payment.

1.1.21 The Architect shall not be responsible for the acts or omissions of the Contractor, or any Subcontractors, or any of the Contractor's or Subcontractors' agents or employees, or any other persons performing any of the Work.

1.2 PROJECT REPRESENTATION BEYOND BASIC SERVICES

1.2.1 If more extensive representation at the site than is described under Subparagraphs 1.1.10 through 1.1.21 inclusive is required, and if the Owner and Architect agree, the Architect shall provide one or more Full-time Project Representatives to assist the Architect.

1.2.2 Such Full-time Project Representatives shall be selected, employed and directed by the Architect, and the Architect shall be compensated therefor as mutually agreed between the Owner and the Architect as set forth in an exhibit appended to this Agreement.

1.2.3 The duties, responsibilities and limitations of authority of such Full-time Project Representatives shall be set forth in an exhibit appended to this Agreement.

1.2.4 Through the on-site observations by Full-time Project Representatives of the Work in progress, the Architect shall endeavor to provide further protection for the Owner against defects in the Work, but the furnishing of such project representation shall not make the Architect responsible for the Contractor's failure to perform the Work in accordance with the Contract Documents.

1.3 ADDITIONAL SERVICES

The following services are not covered in Paragraphs 1.1 or 1.2. If any of these Additional Services are authorized by the Owner, they shall be paid for by the Owner as hereinbefore provided.

1.3.1 Providing special analyses of the Owner's needs, and programming the requirements of the Project.

1.3.2 Providing financial feasibility or other special studies.

1.3.3 Providing planning surveys, site evaluations, or comparative studies of prospective sites.

1.3.4 Making measured drawings of existing construction when required for planning additions or alterations thereto.

1.3.5 Revising previously approved Drawings, Specifications or other documents to accomplish changes not initiated by the Architect.

1.3.6 Preparing Change Orders and supporting data where the change in the Basic Fee resulting from the adjusted Contract Sum is not commensurate with the Architect's services required.

1.3.7 Preparing documents for alternate bids requested by the Owner.

1.3.8 Providing Detailed Estimates of Construction Costs.

1.3.9 Providing consultation concerning replacement of any Work damaged by fire or other cause during construction, and furnishing professional services of the type set forth in Paragraph 1.1 as may be required in connection with the replacement of such Work.

1.3.10 Providing professional services made necessary by the default of the Contractor in the performance of the Construction Contract.

1.3.11 Providing Contract Administration and observation of construction after the Contract Time has been exceeded by more than twenty per cent through no fault of the Architect.

1.3.12 Furnishing the Owner a set of reproducible record prints of drawings showing significant changes made during the construction process, based on marked up prints, drawings and other data furnished by the Contractor to the Architect.

1.3.13 Providing services after final payment to the Contractor.

1.3.14 Providing interior design and other services required for or in connection with the selection of furniture and furnishings.

1.3.15 Providing services as an expert witness in connection with any public hearing, arbitration proceeding, or the proceedings of a court of record.

1.3.16 Providing services for planning tenant or rental spaces.

ARTICLE 2

THE OWNER'S RESPONSIBILITIES

2.1 The Owner shall provide full information regarding his requirements for the Project.

2.2 The Owner shall designate, when necessary, a representative authorized to act in his behalf with respect to the Project. The Owner or his representative shall examine documents submitted by the Architect and shall render decisions pertaining thereto promptly, to avoid unreasonable delay in the progress of the Architect's work.

2.3 The Owner shall furnish a certified land survey of the site giving, as applicable, grades and lines of streets, alleys pavements and adjoining property; rights-of-way, restrictions, easements, encroachments, zoning, deed restrictions, boundaries and contours of the site; locations, dimensions and complete data pertaining to existing buildings, other improvements and trees; and full information concerning available service and utility lines both public and private.

2.4 The Owner shall furnish the services of a soils engineer, when such services are deemed necessary by the Architect, including reports, test borings, test pits, soil bearing values and other necessary operations for determining subsoil conditions.

2.5 The Owner shall furnish structural, mechanical, chemical and other laboratory tests, inspections and reports as required by law or the Contract Documents.

2.6 The Owner shall furnish such legal, accounting and insurance counselling services as may be necessary for the Project, and such auditing services as he may require to ascertain how or for what purposes the Contractor has used the moneys paid to him under the Construction Contract.

2.7 The services, information, surveys and reports required by Paragraphs 2.3 through 2.6 inclusive shall be furnished at the Owner's expense, and the Architect shall be entitled to rely upon the accuracy thereof.

2.8 If the Owner observes or otherwise becomes aware of any fault or defect in the Project or non-conformance with the Contract Documents, he shall give prompt written notice thereof to the Architect.

2.9 The Owner shall furnish information required of him as expeditiously as necessary for the orderly progress of the Work.

ARTICLE 3

CONSTRUCTION COST

3.1 Construction Cost to be used as a basis for determining the Architect's Fee for all Work designed or specified by the Architect, including labor, materials, equipment and furnishings, shall be determined as follows, with precedence in the order listed:

3.1.1 For completed construction, the total cost of all such Work;

3.1.2 For work not constructed, the lowest bona fide bid received from a qualified bidder for any or all of such work; or

3.1.3 For work for which bids are not received, (1) the latest Detailed Cost Estimate, or (2) the Architect's latest Statement of Probable Construction Cost.

3.2 Construction Cost does not include the fees of the Architect and consultants, the cost of the land, rights-of-way, or other costs which are the responsibility of the Owner as provided in Paragraphs 2.3 through 2.6 inclusive.

3.3 Labor furnished by the Owner for the Project shall be included in the Construction Cost at current market rates. Materials and equipment furnished by the Owner shall be included at current market prices, except that used materials and equipment shall be included as if purchased new for the Project.

3.4 Statements of Probable Construction Cost and Detailed Cost Estimates prepared by the Architect represent his best judgment as a design professional familiar with the construction industry. It is recognized, however, that neither the Architect nor the Owner has any control over the cost of labor, materials or equipment, over the contractors' methods of determining bid prices, or over competitive bidding or market conditions. Accordingly, the Architect cannot and does not guarantee that bids will not vary from any Statement of Probable Construction Cost or other cost estimate prepared by him.

3.5 When a fixed limit of Construction Cost is established as a condition of this Agreement, it shall include a bidding contingency of ten per cent unless another amount is agreed upon in writing. When such a fixed limit is established, the Architect shall be permitted to determine what materials, equipment, component systems and types of construction are to be included in the Contract Documents, and to make reasonable adjustments in the scope of the Project to bring it within the fixed limit. The Architect may also include in the Contract Documents alternate bids to adjust the Construction Cost to the fixed limit.

3.5.1 If the lowest bona fide bid, the Detailed Cost Estimate or the Statement of Probable Construction Cost exceeds such fixed limit of Construction Cost (including the bidding contingency) established as a condition of this Agreement, the Owner shall (1) give written approval of an increase in such fixed limit, (2) authorize rebidding the Project within a reasonable time, or (3) cooperate in revising the Project scope and quality as required to reduce the Probable Construction Cost. In the case of (3) the Architect, without additional charge, shall modify the Drawings and Specifications as necessary to bring the Construction Cost within the fixed limit. The providing of this service shall be the limit of the Architect's responsibility in this regard, and having done so, the Architect shall be entitled to his fees in accordance with this Agreement.

ARTICLE 4

DIRECT PERSONNEL EXPENSE

4.1 Direct Personnel Expense of employees engaged on the Project by the Architect includes architects, engineers, designers, job captains, draftsmen, specification writers and typists, in consultation, research and design, in producing Drawings, Specifications and other documents pertaining to the Project, and in services during construction at the site.

4.2 Direct Personnel Expense includes cost of salaries and of mandatory and customary benefits such as statutory employee benefits, insurance, sick leave, holidays and vacations, pensions and similar benefits.

ARTICLE 5

REIMBURSABLE EXPENSES

5.1 Reimbursable Expenses are in addition to the Fees for Basic and Additional Services and include actual expenditures made by the Architect, his employees, or his consultants in the interest of the Project for the following incidental expenses listed in the following Subparagraphs:

5.1.1 Expense of transportation and living when traveling in connection with the Project and for long distance calls and telegrams.

5.1.2 Expense of reproductions, postage and handling of Drawings and Specifications, excluding copies for Architect's office use and duplicate sets at each phase for the Owner's review and approval; and fees paid for securing approval of authorities having jurisdiction over the Project.

5.1.3 If authorized in advance by the Owner, the expense of overtime work requiring higher than regular rates; perspectives or models for the Owner's use; and fees of special consultants for other than the normal structural, mechanical and electrical engineering services.

ARTICLE 6

PAYMENTS TO THE ARCHITECT

6.1 Payments on account of the Architect's Basic Services shall be made as follows:

6.1.1 An initial payment of five per cent of the Basic Fee calculated upon an agreed estimated cost of the Project, payable upon execution of this Agreement, is the minimum payment under this Agreement.

6.1.2 Subsequent payments shall be made monthly in proportion to services performed to increase the compensation for Basic Services to the following percentages of the Basic Fee at the completion of each phase of the Work:

Schematic Design Phase	15%
Design Development Phase	35%
Construction Documents Phase	75%
Bidding or Negotiation Phase	80%
Construction Phase	100%

6.2 Payments for Additional Services of the Architect as defined in Paragraph 1.3, and for Reimbursable Expenses as defined in Article 5, shall be made monthly upon presentation of the Architect's statement of services rendered.

6.3 No deductions shall be made from the Architect's compensation on account of penalty, liquidated damages, or other sums withheld from payments to contractors.

6.4 If the Project is suspended for more than three months or abandoned in whole or in part, the Architect shall be paid his compensation for services performed prior to receipt of written notice from the Owner of such suspension or abandonment, together with Reimbursable Expenses then due and all terminal expenses resulting from such suspension or abandonment.

ARTICLE 7

ARCHITECT'S ACCOUNTING RECORDS

Records of the Architect's Direct Personnel, Consultant and Reimbursable Expenses pertaining to the Project, and records of accounts between the Owner and the Contractor, shall be kept on a generally recognized accounting basis and shall be available to the Owner or his authorized representative at mutually convenient times.

ARTICLE 8

TERMINATION OF AGREEMENT

This Agreement may be terminated by either party upon seven days' written notice should the other party fail substantially to perform in accordance with its terms through no fault of the other. In the event of termination due to the fault of others than the Architect, the Architect shall be paid his compensation for services performed to termination date, including Reimbursable Expenses then due and all terminal expenses.

ARTICLE 9

OWNERSHIP OF DOCUMENTS

Drawings and Specifications as instruments of service are and shall remain the property of the Architect whether the Project for which they are made is executed or not. They are not to be used by the Owner on other projects or extensions to this Project except by agreement in writing and with appropriate compensation to the Architect.

ARTICLE 10

SUCCESSORS AND ASSIGNS

The Owner and the Architect each binds himself, his partners, successors, assigns and legal representatives to the other party to this Agreement and to the partners, successors, assigns and legal representatives of such other party with respect to all covenants of this Agreement. Neither the Owner nor the Architect shall assign, sublet or transfer his interest in this Agreement without the written consent of the other.

ARTICLE 11

ARBITRATION

11.1 All claims, disputes and other matters in question arising out of, or relating to, this Agreement or the breach thereof shall be decided by arbitration in accordance with the Construction Industry Arbitration Rules of the American Arbitration Association then obtaining. This agreement so to arbitrate shall be specifically enforceable under the prevailing arbitration law.

11.2 Notice of the demand for arbitration shall be filed in writing with the other party to this Agreement and with the American Arbitration Association. The demand shall be made within a reasonable time after the claim, dispute or other matter in question has arisen. In no event shall the demand for arbitration be made after institution of legal or equitable proceedings based on such claim, dispute or other matter in question would be barred by the applicable statute of limitations.

11.3 The award rendered by the arbitrators shall be final, and judgment may be entered upon it in any court having jurisdiction thereof.

ARTICLE 12

EXTENT OF AGREEMENT

This Agreement represents the entire and integrated agreement between the Owner and the Architect and supersedes all prior negotiations, representations or agreements, either written or oral. This Agreement may be amended only by written instrument signed by both Owner and Architect.

ARTICLE 13

APPLICABLE LAW

Unless otherwise specified, this Agreement shall be governed by the law of the principal place of business of the Architect.

This Agreement executed the day and year first written above.

OWNER

ARCHITECT

Architect's Registration No.

[A111]

APPENDIX B

AIA Document C131*

Standard Form of Agreement Between the Architect and the Engineer

on a basis of a

PERCENTAGE OF CONSTRUCTION COST

AGREEMENT

made this day of in the year of Nineteen Hundred and

BETWEEN

the Architect, and

the Engineer.

The Architect has made an agreement dated with

The Owner, a copy of the Terms and Conditions and any other pertinent portions of which is attached, made a part hereof and marked Exhibit A, and is hereinafter referred to as the Prime Agreement and provides for furnishing professional services in connection with the Project described therein as follows:

The Architect and Engineer agree as set forth below.

* Reprinted with permission

I. THE ENGINEER shall provide the following professional services for the Architect, in accordance with the Terms and Conditions of this Agreement, which the Architect is required to provide for the Owner under the Prime Agreement:
(Describe services)

The Part of the Project for which the Engineer is to provide such services is hereinafter called This Part of the Project.

II. THE ARCHITECT shall compensate the Engineer, in accordance with the Terms and Conditions of this Agreement, as follows:

a. *FOR THE ENGINEER'S BASIC SERVICES,* as described in Paragraph 1.2, a Basic Fee of per cent (%) of the Construction Cost of the Project, or per cent (%) of the Construction Cost of This Part of the Project.

b. *FOR THE ENGINEER'S ADDITIONAL SERVICES* when authorized by the Architect, as described in Paragraph 1.4, a fee computed as follows:

Principals' time at the fixed rate of dollars ($) per hour. For the purposes of this Agreement, the Principals are:

Employees' time computed at a multiple of ( ) times the employees' Direct Personnel Expense as defined in Article 4.

c. *FOR THE ENGINEER'S REIMBURSABLE EXPENSES,* amounts expended as defined in Article 5 when authorized in advance by the Architect.

d. *THE TIMES AND FURTHER CONDITIONS OF PAYMENT* shall be as described in Article 6.

III. *THE ARCHITECT* shall be the Project Coordinator. The relationship of the Engineer to the Architect shall be that of an independent contractor.

TERMS AND CONDITIONS OF AGREEMENT BETWEEN ARCHITECT AND ENGINEER

ARTICLE 1

ENGINEER'S SERVICES

1.1 GENERAL

The Engineer shall collaborate with the Architect for This Part of the Project and shall be bound to perform the services undertaken hereunder for the Architect in the same manner and to the same extent that the Architect is bound by the Prime Agreement to perform such services for the Owner so that his duties and responsibilities with respect to This Part of the Project shall be co-extensive with those of the Architect to the Owner under the Prime Agreement. Except as set forth herein, the Engineer shall not have any duties or responsibilities for any other part of the Project. The Engineer will perform his work in character, sequence and timing so that it will be coordinated with that of the Architect and other consultants for the Project. The Engineer agrees to a mutual exchange of Drawings with the Architect and other consultants in accordance with a schedule provided by the Architect.

1.2 BASIC SERVICES

The Engineer's Basic Services consist of the five phases described below.

SCHEMATIC DESIGN PHASE

1.2.1 The Engineer shall consult with the Architect to ascertain the requirements of the Project and shall confirm such requirements to the Architect.

1.2.2 The Engineer shall make recommendations regarding basic systems, attend necessary conferences, prepare necessary analyses and be available for general consultation. When necessary the Engineer shall consult with public agencies and other organizations concerning utility services and requirements.

1.2.3 The Engineer shall prepare and submit to the Architect a Statement of the Probable Construction Cost of This Part of the Project based on current area, volume or other unit costs.

1.2.4 The Engineer shall recommend to the Architect the obtaining of such investigations, surveys, tests and analyses as may be necessary for the proper execution of the Engineer's work.

DESIGN DEVELOPMENT PHASE

1.2.5 The Engineer shall prepare from the approved Schematic Design Studies, for approval by the Architect, the Design Development Documents consisting of drawings and other documents to fix and describe This Part of the Project.

1.2.6 The Engineer shall submit to the Architect a further Statement of Probable Construction Cost of This Part of the Project.

CONSTRUCTION DOCUMENTS PHASE

1.2.7 The Engineer shall prepare from the approved Design Development Documents, for approval by the Architect, Working Drawings and Specifications setting forth in detail the requirements for the construction of This Part of the Project and shall deliver the original Drawings and Specifications to the Architect. The original Drawings and Specifications shall be in such form as the Architect may reasonably require.

1.2.8 The Engineer shall advise the Architect of any adjustments to previous Statements of Probable Construction Cost of This Part of the Project indicated by changes in requirements or general market conditions.

1.2.9 The Engineer shall assist the Architect in filing the required documents with respect to This Part of the Project for the approval of governmental authorities having jurisdiction over the Project.

BIDDING OR NEGOTIATION PHASE

1.2.10 If required by the Architect, the Engineer shall assist the Architect and the Owner in obtaining bids or negotiated proposals, and in awarding and preparing construction contracts.

CONSTRUCTION PHASE—ADMINISTRATION OF THE CONSTRUCTION CONTRACT

1.2.11 The Construction Phase will commence with the award of the Construction Contract and will terminate when final payment is made by the Owner to the Contractor.

1.2.12 The Engineer shall assist the Architect in the administration of the construction contract with respect to This Part of the Project.

1.2.13 The Engineer shall at all times have access to the Work of This Part of the Project wherever it is in preparation or progress.

1.2.14 The Engineer shall make periodic visits to the site to familiarize himself generally with the progress and quality of the Work for This Part of the Project to determine in general if such Work is proceeding in accordance with the Contract Documents. On the basis of his on-site observations as an engineer, he shall endeavor to guard the Owner and the Architect against defects and deficiencies in the Work of the Contractor. The Engineer shall not be required to make exhaustive or continuous on-site inspections to check the quality or quantity of the Work. The Engineer shall not be responsible for construction means, methods, techniques, sequences or procedures, or for safety precautions and programs, and he shall not be responsible for the Contractor's failure to carry out the Work for This Part of the Project in accordance with the Contract Documents.

1.2.15 Based on such observations at the site and on the Contractor's Applications for Payment, the Engineer shall assist the Architect in determining the amount owing to the Contractor for This Part of the Project. If requested, he shall certify such amounts to the Architect. A certification by the Engineer to the Architect of an amount owing to the Contractor shall constitute a representation by the Engineer to the Architect and through him to the Owner that, based on the Engineer's observations at the site as provided in Subparagraph 1.2.14 and the data comprising the Application for Payment, the Work for This Part of the Project has progressed to the point indicated; that to the best of his knowledge, information and belief, the quality of such Work is in accordance with the Contract Documents (subject to an evaluation of such Work as a functioning whole upon Substantial Completion, to the results of any subsequent tests called for in the Contract Documents, to minor deviations from the Contract Documents correctable prior to completion, and to any specific qualifications stated by the Engineer); and that the Contractor is entitled to payment in the amount certified.

1.2.16 The Engineer shall assist the Architect in making decisions on all claims of the Owner or Contractor relating to the execution and progress of the Work on This Part of the Project and on all other matters or questions related thereto. The Engineer shall not be liable for the results of any interpretation or decision rendered in good faith.

1.2.17 The Engineer shall assist the Architect in determining whether the Architect shall reject Work for This Part of the Project which does not conform to the Contract Documents. The Engineer shall also assist the Architect in determining whether to require the Contractor to stop the Work with respect to This Part of the Project whenever such action may be necessary for the proper performance of the Contract. The Engineer shall not be liable to the Owner or Architect for the consequences of any recommendation made by him to the Architect in good faith with reference to stopping the Work.

1.2.18 The Engineer shall check and approve shop drawings, samples and other submissions of the Contractor with respect to This Part of the Project only for conformance with the design concept and for compliance with the information given in the Contract Documents. All comments and approvals shall be submitted to the Architect.

1.2.19 The Engineer shall assist the Architect in preparing Change Orders for This Part of the Project.

1.2.20 The Engineer, shall assist the Architect in conducting inspections with respect to This Part of the Project to determine the Dates of Substantial Completion and Final Completion and in receiving written guarantees and related documents assembled by the Contractor with respect to This Part of the Project.

1.2.21 The Engineer shall not be responsible for the acts or omissions of the Contractor, or any Subcontractors, or any of the Contractor's or Subcontractors' agents or employees, or any other persons performing any of the Work.

1.3 PROJECT REPRESENTATION BEYOND BASIC SERVICES

1.3.1 If more extensive representation at the site than is described under Subparagraphs 1.2.11 through 1.2.21 inclusive is required for This Part of the Project and if the Architect and Engineer agree, the Engineer shall provide one or more Full-time Project Representatives to assist the Engineer.

1.3.2 Such Full-time Project Representatives shall be selected, employed and directed by the Engineer and the Engineer shall be compensated therefor as mutually agreed between the Architect and the Engineer.

1.3.3 The duties, responsibilities and limitations of authority of such Full-time Project Representatives shall be as set forth in an exhibit appended to this Agreement.

1.3.4 Through the on-site observations by Full-time Project Representatives of the Work in progress, the Engineer shall endeavor to provide further protection for the Owner against defects in the Work for This Part of the Project, but the furnishing of such project representation shall not make the Engineer responsible for the Contractor's failure to perform the Work in accordance with the Contract Documents.

1.4 ADDITIONAL SERVICES

The following services for This Part of the Project are not covered in Paragraphs 1.2 or 1.3. If any of these Additional Services are authorized by the Architect for This Part of the Project and if the Architect is additionally compensated therefor by the Owner, they shall be paid for by the Architect as hereinbefore provided.

1.4.1 Revising Drawings, Specifications or other documents previously approved by the Owner to accomplish changes not initiated by the Engineer.

1.4.2 Preparing supporting data for Change Orders where the change in the Basic Fee resulting from the adjusted Contract Sum is not commensurate with the Engineer's services required.

1.4.3 Preparing documents for alternate bids requested by the Owner.

1.4.4 Providing Detailed Estimates of Construction Costs.

1.4.5 Providing consultation concerning replacement of any Work damaged by fire or other cause during construction, and furnishing professional services of the type set forth in Paragraph 1.2 as may be required in connection with the replacement of such Work.

1.4.6 Providing professional services made necessary by the default of the Contractor in the performance of the Construction Contract.

1.4.7 Providing contract administration and observation of construction after the Contract Time has been exceeded by more than 20% through no fault of the Engineer.

1.4.8 Furnishing the Architect a set of reproducible record prints of drawings showing significant changes in This Part of the Work made during the construction process, based on marked up prints, drawings and other data furnished by the Contractor.

1.4.9 Providing services after final payment to the Contractor.

1.4.10 Providing services as an expert witness in connection with any public hearing, arbitration proceeding, or the proceedings of a court of record.

ARTICLE 2

THE ARCHITECT'S RESPONSIBILITIES

2.1 The Architect shall provide full information regarding the requirements for This Part of the Project.

2.2 The Architect shall designate, when necessary, a representative authorized to act in his behalf with respect to This Part of the Project. The Architect or his representative shall examine documents submitted by the Engineer and shall render decisions pertaining thereto promptly, to avoid unreasonable delay in the progress of the Engineer's work.

2.3 The Architect shall furnish to the Engineer a copy of the Owner's certified survey of the site.

2.4 The Architect shall request the Owner to furnish the services of a soils engineer, when such services are deemed necessary for This Part of the Project by the Engineer, including reports, test borings, test pits and other necessary operations for determining subsoil conditions.

2.5 The services, information, surveys and reports required by Paragraphs 2.3 and 2.4 shall be furnished at the Owner's expense, and the Engineer shall be entitled to rely upon the accuracy thereof.

2.6 If the Owner has given written notice to the Architect of any fault or defect with respect to This Part of the Project or non-conformance with the Contract Documents, the Architect shall give prompt written notice thereof to the Engineer.

ARTICLE 3

CONSTRUCTION COST

3.1 The Construction Cost of the Project or the Construction Cost of This Part of the Project to be used as a basis for determining the Engineer's Basic Fee for all Work designed or specified by the Engineer, including labor, materials, equipment and furnishings, shall be determined as follows, with precedence in the order listed:

3.1.1 For completed construction, the total cost of all such Work;

3.1.2 For work not constructed, the lowest bona fide bid received from a qualified bidder for any or all of such work; or

3.1.3 For work for which bids are not received, 1) the latest Detailed Cost Estimate, or 2) the Engineer's latest Statement of Probable Construction Cost.

3.2 Construction Cost does not include the fees of the Architect, the Engineer and other consultants, the cost of the land, rights-of-way, or other costs which are the responsibility of the Owner as provided in Paragraphs 2.3 through 2.5 inclusive.

3.3 Labor furnished by the Owner for the Project shall be included in the Construction Cost at current market rates. Materials and equipment furnished by the Owner shall be included at current market prices, except that used materials and equipment shall be included as if purchased new for the Project.

3.4 Statements of Probable Construction Cost and Detailed Cost Estimates prepared by the Engineer represent his best judgment as a design professional familiar with the construction industry. It is recognized, however, that neither the Engineer nor the Architect has any control over the cost of labor, materials or equipment, over the contractors' methods of determining bid prices, or over competitive bidding or market conditions. Accordingly, the Engineer cannot and does not guarantee that bids will not vary from any Statement of Probable Construction Cost or other cost estimate prepared by him.

3.5 When a fixed limit of Construction Cost is established as a condition of the Prime Agreement, the Architect may establish a fixed limit of Construction Cost for This Part of the Project which shall include a bidding contingency of ten per cent unless another amount is agreed upon in writing. When such a fixed limit is established, the Engineer shall be permitted to determine what materials, equipment, component systems and types of construction are to be included in the Contract Documents with respect to This Part of the Project, and to make reasonable adjustments in the scope of This Part of the Project to bring it within the fixed limit. If required, the Engineer shall assist the Architect in including in the Contract Documents alternate bids to adjust the Construction Cost to the fixed limit.

3.5.1 If the lowest bona fide bid, the Detailed Cost Estimate or the Statement of Probable Construction Cost exceeds such fixed limit of Construction Cost for This Part of the Project (including the bidding contingency), the Architect may require the Engineer, without additional charge, to modify the Drawings and Specifications for This Part of the Project as necessary to bring the Construction Cost thereof within such fixed limit for This Part of the Project. The providing of this service shall be the limit of the Engineer's responsibility in this regard, and having done so, he shall be entitled to his fees in the same proportion that the Architect receives payment of his fee from the Owner for This Part of the Project.

ARTICLE 4

DIRECT PERSONNEL EXPENSE

4.1 Direct Personnel Expense of employees engaged on This Part of the Project by the Engineer includes engineers, designers, job captains, draftsmen, specification writers and typists, in consultation, research and design, in producing Drawings, Specifications and other documents pertaining to This Part of the Project, and in services during construction at the site.

4.2 Direct Personnel Expense includes cost of salaries and of mandatory and customary benefits such as statutory employee benefits, insurance, sick leave, holidays and vacations, pensions and similar benefits.

ARTICLE 5

REIMBURSABLE EXPENSES

5.1 Reimbursable Expenses are in addition to the Fees for Basic and Additional Services and include actual expenditures made by the Engineer, his employees, or his consultants in the interest of This Part of the Project for the incidental expenses listed in the following Subparagraphs:

5.1.1 Expense of transportation and living when traveling in connection with This Part of the Project, long distance calls and telegrams, and fees paid for securing approval of authorities having jurisdiction over the Project.

5.1.2 If authorized in advance by the Architect, the expense of overtime work requiring higher than regular rates.

ARTICLE 6

PAYMENTS TO THE ENGINEER

6.1 Upon receipt of payment by the Architect from the Owner, the Architect shall pay the Engineer for services rendered for This Part of the Project in accordance with this Article 6.

6.2 Payments for Basic Services shall be made monthly in proportion to services performed so that the compensation at the completion of each phase of the Work shall equal the following percentages of the Basic Fee:

Schematic Design Phase	15%
Design Development Phase	35%
Construction Documents Phase	75%
Bidding and Negotiation Phase	80%
Construction Phase	100%

6.3 Payments for Additional Services of the Engineer as defined in Paragraph 1.4, and for Reimbursable Expenses as defined in Article 5, shall be made monthly upon presentation of the Engineer's statement of services rendered.

6.4 No deductions shall be made from the Engineer's compensation on account of penalty, liquidated damages, or other sums withheld from payments to contractors.

6.5 If the Project is suspended for more than three months or abandoned in whole or in part, the Engineer shall be paid his compensation for services performed prior to receipt of written notice from the Architect of such suspension or abandonment, together with Reimbursable Expenses then due and all terminal expenses resulting from such suspension or abandonment.

ARTICLE 7

ENGINEER'S RECORDS

7.1 Records of the Engineer's Direct Personnel and Reimbursable Expenses pertaining to This Part of the Project shall be kept on a generally recognized accounting basis and shall be available to the Architect or his authorized representative at mutually convenient times.

7.2 The Engineer shall maintain his design calculations on file in legible form and available to the Architect.

ARTICLE 8

TERMINATION OF AGREEMENT

8.1 This Agreement is terminated if and when the Prime Agreement is terminated. The Architect shall promptly notify the Engineer of such termination.

8.2 This Agreement may be terminated by either party upon seven days' written notice should the other party fail substantially to perform in accordance with its terms through no fault of the other. In the event of termination due to the fault of others than the Engineer, the Engineer shall be paid his compensation for services performed to termination date, including Reimbursable Expenses then due and all terminal expenses, contingent upon comparable adjustment by the Owner of the Architect's compensation.

ARTICLE 9

INSURANCE

9.1 The Architect and the Engineer shall each effect and maintain insurance to protect himself from claims under workmen's compensation acts; claims for damages because of bodily injury including personal injury, sickness or disease, or death of any of his employees or of any person other than his employees; and from claims for damages because of injury to or destruction of tangible property including loss of use resulting therefrom; and from claims arising out of the performance of professional services caused by any errors, omissions or negligent acts for which he is legally liable.

ARTICLE 10

SUCCESSORS AND ASSIGNS

The Architect and the Engineer each binds himself, his partners, successors, assigns and legal representatives to the other party to this Agreement and to the partners, successors, assigns and legal representatives of such other party with respect to all covenants of this Agreement. Neither the Architect nor the Engineer shall assign, sublet or transfer his interest in this Agreement without the written consent of the other.

ARTICLE 11

ARBITRATION

11.1 All claims, disputes and other matters in question arising out of, or relating to, this Agreement, or the breach thereof, shall be decided by arbitration in accordance with the Construction Industry Arbitration Rules of the American Arbitration Association then obtaining unless the parties mutually agree otherwise. This agreement so to arbitrate shall be specifically enforceable under the prevailing arbitration law.

11.2 Notice of the demand for arbitration shall be filed in writing with the other party to this Agreement and with the American Arbitration Association. The demand shall be made within a reasonable time after the claim, dispute or other matter in question has arisen. In no event shall the demand for arbitration be made after institution of legal or equitable proceedings based on such claim, dispute or other matter in question would be barred by the applicable statute of limitations.

11.3 The award rendered by the arbitrators shall be final, and judgment may be entered upon it in accordance with applicable law in any court having jurisdiction thereof.

ARTICLE 12

EXTENT OF AGREEMENT

This Agreement represents the entire and integrated agreement between the Architect and the Engineer and supersedes all prior negotiations, representations or agreements, either written or oral. This Agreement may be amended only by written instrument signed by both Architect and Engineer.

ARTICLE 13

APPLICABLE LAW

Unless otherwise specified, this Agreement shall be governed by the law of the principal place of business of the Architect.

This Agreement executed the day and year first written above.

ARCHITECT

ENGINEER

Architect's Registration No.

Engineer's Registration No.

APPENDIX C

AIA Document A101 *

Standard Form of Agreement Between Owner and Contractor

where the basis of payment is a

STIPULATED SUM

Use only with the latest Edition of AIA Document A201, General Conditions of the Contract for Construction.

AGREEMENT

made this day of in the year of Nineteen Hundred and

BETWEEN

the Owner, and

the Contractor.

The Owner and the Contractor agree as set forth below.

* Reprinted with permission

ARTICLE 1

THE CONTRACT DOCUMENTS

The Contract Documents consist of this Agreement, Conditions of the Contract (General, Supplementary and other Conditions), Drawings, Specifications, all Addenda issued prior to execution of this Agreement and all Modifications issued subsequent thereto. These form the Contract, and all are as fully a part of the Contract as if attached to this Agreement or repeated herein. An enumeration of the Contract Documents appears in Article 8.

ARTICLE 2

THE WORK

The Contractor shall perform all the Work required by the Contract Documents for

(Here insert the caption descriptive of the Work as used on other Contract Documents.)

ARTICLE 3

ARCHITECT

The Architect for this Project is

ARTICLE 4

TIME OF COMMENCEMENT AND COMPLETION

The Work to be performed under this Contract shall be commenced

and completed

(Here insert any special provisions for liquidated damages relating to failure to complete on time.)

ARTICLE 5

CONTRACT SUM

The Owner shall pay the Contractor for the performance of the Work, subject to additions and deductions by Change Order as provided in the Conditions of the Contract, in current funds, the Contract Sum of

(State here the lump sum amount, unit prices, or both, as desired.)

ARTICLE 6

PROGRESS PAYMENTS

Based upon Applications for Payment submitted to the Architect by the Contractor and Certificates for Payment issued by the Architect, the Owner shall make progress payments on account of the Contract Sum to the Contractor as provided in the Conditions of the Contract as follows:

On or about the day of each month per cent of the proportion of the Contract Sum properly allocable to labor, materials and equipment incorporated in the Work and per cent of the portion of the Contract Sum properly allocable to materials and equipment suitably stored at the site or at some other location agreed upon in writing by the parties, up to the day of that month, less the aggregate of previous payments in each case; and upon Substantial Completion of the entire Work, a sum sufficient to increase the total payments to per cent of the Contract Sum, less such retainages as the Architect shall determine for all incomplete Work and unsettled claims.

(Here insert any provisions made for limiting or reducing the amount retained after the Work reaches a certain stage of completion.)

ARTICLE 7

FINAL PAYMENT

Final payment, constituting the entire unpaid balance of the Contract Sum, shall be paid by the Owner to the Contractor days after Substantial Completion of the Work unless otherwise stipulated in the Certificate of Substantial Completion, provided the Work has then been completed, the Contract fully performed, and a final Certificate for Payment has been issued by the Architect.

ARTICLE 8

MISCELLANEOUS PROVISIONS

8.1 Terms used in this Agreement which are defined in the Conditions of the Contract shall have the meanings designated in those Conditions.

8.2 The Contract Documents, which constitute the entire agreement between the Owner and the Contractor, are listed in Article 1 and, except for Modifications issued after execution of this Agreement, are enumerated as follows:

(List below the Agreement, Conditions of the Contract (General, Supplementary, other Conditions), Drawings, Specifications, Addenda and accepted Alternates, showing page or sheet numbers in all cases and dates where applicable.)

This Agreement executed the day and year first written above.

OWNER ______________________ CONTRACTOR ______________________

LA11153

APPENDIX D

AIA Document A201 *

General Conditions of the Contract for Construction

TABLE OF ARTICLES

AIA DOCUMENT A 201 • GENERAL CONDITIONS OF THE CONTRACT FOR CONSTRUCTION • ELEVENTH EDITION • AIA ®
SEPT. 1967 © 1967 THE AMERICAN INSTITUTE OF ARCHITECTS, 1735 NEW YORK AVENUE, N.W., WASHINGTON, D.C. 20006

* Reprinted with permission

INDEX

GENERAL CONDITIONS OF THE CONTRACT FOR CONSTRUCTION

ARTICLE 1

CONTRACT DOCUMENTS

1.1 DEFINITIONS

1.1.1 THE CONTRACT DOCUMENTS

The Contract Documents consist of the Agreement, the Conditions of the Contract (General, Supplementary and other Conditions), the Drawings, the Specifications, all Addenda issued prior to execution of the Agreement, and all Modifications thereto. A Modification is (1) a written amendment to the Contract signed by both parties, (2) a Change Order, (3) a written interpretation issued by the Architect pursuant to Subparagraph 1.2.5, or (4) a written order for a minor change in the Work issued by the Architect pursuant to Paragraph 12.3. A Modification may be made only after execution of the Contract.

1.1.2 THE CONTRACT

The Contract Documents form the Contract. The Contract represents the entire and integrated agreement between the parties hereto and supersedes all prior negotiations, representations, or agreements, either written or oral, including the bidding documents. The Contract may be amended or modified only by a Modification as defined in Subparagraph 1.1.1.

1.1.3 THE WORK

The term Work includes all labor necessary to produce the construction required by the Contract Documents, and all materials and equipment incorporated or to be incorporated in such construction.

1.1.4 THE PROJECT

The Project is the total construction designed by the Architect of which the Work performed under the Contract Documents may be the whole or a part.

1.2 EXECUTION, CORRELATION, INTENT AND INTERPRETATIONS

1.2.1 The Contract Documents shall be signed in not less than triplicate by the Owner and Contractor. If either the Owner or the Contractor or both do not sign the Conditions of the Contract, Drawings, Specifications, or any of the other Contract Documents, the Architect shall identify them.

1.2.2 By executing the Contract, the Contractor represents that he has visited the site, familiarized himself with the local conditions under which the Work is to be performed, and correlated his observations with the requirements of the Contract Documents.

1.2.3 The Contract Documents are complementary, and what is required by any one shall be as binding as if required by all. The intention of the Documents is to include all labor, materials, equipment and other items as provided in Subparagraph 4.4.1 necessary for the proper execution and completion of the Work. It is not intended that Work not covered under any heading, section, branch, class or trade of the Specifications shall be supplied unless it is required elsewhere in the Contract Documents or is reasonably inferable therefrom as being necessary to produce the intended results. Words which have well-known technical or trade meanings are used herein in accordance with such recognized meanings.

1.2.4 The organization of the Specifications into divisions, sections and articles, and the arrangement of Drawings shall not control the Contractor in dividing the Work among Subcontractors or in establishing the extent of Work to be performed by any trade.

1.2.5 Written interpretations necessary for the proper execution or progress of the Work, in the form of drawings or otherwise, will be issued with reasonable promptness by the Architect and in accordance with any schedule agreed upon. Such interpretations shall be consistent with and reasonably inferable from the Contract Documents, and may be effected by Field Order.

1.3 COPIES FURNISHED AND OWNERSHIP

1.3.1 Unless otherwise provided in the Contract Documents, the Contractor will be furnished, free of charge, all copies of Drawings and Specifications reasonably necessary for the execution of the Work.

1.3.2 All Drawings, Specifications and copies thereof furnished by the Architect are and shall remain his property. They are not to be used on any other project, and, with the exception of one contract set for each party to the Contract, are to be returned to the Architect on request at the completion of the Work.

ARTICLE 2

ARCHITECT

2.1 DEFINITION

2.1.1 The Architect is the person or organization identified as such in the Agreement and is referred to throughout the Contract Documents as if singular in number and masculine in gender. The term Architect means the Architect or his authorized representative.

2.1.2 Nothing contained in the Contract Documents shall create any contractual relationship between the Architect and the Contractor.

2.2 ADMINISTRATION OF THE CONTRACT

2.2.1 The Architect will provide general Administration of the Construction Contract, including performance of the functions hereinafter described.

2.2.2 The Architect will be the Owner's representative during construction and until final payment. The Architect will have authority to act on behalf of the Owner to the extent provided in the Contract Documents, unless otherwise modified by written instrument which will be shown to the Contractor. The Architect will advise and consult with the Owner, and all of the Owner's instructions to the Contractor shall be issued through the Architect.

2.2.3 The Architect shall at all times have access to the Work wherever it is in preparation and progress. The Contractor shall provide facilities for such access so the Architect may perform his functions under the Contract Documents.

2.2.4 The Architect will make periodic visits to the site to familiarize himself generally with the progress and quality of the Work and to determine in general if the Work is proceeding in accordance with the Contract Documents. On the basis of his on-site observations as an architect, he will keep the Owner informed of the progress of the Work, and will endeavor to guard the Owner against defects and deficiencies in the Work of the Contractor. The Architect will not be required to make exhaustive or continuous on-site inspections to check the quality or quantity of the Work. The Architect will not be responsible for construction means, methods, techniques, sequences or procedures, or for safety precautions and programs in connection with the Work, and he will not be responsible for the Contractor's failure to carry out the Work in accordance with the Contract Documents.

2.2.5 Based on such observations and the Contractor's Applications for Payment, the Architect will determine the amounts owing to the Contractor and will issue Certificates for Payment in such amounts, as provided in Paragraph 9.4.

2.2.6 The Architect will be, in the first instance, the interpreter of the requirements of the Contract Documents and the judge of the performance thereunder by both the Owner and Contractor. The Architect will, within a reasonable time, render such interpretations as he may deem necessary for the proper execution or progress of the Work.

2.2.7 Claims, disputes and other matters in question between the Contractor and the Owner relating to the execution or progress of the Work or the interpretation of the Contract Documents shall be referred initially to the Architect for decision which he will render in writing within a reasonable time.

2.2.8 All interpretations and decisions of the Architect shall be consistent with the intent of the Contract Documents. In his capacity as interpreter and judge, he will exercise his best efforts to insure faithful performance by both the Owner and the Contractor and will not show partiality to either.

2.2.9 The Architect's decisions in matters relating to artistic effect will be final if consistent with the intent of the Contract Documents.

2.2.10 Any claim, dispute or other matter that has been referred to the Architect, except those relating to artistic effect as provided in Subparagraph 2.2.9 and except any which have been waived by the making or acceptance of final payment as provided in Subparagraphs 9.7.5 and 9.7.6, shall be subject to arbitration upon the written demand of either party. However, no demand for arbitration of any such claim, dispute or other matter may be made until the earlier of:

.1 the date on which the Architect has rendered his decision, or

.2 the tenth day after the parties have presented their evidence to the Architect or have been given a reasonable opportunity to do so, if the Architect has not rendered his written decision by that date.

2.2.11 If a decision of the Architect is made in writing and states that it is final but subject to appeal, no demand for arbitration of a claim, dispute or other matter covered by such decision may be made later than thirty days after the date on which the party making the demand received the decision. The failure to demand arbitration within said thirty days' period will result in the Architect's decision becoming final and binding upon the Owner and the Contractor. If the Architect renders a decision after arbitration proceedings have been initiated, such decision may be entered as evidence but will not supersede any arbitration proceedings except where the decision is acceptable to the parties concerned.

2.2.12 The Architect will have authority to reject Work which does not conform to the Contract Documents. Whenever, in his reasonable opinion, he considers it necessary or advisable to insure the proper implementation of the intent of the Contract Documents, he will have authority to require the Contractor to stop the Work or any portion thereof, or to require special inspection or testing of the Work as provided in Subparagraph 7.8.2 whether or not such Work be then fabricated, installed or completed. However, neither the Architect's authority to act under this Subparagraph 2.2.12, nor any decision made by him in good faith either to exercise or not to exercise such authority, shall give rise to any duty or responsibility of the Architect to the Contractor, any Subcontractor, any of their agents or employees, or any other person performing any of the Work.

2.2.13 The Architect will review Shop Drawings and Samples as provided in Subparagraphs 4.13.1 through 4.13.8 inclusive.

2.2.14 The Architect will prepare Change Orders in accordance with Article 12, and will have authority to order minor changes in the Work as provided in Subparagraph 12.3.1.

2.2.15 The Architect will conduct inspections to determine the dates of Substantial Completion and final completion, will receive written guarantees and related documents required by the Contract and assembled by the Contractor, and will issue a final Certificate for Payment.

2.2.16 If the Owner and Architect agree, the Architect will provide one or more Full-time Project Representatives to assist the Architect in carrying out his responsibilities at the site. The duties, responsibilities and limitations of authority of any such Project Representative shall be as set forth in an exhibit to be incorporated in the Contract Documents.

2.2.17 The duties, responsibilities and limitations of authority of the Architect as the Owner's representative during construction as set forth in Articles 1 through 14 inclusive of these General Conditions will not be modified or extended without written consent of the Owner and the Architect which will be shown to the Contractor.

2.2.18 The Architect will not be responsible for the acts or omissions of the Contractor, any Subcontractors, or any of their agents or employees, or any other persons performing any of the Work.

2.2.19 In case of the termination of the employment of the Architect, the Owner shall appoint an architect against whom the Contractor makes no reasonable objection, whose status under the Contract Documents shall be that of the former architect. Any dispute in connection with such appointment shall be subject to arbitration.

ARTICLE 3

OWNER

3.1 DEFINITION

3.1.1 The Owner is the person or organization identified as such in the Agreement and is referred to throughout the Contract Documents as if singular in number and masculine in gender. The term Owner means the Owner or his authorized representative.

3.2 INFORMATION AND SERVICES REQUIRED OF THE OWNER

3.2.1 The Owner shall furnish all surveys describing the physical characteristics, legal limits and utility locations for the site of the Project.

3.2.2 The Owner shall secure and pay for easements for permanent structures or permanent changes in existing facilities.

3.2.3 Information or services under the Owner's control shall be furnished by the Owner with reasonable promptness to avoid delay in the orderly progress of the Work.

3.2.4 The Owner shall issue all instructions to the Contractor through the Architect.

3.2.5 The foregoing are in addition to other duties and responsibilities of the Owner enumerated herein and especially those in respect to Payment and Insurance in Articles 9 and 11 respectively.

ARTICLE 4

CONTRACTOR

4.1 DEFINITION

4.1.1 The Contractor is the person or organization identified as such in the Agreement and is referred to throughout the Contract Documents as if singular in number and masculine in gender. The term Contractor means the Contractor or his authorized representative.

4.2 REVIEW OF CONTRACT DOCUMENTS

4.2.1 The Contractor shall carefully study and compare the Agreement, Conditions of the Contract, Drawings, Specifications, Addenda and Modifications and shall at once report to the Architect any error, inconsistency or omission he may discover; but the Contractor shall not be liable to the Owner or the Architect for any damage resulting from any such errors, inconsistencies or omissions. The Contractor shall do no Work without Drawings, Specifications or interpretations.

4.3 SUPERVISION AND CONSTRUCTION PROCEDURES

4.3.1 The Contractor shall supervise and direct the Work, using his best skill and attention. He shall be solely responsible for all construction means, methods, techniques, sequences and procedures and for coordinating all portions of the Work under the Contract.

4.4 LABOR AND MATERIALS

4.4.1 Unless otherwise specifically noted, the Contractor shall provide and pay for all labor, materials, equipment, tools, construction equipment and machinery, water, heat, utilities, transportation, and other facilities and services necessary for the proper execution and completion of the Work.

4.4.2 The Contractor shall at all times enforce strict discipline and good order among his employees and shall not employ on the Work any unfit person or anyone not skilled in the task assigned to him.

4.5 WARRANTY

4.5.1 The Contractor warrants to the Owner and the Architect that all materials and equipment furnished under this Contract will be new unless otherwise specified, and that all Work will be of good quality, free from faults and defects and in conformance with the Contract Documents. All Work not so conforming to these standards may be considered defective. If required by the Architect, the Contractor shall furnish satisfactory evidence as to the kind and quality of materials and equipment.

4.5.2 The warranty provided in this Paragraph 4.5 shall be in addition to and not in limitation of any other warranty or remedy required by law or by the Contract Documents.

4.6 TAXES

4.6.1 The Contractor shall pay all sales, consumer, use and other similar taxes required by law.

4.7 PERMITS, FEES AND NOTICES

4.7.1 The Contractor shall secure and pay for all permits, governmental fees and licenses necessary for the proper execution and completion of the Work.

4.7.2 The Contractor shall give all notices and comply with all laws, ordinances, rules, regulations and orders of any public authority bearing on the performance of the Work. If the Contractor observes that any of the Contract Documents are at variance therewith in any respect, he shall promptly notify the Architect in writing, and any necessary changes shall be adjusted by appropriate Modification. If the Contractor performs any Work knowing it to be contrary to such laws, ordinances, rules and regulations, and without such notice to the Architect, he shall assume full responsibility therefor and shall bear all costs attributable thereto.

4.8 CASH ALLOWANCES

4.8.1 The Contractor shall include in the Contract Sum all allowances stated in the Contract Documents. These allowances shall cover the net cost of the materials and equipment delivered and unloaded at the site, and all applicable taxes. The Contractor's handling costs on the site, labor, installation costs, overhead, profit and other expenses contemplated for the original allowance shall be included in the Contract Sum and not in the allowance. The Contractor shall cause the Work covered by these allowances to be performed for such amounts and by such persons as the Architect may direct, but he will not be required to employ persons against whom he makes a reasonable objection. If the cost, when determined, is more than or less than the allowance, the Contract Sum shall be adjusted accordingly by Change Order which will include additional handling costs on the site, labor, installation costs, overhead, profit and other expenses resulting to the Contractor from any increase over the original allowance.

4.9 SUPERINTENDENT

4.9.1 The Contractor shall employ a competent superintendent and necessary assistants who shall be in attendance at the Project site during the progress of the Work. The superintendent shall be satisfactory to the Architect, and shall not be changed except with the consent of the Architect, unless the superintendent proves to be unsatisfactory to the Contractor and ceases to be in his employ. The superintendent shall represent the Contractor and all communications given to the superintendent shall be as binding as if given to the Contractor. Important communications will be confirmed in writing. Other communications will be so confirmed on written request in each case.

4.10 RESPONSIBILITY FOR THOSE PERFORMING THE WORK

4.10.1 The Contractor shall be responsible to the Owner for the acts and omissions of all his employees and all Subcontractors, their agents and employees, and all other persons performing any of the Work under a contract with the Contractor.

4.11 PROGRESS SCHEDULE

4.11.1 The Contractor, immediately after being awarded the Contract, shall prepare and submit for the Architect's approval an estimated progress schedule for the Work. The progress schedule shall be related to the entire Project to the extent required by the Contract Documents. This schedule shall indicate the dates for the starting and completion of the various stages of construction and shall be revised as required by the conditions of the Work, subject to the Architect's approval.

4.12 DRAWINGS AND SPECIFICATIONS AT THE SITE

4.12.1 The Contractor shall maintain at the site for the Owner one copy of all Drawings, Specifications, Addenda, approved Shop Drawings, Change Orders and other Modifications, in good order and marked to record all changes made during construction. These shall be available to the Architect. The Drawings, marked to record all changes made during construction, shall be delivered to him for the Owner upon completion of the Work.

4.13 SHOP DRAWINGS AND SAMPLES

4.13.1 Shop Drawings are drawings, diagrams, illustrations, schedules, performance charts, brochures and other data which are prepared by the Contractor or any Subcontractor, manufacturer, supplier or distributor, and which illustrate some portion of the Work.

4.13.2 Samples are physical examples furnished by the Contractor to illustrate materials, equipment or workmanship, and to establish standards by which the Work will be judged.

4.13.3 The Contractor shall review, stamp with his approval and submit, with reasonable promptness and in orderly sequence so as to cause no delay in the Work or in the work of any other contractor, all Shop Drawings and Samples required by the Contract Documents or subsequently by the Architect as covered by Modifications. Shop Drawings and Samples shall be properly identified as specified, or as the Architect may require. At the time of submission the Contractor shall inform the Architect in writing of any deviation in the Shop Drawings or Samples from the requirements of the Contract Documents.

4.13.4 By approving and submitting Shop Drawings and Samples, the Contractor thereby represents that he has determined and verified all field measurements, field construction criteria, materials, catalog numbers and similar data, or will do so, and that he has checked and coordinated each Shop Drawing and Sample with the requirements of the Work and of the Contract Documents.

4.13.5 The Architect will review and approve Shop Drawings and Samples with reasonable promptness so as to cause no delay, but only for conformance with the design concept of the Project and with the information given in the Contract Documents. The Architect's approval of a separate item shall not indicate approval of an assembly in which the item functions.

4.13.6 The Contractor shall make any corrections required by the Architect and shall resubmit the required number of corrected copies of Shop Drawings or new Samples until approved. The Contractor shall direct specific attention in writing or on resubmitted Shop Drawings to revisions other than the corrections requested by the Architect on previous submissions.

4.13.7 The Architect's approval of Shop Drawings or Samples shall not relieve the Contractor of responsibility for any deviation from the requirements of the Contract Documents unless the Contractor has informed the Architect in writing of such deviation at the time of submission and the Architect has given written approval to the specific deviation, nor shall the Architect's approval relieve the Contractor from responsibility for errors or omissions in the Shop Drawings or Samples.

4.13.8 No portion of the Work requiring a Shop Drawing or Sample submission shall be commenced until the submission has been approved by the Architect. All such portions of the Work shall be in accordance with approved Shop Drawings and Samples.

4.14 USE OF SITE

4.14.1 The Contractor shall confine operations at the site to areas permitted by law, ordinances, permits and the Contract Documents and shall not unreasonably encumber the site with any materials or equipment.

4.15 CUTTING AND PATCHING OF WORK

4.15.1 The Contractor shall do all cutting, fitting or patching of his Work that may be required to make its several parts fit together properly, and shall not endanger any Work by cutting, excavating or otherwise altering the Work or any part of it.

4.16 CLEANING UP

4.16.1 The Contractor at all times shall keep the premises free from accumulation of waste materials or rubbish caused by his operations. At the completion of the Work he shall remove all his waste materials and rubbish from and about the Project as well as all his tools, construction equipment, machinery and surplus materials, and shall clean all glass surfaces and leave the Work "broom-clean" or its equivalent, except as otherwise specified.

4.16.2 If the Contractor fails to clean up, the Owner may do so and the cost thereof shall be charged to the Contractor as provided in Paragraph 7.6.

4.17 COMMUNICATIONS

4.17.1 The Contractor shall forward all communications to the Owner through the Architect.

4.18 INDEMNIFICATION

4.18.1 The Contractor shall indemnify and hold harmless the Owner and the Architect and their agents and employees from and against all claims, damages, losses and expenses including attorneys' fees arising out of or resulting from the performance of the Work, provided that any such claim, damage, loss or expense (a) is attributable to bodily injury, sickness, disease or death, or to injury to or destruction of tangible property (other than the Work itself) including the loss of use resulting therefrom, and (b) is caused in whole or in part by any negligent act or omission of the Contractor, any Subcontractor, anyone directly or indirectly employed by any of them or anyone for whose acts any of them may be liable, regardless of whether or not it is caused in part by a party indemnified hereunder.

4.18.2 In any and all claims against the Owner or the Architect or any of their agents or employees by any employee of the Contractor, any Subcontractor, anyone directly or indirectly employed by any of them or anyone for whose acts any of them may be liable, the indemnification obligation under this Paragraph 4.18 shall not be limited in any way by any limitation on the amount or type of damages, compensation or benefits payable by or for the Contractor or any Subcontractor under workmen's compensation acts, disability benefit acts or other employee benefit acts.

4.18.3 The obligations of the Contractor under this Paragraph 4.18 shall not extend to the liability of the Architect, his agents or employees arising out of (1) the preparation or approval of maps, drawings, opinions, reports, surveys, Change Orders, designs or specifications, or (2) the giving of or the failure to give directions or instructions by the Architect, his agents or employees provided such giving or failure to give is the primary cause of the injury or damage.

ARTICLE 5

SUBCONTRACTORS

5.1 DEFINITION

5.1.1 A Subcontractor is a person or organization who has a direct contract with the Contractor to perform any of the Work at the site. The term Subcontractor is referred to throughout the Contract Documents as if singular in number and masculine in gender and means a Subcontractor or his authorized representative.

5.1.2 A Sub-subcontractor is a person or organization who has a direct or indirect contract with a Subcontractor to perform any of the Work at the site. The term Sub-subcontractor is referred to throughout the Contract Documents as if singular in number and masculine in gender and means a Sub-subcontractor or an authorized representative thereof.

5.1.3 Nothing contained in the Contract Documents shall create any contractual relation between the Owner or the Architect and any Subcontractor or Sub-subcontractor.

5.2 AWARD OF SUBCONTRACTS AND OTHER CONTRACTS FOR PORTIONS OF THE WORK

5.2.1 As soon as practicable after bids are received and prior to the award of the Contract, the successful bidder shall furnish to the Architect in writing for acceptance by the Owner and the Architect a list of the names of the subcontractors or other persons or organizations (including those who are to furnish materials or equipment fabricated to a special design) proposed for such portions of the Work as may be designated in the bidding requirements, or, if none is so designated, the names of the Subcontractors proposed for the principal portions of the Work. Prior to the award of the Contract, the Architect shall notify the successful bidder in writing if either the Owner or the Architect, after due investigation, has reasonable objection to any person or organization on such list. Failure of the Owner or Architect to make an objection to any person or organization on the list prior to the award shall constitute acceptance of such person or organization.

5.2.2 If, prior to the award of the Contract, the Owner or Architect has a reasonable and substantial objection to any person or organization on such list, and refuses in writing to accept such person or organization, the successful bidder may, prior to the award, withdraw his bid without forfeiture of bid security. If the successful bidder submits an acceptable substitute with an increase in his bid price to cover the difference in cost occasioned by such substitution, the Owner may, at his discretion, accept the increased bid price or he may disqualify the bid. If, after the award, the Owner or Architect refuses to accept any person or organization on such list, the Contractor shall submit an acceptable substitute and the Contract Sum shall be increased or decreased by the difference in cost occasioned by such substitution and an appropriate Change Order shall be issued; however, no increase in the Contract Sum shall be allowed for any such substitution unless the Contractor has acted promptly and responsively in submitting a name with respect thereto prior to the award.

5.2.3 The Contractor shall not contract with any Subcontractor or any person or organization proposed for portions of the Work designated in the bidding requirements or, if none is so designated, with any Subcontractor proposed for the principal portions of the Work who has not been accepted by the Owner and the Architect. The Contractor will not be required to contract with any subcontractor or person or organization against whom he has a reasonable objection.

5.2.4 If the Owner or the Architect requires a change of any proposed Subcontractor or person or organization previously accepted by them, the Contract Sum shall be increased or decreased by the difference in cost occasioned by such change and an appropriate Change Order shall be issued.

5.2.5 The Contractor shall not make any substitution for any Subcontractor or person or organization who has been accepted by the Owner and the Architect, unless the substitution is acceptable to the Owner and the Architect.

5.3 SUBCONTRACTUAL RELATIONS

5.3.1 All work performed for the Contractor by a Subcontractor shall be pursuant to an appropriate agreement between the Contractor and the Subcontractor (and where appropriate between Subcontractors and Sub-subcontractors) which shall contain provisions that:

.1 preserve and protect the rights of the Owner and the Architect under the Contract with respect to the Work to be performed under the subcontract so that the subcontracting thereof will not prejudice such rights;

.2 require that such Work be performed in accordance with the requirements of the Contract Documents;

.3 require submission to the Contractor of applications for payment under each subcontract to which the Contractor is a party, in reasonable time to enable the Contractor to apply for payment in accordance with Article 9;

.4 require that all claims for additional costs, extensions of time, damages for delays or otherwise with respect to subcontracted portions of the Work shall be submitted to the Contractor (via any Subcontractor or Sub-subcontractor where appropriate) in the manner provided in the Contract Documents for like claims by the Contractor upon the Owner;

.5 waive all rights the contracting parties may have against one another for damages caused by fire or other perils covered by the property insurance described in Paragraph 11.3, except such rights as they may have to the proceeds of such insurance held by the Owner as trustee under Paragraph 11.3; and

.6 obligate each Subcontractor specifically to consent to the provisions of this Paragraph 5.3.

5.4 PAYMENTS TO SUBCONTRACTORS

5.4.1 The Contractor shall pay each Subcontractor, upon receipt of payment from the Owner, an amount equal to the percentage of completion allowed to the Contractor on account of such Subcontractor's Work. The Contractor shall also require each Subcontractor to make similar payments to his subcontractors.

5.4.2 If the Architect fails to issue a Certificate for Payment for any cause which is the fault of the Contractor and not the fault of a particular Subcontractor, the Contractor shall pay that Subcontractor on demand, made at any time after the Certificate for Payment should otherwise have been issued, for his Work to the extent completed, less the retained percentage.

5.4.3 The Contractor shall pay each Subcontractor a just share of any insurance moneys received by the Contractor under Article 11, and he shall require each Subcontractor to make similar payments to his subcontractors.

5.4.4 The Architect may, on request and at his discretion, furnish to any Subcontractor, if practicable, information regarding percentages of completion certified to the Contractor on account of Work done by such Subcontractors.

5.4.5 Neither the Owner nor the Architect shall have any obligation to pay or to see to the payment of any moneys to any Subcontractor except as may otherwise be required by law.

ARTICLE 6

SEPARATE CONTRACTS

6.1 OWNER'S RIGHT TO AWARD SEPARATE CONTRACTS

6.1.1 The Owner reserves the right to award other contracts in connection with other portions of the Project under these or similar Conditions of the Contract.

6.1.2 When separate contracts are awarded for different portions of the Project, "the Contractor" in the contract documents in each case shall be the contractor who signs each separate contract.

6.2 MUTUAL RESPONSIBILITY OF CONTRACTORS

6.2.1 The Contractor shall afford other contractors reasonable opportunity for the introduction and storage of their materials and equipment and the execution of their work, and shall properly connect and coordinate his Work with theirs.

6.2.2 If any part of the Contractor's Work depends for proper execution or results upon the work of any other separate contractor, the Contractor shall inspect and promptly report to the Architect any apparent discrepancies or defects in such work that render it unsuitable for such proper execution and results. Failure of the Contractor so to inspect and report shall constitute an acceptance of the other contractor's work as fit and proper to receive his Work, except as to defects which may develop in the other separate contractor's work after the execution of the Contractor's Work.

6.2.3 Should the Contractor cause damage to the work or property of any separate contractor on the Project, the Contractor shall, upon due notice, settle with such other contractor by agreement or arbitration, if he will so settle. If such separate contractor sues the Owner on account of any damage alleged to have been so sustained, the Owner shall notify the Contractor who shall defend such proceedings at the Owner's expense, and if any judgment against the Owner arises therefrom the Contractor shall pay or satisfy it and shall reimburse the Owner for all attorneys' fees and court costs which the Owner has incurred.

6.3 CUTTING AND PATCHING UNDER SEPARATE CONTRACTS

6.3.1 The Contractor shall do all cutting, fitting or patching of his Work that may be required to fit it to receive or be received by the work of other contractors shown in the Contract Documents. The Contractor shall not endanger any work of any other contractors by cutting, excavating or otherwise altering any work and shall not cut or alter the work of any other contractor except with the written consent of the Architect.

6.3.2 Any costs caused by defective or ill-timed work shall be borne by the party responsible therefor.

6.4 OWNER'S RIGHT TO CLEAN UP

6.4.1 If a dispute arises between the separate contractors as to their responsibility for cleaning up as required by Paragraph 4.16, the Owner may clean up and charge the cost thereof to the several contractors as the Architect shall determine to be just.

ARTICLE 7

MISCELLANEOUS PROVISIONS

7.1 LAW OF THE PLACE

7.1.1 The Contract shall be governed by the law of the place where the Project is located.

7.2 SUCCESSORS AND ASSIGNS

7.2.1 The Owner and the Contractor each binds himself, his partners, successors, assigns and legal representatives to the other party hereto and to the partners, successors, assigns and legal representatives of such other party in respect to all covenants, agreements and obligations contained in the Contract Documents. Neither party to the Contract shall assign the Contract or sublet it as a whole without the written consent of the other, nor shall the Contractor assign any moneys due or to become due to him hereunder, without the previous written consent of the Owner.

7.3 WRITTEN NOTICE

7.3.1 Written notice shall be deemed to have been duly served if delivered in person to the individual or member of the firm or to an officer of the corporation for whom it was intended, or if delivered at or sent by registered or certified mail to the last business address known to him who gives the notice.

7.4 CLAIMS FOR DAMAGES

7.4.1 Should either party to the Contract suffer injury or damage to person or property because of any act or omission of the other party or of any of his employees, agents or others for whose acts he is legally liable, claim shall be made in writing to such other party within a reasonable time after the first observance of such injury or damage.

7.5 PERFORMANCE BOND AND LABOR AND MATERIAL PAYMENT BOND

7.5.1 The Owner shall have the right, prior to signing the Contract, to require the Contractor to furnish bonds covering the faithful performance of the Contract and the payment of all obligations arising thereunder in such form and amount as the Owner may prescribe and with such sureties as may be agreeable to the parties. If such bonds are stipulated in the bidding requirements, the premiums shall be paid by the Contractor; if required subsequent to the submission of quotations or bids, the cost shall be reimbursed by the Owner. The Contractor shall deliver the required bonds to the Owner not later than the date of execution of the Contract, or if the Work is commenced prior thereto in response to a notice to proceed, the Contractor shall, prior to commencement of the Work, submit evidence satisfactory to the Owner that such bonds will be issued.

7.6 OWNER'S RIGHT TO CARRY OUT THE WORK

7.6.1 If the Contractor defaults or neglects to carry out the Work in accordance with the Contract Documents or fails to perform any provision of the Contract, the Owner may, after seven days' written notice to the Contractor and without prejudice to any other remedy he may have, make good such deficiencies. In such case an appropriate Change Order shall be issued deducting from the payments then or thereafter due the Contractor the cost of correcting such deficiencies, including the cost of the Architect's additional services made necessary by such default, neglect or failure. The Architect must approve both such action and the amount charged to the Contractor. If the payments then or thereafter due the Contractor are not sufficient to cover such amount, the Contractor shall pay the difference to the Owner.

7.7 ROYALTIES AND PATENTS

7.7.1 The Contractor shall pay all royalties and license fees. He shall defend all suits or claims for infringement of any patent rights and shall save the Owner harmless from loss on account thereof, except that the Owner shall be responsible for all such loss when a particular design, process or the product of a particular manufacturer or manufacturers is specified, but if the Contractor has reason to believe that the design, process or product specified is an infringement of a patent, he shall be responsible for such loss unless he promptly gives such information to the Architect.

7.8 TESTS

7.8.1 If the Contract Documents, laws, ordinances, rules, regulations or orders of any public authority having jurisdiction require any Work to be inspected, tested or approved, the Contractor shall give the Architect timely notice of its readiness and of the date arranged so the Architect may observe such inspection, testing or approval. The Contractor shall bear all costs of such inspections, tests and approvals unless otherwise provided.

7.8.2 If after the commencement of the Work the Architect determines that any Work requires special inspection, testing or approval which Subparagraph 7.8.1 does not include, he will, upon written authorization from the Owner, instruct the Contractor to order such special inspection, testing or approval, and the Contractor shall give notice as in Subparagraph 7.8.1. If such special inspection or testing reveals a failure of the Work to comply (1) with the requirements of the Contract Documents or (2), with respect to the performance of the Work, with laws, ordinances, rules, regulations or orders of any public authority having jurisdiction, the Contractor shall bear all costs thereof, including the Architect's additional services made necessary by such failure; otherwise the Owner shall bear such costs, and an appropriate Change Order shall be issued.

7.8.3 Required certificates of inspection, testing or approval shall be secured by the Contractor and promptly delivered by him to the Architect.

7.8.4 If the Architect wishes to observe the inspections, tests or approvals required by this Paragraph 7.8, he will do so promptly and, where practicable, at the source of supply.

7.8.5 Neither the observations of the Architect in his Administration of the Construction Contract, nor inspections, tests or approvals by persons other than the Contractor shall relieve the Contractor from his obligations to perform the Work in accordance with the Contract Documents.

7.9 INTEREST

7.9.1 Any moneys not paid when due to either party under this Contract shall bear interest at the legal rate in force at the place of the Project.

7.10 ARBITRATION

7.10.1 All claims, disputes and other matters in question arising out of, or relating to, this Contract or the breach thereof, except as set forth in Subparagraph 2.2.9 with respect to the Architect's decisions on matters relating to artistic effect, and except for claims which have been waived by the making or acceptance of final payment as provided by Subparagraphs 9.7.5 and 9.7.6, shall be decided by arbitration in accordance with the Construction Industry Arbitration Rules of the American Arbitration Association then obtaining unless the parties mutually agree otherwise. This agreement so to arbitrate shall be specifically enforceable under the prevailing arbitration law. The award rendered by the arbitrators shall be final, and judgment may be entered upon it in accordance with applicable law in any court having jurisdiction thereof.

7.10.2 Notice of the demand for arbitration shall be filed in writing with the other party to the Contract and with the American Arbitration Association, and a copy shall be filed with the Architect. The demand for arbitration shall be made within the time limits specified in Subparagraphs 2.2.10 and 2.2.11 where applicable, and in all other cases within a reasonable time after the claim, dispute or other matter in question has arisen, and in no event shall it be made after institution of legal or equitable proceedings based on such claim, dispute or other matter in question would be barred by the applicable statute of limitations.

7.10.3 The Contractor shall carry on the Work and maintain the progress schedule during any arbitration proceedings, unless otherwise agreed by him and the Owner in writing.

ARTICLE 8

TIME

8.1 DEFINITIONS

8.1.1 The Contract Time is the period of time allotted in the Contract Documents for completion of the Work.

8.1.2 The date of commencement of the Work is the date established in a notice to proceed. If there is no notice to proceed, it shall be the date of the Agreement or such other date as may be established therein.

8.1.3 The Date of Substantial Completion of the Work or designated portion thereof is the Date certified by the Architect when construction is sufficiently complete, in accordance with the Contract Documents, so the Owner may occupy the Work or designated portion thereof for the use for which it is intended.

8.2 PROGRESS AND COMPLETION

8.2.1 All time limits stated in the Contract Documents are of the essence of the Contract.

8.2.2 The Contractor shall begin the Work on the date of commencement as defined in Subparagraph 8.1.2. He shall carry the Work forward expeditiously with adequate forces and shall complete it within the Contract Time.

8.3 DELAYS AND EXTENSIONS OF TIME

8.3.1 If the Contractor is delayed at any time in the progress of the Work by any act or neglect of the Owner or the Architect, or by any employee of either, or by any separate contractor employed by the Owner, or by changes ordered in the Work, or by labor disputes, fire, unusual delay in transportation, unavoidable casualties or any causes beyond the Contractor's control, or by delay authorized by the Owner pending arbitration, or by any cause which the Architect determines may justify the delay, then the Contract Time shall be extended by Change Order for such reasonable time as the Architect may determine.

8.3.2 All claims for extension of time shall be made in writing to the Architect no more than fifteen days after the occurrence of the delay; otherwise they shall be waived. In the case of a continuing cause of delay only one claim is necessary.

8.3.3 If no schedule or agreement is made stating the dates upon which written interpretations as set forth in Subparagraph 1.2.5 shall be furnished, then no claim for delay shall be allowed on account of failure to furnish such interpretations until fifteen days after demand is made for them, and not then unless such claim is reasonable.

8.3.4 This Paragraph 8.3 does not exclude the recovery of damages for delay by either party under other provisions of the Contract Documents.

ARTICLE 9

PAYMENTS AND COMPLETION

9.1 CONTRACT SUM

9.1.1 The Contract Sum is stated in the Agreement and is the total amount payable by the Owner to the Contractor for the performance of the Work under the Contract Documents.

9.2 SCHEDULE OF VALUES

9.2.1 Before the first Application for Payment, the Contractor shall submit to the Architect a schedule of values of the various portions of the Work, including quantities if required by the Architect, aggregating the total Contract Sum, divided so as to facilitate payments to Subcontractors in accordance with Paragraph 5.4, prepared in such form as specified or as the Architect and the Contractor may agree upon, and supported by such data to substantiate its correctness as the Architect may require. Each item in the schedule of values shall include its proper share of overhead and profit. This schedule, when approved by the Architect, shall be used only as a basis for the Contractor's Applications for Payment.

9.3 PROGRESS PAYMENTS

9.3.1 At least ten days before each progress payment falls due, the Contractor shall submit to the Architect an itemized Application for Payment, supported by such data substantiating the Contractor's right to payment as the Owner or the Architect may require.

9.3.2 If payments are to be made on account of materials or equipment not incorporated in the Work but delivered and suitably stored at the site, or at some other location agreed upon in writing, such payments shall be conditioned upon submission by the Contractor of bills of sale or such other procedures satisfactory to the Owner to establish the Owner's title to such materials or equipment or otherwise protect the Owner's interest including applicable insurance and transportation to the site.

9.3.3 The Contractor warrants and guarantees that title to all Work, materials and equipment covered by an Application for Payment, whether incorporated in the Project or not, will pass to the Owner upon the receipt of such payment by the Contractor, free and clear of all liens, claims, security interests or encumbrances, hereinafter referred to in this Article 9 as "liens"; and that no Work, materials or equipment covered by an Application for Payment will have been acquired by the Contractor, or by any other person performing the Work at the site or furnishing materials and equipment for the Project, subject to an agreement under which an interest therein or an encumbrance thereon is retained by the seller or otherwise imposed by the Contractor or such other person.

9.4 CERTIFICATES FOR PAYMENT

9.4.1 If the Contractor has made Application for Payment as above, the Architect will, with reasonable promptness but not more than seven days after the receipt of the Application, issue a Certificate for Payment to the Owner, with a copy to the Contractor, for such amount as he determines to be properly due, or state in writing his reasons for withholding a Certificate as provided in Subparagraph 9.5.1.

9.4.2 The issuance of a Certificate for Payment will constitute a representation by the Architect to the Owner, based on his observations at the site as provided in Subparagraph 2.2.4 and the data comprising the Application for Payment, that the Work has progressed to the point indicated; that, to the best of his knowledge, information and belief, the quality of the Work is in accordance with the Contract Documents (subject to an evaluation of the Work as a functioning whole upon Substantial Completion, to the results of any subsequent tests required by the Contract Documents, to minor deviations from the Contract Documents correctable prior to completion, and to any specific qualifications stated in his Certificate); and that the Contractor is entitled to payment in the amount certified. In addition, the Architect's final Certificate for Payment will constitute a further representation that the conditions precedent to the Contractor's being entitled to final payment as set forth in Subparagraph 9.7.2 have been fulfilled. However, by issuing a Certificate for Payment, the Architect shall not thereby be deemed to represent that he has made exhaustive or continuous on-site inspections to check the quality or quantity of the Work or that he has reviewed the construction means, methods, techniques, sequences or procedures, or that he has made any examination to ascertain how or for what purpose the Contractor has used the moneys previously paid on account of the Contract Sum.

9.4.3 After the Architect has issued a Certificate for Payment, the Owner shall make payment in the manner provided in the Agreement.

9.4.4 No Certificate for a progress payment, nor any progress payment, nor any partial or entire use or occupancy of the Project by the Owner, shall constitute an acceptance of any Work not in accordance with the Contract Documents.

9.5 PAYMENTS WITHHELD

9.5.1 The Architect may decline to approve an Application for Payment and may withhold his Certificate in whole or in part if in his opinion he is unable to make representations to the Owner as provided in Subparagraph 9.4.2. The Architect may also decline to approve any Applications for Payment or, because of subsequently discovered evidence or subsequent inspections, he may nullify the whole or any part of any Certificate for Payment previously issued to such extent as may be necessary in his opinion to protect the Owner from loss because of:

.1 defective work not remedied,

.2 claims filed or reasonable evidence indicating probable filing of claims,

.3 failure of the Contractor to make payments properly to Subcontractors or for labor, materials or equipment,

.4 reasonable doubt that the Work can be completed for the unpaid balance of the Contract Sum,

.5 damage to another contractor,

.6 reasonable indication that the Work will not be completed within the Contract Time, or

.7 unsatisfactory prosecution of the Work by the Contractor.

9.5.2 When the above grounds in Subparagraph 9.5.1 are removed, payment shall be made for amounts withheld because of them.

9.6 FAILURE OF PAYMENT

9.6.1 If the Architect should fail to issue any Certificate for Payment, through no fault of the Contractor, within seven days after receipt of the Contractor's Application for Payment, or if the Owner should fail to pay the Contractor within seven days after the date of payment established in the Agreement any amount certified by the Architect or awarded by arbitration, then the Contractor may, upon seven additional days' written notice to the Owner and the Architect, stop the Work until payment of the amount owing has been received.

9.7 SUBSTANTIAL COMPLETION AND FINAL PAYMENT

9.7.1 When the Contractor determines that the Work or a designated portion thereof acceptable to the Owner is substantially complete, the Contractor shall prepare for submission to the Architect a list of items to be completed or corrected. The failure to include any items on such list does not alter the responsibility of the Contractor to complete all Work in accordance with the Contract Documents. When the Architect on the basis of an inspection determines that the Work is substantially complete, he will then prepare a Certificate of Substantial Completion which shall establish the Date of Substantial Completion, shall state the responsibilities of the Owner and the Contractor for maintenance, heat, utilities, and insurance, and shall fix the time within which the Contractor shall complete the items listed therein, said time to be within the Contract Time unless extended pursuant to Paragraph 8.3. The Certificate of Substantial Completion shall be submitted to the Owner and the Contractor for their written acceptance of the responsibilities assigned to them in such Certificate.

9.7.2 Upon receipt of written notice that the Work is ready for final inspection and acceptance and upon receipt of a final Application for Payment, the Architect will promptly make such inspection and, when he finds the Work acceptable under the Contract Documents and the Contract fully performed, he will promptly issue a final Certificate for Payment stating that to the best of his knowledge, information and belief, and on the basis of his observations and inspections, the Work has been completed in accordance with the terms and conditions of the Contract Documents and that the entire balance found to be due the Contractor, and noted in said final Certificate, is due and payable.

9.7.3 Neither the final payment nor the remaining retained percentage shall become due until the Contractor submits to the Architect (1) an Affidavit that all payrolls, bills for materials and equipment, and other indebtedness connected with the Work for which the Owner or his property might in any way be responsible, have been paid or otherwise satisfied, (2) consent of surety, if any, to final payment and (3), if required by the Owner, other data establishing payment or satisfaction of all such obligations, such as receipts, releases and waivers of liens arising out of the Contract, to the extent and in such form as may be designated by the Owner. If any Subcontractor refuses to furnish a release or waiver required by the Owner, the Contractor may furnish a bond satisfactory to the Owner to indemnify him against any such lien. If any such lien remains unsatisfied after all payments are made, the Contractor shall refund to the Owner all moneys that the latter may be compelled to pay in discharging such lien, including all costs and reasonable attorneys' fees.

9.7.4 If after Substantial Completion of the Work final completion thereof is materially delayed through no fault of the Contractor, and the Architect so confirms, the Owner shall, upon certification by the Architect, and without terminating the Contract, make payment of the balance due for that portion of the Work fully completed and accepted. If the remaining balance for Work not fully completed or corrected is less than the retainage stipulated in the Agreement, and if bonds have been furnished as required in Subparagraph 7.5.1, the written consent of the surety to the payment of the balance due for that portion of the Work fully completed and accepted shall be submitted by the Contractor to the Architect prior to certification of such payment. Such payment shall be made under the terms and conditions governing final payment, except that it shall not constitute a waiver of claims.

9.7.5 The making of final payment shall constitute a waiver of all claims by the Owner except those arising from:

.1 unsettled liens,

.2 faulty or defective Work appearing after Substantial Completion,

.3 failure of the Work to comply with the requirements of the Contract Documents, or

.4 terms of any special guarantees required by the Contract Documents.

9.7.6 The acceptance of final payment shall constitute a waiver of all claims by the Contractor except those previously made in writing and still unsettled.

ARTICLE 10

PROTECTION OF PERSONS AND PROPERTY

10.1 SAFETY PRECAUTIONS AND PROGRAMS

10.1.1 The Contractor shall be responsible for initiating, maintaining and supervising all safety precautions and programs in connection with the Work.

10.2 SAFETY OF PERSONS AND PROPERTY

10.2.1 The Contractor shall take all reasonable precautions for the safety of, and shall provide all reasonable protection to prevent damage, injury or loss to:

.1 all employees on the Work and all other persons who may be affected thereby;

.2 all the Work and all materials and equipment to be incorporated therein, whether in storage on or off the site, under the care, custody or control of the Contractor or any of his Subcontractors or Sub-subcontractors; and

.3 other property at the site or adjacent thereto, including trees, shrubs, lawns, walks, pavements, roadways, structures and utilities not designated for removal, relocation or replacement in the course of construction.

10.2.2 The Contractor shall comply with all applicable laws, ordinances, rules, regulations and orders of any public authority having jurisdiction for the safety of persons or property or to protect them from damage, injury or loss. He shall erect and maintain, as required by existing conditions and progress of the Work, all reasonable safeguards for safety and protection, including posting danger signs and other warnings against hazards, promulgating safety regulations and notifying owners and users of adjacent utilities.

10.2.3 When the use or storage of explosives or other hazardous materials or equipment is necessary for the execution of the Work, the Contractor shall exercise the utmost care and shall carry on such activities under the supervision of properly qualified personnel.

10.2.4 All damage or loss to any property referred to in Clauses 10.2.1.2 and 10.2.1.3 caused in whole or in part by the Contractor, any Subcontractor, any Sub-subcontractor, or anyone directly or indirectly employed by any of them, or by anyone for whose acts any of them may be liable, shall be remedied by the Contractor, except damage or loss attributable to faulty Drawings or Specifications or to the acts or omissions of the Owner or Architect or anyone employed by either of them or for whose acts either of them may be liable, and not attributable to the fault or negligence of the Contractor.

10.2.5 The Contractor shall designate a responsible member of his organization at the site whose duty shall be the prevention of accidents. This person shall be the Contractor's superintendent unless otherwise designated in writing by the Contractor to the Owner and the Architect.

10.2.6 The Contractor shall not load or permit any part of the Work to be loaded so as to endanger its safety.

10.3 EMERGENCIES

10.3.1 In any emergency affecting the safety of persons or property, the Contractor shall act, at his discretion, to prevent threatened damage, injury or loss. Any additional compensation or extension of time claimed by the Contractor on account of emergency work shall be determined as provided in Article 12 for Changes in the Work.

ARTICLE 11

INSURANCE

11.1 CONTRACTOR'S LIABILITY INSURANCE

11.1.1 The Contractor shall purchase and maintain such insurance as will protect him from claims set forth below which may arise out of or result from the Contractor's operations under the Contract, whether such operations be by himself or by any Subcontractor or by anyone directly or indirectly employed by any of them, or by anyone for whose acts any of them may be liable:

.1 claims under workmen's compensation, disability benefit and other similar employee benefit acts;

.2 claims for damages because of bodily injury, occupational sickness or disease, or death of his employees, and claims insured by usual personal injury liability coverage;

.3 claims for damages because of bodily injury, sickness or disease, or death of any person other than his employees, and claims insured by usual personal injury liability coverage; and

.4 claims for damages because of injury to or destruction of tangible property, including loss of use resulting therefrom.

11.1.2 The insurance required by Subparagraph 11.1.1 shall be written for not less than any limits of liability specified in the Contract Documents, or required by law, whichever is greater, and shall include contractual liability insurance as applicable to the Contractor's obligations under Paragraph 4.18.

11.1.3 Certificates of Insurance acceptable to the Owner shall be filed with the Owner prior to commencement of the Work. These Certificates shall contain a provision that coverages afforded under the policies will not be cancelled until at least fifteen days' prior written notice has been given to the Owner.

11.2 OWNER'S LIABILITY INSURANCE

11.2.1 The Owner shall be responsible for purchasing and maintaining his own liability insurance and, at his option, may purchase and maintain such insurance as will protect him against claims which may arise from operations under the Contract.

11.3 PROPERTY INSURANCE

11.3.1 Unless otherwise provided, the Owner shall purchase and maintain property insurance upon the entire Work at the site to the full insurable value thereof. This insurance shall include the interests of the Owner, the Contractor, Subcontractors and Sub-subcontractors in the Work and shall insure against the perils of Fire, Extended Coverage, Vandalism and Malicious Mischief.

11.3.2 The Owner shall purchase and maintain such steam boiler and machinery insurance as may be required by the Contract Documents or by law. This insurance shall include the interests of the Owner, the Contractor, Subcontractors and Sub-subcontractors in the Work.

11.3.3 Any insured loss is to be adjusted with the Owner and made payable to the Owner as trustee for the insureds, as their interests may appear, subject to the requirements of any applicable mortgagee clause and of Subparagraph 11.3.8.

11.3.4 The Owner shall file a copy of all policies with the Contractor before an exposure to loss may occur. If the Owner does not intend to purchase such insurance, he shall inform the Contractor in writing prior to commencement of the Work. The Contractor may then effect insurance which will protect the interests of himself, his Subcontractors and the Sub-subcontractors in the Work, and by appropriate Change Order the cost thereof shall be charged to the Owner. If the Contractor is damaged by failure of the Owner to purchase or maintain such insurance and so to notify the Contractor, then the Owner shall bear all reasonable costs properly attributable thereto.

11.3.5 If the Contractor requests in writing that other special insurance be included in the property insurance policy, the Owner shall, if possible, include such insurance, and the cost thereof shall be charged to the Contractor by appropriate Change Order.

11.3.6 The Owner and Contractor waive all rights against each other for damages caused by fire or other perils to the extent covered by insurance provided under this Paragraph 11.3, except such rights as they may have to the proceeds of such insurance held by the Owner as trustee. The Contractor shall require similar waivers by Subcontractors and Sub-subcontractors in accordance with Clause 5.3.1.5.

11.3.7 If required in writing by any party in interest, the Owner as trustee shall, upon the occurrence of an insured loss, give bond for the proper performance of his duties. He shall deposit in a separate account any money so received, and he shall distribute it in accordance with such agreement as the parties in interest may reach, or in accordance with an award by arbitration in which case the procedure shall be as provided in Paragraph 7.10. If after such loss no other special agreement is made, replacement of damaged work shall be covered by an appropriate Change Order.

11.3.8 The Owner as trustee shall have power to adjust and settle any loss with the insurers unless one of the parties in interest shall object in writing within five days after the occurrence of loss to the Owner's exercise of this power, and if such objection be made, arbitrators shall be chosen as provided in Paragraph 7.10. The Owner as trustee shall, in that case, make settlement with the insurers in accordance with the directions of such arbitrators. If distribution of the insurance proceeds by arbitration is required, the arbitrators will direct such distribution.

11.4 LOSS OF USE INSURANCE

11.4.1 The Owner, at his option, may purchase and maintain such insurance as will insure him against loss of use of his property due to fire or other hazards, however caused.

ARTICLE 12

CHANGES IN THE WORK

12.1 CHANGE ORDERS

12.1.1 The Owner, without invalidating the Contract, may order Changes in the Work within the general scope of the Contract consisting of additions, deletions or other revisions, the Contract Sum and the Contract Time being adjusted accordingly. All such Changes in the Work shall be authorized by Change Order, and shall be executed under the applicable conditions of the Contract Documents.

12.1.2 A Change Order is a written order to the Contractor signed by the Owner and the Architect, issued after the execution of the Contract, authorizing a Change in the Work or an adjustment in the Contract Sum or the Contract Time. Alternatively, the Change Order may be signed by the Architect alone, provided he has written authority from the Owner for such procedure and that a copy of such written authority is furnished to the Contractor upon request. The Contract Sum and the Contract Time may be changed only by Change Order.

12.1.3 The cost or credit to the Owner resulting from a Change in the Work shall be determined in one or more of the following ways:

- **.1** by mutual acceptance of a lump sum properly itemized;
- **.2** by unit prices stated in the Contract Documents or subsequently agreed upon; or
- **.3** by cost and a mutually acceptable fixed or percentage fee.

12.1.4 If none of the methods set forth in Subparagraph 12.1.3 is agreed upon, the Contractor, provided he receives a Change Order, shall promptly proceed with the Work involved. The cost of such Work shall then be determined by the Architect on the basis of the Contractor's reasonable expenditures and savings, including, in the case of an increase in the Contract Sum, a reasonable allowance for overhead and profit. In such case, and also under Clause 12.1.3.3 above, the Contractor shall keep and present, in such form as the Architect may prescribe, an itemized accounting together with appropriate supporting data. Pending final determination of cost to the Owner, payments on account shall be made on the Architect's Certificate for Payment. The amount of credit to be allowed by the Contractor to the Owner for any deletion or change which results in a net decrease in cost will be the amount of the actual net decrease as confirmed by the Architect. When both additions and credits are involved in any one change, the allowance for overhead and profit shall be figured on the basis of net increase, if any.

12.1.5 If unit prices are stated in the Contract Documents or subsequently agreed upon, and if the quantities originally contemplated are so changed in a proposed Change Order that application of the agreed unit prices to the quantities of Work proposed will create a hardship on the Owner or the Contractor, the applicable unit prices shall be equitably adjusted to prevent such hardship.

12.1.6 Should concealed conditions encountered in the performance of the Work below the surface of the ground be at variance with the conditions indicated by the Contract Documents or should unknown physical conditions below the surface of the ground of an unusual nature, differing materially from those ordinarily encountered and generally recognized as inherent in work of the character provided for in this Contract, be encountered, the Contract Sum shall be equitably adjusted by Change Order upon claim by either party made within a reasonable time after the first observance of the conditions.

12.1.7 If the Contractor claims that additional cost or time is involved because of (1) any written interpretation issued pursuant to Subparagraph 1.2.5, (2) any order by the Architect to stop the Work pursuant to Subparagraph 2.2.12 where the Contractor was not at fault, or (3) any written order for a minor change in the Work issued pursuant to Paragraph 12.3, the Contractor shall make such claim as provided in Paragraph 12.2.

12.2 CLAIMS FOR ADDITIONAL COST OR TIME

12.2.1 If the Contractor wishes to make a claim for an increase in the Contract Sum or an extension in the Contract Time, he shall give the Architect written notice thereof within a reasonable time after the occurrence of the event giving rise to such claim. This notice shall be given by the Contractor before proceeding to execute the Work, except in an emergency endangering life or property in which case the Contractor shall proceed in accordance with Subparagraph 10.3.1. No such claim shall be valid unless so made. If the Owner and the Contractor cannot agree on the amount of the adjustment in the Contract Sum or the Contract Time, it shall be determined by the Architect. Any change in the Contract Sum or Contract Time resulting from such claim shall be authorized by Change Order.

12.3 MINOR CHANGES IN THE WORK

12.3.1 The Architect shall have authority to order minor changes in the Work not involving an adjustment in the Contract Sum or an extension of the Contract Time and not inconsistent with the intent of the Contract Documents. Such changes may be effected by Field Order or by other written order. Such changes shall be binding on the Owner and the Contractor.

12.4 FIELD ORDERS

12.4.1 The Architect may issue written Field Orders which interpret the Contract Documents in accordance with Subparagraph 1.2.5 or which order minor changes in the Work in accordance with Paragraph 12.3 without change in Contract Sum or Contract Time. The Contractor shall carry out such Field Orders promptly.

ARTICLE 13

UNCOVERING AND CORRECTION OF WORK

13.1 UNCOVERING OF WORK

13.1.1 If any Work should be covered contrary to the request of the Architect, it must, if required by the Architect, be uncovered for his observation and replaced, at the Contractor's expense.

13.1.2 If any other Work has been covered which the Architect has not specifically requested to observe prior to being covered, the Architect may request to see such Work and it shall be uncovered by the Contractor. If such Work be found in accordance with the Contract Documents, the cost of uncovering and replacement shall, by appropriate Change Order, be charged to the Owner. If such Work be found not in accordance with the Contract Documents, the Contractor shall pay such costs unless it be found that this condition was caused by a separate contractor employed as provided in Article 6, and in that event the Owner shall be responsible for the payment of such costs.

13.2 CORRECTION OF WORK

13.2.1 The Contractor shall promptly correct all Work rejected by the Architect as defective or as failing to conform to the Contract Documents whether observed before or after Substantial Completion and whether or not fabricated, installed or completed. The Contractor shall bear all costs of correcting such rejected Work, including the cost of the Architect's additional services thereby made necessary.

13.2.2 If, within one year after the Date of Substantial Completion or within such longer period of time as may be prescribed by law or by the terms of any applicable special guarantee required by the Contract Documents, any of the Work is found to be defective or not in accordance with the Contract Documents, the Contractor shall correct it promptly after receipt of a written notice from the Owner to do so unless the Owner has previously given the Contractor a written acceptance of such condition. The Owner shall give such notice promptly after discovery of the condition.

13.2.3 All such defective or non-conforming Work under Subparagraphs 13.2.1 and 13.2.2 shall be removed from the site where necessary, and the Work shall be corrected to comply with the Contract Documents without cost to the Owner.

13.2.4 The Contractor shall bear the cost of making good all work of separate contractors destroyed or damaged by such removal or correction.

13.2.5 If the Contractor does not remove such defective or non-conforming Work within a reasonable time fixed by written notice from the Architect, the Owner may remove it and may store the materials or equipment at the expense of the Contractor. If the Contractor does not pay the cost of such removal and storage within ten days thereafter, the Owner may upon ten additional days' written notice sell such Work at auction or at private sale and shall account for the net proceeds thereof, after deducting all the costs that should have been borne by the Contractor including compensation for additional architectural services. If such proceeds of sale do not cover all costs which the Contractor should have borne, the difference shall be charged to the Contractor and an appropriate Change Order shall be issued. If the payments then or thereafter due the Contractor are not sufficient to cover such amount, the Contractor shall pay the difference to the Owner.

13.2.6 If the Contractor fails to correct such defective or non-conforming Work, the Owner may correct it in accordance with Paragraph 7.6.

13.2.7 The obligations of the Contractor under this Paragraph 13.2 shall be in addition to and not in limitation of any obligations imposed upon him by special guarantees required by the Contract Documents or otherwise prescribed by law.

13.3 ACCEPTANCE OF DEFECTIVE OR NON-CONFORMING WORK

13.3.1 If the Owner prefers to accept defective or non-conforming Work, he may do so instead of requiring its removal and correction, in which case a Change Order will be issued to reflect an appropriate reduction in the Contract Sum, or, if the amount is determined after final payment, it shall be paid by the Contractor.

ARTICLE 14

TERMINATION OF THE CONTRACT

14.1 TERMINATION BY THE CONTRACTOR

14.1.1 If the Work is stopped for a period of thirty days under an order of any court or other public authority having jurisdiction, through no act or fault of the Contractor or a Subcontractor or their agents or employees or any other persons performing any of the Work under a contract with the Contractor, or if the Work should be stopped for a period of thirty days by the Contractor for the Architect's failure to issue a Certificate for Payment as provided in Paragraph 9.6 or for the Owner's failure to make payment thereon as provided in Paragraph 9.6, then the Contractor may, upon seven days' written notice to the Owner and the Architect, terminate the Contract and recover from the Owner payment for all Work executed and for any proven loss sustained upon any materials, equipment, tools, construction equipment and machinery, including reasonable profit and damages.

14.2 TERMINATION BY THE OWNER

14.2.1 If the Contractor is adjudged a bankrupt, or if he makes a general assignment for the benefit of his creditors, or if a receiver is appointed on account of his insolvency, or if he persistently or repeatedly refuses or fails, except in cases for which extension of time is provided, to supply enough properly skilled workmen or proper materials, or if he fails to make prompt payment to Subcontractors or for materials or labor, or persistently disregards laws, ordinances, rules, regulations or orders of any public authority having jurisdiction, or otherwise is guilty of a substantial violation of a provision of the Contract Documents, then the Owner, upon certification by the Architect that sufficient cause exists to justify such action, may, without prejudice to any right or remedy and after giving the Contractor and his surety, if any, seven days' written notice, terminate the employment of the Contractor and take possession of the site and of all materials, equipment, tools, construction equipment and machinery thereon owned by the Contractor and may finish the Work by whatever method he may deem expedient. In such case the Contractor shall not be entitled to receive any further payment until the Work is finished.

14.2.2 If the unpaid balance of the Contract Sum exceeds the costs of finishing the Work, including compensation for the Architect's additional services, such excess shall be paid to the Contractor. If such costs exceed such unpaid balance, the Contractor shall pay the difference to the Owner. The costs incurred by the Owner as herein provided shall be certified by the Architect.

APPENDIX E

AIA Document A311*

Performance Bond

KNOW ALL MEN BY THESE PRESENTS: that (Here insert full name and address or legal title of Contractor)

as Principal, hereinafter called Contractor, and, (Here insert full name and address or legal title of Surety)

as Surety, hereinafter called Surety, are held and firmly bound unto (Here insert full name and address or legal title of Owner)

as Obligee, hereinafter called Owner, in the amount of

Dollars ($),

for the payment whereof Contractor and Surety bind themselves, their heirs, executors, administrators, successors and assigns, jointly and severally, firmly by these presents.

WHEREAS,

Contractor has by written agreement dated 19 , entered into a contract with Owner for

in accordance with Drawings and Specifications prepared by (Here insert full name and address or legal title of Architect)

which contract is by reference made a part hereof, and is hereinafter referred to as the Contract.

* Reprinted with permission

NOW, THEREFORE, THE CONDITION OF THIS OBLIGATION is such that, if Contractor shall promptly and faithfully perform said Contract, then this obligation shall be null and void; otherwise it shall remain in full force and effect.

The Surety hereby waives notice of any alteration or extension of time made by the Owner.

Whenever Contractor shall be, and declared by Owner to be in default under the Contract, the Owner having performed Owner's obligations thereunder, the Surety may promptly remedy the default, or shall promptly

1) Complete the Contract in accordance with its terms and conditions, or

2) Obtain a bid or bids for completing the Contract in accordance with its terms and conditions, and upon determination by Surety of the lowest responsible bidder, or, if the Owner elects, upon determination by the Owner and the Surety jointly of the lowest responsible bidder, arrange for a contract between such bidder and Owner, and make available as Work progresses (even though there should be a default or a succession of defaults under the contract or contracts of completion arranged under this paragraph) sufficient funds to pay the cost of completion less the balance of the contract price; but not exceeding, including other costs and damages for which the Surety may be liable hereunder, the amount set forth in the first paragraph hereof. The term "balance of the contract price," as used in this paragraph, shall mean the total amount payable by Owner to Contractor under the Contract and any amendments thereto, less the amount properly paid by Owner to Contractor.

Any suit under this bond must be instituted before the expiration of two (2) years from the date on which final payment under the Contract falls due.

No right of action shall accrue on this bond to or for the use of any person or corporation other than the Owner named herein or the heirs, executors, administrators or successors of Owner.

Principal (Seal)

Title

Surety (Seal)

Title

Subscribed and sworn to before me this

day of 19

Notary Public:

My Commission expires:

[A1117]

APPENDIX F

*AIA Document A311**

Labor and Material Payment Bond

THIS BOND IS ISSUED SIMULTANEOUSLY WITH PERFORMANCE BOND IN FAVOR OF THE OWNER CONDITIONED ON THE FULL AND FAITHFUL PERFORMANCE OF THE CONTRACT

KNOW ALL MEN BY THESE PRESENTS: that (Here insert full name and address or legal title of Contractor)

as Principal, hereinafter called Contractor, and, (Here insert full name and address or legal title of Surety)

as Surety, hereinafter called Surety, are held and firmly bound unto (Here insert full name and address or legal title of Owner)

as Obligee, hereinafter called Owner, for the use and benefits of claimants as hereinbelow defined, in the amount of (Here insert a sum equal to at least one-half of the contract price) Dollars ($), for the payment whereof Principal and Surety bind themselves, their heirs, executors, administrators, successors and assigns, jointly and severally, firmly by these presents.

WHEREAS,

Principal has by written agreement dated 19 , entered into a contract with Owner for

in accordance with Drawings and Specifications prepared by (Here insert full name and address or legal title of Architect)

which contract is by reference made a part hereof, and is hereinafter referred to as the Contract.

NOW, THEREFORE, THE CONDITION OF THIS OBLIGATION is such that, if Principal shall promptly make payment to all claimants as hereinafter defined, for all labor and material used or reasonably required for use in the performance of the Contract, then this obligation shall be void; otherwise it shall remain in full force and effect, subject, however, to the following conditions:

1. A claimant is defined as one having a direct contract with the Principal or with a Subcontractor of the Principal for labor, material, or both, used or reasonably required for use in the performance of the Contract, labor and material being construed to include that part of water, gas, power, light, heat, oil, gasoline, telephone service or rental of equipment directly applicable to the Contract. •

2. The above named Principal and Surety hereby jointly and severally agree with the Owner that every claimant as herein defined, who has not been paid in full before the expiration of a period of ninety (90) days after the date on which the last of such claimant's work or labor was done or performed, or materials were furnished by such claimant, may sue on this bond for the use of such claimant, prosecute the suit to final judgment for such sum or sums as may be justly due claimant, and have execution thereon. The Owner shall not be liable for the payment of any costs or expenses of any such suit.

3. No suit or action shall be commenced hereunder by any claimant:

a) Unless claimant, other than one having a direct contract with the Principal, shall have given written notice to any two of the following: The Principal, the Owner, or the Surety above named, within ninety (90) days after such claimant did or performed the last of the work or labor, or furnished the last of the materials for which said claim is made, stating with substantial accuracy the amount claimed and the name of the party to whom the materials were furnished, or for whom the work or labor was done or performed. Such notice shall be served by mailing the same by registered mail or certified mail, postage prepaid, in an envelope addressed to the Principal, Owner or Surety, at any place where an office is regularly maintained for the transaction of business, or served in any manner in which legal process may be served in the state in which the aforesaid project is located, save that such service need not be made by a public officer.

b) After the expiration of one (1) year following the date on which Principal ceased Work on said Contract, it being understood, however, that if any limitation embodied in this bond is prohibited by any law controlling the construction hereof such limitation shall be deemed to be amended so as to be equal to the minimum period of limitation permited by such law.

c) Other than in a state court of competent jurisdiction in and for the county or other poliical subdivision of the state in which the Project, or any part thereof, is situated, or in the United States District Court for the district in which the Project, or any part thereof, is situated, and not elsewhere.

4. The amount of this bond shall be reduced by and to the extent of any payment or payments made in good faith hereunder, inclusive of the payment by Surety of mechanics' liens which may be filed of record against said improvement, whether or not claim for the amount of such lien be presented under and against this bond.

Principal (Seal)

Title

Surety (Seal)

Title

Subscribed and sworn to before me this

day of 19

Notary Public:

My Commission expires:

APPENDIX G

CONSTRUCTION INDUSTRY ARBITRATION RULES

Effective Date March 8, 1966

Section 1. AGREEMENT OF PARTIES—The parties shall be deemed to have made these Rules a part of their arbitration agreement whenever they have provided for arbitration under the Construction Industry Arbitration Rules. These Rules and any amendment thereof shall apply in the form obtaining at the time the arbitration is initiated.

Section 2. NAME OF TRIBUNAL—Any Tribunal constituted by the parties for the settlement of their dispute under these Rules shall be called the Construction Industry Arbitration Tribunal, hereinafter called the Tribunal.

Section 3. ADMINISTRATOR—When parties agree to arbitrate under these Rules, or when they provide for arbitration by the American Arbitration Association, hereinafter called AAA, and an arbitration is initiated hereunder, they thereby constitute AAA the administrator of the arbitration. The authority and duties of the administrator are prescribed in the agreement of the parties and in these Rules.

Section 4. DELEGATION OF DUTIES—The duties of the AAA under these Rules may be carried out through Tribunal Administrators, or such other officers or committees as the AAA may direct.

Section 5. NATIONAL PANEL OF ARBITRATORS—In cooperation with the Construction Industry Arbitration Committee, the AAA shall establish and maintain a National Panel of Construction Arbitrators, hereinafter called the Panel, and shall appoint an arbitrator or arbitrators therefrom as hereinafter provided. A neutral arbitrator selected by mutual choice of both parties or their appointees, or appointed by the AAA, is hereinafter called the arbitrator, whereas an arbitrator selected unilaterally by one party is hereinafter called the party-appointed arbitrator. The term Arbitrator may hereinafter be used to refer to one arbitrator or to a Tribunal of multiple arbitrators.

Section 6. OFFICE OF TRIBUNAL—The general office of a Tribunal is the headquarters of the AAA, which may, however, assign the administration of an arbitration to any of its Regional Offices.

Section 7. INITIATION UNDER AN ARBITRATION PROVISION IN A CONTRACT—Arbitration under an arbitration provision in a contract shall be initiated in the following manner:

The initiating party shall, within the time specified by the contract, if any, file with the other party a notice of his intention to arbitrate (Demand), which notice shall contain a statement setting forth the nature of the dispute, the amount involved, if any, and the remedy sought; and shall file two copies of said notice with any Regional Office of the AAA, together with two copies of the arbitration provisions of the contract and the appropriate filing fee as provided in Section 47 hereunder.

The AAA shall give notice of such filing to the other party. If he so desires, the party upon whom the demand for arbitration is made may file an answering statement in duplicate with the AAA within seven days after notice from the AAA, in which event he shall simultaneously send a copy of his answer to the other party. If a monetary claim is made in the answer the appropriate administrative fee provided in the Fee Schedule shall be forwarded to the AAA with the answer. If no answer is filed within the stated time, it will be treated as a denial of the claim. Failure to file an answer shall not operate to delay the arbitration.

Section 8. CHANGE OF CLAIM—After filing of the claim, if either party desires to make any new or different claim, such claim shall be made in writing and filed with the AAA, and a copy thereof shall be mailed to the other party who shall have a period of seven days from the date of such mailing within which to file an answer with the AAA. However, after the Arbitrator is appointed no new or different claim may be submitted to him except with his consent.

Section 9. INITIATION UNDER A SUBMISSION—Parties to any existing dispute may commence an arbitration under these Rules by filing at any Regional Office two (2) copies of a written agreement to arbitrate under these Rules (Submission), signed by the parties. It shall contain a statement of the matter in dispute, the amount of money involved, if any, and the remedy sought, together with the appropriate filing fee as provided in the Fee Schedule.

Section 10. FIXING OF LOCALE—The parties may mutually agree on the locale where the arbitration is to be held. If any party requests that the hearing be held in a specific locale and the other party files no objection thereto within seven days after notice of the request is mailed to such party, the locale shall be the one requested. If a party objects to the locale requested by the other party, the AAA shall have power to determine the locale and its decision shall be final and binding.

Section 11. QUALIFICATIONS OF ARBITRATOR—No person shall serve as an Arbitrator in any arbitration if he has any financial or personal interest in the result of the arbitration, unless the parties, in writing, waive such disqualification.

Section 12. APPOINTMENT FROM PANEL—If the parties have not appointed an Arbitrator and have not provided any other method of appointment, the Arbitrator shall be appointed in the following manner: Immediately after the filing of the Demand or Submission, the AAA shall submit simultaneously to each party to the dispute an identical list of names of persons chosen from the Panel. Each party to the dispute shall have seven days from the mailing date in which to cross off any names to which he objects, number the remaining names indicating the order of his preference, and return the list to the AAA. If a party does not return the list within the time specified, all persons named therein shall be deemed acceptable. From among the persons who have been approved on both lists, and in accordance with the designated order of mutual preference, the AAA shall invite the acceptance of an Arbitrator to serve. If the parties fail to agree upon any of the persons named, or if acceptable Arbitrators are unable to act, or if for any other reason the appointment cannot be made from the submitted lists, the AAA shall have the power to make the appointment from other members of the Panel without the submission of any additional lists.

Section 13. DIRECT APPOINTMENT BY PARTIES—If the agreement of the parties names an Arbitrator or specifies a method of appointing an Arbitrator, that designation or method shall be followed. The notice of appointment, with name and address of such Arbitrator, shall be filed with the AAA by the appointing party. Upon the request of any such appointing party, the AAA shall submit a list of members from the Panel from which the party may, if he so desires, make the appointment.

If the agreement specifies a period of time within which an Arbitrator shall be appointed, and any party fails to make such appointment within that period, the AAA shall make the appointment.

If no period of time is specified in the agreement, the AAA shall notify the parties to make the appointment and if within seven days after mailing of such notice such Arbitrator has not been so appointed, the AAA shall make the appointment.

Section 14. APPOINTMENT OF ARBITRATOR BY PARTY-APPOINTED ARBITRATORS—If the parties have appointed their party-appointed Arbitrators or if either or both of them have been appointed as provided in Section 13, and have authorized such Arbitrators to appoint an Arbitrator within a specified time and no appointment is made within such time or any agreed extension thereof, the AAA shall appoint an Arbitrator who shall act as Chairman.

If no period of time is specified for appointment of the third Arbitrator and the party-appointed Arbitrators do not make the appointment within seven days from the date of the appointment of the last party-appointed Arbitrator, the AAA shall appoint the Arbitrator who shall act as Chairman.

If the parties have agreed that their party-appointed Arbitrators shall appoint the Arbitrator from the Panel, the AAA shall furnish to the party-appointed Arbitrators, in the manner prescribed in Section 12, a list selected from the Panel, and the appointment of the Arbitrator shall be made as prescribed in such Section.

Section 15. NATIONALITY OF ARBITRATOR IN INTERNATIONAL ARBITRATION—If one of the parties is a national or resident of a country other than the United States, the Arbitrator shall, upon the request of either party, be appointed from among the nationals of a country other than that of any of the parties.

Section 16. NUMBER OF ARBITRATORS—If the arbitration agreement does not specify or the parties are unable to agree as to the number of Arbitrators, the dispute shall be heard and determined by three Arbitrators, unless the AAA, in its discretion, directs that a single Arbitrator or a greater number of Arbitrators be appointed.

Section 17. NOTICE TO ARBITRATOR OF HIS APPOINTMENT—Notice of the appointment of the Arbitrator, whether mutually appointed by the parties or by the AAA, shall be mailed to the Arbitrator by the AAA, together with a copy of these Rules, and the signed acceptance of the Arbitrator shall be filed prior to the opening of the first hearing.

Section 18. DISCLOSURE BY ARBITRATOR OF DISQUALIFICATION—Prior to accepting his appointment, the prospective Arbitrator shall disclose any circumstances likely to create a presumption of bias or which he believes might disqualify him as an impartial Arbitrator. Upon receipt of such information, the AAA shall immediately disclose it to the parties who, if willing to proceed under the circumstances disclosed, shall so advise the AAA in writing. If either party declines to waive the presumptive disqualification, the vacancy thus created shall be filled in accordance with the applicable provisions of these Rules.

Section 19. VACANCIES—If any Arbitrator should resign, die, withdraw, refuse, be disqualified or be unable to perform the duties of his office, the AAA shall, on proof satisfactory to it, declare the office vacant. Vacancies shall be filled in accordance with the applicable provisions of these Rules and the matter shall be reheard unless the parties shall agree otherwise.

Section 20. TIME AND PLACE—The Arbitrator shall fix the time and place for each hearing. The AAA shall mail to each party notice thereof at least five days in advance, unless the parties by mutual agreement waive such notice or modify the terms thereof.

Section 21. REPRESENTATION BY COUNSEL—Any party may be represented by counsel. A party intending to be so represented shall notify the other party and the AAA of the name and address of counsel at least three days prior to the date set for the hearing at which counsel is first to appear. When an arbitration is initiated by counsel, or where an attorney replies for the other party, such notice is deemed to have been given.

Section 22. STENOGRAPHIC RECORD—The AAA shall make the necessary arrangements for the taking of a stenographic record whenever such record is requested by a party. The requesting party or parties shall pay the cost of such record as provided in Section 49.

Section 23. INTERPRETER—The AAA shall make the necessary arrangements for the services of an interpreter upon the request of one or both parties, who shall assume the cost of such service.

Section 24. ATTENDANCE AT HEARINGS—Persons having a direct interest in the arbitration are entitled to attend hearings. The Arbitrator shall otherwise have the power to require the retirement of any witness or witnesses during the testimony of other witnesses. It shall be discretionary with the Arbitrator to determine the propriety of the attendance of any other persons.

Section 25. ADJOURNMENTS—The Arbitrator may take adjournments upon the request of a party or upon his own initiative and shall take such adjournment when all of the parties agree thereto.

Section 26. OATHS—Before proceeding with the first hearing or with the examination of the file, each Arbitrator may take an oath of office, and if required by law, shall do so. The Arbitrator may, in his discretion, require witnesses to testify under oath administered by any duly qualified person or, if required by law or demanded by either party, shall do so.

Section 27. MAJORITY DECISION—Whenever there is more than one Arbitrator, all decisions of the Arbitrators must be by at least a majority. The award must also be made by at least a majority unless the concurrence of all is expressly required by the arbitration agreement or by law.

Section 28. ORDER OF PROCEEDINGS—A hearing shall be opened by the filing of the oath of the Arbitrator, where required, and by the recording of the place, time and date of the hearing, the presence of the Arbitrator and parties, and counsel, if any, and by the receipt by the Arbitrator of the statement of the claim and answer, if any.

The Arbitrator may, at the beginning of the hearing, ask for statements clarifying the issues involved.

The complaining party shall then present his claim and proofs and his witnesses, who shall submit to questions or other examination. The defending party shall then present his defense and proofs and his witnesses, who shall submit to questions or other examination. The Arbitrator may in his discretion vary this procedure but he shall afford full and equal opportunity to the parties for the presentation of any material or relevant proofs.

Exhibits, when offered by either party, may be received in evidence by the Arbitrator.

The names and addresses of all witnesses and exhibits in order received shall be made a part of the record.

Section 29. ARBITRATION IN THE ABSENCE OF A PARTY—Unless the law provides to the contrary, the arbitration may proceed in the absence of any party, who, after due notice, fails to be present or fails to obtain an adjournment. An award shall not be made solely on the default of a party. The Arbitrator shall require the party who is present to submit such evidence as he may require for the making of an award.

Section 30. EVIDENCE—The parties may offer such evidence as they desire and shall produce such additional evidence as the Arbitrator may deem necessary to an understanding and determination of the dispute. When the Arbitrator is authorized by law to subpoena witnesses or documents, he may do so upon his own initiative or upon the request of any party. The Arbitrator shall be the judge of the admissibility of the evidence offered and conformity to legal rules of evidence shall not be necessary. All evidence shall be taken in the presence of all of the Arbitrators and all of the parties, except where any of the parties is absent in default or has waived his right to be present.

Section 31. EVIDENCE BY AFFIDAVIT AND FILING OF DOCUMENTS—The Arbitrator may receive and consider the evidence of witnesses by affidavit, but shall give it only such weight as he deems it entitled to after consideration of any objections made to its admission.

All documents not filed with the Arbitrator at the hearing, but arranged for at the hearing or subsequently by agreement of the parties, shall be filed with the AAA for transmission to the Arbitrator. All parties shall be afforded opportunity to examine such documents.

Section 32. INSPECTION OR INVESTIGATION—Whenever the Arbitrator deems it necessary to make an inspection or investigation in connection with the arbitration, he shall direct the AAA to advise the parties of his intention. The Arbitrator shall set the time and the AAA shall notify the parties thereof. Any party who so desires may be present at such inspection or investigation. In the event that one or both parties are not present at the inspection or investigation, the Arbitrator shall make a verbal or written report to the parties and afford them an opportunity to comment.

Section 33. CONSERVATION OF PROPERTY—The Arbitrator may issue such orders as may be deemed necessary to safeguard the property which is the subject matter of the arbitration without prejudice to the rights of the parties or to the final determination of the dispute.

Section 34. CLOSING OF HEARINGS—The Arbitrator shall specifically inquire of the parties whether they have any further proofs to offer or witnesses to be heard. Upon receiving negative replies, the Arbitrator shall declare the hearings closed and a minute thereof shall be recorded. If briefs are to be filed, the hearings shall be declared closed as of the final date set by the Arbitrator for the receipt of briefs. If documents are to be filed as provided for in Section 31 and the date set for their receipt is later than that set for the receipt of briefs, the later date shall be the date of closing the hearing. The time limit within which the Arbitrator is required to make his award shall commence to run, in the absence of other agreements by the parties, upon the closing of the hearings.

Section 35. REOPENING OF HEARINGS—The hearings may be reopened by the Arbitrator on his own motion, or upon application of a party at any time before the award is made. If the reopening of the hearing would prevent the making of the award within the specific time agreed upon by the parties in the contract out of which the controversy has arisen, the matter may not be reopened, unless the parties agree upon the extension of such time limit. When no specific date is fixed in the contract, the Arbitrator may reopen the hearings, and the Arbitrator shall have thirty days from the closing of the reopened hearings within which to make an award.

Section 36. WAIVER OF ORAL HEARING—The parties may provide, by written agreement, for the waiver of oral hearings. If the parties are unable to agree as to the procedure, the AAA shall specify a fair and equitable procedure.

Section 37. WAIVER OF RULES—Any party who proceeds with the arbitration after knowledge that any provision or requirement of these Rules has not been complied with and who fails to state his objection thereto in writing, shall be deemed to have waived his right to object.

Section 38. EXTENSIONS OF TIME—The parties may modify any period of time by mutual agreement. The AAA for good cause may extend any period of time established by these Rules, except the time for making the award. The AAA shall notify the parties of any such extension of time and its reason therefor.

Section 39. COMMUNICATION WITH ARBITRATOR AND SERVING OF NOTICES—There shall be no communication between the parties and an Arbitrator other than at oral hearings. Any other oral or written communications from the parties to the Arbitrator shall be directed to the AAA for transmittal to the Arbitrator.

Each party to an agreement which provides for arbitration under these Rules shall be deemed to have consented that any papers, notices or process necessary or proper for the initiation or continuation of an arbitration under these Rules and for any court action in connection therewith or for the entry of judgment on any award made thereunder may be served upon such party by mail addressed to such party or his attorney at his last known address or by personal service, within or without the state wherein the arbitration is to be held (whether such party be within or without the United States of America), provided that reasonable opportunity to be heard with regard thereto has been granted such party.

Section 40. TIME OF AWARD—The award shall be made promptly by the Arbitrator and, unless otherwise agreed by the parties, or specified by law, not later than thirty days from the date of closing the hearings, or if oral hearings have been waived, from the date of transmitting the final statements and proofs to the Arbitrator.

Section 41. FORM OF AWARD—The award shall be in writing and shall be signed either by the sole Arbitrator or by at least a majority if there be more than one. It shall be executed in the manner required by law.

Section 42. SCOPE OF AWARD—The Arbitrator may grant any remedy or relief which he deems just and equitable and within the terms of the agreement of the parties. The Arbitrator, in his award, shall assess arbitration fees and expenses as provided in §§ 47 and 49 equally or in favor of any party and, in the event any administrative fees or expenses are due the AAA, in favor of the AAA.

Section 43. AWARD UPON SETTLEMENT—If the parties settle their dispute during the course of the arbitration, the Arbitrator, upon their request, may set forth the terms of the agreed settlement in an award.

Section 44. DELIVERY OF AWARD TO PARTIES—Parties shall accept as legal delivery of the award the placing of the award or a true copy thereof in the mail by the AAA, addressed to such party at his last known address or to his attorney, or personal service of the award, or the filing of the award in any manner which may be prescribed by law.

Section 45. RELEASE OF DOCUMENTS FOR JUDICIAL PROCEEDINGS—The AAA shall, upon the written request of a party, furnish to such party, at his expense, certified facsimiles of any papers in the AAA's possession that may be required in judicial proceedings relating to the arbitration.

Section 46. APPLICATIONS TO COURT—No judicial proceedings by a party relating to the subject matter of the arbitration shall be deemed a waiver of the party's right to arbitrate.

The AAA is not a necessary party in judicial proceedings relating to the arbitration.

Section 47. ADMINISTRATIVE FEES—As a nonprofit organization, the AAA shall prescribe an administrative fee schedule and a refund schedule to compensate it for the cost of providing administrative services. The schedule in effect at the time of filing or the time of refund shall be applicable.

The administrative fees shall be advanced by the initiating party or parties in accordance with the administrative fee schedule, subject to final apportionment by the Arbitrator in his award.

When a matter is withdrawn or settled, the refund shall be made in accordance with the refund schedule.

The AAA, in the event of extreme hardship on the part of any party, may defer or reduce the administrative fee.

Section 48. FEE WHEN ORAL HEARINGS ARE WAIVED—Where all Oral Hearings are waived under Section 36 the Administrative Fee Schedule shall apply.

Section 49. EXPENSES—The expenses of witnesses for either side shall be paid by the party producing such witnesses.

The cost of the stenographic record, if any is made, and all transcripts thereof, shall be prorated equally between the parties ordering copies unless they shall otherwise agree and shall be paid for by the responsible parties directly to the reporting agency.

All other expenses of the arbitration, including required traveling and other expenses of the Arbitrator and of AAA representatives, and the expenses of any witness or the cost of any proofs produced at the direct request of the Arbitrator, shall be borne equally by the parties, unless they agree otherwise, or unless the Arbitrator in his award assesses such expenses or any part thereof against any specified party or parties.

Section 50. ARBITRATOR'S FEE—Unless the parties agree to the terms of compensation, members of the National Panel of Construction Arbitrators will serve without compensation for the first two days of service. Thereafter, unless the parties agree as to the terms of compensation of Arbitrators, compensation shall be based upon the amount of service involved and the number of hearings. An appropriate daily rate and other arrangements shall be discussed with the Arbitrators and submitted to the parties prior to the appointment of the Arbitrators.

Any arrangements for the compensation of an Arbitrator shall be made through the AAA and not directly by him with the parties. The terms of compensation of Arbitrators on a Tribunal shall be identical.

Section 51. DEPOSITS—The AAA may require the parties to deposit in advance such sums of money as it deems necessary to defray the expense of the arbitration, including the Arbitrator's fee if any, and shall render an accounting to the parties and return any unexpended balance.

Section 52. INTERPRETATION AND APPLICATION OF RULES—The Arbitrator shall interpret and apply these Rules insofar as they relate to his powers and duties. When there is more than one Arbitrator and a difference arises among them concerning the meaning or application of any such Rules, it shall be decided by a majority vote. If that is unobtainable, either an Arbitrator or a party may refer the question to the AAA for final decision. All other Rules shall be interpreted and applied by the AAA.

*

INDEX

References are to Pages

WEST PUBLISHING CO